D0444642

Collins
Latin
Dictionary

HarperCollins Publishers
Westerhill Road
Bishopbriggs
Glasgow
G64 2QT
Great Britain

First Edition 1997

Latest Reprint 2005

© HarperCollins Publishers 1997

ISBN-13   978-0-00-722439-5
ISBN-10   0-00-722439-7

Collins® is a registered trademark of
HarperCollins Publishers Limited

www.collins.co.uk

A catalogue record for this book is available
from the British Library

HarperCollins Publishers, 10 East 53rd Street,
New York, NY 10022

ISBN-13   978-0-06-053690-9
ISBN-10   0-06-053690-x

Library of Congress Cataloging-in-
Publication Data has been applied for

www.harpercollins.com

HARPERCOLLINS LATIN CONCISE DICTIONARY.
First HarperCollins edition published 2003

HarperCollins books may be purchased for
educational, business, or sales promotional
use. For information, please write to:
Special Markets Department, HarperCollins
Publishers, 10 East 53rd Street, New York,
NY 10022

Dictionary text typeset by Tradespools Ltd,
Somerset

Grammar text typeset by Latimer Trend Ltd,
Plymouth

Printed in Italy by Legoprint S.P.A.

Dictionary based on the Collins Latin Gem © 1957 *by*
Professor D.A. Kidd
Canterbury University

Grammar text and dictionary supplements by
Mary Wade

Editorial coordinator
Joyce Littlejohn

Latin consultants
Ian Brookes
Denis Bruce
Michael D. Igoe

Series editor
Lorna Sinclair

Editorial management
Vivian Marr

CONTENTS

ABBREVIATIONS

adj	adjective	*MED*	medicine
abl	ablative	*MIL*	military
acc	accusative	*mod*	modern
adv	adverb	*n*	noun
AGR	agriculture	*NAUT*	nautical
ARCH	architecture	*neg*	negative
art	article	*nom*	nominative
ASTR	astronomy	*nt*	neuter
AUG	augury	*num*	numeral
COMM	business	*occ*	occasionally
CIRCS	circumstances	*p*	participle
compar	comparative	*pass*	passive
conj	conjunction	*perf*	perfect
cpd	compound	*perh*	perhaps
dat	dative	*pers*	person
defec	defective	*PHILOS*	philosophy
ECCL	ecclesiastical	*pl*	plural
esp	especially	*POL*	politics
excl	exclamatory	*ppa*	perfect participle active
f	feminine	*ppp*	perfect participle passive
fig	figurative	*prep*	preposition
fut	future	*pres*	present
gen	genitive	*pron*	pronoun
GEOG	geography	*prop*	properly
GRAM	grammar	*PROV*	proverb
impers	impersonal	*relat*	relative
imperf	imperfect	*RHET*	rhetoric
impv	imperative	*sg*	singular
indecl	indeclinable	*sim*	similarly
indic	indicative	*subj*	subjunctive
inf	informal	*superl*	superlative
infin	infinitive	*THEAT*	theatre
interj	interjection	*UNIV*	university
interrog	interrogative	*usu*	usually
LIT	literature	*vi*	intransitive verb
loc	locative	*voc*	vocative
m	masculine	*vt*	transitive verb
MATH	mathematics		

INTRODUCTION

Whether you are learning Latin for the first time or wish to "brush up" what you learned some time ago, this dictionary is designed to help you understand Latin and to express yourself in Latin, if you so wish.

HOW TO USE THE DICTIONARY

Entries are laid out as follows:

Headword

This is shown in bold type. On the Latin-English side all long vowels are shown by placing a ‾ above them. Latin nouns show the genitive singular form in bold. Latin verbs show the first person singular of the present indicative as the headword, followed by the infinitive, the first person singular of the perfect indicative and usually the past participle, all in bold type:

elegīa, -ae
elementum, -ī
ēlevō, āre
ēmātūrēscō, -ēscere, -uī

Part of Speech

Next comes the part of speech (noun, verb, adjective etc), shown in *italics*. Part of speech abbreviations used in the dictionary are shown in the abbreviations list (*p iv*). Where a word has more than one part of speech, each new part of speech is preceded by a black lozenge (♦). If a Latin headword is a preposition, the case taken by the preposition comes immediately after the part of speech, in *italics* and in brackets.

era, -ae *f*
ticklish *adj*
thunder *n* tonitrus *m* ♦ *vi* tonare, intonare.
ērgā *prep* (*with acc*) towards; against.

Meanings

Where a word or a part of speech has only one meaning, the translation comes immediately after the part of speech. However, many words have more than one meaning. Where the context is likely to show which translation is correct, variations in meaning are simply separated by a semi-colon. But usually there will also be an "indicator" in *italics* and in brackets. Some meanings relate to specific subject areas, for example religion, politics, military matters etc –

v

these indicators are in small italic capitals.

ēnsiger, -ī *adj* with his sword.
toy *n* crepundia *ntpl* ♦ *vi* ludere.
toll collector *n* exactor *m*; portitor *m*.
eō, -īre, īvī *and* **iī, itum** *vi* to go; (*MIL*) to march; (*time*) to pass; (*event*) to proceed, turn out.

Translations

Most words can be translated directly. On the English-Latin side, translations of nouns include the gender of the Latin noun in *italics*. However, sometimes a phrase is needed to show how a word is used, but in some cases a direct translation of a phrase would be meaningless: the symbol ~ in front of a translation shows that the translation is natural English, but does not mean word for word what the Latin means. Sometimes, even an approximate translation would not be very helpful (for place names, for example) – in these cases, an explanation in *italics* is given instead. In other cases, the user will need more information than simply the translation; in these cases, "indicators" are included in the translation(s), giving, for instance, the case required by a Latin verb or preposition or further details about a place or person.

thumb *n* pollex *m*; **have under one's** ~ in potestate sua habere.
elephantomacha, -ae *m fighter mounted on an elephant.*
Erymanthus, -ī *m* mountain range in Arcadia (*where Hercules killed the bear*).
thwart *vt* obstare (*dat*), officere (*dat*).

Pronunciation

Since Latin pronunciation is regular, once the basic rules have been learned (*see pp viii, ix*), the dictionary does not show phonetic transcriptions against each headword, but does show all long vowels.

Other Information

The dictionary also includes:
- a basic grammar section
- information about life in Roman times:
  – how government and the army were organized – how numbers and dates were calculated and expressed – family relationships – geographical names – major Roman authors – key events in Roman history – (*important historical and mythological characters and events are listed within the body of the main text*).
- a section on Latin poetry and scansion
- a list of Latin expressions commonly used in English today

LATIN ALPHABET

The Latin alphabet is the one which has been almost universally adopted by the modern languages of Europe and America. In the Classical period it had 23 letters, namely the English alphabet without letters j, v and w.

Letter v

The symbol v was the capital form of the letter u, but in a later age the small v came into use to represent the consonantal u, and as it is commonly so employed in modern editions of Latin authors, it has been retained as a distinct letter in this dictionary for convenience.

Letter j

The symbol j came to be used as the consonantal i, and is found in older editions of the Classics, but as it has been almost entirely discarded in modern texts, it is not used in this dictionary, and words found spelt with a j must therefore be looked up under i.

Letters w, y, z

The letter w may be seen in the Latinized forms of some modern names, e.g. Westmonasterium Westminster. The letters y and z occur only in words of Greek origin.

ORTHOGRAPHY

Many Latin words which begin with a prefix can be spelled in two ways. The prefix can retain its original spelling, or it can be assimilated, changing a letter depending on the letter which follows it. Compare the following:

ad before g, l, r and p:

adpropinquare	appropinquare
adgredi	aggredi
adloquor	alloquor
adrogans	arrogans

ad is also often assimilated before f and n:

adfectus	affectus
adnexus	annexus

and **ad** is often shortened to a before sc:

adscendere	ascendere

in changes to **il** before l, to **im** before m or p and to **ir** before r.

con becomes **cor** when followed by another r and **col** when followed by l.

We have provided cross-references in the text to draw your attention to the alternative forms of words. Thus, although **arrogantia** does not appear in the Latin-English section, the cross-reference at **arr-** will point you to the entry for **adrogantia**, where the translation is given.

PRONUNCIATION

The ancient pronunciation of Latin has been established with a fair degree of certainty from the evidence of ancient authorities and inscriptions and inferences from the modern Romance languages. It is not possible, of course, to recapture the precise nuances of Classical Latin speech, but what follows is now generally accepted and generally understood as a reasonably accurate guide to the sounds of Latin as spoken by educated Romans during the two centuries from Cicero to Quintilian.

ACCENT

The Latin accent in the Classical period was a weak stress, perhaps with an element of pitch in it. It falls, as in English, on the second last syllable of the word, if that syllable is long, and on the third last syllable if the second last is short. Disyllabic words take the accent on the first syllable, unless they have already lost a final syllable, *e.g.* **illīc(e)**.

Inflected words are commonly learned with the accent wrongly placed on the last syllable, for convenience in memorizing the inflexions. But it is advisable to get the accent as well as the ending right.

The correct accent of other words can easily be found by noting carefully the quantity of the second last syllable and then accenting the word as in English, according to the rule given above. Thus **fuērunt** is accented on the second last syllable because the e is long, whereas **fuerant** is accented on the third last, because the e is short.

VOWELS

Vowels are pure and should not be diphthongized as in certain sounds of Southern English. They may be long or short. Throughout this Dictionary all vowels known or believed by the best authorities to be long are marked with a line above them; those unmarked are either known to be short or of uncertain quantity.

	Short		*Long*	
agricolạ	rạt	rāmus	rạther
hederā	pẹn	avē	pạy
ītaque	kīn	cīvis	kẹen
favọr	rọb	ampliō	rọbe
nebulạ	fụll	lūna	fọol

y is a Greek sound and is pronounced (both short and long) as **u** in French *ie* rụe.

DIPHTHONGS

_ae_stas	tr_y_	
_au_diō	to_w_n	
h_ei_	p_ay_ee	
m_eu_s	_ay-oo_	*with the accent on first sound*
m_oe_cha	t_oy_	
t_ui_tus	L_ou_is	

CONSONANTS

_b_alneae	_b_a_b_y	
a_bs_tēmius	a_ps_e	
su_bt_ractus	a_pt_	
_c_astra	_c_ar	
_ch_orda	sepul_ch_re	
inter_d_o	_d_og	
cōn_f_lō	_f_ortune	
in_g_redior	_g_o	
_h_abeō	_h_and	(*but faintly*)
_i_aceō	_y_es	(*consonantal i = j*)
_K_alendae	oa_k_	
con_g_elō	_l_et	
co_m_es	_m_an	(*final m was hardly sounded and may have simply nasalized the preceding vowel*)
pā_n_is	_n_o	
pa_ng_o	fi_ng_er	
stu_p_eō	a_p_t	
rap_h_anus	_p_ill	
exse_qu_or	_qu_ite	
suprēm_us	_br_ae	(*Scottish*)
mā_gn_us	_s_ister	(*never as in rose*)
lae_t_us	s_t_op	
_th_eātrum	_t_ake	
_v_apor	_w_in	
	(and consonantal u)	
de_x_tra	si_x_	(*ks, not gs*)
_z_ōna	_z_ero	

Double consonants lengthen the sound of the consonant.

Quick Reference Grammar

DECLENSIONS OF NOUNS

1st Declension

mainly f   *m*

SING

Nom.	terra	crambē	Aenēās	Anchīsēs
Voc.	terra	crambē	Aenēā	Anchīsā, -ē
Acc.	terram	crambēn	Aenēam, -ān	Anchīsam, -ēn
Gen.	terrae	crambēs	Aenēae	Anchīsae
Dat.	terrae	crambae	Aenēae	Anchīsae
Abl.	terrā	cramba	Aenēā	Anchīsā

PLURAL

Nom.	terrae	crambae
Voc.	terrae	crambae
Acc.	terrās	crambās
Gen.	terrārum	crambārum
Dat.	terrīs	crambīs
Abl.	terrīs	crambīs

2nd Declension

mainly m

SING

Nom.	modus	Lūcius	Dēlos (f)	puer	liber
Voc.	mode	Lūcī	Dēle	puer	liber
Acc.	modum	Lūcium	Dēlon	puerum	librum
Gen.	modī	Lūcī	Dēlī	puerī	librī
Dat.	modō	Lūciō	Dēlō	puerō	librō
Abl.	modō	Lūciō	Dēlō	puerō	librō

PLURAL

Nom.	modī	puerī	librī
Voc.	modī	puerī	librī
Acc.	modōs	puerōs	librōs
Gen.	modōrum	puerōrum	librōrum
Dat.	modīs	puerīs	librīs
Abl.	modīs	puerīs	librīs

nt

	SING
Nom.	dōnum
Voc.	dōnum
Acc.	dōnum
Gen.	dōnī
Dat.	dōnō
Abl.	dōnō

	PLURAL
Nom.	dōna
Voc.	dōna
Acc.	dōna
Gen.	dōnōrum
Dat.	dōnīs
Abl.	dōnīs

3rd Declension

Group I: *Vowel stems, with gen pl in* -ium

	m and f		*nt*	
SING				
Nom.	clādēs	nāvis	rēte	animal
Voc.	clādēs	nāvis	rēte	animal
Acc.	clādem	nāvem, -im	rēte	animal
Gen.	clādis	nāvis	rētis	animālīs
Dat.	clādī	nāvī	rētī	animālī
Abl.	clāde	nāve, -ī	rētī	animālī
PLURAL				
Nom.	clādēs	nāvēs	rētia	animālia
Voc.	clādēs	nāvēs	rētia	animālia
Acc.	clādēs, -īs	nāvēs, -īs	rētia	animālia
Gen.	clādium	nāvium	rētium	animālium
Dat.	clādibus	nāvibus	rētibus	animālibus
Abl.	clādibus	nāvibus	rētibus	animālibus

Group II: *Consonant stems, some with gen pl in* -ium, *some in* -um *and some in either. Monosyllabic nouns ending in two consonants (e.g.* **urbs** *below) regularly have* -ium.

	m and f			*f*	*nt*
SING					
Nom.	urbs	amāns	laus	aetās	os
Voc.	urbs	amāns	laus	aetās	os
Acc.	urbem	amantem	laudem	aetātem	os
Gen.	urbis	amantis	laudis	aetātis	ossis
Dat.	urbī	amantī	laudī	aetātī	ossī
Abl.	urbe	amante	laude	aetāte	osse
PLURAL					
Nom.	urbēs	amantēs	laudēs	aetātēs	ossa
Voc.	urbēs	amantēs	laudēs	aetātēs	ossa

Acc.	urbēs	amantēs	laudēs	aetātēs	ossa
Gen.	urbium	amantium,	laudum,	aetātum,	ossium
		-um	-ium	-ium	
Dat.	urbibus	amantibus	laudibus	aetātibus	ossibus
Abl.	urbibus	amantibus	laudibus	aetātibus	ossibus

Group III: *Consonant stems, with gen pl in* **-um**

		m and f			nt	
SING						
Nom.	mōs	ratiō	pater	nōmen	opus
Voc.	mōs	ratiō	pater	nōmen	opus
Acc.	mōrem	ratiōnem	patrem	nōmen	opus
Gen.	mōris	ratiōnis	patris	nōminis	operis
Dat.	mōrī	ratiōnī	patrī	nōminī	operī
Abl.	mōre	ratiōne	patre	nōmine	opere
PLURAL						
Nom.	mōrēs	ratiōnēs	patrēs	nōmina	opera
Voc.	mōrēs	ratiōnēs	patrēs	nōmina	opera
Acc.	mōrēs	ratiōnēs	patrēs	nōmina	opera
Gen.	mōrum	ratiōnum	patrum	nōminum	operum
Dat.	mōribus	ratiōnibus	patribus	nōminibus	operibus
Abl.	mōribus	ratiōnibus	patribus	nōminibus	operibus

Group IV: *Greek nouns*

	m		f	nt
SING				
Nom.	āēr	hērōs	Periclēs	Naias	poēma
Voc.	āēr	hērōs	Periclē	Naias	poēma
Acc.	āera	hērōa	Periclem,	Naiada	poēma
			Periclea		
Gen.	āeris	hērōis	Periclis, -ī	Naiadis, -os	poēmatis
Dat.	āerī	hērōī	Periclī	Naiadī	poēmatī
Abl.	āere	hērōe	Periclē	Naiade	poēmate
PLURAL					
Nom.	āeres	hērōes		Naiades	poēmata
Voc.	āeres	hērōes		Naiades	poēmata
Acc.	āeras	hērōas		Naiadas	poēmata
Gen.	āerum	hērōum		Naiadum	poēmatōrum
Dat.	āeribus	hērōibus		Naiadibus	poēmatīs
Abl.	āeribus	hērōibus		Naiadibus	poēmatīs

	4th Declension		5th Declension	
	mainly m	*nt*	*mainly f*	
SING				
Nom.	portus	genū	diēs	rēs
Voc.	portus	genū	diēs	rēs
Acc.	portum	genū	diem	rem
Gen.	portūs	genūs	diēī	reī
Dat.	portuī	genū	diēī	reī
Abl.	portū	genū	diē	rē
PLURAL				
Nom.	portūs	genua	diēs	rēs
Voc.	portūs	genua	diēs	rēs
Acc.	portūs	genua	diēs	rēs
Gen.	portuum	genuum	diērum	rērum
Dat.	portibus, -ubus	genibus, -ubus	diēbus	rēbus
Abl.	portibus, -ubus	genibus, -ubus	diēbus	rēbus

CONJUGATIONS OF VERBS

ACTIVE

PRESENT TENSE

	First parāre *prepare*	Second habēre *have*	Third sūmere *take*	Fourth audīre *hear*
Indicative				
SING				
1st pers	parō	habeō	sūmō	audiō
2nd pers	parās	habēs	sūmis	audīs
3rd pers	parat	habet	sūmit	audit
PLURAL				
1st pers	parāmus	habēmus	sūmimus	audīmus
2nd pers	parātis	habētis	sūmitis	audītīs
3rd pers	parant	habent	sūmunt	audiunt
Subjunctive				
SING				
1st pers	parem	habeam	sūmam	audiam
2nd pers	parēs	habeās	sūmās	audiās
3rd pers	paret	habeat	sūmat	audiat
PLURAL				
1st pers	parēmus	habeāmus	sūmāmus	audiāmus
2nd pers	parētis	habeātis	sūmātis	audiātis
3rd pers	parent	habeant	sūmant	audiant

xvii

IMPERFECT TENSE
Indicative

SING				
1st pers	parābam	habēbam	sūmēbam	audiēbam
2nd pers	parābās	habēbās	sūmēbās	audiēbās
3rd pers	parābat	habēbat	sūmēbat	audiēbat
PLURAL				
1st pers	parābāmus	habēbāmus	sūmēbāmus	audiēbāmus
2nd pers	parābātis	habēbātis	sūmēbātis	audiēbātis
3rd pers	parābant	habēbant	sūmēbant	audiēbant

Subjunctive

SING				
1st pers	parārem	habērem	sūmerem	audīrem
2nd pers	parārēs	habērēs	sūmerēs	audīrēs
3rd pers	parāret	habēret	sūmeret	audīret
PLURAL				
1st pers	parārēmus	habērēmus	sūmerēmus	audīrēmus
2nd pers	parārētis	habērētis	sūmerētis	audīrētis
3rd pers	parārent	habērent	sūmerent	audīrent

FUTURE TENSE
Indicative

SING				
1st pers	parābō	habēbō	sūmam	audiam
2nd pers	parābis	habēbis	sūmēs	audiēs
3rd pers	parābit	habēbit	sūmet	audiet
PLURAL				
1st pers	parābimus	habēbimus	sūmēmus	audiēmus
2nd pers	parābitis	habēbitis	sūmētis	audiētis
3rd pers	parābunt	habēbunt	sūment	audient

Subjunctive

SING

parātūrus, -a, -um		
habitūrus, -a, -um	sim	*or* essem
sūmptūrus, -a, -um	sīs	essēs
audītūrus, -a, -um	sit	esset

PLURAL

parātūrī, -ae, -a		
habitūrī, -ae, -a	simus	*or* essēmus
sūmptūrī, -ae, -a	sītis	essētis
audītūrī, -ae, -a	sint	essent

PERFECT TENSE
Indicative

SING

1st pers	parāvī	habuī	sūmpsī	audīvī
2nd pers	parāvistī	habuistī	sūmpsistī	audīvistī
3rd pers	parāvit	habuit	sūmpsit	audīvit

PLURAL

1st pers	parāvimus	habuimus	sūmpsimus	audīvimus
2nd pers	parāvistis	habuistis	sūmpsistis	audīvistis
3rd pers	parāvērunt, -e	habuērunt, -e	sūmpsērunt, -e	audīvērunt, -e

Subjunctive

SING

1st pers	parāverim	habuerim	sūmpserim	audīverim
2nd pers	parāveris	habueris	sūmpseris	audīveris
3rd pers	parāverit	habuerit	sūmpserit	audīverit

PLURAL

1st pers	parāverimus	habuerimus	sūmpserimus	audīverimus
2nd pers	parāveritis	habueritis	sūmpseritis	audīveritis
3rd pers	parāverint	habuerint	sūmpserint	audīverint

PLUPERFECT TENSE
Indicative

SING

1st pers	parāveram	habueram	sūmpseram	audīveram
2nd pers	parāverās	habuerās	sūmpserās	audīverās
3rd pers	parāverat	habuerat	sūmpserat	audīverat

PLURAL

1st pers	parāverāmus	habuerāmus	sūmpserāmus	audīverāmus
2nd pers	parāverātis	habuerātis	sūmpserātis	audīverātis
3rd pers	parāverant	habuerant	sūmpserant	audīverant

Subjunctive

SING

1st pers	parāvissem	habuissem	sūmpsissem	audīvissem
2nd pers	parāvissēs	habuissēs	sūmpsissēs	audīvissēs
3rd pers	parāvisset	habuisset	sūmpsisset	audīvisset

PLURAL

1st pers	parāvissēmus	habuissēmus	sūmpsissēmus	audīvissēmus
2nd pers	parāvissētis	habuissētis	sūmpsissētis	audīvissētis
3rd pers	parāvissent	habuissent	sūmpsissent	audīvissent

FUTURE PERFECT TENSE
Indicative

SING				
1st pers	parāverō	habuerō	sūmpserō	audīverō
2nd pers	parāveris	habueris	sūmpseris	audīveris
3rd pers	parāverit	habuerit	sūmpserit	audīverit
PLURAL				
1st pers	parāverimus	habuerimus	sūmpserimus	audīverimus
2nd pers	parāveritis	habueritis	sūmpseritis	audīveritis
3rd pers	parāverint	habuerint	sūmpserint	audīverint

IMPERATIVE
Present

SING	parā	habē	sūme	audī
PLURAL	parāte	habēte	sūmite	audīte

Future

SING				
2nd pers	parātō	habētō	sūmitō	audītō
3rd pers	parātō	habētō	sūmitō	audītō
PLURAL				
2nd pers	parātōte	habētōte	sūmitōte	audītōte
3rd pers	parantō	habentō	sūmuntō	audiuntō

INFINITIVE
Present

parāre	habēre	sūmere	audīre

Perfect

parāvisse	habuisse	sūmpsisse	audīvisse

Future

parātūrus,	-a, -um, esse
habitūrus,	-a, -um, esse
sūmptūrus,	-a, -um, esse
audītūrus,	-a, -um, esse

PASSIVE

PRESENT TENSE
Indicative

SING				
1st pers	paror	habeor	sūmor	audior
2nd pers	parāris	habēris	sūmeris	audīris
3rd pers	parātur	habētur	sūmitur	audītur
PLURAL				
1st pers	parāmur	habēmur	sūmimur	audīmur
2nd pers	parāminī	habēminī	sūmiminī	audīminī
3rd pers	parantur	habentur	sūmuntur	audiuntur

Subjunctive

SING				
1st pers	parer	habear	sūmar	audiar
2nd pers	parēris	habeāris	sūmāris	audiāris
3rd pers	parētur	habeātur	sūmātur	audiātur
PLURAL				
1st pers	parēmur	habeāmur	sūmāmur	audiāmur
2nd pers	parēminī	habeāminī	sūmāminī	audiāminī
3rd pers	parentur	habeantur	sūmantur	audiantur

IMPERFECT TENSE
Indicative

SING				
1st pers	parābar	habēbar	sūmēbar	audiēbar
2nd pers	parābāris	habēbāris	sūmēbāris	audiēbāris
3rd pers	parābātur	habēbātur	sūmēbātur	audiēbātur
PLURAL				
1st pers	parābāmur	habēbāmur	sūmēbāmur	audiēbāmur
2nd pers	parābāmini	habēbāmini	sūmēbāminī	audiēbāminī
3rd pers	parābārtur	habēbantur	sūmēbantur	audiēbantur

Subjunctive

SING				
1st pers	parārer	habērer	sūmerer	audīrer
2nd pers	parārēris	habērēris	sūmerēris	audīrēris
3rd pers	parārētur	habērētur	sūmerētur	audīrētur

PLURAL				
1st pers	parārēmur	habērēmur	sūmerēmur	audīrēmur
2nd pers	parārēminī	habērēminī	sūmerēminī	audīrēminī
3rd pers	parārentur	habērentur	sūmerentur	audīrentur

FUTURE TENSE

Indicative

SING				
1st pers	parābor	habēbor	sūmar	audiar
2nd pers	parāberis	habēberis	sūmeris	audiēris
3rd pers	parābitur	habēbitur	sūmetur	audiētur

PLURAL				
1st pers	parābimur	habēbimur	sūmemur	audiēmur
2nd pers	parābiminī	habēbiminī	sūmeminī	audiēminī
3rd pers	parābuntur	habēbuntur	sūmentur	audientur

PERFECT TENSE

Indicative

SING		PLURAL	
parātus, -a, -um	sum/es/est	parātī, -ae, -a	sumus/estis/sunt
habitus, -a, -um	sum/es/est	habitī, -ae, -a	sumus/estis/sunt
sūmptus, -a, -um	sum/es/est	sūmptī, -ae, -a	sumus/estis/sunt
audītus, -a, -um	sum/es/est	audītī, -ae, -a	sumus/estis/sunt

Subjunctive

SING		PLURAL	
parātus, -a, -um	sim/sīs/sit	parātī, -ae, -a	sīmus/sītis/sint
habitus, -a, -um	sim/sīs/sit	habitī, -ae, -a	sīmus/sītis/sint
sūmptus, -a, -um	sim/sīs/sit	sūmptī, -ae, -a	sīmus/sītis/sint
audītus, -a, -um	sim/sīs/sit	audītī, -ae, -a	sīmus/sītis/sint

PLUPERFECT TENSE

Indicative

SING		PLURAL	
parātus, -a, -um	eram/eras/erat	parātī, -ae, -a	eramus/eratis/erant
habitus, -a, -um	eram/eras/erat	habitī, -ae, -a	eramus/eratis/erant
sūmptus, -a, -um	eram/eras/erat	sūmptī, -ae, -a	eramus/eratis/erant
audītus, -a, -um	eram/eras/erat	audītī, -ae, -a	eramus/eratis/erant

Subjunctive

SING		PLURAL
parātus, -a, -um	essem/essēs/esset	parātī, -ae, -a essēmus/essētis/essent
habitus, -a, -um	essem/essēs/esset	habītī, -ae, -a essēmus/essētis/essent
sūmptus, -a, -um	essem/essēs/esset	sūmptī, -ae, -a essēmus/essētis/essent
audītus, -a, -um	essem/essēs/esset	audītī, -ae, -a essēmus/essētis/essent

FUTURE PERFECT TENSE

Indicative

SING		PLURAL
parātus, -a, -um	erō/eris/erit	parātī, -ae, -a erimus/eritis/erunt
habitus, -a, -um	erō/eris/erit	habītī, -ae, -a erimus/eritis/erunt
sūmptus, -a, -um	erō/eris/erit	sūmptī, -ae, -a erimus/eritis/erunt
audītus, -a, -um	erō/eris/erit	audītī, -ae, -a erimus/eritis/erunt

IMPERATIVE

Present

SING	parāre	habēre	sūmere	audīre
PLURAL	parāminī	habēminī	sūmiminī	audīminī

Future

SING				
2nd pers	parātor	habētor	sūmitor	audītor
3rd pers	parātor	habētor	sūmitor	audītor
PLURAL				
3rd pers	parantor	habentor	sūmuntor	audiuntor

INFINITIVE

Present

parārī	habērī	sūmī	audīrī

Perfect

parātus -a, -um, esse	habitus -a, -um, esse	sūmptus -a, -um, esse	audītus, -a, -um, esse

Future

parātum īrī	habitum īrī	sūmptum īrī	audītum īrī

VERBAL NOUNS AND ADJECTIVES

Present Participle Active

parāns	habēns	sūmēns	audiēns

Perfect Participle Passive

parātus	habitus	sūmptus	audītus

Future Participle Active

parātūrus	habitūrus	sūmptūrus	audītūrus

Gerund
(acc, gen, dat and abl)

parandum, -ī, -ō	habendum, -ī, -ō	sūmendum, -ī, -ō	audiendum, -ī, -ō

Gerundive

parandus	habendus	sūmendus	audiendus

Supines

1st	parātum	habitum	sūmptum	audītum
2nd	parātū	habitū	sūmptū	audītū

Note. *Some verbs of the 3rd conjugation have the present indicative ending in -io; e.g.* **capio,** *I capture.*

PRESENT TENSE

INDICATIVE		SUBJUNCTIVE	
Active	**Passive**	**Active**	**Passive**
capio	capior	capiam	capiar
capis	caperis	capias	capiāris
capit	capitur	capiat	capiātur
capimus	capimur	capiāmus	capiāmur
capitis	capiminī	capiātis	capiāminī
capiunt	capiuntur	capiant	capiantur

IMPERFECT TENSE

capiēbam *etc.*	capiēbar *etc.*	caperem *etc.*	caperer *etc.*

FUTURE TENSE

capiam	capiar
capiēs *etc.*	capiēris *etc.*

INFINITIVE MOOD

Present Active	capere
Present Passive	capī

PRESENT IMPERATIVE

	Active		Passive
cape	capite	capere	capiminī

	PARTICIPLE	*GERUND*	*GERUNDIVE*
Pres.	capiēns	capiendum	capiendus, -a, um

In all other tenses and moods **capere** *is similar to* **sumere.**

IRREGULAR VERBS

	Esse *be*	**Posse** *be able*	**Velle** *wish*	**Ire** *go*
		Present Indicative		
SING				
1st Pers	sum	possum	volō	eō
2nd Pers	es	potes	vīs	īs
3rd Pers	est	potest	vult, volt	it
PLURAL				
1st Pers	sumus	possumus	volumus	īmus
2nd Pers	estis	potestis	vultis, voltis	ītis
3rd Pers	sunt	possunt	volunt	eunt
		Present Subjunctive		
SING				
1st Pers	sim	possim	velim	eam
2nd Pers	sīs	possīs	velīs	eās
3rd Pers	sit	possit	velit	eat
PLURAL				
1st Pers	sīmus	possīmus	velīmus	eāmus
2nd Pers	sītis	possītis	velītis	eātis
3rd Pers	sint	possint	velint	eant
		Imperfect Indicative		
1st Pers	eram	poteram	volēbam	ībam
		Imperfect Subjunctive		
1st Pers	essem	possem	vellem	īrem
		Future Indicative		
1st Pers	erō	poterō	volam	ībō
		Future Subjunctive		
1st Pers	futūrus, -a, -um sim *or* essem	—	—	itūrus, -a, -um sim *or* essem
		Perfect Indicative		
1st Pers	fuī	potuī	voluī	īvī, iī
		Perfect Subjunctive		
1st Pers	fuerim	potuerim	voluerim	īverim, ierim

Pluperfect Indicative

| 1st Pers | fueram | potueram | volueram | īveram, ieram |

Pluperfect Subjunctive

| 1st Pers | fuissem | potuissem | voluissem | īvissem, iissem |

Future Perfect Indicative

| 1st Pers | fuerō | potuerō | voluerō | īverō, ierō |

Present Imperative

| SING | es | — | — | ī |
| PLURAL | este | — | — | īte |

Future Imperative

| SING | estō | — | — | ītō |
| PLURAL | estōte | — | — | ītōte |

Infinitives

PRES	esse	posse	velle	īre
PERF	fuisse	potuisse	voluisse	īvisse, iisse
FUT	futūrus, -a, -um, esse	—	—	itūrus, -a, -um, esse

Participles

| PRES | — | — | — | iēns, euntis |
| FUT | futūrus | — | — | itūrus |

Gerund and Supine

| GERUND | — | — | — | eundum |
| SUPINE | — | — | — | itum |

Latin-English

A, a

ā *prep (with abl)* from; after, since; by, in respect of; **ab epistulīs, ā manū** secretary; **ab hāc parte** on this side; **ab integrō** afresh; **ā nōbīs** on our side; **ā tergō** in the rear; **cōpiōsus ā frūmentō** rich in corn; **usque ab** ever since.

ā *interj* ah!

ab *prep see* **ā**.

abāctus *ppp of* **abigō**.

abacus, -ī *m* tray; sideboard; gaming board; panel; counting table.

abaliēnō, -āre, -āvī, -ātum *vt* to dispose of; to remove, estrange.

Abantiadēs *m* Acrisius *or* Perseus.

Abās, -antis *m a king of Argos*.

abavus, -ī *m* great-great-grandfather.

abbās, -ātis *m* abbot.

abbātia *f* abbey.

abbātissa *f* abbess.

Abdēra, -ōrum *or* **-ae** *ntpl or f a town in Thrace*.

Abdērītānus *adj see n.*

Abdērītēs *m* Democritus *or* Protagoras.

abdicātiō, -ōnis *f* disowning, abdication.

abdicō, -āre, -āvī, -ātum *vt* to disown; to resign; **sē ~** abdicate

abdīcō, -īcere, -īxī, -ictum *vt (*of omens*)* to be unfavourable to.

abditus *ppp of* **abdō**.

abdō, -ere, -idī, -itum *vt* to hide; to remove.

abdōmen, -inis *nt* paunch, belly; gluttony.

abdūcō, -ūcere, -ūxī, -uctum *vt* to lead away, take away; to seduce.

abductus *ppp of* **abdūcō**.

abecedārium, -iī *nt* alphabet.

abēgī *perf of* **abigō**.

abeō, -īre, -iī, -itum *vt* to go away, depart; to pass away; to be changed; to retire *(from an office)*; **sīc ~** turn out like this.

abequitō, -āre, -āvī, -ātum *vt* to ride away.

aberrātiō, -ōnis *f* relief *(from trouble)*.

aberrō, -āre, -āvī, -ātum *vt* to stray; to deviate; to have respite.

abfore *fut infin of* **absum**.

abfuī *perf of* **absum**.

abfutūrus *fut p of* **absum**.

abhinc *adv* since, ago.

abhorreō, -ēre, -uī *vi* to shrink from; to differ; to be inconsistent.

abiciō, -icere, -iēcī, -iectum *vt* to throw away, throw down; to abandon, degrade.

abiectus *ppp of* **abiciō** ♦ *adj* despondent; contemptible.

abiēgnus *adj* of fir.

abiēns, -euntis *pres p of* **abeō**.

abiēs, -etis *f* fir; ship.

abigō, -igere, -ēgī, -āctum *vt* to drive away.

abitus, -ūs *m* departure; exit.

abiūdicō, -āre, -āvī, -ātum *vt* to take away *(by judicial award)*.

abiūnctus *ppp of* **abiungō**.

abiungō, -ungere, -ūnxī, -ūnctum *vt* to unyoke; to detach.

abiūrō, -āre, -āvī, -ātum *vt* to deny on oath.

ablātus *ppp of* **auferō**.

ablēgātiō, -ōnis *f* sending away.

ablēgō, -āre, -āvī, -ātum *vt* to send out of the way.

abligurriō, -īre, -īvī, -ītum *vt* to spend extravagantly.

ablocō, -āre, -āvī, -ātum *vt* to let (a house).

ablūdō, -dere, -sī, -sum *vi* to be unlike.

abluō, -uere, -uī, -ūtum *vt* to wash clean; to remove.

abnegō, -āre, -āvī, -ātum *vt* to refuse.

abnepōs, -ōtis *m* great-great-grandson.

abneptis *f* great-great-granddaughter.

abnoctō, -āre *vi* to stay out all night.

abnōrmis *adj* unorthodox.

abnuō, -uere, -uī, -ūtum *vt* to refuse; to deny.

aboleō, -ēre, -ēvī, -itum *vt* to abolish.

abolēscō, -ēscere, -ēvī *vi* to vanish.

abolitiō, -ōnis *f* cancelling.

abolla, -ae *f* greatcoat.

abōminātus *adj* accursed.

abōminor, -ārī, -ātus *vt* to deprecate; to detest.

Aborīginēs, -um *mpl* original inhabitants.

aborior, -īrī, -tus *vi* to miscarry.

abortiō, -ōnis *f* miscarriage.

abortīvus *adj* born prematurely.

abortus, -ūs *m* miscarriage.

abrādō, -dere, -sī, -sum *vt* to scrape off, shave.

abrāsus *ppp of* **abrādō**.

abreptus *ppp of* **abripiō**.

abripiō, -ipere, -ipuī, -eptum *vt* to drag away, carry off.

Noun declensions and verb conjugations are shown on pp xiii to xxv. The present infinitive ending of a verb shows to which conjugation it belongs -**āre** = 1st; -**ēre** = 2nd; -**ere** = 3rd and -**īre** = 4th. Irregular verbs are shown on p xxvi

abrogātiō, -ōnis f repeal.
abrogō, -āre, -āvī, -ātum vt to annul.
abrotonum, -ī nt southernwood.
abrumpō, -umpere, -ūpī, -uptum vt to break off.
abruptus ppp of **abrumpō** ♦ adj steep; abrupt, disconnected.
abs etc see **ā**.
abscēdō, -ēdere, -essi, -essum vi to depart, withdraw; to cease.
abscīdō, -dere, -dī, -sum vt to cut off.
abscindō, -ndere, -dī, -ssum vt to tear off, cut off.
abscissus ppp of **abscindō**.
abscīsus ppp of **abscīdō** ♦ adj steep; abrupt.
abscondō, -ere, -ī and **idī, -itum** vt to conceal; to leave behind.
absēns, -entis pres p of **absum** ♦ adj absent.
absentia, -ae f absence.
absiliō, -īre, -iī and **uī** vi to spring away.
absimilis adj unlike.
absinthium, -ī and **iī** nt wormwood.
absis, -īdis f vault; (ECCL) chancel.
absistō, -istere, -titī vi to come away; to desist.
absolūte adv fully, unrestrictedly.
absolūtiō, -ōnis f acquittal; perfection.
absolūtus ppp of **absolvō** ♦ adj complete; (RHET) unqualified.
absolvō, -vere, -vī, -ūtum vt to release, set free; (law) to acquit; to bring to completion, finish off; to pay off, discharge.
absonus adj unmusical; incongruous; ~ **ab** not in keeping with.
absorbeō, -bēre, -buī, -ptum vt to swallow up; to monopolize.
absp- etc see **asp-**.
absque prep (with abl) without, but for.
abstēmius adj temperate.
abstergeō, -gēre, -sī, -sum vt to wipe away; (fig) to banish.
absterreō, -ēre, -ui, -itum vt to scare away, deter.
abstinēns, -entis adj continent.
abstinenter adv with restraint.
abstinentia, -ae f restraint, self-control; fasting.
abstineō, -inēre, -inuī, -entum vt to withhold, keep off ♦ vi to abstain, refrain; **sē** ~ refrain.
abstitī perf of **absistō**.
abstō, -āre vi to stand aloof.
abstractus ppp of **abstrahō**.
abstrahō, -here, -xī, -ctum vt to drag away, remove; to divert.
abstrūdō, -dere, -sī, -sum vt to conceal.
abstrūsus ppp of **abstrūdō** ♦ adj deep, abstruse; reserved.
abstulī perf of **auferō**.
absum, abesse, āfuī vi to be away, absent, distant; to keep clear of; to be different; to be missing, fail to assist; **tantum abest ut** so far from; **haud multum āfuit quīn** I was (they

were etc) within an ace of.
absūmō, -ere, -psī, -ptum vt to consume; to ruin, kill; (time) to spend.
absurdē adv out of tune; absurdly.
absurdus adj unmusical; senseless, absurd.
Absyrtus, -ī m brother of Medea.
abundāns, -antis adj overflowing; abundant; rich; abounding in.
abundanter adv copiously.
abundantia, -ae f abundance, plenty; wealth.
abundē adv abundantly, more than enough.
abundō, -āre, -āvī, -ātum vi to overflow; to abound, be rich in.
abūsiō, -ōnis f (RHET) catachresis.
abusque prep (with abl) all the way from.
abūtor, -tī, -sus vi (with abl) to use up; to misuse.
Abȳdēnus adj see n.
Abȳdos, Abȳdus, -ī m a town on Dardanelles.
ac etc see **atque**.
Acadēmia, -ae f Plato's Academy at Athens; Plato's philosophy; Cicero's villa.
Acadēmica ntpl Cicero's book on the Academic philosophy.
Acadēmus, -ī m an Athenian hero.
acalanthis, -dis f thistlefinch.
acanthus, -ī m bear's-breech.
Acarnānes, -um mpl the Acarnanians.
Acarnānia, -iae f a district of N.W. Greece.
Acarnānicus adj see n.
Acca Lārentia, -ae, -ae f Roman goddess.
accēdō, -ēdere, -essī, -essum vi to come, go to, approach; to attack; to be added; to agree with; (duty) to take up; **ad rem pūblicam** ~ to enter politics; **prope** ~ **ad** to resemble; **~ēdit quod, hūc ~ēdit ut** moreover.
accelerō, -āre, -āvī, -ātum vt, vi to hasten.
accendō, -endere, -endī, -ēnsum vt to set on fire, light; to illuminate; (fig) to inflame, incite.
accēnseō, -ēre, -uī, -um vt to assign.
accēnsī mpl (MIL) supernumeraries.
accēnsus ppp of **accendō** and **accēnseō**.
accēnsus, -ī m officer attending a magistrate.
accentus, -ūs m accent.
accēpī perf of **accipiō**.
acceptiō, -ōnis f receiving.
acceptum nt credit side (of ledger); **in** ~ **referre** place to one's credit.
acceptus ppp of **accipiō** ♦ adj acceptable.
accersō etc see **arcessō**.
accessiō, -ōnis f coming, visiting; attack; increase, addition.
accessus, -ūs m approach, visit; flood tide; admittance, entrance.
Acciānus adj see **Accius**.
accīdō, -dere, -dī, -sum vt to fell, cut into; to eat up, impair.
accidō, -ere, -ī vi to fall (at, on); (senses) to strike; (usu misfortune) to befall, happen.
accingō, -gere, -xī, -ctum vt to gird on, arm; (fig) to make ready.
acciō, -īre, -īvī, -ītum vt to summon; to

procure.
accipiō, -ipere, -ēpī, -eptum vt to take,
receive, accept; (guest) to treat; (information)
to hear; to interpret, take as; to suffer; to
approve.
accipiter, -ris m hawk.
accīsus ppp of **accīdō**.
accītus ppp of **acciō**.
accītus, -ūs m summons.
Accius, -ī m Roman tragic poet.
acclāmātiō, -ōnis f shout (of approval or
disapproval).
acclāmō, -āre, -āvī, -ātum vi to cry out
against; to hail.
acclārō, -āre, -āvī, -ātum vt to make known.
acclinātus adj sloping.
acclīnis adj leaning against; inclined.
acclīnō, -āre, -āvī, -ātum vt to lean against;
sē ~ incline towards.
acclīvis adj uphill.
acclīvitās, -ātis f gradient.
accola, -ae m neighbour.
accolō, -olere, -oluī, -ultum vt to live near.
accommodātē adv suitably.
accommodātiō, -ōnis f fitting together;
compliance.
accommodātus adj suited.
accommodō, -āre, -āvī, -ātum vt to fit, put
on; to adjust, adapt, bring to; to apply; **sē ~**
devote oneself.
accommodus adj suitable.
accrēdō, -ere, -idī, -itum v to believe.
accrēscō, -ēscere, -ēvī, -ētum vi to increase,
be added.
accrētiō, -ōnis f increasing.
accubitiō, -ōnis f reclining (at meals).
accubō, -āre vi to lie near; to recline (at
meals).
accumbō, -mbere, -buī, -bitum vi to recline
at table; **in sinū ~ sit** next to.
accumulātē adv copiously.
accumulō, -āre, -āvī, -ātum vt to pile up,
amass; to load.
accūrātē adv painstakingly.
accūrātiō, -ōnis f exactness.
accūrātus adj studied.
accūrō, -āre, -āvī, -ātum v to attend to.
accurrō, -rrere, -currī and **rrī, -rsum** vi to
hurry to.
accursus, -ūs m hurrying.
accūsābilis adj reprehensible.
accūsātiō, -ōnis f accusation.
accūsātor, -ōris m accuser, prosecutor.
accūsātōriē adv like an accuser.
accūsātōrius adj of the accuser.
accūsō, -āre, -āvī, -ātum vt to accuse,
prosecute; to reproach; **ambitūs ~** prosecute
for bribery.
acer, -is nt maple.
ācer, -ris adj sharp; (sensation) keen, pungent;

(emotion) violent; (mind) shrewd; (conduct)
eager, brave; hasty, fierce; (circumstances)
severe.
acerbē adv see **acerbus**.
acerbitās, -ātis f bitterness; (fig) harshness,
severity; sorrow.
acerbō, -āre, -āvī, -ātum vt to aggravate.
acerbus adj bitter, sour; harsh; (fig)
premature; (person) rough, morose, violent;
(things) troublesome, sad.
acernus adj of maple.
acerra, -ae f incense box.
acervātim adv in heaps.
acervō, -āre, -āvī, -ātum vt to pile up.
acervus, -ī m heap.
acēscō, -ere, acuī vt to turn sour.
Acestēs, -ae m a mythical Sicilian.
acētum, -ī nt vinegar; (fig) wit.
Achaemenēs, -is m first Persian king; type of
Oriental wealth.
Achaeus adj Greek.
Achāia, -ae f a district in W. Greece; Greece;
Roman province.
Achāicus adj see n.
Achātēs, -ae m companion of Aeneas.
Achelōius adj see n.
Achelōus, -ī m river in N.W. Greece; river god.
Acherōn, -ontis m river in Hades.
Acherūsius adj see **Acherōn**.
Achillēs, -is m Greek epic hero.
Achillēus adj see n.
Achīvus adj Greek.
Acidalia, -ae f Venus.
Acidālius adj see n.
acidus adj sour, tart; (fig) disagreeable.
aciēs, -ēī f sharp edge or point; (eye) sight,
keen glance, pupil; (mind) power,
apprehension; (ML) line of troops, battle
order, army, battle; (fig) debate; **prīma ~**
van; **novissima ~** rearguard.
acīnacēs, -is m scimitar.
acinum, -ī nt berry, grape; fruit seed.
acinus, -ī m berry, grape; fruit seed.
acipēnser, -eris m sturgeon.
acipēnsis, -is m sturgeon.
aclys, -dis f javelin.
aconītum, -ī nt monkshood; poison.
acor, -ōris m sour taste.
acquiēscō, -ēscere, -ēvī, -ētum vi to rest,
die; to find pleasure (in); to acquiesce.
acquīrō, -rere, -sīvī, -sītum vt to get in
addition, acquire.
Acragās, -antis m see **Agrigentum**.
acrātophorum, -ī nt wine jar.
acrēdula, -ae f a bird (unidentified).
ācriculus adj peevish.
ācrimōnia, -ae f pungent taste; (speech,
action) briskness, go.
Acrisiōniadēs, -ae m Perseus.
Acrisius, -ī m father of Danae.

ācriter _adv see_ **ācer.**
ācroāma, -tis _nt_ entertainment, entertainer.
ācroāsis, -is _f_ public lecture.
Ācroceraunia, -ōrum _ntpl_ a promontory in
N.W. Greece.
Ācrocorinthus, -ī _f_ fortress of Corinth.
acta, -ae _f_ beach.
ācta, -ōrum _ntpl_ public records, proceedings;
~ **diurna,** ~ **pūblica** daily gazette.
Actaeus _adj_ Athenian.
āctiō, -ōnis _f_ action, doing; official duties,
negotiations; (_law_) action, suit, indictment,
pleading, case, trial; (_RHET_) delivery; (_drama_)
plot; ~ **grātiārum** expression of thanks;
~**ōnem intendere, īnstituere** bring an action.
āctitō, -āre, -āvī, -ātum _vt_ to plead, act often.
Actium, -ī _and_ **ī ī** _nt_ a town in N.W. Greece;
Augustus's great victory.
Actius, -iacus _adj see n._
āctivus _adj_ of action, practical.
āctor, -ōris _m_ driver, performer; (_law_)
plaintiff, pleader; (_COMM_) agent; (_RHET_) orator;
(_drama_) actor; ~ **pūblicus** manager of public
property; ~ **summārum** cashier.
āctuāria _f_ pinnace.
āctuāriolum, -ī _m_ small barge.
āctuārius _adj_ fast (ship).
āctuōsē _adv_ actively.
āctuōsus _adj_ very active.
āctus _ppp of_ **agō.**
āctus, -ūs _m_ moving, driving; right of way for
cattle _or_ vehicles; performance; (_drama_)
playing a part, recital, act of a play.
āctūtum _adv_ immediately.
acuī _perf of_ **acēscō;** _perf of_ **acuō.**
acula, -ae _f_ small stream.
aculeātus _adj_ prickly; (_words_) stinging;
quibbling.
aculeus, -ī _m_ sting, prickle barb; (_fig_) sting.
acūmen, -inis _nt_ point, sting; (_fig_)
shrewdness, ingenuity; trickery.
acuō, -uere, -uī, -ūtum _vt_ to sharpen; to
exercise; (_the mind_) to stimulate; to rouse (to
action).
acus, -ūs _f_ needle, pin; **acū pingere**
embroider; **rem acū tangere** = _hit the nail on
the head._
acūtē _adv see_ **acūtus.**
acūtulus _adj_ rather subtle.
acūtus _adj_ sharp, pointed; (_senses_) keen;
(_sound_) high-pitched; severe; intelligent.
ad _prep_ (_with acc_) to, towards, against; near, at;
until; (_num_) about; with regard to, according
to; for the purpose of, for; compared with;
besides; **ad Castoris** to the temple of Castor;
ad dextram on the right; **ad hōc** besides; **ad
locum** on the spot; **ad manum** at hand; **ad
rem** to the point; **ad summam** in short; **ad
tempus** in time; **ad ūnum omnes** all without
exception; **ad urbem esse** wait outside the
city gates; **ad verbum** literally; **nīl ad**
nothing to do with; **usque ad** right up to.
adāctiō, -ōnis _f_ enforcing.

adāctus _ppp of_ **adigō.**
adāctus, -ūs _m_ snapping (_of teeth_).
adaequē _adv_ equally.
adaequō, -āre, -āvī, -ātum _vt_ to make equal,
level; to equal, match ♦ _vi_ to be equal.
adamantēus, adamantinus _adj see_ **adamās.**
adamās, -antis _m_ adamant, steel; diamond.
adamō, -āre, -āvī, -ātum _vt_ to fall in love
with.
adaperiō, -īre, -uī, -tum _vt_ to throw open.
adapertilis _adj_ openable.
adaquō, -āre, -āvī, -ātum _vt_ (_plants, animals_)
to water.
adaquor _vi_ to fetch water.
adauctus, -ūs _m_ growing.
adaugeō, -gēre, -xī, -ctum _vt_ to aggravate;
(_sacrifice_) to consecrate.
adaugēscō, -ere _vi_ to grow bigger.
adbibō, -ere, -ī _vt_ to drink; (_fig_) to drink in.
adbītō, -ere _vi_ to come near.
adc- _etc see_ **acc-.**
addecet, -ēre _vt_ it becomes.
addēnseō, -ēre _vt_ to close (ranks).
addīcō, -īcere, -īxī, -ictum _vi_ (_AUG_) to be
favourable ♦ _vt_ (_law_) to award; (_auction_) to
knock down; (_fig_) to sacrifice, devote.
addictiō, -ōnis _f_ award (_at law_).
addictus _ppp of_ **addīcō** ♦ _m_ bondsman.
addiscō, -scere, -dicī _vt_ to learn more.
additāmentum, -ī _nt_ increase.
additus _ppp of_ **addō.**
addō, -ere, -idī, -itum _vt_ to add, put to, bring
to; to impart; to increase; ~ **gradum** quicken
pace; ~**e quod** besides.
addoceō, -ēre, -uī, -tum _vt_ to teach new.
addubitō, -āre, -āvī, -ātum _vi_ to be in doubt
♦ _vt_ to question.
addūcō, -ūcere, -ūxī, -uctum _vt_ to take,
bring to; to draw together, pull taut,
wrinkle; (_fig_) to induce; (_pass_) to be led to
believe.
adductus _ppp of_ **addūcō** ♦ _adj_ contracted; (_fig_)
severe.
adedō, -edere, -ēdī, -ēsum _vt_ to begin to eat;
to eat up; to use up; to wear away.
adēmī _perf of_ **adimō.**
ademptiō, -ōnis _f_ taking away.
ademptus _ppp of_ **adimō.**
adeō, -īre, -iī, -itum _vt, vi_ to go to, approach;
to address; to undertake, submit to, enter
upon.
adeō _adv_ so; (_after pron_) just; (_after conj, adv,
adj: for emphasis_) indeed, very; (_adding an
explanation_) for, in fact, thus; or rather; ~
nōn ... ut so far from; **atque** ~, **sīve** ~ or
rather; **usque** ~ so far, so long, so much.
adeps, -ipis _m/f_ fat; corpulence.
adeptiō, -ōnis _f_ attainment.
adeptus _ppa of_ **adipīscor.**
adequitō, -āre, -āvī, -ātum _vi_ to ride up (to).
adesdum come here!
adesse _infin of_ **adsum.**
adēsus _ppp of_ **adedō.**

adfābilis *adj* easy to talk to.
adfābilitās, -ātis *f* courtesy.
adfabrē *adv* ingeniously.
adfatim *adv* to one's satisfaction, enough, ad nauseam.
adfātur, -rī, -tus *vt* (*defect*) to speak to.
adfātus *ppa of* **adfātur**.
adfātus, -ūs *m* speaking to.
adfectātiō, -ōnis *f* aspiring; (*RHET*) affectation.
adfectātus *adj* (*RHET*) studied.
adfectiō, -ōnis *f* frame of mind, mood; disposition; goodwill; (*ASTRO*) relative position.
adfectō, -āre, -āvī, -ātum *vt* to aspire to, aim at; to try to win over to make pretence of; **viam ~ ad** try to get to.
adfectus *ppp of* **adficiō** ♦ *adj* affected with, experienced (*abl*); (*person*) disposed; (*things*) weakened; (*undertakings*) well-advanced.
adfectus, -ūs *m* disposition, mood; fondness; (*pl*) loved ones.
adferō, adferre, attulī, adlātum *and* **allātum** *vt* to bring, carry to; to bring to bear, use against; to bring news; (*explanation*) to bring forward; to contribute (*something useful*).
adficiō, -icere, -ēcī, -ectum *vt* to affect; to endow, afflict with (*abl*; **exsiliō ~** banish; **honōre ~** honour; *also used with other nouns to express the corresponding verbs*.
adfictus *ppp of* **adfingō**.
adfīgō, -gere, -xi, -xum *vt* to fasten, attach; to impress (*on the mind*).
adfingō, -ngere, -nxī, -ctum *vt* to make, form (as part of); to invent.
adfinis, -is *m/f* neighbour; relation (*by marriage*) ♦ *adj* neighbouring; associated with (*dat or gen*).
adfinitās, -ātis *f* relationship (*by marriage*).
adfirmātē *adv* with assurance.
adfirmātiō, -ōnis *f* declaration.
adfirmō, -āre, -āvī, -ātum *v* to declare; to confirm.
adfīxus *ppp of* **adfīgō**.
adflātus, -ūs *m* breath, exhalation; (*fig*) inspiration.
adfleō, -ēre *vi* to weep (*at*).
adflīctātiō, -ōnis *f* suffering.
adflīctō, -āre, -āvī, -ātum *vt* to harass, distress.
adflīctor, -ōris *m* destroyer.
adflīctus *ppp of* **adflīgō** ♦ *adj* distressed, ruined; dejected; depraved.
adflīgō, -īgere, -īxī, -ictum *vt* to dash against, throw down, (*fig*) to impair, crush.
adflō, -āre, -āvī, -ātum *vt, vi* to blow on, breathe upon.
adfluēns, -entis *adj* rich (in).
adfluenter *adv* copiously.

adfluentia, -ae *f* abundance.
adfluō, -ere, -xī, -xum *vi* to flow; (*fig*) to flock in, abound in.
adfore *fut infin of* **adsum**.
adforem *imperf subj of* **adsum**.
adfuī *perf of* **adsum**.
adfulgeō, -gēre, -sī *vi* to shine on; to appear.
adfundō, -undere, -ūdī, -ūsum *vt* to pour in; to rush (troops) to.
adfūsus *adj* prostrate.
adfutūrus *fut p of* **adsum**.
adgemō, -ere *vi* to groan at.
adglomerō, -āre *vt* to add on.
adglūtinō, -āre *vt* to stick on.
adgravēscō, -ere *vi* to become worse.
adgravō, -āre, -āvī, -ātum *vt* to aggravate.
adgredior, -dī, -ssus *vt* to approach, accost; to attack; (*a task*) to undertake, take up.
adgregō, -āre, -āvī, -ātum *vt* to add, attach.
adgressiō, -ōnis *f* introductory remarks.
adgressus *ppa of* **adgredior**.
adhaereō, -rēre, -sī, -sum *vi* to stick to; (*fig*) to cling to, keep close to.
adhaerēscō, -ere *vi* to stick to or in; (*speech*) to falter.
adhaesiō, -ōnis *f* clinging.
adhaesus, -ūs *m* adhering.
adhibeō, -ēre, -uī, -itum *vt* to bring, put, add; to summon, consult, treat; to use, apply (*for some purpose*).
adhinniō, -īre, -īvī, -ītum *vi* to neigh to; (*fig*) to go into raptures over.
adhortātiō, -ōnis *f* exhortation.
adhortātor, -ōris *m* encourager.
adhortor, -ārī, -ātus *vt* to encourage, urge.
adhūc *adv* so far; as yet, till now; still ~ **nōn** not yet.
adiaceō, -ēre, -uī *vi* to lie near, border on.
adiciō, -icere, -iēcī, -iectum *vt* to throw to; to add; to turn (mind, eyes) towards.
adiectiō, -ōnis *f* addition.
adiectus *ppp of* **adiciō**.
adiectus, -ūs *m* bringing close.
adigō, -igere, -ēgī, -āctum *vt* to drive (to); to compel; **iūs iūrandum ~** put on oath; **in verba ~** force to owe allegiance.
adimō, -imere, -ēmī, -emptum *vt* to take away (from *dat*).
adipātum *nt* pastry.
adipātus *adj* fatty; (*fig*) florid.
adipīscor, -ipīscī, -eptus *vt* to overtake; to attain, acquire.
aditus, -ūs *m* approach, access (*to a person*); entrance; (*fig*) avenue.
adiūdicō, -āre, -āvī, -ātum *vt* to award (*in arbitration*); to ascribe.
adiūmentum, -ī *nt* aid, means of support.
adiūncta *ntpl* collateral circumstances.
adiūnctiō, -ōnis *f* uniting; addition; (*RHET*) proviso; repetition.

Noun declensions and verb conjugations are shown on pp xiii to xxv. The present infinitive ending of a verb shows to which conjugation it belongs: **-āre** = 1st; **-ēre** = 2nd; **-ere** = 3rd and **-īre** = 4th. Irregular verbs are shown on p xxvi

adiŭnctus _ppp of_ **adiungō ♦** _adj_ connected.
adiungō, -ungere, -ŭnxī, -ŭnctum _vt_ to yoke; to attach; (_suspicion etc_) to direct; (_remark_) to add.
adiŭrō, -āre, -āvī, -ātum _vt, vi_ to swear, swear by.
adiŭtō, -āre, -āvī, -ātum _vt_ to help.
adiŭtor, -ōris _m_ helper; (_MIL_) adjutant; (_POL_) official; (_THEAT_) supporting cast.
adiŭtrīx, -rīcis _f see_ **adiŭtor.**
adiŭtus _ppp of_ **adiuvō.**
adiuvō, -uvāre, -ūvī, -ūtum _vt_ to help; to encourage.
adj- _etc see_ **adi-.**
adlābor, -bī, -psus _vi_ to fall, move towards, come to.
adlabōrō, -āre, -āvī, -ātum _vi_ to work hard; to improve by taking trouble.
adlacrimō, -āre, -āvī, -ātum _vi_ to shed tears.
adlāpsus _ppa of_ **adlābor.**
adlāpsus, -ūs _m_ stealthy approach.
adlātrō, -āre, -āvī, -ātum _vt_ to bark at; (_fig_) to revile.
adlātus _ppp of_ **adferō.**
adlaudō, -āre, -āvī, -ātum _vt_ to praise highly.
adlectō, -āre, -āvī, -ātum _vt_ to entice.
adlēctus _ppp of_ **adlegō.**
adlectus _ppp of_ **adliciō.**
adlēgātī _mpl_ deputies.
adlēgātiō, -ōnis _f_ mission.
adlēgō, -āre, -āvī, -ātum _vt_ to despatch, commission; to mention.
adlegō, -egere, -ēgī, -ēctum _vt_ to elect.
adlevāmentum, -ī _nt_ relief.
adlevātiō, -ōnis _f_ easing.
adlevō, -āre, -āvī, -ātum _vt_ to lift up; to comfort; to weaken.
adliciō, -icere, -exī, -ectum _vt_ to attract.
adlīdō, -dere, -sī, -sum _vt_ to dash (against); (_fig_) to hurt.
adligō, -āre, -āvī, -ātum _vt_ to tie up, bandage; (_fig_) to bind, lay under an obligation.
adlinō, -inere, -ēvī, -itum _vt_ to smear; (_fig_) to attach.
adlīsus _ppp of_ **adlīdō.**
adlocūtiō, -ōnis _f_ address; comforting words.
adlocūtus _ppa of_ **adloquor.**
adloquium, -ī _and_ **iī** _nt_ talk; encouragement.
adloquor, -quī, -cūtus _vt_ to speak to, address.
adlūdiō, -āre, -āvī, -ātum _vi_ to play (with).
adlūdō, -dere, -sī, -sum _vi_ to joke, play.
adluō, -ere, -ī _vt_ to wash.
adluviēs, -ēī _f_ pool left by flood water.
adluviō, -ōnis _f_ alluvial land.
admātūrō, -āre, -āvī, -atum _vt_ to hurry on.
admētior, -tīrī, -nsus _vt_ to measure out.
adminiculor, -ārī, -ātus _vt_ to prop.
adminiculum, -ī _nt_ (_AGR_) stake; (_fig_) support.
administer, -rī _m_ assistant.

administrātiō, -ōnis _f_ services; management.
administrātor, -ōris _m_ manager.
administrō, -āre, -āvī, -ātum _vt_ to manage, govern.
admīrābilis _adj_ wonderful, surprising.
admīrābilitās, -ātis _f_ wonderfulness.
admīrābiliter _adv_ admirably; paradoxically.
admīrātiō, -ōnis _f_ wonder, surprise, admiration.
admīror, -ārī, -ātus _vt_ to wonder at, admire; to be surprised at.
admisceō, -scēre, -scuī, -xtum _vt_ to mix in with, add to; (_fig_) to involve; **sē ~** interfere.
admissārius, -ī _and_ **iī** _m_ stallion.
admissum, -ī _nt_ crime.
admissus _ppp of_ **admittō.**
admittō, -ittere, -īsī, -issum _vt_ to let in, admit; to set at a gallop; to allow; to commit (a crime); **equō ~issō** charging.
admixtiō, -ōnis _f_ admixture.
admixtus _ppp of_ **admisceō.**
admoderātē _adv_ suitably.
admoderor, -ārī, -ātus _vt_ to restrain.
admodum _adv_ very, quite; fully; yes; (_with neg_) at all.
admoneō, -ēre, -uī, -itum _vt_ to remind, suggest, advise, warn.
admonitiō, -ōnis _f_ reminder, suggestion, admonition.
admonitor, -ōris _m_ admonisher (_male_).
admonitrīx, -rīcis _f_ admonisher (_female_).
admonitū _at_ the suggestion, instance.
admordeō, -dēre, -sum _vt_ to bite into; (_fig_) to cheat.
admorsus _ppp of_ **admordeō.**
admōtiō, -ōnis _f_ applying.
admōtus _ppp of_ **admoveō.**
admoveo, -ovēre, -ōvī, -ōtum _vt_ to move, bring up, apply; to lend (an ear), direct (the mind).
admurmurātiō, -ōnis _f_ murmuring.
admurmurō, -āre, -āvī, -ātum _vi_ to murmur (_of a crowd approving or disapproving_).
admutilō, -āre, -āvī, -ātum _vt_ to clip close; (_fig_) to cheat.
adnectō, -ctere, -xuī, -xum _vt_ to connect, tie.
adnexus, -ūs _m_ connection.
adnīsus _ppp ef_ **adnītor.**
adnītor, -tī, -sus _and_ **-xus** _vi_ to lean on; to exert oneself.
adnīxus _ppp of_ **adnītor.**
adnō, -āre _v-, vi_ to swim to.
adnotō, -āre, -āvī, -ātum _vt_ to comment on.
adnumerō, -āre, -āvī, -ātum _vt_ to pay out; to reckon along with.
adnuō, -uere, -uī, -ūtum _vi_ to nod; to assent, promise; to indicate.
adoleō, -olēre, -oluī, -ultum _vt_ to burn; to pile with gifts.
adolēscen- _etc see_ **adulēscen-.**
adolēscō, -ēscere, -ēvī _vi_ to grow up, increase; to burn.

Adōnis, -is and **idis** m a beautiful youth loved by Venus.
adopertus adj covered.
adoptātiō, -ōnis f adopting.
adoptiō, -ōnis f adoption.
adoptīvus adj by adoption.
adoptō, -āre, -āvī, -ātum vt to choose; to adopt.
ador, -ōris and **oris** nt spelt.
adōreus adj see n.
adōrea f glory.
adorior, -īrī, -tus vt to accost; to attack; to set about.
adōrnō, -āre, -āvī, -ātum vt to get ready.
adōrō, -āre, -āvī, -ātum vt to entreat; to worship, revere.
adortus ppa of **adorior**.
adp- etc see **app-**.
adrādō, -dere, -sī, -sum vt to shave close.
Adrastus, -ī m a king of Argos
adrāsus ppp of **adrādō**.
adrēctus ppp of **adrigō** ♦ adj steep.
adrēpō, -ere, -sī, -tum vt to creep, steal into.
adreptus ppp of **adripiō**
Adria etc see **Hadria** etc.
adrīdeō, -dēre, -sī, -sum vt, vi to laugh, smile at; to please.
adrigō, -igere, -ēxī, -ēctum vt to raise; (fig) to rouse.
adripiō, -ipere, -ipuī, -eptum vt to seize; to appropriate; to take hold of; to learn quickly; (law) to arrest; to satirize.
adrōdō, -dere, -sī, -sum vt to gnaw, nibble at.
adrogāns, -antis adj arrogant, insolent.
adroganter adv see **adrogāns**.
adrogantia, -ae f arrogance, presumption, haughtiness.
adrogātiō, -ōnis f adoption.
adrogō, -āre, -āvī, -ātum vt to ask; to associate; to claim, assume; (fig) to award.
adsc- etc see **asc-**.
adsecla etc see **adsecula**.
adsectātiō, -ōnis f attendance.
adsectātor, -ōris m follower.
adsector, -ārī, -ātus vt to attend on, follow (esp a candidate).
adsecula, -ae m follower (derogatory).
adsēdī perf of **adsideō**; perf of **adsīdō**.
adsēnsiō, -ōnis f assent, applause; (PHILOS) acceptance of the evidence of the senses.
adsēnsor, -ōris m one in agreement.
adsēnsus ppa of **adsentior**.
adsēnsus, -ūs m assent, approval; echo; (PHILOS) acceptance of the evidence of the senses.
adsentātiō, -ōnis f flattery.
adsentātiuncula f trivial compliments.
adsentātor, -ōris m flatterer (male).
adsentātōriē adv ingratiatingly.

adsentātrīx, -rīcis f flatterer (female).
adsentiō, -entīre, -ēnsī, -ēnsum; -entior, -entīrī, -ēnsus vi to agree, approve.
adsentor, -ārī, -ātus vi to agree, flatter.
adsequor, -quī, -cūtus vt to overtake; to attain; to grasp (by understanding).
adserō, -ere, -uī, -tum vt (law) to declare free (usu with manū), liberate (a slave); to lay claim to, appropriate; ~ **in servitūtem** claim as a slave.
adserō, -erere, -ēvī, -itum vt to plant near.
adsertiō, -ōnis f declaration of status.
adsertor, -ōris m champion.
adserviō, -īre vi to assist.
adservō, -āre, -āvī, -ātum vt to watch carefully; to keep, preserve.
adsessiō, -ōnis f sitting beside.
adsessor, -ōris m counsellor.
adsessus, -ūs m sitting beside.
adsevēranter adv emphatically.
adsevērātiō, -ōnis f assertion; earnestness.
adsevērō, -āre, -āvī, -ātum vt to do in earnest; to assert strongly.
adsideō, -idēre, -ēdī, -essum vi to sit by; to attend, assist; to besiege; to resemble.
adsīdō, -īdere, -ēdī vi to sit down.
adsiduē adv continually.
adsiduitās, -ātis f constant attendance; continuance, frequent recurrence.
adsiduō adv continually.
adsiduus adj constantly in attendance, busy; continual, incessant.
adsiduus, -ī m taxpayer.
adsignātiō, -ōnis f allotment (of land).
adsignō, -āre, -āvī, -ātum vt to allot (esp land); to assign; to impute, attribute; to consign.
adsiliō, -īlīre, -iluī, -ultum vi to leap at or on to.
adsimilis adj like.
adsimiliter adv similarly.
adsimulātus adj similar; counterfeit.
adsimulō, -āre, -āvī, -ātum vt, vi to compare; to pretend, imitate.
adsistō, -istere, -titī vi to stand (by); to defend.
adsitus ppp of **adserō**.
adsoleō, -ēre vi to be usual.
adsonō, -āre vi to respond.
adsp- etc see **asp-**.
adsternō, -ere vt to prostrate.
adstipulātor, -ōris m supporter.
adstipulor, -ārī, -ātus vi to agree with.
adstitī perf of **adsistō**; perf of **adstō**.
adstō, -āre, -itī vi to stand near, stand up; to assist.
adstrepō, -ere vi to roar.
adstrictē adv concisely.
adstrictus ppp of **adstringō** ♦ adj tight, narrow; concise; stingy.

adstringō, -ngere, -nxī, -ctum *vt* to draw close, tighten; to bind, oblige; to abridge.
adstruō, -ere, -xī, -ctum *vt* to build on; to add.
adstupeō, -ēre *vi* to be astonished.
adsuēfaciō, -acere, -ēcī, -actum *vt* to accustom, train.
adsuēscō, -scere, -vī, -tum *vi* to accustom, train.
adsuētūdō, -inis *f* habit.
adsuētus *ppp of* **adsuēscō ♦** *adj* customary.
adsultō, -āre, -āvī, -ātum *vi* to jump; to attack.
adsultus, -ūs *m* attack.
adsum, -esse, -fuī *vi* to be present; to support, assist (*esp at law*); to come; to appear before (a tribunal); **animō ~ pay** attention; **iam aderō** I'll be back soon.
adsūmō, -ere, -psī, -ptum *vt* to take for oneself, receive; to take also.
adsūmptiō, -ōnis *f* taking up; (*logic*) minor premise.
adsūmptīvus *adj* (*law*) which takes its defence from extraneous circumstances.
adsūmptum, -ī *nt* epithet.
adsūmptus *ppp of* **adsūmō**.
adsuō, -ere *vt* to sew on.
adsurgō, -gere, -rēxī, -rēctum *vi* to rise, stand up; to swell, increase.
adt- *etc see* **att-**.
adulātiō, -ōnis *f* (*dogs*) fawning; servility.
adulātor, -ōris *m* sycophant.
adulātōrius *adj* flattering.
adulēscēns, -entis *m/f* young man *or* woman (*usu from 15 to 30 years*).
adulēscentia, -ae *f* youth (*age 15 to 30*).
adulēscentula, -ae *f* girl.
adulēscentulus, -ī *m* quite a young man.
adulō, -āre, -āvī, -ātum; adulor, -ārī, -ātus *vt, vi* to fawn upon, flatter, kowtow.
adulter, -ī *m*, **-a, -ae** *f* adulterer, adulteress ♦ *adj* adulterous.
adulterīnus *adj* forged.
adulterium, -ī *and* **iī** *nt* adultery.
adulterō, -āre, -āvī, -ātum *vt, vi* to commit adultery; to falsify.
adultus *ppp of* **adolēscō ♦** *adj* adult, mature.
adumbrātim *adv* in outline.
adumbrātiō, -ōnis *f* sketch; semblance.
adumbrātus *adj* false.
adumbrō, -āre, -āvī, -ātum *vt* to sketch; to represent, copy.
aduncitās, -ātis *f* curvature.
aduncus *adj* hooked, curved.
adurgeō, -ēre *vt* to pursue closely.
adūrō, -rere, -ssī, -stum *vt* to burn; to freeze; (*fig*) to fire.
adusque *prep* (*with acc*) right up to ♦ *adv* entirely.
adūstus *ppp of* **adūrō ♦** *adj* brown.
advectīcius *adj* imported.
advectō, -āre *vt* to carry frequently.
advectus *ppp of* **advehō**.

advectus, -ūs *m* bringing.
advehō, -here, -xī, -ctum *vt* to carry, convey; (*pass*) to ride.
advēlō, -āre *vt* to crown.
advena, -ae *m/f* stranger ♦ *adj* foreign.
adveniō, -enīre, -ēnī, -entum *vi* to arrive, come.
adventīcius *adj* foreign, extraneous; unearned.
adventō, -āre, -āvī, -ātum *vi* to come nearer and nearer, advance rapidly.
adventor, -ōris *m* visitor.
adventus, -ūs *m* arrival, approach.
adversāria *ntpl* daybook.
adversārius, -ī *and* **iī** *m* opponent ♦ *adj* opposing.
adversātrīx, -īcis *f* antagonist.
adversiō, -ōnis *f* turning (the attention).
adversor, -ārī, -ātus *vi* to oppose, resist.
adversum, -ī *nt* opposite; misfortune ♦ *prep* (*+ acc*) towards, against ♦ *adv* to meet.
adversus *ppp of* **advertō ♦** *adj* opposite, in front; hostile; **~ō flūmine** upstream; **~ae rēs** misfortune ♦ *prep* (*+ acc*) towards, against ♦ *adv* to meet.
advertō, -tere, -tī, -sum *vt* to turn, direct towards; to call attention; **animum ~ notice**, perceive; (*with* **ad**) to attend to; (*with* **in**) to punish.
advesperāscit, -scere, -vit *vi* it is getting dark.
advigilō, -āre *vi* to keep watch.
advocātiō, -ōnis *f* legal assistance, counsel.
advocātus, -ī *m* supporter in a lawsuit; advocate, counsel.
advocō, -āre, -āvī, -ātum *vt* to summon; (*law*) to call in the assistance of.
advolō, -āre, -āvī, -ātum *vi* to fly to, swoop down upon.
advolvō, -vere, -vī, -ūtum *vt* to roll to; to prostrate.
advor- *etc see* **adver-**.
adytum, -ī *nt* sanctuary.
Aeacidēs, -idae *m* Achilles; Pyrrhus.
Aeacus, -ī *m* father of Peleus, and judge of the dead.
Aeaea, -ae *f* Circe's island.
Aeaeus *adj of* Circe.
aedēs, -is *f* temple; (*pl*) house.
aedicula, -ae *f* shrine; small house, room.
aedificātiō, -ōnis *f* building.
aedificātiuncula, -ae *f* little house.
aedificātor, -ōris *m* builder.
aedificium, -ī *and* **iī** *nt* building.
aedificō, -āre, -āvī, -ātum *vt* to build, construct.
aedīlicius *adj* aedile's ♦ *m* ex-aedile.
aedīlis, -is *m* aedile.
aedīlitās, -ātis *f* aedileship.
aedis, -is *see* **aedēs**.
aeditumus, aedituus, -ī *m* temple-keeper.
Aeduī, -ōrum *mpl* a tribe of central Gaul.
Aeētēs, -ae *m* father of Medea.

Aegaeus adj Aegean ♦ nt Aegean Sea.
Aegātēs, -um fpl islands off Sicily.
aeger, -rī adj ill, sick; sorrowful; weak.
Aegīna, -ae f a Greek island.
Aegīnēta, -ae m inhabitant of Aegina.
aegis, -dis f shield of Jupiter or Athena, aegis.
Aegisthus, -ī m paramour of Clytemnestra.
aegocerōs, -ōtis m Capricorn.
aegrē adv painfully; with displeasure; with
difficulty; hardly; ~ **ferre** be annoyed.
aegrēscō, -ere vi to become ill; to be
aggravated.
aegrimōnia, -ae f distress of mind.
aegritūdō, -inis f sickness; sorrow.
aegror, -ōris m illness.
aegrōtātiō, -ōnis f illness, disease.
aegrōtō, -āre, -āvī, -ātum vi to be ill.
aegrōtus adj ill, sick.
Aegyptius adj see n.
Aegyptus, -ī f Egypt ♦ m brother of Danaus.
aelinos, -ī m dirge.
Aemiliānus adj esp Scipio destroyer of Carthage.
Aemilius, -ī Roman family name; **Via ~ia** road in
N. Italy.
aemulātiō, -ōnis f rivalry (good or bad);
jealousy.
aemulātor, -ōris m zealous imitator.
aemulor, -ārī, -ātus vt to rival, copy; to be
jealous.
aemulus, -ī m rival ♦ adj rivalling; jealous.
Aeneadēs, -ae m Trojan Roman.
Aenēās, -ae m Trojan leader and hero of Virgil's
epic.
Aenēis, -idis and **idos** f Aeneid.
Aenēius adj see n.
aēneus adj of bronze.
aenigma, -tis nt riddle, mystery.
aēnum, -ī nt bronze vessel.
aēnus adj of bronze.
Aeolēs, -um mpl the Aeolians.
Aeolia f Lipari Island.
Aeolidēs m a descendant of Aeolus.
Aeolis, -idis f Aeolia (N. W. of Asia Minor).
Aeolis, -idis f daughter of Aeolus.
Aeolius adj see n.
Aeolus, -ī m king of the winds.
aequābilis adj equal; consistent, even;
impartial.
aequābilitās, -ātis f uniformity; impartiality.
aequābiliter adv uniformly.
aequaevus adj of the same age.
aequālis adj equal, like; of the same age,
contemporary; uniform.
aequālitās, -ātis f evenness; (in politics, age)
equality, similarity.
aequāliter adv evenly.
aequanimitās, -ātis f goodwill; calmness.
aequātiō, -ōnis f equal distribution.
aequē adv equally; just as (with ac, atque, et,
quam); justly.
Aequī, -ōrum mpl a people of central Italy.

Aequicus, Aequiculus adj see n.
Aequimaelium, -ī and **iī** nt an open space in
Rome.
aequinoctiālis adj see n.
aequinoctium, -ī and **iī** nt equinox.
aequiperābilis adj comparable.
aequiperō, -āre, -āvī, -ātum vt to compare;
to equal.
aequitās, -ātis f uniformity; fair dealing,
equity; calmness of mind.
aequō, -āre, -āvī, -ātum vt to make equal,
level; to compare; to equal; **solō ~** raze to the
ground.
aequor, -is nt a level surface, sea.
aequoreus adj of the sea.
aequum, -ī nt plain; justice.
aequus adj level, equal; favourable, friendly,
fair, just; calm; **~ō animō** patiently; **~ō Marte**
without deciding the issue; **~um est** it is
reasonable; **ex ~ō** equally.
āēr, āeris m air, weather; mist.
aerāria f mine.
aerārium nt treasury
aerārius adj of bronze; of money ♦ m a citizen
of the lowest class at Rome; **tribūnī ~ī**
paymasters; a wealthy middle class at Rome.
aerātus adj of bronze
aereus adj of copper or bronze.
aerifer, -ī adj carrying cymbals.
aeripēs, -edis adj bronze-footed.
āerius adj of the air; lofty.
aerūgō, -inis f rust; (fig) envy, avarice.
aerumna, -ae f trouble, hardship.
aerumnōsus adj wretched.
aes, aeris nt copper, bronze; money; (pl)
objects made of copper or bronze (esp
statues, instruments, vessels; soldiers' pay); **~**
aliēnum debt; **~ circumforāneum** borrowed
money; **~ grave** Roman coin, as.
Aeschylus, -ī m Greek tragic poet.
Aesculāpius, -ī m god of medicine.
aesculētum, -ī nt oak forest.
aesculeus adj see **aesculus.**
aesculus, -ī f durmast oak.
Aesōn, -onis m father of Jason.
Aesonidēs, -ae m Jason.
Aesōpius adj see n.
Aesōpus, -ī m Greek writer of fables.
aestās, -ātis f summer.
aestifer, -ī adj heat-bringing.
aestimātiō, -ōnis f valuation, assessment;
lītis ~ assessment of damages.
aestimātor, -ōris m valuer.
aestimō, -āre, -āvī, -ātum vt to value,
estimate the value of; **magnī ~** think highly
of.
aestīva, -ōrum ntpl summer camp, campaign.
aestīvus adj summer
aestuārium, -ī and **iī** nt tidal waters, estuary.
aestuō, -āre, -āvī, -ātum vi to boil, burn;

(*movement*) to heave, toss; (*fig*) to be excited; to waver.
aestuōsus *adj* very hot; agitated.
aestus, -ūs *m* heat; surge of the sea; tide; (*fig*) passion; hesitation.
aetās, -ātis *f* age, life; time.
aetātem *adv* for life.
aetātula, -ae *f* tender age.
aeternitās, -ātis *f* eternity.
aeternō, -āre *vt* to immortalize.
aeternus *adj* eternal, immortal; lasting; in ~um for ever.
aethēr, -eris *m* sky, heaven; air.
aetherius *adj* ethereal, heavenly; of air.
Aethiops, -is *adj* Ethiopian; (*fig*) stupid.
aethra, -ae *f* sky.
Aetna, -ae *f* Etna (*in Sicily*).
Aetnaeus, Aetnēnsis *adj see* n.
Aetōlia, -iae *f* a district of N. Greece.
Aetōlus, -icus *adj see* n.
aevitās, -ātis old form of **aetās**.
aevum, -ī *nt* age, lifetime; eternity; in ~ for ever.
Āfer, -rī *adj* African.
āfore *fut infin of* **absum**.
Āfrānius, -ī *m* Latin comic poet.
Āfrica, -ae *f* Roman province (*now* Tunisia).
Āfricānae *fpl* panthers.
Āfricānus *adj* name of two Scipios.
Āfricus *adj* African ♦ *m* south-west wind.
āfuī, āfutūrus *perf, fut p of* **absum**.
Agamēmnōn, -onis *m* leader of Greeks against Troy.
Agamēmnonius *adj see* n.
Aganippē, -ēs *f* a spring on Helicon.
agāsō, -ōnis *m* ostler, footman.
age, agedum come on!, well then.
agellus, -ī *m* plot of land.
Agēnōr, -oris *m* father of Europa.
Agēnoreus *adj see* n.
Agēnoridēs, -ae *m* Cadmus; Perseus.
agēns, -entis *adj* (*RHET*) effective.
ager, -rī *m* land, field; countryside; territory.
agg- *etc see* **adg-**.
agger, -is *m* rampart; mound, embankment, any built-up mass.
aggerō, -āre, -āvī, -ātum *vt* to pile up; to increase.
aggerō, -rere, -ssī, -stum *vt* to carry, bring.
aggestus, -ūs *m* accumulation.
agilis *adj* mobile; nimble, busy.
agilitās, -ātis *f* mobility.
agitābilis *adj* light.
agitātiō, -ōnis *f* movement, activity.
agitātor, -ōris *m* driver, charioteer.
agitō, -āre, -āvī, -ātum *vt* (*animals*) to drive; to move, chase, agitate; (*fig*) to excite (to action); to persecute, ridicule; to keep (*a ceremony*) ♦ *vi* to live; to deliberate.
agmen, -inis *nt* forward movement, procession, train; army on the march; ~ claudere bring up the rear; novissimum ~ rearguard; prīmum ~ van.

agna, -ae *f* ewe lamb; lamb (flesh).
agnāscor, -scī, -tus *vi* to be born after.
agnātus, -ī *m* relation (*by blood on father's side*).
agnellus, -ī *m* little lamb.
agnīnus *adj* of lamb.
agnitiō, -ōnis *f* recognition, knowledge.
agnitus *ppp of* **agnōscō**.
agnōmen, -inis *nt* an extra surname (*eg* Africanus).
agnōscō, -ōscere, -ōvī, -itum *vt* to recognize; to acknowledge, allow; to understand.
agnus, -ī *m* lamb.
agō, agere, ēgī, āctum *vt* to drive, lead; to plunder; to push forward, put forth; (*fig*) to move, rouse, persecute; to do, act, perform; (*time*) to pass, spend; (*undertakings*) to manage, wage; (*public speaking*) to plead, discuss; to negotiate, treat; (*THEAT*) to play, act the part of; ~ **cum populō** address the people; **age** come on!, well then; **age age** all right!; **āctum est dē** it is all up with; **aliud ~** not attend; **animam ~** expire; **annum quartum ~** be three years old; **causam ~** plead a cause; **hōc age** pay attention; **id ~ ut** aim at; **lēge ~** go to law; **nīl agis** it's no use; **quid agis?** how are you?; **rēs agitur** interests are at stake; **sē ~** go, come.
agrāriī *mpl* the land reform party.
agrārius *adj* of public land; **lēx ~a** land law.
agrestis *adj* rustic; boorish, wild, barbarous ♦ *m* countryman.
agricola, -ae *m* countryman, farmer.
Agricola, -ae *m* a Roman governor of Britain; his biography by Tacitus.
Agrigentīnus *adj see* n.
Agrigentum, -ī *nt* a town in Sicily.
agripeta, -ae *m* landgrabber.
Agrippa, -ae *m* Roman surname (*esp Augustus's minister*).
Agrippīna, -ae *f* mother of Nero; **Colōnia ~a** or **~ēnsis** Cologne.
Agyīeus, -eī *and* **eos** *m* Apollo.
āh *interj* ah! (*in sorrow or joy*).
aha *interj* expressing reproof *or* laughter.
ahēn- *etc see* **aēn-**.
Āiāx, -ācis *m* Ajax (*name of two Greek heroes at Troy*).
āiō *vt* (*defec*) to say, speak; **ain tū?/ain vērō?** really?; **quid ais?** I say!
āla, -ae *f* wing; armpit; (*MIL*) wing of army.
alabaster, -rī *m* perfume box.
alacer, -ris *adj* brisk, cheerful.
alacritās, -ātis *f* promptness, liveliness; joy, rapture.
alapa, -ae *f* slap on the face; a slave's freedom.
ālāriī *mpl* allied troops.
ālārius *adj* (*MIL*) on the wing.
ālātus *adj* winged.
alauda, -ae *f* lark; name of a legion of Caesar's.
alāzōn, -onis *m* braggart.

Alba Longa, -ae, -ae *f a Latin town (precursor of Rome).*
Albānus *adj* Alban; **Lacus ~, Mōns ~** *lake and mountain near Alba Longa.*
albātus *adj* dressed in white.
albeō, -ēre *vi* to be white to dawn.
albēscō, -ere *vi* to become white; to dawn.
albicō, -āre *vi* to be white.
albidus *adj* white.
Albiōn, -ōnis *f ancient name for Britain.*
albitūdō, -inis *f* whiteness.
Albula, -ae *f old name for the Tiber.*
albulus *adj* whitish.
album, -ī *nt* white; records.
Albunea, -ae *f a spring at Tibur; a sulphur spring near Alban Lake.*
albus *adj* white, bright
Alcaeus, -ī *m Greek lyric poet.*
alcēdō, -inis *f* kingfisher
alcēdōnia *ntpl* halcyon days.
alcēs, -is *f* elk.
Alcibiadēs, -is *m brilliant Athenian politician.*
Alcīdēs, -ae *m* Hercules.
Alcinous, -ī *m king of Phaeacians in the Odyssey.*
ālea, -ae *f* gambling, dice; *(fig)* chance, hazard; **iacta ~ est** the die is cast; **in ~am dare** to risk.
āleātor, -ōris *m* gambler.
āleātōrius *adj* in gambling.
ālēc *etc see* **allēc.**
āleō, -ōnis *m* gambler
āles, -itis *adj* winged; swift ♦ *m/f* bird; omen.
alēscō, -ere *vi* to grow up.
Alexander, -rī *m a Greek name; Paris (prince of Troy); Alexander the Great (king of Macedon).*
Alexandrēa *(later* **-īa)** **-eae** *f Alexandria in Egypt.*
alga, -ae *f* seaweed.
algeō, -gēre, -sī *vi* to feel cold; *(fig)* to be neglected.
algēscō, -ere *vi* to catch cold.
Algidus, -ī *m mountain in Latium.*
algidus *adj* cold.
algor, -ōris *m* cold.
algū *abl sg m* with cold.
aliā *adv* in another way.
aliās *adv* at another time; at one time ... at another.
alibī *adv* elsewhere; otherwise; in one place ... in another.
alicubī *adv* somewhere.
alicunde *adv* from somewhere.
alid *old form of* **aliud.**
aliēnātiō, -ōnis *f* transfer; estrangement.
aliēnigena, -ae *m* foreigner
aliēnigenus *adj* foreign; heterogeneous.
aliēnō, -āre, -āvī, -ātum *vt* to transfer (property by sale); to alienate, estrange; *(mind)* to derange.

aliēnus *adj* of another, of others; alien, strange; *(with abl or ab)* unsuited to, different from; hostile ♦ *m* stranger.
āliger, -ī *adj* winged.
alimentārius *adj* about food.
alimentum, -ī *nt* nourishment, food; obligation of children to parents; *(fig)* support.
alimōnium, -i *and* **ī** *nt* nourishment.
aliō *adv* in another direction, elsewhere; one way ... another way.
alioquī, aliōquin *adv* otherwise, else; besides.
aliōrsum *adv* in another direction; differently.
ālipēs, -edis *adj* wing-footed; fleet.
alīptēs, -ae *m* sports trainer.
aliquā *adv* some way or other.
aliquam *adv:* **~ diū** for sometime; **~ multī** a considerable number.
aliquandō *adv* sometime, ever; sometimes; once, for once; now at last.
aliquantisper *adv* for a time.
aliquantō *adv (with comp)* somewhat.
aliquantulum *nt* a very little ♦ *adv* somewhat.
aliquantulus *adj* quite small.
aliquantum *acj* a good deal ♦ *adv* somewhat.
aliquantus *adj* considerable.
aliquātenus *adv* to some extent.
aliquī, -qua, -quod *adj* some, any; some other.
aliquid *adv* at all.
aliquis, -quid *pron* somebody, something; someone *or* something important.
aliquō *adv* to some place, somewhere else.
aliquot *adj (indecl)* some.
aliquotiēns *adv* several times.
aliter *adv* otherwise, differently; in one way ... in another.
alitus *ppp of* **alō.**
ālium, -i *and* **ī** *nt* garlic.
aliunde *adv* from somewhere else.
alius, alia, aliud *adj* other, another; different; **alius ... alius** some .. others; **alius ex aliō** one after the other; **in alia omnia īre** oppose a measure; **nihil aliud quam** only.
all- *etc see* **adl-.**
allēc, -is *nt* fish pickle.
allex, -icis *m* big toe.
Allia, -ae *f* tributary of the Tiber *(scene of a great Roman defeat).*
Alliēnsis *adj see* **Allia**
Allobrogēs, -um *mpl a people of S.E. Gaul.*
Allobrogicus *adj see* **a.**
almus *adj* nourishing; kindly.
alnus, -ī *f* alder.
alō, -ere, -uī, -tum *cnd* **-itum** *vt* to nourish, rear; to increase, promote.
Alpēs, -ium *fpl* Alps.
Alphēus, -ī *m river of Olympia in S.W. Greece.*
Alpīnus *adj see* **n.**

Noun declensions and verb conjugations are shown on pp xiii to xxv. The present infinitive ending of a verb shows to which conjugation it belongs: **-āre** = 1st; **-ēre** = 2nd; **-ere** = 3rd and **-īre** = 4th. Irregular verbs are shown on p xxvi

alsī *perf of* **algeō.**
alsius, alsus *adj* cold.
altāria, -ium *ntpl* altars, altar; altar top.
altē *adv* on high, from above; deep; from afar.
alter, -īus *adj* the one, the other (*of two*); second, the next; fellow man; different; ~ **ego**, ~ **īdem** a second self; ~**um tantum** twice as much; **ūnus et** ~ one or two.
altercātiō, -ōnis *f* dispute, debate.
altercor, -ārī, -ātus *vi* to wrangle, dispute; to cross-examine.
alternis *adv* alternately.
alternō, -āre, -āvī, -ātum *vt* to do by turns, alternate.
alternus *adj* one after the other, alternate; elegiac (*verses*).
alteruter, -īusutrīus *adj* one or the other.
altilis *adj* fat (*esp fowls*).
altisonus *adj* sounding on high.
altitonāns, -antis *adj* thundering on high.
altitūdō, -inis *f* height, depth; (*fig*) sublimity, (*mind*) secrecy.
altivolāns, -antis *adj* soaring on high.
altor, -ōris *m* foster father.
altrīnsecus *adv* on the other side.
altrīx, -īcis *f* nourisher, foster mother.
altum, -ī *nt* heaven; sea (*usu out of sight of land*); **ex** ~**ō repetītus** far-fetched.
altus *adj* high, deep; (*fig*) noble; profound.
ālūcinor, -ārī, -ātus *vi* to talk wildly; (*mind*) to wander.
aluī *perf of* **alō.**
alumnus, -ī *m/f* foster child; pupil.
alūta, -ae *f* soft leather; shoe, purse, face patch.
alveārium, -ī *and* **iī** *nt* beehive.
alveolus, -ī *m* basin.
alveus, -eī *m* hollow; trough; (*ship*) hold; bath tub; riverbed.
alvus, -ī *f* bowels; womb; stomach.
amābilis *adj* lovely, lovable.
amābilitās, -ātis *f* charm.
amābiliter *adv see* **amābilis.**
Amalthēa, -ae *f* nymph or she-goat; **cornū** ~**ae** horn of plenty.
Amalthēum, -ī *nt* Atticus's library.
āmandātiō *f* sending away.
āmandō, -āre, -āvī, -ātum *vt* to send away.
amāns, -antis *adj* fond ♦ *m* lover.
amanter *adv* affectionately.
āmanuēnsis, -is *m* secretary.
amāracinum, -inī *nt* marjoram ointment.
amāracum, -i *nt*, **amāracus, -ī** *m/f* sweet marjoram.
amārē *adv see* **amārus.**
amāritiēs, -ēī *f*, **amāritūdō, -inis** *f*, **amāror, -ōris** *m* bitterness.
amārus *adj* bitter; (*fig*) sad; ill-natured.
amāsius, -ī *and* **iī** *m* lover.
Amathūs, -ūntis *f* town in Cyprus.
Amathūsia *f* Venus.
amātiō, -ōnis *f* lovemaking.
amātor, -ōris *m* lover, paramour.

amātorculus *m* poor lover.
amatōriē *adv* amorously.
amatōrius *adj* of love, erotic.
amātrīx, -rīcis *f* mistress.
Amāzōn, -onis *f* Amazon, warrior woman.
Amāzonides *fpl* Amazons.
Amāzonius *adj see n.*
ambāctus, -ī *m* vassal.
ambāgēs, -is *f* windings; (*speech*) circumlocution, quibbling; enigma.
ambedō, -edere, -ēdī, -ēsum *vt* to consume.
ambēsus *ppp of* **ambedō.**
ambigō, -ere *vt, vi* to wander about; to be in doubt; to argue; to wrangle.
ambiguē *adv* doubtfully.
ambiguitās, -ātis *f* ambiguity.
ambiguus *adj* changeable, doubtful, unreliable; ambiguous.
ambiō, -īre, -iī, -ītum *vt* to go round, encircle; (*POL*) to canvass for votes; (*fig*) to court (for a favour).
ambitiō, -ōnis *f* canvassing for votes; currying favour; ambition.
ambitiōsē *adv* ostentatiously.
ambitiōsus *adj* winding; ostentatious, ambitious.
ambitus *ppp of* **ambiō.**
ambitus, -ūs *m* circuit, circumference; circumlocution; canvassing, bribery; **lēx de** ~**ū** a law against bribery.
ambō, ambae, ambō *num* both, two.
Ambracia, -ae *f* district of N.W. Greece.
Ambraciēnsis, -us *adj see n.*
ambrosia, -ae *f* food of the gods.
ambrosius *adj* divine.
ambūbāia, -ae *f* Syrian flute-girl.
ambulācrum, -ī *nt* avenue.
ambulātiō, -ōnis *f* walk, walking; walk (*place*).
ambulātiuncula *f* short walk.
ambulō, -āre, -āvī, -ātum *vi* to walk, go; to travel.
ambūrō, -rere, -ssī, -stum *vt* to burn up; to make frostbitten; (*fig*) to ruin.
ambūstus *ppp of* **ambūrō.**
amellus, -ī *m* Michaelmas daisy.
āmēns, -entis *adj* mad, frantic; stupid.
āmentia, -ae *f* madness; stupidity.
āmentum, -ī *nt* strap (for throwing javelin).
ames, -itis *m* fowler's pole.
amfr- *etc see* **anfr-.**
amīca, -ae *f* friend; mistress.
amiciō, -īre, -tus *vt* to clothe, cover.
amīciter, -ē *adv see* **amīcus.**
amīcitia, -ae *f* friendship; alliance.
amictus *ppp of* **amiciō.**
amictus, -ūs *m* (manner of) dress; clothing.
amiculum, -ī *nt* cloak.
amīculus, -ī *m* dear friend.
amīcus, -ī *m* friend ♦ *adj* friendly, fond.
āmissiō, -ōnis *f* loss.
āmissus *ppp of* **āmittō.**
amita, -ae *f* aunt (*on father's side*).

āmittō, -ittere, -īsī, -issum vt to let go, lose.
Ammōn, -is m Egyptian god identified with Jupiter.
Ammōniacus adj see n.
amnicola, -ae m/f sth growing by a river.
amniculus m brook.
amnicus adj see n.
amnis, -is m river.
amō, -āre, -āvī, -ātum vt to love, like; (colloq) to be obliged to; **ita mē dī ament!** ≈ bless my soul!; **amābō** please!
amoenitās, -ātis f delightfulness (esp of scenery).
amoenus adj delightful.
āmōlior, -īrī, -ītus vt to remove.
amōmum, -ī nt cardamom.
amor, -ōris m love; (fig) strong desire; term of endearment; Cupid; (pl) love affairs.
āmōtiō, -ōnis f removal.
āmōtus ppa of **āmoveō**.
āmoveō, -ovēre, -ōvī, -ōtum vt to remove; to banish.
amphibolia, -ae f ambiguity.
Amphīōn, -onis m musician and builder of Thebes.
Amphīonius adj see n.
amphitheātrum, -ī nt amphitheatre.
Amphitrītē, -ēs f sea goddess; the sea.
Amphitryō, -ōnis m husband of Alcmena.
Amphitryōniadēs m Hercules.
amphora, -ae f a two-handled jar; liquid measure; (NAUT) measure of tonnage.
Amphrȳsius adj of Apollo.
Amphrȳsus, -ī m river in Thessaly.
ample adv see **amplūs**.
amplector, -ctī, -xus vt to embrace, encircle; (mind) to grasp; (speech) to deal with; (fig) to cherish.
amplexor, -ārī, -ātus vt to embrace, love.
amplexus ppa of **amplector**.
amplexus, -ūs m embrace, encircling.
amplificātiō, -ōnis f enlargement; (RHET) a passage elaborated for effect.
amplificē adv splendidly.
amplificō, -āre, -āvī, -ātum vt to increase, enlarge; (RHET) to enlarge upon.
ampliō, -āre, -āvī, -ātum vt to enlarge; (law) to adjourn.
ampliter adv see **amplūs**.
amplitūdō, -inis f size; (fig) distinction; (RHET) fullness.
amplius adv more (esp amount or number), further, longer; ~ **ducentī** more than 200; ~ **nōn petere** take no further legal action; ~ **prōnūntiāre** adjourn a case.
amplus adj large, spacious; great, abundant; powerful, splendid, eminent; (sup) distinguished.
ampulla, -ae f a two-handled flask; (fig) high-flown language.

ampullārius, -ārī m flask-maker.
ampullor, -ārī vi to use high-flown language.
amputātiō, -ōnis f pruning.
amputatus adj (RHET) disconnected.
amputō, -āre, -āvī, -ātum vt to cut off, prune; (fig) to lop off.
Amūlius, -ī m king of Alba Longa, grand-uncle of Romulus.
amurca, -ae f lees of olive oil.
amussitātus adj nicely adjusted.
Amȳclae, -ārum fpl town in S. Greece.
Amȳclaeus adj see n.
amygdalum, -ī nt almond.
amystis, -dis f emptying a cup at a draught.
an conj or; perhaps; (with single question) surely not; **haud sciō** ~ I feel sure.
Anacreōn, -ontis m Greek lyric poet.
anadēma, -tis nt headband.
anagnōstēs, -ae m reader.
anapaestum, -ī nt poem in anapaests.
anapaestus adj: ~ **pēs** anapaest.
anas, -tis f duck.
anaticula f duckling.
anatīnus adj see n.
anatocismus, -ī m compound interest.
Anaxagorās, -ae m early Greek philosopher.
Anaximander, -rī m early Greek philosopher.
anceps, -ipitis adj two-headed; double; wavering, doubtful; dangerous ♦ nt danger.
Anchīsēs, -ae m father of Aeneas.
Anchīsēus adj Aeneas.
Anchīsiadēs m Aeneas.
ancīle, -is nt oval shield (esp one said to have fallen from heaven in Numa's reign).
ancilla, -ae f servant.
ancillāris adj of a young servant.
ancillula f young servant.
ancīsus adj cut round.
ancora, -ae f anchor.
ancorārius adj see n.
ancorāle, -is nt cable.
Ancus Marcius, -ī, -ī m 4th king of Rome.
Ancȳra, -ae f Ankara (capital of Galatia).
andabata, -ae m blindfold gladiator.
Andrius adj see **Andros**.
androgynē, -ēs f hermaphrodite.
androgynus, -ī m hermaphrodite.
Andromachē, -ēs f wife of Hector.
Andromeda, -ae f wife of Perseus; a constellation.
Andronicus, -ī m Livius (earliest Latin poet).
Andros (-us), -ī m Aegean island.
ānellus, -ī m little ring.
anēthum, -ī nt fennel.
ānfrāctus, -ūs m bend, orbit; roundabout way; (words) digression, prolixity.
angelus, -ī m angel.
angina, -ae f quinsy.
angiportum, -ī nt alley.
angiportus, -ūs m alley.

Noun declensions and verb conjugations are shown on pp xiii to xxv. The present infinitive ending of a verb shows to which conjugation it belongs: **-āre** = 1st; **-ēre** = 2nd; **-ere** = 3rd and **-īre** = 4th. Irregular verbs are shown on p xxvi

ango̅, -ere *vt* to throttle; (*fig*) to distress, torment.
angor, -o̅ris *m* suffocation; (*fig*) anguish, torment.
anguicomus *adj* with snakes for hair.
anguiculus, -ī *m* small snake.
anguifer, -ī *adj* snake-carrying.
anguigena, -ae *m* one born of serpents; Theban.
anguilla, -ae *f* eel.
anguimanus *adj* with a trunk.
anguipe̅s, -edis *adj* serpent-footed.
anguis, -is *m/f* snake, serpent; (*constellation*) Draco.
Anguitene̅ns, -entis *m* Ophiuchus.
angula̅tus *adj* angular.
angulus, -ī *m* angle, corner; out-of-the-way place; **ad pare̅s ~o̅s** at right angles.
anguste̅ *adv* close, within narrow limits; concisely.
angustiae, -a̅rum *fpl* defile, strait; (*time*) shortness; (*means*) want; (*circs*) difficulty; (*mind*) narrowness; (*words*) subtleties.
angusticla̅vius *adj* wearing a narrow purple stripe.
angusto̅, -a̅re *vt* to make narrow.
angustum, -ī *nt* narrowness; danger.
angustus *adj* narrow, close; (*time*) short; (*means*) scanty; (*mind*) mean; (*argument*) subtle; (*circs*) difficult.
anhe̅litus, -ūs *m* panting; breath, exhalation.
anhe̅lo̅, -a̅re, -a̅vī, -a̅tum *vi* to breathe hard, pant; to exhale.
anhe̅lus *adj* panting.
anicula, -ae *f* poor old woman.
Anie̅nsis, Anie̅nus *adj* of the river Anio.
Anie̅nus *m* Anio.
anīlis *adj* of an old woman.
anīlita̅s, -ta̅tis *f* old age.
anīliter *adv* like an old woman.
anima, -ae *f* wind, air; breath; life; soul, mind; ghost, spirit; **~am agere, effla̅re** expire; **~am comprimere** hold one's breath.
animadversio̅, -o̅nis *f* observation; censure, punishment.
animadversor, -o̅ris *m* observer.
animadverto̅, -tere, -tī, -sum *vt* to pay attention to, notice; to realise; to censure, punish; **~ in** punish.
animal, -a̅lis *nt* animal; living creature.
anima̅lis *adj* of air; animate.
anima̅ns, -antis *m/f/nt* living creature; animal.
anima̅tio̅, -o̅nis *f* being.
anima̅tus *adj* disposed, in a certain frame of mind; courageous.
animo̅, -a̅re, -a̅vī, -a̅tum *vt* to animate; to give a certain temperament to.
animo̅se̅ *adv* boldly, eagerly.
animo̅sus *adj* airy; lifelike; courageous, proud.
animula, -ae *f* little soul.
animulus, -ī *m* darling.
animus, -ī *m* mind, soul; consciousness;

reason, thought, opinion, imagination; heart, feelings, disposition; courage, spirit, pride, passion; will, purpose; term of endearment; **~ī in** mind, in heart; **~ī causa̅** for amusement; **~o̅ fingere** imagine; **~o̅ male est** I am fainting; **aequo̅ ~o̅ esse** be patient, calm; **bono̅ ~o̅ esse** take courage; be well-disposed; **ex ~o̅** sincerely; **ex ~o̅ effluere** be forgotten; **in ~o̅ habe̅re** purpose; **meo̅ ~o̅ in** my opinion.
Anio̅, -e̅nis *m* tributary of the Tiber.
Anna Perenna, -ae, -ae *f* Roman popular goddess.
anna̅le̅s, -ium *mpl* annals, chronicle.
anna̅lis *adj* of a year; **le̅x ~** law prescribing ages for public offices.
anne *etc see* **an.**
anniculus *adj* a year old.
anniversa̅rius *adj* annual.
anno̅n or not.
anno̅na, -ae *f* year's produce; grain; price of corn; the market.
anno̅sus *adj* aged.
anno̅tinus *adj* last year's.
annus, -ī *m* year; **~ ma̅gnus** astronomical great year; **~ solidus** a full year.
annuus *adj* a year's; annual.
anquīro̅, -rere, -sīvī, -sītum *vt* to search for; to make inquiries; (*law*) to institute an inquiry (*de̅*) *or* prosecution (*abl or gen*).
a̅nsa, -ae *f* handle; (*fig*) opportunity.
a̅nsa̅tus *adj* with a handle; (*comedy*) with arms akimbo.
a̅nser, -is *m* goose.
a̅nserīnus *adj see* **n.**
ante *prep* (*with acc*) before (*in time, place, comparison*) ♦ *adv* (*place*) in front; (*time*) before.
antea̅ *adv* before, formerly.
antecapio̅, -apere, -e̅pī, -eptum *vt* to take beforehand, anticipate.
antece̅do̅, -e̅dere, -essī, -essum *vt* to precede; to surpass.
antecello̅, -ere *vi* to excel, be superior.
anteceptus *ppp of* **antecapio̅.**
antecessio̅, -o̅nis *f* preceding; antecedent cause.
antecessor, -o̅ris *m* forerunner.
antecursor, -o̅ris *m* forerunner, pioneer.
anteeo̅, -īre, -īī *vi* to precede, surpass.
antefero̅, -ferre, -tulī, -la̅tum *vt* to carry before; to prefer; to anticipate.
antefīxus *adj* attached (in front) ♦ *ntpl* ornaments on roofs of buildings.
antegredior, -dī, -ssus *vt* to precede.
antehabeo̅, -e̅re *vt* to prefer.
antehac *adv* formerly, previously.
antela̅tus *ppp of* **antefero̅.**
antelu̅ca̅nus *adj* before dawn.
antemerīdia̅nus *adj* before noon.
antemitto̅, -ittere, -īsī, -issum *vt* to send on in front.
antenna, -ae *f* yardarm.

antepīlānī, -ōrum mpl (MIL) the front ranks.
antepōnō, -ōnere, -osuī, -ositum vt to set
before; to prefer.
antequam conj before.
Anterōs, -ōtis m avenger of slighted love.
antēs, -ium mpl rows.
antesignānus, -ī m (MIL) eader; (pl) defenders
of the standards.
antestō, antistō, -āre, -ētī vi to excel,
distinguish oneself.
antestor, -ārī, -ātus vi to call a witness.
anteveniō, -enīre, -ēnī, -entum vt, vi to
anticipate; to surpass.
antevertō, -tere, -tī, -sum vt to precede; to
anticipate; to prefer.
anticipātiō, -ōnis f foreknowledge.
anticipō, -āre, -āvī, -ātum vt to take before,
anticipate.
antīcus adj in front.
Antigonē, -ēs f daughter of Oedipus.
Antigonus, -ī m name of Macedonian kings.
Antiochēnsis adj see n.
Antiochīa, -iae f Antioch (capita of Syria).
Antiochus, -ī m name of kings of Syria.
antīquārius, -ī and īī m artiquary.
antīquē adv in the old style.
antīquitās, -ātis f antiquity, the ancients;
integrity.
antīquitus adv long ago, from ancient times.
antīquō, -āre, -āvī, -ātum vt to vote against
(a bill).
antīquus adj ancient, former, old; good old-
fashioned, honest, illustrious; antīquior
more important; antīquissimus most
important.
antistēs, -itis m/f high priest, chief priestess;
(fig) master (in any art).
Antisthenēs, -is and ae m founder of Cynic
philosophy.
antistita, -ae f chief priestess.
antistō etc see antestō.
antitheton, -ī nt (RHET) antithesis.
Antōnīnus, -ī m name of Roman emperors (esp
Pius and Marcus Aurelius)
Antōnius, -ī m Roman name (esp the famous
orator, and Mark Antony).
antrum, -ī nt cave, hollow.
ānulārius, -ī m ringmaker.
ānulātus adj with rings on.
ānulus, -ī m ring; equestr an rank.
ānus, -ī m rectum; ring.
anus, -ūs f old woman ♦ adj old.
ānxiē adv see anxius.
ānxietās, -ātis f anxiety, trouble (of the mind).
ānxifer, -ī adj disquieting.
ānxitūdō, -inis f anxiety.
ānxius adj (mind) troubled, disquieting.
Āones, -um adj Boeotian.
Āonia f part of Boeotia.
Āonius adj of Boeotia, of Helicon.

Aornos, -ī m lake Avernus.
apage interj away with!, go away!
apēliōtēs, -ae m east wind.
Apellēs, -is m Greek painter.
aper, -rī m boar.
aperiō, -īre, -uī, -tum vt to uncover, disclose,
open; (country) to open up; (fig) to unfold,
explain, reveal.
apertē adv clearly, openly.
apertum, -ī nt open space; in ~ō esse be well
known; be easy.
apertus ppp of aperiō ♦ adj open, exposed;
clear, manifest; (person) frank.
aperuī perf of aperiō.
apex, -icis m summit; crown, priest's cap; (fig)
crown.
aphractus, -ī f a long open boat.
apiārius, -ī and īī m beekeeper.
Apicius, -ī m Roman epicure.
apicula, -ae f little bee.
apis, -is f bee.
apīscor, -īscī, -tus vt to catch, get, attain.
apium, -ī and īī nt celery.
aplustre, -is nt decorated stern of a ship.
apoclētī, -ōrum mpl committee of the Aetolian
League.
apodytērium, -ī and īī nt dressing room.
Apollināris, -ineus adj: lūdī ~ināres Roman
games in July.
Apollō, -inis m Greek god of music, archery,
prophecy, flocks and herds, and often identified
with the sun.
apologus, -ī m narrative, fable.
apophorēta, -ōrum ntpl presents for guests to
take home.
apoproēgmena, -ōrum ntpl (PHILOS) what is
rejected.
apostolicus adj see n.
apostolus, -ī m (ECCL) apostle.
apothēca, -ae f storehouse, wine store.
apparātē adv see apparātus.
apparātiō, -ōnis f preparation.
apparātus adj ready, well-supplied,
sumptuous.
apparātus, -ūs m preparation; equipment,
munitions; pomp, ostentation.
appāreō, -ēre, -uī, -itum vi to come in sight,
appear; to be seen, show oneself; to wait
upon (an official); ~et it is obvious.
appāritiō, -ōnis f service; domestic servants.
appāritor, -ōris m attendant.
apparō, -āre, -āvī, -ātum vt to prepare,
provide.
appellātiō, -ōnis f accosting, appeal; title;
pronunciation.
appellātor, -ōris m appellant.
appellitātus adj usually called.
appellō, -āre, -āvī, -ātum vt to speak to; to
appeal to; (for money) to dun; (law) to sue; to
call, name; to pronounce.

appellō, -ellere, -ulī, -ulsum vt to drive, bring (to); (_NAUT_) to bring to land.

appendicula, -ae f small addition.

appendix, -icis f supplement.

appendō, -endere, -endī, -ensum vt to weigh, pay.

appetēns, -entis adj eager; greedy.

appetenter adv see **appetēns.**

appetentia, -ae f craving.

appetītiō, -ōnis f grasping, craving.

appetītus ppp of **appetō.**

appetītus, -ūs m craving; natural desire (as _opposed to reason_).

appetō, -ere, -īvī, -ītum vt to grasp, try to get at; to attack; to desire ♦ vi to approach.

appingō, -ere vt to paint (in); (_colloq_) to write more.

Appius, -ī m Roman first name; **Via ~ia** _main road from Rome to Capua and Brundisium._

applaudō, -dere, -sī, -sum vt to strike, clap ♦ vi to applaud.

applicātiō, -ōnis f applying (_of the mind_); **iūs ~ōnis** _the right of a patron to inherit a client's effects._

applicātus and **ītus** ppp of **applicō.**

applicō, -āre, -āvī and **uī, -ātum** and **itum** vt to attach, place close (to); (_NAUT_) to steer, bring to land; **sē, animum ~** devote self, attention (to).

applōrō, -āre vt to deplore.

appōnō, -ōnere, -osuī, -ositum vt to put (to, beside); (_meal_) to serve; to add, appoint; to reckon.

apporrēctus adj stretched nearby.

apportō, -āre, -āvī, -ātum vt to bring, carry (to).

apposcō, -ere vt to demand also.

appositē adv suitably.

appositus ppp of **appōnō** ♦ adj situated near; (_fig_) bordering on; suitable.

apposuī perf of **appōnō.**

appōtus adj drunk.

apprecor, -ārī, -ātus vt to pray to.

apprehendō, -endere, -endī, -ēnsum vt to take hold of; (_MIL_) to occupy; (_argument_) to bring forward.

apprīmē adv especially.

apprimō, -imere, -essī, -essum vt to press close.

approbātiō, -ōnis f acquiescence; proof.

approbātor, -ōris m approve.

approbē adv very well.

approbō, -āre, -āvī, -ātum vt to approve; to prove; to perform to someone's satisfaction.

apprōmittō, -ere vt to promise also.

approperō, -āre, -āvī, -ātum vt to hasten ♦ vi to hurry up.

appropinquātiō, -ōnis f approach.

appropinquō, -āre, -āvī, -ātum vi to approach.

appugnō, -āre vt to attack.

appulsus ppp of **appellō.**

appulsus, -ūs m landing; approach.

aprīcātiō, -ōnis f basking.

aprīcor, -ārī vi to bask.

aprīcus adj sunny; basking; **in ~um prōferre** bring to light.

Aprīlis adj April, of April.

aprūgnus adj of the wild boar.

aps- etc see **abs-.**

aptē adv closely; suitably, rightly.

aptō, -āre, -āvī, -ātum vt to fit, put on; (_fig_) to adapt; to prepare, equip.

aptus adj attached, joined together, fitted (with); suitable.

apud prep (_with acc_) 1. (_with persons_) beside, by, with, at the house of, among, in the time of; (_speaking_) in the presence of, to; (_judgment_) in the opinion of; (_influence_) with; (_faith_) in; (_authors_) in 2. (_with places_) near, at, in; **est ~ mē** I have; **sum ~ mē** I am in my senses.

Āpūlia, -iae f district of S.E. Italy.

Āpūlus adj see n.

aput prep see **apud.**

aqua, -ae f water; **~ mihī haeret** I am in a fix; **~ intercus** dropsy; **~m adspergere** revive; **~m praebēre** entertain; **~m et terram petere** demand submission; **~ā et ignī interdīcere** outlaw.

aquae fpl medicinal waters, spa.

aquaeductus, -ūs m aqueduct; right of leading water.

aquāliculus m belly.

aquālis, -is n/f washbasin.

aquārius ad of water ♦ m water carrier, water inspector; a constellation.

aquāticus adj aquatic; humid.

aquātilis ad aquatic.

aquātiō, -ōnis f fetching water; watering place.

aquātor, -ōris m water carrier.

aquila, -ae f eagle; standard of a legion; (_ARCH_) gable; a constellation; **~ae senectūs** a vigorous old age.

Aquileia, -ae f town in N. Italy.

Aquileiēnsis adj see n.

aquilifer, -ī m chief standard-bearer.

aquilīnus adj eagle's.

aquilō, -ōnis m north wind; north.

aquilōnius adj northerly.

aquilus adj swarthy.

Aquīnās, ātis adj see n.

Aquīnum, -ī nt town in Latium.

Aquītānia, -iae f district of S.W. Gaul.

Aquītānus adj see n.

aquor, -ārī, -ātus vi to fetch water.

aquōsus adj humid, rainy.

aquula, -ae f little stream.

āra, -ae f altar; (_fig_) refuge; a constellation; **~ae et focī** hearth and home.

arabarchēs, -ae m customs officer in Egypt.

Arabia, -iae f Arabia.

Arabicē adv with all the perfumes of Arabia.

Arabicus, Arabicius, Arabus adj see n.

Arachnē, -s f Lydian woman changed into a spider.

aranea, -ae f spider; cobweb.
araneola f, **-olus** m small spider
araneōsus adj full of spiders' webs.
araneum, -ī nt spider's web.
araneus, -i m spider ♦ adj of spiders.
Arar, -is m river Saône.
Arātēus adj see **Arātus.**
aratiō, -ōnis f ploughing, farming; arable land.
aratiuncula f small plot.
arator -ōris m ploughman, farmer; (pl) cultivators of public land.
aratrum, -ī nt plough.
Arātus, -ī m Greek astronomical poet.
Araxēs, -is m river in Armenia.
arbiter, -rī m witness; arbiter, judge, umpire; controller; ~ **bibendī** president of a drinking party.
arbitra, -ae f witness.
arbitrāriō adv with some uncertainty.
arbitrārius adj uncertain
arbitrātus, -ūs m decision; meō -ū in my judgment.
arbitrium, -ī and **iī** nt decision (of an arbitrator), judgment; mastery, control.
arbitror, -ārī, -ātus vt, vi to be a witness of; to testify; to think, suppose.
arbor, (arbōs), -oris f tree; ship, mast, oar; ~ **īnfēlīx** gallows.
arboreus adj of trees, like a tree.
arbustum, -ī nt plantation, orchard; (pl) trees.
arbustus adj wooded
arbuteus adj of the strawberry tree.
arbutum, -ī nt fruit of strawberry tree.
arbutus, -ī f strawberry tree.
arca, -ae f box; moneybox, purse; coffin; prison cell; **ex ~ā absolvere** pay cash.
Arcades, -um mpl Arcadians.
Arcadia, -iae f district of S. Greece.
Arcadicus, -ius adj see **Arcadia.**
arcānō adv privately.
arcānum, -ī nt secret, mystery.
arcānus adj secret; able to keep secrets.
arceō, -ēre, -uī, -tum vt to enclose; to keep off, prevent.
accessītū abl sg m at the summons
accessītus ppp of **accessō** ♦ adj far-fetched.
accessō, -ere, -īvī, -ītum vt to send for, fetch; (law) to summon, accuse; (fig) to derive.
archetypus, -ī m original.
Archilochus, -ī m Greek iambic and elegiac poet.
archimagīrus, -ī m chief cook.
Archimēdēs, -is m famous mathematician of Syracuse.
archipīrāta, -ae m pirate chief.
architectōn, -onis m master builder; master in cunning.
architector, -ārī, -ātus vi to construct; (fig) to devise.
architectūra, -ae f architecture.

architectus, -ī m architect; (fig) author.
archōn, -ontis m Athenian magistrate.
Archytās, -ae m Pythagorean philosopher of Tarentum.
arcitenēns, -entis adj holding a bow ♦ m Apollo.
Arctophylax, -cis m (constellation) Bootes.
arctos, -ī f Great Bear, Little Bear; north, north wind; night.
Arctūrus, -ī m brightest star in Boôtes.
arctus etc see **artus** etc.
arcuī perf of **arceō.**
arcula, -ae f casket; (RHET) ornament.
arcuō, -āre, -āvī, -ātum vt to curve.
arcus, -ūs m bow; rainbow; arch, curve; (MATH) arc.
ardea, -ae f heron.
Ardea, -ae f town in Latium.
ardeliō, -ōnis m busybody.
ardēns, -entis adj hot, glowing, fiery; (fig) eager, ardent.
ardenter adv passionately.
ardeō, -dēre, -sī, -sum vi to be on fire, burn, shine; (fig) to be fired, burn.
ardēscō, -ere vi to catch fire, gleam; (fig) to become inflamed, wax hotter.
ardor, -ōris m heat, brightness; (fig) ardour, passion.
arduum, -ī nt steep slope; difficulty.
arduus adj steep, high; difficult, troublesome.
area, -ae f vacant site, open space, playground; threshing-floor; (fig) scope (for effort).
arefaciō, -acere, -ēcī, -actum vt to dry.
arēna etc see **harēna.**
arēns, -entis adj arid; thirsty.
areō, -ēre vi to be dry.
areola, -ae f small open space.
Arēopagītēs m member of the court.
Arēopagus, -ī m Mars' Hill in Athens; a criminal court.
Arēs, -is m Greek god of war.
ārēscō, -ere vi to dry, dry up.
Arestoridēs, -ae m Argus.
aretālogus, -ī m braggart.
Arethūsa, -ae f spring near Syracuse.
Arethūsis adj Syracusan.
Argēī, -ōrum mpl sacred places in Rome; effigies thrown annually into the Tiber.
argentāria, -ae f bank, banking; silver mine.
argentārius adj of silver, of money ♦ m banker.
argentātus adj silver-plated; backed with money.
argenteus adj of silver, adorned with silver; silvery (in colour); of the silver age.
argentum, -ī nt silver, silver plate; money.
Argēus, -īvus, -olicus adj Argive; Greek.
Argīlētānus adj see n.
Argīlētum, -ī nt part of Rome (noted for

bookshops).
argilla, -ae _f_ clay.
Argō, -ūs _f_ Jason's ship.
Argolis, -olidis _f_ district about Argos.
Argonautae, -ārum _mpl_ Argonauts.
Argonauticus _adj see n._
Argos _nt, -ī, -ōrum_ _mpl_ town in S.E. Greece.
Argōus _adj see_ **Argō.**
argūmentātiō, -ōnis _f_ adducing proofs.
argūmentor, -ārī, -ātus _vt, vi_ to prove,
 adduce as proof; to conclude.
argūmentum, -ī _nt_ evidence, proof; (_LIT_)
 subject matter, theme, plot (_of a play_); (_art_)
 subject, motif.
arguō, -uere, -uī, -ūtum _vt_ to prove, make
 known; to accuse, blame, denounce.
Argus, -ī _m_ monster with many eyes.
argūtē _adv_ subtly.
argūtiae, -ārum _fpl_ nimbleness, liveliness;
 wit, subtlety, slyness.
argūtor, -ārī, -ātus _vi_ to chatter.
argūtulus _adj_ rather subtle.
argūtus _adj_ (_sight_) clear, distinct, graceful;
 (_sound_) clear, melodious, noisy; (_mind_)
 acute, witty, sly.
argyraspis, -dis _adj_ silver-shielded.
Ariadna, -ae _f_ daughter of Minos of Crete.
Ariadnaeus _adj see n._
āridulus _adj_ rather dry.
āridum, -ī _nt_ dry land.
āridus _adj_ dry, withered; meagre; (_style_) flat.
ariēs, -etis _m_ ram; 1st sign of Zodiac;
 battering ram; beam used as a breakwater.
arietō, -āre _vt, vi_ to butt, strike hard.
Ariōn, -onis _m_ early Greek poet and musician.
Ariōnius _adj see n._
arista, -ae _f_ ear of corn.
Aristaeus, -ī _m_ legendary founder of beekeeping.
Aristarchus, -ī _m_ Alexandrian scholar; a severe
 critic.
Aristīdēs, -is _m_ Athenian statesman noted for
 integrity.
Aristippēus _adj see n._
Aristippus, -ī _m_ Greek hedonist philosopher.
aristolochia, -ae _f_ birthwort.
Aristophanēs, -is _m_ Greek comic poet.
Aristophanēus, _and_ **īus** _adj see n._
Aristotelēs, -is _m_ Aristotle (_founder of_
 Peripatetic school of philosophy).
Aristotelēus, _and_ **īus** _adj see n._
arithmētica, -ōrum _ntpl_ arithmetic.
āritūdō, -inis _f_ dryness.
Ariūsius _adj_ of Ariusia in Chios.
arma, -ōrum _ntpl_ armour, shield; arms,
 weapons (_of close combat only_); warfare,
 troops; (_fig_) defence, protection;
 implements, ship's gear.
armāmenta, -ōrum _ntpl_ implements, ship's
 gear.
armāmentārium, -ī _and_ **iī** _nt_ arsenal.
armāriolum, -ī _nt_ small chest.
armārium, -ī _and_ **iī** _nt_ chest, safe.
armātū _m abl_ armour; **gravī ~** with heavy-

armed troops.
armatūra, -ae _f_ armour, equipment; **levis ~**
 light-armed troops.
armatus _adj_ armed.
Armenia, -ae _f_ Armenia.
Armeniaca, -acae _f_ apricot tree.
Armeniacum, -acī _nt_ apricot.
Armenius _adj see_ **Armenia.**
armentālis _adj_ of the herd.
armentārius, -ī _and_ **iī** _m_ cattle herd.
armentum, -ī _nt_ cattle (_for ploughing_), herd
 (_cattle etc_).
armifer, -ī _adj_ armed.
armiger, -ī _m_ armour-bearer ♦ _adj_ armed;
 productive of warriors.
armilla, -ae _f_ bracelet.
armillātus _adj_ wearing a bracelet.
armipotēns, -entis _adj_ strong in battle.
armisonus _adj_ resounding with arms.
armō, -āre, -āvī, -ātum _vt_ to arm, equip; to
 rouse to arms (against).
armus, -ī _m_ shoulder (_esp of animals_).
Arniēnsis _adj see_ **Arnus.**
Arnus, -ī _m_ river Arno.
arō, -āre, -āvī, -ātum _vt_ to plough, cultivate;
 to live by farming; (_fig: sea, brow_) to furrow.
Arpīnās, -ātis _adj see n._
Arpīnum, -ī _nt_ town in Latium (_birthplace of_
 Cicero).
arquātus _adj_ jaundiced.
arr- _etc see_ **adr-.**
arrabō, -ōnis _m_ earnest money.
ars, artis _f_ skill (_in any craft_); the art (_of any_
 profession); science, theory; handbook; work
 of art; moral quality, virtue; artifice, fraud.
ārsī _perf of_ **ārdeō.**
ārsus _ppp of_ **ārdeō.**
artē _adv_ closely, soundly, briefly.
artēria, -ae _f_ windpipe; artery.
artēria, -ōrum _ntpl_ trachea.
arthrīticus _adj_ gouty.
articulātim _adv_ joint by joint; (_speech_)
 distinctly.
articulō, -āre, -āvī, -ātum _vt_ to articulate.
articulōsus _adj_ minutely subdivided.
articulus, -ī _m_ joint, knuckle; limb; (_words_)
 clause; (_time_) point, turning point; **in ipsō ~ō**
 temporis in the nick of time.
artifex, -ic _s m_ artist, craftsman, master; (_fig_)
 maker, author ♦ _adj_ ingenious, artistic,
 artificial.
artificiōsē _adv_ skilfully.
artificiōsus _adj_ ingenious, artistic, artificial.
artificium, -ī _and_ **iī** _nt_ skill, workmanship; art,
 craft; theory, rule of an art; ingenuity,
 cunning.
artō, -āre _vt_ to compress, curtail.
artolaganus, -ī _m_ kind of cake.
artopta, -ae _m_ baker; baking tin.
artus _adj_ close, narrow, tight; (_sleep_) deep;
 (_fig_) strict, straitened.
artus, -ūs _m_ joint; (_pl_) limbs, body; (_fig_)
 strength

ārula, -ae f small altar.
arundō etc see **harundō** etc.
arvīna, -ae f grease.
arvum, -ī nt field; land, country, plain.
arvus adj ploughed.
arx, arcis f fortress, castle, height, summit; (fig) bulwark, stronghold; **arcem facere ē cloācā** make a mountain out of a molehill.
ās, assis m (weight) pound; (coin) bronze unit, of low value; (inheritance) the whole (subdivided into 12 parts ; **ad assem** to the last farthing; **hērēs ex asse** sole heir.
Ascānius, -ī m son of Aeneas.
ascendō, -endere, -endī, -ēnsum vt, vi to go up, climb, embark; (fig) to rise.
ascēnsiō, -ōnis f ascent (fig) sublimity.
ascēnsus, -ūs m ascent, rising; way up.
ascia, -ae f axe; mason's trowel.
ascīō, -īre vt to admit.
ascīscō, -īscere, -īvī, -ītum vt to receive with approval; to admit (to somekind of association); to appropriate, adopt (esp customs); to arrogate to oneself.
ascītus adj acquired, alien.
Ascra, -ae f birthplace of Hesiod in Boeotia.
Ascraeus adj of Ascra; of Hesiod; of Helicon.
ascrībō, -bere, -psī, -ptum vt to add (in writing); to attribute, ascribe; to apply (an illustration); to enrol, include.
ascrīptīcius adj enrolled
ascrīptiō, -ōnis f addition (in writing).
ascrīptīvus adj (MIL) supernumerary.
ascriptor, -ōris m supporter.
ascrīptus ppp of **ascrībō**.
asella, -ae f young ass.
asellus, -ī m young ass.
Āsia, -ae f Roman province; Asia Minor; Asia.
asīlus, -ī m gad fly.
asinus, -ī m ass; fool.
Āsis, -dis f Asia.
Āsius (Āsiānus, Āsiāticus) adj see n.
Āsōpus, -ī m river in Boeotia.
asōtus, -ī m libertine.
asparagus, -ī m asparagus.
aspargō etc see **aspergō**.
aspectābilis adj visible.
aspectō, -āre vt to look at, gaze at; to pay heed to; (places) to face.
aspectus ppp of **aspiciō**.
aspectus, -ūs m look, sight; glance, sense of sight; aspect, appearance
aspellō, -ere vt to drive away.
asper, -ī adj rough; (taste) bitter; (sound) harsh; (weather) severe; (fig) rugged; (person) violent, exasperated, unkind, austere; (animal) savage; (circs) difficult.
asperē adv see adj.
aspergō, -gere, -sī, -sum vt to scatter, sprinkle; to bespatter, besprinkle; **aquam ~** revive.
aspergō, -inis f sprinkling; spray.

asperitās, -ātis f roughness, unevenness, harshness, severity; (fig) ruggedness, fierceness; trouble, difficulty.
aspernātiō, -ōnis f disdain.
aspernor, -ārī, -ātus vt to reject, disdain.
asperō, -āre, -āvī, -ātum vt to roughen, sharpen; to exasperate.
aspersiō, -ōnis f sprinkling.
aspersus ppp of **aspergō**.
aspiciō, -icere, -exī, -ectum vt to catch sight of, look at; (places) to face; (fig) to examine, consider.
aspīrātiō, -ōnis f breathing (on); evaporation; pronouncing with an aspirate.
aspīrō, -āre, -āvī, -ātum vi to breathe, blow; to favour; to aspire, attain (to) ♦ vt to blow, instil.
aspis, -dis f asp.
asportātiō, -ōnis f removal.
asportō, -āre vt to carry off.
asprēta, -ōrum ntpl rough country.
ass- etc see **ads-**.
Assaracus, -ī m Trojan ancestor of Aeneas.
asser, -is m pole, stake.
assula, -ae f splinter.
assulātim adv in splinters.
assum, -ī nt roast; (pl) sweating-bath.
āssus adj roasted.
Assyria, -ae f country in W. Asia.
Assyrius adj Assyrian; oriental.
ast conj (laws) and then; (vows) then; (strong contrast) and yet.
ast- etc see **adst-**.
Astraea, -ae f goddess of Justice.
Astraeus, -ī m father of winds; **~ī frātrēs** the winds.
astrologia, -ae f astronomy.
astrologus, -ī m astronomer; astrologer.
astrum, -ī nt star, heavenly body, constellation; a great height; heaven, immortality, glory.
astu nt (indecl) city (esp Athens).
astus, -ūs m cleverness, cunning.
astūtē adv cleverly.
astūtia, -ae f slyness, cunning.
astūtus adj artful, sly.
Astyanax, -ctis m son of Hector and Andromache.
asȳlum, -ī nt sanctuary.
asymbolus adj with no contribution.
at conj (adversative) but, on the other hand; (objecting) but it may be said; (limiting) at least, but at least; (continuing) then, thereupon; (transitional) now; (with passionate appeals) but oh!, look now!; **~ enim** yes, but; **~ tamen** nevertheless.
Atābulus, -ī m sirocco.
atat interj (expressing fright, pain, surprise) oh!
atavus, -ī m great-great-great-grandfather; ancestor.

Atella, -ae *f Oscan town in Campania.*
Atellānicus, Atellānius *adj see n.*
Atellānus *adj:* **fābula ~āna** *kind of comic show popular in Rome.*
āter, -rī *adj* black, dark; gloomy, dismal; malicious; **diēs ~rī** unlucky days.
Athamantēus *adj see* **Athamās.**
Athamantiadēs *m* Palaemon.
Athamantis *f* Helle.
Athamās, -antis *m* king of Thessaly (*who went mad*).
Athēnae, -ārum *fpl* Athens.
Athēnaeus, -iēnsis *adj see n.*
atheos, -ī *m* atheist.
athlēta, -ae *m* wrestler, athlete.
athlēticē *adv* athletically.
Athos (*dat* -ō, *acc* -ō, -on, -ōnem) *m mount Athos in Macedonia.*
Atlanticus *adj:* **mare ~anticum** Atlantic Ocean.
Atlantiadēs *m* Mercury.
Atlantis *f* lost Atlantic island; a Pleiad.
Atlās, -antis *m giant supporting the sky;* Atlas mountains.
atomus, -ī *m* atom.
atque (*before consonants* **ac**) *conj* (*connecting words*) and, and in fact; (*connecting clauses*) and moreover, and then, and so, and yet; (*in comparison*) as, than, to, from; **~ adeō** and that too; or rather; **~ nōn** and not rather; **~ sī** as if; **alius ~** different from; **contrā ~** opposite to; **īdem ~** same as; **plūs ~** more than.
atquī *conj* (*adversative*) and yet, nevertheless, yes but; (*confirming*) by all means; (*minor premise*) now; **~ sī** if now.
ātrāmentum, -ī *nt* ink; blacking.
ātrātus *adj* in mourning.
Atreus, -eī *m* son of Pelops (*king of Argos*).
Atrīdēs *m* Agamemnon; Meneleaus.
ātriēnsis, -is *m* steward, major-domo.
ātriolum, -ī *nt* anteroom.
ātrium, -ī *and* **īī** *nt* hall, *open central room in Roman house; forecourt of a temple;* hall (*in other buildings*).
atrōcitās, -ātis *f* hideousness; (*mind*) brutality; (PHILOS) severity.
atrōciter *adv* savagely.
Atropos, -ī *f* one of the Fates.
atrōx, -ōcis *adj* hideous, dreadful; fierce, brutal, unyielding.
attāctus ppp *of* **attingō.**
attāctus, -ūs *m* contact.
attagēn, -is *m* heathcock.
Attalica *ntpl* garments of woven gold.
Attalicus *adj* of Attalus; of Pergamum; ornamented with gold cloth.
Attalus, -ī *m* king of Pergamum (*who bequeathed his kingdom to Rome*).
attamen *conj* nevertheless.
attat *etc see* **atat.**
attegia, -ae *f* hut.
attemperātē *adv* opportunely.
attempto *etc see* **attentō.**

attendō, -dere, -dī, -tum *vt* to direct (*the attention*); to attend to, notice.
attenē *adv* carefully.
attentiō, -ōnis *f* attentiveness.
attentō, -āre, -āvī, -ātum *vt* to test, try; (*loyalty*) to tamper with; to attack.
attentus ppp *of* **attendō** ♦ *adj* attentive, intent; businesslike, careful (*esp about money*).
attentus ppp *of* **attineō.**
attenuātē *adv* simply.
attenuātus *adj* weak; (*style*) brief; refined; plain.
attenuō, -āre, -āvī, -ātum *vt* to weaken, reduce; to diminish; to humble.
atterō, -erere, -rīvī, -rītum *vt* to rub; to wear away; (*fig*) to impair, exhaust.
attestor, -ārī, -ātus *vt* to confirm.
attexō, -ere, -uī, -tum *vt* to weave on; (*fig*) to add on.
Atthis, -dis *f* Attica.
Attiānus *adj see* **Attius.**
Attica, -ae *f* district of Greece about Athens.
Atticē *adv* in the Athenian manner.
Atticissō *vi* to speak in the Athenian manner.
Atticus *adj* Attic, Athenian; (RHET) of a plain and direct style.
attigī *perf of* **attingō.**
attigō *see* **attingō.**
attineō, -inēre, -inuī, -entum *vt* to hold fast, detain; to guard; to reach for ♦ *vi* to concern, pertain, be of importance, avail.
attingō, -ingere, -igī, -āctum *vt* to touch; to strike, assault; to arrive at; to border on; to affect; to mention; to undertake; to concern, resemble.
Attis, -dis *m* Phrygian priest of Cybele.
Attius, -ī *m* Latin tragic poet.
attollō, -ere *vt* to lift up, erect; (*fig*) to exalt, extol.
attondeō, -ondēre, -ondī, -ōnsum *vt* to shear, prune, crop; (*fig*) to diminish; (*comedy*) to fleece.
attonitus *adj* thunderstruck, terrified, astonished; inspired.
attonō, -āre, -uī, -itum *vt* to stupefy.
attōnsus ppp *of* **attondeō.**
attorqueō, -ēre *vt* to hurl upwards.
attractus ppp *of* **attrahō.**
attrahō, -here, -xī, -ctum *vt* to drag by force, attract; (*fig*) to draw, incite.
attrectō, -āre *vt* to touch, handle; to appropriate.
attrepidō, -āre *vi* to hobble along.
attribuō, -uere, -uī, -ūtum *vt* to assign, bestow; to add; to impute, attribute; to lay as a tax.
attribūtiō, -ōnis *f* (*money*) assignment; (GRAM) predicate.
attribūtum, -ī *nt* (GRAM) predicate.
attribūtus ppp *of* **attribuō** ♦ *adj* subject.
attrītus ppp *of* **atterō** ♦ *adj* worn; bruised; (*fig*) impudent.
attulī *perf of* **adferō.**

au *interj* (*expressing pain, surprise*) oh!

auceps, -upis *m* fowler; (*fig*) eavesdropper; a pedantic critic.

auctārium, -ī *and* **iī** *nt* extra.

auctilicus *adj* increasing.

auctiō, -ōnis *f* increase; auction sale.

auctiōnārius *adj* auction; **tabulae -ae** catalogues.

auctiōnor, -ārī, -ātus *vi* to hold an auction.

auctitō, -āre *vt* to greatly increase.

auctō, -āre *vt* to increase.

auctor, -ōris *m/f* 1. (*originator of families*) progenitor; (: *of buildings*) founder; (: *of deeds*) doer. 2. (*composer of writings*) author, historian; (: *of knowledge*) investigator, teacher; (: *of news*) informant. 3. (*instigator of action*) adviser; (: *of measures*) promoter; (: *of laws*) proposer, supporter; ratifier. 4. (*person of influence: in public life*) leader; (: *of conduct*) model; (: *of guarantees*) witness, bail; (: *of property*) seller; (: *of women and minors*) guardian; (: *of others' welfare*) champion; **mē ~ōre** at my suggestion.

auctōrāmentum, -ī *nt* contract; wages.

auctōrātus *adj* bound (*by a pledge*); hired out (*for wages*).

auctōritās, -ātis *f* 1. source; lead, responsibility. 2. judgment; opinion; advice, support; bidding, gudance; (*of senate*) decree; (*of people*) will. 3. power; (*person*) influence, authority prestige; (*things*) importance, worth; (*conduct*) example; (*knowledge*) warrant document, authority; (*property*) right of possession.

auctumn- *etc see* **autumn-**.

auctus *ppp of* **augeō** ♦ *adj* enlarged, great.

auctus, -ūs *m* growth, increase.

aucupium, -ī *and* **iī** *nt* fowling; birds caught; (*fig*) hunting (after), quibbling.

aucupō, -āre *vt* to watch for.

aucupor, -ārī, -ātus *vi* to go fowling ♦ *vt* to chase; (*fig*) to try to catch.

audācia, -ae *f* daring, courage; audacity, impudence; (*pl*) deeds of daring.

audācter, audāciter *adv see* **audāx**.

audāx, -ācis *adj* bold, daring; rash, audacious; proud.

audēns, -entis *adj* bold, brave.

audenter *adv see* **audēns**.

audentia, -ae *f* boldness, courage.

audeō, -dēre, -sus *vt, vi* to dare, venture; to be brave.

audiēns, -entis *m* hearer ♦ *adj* obedient.

audientia, -ae *f* hearing; ~ **m facere** gain a hearing.

audiō, -īre, -īvī *and* **iī, -ītum** *vt* to hear; to learn, be told; to be called; to listen, attend to, study under (a teacher); to examine a case; to agree with; to obey, heed; **bene/ male ~** have a good/bad reputation.

audītiō, -ōnis *f* listening; hearsay, news.

audītor, -ōris *m* hearer; pupil.

audītōrium, -ī *and* **iī** *nt* lecture room, law court; audience.

audītus, -ūs *m* (sense of) hearing; a hearing; rumour.

auferō, auferre, abstulī, ablātum *vt* to take away, carry away; to mislead, lead into a digression; to take by force, steal; to win, obtain (*as the result of effort*); **aufer** away with!

Aufidus, -ō *m* river in Apulia.

aufugiō, -ugere, -ūgī *vi* to run away ♦ *vt* to flee from.

Augeās, -ae *m* king of Elis (*whose stables Hercules cleaned*).

augeō, -gēre, -xī, -ctum *vt* to increase; to enrich, bless (with); to praise, worship ♦ *vi* to increase.

augēscō, -ere *vi* to begin to grow, increase.

augmen, -inis *nt* growth.

augur, -is *m/f* augur; prophet, interpreter.

augurāle, -is *nt* part of camp where auspices were taken.

augurālis *adj* augur's.

augurātiō, -ōnis *f* soothsaying.

augurātō *adv* after taking auspices.

augurātus, -ūs *m* office of augur.

augurium, -ī *and* **iī** *nt* augury; an omen; prophecy, interpretation; presentiment.

augurius *adj* of augurs.

augurō, -āre *vt, vi* to take auguries; to consecrate by auguries; to forebode.

auguror, -ārī, -ātus *vt, vi* to take auguries; to foretell by omens; to predict, conjecture.

Augusta, -ae *f* title of the emperor's wife, mother, daughter *or* sister.

Augustālis *adj* of Augustus; **lūdī ~ēs** games in October; **praefectus ~is** governor of Egypt; **sodālēs ~ēs** priests of deified Augustus.

augustē *adv see* **augustus**.

augustus *adj* venerable, august, majestic.

Augustus, -ī *m* title given to C Octavius, first Roman emperor, and so to his successors ♦ *adj* imperial; (*month*) August, of August.

aula, -ae *f* courtyard of a Greek house; hall of a Roman house; palace, royal court; courtiers; royal power.

aula *etc see* **olla**.

aulaeum, -ī *nt* embroidered hangings, canopy, covering; (*THEAT*) curtain.

aulicī, -ōrum *mpl* courtiers.

aulicus *adj* of the court.

Aulis, -idis *and* **is** *f* port in Boeotia from which the Greeks sailed for Troy.

auloedus, -ī *m* singer accompanied by flute.

aura, -ae *f* breath of air, breeze, wind; air, upper world; vapour, odour, sound, gleam; (*fig*) winds (*of public favour*), breeze (*of prosperity*); air (*of freedom*), daylight (*of*

Noun declensions and verb conjugations are shown on pp xiii to xxv. The present infinitive ending of a verb shows to which conjugation it belongs **-āre** = 1st; **-ēre** = 2nd; **-ere** = 3rd and **-īre** = 4th. Irregular verbs are shown on p xxvi

publ*i*city).
aurāria, -ae *f* gold mine.
aurārius *adj* of gold.
aurātus *adj* gilt, ornamented with gold; gold.
Aurēlius, -ī *m* Roman name; **lēx ~ia** *law on the composition of juries*; **via ~ia** *main road running NW from Rome.*
aureolus *adj* gold; beautiful, splendid.
aureus *adj* gold, golden; gilded; (*fig*) beautiful splendid ♦ *m* gold coin.
aurichalcum, -ī *nt* a precious metal.
auricomus *adj* golden-leaved.
auricula, -ae *f* the external ear; ear.
aurifer, -ī *adj* gold-producing.
aurifex, -icis *m* goldsmith.
aurīga, -ae *m* charioteer, driver; groom; helmsman; a constellation.
aurigena, -ae *adj* gold-begotten.
auriger, -ī *adj* gilded.
aurīgō, -āre *vi* to compete in the chariot race.
auris, -is *f* ear; (*RHET*) judgment; (*AGR*) earthboard (*of a plough*); **ad ~em admonēre** whisper; **in utramvis ~em dormīre** sleep soundly.
aurītulus, -ī *m* "Long-Ears".
aurītus *adj* long-eared; attentive.
aurōra, -ae *f* dawn, morning; *goddess of dawn*; the East.
aurum, -i *nt* gold; gold plate, jewellery, bit, fleece *etc*; money; lustre; the Golden Age.
auscultātiō, -ōnis *f* obedience.
auscultātor, -ōris *m* listener.
auscultō, -āre, -āvī, -ātum *vt* to listen to; to overhear ♦ *vi* (*of servants*) to wait at the door; to obey.
ausim *subj of* **audeō.**
Ausones, -um *mpl* *indigenous people of central Italy.*
Ausonia *f* Italy.
Ausonidae *mpl* Italians.
Ausonius, -is *adj* Italian.
auspex, -icis *m* augur, soothsayer; patron, commander; witness of a marriage contract.
auspicātō *adv* after taking auspices; at a lucky moment.
auspicātus *adj* consecrated; auspicious, lucky.
auspicium, -ī *and* **iī** *nt* augury, auspices; right of taking auspices; power, command; omen; **~ facere** give a sign.
auspicō, -āre *vi* to take the auspices.
auspicor, -ārī, -ātus *vi* to take the auspices; to make a beginning ♦ *vt* to begin, enter upon.
auster, -rī *m* south wind; south.
austērē *adv see* **austērus.**
austēritās, -ātis *f* severity.
austērus *adj* severe, serious; gloomy, irksome.
austrālis *adj* southern.
austrīnus *adj* from the south.
ausum, -ī *nt* enterprise.

ausus *ppa of* **audeō.**
aut *conj* or; either ... or; or else *or* at least, or rather.
autem *conj* (*adversative*) but, on the other hand; (*in transitions, parentheses*) moreover, now, and; (*in dialogue*) indeed.
authepsa, -ae *f* stove.
autographus *adj* written with his own hand.
Autolycus, -ī *m* a robber.
automaton, -ī *nt* automaton.
automatus *adj* spontaneous.
Automedōn, -ontis *m* a charioteer.
autumnālis *adj* autumn, autumnal.
autumnus, -ī *m* autumn ♦ *adj* autumnal.
autumō, -āre *vt* to assert.
auxī *perf of* **augeō.**
auxilia, -iōrum *ntpl* auxiliary troops; military force.
auxiliāris *adj* helping, auxiliary; of the auxiliaries ♦ *mpl* auxiliary troops.
auxiliārius *adj* helping; auxiliary.
auxiliātor, -ōris *m* helper.
auxiliātus, -ūs *m* aid.
auxilior, -ārī, -ātus *vi* to aid, support.
auxilium, -ī *and* **iī** *nt* help, assistance.
avārē, avāiter *adv see* **avārus.**
avāritia, -ae *f* greed, selfishness.
avāritiēs, -ēī *f* avarice.
avārus *adj* greedy, covetous; eager.
avē, avēte, avētō *impv* hail!, farewell!
āvehō, -here, -xī, -ctum *vt* to carry away; (*pass*) to ride away.
āvellō, -ellere, -ellī *and* **ulsī (-olsī), -ulsum (-olsum)** *vt* to pull away, tear off; to take away (by force), remove.
avēna, -ae *f* oats; (*music*) reed, shepherd's pipe.
Aventīnum, -ī *nt* Aventine hill.
Aventīnus, -ī *m* Aventine hill in Rome ♦ *adj* of Aventine.
avēns, -entis *adj* eager.
aveō, -ēre *vt* to desire, long for.
Avernālis *adj* of lake Avernus.
Avernus, -ī *m* lake near Cumae (*said to be an entrance to the lower world*); the lower world ♦ *adj* birdless; of Avernus; infernal.
āverruncō, -āre *vt* to avert.
āversābilis *adj* abominable.
āversor, -ārī, -ātus *vi* to turn away ♦ *vt* to repulse, decline.
āversor, -ōris *m* embezzler.
āversum, -ī *nt* back.
āversus *ppp of* **āvertō** ♦ *adj* in the rear, behind, backwards; hostile, averse.
āvertō, -tere, -tī, -sum *vt* to turn aside, avert; to divert; to embezzle; to estrange ♦ *vi* to withdraw.
avia, -ae *f* grandmother.
avia, -ōrum *ntpl* wilderness.
aviārium, -ī *nt* aviary, haunt of birds.
aviārius *adj* of birds.
avidē *adv see* **avidus.**
aviditās, -ātis *f* eagerness, longing; avarice.

avidus adj eager, covetous; avaricious, greedy; hungry; vast.
avis, -is f bird; omen; - alba a rarity.
avītus adj of a grandfather; ancestral.
āvius adj out of the way, lonely, untrodden; wandering, astray.
āvocāmentum, -ī nt relaxation.
āvocātiō, -ōnis f diversion.
āvocō, -āre vt to call off; to divert, distract; to amuse.
āvolō, -āre vi to fly away, hurry away; to depart, vanish.
āvolsus, avulsus ppp of **āvellō**.
avunculus, -ī m uncle (on mother's side); ~ **māgnus** great-uncle.
avus, -ī m grandfather; ancestor.
Axenus, -ī m Black Sea.
axicia, axitia, -ae f scissors
āxilla -ae f armpit.
axis, -is m axle, chariot; axis, pole, sky, clime; plank.
azȳmus adj unleavened.

B, b

babae interj (expressing wonder or joy) oho!
Babylōn, -ōnis f ancient city on the Euphrates.
Babylōnia f the country under Babylon.
Babylōnicus, (-)ōniēns is adj see a.
Babylōnius adj Babylonian; Chaldaean, versed in astrology.
bāca, -ae f berry; olive; fruit; pearl.
bācātus adj of pearls.
bacca etc see **bāca**.
baccar, -is nt cyclamen.
Baccha, -ae f Bacchante.
Bacchānal, -ālis nt place consecrated to Bacchus; (pl) festival of Bacchus.
bacchātiō, -ōnis f revel.
Bacchēus, -icus, -ius adj see a.
Bacchiadae, -ārum mpl kings of Corinth (founders of Syracuse).
bacchor, -ārī, -ātus vi to celebrate the festival of Bacchus; to revel, rave; to rage.
Bacchus, -ī m god of wine, vegetation, poetry, and religious ecstasy; vine, wine.
bācifer, -ī adj olive-bearing.
bacillum, -ī nt stick, lictor's staff
Bactra, -ōrum ntpl capital of Bactria in central Asia (now Balkh).
Bactriāna f Bactria.
Bactriānus and ius adj Bactrian.

baculum, -ī nt, **-us, -ī** m stick, staff.
Baetica f Roman province (now Andalusia).
Baeticus adj see **Baetis**.
Baetis, -is m river in Spain (now Guadalquivir).
Bagrada, -ae m river in Africa (now Mejerdah).
Bāiae, -ārum fpl Roman spa on Bay of Naples.
Bāiānus adj see n.
bāiulō, -āre vt to carry (something heavy).
bāiulus, -ī m porter.
bālaena, -ae f whale.
balanus, -ī f balsam (from an Arabian nut); a shellfish.
balatrō, -ōnis m jester.
bālātus, -ūs m bleating.
balbus adj stammering.
balbūtiō, -īre vt, vi to stammer, speak indistinctly; (fig) to speak obscurely.
Baliārēs, -ium fpl Balearic islands.
Baliāris, Baliāricus adj see n.
balineum etc see **balneum** etc.
ballista, -ae f (MIL) catapult for shooting stones and other missiles; (fig) weapon.
ballistārium, -ī and **iī** nt catapult.
balneae, -ārum fpl bath, baths.
balneāria, -ōrum ntpl bathroom.
balneārius adj of the baths.
balneātor, -ōris m bath superintendent.
balneolum, -ī nt small bath.
balneum, -ī nt bath.
bālō, -āre vi to bleat.
balsamum, -ī nt balsam, balsam tree.
baltea, -ōrum ntpl belt (esp swordbelt; woman's girdle; strapping).
balteus, -ī m belt (esp swordbelt; woman's girdle; strapping).
Bandusia, -ae f spring near Horace's birthplace.
baptisma, -tis nt baptism.
baptizō, -āre vt (ECCL) to baptize.
barathrum, -ī nt abyss; the lower world; (fig) a greedy person.
barba, -ae f beard.
barbarē adv in a foreign language, in Latin; in an uncivilized way; roughly, cruelly.
barbaria, -ae, -ēs acc, and **-em** f a foreign country (outside Greece or Italy); (words) barbarism; (manners) rudeness, stupidity.
barbaricus adj foreign, outlandish; Italian.
barbarus adj foreign, barbarous; (to a Greek) Italian; rude, uncivilized; savage, barbarous ♦ m foreigner, barbarian.
barbātulus adj with a little beard.
barbātus adj bearded, adult; ancient (Romans); of philosophers.
barbiger, -ī adj bearded.
barbitos (acc **-on**) m lyre, lute.
barbula, -ae f little beard.
Barcās, -ae m ancestor of Hannibal.

Noun declensions and verb conjugations are shown on pp xiii to xxv. The present infinitive ending of a verb shows to which conjugation it belongs: **-āre** = 1st; **-ēre** = 2nd; **-ere** = 3rd and **-īre** = 4th. Irregular verbs are shown on p xxvi

Barcīnus *adj see* **n.**
bardus *adj* dull, stupid.
bardus, -ī *m* Gallic minstrel.
bārō, -ōnis *m* dunce.
barrus, -ī *m* elephant.
bascauda, -ae *f* basket (*for the table*).
bāsiātiō, -ōnis *f* kiss.
basilica, -ae *f public building used as exchange and law court.*
basilicē *adv* royally, in magnificent style.
basilicum, -ī *nt* regal robe.
basilicus *adj* royal, magnificent ♦ *m* highest throw at dice.
bāsiō, -āre *vt* to kiss.
basis, -is *f* pedestal, base.
bāsium, -ī *and* **iī** *nt* kiss.
Bassareus, -eī *m* Bacchus.
Batāvī, -ōrum *mpl* people of Batavia (*now* Holland).
batillum, -ī *nt* firepan.
Battiadēs, -ae *m* Callimachus.
bātuō, -ere, -ī *vt* to beat.
baubor, -ārī *vi* (*of dogs*) to howl.
Baucis, -idis *f wife of Philemon.*
beātē *adv see* **beātus.**
beātitās, -ātis *f* happiness.
beātitūdō, -inis *f* happiness.
beātulus, -ī *m* the blessed man.
beātus *adj* happy; prosperous, well-off; rich, abundant.
Bēdriacēnsis *adj see* **n.**
Bēdriācum, -ī *nt village in N. Italy.*
Belgae, -ārum *mpl* people of N. Gaul (*now* Belgium).
Bēlīdēs, -īdae *m* Danaus, Aegyptus, Lynceus.
Bēlides, -um *fpl* Danaids.
bellāria, -ōrum *ntpl* dessert, confectionery.
bellātor, -ōris *m* warrior, fighter ♦ *adj* warlike.
bellātōrius *adj* aggressive.
bellātrīx, -īcis *f* warrioress ♦ *adj* warlike.
bellē *adv* well, nicely; ~ **habēre** be well (in health).
Bellerophōn, -ontis *m slayer of Chimaera, rider of Pegasus.*
Bellerophontēus *adj see* **n.**
bellicōsus *adj* warlike.
bellicus *adj* of war, military; ~**um canere** give the signal for marching or attack.
belliger, -ī *adj* martial.
belligerō, -āre, -āvī, -ātum *vi* to wage war.
bellipotēns, -entis *adj* strong in war.
bellō, -āre, -āvī, -ātum *vi* to fight, wage war.
Bellōna, -ae *f goddess of war.*
bellor, -ārī *vi* to fight.
bellulus *adj* pretty.
bellum, -ī *nt* war, warfare; battle; ~ **gerere** wage war; ~**ī** in war.
bellus *adj* pretty, handsome; pleasant, nice.
bēlua, -ae *f* beast, monster (*esp large and fierce*); any animal; (*fig*) brute; ~ **Gaetula** India elephant.
bēluātus *adj* embroidered with animals.

bēluōsus *adj* full of monsters.
Bēlus, -ī *m* Baal; an oriental king.
Bēnācus, -ī *m* lake in N. Italy (*now* Garda).
bene *adv* (*compar* **melius**, *superl* **optimē**) well; correctly; profitably; very ♦ *interj* bravo!, good!; ~ **dīcere** speak well; speak well of, praise; ~ **emere** buy cheap; ~ **est tibi** you are well off; ~ **facere** do well; do good to; ~ **facis** thank you; **rem** ~ **gerere** be successful; ~ **sē habēre** have a good time; ~ **habet** all is well, it's all right; ~ **merērī dē** do a service to; ~ **partum** honestly acquired; ~ **tēl** your health!; ~ **vēndere** sell at a high price; ~ **vīvere** live a happy life.
benedīcō, -īcere, -īxī, -ictum *vt* to speak well of, praise; (*ECCL*) to bless.
benedictiō, -ōnis *f* (*ECCL*) blessing.
beneficentia, -ae *f* kindness.
beneficiāriī, -ōrum *mpl* privileged soldiers.
beneficium, -ī *and* **iī** *nt* benefit, favour; (*POL, MIL*) promotion; ~**ō tuō** thanks to you.
beneficus *adj* generous, obliging.
Beneventānus *adj see* **n.**
Beneventum, -ī *nt* town in S. Italy (*now* Benevento).
benevolē *adv see* **benevolus.**
benevolēns, -entis *adj* kind-hearted.
benevolentia, -ae *f* goodwill, friendliness.
benevolus *adj* kindly, friendly; (*of servants*) devoted.
benīgnē *adv* willingly, courteously; generously; (*colloq*) no thank you; ~ **facere** do a favour.
benīgnitās, -ātis *f* kindness; liberality, bounty.
benīgnus *adj* kind, friendly; favourable; liberal, lavish; fruitful, bounteous.
beō, -āre, -āvī, -ātum *vt* to gladden, enrich.
Berecyntia *f* Cybele.
Berecyntius *adj* of Berecyntus; of Cybele.
Berecyntus, -ī *m mountain in Phrygia sacred to Cybele.*
Berenīcē, -ēs *f a queen of Egypt*; **coma ~ēs** a constellation.
bēryllus, -ī *m* beryl.
bēs, bessis *m* two-thirds of the *as*; two-thirds.
bēstia, -ae *f* beast; wild animal for the arena.
bēstiārius *adj* of beasts ♦ *m* beast fighter in the arena.
bēstiola, -ae *f* small animal.
bēta, -ae *f* beet.
bēta *nt indecl* Greek letter beta.
bibī *perf of* **bibō.**
bibliopōla, -ae *m* bookseller.
bibliothēca, -ae, -ē, -ēs *f* library.
bibō, -ere, -ī *vt* to drink; to live on the banks of (a river); to drink in, absorb; (*fig*) to listen attentively, be imbued; ~ **aquas** be drowned; **Graecō mōre** ~ drink to one's health.
bibulus *adj* fond of drink, thirsty; (*things*) thirsty.
Bibulus, -ī *m consul with Caesar in 59 BC.*

biceps, -ipitis adj two-headed.
biclīnium, -ī and **iī** nt dining couch for two.
bicolor, -ōris adj two-coloured.
bicorniger, -ī adj two-horned.
bicornis adj two-horned, two-pronged; (rivers) two-mouthed.
bicorpor, -is adj two-bodied.
bidēns, -entis adj with two teeth or prongs ♦ m hoe ♦ f sheep (or other sacrificial animal).
bidental, -ālis nt a place struck by lightning.
biduum, -ī nt two days.
biennium, -ī and **iī** nt two years.
bifāriam adv in two parts, twice.
bifer, -ī adj flowering twice a year.
bifidus adj split in two.
biforis adj double-doored; double.
biförmātus, biförmis adj with two forms.
bifröns, -ontis adj two-headed.
bifurcus adj two-pronged, forked.
bīgae, -ārum fpl chariot and pair.
bīgātus adj stamped with a chariot and pair.
biiugī, -ōrum mpl two horses yoked abreast; chariot with two horses.
biiugis, biiugus adj yoked.
bilībra, -ae f two pounds.
bilībris adj holding two pounds.
bilinguis adj double-tongued; bilingual; deceitful.
bīlis, -is f bile, gall; (fig) anger, displeasure; ~ ātra, nigra melancholy; madness.
bilīx, -īcis adj double-stranded.
bilūstris adj ten years.
bimaris adj between two seas.
bimarītus, -ī m bigamist.
bimāter, -ris adj having two mothers.
bimembris adj half man, half beast; (pl) Centaurs.
bimēstris adj of two months, two months old.
bimulus adj only two years old.
bīmus adj two years old, for two years.
bīnī, bīnae, bīna num two each, two by two; a pair; (with pl nouns having a meaning) two.
binoctium, -ī and **iī** nt two nights.
binōminis adj with two names.
Biōn, -ōnis m satirical philosopher.
Biōnēus adj satirical.
bipalmis adj two spans long.
bipartītō adv in two parts, in two directions.
bipartītus adj divided in two.
bipatēns, -entis adj double-opening.
bipedālis adj two feet long, broad or thick.
bipennifer, -ī adj wielding a battle-axe.
bipennis, -is adj two-edged ♦ f battle-axe.
bipertītō etc see **bipartītō**
bipēs, -edis adj two-footed ♦ m biped.
birēmis adj two-oared; with two banks of oars ♦ f two-oared skiff; galley with two banks of oars.
bis adv twice, double; ~ ad eundem make the same mistake twice; ~ diē, in diē twice a day;

~ tantō, tantum twice as much; ~ terque frequently; ~ terve seldom.
bissextus, -ī m intercalary day after 24th Feb.
Bistones, -um mpl people of Thrace.
Bistonis f Thracian woman, Bacchante.
Bistonius adj Thracian.
bisulcilingua, -ae adj fork-tongued, deceitful.
bisulcus adj cloven.
Bīthȳnia, -iae f province of Asia Minor.
Bīthȳnicus, Bīthȳnius, -us adj see **Bīthȳnia**.
bītō, -ere vi to go.
bitūmen, -inis nt bitumen, a kind of pitch.
bitūmineus adj see **bitūmen**.
bivium nt two ways.
bivius adj two-way.
blaesus adj lisping, indistinct.
blandē adv see **blandus**.
blandidicus adj fair-spoken.
blandiloquentia, -ae f attractive language.
blandiloquus, -entulus adj fair-spoken.
blandīmentum, -ī nt compliment, allurement.
blandior, -īrī, -ītus vi to coax, caress; to flatter, pay compliments; (things) to please, entice.
blanditia, -ae f caress, flattery; charm, allurement.
blandītim adv caressingly.
blandus adj smooth-tongued, flattering; fawning; charming, winsome.
blaterō, -āre vi to babble.
blatiō, -īre vt to babble.
blatta, -ae f cockroach.
blennus, -ī m idiot.
bliteus adj silly.
blitum, -ī nt kind of spinach.
boārius adj of cattle; forum -um cattle market in Rome.
Bodotria, -ae f Firth of Forth.
Boeōtarchēs m chief magistrate of Boeotia.
Boeotia, -iae f district of central Greece.
Boeōtius, -us adj see n.
boiae, -ārum fpl collar.
Boiī, -ōrum mpl people of S.E. Gaul.
Boiohaemī, -ōrum mpl Bohemians.
bōlētus, -ī m mushroom.
bolus, -ī m (dice) throw; (net) cast; (fig) haul, piece of good luck; titbit.
bombus, -ī m booming, humming, buzzing.
bombȳcinus adj of silk.
bombȳx, -ȳcis m silkworm; silk.
Bona Dea, -ae, -ae f goddess worshipped by women.
bonitās, -ātis f goodness; honesty, integrity; kindness, affability.
Bonōnia, -ae f town in N. Italy (now Bologna).
Bonōniēnsis adj see n.
bonum, -ī nt a moral good; advantage, blessing; (pl) property; cuī ~ō? who was the

---

Noun declensions and verb conjugations are shown on pp xiii to xxv. The present infinitive ending of a verb shows to which conjugation it belongs: -āre = 1st; -ēre = 2nd; -ere = 3rd and -īre = 4th. Irregular verbs are shown on p xxvi

gainer?

bonus adj (compar **melior**, superl **optimus**) good; kind; brave; loyal; beneficial; lucky ♦ mpl upper class party, conservatives; ~**a aetās** prime of life; ~**ō animō** of good cheer; well-disposed; ~**ae artēs** integrity; culture, liberal education; ~ **a dicta** witticisms; ~**a fidēs** good faith; ~**ī mōrēs** morality; ~**ī nummī** genuine money; ~**a pars** large part; conservative party; ~**ae rēs** comforts, luxuries; prosperity; morality; ~**ā veniā** with kind permission; ~**a verba** words of good omen; well-chosen diction; ~**a vōx** loud voice.

boō, -āre vi to cry aloud.

Boōtēs, -ae nt constellation containing Arcturus.

Boreās, -ae m north wind; north.

Boreus adj see n.

Borysthenēs, -is m river Dnieper.

Borysthenidae mpl dwellers near the Dnieper.

Borysthenius adj see **Borysthenidae**.

bōs, bovis m/f ox, cow; kind of turbot; ~ **Lūca** elephant; **bovī clitellās impōnere** ≈ put a round peg in a square hole.

Bosporānus adj see n.

Bosporius adj: ~ **Cimmerius** strait from Sea of Azov to Black Sea.

Bosporus, -ī m strait from Black Sea to Sea of Marmora.

Boudicca, -ae f British queen (falsely called Boadicea).

bovārius etc see **boārius**.

Bovillae, -ārum fpl ancient Latin town.

Bovillānus adj see n.

bovillus adj of oxen.

brācae, -ārum fpl trousers.

brācātus adj trousered; barbarian (esp of tribes beyond the Alps).

bracchiālis adj of the arm.

bracchiolum, -ī nt dainty arm.

bracchium, -ī and **iī** nt arm, forearm; (shellfish) claw; (tree) branch; (sea) arm; (NAUT) yardarm; (MIL) outwork, mole; **levī, mollī bracchiō** casually.

bractea etc see **brattea**.

brassica, -ae f cabbage.

brattea, -ae f gold leaf.

bratteola, -ae f very fine gold leaf.

Brennus, -ī m Gallic chief who defeated the Romans.

brevī adv shortly, soon; briefly, in a few words.

brevia, -ium ntpl shoals.

breviārium, -ī and **iī** nt summary, statistical survey, official report.

breviculus adj shortish.

breviloquēns, -entis adj brief.

brevis adj short, small, shallow; brief, short-lived; concise.

brevitās, -ātis f shortness, smallness; brevity, conciseness.

breviter adv concisely.

Brigantēs, -um mpl British tribe in N. England.

Briganticus adj see n.

Brisēis, -idos f captive of Achilles.

Britannia, -iae f Britain; the British Isles.

Britannicus m son of emperor Claudius.

Britannus, (-icus) adj see n.

Bromius, -ī and **iī** m Bacchus.

brūma, -ae f winter solstice, midwinter; winter.

brūmālis adj of the winter solstice; wintry; ~ **flexus** tropic of Capricorn.

Brundisīnus adj see n.

Brundisium, -ī and **iī** nt port in S.E. Italy (now Brindisi).

Bruttiī, -ōrum mpl people of the toe of Italy.

Bruttius adj see n.

brūtus adj heavy, unwieldy; stupid, irrational.

Brūtus, -ī m liberator of Rome from kings; murderer of Caesar.

bubīle, -is nt stall.

būbō, -ōnis m/f owl.

būbula, -ae f beef.

bubulcitor, -ārī vi to drive oxen.

bubulcus, -ī m ploughman.

būbulus adj of cattle.

būcaeda, -ae m flogged slave.

bucca, -ae f cheek; mouth; ranter.

buccō, -ōnis m babbler.

buccula, -ae f visor.

bucculentus adj fat-cheeked.

būcerus adj horned.

būcina, -ae f shepherd's horn; military trumpet; night watch.

būcinātor, -ōris m trumpeter.

būcolica, -ōrum ntpl pastoral poetry.

būcula, -ae f young cow.

būfō, -ōnis m toad.

bulbus, -ī m bulb; onion.

būlē, -es f Greek senate.

būleuta m senator.

būleutērium nt senate house.

bulla, -ae f bubble; knob, stud; gold charm worn round the neck by children of noblemen.

bullātus adj wearing the bulla; still a child.

būmastus, -ī f kind of vine.

būris, -is m plough-beam.

Burrus old form of **Pyrrhus**.

Busīris, -idis m Egyptian king killed by Hercules.

bustirapus, -ī m graverobber.

bustuārius adj at a funeral.

bustum, -ī nt funeral place; tomb, grave.

buxifer, -ī adj famed for its box trees.

buxum, -ī nt boxwood; flute, top, comb, tablet.

buxus, -ī f box tree; flute.

Byzantium, -ī and **iī** nt city on Bosporus (later Constantinople, now Istanbul).

Byzantius adj see n.

C, c

caballīnus adj horse's.
caballus, -ī m horse.
cacātus adj impure.
cachinnātiō, -ōnis f loud laughter.
cachinnō, -āre vi to laugh, guffaw.
cachinnō, -ōnis m scoffer.
cachinnus, -ī m laugh, derisive laughter; (waves) splashing.
cacō, -āre vi to evacuate the bowels.
cacoēthes, -is nt (fig) itch.
cacula, -ae m soldier's slave.
cacūmen, -inis nt extremity, point, summit, treetop; (fig) height, limit.
cacūminō, -āre vt to make pointed.
Cācus, -ī m giant robber, son of Vulcan.
cadāver, -is nt corpse, carcass.
cadāverōsus adj ghastly.
Cadmēa, -ēae f fortress of Thebes.
Cadmēis, -ēidis f Agave; Ino; Semele.
Cadmēus, (-ēius) adj of Cadmus, Theban.
Cadmus, -ī m founder of Thebes.
cadō, -ere, cecidī, cāsum vi to fall; to droop, die, be killed; (ASTRO) to set; (dice) to be thrown; (events) to happen, turn out; (money) to be due; (strength, speech, courage) to diminish, cease, fail; (wind, rage) to subside; (words) to end; ~ **in** suit, agree with; come under; ~ **sub** be exposed to; animis ~ be disheartened; **causā** ~ lose one's case.
cādūceātor, -ōris m officer with flag of truce.
cādūceus, -ī m herald's staff; Mercury's wand.
cādūcifer, -ī adj with herald's staff.
cādūcus adj falling, fallen; (fig) perishable, fleeting, vain; (law) without an heir ♦ nt property without an heir.
Cadurcī, -ōrum mpl Gallic tribe.
Cadurcum, -ī nt linen coverlet.
cadus, -ī m jar, flask (esp for wine); urn.
caecigenus adj born blind.
Caeciliānus adj see n.
Caecilius, -ī m Roman name (esp early Latin comic poet).
caecitās, -ātis f blindness.
caecō, -āre, -āvī, -ātum vt to blind; to make obscure.
Caecubum, -ī nt choice wine from ~ e Ager Caecubus in S. Latium.
caecus adj blind; invisible, secret; dark, obscure; (fig) aimless, unknown, uncertain; **appāret ~ō** ≈ it's as clear as daylight; **domus ~a** a house with no windows; **~ā die emere** buy

on credit; **~um corpus** the back.
caedēs, -is f murder, massacre; gore; the slain.
caedō, -ere, cecīdī, caesum vt to cut; to strike; to kill, cut to pieces; (animals) to sacrifice.
caelāmen, -inis nt engraved work.
caelātor, -ōris m engraver.
caelātūra, -ae f engraving in bas-relief.
caelebs, -ibis adj unmarried (bachelor or widower); (trees) with no vine trained on.
caeles, -itis adj celestial ♦ mpl the gods.
caelestis, -is adj of the sky, heavenly; divine; glorious ♦ mpl the gods ♦ ntpl the heavenly bodies.
Caeliānus adj see n.
caelibātus, -ūs m celibacy.
caelicola, -ae m god.
caelifer, -ī adj supporting the sky.
Caelius, -ī m Roman name; Roman hill.
caelō, -āre, -āvī, -ātum vt to engrave (in relief on metals), carve (on wood); (fig) to compose.
caelum, -ī nt engraver's chisel.
caelum, -ī nt sky, heaven; air, climate, weather; (fig) height of success, glory; **~um ac terrās miscēre** create chaos; **ad ~um ferre** extol; **dē ~ō dēlāpsus** a messiah; **dē ~ō servāre** watch for omens; **dē ~ō tangī** be struck by lightning; **digitō ~um attingere** ≈ be in the seventh heaven; **in ~ō esse** be overjoyed.
caementum, -ī nt quarrystone, rubble.
caenōsus adj muddy.
caenum, -ī nt mud, filth.
caepa, -ae f, **caepe, -is** nt onion.
Caere nt indecl (gen -itis, abl -ēte) f ancient Etruscan town.
Caeres, -itis and **ētis** adj: **~ite cērā dignī** like the disfranchised masses.
caerimōnia, -ae f sanctity; veneration (for gods); religious usage, ritual.
caeruleus, caerulus adj blue, dark blue, dark green, dusky ♦ ntpl the sea.
Caesar, -is m Julius (great Roman soldier, statesman, author); Augustus; the emperor.
Caesareus, and iānus, and īnus adj see n.
caesariātus adj bushy-haired.
caesariēs, -ēī f hair.
caesīcius adj bluish.
caesim adv with the edge of the sword; (RHET) in short clauses.
caesius adj bluish grey, blue-eyed.
caespes, -itis m sod, turf; mass of roots.
caestus, -ūs m boxing glove.
caesus ppp of **caedō**.
caetra, -ae f targe.
caetrātus adj armed with a targe.
Caīcus, -ī m river in Asia Minor.
Caiēta, -ae, -ē, -ēs f town in Latium.
Cāius etc see Gaius.

Noun declensions and verb conjugations are shown on pp xiii to xxv. The present infinitive ending of a verb shows to which conjugation it belongs: -āre = 1st; -ēre = 2nd; -ere = 3rd and -īre = 4th. Irregular verbs are shown on p xxvi

Calaber, -rī _adj_ Calabrian.
Calabria _f S.E. peninsula of Italy._
Calamis, -idis _m Greek sculptor._
calamister, -rī _m_, **-rum, -rī** _nt_ curling iron;
(_RHET_) flourish.
calamistrātus _adj_ curled; foppish.
calamitās, -ātis _f_ disaster; (_MIL_) defeat; (_AGR_)
damage, failure.
calamitōsē _adv see_ **calamitōsus.**
calamitōsus _adj_ disastrous, ruinous; blighted,
unfortunate.
calamus, -ī _m_ reed; stalk; pen, pipe, arrow,
fishing rod.
calathiscus, -ī _m_ small basket.
calathus, -ī _m_ wicker basket; bowl, cup.
calātor, -ōris _m_ servant.
calcāneum, -ī _nt_ heel.
calcar, -āris _nt_ spur.
calceāmentum, -ī _nt_ shoe.
calceātus _ppp_ shod.
calceolārius, -ī _and_ **iī** _m_ shoemaker.
calceolus, -ī _m_ small shoe.
calceus, -ī _m_ shoe.
Calchās, -antis _m Greek prophet at Troy._
calcitrō, -āre _vi_ to kick; (_fig_) to resist.
calcō, -āre, -āvī, -ātum _vt_ to tread, trample
on; (_fig_) to spurn.
calculus, -ī _m_ pebble, stone; draughtsman,
counting stone, reckoning, voting stone;
~um redūcere take back a move; **~ōs**
subdūcere compute; **ad ~ōs vocāre** subject to
a reckoning.
caldārius _adj_ with warm water.
caldus _etc see_ **calidus.**
Calēdonia, -ae _f_ the Scottish Highlands.
Calēdonius _adj see n._
calefaciō, (calfacio), -facere, -fēcī, -factum
_vt_ to warm, heat; (_fig_) to provoke, excite.
calefactō, -āre _vt_ to warm.
Calendae _see_ **Kalendae.**
Calēnus _adj_ of Cales ♦ _nt_ wine of Cales.
caleō, -ēre _vi_ to be warm, be hot, glow; (_mind_)
to be inflamed; (_things_) to be pursued with
enthusiasm; to be fresh.
Calēs, -ium _fpl town in Campania._
calēscō, -ere, -uī _vi_ to get hot; (_fig_) to become
inflamed.
calidē _adv_ promptly.
calidus _adj_ warm, hot; (_fig_) fiery, eager; hasty;
prompt ♦ _f_ warm water ♦ _nt_ warm drink.
caliendrum, -ī _nt_ headdress of hair.
caliga, -ae _f_ soldier's boot.
caligātus _adj_ heavily shod.
cālīginōsus _adj_ misty, obscure.
cālīgō, -inis _f_ mist, fog; dimness, darkness;
(_mind_) obtuseness; (_CIRCS_) trouble.
cālīgō, -āre _vi_ to be misty, be dim; to cause
dizziness.
Caligula, -ae _m emperor Gaius._
calix, -cis _m_ wine cup; cooking pot.
calleō, -ēre _vi_ to be thick-skinned; (_fig_) to be
unfeeling; to be wise, be skilful ♦ _vt_ to know,
understand.

callidē _adv see_ **callidus.**
calliditās, -ātis _f_ skill; cunning.
callidus _adj_ skilful, clever; crafty.
Callimachus, -ī _m Greek poet of Alexandria._
Calliopē, -ēs, _and_ **ēa, -ēae** _f Muse of epic_
poetry.
callis, -is _m_ footpath, mountain track; pass;
hill pastures.
Callistō, -ūs _f daughter of Lycaon;_ (_constellation_)
Great Bear.
callōsus _adj_ hard-skinned; solid.
callum, -ī _nt_ hard _or_ thick skin; firm flesh; (_fig_)
callousness.
calō, -āre, -āvī, -ātum _vt_ to convoke.
cālō, -ōnis _m_ soldier's servant; drudge.
calor, -ōris _m_ warmth, heat; (_fig_) passion,
love.
Calpē, -ēs _f_ Rock of Gibraltar.
Calpurniānus _adj see n._
Calpurnius, -ī _m Roman name._
caltha, -ae _f_ marigold.
calthula, -ae _f_ yellow dress.
caluī _perf of_ **calēscō.**
calumnia, -ae _f_ chicanery, sharp practice;
subterfuge; misrepresentation; (_law_)
dishonest accusation, blackmail; being
convicted of malicious prosecution; **~am**
iūrāre swear that an action is brought in
good faith.
calumniātor, -ōris _m_ legal trickster,
slanderer.
calumnior, -ārī, -ātus _vt_ to misrepresent,
slander; (_law_) to bring an action in bad faith;
sē ~ deprecate oneself.
calva, -ae _f_ bald head.
calvitium, -ī _and_ **iī** _nt_ baldness.
calvor, -ārī _vt_ to deceive.
calvus _adj_ bald.
calx, -cis _f_ heel; foot; **~ce petere, ferīre** kick;
adversus stimulum ~cēs ≈ _kicking against the_
pricks.
calx, -cis _f_ pebble; lime, chalk; finishing line,
end; **ad carceres ā ~ce revocārī** have to begin
all over again.
Calydōn, -ōnis _f town in Aetolia._
Calydōnis _adj_ Calydonian.
Calydōnius _f_ Deianira; **~ōnius amnis**
Achelous; **~ hērōs** Meleager; **~ōnia rēgna**
Daunia in S. Italy.
Calypsō, -ūs (_acc_ **-ō**) _f nymph who detained_
Ulysses in Ogygia.
camēlīnus _adj_ camel's.
camella, -ae _f_ wine cup.
camēlus, -ī _m_ camel.
Camēna, -ae _f_ Muse; poetry.
camera, -ae _f_ arched roof.
Camerīnum, -ī _nt town in Umbria._
Camers, -tis, _and_ **tīnus** _adj_ of Camerinum.
Camillus, -ī _m_ Roman hero (_who saved Rome_
from the Gauls).
camīnus, -ī _m_ furnace, fire; forge; **oleum**
addere ~ō ≈ _add fuel to the flames._
cammarus, -ī _m_ lobster.

Campānia, -iae f district of W. Italy.
Campānicus, and ius, and us adj Campanian, Capuan.
campē, -ēs f evasion.
campester, -ris adj cf the plain; cf the Campus Martius ♦ nt loincloth ♦ ntpl level ground.
campus, -ī m plain; sports field; any level surface; (fig) theatre, arena (of action, debate); ~ **Martius** level ground by the Tiber (used for assemblies sports, military drills).
Camulodūnum, -ī nt town of Trinobantes (now Colchester).
camur, -ī adj crooked.
canālis, -is m pipe, conduit, canal.
cancellī, -ōrum mpl grating, enclosure; barrier (in public places), bar of law court.
cancer, -rī m crab; (constellation) Cancer; south, tropical heat; (MED) cancer.
candefaciō, -ere vt to make dazzlingly white.
candēla, -ae f taper, tallow candle; waxed cord; ~**am appōnere valvīs** set the house on fire.
candēlābrum, -ī nt candlestick, chandelier, lampstand.
candēns, -entis adj dazzling white; white-hot.
candeō, -ēre vi to shine, be white; to be white-hot.
candēscō, -ere vi to become white; to grow white-hot.
candidātōrius adj of a candidate
candidātus adj dressed in white ♦ m candidate for office.
candidē adv in white sincerely.
candidulus adj pretty white.
candidus adj white, bright; radiant, beautiful; clothed in white; (style) clear; (wind) candid, frank; (CIRCS) happy; ~**a sententia** acquittal.
candor, -ōris m whiteness, brightness, beauty; (fig) brilliance, sincerity.
cānēns, -entis adj white.
cāneō, -ēre, -uī vi to be grey, be white.
cānescō, -ere vi to grow white; to grow old.
canīcula, -ae f bitch; Dog Star, Sirius.
canīnus adj dog's, canine; snarling, spiteful; ~ **littera** letter R.
canis, -is m/f dog, bitch; (fig) shameless or angry person; hanger-on; (dice) lowest throw; (ASTRO) Canis Major, Canis Minor; (myth) Cerberus.
canistrum, -ī nt wicker basket.
cānitiēs, -ēī f greyness; grey hair, old age.
canna, -ae f reed; pipe; gondola.
cannabis, -is f hemp.
Cannae, -ārum fpl village in Apulia (scene of great Roman defeat by Hannibal)
Cannēnsis adj see n.
canō, canere, cecinī vt vi to sing; to play; to sing about, recite, celebrate; to prophesy; (MIL) to sound; (birds) to sing crow.

canor, -ōris m song, tune, sound.
canōrus adj musical, melodious; singsong ♦ nt melodiousness.
Cantaber, -rī m Cantabrian.
Cantabria, -riae f district of N Spain.
Cantabricus adj see n.
cantāmen, -inis nt charm.
cantharis, -idis f beetle; Spanish fly.
cantharus, -ī m tankard.
canthērīnus adj of a horse.
canthērius, -ī and iī m gelding.
canticum, -ī nt aria in Latin comedy; song.
cantilēna, -ae f old song, gossip; ~**am eandem canere** keep harping on the same theme.
cantiō, -ōnis f song; charm.
cantitō, -āre, -āvī, -atum vt to sing or play often.
Cantium, -ī and **iī** nt Kent.
cantiunculae, -ārum fpl fascinating strains.
cantō, -āre, -āvī, -ātum vt, vi to sing; to play; to sing about, recite, celebrate; to proclaim, harp on; to use magic spells; to sound; to drawl.
cantor, -ōris m, -**rīx, -rīcis** f singer, musician, poet; actor.
cantus, -ūs m singing, playing, music; prophecy; magic spell.
cānus adj white, grey, hoary; old ♦ mpl grey hairs.
Canusīnus adj see n.
Canusium, -ī nt town in Apulia (famous for wool).
capācitās, -ātis f spaciousness.
capāx, -ācis adj capable of holding, spacious, roomy; capable, able, fit.
capēdō, -inis f sacrificial dish.
capēduncula f small dish.
capella, -ae f she-goat; (ASTRO) bright star in Auriga.
Capēna, -ae f old Etruscan town.
Capēnās, -us adj: **Porta ~a** Roman gate leading to the Via Appia.
caper, -rī m goat; odour of the armpits.
caperrō, -āre vi to wrinkle.
capessō, -ere, -īvī, -ītum vt to seize, take hold of, try to reach, make for; to take in hand, engage in; **rem pūblicam** ~ go in for politics.
capillātus adj long-haired; ancient.
capillus, -ī m hair (of head or beard); a hair.
capiō, -ere, cēpī, captum vt to take, seize; to catch, capture; (MIL) to occupy, take prisoner; (NAUT) to make, reach (a goal); (fig) to captivate, charm, cheat; (pass) to be maimed, lose the use of; to choose; (appearance) to assume; (habit) to cultivate; (duty) to undertake; (ideas) to conceive, form; (feeling) to experience; (harm) to suffer; to receive, get, inherit; to contain, hold; (fig) to bear; (mind) to grasp; **cōnsilium**

Noun declensions and verb conjugations are shown on pp xiii to xxv. The present infinitive ending of a verb shows to which conjugation it belongs: **-āre** = 1st; **-ēre** = 2nd; **-ere** = 3rd and **-īre** = 4th. Irregular verbs are shown on p xxvi

~ come to a decision; **impetum** ~ gather momentum; **initium** ~ start; **oculō capī** lose an eye; **mente captus** insane; **cupīdō eum cēpit** he felt a desire.
capis, -dis _f sacrificial bowl with one handle._
capistrātus _adj_ haltered.
capistrum, -ī _nt_ halter, muzzle.
capital, -ālis _nt_ capital crime.
capitālis _adj_ mortal, deadly, dangerous; (_law_) capital; important, excellent.
capitō, -ōnis _m_ bighead.
Capitōlīnus _adj_ of the Capitol; of Jupiter.
Capitōlium, -ī _nt_ Roman hill with temple of Jupiter.
capitulātim _adv_ summarily.
capitulum, -ī _nt_ small head; person, creature.
Cappadocia, -ae _f country of Asia Minor._
capra, -ae _f_ she-goat; odour of armpits; (_ASTRO_) Capella.
caprea, -ae _f_ roe.
Capreae, -ārum _fpl_ island of Capri.
capreolus, -ī _m_ roebuck; (_pl_) crossbeams.
Capricornus, -ī _m_ (_constellation_) Capricorn (_associated with midwinter_).
caprifīcus, -ī _f_ wild fig tree.
caprigenus _adj_ of goats.
caprimulgus, -ī _m_ goatherd, rustic.
caprīnus _adj_ of goats.
capripēs, -edis _adj_ goat-footed.
capsa, -ae _f_ box (_esp for papyrus rolls_).
capsō _archaic fut of_ **capiō.**
capsula, -ae _f_ small box; **dē ~ā tōtus** ≈ _out of a bandbox._
Capta, -ae _f_ Minerva.
captātiō, -ōnis _f_ catching at.
captātor, -ōris _m_ one who courts; legacy hunter.
captiō, -ōnis _f_ fraud; disadvantage; (_argument_) fallacy, sophism.
captiōsē _adv see_ **captiōsus.**
captiōsus _adj_ deceptive; dangerous; captious.
captiuncula, -ae _f_ quibble.
captīvitās, -ātis _f_ captivity; capture.
captīvus _adj_ captive, captured; of captives ♦ _m/f_ prisoner of war.
captō, -āre, -āvī, -ātum _vt_ to try to catch, chase; to try to win, court, watch for; to deceive, trap.
captus _ppp of_ **capiō** ♦ _m_ prisoner.
captus, -ūs _m_ grasp, notion.
Capua, -ae _f chief town of Campania._
capulāris _adj_ due for a coffin.
capulus, -ī _m_ coffin; handle, hilt.
caput, -itis _nt_ head; top, extremity; (_rivers_) source; (_more rarely_) mouth; person, individual; life; civil rights; (_person_) chief, leader; (_towns_) capital; (_money_) principal; (_writing_) substance, chapter; principle, main point, the great thing; ~ **cēnae** main dish; ~**itis accūsāre** charge with a capital offence; ~**itis damnāre** condemn to death; ~**itis dēminūtiō** loss of political rights; ~**itis poena** capital punishment; ~**ita cōnferre** confer in

secret; **in ~ita** per head; **suprā ~ut esse** be imminent.
Cār, -is _m_ Carian.
carbaseus _adj_ linen, canvas.
carbasus, -ī _f_ (_pl_ **-a, -ōrum** _nt_) Spanish flax, fine linen; garment, sail, curtain.
carbō, -ōnis _m_ charcoal, embers.
carbōnārius, -ī _and_ **iī** _m_ charcoal burner.
carbunculus, -ī _m_ small coal; precious stone.
carcer, -is _m_ prison; jailbird; barrier, starting place (_for races_); **ad ~ēs ā calce revocārī** have to begin all over again.
carcerārius _adj_ of a prison.
carchēsium, -ī _and_ **iī** _nt_ drinking cup; (_NAUT_) masthead.
cardiacus, -ī _m_ dyspeptic.
cardō, -inis _m_ hinge; (_ASTRO_) pole, axis, cardinal point; (_fig_) juncture, critical moment.
carduus, -ī _m_ thistle.
cārē _adv see_ **cārus.**
cārectum, -ī _nt_ sedge.
cāreō, -ēre, -uī _vi_ (_with abl_) to be free from, not have, be without; to abstain from, be absent from; to want, miss.
cārex, -icis _f_ sedge.
Cāria, -ae _f district of S.W. Asia Minor._
Cāricus _adj_ Carian ♦ _f_ dried fig.
cariēs (_acc_ **-em,** _abl_ **-ē**) _f_ dry rot.
carīna, -ae _f_ keel; ship.
Carīnae, -ārum _fpl_ district of Rome.
carīnārius, -ī _and_ **iī** _m_ dyer of yellow.
cariōsus _adj_ crumbling; (_fig_) withered.
cāris, -idis _f_ kind of crab.
cāritās, -ātis _f_ dearness, high price; esteem, affection.
carmen, -inis _nt_ song, tune; poem, poetry, verse; prophecy; (_in law, religion_) formula; moral text.
Carmentālis _adj see n._
Carmentis, -is, _and_ **a, -ae** _f_ prophetess, mother of Evander.
carnārium, -ī _and_ **iī** _nt_ fleshhook; larder.
Carneadēs, -is _m_ Greek philosopher (_founder of the New Academy_).
Carneadēus _adj see n._
carnifex, -icis _m_ executioner, hangman; scoundrel; murderer.
carnificīna, -ae _f_ execution; torture; ~**am facere** be an executioner.
carnificō, -āre _vt_ to behead, mutilate.
carnuf- _etc see_ **carnif-.**
carō, -nis _f_ flesh.
cārō, -ere _vt_ to card.
Carpathus _adj see n._
Carpathus, -ī _f_ island between Crete and Rhodes.
carpatina, -ae _f_ leather shoe.
carpentum, -ī _nt_ two-wheeled coach.
carpō, -ere, -sī, -tum _vt_ to pick, pluck, gather; to tear off; to browse, graze on; (_wool_) to card; (_fig_) to enjoy, snatch; to carp at, slander; to weaken, wear down; to divide

up; (journey) to go, travel.
carptim adv in parts, at different points; at
different times.
carptor, -ōris m carver.
carptus ppp of **carpō.**
carrus, -ī m waggon.
Carthāginiēnsis adj see n.
Carthāgō, -inis f Carthage (near Tunis); ~
Nova town in Spain (now Cartagena).
caruncula, -ae f piece of flesh.
cārus adj dear, costly; dear, beloved.
Carystēus adj see n.
Carystos, -ī f town in Euboea (famous for
marble).
casa, -ae f cottage, hut.
cascus adj old.
cāseolus, -ī m small cheese.
cāseus, -ī m cheese.
casia, -ae f cinnamon; spurge laurel.
Caspius adj Caspian.
Cassandra, -ae f Trojan princess and
prophetess, doomed never to be believed.
cassēs, -ium mpl net, snare; spider's web.
Cassiānus adj see n.
cassida, -ae f helmet
Cassiepēa, -ae, Cassiopē, -ēs f mother of
Andromeda; a constellation.
cassis, -idis f helmet.
Cassius, -ī m Roman family name.
cassō, -āre vi to shake.
cassus adj empty; devoid of, without (abl);
vain, useless; ~ lūmine dead; in ~um in vain.
Castalia, -ae f spring on Parnassus, (sacred to
Apollo and the Muses).
Castalides, -dum fpl Muses.
Castalius, -s adj see n.
castanea, -ae f chestnut tree; chestnut.
castē adv see **castus.**
castellānus adj of a fortress ♦ mpl garrison.
castellātim adv in different fortresses.
castellum, -ī nt fortress, castle; (fig) defence,
refuge.
castēria, -ae f rowers' quarters.
castīgābilis adj punishable.
castīgātiō, -ōnis f correction, reproof.
castīgātor, -ōris m reprover.
castīgātus adj small, slender.
castīgō, -āre, -āvī, -ātum vt to correct,
punish; to reprove; to restrain.
castimōnia, -ae f purity, morality; chastity,
abstinence.
castitās, -ātis f chastity.
castor, -oris m beaver.
Castor, -oris m twin brother of Pollux (patron
of sailors); star in Gemini.
castoreum, -ī nt odorous secretion of the beaver.
castra, -ōrum ntpl camp; day's march; army
life; (fig) party, sect; ~ movēre strike camp;
~ mūnīre construct a camp; ~ pōnere pitch
camp; **bīna** ~ two camps.

castrēnsis adj of the camp, military.
castrō, -āre vt to castrate; (fig) to weaken.
castrum, -ī nt fort.
castus adj clean, pure, chaste, innocent; holy,
pious.
cāsū adv by chance.
casula, -ae f little cottage.
cāsus, -ūs m fall, downfall; event, chance,
accident; misfortune, death; opportunity;
(time) end; (GRAM) case.
Catadūpa, -ōrum ntpl Nile cataract near Syene.
catagraphus adj painted.
Catamītus, -ī m Ganymede.
cataphractēs, -ae m coat of mail.
cataphractus adj wearing mail.
cataplus, -ī m ship arriving.
catapulta, -ae f (MIL) catapult; (fig) missile.
catapultārius adj thrown by catapult.
cataracta, -ae f waterfall; sluice; drawbridge.
catasta, -ae f stage, scaffold.
catē adv see **catus.**
catēia, -ae f javelin.
catella, -ae f small chain.
catellus, -ī m puppy.
catēna, -ae f chain; fetter; (fig) bond,
restraint; series.
catēnātus adj chained, fettered.
caterva, -ae f crowd, band; flock; (MIL) troop,
body; (THEAT) company.
catervātim adv in companies.
cathedra, -ae f armchair, sedan chair;
teacher's chair.
catholicus adj (ECCL) orthodox, universal.
Catilīna, -ae m Catiline (conspirator suppressed
by Cicero).
Catilīnārius adj see n.
catillō, -āre vt to lick a plate.
catillus, -ī m small dish.
catīnus, -ī m dish, pot.
Catō, -ōnis m famous censor and author,
idealised as the pattern of an ancient Roman;
famous Stoic and republican leader against
Caesar.
Catōniānus adj see n.
Catōnīnī mpl Cato's supporters.
catōnium, -ī and **iī** nt the lower world.
Catullus, -ī m Latin lyric poet.
catulus, -ī m puppy; cub, young of other
animals.
catus adj clever, wise; sly, cunning.
Caucasius adj see n.
Caucasus, -ī m Caucasus mountains.
cauda, -ae f tail; ~am iactāre fawn; ~am
trahere be made a fool of.
caudeus adj wooden.
caudex, -icis m trunk; block of wood; book,
ledger; (fig) blockhead.
caudicālis adj of woodcutting.
Caudīnus adj see n.

Caudium, -ī *nt Samnite town.*
caulae, -ārum *fpl* opening; sheepfold.
caulis, -is *m* stalk; cabbage.
Cauneus *adj* Caunian.
Caunus, -ī *f town in Caria* ♦ *fpl* dried figs.
caupō, -ōnis *m* shopkeeper, innkeeper.
caupōna, -ae *f* shop, inn.
caupōnius *adj see n.*
caupōnor, -ārī *vt* to trade in.
caupōnula, -ae *f* tavern.
Caurus, -ī *m* north-west wind.
causa, -ae *f* cause, reason; purpose, sake; excuse, pretext; opportunity; connection, case, position; (*law*) case, suit; (*POL*) cause, party; (*RHET*) subject matter; **~am agere, ōrāre** plead a case; **~am dēfendere** speak for the defence; **~am dīcere** defend oneself; **~ā** for the sake of; **cum ~ā** with good reason; **quā dē ~ā** for this reason; **in ~ā esse** be responsible; **per ~am** under the pretext.
causārius *adj* (*MIL*) unfit for service.
causia, -ae *f* Macedonian hat.
causidicus, -ī *m* advocate.
causificor, -ārī *vi* to make a pretext.
causor, -ārī, -ātus *vt, vi* to pretend, make an excuse of.
caussa *etc see* **causa.**
causula, -ae *f* petty lawsuit; slight cause.
cautē *adv* carefully, cautiously; with security.
cautēla, -ae *f* caution.
cautēs, -is *f* rock, crag.
cautim *adv* warily.
cautiō, -ōnis *f* caution, wariness; (*law*) security, bond, bail; **mihi ~ est** I must take care; **mea ~ est** I must see to it.
cautor, -ōris *m* wary person; surety.
cautus *ppp of* **caveō** ♦ *adj* wary, provident; safe, secure.
cavaedium, -ī *and* **iī** *nt* inner court of a house.
cavea, -ae *f* cage, stall, coop, hive; (*THEAT*) auditorium; theatre; **prīma ~** upper class seats; **ultima ~** lower class seats.
caveō, -ēre, cāvī, cautum *vt* to beware of, guard against ♦ *vi* (*with ab or abl*) to be on one's guard against; (*with dat*) to look after; (*with nē*) to take care that ... not; (*with ut*) to take good care that; (*with subj or inf*) to take care not to, do not; (*law*) to stipulate, decree; (*COMM*) to get a guarantee, give a guarantee, stand security; **cavē!** look out!
caverna, -ae *f* hollow, cave, vault; (*NAUT*) hold.
cavilla, -ae *f* jeering.
cavillātiō, -ōnis *f* jeering, banter; sophistry.
cavillātor, -ōris *m* scoffer.
cavillor, -ārī, -ātus *vt* to scoff at ♦ *vi* to jeer, scoff; to quibble.
cavō, -āre, -āvī, -ātum *vt* to hollow, excavate.
cavus *adj* hollow, concave, vaulted; (*river*) deep-channelled ♦ *nt* cavity, hole.
Caystros, -us, -ī *m* river in Lydia (*famous for swans*).
-ce *demonstrative particle appended to pronouns and adverbs.*

Cēa, -ae *f* Aegean island (*birthplace of Simonides*).
cecidī *perf of* **cadō.**
cecīdī *perf of* **caedō.**
cecinī *perf of* **canō.**
Cecropidēs, -idae *m* Theseus; Athenian.
Cecropis, -idis *f* Aglauros; Procne; Philomela; Athenian, Attic.
Cecropius *adj* Athenian ♦ *f* Athens.
Cecrops, -is *m ancient king of Athens.*
cēdō, -ere, cessī, cessum *vi* to go, walk; to depart, withdraw, retreat; to pass away, die; (*events*) to turn out; to be changed (into); to accrue (to) to yield, be inferior (to) ♦ *vt* to give up, concede, allow; **~ bonīs, possessiōne** make over property (to); **~ forō** go bankrupt; **~ locō** leave one's post; **~ memoriā** be forgotten.
cedo (*pl* **cette**) *impv* give me, bring here; tell me; let me; look at!
cedrus, -ī *f* cedar, perfumed juniper; cedar oil.
Celaenō, -ūs *f* a Harpy; a Pleiad.
cēlāta *ntpl* secrets.
celeber, -ris *adj* crowded, populous; honoured, famous; repeated.
celebrātiō, -ōnis *f* throng; celebration.
celebrātus *adj* full, much used; festive; famous.
celebritās, -ātis *f* crowd; celebration; fame.
celebrō, -āre, -āvī, -ātum *vt* to crowd, frequent; to repeat, practise; to celebrate, keep (*a festival*); to advertise, glorify.
celer, -is *adj* quick, swift, fast; hasty.
Celerēs, -um *mpl* royal bodyguard.
celeripēs, -edis *adj* swift-footed.
celeritās, -ātis *f* speed, quickness.
celeriter *adv see* **celer.**
celerō, -āre *vt* to quicken ♦ *vi* to make haste.
cella, -ae *f* granary, stall, cell; garret, hut, small room; sanctuary of a temple.
cellārius *adj* of the storeroom ♦ *m* steward.
cellula, -ae *f* little room.
cēlō, -āre, -āvī, -ātum *vt* to hide, conceal, keep secret; **id mē ~at** he keeps me in the dark about it.
celōx, -ōcis *adj* swift ♦ *f* fast ship, yacht.
celsus *adj* high, lofty; (*fig*) great, eminent; haughty.
Celtae, -ārum *mpl* Celts (*esp of central Gaul*) ♦ *nt* the Celtic nation.
Celtibērī, -ērum *mpl* people of central Spain.
Celtibēria, -iae *f* Central Spain.
Celtibēricus *adj see n.*
Celticus *adj* Celtic.
cēna, -ae *f* dinner (*the principal Roman meal*); **inter ~am** at table.
cēnāculum, -ī *nt* dining-room; upper room, garret.
cēnāticus *adj* of dinner.
cēnātiō, -ōnis *f* dining-room.
cēnātus *ppc* having dined, after dinner ♦ *ppp* spent in feasting.

Cenchreae, -ārum *fpl* harbour of Corinth.
cēnitō, -āre *vi* to be accustomed to dine.
cēnō, -āre, -āvī, -ātum *vi* to dine; *vt* to eat, dine on.
cēnseō, -ēre, -uī, -um *vt* (*census*) to assess, rate, take a census, make a property return; (*fig*) to estimate, appreciate, celebrate; (*senate or other body*) to decree, resolve; (*member*) to express an opinion, move, vote; to advise; to judge, think, suppose, consider; **cēnsuī ~endō** for census purposes.
cēnsiō, -ōnis *f* punishment; expression of opinion.
cēnsor, -ōris *m* censor; (*fig*) severe judge, critic.
cēnsōrius *adj* of the censors, to be dealt with by the censors; (*fig*) severe; **~ ō ~ an** ex-censor.
cēnsūra, -ae *f* censorship; criticism.
cēnsus *ppp of* **cēnseō; capite ~** the poorest class of Roman citizens.
cēnsus, -ūs *m* register of Roman citizens and their property, census; registered property; wealth; **~um agere, habēre** to hold a census; **sine ~ū** poor.
centaurēum, -ī *nt* centaury.
Centaurēus *adj see n.*
Centaurus, -ī *m* Centaur, half man half horse.
centēnī, -um *num* a hundred each, a hundred.
centēsimus *adj* hundredth; **~** hundredth part; (*interest*) 1 per cent monthly (*12 per cent per annum*).
centiceps *adj* hundred-headed.
centiēns, -ēs *adv* a hundred times.
centimanus *adj* hundred-handed.
centō, -ōnis *m* patchwork; **~ōnēs sarcīre** ≈ *tell tall stories*.
centum *num* a hundred.
centumgeminus *adj* hundred-fold.
centumplex *adj* hundred-fold.
centumpondium, -ī *and* **iī** *nt* a hundred pounds.
centumvirālis *adj* of the centumviri.
centumvirī, -ōrum *mpl* a bench of judges who heard special civil cases in Rome.
centunculus, -ī *m* piece of patchwork, saddlecloth.
centuria, -ae *f* (*MIL*) company; (*POL*) century (*a division of the Roman people according to property*).
centuriātim *adv* by companies, by centuries.
centuriātus *adj* divided by centuries; **comitia ~a** assembly which voted by centuries.
centuriātus, -ūs *m* division into centuries; rank of centurion.
centuriō, -āre, -āvī, -ātum *v* (*MIL*) to assign to companies; (*POL*) to divide by centuries.
centuriō, -ōnis *m* (*MIL*) captain, centurion.
centussis, -is *m* a hundred asses.
cēnula, -ae *f* little dinner.

Ceōs, acc -ō *see* **Cea.**
Cēphēis *f* Andromeda.
Cēphēius *adj* of Cepheus.
Cēphēus *adj* Ethiopian.
Cēpheus, -eī (*acc -ea*) *m* king of Ethiopia (*father of Andromeda*).
Cēphīsis *adj see n.*
Cēphīsius *m* Narcissus.
Cēphīsus, -ī *m* river in central Greece.
cēpī *perf of* **capiō.**
cēra, -ae *f* wax; honey cells; writing tablet, notebook; seal; portrait of an ancestor; **prīma ~** first page.
Ceramīcus, -ī *m* Athenian cemetery.
cērārium, -ī *and* **iī** *nt* seal-duty.
cerastēs, -ae *m* a horned serpent.
cerasus, -ī *f* cherry tree; cherry.
cērātus *adj* waxed.
Ceraunia, -ōrum *nt,* **Cerauniī** *m* mountains in Epirus.
Cerbereus *adj see n.*
Cerberus, -ī *m* three-headed watchdog of Hades.
cercopithēcus, -ī *m* monkey.
cercūrus, -ī *m* Cyprian type of ship.
cerdō, -ōnis *m* tradesman.
Cereālia, -ium *ntpl* festival of Ceres.
Cereālis *adj* of Ceres; of corn, of meal.
cerebrōsus *adj* hot-headed.
cerebrum, -ī *nt* brain; understanding; quick temper.
Cerēs, -eris *f* goddess of grain; (*fig*) grain, bread.
cēreus *adj* waxen; wax-coloured; (*fig*) supple, easily led; **~** *m* taper.
cēriāria, -ae *f* taper maker.
cērina, -ōrum *ntpl* wax-coloured clothes.
cērintha, -ae *f* honeywort.
cernō, -ere, -crēvī, crētum *vt* to see, discern; to understand, perceive; to decide, determine; (*law*) to decide to take up (an inheritance).
cernuus *adj* face downwards.
cērōma, -atis *nt* wrestlers' ointment.
cērōmaticus *adj* smeared with wax ointment.
cerrītus *adj* crazy.
certāmen, -inis *nt* contest, match; battle, combat; (*fig*) struggle, rivalry.
certātim *adv* emulously.
certātiō, -ōnis *f* contest; debate; rivalry.
certē *adv* assuredly, of course; at least.
certō *adv* certainly, really.
certō, -āre, -āvī, -ātum *vi* to contend, compete; (*MIL*) to fight it out; (*law*) to dispute; (*with inf*) to try hard.
certus *adj* determined, fixed, definite; reliable, unerring; sure, certain; **mihi ~um est** I have made up my mind; **~um scīre, prō ~ō habēre** know for certain, be sure; **~iōrem facere** inform.
cērula, -ae *f* piece of wax; **~ miniāta** red

Noun declensions and verb conjugations are shown on pp xiii to xxv. The present infinitive ending of a verb shows to which conjugation it belongs: **-āre** = 1st; **-ēre** = 2nd; **-ere** = 3rd and **-īre** = 4th. Irregular verbs are shown on p xxvi

pencil.
cērussa, -ae f white lead.
cērussātus adj painted with white lead.
cerva, -ae f hind, deer.
cervical, -ālis nt pillow.
cervīcula, -ae f slender neck.
cervīnus adj deer's.
cervīx, -īcis f neck; in ~**īcibus esse** be a burden (to), threaten.
cervus, -ī m stag, deer; (MIL) palisade.
cessātiō, -ōnis f delaying; inactivity, idleness.
cessātor, -ōris m idler.
cessī perf of **cēdō**.
cessiō, -ōnis f giving up.
cessō, -āre, -āvī, -ātum vi to be remiss, stop; to loiter, delay; to be idle, rest, do nothing; (land) to lie fallow; to err.
cestrosphendonē, -ēs f (MIL) engine for shooting stones.
cestus, -ī m girdle (esp of Venus).
cētārium, -ī and **iī** nt fishpond.
cētārius, -ī and **iī** m fishmonger.
cētera adv in other respects.
cēterī, -ōrum adj the rest, the others; (sg) the rest of.
cēterōquī, -n adv otherwise.
cēterum adv for the rest, otherwise; but for all that; besides.
Cethēgus, -ī m a conspirator with Catiline.
cētr- etc see **caetr-**.
cette etc see **cedo**.
cētus, -ī m (-**ē** ntpl) sea monster, whale.
ceu adv just as, as if.
Cēus adj see **Cēa**.
Cēyx, -ycis m husband of Alcyone, changed to a kingfisher.
Chalcidēnsis, (-discus) adj see n.
Chalcis, -dis f chief town of Euboea.
Chaldaeī, -aeōrum mpl Chaldeans; astrologers.
Chaldāicus adj see n.
chalybēius adj of steel.
Chalybes, -um mpl a people of Pontus (famous as ironworkers).
chalybs, -is m steel.
Chāones, -um mpl a people of Epirus.
Chāonia, -iae f Epirus.
Chāonius, -is adj see n.
Chaos (abl -**ō**) nt empty space, the lower world, chaos.
chara, -ae f an unidentified vegetable.
charistia, -ōrum ntpl a Roman family festival.
Charites, -um fpl the Graces.
Charōn, -ontis m Charon (ferryman of Hades).
charta, -ae f sheet of papyrus, paper; writing.
chartula, -ae f piece of paper.
Charybdis, -is f monster personifying a whirlpool in the Straits of Messina; (fig) peril.
Chattī, -ōrum mpl a people of central Germany.
Chēlae, -ārum fpl (ASTRO) the Claws (of Scorpio), Libra.
chelydrus, -ī m watersnake.

chelys (acc -**yn**) f tortoise; lyre.
cheragra, -ae f gout in the hands.
Cherronēsus, Chersonēsus, -ī f Gallipoli peninsula; Crimea.
chīliarchus, -ī m officer in charge of 1000 men; chancellor of Persia.
Chimaera, -ae f fire-breathing monster formed of lion, goat and serpent.
Chimaeriferus adj birthplace of Chimaera.
Chios, -ī f Aegean island (famous for wine).
Chīus adj Chian ♦ nt Chian wine; Chian cloth.
chīrographum, -ī nt handwriting; document.
Chīrōn, -ōnis m a learned Centaur (tutor of heroes).
chīronomos, -ī m/f, **chīronomōn, -untis** m mime actor.
chiūrūrgia, -ae f surgery; (fig) violent measures.
chlamydātus adj wearing a military cloak.
chlamys, -dis f Greek military cloak.
Choerilus, -ī m inferior Greek poet.
chorāgium, -ī and **iī** nt producing of a chorus.
chorāgus, -ī m one who finances a chorus.
choraulēs, -ae m flute-player (accompanying a chorus).
chorda, -ae f string (of an instrument); rope.
chorēa, -ae f dance.
chorēus, -ī m trochee.
chorus, -ī m choral dance; chorus, choir of singers or dancers; band, troop.
Christiānismus, -ī m Christianity.
Christiānus adj Christian.
Christus, -ī m Christ.
Chrȳsēis, -ēidis f daughter of Chrȳsēs.
Chrȳsēs, -ae m priest of Apollo in the Iliad.
Chrȳsippēus adj see n.
Chrȳsippus, -ī m Stoic philosopher.
chrȳsolithos, -ī m/f topaz.
chrȳsos, -ī m gold.
cibārius adj food (in cpds); common ♦ ntpl rations.
cibātus, -ūs m food.
cibōrium, -ī and **iī** nt kind of drinking cup.
cibus, -ī m food, fodder, nourishment.
cicāda, -ae f cicada, cricket.
cicātrīcōsus adj scarred.
cicātrīx, -īcis f scar; (plants) mark of an incision.
ciccus, -ī m pomegranate pip.
cicer, -is nt chickpea.
Cicerō, -ōnis m great Roman orator and author.
Cicerōniānus adj see n.
cichorēum, -ī nt chicory.
Cicōnes, -um mpl people of Thrace.
ciconia, -ae f stork.
cicur, -is adj tame.
cicūta, -ae f hemlock; pipe.
cieō, ciēre, cīvī, citum vt to move, stir, rouse; to call, invoke; (fig) to give rise to, produce; **calcem** ~ make a move (in chess).
Cilicia, -ae f country in S. Asia Minor (famous for piracy).
Ciliciēnsis, (-us) adj see n.

Cilix, -cis, -ssa adj Cilician ♦ nt goats' hair garment.

Cimbrī, -ōrum mpl people of N. Germany.

Cimbricus adj see n.

cīmex, -icis m bug.

Cimmeriī, -ōrum mpl people of the Crimea; mythical race in caves near Cumae.

Cimmerius adj see n.

cinaedius adj lewd.

cinaedus, -ī m sodomite; lewd dancer.

cincinnātus adj with curled hair.

Cincinnātus, -ī m ancient Roman dictator.

cincinnus, -ī m curled hair; (fig) rhetorical ornament.

Cincius, -ī m Roman tribune; Roman historian.

cincticulus, -ī m small girdle

cinctus ppp of **cingō**.

cinctus, -ūs m girding; ~ Gabīnus a ceremonial style of wearing the toga.

cinctūtus adj girded.

cinefactus adj reduced to ashes

cinerārius, -ī and **iī** m hair curler.

cingō, -gere, -xī, -ctum vt to surround, enclose; to gird, crown; (MIL) to besiege; fortify; to cover, escort; **ferrum ~or** I put on my sword.

cingula, -ae f girth (of animals).

cingulum, -ī nt belt.

cingulus, -ī m zone.

ciniflō, -ōnis m hair curler.

cinis, -eris m ashes; (fig) ruin.

Cinna, -ae m colleague of Marius, poet friend of Catullus.

cinnamōmum, cinnamum -ī nt cinnamon.

cinxī perf of **cingō**.

Cīnyphius adj of the Cinyps, river of N. Africa; African.

Cinyrās, -ae m father of Adonis.

Cinyrēius adj see n.

cippus, -ī m tombstone; (pl) palisade.

circā adv around, round about ♦ prep (with acc) (place) round, in the vicinity of, in; (time, number) about; with regard to.

Circaeus adj see **Circē**.

circamoerium, -ī and **iī** nt space on both sides of a wall.

Circē, -ēs and **ae** f goddess with magic powers living in Aeaea.

circēnsēs, -ium mpl the games.

circēnsis adj of the Circus.

circinō, -āre vt to circle through.

circinus, -ī m pair of compasses.

circiter adv (time, number) about ♦ prep (with acc) about, near.

circueō, circumeō, -ire, -īvī and **iī, -itum** vt, vi to go round, surround; (MIL) to encircle; to visit, go round canvassing; to deceive.

circuitiō, -ōnis f (MIL) rounds; (speech) evasiveness.

circuitus ppp of **circueō**.

circuitus, -ūs m revolution; way round, circuit; (RHET) period, periphrasis.

circulātor, -ōris m pedlar.

circulor, -ārī vi to collect in crowds.

circulus, -ī m circle; orbit; ring; social group.

circum adv round about ♦ prep (with acc) round, about; near; ~ **īnsulās mittere** send to the islands round about.

circumagō, -agere, -ēgī, -āctum vt to turn, move in a circle, wheel; (pass: time) to pass; (: mind) to be swayed.

circumarō, -āre vt to plough round.

circumcaesūra, -ae f outline.

circumcīdō, -dere, -dī, -sum vt to cut round, trim; to cut down, abridge.

circumcircā adv all round.

circumcīsus ppp of **circumcīdō** ♦ adj precipitous.

circumclūdō, -dere, -sī, -sum vt to shut in, hem in.

circumcolō, -ere vt to live round about.

circumcursō, -āre vi to run about.

circumdō, -are, -edī, -atum vt to put round; to surround, enclose.

circumdūcō, -ūcere, -ūxī, -uctum vt to lead round, draw round; to cheat; (speech) to prolong, drawl.

circumductus ppp of **circumdūcō**.

circumeō etc see **circueō**.

circumequitō, -āre vt to ride round.

circumferō, -ferre, -tulī, -lātum vt to carry round, pass round; to spread, broadcast; to purify; (pass) to revolve.

circumflectō, -ctere, -xī, -xum vt to wheel round.

circumflō, -āre vt (fig) to buffet.

circumfluō, -ere, -xī vt, vi to flow round; (fig) to overflow, abound.

circumfluus adj flowing round; surrounded (by water).

circumforāneus adj itinerant; (money) borrowed.

circumfundō, -undere, -ūdī, -ūsum vt to pour round, surround; (fig) to crowd round, overwhelm; (pass) to flow round.

circumgemō, -ere vt to growl round.

circumgestō, -āre vt to carry about.

circumgredior, -dī, -ssus vt, vi to make an encircling move, surround.

circumiaceō, -ēre vi to be adjacent.

circumiciō, -icere, -iēcī, -iectum vt to throw round, put round; to surround.

circumiecta ntpl neighbourhood.

circumiectus adj surrounding.

circumiectus, -ūs m enclosure; embrace.

circumit- etc see **circuit-**.

circumitiō, -ōnis f see **circuitiō**.

circumitus, -ūs m see **circuitus**.

circumlātus ppp of **circumferō**.

circumligō, -āre, -āvī, -ātum vt to tie to, bind

round.

circumlinō, -ere, -tum *vt* to smear all over, bedaub.

circumluō, -ere *vt* to wash.

circumluviō, -ōnis *f* alluvial land.

circummittō, -ittere, -īsī, -issum *vt* to send round.

circummoeniō (circummūniō), -īre, -īvī, -ītum *vt* to fortify.

circummūnītiō, -ōnis *f* investing.

circumpadānus *adj* of the Po valley.

circumpendeō, -ēre *vi* to hang round.

circumplaudō, -ere *vt* to applaud on all sides.

circumplector, -ctī, -xus *vt* to embrace, surround.

circumplicō, -āre, -āvī, -ātum *vt* to wind round.

circumpōnō, -pōnere, -posuī, -positum *vt* to put round.

circumpōtātiō, -ōnis *f* passing drinks round.

circumrētiō, -īre, -īvī, -ītum *vt* to ensnare.

circumrōdō, -rosī, -rodere *vt* to nibble round about; (*fig*) to slander.

circumsaepiō, -īre, -sī, -tum *vt* to fence round.

circumscindō, -ere *vt* to strip.

circumscrībō, -bere, -psī, -ptum *vt* to draw a line round; to mark the limits of; to restrict, circumscribe; to set aside; to defraud.

circumscrīptē *adv* in periods.

circumscrīptiō, -ōnis *f* circle, contour; fraud; (*RHET*) period.

circumscrīptor, -ōris *m* defrauder.

circumscrīptus *ppp of* **circumscrībō** ♦ *adj* restricted; (*RHET*) periodic.

circumsecō, -āre *vt* to cut round.

circumsedeō, -edēre, -ēdī, -essum *vt* to blockade, beset.

circumsēpiō *etc see* **circumsaepiō.**

circumsessiō, -ōnis *f* siege.

circumsessus *ppp of* **circumsedeō.**

circumsīdō, -ere *vt* to besiege.

circumsiliō, -īre *vi* to hop about; (*fig*) to be rampant.

circumsistō, -sistere, -stetī surround.

circumsonō, -āre *vi* to resound on all sides ♦ *vt* to fill with sound.

circumsonus *adj* noisy.

circumspectātrīx, -īcis *f* spy.

circumspectiō, -ōnis *f* caution.

circumspectō, -āre *vt, vi* to look all round, search anxiously, be on the lookout.

circumspectus *ppp of* **circumspiciō** ♦ *adj* carefully considered, cautious.

circumspectus, -ūs *m* consideration; view.

circumspiciō, -icere, -exī, -ectum *vi* to look all round; to be careful ♦ *vt* to survey; (*fig*) to consider, search for.

circumstantēs, -antium *mpl* bystanders.

circumstetī *perf of* **circumsistō;** *perf of* **circumstō.**

circumstō, -āre, -etī *vt, vi* to stand round; to

besiege; (*fig*) to encompass.

circumstrepō, -ere *vt* to make a clamour round.

circumsurgēns, -entis *pres p* rising on all sides.

circumtentus *adj* covered tightly.

circumterō, -ere *vt* to crowd round.

circumtextus *adj* embroidered round the edge.

circumtonō, -āre, -uī *vt* to thunder about.

circumvādō, -dere, -sī *vt* to assail on all sides.

circumvagus *adj* encircling.

circumvallō, -āre, -āvī, -ātum *vt* to blockade, beset.

circumvectiō, -ōnis *f* carrying about; (*sun*) revolution.

circumvector, -ārī *vi* to travel round, cruise round; (*fig*) describe.

circumvehor, -hī, -ctus *vt, vi* to ride round, sail round; (*fig*) to describe.

circumvēlō, -āre *vt* to envelop.

circumveniō, -enīre, -ēnī, -entum *vt* to surround, beset; to oppress; to cheat.

circumvertō, circumvortō, -ere *vt* to turn round.

circumvestiō, -īre *vt* to envelop.

circumvinciō, -īre *vt* to lash about.

circumvīsō, -ere *vt* to look at all round.

circumvolitō, -āre, -āvī, -ātum *vt, vi* to fly round; to hover around.

circumvolō, -āre *vt* to fly round.

circumvolvō, -vere *vt* to roll round.

circus, -ī *m* circle; the Circus Maximus (*famous Roman racecourse*); a racecourse.

Cirrha, -ae *f* town near Delphi (*sacred to Apollo*).

Cirrhaeus *adj see n.*

cirrus, -ī *m* curl of hair; fringe.

cis *prep* (*with acc*) on this side of; (*time*) within.

Cisalpīnus *adj* on the Italian side of the Alps, Cisalpine.

cisium, -ī *and* **iī** *nt* two-wheeled carriage.

Cissēis, -dis *f* Hecuba.

cista, -ae *f* box, casket; ballot box.

cistella, -ae *f* small box.

cistellātrīx, -īcis *f* keeper of the moneybox.

cistellula, -ae *f* little box.

cisterna, -ae *f* reservoir.

cistophorus, -ī *m* an Asiatic coin.

cistula, -ae *f* little box.

citātus *adj* quick, impetuous.

citerior (*sup* **-imus**) *adj* on this side, nearer.

Cithaerōn, -ōnis *m* mountain range between Attica and Boeotia.

cithara, -ae *f* lute.

citharista, -ae *m,* **citharistria, -ae** *f* lute player.

citharizō, -āre *vi* to play the lute.

citharoedus, -ī *m* a singer who accompanies himself on the lute.

citimus *adj* nearest.

cito (*com* **-ius,** *sup* **-issimē**) *adv* quickly, soon;

nōn ~ not easily.
citō, -āre, -āvī, -ātum vt to set in motion, rouse; to call (by name), appeal to, cite, mention.
citrā adv on this side, this way, not so far ♦ prep (with acc) on this side of, short of; (time) before, since; apart from; **~ quem** before.
citreus adj of citrus wood.
citrō adv hither, this way; **ultrō ~ citue** to and fro.
citrus, -ī f citrus tree; citron tree.
citus ppp of **cieō** ♦ adj quick.
cīvicus adj civic, civil; **corōna ~a** civic crown for saving a citizen's life in war.
cīvīlis adj of citizens, civil; political, civilian; courteous, democratic; **iūs ~e** civil rights; Civil Law; code of legal procedure.
cīvīlitās, -ātis f politics; politeness.
cīvīliter adv like citizens; courteously.
cīvis, -is m/f citizen, fellow citizen.
cīvitās, -ātis f citizenship; community; state; city; **~āte dōnāre** naturalize.
clādēs, -is f damage, disaster, ruin; defeat; (fig) scourge; **dare ~em** make havoc.
clam adv secretly; unknown ♦ prep (with acc) unknown to; **~ mē habēre** keep from me.
clāmātor, -ōris m bawler.
clāmitātiō, -ōnis f bawling.
clāmitō, -āre, -āvī, -ātum vt, vi to bawl, screech, cry out.
clāmō, -āre, -āvī, -ātum vt, vi to shout, cry out; to call upon, proclaim.
clāmor, -ōris m shout, cry; acclamation.
clāmōsus adj noisy.
clanculum adv secretly ♦ prep (with acc) unknown to.
clandestīnō adv see **clandestīnus.**
clandestīnus adj secret.
clangor, -ōris m clang, noise.
clārē adv brightly, loudly, clearly, with distinction.
clāreō, -ēre vi to be bright, be clear; to be evident; to be renowned.
clārēscō, -ere, clāruī vi to brighten, sound clear; to become obvious; to become famous.
clārigātiō, -ōnis f formal ultimatum to an enemy; fine for trespass.
clārigō, -āre vi to deliver a formal ultimatum.
clārisonus adj loud and clear.
clāritās, -ātis f distinctness; (RHET) lucidity; celebrity.
clāritūdō, -inis f brightness; (fig) distinction.
Clarius adj of Claros ♦ m Apollo.
clārō, -āre vt to illuminate; to explain; to make famous.
Claros, -ī f town in Ionia (famous for worship of Apollo).
clārus adj (sight) bright; (sound) loud; (mind) clear; (person) distinguished; **~ntonāre**

thunder from a clear sky; vir ~issimus a courtesy title for eminent men.
classiārius adj naval ♦ mpl marines.
classicula, -ae f flotilla.
classicum, -ī nt battle-signal; trumpet.
classicus adj of the first class; naval ♦ mpl marines.
classis, -is f a political class; army; fleet.
clāthrī, -ōrum mpl cage.
clātrātus adj barred.
clātrī, -ōrum mpl see **clāthrī.**
claudeō, -ēre vi to limp; (fig) to be defective.
claudicātiō, -ōnis f limping.
claudicō, -āre vi to be lame; to waver, be defective.
Claudius, -ī m patrician family name (esp Appius Claudius Caecus, famous censor); the Emperor Claudius.
Claudius, -iānus, -iālis adj see n.
claudō, -dere, -sī, -sum vt to shut, close; to cut off, block; to conclude; to imprison, confine, blockade; **agmen ~** bring up the rear.
claudō, -ere etc see **claudeō.**
claudus adj lame, crippled; (verse) elegiac; (fig) wavering.
clausī perf of **claudō.**
claustra, -ōrum ntpl bar, bolt, lock; barrier, barricade, dam.
clausula, -ae f conclusion; (RHET) ending of a period.
clausum, -ī nt enclosure.
clausus ppp of **claudō.**
clāva, -ae f club, knotty branch; (MIL) foil.
clāvārium, -ī and **ii** nt money for buying shoe nails.
clāvātor, -ōris m cudgel-bearer.
clāvicula, -ae f vine tendril.
clāviger, -ī m (Hercules) club bearer; (Janus) key-bearer.
clāvis, -is f key.
clāvus, -ī m nail; tiller, rudder; purple stripe on the tunic (broad for senators, narrow for equites); **~um annī movēre** reckon the beginning of the year.
Cleanthēs, -is m Stoic philosopher.
clēmēns, -entis adj mild, gentle, merciful; (weather, water) mild, calm.
clēmenter adv gently, indulgently; gradually.
clēmentia, -ae f mildness, forbearance, mercy.
Cleopatra, -ae f queen of Egypt.
clepō, -ere, -sī, -tum vt to steal.
clepsydra, -ae f waterclock (used for timing speakers); **~am dare** give leave to speak; **~am petere** ask leave to speak.
clepta, -ae m thief.
cliēns, -entis m client, dependant; follower; vassal-state.
clienta, -ae f client.

clientēla, -ae f clientship, protection; clients.
clientulus, -ī m insignificant client.
clīnāmen, -inis nt swerve.
clīnātus adj inclined.
Clīō, -ūs f Muse of history.
clipeātus adj armed with a shield.
clipeus, -ī m, **-um, -ī** nt round bronze shield; disc; medallion on a metal base.
clitellae, -ārum fpl packsaddle, attribute of an ass.
clitellārius adj carrying packsaddles.
Clitumnus, -ī m river in Umbria.
clīvōsus adj hilly.
clīvus, -ī m slope, hill; ~ **sacer** part of the Via Sacra.
cloāca, -ae f sewer, drain.
Cloācīna, -ae f Venus.
Clōdius, -ī m Roman plebeian name (esp the tribune, enemy of Cicero).
Cloelia, -ae f Roman girl hostage (who escaped by swimming the Tiber).
Clōthō (acc -ō) f one of the Fates.
clueō, -ēre, -eor, -ērī vi to be called, be famed.
clūnis, -is m/f buttock.
clūrīnus adj of apes.
Clūsīnus adj see n.
Clūsium, -ī nt old Etruscan town (now Chiusi).
Clūsius, -ī m Janus.
Clytaemnēstra, -ae f wife of Agamemnon (whom she murdered).
Cnidius adj see n.
Cnidus, -ī f town in Caria (famous for worship of Venus).
coacervātiō, -ōnis f accumulation.
coacervō, -āre vt to heap, accumulate.
coacēscō, -ēscere, -uī vi to become sour.
coāctō, -āre vt to force.
coāctor, -ōris m collector (of money).
coāctōrēs agminis rearguard.
coāctum, -ī nt thick coverlet.
coāctus adj forced.
coāctus ppp of **cōgō**.
coāctus, -ūs m compulsion.
coaedificō, -āre, -ātum vt to build on.
coaequō, -āre, -āvī, -ātum vt to make equal, bring down to the same level.
coagmentātiō, -ōnis f combination.
coagmentō, -āre, -āvī, -ātum vt to glue, join together.
coagmentum, -ī nt joining, joint.
coāgulum, -ī nt rennet.
coalēscō, -ēscere, -uī, -itum vi to grow together; (fig) to agree together; to flourish.
coangustō, -āre vt to restrict.
coarct- etc see **coart-**.
coarguō, -ere, -ī vt to convict, prove conclusively.
coartātiō, -ōnis f crowding together.
coartō, -āre, -āvī, -ātum vt to compress, abridge.
coccineus, coccinus adj scarlet.
coccum, -ī nt scarlet.

cochlea, coclea, -ae f snail.
cocleāre, -is nt spoon.
cocles, -itis m man blind in one eye; surname of Horatius who defended the bridge.
coctilis adj baked; of bricks.
coctus ppp of **coquō** ♦ adj (fig) well considered.
cocus etc see **coquus**.
Cōcȳtius adj see n.
Cōcȳtos, -us, -ī m river in the lower world.
cōda etc see **cauda**.
cōdex etc see **caudex**.
cōdicillī, -ōrum mpl letter, note, petition; codicil.
Codrus, -ī m last king of Athens.
coēgī perf of **cōgō**.
coel- etc see **cael-**.
coemō, -emere, -ēmī, -emptum vt to buy up.
coemptiō, -ōnis f a form of Roman marriage; mock sale of an estate.
coemptiōnālis adj used in a mock sale; worthless.
coen- etc see **caen-** or **cēn-**.
coeō, -īre, -īvī and **iī, -itum** vi to meet, assemble; to encounter; to combine, mate; (wounds) to close; to agree, conspire ♦ vt: ~ **societātem** make a compact.
coepiō, -ere, -ī, -tum vt, vi begin (esp in perf tenses); **rēs agī ~tae sunt** things began to be done; **coepisse** to have begun.
coeptō, -āre, -āvī, -ātum vt, vi to begin, attempt.
coeptum, -ī nt beginning, undertaking.
coeptus ppp of **coepiō**.
coeptus, -ūs m beginning.
coepulōnus, -ī m fellow-banqueter.
coerātor etc see **cūrātor**.
coerceō, -ēre, -uī, -itum vt to enclose; to confine, repress; (fig) to control, check, correct.
coercitiō, -ōnis f coercion, punishment.
coetus, coitus, -ūs m meeting, joining together; assembly, crowd.
cōgitātē adv deliberately.
cōgitātiō, -ōnis f thought, reflection; idea, plan; faculty of thought, imagination.
cōgitātus adj deliberate ♦ ntpl ideas.
cōgitō, -āre, -āvī, -ātum vt, vi to think, ponder, imagine; to feel disposed; to plan, intend.
cognātiō, -ōnis f relationship (by blood); kin, family; (fig) affinity, resemblance.
cognātus, -ī m, **-a, -ae** f relation ♦ adj related; (fig) connected, similar.
cognitiō, -ōnis f acquiring of knowledge, knowledge; idea, notion; (law) judicial inquiry; (comedy) recognition.
cognitor, -ōris m (law) attorney; witness of a person's identity; (fig) defender.
cognitus adj acknowledged.
cognitus ppp of **cognōscō**.
cognōmen, -inis nt surname; name.
cognōmentum, -ī nt surname, name.

cognōminis adj with the same name.

cognōminō, -āre, -āvī, -ātum vt to give a surname to; **verba ~āta** synonyms.

cognōscō, -ōscere, -ōvī, -itum vt to get to know, learn, understand; to know, recognize, identify; (law) to investigate; (MIL) to reconnoitre.

cōgō, -ere, coēgī, coāctum vt to collect, gather together; (liquids) to thicken, curdle; to contract, confine; to compel, force; to infer; **agmen ~** bring up the rear; **senātum ~** call a meeting of the senate.

cohaerentia, -ae f coherence.

cohaereō, -rēre, -sī, -sum vi to stick together, cohere; to cling to; (fig) to be consistent, harmonize; to agree, be consistent with.

cohaerēscō, -ere vi to stick together.

cohaesus ppp of **cohaereō**.

cohērēs, -ēdis m/f co-heir.

cohibeō, -ēre, -uī, -itum vt to hold together, encircle; to hinder, stop; (fig) to restrain, repress.

cohonestō, -āre vt to do honour to.

cohorrēscō, -ēscere. -uī vi to shudder all over.

cohors, -tis f courtyard; (MIL) cohort (about 600 men); retinue (esp of the praetor in a province); (fig) company.

cohortātiō, -ōnis f encouragement.

cohorticula, -ae f small cohort.

cohortor, -ārī, -ātus vt to encourage, urge.

coitiō, -ōnis f encounter; conspiracy.

coitus etc see **coetus**.

colaphus, -ī m blow with the fist, box.

Colchis, -idis f Medea's country (at the E. end of the Black Sea).

Colchis, -us, -icus adj Colchian.

cōleus etc see **culleus**.

cōlis etc see **caulis**.

collābāscō, -ere vi to waver also.

collabefactō, -āre vt to shake violently.

collabefīō, -fierī, -factus vi to be destroyed.

collābor, -bī, -psus vi to fall in ruin, collapse.

collacerātus adj torn to pieces.

collacrimātiō, -ōnis f weeping.

collactea, -ae f foster-sister.

collāpsus ppa of **collābor**.

collāre, -is nt neckband.

Collātia, -iae f ancient town near Rome ♦ m husband of Lucretia.

Collātīnus adj of Collatia.

collātiō, -ōnis f bringing together, combination; (money) contribution; (RHET) comparison; (PHILOS) analogy.

collātor, -ōris m contributor.

collātus ppp of **cōnferō**.

collaudātiō, -ōnis f praise.

collaudō, -āre, -āvī, -ātum vt to praise highly.

collaxō, -āre vt to make porous.

collēcta, -ae f money contribution.

collēctīcius adj hastily gathered.

collēctiō, -ōnis f gathering up; (RHET) recapitulation.

collēctus ppp of **colligō**.

collēctus, -ūs m accumulation.

collēga, -ae m colleague; associate.

collēgī perf of **colligō**.

collēgium, -ī and ī ī nt association in office; college, guild (of magistrates, etc).

collībertus, -ī m fellow freedman.

collibet, collubet, -uit and **itum est** vi it pleases.

collīdō, -dere, -sī, -sum vt to beat together, strike, bruise; (fig) to bring into conflict.

colligātiō, -ōnis f connection.

colligō, -āre, -āvī, -ātum vt to fasten, tie up; (fig) to combine; to restrain, check.

colligō, -igere, -ēgī, -ēctum vt to gather, collect; to compress, draw together; to check; (fig) to acquire; to think about; to infer, conclude; **animum, mentem ~** recover, rally; **sē ~** crouch; recover one's courage; **vāsa ~** (MIL) pack up.

Collīna Porta gate in N.E. of Rome.

collīneō, -āre vt, vi to aim straight.

collinō, -inere, -ēvī, -itum vt to besmear; (fig) to deface.

colliquefactus adj dissolved.

collis, -is m hill, slope.

collīsī perf of **collīdō**.

collīsus ppp of **collīdō**.

collitus ppp of **collinō**.

collocātiō, -ōnis f arrangement; giving in marriage.

collocō, -āre, -āvī, -ātum vt to place, station, arrange; to give in marriage; (money) to invest; (fig) to establish; to occupy, employ.

collocuplētō, -āre, -āvī vt to enrich.

collocūtiō, -ōnis f conversation.

colloquium, -ī and ī ī nt conversation, conference.

colloquor, -quī, -cūtus vi to converse, hold a conference ♦ vt to talk to.

collubet etc see **collibet**.

collūceō, -ēre vi to shine brightly; (fig) to be resplendent.

collūdō, -dere, -sī, -sum vi to play together or with; to practise collusion.

collum, -ī nt neck; **~ torquēre, obtorquēre, obstringere** arrest.

colluō, -uere, -uī, -ūtum vt to rinse, moisten.

collus etc see **collum**.

collūsiō, -ōnis f secret understanding.

collūsor, -ōris m playmate, fellow gambler.

collūstrō, -āre, -āvī, -ātum vt to light up; to survey.

colluviō, -ōnis, -ēs, -em, -ē f sweepings, filth; (fig) dregs, rabble.

Noun declensions and verb conjugations are shown on pp xiii to xxv. The present infinitive ending of a verb shows to which conjugation it belongs: **-āre** = 1st; **-ēre** = 2nd; **-ere** = 3rd and **-īre** = 4th. Irregular verbs are shown on p xxvi

collybus, -ī m money exchange, rate of exchange.

collȳra, -ae f vermicelli.

collȳricus adj see n.

collȳrium, -ī and **iī** nt eye lotion.

colō, -ere, -uī, cultum vt (AGR) to cultivate, work; (place) to live in; (human affairs) to cherish, protect, adorn; (qualities, pursuits) to cultivate, practise; (gods) to worship; (men) to honour, court; **vītam ~** live.

colocāsia, -ae f, **-a, -ōrum** ntpl Egyptian bean, caladium.

colōna, -ae f country-woman.

colōnia, -ae f settlement, colony; settlers.

colōnicus adj colonial.

colōnus, -ī m crofter, farmer; settler, colonist.

color (colōs), -ōris m colour; complexion; beauty, lustre; (fig) outward show; (RHET) style, tone; colourful excuse; **~ōrem mūtāre** blush, go pale; **homō nullīus ~ōris** an unknown person.

colōrātus adj healthily tanned.

colōrō, -āre, -āvī, -ātum vt to colour, tan; (fig) to give a colour to.

colossus, -ī m gigantic statue (esp that of Apollo at Rhodes).

colostra, colustra, -ae f beestings.

coluber, -rī m snake.

colubra, -ae f snake.

colubrifer, -ī adj snaky.

colubrīnus adj wily.

coluī perf of **colō**.

cōlum, -ī nt strainer.

columba, -ae f dove, pigeon.

columbar, -āris nt kind of collar.

columbārium, -ī and **iī** nt dovecote.

columbīnus adj pigeon's ♦ m little pigeon.

columbus, -ī m dove, cock-pigeon.

columella, -ae f small pillar.

columen, -inis nt height, summit; pillar; (fig) chief; prop.

columna, -ae f column, pillar; a pillory in the Forum Romanum; waterspout.

columnārium, -ī and **iī** nt pillar tax.

columnārius, -ī m criminal.

columnātus adj pillared.

colurnus adj made of hazel.

colus, -ī and **ūs** f (occ m) distaff.

cōlyphia, -ōrum ntpl food of athletes.

coma, -ae f hair (of the head); foliage.

comāns, -antis adj hairy, plumed; leafy.

cōmarchus, -ī m burgomaster.

comātus adj long-haired; leafy; **Gallia ~ Transalpine** Gaul.

combibō, -ere, -ī vt to drink to the full, absorb.

combibō, -ōnis m fellow-drinker.

combūrō, -rere, -ssī, -stum vt to burn up; (fig) to ruin.

combūstus ppp of **combūrō**.

comedō, -ēsse, -ēdī, -ēsum and **-ēstum** vt to eat up, devour; (fig) to waste, squander; **sē ~** pine away.

Cōmēnsis adj see **Cōmum**.

comes, -itis m/f companion, partner; attendant, follower; one of a magistrate's or emperor's retinue; (medieval title) count.

comēs, comēst pres tense of **comedō**.

comēstus, comēsus ppp of **comedō**.

comētēs, -ae m comet.

cōmicē adv in the manner of comedy.

cōmicus, -ī m comedy actor, comedy writer ♦ adj of comedy, comic.

cōmis adj courteous, friendly.

cōmissābundus adj carousing.

cōmissātiō, -ōnis f Bacchanalian revel.

cōmissātor, -ōris m reveller.

cōmissor, -ārī, -ātus vi to carouse, make merry.

cōmitās, -ātis f kindness, affability.

comitātus, -ūs m escort, retinue; company.

cōmiter adv see **cōmis**.

comitia, -iōrum ntpl assembly for the election of magistrates and other business (esp the ~ centuriāta); elections.

comitiālis adj of the elections; **~ morbus** epilepsy.

comitiātus, -ūs m assembly at the elections.

comitium, -ī and **iī** nt place of assembly.

comitō, -āre, -āvī, -ātum vt to accompany.

comitor, -ārī, -ātus vt, vi to attend, follow.

commaculō, -āre, -āvī, -ātum vt to stain, defile.

commanipulāris, -is m soldier in the same company.

commeātus, -ūs m passage; leave, furlough; convoy (of troops or goods); (MIL) lines of communication, provisions, supplies.

commeditor, -ārī vt to practise.

commeminī, -isse vt, vi to remember perfectly.

commemorābilis adj memorable.

commemorātiō, -ōnis f recollection, recounting.

commemorō, -āre, -āvī, -ātum vt to recall, remind; to mention, relate.

commendābilis adj praiseworthy.

commendātīcius adj of recommendation or introduction.

commendātiō, -ōnis f recommendation; worth, excellence.

commendātor, -ōris m commender (male).

commendātrīx, -rīcis f commender (female).

commendātus adj approved, valued.

commendō, -āre, -āvī, -ātum vt to entrust, commit, commend (to one's care or charge); to recommend, set off to advantage.

commēnsus ppa of **commētior**.

commentāriolum, -ī nt short treatise.

commentārius, -ī and **iī** m, **-ium, -ī** and **iī** nt notebook; commentary, memoir; (law) brief.

commentātiō, -ōnis f studying, meditation.

commentīcius adj fictitious, imaginary; false.

commentor, -ārī, -ātus vt, vi to study, think

over, prepare carefully; to invent, compose, write.

commentor, -ōris m inventor.

commentum, -ī nt invention, fiction; contrivance.

commentus ppa of **comminīscor** ✦ adj feigned, fictitious.

commeō, -āre vi to pass to and fro; to go or come often.

commercium, -ī and **iī** nt trade, commerce; right to trade; dealings, communication.

commercor, -ārī, -ātus vt to buy up.

commereō, -ēre, -uī, -itum; -eor, -ērī, -itus vt to deserve; to be guilty of.

commētior, -tīrī, -nsus vt to measure.

commētō, -āre vi to go often.

commictus ppp of **commingō**.

commigrō, -āre, -āvī, -ātum vi to remove, migrate.

commīlitium, -ī and **iī** nt service together.

commīlitō, -ōnis m fellow soldier.

comminātiō, -ōnis f threat.

commingō, -ingere, -īnxī, -ictum vt to pollute.

comminīscor, -ī, commentus v- to devise, contrive.

comminor, -ārī, -ātus vt to threaten.

comminuō, -uere, -uī, -ūtum v: to break up, smash; to diminish; to impair.

comminus adv hand to hand; near at hand.

commīsceō, -scēre, -scuī, -xtum vt to mix together, join together.

commiserātiō, -ōnis (RHET) passage intended to arouse pity.

commiserēscō, -ere ut to pity.

commiseror, -ārī vt to bewail ✦ v (RHET) to try to excite pity.

commissiō, -ōnis f start (of a contest).

commissum, -ī nt enterprise; offence, crime; secret.

commissūra, -ae f joint, connection.

commissus ppp of **committō**.

committō, -ittere, -īsī, -issum v: to join, connect, bring together; to begin, undertake; (battle) to join, engage in; (offence) to commit, be guilty of; (punishment) to incur, forfeit; to entrust, trust; **sē urbī** ~ venture into the city.

commīxtus ppp of **commīsceō**.

commodē adv properly, well; apt-y, opportunely; pleasantly.

commoditās, -ātis f convenience, ease, fitness; advantage; (person) kindliness; (RHET) apt expression.

commodō, -āre, -āvī, -ātum vi to adjust, adapt; to give, lend, oblige with (with dat) to oblige.

commodulē, -um adv conveniently.

commodum, -ī nt convenience; advantage, interest; pay, salary; loan; **~ō tuō** at your

leisure; **~a vītae** the good things of life.

commodum adv opportunely; just.

commodus adj proper, fit, full; suitable, easy, opportune; (person) pleasant, obliging.

commōlior, -īrī v: to set in motion.

commonefaciō, -facere, -fēcī, -factum vt to remind, recall.

commoneō, -ēre, -uī, -itum vt to remind, impress upon.

commōnstrō, -āre vt to point out.

commorātiō, -ōnis f delay, residence; (RHET) dwelling (on a topic).

commoror, -ārī, -ātus vi to sojourn, wait; (RHET) to dwell ✦ r to detain.

commōtiō, -ōnis excitement.

commōtiuncula f slight indisposition.

commōtus ppp of **commoveō** ✦ adj excited, emotional.

commoveō, -ovēre, -ōvī, -ōtum vt to set in motion, move, dislodge, agitate; (mind) to unsettle, shake, excite, move, affect; (emotions) to stir up, provoke.

commūne, -is nt common property; state; in ~e for a common end; equally; in general.

commūnicātiō, -ōnis f imparting; (RHET) making the audience appear to take part in the discussion.

commūnicō, -āre, -āvī, -ātum vt to share (by giving or receiving); to impart, communicate; **cōnsilia ~ cum** make common cause with.

commūniō, -īre, -īvī and **iī, -ītum** vt to build (a fortification); to fortify, strengthen.

commūniō, -ōnis f sharing in common, communion.

commūnis adj common, general, universal; (person) affable, democratic; **~ia loca** public places; **~ēs locī** general topics; **~is sēnsus** popular sentiment; **aliquid ~e habēre** have something in common.

commūnitās, -ātis f fellowship; sense of fellowship; affability.

commūniter adv in common, jointly.

commūnītiō, -ōnis f preparing the way.

commurmuror, -ārī, -ātus vi to mutter to oneself.

commūtābilis adj changeable.

commūtātiō, -iōnis f change.

commūtātus, -ūs m change.

commūtō, -āre, -āvī, -ātum vt to change, exchange, interchange.

cōmō, -ere, -psī, -ptum vt to arrange, dress, adorn.

cōmoedia, -ae f comedy.

cōmoedicē adv as in comedy.

cōmoedus, -ī m comic actor.

cōmōsus adj shaggy.

compāctiō, -ōnis f joining together.

compāctus ppp of **compingō**.

compāgēs, -is, -ō, -inis f joint, structure,

Noun declensions and verb conjugations are shown on pp xiii to xxv. The present infinitive ending of a verb shows to which conjugation it belongs: **-āre** = 1st; **-ēre** = 2nd; **-ere** = 3rd and **-īre** = 4th. Irregular verbs are shown on p xxvi

framework.

compār, -aris *m/f* comrade, husband, wife ♦ *adj* equal.

comparābilis *adj* comparable.

comparātē *adv* by bringing in a comparison.

comparātiō, -ōnis *f* comparison; (*ASTRO*) relative positions; agreement; preparation, procuring.

comparātīvus *adj* based on comparison.

compāreō, -ēre *vi* to be visible; to be present, be realised.

comparō, -āre, -āvī, -ātum *vt* to couple together, match; to compare; (*POL*) to agree (about respective duties); to prepare, provide; (*custom*) to establish; to procure, purchase, get.

compāscō, -ere *vt* to put (cattle) to graze in common.

compāscuus *adj* for common pasture.

compecīscor, -īscī, -tus *vi* to come to an agreement.

compectum, -tī *nt* agreement.

compedīō, -īre, -ītum *vt* to fetter.

compēgī *perf of* **compingō**.

compellātiō, -ōnis *f* reprimand.

compellō, -āre, -āvī, -ātum *vt* to call, address; to reproach; (*law*) to arraign.

compellō, -ellere, -ulī, -ulsum *vt* to drive, bring together, concentrate; to impel, compel.

compendiārius *adj* short.

compendium, -ī *and* **iī** *nt* saving; abbreviating; short cut; **~ī facere** save; abridge; **~ī fierī** be brief.

compēnsātiō, -ōnis *f* (*fig*) compromise.

compēnsō, -āre, -āvī, -ātum *vt* to balance (against), make up for.

compercō, -cere, -sī *vt, vi* to save; to refrain.

comperendinātiō, -iōnis *f* adjournment for two days.

comperendinātus, -ūs *m* adjournment for two days.

comperendinō, -āre *vt* to adjourn for two days.

comperiō, -īre, -ī, -tum (*occ* **-ior**) *vt* to find out, learn; **~tus** detected; found guilty; **~tum habēre** know for certain.

compēs, -edis *f* fetter, bond.

compēscō, -ere, -uī *vt* to check, suppress.

competītor, -ōris *m*, **-rīx, -rīcis** *f* rival candidate.

competō, -ere, -īvī *and* **iī, -ītum** *vi* to coincide, agree; to be capable.

compīlātiō, -ōnis *f* plundering; compilation.

compīlō, -āre, -āvī, -ātum *vt* to pillage.

compingō, -ingere, -ēgī, -āctum *vt* to put together, compose; to lock up, hide away.

compitālia, -ium *and* **iōrum** *ntpl* festival in honour of the Lares Compitales.

compitālicius *adj* of the Compitalia.

compitālis *adj* of crossroads.

compitum, -ī *nt* crossroads.

complaceō, -ēre, -uī *and* **itus sum** *vi* to

please (someone else) as well, please very much.

complānō, -āre *vt* to level, raze to the ground.

complector, -ctī, -xus *vt* to embrace, clasp; to enclose; (*speech, writing*) to deal with, comprise; (*mind*) to grasp, comprehend; to honour, be fond of.

complēmentum, -ī *nt* complement.

compleō, -ēre, -ēvī, -ētum *vt* to fill, fill up; (*MIL*) to man, make up the complement of; (*time, promise, duty*) to complete, fulfil, finish.

complētus *adj* perfect.

complexiō, -ōnis *f* combination; (*RHET*) period; (*logic*) conclusion of an argument; dilemma.

complexus, -ūs *m* embrace; (*fig*) affection, close combat; (*speech*) connection.

complicō, -āre *vt* to fold up.

complōrātiō, -iōnis *f*, **-us, -ūs** *m* loud lamentation.

complōrō, -āre, -āvī, -ātum *vt* to mourn for.

complūrēs, -ium *adj* several, very many.

complūriēns *adv* several times.

complūsculī, -ōrum *adj* quite a few.

compluvium, -ī *and* **iī** *nt* roof opening in a Roman house.

compōnō, -ōnere, -osuī, -ositum *vt* to put together, join; to compose, construct; to compare, contrast; to match, oppose; to put away, store up, stow; (*dead*) to lay out, inter; to allay, quieten, reconcile; to adjust, settle, arrange; to devise, prepare ♦ *vi* to make peace.

comportō, -āre *vt* to collect, bring in.

compos, -tis *adj* in control, in possession; sharing; **vōtī ~** having got one's wish.

compositē *adv* properly, in a polished manner.

compositiō, -ōnis *f* compounding, system; (*words*) arrangement; reconciliation; matching (of fighters).

compositor, -ōris *m* arranger.

compositūra, -ae *f* connection.

compositus *ppp of* **compōnō** ♦ *adj* orderly, regular; adapted, assumed, ready; calm, sedate; (*words*) compound; **compositō, ex compositō** as agreed.

compōtātiō, -ōnis *f* drinking party.

compotiō, -īre *vt* to put in possession (of).

compōtor, -ōris *m*, **-rīx, -rīcis** *f* fellow drinker.

comprānsor, -ōris *m* fellow guest.

comprecātiō, -ōnis *f* public supplication.

comprecor, -ārī, -ātus *vt, vi* to pray to; to pray for.

comprehendō (comprendō), -endere, -endī, -ēnsum *vt* to grasp, catch; to seize, arrest, catch in the act; (*words*) to comprise, recount; (*thought*) to grasp, comprehend; to hold in affection; **numerō ~** count.

comprehēnsibilis *adj* conceivable.

comprehēnsiō, -ōnis *f* grasping, seizing;

perception, idea; (RHET) period.
comprehēnsus, comprēnsus ppp of
comprehendō.
comprendō etc see **comprehendō.**
compressī perf of **comprimō**
compressiō, -ōnis f embrace; (RHET)
compression.
compressus ppp of **comprimō.**
compressus, -ūs m compression, embrace.
comprimō, -imere, -essī, -essum vt to
squeeze, compress; to check, restrain; to
suppress, withhold; **animam ~** hold one's
breath; **~essīs manibus** with hands folded,
idle.
comprobātiō, -ōnis f approval.
comprobātor, -ōris m supporter.
comprobō, -āre, -āvī, -ātum vt to prove,
make good; to approve.
comprōmissum, -ī nt mutual agreement to
abide by an arbitrator's decision.
comprōmittō, -ittere, -īsī, -issum vt to
undertake to abide by an arbitrator's
decision.
cōmpsī perf of **cōmō.**
cōmptus ppp of **cōmō** ♦ adj elegant.
cōmptus, -ūs m coiffure; union.
compulī perf of **compellō.**
compulsus ppp of **compellō.**
compungō, -ungere, -ūnxī, -ūnctum vt to
prick, sting, tattoo.
computō, -āre, -āvī, -ātum vt to reckon,
number.
Cōmum, -ī nt (also **Novum Cōmum**) town in N.
Italy (now Como).
cōnāmen, -inis nt effort; support.
cōnāta, -ōrum ntpl undertaking, venture.
cōnātus, -ūs m effort; endeavour; inclination,
impulse.
concaedēs, -ium fpl barricade of felled trees.
concalefaciō, -facere, -fēcī, -factum vt to
warm well.
concaleō, -ēre vi to be hot.
concalēscō, -ēscere, -uī vi to become hot,
glow.
concallēscō, -ēscere, -uī vi to become
shrewd; to become unfeeling.
concastīgō, -āre vt to punish severely.
concavō, -āre vt to curve.
concavus adj hollow; vaulted, bent.
concēdō, -ēdere, -essī, -essum vi to
withdraw, depart; to disappear, pass away,
pass; to yield, submit, give precedence,
comply ♦ vt to give up, cede; to grant, allow;
to pardon, overlook.
concelebrō, -āre, -āvī, -ātum v to frequent,
fill, enliven; (study) to pursue eagerly; to
celebrate; to make known.
concēnātiō, -ōnis f dining together.
concentiō, -ōnis f chorus.
concenturiō, -āre vt to marshal.

concentus, -ūs m chorus, concert; (fig)
concord, harmony.
conceptiō, -ōnis f conception; drawing up
legal formulae.
conceptīvus adj (holidays) movable.
conceptus ppp of **concipiō.**
conceptus, -ūs m conception.
concerpō, -ere, -sī, -tum vt to tear up; (fig) to
abuse.
concertātiō, -ōnis f controversy.
concertātor, -ōris m rival.
concertātōrius adj controversial.
concertō, -āre, -āvī, -ātum vi to fight; to
dispute.
concessiō, -ōnis f grant, permission; (law)
pleading guilty and asking indulgence.
concessō, -āre vi to stop, loiter.
concessus ppp of **concēdō.**
concessus, -ūs m permission.
concha, -ae f mussel, oyster, murex; mussel
shell, oyster shell, pearl; purple dye;
trumpet, perfume dish.
conchis, -is f kind of bean.
conchīta, -ae m catcher of shellfish.
conchȳliātus adj purple.
conchȳlium, -ī and **iī** nt shellfish, oyster,
murex; purple.
concidō, -ere, -ī vi to fall, collapse; to subside,
fail, perish.
concīdō, -dere, -dī, -sum vt to cut up, cut to
pieces, kill; (fig) to ruin, strike down; (RHET)
to dismember, enfeeble.
**concieō, -iēre, -īvī, -itum; conciō, -īre,
-ītum** vt to rouse, assemble; to stir up,
shake; (fig) to rouse, provoke.
conciliābulum, -ī nt place for public
gatherings.
conciliātiō, -ōnis f union; winning over
(friends, hearers); (PHILOS) inclination.
conciliātor, -ōris m promoter.
conciliātrīx, -īcis m, **-īcula, -ae** f promoter,
matchmaker.
conciliātus, -ūs m combination.
conciliātus adj beloved; favourable.
conciliō, -āre, -āvī, -ātum vt to unite; to win
over, reconcile; to procure, purchase, bring
about, promote.
concilium, -ī and **iī** nt gathering, meeting;
council; (things) union.
concinnē adv see **concinnus.**
concinnitās, -ētis, -ūdō, -ūdinis f (RHET)
rhythmical style.
concinnō, -āre, -āvī, -ātum vt to arrange; to
bring about, produce; (with adj) to make.
concinnus adj symmetrical, beautiful; (style)
polished, rhythmical; (person) elegant,
courteous; (things) suited, pleasing.
concinō, -ere, -uī vi to sing, play, sound
together; (fig) to agree, harmonize ♦ vt to
sing about, celebrate, prophesy.

conciō *etc see* **concieō.**
concio- *etc see* **contio-.**
concipiō, -ipere, -ēpī, -eptum *vt* to take to oneself, absorb; (*women*) to conceive; (*senses*) to perceive; (*mind*) to conceive, imagine, understand; (*feelings, acts*) to harbour, foster, commit; (*words*) to draw up, intimate formally.
concīsiō, -ōnis *f* breaking up into short clauses.
concīsus *ppp of* **concīdō** ♦ *adj* broken up, concise.
concitātē *adv see* **concitātus.**
concitātiō, -ōnis *f* acceleration; (*mind*) excitement, passion; riot.
concitātor, -ōris *m* agitator.
concitātus *ppp of* **concitō** ♦ *adj* fast; excited.
concitō, -āre, -āvī, -ātum *vt* to move rapidly, bestir, hurl; to urge, rouse, impel; to stir up, occasion.
concitor, -ōris *m* instigator.
concitus, concītus *ppp of* **concieō;** *ppp of* **conciō.**
conclāmātiō, -ōnis *f* great shout.
conclāmitō, -āre *vi* to keep on shouting.
conclāmō, -āre, -āvī, -ātum *vt, vi* to shout, cry out; to call to help; (*MIL*) to give the signal; (*dead*) to call by name in mourning; **vāsa ~** give the order to pack up; **~ātum est** it's all over.
conclāve, -is *nt* room.
conclūdō, -dere, -sī, -sum *vt* to shut up, enclose; to include, comprise; to end, conclude, round off (*esp with a rhythmical cadence*); (*PHILOS*) to infer, demonstrate.
conclūsē *adv* with rhythmical cadences.
conclūsiō, -ōnis *f* (*MIL*) blockade; end, conclusion; (*RHET*) period, peroration; (*logic*) conclusion.
conclūsiuncula, -ae *f* quibble.
conclūsum, -ī *nt* logical conclusion.
conclūsus *ppp of* **conclūdō.**
concoctus *ppp of* **concoquō.**
concolor, -ōris *adj* of the same colour.
concomitātus *adj* escorted.
concoquō, -quere, -xī, -ctum *vt* to boil down; to digest; (*fig*) to put up with, stomach; (*thought*) to consider well, concoct.
concordia, -ae *f* friendship, concord, union; *goddess of Concord.*
concorditer *adv* amicably.
concordō, -āre *vi* to agree, be in harmony.
concors, -dis *adj* concordant, united, harmonious.
concrēbrēscō, -ēscere, -uī *vi* to gather strength.
concrēdō, -ere, -idī, -itum *vt* to entrust.
concremō, -āre, -āvī, -ātum *vt* to burn.
concrepō, -āre, -uī, -itum *vt* to rattle, creak, clash, snap (*fingers*) ♦ *vt* to beat.
concrēscō, -scere, -vī, -tum *vi* to harden, curdle, congeal, clot; to grow, take shape.
concrētiō, -ōnis *f* condensing; matter.

concrētum, -ī *nt* solid matter, hard frost.
concrētus *ppa of* **concrēscō** ♦ *adj* hard, thick, stiff, congealed; compounded.
concrīminor, -ārī, -ātus *vi* to bring a complaint.
concruciō, -āre *vt* to torture.
concubīna, -ae *f* (*female*) concubine.
concubīnātus, -ūs *m* concubinage.
concubīnus, -ī *m* (*male*) concubine.
concubitus, -ūs *m* reclining together (at table); sexual union.
concubius *adj*: **~iā nocte** during the first sleep ♦ *nt* the time of the first sleep.
conculcō, -āre *vt* to trample under foot, treat with contempt.
concumbō, -mbere, -buī, -bitum *vi* to lie together, lie with.
concupīscō, -īscere, -īvī, -ītum *vt* to covet, long for, aspire to.
concūrō, -āre *vt* to take care of.
concurrō, -rere, -rī, -sum *vi* to flock together, rush in; (*things*) to clash, meet; (*MIL*) to join battle, charge; (*events*) to happen at the same time, concur.
concursātiō, -ōnis *f* running together, rushing about; (*MIL*) skirmishing; (*dreams*) coherent design.
concursātor, -ōris *m* skirmisher.
concursiō, -ōnis *f* meeting, concourse; (*RHET*) repetition for emphasis.
concursō, -āre *vi* to collide; to rush about, travel about; (*MIL*) to skirmish ♦ *vt* to visit, go from place to place.
concursus, -ūs *m* concourse, gathering, collision; uproar; (*fig*) combination; (*MIL*) assault, charge.
concussī *perf of* **concutiō.**
concussus *ppp of* **concutiō.**
concussus, -ūs *m* shaking.
concutiō, -tere, -ssī, -ssum *vt* to strike, shake, shatter; (*weapons*) to hurl; (*power*) to disturb, impair; (*person*) to agitate, alarm; (*self*) to search, examine; to rouse.
condalium, -ī *and* **iī** *nt* slave's ring.
condecet, -ēre *vt impers* it becomes.
condecorō, -āre *vt* to enhance.
condemnō, -āre, -āvī, -ātum *vt* to condemn, sentence; to urge the conviction of; to blame, censure; **ambitūs ~** convict of bribery; **capitis ~** condemn to death; **vōtī ~ātus** obliged to fulfil a vow.
condēnsō, -āre, -eō, -ēre *vt* to compress, move close together.
condēnsus *adj* very dense, close, thick.
condiciō, -ōnis *f* arrangement, condition, terms; marriage contract, match; situation, position, circumstances; manner, mode; **eā ~ōne ut** on condition that; **sub ~ōne** conditionally; **hīs ~ōnibus** on these terms; **vītae ~** way of life.
condīcō, -īcere, -īxī, -ictum *vt, vi* to talk over, agree upon, promise; **ad cēnam ~** have a

dinner engagement.
condidī *perf of* **condō.**
condignē *adv see* **condignus.**
condignus *adj* very worthy.
condīmentum, -ī *nt* spice, seasoning.
condiō, -īre, -īvī, -ītum *vt* to pickle, preserve, embalm; to season; (*fig*) to give zest to, temper.
condiscipulus, -ī *m* school-fellow
condiscō, -scere, -dicī *vt* to learn thoroughly, learn by heart.
conditiō *etc see* **condiciō.**
condītiō, -ōnis *f* preserving, seasoning.
conditor, -ōris *m* founder, author, composer.
conditōrium, -ī *and* **iī** *nt* coffin, urn, tomb.
condītus *adj* savoury; (*fig*) polished.
conditus *ppp of* **condō.**
condītus *ppp of* **condiō.**
condō, -ere, -idī, -itum *vt* 1. (*build, found: arts*) to make, compose, write; (: *institutions*) to establish 2. (*put away for keeping, store up: fruit*) to preserve; (: *person*) to imprison; (: *dead*) to bury; (: *memory*) to lay up; (: *time*) to pass, bring to a close 3. (*put out of sight, conceal: eyes*) to close; (: *sword*) to sheathe, plunge; (: *troops*) to place in ambush.
condocefaciō, -ere *vt* to train.
condoceō, -ēre, -uī, -tum *vt* to train.
condolēscō, -ēscere, -uī *vi* to begin to ache, feel very sore.
condōnātiō, -ōnis *f* giving away.
condōnō, -āre, -āvī, -ātum *vt* to give, present, deliver up; (*debt*) to remit; (*offence*) to pardon, let off.
condormīscō, -īscere, -īvī *vi* to fall fast asleep.
condūcibilis *adj* expedient.
condūcō, -ūcere, -ūxī, -uctum *vt* to bring together, assemble, connect; to hire, rent, borrow; (*public work*) to undertake, get the contract for; (*taxes*) to farm ♦ *vi* to be of use, profit.
conductī, -ōrum *mpl* hirelings, mercenaries.
conductīcius *adj* hired.
conductiō, -ōnis *f* hiring, farming.
conductor, -ōris *m* hirer, tenant; contractor.
conductum, -ī *nt* anything hired or rented.
conductus *ppp of* **condūcō.**
conduplicō, -āre *vt* to couple.
condūrō, -āre *vt* to make very hard.
condus, -ī *m* steward.
cōnectō, -ctere, -xuī, -xum *vt* to tie, fasten, link, join; (*logic*) to state a conclusion.
cōnexum, -ī *nt* logical inference.
cōnexus *ppp of* **cōnectō** ♦ *adj* connected; (*time*) following.
cōnexus, -ūs *m* combination.
cōnfābulor, -ārī, -ātus *vi* to talk (to), discuss.
cōnfarreātiō, -ōnis *f* the most solemn of Roman marriage ceremonies.

cōnfarreō, -āre, -ātum *vt* to marry by confarreatio.
cōnfātālis *adj* bound by the same destiny.
cōnfēcī *perf of* **cōnficiō.**
cōnfectiō, -ōnis *f* making, completion; (*food*) chewing.
cōnfector, -ōris *m* maker, finisher; destroyer.
cōnfectus *ppp of* **cōnficiō.**
cōnferciō, -cīre, -tum *vt* to stuff, cram, pack closely.
cōnferō, -ferre, -tulī, -lātum *vt* to gather together, collect; to contribute; to confer, talk over; (*MIL*) to oppose, engage in battle; to compare; (*words*) to condense; to direct, transfer; to transform (into), turn (to); to devote, bestow; to ascribe, assign, impute; (*time*) to postpone; **capita ~** put heads together, confer; **gradum ~ cum** walk beside; **sē ~ go**, turn (to); **sermōnēs ~** converse; **signa ~** join battle.
cōnfertim *adv* in close order.
cōnfertus *ppp of* **cōnferciō** ♦ *adj* crowded, full; (*MIL*) in close order.
cōnfervēscō, -vēscere, -buī *vi* to boil up, grow hot.
cōnfessiō, -ōnis *f* acknowledgement, confession.
cōnfessus *ppa of* **cōnfiteor** ♦ *adj* acknowledged, certain; **in ~ō esse/in ~um venīre** be generally admitted.
cōnfestim *adv* immediately.
cōnficiō, -icere, -ēcī, -ectum *vt* to make, effect, complete, accomplish; to get together, procure; to wear out, exhaust, consume, destroy; (*comm*) to settle; (*space*) to travel; (*time*) to pass, complete; (*philos*) to be an active cause; (*logic*) to deduce; (*pass*) it follows.
cōnfictiō, -ōnis *f* fabrication.
cōnfictus *ppp of* **cōnfingō.**
cōnfīdēns, -entis *pres p of* **cōnfīdō** ♦ *adj* self-confident, bold, presumptuous.
cōnfīdenter *adv* fearlessly, insolently.
cōnfīdentia, -ae *f* confidence, self-confidence; impudence.
cōnfīdentiloquus *adj* outspoken.
cōnfīdō, -dere, -sus sum *vi* to trust, rely, be sure; **sibi ~** be confident.
cōnfīgō, -gere, -xī, -xum *vt* to fasten together; to pierce, shoot; (*fig*) to paralyse.
cōnfingō, -ingere, -inxī, -ictum *vt* to make, invent, pretend.
cōnfīnis *adj* adjoining; (*fig*) akin.
cōnfīnium, -ī *nt* common boundary; (*pl*) neighbours; (*fig*) close connection, borderland between.
cōnfīō, -fierī *occ pass of* **cōnficiō.**
cōnfirmātiō, -ōnis *f* establishing; (*person*) encouragement; (*fact*) verifying; (*rhet*) adducing of proofs.

cōnfirmātor, -ōris *m* guarantor (*of money*).
cōnfirmātus *adj* resolute; proved, certain.
cōnfirmō, -āre, -āvī, -ātum *vt* to strengthen, reinforce; (*decree*) to confirm, ratify; (*mind*) to encourage; (*fact*) to corroborate, prove, assert; **sē ~** recover; take courage.
cōnfiscō, -āre *vt* to keep in a chest; to confiscate.
cōnfisiō, -ōnis *f* assurance.
cōnfisus *ppa of* **cōnfīdō.**
cōnfiteor, -itērī, -essus *vt, vi* to confess, acknowledge; to reveal.
cōnfixus *ppp of* **cōnfīgō.**
cōnflagrō, -āre, -āvī, -ātum *vi* to burn, be ablaze.
cōnflīctiō, -ōnis *f* conflict.
cōnflīctō, -āre, -āvī, -ātum *vt* to strike down, contend (with); (*pass*) to fight, be harassed, be afflicted.
cōnflīctus, -ūs *m* striking together.
cōnflīgō, -gere, -xī, -ctum *vt* to dash together; (*fig*) to contrast ♦ *vi* to fight, come into conflict.
cōnflō, -āre, -āvī, -ātum *vt* to ignite; (*passion*) to inflame; to melt down; (*fig*) to produce, procure, occasion.
cōnfluēns, -entis, -entēs, -entium *m* confluence of two rivers.
cōnfluō, -ere, -xī *vi* to flow together; (*fig*) to flock together, pour in.
cōnfodiō, -odere, -ōdī, -ossum *vt* to dig; to stab.
cōnfore *fut infin of* **cōnsum.**
cōnfōrmātiō, -ōnis *f* shape, form; (*words*) arrangement; (*voice*) expression; (*mind*) idea; (*RHET*) figure.
cōnfōrmō, -āre, -āvī, -ātum *vt* to shape, fashion.
cōnfossus *ppp of* **cōnfodiō** ♦ *adj* full of holes.
cōnfrāctus *ppp of* **cōnfringō.**
cōnfragōsus *adj* broken, rough; (*fig*) hard.
cōnfrēgī *pvrf of* **cōnfringō.**
cōnfremō, -ere, -uī *vi* to murmur aloud.
cōnfricō, -āre *vt* to rub well.
cōnfringō, -ingere, -ēgī, -āctum *vt* to break in pieces, wreck; (*fig*) to ruin.
cōnfugiō, -ugere, -ūgī *vi* to flee for help (to), take refuge (with); (*fig*) to have recourse (to).
cōnfugium, -ī *and* **iī** *nt* refuge.
cōnfundō, -undere, -ūdī, -ūsum *vt* to mix, mingle, join; to mix up, confuse, throw into disorder; (*mind*) to perplex, bewilder; to diffuse, spread over.
cōnfūsē *adv* confusedly.
cōnfūsiō, -ōnis *f* combination; confusion, disorder; **ōris ~** going red in the face.
cōnfūsus *ppp of* **cōnfundō** ♦ *adj* confused, disorderly, troubled.
cōnfūtō, -āre, -āvī, -ātum *vt* to keep from boiling over; to repress; to silence, confute.
congelō, -āre, -āvī, -ātum *vt* to freeze, harden ♦ *vi* to freeze over, grow numb.

congeminō, -āre, -āvī, -ātum *vt* to double.
congemō, -ere, -uī *vi* to groan, sigh ♦ *vt* to lament.
conger, -rī *m* sea eel.
congeriēs, -ēī *f* heap, mass, accumulation.
congerō, -rere, -ssī, -stum *vt* to collect, accumulate, build; (*missiles*) to shower; (*speech*) to comprise; (*fig*) to heap (upon), ascribe.
congerō, -ōnis *m* thief.
congerrō, -ōnis *m* companion in revelry.
congestīcius *adj* piled up.
congestus *ppp of* **congerō.**
congestus, -ūs *m* accumulating; heap, mass.
congiālis *adj* holding a congius.
congiārium, -ī *and* **iī** *nt* gift of food to the people, gratuity to the army.
congius, -ī *and* **iī** *m* Roman liquid measure (*about 6 pints*).
conglaciō, -āre *vi* to freeze up.
conglīscō, -ere *vi* to blaze up.
conglobātiō, -ōnis *f* mustering.
conglobō, -āre, -āvī, -ātum *vt* to make round; to mass together.
conglomerō, -āre *vt* to roll up.
conglūtinātiō, -ōnis *f* gluing, cementing; (*fig*) combination.
conglūtinō, -āre, -āvī, -ātum *vt* to glue, cement; (*fig*) to join, weld together; to contrive.
congraecō, -āre *vt* to squander on luxury.
congrātulor, -ārī, -ātus *vi* to congratulate.
congredior, -dī, -ssus *vt, vi* to meet, accost; to contend, fight.
congregābilis *adj* gregarious.
congregātiō, -ōnis *f* union, society.
congregō, -āre, -āvī, -ātum *vt* to collect, assemble, unite.
congressiō, -ōnis *f* meeting, conference.
congressus *ppa of* **congredior.**
congressus, -ūs *m* meeting, association, union; encounter, fight.
congruēns, -entis *adj* suitable, consistent, proper; harmonious.
congruenter *adv* in conformity.
congruō, -ere, -ī *vi* to coincide; to correspond, suit; to agree, sympathize.
congruus *adj* agreeable.
coniciō, -icere, -iēcī, -iectum *vt* to throw together; to throw, hurl; to put, fling, drive, direct; to infer, conjecture; (*augury*) to interpret; **sē ~** rush, fly; devote oneself.
coniectiō, -ōnis *f* throwing; conjecture, interpretation.
coniectō, -āre *vt* to infer, conjecture, guess.
coniector, -ōris *m* (male) interpreter, diviner.
coniectrīx, -rīcis *f* (female) interpreter, diviner.
coniectūra, -ae *f* inference, conjecture, guess; interpretation.
coniectūrālis *adj* (*RHET*) involving a question of fact.

coniectus *ppp of* **coniciō.**

coniectus, -ūs *m* heap mass concourse; throwing, throw, range; (*eyes, mind*) turning, directing.

cōnifer, cōniger, -ī *adj* cone-bearing.

cōnītor, -tī, -sus *and* **-xus** *vi* to lean on; to strive, struggle on; to labour.

coniugālis *adj* of marriage, conjugal.

coniugātiō, -ōnis *f* etymological relationship.

coniugātor, -ōris *m* uniter.

coniugiālis *adj* marriage- (*in cpds*).

coniugium, -ī *and* **iī** *nt* union, marriage; husband, wife.

coniugō, -āre *vt* to form (*a friendship*); **~āta verba** words related etymologically.

coniūnctē *adv* jointly; on familiar terms; (*logic*) hypothetically.

coniūnctim *adv* together, jointly.

coniūnctiō, -ōnis *f* union, connection, association; (*minds*) sympathy, affinity; (*GRAM*) conjunction.

coniūnctum, -ī *nt* (*RHET*) connection; (*PHILOS*) inherent property (*of a body*).

coniūnctus *ppp of* **coniungō ♦** *adj* near; connected, agreeing, conforming; related, friendly, intimate.

coniungō, -ūngere, -ūnxī, -ūnctum *vt* to yoke, join together, connect; (*war*) to join forces in; to unite in love, marriage, friendship; to continue without a break.

coniūnx, -ugis *m/f* consort, wife, husband, bride.

coniūrātī, -ōrum *mpl* conspirators.

coniūrātiō, -ōnis *f* conspiracy, plot; alliance.

coniūrātus *adj* (*MIL*) after taking the oath.

coniūrō, -āre, -āvī, -ātum *vi* to take an oath; to conspire, plot.

coniux *etc see* **coniūnx**

cōnīveō, -vēre, -vī *and* **xī** *vi* to shut the eyes, blink; (*fig*) to be asleep; to connive at.

conj- *etc see* **coni-.**

conl- *etc see* **coll-.**

conm- *etc see* **comm-.**

conn- *etc see* **cōn-.**

Conōn, -is *m* Athenian commander; Greek astronomer.

cōnōpēum (-eum), -ēī *nt* mosquito net.

cōnor, -ārī, -ātus *vt* to try, attempt, venture.

conp- *etc see* **comp-.**

conquassātiō, -ōnis *f* severe shaking.

conquassō, -āre, -ātum *vt* to shake, upset, shatter.

conqueror, -rī, -stus *vt* *vi* to complain bitterly of, bewail.

conquestiō, -ōnis *f* complaining (*RHET*) appeal to pity.

conquestus *ppa of* **conqueror.**

conquestus, -ūs *m* outcry.

conquiēscō, -scere, -vī, -tum *vi* to rest, take

a respite; (*fig*) to be at peace, find recreation; (*things*) to stop, be quiet.

conquīnīscō, -ere *vi* to cower, squat, stoop down.

conquīrō, -rere, -sīvī, -sītum *vt* to search for, collect.

conquīsītē *adv* carefully.

conquīsītiō, -ōnis *f* search; (*MIL*) levy.

conquīsītor, -ōris *m* recruiting officer; (*THEATRE*) claqueur.

conquīsītus *ppp of* **conquīrō ♦** *adj* select, costly.

conr- *etc see* **corr-.**

cōnsaepiō, -īre, -sī, -tum *vt* to enclose, fence round.

cōnsaeptum, -tī *nt* enclosure.

cōnsalūtātiō, -ōnis *f* mutual greeting.

cōnsalūtō, -āre, -āvī, -ātum *vt* to greet, hail.

cōnsānēscō, -ēscere, -uī *vi* to heal up.

cōnsanguineus *adj* brother, sister, kindred ♦ *mpl* relations.

cōnsanguinitās, -ātis *f* relationship.

cōnscelerātus *adj* wicked.

cōnscelerō, -āre, -āvī, -ātum *vt* to disgrace.

cōnscendō, -endere, -endī, -ēnsum *vt, vi* to climb, mount, embark.

cōnscēnsiō, -ōnis *f* embarkation.

cōnscēnsus *ppp of* **cōnscendō.**

cōnscientia, -ae *f* joint knowledge, being in the know; (*sense of*) consciousness; moral sense, conscience, guilty conscience.

cōnscindō, -ndere, -dī, -ssum *vt* to tear to pieces; (*fig*) to abuse.

cōnsciō, -īre *vt* to be conscious of guilt.

cōnscīscō, -scere, -vī *and* **iī, -ītum** *vt* to decide on publicly; to inflict on oneself; **mortem (sibi) ~** commit suicide.

cōnscīssus *ppp of* **cōnscindō.**

cōnscītus *ppp of* **cōnscīscō.**

cōnscius *adj* sharing knowledge, privy, in the know; aware, conscious (of); conscious of guilt ♦ *m/f* confederate, confidant.

cōnscreor, -ārī *vi* to clear the throat.

cōnscrībō, -bere, -psī, -ptum *vt* to enlist, enrol; to write, compose, draw up, prescribe.

cōnscrīptiō, -ōnis *f* document, draft.

cōnscrīptus *ppp of* **cōnscrībō; patrēs ~ī** *patrician and elected plebeian members*; senators.

cōnsecō, -āre, -uī, -tum *vt* to cut up.

cōnsecrātiō, -ōnis *f* consecration, deification.

cōnsecrō, -āre, -āvī, -ātum *vt* to dedicate, consecrate, deify; (*fig*) to devote; to immortalise; **caput ~** doom to death.

cōnsectārius *adj* logical, consequent ♦ *ntpl* inferences.

cōnsectātiō, -ōnis *f* pursuit.

cōnsectātrīx, -īcis *f* (*fig*) follower.

cōnsectiō, -ōnis f cutting up.

cōnsector, -ārī, -ātus vt to follow, go after, try to gain; to emulate, imitate; to pursue, chase.

cōnsecūtiō, -ōnis f (PHILOS) consequences, effect; (RHET) sequence.

cōnsēdī perf of **cōnsīdō.**

cōnsenēscō, -ēscere, -uī vi to grow old, grow old together; (fig) to fade, pine, decay, become obsolete.

cōnsēnsiō, -ōnis f agreement, accord; conspiracy, plot.

cōnsēnsū adv unanimously.

cōnsēnsus ppp of **cōnsentiō.**

cōnsēnsus, -ūs m agreement, concord; conspiracy; (PHILOS) common sensation; (fig) harmony.

cōnsentāneus adj agreeing, in keeping with; **~um est** it is reasonable.

cōnsentiō, -entīre, -ēnsī, -ēnsum vi to agree, determine together; to plot, conspire; (PHILOS) to have common sensations; (fig) to harmonize, suit, be consistent (with); **bellum** ~ vote for war.

cōnsequēns, -entis pres p of **cōnsequor** ♦ adj coherent, reasonable; logical, consequent ♦ nt consequence.

cōnsequor, -quī, -cūtus vt to follow, pursue; to overtake, reach; (time) to come after; (example) to follow, copy; (effect) to result, be the consequence of; (aim) to attain, get; (mind) to grasp, learn; (events) to happen to, come to; (standard) to equal, come up to; (speech) to do justice to.

cōnserō, -erere, -ēvī, -itum vt to sow, plant; (ground) to sow with, plant with; (fig) to cover, fill.

cōnserō, -ere, -uī, -tum vt to join, string together, twine; (MIL) to join battle; **manum/ manūs** ~ engage in close combat; **ex iūre manum** ~ lay claim to (in an action for possession).

cōnsertē adv connectedly.

cōnsertus ppp of **cōnserō.**

cōnserva, -ae f fellow slave.

cōnservātiō, -ōnis f preserving.

cōnservātor, -ōris m preserver.

cōnservitium, -ī and **iī** nt being fellow slaves.

cōnservō, -āre, -āvī, -ātum vt to preserve, save, keep.

cōnservus, -ī m fellow slave.

cōnsessor, -ōris m companion at table, fellow spectator; (law) assessor.

cōnsessus, -ūs m assembly; (law) court.

cōnsēvī perf of **cōnserō.**

cōnsīderātē adv cautiously, deliberately.

cōnsīderātiō, -ōnis f contemplation.

cōnsīderātus adj (person) circumspect; (things) well-considered.

cōnsīderō, -āre, -āvī, -ātum vt to look at, inspect; to consider, contemplate.

cōnsīdō, -īdere, -ēdī, -essum vi to sit down, take seats; (courts) to be in session; (MIL) to

take up a position; (residence) to settle; (places) to subside, sink; (fig) to sink, settle down, subside.

cōnsignō, -āre, -āvī, -ātum vt to seal, sign; to attest, vouch for; to record, register.

cōnsilēscō, -ere vi to calm down.

cōnsiliārius, -ī and **iī** m adviser, counsellor; spokesman ♦ adj counselling.

cōnsiliātor, -ōris m counsellor.

cōnsilior, -ārī, -ātus vi to consult; (with dat) to advise.

cōnsilium, -ī and **iī** nt deliberation, consultation; deliberating body, council; decision, purpose; plan, measure, stratagem; advice, counsel; judgement, insight, wisdom; **~ium capere, inīre** come to a decision, resolve; **~i esse** be an open question; **~iō** intentionally; **eō ~iō ut** with the intention of; **prīvātō ~iō** for one's own purposes.

cōnsimilis adj just like.

cōnsipiō, -ere vi to be in one's senses.

cōnsistō, -istere, -titī vi to stand, rest, take up a position; to consist (of), depend (on); to exist, be; (fig) to stand firm, endure; (liquid) to solidify, freeze; to stop, pause, halt, come to rest; (fig) to come to a standstill, come to an end.

cōnsitiō, -ōnis f sowing, planting.

cōnsitor, -ōris m sower, planter.

cōnsitus ppp of **cōnserō.**

cōnsōbrīnus, -ī m, **-a, -ae** f cousin.

cōnsociātiō, -ōnis f society.

cōnsociō, -āre, -āvī, -ātum vt to share, associate, unite.

cōnsōlābilis adj consolable.

cōnsōlātiō, -ōnis f comfort, encouragement, consolation.

cōnsōlātor, -ōris m comforter.

cōnsōlātōrius adj of consolation.

cōnsōlor, -ārī, -ātus vt to console, comfort, reassure; (things) to relieve, mitigate.

cōnsomniō, -āre vt to dream about.

cōnsonō, -āre, -uī vi to resound; (fig) to accord.

cōnsonus adj concordant; (fig) suitable.

cōnsōpiō, -īre, -ītum vt to put to sleep.

cōnsors, -tis adj sharing in common; (things) shared in common ♦ m/f partner, colleague.

cōnsortiō, -ōnis f partnership, fellowship.

cōnsortium, -ī and **iī** nt society, participation.

cōnspectus ppp of **cōnspiciō** ♦ adj visible; conspicuous.

cōnspectus, -ūs m look, view, sight; appearing on the scene; (fig) mental picture, survey; **in ~um venīre** come in sight, come near.

cōnspergō, -gere, -sī, -sum vt to besprinkle; (fig) to spangle.

cōnspiciendus adj noteworthy, distinguished.

cōnspiciō, -icere, -exī, -ectum vt to observe, catch sight of; to look at (esp with admiration),

contemplate; (*pass*) to attract attention, be
conspicuous, be notorious; (*mina*) to see,
perceive.

cōnspicor, -ārī, -ātus *vt* to observe, see,
catch sight of.

cōnspicuus *adj* visible, conspicuous,
distinguished.

cōnspīrātiō, -ōnis *f* concord, unanimity;
plotting, conspiracy.

cōnspīrō, -āre, -āvī, -ātum *vi* to agree, unite;
to plot, conspire; (*music*) to sound together.

cōnspōnsor, -ōris *m* co-guarantor.

cōnspuō, -ere *vt* to spit upon.

cōnspurcō, -āre *vt* to pollute.

cōnspūtō, -āre *vt* to spit upon (*with contempt*).

cōnstabiliō, -īre, -īvī, -itum *vt* to establish.

cōnstāns, -antis *pres p of* **cōnstō** ♦ *adj* steady,
stable, constant; consistent; faithful,
steadfast.

cōnstanter *adv* steadily, firmly, calmly;
consistently.

cōnstantia, -ae *f* steadiness, firmness;
consistency, harmony; self-possession,
constancy.

cōnsternātiō, -ōnis *f* disorder, tumult;
(*horses*) stampede; (*mind*) dismay, alarm.

cōnsternō, -ernere, -rāvī, -rātum *vt* to
spread, cover, thatch, pave; **~rāta nāvis**
decked ship.

cōnsternō, -āre, -āvī, -ātum *vt* tc startle,
stampede; to alarm, throw into confusion.

cōnstipō, -āre *vt* to crowd together.

cōnstitī *perf of* **cōnsistō**.

cōnstituō, -uere, -uī, -ūtum *vt* to put, place,
set down; (*MIL*) to station, post, halt; to
establish, build, create; to settle, arrange,
organize; to appoint, determine, fix; to
resolve, decide; **bene ~ūtum corpus** a good
constitution.

cōnstitūtiō, -ōnis *f* state, condition;
regulation, decree; definition, point at issue.

cōnstitūtum, -ūtī *nt* agreement.

cōnstō, -āre, -itī, -ātum *vi* to stand together;
to agree, correspond, tally; to stand firm,
remain constant; to exist, be; to consist (of),
be composed (of); (*facts*) to be established,
be well-known; (*comm*) to cost; **sibi ~** be
consistent; **inter omnēs ~at** it is common
knowledge; **mihi ~at** I am determined; **ratiō
~at** the account is correct.

cōnstrātum, -ī *nt* flooring, deck.

cōnstrātus *ppp of* **cōnsternō**.

cōnstringō, -ingere, -inxī, -ictum *vt* to tie
up, bind, fetter; (*fig*) to restrain, restrict;
(*speech*) to compress, condense.

cōnstructiō, -ōnis *f* building up; (*words*)
arrangement, sequence.

cōnstruō, -ere, -xī, -ctum *vt* to heap up; to
build, construct.

cōnstuprātor, -ōris *m* debaucher.

cōnstuprō, -āre *vt* to debauch, rape.

cōnsuādeō, -ēre *vi* to advise strongly.

Cōnsuālia, -ium *ntpl* festival of Consus.

cōnsuāsor, -ōris *m* earnest adviser.

cōnsūdō, -āre *vi* to sweat profusely.

cōnsuēfaciō, -facere, -fēcī, -factum *vt* to
accustom.

cōnsuēscō, -scere, -vī, -tum *vt* to accustom,
inure ♦ *vi* to get accustomed; to cohabit
(with); (*perf tenses*) to be accustomed, be in
the habit of.

cōnsuētūdō, -inis *f* custom, habit;
familiarity, social intercourse; love affair;
(*language*) usage, idiom; **~ine/ex ~ine** as
usual; **epistulārum** ~ correspondence.

cōnsuētus *ppp of* **cōnsuēscō** ♦ *adj* customary,
usual.

cōnsuēvī *perf of* **cōnsuēscō**.

cōnsul, -is *m* consul; **~ dēsignātus** consul
elect; **~ ōrdinārius** regular consul; **~
suffectus** *successor to a consul who has died
during his term of office*; **~ iterum/tertium**
consul for the second/third time; **~em**
creāre, dīcere, facere elect to the consulship;
L. Domitiō App. Claudiō ~ibus in the year 54
B.C.

cōnsulāris *adj* consular, consul's; of consular
rank ♦ *m* ex-consul.

cōnsulāriter *adv* in a manner worthy of a
consul.

cōnsulātus, -ūs *m* consulship; **~um petere**
stand for the consulship.

cōnsulō, -ere, -uī, -tum *vi* to deliberate, take
thought; (*with dat*) to look after, consult the
interests of; (*with dē or* in) to take measures
against, pass sentence on ♦ *vt* to consult, ask
advice of; to consider; to advise
(something); to decide; **boni/optimī ~** take in
good part, be satisfied with.

cōnsultātiō, -ōnis *f* deliberation; inquiry;
case.

cōnsultē *adv* deliberately.

cōnsultō *adv* deliberately.

cōnsultō, -āre, -āvī, -ātum *vt, vi* to
deliberate, reflect; to consult; (*with dat*) to
consult the interests of.

cōnsultor, -ōris *m* counsellor; consulter,
client.

cōnsultrīx, -īcis *f* protectress.

cōnsultum, -ī *nt* decree (*esp of the Senate*);
consultation; response (*from an oracle*).

cōnsultus *ppp of* **cōnsulō** ♦ *adj* considered;
experienced, skilled ♦ *m* lawyer; **iūris ~us**
lawyer.

cōnsuluī *perf of* **cōnsulō**.

(cōnsum), futūrum, fore *vi* to be all right.

cōnsummātus *adj* perfect.

cōnsummō, -āre *vt* to sum up; to complete,
perfect.

cōnsūmō, -ere, -psī, -ptum *vt* to consume,

Noun declensions and verb conjugations are shown on pp xiii to xxv. The present infinitive ending of a verb shows
to which conjugation it belongs: -**āre** = 1st; -**ēre** = 2nd; -**ere** = 3rd and -**īre** = 4th. Irregular verbs are shown on p xxvi

use up, eat up; to waste, squander; to
exhaust, destroy, kill; to spend, devote.
cōnsūmptiō, -ōnis *f* wasting.
cōnsūmptor, -ōris *m* destroyer.
cōnsūmptus *ppp of* cōnsūmō.
cōnsuō, -uere, -uī, -ūtum *vt* to sew up; (*fig*)
to contrive.
cōnsurgō, -gere, -rēxī, -rēctum *vi* to rise,
stand up; to be roused (to); to spring up,
start.
cōnsurrēctiō, -ōnis *f* standing up.
Cōnsus, -ī *m* ancient Roman god (*connected
with harvest*).
cōnsusurrō, -āre *vi* to whisper together.
cōnsūtus *ppp of* cōnsuō.
contābefaciō, -ere *vt* to wear out.
contābēscō, -ēscere, -uī *vi* to waste away.
contabulātiō, -ōnis *f* flooring, storey.
contabulō, -āre, -āvī, -ātum *vt* to board
over, build in storeys.
contāctus *ppp of* contingō.
contāctus, -ūs *m* touch, contact; contagion,
infection.
contāgēs, -is *f* contact, touch.
contāgiō, -ōnis *f*, contāgium, -ī *and* iī *nt*
contact; contagion, infection; (*fig*)
contamination, bad example.
contāminātus *adj* impure, vicious.
contāminō, -āre, -āvī, -ātum *vt* to defile; (*fig*)
to mar, spoil.
contechnor, -ārī, -ātus *vi* to think out plots.
contegō, -egere, -ēxī, -ēctum *vt* to cover up,
cover over; to protect; to hide.
contemerō, -āre *vt* to defile.
contemnō, -nere, -psī, -ptum *vt* to think
light of, have no fear of, despise, defy; to
disparage.
contemplātiō, -ōnis *f* contemplation,
surveying.
contemplātor, -ōris *m* observer.
contemplātus, -ūs *m* contemplation.
contemplō, -āre, -āvī, -ātum, -or, -ārī,
-ātus *vt* to look at, observe, contemplate.
contempsī *perf of* contemnō.
contemptim *adv* contemptuously,
slightingly.
contemptiō, -ōnis *f* disregard, scorn,
despising.
contemptor, -ōris *m* (male) despiser, defiler.
contemptrīx, -rīcis *f* (female) despiser,
defiler.
contemptus *ppp of* contemnō ♦ *adj*
contemptible.
contemptus, -ūs *m* despising, scorn; being
slighted; ~uī esse be despised.
contendō, -dere, -dī, -tum *vt* to stretch,
draw, tighten; (*instrument*) to tune; (*effort*) to
strain, exert; (*argument*) to assert, maintain;
(*comparison*) to compare, contrast; (*course*)
to direct ♦ *vi* to exert oneself, strive; to
hurry; to journey, march; to contend,
compete, fight; to entreat, solicit.
contentē *adv* (*from* contendō) earnestly,

intensely.
contentē *adv* (*from* contineō) closely.
contentiō, -ōnis *f* straining, effort; striving
(after); struggle, competition, dispute;
comparison, contrast, antithesis.
contentus *ppp of* contendō ♦ *adj* strained,
tense; (*fig*) intent.
contentus *ppp of* contineō ♦ *adj* content,
satisfied.
conterminus *adj* bordering, neighbouring.
conterō, -erere, -rīvī, -rītum *vt* to grind,
crumble; to wear out, waste; (*time*) to spend,
pass; (*fig*) to obliterate.
conterreō, -ēre, -uī, -itum *vt* to terrify.
contestātus *adj* proved.
contestor, -ārī, -ātus *vt* to call to witness;
lītem ~ open a lawsuit by calling witnesses.
contexō, -ere, -uī, -tum *vt* to weave,
interweave; to devise, construct; (*recital*) to
continue.
contextē *adv* in a connected fashion.
contextus *adj* connected.
contextus, -ūs *m* connection, coherence.
conticēscō (-īscō), -ēscere, -uī *vi* to become
quiet, fall silent; (*fig*) to cease, abate.
contigī *perf of* contingō.
contignātiō, -ōnis *f* floor, storey.
contignō, -āre *vt* to floor.
contiguus *adj* adjoining, near; within reach.
continēns, -entis *pres p of* contineō ♦ *adj*
bordering, adjacent; unbroken, continuous;
(*time*) successive, continual, uninterrupted;
(*person*) temperate, continent ♦ *nt* mainland,
continent; essential point (*in an argument*).
continenter *adv* (*place*) in a row; (*time*)
continuously; (*person*) temperately.
continentia, -ae *f* moderation, self-control.
contineō, -inēre, -inuī, -entum *vt* to hold,
keep together; to confine, enclose; to
contain, include, comprise; (*pass*) to consist
of, rest on; to control, check, repress.
contingō, -ingere, -igī, -āctum *vt* to touch,
take hold of, partake of; to be near, border
on; to reach, come to; to contaminate; (*mind*)
to touch, affect, concern ♦ *vi* to happen,
succeed.
contingō, -ere *vt* to moisten, smear.
continuātiō, -ōnis *f* unbroken, succession,
series; (*RHET*) period.
continuī *perf of* contineō.
continuō *adv* immediately, without delay;
(*argument*) necessarily.
continuō, -āre, -āvī, -ātum *vt* to join
together, make continuous; to continue
without a break; verba ~ form a sentence.
continuus *adj* joined (to); continuous,
successive, uninterrupted; ~ā nocte the
following night; triduum ~um three days
running.
cōntiō, -ōnis *f* public meeting; speech,
address; rostrum; ~ōnem habēre hold a
meeting; deliver an address; prō ~ōne in
public.

cōntiōnābundus *adj* delivering a harangue, playing the demagogue.

cōntiōnālis *adj* suitable for a public meeting, demagogic.

cōntiōnārius *adj* fond of public meetings.

cōntiōnātor, -ōris *m* demagogue.

cōntiōnor, -ārī, -ātus *vi* to address a public meeting, harangue; to declare in public; to come to a meeting.

cōntiuncula, -ae *f* short speech.

contorqueō, -quēre, -sī, -tum *vt* to twist, turn; (*weapons*) to throw, brandish; (*words*) to deliver forcibly.

contortē *adv* intricately.

contortiō, -ōnis *f* intricacy.

contortor, -ōris *m* perverter.

contortulus *adj* somewhat complicated.

contortuplicātus *adj* very complicated.

contortus *ppp of* **contorqueō** ♦ *adj* vehement; intricate.

contrā *adv* (place) opposite, face to face; (*speech*) in reply; (*action*) to fight, in opposition, against someone; (*result, with esse*) adverse, unsuccessful; (*comparison*) the contrary, conversely, differently; (*argument*) on the contrary, on the other hand; ~ **atque, quam** contrary to what, otherwise than ♦ *prep* (*with acc*) facing, opposite to; against; contrary to, in violation of.

contractiō, -ōnis *f* contracting; shortening; despondency.

contractiuncula, -ae *f* slight despondency.

contractus *ppp of* **contrahō** ♦ *adj* contracted, narrow; short; in seclusion.

contrādīcō, -dīcere, -dīxī, -dictum (*usu two words*) *vt, vi* to oppose, object; (*law*) to be counsel for the other side.

contrādictiō, -ōnis *f* objection.

contrahō, -here, -xī, -ctum *vt* to draw together, assemble; to bring about, achieve; (*comm*) to contract, make a bargain; to shorten, narrow; to limit, depress; (*blame*) to incur; (*brow*) to wrinkle; (*sail*) to shorten; (*sky*) to overcast.

contrāriē *adv* differently.

contrārius *adj* opposite, from opposite; contrary; hostile, harmful ♦ *nt* opposite, reverse; **ex ~ō** on the contrary.

contrectābiliter *adv* so as to be felt.

contrectātiō, -ōnis *f* touching.

contrectō, -āre, -āvī, -ātum *vt* to touch, handle; (*fig*) to consider.

contremīscō, -īscere, -uī *vi* to tremble all over; (*fig*) to waver ♦ *vt* to be afraid of.

contremō, -ere *vi* to quake.

contribuō, -uere, -uī, -ūtum *vt* to bring together, join, incorporate.

contristō, -āre, -āvī, -ātum *vt* to sadden, darken, cloud.

contrītus *ppp of* **conterō** ♦ *adj* trite, well-worn.

contrōversia, -ae *f* dispute, argument, debate, controversy.

contrōversiōsus *adj* much disputed.

contrōversus *adj* disputed, questionable.

contrucīdō, -āre, -āvī, -ātum *vt* to massacre.

contrūdō, -dere, -sī, -sum *vt* to crowd together.

contruncō, -āre *vt* to hack to pieces.

contrūsus *ppp of* **contrūdō**.

contubernālis, -is *m/f* tent companion; junior officer serving with a general; (*fig*) companion, mate

contubernium, -ī *and* **iī** *nt* service in the same tent, mess; service as junior officer with a general; common tent; slaves' home.

contueor, -ērī, -itus *vt* to look at, consider, observe.

contuitus, -ūs *m* observing, view.

contulī *perf of* **cōnferō**.

contumācia, -ae *f* obstinacy, defiance.

contumāciter *adv see* **contumāx**.

contumāx, -ācis *adj* stubborn, insolent, pigheaded.

contumēlia, -ae *f* (*verbal*) insult, libel, invective; (*physical*) assault, ill-treatment.

contumēliōsē *adv* insolently.

contumēliōsus *adj* insulting, outrageous.

contumulō, -āre *vt* to bury.

contundō, -undere, -udī, -ūsum *vt* to pound, beat, bruise; (*fig*) to suppress, destroy.

contuor *etc see* **contueor**.

conturbātiō, -ōnis *f* confusion, mental disorder.

conturbātus *adj* distracted, diseased.

conturbō, -āre, -āvī, -ātum *vt* to throw into confusion; (*mind*) to derange, disquiet; (*money*) to embarrass.

contus, -ī *m* pole.

contūsus *ppp of* **contundō**.

contūtus *see* **contuitus**.

cōnūbiālis *adj* conjugal.

cōnūbium, -ī *and* **iī** *nt* marriage; **iūs ~ī** right of intermarriage.

cōnus, -ī *m* cone; (*helmet*) apex.

convador, -ārī, -ātus *vt* (*law*) to bind over.

convalēscō, -ēscere, -uī *vi* to recover, get better; (*fig*) to grow stronger, improve.

convallis, -is *f* valley with hills on all sides.

convāsō, -āre *vt* to pack up.

convectō, -āre *vt* to bring home.

convector, -ōris *m* fellow passenger.

convehō, -here, -xī, -ctum *vt* to bring in, carry.

convellō, -ellere, -ellī, -ulsum *and* **olsum** *vt* to wrench, tear away; to break up; (*fig*) to destroy, overthrow; **signa ~** decamp.

convena, -ae *adj* meeting.

convenae, -ārum *m/f* crowd of strangers, refugees.

Noun declensions and verb conjugations are shown on pp xiii to xxv. The present infinitive ending of a verb shows to which conjugation it belongs: **-āre** = 1st; **-ēre** = 2nd; **-ere** = 3rd and **-īre** = 4th. Irregular verbs are shown on p xxvi

conveniēns, -entis *pres p of* **conveniō** ♦ *adj* harmonious, consistent; fit, appropriate.
convenienter *adv* in conformity (with), consistently; aptly.
convenientia, -ae *f* conformity, harmony.
conveniō, -enīre, -ēnī, -entum *vi* to meet, assemble; (*events*) to combine, coincide; (*person*) to agree, harmonize; (*things*) to fit, suit; (*impers*) to be suitable, be proper ♦ *vt* to speak to, interview.
conventīcium, -ī *and* **iī** *nt* payment for attendance at assemblies.
conventīcius *adj* visiting regularly.
conventiculum, -ī *nt* gathering; meeting place.
conventiō, -ōnis *f* agreement.
conventum, -ī *nt* agreement.
conventus *ppp of* **conveniō**.
conventus, -ūs *m* meeting; (*law*) local assizes; (*comm*) corporation; agreement; **~ūs agere** hold the assizes.
converrō, -rere, -rī, -sum *vt* to sweep up, brush together; (*comedy*) to give a good beating to.
conversātiō, -ōnis *f* associating (with).
conversiō, -ōnis *f* revolution, cycle; change over; (*rhet*) well-rounded period; verbal repetition at end of clauses.
conversō, -āre *vt* to turn round.
conversus *ppp of* **converrō**; *ppp of* **convertō**.
convertō, -tere, -tī, -sum *vt* to turn round, turn back; (*mil*) to wheel; to turn, direct; to change, transform; (*writings*) to translate ♦ *vi* to return, turn, change.
convestiō, -īre, -īvī, -ītum *vt* to clothe, encompass.
convexus *adj* vaulted, rounded; hollow; sloping ♦ *nt* vault, hollow.
convīciātor, -ōris *m* slanderer.
convīcior, -ārī, -ātus *vt* to revile.
convīcium, -ī *and* **iī** *nt* loud noise, outcry; invective, abuse; reproof, protest.
convīctiō, -ōnis *f* companionship.
convīctor, -ōris *m* familiar friend.
convīctus *ppp of* **convincō**.
convīctus, -ūs *m* community life, intercourse; entertainment.
convincō, -incere, -īcī, -ictum *vt* to refute, convict, prove wrong; to prove, demonstrate.
convīsō, -ere *vt* to search, examine; to pervade.
convītium *see* **convīcium**.
convīva, -ae *m/f* guest.
convīvālis *adj* festive, convivial.
convīvātor, -ōris *m* host.
convīvium, -ī *and* **iī** *nt* banquet, entertainment; guests.
convīvor, -ārī, -ātus *vi* to feast together, carouse.
convocātiō, -ōnis *f* assembling.
convocō, -āre, -āvī, -ātum *vt* to call a meeting of, muster.

convolnerō *see* **convulnerō**.
convolō, -āre, -āvī, -ātum *vi* to flock together.
convolsus *see* **convulsus**.
convolvō, -vere, -vī, -ūtum *vt* to roll up, coil up; to intertwine.
convomō, -ere *vt* to vomit over.
convorrō *see* **converrō**.
convortō *see* **convertō**.
convulnerō, -āre *vt* to wound seriously.
convulsus *ppp of* **convellō**.
cooperiō, -īre, -uī, -tum *vt* to cover over, overwhelm.
cooptātiō, -ōnis *f* electing, nominating (of new members).
cooptō, -āre, -āvī, -ātum *vt* to elect (as a colleague).
coorior, -īrī, -tus *vi* to rise, appear; to break out, begin.
coortus, -ūs *m* originating.
cōpa, -ae *f* barmaid.
cophinus, -ī *m* basket.
cōpia, -ae *f* abundance, plenty, number; resources, wealth, prosperity; (*mil, usu pl*) troops, force; (*words, thought*) richness, fulness, store; (*action*) opportunity, facility, means, access; **prō ~ā** according to one's resources, as good as possible considering.
cōpiolae, -ārum *fpl* small force.
cōpiōsē *adv* abundantly, fully, at great length.
cōpiōsus *adj* abounding, rich, plentiful; (*speech*) eloquent, fluent.
cōpis *adj* rich.
cōpula, -ae *f* rope, leash, grapnel; (*fig*) bond.
cōpulātiō, -ōnis *f* coupling, union.
cōpulātus *adj* connected, binding.
cōpulō, -āre, -āvī, -ātum *vt* to couple, join; (*fig*) to unite, associate.
coqua, -ae *f* cook.
coquīnō, -āre *vi* to be a cook.
coquīnus *adj* of cooking.
coquō, -quere, -xī, -ctum *vt* to cook, boil, bake; to parch, burn; (*fruit*) to ripen; (*stomach*) to digest; (*thought*) to plan, concoct; (*care*) to disquiet, disturb.
coquus (cocus), -ī *m* cook.
cor, cordis *nt* heart; (*feeling*) heart, soul; (*thought*) mind, judgement; **cordī esse** please, be agreeable.
cōram *adv* in one's presence; in person ♦ *prep* (*with abl*) in the presence of, before.
corbis, -is *m/f* basket.
corbīta, -ae *f* slow boat.
corbula, -ae *f* little basket.
corculum, -ī *nt* dear heart.
Corcӯra, -ae *f* island off W. coast of Greece (*now* Corfu).
Corcӯraeus *adj see n.*
cordātē *adv see* **cordātus**.
cordātus *adj* wise.
cordolium, -ī *and* **iī** *nt* sorrow.
Corfiniēnsis *adj see n.*
Corfinium, -ī *nt* town in central Italy.

coriandrum, -ī nt coriander.
Corinthiacus, -iēnsis, -ius adj: ~ium aes
Corinthian brass (an alloy of gold, silver and
copper).
Corinthus, -ī f Corinth.
corium (corius m) **-ī** and **ī ī** nt hide, skin;
leather, strap.
Cornēlia, -iae f mother of the Gracchi.
Cornēliānus, -ius adj lēgēs ~iae Sulla's laws.
Cornēlius, -ī m famous Roman family name
(esp Scipios, Gracchi, Sulla).
corneolus adj horny.
corneus adj of horn.
corneus adj of the cornel tree, of cornel wood.
cornicen, -cinis m horn-blower.
cornīcula, -ae f little crow.
corniculārius, -ī and **ī ī** m adjutant
corniculum, -ī nt a horn-shaped decoration.
corniger, -ī adj horned.
cornipēs, -edis adj horn-footed.
cornīx, -īcis f crow.
cornū, -ūs, -um, -ī nt horn; anything horn-
shaped; (army) wing; (bay) arm; (book)
roller-end; (bow) tip; (helmet) crest-socket;
(land) tongue, spit; (lyre) arm; (moon) horn;
(place) side; (river) branch; (yardarm) point;
anything made of horn: bow, funnel,
lantern; (music) horn; (oil) cruet; anything
like horn; beak, hoof, wart; (fig) strength,
courage; ~ cōpiae Amalthea's horn, symbol of
plenty.
cornum, -ī nt cornelian cherry.
cornum see **cornū.**
cornus, -ī f cornelian cherry tree; javelin.
corōlla, -ae f small garland.
corōllārium, -ī and **ī ī** nt garland for actors;
present, gratuity.
corōna, -ae f garland, crown; (ASTRO) Corona
Borealis; (people) gathering, bystanders;
(MIL) cordon of besiegers or defenders; sub
~ā vēndere, vēnīre sell, be sold as slaves.
Corōnaeus, -ēus, -ēnsis adj see **Corōnēa.**
corōnārium aurum gold collected in the
provinces for a victorious general.
Corōnēa, -ēae f town in central Greece.
corōnō, -āre, -āvī, -ātum vt to put a garland
on, crown; to encircle.
corporeus adj corporeal; of flesh.
corpulentus adj corpulent.
corpus, -oris nt body; substance, flesh;
corpse; trunk, torso; person, individual; (fig)
structure, corporation, body politic.
corpusculum, -ī nt particle; term of
endearment.
corrādō, -dere, -sī, -sum vt to scrape
together, procure.
corrēctiō, -ōnis f amending, improving.
corrēctor, -ōris m reformer, critic.
corrēctus ppp of **corrigō.**
correpō, -ere, -sī vi to creep, slink, cower.

correptē adv briefly.
correptus ppp of **corripiō.**
corrīdeō, -ēre vi to laugh aloud.
corrigia, -ae f shoelace.
corrigō, -igere, -ēxī, -ēctum vt to make
straight; to put right, improve, correct.
corripiō, -ipere, -ipuī, -eptum vt to seize,
carry off, get along quickly; (speech) to
reprove, reproach, accuse; (passion) to seize
upon, attack; (time, words) to cut short; sē
gradum, viam ~ hasten, rush.
corrōborō, -āre -āvī, -ātum vt to make
strong, invigorate.
corrōdō, -dere, -sī, -sum vt to nibble away.
corrogō, -āre vt to gather by requesting.
corrūgō, -āre vt to wrinkle.
corrumpō, -umpere, -ūpī, -uptum vt to
break up, ruin, waste; to mar, adulterate,
falsify; (person) to corrupt, seduce, bribe.
corruō, -ere, -ī v to fall, collapse ♦ vt to
overthrow, heap up.
corruptē adv perversely; in a lax manner.
corruptēla, -ae f corruption, bribery;
seducer.
corruptiō, -ōn s f bribing, seducing; corrupt
state.
corruptor, -ōris m, **-rīx, -rīcis** f corrupter,
seducer.
corruptus ppp of **corrumpō** ♦ adj spoiled,
corrupt, bad.
Corsus adj Corsican.
cortex, -icis m/f bark, rind; cork.
cortīna, -ae f kettle, cauldron; tripod of
Apollo; (fig) vault, circle.
corulus, -ī f hazel.
Cōrus see **Caurus.**
coruscō, -āre vi to butt; to shake, brandish ♦
vi to flutter, flash, quiver.
coruscus adj tremulous, oscillating;
shimmering, glittering.
corvus, -ī m raven; (MIL) grapnel.
Corybantēs, -ium mpl priests of Cybele.
Corybantius adj see n.
cōrycus, -ī m punchball.
corylētum, -ī nt hazel copse.
corylus, -ī f hazel.
corymbifer m Bacchus.
corymbus, -ī m cluster (esp of ivy berries).
coryphaeus, -ī m leader.
cōrytos, -us, -ī m quiver.
cōs f hard rock, flint; grindstone.
Cōs, Cōī f Aegean island (famous for wine and
weaving) ♦ nt Coan wine ♦ ntpl Coan clothes.
cosmēta, -ae m master of the wardrobe.
costa, -ae f rib; side, wall.
costum, -ī nt an aromatic plant, perfume.
cothurnātus adj buskined, tragic.
cothurnus, -ī m buskin, hunting boot;
tragedy, elevated style.
cotīd see **cottīd-**

Noun declensions and verb conjugations are shown on pp xiii to xxv. The present infinitive ending of a verb shows
to which conjugation it belongs: **-āre** = 1st; **-ēre** = 2nd; **-ere** = 3rd and **-īre** = 4th. Irregular verbs are shown on p xxvi

cōtis *f see* **cōs.**

cottabus, -ī *m* game of throwing drops of wine.

cottana, -ōrum *ntpl* Syrian figs.

cottīdiānō *adv* daily.

cottīdiānus *adj* daily; everyday, ordinary.

cottīdiē *adv* every day, daily.

coturnīx, -īcis *f* quail.

Cotyttia, -ōrum *ntpl festival of Thracian goddess Cotytto.*

Cōus *adj* Coan.

covinnārius, -ī *and* **ī ī** *m* chariot fighter.

covinnus, -ī *m* war chariot; coach.

coxa, -ae, coxendīx, -īcis *f* hip.

coxī *perf of* **coquō.**

crābrō, -ōnis *m* hornet.

crambē-, -ēs *f* cabbage; ~ **repetīta stale** repetitions.

Crantor, -oris *m Greek Academic philosopher.*

crāpula, -ae *f* intoxication, hangover.

crāpulārius *adj* for intoxication.

crās *adv* tomorrow.

crassē *adv* grossly, dimly.

Crassiānus *adj see* **Crassus.**

crassitūdō, -inis *f* thickness, density.

crassus *adj* thick, gross, dense; (*fig*) dull, stupid.

Crassus, -ī *m* famous orator; wealthy politician, triumvir with Caesar and Pompey.

crāstinum, -ī *nt* the morrow.

crāstinus *adj* of tomorrow; **diē ~ī** tomorrow.

crātēr, -is *m*, **-a, -ae** *f* bowl (*esp for mixing wine and water*); crater; a constellation.

crātis, -is *f* wickerwork, hurdle; (*AGR*) harrow; (*MIL*) faggots for lining trenches; (*shield*) ribs; (*fig*) frame, joints.

creātiō, -ōnis *f* election.

creātor, -ōris *m*, **-rīx, -rīcis** *f* creator, father, mother.

creātus *m* (*with abl*) son of.

crēber, -rī *adj* dense, thick, crowded; numerous, frequent; (*fig*) prolific, abundant.

crēbrēscō, -ēscere, -uī *vi* to increase, become frequent.

crēbritās, -ātis *f* frequency.

crēbrō *adv* repeatedly.

crēdibilis *adj* credible.

crēdibiliter *adv see* **crēdibilis.**

crēditor, -ōris *m* creditor.

crēditum, -ītī *nt* loan.

crēdō, -ere, -idī, -itum *vt, vi* to entrust, lend; to trust, have confidence in; to believe; to think, suppose; **~erēs** one would have thought.

crēdulitās, -ātis *f* credulity.

crēdulus *adj* credulous, trusting.

cremō, -āre, -āvī, -ātum *vt* to burn, cremate.

Cremōna, -ae *f town in N. Italy.*

Cremōnēnsis *adj see n.*

cremor, -ōris *m* juice, broth.

creō, -āre, -āvī, -ātum *vt* to create, produce, beget; to elect (to an office); to cause, occasion.

creper, -ī *adj* dark; doubtful.

crepida, -ae *f* sandal; **nē sūtor suprā ~am** ≈ *let the cobbler stick to his last.*

crepidātus *adj* wearing sandals.

crepīdō, -inis *f* pedestal, base; bank, pier, dam.

crepidula, -ae *f* small sandal.

crepitācillum, -ī *nt* rattle.

crepitō, -āre *vi* to rattle, chatter, rustle, creak.

crepitus, -ūs *m* rattling, chattering, rustling, creaking.

crepō, -āre, -uī, -itum *vi* to rattle, creak, snap (fingers) ♦ *vt* to make rattle, clap; to chatter about.

crepundia, -ōrum *ntpl* rattle, babies' toys.

crepusculum, -ī *nt* twilight, dusk; darkness.

Crēs, -ētis *m* Cretan.

crēscō, -scere, -vī, -tum *vi* to arise, appear, be born; tc grow up, thrive, increase, multiply; to prosper, be promoted, rise in the world.

Crēsius *adj* Cretan.

Crēssa, -ae *f* Cretan.

Crēta, -ae *f* Crete.

crēta, -ae *f* chalk; good mark.

Crētaeus *and* **-icus** *and* **-is, -idis** *adj see n.*

crētātus *ad* chalked; dressed in white.

Crētē *see* **Crēta.**

crēteus *adj* of chalk, of clay.

crētiō, -ōnis *f* declaration of accepting an inheritance.

crētōsus *adj* chalky, clayey.

crētula, -ae *f* white clay for sealing.

crētus *ppp of* **cernō** ♦ *ppa of* **crēscō** ♦ *adj* descended, born.

Creūsa, -ae *f wife of Jason; wife of Aeneas.*

crēvī *perf of* **cernō;** *perf of* **crēscō.**

crībrum, -ī *nt* sieve.

crīmen, -iris *nt* accusation, charge, reproach; guilt, crime; cause of offence; **esse in ~ine** stand accused.

crīminātiō, -ōnis *f* complaint, slander.

crīminātor, -ōris *m* accuser.

crīminō, -āre *vt* to accuse.

crīminor, -ārī, -ātus *dep* to accuse, impeach; (*things*) tc complain of, charge with.

crīminōsē *adv* accusingly, slanderously.

crīminōsus *adj* reproachful, slanderous.

crīnālis *adj* for the hair, hair- (*in cpds*) ♦ *nt* hairpin.

crīnis, -is *m* hair; (*comet*) tail.

crīnītus *ad* long-haired; crested; **stēlla ~a** comet.

crīspāns, -antis *adj* wrinkled.

crīspō, -āre *vt* to curl, swing, wave.

crīspus *adj* curled; curly-headed; wrinkled; tremulous.

crista, -ae *f* cockscomb, crest; plume.

cristātus *adj* crested, plumed.

criticus, -ī *m* critic.

croceus *adj* of saffron, yellow.

crocinus *adj* yellow ♦ *nt* saffron oil.

crōciō, -īre vi to croak.
crocodīlus, -ī m crocodile.
crocōtārius adj of saffron clothes.
crocōtula, -ae f saffron dress.
crocus, -ī m, **-um, -ī** nt saffron yellow.
Croesus, -ī m king of Lydia (famed for wealth).
crotalistria, -ae f castanet dancer.
crotalum, -ī nt rattle, castanet.
cruciābilitās, -ātis f tormen .
cruciāmentum, -ī nt torture
cruciātus, -ūs m torture; instrument of torture; (fig) ruin, misfortune.
cruciō, -āre, -āvī, -ātum vt to torture; to torment.
crūdēlis adj hard-hearted, cruel
crūdēlitās, -ātis f cruelty, severity.
crūdēliter adv see **crūdēlis**.
crūdēscō, -ēscere, -uī vi to grow violent, grow worse.
crūditās, -ātis f indigestion.
crūdus adj bleeding; (food) raw, undigested; (person) dyspeptic; (leather raw-hide; (fruit) unripe; (age) immature, fresh; (voice) hoarse; (fig) unfeeling, cruel, merciless.
cruentō, -āre vt to stain with blood, wound.
cruentus adj bloody, gory; blood-thirsty, cruel; blood-red.
crumēna, -ae f purse; money.
crumilla, -ae f purse.
cruor, -ōris m blood; bloodshed.
cruppellāriī, -ōrum mpl mail-clad fighters.
crūrifragius, -ī and **iī** m one whose legs have been broken.
crūs, -ūris nt leg, shin.
crūsta, -ae f hard surface, crust; stucco, embossed or inlaid work.
crūstulum, -ī nt small pastry.
crūstum, -ī nt pastry.
crux, -ucis f gallows, cross; (fig) torment; **abī in malam ~cem** ≈ go and be hanged!
crypta, -ae f underground passage, grotto.
cryptoporticus, -ūs f covered walk.
crystallinus adj of crystal ♦ ntpl crystal vases.
crystallum, -ī nt, **-us, -ī** m crystal.
cubiculāris, cubiculārius adj of the bedroom ♦ m valet de chambre.
cubiculum, -ī nt bedroom.
cubīle, -is nt bed, couch; (animals) lair, nest; (fig) den.
cubital, -ālis nt cushion.
cubitālis adj a cubit long.
cubitō, -āre vi to lie (in bed)
cubitum, -ī nt elbow; cubit.
cubitus, -ūs m lying in bed.
cubō, -āre, -uī, -itum vi to lie in bed; to recline at table; (places) to lie on a slope.
cucullus, -ī m hood, cowl.
cucūlus, -ī m cuckoo.
cucumis, -eris m cucumber
cucurbita, -ae f gourd; cupping glass.

cucurrī perf of **currō**.
cūdō, -ere vt to beat, thresh; (metal) to forge; (money) to coin.
cūiās, -tis pron of what country?, of what town?
cuicuimodī (gen of **quisquis** and **mōdus**) of whatever kind, whatever like.
cūius pron (interrog) whose?; (rel) whose.
culcita, -ae f mattress, pillow; eyepatch.
cūleus see **culleus**.
culex, -icis m gnat.
culīna, -ae f kitchen; food.
culleus, cūleus, -ī m leather bag for holding liquids; a fluid measure.
culmen, -inis nt stalk; top, roof, summit; (fig) height, acme.
culmus, -ī m stalk, straw.
culpa, -ae f blame, fault; mischief; **in ~ā sum, mea ~a est** I am at fault or to blame.
culpātus adj blameworthy.
culpitō, -āre vt to find fault with.
culpō, -āre, -āvī, -ātum vt to blame, reproach.
cultē adv in a refined manner.
cultellus, -ī m. small knife.
culter, -rī m knife, razor.
cultiō, -ōnis f cultivation.
cultor, -ōris m cultivator, planter, farmer; inhabitant; supporter, upholder; worshipper
cultrīx, -īcis f inhabitant; (fig) nurse, fosterer.
cultūra, -ae f cultivation, agriculture; (mind) care, culture; (person) courting.
cultus ppp of **colō** ♦ adj cultivated; (dress) well-dressed; (mind) polished, cultured ♦ ntpl cultivated land.
cultus, -ūs m cultivation, care; (mind) training, culture; (dress) style, attire; (way of life) refinement, civilization; (gods) worship; (men) honouring.
culullus, -ī m goblet.
cūlus, -ī m buttocks.
cum prep (with abl) with; (denoting accompaniment, resulting circumstances, means, dealings, comparison, possession); **~ decimō** tenfold; **~ eō quod, ut** with the proviso that ~ **prīmīs** especially; **~ magnā calamitāte cīvitātis** to the great misfortune of the community; **~ perīculō suō** at one's own peril.
cum conj (time) when, whenever, while, as, after, since; (cause) since, as, seeing that; (concession) although; (condition) if; (contrast) while, whereas; **multī annī sunt ~ in aere meō est** for many years now he has been in my debt; **aliquot sunt annī ~ vōs dēlēgī** it is now some years since I chose you; **~ māximē** just when; just then, just now; **~ prīmum** as soon as; **~ ... tum** not only ... but also; both ... and.

Cūmae, -ārum _fpl_ town near Naples (_famous for its Sibyl_).

Cūmaeānum, -āni _nt Cicero's Cumaean residence._

Cūmaeus, -ānus _adj see n._

cumba, cymba, -ae _f_ boat, skiff.

cumera, -ae _f_ grain chest.

cumīnum, -ī _nt_ cumin.

cumque (quomque) _adv_ -ever, -soever; at any time.

cumulātē _adv_ fully, abundantly.

cumulātus _adj_ increased; complete.

cumulō, -āre, -āvī, -ātum _vt_ to heap up; to amass, increase; to fill up, overload; (_fig_) to fill, overwhelm, crown, complete.

cumulus, -ī _m_ heap, mass; crowning addition, summit.

cūnābula, -ōrum _ntpl_ cradle.

cūnae, -ārum _fpl_ cradle.

cunctābundus _adj_ hesitant, dilatory.

cunctāns, -antis _adj_ dilatory, reluctant; sluggish, tough.

cunctanter _adv_ slowly.

cunctātiō, -ōnis _f_ delaying, hesitation.

cunctātor, -ōris _m_ loiterer; one given to cautious tactics (_esp Q Fabius Maximus_).

cunctor, -ārī, -ātus _vi_ to linger, delay, hesitate; to move slowly.

cūnctus _adj_ the whole of; (_pl_) all together, all.

cuneātim _adv_ in the form of a wedge.

cuneātus _adj_ wedge-shaped.

cuneus, -ī _m_ wedge; (_MIL_) wedge-shaped formation of troops; (_THEATRE_) block of seats.

cunīculus, -ī _m_ rabbit; underground passage; (_MIL_) mine.

cunque _see_ **cumque**.

cūpa, -ae _f_ vat, tun.

cupidē _adv_ eagerly, passionately.

Cupīdineus _adj see_ **Cupīdō**.

cupiditās, -ātis _f_ desire, eagerness, enthusiasm; passion, lust; avarice, greed; ambition; partisanship.

cupīdō, -inis _f_ desire, eagerness; passion, lust; greed.

Cupīdō, -inis _m_ Cupid (_son of Venus_).

cupidus _adj_ desirous, eager; fond, loving; passionate, lustful; greedy, ambitious; partial.

cupiēns, -entis _pres p of_ **cupiō** ♦ _adj_ eager, desirous.

cupienter _adv see_ **cupiēns**.

cupiō, -ere, -īvī _and_ **iī, -ītum** _vt_ to wish, desire, long for; (_with dat_) to wish well.

cupītor, -ōris _m_ desirer.

cupītus _ppp of_ **cupiō**.

cuppēdia, -ae _f_ fondness for delicacies.

cuppēdia, -ōrum _ntpl_ delicacies.

cuppēdinārius, -ī _m_ confectioner.

cuppēdō, -inis _f_ longing, passion.

cuppes, -dis _adj_ fond of delicacies.

cupressētum, -ī _nt_ cypress grove.

cupresseus _adj_ of cypress wood.

cupressifer, -ī _adj_ cypress-bearing.

cupressus, -ī _f_ cypress.

cūr _adv_ why?; (_indirect_) why, the reason for.

cūra, -ae _f_ care, trouble, pains (bestowed); anxiety, concern, sorrow (felt); attention (to), charge (of), concern (for); (_MED_) treatment, cure; (_writing_) work; (_law_) trusteeship; (_poet_) love; (_person_) mistress, guardian; ~ **est** I am anxious; ~**ae esse** be attended to, looked after.

cūrābilis _adj_ troublesome.

cūralium, -ī _and_ **iī** _nt_ red coral.

cūrātē _adv_ carefully.

cūrātiō, -ōnis _f_ charge, management; office; treatment, healing.

cūrātor, -ōris _m_ manager, overseer; (_law_) guardian.

cūrātūra, -ae _f_ dieting.

cūrātus _adj_ cared for; earnest, anxious.

curculiō, -ōnis _m_ weevil.

curculiunculus, -ī _m_ little weevil.

Curēnsis _adj see n._

Curēs, -ium _mpl_ ancient Sabine town.

Cūrētēs, -um _mpl_ attendants of Jupiter in Crete.

Cūrētis, -idis _adj_ Cretan.

cūria, -ae _f_ earliest division of the Roman people; meeting-place of a curia; senate house; senate.

cūriālis, -is _m_ member of a curia.

cūriātim _adv_ by curiae.

cūriātus _adj_ of the curiae; **comitia ~a** earliest Roman assembly.

cūriō, -ōnis _m_ president of a curia; ~ **māximus** head of all the curiae.

cūriō, -ōnis _adj_ emaciated.

cūriōsē _adv_ carefully; inquisitively.

cūriōsitās, -ātis _f_ curiosity.

cūriōsus _adj_ careful, thoughtful, painstaking; inquiring, inquisitive, officious; careworn.

curis, -ītis _f_ spear.

cūrō, -āre, -āvī, -ātum _vt_ to take care of, attend to; to bother about; (_with gerundive_) to get something done; (_with inf_) to take the trouble; (_with ut_) to see to it that; (_public life_) to be in charge of, administer; (_MED_) to treat, cure; (_money_) to pay, settle up; **aliud ~ā** never mind; **corpus/cutem** ~ take it easy; **prōdigia** ~ avert portents.

curriculum, -ī _nt_ running, race; course, lap; (_fig_) career; ~**ō** at full speed.

currō, -ere cucurrī, cursum _vi_ to run; to hasten, fly ♦ _vt_ to run through, traverse; ~**entem incitāre** ≈ spur a willing horse.

currus, -ūs _m_ car, chariot; triumph; team of horses; ploughwheels.

cursim _adv_ quickly, at the double.

cursitō, -āre _vi_ to run about, fly hither and thither.

cursō, -āre _vi_ to run about.

cursor, -ōris _m_ runner, racer; courier.

cursūra, -ae _f_ running.

cursus, -ūs _m_ running, speed; passage, journey; course, direction; (_things_) movement, flow; (_fig_) rapidity, flow, progress; ~ **honōrum** succession of magistracies; ~ **rērum** course of events; ~**um tenēre** keep on one's course; ~**ū** at a run; **māgnō** ~**ū** at full speed

curtō, -āre *vt* to shorten.

curtus *adj* short, broken off; incomplete.

curūlis *adj* official, curule; **aedīlis** ~ patrician, aedile; **sella** ~ magistrates' chair; **equī** ~ horses provided for the games by the state.

curvāmen, -inis *nt* bend.

curvātūra, -ae *f* curve.

curvō, -āre, -āvī, -ātum *vt* to curve, bend, arch; (*fig*) to move.

curvus *adj* bent, curved, crooked; (*person*) aged; (*fig*) wrong.

cuspis, -dis *f* point; spear, javelin, trident, sting.

custōdēla, -ae *f* care, guard.

custōdia, -ae *f* watch, guard care; (*person*) sentry, guard; (*place*) sentry's post, guardhouse; custody, confinement, prison; **lībera** ~ confinement in one's own house.

custōdiō, -īre, -īvī *and* **iī, -ītum** *vt* to guard, defend; to hold in custody, keep watch on; to keep, preserve, observe.

custōs, -ōdis *m/f* guard, bodyguard, protector, protectress; jailer, warder; (*MIL*) sentry, spy; container.

cutīcula, -ae *f* skin.

cutis, -is *f* skin; ~**em cūrāre** ≈ take it easy.

cyathissō, -āre *vi* to serve wine.

cyathus, -ī *m* wine ladle; (*measure*) one-twelfth of a pint.

cybaea, -ae *f* kind of merchant ship.

Cybēbē, Cybelē, -ēs *f* Phrygian mother-goddess, Magna Mater.

Cybelēius *adj see n.*

Cyclades, -um *fpl* group of Aegean islands.

cyclas, -adis *f* formal dress with a border.

cyclicus *adj* of the traditional epic stories.

Cyclōpius *adj see n.*

Cyclōps, -is *m* one-eyed giant (*esp* Polyphemus).

cycnēus *adj* of a swan, swan's.

cycnus, -ī *m* swan.

Cydōnius *adj* Cretan ♦ *ntpl* quinces.

cygnus *see* cycnus.

cylindrus, -ī *m* cylinder; roller.

Cyllēnē, -ēs *and* **ae** *f* mountain in Arcadia.

Cyllēnēus, -is, -ius *adj see n.*

Cyllēnius, -ī *m* Mercury.

cymba *see* cumba.

cymbalum, -ī *nt* cymbal.

cymbium, -ī *and* **iī** *nt* cup

Cynicē *adv* like the Cynics.

Cynicus, -ī *m* a Cynic philosopher (*esp* Diogenes) ♦ *adj* Cynic.

cynocephalus, -ī *m* dog-headed ape.

Cynosūra, -ae *f* constellation of Ursa Minor.

Cynosūris, -idis *adj see n.*

Cynthia, -iae *f* Diana.

Cynthius, -ī *m* Apollo.

Cynthus, -ī *m* hill in Delos (*birthplace of Apollo and Diana*).

cyparissus, -ī *f* cypress.

Cypris, -idis *f* Venus.

Cyprius *adj* Cyprian; copper.

Cyprus, -ī *f* island of Cyprus (*famed for its copper and the worship of Venus*).

Cyrēnaeī, -ōrum *mpl* followers of Aristippus.

Cyrēnaeus, -aicus, -ēnsis *adj see n.*

Cyrēnē, -ēs *f*, **-ae, -ārum** *fpl* town and province of N. Africa.

Cyrnēus *adj* Corsican.

Cȳrus, -ī *m* Persian king.

Cytaeis, -idis *f* Medea.

Cythēra, -ae *f* island S. of Greece (*famed for its worship of Venus*).

Cytherēa, -ēae *and* **-ēia, -ēiae** *and* **-ēis, -ēidis** *f* Venus.

Cythereūs, Cythēriacus *adj* Cytherean; of Venus.

cytisus, -ī *m/f* cytisus (*a kind of clover*).

Cyzicēnus *adj see* Cyzicum.

Cyzicum, -ī *n*, **-us, -os, -ī** *f* town on Sea of Marmora.

D, d

Dācī, -ōrum *mpl* Dacians, a people on the lower Danube.

Dācia, -iae *f* the country of the Dācī (*now Romania*).

Dācicus, -icī *m* gold coin of Domitian's reign.

dactylicus *adj* dactylic.

dactylus, -ī *m* dactyl.

Daedalēus *adj see n.*

daedalus *adj* artistic, skilful in creating; skilfully made, variegated.

Daedalus, -ī *m* mythical Athenian craftsman and inventor.

Dalmatae, -ārum *mpl* Dalmatians (*a people on the East coast of the Adriatic*).

Dalmatia, -iae *f* Dalmatia.

Dalmaticus *adj see n.*

dāma, -ae *f* deer; venison.

Damascēnus *adj see n.*

Damascus, -ī *f* Damascus.

damma *f see* dāma.

damnātiō, -ōnis *f* condemnation.

damnātōrius *adj* condemnatory.

damnātus *adj* criminal; miserable.

damnificus *adj* pernicious.

Noun declensions and verb conjugations are shown on pp xiii to xxv. The present infinitive ending of a verb shows to which conjugation it belongs: -**āre** = 1st; -**ēre** = 2nd; -**ere** = 3rd and -**īre** = 4th. Irregular verbs are shown on p xxvi

damnō, -āre, -āvī, -ātum _vt_ to condemn, sentence; to procure the conviction of; (_heirs_) to oblige; to censure; **capitis/capite ~** condemn to death; **māiestātis, dē māiestāte ~** condemn for treason; **vōtī ~** oblige to fulfil a vow.

damnōsē _adv_ ruinously.

damnōsus _adj_ harmful, ruinous; spendthrift; wronged.

damnum, -ī _nt_ loss, harm, damage; (_law_) fine, damages; **~ facere** suffer loss.

Danaē, -ēs _f_ mother of Perseus.

Danaēius _adj_ see n.

Danaī, -ōrum and **um** _mpl_ the Greeks.

Danaidēs, -idum _fpl_ daughters of Danaus.

Danaus, -ī _m_ king of Argos and father of 50 daughters.

Danaus _adj_ Greek.

danīsta, -ae _m_ moneylender.

danīsticus _adj_ moneylending.

danō see **dō**.

Dānuvius, -ī _m_ upper Danube.

Daphnē, -ēs _f_ nymph changed into a laurel tree.

Daphnis, -idis (_acc_ -im and -in) _m_ mythical Sicilian shepherd.

dapinō, -āre _vt_ to serve (food).

daps, dapis _f_ religious feast; meal, banquet.

dapsilis _adj_ sumptuous, abundant.

Dardania, -iae _f_ Troy.

Dardanidēs, -idae _m_ Trojan (_esp_ Aeneas).

Dardanus, -ī _m_ son of Jupiter and ancestor of Trojan kings.

Dardanus, -ius, -is, -idis _adj_ Trojan.

Darēus, -ī _m_ Persian king.

datārius _adj_ to give away.

datātim _adv_ passing from one to the other.

datiō, -ōnis _f_ right to give away; (_laws_) making.

datō, -āre _vt_ to be in the habit of giving.

dator, -ōris _m_ giver; (_sport_) bowler.

Daulias, -adis _adj_ see n.

Daulis, -dis _f_ town in central Greece (_noted for the story of Procne and Philomela_).

Daunias, -iadis _f_ Apulia.

Daunius _adj_ Rutulian; Italian.

Daunus, -ī _m_ legendary king of Apulia (_ancestor of Turnus_).

dē _prep_ (_with abl: movement_) down from, from; (_origin_) from, of, out of; (_time_) immediately after, in; (_thought, talk, action_) about, concerning; (_reason_) for, because of; (_imitation_) after, in accordance with; **~ industriā** on purpose; **~ integrō** afresh; **~ nocte** during the night; **diem ~ diē** from day to day.

dea, -ae _f_ goddess.

dealbō, -āre _vt_ to whitewash, plaster.

deambulātiō, -ōnis _f_ walk.

deambulō, -āre, -āvī, -ātum _vi_ to go for a walk.

deamō, -āre, -āvī, -ātum _vt_ to be in love with; to be much obliged to.

dearmātus _adj_ disarmed.

deartuō, -āre, -āvī, -ātum _vt_ to dismember, ruin.

deasciō, -āre _vt_ to smooth with an axe; (_fig_) to cheat.

dēbacchor, -ārī, -ātus _vi_ to rage furiously.

dēbellātor, -ōris _m_ conqueror.

dēbellō, -āre, -āvī, -ātum _vi_ to bring a war to an end ♦ _vt_ to subdue; to fight out.

dēbeō, -ēre, -uī, -itum _vt_ to owe; (_with inf_) to be bound, ought, should, must; to have to thank for, be indebted for; (_pass_) to be destined.

dēbilis _adj_ frail, weak, crippled.

dēbilitās, -ātis _f_ weakness, infirmity.

dēbilitātiō, -ōnis _f_ weakening.

dēbilitō, -āre, -āvī, -ātum _vt_ to cripple, disable; (_fig_) to paralyse, unnerve.

dēbitiō, -ōnis _f_ owing.

dēbitor, -ōris _m_ debtor.

dēbitum, -ī _nt_ debt.

dēblaterō, -āre _vt_ to blab.

dēcantō, -āre, -āvī, -ātum _vt_ to keep on repeating ♦ _vi_ to stop singing.

dēcēdō, -ēdere, -essī, -essum _vi_ to withdraw, depart; to retire from a province (_after term of office_); to abate, cease, die; (_rights_) to give up, forgo; (_fig_) to go wrong, swerve (from duty); **dē viā ~** get out of the way.

decem _num_ ten.

December, -ris _adj_ of December ♦ _m_ December.

decempeda, -ae _f_ ten-foot rule.

decempedātor, -ōris _m_ surveyor.

decemplex, -icis _adj_ tenfold.

decemprīmī, -ōrum _mpl_ civic chiefs of Italian towns.

decemscalmus _adj_ ten-oared.

decemvirālis _adj_ of the decemviri.

decemvirātus, -ūs _m_ office of decemvir.

decemvirī, -ōrum and **um** _mpl_ commission of ten men (_for public or religious duties_).

decennis _adj_ ten years'.

decēns, -entis _adj_ seemly, proper; comely, handsome.

decenter _adv_ with propriety.

decentia, -ae _f_ comeliness.

dēceptus _ppp of_ dēcipiō.

dēcernō, -ernere, -rēvī, -rētum _vt_ to decide, determine; to decree; to fight it out, decide the issue.

dēcerpō, -ere, -sī, -tum _vt_ to pluck off, gather; (_fig_) to derive, enjoy.

dēcertātiō, -ōnis _f_ deciding the issue.

dēcertō, -āre, -āvī, -ātum _vi_ to fight it out, decide the issue.

dēcessiō, -ōnis _f_ departure; retirement (from a province); deduction, disappearance.

dēcessor, -ōris _m_ retiring magistrate.

dēcessus, -ūs _m_ retirement (from a province); death; (_tide_) ebbing.

decet, -ēre, -uīt _vt, vi_ it becomes, suits; it is

right, proper.

dēcidō, -ere, -ī vi to fall down, fall off; to die; (fig) to fail, come down.

dēcīdō, -dere, -dī, -sum vt to cut off; to settle, put an end to.

deciēns, deciēs adv ten times.

decimus, decumus adj tenth; ~um ~ō tenfold; ~um for the tenth time.

dēcipiō, -ipere, -ēpī, -eptum vt to ensnare; to deceive, beguile, disappoint.

dēcīsiō, -ōnis f settlement.

dēcīsus ppp of **dēcīdō**.

Decius, -ī m Roman plebeian name (esp P Decius Mus, father and son, who devoted their lives in battle).

Decius, -iānus adj see n.

dēclāmātiō, -ōnis f loud talking; rhetorical exercise on a given theme.

dēclāmātor, -ōris m apprentice in public speaking.

dēclāmātōrius adj rhetorical.

dēclāmitō, -āre vi to practise rhetoric; to bluster ♦ vt to practise pleading.

dēclāmō, -āre, -āvī, -ātum vi to practise public speaking, declaim; to bluster.

dēclārātiō, -ōnis f expression, making known.

dēclārō, -āre, -āvī, -ātum vt to make known; to proclaim, announce, reveal, express, demonstrate.

dēclīnātiō, -ōnis f swerving avoidance; (RHET) digression; (GRAM) inflection.

dēclīnō, -āre, -āvī, -ātum vt to turn aside, deflect; (eyes) to close; to evade, shun ♦ vi to turn aside, swerve; to digress.

declive nt slope, decline.

dēclīvis adj sloping, steep, downhill.

dēclīvitās, -ātis f sloping ground.

dēcocta, -ae f a cold drink.

dēcoctor, -ōris m bankrupt.

dēcoctus ppp of **dēcoquō** ♦ adj (style) ripe, elaborated.

dēcōlō, -āre vi to run off; (fig) to fail.

dēcolor, -ōris adj discoloured, faded; ~ aetās a degenerate age.

dēcolōrātiō, -ōnis f discolouring.

dēcolōrō, -āre, -āvī, -ātum vt to discolour, deface.

dēcoquō, -quere, -xī, -ctum vt to boil down; to cook ♦ vi to go bankrupt.

decor, -ōris m comeliness, ornament, beauty.

decōrē adv becomingly, beautifully.

decōrō, -āre, -āvī, -ātum vt to adorn, embellish; (fig) to distinguish, honour.

decōrum, -ī nt propriety.

decōrus adj becoming, proper, beautiful, noble; adorned.

dēcrepitus adj decrepit

dēcrēscō, -scere, -vī, -tum vi to decrease, wane, wear away; to disappear.

dēcrētum, -ī nt decree, resolution; (PHILOS) doctrine.

dēcrētus ppp of **dēcernō**.

dēcrēvī perf of **dēcernō**; perf of **dēcrēscō**.

decuma, -ae f tithe; provincial land tax; largess.

decumāna, -ae f wife of a tithe-collector.

decumānus adj paying tithes; (MIL) of the 10th cohort or legion ♦ m collector of tithes; ~ī, ~ōrum mpl men of the 10th legion; porta ~a main gate of a Roman camp.

decumātēs, -ium adj pl subject to tithes.

dēcumbō, -mbere, -buī vi to lie down; to recline at table; to fall (in fight).

decumus see **decimus**.

decuria, -ae f group of ten; panel of judges; social club.

decuriātiō, -ōnis f, **decuriātus, -ūs** m dividing into decuriae.

decuriō, -āre, -āvī, -ātum vt to divide into decuriae or groups.

decuriō, -ōnis m head of a decuria; (MIL) cavalry officer; senator of a provincial town or colony.

dēcurrō, -rrere, -currī and **rrī, -rsum** vt, vi to run down, hurry, flow, sail down; to traverse; (MIL) to parade, charge; (time) to pass through; (fig) to have recourse to.

dēcursiō, -ōnis f military manoeuvre.

dēcursus ppp of **dēcurrō**.

dēcursus, -ūs m descent, downrush; (MIL) manoeuvre, attack; (time) career.

dēcurtātus adj mutilated.

decus, -oris nt ornament, glory, beauty; honour, virtue; (pl) heroic deeds.

dēcussō, -āre vt to divide crosswise.

dēcutiō, -tere, -ssī, -ssum vt to strike down, shake off.

dēdecet, -ēre, -uit vt it is unbecoming to, is a disgrace to.

dēdecorō, -āre vt to disgrace.

dēdecōrus adj dishonourable.

dēdecus, -oris nt disgrace, shame; vice, crime.

dedī perf of **dō**.

dēdicātiō, -ōnis f consecration.

dēdicō, -āre, -āvī, -ātum vt to consecrate, dedicate; to declare (property in a census return).

dēdidī perf of **dēdō**.

dēdignor, -ārī, -ātus vt to scorn, reject.

dēdiscō, -scere, -didicī vt to unlearn, forget.

dēditīcius, -ī and **iī** m one who has capitulated.

dēditiō, -ōnis f surrender, capitulation.

dēditus ppp of **dēdō** ♦ adj addicted, devoted; ~ā operā intentionally.

dēdō, -ere, -idī, -itum vt to give up, yield, surrender; to devote.

dēdoceō, -ēre vt to teach not to.

dēdoleō, -ēre, -uī vi to cease grieving.

dēdūcō, -ūcere, -ūxī, -uctum *vt* to bring down, lead away, deflect; (*MIL*) to lead, withdraw; (*bride*) to bring home; (*colony*) to settle; (*hair*) to comb out; (*important person*) to escort; (*law*) to evict, bring to trial; (*money*) to subtract; (*sail*) to unfurl; (*ship*) to launch; (*thread*) to spin out; (*writing*) to compose; (*fig*) to bring, reduce, divert, derive.

dēductiō, -ōnis *f* leading off; settling a colony; reduction; eviction; inference.

dēductor, -ōris *m* escort.

dēductus *ppp of* **dēdūcō** ♦ *adj* finely spun.

deerrō, -āre, -āvī, -ātum *vi* to go astray.

deesse *infin of* **dēsum**.

dēfaecō, -āre, -āvī, -ātum *vt* to clean; (*fig*) to make clear, set at ease.

dēfatigātiō, -ōnis *f* tiring out; weariness.

dēfatīgō, -āre, -āvī, -ātum *vt* to tire out, exhaust.

dēfatīscor *etc see* **dēfetīscor**.

dēfectiō, -ōnis *f* desertion; failure, faintness; (*ASTRO*) eclipse.

dēfector, -ōris *m* deserter, rebel.

dēfectus *ppp of* **dēficiō** ♦ *adj* weak, failing.

dēfectus, -ūs *m* failure; eclipse.

dēfendō, -dere, -dī, -sum *vt* to avert, repel; to defend, protect; (*law*) to speak in defence, urge, maintain; (*THEATRE*) to play (a part); **crīmen ~** answer an accusation.

dēfēnsiō, -ōnis *f* defence, speech in defence.

dēfēnsitō, -āre *vt* to defend often.

dēfēnsō, -āre *vt* to defend.

dēfēnsor, -ōris *m* averter; defender, protector, guard.

dēferō, -ferre, -tulī, -lātum *vt* to bring down, bring, carry; to bear away; (*power, honour*) to offer, confer; (*information*) to report; (*law*) to inform against, indict; to recommend (for public services); **ad cōnsilium ~** take into consideration.

dēfervēscō, -vēscere, -vī *and* **buī** *vi* to cool down, calm down.

dēfessus *adj* tired, exhausted.

dēfetīgō *etc see* **dēfatīgō**.

dēfetīscor, -tīscī, -ssus *vi* to grow weary.

dēficiō, -icere, -ēcī, -ectum *vt, vi* to desert, forsake, fail; to be lacking, run short, cease; (*ASTRO*) to be eclipsed; **animō ~** lose heart.

dēfīgō, -gere, -xī, -xum *vt* to fix firmly; to drive in, thrust; (*eyes, mind*) to concentrate; (*fig*) to stupefy, astound; (*magic*) to bewitch.

dēfingō, -ere *vt* to make, portray.

dēfīniō, -īre, -īvī, -ītum *vt* to mark the limit of, limit; to define, prescribe; to restrict; to terminate.

dēfinītē *adv* precisely.

dēfīnītiō, -ōnis *f* limiting, prescribing, definition.

dēfīnītīvus *adj* explanatory.

dēfīnītus *adj* precise.

dēfīō, -ierī *vi* to fail.

dēflagrātiō, -ōnis *f* conflagration.

dēflagrō, -āre, -āvī, -ātum *vi* to be burned down, perish; to cool down, abate ♦ *vt* to burn down.

dēflectō, -ctere, -xī, -xum *vt* to bend down, turn aside; (*fig*) to pervert ♦ *vi* to turn aside, deviate.

dēfleō, -ēre. -ēvī, -ētum *vt* to lament bitterly, bewail ♦ *vi* to weep bitterly.

dēflexus *ppp of* **dēflectō**.

dēflōrēscō, -ēscere, -uī *vi* to shed blooms; (*fig*) to fade.

dēfluō, -ere, -xī, -xum *vi* to flow down, float down; to fall, drop, droop; (*fig*) to come from, be derived; to flow past; (*fig*) to pass away, fail.

dēfodiō, -ōdere, -ōdī, -ossum *vt* to dig, dig out; to bury; (*fig*) to hide away.

dēfore *fut infin of* **dēsum**.

dēfōrmis *adj* misshapen, disfigured, ugly; shapeless; (*fig*) disgraceful, disgusting.

dēfōrmitās, -ātis *f* deformity, hideousness; baseness.

dēfōrmō, -āre, -āvī, -ātum *vt* to form, sketch; to deform, disfigure; to describe; to mar, disgrace.

dēfossus *ppp of* **dēfodiō**.

dēfraudō, -āre *vt* to cheat, defraud; **genium ~** deny oneself.

dēfrēnātus *adj* unbridled.

dēfricō, -āre, -uī, -ātum *and* **tum** *vt* to rub down; (*fig*) to satirize.

dēfringō, -ingere, -ēgī, -āctum *vt* to break off, break down.

dēfrūdō *etc see* **dēfraudō**.

dēfrutum, -ī *nt* new wine boiled down.

dēfugiō, -ugere, -ūgī *vt* to run away from, shirk ♦ *vi* to flee.

dēfuī *perf of* **dēsum**.

dēfūnctus *ppa of* **dēfungor** ♦ *adj* discharged; dead.

dēfundō, -undere, -ūdī, -ūsum *vt* to pour out.

dēfungor, -ungī, -ūnctus *vi* (*with abl*) to discharge, have done with; to die.

dēfutūrus *fut p of* **dēsum**.

dēgener, -is *adj* degenerate, unworthy, base.

dēgenerātum, -ātī *nt* degenerate character.

dēgenerō, -āre, -āvī, -ātum *vi* to degenerate, deteriorate ♦ *vt* to disgrace.

dēgerō, -ere *vt* to carry off.

dēgō, -ere. -ī *vt* (*time*) to pass, spend; (*war*) wage ♦ *vi* to live.

dēgrandinat it is hailing heavily.

dēgravō, -āre *vt* to weigh down, overpower.

dēgredior, -dī, -ssus *vi* to march down, descend, dismount.

dēgrunniō, -īre *vi* to grunt hard.

dēgustō, -āre *vt* to taste, touch; (*fig*) to try, experience.

dehinc *adv* from here; from now, henceforth; then, next.

dehīscō, -ere *vi* to gape, yawn.

dehonestāmentum, -ī *nt* disfigurement.

dehonestō, -āre vt to disgrace.
dehortor, -ārī, -ātus vt to dissuade, discourage.
Dēianīra, -ae f wife of Hercules.
dēiciō, -icere, -iēcī, -iectum vt to throw down, hurl, fell; to overthrow kill; (eyes) to lower, avert; (law) to evict; (mil) to dislodge; (ship) to drive off its course; (hopes, honours) to foil, disappoint.
dēiectiō, -ōnis f eviction.
dēiectus ppp of **dēiciō** ♦ adj low-lying; disheartened.
dēiectus, -ūs m felling; steep slope.
dēierō, -āre, -āvī, -ātum vi to swear solemnly.
dein etc see **deinde.**
deinceps adv successively, in order.
deinde, dein adv from there, next; then, thereafter; next in order.
Dēiotarus, -ī m king of Galatia (defended by Cicero).
Dēiphobus, -ī m son of Priam second husband of Helen).
dēiungō, -ere vt to sever.
dēiuvō, -āre vt to fail to help.
dej- etc see **dei-.**
dēlābor, -bī, -psus vi to fall down, fly down, sink; (fig) to come down, fall into.
dēlacerō, -āre vt to tear to pieces.
dēlāmentor, -ārī vt to mourn bitterly for.
dēlāpsus ppa of **dēlābor.**
dēlassō, -āre vt to tire out.
dēlātiō, -ōnis f accusing, informing.
dēlātor, -ōris m informer, denouncer.
dēlectābilis adj enjoyable.
dēlectāmentum, -ī nt amusement.
dēlectātiō, -ōnis f delight.
dēlectō, -āre vt to charm, delight, amuse.
dēlēctus ppp of **dēligō.**
dēlēctus, -ūs m choice; see also **dilēctus.**
dēlēgātiō, -ōnis f assignment.
dēlēgī perf of **dēligō.**
dēlēgō, -āre, -āvī, -ātum vt to assign, transfer, make over; to ascribe.
dēlēnificus adj charming.
dēlēnīmentum, -ī nt solace, allurement.
dēlēniō, -īre, -īvī, -ītum vt to soothe, solace; to seduce, win over.
dēlēnītor, -ōris m cajoler.
dēleō, -ēre, -ēvī, -ētum vt to destroy, annihilate; to efface, blot out.
Dēlia, -ae f Diana.
Dēliacus adj of Delos.
dēlīberābundus adj deliberating.
dēlīberātiō, -ōnis f deliberating, consideration.
dēlīberātīvus adj deliberative.
dēlīberātor, -ōris m consulter.
dēlīberātus adj determined.
dēlīberō, -āre, -āvī, -ātum vt, vi to consider,

deliberate, consult; to resolve, determine; ~ārī potest it is in doubt.
dēlībō, -āre, -āvī, -ātum vt to taste, sip; to pick, gather; to detract from, mar.
dēlībrō, -āre vt to strip the bark off.
dēlībuō, -uere, -uī, -ūtum vt to smear, steep.
dēlicātē adv luxuriously.
dēlicātus adj delightful; tender, soft; voluptuous, spoiled, effeminate; fastidious.
dēliciae, -ārum fpl delight, pleasure; whimsicalities, sport; (person) sweetheart, darling.
dēliciolae, -ārum fpl darling.
dēlicium, -ī and **iī** nt favourite.
dēlicō, -āre vt to explain.
dēlictum, -ī nt offence, wrong.
dēlicuus adj lacking.
dēligō, -igere, -ēgī, -ēctum vt to select, gather; to set aside.
dēligō, -āre, -āvī, -ātum vt to tie up, make fast.
dēlingō, -ere vt to have a lick of.
dēlīnī- etc see **dēlēnī-.**
dēlinquō, -inquere, -īquī, -ictum vi to fail, offend, do wrong.
dēliquēscō, -quēscere, -cuī vi to melt away; (fig) to pine away.
dēliquiō, -ōnis f lack.
dēlīrāmentum, -ī nt nonsense.
dēlīrātiō, -ōnis f dotage.
dēlīrō, -āre vi to be crazy, drivel.
dēlīrus adj crazy.
dēlitēscō, -ēscere, -uī vi to hide away, lurk; (fig) to skulk, take shelter under.
dēlītigō, -āre vi to scold.
Dēlius, -iacus adj see n.
Delmatae see **Dalmatae.**
Dēlos, -ī f sacred Aegean island (birthplace of Apollo and Diana).
Delphī, -ōrum mpl town in central Greece (famous for its oracle of Apollo); the Delphians.
Delphicus adj see n.
delphīnus, -ī and **delphīn, -is** m dolphin.
Deltōton, -ī nt (constellation) Triangulum.
dēlubrum, -ī nt sanctuary, temple.
dēluctō, -āre, -or, -ārī vi to wrestle.
dēlūdificō, -āre vt to make fun of.
dēlūdō, -dere, -sī, -sum vt to dupe, delude.
dēlumbis adj feeble.
dēlumbō, -āre vt to enervate.
dēmadēscō, -ēscere, -uī vi to be drenched.
dēmandō, -āre vt to entrust, commit.
dēmarchus, -ī m demarch (chief of a village in Attica).
dēmēns, -entis adj mad, foolish.
dēmēnsum, -ī nt ration.
dēmēnsus ppa of **dēmētior.**
dēmenter adv see **dēmēns.**
dēmentia, -ae f madness, folly.
dēmentiō, -īre vi to rave.

Noun declensions and verb conjugations are shown on pp xiii to xxv. The present infinitive ending of a verb shows to which conjugation it belongs: **-āre** = 1st; **-ēre** = 2nd; **-ere** = 3rd and **-īre** = 4th. Irregular verbs are shown on p xxvi

dēmereō, -ēre, -uī, -itum, -eor, -ērī _vt_ to earn, deserve; to do a service to.

dēmergō, -gere, -sī, -sum _vt_ to submerge, plunge, sink; (_fig_) to overwhelm.

dēmessus _ppp of_ **dēmetō**.

dēmētior, -tīrī, -nsus _vt_ to measure out.

dēmetō, -tere, -ssuī, -ssum _vt_ to reap, harvest; to cut off.

dēmigrātiō, -ōnis _f_ emigration.

dēmigrō, -āre _vi_ to move, emigrate.

dēminuō, -uere, -uī, -ūtum _vt_ to make smaller, lessen, detract from; **capite ~** deprive of citizenship.

dēminūtiō, -ōnis _f_ decrease, lessening; (_law_) right to transfer property; **capitis ~** loss of political rights.

dēmīror, -ārī, -ātus _vt_ to marvel at, wonder.

dēmisse _adv_ modestly, meanly.

dēmissīcius _adj_ flowing.

dēmissiō, -ōnis _f_ letting down; (_fig_) dejection.

dēmissus _ppp of_ **dēmittō** ♦ _adj_ low-lying; drooping; humble, unassuming; dejected; (_origin_) descended.

dēmītigō, -āre _vt_ to make milder.

dēmittō, -ittere, -īsī, -issum _vt_ to let down, lower, sink; to send down, plunge; (_beard_) to grow; (_ship_) to bring to land; (_troops_) to move down; (_fig_) to cast down, dishearten, reduce, impress; **sē ~** stoop; descend; be disheartened.

dēmiūrgus, -ī _m_ _chief magistrate in a Greek state._

dēmō, -ere, -psī, -ptum _vt_ to take away, subtract.

Dēmocriticus, -ius, -ēus _adj see n._

Dēmocritus, -ī _m_ _Greek philosopher (author of the atomic theory)._

dēmōlior, -īrī _vt_ to pull down, destroy.

dēmōlītiō, -ōnis _f_ pulling down.

dēmōnstrātiō, -ōnis _f_ pointing out, explanation.

dēmōnstrātīvus _adj_ (_RHET_) for display.

dēmōnstrātor, -ōris _m_ indicator.

dēmōnstrō, -āre, -āvī, -ātum _vt_ to point out; to explain, represent, prove.

dēmorior, -ī, -tuus _vi_ to die, pass away ♦ _vt_ to be in love with.

dēmoror, -ārī, -ātus _vi_ to wait ♦ _vt_ to detain, delay.

dēmortuus _ppa of_ **dēmorior**.

Dēmosthenēs, -is _m_ _greatest Athenian orator._

dēmoveō, -ovēre, -ōvī, -ōtum _vt_ to remove, turn aside, dislodge.

dēmpsī _perf of_ **dēmō**.

dēmptus _ppp of_ **dēmō**.

dēmūgītus _adj_ filled with lowing.

dēmulceō, -cēre, -sī _vt_ to stroke.

dēmum _adv_ (_time_) at last, not till; (_emphasis_) just, precisely; **ibi ~** just there; **modo ~** only now; **nunc ~** now at last; **post ~** not till after; **tum ~** only then.

dēmurmurō, -āre _vt_ to mumble through.

dēmūtātiō, -ōnis _f_ change.

dēmūtō, -āre _vt_ to change, make worse ♦ _vi_ to change one's mind.

dēnārius, -ī _and_ **iī** _m_ _Roman silver coin._

dēnārrō, -āre _vt_ to relate fully.

dēnāsō, -āre _vt_ to take the nose off.

dēnatō, -āre _vi_ to swim down.

dēnegō, -āre, -āvī, -ātum _vt_ to deny, refuse, reject ♦ _vi_ to say no.

dēnī, -ōrum _adj_ ten each, in tens; ten; tenth.

dēnicālis _adj_ for purifying after a death.

dēnique _adv_ at last, finally; (_enumerating_) lastly, next; (_summing up_) in short, briefly; (_emphasis_) just, precisely.

dēnōminō, -āre _vt_ to designate.

dēnōrmō, -āre _vt_ to make irregular.

dēnotō, -āre, -āvī, -ātum _vt_ to point out, specify; to observe.

dēns, dentis _m_ tooth; ivory; prong, fluke.

dēnsē _adv_ repeatedly.

dēnsō, -āre, -āvī, -ātum, dēnseō, -ēre _vt_ to thicken; (_ranks_) to close.

dēnsus _adj_ thick, dense, close; frequent; (_style_) concise.

dentālia, -ium _ntpl_ ploughbeam.

dentātus _adj_ toothed; (_paper_) polished.

dentiō, -īre _vi_ to cut one's teeth; (_teeth_) to grow.

dēnūbō, -bere, -psī, -ptum _vi_ to marry, marry beneath one.

dēnūdō, -āre, -āvī, -ātum _vt_ to bare, strip; (_fig_) to disclose.

dēnūntiātiō, -ōnis _f_ intimation, warning.

dēnūntiō, -āre, -āvī, -ātum _vt_ to intimate, give notice of, declare; to threaten, warn; (_law_) to summon as witness.

dēnuō _adv_ afresh, again, once more.

deonerō, -āre _vt_ to unload.

deorsum, deorsus _adv_ downwards.

deōsculor, -ārī _vt_ to kiss warmly.

dēpaciscor _etc see_ **dēpeciscor**.

dēpāctus _adj_ driven in firmly.

dēpāscō, -scere, -vī, -stum, -scor, -scī _vt_ to feed on, eat up; (_fig_) to devour, destroy, prune away.

dēpeciscor, -īscī, -tus _vt_ to bargain for, agree about.

dēpectō, -ctere, -xum _vt_ to comb; (_comedy_) to flog.

dēpectus _ppa of_ **dēpeciscor**.

dēpecūlātor, -ōris _m_ embezzler.

dēpecūlor, -ārī, -ātus _vt_ to plunder.

dēpellō, -ellere, -ulī, -ulsum _vt_ to expel, remove, cast down; (_MIL_) to dislodge; (_infants_) to wean; (_fig_) to deter, avert.

dēpendeō, -ēre _vi_ to hang down, hang from; to depend on; to be derived.

dēpendō, -endere, -endī, -ēnsum _vt_ to weigh, pay up.

dēperdō, -ere, -idī, -itum _vt_ to lose completely, destroy, ruin.

dēpereō, -īre, -iī _vi_ to perish, be completely destroyed; to be undone ♦ _vt_ to be hopelessly

in love with.
dēpexus *ppp of* **dēpectō**.
dēpingō, -ingere, -inxī, -ictum *vt* to paint;
(*fig*) to portray, describe.
dēplangō, -gere, -xī *vt* to bewail frantically.
dēplexus *adj* grasping.
dēplōrābundus *adj* weeping bitterly.
dēplōrō, -āre, -āvī, -ātum *vi* to weep bitterly
♦ *vt* to bewail bitterly, mourn; to despair of.
dēpluit, -ere *vi* to rain down.
dēpōnō, -ōnere, -osuī, -ositum *vt* to lay
down; to set aside, put away, get rid of; to
wager; to deposit, entrust, commit to the
care of; (*fig*) to give up.
dēpopulātiō, -ōnis *f* ravaging.
dēpopulātor, -ōris *m* marauder.
dēpopulor, -ārī, -ātus; -ō, -āre *vt* to ravage,
devastate; (*fig*) to waste, destroy.
dēportō, -āre, -āvī, -ātum *vt* to carry down,
carry off; to bring home (from a province);
(*law*) to banish for life; (*fig*) to win.
dēposcō, -scere, -poscī *vt* to demand,
require, claim.
dēpositum, -ī *nt* trust, deposit.
dēpositus *ppp of* **dēpōnō** ♦ *adj* dying, dead,
despaired of.
dēprāvātē *adv* perversely.
dēprāvātiō, -ōnis *f* distorting.
dēprāvō, -āre, -āvī, -ātum *vt* to distort; (*fig*)
to pervert, corrupt.
dēprecābundus *adj* imploring.
dēprecātiō, -ōnis *f* averting by prayer;
imprecation, invocation; pleafor
indulgence.
dēprecātor, -ōris *m* intercessor.
dēprecor, -ārī, -ātus *vt* to avert (by prayer);
to deprecate, intercede for
**dēprehendō, dēprendō, -endere, -endī,
-ēnsum** *vt* to catch, intercept to overtake,
surprise; to catch in the act, detect; (*fig*) to
perceive, discover.
dēprehēnsiō, -ōnis *f* detection.
dēprehēnsus, dēprēnsus *ppp of*
dēprehendō.
dēpressī *perf of* **dēprimō**.
dēpressus *ppp of* **dēprimō** ♦ *adj* low.
dēprimō, -imere, -essī, -essum *vt* to press
down, weigh down; to dig deep; (*ship*) to
sink; (*fig*) to suppress, keep down.
dēproelior, -ārī *vi* to fight it out.
dēprōmō, -ere, psī, -ptum *vt* to fetch, bring
out, produce.
dēproperō, -āre *vi* to hurry up ♦ *vt* to hurry
and make.
depsō, -ere *vt* to knead.
dēpudet, -ēre, -uit *v impers* not to be ashamed.
dēpūgis *adj* thin-buttocked.
dēpugnō, -āre, -āvī, -ātum *v* to fight it out,
fight hard.
dēpulī *perf of* **dēpellō**.

dēpulsiō, -ōnis *f* averting; defence.
dēpulsō, -āre *vt* to push out of the way.
dēpulsor, -ōris *m* repeller.
dēpulsus *ppp of* **dēpellō**.
dēpūrgō, -āre *vt* to clean.
dēputō, -āre *vt* to prune; to consider, reckon.
dēpȳgis *etc see* **dēpūgis**.
dēque *adv* down.
dērēctā, -ē, -ō *adv* straight.
dērēctus *ppp of* **dērigō** ♦ *adj* straight, upright,
at right angles; straightforward.
dērelictiō, -ōnis *f* disregarding.
dērelinquō, -inquere, -īquī, -ictum *vt* to
abandon, forsake.
dērepente *adv* suddenly.
dērēpō, -ere *vi* to creep down.
dēreptus *ppp of* **dēripiō**.
dērīdeō, -dēre, -sī, -sum *vt* to laugh at,
deride.
dērīdiculum. -ī *nt* mockery, absurdity; object
of derision.
dērīdiculus *adj* laughable.
dērigēscō, -ēscere, -uī *vi* to stiffen, curdle.
dērigō, -igere, -ēxī, -ēctum *vt* to turn, aim,
direct; (*fig*) to regulate.
dēripiō, -ipere, -ipuī. -eptum *vt* to tear off,
pull down.
dērīsor, -ōris *m* scoffer.
dērīsus *ppp of* **dērīdeō**
dērīsus, -ūs *m* scorn, derision.
dērīvātiō, -ōnis *f* diverting.
dērīvō, -āre, -āvī, -ātum *vt* to lead off, draw
off.
dērogō, -āre *vt* (*law*) to propose to amend;
(*fig*) to detract from.
dērōsus *adj* gnawed away.
dēruncinō, -āre *vt* to plane off; (*comedy*) to
cheat.
dēruō, -ere, -ī *vt* to demolish.
dēruptus *adj* steep ♦ *r tpl* precipice.
dēsaeviō, -īre *vi* to rage furiously; to cease
raging.
dēscendō, -endere, -endī, -ēnsum *vi* to
come down, go down, descend, dismount;
(*MIL*) to march down; (*things*) to fall, sink,
penetrate; (*fig*) to stoop (to), lower oneself.
dēscēnsiō, -ōnis *f* going down.
dēscēnsus, -ūs *m* way down.
dēscīscō, -īscere, -īvī *and* **iī, -ītum** *vi* to
desert, revolt; to deviate, part company.
dēscrībō, -bere, -psī. -ptum *vt* to copy out; to
draw, sketch; to describe; *see also* **discrībō**.
dēscrīptiō, -ōnis *f* copy; drawing, diagram;
description.
dēscrīptus *ppp of* **dēscrībō**; *see also* **discrīptus**.
dēsecō, -āre, -uī, -tum *vt* to cut off.
dēserō, -ere, -uī, -tum *vt* to desert, abandon,
forsake; (*bail*) to forfeit.
dēsertor, -ōris *m* deserter.
dēsertus *ppp of* **dēserō** ♦ *adj* desert,

Noun declensions and verb conjugations are shown on pp xiii to xxv. The present infinitive ending of a verb shows
to which conjugation it belongs: -āre = 1st; -ēre = 2nd; -ere = 3rd and -īre = 4th. Irregular verbs are shown on p xxvi

uninhabited ♦ *ntpl* deserts.
dēserviō, -īre *vi* to be a slave (to), serve.
dēses, -idis *adj* idle, inactive.
dēsiccō, -āre *vt* to dry, drain.
dēsideō, -idēre, -ēdī *vi* to sit idle.
dēsīderābilis *adj* desirable.
dēsīderātiō, -ōnis *f* missing.
dēsīderium, -ī *and* **iī** *nt* longing, sense of loss;
want; petition; **mē ~ tenet urbis** I miss Rome.
dēsīderō, -āre, -āvī, -ātum *vt* to feel the
want of, miss; to long for, desire; (*casualties*)
to lose.
dēsidia, -ae *f* idleness, apathy.
dēsidiōsē *adv* idly.
dēsidiōsus *adj* lazy, idle; relaxing.
dēsīdō, -īdere, -ēdī *vi* to sink, settle down;
(*fig*) to deteriorate.
dēsignātiō, -ōnis *f* specifying; election (of
magistrates).
dēsignātor *etc see* **dissignātor**.
dēsignātus *adj* elect.
dēsignō, -āre, -āvī, -ātum *vt* to trace out; to
indicate, define; (*POL*) to elect; (*art*) to depict.
dēsiī *perf of* **dēsinō**.
dēsiliō, -ilīre, -iluī, -ultum *vi* to jump down,
alight.
dēsinō, -nere, -ī *vt* to leave off, abandon ♦ *vi*
to stop, desist; to end (in).
dēsipiēns, -ientis *adj* silly.
dēsipientia, -ae *f* folly.
dēsipiō, -ere *vi* to be stupid, play the fool.
dēsistō, -istere, -titī, -titum *vi* to stop, leave
off, desist.
dēsitus *ppp of* **dēsinō**.
dēsōlō, -āre, -āvī, -ātum *vt* to leave desolate,
abandon.
dēspectō, -āre *vt* to look down on, command a
view of; to despise.
dēspectus *ppp of* **dēspiciō** ♦ *adj* contemptible.
dēspectus, -ūs *m* view, prospect.
dēspēranter *adv* despairingly.
dēspērātiō, -ōnis *f* despair.
dēspērātus *adj* despaired of, hopeless;
desperate, reckless.
dēspērō, -āre, -āvī, -ātum *vt*, *vi* to despair,
give up hope of.
dēspexī *perf of* **dēspiciō**.
dēspicātiō, -ōnis *f* contempt.
dēspicātus *adj* despised, contemptible.
dēspicātus, -ūs *m* contempt.
dēspicientia, -ae *f* contempt.
dēspiciō, -icere, -exī, -ectum *vt* to look down
on; to despise ♦ *vi* to look down.
dēspoliātor, -ōris *m* robber.
dēspoliō, -āre *vt* to rob, plunder.
dēspondeō, -ondēre, -ondī *and* **opondī,
-ōnsum** *vt* to pledge, promise; to betroth; to
devote; to give up, despair of; **animum ~**
despair.
dēspūmō, -āre *vt* to skim off.
dēspuō, -ere *vi* to spit on the ground ♦ *vt* to
reject.
dēsquāmō, -āre *vt* to scale, peel.

dēstillō, -āre *vi* to drop down ♦ *vt* to distil.
dēstimulō, -āre *vt* to run through.
dēstinātiō, -ōnis *f* resolution, appointment.
dēstinātus *adj* fixed, decided.
dēstinō, -āre, -āvī, -ātum *vt* to make fast; to
appoint, determine, resolve; (*archery*) to aim
at; (*fig*) to intend to buy ♦ *nt* mark; intention;
~ātum est mihi I have decided.
dēstitī *perf of* **dēsistō**.
dēstituō, -uere, -uī, -ūtum *vt* to set apart,
place; to forsake, leave in the lurch.
dēstitūtiō, -ōnis *f* defaulting.
dēstitūtus *ppp of* **dēstituō**.
dēstrictus *ppp of* **dēstringō** ♦ *adj* severe.
dēstringō, -ingere, -inxī, -ictum *vt* (*leaves*)
to strip; (*body*) to rub down; (*sword*) to draw;
to graze, skim; (*fig*) to censure.
dēstruō, -ere, -xī, -ctum *vt* to demolish; to
destroy.
dēsubitō *adv* all of a sudden.
dēsūdāscō, -ere *vi* to sweat all over.
dēsūdō, -āre *vi* to exert oneself.
dēsuēfactus *adj* unaccustomed.
dēsuētūdō, -inis *f* disuse.
dēsuētus *adj* unaccustomed, unused.
dēsultor, -ōris *m* circus rider; (*fig*) fickle
lover.
dēsultūra, -ae *f* jumping down.
dēsum, deesse, -fuī *vi* to be missing, fail, fail
in one's duty.
dēsūmō, -ere, -psī, -ptum *vt* to select.
dēsuper *adv* from above.
dēsurgō, -ere *vi* to rise.
dētegō, -egere, -ēxī, -ēctum *vt* to uncover,
disclose; (*fig*) to reveal, detect.
dētendō, -endere, -ēnsum *vt* (*tent*) to strike.
dētentus *ppp of* **dētineō**.
dētergō, -gere, -sī, -sum *vt* to wipe away,
clear away; to clean; to break off.
dēterior, -ōris *adj* lower; inferior, worse.
dēterius *adv* worse.
dēterminātiō, -ōnis *f* boundary, end.
dēterminō, -āre, -āvī, -ātum *vt* to bound,
limit; to settle.
dēterō, -erere, -rīvī, -rītum *vt* to rub, wear
away; (*style*) to polish; (*fig*) to weaken.
dēterreō, -ēre, -uī, -itum *vt* to frighten away;
to deter, discourage, prevent.
dētersus *ppp of* **dētergeō**.
dētestābilis *adj* abominable.
dētestātiō, -ōnis *f* execration, curse;
averting.
dētestor, -ārī, -ātus *vt* to invoke, invoke
against; to curse, execrate; to avert,
deprecate.
dētexō, -ere, -uī, -tum *vt* to weave, finish
weaving; (*comedy*) to steal; (*fig*) to describe.
dētineō, -inēre, -inuī, -entum *vt* to hold
back, detain; to keep occupied.
dētondeō, -ondēre, -ondī, -ōnsum *vt* to
shear off, strip.
dētonō, -āre, -uī *vi* to cease thundering.
dētorqueō, -quēre, -sī, -tum *vt* to turn aside,

direct; to distort, misrepresent
dētractātiō, -ōnis f declining.
dētrectātor, -ōris m disparager.
dētractiō, -ōnis f removal, departure.
dētractō etc see **dētrectō.**
dētractus ppp of **dētrahō.**
dētrahō, -here, -xī, -ctum vt to draw off, take away, pull down; to withdraw, force to leave; to detract, disparage.
dētrectō, -āre, -āvī, -ātum vt to decline, shirk; to detract from, disparage.
dētrīmentōsus adj harmful.
dētrīmentum, -ī nt loss, harm (vut) defeat; ~ **capere** suffer harm.
dētrītus ppp of **dēterō.**
dētrūdō, -dere, -sī, -sum vt to push down, thrust away; to dislodge, evict; to postpone; (fig) to force.
dētruncō, -āre, -āvī, -ātum vt to cut off, behead, mutilate.
dētrūsus ppp of **dētrūdō.**
dēturbō, -āre, -āvī, -ātum vt to dash down, pull down; (fig) to cast down, deprive.
Deucaliōn, -ōnis m son of Prometheus (survivor of the Flood).
Deucaliōnēus adj see **Deucaliōn.**
deūnx, -cis m eleven twelfths
deūrō, -rere, -ssī, -stum vt to burn up; to frost.
deus, -ī (voc deus, pl dī, deos, deum, dis) m god; **dī meliōra!** Heaven forbid!; **dī tē ament!** bless you!
deūstus ppp of **deūrō.**
deūtor, -ī vi to maltreat
dēvastō, -āre vt to lay waste.
dēvehō, -here, -xī, -ctum vt to carry down, convey; (pass) to ride down, sail down.
dēvellō, -ellere, -ellī and **olsī, -ulsum** vt to pluck, pull out.
dēvēlō, -āre vt to unveil.
dēveneror, -ārī vt to worship; to avert by prayers.
dēveniō, -enīre, -ēnī, -entum vi to come, reach, fall into.
dēverberō, -āre, -āvī, -ātum vt to thrash soundly.
dēversor, -ārī vi to lodge, stay (as guest).
dēversor, -ōris m guest
dēversōriolum, -ī nt small lodging.
dēversōrium, -ī and **iī** n inn, lodging.
dēversōrius adj for lodging
dēverticulum, -ī nt by-road, by-pass; digression; lodging place; (fig) refuge.
dēvertō, -tere, -tī, -sum vi to turn aside, put up; to have recourse to; to digress.
dēvertor, -tī, versus vi see **dēvertō.**
dēvexus adj sloping, going down, steep.
dēvinciō, -cīre, -xī, -ctum vt to tie up; (fig) to bind, lay under an obligation.
dēvincō, -incere, -īcī, -ictum vt to defeat

completely, win the day.
dēvītātiō, -ōnis f avoiding.
dēvītō, -āre vt to avoid.
dēvius adj out of the way, devious; (person) solitary, wandering off the beaten track; (fig) inconstant.
dēvocō, -āre, -āvī, -ātum vt to call down, fetch; to entice away.
dēvolō, -āre vi to fly down.
dēvolvō, -vere, -vī, -ūtum vt to roll down, fall; (wool) to spin off.
dēvorō, -āre, -āvī, -ātum vt to swallow, gulp down; to engulf, devour; (money) to squander; (tears) to repress; (trouble) to endure patiently.
dēvors-, dēvort- see **dēvers-, dēvert-.**
dēvortia, -ōrum ntpl byways.
dēvōtiō, -ōnis f devoting; (magic) spell.
dēvōtō, -āre vt to bewitch.
dēvōtus ppp of **dēvoveō** ♦ adj faithful; accursed.
dēvoveō, -ovēre, -ōvī, -ōtum vt to devote, vow, dedicate; to give up; to curse; to bewitch.
dēvulsus ppp of **dēvellō.**
dextella, -ae f little right hand.
dexter, -erī and **rī** adj right, right-hand; handy, skilful; favourable.
dexteritās, -ātis f adroitness.
dextra f right hand, right-hand side; hand; pledge of friendship.
dextrā prep (with acc) on the right of.
dextrē (compar -erius) adv adroitly.
dextrōrsum, -rsus, -vorsum adv to the right.
dī pl of **deus.**
diabathrāriu̇s, -ī and **iī** m slipper maker.
diabolus, -ī m devil.
diāconus, -ī m (ECCL) deacon.
diadēma, -tis nt royal headband, diadem.
diaeta, -ae f diet; living room.
dialectica, -ae, -ē, -ēs f dialectic, logic ♦ ntpl logical questions.
dialecticē adv dialectically.
dialecticus adj dialectical ♦ m logician.
Diālis adj of Jupiter ♦ m high priest of Jupiter.
dialogus, -ī m dialogue, conversation.
Diāna, -ae f virgin goddess of hunting (also identified with the moon and Hecate, and patroness of childbirth).
Diānius adj of Diana ♦ nt sanctuary of Diana.
diāria, -ōrum ntpl daily allowance of food or pay.
dibaphus, -ī f Roman state robe.
dica, -ae f lawsuit.
dicācitās, -ātis f raillery, repartee.
dicāculus adj pert.
dicātiō, -ōnis f declaration of citizenship.
dicāx, -ācis adj witty, smart.
dichorēus, -ī m double trochee.
diciō, -ōnis f power, sway, authority.

dicis causā for the sake of appearance.
dicō, -āre, -āvī, -ātum *vt* to dedicate, consecrate; to deify; to devote, give over.
dīcō, -cere, -xī, dictum *vt* to say, tell; to mention, mean, call, name; to pronounce; (*RHET*) to speak, deliver; (*law*) to plead; (*poetry*) to describe, celebrate; (*official*) to appoint; (*time, place*) to settle, fix ♦ *vi* to speak (in public); **causam ~** plead; **iūs ~** deliver judgment; **sententiam ~** vote; **~cō** namely; **~xī** I have finished; **dictum factum** no sooner said than done.
dicrotum, -ī *nt* bireme.
Dictaeus *adj* Cretan.
dictamnus, -ī *f* dittany (*a kind of wild marjoram*).
dictāta, -ōrum *ntpl* lessons, rules.
dictātor, -ōris *m* dictator.
dictātōrius *adj* dictator's.
dictātūra, -ae *f* dictatorship.
Dictē, -ēs *f* mountain in Crete (*where Jupiter was brought up*).
dictiō, -ōnis *f* speaking, declaring; style, expression, oratory; (*oracle*) response.
dictitō, -āre *vt* to keep saying, assert; to plead often.
dictō, -āre, -āvī, -ātum *vt* to say repeatedly; to dictate; to compose.
dictum, -ī *nt* saying, word; proverb; bon mot, witticism; command.
dictus *ppp of* **dīcō.**
Dictynna, -ae *f* Britomartis; Diana.
Dictynnaeus *adj see n.*
didicī *perf of* **discō.**
dīdō, -ere, -idī, -itum *vt* to distribute, broadcast.
Dīdō, -ūs *and* **-ōnis** (*acc* -ō) *f* Queen of Carthage.
dīdūcō, -ūcere, -ūxī, -uctum *vt* to separate, split, open up; (*MIL*) to disperse; (*fig*) to part, divide.
diēcula, -ae *f* one little day.
diērēctus *adj* crucified; **abī ~** go and be hanged.
diēs, -ēī *m/f* day; set day (*usu fem*); a day's journey; (*fig*) time; **~ meus** my birthday; **~em dīcere** impeach; **~em obīre** die; **~em dē ~ē, ~em ex ~ē** from day to day; **in ~em** to a later day; for today; **in ~ēs** daily.
Diēspiter, -ris *m* Jupiter.
diffāmō, -āre, -āvī, -ātum *vt* to divulge; to malign.
differentia, -ae *f* difference, diversity; species.
differitās, -ātis *f* difference.
differō, -erre, distulī, dīlātum *vt* to disperse; to divulge, publish; (*fig*) to distract, disquiet; (*time*) to put off, delay ♦ *vi* to differ, be distinguished.
differtus *adj* stuffed, crammed.
difficilis *adj* difficult; (*person*) awkward, surly.
difficiliter *adv* with difficulty.
difficultās, -ātis *f* difficulty, distress, hardship; surliness.

difficulter *adv* with difficulty.
diffīdēns, -entis *adj* nervous.
diffīdenter *adv* without confidence.
diffīdentia, -ae *f* mistrust, diffidence.
diffīdō, -dere, -sus *vi* to distrust, despair.
diffindō, -ndere, -dī, -ssum *vt* to split, open up; (*fig*) to break off.
diffingō, -ere *vt* to remake.
diffissus *ppp of* **diffindō.**
diffīsus *ppa of* **diffīdō.**
diffiteor, -ērī *vt* to disown.
diffluēns, -entis *adj* (*RHET*) loose.
diffluō, -ere *vi* to flow away; to melt away; (*fig*) to wallow.
diffringō, -ere *vt* to shatter.
diffugiō, -ugere, -ūgī *vi* to disperse, disappear.
diffugium, -ī and iī *nt* dispersion.
diffunditō, -āre *vt* to pour out, waste.
diffundō, -undere, -ūdī, -ūsum *vt* to pour off; to spread, diffuse; to cheer, gladden.
diffūsē *adv* expansively.
diffūsilis *adj* diffusive.
diffūsus *ppp of* **diffundō** ♦ *adj* spreading; (*writing*) loose.
Dīgentia, -ae *f* tributary of the Anio (*near Horace's villa*).
dīgerō, -rere, -ssī, -stum *vt* to divide, distribute; to arrange, set out; to interpret.
dīgestiō, -ōnis *f* (*RHET*) enumeration.
dīgestus *ppp of* **dīgerō.**
digitulus, -ī *m* little finger.
digitus, -ī *m* finger; toe; inch; (*pl*) skill in counting; **~um porrigere, prōferre** take the slightest trouble; **~um trānsversum nōn discēdere** not swerve a finger's breadth; **attingere caelum ~ō** reach the height of happiness; **licērī ~ō** bid at an auction; **mōnstrārī ~ō** be a celebrity; **extrēmī, summī ~ī** the fingertips; **concrepāre ~īs** snap the fingers.
dīgladior, -ārī *vi* to fight fiercely.
dignātiō, -ōnis *f* honour, dignity.
dignē *adv see* **dignus.**
dignitās, -ātis *f* worth, worthiness; dignity, rank, position; political office.
dignō, -āre *vt* to think worthy.
dignor, -ārī *vt* to think worthy; to deign.
dignōscō, -ere *vt* to distinguish.
dignus *adj* worth, worthy; (*things*) fitting, proper.
dīgredior, -dī, -ssus *vi* to separate, part; to deviate, digress.
dīgressiō, -ōnis *f* parting; deviation, digression.
dīgressus *ppa of* **dīgredior.**
dīgressus, -ūs *m* parting.
dīiūdicātiō, -ōnis *f* decision.
dīiūdicō, -āre *vt* to decide; to discriminate.
dīiun- *etc see* **disiun-.**
dīlābor, -bī, -psus *vi* to dissolve, disintegrate; to flow away; (*troops*) to disperse; (*fig*) to decay, vanish.

dīlacerō, -āre *vt* to tear to pieces.
dīlāminō, -āre *vt* to split in two.
dīlaniō, -āre, -āvī, -ātum *vt* to tear to shreds.
dīlapidō, -āre *vt* to demolish.
dīlāpsus *ppa of* dīlābor.
dīlargior, -īrī *vt* to give away liberally.
dīlātiō, -ōnis *f* putting off, adjournment.
dīlātō, -āre, -āvī, -ātu~ *vt* to expand;
   (*pronunciation*) to broaden.
dīlātor, -ōris *m* procrastinator
dīlātus *ppp of* differō.
dīlaudō, -āre *vt* to praise extravagantly.
dīlēctus *ppp of* dīligō ♦ *adj* beloved.
dīlēctus, -ūs *m* selection, picking; (*MIL*) levy;
   ~um habēre hold a levy, recruit
dīlēxī *perf of* dīligō.
dīligēns, -entis *adj* painstaking,
   conscientious, attentive (to); thrifty.
dīligenter *adv see* dīligēns.
dīligentia, -ae *f* careful ness, attentiveness;
   thrift.
dīligō, -igere, -ēxī, -ēctum *vt* to prize
   especially, esteem, love.
dīlōrīcō, -āre *vt* to tear open.
dīlūceō, -ēre *vi* to be evident.
dīlūcēscit, -cēscere, -xit *vi* to dawn, begin to
   grow light.
dīlūcidē *adv see* dīlūcidus.
dīlūcidus *adj* clear, distinct.
dīlūculum, -ī *nt* dawn.
dīlūdium, -ī *and* iī *nt* interval.
dīluō, -uere, -uī, -ūtum *vt* to wash away,
   dissolve, dilute; to explain; (*fig*) to weaken,
   do away with.
dīluviēs, -iēī *f*, -ium, -ī *and* iī *nt* flood, deluge.
dīluviō, -āre *vt* to inundate.
dīmānō, -āre *vi* to spread abroad.
dīmēnsiō, -ōnis *f* measuring.
dīmēnsus *adj* measured.
dīmētior, -tīrī, -nsus *vt* to measure out.
dīmētō, -āre, -or, -ārī *v* to mark out.
dīmicātiō, -ōnis *f* fighting, struggle.
dīmicō, -āre, -āvī, -ātu~ *vi* to fight, struggle,
   contend.
dīmidiātus *adj* half, halved.
dīmidius *adj* half ♦ *nt* half.
dīmissiō, -ōnis *f* sending away; discharging.
dīmissus *ppp of* dīmittō.
dīmittō, -ittere, -īsī, -issum *vi* to send away,
   send round; to let go, let down (*meeting*) to
   dismiss; (*MIL*) to disband, detach; (*fig*) to
   abandon, forsake.
dimminuō, -ere *vt* to dash to pieces.
dīmoveō, -ovēre, -ōvī, -ōtum *vt* to part,
   separate; to disperse; to entice away.
Dindymēnē, -ēnēs *f* Cybele.
Dindymus, -ī *m* mountain in Mysia (*sacred to
   Cybele*).
dīnōscō *see* dīgnōscō.
dīnumerātiō, -ōnis *f* reckoning up.

dīnumerō, -āre *vt* to count, reckon up; to pay
   out.
diōbolāris *adj* costing two obols.
dioecēsis, -is *f* district; (*ECCL*) diocese.
dioecētēs, -ae *m* treasurer.
Diogenēs, -is *m* famous Cynic philosopher; a
   Stoic philosopher.
Diomēdēs, -is *m* Greek hero at the Trojan War.
Diomēdēus *adj see* n.
Diōnaeus *adj see* Diōnē.
Diōnē, -ēs *and* -a, -ae *f* mother of Venus; Venus.
Dionȳsius, -ī *m* tyrant of Syracuse.
Dionȳsus, -ī *m* Bacchus; -ia, -iōrum *ntpl* Greek
   festival of Bacchus.
diōta, -ae *f* a two-handled wine jar.
diplōma, -tis *nt* letter of recommendation.
Dipylon, -ī *nt* Athenian gate.
Dircaeus *adj* Boeotian.
Dircē, -ēs *f* famous spring in Boeotia.
dīrēctus *ppp of* dīrigō ♦ *adj* straight;
   straightforward, simple; *see also* dērēctus.
dirēmī *perf of* dirimō.
diremptus *ppp of* dirimō.
diremptus, -ūs *m* separation.
dīreptiō, -ōnis *f* plundering.
dīreptor, -ōris *m* plunderer.
dīreptus *ppp of* dīripiō.
dīrēxī *perf of* dīrigō.
dīribeō, -ēre *vt* to sort out (*votes taken from
   ballot-boxes*)
dīribitiō, -ōnis *f* sorting.
dīribitor, -ōris *m* ballot-sorter.
dīrigō, -igere, -ēxī, -ēctum *vt* to put in line,
   arrange; *see also* dērigō.
dirimō, -imere, -ēmī, -emptum *vt* to part,
   divide; to interrupt, break off; to put an end
   to.
dīripiō, -ipere, -ipuī, -eptum *vt* to tear in
   pieces; to plunder, ravage; to seize; (*fig*) to
   distract.
dīritās, -ātis *f* mischief, cruelty.
dīrumpō, disrumpō, -umpere, -ūpī,
   -uptum *vt* to burst, break in pieces; (*fig*) to
   break off; (*pass*) to burst (with passion).
dīruō, -ere, -ī, -tum *vt* to demolish; to scatter;
   aere ~tus having one's pay stopped.
dīruptus *ppp of* dīrumpō.
dīrus *adj* ominous, fearful; (*pers*) dread,
   terrible ♦ *fpl* bad luck; the Furies ♦ *ntpl*
   terrors.
dīrutus *ppp of* dīruō ♦ *adj* bankrupt.
dīs, dītis *adj* rich.
Dīs, Dītis *m* Pluto.
discēdō, -ēdere, -ēssī, -essum *vi* to go away,
   depart; to part, disperse; (*MIL*) to march
   away; (*result of battle*) to come off; (*POL*) to go
   over (to a different policy); to pass away,
   disappear; to leave out of consideration; ab
   signīs ~ break the ranks; victor ~ come off
   best.

Noun declensions and verb conjugations are shown on pp xii. to xxv. The present infinitive ending of a verb shows
to which conjugation it belongs: -āre =1st; -ēre = 2nd; -ere = 3rd and -īre = 4th. Irregular verbs are shown on p xxvi

disceptātiō, -ōnis *f* discussion, debate.
disceptātor, -ōris *m*, **-rīx, -rīcis** *f* arbitrator.
disceptō, -āre *vt* to debate, discuss; (*law*) to decide.
discernō, -ernere, -rēvī, -rētum *vt* to divide, separate; to distinguish between.
discerpō, -ere, -sī, -tum *vt* to tear apart, disperse; (*fig*) to revile.
discessiō, -ōnis *f* separation, departure; (*senate*) division.
discessus, -ūs *m* parting; departure; marching away.
discidium, -i *and* **ī ī** *nt* disintegration; separation, divorce; discord.
discīdō, -ere *vt* to cut in pieces.
discinctus *ppp of* **discingō** ♦ *adj* ungirt; negligent; dissolute.
discindō, -ndere, -dī, -ssum *vt* to tear up, cut open.
discingō, -gere, -xī, -ctum *vt* to ungird.
disciplīna, -ae *f* teaching, instruction; learning, science, school, system; training, discipline; habits.
discipulus, -ī *m*, **-a, -ae** *f* pupil, apprentice.
discissus *ppp of* **discindō**.
disclūdō, -dere, -sī, -sum *vt* to keep apart, separate out.
discō, -ere, didicī *vt* to learn, be taught, be told.
discolor, -ōris *adj* of a different colour; variegated; different.
discondūcit it is not worthwhile.
disconveniō, -īre *vi* to disagree, be inconsistent.
discordābilis *adj* disagreeing.
discordia, -ae *f* discord, disagreement.
discordiōsus *adj* seditious.
discordō, -āre *vi* to disagree, quarrel; to be unlike.
discors, -dis *adj* discordant, at variance; inconsistent.
discrepantia, -ae *f* disagreement.
discrepātiō, -ōnis *f* dispute.
discrepitō, -āre *vi* to be quite different.
discrepō, -āre, -uī *vi* to be out of tune; to disagree, differ; to be disputed.
discrētus *ppp of* **discernō**.
dīscrībō, -bere, -psī, -ptum *vt* to distribute, apportion, classify.
discrīmen, -inis *nt* interval, dividing line; distinction, difference; turning point, critical moment; crisis, danger.
discrīminō, -āre *vt* to divide.
dīscrīptē *adv* in good order.
dīscrīptiō, -ōnis *f* apportioning, distributing.
dīscrīptus *ppp of* **dīscrībō** ♦ *adj* secluded; well-arranged.
discruciō, -āre *vt* to torture; (*fig*) to torment, trouble.
discumbō, -mbere, -buī, -bitum *vi* to recline at table; to go to bed.
discupiō, -ere *vi* to long.
discurrō, -rrere, -currī *and* **rrī, -rsum** *vi* to

run about, run different ways.
discursus, -ūs *m* running hither and thither.
discus, -ī *m* quoit.
discussus *ppp of* **discutiō**.
discutiō, -tere, -ssī, -ssum *vt* to dash to pieces, smash; to scatter; to dispel.
disertē, -im *adv* distinctly; eloquently.
disertus *adj* fluent, eloquent; explicit.
disiciō, -icere, -iēcī, -iectum *vt* to scatter, cast asunder; to break up, destroy; (*MIL*) to rout.
disiectō, -āre *vt* to toss about.
disiectus *ppp of* **disiciō**.
disiectus, -ūs *m* scattering.
disiūnctiō, -ōnis *f* separation, differing; (*logic*) statement of alternatives; (*RHET*) a sequence of short co-ordinate clauses.
disiūnctius *adv* rather in the manner of a dilemma.
disiūnctus *ppp of* **disiungō** ♦ *adj* distinct, distant, removed; (*speech*) disjointed; (*logic*) opposite.
disiungō, -ungere, -ūnxī, -ūnctum *vt* to unyoke; to separate, remove.
dispālēscō, -ere *vi* to be noised abroad.
dispandō, -āndere, -ānsum *and* **-essum** *vt* to spread out.
dispār, -aris *adj* unlike, unequal.
disparilis *adj* dissimilar.
disparō, -āre, -āvī, -ātum *vt* to segregate.
dispart- *etc see* **dispert-**.
dispectus *ppp of* **dispiciō**.
dispellō, -ellere, -ulī, -ulsum *vt* to scatter, dispel.
dispendium, -ī *and* **ī ī** *nt* expense, loss.
dispennō *etc see* **dispandō**.
dispēnsātiō, -ōnis *f* management, stewardship.
dispēnsātor, -ōris *m* steward, treasurer.
dispēnsō, -āre, -āvī, -ātum *vi* to weigh out, pay out; to manage, distribute; (*fig*) to regulate.
dispercutiō, -ere *vt* to dash out.
disperdō, -ere, -idī, -itum *vt* to ruin, squander.
dispereō, -īre, -iī *vi* to go to ruin, be undone.
dispergō, -gere, -sī, -sum *vt* to disperse, spread over, space out.
dispersē *adv* here and there.
dispersus *ppp of* **dispergō**.
dispertiō, -īre, -īvī, -ītum; -ior, -īrī *vt* to apportion, distribute.
dispertītiō, -ōnis *f* division.
dispessus *ppp of* **dispandō**.
dispiciō, -icere, -exī, -ectum *vt* to see clearly, see through; to distinguish, discern; (*fig*) to consider.
displiceō, -ēre *vi* (*with dat*) to displease; **sibi ~** be in a bad humour.
displōdō, -dere, -sum *vt* to burst with a crash.
dispōnō, -ōnere, -osuī, -ositum *vt* to set out, arrange; (*MIL*) to station.

dispositē *adv* methodically.
dispositiō, -ōnis *f* arrangement.
dispositūra, -ae *f* arrangement.
dispositus *ppp of* **dispōnō** ♦ *adj* orderly.
dispositus, -ūs *m* arranging.
dispudet, -ēre, -uit *v impers* to be very ashamed.
dispulsus *ppp of* **dispellō**.
disputātiō, -ōnis *f* argument.
disputātor, -ōris *m* debater.
disputō, -āre, -āvī, -ātum *vt* to calculate; to examine, discuss.
disquīrō, -ere *vt* to investigate.
disquīsītiō, -ōnis *f* inquiry.
disrumpō *etc see* **dīrumpō**.
dissaepiō, -īre, -sī, -tum *vt* to fence off, separate off.
dissaeptum, -ī *nt* partition.
dissāvior, -ārī *vt* to kiss passionately.
dissēdī *perf of* **dissideō**.
dissēminō, -āre *vt* to sow, broadcast.
dissēnsiō, -ōnis *f* disagreement, conflict.
dissēnsus, -ūs *m* dissension.
dissentāneus *adj* contrary.
dissentiō, -entīre, -ēnsī, -ēnsum *vi* to disagree, differ; to be unlike, be inconsistent.
dissēp- *etc see* **dissaep-**.
disserēnō, -āre *vi* to clear up.
disserō, -erere, -ēvī, -itum *vt* to sow, plant at intervals.
disserō, -ere, -uī, -tum *vt* to set out in order, arrange; to examine, discuss.
disserpō, -ere *vi* to spread imperceptibly.
dissertō, -āre *vt* to discuss, dispute.
dissideō, -idēre, -ēdī, -essum *vi* to be distant; to disagree, quarrel to differ, be unlike, be uneven.
dissignātiō, -ōnis *f* arrangement.
dissignātor, -ōris *m* master of ceremonies; undertaker.
dissignō, -āre *vt* to arrange, regulate; *see also* **dēsignō**.
dissiliō, -īre, -uī *vi* to fly apart break up.
dissimilis *adj* unlike, different.
dissimiliter *adv* differently.
dissimilitūdō, -inis *f* unlikeness.
dissimulanter *adv* secretly.
dissimulantia, -ae *f* dissembling.
dissimulātiō, -ōnis *f* disguising; dissembling; Socratic irony.
dissimulātor, -ōris *m* dissembler.
dissimulō, -āre, -āvī, -ātum *vt* to dissemble, conceal, pretend that … not, ignore.
dissipābilis *adj* diffusible.
dissipātiō, -ōnis *f* scattering, dispersing.
dissipō, dissupō, -āre, -āvī, -ātum *vt* to scatter, disperse; to spread, broadcast; to squander, destroy; (*MIL*) to put to flight.
dissitus *ppp of* **disserō**.

dissociābilis *adj* disuniting; incompatible.
dissociātiō, -ōnis *f* separation.
dissociō, -āre, -āvī, -ātum *vt* to disunite, estrange.
dissolūbilis *adj* dissoluble.
dissolūtē *adv* loosely, negligently.
dissolūtiō, -ōnis *f* breaking up, destruction; looseness; (*law*) refutation; (*person*) weakness.
dissolūtum, -ī *nt* asyndeton.
dissolūtus *ppp of* **dissolvō** ♦ *adj* loose; lax, careless; licentious.
dissolvō, -vere, -vī, -ūtum *vt* to unloose, dissolve; to destroy, abolish; to refute; to pay up, discharge (debt); to free, release.
dissonus *adj* discordant, jarring, disagreeing, different.
dissors, -tis *adj* not shared.
dissuādeō, -dēre, -sī, -sum *vt* to advise against, oppose.
dissuāsiō, -ōr is *f* advising against.
dissuāsor, -ōris *m* opposer.
dissultō, -āre *vi* to fly asunder.
dissuō, -ere *vt* to undo, open up.
dissupō *etc see* **dissipō**.
distaedet, -ēre *v impers* to weary, disgust.
distantia, -ae *f* diversity.
distendō (-nō , -dere, -dī, -tum *vt* to stretch out, swell.
distentus *ppp of* **distendō** ♦ *adj* full ♦ *ppp of* **distineō** ♦ *adj* busy.
disterminō, -āre *vt* to divide, limit.
distichon, -ī *nt* couplet.
distinctē *adv* distinctly, lucidly.
distinctiō, -ōnis *f* differentiating, difference; (*GRAM*) punctuation; (*RHET*) distinction between words.
distinctus *ppp of* **distinguō** ♦ *adj* separate, distinct; ornamented, set off; lucid.
distinctus, -ūs *m* difference.
distineō, -inēre, -inuī, -entum *vt* to keep apart, divide; to distract; to detain, occupy; to prevent.
distinguō, -guere, -xī, -ctum *vt* to divide, distinguish, discriminate; to punctuate; to adorn, set off.
distō, -āre *vi* to be apart, be distant; to be different.
distorqueō, -quēre, -sī, -tum *vt* to twist, distort.
distortiō, -ōnis *f* contortion.
distortus *ppp of* **distorqueō** ♦ *adj* deformed.
distractiō, -ōnis *f* parting, variance.
distractus *ppp of* **distrahō** ♦ *adj* separate.
distrahō, -here, -xī, -ctum *vt* to tear apart, separate, estrange; to sell piecemeal, retail; (*mind*) to distract, perplex; **aciem ~** break up a formation; **contrōversiās ~** end a dispute; **vōcēs ~** leave a hiatus.
distribuō, -uere, -uī, -ūtum *vt* to distribute,

Noun declensions and verb conjugations are shown on pp xiii to xxv. The present infinitive ending of a verb shows to which conjugation it belongs: **-āre** =1st; **-ēre** = 2nd; **-ere** = 3rd and **-īre** = 4th. Irregular verbs are shown on p xxvi

divide.
distribūtē adv methodically.
distribūtiō, -ōnis f distribution, division.
districtus ppp of **distringō** ♦ adj busy, occupied; perplexed; severe.
distringō, -ngere, -nxī, -ctum vt to draw apart; to engage, distract; (MIL) to create a diversion against.
distruncō, -āre vt to cut in two.
distulī perf of **differō**.
disturbō, -āre, -āvī, -ātum vt to throw into confusion; to demolish; to frustrate, ruin.
dītēscō, -ere vi to grow rich.
dīthyrambicus adj dithyrambic.
dīthyrambus, -ī m dithyramb.
dītiae, -ārum fpl wealth.
dītiō etc see **diciō**.
dītō, -āre vt to enrich.
diū (comp **diūtius**, sup **diūtissimē**) adv long, a long time; long ago; by day.
diurnum, -ī nt day-book; **ācta ~a** Roman daily gazette.
diurnus adj daily, for a day; by day, day- (in cpds).
dīus adj divine, noble.
diūtinē adv long.
diūtinus adj long, lasting.
diūtissimē, -ius etc see **diū**.
diūturnitās, -ātis f long time, long duration.
diūturnus adj long, lasting.
dīva, -ae f goddess.
dīvāricō, -āre vt to spread.
dīvellō, -ellere, -ellī, -ulsum vt to tear apart, tear in pieces; (fig) to tear away, separate, estrange.
dīvēndō, -ere, -itum vt to sell in lots.
dīverberō, -āre vt to divide, cleave.
dīverbium, -ī and **iī** nt (comedy) passage in dialogue.
dīversē adv in different directions, variously.
dīversitās, -ātis f contradiction, disagreement, difference.
dīversus, dīvorsus ppp of **dīvertō** ♦ adj in different directions, apart; different; remote; opposite, conflicting; hostile ♦ mpl individuals.
dīvertō, -tere, -tī, -sum vi to turn away; differ.
dīves, -itis adj rich.
dīvexō, -āre vt to pillage.
dīvidia, -ae f worry, concern.
dīvidō, -idere, -īsī, -īsum vt to divide, break open; to distribute, apportion; to separate, keep apart; to distinguish; (jewel) to set off; **sententiam ~** take the vote separately on the parts of a motion.
dīviduus adj divisible; divided.
dīvīnātiō, -ōnis f foreseeing the future, divination; (law) inquiry to select the most suitable prosecutor.
dīvīnē adv by divine influence; prophetically; admirably.
dīvīnitās, -ātis f divinity; divination; divine quality.
dīvīnitus adv from heaven, by divine influence; excellently.
dīvīnō, -āre, -āvī, -ātum vt to foresee, prophesy.
dīvīnus adj divine, of the gods; prophetic; superhuman, excellent ♦ m soothsayer ♦ nt sacrifice; oath; **rēs ~a** religious service, sacrifice; **~a hūmānaque** all things in heaven and earth; **~ī crēdere** believe on oath.
dīvīsī perf of **dīvidō**.
dīvīsiō, -ōnis f division; distribution.
dīvīsor, -ōris m distributor; bribery agent.
dīvīsus ppp of **dīvidō** ♦ adj separate.
dīvīsus, -ūs m division.
dīvitiae, -ārum fpl wealth; (fig) richness.
dīvor- etc see **dīver-**.
dīvortium, -ī and **iī** nt separation; divorce (by consent); road fork, watershed.
dīvulgātus adj widespread.
dīvulgō, -āre, -āvī, -ātum vt to publish, make public.
dīvulsus ppp of **dīvellō**.
dīvum, -ī nt sky; **sub ~ō** in the open air.
dīvus adj divine; deified ♦ m god.
dīxī perf of **dīcō**.
dō, dare, dedī, datum vt to give; to permit, grant; to put, bring, cause, make; to give up, devote; to tell; to impute; **fābulam ~** produce a play; **in fugam ~** put to flight; **litterās ~** post a letter; **manūs ~** surrender; **nōmen ~** enlist; **operam ~** take pains, do one's best; **poenās ~** pay the penalty; **vēla ~** set sail; **verba ~** cheat.
doceō, -ēre, -uī, -tum vt to teach; to inform, tell; **fābulam ~** produce a play.
dochmius, -ī and **iī** m dochmiac foot.
docilis adj easily trained, docile.
docilitās, -ātis f aptness for being taught.
doctē adv skilfully, cleverly.
doctor, -ōris m teacher, instructor.
doctrīna, -ae f instruction, education, learning; science.
doctus ppp of **doceō** ♦ adj learned, skilled; cunning, clever.
documentum, -ī nt lesson, example, proof.
Dōdōna, -ae f town in Epirus (famous for its oracle of Jupiter).
Dōdōnaeus, -is, -idis adj see **Dōdōna**.
dōdrāns, -antis m three-fourths.
dogma, -tis nt philosophical doctrine.
dolābra, -ae f pickaxe.
dolēns, -entis pres p of **doleō** ♦ adj painful.
dolenter adv sorrowfully.
doleō, -ēre, -uī, -itum vt, vi to be in pain, be sore; to grieve, lament, be sorry (for); to pain; **cuī ~et meminit** ≈ once bitten, twice shy.
dōliāris adj tubby.
dōliolum, -ī nt small cask.
dōlium, -ī and **iī** nt large wine jar.
dolō, -āre, -āvī, -ātum vt to hew, shape with an axe.
dolō, -ōnis m pike; sting; fore-topsail.

Dolopes, -um *mpl people of Thessaly.*
Dolopia, -iae *f the country of the people of Thessaly.*
dolor, -ōris *m* pain, pang; sorrow, trouble; indignation, resentment; (*RHET*) pathos.
dolōsē *adv see* **dolōsus**.
dolōsus *adj* deceitful, crafty.
dolus, -ī *m* deceit, guile, trick; ~ **malus** wilful fraud.
domābilis *adj* tameable.
domesticus *adj* domestic, household; personal, private; of one's own country, internal ♦ *mpl* members of a household; **bellum** ~ civil war.
domī *adv* at home.
domicilium, -ī *and* **iī** *nt* dwelling.
domina, -ae *f* mistress, lady of the house; wife, mistress; (*fig*) lady.
domināns, -antis *pres p of* **domi nor** ♦ *adj* (*words*) literal ♦ *m* tyrant.
dominātiō, -ōnis *f* mastery, tyranny.
dominātor, -ōris *m* lord.
dominātrīx, -rīcis *f* queen.
dominātus, -ūs *m* mastery, sovereignty.
dominicus *adj* (*ECCL*) the Lord's.
dominium, -ī *and* **iī** *nt* absolute ownership; feast.
dominor, -ārī, -ātus *vi* to rule, be master; (*fig*) to lord it.
dominus, -ī *m* master, lord; owner; host; despot; (*ECCL*) the Lord.
Domitiānus *adj m Roman Emperor.*
Domitius, -ī *m* Roman plebeian name (*esp with surname Ahenobarbus*).
domitō, -āre *vt* to break in.
domitor, -ōris *m*, **-rīx, -rīcis** *f* tamer; conqueror.
domitus *ppp of* **domō**.
domitus, -ūs *m* taming.
domō, -āre, -uī, -itum *vt* to tame, break in; to conquer.
domus, -ūs *and* **ī** *f* house (*esp in town*); home, native place; family; (*PHILOS*) sect; **-ī** at home; in peace; **-ī habēre** have of one's own, have plenty of; **~um** home(wards); **-ō** from home.
dōnābilis *adj* deserving a present.
dōnārium, -ī *and* **iī** *nt* offering; altar temple.
dōnātiō, -ōnis *f* presenting.
dōnātīvum, -ī *nt* largess, gratuity.
dōnec (**dōnicum, dōnique**) *conj* until; while, as long as.
dōnō, -āre, -āvī, -ātum *vt* to present, bestow; to remit, condone (for another's sake); (*fig*) to sacrifice.
dōnum, -ī *nt* gift; offering.
dorcas, -dis *f* gazelle.
Dōrēs, -um *mpl* Dorians (*mostly the Greeks of the Peloponnese*).
Dōricus *adj* Dorian; Greek.
Dōris, -dis *f* a sea nymph; the sea.

dormiō, -īre, -īvī, -ītum *vi* to sleep, be asleep.
dormītātor, -ōris *m* dreamer.
dormītō, -āre *vi* to be drowsy, nod.
dorsum, -ī *nt* back; mountain ridge.
dōs, dōtis *f* dowry; (*fig*) gift, talent.
Dossēnus, -ī *m* hunchback, clown.
dōtālis *adj* dowry (*in cpds*), dotal.
dōtātus *adj* richly endowed.
dōtō, -āre *vt* to endow.
drachma (**drachuma**), **-ae** *f a Greek silver coin.*
dracō, -ōnis *m* serpent, dragon; (*ASTRO*) Draco.
dracōnigena, **-ae** *cdj* sprung from dragon's teeth.
drāpeta, -ae *m* runaway slave.
Drepanum, -ī, -a, -ōrum *nt* town in W. Sicily.
dromas, -dis *m* dromedary.
dromos, -ī *m* racecourse at Sparta.
Druidēs, -um, -ae, -ārum *mpl* Druids.
Drūsiānus *adj see* **Drūsus**.
Drūsus, -ī *m* Roman surname (*esp famous commander in Germany under Augustus*).
Dryades, -um *fpl* woodnymphs, Dryads.
Dryopes, -um *mpl a people of Epirus.*
dubiē *adv* doubtfully.
dubitābilis *adj* doubtful.
dubitanter *adv* doubtingly, hesitatingly.
dubitātiō, -ōn s *f* wavering, uncertainty, doubting; hesitancy, irresolution; (*RHET*) misgiving.
dubitō, -āre, -āvī, -ātum *vt, vi* to waver, be in doubt, wonder, doubt; to hesitate, stop to think.
dubium *nt* doubt.
dubius *adj* wavering, uncertain; doubtful, indecisive; precarious; irresolute ♦ *nt* doubt; **in ~um vocāre** call in question; **in ~um venīre** be called in question; **sine ~ō, haud ~ē** undoubtedly.
ducēnī, -ōrum *adj* 200 each.
ducentēsima, **-ae** *f* one-half per cent.
ducentī, -ōrum *num* two hundred.
ducentiēs, -iēns *adv* 200 times.
dūcō, -cere, -xī, ductum *vt* to lead, guide, bring, take; to draw, draw out; to reckon, consider; (*MIL*) to lead, march, command; (*breath*) to inhale; (*ceremony*) to conduct; (*changed aspect*) to take on, receive; (*dance*) to perform; (*drink*) to quaff; (*metal*) to shape, beat out; (*mind*) to attract, induce, deceive; (*oars*) to pull; (*origin*) to derive, trace; (*time*) to prolong, put off, pass; (*udders*) to milk; (*wool*) to spin; (*a work*) to construct, compose, make; (*comm*) to calculate; **īlia** ~ become broken-winded; **in numerō hostium** ~ regard as an enemy; **ōs** ~ make faces; **parvī** ~ think little of; **ratiōnem** ~ have regard for; **uxōrem** ~ marry.
ductim *adv* in streams.
ductitō, -āre *vt* to lead on, deceive; to marry.

ductō, -āre *vt* to lead, draw; to take home; to cheat.

ductor, -ōris *m* leader, commander; guide, pilot.

ductus *ppp of* **dūcō**.

ductus, -ūs *m* drawing, drawing off; form; command, generalship.

dūdum *adv* a little while ago, just now; for long; **haud ~** not long ago; **iam ~ adsum** I have been here a long time; **quam ~** how long.

duellum *etc see* **bellum**.

Duillius, -ī *m consul who defeated the Carthaginians at sea*.

duim *pres subj of* **dō**.

dulce, -iter *adv see* **dulcis**.

dulcēdō, -inis *f* sweetness; pleasantness, charm.

dulcēscō, -ere *vi* to become sweet.

dulciculus *adj* rather sweet.

dulcifer, -ī *adj* sweet.

dulcis *adj* sweet; pleasant, lovely; kind, dear.

dulcitūdō, -inis *f* sweetness.

dūlicē *adv* like a slave.

Dūlichium, -ī *nt island in the Ionian Sea near Ithaca*.

Dūlichius *adj* of Dulichium; of Ulysses.

dum *conj* while, as long as; provided that, if only; until ♦ *adv (enclitic)* now, a moment; *(with neg)* yet.

dūmētum, -ī *nt* thicket, thornbushes.

dummodo *conj* provided that.

dūmōsus *adj* thorny.

dumtaxat *adv* at least; only, merely.

dūmus, -ī *m* thornbush.

duo, duae, duo *num* two.

duodeciēns, -ēs *adv* twelve times.

duodecim *num* twelve.

duodecimus *adj* twelfth.

duodēnī, -ōrum *adj* twelve each, in dozens.

duodēquadrāgēsimus *adj* thirty-eighth.

duodēquadrāgintā *num* thirty-eight.

duodēquīnquāgēsimus *adj* forty-eighth.

duodētrīciēns *adv* twenty-eight times.

duodētrīgintā *num* twenty-eight.

duodēvīcēnī *adj* eighteen each.

duodēvīgintī *num* eighteen.

duoetvīcēsimānī, -ānōrum *mpl* soldiers of the 22nd legion.

duoetvīcēsimus *adj* twenty-second.

duovirī, duumvirī, -ōrum *mpl* a board of two men; colonial magistrates; **~ nāvālēs** naval commissioners (for supply and repair); **~ sacrōrum** keepers of the Sibylline Books.

duplex, -icis *adj* double, twofold; both; *(person)* false.

duplicārius, -ī *and* **iī** *m* soldier receiving double pay.

dupliciter *adv* doubly, on two accounts.

duplicō, -āre, -āvī, -ātum *vt* to double, increase; to bend.

duplus *adj* double, twice as much ♦ *nt* double ♦ *f* double the price.

dupondius, -ī *and* **iī** *m* coin worth two asses.

dūrābilis *adj* lasting.

dūrāmen, -inis *nt* hardness.

dūrateus *adj* wooden.

dūrē, -iter *adv* stiffly; hardily; harshly, roughly.

dūrēscō, -ēscere, -uī *vi* to harden.

dūritās, -ātis *f* harshness.

dūritia, -ae, -ēs, -em *f* hardness; hardiness; severity; want of feeling.

dūrō, -āre, -āvī, -ātum *vt* to harden, stiffen; to make hardy, inure; *(mind)* to dull ♦ *vi* to harden; to be patient, endure; to hold out, last; *(mind)* to be steeled.

dūruī *perf of* **dūrēscō**.

dūrus *adj* hard, harsh, rough; hardy, tough; rude, uncultured; *(character)* severe, unfeeling, impudent, miserly; *(circs)* hard, cruel.

duumvirī *etc see* **duovirī**.

dux, ducis *m* leader, guide; chief, head; *(mil)* commander, general.

dūxī *perf of* **dūcō**.

Dymantis, -antidis *f* Hecuba.

Dymās, -antis *m father of Hecuba*.

dynamis, -is *f* plenty.

dynastēs, -ae *m* ruler, prince.

Dyrrhachīnus *adj see n*.

Dyrrhachium (Dyrrachium), -ī *nt* Adriatic port (*now* Durazzo).

E, e

ē *prep see* **ex**.

ea *f pron* she, it ♦ *adj see* **is**.

eā *adv* there, that way.

eādem *adv* the same way; at the same time.

eadem *f adj see* **idem**.

eaīdem, eapse *f of* **ipse**.

eapse *f of* **ipse**.

eātenus *adv* so far.

ebenus *etc see* **hebenus**.

ēbibō, -ere, -ī *vt* to drink up, drain; to squander; to absorb.

ēblandior, -īrī *vt* to coax out, obtain by flattery; **~ītus** obtained by flattery.

Eborācum, -ī *nt* York.

ēbrietās, ātis *f* drunkenness.

ēbriolus *adj* tipsy.

ēbriōsitās, -ātis *f* addiction to drink.

ēbriōsus *adj* drunkard; *(berry)* juicy.

ēbrius *adj* drunk; full; *(fig)* intoxicated.

ēbulliō, -īre *vi* to bubble up ♦ *vt* to brag about.

ebulus, -ī *m*, **-um, -ī** *nt* danewort, dwarf elder.

ebur, -is *nt* ivory; ivory work.

Eburācum, -ī *nt* York.
eburātus *adj* inlaid with ivory.
eburneolus *adj* of ivory.
eburneus, eburnus *adj* of ivory; *very*-white.
ēcastor *interj* by Castor!
ecce *adv* look!, here is!, there is!; ⅅ and
behold!; ~a, ~am, ~illam, ~istam ⅼere she is!;
~um, ~illum here he is!; ~ōs, ~ās here they
are!
eccerē *interj* there now!
eccheuma, -tis *nt* pouring out.
ecclēsia, -ae *f* a Greek assembly; (*ec*)
congregation, church.
eccum *etc see* **ecce.**
ecdicus, -ī *m* civic lawyer.
ecf- *see* **eff-**.
echidna, -ae *f* viper; ~ **Lernaea** hydra.
echīnus, -ī *m* sea-urchin; hedgehog; a rinsing
bowl.
Echīōn, -onis *m* Theban hero.
Echīonidēs *m* Pentheus.
Echīonius *adj* Theban.
Echō, -us *f* wood nymph; echo.
ecloga, -ae *f* selection; eclogue.
ecquandō *adv* ever.
ecquī, -ae, -od *adj interrog* any.
ecquid, -ī *adv* whether.
ecquis, -id *pron interrog* anyone, anything.
ecquō *adv* anywhere.
eculeus, -ī *m* foal; rack.
edācitās, -ātis *f* gluttony.
edāx, -ācis *adj* gluttonous; (*fig*) devouring,
carking.
ēdentō, -āre *vt* to knock the teeth out of.
ēdentulus *adj* toothless; old.
edepol *interj* by Pollux, indeed.
ēdī *perf of* **edō.**
ēdīcō, -īcere, -īxī, -ictum *vt* to declare; to
decree, publish an edict.
ēdictiō, -ōnis *f* decree.
ēdictō, -āre *vt* to proclaim.
ēdictum, -ī *nt* proclamation, edict *esp a
praetor's*).
ēdidī *perf of* **ēdō.**
ēdiscō, -ere, ēdidicī *vt* to learn well, learn by
heart.
ēdisserō, -ere, -uī, -tum *vt* to explain in
detail.
ēdissertō, -āre *vt* to explain fully.
ēditīcius *adj* chosen by the plaintiff.
ēditiō, -ōnis *f* publishing, edition; statement;
(*law*) designation of a suit.
ēditus *ppp of* **ēdō** ♦ *adj* high; descended ♦ *nt*
height; order.
edō, edere *and* **ēsse, ēdī, ēsum** *vt* tc eat; (*fig*)
to devour.
ēdō, -ere, -idī, -itum *vt* to put forth,
discharge; to emit; to give birth to, produce;
(*speech*) to declare, relate, utter; (*action*) to
cause, perform; (*book*) to publish; (*nol*) to

promulgate; ⅼūdōs ~ put on a show; **tribūs** ~
nominate tribes of jurors.
ēdoceō, -ere, -uī, -ctum *vt* to instruct
clearly, teach thoroughly.
ēdomō, -āre, -uī, -itum *vt* to conquer,
overcome.
Ēdōnus *adj* Thracian.
ēdormiō, -īre *vi* to have a good sleep ♦ *vt* to
sleep off.
ēdormīscō, -ere *vt* to sleep off.
ēducātiō, -ōr is *f* bringing up, rearing.
ēducātor, -ōr is *m* foster father, tutor.
ēducātrīx, -īcis *f* nurse.
ēducō, -āre, -āvī, -ātum *vt* to bring up, rear,
train; to produce.
ēdūcō, -ūcere, -ūxī, -uctum *vt* to draw out,
bring away; to raise up, erect; (*law*) to
summon; (*Mr*) to lead out, march out; (*ship*)
to put to sea; (*young*) to hatch, rear, train.
edūlis *adj* edible.
ēdūrō, -āre *vi* to last out.
ēdūrus *adj* very hard.
effarciō *etc see* **efferciō.**
effātus *ppa of* **effor** ♦ *adj* solemnly pronounced,
declared ♦ *n* axiom; (*pl*) predictions.
effectiō, -ōnis *f* performing; efficient cause.
effector, -ōris *m*, **-rīx, -rīcis** *f* producer,
author.
effectus *ppp of* **efficiō.**
effectus, -ūs *m* completion, performance;
effect.
effēminātē *adv see* **effēminātus.**
effēminātus *adj* effeminate.
effēminō, -āre, -āvī, -ātum *vt* to make a
woman of; to enervate.
efferātus *adj* savage.
efferciō, -cīre, -tum *vt* to cram full.
efferitās, -ātis *f* wildness.
efferō, -āre, -āvī, -ātum *vt* to make wild; (*fig*)
to exasperate.
efferō (ecferō-, -re, extulī, ēlātum *vt* to
bring out, carry out; to lift up, raise; (*dead*)
to carry to the grave; (*emotion*) to transport;
(*honour*) to exalt; (*news*) to spread abroad;
(*soil*) to produce; (*trouble*) to endure to the
end; **sē** ~ rise, be conceited.
effertus *ppp of* **efferciō** ♦ *adj* full, bulging.
efferus *adj* savage.
effervēscō, -vēscere, -buī *vi* to boil over; (*fig*)
to rage.
effervō, -ere *vi* to boil up.
effētus *adj* exhausted.
efficācitās, -ātis *f* power.
efficāciter *adv* effectually.
efficāx, -ācis *adj* capable, effective.
efficiēns, -entis *pres p of* **efficiō** ♦ *adj* effective,
efficient.
efficienter *adv* efficiently.
efficientia, -ae *f* power, efficacy.
efficiō, -icere, -ēcī, -ectum *vt* to make,

Noun declensions and verb conjugations are shown on pp xiii to xxv. The present infinitive ending of a verb shows
to which conjugation it belongs: **-āre** = 1st, **-īre** = 2nd, **-ere** = 3rd and **-īre** = 4th. Irregular verbs are shown on p xxvi

accomplish; to cause, bring about; (*numbers*) to amount to; (*soil*) to yield; (*theory*) to make out, try to prove.

effictus *ppp of* **effingō**.

effigiēs, -ēī, -a, -ae *f* likeness, copy; ghost; portrait, statue; (*fig*) image, ideal.

effingō, -ngere, -nxī, -ctum *vt* to form, fashion; to portray, represent; to wipe clean; to fondle.

efflāgitātiō, -ōnis *f* urgent demand.

efflāgitātus, -ūs *m* urgent request.

efflāgitō, -āre *vt* to demand urgently.

efflīctim *adv* desperately.

efflīctō, -āre *vt* to strike dead.

efflīgō, -gere, -xī, -ctum *vt* to exterminate.

efflō, -āre, -āvī, -ātum *vt* to breathe out, blow out ♦ *vi* to billow out; **animam ~ expire.**

efflōrēscō, -ēscere, -uī *vi* to blossom forth.

effluō, -ere, -xī *vi* to run out, issue, emanate; (*fig*) to pass away, vanish; (*rumour*) to get known; **ex animō ~ become forgotten.**

effluvium, -ī *and* **iī** *nt* outlet.

effodiō, -odere, -ōdī, -ossum *vt* to dig up; (*eyes*) to gouge out; (*house*) to ransack.

effor, -ārī, -ātus *vt* to speak, utter; (*augury*) to ordain; (*logic*) to state a proposition.

effossus *ppp of* **effodiō**.

effrēnātē *adv see* **effrēnātus**.

effrēnātiō, -ōnis *f* impetuousness.

effrēnātus *adj* unbridled, violent, unruly.

effrēnus *adj* unbridled.

effringō, -ingere, -ēgī, -āctum *vt* to break open, smash.

effugiō, -ugere, -ūgī *vi* to run away, escape ♦ *vt* to flee from, escape; to escape the notice of.

effugium, -ī *and* **iī** *nt* flight, escape; means of escape.

effulgeō, -gēre, -sī *vi* to shine out, blaze.

effultus *adj* supported.

effundō, -undere, -ūdī, -ūsum *vt* to pour forth, pour out; (*crops*) to produce in abundance; (*missiles*) to shoot; (*rider*) to throw; (*speech*) to give vent to; (*effort*) to waste; (*money*) to squander; (*reins*) to let go; **sē ~, ~undī** rush out; indulge (in).

effūsē *adv* far and wide; lavishly, extravagantly.

effūsiō, -ōnis *f* pouring out, rushing out; profusion, extravagance; exuberance.

effūsus *ppp of* **effundō** ♦ *adj* vast, extensive; loose, straggling; lavish, extravagant.

effūtiō, -īre *vt* to blab, chatter.

ēgelidus *adj* mild, cool.

egēns, -entis *pres p of* **egeō** ♦ *adj* needy.

egēnus *adj* destitute.

egeō, -ēre, -uī *vi* to be in want; (*with abl or gen*) to need, want.

Ēgeria, -ae *f* nymph who taught Numa.

ēgerō, -rere, -ssī, -stum *vt* to carry out; to discharge, emit.

egestās, -ātis *f* want, poverty.

ēgestus *ppp of* **ēgerō**.

ēgī *perf of* **agō**.

ego *pron* I; **~met** I (*emphatic*).

ēgredior, -dī, -ssus *vi* to go out, come out; to go up, climb; (*MIL*) to march out; (*NAUT*) to disembark, put to sea; (*speech*) to digress ♦ *vt* to go beyond, quit; (*fig*) to overstep, surpass.

ēgregiē *adv* uncommonly well, singularly.

ēgregius *adj* outstanding, surpassing; distinguished, illustrious.

ēgressus *ppa of* **ēgredior**.

ēgressus, -ūs *m* departure; way out; digression; (*NAUT*) landing; (*river*) mouth.

eguī *perf of* **egeō**.

ēgurgitō, -āre *vt* to lavish.

ehem *interj* (*expressing surprise*) ha!, so!

ēheu *interj* (*expressing pain*) alas!

eho *interj* (*expressing rebuke*) look here!

ei *dat of* **is**.

ei *interj* (*expressing alarm*) oh!

eia *interj* (*expressing delight, playful remonstrance, encouragement*) aha!, come now!, come on!

ēiaculor, -ārī *vt* to shoot out.

ēiciō, -icere, -iēcī, -iectum *vt* to throw out, drive out, put out; (*joint*) to dislocate; (*mind*) to banish; (*NAUT*) to bring to land, run aground, wreck; (*rider*) to throw; (*speech*) to utter; (*THEAT*) to hiss off; **sē ~** rush out, break out.

ēiectāmenta, -ōrum *ntpl* refuse.

ēiectiō, -ōnis *f* banishment.

ēiectō, -āre *vt* to throw up.

ēiectus *ppp of* **ēiciō** ♦ *adj* shipwrecked.

ēiectus, -ūs *m* emitting.

ēierō, ēiūrō, -āre *vt* to abjure, reject on oath, forswear; (*office*) to resign; **bonam cōpiam ~** declare oneself bankrupt.

ēiulātiō, -ōnis *f*, **ēiulātus, -ūs** *m* wailing.

ēiulō, -āre *vi* to wail, lament.

ēius *pron* his, her, its; **~modī** such.

ej- *etc see* **ei-**.

ēlābor, -bī, -psus *vi* to glide away, slip off; to escape, get off; to pass away.

ēlabōrātus *adj* studied.

ēlabōrō, -āre, -āvī, -ātum *vi* to exert oneself, take great pains ♦ *vt* to work out, elaborate.

ēlāmentābilis *adj* very mournful.

ēlanguēscō, -ēscere, -ī *vi* to grow faint; to relax.

ēlapsus *ppa of* **ēlābor**.

ēlātē *adv* proudly.

ēlātiō, -ōnis *f* ecstasy, exaltation.

ēlātrō, -āre *vt* to bark out.

ēlātus *ppp of* **efferō** ♦ *adj* high; exalted.

ēlavō, -avāre, -āvī, -autum *and* **-ōtum** *vt* to wash clean; (*comedy*) to rob.

Elea, -ae *f* town in S. Italy (*birthplace of Parmenides*).

Eleātēs, -āticus *adj see n.*

ēlecebra, -ae *f* snare.

ēlēctē *adv* choicely.

ēlēctilis *adj* choice.

ēlectiō, -ōnis f choice, option.
ēlectō, -āre vt to coax out.
ēlēctō, -āre vt to select.
Ēlectra, -ae f a Pleiad (daughter of Atlas; sister of Orestes).
ēlectrum, -ī nt amber; an alloy of gold and silver.
ēlēctus ppp of ēligō ♦ adj select, choice.
ēlēctus, -ūs m choice.
ēlegāns, -antis adj tasteful, refined, elegant; fastidious; (things) fine, choice.
ēleganter adv with good taste.
ēlegantia, -ae f taste, finesse, elegance; fastidiousness.
ēlēgī perf of ēligō.
elegī, -ōrum mpl elegiac verses.
elegīa, -ae f elegy.
Eleleides, -eidum fpl Bacchantes.
Eleleus, -eī m Bacchus.
elementum, -ī nt element; (pl) first principles, rudiments; beginnings; letters (of alphabet).
elenchus, -ī m a pear-shaped pearl.
elephantomacha, -ae m fighter mounted on an elephant.
elephantus, -ī, elephās, -antis m elephant; ivory.
Ēlēus, -ius, -ias adj Elean; Olympian.
Eleusīn, -is f Eleusis (Attic town famous for its mysteries of Demeter).
Eleusīus adj see Eleusīn.
eleutheria, -ae f liberty.
ēlevō, -āre vt to lift, raise; to alleviate; to make light of, lessen, disparage.
ēliciō, -ere, -uī, -itum vt to lure out, draw out; (god) to call down; (spirit) to conjure up; (fig) to elicit, draw.
ēlīdō, -dere, -sī, -sum vt to dash out, squeeze out; to drive out; to crush, destroy.
ēligō, -igere, -ēgī, -ēctum vt to pick, pluck out; to choose.
ēlīminō, -āre vt to carry outside.
ēlīmō, -āre vt to file; (fig) to perfect.
ēlinguis adj speechless; not eloquent.
ēlinguō, -āre vt to tear the tongue out of.
Ēlis, -idis f district and town in the Peloponnese (famous for Olympia).
Elissa, -ae f Dido.
ēlīsus ppp of ēlīdō.
ēlixus adj boiled.
elleborōsus adj quite mad.
elleborus, -ī m, -um, -ī nt hellebore.
ellum, ellam there he (she) is!
ēlocō, -āre vt to lease, farm out.
ēlocūtiō, -ōnis f delivery, style.
ēlocūtus ppa of ēloquor.
elogium, -ī and iī nt short saying; inscription; (will) clause.
ēloquēns, -entis adj eloquent.
ēloquenter adv see adj.

ēloquentia, -ae f eloquence.
ēloquium, -ī and iī nt eloquence.
ēloquor, -quī, -cūtus vt, vi to speak out, speak eloquently.
ēlūceō, -cēre, -xī vi to shine out, glitter.
ēluctor, -ārī, -ātus vi to struggle, force a way out ♦ vt to struggle out of, surmount.
ēlūcubrō, -āre, -or, -ārī, -ātus vt to compose by lamplight.
ēlūdificor, -ārī, -ātus vt to cheat, play up.
ēlūdō, -dere, -sī, -sum vt to parry, ward off, foil; to win off at play; to outplay, outmanoeuvre; to cheat, make fun of ♦ vi to finish one's sport.
ēlūgeō, -gēre, -xī vt to mourn for.
ēlumbis adj feeble.
ēluō, -uere, -uī, -ūtum vt to wash clean; (money) to squander; (fig) to wash away, get rid of.
ēlūsus ppp of ēlūdō.
ēlūtus ppp of ēluō ♦ adj insipid.
ēluviēs, -em -ēf discharge; overflowing.
ēluviō, -ōnis f deluge.
Ēlysium, -ī nt Elysium.
Ēlysius adj Elysian.
em interj there you are!
ēmancipātiō, -ōnis f giving a son his independence; conveyance of property.
ēmancipō, -āre vt to declare independent; to transfer, give up, sell.
ēmānō, -āre, -āvī, -ātum vi to flow out; to spring (from); (news) to leak out, become known.
Ēmathia, -ae f district of Macedonia; Macedonia, Thessaly.
Ēmathius adj Macedonian, Pharsalian; -des, -dum fpl Muses.
ēmātūrēscō, -ēscere, -uī vi to soften.
emāx, -ācis adj fond of buying.
emblēma, -tis nt inlaid work, mosaic.
embolium, -ī and iī nt interlude.
ēmendābilis adj corrigible.
ēmendātē adv see ēmendātor.
ēmendātiō, -ōnis f correction.
ēmendātor, -ōris m, -rīx, -rīcis f corrector.
ēmendātus adj faultless.
ēmendō, -āre, -āvī, -ātum vt to correct, improve.
ēmēnsus ppa of ēmētior ♦ adj traversed.
ēmentior, -īrī, -ītus vi to tell lies ♦ vt to pretend, fabricate; -ītus pretended.
ēmercor, -ārī vt to purchase.
ēmereō, -ēre, -uī, -itum, -eor, -ērī vt to earn fully, deserve; to lay under an obligation; to complete one's term of service.
ēmergō, -gere, -sī, -sum vt to raise out; (fig) to extricate ♦ vi to rise, come up, emerge; (fig) to get clear, extricate oneself; (impers) it becomes evident.
ēmeritus ppa of ēmereor ♦ adj superannuated,

worn-out ♦ *m* veteran.
ēmersus *ppp of* **ēmergō.**
emetica, -ae *f* emetic.
ēmētior, -tīrī, -nsus *vt* to measure out; to traverse, pass over; (*time*) to live through; (*fig*) to impart.
ēmetō, -ere *vt* to harvest.
ēmī *perf of* **emō.**
ēmicō, -āre, -uī, -ātum *vi* to dart out, dash out, flash out; (*fig*) to shine.
ēmigrō, -āre, -āvī, -ātum *vi* to remove, depart.
ēminēns, -entis *pres p of* **ēmineō** ♦ *adj* high, projecting; (*fig*) distinguished, eminent.
ēminentia, -ae *f* prominence; (*painting*) light.
ēmineō, -ēre, -uī *vi* to stand out, project; to be prominent, be conspicuous, distinguish oneself.
ēminor, -ārī *vi* to threaten.
ēminus *adv* at *or* from a distance.
ēmīror, -ārī *vt* to marvel at.
ēmissārium, -ī *and* **iī** *nt* outlet.
ēmissārius, -ī *and* **iī** *m* scout.
ēmissīcius *adj* prying.
ēmissiō, -ōnis *f* letting go, discharge.
ēmissus *ppp of* **ēmittō.**
ēmissus, -ūs *m* emission.
ēmittō, -ittere, -īsī, -issum *vt* to send out, let out; to let go, let slip; (*missile*) to discharge; (*person*) to release, free; (*sound*) to utter; (*writing*) to publish.
emō, -ere, ēmī, emptum *vt* to buy, procure; to win over; **bene ~** buy cheap; **male ~** buy dear; **in diem ~** buy on credit.
ēmoderor, -ārī *vt* to give expression to.
ēmodulor, -ārī *vt* to sing through.
ēmōlior, -īrī *vt* to accomplish.
ēmolliō, -īre, -iī, -ītum *vt* to soften; to mollify; to enervate.
ēmolumentum, -ī *nt* profit, advantage.
ēmoneō, -ēre *vt* to strongly advise.
ēmorior, -ī, -tuus *vi* to die; (*fig*) to pass away.
ēmortuālis *adj* of death.
ēmoveō, -ovēre, -ōvī, -ōtum *vt* to remove, drive away.
Empedoclēs, -is *m* Sicilian philosopher.
Empedoclēus *adj see n.*
empīricus, -ī *m* empirical doctor.
emporium, -ī *and* **iī** *nt* market, market town.
emptiō, -ōnis *f* buying; a purchase.
emptitō, -āre *vt* to often buy.
emptor, -ōris *m* purchaser.
emptus *ppp of* **emō.**
ēmulgeō, -ēre *vt* to drain.
ēmunctus *ppp of* **ēmungō** ♦ *adj* discriminating.
ēmungō, -gere, -xī, -ctum *vt* to blow the nose of; (*comedy*) to cheat.
ēmūniō, -īre, -īvī, -ītum *vt* to strengthen, secure; to build up; to make roads through.
ēn *interj* (*drawing attention*) look!, see!; (*excited question*) really, indeed!; (*command*) come now!

ēnārrābilis *adj* describable.
ēnārrō, -āre, -āvī, -ātum *vt* to describe in detail.
ēnāscor, -scī, -tus *vi* to sprout, grow.
ēnatō, -āre *vi* to swim ashore; (*fig*) to escape.
ēnātus *ppa of* **ēnāscor.**
ēnāvigō, -āre *vi* to sail clear, clear ♦ *vt* to sail over.
Enceladus, -ī *m* giant under Etna.
endromis, -dis *f* sports wrap.
Endymiōn, -ōnis *m* a beautiful youth loved by the Moon, and doomed to lasting sleep.
ēnecō, -āre, -uī *and* **-āvī, -tum** *and* **ātum** *vt* to kill; to wear out; to torment.
ēnervātus *adj* limp.
ēnervis *adj* enfeebled.
ēnervō, -āre, -āvī, -ātum *vt* to weaken, unman.
ēnicō *etc see* **ēnecō.**
enim *conj* (*affirming*) yes, truly, in fact; (*explaining*) for, for instance, of course; **at ~** but it will be objected; **quid ~** well?; **sed ~** but actually.
enimvērō *conj* certainly, yes indeed.
Enīpeus, -eī *m* river in Thessaly.
ēnīsus *ppa of* **ēnītor.**
ēniteō, -ēre, -uī *vi* to shine, brighten up; (*fig*) to be brilliant, distinguish oneself.
ēnitēscō, -ēscere, -uī *vi* to shine, be brilliant.
ēnītor, -tī, -sus *and* **xus** *vi* to struggle up, climb; to strive, make a great effort ♦ *vt* to give birth to; to climb.
ēnīxē *adv* earnestly.
ēnīxus *ppa of* **ēnītor** ♦ *adj* strenuous.
Enniānus *adj see n.*
Ennius, -ī *m* greatest of the early Latin poets.
Ennosigaeus, -ī *m* Earthshaker, Neptune.
ēnō, -āre, -āvī *vi* to swim out, swim ashore; to fly away.
ēnōdātē *adv* lucidly.
ēnōdātiō, -ōnis *f* unravelling.
ēnōdis *adj* free from knots; plain.
ēnōdō, -āre, -āvī, -ātum *vt* to elucidate.
ēnōrmis *adj* irregular; immense.
ēnōtēscō, -ēscere, -uī *vi* to get known.
ēnotō, -āre *vt* to make a note of.
ensiculus, -ī *m* little sword.
ēnsiger, -ī *adj* with his sword.
ēnsis, -is *m* sword.
enthymēma, -tis *nt* argument.
ēnūbō, -bere, -psī *vi* to marry out of one's station; to marry and go away.
ēnucleātē *adv* plainly.
ēnucleātus *adj* (*style*) straightforward; (*votes*) honest.
ēnucleō, -āre *vt* to elucidate.
ēnumerātiō, -ōnis *f* enumeration; (*RHET*) recapitulation.
ēnumerō, -āre *vt* to count up; to pay out; to relate.
ēnūntiātiō, -ōnis *f* proposition.
ēnūntiātum, -ī *nt* proposition.
ēnūntiō, -āre *vt* to disclose, report; to

express; to pronounce.
ēnūptiō, -ōnis f marrying out ʃ ɔ ɒ e's
station.
ēnūtriō, -īre vt to feed, bring up
eō, īre, īvī and **iī, itum** vi to go (vi) to march;
(time) to pass; (event) to proceed, turn out; in
alia omnia ~ vote against a bill; in sententiam
~ support a motion; sīc eat so may he fare!; ī
(mocking) go on!
eō adv (place) thither, there; (purpose) with a
view to; (degree) so far, to such a pitch;
(time) so long; (cause) on that account, for
the reason; (with compar) the; accēdit eō
besides; rēs erat eō locī such was the state of
affairs; eō magis all the more
eōdem adv to the same place, purpose or
person; ~ locī in the same place.
Ēōs f dawn ♦ m morning star; Oriental.
Ēous adj at dawn, eastern.
Ēpamīnōndās, -ae m Theban general
ēpāstus adj eaten up.
ephēbus, -ī m youth (18 to 20).
ephēmeris, -idis f diary.
Ephesius adj see n.
Ephesus, -ī f Ionian town in Asia Minor
ephippiātus adj riding a saddled horse.
ephippium, -ī and **iī** nt saddle.
ephorus, -ī m a Spartan magistrate ephor.
Ephyra, -ae, -ē, -ēs f Corinth.
Ephyrēius adj see **Ephyra.**
Epicharmus, -ī m Greek philosopher and comic
poet.
epichysis, -is f kind of jug.
epicōpus adj rowing.
Epicūrēus, epicus adj epic.
Epicūrus, -ī m famous Greek philosopher.
Epidaurius adj see n.
Epidaurus, -ī f town in E. Peloponnese.
epidīcticus adj (RHET) for display.
epigramma, -tis nt inscription; epigram.
epilogus, -ī m peroration.
epimēnia, -ōrum ntpl a month' rations.
Epimēthis, -dis f Pyrrha (daughter of
Epimetheus).
epirēdium, -ī and **iī** nt trace.
Ēpīrōtēs, -ōtae m native of Epirus.
Ēpīrōticus, -ēnsis adj see n.
Ēpīrus, -os, -ī f district of N.W. Greece.
episcopus, -ī m bishop.
epistolium, -ī and **iī** nt short note.
epistula, -ae f letter; ab ~is secretary.
epitaphium, -ī and **iī** nt funeral oration.
epithēca, -ae f addition.
epitoma, -ae, -ē, -ēs f abridgement.
epityrum, -ī nt olive salad.
epops, -is m hoopoe.
epos (pl -ē) nt epic.
ēpōtō, -āre, -āvī, -um vt to drink up, drain; to
waste in drink; to absorb.
epulae, -ārum fpl dishes; feast, banquet.

epulāris adj at a banquet.
epulō, -ōnis m guest at a feast; priest in
charge of religious banquets.
epulor, -ārī, -ātus vi to be at a feast ♦ vt to
feast on.
epulum, -ī nt banquet.
equa, -ae f mare.
eques, -itis m horseman, trooper; (pl)
cavalry; knight, member of the equestrian
order.
equester, -ris adj equestrian; cavalry- (in
cpds).
equidem adv (affirming) indeed, of course, for
my part; (concessive) to be sure.
equīnus adj horse's.
equīria, -ōrum ntpl horseraces.
equitātus, -ūs m cavalry.
equitō, -āre vi to ride
equuleus etc see **eculeus.**
equulus, -ī m colt.
equus, -ī m horse; (ASTRO) Pegasus; ~ bipēs
seahorse; ~ō merēre serve in the cavalry; ~īs
virīsque with air ight and main.
era, -ae f mistress (of the house); (goddess)
Lady.
ērādīcō, -āre vt to root out, destroy.
ērādō, -dere, -sī, -sum vt to erase, obliterate.
Eratō f Muse of lyric poetry.
Eratosthenēs, -is m famous Alexandrian
geographer.
Erebēus adj see n.
Erebus, -ī m god of darkness; the lower world.
Erechtheus, -ēī m legendary king of Athens.
Erechthēus adj see n.
Erechthīdae mp Athenians
Erechthis, -idis f Orithyia; Procris.
ērēctus ppp of **ērigō** ♦ adj upright, lofty; noble,
haughty; alert, tense; resolute.
ērēpō, -ere, -sī vi to creep out, clamber up ♦
vt to crawl over, climb.
ēreptiō, -ōnis seizure, robbery.
ēreptor, -ōris m robber.
ēreptus ppp of **ēripiō.**
ergā prep (with acc) towards; against.
ergastulum, -ī nt prison (esp for slaves); (pl)
convicts.
ergō adv therefore, consequently; (questions,
commands) then, so; (resuming) well then;
(with gen) for the sake of, because of.
Erichthonius, -ī m a king of Troy; a king of
Athens ♦ adj Trojan; Athenian.
ēricius, -ī and **iī** m hedgehog; (MIL) beam with
iron spikes.
Ēridanus, -ī m mythical name of river Po.
erifuga, -ae m runaway slave.
ērigō, -igere, -ēxī, -ēctum vt to make
upright, raise up, erect; to excite; to
encourage.
Ērigonē, -ēs f (constellation) Virgo.
Ērigonēius adj see n.

erīlis _adj_ the master's, the mistress's.

Erīnȳs, -yos _f_ Fury; (_fig_) curse, frenzy.

Eriphȳla, -ae _f_ mother of Alcmaeon (_who killed her_).

ēripiō, -ipere, -ipuī, -eptum _vt_ to tear away, pull away, take by force; to rob; to rescue; **sē ~ escape.**

ērogātiō, -ōnis _f_ paying out.

ērogitō, -āre _vt_ to enquire.

ērogō, -āre, -āvī, -ātum _vt_ to pay out, expend; to bequeath.

errābundus _adj_ wandering.

errāticus _adj_ roving, shifting.

errātiō, -ōnis _f_ wandering, roving.

errātum, -ī _nt_ mistake, error.

errātus, -ūs _m_ wandering.

errō, -āre, -āvī, -ātum _vi_ to wander, stray, lose one's way; to waver; to make a mistake, err ♦ _vt_ to traverse; **stēllae ~antēs** planets.

errō, -ōnis _m_ vagabond.

error, -ōris _m_ wandering; meander, maze; uncertainty; error, mistake, delusion; deception.

ērubēscō, -ēscere, -uī _vi_ to blush; to feel ashamed ♦ _vt_ to blush for, be ashamed of; to respect.

ērūca, -ae _f_ colewort.

ēructō, -āre _vt_ to belch, vomit; to talk drunkenly about; to throw up.

ērudiō, -īre, -iī, -ītum _vt_ to educate, instruct.

ērudītē _adv_ learnedly.

ērudītiō, -ōnis _f_ education, instruction; learning, knowledge.

ērudītulus _adj_ somewhat skilled.

ērudītus _ppp of_ **ērudiō** ♦ _adj_ learned, educated, accomplished.

ērumpō, -umpere, -ūpī, -uptum _vt_ to break open; to make break out ♦ _vi_ to burst out, break through; to end (in).

ēruō, -ere, -ī, -tum _vt_ to uproot, tear out; to demolish, destroy; to elicit, draw out; to rescue.

ēruptiō, -ōnis _f_ eruption; (_MIL_) sally.

ēruptus _ppp of_ **ērumpō**.

erus, -ī _m_ master (of the house); owner.

ērutus _ppp of_ **ēruō**.

ervum, -ī _nt_ vetch.

Erycīnus _adj_ of Eryx; of Venus; Sicilian ♦ _f_ Venus.

Erymanthius, -is _adj see n._

Erymanthus _and_ **-ī** _m_ mountain range in Arcadia, (_where Hercules killed the bear_).

Eryx, -cis _m_ town and mountain in the extreme W. of Sicily.

esca, -ae _f_ food, tit-bits; bait.

escārius _adj_ of food; of bait ♦ _ntpl_ dishes.

ēscendō, -endere, -endī, -ēnsum _vi_ to climb up, go up ♦ _vt_ to mount.

ēscēnsiō, -ōnis _f_ raid (from the coast); disembarkation.

esculentus _adj_ edible, tasty.

Esquiliae, -iārum _fpl_ Esquiline hill in Rome.

Esquilīnus _adj_ Esquiline ♦ _f_ Esquiline gate.

essedārius, -ī _and_ **ī** _m_ chariot fighter.

essedum, -ī _nt_ war chariot.

essitō, -āre _vt_ to usually eat.

ēst _pres of_ **edō**.

ēstrix, -īcis _f_ glutton.

ēsuriālis _adj_ of hunger.

ēsuriō, -īre, -ītum _vi_ to be hungry ♦ _vt_ to hunger for.

ēsurītiō, -ōnis _f_ hunger.

ēsus _ppp of_ **edō**.

et _conj_ and; (_repeated_) both ... and; (_adding emphasis_) in fact, yes; (_comparing_) as, than ♦ _adv_ also, too; even.

etenim _conj_ (_adding an explanation_) and as a matter of fact, in fact.

etēsiae, -ārum _fpl_ Etesian winds.

etēsius _adj see n._

ēthologus, -ī _m_ mimic.

etiam _adv_ also, besides; (_emphatic_) even, actually; (_affirming_) yes, certainly; (_indignant_) really!; (_time_) still, as yet; again; ~ atque ~ again and again; ~ cavēs! do be careful!; **nihil ~** nothing at all.

etiamdum _adv_ still, as yet.

etiamnum, etiamnunc _adv_ still, till now, till then; besides.

etiamsī _conj_ even if, although.

etiamtum, etiamtunc _adv_ till then, still.

Etrūria, -ae _f_ district of Italy north of Rome.

Etruscus _adj_ Etruscan.

etsī _conj_ even if, though; and yet.

etymologia, -ae _f_ etymology.

eu _interj_ well done!, bravo!

Euan _m_ Bacchus.

Euander _and_ **rus, -rī** _m_ Evander (_ancient king on the site of Rome_).

Euandrius _adj see n._

euax _interj_ hurrah!

Euboea, -oeae _f_ Greek island.

Euboicus _adj_ Euboean.

euge, eugepae _interj_ bravo!, cheers!

Euhan _m_ Bacchus.

euhāns, -antis _adj_ shouting the Bacchic cry.

Euhias _f_ Bacchante.

Euhius, -ī _m_ Bacchus.

euhoe _interj_ ecstatic cry of Bacchic revellers.

Euius, -ī _m_ Bacchus.

Eumenidēs, -um _fpl_ Furies.

eunūchus, -ī _m_ eunuch.

Euphrātēs, -is _m_ river Euphrates.

Eupolis, -dis _m_ Athenian comic poet.

Eurīpidēs, -is _m_ Athenian tragic poet.

Eurīpidēus _adj see n._

Eurīpus, -ī _m_ strait between Euboea and mainland; a channel, conduit.

Eurōpa, -ae _and_ **ē, -ēs** _f_ mythical princess of Tyre (_who was carried by a bull to Crete_); continent of Europe.

Eurōpaeus _adj see n._

Eurōtās, -ae _m_ river of Sparta.

Eurōus _adj_ eastern.

Eurus, -ī _m_ east wind; south-east wind.

Eurydicē, -ēs _f_ wife of Orpheus.

Eurystheus, -eī m king of Mycenae (who imposed the labours on Hercules).
euschēmē adv gracefully.
Euterpē, -ēs f Muse of music.
Euxīnus m the Black (Sea).
ēvādō, -dere, -sī, -sum vi to come out; to climb up; to escape; to turn out: result, come true ♦ vt to pass, mount; to escape from.
ēvagor, -ārī, -ātus vi (MIL) to manœuvre; (fig) to spread ♦ vt to stray beyond
ēvalēscō, -ēscere, -uī vi to grow, ir crease; to be able; to come into vogue.
Ēvander etc see **Euander.**
ēvānēscō, -ēscere, -uī vi to vanish die away, lose effect.
ēvangelium, -ī and **iī** nt (ECCL) Gospel.
ēvānidus adj vanishing.
ēvāsī perf of **ēvādō.**
ēvastō, -āre vt to devastate.
ēvehō, -here, -xī, -ctum vt to carry, cut; to raise up, exalt; to spread abroad ± (pass) to ride, sail, move out.
ēvellō, -ellere, -ellī, -ulsum v - out, pull out; to eradicate.
ēveniō, -enīre, -ēnī, -entum vi to come out; to turn out, result; to come to pass: happen, befall.
ēventum, -ī nt result, issue; occurrence, event; fortune, experience.
ēventus, -ūs m result, issue; success; fortune, fate.
ēverberō, -āre vt to beat violently.
ēverriculum, -ī nt dragnet.
ēverrō, -rere, -rī, -sum vt to sweep out, clean out.
ēversiō, -ōnis f overthrow, destruction.
ēversor, -ōris m destroyer.
ēversus ppp of **ēverrō;** ppp of **ēvertō.**
ēvertō, -tere, -tī, -sum vt to turn out, eject; to turn up, overturn; to overthrow, ruin, destroy.
ēvestīgātus adj tracked down.
ēvictus ppp of **ēvincō.**
ēvidēns, -entis adj visible, plain, evident.
ēvidenter adv see **evidēns.**
ēvidentia, -ae f distinctness.
ēvigilō, -āre, -āvī, -ātum vi to be wide awake ♦ vt to compose carefully.
ēvīlēscō, -ere vi to become worthless
ēvinciō, -cīre, -xī, -ctum vt to garland, crown.
ēvincō, -incere, -īcī, -ictum vt to overcome, conquer; to prevail over; to prove.
ēvirō, -āre vt to castrate.
ēviscerō, -āre vt to disembowel, tear to pieces.
ēvītābilis adj avoidable.
ēvītō, -āre, -āvī, -ātum vt to avoid, clear.
ēvocātī, -ōrum mpl veteran volunteers.
ēvocātor, -ōris m enlister.

ēvocō, -āre, -āvī, -ātum vt to call out, summon; to challenge; to call up; to call forth, evoke.
ēvolō, -āre, -āvī, -ātum vi to fly out, fly away; to rush out; (fig) to rise, soar.
ēvolūtiō, -ōnis f unrolling (a book).
ēvolvō, -vere, -vī, -ūtum vt to roll out, roll along; to unroll, unfold; (book) to open, read; (fig) to disclose, unravel, disentangle.
ēvomō, -ere, -uī, -itum vt to vomit up, disgorge.
ēvulgō, -āre, -āvī, -ātum vt to divulge, make public.
ēvulsiō, -ōnis f pulling out.
ēvulsus ppp of **ēvellō.**
ex, ē prep (with abl) (place) out of, from, down from; (person) from; (time) after, immediately after, since; (change) from being; (source, material) of; (cause) by reason of, through; (conformity) in accordance with; **ex itinere** on the march; **ex parte** in part; **ex quō** since; **ex rē, ex ūsū** for the good of; **ē rē pūblicā** constitutionally; **ex sententiā** to one's liking; **aliud ex aliō** one thing after another; **ūnus ex** one of.
exacerbō, -āre vt to exasperate.
exāctiō, -ōnis f expulsion; supervision; tax; (debts) calling in.
exāctor, -ōris m expeller; superintendent; tax collector.
exāctus ppp cf **exigō** ♦ adj precise, exact.
exacuō, -uere, -uī, -ūtum vt to sharpen; (fig) to quicken, inflame.
exadversum, -us adv, prep (with acc) right opposite.
exaedificātiō, -ōnis f construction.
exaedificō, -āre vt to build up; to finish the building of.
exaequātiō, -ōnis f levelling.
exaequō, -āre, -āvī, -ātum vt to level out; to compensate; to put on an equal footing; to equal.
exaestuō, -āre vi to boil up.
exaggerātiō, -ōnis f exaltation.
exaggerō, -āre, -āvī, -ātum vt to pile up; (fig) to heighten, enhance.
exagitātor, -ōris m critic.
exagitō, -āre, -āvī, -ātum vt to disturb, harass; to scold, censure; to excite, incite.
exagōga, -ae f export.
exalbēscō, -ēscere, -uī vi to turn quite pale.
exāmen, -inis nt swarm, crowd; tongue of a balance; examining.
examinō, -āre, -āvī, -ātum vt to weigh; to consider, test.
examussim adv exactly, perfectly.
exanclō, -āre vt to drain; to endure to the end.
exanimālis adj dead; deadly.
exanimātiō, -ōnis f panic.
exanimis adj lifeless, breathless, terrified.

Noun declensions and verb conjugations are shown on pp xiii to xxv. The present infinitive ending of a verb shows to which conjugation it belongs: -**āre** = 1st; -**ēre** = 2nd; -**ere** = 3rd and -**īre** = 4th. Irregular verbs are shown on p xxvi

exanimō, -āre, -āvī, -ātum *vt* to wind; to kill; to terrify, agitate; (*pass*) to be out of breath.

exanimus *see* **exanimis.**

exārdēscō, -dēscere, -sī, -sum *vi* to catch fire, blaze up; (*fig*) to be inflamed, break out.

exārēscō, -ēscere, -uī *vi* to dry, dry up.

exarmō, -āre *vt* to disarm.

exarō, -āre, -āvi, -ātum *vt* to plough up; to cultivate, produce; (*brow*) to furrow; (*writing*) to pen.

exārsī *perf of* **exārdēscō.**

exasciātus *adj* hewn out.

exasperō, -āre, -āvī, -ātum *vt* to roughen; (*fig*) to provoke.

exauctōrō, -āre, -āvī, -ātum *vt* (*MIL*) to discharge, release; to cashier.

exaudiō, -īre, -īvī, -ītum *vt* to hear clearly; to listen to; to obey.

exaugeō, -ēre *vt* to increase.

exaugurātiō, -ōnis *f* desecrating.

exaugurō, -āre *vt* to desecrate.

exauspicō, -āre *vi* to take an omen.

exbibō *etc see* **ēbibō.**

excaecō, -āre *vt* to blind; (*river*) to block up.

excandēscentia, -ae *f* growing anger.

excandēscō, -ēscere, -uī *vi* to burn, be inflamed.

excantō, -āre *vt* to charm out, spirit away.

excarnificō, -āre *vt* to tear to pieces.

excavō, -āre *vt* to hollow out.

excēdō, -ēdere, -essī, -essum *vi* to go out, go away; to die, disappear; to advance, proceed (to); to digress ◆ *vt* to leave; to overstep, exceed.

excellēns, -entis *pres p of* **excellō** ◆ *adj* outstanding, excellent.

excellenter *adv see* **excellēns.**

excellentia, -ae *f* superiority, excellence.

excellō, -ere *vi* to be eminent, excel.

excelsē *adv* loftily.

excelsitās, -ātis *f* loftiness.

excelsum, -ī *nt* height.

excelsus *adj* high, elevated; eminent, illustrious.

exceptiō, -ōnis *f* exception, restriction; (*law*) objection.

exceptō, -āre *vt* to catch, take out.

exceptus *ppp of* **excipiō.**

excernō, -ernere, -rēvī, -rētum *vt* to sift out, separate.

excerpō, -ere, -sī, -tum *vt* to take out; to select, copy out extracts; to leave out, omit.

excessus, -ūs *m* departure, death.

excetra, -ae *f* snake.

excidiō, -ōnis *f* destruction.

excidium, -ī *and* **iī** *nt* overthrow, destruction.

excidō, -ere, -ī *vi* to fall out, fall; (*speech*) to slip out, escape; (*memory*) to get forgotten, escape; (*person*) to fail, lose; (*things*) to disappear, be lost.

excīdō, -dere, -dī, -sum *vt* to cut off, hew out, fell; to raze; (*fig*) to banish.

excieō *vt see* **exciō.**

exciō, -īre, -īvī *and* **iī, -itum** *and* **ītum** *vt* to call out, rouse, summon; to occasion, produce; to excite.

excipiō, -ipere, -ēpī, -eptum *vt* to take out, remove; to exempt, make an exception of, mention specifically; to take up, catch, intercept, overhear; to receive, welcome, entertain; to come next to, follow after, succeed.

excīsiō, -ōnis *f* destroying.

excīsus *ppp of* **excīdō.**

excitātus *adj* loud, strong.

excitō, -āre, -āvī, -ātum *vt* to rouse, wake up, summon; to raise, build; to call on (to stand up); (*fig*) to encourage, revive, excite.

excitus, excītus *ppp of* **exciō.**

exclāmātiō, -ōnis *f* exclamation.

exclāmō, -āre, -āvī, -ātum *vi* to cry out, shout ◆ *vt* to exclaim, call.

exclūdō, -dere, -sī, -sum *vt* to shut out, exclude; to shut off, keep off; (*egg*) to hatch out; (*eye*) to knock out; (*fig*) to prevent, except.

exclūsiō, -ōnis *f* shutting out.

exclūsus *ppp of* **exclūdō.**

excoctus *ppp of* **excoquō.**

excōgitātiō, -ōnis *f* thinking out, devising.

excōgitō, -āre, -āvī, -ātum *vt* to think out, contrive.

excolō, -olere, -oluī, -ultum *vt* to work carefully; to perfect, refine.

excoquō, -quere, -xī, -ctum *vt* to boil away; to remove with heat, make with heat; to dry up.

excors, -dis *adj* senseless, stupid.

excrēmentum, -ī *nt* excretion.

excreō *etc see* **exscreō.**

excrēscō, -scere, -vī, -tum *vi* to grow, rise up.

excrētus *ppp of* **excernō.**

excruciō, -āre, -āvī, -ātum *vt* to torture, torment.

excubiae, -ārum *fpl* keeping guard, watch; sentry.

excubitor, -ōris *m* sentry.

excubō, -āre, -uī, -itum *vi* to sleep out of doors; to keep watch; (*fig*) to be on the alert.

excūdō, -dere, -dī, -sum *vt* to strike out, hammer out; (*egg*) to hatch; (*fig*) to make, compose.

exculcō, -āre *vt* to beat, tramp down.

excultus *ppp of* **excolō.**

excurrō, -rrere, -currī *and* **rrī, -rsum** *vi* to run out, hurry out; to make an excursion; (*MIL*) to make a sortie; (*place*) to extend, project; (*fig*) to expand.

excursiō, -ōnis *f* raid, sortie; (*gesture*) stepping forward; (*fig*) outset.

excursor, -ōris *m* scout.

excursus, -ūs *m* excursion, raid, charge.

excūsābilis *adj* excusable.

excūsātē *adv* excusably.

excūsātiō, -ōnis *f* excuse, plea.

excūsō, -āre, -āvī, -ātum vt to excuse; to apologize for; to plead as an excuse.

excussus ppp of **excutiō**.

excūsus ppp of **excūdō**.

excutiō, -tere, -ssī, -ssum vt to shake out, shake off; to knock out, drive out, cast off; (fig) to discard, banish; to examine, inspect.

exdorsuō, -āre vt to fillet.

exec- etc see **exsec-**.

exedō, -esse, -ēdī, -ēsum vt to eat up; to wear away, destroy; (feelings) to prey on.

exedra, -ae f hall, lecture room.

exedrium, -ī and **iī** nt sitting room.

exēmī perf of **eximō**.

exemplar, -āris nt copy; likeness; model, ideal.

exemplārēs mpl copies.

exemplum, -ī nt copy; example, sample, precedent, pattern; purport, example; warning, object lesson; ~ dare set an example; ~ī causā, gratiā for instance.

exemptus ppp of **eximō**.

exenterō, -āre vt (comedy) to empty, clean out; to torture.

exeō, -īre, -iī, -itum vi to go out, leave; to come out, issue; (MIL) to march out; (time) to expire; to spring up, rise ♦ vt to pass beyond; to avoid; ~ ex potestāte lose control.

exeq- etc see **exseq-**.

exerceō, -ēre, -uī, -itum vt to keep busy, supervise; (ground) to work, cultivate; (MIL) to drill, exercise; (mind) to engage, employ; (occupation) to practise, follow, carry on; (trouble) to worry, harass; sē ~ practise, exercise.

exercitātiō, -ōnis f practice, exercise, experience.

exercitātus adj practised, trained, versed; troubled.

exercitium, -ī and **iī** nt exercising.

exercitō, -āre vt to exercise.

exercitor, -ōris m trainer.

exercitus ppp of **exerceō** ♦ adj disciplined; troubled; troublesome.

exercitus, -ūs m army (esp the infantry); assembly; troop, flock; exercise.

exerō etc see **exserō**.

exēsor, -ōris m corroder.

exēsus ppp of **exedō**.

exhālātiō, -ōnis f vapour.

exhālō, -āre vt to exhale, breathe out ♦ vi to steam; to expire.

exhauriō, -rīre, -sī, -stum vt to drain off; to empty; to take away, remove; (fig) to exhaust, finish; (trouble) to undergo, endure to the end.

exhērēdō, -āre vt to disinherit.

exhērēs, -ēdis adj disinherited.

exhibeō, -ere, -uī, -itum vt to hold out, produce (in public); to display, show; to

cause, occasion.

exhilarātus adj delighted.

exhorrēscō, -ēscere, -uī vi to be terrified ♦ vt to be terrified at.

exhortātiō, -ōnis f encouragement.

exhortor -ārī, -ātus vt to encourage.

exigō, -igere, -ēgī, -āctum vt to drive out, thrust; (payment) to exact, enforce; to demand, claim; (goods) to dispose of; (time) to pass, complete; (work) to finish; (news) to ascertain; to test, examine, consider.

exiguē adv briefly, slightly, hardly.

exiguitās, -ātis f smallness, meagreness.

exiguus adj small, short, meagre ♦ nt a little bit.

exiliō etc see **exsiliō**.

exīlis adj thin, small, meagre; poor; (style) flat, insipid.

exīlitās, -ātis f thinness, meagreness.

exīliter adv feebly.

exilium etc see **exsilium**.

exim see **exinde**.

eximiē adv exceptionally.

eximius adj exempt; select; distinguished, exceptional.

eximō, -imere, -ēmī, -emptum vt to take out, remove; to release, free; to exempt; (time) to waste; (fig) to banish.

exin see **exinde**.

exināniō, -īre, -iī, -ītum vt to empty; to pillage.

exinde adv (place) from there, next; (time) then, thereafter, next; (measure) accordingly.

exīstimātiō, -ōnis f opinion, judgment; reputation, character; (money) credit.

exīstimātor, -ōris m judge, critic.

exīstimō, -āre, -āvī, -ātum vt to value, estimate, judge, think, consider.

existō etc see **exsistō**.

exīstumō vt see **exīstimō**.

exitiābilis adj deadly, fatal.

exitiālis adj deadly.

exitiōsus adj pernicious, fatal.

exitium, -ī and **iī** nt destruction, ruin.

exitus, -ūs m departure; way out, outlet; conclusion, end; death; outcome, result.

exlēx, -ēgis adj above the law, lawless.

exoculō, -āre vt to knock the eyes out of.

exodium, -ī and **iī** nt afterpiece.

exolēscō, -scere, -vī, -tum vi to decay, become obsolete.

exolētus adj full-grown.

exonerō, -āre, -āvī, -ātum vt to unload, discharge; (fig) to relieve, exonerate.

exoptātus adj welcome.

exoptō, -āre, -āvī, -ātum vt to long for, desire.

exōrābilis adj sympathetic.

exōrātor, -ōris m successful pleader.

Noun declensions and verb conjugations are shown on pp xiii to xxv. The present infinitive ending of a verb shows to which conjugation it belongs: **-āre** = 1st; **-ēre** = 2nd; **-ere** = 3rd and **-īre** = 4th. Irregular verbs are shown on p xxvi

exōrdior, -dīrī, -sus *vt* to lay the warp; to begin.

exōrdium, -ī *and* **iī** *nt* beginning; (*RHET*) introductory section.

exorior, -īrī, -tus *vi* to spring up, come out, rise; to arise, appear, start.

exōrnātiō, -ōnis *f* embellishment.

exōrnātor, -ōris *m* embellisher.

exōrnō, -āre, -āvī, -ātum *vt* to equip, fit out; to embellish, adorn.

exōrō, -āre, -āvī, -ātum *vt* to prevail upon, persuade; to obtain, win by entreaty.

exōrsus *ppa of* **exōrdior** ♦ *adj* begun ♦ *ntpl* preamble.

exōrsus, -ūs *m* beginning.

exortus *ppa of* **exorior.**

exortus, -ūs *m* rising; east.

exos, -ossis *adj* boneless.

exōsculor, -ārī, -ātus *vt* to kiss fondly.

exossō, -āre *vt* to bone.

exōstra, -ae *f* stage mechanism; (*fig*) public.

exōsus *adj* detesting.

exōticus *adj* foreign.

expallēscō, -ēscere, -uī *vi* to turn pale, be afraid.

expalpō, -āre *vt* to coax out.

expandō, -ere *vt* to unfold.

expatrō, -āre *vt* to squander.

expavēscō, -ere, expāvī *vi* to be terrified ♦ *vt* to dread.

expect- *etc see* **exspect-.**

expediō, -īre, -īvī *and* **iī, -ītum** *vt* to free, extricate, disentangle; to prepare, clear (for action); to put right, settle; to explain, relate; (*impers*) it is useful, expedient.

expedītē *adv* readily, freely.

expedītiō, -ōnis *f* (*MIL*) expedition, enterprise.

expedītus *ppp of* **expediō** ♦ *adj* light-armed; ready, prompt; at hand ♦ *m* light-armed soldier; **in ~ō esse, habēre** be, have in readiness.

expellō, -ellere, -ulī, -ulsum *vt* to drive away, eject, expel; to remove, repudiate.

expendō, -endere, -endī, -ēnsum *vt* to weigh out; to pay out; (*penalty*) to suffer; (*mind*) to ponder, consider, judge.

expēnsum, -ī *nt* payment, expenditure.

expergēfaciō, -facere, -fēcī, -factum *vt* to rouse, excite.

expergīscor, -gīscī, -rēctus *vi* to wake up; to bestir oneself.

expergō, -ere, -ī, -itum *vt* to awaken.

experiēns, -entis *pres p of* **experior** ♦ *adj* enterprising.

experientia, -ae *f* experiment; endeavour; experience, practice.

experimentum, -ī *nt* proof, test; experience.

experior, -īrī, -tus *vt* to test, make trial of; to attempt, experience; (*law*) to go to law; (*perf tenses*) to know from experience.

experrēctus *ppa of* **expergīscor.**

expers, -tis *adj* having no part in, not sharing; free from, without.

expertus *ppa of* **experior** ♦ *adj* proved, tried; experienced.

expetessō, -ere *vt* to desire.

expetō, -ere, -īvī *and* **iī, -ītum** *vt* to aim at, tend towards; to desire, covet; to attack; to demand, require ♦ *vi* to befall, happen.

expiātiō, -ōnis *f* atonement.

expictus *ppr of* **expingō.**

expīlātiō, -ōnis *f* pillaging.

expīlātor, -ōris *m* plunderer.

expīlō, -āre, -āvī, -ātum *vt* to rob, plunder.

expingō, -ingere, -inxī, -ictum *vt* to portray.

expiō, -āre, -āvī, -ātum *vt* to purify; to atone for, make amends for; to avert (evil).

expīrō *etc see* **exspīrō.**

expiscor, -ērī, -ātus *vt* to try to find out, ferret out.

explānātē *adv see* **explānātus.**

explānātiō, -ōnis *f* explanation.

explānātor, -ōris *m* interpreter.

explānātus *adj* distinct.

explānō, -āre, -āvī, -ātum *vt* to state clearly, explain; to pronounce clearly.

explaudō *etc see* **explōdō.**

explēmentum, -ī *nt* filling.

expleō, -ēre, -ēvī, -ētum *vt* to fill up; to complete; (*desire*) to satisfy, appease; (*duty*) to perform, discharge; (*loss*) to make good; (*time*) to fulfil, complete.

explētiō, -ōnis *f* satisfying.

explētus *ppp of* **expleō** ♦ *adj* complete.

explicātē *adv* plainly.

explicātiō, -ōnis *f* uncoiling; expounding, analyzing.

explicātor, -ōris *m*, **-rīx, -rīcis** *f* expounder.

explicātus *adj* spread out; plain, clear.

explicātus, -ūs *m* explanation.

explicitus *adj* easy.

explicō, -āre, -āvī *and* **uī, -ātum** *and* **itum** *vt* to unfold, undo, spread out; (*book*) to open; (*MIL*) to deploy, extend; (*difficulty*) to put in order, settle; (*speech*) to develop, explain; to set free.

explōdō, -dere, -sī, -sum *vt* to hiss off, drive away; (*fig*) to reject.

explōrātē *adv* with certainty.

explōrātiō, -ōnis *f* spying.

explōrātor, -ōris *m* spy, scout.

explōrātus *adj* certain, sure.

explōrō, -āre, -āvī, -ātum *vt* to investigate, reconnoitre; to ascertain; to put to the test.

explōsī *perf of* **explōdō.**

explōsiō, -ōnis *f* driving off (the stage).

explōsus *ppp of* **explōdō.**

expoliō, -īre, -īvī, -ītum *vt* to smooth off, polish; (*fig*) to refine, embellish.

expolītiō, -ōnis *f* smoothing off; polish, finish.

expōnō, -ēnere, -osuī, -ositum *vt* to set out, put out; (*child*) to expose; (*NAUT*) to disembark; (*money*) to offer; (*fig*) to set forth, expose, display; (*speech*) to explain, expound.

exporrigō, -igere, -ēxī, -ēctum *vt* to extend, smooth out.

exportātiō, -ōnis *f* exporting

exportō, -āre, -āvī, -ātum *vt* to carry out, export.

exposcō, -ere, expoposcī *vt* to implore, pray for; to demand.

expositīcius *adj* foundling.

expositiō, -ōnis *f* narration, explanation.

expositus *ppp of* **expōnō ♦** *adj* open, affable; vulgar.

expostulātiō, -ōnis *f* complaint

expostulō, -āre, -āvī, -ātum *vt* to demand urgently; to complain of, expostulate.

expōtus *ppp of* **ēpōtō.**

expressus *ppp of* **exprimō ♦** *adj* distinct, prominent.

exprimō, -imere, -essī, -essum *vt* to squeeze out, force out; to press up; (*fig*) to extort, wrest; (*art*) to mould, model; (*words*) to imitate, portray, translate pronounce.

exprobrātiō, -ōnis *f* reproach.

exprobrō, -āre, -āvī, -ātum *vt* to reproach, cast up.

exprōmō, -ere, -psī, -ptum *vt* to bring out, fetch out; (*acts*) to exhibit, practise; (*feelings*) to give vent to; (*speech*) to disclose, state.

expugnābilis *adj* capable of being taken by storm.

expugnācior, -ōris *adj* more effective.

expugnātiō, -ōnis *f* storming, assault.

expugnātor, -ōris *m* stormer.

expugnō, -āre, -āvī, -ātum *vt* to storm, reduce; to conquer; (*fig*) to overcome, extort.

expulī *perf of* **expellō.**

expulsiō, -ōnis *f* expulsion.

expulsor, -ōris *m* expeller.

expulsus *ppp of* **expellō.**

expultrīx, -īcis *f* expeller.

expungō, -ungere, -ūnxī, -ūnctum *vt* to prick out, cancel.

expūrgātiō, -ōnis *f* excuse.

expūrgō, -āre *vt* to purify; to justify.

exputō, -āre *vt* to consider, comprehend.

exquīrō, -rere, -sīvī, -sītum *vt* to search out, investigate; to inquire; to devise.

exquīsītē *adv* with particular care.

exquīsītus *ppp of* **exquīrō ♦** *adj* well thought out, choice.

exsaeviō, -īre *vi* to cease raging.

exsanguis *adj* bloodless, pale; feeble.

exsarciō, -cīre, -tum *vt* to repair.

exsatiō, -āre *vt* to satiate, satisfy.

exsaturābilis *adj* appeasable.

exsaturō, -āre *vt* to satiate.

exsce- *etc see* **esce-.**

exscindō, -ndere, -dī, -ssum *vt* to extirpate.

exscreō, -āre *vt* to cough up.

exscrībō, -bere, -psī, -ptum *vt* to copy out; to note down.

exsculpō, -ere, -sī, -tum *vt* to carve out; to erase; (*fig*) to extort.

exsecō, -āre, -uī, -tum *vt* to cut out; to castrate.

exsecrābilis *adj* cursing, deadly.

exsecrātiō, -ōnis *f* curse; solemn oath.

exsecrātus *adj* accursed.

exsecror, -ārī, -ātus *vt* to curse; to take an oath.

exsectiō, -ōnis *f* cutting out.

exsecūtiō, -ōnis *f* management; discussion.

exsecūtus *ppa of* **exsequor.**

exsequiae, -ārum *fpl* funeral, funeral rites.

exsequiālis *adj* funeral.

exsequor, -quī, -cūtus *vt* to follow, pursue; to follow to the grave; (*duty*) to carry out, accomplish; (*speech*) to describe, relate; (*suffering*) to undergo; (*wrong*) to avenge, punish.

exserciō *vt see* **exsarciō.**

exserō, -ere, -uī, -tum *vt* to put out, stretch out; to reveal.

exsertō, -āre *vt* to stretch out repeatedly.

exsertus *ppp of* **exserō ♦** *adj* protruding.

exsībilō, -āre *vt* to hiss off.

exsiccātus *adj* (*style*) uninteresting.

exsiccō, -āre, -āvī, -ātum *vt* to dry up; to drain.

exsicō *etc see* **exsecō.**

exsignō, -āre *vt* to write down in detail.

exsiliō, -īre, -uī *vi* to jump up, spring out; to start.

exsilium, -ī *and* **iī** *nt* banishment, exile; retreat.

exsistō, -istere, -titī, -titum *vi* to emerge, appear; to arise, spring (from); to be, exist.

exsolvō, -vere, -vī, -ūtum *vt* to undo, loosen, open; to release, free; to get rid of, throw off; (*debt, promise*) to discharge, fulfil, pay up; (*words*) to explain.

exsomnis *adj* sleepless, watchful.

exsorbeō, -ēre, -uī *vt* to suck, drain; to devour, endure.

exsors, -tis *adj* chosen, special; free from.

exspargō *etc see* **exspergō.**

exspatior, -ārī, -ātus *vi* to go off the course.

exspectābilis *adj* to be expected.

exspectātiō, -ōnis *f* waiting, expectation.

exspectātus *adj* looked for, welcome.

exspectō, -āre, -āvī, -ātum *vt* to wait for, till; to see; to expect; to hope for, dread; to require.

exspergō, -gere, -sum *vt* to scatter; to diffuse.

exspēs *adj* despairing.

exspīrātiō, -ōnis *f* exhalation.

exspīrō, -āre, -āvī, -ātum *vt* to breathe out, exhale; to emit **♦** *vi* to rush out; to expire, come to an end.

exsplendēscō, -ere *vi* to shine.

exspoliō, -āre *vt* to pillage.

exspuō, -uere, -uī, -ūtum *vt* to spit out, eject; (*fig*) to banish.

exsternō, -āre *vt* to terrify.

exstillō, -āre *vi* to drip.

exstimulātor, -ōris *m* instigator.

exstimulō, -āre *vt* to goad on; to excite.

exstinctiō, -ōnis *f* annihilation.

exstinctor, -ōris *m* extinguisher; destroyer.

exstinguō, -guere, -xī, -ctum *vt* to put out, extinguish; to kill, destroy, abolish.

exstirpō, -āre *vt* to root out, eradicate.

exstitī *perf of* **exsistō**.

exstō, -āre *vi* to stand out, project; to be conspicuous, be visible; to be extant, exist, be.

exstructiō, -ōnis *f* erection.

exstruō, -ere, -xī, -ctum *vt* to heap up; to build up, construct.

exsūdō, -āre *vi* to come out in sweat ♦ *vt* (*fig*) to toil through.

exsūgō, -gere, -xī, -ctum *vt* to suck out.

exsul, -is *m/f* exile.

exsulō, -āre, -āvī, -ātum *vi* to be an exile.

exsultātiō, -ōnis *f* great rejoicing.

exsultim *adv* friskily.

exsultō, -āre, -āvī, -ātum *vi* to jump up, prance; (*fig*) to exult, run riot, boast; (*speech*) to range at will.

exsuperābilis *adj* superable.

exsuperantia, -ae *f* superiority.

exsuperō, -āre, -āvi, -ātum *vi* to mount up; to gain the upper hand, excel ♦ *vt* to go over; to surpass; to overpower.

exsurdō, -āre *vt* to deafen; (*fig*) to dull.

exsurgō, -gere, -rēxī, -rēctum *vi* to rise, stand up; to recover.

exsuscitō, -āre *vt* to wake up; (*fire*) to fan; (*mind*) to excite.

exta, -ōrum *ntpl* internal organs.

extābēscō, -ēscere, -uī *vi* to waste away; to vanish.

extāris *adj* sacrificial.

extemplō *adv* immediately, on the spur of the moment; **quom ~** as soon as.

extemporālis *adj* extempore.

extempulō *see* **extemplō**.

extendō, -dere, -dī, -tum *and* **extēnsum** *vt* to stretch out, spread, extend; to enlarge, increase; (*time*) to prolong; **sē ~** exert oneself; **īre per ~tum fūnem** walk the tightrope.

extēnsus *ppp of* **extendō**.

extentō, -āre *vt* to strain, exert.

extentus *ppp of* **extendō** ♦ *adj* broad.

extenuātiō, -ōnis *f* (*RHET*) diminution.

extenuō, -āre, -āvī, -ātum *vt* to thin out, rarefy; to diminish, weaken.

exter *adj* from outside; foreign.

exterebrō, -āre *vt* to bore out; to extort.

extergeō, -gere, -sī, -sum *vt* to wipe off,

clean; to plunder.

exterior, -ōris *adj* outer, exterior.

exterius *adv* on the outside.

exterminō, -āre *vt* to drive out, banish; (*fig*) to put aside.

externus *adj* outward, external; foreign, strange.

exterō, -erere, -rīvī, -rītum *vt* to rub out, wear away

exterreō, -ēre, -uī, -itum *vt* to frighten.

extersus *ppp of* **extergeō**.

exterus *see* **exter**.

extexō, -ere *vt* to unweave; (*fig*) to cheat.

extimēscō, -ēscere, -uī *vi* to be very frightened ♦ *vt* to be very afraid of.

extimus *adj* outermost, farthest.

extin- *etc see* **exstin-**.

extispex, -icis *m* diviner.

extollō, -ere *vt* to lift up, raise; (*fig*) to exalt, beautify; (*time*) to defer.

extorqueō, -quēre, -sī, -tum *vt* to wrench out, wrest; to dislocate; (*fig*) to obtain by force, extort.

extorris *adj* banished, in exile.

extortor, -ōris *m* extorter.

extortus *ppp of* **extorqueō**.

extrā *adv* outside; **~ quam** except that, unless ♦ *prep* (*with acc*) outside, beyond; free from; except.

extrahō, -here, -xī, -ctum *vt* to draw out, pull out; to extricate, rescue; to remove; (*time*) to prolong, waste.

extrāneus, -ī *m* stranger ♦ *adj* external, foreign.

extraōrdinārius *adj* special, unusual.

extrārius *adj* external; unrelated ♦ *m* stranger.

extrēmitās, -ātis *f* extremity, end.

extrēmum, -ī *nt* end; **ad ~** at last.

extrēmum *adv* for the last time.

extrēmus *adj* outermost, extreme; last; utmost, greatest, meanest.

extrīcō, -āre, -āvī, -ātum *vt* to disentangle, extricate; to clear up.

extrīnsecus *adv* from outside, from abroad; on the outside.

extrītus *ppp of* **exterō**.

extrūdō, -dere, -sī, -sum *vt* to drive out; to keep out; (*sale*) to push.

extulī *perf of* **efferō**.

extumeō, -ēre *vi* to swell up.

extundō, -undere, -udī, -ūsum *vt* to beat out, hammer out; (*comedy*) to extort; (*fig*) to form, compose.

exturbō, -āre, -āvī, -ātum *vt* to drive out, throw out, knock out; (*wife*) to put away; (*fig*) to banish, disturb.

exūberō, -āre *vi* to abound.

exul *etc see* **exsul**.

exulcerō, -āre, -āvī, -ātum *vt* to aggravate.

exululō, -āre *vi* to howl wildly ♦ *vt* to invoke with cries.

exūnctus *ppp of* **exungō**.

exundō, -āre vi to overflow; to be washed up.
exungō, -ere vt to anoint liberally.
exuō, -uere, -uī, -ūtum vt to draw out, put off; to lay aside; to strip.
exūrō, -rere, -ssī, -stum vt to burn up; to dry up; to burn out; (*fig*) to inflame.
exūstiō, -ōnis f conflagration.
exūtus ppp of **exuō**.
exuviae, -ārum fpl clothing, arms; hide; spoils.

F, f

faba, -ae f bean.
fabālis adj bean- (*in cpds*).
fābella, -ae f short story, fable; play.
faber, -rī m craftsman (*in metal, stone, wood*), tradesman, smith; (*MIL*) artisan; **~ errārius** blacksmith; **~ tignārius** carpenter ♦ adj skilful.
Fabius, -ī m Roman family name (*esp Q F Maximus Cunctator, dictator against Hannibal*).
Fabius, -iānus adj see n.
fabrē adv skilfully.
fabrēfaciō, -facere, -fēcī, -factum vt to make, build, forge.
fabrica, -ae f art, trade; work of art, workshop; (*comedy*) trick.
fabricātiō, -ōnis f structure.
fabricātor, -ōris m artificer.
Fabricius, -ī m Roman family name (*esp C F Luscinus, incorruptible commander against Pyrrhus*).
Fabricius, -iānus adj see n.
fabricō, -āre; -or, -ārī, -ātus vt, vi to make, build, forge.
fabrīlis adj artificer's ♦ ntpl tools.
fābula, -ae f story; common talk; play, drama; fable; **~ae!** nonsense!; **lupus in ~ā** = talk of the devil!
fābulor, -ārī, -ātus vi to talk, converse ♦ vt to say, invent.
fābulōsus adj legendary.
facessō, -ere, -īvī, -ītum vt to perform, carry out; to cause (trouble) ♦ vi to go away, retire.
facētē adv humorously; brilliantly.
facētiae, -ārum fpl wit, cleverness, humour.
facētus adj witty, humorous; fine, genteel, elegant.
faciēs, -ēī f form, shape; face, looks; appearance, aspect, character.

facile adv easily; unquestionably; readily; pleasantly.
facilis adj easy; well-suited; ready, quick; (*person*) good-natured, approachable; (*fortune*) prosperous.
facilitās, -ātis f ease, readiness; (*speech*) fluency; (*person*) good nature, affability.
facinorōsus adj criminal.
facinus, -oris nt deed, action; crime.
faciō, -ere, fēcī, factum (*imp* **fac**, *pass* **fīō**) vt to make, create, compose, cause; to do, perform; (*profession*) to practise; (*property*) to put under; (*value*) to regard, think of; (*words*) to represent, pretend, suppose ♦ vi to do, act; (*religion*) to offer sacrifice; (*with* **ad** *or* **dat**) to be of use; **cōpiam ~** afford an opportunity; **damnum ~** suffer loss; **metum ~** excite fear; **proelium ~** join battle; **rem ~** make money; **verba ~** talk; **māgnī ~** think highly of; **quid tibi faciam?** how am I to answer you?; **quid tē faciam?** what am I to do with you?; **fac sciam** let me know; **fac potuisse** suppose one could have.
factiō, -ōnis f making, doing; group, party, faction (*esp in politics and chariot racing*).
factiōsus adj facticus, oligarchical.
factitō, -āre, -āvī, -ātum vt to keep making or doing; to practise; to declare (to be).
factor, -ōris m (*sport*) batsman.
factum, -ī nt deed, exploit.
factus ppp of **faciō**.
facula, -ae f little torch.
facultās, -ātis f means, opportunity; ability; abundance, supply, resources.
fācundē adv see **fācundus**.
fācundia, -ae f eloquence.
fācundus adj fluent, eloquent.
faeceus adj impure.
faecula, -ae f wine lees.
faenebris adj of usury.
faenerātiō, -ōnis f usury.
faenerātō adv with interest.
faenerātor, -ōris m moneylender.
faenerō, -āre; -or, -ārī, -ātus vt to lend at interest; to ruin with usury; (*fig*) to trade in.
faenīlia, -um ntpl hayloft.
faenum, -ī nt hay; **~ habet in cornū** he is dangerous.
faenus, -oris nt interest; capital lent at interest; (*fig*) profit, advantage.
faenusculum, -ī nt a little interest.
Faesulae, -ārum fpl town in Etruria (*now Fiesole*).
Faesulānus adj see n.
faex, faecis f sediment, lees; brine (of pickles); (*fig*) dregs.
fāgineus, fāginus adj of beech.
fāgus, -ī f beech.
fala, -ae f siege tower, used in assaults; (*Circus*) pillar.

falārica, -ae *f* a missile, firebrand.
falcārius, -ī *and* **iī** *m* sicklemaker.
falcātus *adj* scythed; sickle-shaped.
falcifer, -ī *adj* scythe-carrying.
Falernus *adj* Falernian (*of a district in N.*
**Campania famous for its wine*) ♦ *nt* Falernian
wine.
Faliscī, -ōrum *mpl* a people of S.E. Etruria
(*with chief town Falerii*).
Faliscus *adj see n.*
fallācia, -ae *f* trick, deception.
fallāciter *adv see* **fallāx.**
fallāx, -ācis *adj* deceitful, deceptive.
fallō, -lere, fefellī, -sum *vt* to deceive, cheat,
beguile; to disappoint, fail, betray; (*promise*)
to break; to escape the notice of, be
unknown to; (*pass*) to be mistaken; **mē ~lit** I
am mistaken; I do not know.
falsē *adv* wrongly, by mistake; fraudulently.
falsidicus *adj* lying.
falsificus *adj* deceiving.
falsiiūrius *adj* perjurious.
falsiloquus *adj* lying.
falsiparēns, -entis *adj* with a pretended
father.
falsō *adv see* **falsē.**
falsus *ppp of* **fallō** ♦ *adj* false, mistaken;
deceitful; forged, falsified; sham, fictitious
♦ *nt* falsehood, error.
falx, falcis *f* sickle, scythe; pruning hook; (*MIL*)
siege hook.
fāma, -ae *f* talk, rumour, tradition; public
opinion; reputation, fame; infamy.
famēlicus *adj* hungry.
famēs, -is *f* hunger; famine; (*fig*) greed; (*RHET*)
poverty of expression.
fāmigerātiō, -ōnis *f* rumour.
fāmigerātor, -ōris *m* telltale.
familia, -ae *f* domestics, slaves of a
household; family property, estate; family,
house; school, sect; **pater ~ās** master of a
household; **~am dūcere** be head of a sect,
company *etc.*
familiāris *adj* domestic, household, family;
intimate, friendly; (*entrails*) relating to the
sacrificer ♦ *m* servant; friend.
familiāritās, -ātis *f* intimacy, friendship.
familiāriter *adv* on friendly terms.
fāmōsus *adj* celebrated; infamous;
slanderous.
famula, -ae *f* maidservant, handmaid.
famulāris *adj* of servants.
famulātus, -ūs *m* slavery.
famulor, -ārī *vi* to serve.
famulus, -ī *m* servant, attendant ♦ *adj*
serviceable.
fānāticus *adj* inspired; frantic, frenzied.
fandī *gerund of* **for.**
fandum, -ī *nt* right.
fānum, -ī *nt* sanctuary temple.
fār, farris *nt* spelt; corn; meal.
farciō, -cīre, -sī, -tum *vt* to stuff, fill full.
farīna, -ae *f* meal, flour.

farrāgō, -inis *f* mash, hotch-potch; medley.
farrātus *adj* of corn; filled with corn.
farsī *perf of* **farciō.**
fartem, -im *f acc* filling; mincemeat.
fartor, -ōris *m* fattener, poulterer.
fartus *ppp of* **farciō.**
fās *nt* divine law; right; **~ est** it is lawful,
possible.
fascia, -ae *f* band, bandage; streak of cloud.
fasciculus, -ī *m* bundle, packet.
fascinō, -āre *vt* to bewitch, (*esp with the evil
eye*).
fascinum, -ī *nt*, **-us, -ī** *m* charm.
fasciola, -ae *f* small bandage.
fascis, -is *m* bundle, faggot; soldier's pack,
burden; (*pl*) rods and axe carried before the
highest magistrates; high office (*esp the
consulship*).
fassus *ppa of* **fateor.**
fāstī, -ōrum *mpl* register of days for legal and
public business; calendar; registers of
magistrates and other public records.
fastīdiō, -īre, -iī, -ītum *vt* to loathe, dislike,
despise ♦ *vi* to feel squeamish, be disgusted;
to be disdainful.
fastīdiōsē *adv* squeamishly; disdainfully.
fastīdiōsus *adj* squeamish, disgusted;
fastidious, nice; disagreeable.
fastīdium, -ī *and* **iī** *nt* squeamishness, distaste;
disgust, aversion; disdain, pride.
fastīgātē *adv* in a sloping position.
fastīgātus *adj* sloping up *or* down.
fastīgium, -ī *and* **iī** *nt* gable, pediment; slope;
height, depth; top, summit; (*fig*) highest
degree, acme, dignity; (*speech*) main
headings.
fāstus *adj* lawful for public business.
fastus, -ūs *m* disdain, pride.
Fāta *ntpl* the Fates.
fātālis *adj* fateful, destined; fatal, deadly.
fātāliter *adv* by fate.
fateor, -tērī, -ssus *vt* to confess,
acknowledge; to reveal, bear witness to.
fāticanus, -inus *adj* prophetic.
fātidicus *adj* prophetic ♦ *m* prophet.
fātifer, -ī *adj* deadly.
fatīgātiō, -ōnis *f* weariness.
fatīgō, -āre, -āvī, -ātum *vt* to tire, exhaust; to
worry, importune; to wear down, torment.
fātiloqua, -ae *f* prophetess.
fatīscō, -ere; -or, -ī *vi* to crack, split; (*fig*) to
become exhausted.
fatuitās, -ātis *f* silliness.
fātum, -ī *nt* divine word, oracle; fate, destiny;
divine will; misfortune, doom, death; **~ō**
obīre die a natural death.
fātur, fātus *3rd pers, ppa of* **for.**
fatuus *adj* silly; unwieldy ♦ *m* fool.
faucēs, -ium *fpl* throat; pass, narrow channel,
chasm; (*fig*) jaws.
Faunus, -ī *m* father of Latinus (*god of forests
and herdsmen, identified with Pan*); (*pl*)
woodland spirits, Fauns.

fauste adv see **faustus**.
faustitās, -ātis f good fortune, fertility.
faustus adj auspicious, lucky.
fautor, -ōris m supporter, patron.
fautrīx, -īcis f protectress.
favea, -ae f pet slave.
faveō, -ēre, fāvī, fautum vi (with dat) to favour, befriend, support; ~ **linguīs** keep silence.
favilla, -ae f embers, ashes; (fig) spark.
favitor etc see **fautor**.
Favōnius, -ī m west wind, zephyr.
favor, -ōris m favour, support; applause.
favōrābilis adj in favour; pleasing.
favus, -ī m honeycomb.
fax, facis f torch, wedding torch, funeral torch; marriage, death; (ASTRO) meteor; (fig) flame, fire, instigator; guide; **facem praeferre** act as guide.
faxim, faxō old subj and fut of **faciō**.
febrīcula, -ae f slight fever.
febris, -is f fever.
Februārius, -ī m February ♦ adj of February.
februum, -ī nt purification; **Februa** pl festival of purification in February.
fēcī perf of **faciō**.
fēcunditās, -ātis f fertility; (style) exuberance.
fēcundō, -āre vt to fertilise.
fēcundus adj fertile, fruitful; fertilising; (fig) abundant, rich, prolific.
fefellī perf of **fallō**.
fel, fellis nt gall bladder, bile; poison; (fig) animosity.
fēlēs, -is f cat.
fēlīcitās, -ātis f happiness, good luck.
fēlīciter adv abundantly; favourably, happily.
fēlīx, -īcis adj fruitful; auspicious, favourable; fortunate, successful.
fēmella, -ae f girl.
fēmina, -ae f female, woman.
fēmineus adj woman's, of women; unmanly.
femur, -oris and **inis** nt thigh.
fēn- etc see **faen-**.
fenestra, -ae f window; (fig) loophole.
fera, -ae f wild beast.
ferācius adv more fruitfully.
fērālis adj funereal; of the Feralia; deadly ♦ ntpl festival of the dead in February.
ferāx, -ācis adj fruitful, productive.
ferbuī perf of **ferveō**.
ferculum, -ī nt litter, barrow; dish, course.
ferē adv almost, nearly, about; quite, just; usually, generally, as a rule; (with neg) hardly; **nihil** ~ hardly anything.
ferentārius, -ī and **iī** m a light-armed soldier.
Feretrius, -ī m an epithet of Jupiter.
feretrum, -ī nt bier.
fēriae, -ārum fpl festival, holidays; (fig) peace, rest.

fēriātus adj on holiday, idle.
ferīnus adj of wild beasts ♦ f game.
feriō, -īre vt to strike, hit; to kill, sacrifice; (comedy) to cheat; **foedus** ~ conclude a treaty.
feritās, -ātis f wildness, savagery.
fermē see **ferē**.
fermentum, -ī nt yeast; beer; (fig) passion, vexation.
ferō, ferre, tulī, lātum vt to carry, bring, bear; to bring forth, produce; to move, stir, raise; to carry off, sweep away, plunder; (pass) to rush, hurry, fly, flow, drift; (road) to lead; (trouble) to endure, suffer, sustain; (feelings) to exhibit, show; (speech) to talk about, give out, celebrate; (bookkeeping) to enter; (CIRCS) to allow, require; **sē** ~ rush, move; profess to be, boast; **condiciōnem, lēgem** ~ propose terms, a law; **iūdicem** ~ sue; **sententiam, suffrāgium** ~ vote; **signa** ~ march; attack; **aegrē, graviter** ~ be annoyed at; **laudibus** ~ extol; **in oculīs** ~ be very fond of; **prae sē** ~ show, declare; **fertur, ferunt** it is said, they say; **ut mea fert opīniō** in my opinion.
ferōcia, -ae f courage; spirit; pride, presumption.
ferōcitās, -ātis f high spirits, aggressiveness; presumption.
ferōciter adv bravely; insolently.
Fērōnia, -ae f old Italian goddess.
ferōx, -ōcis adj warlike, spirited, daring; proud, insolent.
ferrāmentum, -ī nt tool, implement.
ferrārius adj of iron; **faber** ~ blacksmith ♦ f iron-mine, iron-works.
ferrātus adj ironclad, ironshod ♦ mpl men in armour.
ferreus adj of iron, iron; (fig) hard, cruel; strong, unyielding.
ferrūgineus adj rust-coloured, dark.
ferrūgō, -inis f rust; dark colour; gloom.
ferrum, -ī nt iron; sword; any iron implement; force of arms; ~ **et ignis** devastation.
fertilis adj fertile, productive; fertilising.
fertilitās, -ātis f fertility.
ferula, -ae f fennel; staff, rod.
ferus adj wild; uncivilised, cruel ♦ m beast.
fervēfaciō, -ere, -tum vt to boil.
fervēns, -entis pres p of **ferveō** ♦ adj hot; raging; (fig) impetuous, furious.
ferventer adv hotly.
ferveō, -vēre, -buī vi to boil, burn; (fig) to rage, bustle, be agitated.
fervēscō, -ere vi to boil up, grow hot.
fervidus adj hot, raging; (fig) fiery, violent.
fervō, -vere, -vī vi see **ferveō**.
fervor, -ōris m seething; heat; (fig) ardour, passion.
Fescennīnus adj Fescennine (a kind of ribald

song, perhaps from Fescennium in Etruria).
fessus adj tired, worn out.
festīnanter adv hastily.
festīnātiō, -ōnis f haste, hurry.
festīnō, -āre vi to hurry, be quick ♦ vt to
 hasten, accelerate.
festīnus adj hasty, quick.
fēstīvē adv gaily; humorously.
fēstīvitās, -ātis f gaiety, merriment; humour,
 fun.
fēstīvus adj gay, jolly; delightful; (speech)
 humorous.
festūca, -ae f rod (with which slaves were
 manumitted).
fēstus adj festal, on holiday ♦ nt holiday; feast.
fētiālis, -is m priest who carried out the ritual in
 making war and peace.
fētūra, -ae f breeding; brood.
fētus adj pregnant; newly delivered; (fig)
 productive, full of.
fētus, -ūs m breeding, bearing, producing;
 brood, young; fruit, produce; (fig)
 production.
fiber, -rī m beaver.
fibra, -ae f fibre; section of lung or liver;
 entrails.
fībula, -ae f clasp, brooch; clamp.
fīcedula, -ae f fig pecker.
fictē adv falsely.
fictilis adj clay, earthen ♦ nt jar; clay figure.
fictor, -ōris m sculptor; maker, inventor.
fictrīx, -īcis f maker.
fictūra, -ae f shaping, invention.
fictus ppp of **fingō** ♦ adj false, fictitious ♦ nt
 falsehood.
fīculnus adj of the fig tree.
fīcus, -ī and **ūs** f fig tree; fig.
fidēle adv faithfully, surely, firmly.
fidēlia, -ae f pot, pail; **dē eādem ~ā duōs
 parietēs dealbāre** ≈ kill two birds with one
 stone.
fidēlis adj faithful, loyal; trustworthy, sure.
fidēlitās, -ātis f faithfulness, loyalty.
fidēliter adv faithfully, surely, firmly.
Fīdēnae, -ārum fpl ancient Latin town.
Fīdēnās, -ātis adj see n.
fīdēns, -entis pres p of **fīdō** ♦ adj bold, resolute.
fīdenter adv see **fidens**.
fīdentia, -ae f self-confidence.
fidēs, -eī f trust, faith, belief; trustworthiness,
 honour, loyalty, truth; promise, assurance,
 word; guarantee, safe-conduct, protection;
 (COMM) credit; (law) good faith; ~ **mala**
 dishonesty; **rēs ~que** entire resources; ~**em
 facere** convince; ~**em servāre ergā** keep faith
 with; **dī vostram ~em!** for Heaven's sake!; **ex
 fidē bonā** in good faith.
fidēs, -is f (usu pl) stringed instrument, lyre,
 lute; (ASTRO) Lyra.
fidī perf of **findō**.
fidicen, -inis m musician; lyric poet.
fidicina, -ae f music girl.
fidicula, -ae f small lute.

Fidius, -ī m an epithet of Jupiter.
fīdō, -dere, -sus vi (with dat or abl) to trust,
 rely on.
fīdūcia, -ae f confidence, assurance; self-
 confidence; (law) trust, security.
fīdūciārius adj to be held in trust.
fīdus adj trusty, reliable; sure, safe.
fīgō, -gere, -xī, -xum vt to fix, fasten, attach;
 to drive in, pierce; (speech) to taunt.
figulāris adj a potter's.
figulus, -ī m potter; builder.
figūra, -ae f shape, form; nature, kind;
 phantom; (RHET) figure of speech.
figūrō, -āre vt to form, shape.
fīlātim adv thread by thread.
fīlia, -ae f daughter.
filicātus adj with fern patterns.
fīliola, -ae f little daughter.
fīliolus, -ī m little son.
fīlius, -ī and **iī** m son; **terrae** ~ a nobody.
filix, -cis f fern.
fīlum, -ī nt thread; band of wool, fillet; string,
 shred, wick; contour, shape; (speech)
 texture, quality.
fimbriae, -ārum fpl fringe, end.
fimus, -ī m dung; dirt.
findō, -ndere, -dī, -ssum vt to split, divide; to
 burst.
fingō, -ere, finxī, fictum vt to form, shape,
 make; to mould, model; to dress, arrange; to
 train; (mind, speech) to imagine, suppose,
 represent, sketch; to invent, fabricate;
 vultum ~ compose the features.
fīniō, -īre, -īvī, -ītum vt to bound, limit; to
 restrain; to prescribe, define, determine; to
 end, finish, complete ♦ vi to finish, die.
fīnis, -is m (occ f) boundary, border; (pl)
 territory; bound, limit; end; death; highest
 point, summit; aim, purpose; ~ **bonōrum** the
 chief good; **quem ad ~em?** how long?; ~**e
 genūs** up to the knee.
fīnītē adv within limits.
fīnitimus adj neighbouring, adjoining; akin,
 like ♦ mpl neighbours.
fīnītor, -ōris m surveyor.
fīnītumus adj see **fīnitimus**.
fīnītus ppp of **fīniō** ♦ adj (RHET) well-rounded.
finxī perf of **fingō**.
fīō, fierī, factus vi to become, arise; to be
 made, be done; to happen; **quī fit ut?** how is it
 that?; **ut fit** as usually happens; **quid mē fiet?**
 what will become of me?
firmāmen, -inis nt support.
firmāmentum, -ī nt support, strengthening;
 (fig) mainstay.
firmātor, -ōris m establisher.
firmē adv powerfully, steadily.
firmitās, -ātis f firmness, strength;
 steadfastness, stamina.
firmiter adv see **firmē**.
firmitūdō, -inis f strength, stability.
firmō, -āre, -āvī, -ātum vt to strengthen,
 support, fortify; (mind) to encourage,

steady; (fact) to confirm, prove, assert.
firmus adj strong, stable, firm; (fig) powerful,
    constant, sure, true.
fiscella, -ae f wicker basket.
fiscina, -ae f wicker basket.
fiscus, -ī m purse, moneybox; public
    exchequer; imperial treasury; the
    emperor's privy purse.
fissilis adj easy to split.
fissiō, -ōnis f dividing.
fissum, -ī nt slit, fissure.
fissus ppp of **findō**.
fistūca, -ae f rammer.
fistula, -ae f pipe, tube; panpipes; (MED) ulcer.
fistulātor, -ōris m panpipe player.
fīsus ppa of **fīdō**.
fīxī perf of **fīgō**.
fīxus ppp of **fīgō** ♦ adj fixed, fast, permanent.
flābellifera, -ae f fanbearer
flābellum, -ī nt fan.
flābilis adj airy.
flābra, -ōrum ntpl blasts, gusts; wind.
flacceō, -ēre vi to flag, lose heart.
flaccēscō, -ere vi to flag, droop.
flaccidus adj flabby, feeble.
flaccus adj flap-eared.
Flaccus, -ī m surname of Horace.
flagellō, -āre vt to whip, lash.
flagellum, -ī nt whip, lash; strap, thong; (vine)
    shoot; (polyp) arm; (feelings) sting.
flāgitātiō, -ōnis f demand.
flāgitātor, -ōris m demander, dun.
flāgitiōsē adv infamously.
flāgitiōsus adj disgraceful, profligate.
flāgitium, -ī and **iī** nt offence, disgrace,
    shame; scoundrel.
flāgitō, -āre, -āvī, -ātum vt to demand,
    importune, dun; (law) to summon.
flagrāns, -antis pres p of **flagrō** ♦ adj hot,
    blazing; brilliant; passionate.
flagranter adv passionately.
flagrantia, -ae f blazing; (fig) shame.
flagrō, -āre vi to blaze, burn, be on fire;
    (feelings) to be excited, be inflamed; (ill-will)
    to be the victim of.
flagrum, -ī nt whip, lash.
flāmen, -inis m priest of a particular deity.
flāmen, -inis nt blast, gale, wind.
flāminica, -ae f wife of a priest.
Flāminīnus, -ī m Roman surname (esp the
    conqueror of Philip V of Macedon).
flāminium, -ī and **iī** nt priesthood.
Flāminius, -ī m Roman family name (esp the
    consul defeated by Hannibal).
Flāminius, -iānus adj: **Via ~** road from Rome
    N.E. to Ariminum.
flamma, -ae f flame, fire; torch, star; fiery
    colour; (fig) passion; danger, disaster.
flammeolum, -ī nt bridal veil.
flammēscō, -ere vi to become fiery.

flammeus adj fiery, blazing; flame-coloured ♦
    nt bridal veil.
flammifer, -ī adj fiery.
flammō, -āre, -āvī, -ātum vi to blaze ♦ vt to
    set on fire, burn; (fig) to inflame, incense.
flammula, -ae f little flame.
flātus, -ūs m blowing, breath; breeze; (fig)
    arrogance.
flāvēns, -entis adj yellow, golden.
flāvēscō, -ere vi to turn yellow.
Flāviānus adj see n.
Flāvius, -ī m Roman family name (esp the
    emperors Vespasian, Titus and Domitian).
flāvus adj yellow, golden.
flēbilis adj lamentable; tearful, mournful.
flēbiliter adv see **flēbilis**.
flectō, -ctere, -xī, -xum vt to bend, turn; to
    turn aside, wheel; (promontory) to round;
    (mind) to direct, persuade, dissuade ♦ vi to
    turn, march.
fleō, -ēre, -ēvī, -ētum vi to weep, cry ♦ vt to
    lament, mourn for.
flētus, -ūs m weeping, tears.
flexanimus adj moving.
flexī perf of **flectō**.
flexibilis adj pliant, flexible; fickle.
flexilis adj pliant.
flexiloquus adj ambiguous.
flexiō, -ōnis f bending, winding, (voice)
    modulation.
flexipēs, -edis adj twining.
flexuōsus adj tortuous.
flexūra, -ae f bending.
flexus ppp of **flectō** ♦ adj winding.
flexus, -ūs m winding, bending; change.
flictus, -ūs m collision.
flō, -āre, -āvī, -ātum vt, vi to blow; (money) to
    coin.
floccus, -ī m bit of wool; triviality; **~ī nōn faciō**
    = I don't care a straw for.
Flōra, -ae f goddess of flowers.
Flōrālis adj see n.
flōrēns, -entis pres p of **flōreō** ♦ adj in bloom;
    bright; prosperous, flourishing.
flōreō, -ēre, -uī vi to blossom, flower; (age) to
    be in one's prime; (wine) to froth; (fig) to
    flourish, prosper; (places) to be gay with.
flōrēscō, -ere vi to begin to flower; to grow
    prosperous.
flōreus adj of flowers, flowery.
flōridulus adj pretty, little.
flōridus adj of flowers, flowery; fresh, pretty;
    (style) florid, ornate.
flōrifer, -ī adj flowery.
flōrilegus adj flower-sipping.
flōrus adj beautiful.
flōs, -ōris m flower, blossom; (wine) bouquet;
    (age) prime, heyday; (youth) downy beard,
    youthful innocence; (fig) crown, glory;
    (speech) ornament.

Noun declensions and verb conjugations are shown on pp xiii to xxv. The present infinitive ending of a verb shows
to which conjugation it belongs: **-āre** = 1st; **-ēre** = 2nd; **-ere** = 3rd and **-īre** = 4th. Irregular verbs are shown on p xxvi

flōsculus, -ī m little flower; (*fig*) pride, ornament.

flūctifragus *adj* surging.

flūctuātiō, -ōnis f wavering.

flūctuō, -āre vi to toss, wave; (*fig*) to rage, swell, waver.

flūctuōsus *adj* stormy.

flūctus, -ūs m wave; flowing, flood; (*fig*) disturbance; ~**ūs** (*pl*) **in simpulō** ≈ *a storm in a teacup.*

fluēns, -entis *pres p of* **fluō** ♦ *adj* lax, loose, enervated; (*speech*) fluent.

fluenta, -ōrum *ntpl* stream, flood.

fluenter *adv* in a flowing manner.

fluentisonus *adj* wave-echoing.

fluidus *adj* flowing, fluid; lax, soft; relaxing.

fluitō, -āre vi to flow, float about; to wave, flap, move unsteadily; (*fig*) to waver.

flūmen, -inis nt stream, river; (*fig*) flood, flow, fluency; **adversō ~ine** upstream; **secundō ~ine** downstream.

flūmineus *adj* river- (*in cpds*).

fluō, -ere, -xī, -xum vi to flow; to overflow, drip; (*fig*) to fall in, fall away, vanish; (*speech*) to run evenly; (*CIRCS*) to proceed, tend.

flūtō *etc see* **fluitō**.

fluviālis *adj* river- (*in cpds*).

fluviātilis *adj* river- (*in cpds*).

flūvidus *etc see* **fluidus**.

fluvius, -ī *and* **iī** m river, stream.

fluxi *perf of* **fluō**.

fluxus *adj* flowing, loose, leaky; (*person*) lax, dissolute; (*thing*) frail, fleeting, unreliable.

fōcāle, -is nt scarf.

foculus, -ī m stove, fire.

focus, -ī m hearth, fireplace; pyre, altar; (*fig*) home.

fodicō, -āre vt to nudge, jog.

fodiō, -ere, fōdī, fossum vt to dig; to prick, stab; (*fig*) to goad.

foedē *adv see* **foedus**.

foederātus *adj* confederated.

foedifragus *adj* perfidious.

foeditās, -ātis f foulness, hideousness.

foedō, -āre, -āvī, -ātum vt to mar, disfigure; to disgrace, sully.

foedus *adj* foul, hideous, revolting; vile, disgraceful.

foedus, -eris nt treaty, league; agreement, compact; law.

foen- *etc see* **faen-**.

foeteō, -ēre vi to stink.

foetidus *adj* stinking.

foetor, -ōris m stench.

foetu- *etc see* **fētu-**.

foliātum, -ī nt nard oil.

folium, -ī *and* **iī** nt leaf.

folliculus, -ī m small bag; eggshell.

follis, -is m bellows; punchball; purse.

fōmentum, -ī nt poultice, bandage; (*fig*) alleviation.

fōmes, -itis m tinder, kindling.

fōns, fontis m spring, source; water; (*fig*) origin, fountainhead.

fontānus *adj* spring- (*in cpds*).

fonticulus, -ī m little spring.

for, fārī, fātus vt, vi to speak, utter.

forābilis *adj* penetrable.

forāmen, -inis nt hole, opening.

forās *adv* out, outside.

forceps, -ipis m/f tongs, forceps.

forda, -ae f cow in calf.

fore, forem *fut infin, imperf subj of* **sum**.

forēnsis *adj* public, forensic; of the marketplace.

foris, -is f (*usu pl*) door; (*fig*) opening, entrance.

forīs *adv* out of doors, outside, abroad; from outside, from abroad; ~ **cēnāre** dine out.

fōrma, -ae f form, shape, appearance; mould, stamp, last; (*person*) beauty; (*fig*) idea, nature, kind.

fōrmāmentum, -ī nt shape.

fōrmātūra, -ae f shaping.

Formiae, -ārum fpl town in S. Latium.

Formiānus *adj* of Formiae ♦ nt villa at Formiae.

formīca, -ae f ant.

formīcinus *adj* crawling.

formīdābilis *adj* terrifying.

formīdō, -āre, -āvī, -ātum vt, vi to fear, be terrified.

formīdō, -inis f terror, awe, horror; scarecrow.

formīdolōsē *adv see* **formīdolōsus**.

formīdolōsus *adj* fearful, terrifying; afraid.

fōrmō, -āre, -āvī, -ātum vt to shape, fashion, form.

fōrmōsitās, -ātis f beauty.

fōrmōsus *adj* beautiful, handsome.

fōrmula, -ae f rule, regulation; (*law*) procedure, formula; (*PHILOS*) principle.

fornācula, -ae f small oven.

fornāx, -ācis f furnace, oven, kiln.

fornicātus *adj* arched.

fornix, -icis m arch, vault; brothel.

forō, -āre vt to pierce.

Foroiūliēnsis *adj see* **Forum Iuli**.

fors, fortis f chance, luck ♦ *adv* perchance; ~**te** by chance, as it happened; perhaps; **nē ~te** in case; **sī ~te** if perhaps; in the hope that.

forsan, forsit, forsitan *adv* perhaps.

fortasse, -is *adv* perhaps, possibly; (*irony*) very likely.

forticulus *adj* quite brave.

fortis *adj* strong, sturdy; brave, manly, resolute.

fortiter *adv* vigorously; bravely.

fortitūdō, -inis f courage, resolution; strength.

fortuītō *adv* by chance.

fortuītus *adj* casual, accidental.

fortūna, -ae f chance, luck, fortune; good luck, success; misfortune; circumstances, lot; (*pl*) possessions; ~**ae fīlius** Fortune's

favourite; ~am habēre be successful.
fortūnātē adv see fortunātus.
fortūnātus adj happy, lucky; well off, rich, blessed.
fortūnō, -āre vt to bless, prosper.
forulī, -ōrum mpl bookcase.
forum, -ī nt public place, market; market town; Roman Forum between the Palatine and Capitol; public affairs, law courts, business; ~ boārium cattle market; ~ olitōrium vegetable market; ~ piscātōrium fish market; ~ agere hold an assize ~ attingere enter public life; cēdere ~ō go bankrupt; utī ~ō take advantage of a situation.
Forum Iūli colony in S. Gaul (now Fréjus).
forus, -ī m gangway; block of seats; (bees) cell frame.
fossa, -ae f ditch, trench.
fossiō, -ōnis f digging.
fossor, -ōris m digger.
fossus ppp of fodiō.
fōtus ppp of foveō.
fovea, -ae f pit, pitfall.
foveō, -ēre, fōvī, fōtum vt to warm, keep warm; (MED) to foment; to fondle, keep; (fig) to cherish, love, foster, pamper, encourage; castra ~ remain in camp.
frāctus ppp of frangō ♦ adj weak, faint.
frāga, -ōrum ntpl strawberries.
fragilis adj brittle, fragile; frail, fleeting.
fragilitās, -ātis f frailness.
fragmen, -inis nt (pl) fragments, ruins, wreck.
fragmentum, -ī nt fragment, remnant.
fragor, -ōris m crash, din; disintegration.
fragōsus adj crashing, roaring, breakable; rough.
frāgrāns, -antis adj fragrant.
framea, -ae f German spear.
frangō, -angere, -ēgī, -āctum vt to break, shatter, wreck; to crush, grind (fig) to break down, weaken, humble; (emotion) to touch, move; cervīcem ~ strangle.
frāter, -ris m brother; cousin; (fig) friend, ally.
frāterculus, -ī m brother.
frāternē adv like a brother.
frāternitās, -ātis f brotherhood.
frāternus adj brotherly, a brother's, fraternal.
frātricīda, -ae m fratricide.
fraudātiō, -ōnis f deceit, fraud.
fraudātor, -ōris m swindler
fraudō, -āre, -āvī, -ātum vt to cheat, defraud; to steal, cancel.
fraudulentus adj deceitful, fraudulent.
fraus, -audis f deceit, fraud delusion, error; offence, wrong; injury, damage; lēgī ~dem facere evade the law; in ~dem incidere be disappointed; sine ~de without harm.
fraxineus, fraxinus adj of ash.
fraxinus, -ī f ash tree; ashen spear.

Fregellae, -ārum fpl town in S. Latium.
Fregellānus adj see n.
frēgī perf of frangō.
fremebundus adj roaring.
fremitus, -ūs m roaring, snorting, noise.
fremō, -ere, -uī, -itum vi to roar, snort, grumble ♦ vt to shout for, complain.
fremor, -ōris m murmuring.
frendō, -ere vi to gnash the teeth.
frēnō, -āre, -āvī, -ātum vt to bridle; (fig) to curb, restrain.
frēnum, -ī nt (pl -a, -ōrum nt, -ī, -ōrum m) bridle, bit; (fig) curb, check; ~ōs dare give vent to; ~um mordēre ≈ take the bit between one's teeth.
frequēns, -entis adj crowded, numerous, populous; regular, repeated, frequent; ~ senatus a crowded meeting of the senate.
frequentātiō, -ōnis f accumulation.
frequenter adv in large numbers; repeatedly, often.
frequentia, -ae f full attendance, throng, crowd.
frequentō, -āre, -āvī, -ātum vt to crowd, populate; to visit repeatedly, frequent; to repeat; (festival) to celebrate, keep.
fretēnsis adj of the Straits of Messina.
fretum, -ī nt strait; sea; (fig) violence; ~ Siciliēnse Straits of Messina.
fretus, -ūs m strait.
frētus adj relying, confident.
frētus adj relying, confident.
fricō, -āre, -uī, -tum vt to rub, rub down.
frictus ppp of frigō.
frigefactō, -āre vt to cool.
frīgeō, -ēre vi to be cold; (fig) to be lifeless, flag; to be coldly received, fall flat.
frīgerāns adj cooling.
frīgēscō, -ere vi to grow cold; to become inactive.
frīgida, -ae f cold water.
frīgidē adv feebly.
frīgidulus adj rather cold, faint.
frīgidus adj cold, cool; chilling; (fig) dull, torpid; (words) flat, uninteresting.
frīgō, -gere, -xī, -ctum vt to roast, fry.
frīgus, -oris nt cold; cold weather, winter; death; (fig) dullness, inactivity; coldness, indifference.
friguttiō, -īre vi to stammer.
friō, -āre vt to crumble.
fritillus, -ī m dice box.
frīvolus adj empty, paltry.
frīxī perf of frigō.
frondātor, -ōris m vinedresser, pruner.
frondeō, -ēre vi to be in leaf.
frondēscō, -ere vi to become leafy, shoot.
frondeus adj leafy.
frondifer, -ī adj leafy.
frondōsus adj leafy.
frōns, -ondis f leaf, foliage; garland of leaves.

Noun declensions and verb conjugations are shown on pp xiii to xxv. The present infinitive ending of a verb shows to which conjugation it belongs: -āre = 1st; -ēre = 2nd; -ere = 3rd and -īre = 4th. Irregular verbs are shown on p xxvi

frōns, -ontis _f_ forehead, brow; front, facade; (_fig_) look, appearance, exterior; **~ontem contrahere** frown; **ā ~onte** in front; **in ~onte** in breadth.
frontālia, -um _ntpl_ frontlet.
frontō, -ōnis _m_ a broad-browed man.
frūctuārius _adj_ productive; paid for out of produce.
fructuōsus _adj_ productive; profitable.
frūctus _ppa of_ **fruor.**
frūctus, -ūs _m_ enjoyment; revenue, income; produce, fruit; (_fig_) consequence, reward; **~uī esse** be an asset (to); **~um percipere** reap the fruits (of).
frūgālis _adj_ thrifty, worthy.
frūgālitās, -ātis _f_ thriftiness, restraint.
frūgāliter _adv_ temperately.
frūgēs _etc see_ **frūx.**
frūgī _adj_ (_indecl_) frugal, temperate, honest; useful.
frūgifer, -ī _adj_ fruitful, fertile.
frūgiferēns, -entis _adj_ fruitful.
frūgilegus _adj_ food-gatherering.
frūgiparus _adj_ fruitful.
frūmentārius _adj_ of corn, corn- (_in cpds_) ♦ _m_ corn dealer; **lēx ~a** law about the distribution of corn; **rēs ~a** commissariat.
frūmentātiō, -ōnis _f_ foraging.
frūmentātor, -ōris _m_ corn merchant, forager.
frūmentor, -ārī, -ātus _vi_ to go foraging.
frūmentum, -ī _nt_ corn, grain, (_pl_) crops.
frūnīscor, -ī _vt_ to enjoy.
fruor, -uī, -ūctus _vt, vi_ (_usu with abl_) to enjoy, enjoy the company of; (_law_) to have the use and enjoyment of.
frūstillātim _adv_ in little bits.
frūstrā _adv_ in vain, for nothing; groundlessly; in error; **~ esse** be deceived; **~ habēre** foil.
frūstrāmen, -inis _nt_ deception.
frūstrātiō, -ōnis _f_ deception, frustration.
frūstrō, -āre; -or, -ārī, -ātus _vt_ to deceive, trick.
frūstulentus _adj_ full of crumbs.
frūstum, -ī _nt_ bit, scrap.
frutex, -icis _m_ bush, shrub; (_comedy_) blockhead.
fruticētum, -ī _nt_ thicket.
fruticor, -ārī _vi_ to sprout.
fruticōsus _adj_ bushy.
frūx, -ūgis _f_, **-ūgēs, -ūgum** fruits of the earth, produce; (_fig_) reward, success; virtue; **sē ad ~ūgem bonam recipere** reform.
fuam _old pres subj of_ **sum.**
fūcātus _adj_ counterfeit, artificial.
fūcō, -āre, -āvī, -ātum _vt_ to paint, dye (_esp red_).
fūcōsus _adj_ spurious.
fūcus, -ī _m_ red dye, rouge; bee glue; (_fig_) deceit, pretence.
fūcus, -ī _m_ drone.
fūdī _perf of_ **fundō.**
fuga, -ae _f_ flight, rout; banishment; speed,

swift passing; refuge; (_fig_) avoidance, escape; **~am facere, in ~am dare** put to flight.
fugācius _adv_ more timidly.
fugāx, -ācis _adj_ timorous, shy, fugitive; swift, transient; (_with gen_) avoiding.
fūgī _perf of_ **fugiō.**
fugiēns, -entis _pres p of_ **fugiō** ♦ _adj_ fleeting, dying; averse (to).
fugiō, -ere, fūgī, -itum _vi_ to flee, run away, escape; to go into exile; (_fig_) to vanish, pass swiftly ♦ _vt_ to flee from, escape from; to shun, avoid; (_fig_) to escape, escape notice of; **~e quaerere** do not ask; **mē ~it** I do not notice _or_ know.
fugitīvus, -ī _m_ runaway slave, truant, deserter ♦ _adj_ fugitive.
fugitō, -āre _vt_ to flee from, shun.
fugō, -āre, -āvī, -ātum _vt_ to put to flight; to banish; to rebuff.
fulcīmen, -inis _nt_ support.
fulciō, -cīre, -sī, -tum _vt_ to prop, support; to strengthen, secure; (_fig_) to sustain, bolster up.
fulcrum, -ī _nt_ bedpost; couch.
fulgeō, -gēre, -sī _vi_ to flash, lighten; to shine; (_fig_) to be illustrious.
fulgidus _adj_ flashing.
fulgō _etc see_ **fulgeō.**
fulgor, -ōris _m_ lightning; flash, brightness; (_fig_) splendour.
fulgur, -is _nt_ lightning; thunderbolt; splendour.
fulgurālis _adj_ on lightning as an omen.
fulgurātor, -ōris _m_ interpreter of lightning.
fulgurītus _adj_ struck by lightning.
fulgurō, -āre _vi_ to lighten.
fulica, -ae _f_ coot.
fūlīgō, -inis _f_ soot; black paint.
fulix, -cis _f_ _see_ **fulica.**
fullō, -ōnis _m_ fuller.
fullōnius _adj_ fuller's.
fulmen, -inis _nt_ thunderbolt; (_fig_) disaster.
fulmenta, -ae _f_ heel of a shoe.
fulmineus _adj_ of lightning; (_fig_) deadly.
fulminō, -āre _vi_ to lighten; (_fig_) to threaten.
fulsī _perf of_ **fulciō;** _perf of_ **fulgeō.**
fultūra, -ae _f_ support.
fultus _ppp of_ **fulciō.**
Fulvia, -iae _f_ wife of M. Antony.
Fulvius, -ī _m_ Roman family name.
fulvus _adj_ yellow, tawny, dun.
fūmeus _adj_ smoking.
fūmidus _adj_ smoky, smoking.
fūmifer, -ī _adj_ smoking.
fūmificō, -āre _vi_ to burn incense.
fūmificus _adj_ steaming.
fūmō, -āre _vi_ to smoke, steam.
fūmōsus _adj_ smoky, smoked.
fūmus, -ī _m_ smoke, steam.
fūnāle, -is _nt_ cord; wax torch; chandelier.
fūnambulus, -ī _m_ tightrope walker.
fūnctiō, -ōnis _f_ performance.
fūnctus _ppa of_ **fungor.**

fūnda, -ae f sling; dragnet.
fundāmen, -inis nt foundation.
fundāmentum, -ī nt foundation; **~a agere,
iacere** lay the foundations.
Fundānus adj see **Fundī.**
fundātor, -ōris m founder.
Fundī, -ōrum mpl coast town in Latium.
funditō, -āre vt to sling.
funditor, -ōris m slinger.
funditus adv utterly, completely; ~ the
bottom.
fundō, -āre, -āvī, -ātum vt to found; to
secure; (fig) to establish, make sure.
fundō, -ere, fūdī, fūsum vt to pour, shed,
spill; (metal) to cast; (solids) to hurl, scatter,
shower; (MIL) to rout; (crops) to produce in
abundance; (speech) to utter; (fig) to spread,
extend.
fundus, -ī m bottom; farm, estate; (law)
authorizer.
fūnebris adj funeral- (in cpds); murderous.
fūnerātus adj killed.
fūnereus adj funeral- (in cpds); fatal.
fūnestō, -āre vt to pollute with murder,
desecrate.
fūnestus adj deadly, fatal; sorrowful, in
mourning.
fungīnus adj of a mushroom.
fungor, -gi, fūnctus vt, vi (usu withabl) to
perform, discharge, do; to be acted on.
fungus, -ī m mushroom, fungus (candle) clot
on the wick.
fūniculus, -ī m cord.
fūnis, -is m rope, rigging; **~em dūcere** be the
master.
fūnus, -eris nt funeral; death; corpse; ruin,
destruction.
fūr, fūris m thief; slave.
fūrācissimē adv most thievishly.
fūrāx, -ācis adj thieving.
furca, -ae f fork; fork-shaped pole; pillory.
furcifer, -ī m gallows rogue.
furcilla, -ae f little fork.
furcillō, -āre vt to prop up.
furcula, -ae f forked prop; **~ae Caudīnae** Pass
of Caudium.
furenter adv furiously.
furfur, -is m bran; scurf.
Furia, -ae f Fury, avenging spirit; madness,
frenzy, rage.
furiālis adj of the Furies; frantic, fearful;
infuriating.
furiāliter adv madly.
furibundus adj mad, frenzied.
furiō, -āre, -āvī, -ātum vt to madden.
furiōsē adv in a frenzy.
furiōsus adj mad, frantic.
furnus, -ī m oven.
furō, -ere vi to rave, rage, be mad, be crazy.
fūror, -ārī, -ātus vt to steal; to pilfer; to

impersonate.
furor, -ōris m madness, frenzy, passion.
fūrtificus adj thievish.
fūrtim adv by stealth, secretly.
fūrtīvē adv secretly.
fūrtīvus adj stolen; secret, furtive.
fūrtō adv secretly.
fūrtum, -ī nt theft, robbery; (pl) stolen goods;
(fig) trick, intrigue.
fūrunculus, -ī m pilferer.
furvus adj black, dark.
fuscina, -ae f trident.
fuscō, -āre vt to blacken.
fuscus adj dark, swarthy; (voice) husky,
muffled.
fūsē adv diffusely.
fūsilis adj molten, softened.
fūsiō, -ōnis f outpouring.
fūstis, -is m stick, club, cudgel; (MIL) beating to
death.
fūstuārium, -ī and **iī** nt beating to death.
fūsus ppp of **fundō** ♦ adj broad, diffuse;
copious.
fūsus, -ī m spindle.
futtile adv in vain.
futtilis adj brittle; worthless.
futtilitās, -ātis f futility.
futūrum, -ī nt future.
futūrus fut p of **sum** ♦ adj future, coming.

G, g

Gabiī, -iōrum mpl ancient town in Latium.
Gabinius, -ī m Roman family name (esp Aulus,
tribune 67 B.C.).
Gabinius, -iānus adj: **lēx ~ia** law giving Pompey
command against the pirates.
Gabīnus adj see **Gabiī.**
Gādēs, -ium fpl town in Spain (now Cadiz).
Gāditānus adj see n.
gaesum, -ī nt Gallic javelin.
Gaetūlī, -ōrum mpl African people N of Sahara.
Gaetūlus, -icus adj Gaetulian; African.
Gāius, -ī m Roman praenomen (esp emperor
Caligula).
Gāius, -ia m/f (wedding ceremony) bridegroom,
bride.
Galatae, -ārum mpl Galatians of Asia Minor.
Galatia, -iae f Galatia.
Galba, -ae m Roman surname (esp emperor
68–9).
galbaneus adj of galbanum, a Syrian plant.

Noun declensions and verb conjugations are shown on pp xiii to xxv. The present infinitive ending of a verb shows
to which conjugation it belongs: -āre = 1st, -ēre = 2nd; -ere = 3rd and -īre = 4th. Irregular verbs are shown on p xxvi

galbinus *adj* greenish-yellow ♦ *ntpl* pale green clothes.

galea, -ae *f* helmet.

galeātus *adj* helmeted.

galērītus *adj* rustic.

galērum, -ī *nt*, **-us, -ī** *m* leather hood, cap; wig.

galla, -ae *f* oak apple.

Gallī, -ōrum *mpl* Gauls (*people of what is now France and N. Italy*).

Gallia, -iae *f* Gaul.

Gallicānus *adj* of Italian Gaul.

Gallicus *adj* Gallic ♦ *f* a Gallic shoe.

gallīna, -ae *f* hen; **~ae albae fīlius** fortune's favourite.

gallīnāceus *adj* of poultry.

gallīnārius, -ī *and* **iī** *m* poultry farmer.

Gallograecī, -ōrum *mpl* Galatians.

Gallograecia, -iae *f* Galatia.

gallus, -ī *m* cock.

Gallus, -ī *m* Gaul; Roman surname (*esp the lyric poet; priest of Cybele*).

ganēa, -ae *f* low eating house.

ganeō, -ōnis *m* profligate.

ganeum, -ī *nt* low eating house.

Gangaridae, -ārum *mpl* a people on the Ganges.

Gangēs, -is *m* river Ganges.

Gangēticus *adj see* n.

ganniō, -īre *vi* to yelp; (*fig*) to grumble.

gannītus, -ūs *m* yelping.

Ganymēdēs, -is *m* Ganymede, (*cup bearer in Olympus*).

Garamantes, -um *mpl* N. African tribe.

Garamantis, -idis *adj see* n.

Gargānus, -ī *m* mountain in E. Italy.

garriō, -īre *vi* to chatter.

garrulitās, -ātis *f* chattering.

garrulus *adj* talkative, babbling.

garum, -ī *nt* fish sauce.

Garumna, -ae *f* river Garonne.

gaudeō, -ēre, gāvīsus *vt, vi* to rejoice, be pleased, delight (in); **in sē, in sinū ~** be secretly pleased.

gaudium, -ī *and* **iī** *nt* joy, delight, enjoyment.

gaulus, -ī *m* bucket.

gausape, -is *nt*, **-a, -ōrum** *pl* a woollen cloth, frieze.

gāvīsus *ppa of* **gaudeō.**

gāza, -ae *f* treasure, riches.

gelidē *adv* feebly.

gelidus *adj* cold, frosty; stiff, numb; chilling ♦ *f* cold water.

gelō, -āre *vt* to freeze.

Gelōnī, -ōrum *mpl* Scythian tribe (*now Ukraine*).

gelū, -ūs *nt* frost, cold; chill.

gemebundus *adj* groaning.

gemellipara, -ae *f* mother of twins.

gemellus *adj* twin, double; alike ♦ *m* twin.

geminātiō, -ōnis *f* doubling.

geminō, -āre, -āvī, -ātum *vt* to double, bring together; to repeat ♦ *vi* to be double.

geminus *adj* twin, double, both; similar ♦ *mpl* twins (*esp Castor and Pollux*).

gemitus, -ūs *m* groan, sigh; moaning sound.

gemma, -ae *f* bud, precious stone, jewel; jewelled cup, signet.

gemmātus *adj* bejewelled.

gemmeus *adj* jewelled; sparkling.

gemmifer, -ī *adj* gem-producing.

gemmō, -āre *vi* to bud, sprout; to sparkle.

gemō, -ere, -uī, -itum *vi* to sigh, groan, moan ♦ *vt* to bewail.

Gemōniae, -ārum *fpl* steps in Rome on which bodies of criminals were thrown.

genae, -ārum *fpl* cheeks; eyes, eye sockets.

geneālogus, -ī *m* genealogist.

gener, -ī *m* son-in-law.

generālis *adj* of the species; universal.

generāliter *adv* generally.

generāscō, -ere *vi* to be produced.

generātim *adv* by species, in classes; in general.

generātor, -ōris *m* producer.

generō, -āre, -āvī, -ātum *vt* to breed, procreate.

generōsus *adj* high-born, noble; well-stocked; generous, chivalrous; (*things*) noble, honourable.

genesis, -is *f* birth; horoscope.

genethliacon, -ī *nt* birthday poem.

genetīvus *adj* native, inborn.

genetrīx, -īcis *f* mother.

geniālis *adj* nuptial; joyful, genial.

geniāliter *adv* merrily.

geniculātus *adj* jointed.

genista, -ae *f* broom.

genitābilis *adj* productive.

genitālis *adj* fruitful, generative; of birth.

genitāliter *adv* fruitfully.

genitor, -ōris *m* father, creator.

genitus *ppp of* **gignō.**

genius, -ī *and* **iī** *m* guardian spirit; enjoyment, inclination; talent; **~iō indulgēre** enjoy oneself.

gēns, gentis *f* clan, family, stock, race; tribe, people, nation; descendant; (*pl*) foreign peoples; **minimē gentium** by no means; **ubi gentium** where in the world.

genticus *adj* national.

gentīlicius *adj* family.

gentīlis *adj* family, hereditary; national ♦ *m* kinsman.

gentīlitās, -ātis *f* clan relationship.

genū, -ūs *nt* knee.

genuālia, -um *ntpl* garters.

genuī *perf of* **gignō.**

genuīnus *adj* natural.

genuīnus *adj* of the cheek ♦ *mpl* back teeth.

genus, -eris *nt* birth, descent, noble birth, descendant; race; kind, class, species, respect, way; (*logic*) genus, general term; **id ~** of that kind; **in omnī ~ere** in all respects.

geōgraphia, -ae *f* geography.

geōmetrēs, -ae *m* geometer.

geōmetria, -ae f geometry.
geōmetricus adj geometrical ♦ ntpl geometry.
germānē adv sincerely.
Germānī, -ōrum mpl Germans.
Germānia, -iae f Germany.
Germānicus adj, m cognomen oī Nero Claudius Drusus and his son.
germānitās, -ātis f brotherhood, sisterhood; relation of sister colonies.
germānus adj of the same parents, full (brother, sister); genuine, true ♦ n full brother ♦ f full sister.
germen, -inis nt bud, shoot; embryo; (fig) germ.
gerō, -rere, -ssī, -stum vt to carry, wear; to bring; (plants) to bear, produce; (feelings) to entertain, show; (activity) to conduct, manage, administer, wage (time) spend; **mōrem ~** comply, humour; **persōram ~** play a part; **sē ~** behave; **sē medium ~** be neutral; **prae sē ~** exhibit; **rēs ~stae** exploits.
gerō, -ōnis nt carrier.
gerrae, -ārum fpl trifles, nonsense.
gerrō, -ōnis m idler.
gerulus, -ī m carrier.
Gēryōn, -onis m mythical three-bodied king killed by Hercules.
gessī perf of **gerō**.
gestāmen, -inis nt arms, ornaments, burden; litter, carriage.
gestiō, -ōnis f performance.
gestiō, -īre vi to jump for joy, be excited; to be very eager.
gestiō, -āre vt to always wear or carry.
gestō, -āre vt to carry about us ually wear; to fondle; to blab; (pass) to go for a ride, drive, sail.
gestor, -ōris m telltale.
gestus ppp of **gerō**.
gestus, -ūs m posture, gesture; gesticulation.
Getae, -ārum mpl Thracian tribe on the lower Danube.
Geticus adj Getan, Thracian.
gibbus, -ī m hump.
Gigantes, -um mpl Giants, sons cf Earth.
Gigantēus adj see n.
gignō, -ere, genuī, genitum vt to beget, bear, produce; to cause.
gilvus adj pale yellow, dun.
gingīva, -ae f gum.
glaber, -rī adj smooth, bald ♦ m favourite slave.
glaciālis adj icy.
glaciēs, -ēī f ice.
glaciō, -āre vt to freeze.
gladiātor, -ōris m gladiator; (pl) gladiatorial show.
gladiātōrius adj of gladiators ♦ nt gladiators' pay.
gladiātūra, -ae f gladiator's profession.

gladius, -ī and **iī** m sword; (fig) murder, death; **~ium stringere** draw the sword; **suō sibi ~iō iugulāre** ≈ beat at his own game.
glaeba, -ae f sod, clod of earth; soil; lump.
glaebula, -ae f small lump; small holding.
glaesum etc see **glēsum**.
glandifer, -ī adj acorn-bearing.
glandium, -ī and **iī** nt glandule (in meat).
glāns, -andis f acorn, nut; bullet.
glārea, -ae f gravel.
glāreōsus adj gravelly.
glaucūma, -ae f cataract; **~am ob oculōs obicere** ≈ throw dust in the eyes of.
glaucus adj bluish grey.
glēba etc see **glaeba**.
glēsum, -ī nt amber.
glīs, -īris m dormouse.
glīscō, -ere vi to grow, swell, blaze up.
globōsus adj spherical.
globus, -ī m ball, sphere; (MIL) troop; mass, crowd, cluster.
glōmerāmen, -inis nt bell.
glomerō, -āre, -āvī, -ātum vt to form into a ball, gather, accumulate.
glomus, -eris nt ball of thread, clue.
glōria, -ae f glory, fame; ambition, pride, boasting; (pl) glorious deeds.
glōriātiō, -ōnis f boasting.
glōriola, -ae f a little glory.
glōrior, -ārī, -ātus vt, v. to boast, pride oneself.
glōriōsē adv see **glōriōsus**.
glōriōsus adj famous, glorious; boastful.
glūten, -inis nt glue.
glūtinātor, -ōris m bookbinder.
gluttiō, -īre vt to gulp down.
gnāruris, gnārus adj knowing, expert; known.
gnātus see **nātus**.
gnāvus see **nāvus**.
Gnōsius and **iacus** and **ias** adj of Cnossos, Cretan.
Gnōsis, -idis f Ariadne
Gnōsus, -ī f Cnossos (ancient capital of Crete) ♦ f Ariadne.
gōbiō, -ōnis, gōbius, -ī and **iī** m gudgeon.
Gorgiās, -ae m Sicilian sophist and teacher of rhetoric.
Gorgō, -ōnis f mythical monster capable of turning men to stone. Medusa.
Gorgoneus adj: equus ~ Pegasus; lacus ~ Hippocrene.
Gortȳna, -ae f Cretan town.
Gortȳnius, -iacus adj Gortynian, Cretan.
gōrytos, -ī m quiver.
grabātus, -ī m camp bed, low couch.
Gracchānus adj see n.
Gracchus, -ī m Roman surname (esp the famous tribunes Tiberius and Gaius).
gracilis adj slender, slight, meagre, poor;

(*style*) plain.

gracilitās, -ātis *f* slimness, leanness; (*style*) simplicity.

grāculus, -ī *m* jackdaw.

gradātim *adv* step by step, gradually.

gradātiō, -ōnis *f* (*RHET*) climax.

gradior, -adī, -essus *vi* to step, walk.

Grādīvus, -ī *m* Mars.

gradus, -ūs *m* step, pace; stage, step towards; firm stand, position, standing; (*pl*) stair, steps; (*hair*) braid; (*MATH*) degree; (*fig*) degree, rank; **citātō, plēnō ~ō** at the double; **suspēnsō ~ū** on tiptoe; **dē ~ū deicī** be disconcerted.

Graecē *adv* in Greek.

Graecia, -iae *f* Greece; **Māgna ~** S. Italy.

graecissō, -āre *vi* to ape the Greeks.

graecor, -ārī *vi* to live like Greeks.

Graeculus *adj* (*contemptuous*) Greek.

Graecus *adj* Greek.

Grāiugena, -ae *m* Greek.

Grāius *adj* Greek.

grallātor, -ōris *m* stiltwalker.

grāmen, -inis *nt* grass; herb.

grāmineus *adj* grassy; of cane.

grammaticus *adj* literary, grammatical ♦ *m* teacher of literature and language ♦ *f/ntpl* grammar, literature, philology.

grānāria, -ōrum *ntpl* granary.

grandaevus *adj* aged, very old.

grandēscō, -ere *vi* to grow.

grandiculus *adj* quite big.

grandifer, -ī *adj* productive.

grandiloquus, -ī *m* grand speaker; boaster.

grandinat, -āre *vi* it hails.

grandis *adj* large, great, tall; old; strong; (*style*) grand, sublime; **~ nātū** old.

granditās, -ātis *f* grandeur.

grandō, -inis *f* hail.

grānifer, -ī *adj* grain-carrying.

grānum, -ī *nt* seed, grain.

graphicē *adv* nicely.

graphicus *adj* fine, masterly.

graphium, -ī and iī *nt* stilus, pen.

grassātor, -ōris *m* vagabond; robber, footpad.

grassor, -ārī, -ātus *vi* to walk about, prowl, loiter; (*action*) to proceed; (*fig*) to attack, rage against.

grātē *adv* with pleasure; gratefully.

grātēs *fpl* thanks.

grātia, -ae *f* charm, grace; favour, influence, regard, friendship; kindness, service; gratitude, thanks; **~am facere** excuse; **~am referre** return a favour; **in ~am redīre cum** be reconciled to; **~ās agere** thank; **~ās habēre** feel grateful; **~ā** (*with gen*) for the sake of; **eā ~ā** on that account; **~īs** for nothing.

Grātiae, -ārum *fpl* the three Graces.

grātificātiō, -ōnis *f* obligingness.

grātificor, -ārī *vi* to do a favour, oblige ♦ *vt* to make a present of.

gratiīs, grātīs *adv* for nothing.

grātiōsus *adj* in favour, popular; obliging.

grātor, -ārī, -ātus *vi* to rejoice, congratulate.

grātuītō *adv* for nothing.

grātuītus *adj* free, gratuitous.

grātulābundus *adj* congratulating.

grātulātiō, -ōnis *f* rejoicing; congratulation; public thanksgiving.

grātulor, -ārī, -ātus *vt, vi* to congratulate; to give thanks.

grātus *adj* pleasing, welcome, dear; grateful, thankful; (*acts*) deserving thanks; **~um facere** do a favour.

gravātē *adv* reluctantly, grudgingly.

gravātim *adv* unwillingly.

gravēdinōsus *adj* liable to colds.

gravēdō, -inis *f* cold in the head.

graveolēns, -entis *adj* strong-smelling.

gravēscō, -ere *vi* to become heavy; to grow worse.

graviditās, -ātis *f* pregnancy.

gravidō, -āre *vt* to impregnate.

gravidus *adj* pregnant; loaded, full.

gravis *adj* heavy; loaded, pregnant; (*smell*) strong, offensive; (*sound*) deep, bass; (*body*) sick; (*food*) indigestible; (*fig*) oppressive, painful, severe; important, influential, dignified.

gravitās, -ātis *f* weight, severity, sickness; importance, dignity, seriousness; **annōnae ~** high price of corn.

graviter *adv* heavily; strongly, deeply; severely, seriously, violently; gravely, with dignity; **~ ferre** be vexed at.

gravō, -āre *vt* to load, weigh down; to oppress, aggravate.

gravor, -ārī *vt, vi* to feel annoyed, object to, disdain.

gregālis *adj* of the herd, common ♦ *m* comrade.

gregārius *adj* common; (*MIL*) private.

gregātim *adv* in crowds.

gremium, -ī *nt* bosom, lap.

gressus *ppa of* gradior.

gressus, -ūs *m* step; course.

grex, -egis *m* flock, herd; company, troop.

grunniō, -īre *vi* to grunt.

grunnītus, -ūs *m* grunting.

grūs, -uis *f* crane.

grȳps, -ȳpis *m* griffin.

gubernāclum (gubernāculum), -ī *nt* rudder, tiller; helm, government.

gubernātiō, -ōnis *f* steering, management.

gubernātor, -ōris *m* steersman, pilot, governor.

gubernātrīx, -īcis *f* directress.

gubernō, -āre, -āvī, -ātum *vt* to steer, pilot; to manage, govern.

gula, -ae *f* gullet, throat; gluttony, palate.

gulōsus *adj* dainty.

gurges, -itis *m* abyss, deep water, flood; (*person*) spendthrift.

gurguliō, -ōnis *f* gullet, windpipe.

gurgustium, -ī and iī *nt* hovel, shack.

gustātus, -ūs m sense of taste; flavour.
gustō, -āre, -āvī, -ātum vt to taste; to have a
snack; (fig) to enjoy, overhear. **prīnīs labrīs**
~ have a superficial knowledge of.
gustus, -ūs m tasting; preliminary dish.
gutta, -ae f drop; spot, speck.
guttātim adv drop by drop.
guttur, -is nt throat, gluttony.
gūtus, -ī m flask.
Gyās, -ae m giant with a hundred arms.
Gȳgaeus adj see n.
Gȳgēs, -is and **ae** m king of Lydia (famed for
his magic ring).
gymnasiarchus, -ī m master of a
gymnasium.
gymnasium, -ī and **iī** nt sports ground, school.
gymnasticus adj gymnastic.
gymnicus adj gymnastic.
gynaecēum, -ēī and **īum, -ī** nt women's
quarters.
gypsātus adj coated with plaster.
gypsum, -ī nt plaster of Paris; a plaster
figure.
gȳrus, -ī m circle, coil, ring; course.

H, h

ha interj (expressing joy or laughter) hurrah!, ha
ha!
habēna, -ae f strap; (pl) reins; (fig) control;
~**ās dare, immittere** allow to run freely.
habeō, -ēre, -uī, -itum vt to have, hold; to
keep, contain, possess; (fact) to know; (with
infin) to be in a position to; (person) to treat,
regard, consider; (action) to make, hold,
carry out ♦ vi to have possessions;
ōratiōnem ~ make a speech; in animō ~
intend; **prō certō** ~ be sure; **sē** ~ fine oneself,
be; **sibi, sēcum** ~ keep to oneself; (fight) ~**et a**
hit!; **bene** ~**et** it is well; **sīc** ~**et** so it is; **sīc**
~**ētō** be sure of this.
habilis adj manageable, handy; suitable,
nimble, expert.
habilitās, -ātis f aptitude.
habitābilis adj habitable.
habitātiō, -ōnis f dwelling, house.
habitātor, -ōris m tenant, inhabitant.
habitō, -āre, -āvī, -ātum vt to inhabit ♦ vi to
live, dwell; to remain, be always (in).
habitūdō, -inis f condition.
habitus ppp of **habeō** ♦ adj stout; in a humour.
habitus, -ūs m condition, appearance; dress;

character, quality; disposition, feeling.
hāc adv this way.
hāctenus adv thus far, so far; till now.
Hadria, -ae f town in N. Italy; Adriatic Sea.
Hadriānus, -ānī m emperor Hadrian.
Hadriāticus and **acus** adj of emperor Hadrian.
haedilia, -ae f little kid.
haedinus adj kid's.
haedulus, -ī m little kid.
haedus, -ī m kid; (ASTRO, usu pl) the Kids (a
cluster in Auriga).
Haemonia, -ae f Thessaly.
Haemonius adj Thessalian.
Haemus, -ī m mountain range in Thrace.
haereō, -rēre, -sī, -sum vi to cling, stick, be
attached; (nearness) to stay close, hang on;
(continuance) to linger, remain (at);
(stoppage) to stick fast, come to a standstill,
be at a loss.
haerēscō, -ere vi to adhere.
haeresis, -is f sect.
haesī perf of **haereō.**
haesitantia, -ae f stammering.
haesitātiō, -ōnis f stammering; indecision.
haesitō, -āre vi to get stuck; to stammer; to
hesitate, be uncertain.
hahae, hahahae see **ha.**
hālitus, -ūs m breath, vapour.
hallex, -icis m big toe.
hallūc- see **alūc-.**
hālō, -āre vi to be fragrant ♦ vt to exhale.
hāluc etc see **alūc.**
halyaeetos, -ī m osprey.
hama, -ae f water bucket.
Hamādryas, -adis f woodnymph.
hāmātilis adj with hooks.
hāmātus adj hooked.
Hamilcar, -is m father of Hannibal.
hāmus, -ī m hook; talons.
Hannibal, -is m famous Carthaginian general in
2nd Punic War.
hara, -ae f stye, pen.
harēna, -ae f sand; desert, seashore; arena (in
the amphitheatre).
harēnōsus adj sandy.
hariola, -ae f, **hariolus, -ī** m soothsayer.
hariolor, -ārī vi to prophesy; to talk nonsense.
harmonia, -ae f concord, melody; (fig)
harmony.
harpagō, -āre vt to steal.
harpagō, -ōnis m grappling hook; (person)
robber.
harpē, -ēs f scimitar.
Harpȳiae, -ārum fpl Harpies (mythical
monsters, half women, half bird).
harundifer, -ī adj reed-crowned.
harundineus adj reedy.
harundinōsus adj abounding in reeds.
harundō, -inis f reed, cane; fishing rod; shaft,
arrow; (fowling) limed twig; (music) pipe,

---

flute; (*toy*) hobbyhorse; (*weaving*) comb; (*writing*) pen.
haruspex, -icis *m* diviner (*from entrails*); prophet.
haruspica, -ae *f* soothsayer.
haruspicīnus *adj of divination by entrails* ♦ *f art of such divination.*
haruspicium, -ī *and* **iī** *nt* divination.
Hasdrubal, -is *m brother of Hannibal.*
hasta, -ae *f* spear, pike; sign of an auction sale; **sub ~ā vēndere** put up for auction.
hastātus *adj* armed with a spear ♦ *mpl first line of Roman army in battle;* **prīmus ~** 1st company of hastati.
hastīle, -is *nt* shaft, spear, javelin; vine prop.
hau, haud *adv* not, not at all.
hauddum *adv* not yet.
haudquāquam *adv* not at all, not by any means.
hauriō, -rīre, -sī, -stum *vt* to draw, draw off, derive; to drain, empty, exhaust; to take in, drink, swallow, devour.
haustus *ppp of* **hauriō.**
haustus, -ūs *m* drawing (water); drinking; drink, draught.
haut *etc see* **haud.**
hebdomas, -dis *f* week.
Hēbē, -ēs *f* goddess of youth (*cup bearer to the gods*).
hebenus, -ī *f* ebony.
hebeō, -ēre *vi* to be blunt, dull, sluggish.
hebes, -tis *adj* blunt, dull, sluggish; obtuse, stupid.
hebēscō, -ere *vi* to grow dim *or* dull.
hebetō, -āre *vt* to blunt, dull, dim.
Hebrus, -ī *m* Thracian river (*now* Maritza).
Hecatē, -ēs *f* goddess of magic (*and often identified with Diana*).
Hecatēius, -ēis *adj see n.*
hecatombē, -ēs *f* hecatomb.
Hector, -is *m* son of Priam (*chief warrior of the Trojans against the Greeks*).
Hectoreus *adj* of Hector; Trojan.
Hecuba, -ae *and* **ē, -ēs** *f* wife of Priam.
hedera, -ae *f* ivy.
hederiger, -ī *adj* wearing ivy.
hederōsus *adj* covered with ivy.
hēdychrum, -ī *nt* a cosmetic perfume.
hei, heia *etc see* **ei, eia.**
Helena, -ae *and* **ē, -ēs** *f* Helen (*wife of Menelaus, abducted by Paris*).
Helenus, -ī *m* son of Priam (*with prophetic powers*).
Hēliades, -um *fpl* daughters of the Sun (*changed to poplars or alders, and their tears to amber*).
Helicē, -ēs *f* the Great Bear.
Helicōn, -ōnis *m* mountain in Greece sacred to Apollo and the Muses.
Helicōniades, -um *fpl* the Muses.
Helicōnius *adj see* **Helicōn.**
Hellas, -dis *f* Greece.
Hellē, -ēs *f* mythical Greek princess (*carried

by the golden-fleeced ram, and drowned in the Hellespont*).
Hellēspontius, -iacus *adj see n.*
Hellēspontus, -ī *m* Hellespont (*now* Dardanelles).
helluō, -ōnis *m* glutton.
helluor, -ārī *vi* to be a glutton.
helvella, -ae *f* a savoury herb.
Helvētiī, -ōrum *mpl* people of E. Gaul (*now* Switzerland).
Helvētius, -cus *adj see n.*
hem *interj* (*expressing surprise*) eh?, well well!
hēmerodromus, -ī *m* express courier.
hēmicillus, -ī *m* mule.
hēmicyclium, -ī *and* **iī** *nt* semicircle with seats.
hēmīna, -ae *f* half a pint.
hendecasyllabī, -ōrum *mpl* hendecasyllabics, verses of eleven syllables.
heptēris, -is *f* ship with seven banks of oars.
hera *etc see* **era.**
Hēra, -ae *f* Greek goddess identified with Juno.
Hēraclītus, -ī *m* early Greek philosopher.
Hēraea, -aeōrum *ntpl* festival of Hera.
herba, -ae *f* blade, young plant; grass, herb, weed.
herbēscō, -ere *vi* to grow into blades.
herbeus *adj* grass-green.
herbidus *adj* grassy.
herbifer, -ī *adj* grassy.
herbōsus *adj* grassy, made of turf; made of herbs.
herbula, -ae *f* little herb.
hercīscō, -ere *vt* to divide an inheritance.
hercle *interj* by Hercules!
herctum, -ī *nt* inheritance.
Hercule *interj* by Hercules!
Herculēs, -is *and* **ī** *m* mythical Greek hero, later deified.
Herculeus *adj:* **arbor ~** poplar; **urbs ~** Herculaneum.
here *etc see* **herī.**
hērēditārius *adj* inherited; about an inheritance.
hērēditās, -ātis *f* inheritance; **~ sine sacrīs** a gift without awkward obligations.
hērēdium, -ī *and* **iī** *nt* inherited estate.
hērēs, -ēdis *m/f* heir, heiress; (*fig*) master, successor.
herī *adv* yesterday.
herīlis *etc see* **erilis.**
Hermēs, -ae *m* Greek god identified with Mercury; Hermes pillar.
Hernicī, -ōrum *mpl* people of central Italy.
Hernicus *adj see n.*
Hērodotus, -ī *m* first Greek historian.
hērōicus *adj* heroic, epic.
hērōīna, -ae *f* demigoddess.
hērōis, -dis *f* demigoddess.
hērōs, -is *m* demigod, hero.
hērōus *adj* heroic, epic.
herus *etc see* **erus.**

Hēsiodēus, -īus adj see n.
Hēsiodus, -ī m Hesiod (Greek didactic poet).
Hesperia, -iae f Italy; Spain.
Hesperides, -idum fpl keepers of a garden in the far West.
Hesperius, -is adj western.
Hesperus, -ī m evening star.
hesternus adj of yesterday.
heu interj (expressing dismay or pain) ah!, alas!
heus interj (calling attention) ho!, hallo!
hexameter, -rī m hexameter verse.
hexēris, -is f ship with six banks of oars.
hiātus, -ūs m opening, abyss; open mouth, gaping; (GRAM) hiatus.
Hibērēs, -um mpl Spaniards.
Hibēria, -iae f Spain.
hīberna, -ōrum ntpl winter quarters.
hībernācula, -ōrum ntpl winter tents.
Hibernia, -ae f Ireland.
hībernō, -āre vi to winter, remain in winter quarters.
hībernus adj winter, wintry.
Hibērus, -icus adj Spanish.
Hibērus, -ī m river Ebro.
hibīscum, -ī nt marsh mallow.
hibrida, hybrida, -ae m/f mongrel, half-breed.
hīc, haec, hōc pron, adj this; he, she, it; my, the latter, the present; **hīc homō** I; **hōc magis** the more; **hōc est** that is.
hīc adv here; herein; (time) at this point.
hīce, haece, hōce emphatic forms of **hīc, haec, hōc.**
hīcine, haecine, hōcine emphatic forms of **hīc, haec, hōc.**
hiemālis adj winter, stormy.
hiemō, -āre vi to pass the winter; to be wintry, stormy.
hiems, (hiemps), -is f winter; stormy weather, cold.
Hierōnymus, -ī m Jerome.
Hierosolyma, -ōrum ntpl Jerusalem.
Hierosolymārius adj see n.
hietō, -āre vi to yawn.
hilare adv see **hilaris.**
hilaris adj cheerful, merry.
hilaritās, -ātis f cheerfulness.
hilaritūdō, -inis f merriment.
hilarō, -āre vt to cheer, gladden.
hilarulus adj a gay little thing.
hilarus etc see **hilaris.**
hīllae, -ārum fpl smoked sausage.
Hīlōtae, -ārum mpl Helots (of Sparta).
hīlum, -ī nt something, a whit.
hinc adv from here, hence; on this side; from this source, for this reason; (time) henceforth.
hinniō, -īre vi to neigh.
hinnītus, -ūs m neighing.
hinnuleus, -ī m fawn.

hiō, -āre vi to be open, gape, yawn; (speech) to be disconnected, leave a hiatus ♦ vt to sing.
hippagōgī, -ōrum fpl cavalry transports.
hippocentaurus, -ī m centaur.
hippodromos, -ī m racecourse.
Hippolytus, -ī m son of Theseus (slandered by stepmother Phaedra).
hippomanes, -is nt mare's fluid; membrane on foal's forehead.
Hippōnactēus adj of Hipponax ♦ m iambic verse used by Hipponax.
Hippōnax, -ctis m Greek satirist.
hippotoxotae, -ārum mpl mounted archers.
hīra, -ae f the empty gut.
hircīnus adj of a goat.
hircōsus adj goatish.
hircus, -ī m he-goat; goatish smell.
hirnea, -ae f jug.
hirq- etc see **hirc-.**
hirsūtus adj shaggy, bristly; uncouth.
hirtus adj hairy, shaggy; rude.
hirūdō, -inis f leech.
hirundinīnus adj swallows'.
hirundō, -inis f swallow.
hīscō, -ere vi to gape; to open the mouth ♦ vt to utter.
Hispānia, -iae f Spain.
Hispāniēnsis, -us adj Spanish.
hispidus adj hairy, rough.
Hister, -rī m lower Danube.
historia, -ae f history, inquiry; story.
historicus adj historical ♦ m historian.
histricus adj of the stage.
histriō, -ōnis m actor.
histriōnālis adj of an actor.
histriōnia, -ae f acting.
hiulcē adv with hiatus.
hiulcō, -āre vt to split open.
hiulcus adj gaping, open; (speech) with hiatus.
hodiē adv today; nowadays, now; up to the present.
hodiernus adj today's.
holitor, -ōris m market gardener.
holitōrius adj for market gardeners.
holus, -eris nt vegetables.
holusculum, -ī nt small cabbage.
Homēricus adj see n.
Homērus, -ī m Greek epic poet, Homer.
homicīda, -ae m killer, murderer.
homicīdium, -ī and **iī** n murder.
homō, -inis m/f human being, man; (pl) people, the world; (derogatory) fellow, creature; **inter -inēs esse** be alive; see the world.
homullus, -ī, homunciō, -ōnis, homunculus, -ī m little man, poor creature, mortal.
honestās, -ātis f good character, honourable reputation; sense of honour, integrity;

(_things_) beauty.
honestē _adv_ decently, virtuously.
honestō, -āre _vt_ to honour, dignify,
embellish.
honestus _adj_ honoured, respectable;
honourable, virtuous; (_appearance_)
handsome ♦ _m_ gentleman ♦ _nt_ virtue, good;
beauty.
honor, -ōris _m_ honour, esteem; public office,
position, preferment; award, tribute,
offering; ornament, beauty; ~**ōris causā** out
of respect; for the sake of; ~**ōrem praefārī**
apologize for a remark.
honōrābilis _adj_ a mark of respect.
honōrārius _adj_ done out of respect, honorary.
honōrātē _adv_ honourably.
honōrātus _adj_ esteemed, distinguished; in
high office; complimentary.
honōrificē _adv_ in complimentary terms.
honōrificus _adj_ complimentary.
honōrō, -āre, -āvī, -ātum _vt_ to do honour to,
embellish.
honōrus _adj_ complimentary.
honōs _etc see_ **honor.**
hōra, -ae _f_ hour; time, season; (_pl_) clock; **in**
~**ās** hourly; **in** ~**am vīvere** ≈ live from hand to
mouth.
hōraeum, -ī _nt_ pickle.
Horātius, -ī _m_ Roman family name (_esp the
defender of Rome against Porsenna); the lyric
poet Horace._
Horātius _adj see n._
hordeum, -ī _nt_ barley.
horia, -ae _f_ fishing smack.
hōrnō _adv_ this year.
hōrnōtinus _adj_ this year's.
hōrnus _adj_ this year's.
hōrologium, -ī _and_ **iī** _nt_ clock.
horrendus _adj_ fearful, terrible; awesome.
horrēns, -entis _pres p of_ **horreō** ♦ _adj_ bristling,
shaggy.
horreō, -ēre, -uī _vi_ to stand stiff, bristle; to
shiver, shudder, tremble ♦ _vt_ to dread; to be
afraid, be amazed.
horrēscō, -ere _vi_ to stand on end, become
rough; to begin to quake; to start, be
terrified ♦ _vt_ to dread.
horreum, -ī _nt_ barn, granary, store.
horribilis _adj_ terrifying; amazing.
horridē _adv see_ **horridus.**
horridulus _adj_ protruding a little; unkempt;
(_fig_) uncouth.
horridus _adj_ bristling, shaggy, rough, rugged;
shivering; (_manners_) rude, uncouth;
frightening.
horrifer, -ī _adj_ chilling; terrifying.
horrificē _adv_ in awesome manner.
horrificō, -āre _vt_ to ruffle; to terrify.
horrificus _adj_ terrifying.
horrisonus _adj_ dread-sounding.
horror, -ōris _m_ bristling; shivering, ague;
terror, fright, awe, a terror.
hōrsum _adv_ this way.

hortāmen, -inis _nt_ encouragement.
hortāmentum, -ī _nt_ encouragement.
hortātiō, -ōnis _f_ harangue, encouragement.
hortātor, -ōris _m_ encourager.
hortātus, -ūs _m_ encouragement.
Hortēnsius, -ī _m_ Roman family name (_esp an
orator in Cicero's time_).
hortor, -ārī, -ātus _vt_ to urge, encourage,
exhort, harangue.
hortulus, -ī _m_ little garden.
hortus, -ī _m_ garden; (_pl_) park.
hospes, -itis _m,_ **hospita, -ae** _f_ host, hostess;
guest, friend; stranger, foreigner ♦ _adj_
strange.
hospitālis _adj_ host's, guest's; hospitable.
hospitālitās, -ātis _f_ hospitality.
hospitāliter _adv_ hospitably.
hospitium, -ī _and_ **iī** _nt_ hospitality, friendship;
lodging, inn.
hostia, -ae _f_ victim, sacrifice.
hostiātus _adj_ provided with victims.
hosticus _adj_ hostile; strange ♦ _nt_ enemy
territory.
hostīlis _adj_ of the enemy, hostile.
hostīliter _adv_ in hostile manner.
hostīmentum, -ī _nt_ recompense.
hostiō, -īre _vt_ to requite.
hostis, -is _m/f_ enemy.
hūc _adv_ hither, here; to this, to such a pitch; ~
illūc hither and thither.
hui _interj_ (_expressing surprise_) ho!, my word!
hūiusmodī such.
hūmānē, -iter _adv_ humanly; gently, politely.
hūmānitās, -ātis _f_ human nature, mankind;
humanity, kindness, courtesy; culture,
refinement.
hūmānitus _adv_ in accordance with human
nature; kindly.
hūmānus _adj_ human, humane, kind,
courteous; cultured, refined, well-educated;
~**ō māior** superhuman.
humātiō, -ōnis _f_ burying.
hūme-, hūmi- _see_ **ūme-, ūmi-.**
humilis _adj_ low, low-lying, shallow; (_condition_)
lowly, humble, poor; (_language_)
commonplace; (_mind_) mean, base.
humilitās, -ātis _f_ low position, smallness,
shallowness; lowliness, insignificance;
meanness, baseness.
humiliter _adv_ meanly, humbly.
humō, -āre, -āvī, -ātum _vt_ to bury.
humus, -ī _f_ earth, ground; land; ~**ī** on the
ground.
hyacinthinus _adj_ of the hyacinthus.
hyacinthus, -ī _m_ iris, lily.
Hyades, -um _fpl_ Hyads (_a group of stars in
Taurus_).
hyaena, -ae _f_ hyena.
hyalus, -ī _m_ glass.
Hybla, -ae _f_ mountain in Sicily (_famous for
bees_).
Hyblaeus _adj see n._
hybrida _etc see_ **hibrida.**

Hydaspēs, -is *m* tributary of river Indus (*now* Jelum).
Hȳdra, -ae *f* hydra (*a mythical dragon with seven heads*).
hydraulus, -ī *m* water organ.
hydria, -ae *f* ewer.
Hydrochous, -ī *m* Aquarius.
hydrōpicus *adj* suffering from dropsy.
hydrōps, -is *m* dropsy.
hydrus, -ī *m* serpent.
Hylās, -ae *m* a youth loved by Hercules.
Hymēn, -enis, Hymenaeus, -ī *m* god of marriage; wedding song; wedding.
Hymettius *adj see n.*
Hymettus, -ī *m* mountain near Athens (*famous for honey and marble*).
Hypanis, -is *m* river of Sarmatia (*now* Bug).
Hyperboreī, -ōrum *mpl* fabulous people in the far North.
Hyperboreus *adj see n.*
Hyperiōn, -onis *m* father of the Sun; the Sun.
hypodidasculus, -ī *m* assistant teacher.
hypomnēma, -tis *nt* memorandum.
Hyrcānī, -ōrum *mpl* people on the Caspian Sea.
Hyrcānus *adj* Hyrcanian.

I, i

Iacchus, -ī *m* Bacchus; wine.
iaceō, -ēre, -uī *vi* to lie; to be ill, be dead; (*places*) to be situated, be flat or low-lying, be in ruins; (*dress*) to hang loose; (*fig*) to be inactive, be downhearted; (*things*) to be dormant, neglected, despised.
iaciō, -ere, iēcī, iactum *vt* to throw; to lay, build; (*seed*) to sow; (*speech*) to cast, let fall, mention.
iactāns, -antis *pres p of* **iactō** ♦ *adj* boastful.
iactanter *adv* ostentatiously.
iactantia, -ae *f* boasting, ostentation
iactātiō, -ōnis *f* tossing, gesticulation; boasting, ostentation; ~ **populāris** publicity.
iactātus, -ūs *m* waving.
iactitō, -āre *vt* to mention, bandy.
iactō, -āre, -āvī, -ātum *vt* to throw, scatter; to shake, toss about; (*mind*) to disquiet; (*ideas*) to consider, discuss, mention; (*speech*) to boast of; **sē** ~ waver, fluctuate; to behave ostentatiously, be officious.
iactūra, -ae *f* throwing overboard; loss, sacrifice.
iactus *ppp of* **iaciō**.

iactus, -ūs *m* throwing, throw; intrā tēlī iactum within spear's range.
iacuī *perf of* **iaceō**
iaculābilis *adj* missile.
iaculātor, -ōris *m* thrower, shooter; light-armed soldier.
iaculātrīx, -īcis *f* huntress.
iaculor, -ārī, -ātus *vt* to throw, hurl, shoot; to throw the javelin; to shoot at, hit; (*fig*) to aim at, attack.
iaculum, -ī *nt* javelin; fishing net.
iāien- *etc see* **iēn-**.
iam *adv* (*past*) already, by then; (*present*) now, already; (*future*) directly, very soon; (*emphasis*) indeed, precisely; (*inference*) therefore, then; surely; (*transition*) moreover, next; **iam dūdum** for a long time, long ago; immediately; **iam iam** right now, any moment now; **nōn ~** no longer; **iam** ... at one time ... at another; **iam nunc** just now; **iam prīdem** long ago, for a long time; **iam tum** even at that time; **sī iam** supposing for the purpose of argument.
iambēus *adj* iambic.
iambus, -ī *m* iambic foot; iambic poetry.
lānālis *adj see* **lānus.**
lāniculum, -ī *nt* Roman hill across the Tiber.
iānitor, -ōris *m* doorkeeper, porter.
iānua, -ae *f* door; entrance; (*fig*) key.
lānuārius *adj of* January ♦ *m* January.
lānus, -ī *m* god of gateways and beginnings; archway, arcade.
lapetīonidēs, -ae *m* Atlas.
lapetus, -ī *m* a Titan (*father of Atlas and Prometheus*).
lāpyx, -gis *adj* Iapygian; Apulian ♦ *m* west-north-west wind from Apulia.
lāsōn, -onis *m* Jason (*leader of Argonauts, husband of Medea*).
lāsonius *adj see n.*
iaspis, -dis *f* jasper.
Ibēr- *etc see* **Hibēr-**.
ibi *adv* there; then; in this, at it.
ibīdem *adv* in the same place; at that very moment.
ibis, -is *and* **idis** *f* ibis.
Icarium, -ī *nt* Icarian Sea.
Icarius *adj see n.*
Icarus, -ī *m* son of Daedalus (*drowned in the Aegean*).
īcō, -ere, -ī, ictum *vt* to strike; **foedus** ~ make a treaty.
ictericus *adj* jaundiced.
ictis, -dis *f* weasel.
ictus *ppp of* **īcō**.
ictus, -ūs *m* stroke, blow; wound; (*metre*) beat.
Ida, -ae, -ē, -ēs *f* mountain in Crete; mountain near Troy.
Idaeus *adj* Cretan; Trojan.
idcircō *adv* for that reason; for the purpose.

Noun declensions and verb conjugations are shown on pp xiii to xxv. The present infinitive ending of a verb shows to which conjugation it belongs: -āre = 1st, -ēre = 2nd; -ere = 3rd and -īre = 4th. Irregular verbs are shown on p xxvi

īdem, eadem, idem pron the same; also, likewise.

identidem adv repeatedly, again and again.

ideō adv therefore, for this reason, that is why.

idiōta, -ae m ignorant person, layman.

īdōlon, -ī nt apparition.

idōneē adv see **idōneus**.

idōneus adj fit, proper, suitable, sufficient.

Īdūs, -uum fpl Ides (the 15th March, May, July, October, the 13th of other months).

iēcī perf of **iaciō**.

iecur, -oris and **inoris** nt liver; (fig) passion.

iecusculum, -ī nt small liver.

iēiūniōsus adj hungry.

iēiūnitās, -ātis f fasting; (fig) meagreness.

iēiūnium, -ī and **iī** nt fast; hunger; leanness.

iēiūnus adj fasting, hungry; (things) barren, poor, meagre; (style) feeble.

iēntāculum, -ī nt breakfast.

igitur adv therefore, then, so.

ignārus adj ignorant, unaware; unknown.

ignāvē, -iter adv without energy.

ignāvia, -ae f idleness, laziness; cowardice.

ignāvus adj idle, lazy, listless; cowardly; relaxing.

ignēscō, -ere vi to take fire, burn.

igneus adj burning, fiery.

igniculus, -ī m spark; (fig) fire, vehemence.

ignifer, -ī adj fiery.

ignigena, -ae m the fireborn (Bacchus).

ignipēs, -edis adj fiery-footed.

ignipotēns, -entis adj fire-working (Vulcan).

ignis, -is m fire, a fire; firebrand, lightning; brightness, redness; (fig) passion, love.

ignōbilis adj unknown, obscure; low-born.

ignōbilitās, -ātis f obscurity; low birth.

ignōminia, -ae f dishonour, disgrace.

ignōminiōsus adj (person) degraded, disgraced; (things) shameful.

ignōrābilis adj unknown.

ignōrantia, -ae f ignorance.

ignōrātiō, -ōnis f ignorance.

ignōrō, -āre, -āvī, -ātum vt to not know, be unacquainted with; to disregard.

ignōscō, -scere, -vī, -tum vt, vi to forgive, pardon.

ignōtus adj unknown; low-born; ignorant.

īlex, -icis f holm oak.

īlia, -um ntpl groin; entrails; ~ dūcere become broken-winded.

Īlia, -ae f mother of Romulus and Remus.

Īliadēs, -adae m son of Ilia; Trojan.

Īlias, -dis f the Iliad; a Trojan woman.

īlicet adv it's all over, let us go; immediately.

īlicō adv on the spot; instantly.

īlignus adj of holm oak.

Īlīthyia, -ae f Greek goddess of childbirth.

Īlium, -on, -ī nt, **-os, -ī** f Troy.

Īlius, -acus adj Trojan.

illā adv that way.

illābefactus adj unbroken.

illābor, -bī, -psus vi to flow into, fall down.

illabōrō, -āre vi to work (at).

illāc adv that way.

illacessītus adj unprovoked.

illacrimābilis adj unwept; inexorable.

illacrimō, -āre; -or, -ārī vi to weep over, lament; to weep.

illaesus adj unhurt.

illaetābilis adj cheerless.

illāpsus ppa of **illābor**.

illaqueō, -āre vt to ensnare.

illātus ppp of **īnferō**.

illaudātus adj wicked.

ille, -a, -ud pron and adj that, that one; he, she, it; the famous; the former, the other; **ex ~ō** since then.

illecebra, -ae f attraction, lure, bait, decoy bird.

illecebrōsus adj seductive.

illectus ppp of **illiciō**.

illēctus adj unread.

illepidē adv see **illepidus**.

illepidus adj inelegant, churlish.

illex, -icis m/f lure.

illēx, -ēgis adj lawless.

illexī perf of **illiciō**.

illībātus adj unimpaired.

illīberālis adj ungenerous, mean, disobliging.

illīberālitās, -ātis f meanness.

illīberāliter adv see **illīberālis**.

illic, -aec, -ūc pron he, she, it; that.

illīc adv there, yonder; in that matter.

illiciō, -icere, -exī, -ectum vt to seduce, decoy, mislead.

illicitātor, -ōris m sham bidder (at an auction).

illicitus adj unlawful.

illīdō, -dere, -sī, -sum vt to strike, dash against.

illigō, -āre, -āvī, -ātum vt to fasten on, attach; to connect; to impede, encumber, oblige.

illim adv from there.

illīmis adj clear.

illinc adv from there; on that side.

illinō, -inere, -ēvī, -itum vt to smear over, cover, bedaub.

illiquefactus adj melted.

illīsī perf of **illīdō**.

illīsus ppp of **illīdō**.

illitterātus adj uneducated, uncultured.

illitus ppp of **illinō**.

illō adv (to) there; to that end.

illōtus adj dirty.

illūc adv (to) there; to that; to him/her.

illūceō, -ēre vi to blaze.

illūcēscō, -cēscere, -xī vi to become light, dawn.

illūdō, -dere, -sī, -sum vt, vi to play, amuse oneself; to abuse; to jeer at, ridicule.

illūminātē adv luminously.

illūminō, -āre, -āvī, -ātum vt to light up; to enlighten; to embellish.

illūsiō, -ōnis f irony.

illūstris adj bright, clear; distinct, manifest;

distinguished, illustrious.
illūstrō, -āre, -āvī, -ātum vt to illuminate; to make clear, explain; to make famous.
illūsus ppp of **illūdō.**
illuviēs, -ēī f dirt, filth; floods.
Illyria, -ae f, **-cum, -cī** nt Illyria.
Illyricus, -us adj see **Illyricum.**
Illyriī, -ōrum mpl people E. of the Adriatic.
Ilva, -ae f Italian island (now Elba).
imāginārius adj fancied.
imāginātiō, -ōnis f fancy.
imāginor, -ārī, vt to picture to oneself.
imāgō, -inis f likeness, picture, statue; portrait of ancestor; apparition, ghost; echo, mental picture, idea; (fig) semblance, mere shadow; (RHET) comparison.
imbēcillē adv faintly.
imbēcillitās, -ātis f weakness, helplessness.
imbēcillus adj weak, frail; helpless.
imbellis adj non-combatant; peaceful; cowardly.
imber, -ris m rain, heavy shower; water; (fig) stream, shower.
imberbis, imberbus adj beardless.
imbibō, -ere, -ī vt (mind) to conceive; to resolve.
imbrex, -icis f tile.
imbricus adj rainy.
imbrifer, -ī adj rainy.
imbuō, -uere, -uī, -ūtum vt to wet, steep, dip; (fig) to taint, fill; to inspire, accustom, train; to begin, be the first to explore
imitābilis adj imitable.
imitāmen, -inis nt imitation; likeness.
imitāmenta, -ōrum ntpl pretence.
imitātiō, -ōnis f imitation.
imitātor,-ōris m, **-rīx,-rīcis** f imitator.
imitātus adj copied.
imitor, -ārī, -ātus vt to copy, portray; to imitate, act like.
immadēscō, -ēscere, -uī vi to become wet.
immāne adv savagely.
immānis adj enormous, vast; monstrous, savage, frightful.
immānitās, -ātis f vastness; savageness, barbarism.
immānsuētus adj wild.
immātūritās, -ātis f over-eagerness.
immātūrus adj untimely.
immedicābilis adj incurable.
immemor, -is adj unmindful, forgetful, negligent.
immemorābilis adj indescribable, not worth mentioning.
immemorātus adj hitherto untold.
immēnsitās, -ātis f immensity.
immēnsum, -ī nt infinity, vast extent ♦ adv exceedingly.
immēnsus adj immeasurable, vast, unending.
immerēns, -entis adj undeserving.

immergō, -gere, -sī, -sum vt to plunge, immerse.
immeritō adv unjustly.
immeritus adj undeserving, innocent; undeserved.
immērsābilis adj never foundering.
immērsus ppp of **immergō.**
immētātus adj unmeasured.
immigrō, -āre, -āvī, -ātum vi to move (into).
immineō, -ēre, -uī vi to overhang, project; to be near, adjoin, impend; to threaten, be a menace to; to long for, grasp at.
imminuō, -uere, -uī, -ūtum vt to lessen, shorten; to impair; to encroach on, ruin.
imminūtiō, -ōnis f mutilation; (RHET) understatement.
immisceō, -scēre, -scuī, -xtum vt to intermingle, blend; sē ~ join, meddle with.
immiserābilis adj unpitied.
immisericorditer adv unmercifully.
immisericors, -dis adj pitiless.
immissiō, -ōnis f letting grow.
immissus ppp of **immittō.**
immītis adj unripe; severe, inexorable.
immittō, -ittere, -īsī, -issum vt to let in, put in; to graft on; to let go, let loose, let grow; to launch, throw; to incite, set on.
immīxtus ppp of **immisceō.**
immo adv (correcting preceding words) no, yes; on the contrary, or rather; ~ sī ah, if only.
immōbilis adj motionless; immovable.
immoderātē adv extravagantly.
immoderātiō, -ōnis f excess.
immoderātus adj limitless; excessive, unbridled.
immodestē adv extravagantly.
immodestia, -ae f license.
immodestus adj immoderate.
immodicē adv see **immodicus.**
immodicus adj excessive, extravagant, unruly.
immodulātus adj unrhythmical.
immolātiō, -ōnis f sacrifice.
immolātor, -ōris m sacrificer.
immolītus adj erected.
immolō, -āre, -āvī, -ātum vt to sacrifice; to slay.
immorior, -ī, -tuus vi to die upon; to waste away.
immorsus adj bitten; (fig) stimulated.
immortālis adj immortal, everlasting.
immortālitās, -ātis f immortality; lasting fame.
immortāliter adv infinitely.
immōtus adj motionless, unmoved, immovable.
immūgiō, -īre, -iī vi to roar (in).
immulgeō, -ēre vt to milk.
immundus adj unclean, dirty.
immūniō, -īre, -īvī vt to strengthen.

immūnis *adj* with no public obligations, untaxed, free from office; exempt, free (from).

immūnitās, -ātis *f* exemption, immunity, privilege.

immūnītus *adj* undefended; (*roads*) unmetalled.

immurmurō, -āre *vi* to murmur (at).

immūtābilis *adj* unalterable.

immūtābilitās, -ātis *f* immutability.

immūtātiō, -ōnis *f* exchange; (*RHET*) metonymy.

immūtātus *adj* unchanged.

immūtō, -āre, -āvī, -ātum *vt* to change; (*words*) to substitute by metonymy.

impācātus *adj* aggressive.

impāctus *ppp of* **impingō**.

impār, -aris *adj* unequal, uneven, unlike; no match for, inferior; (*metre*) elegiac.

imparātus *adj* unprepared, unprovided.

impariter *adv* unequally.

impāstus *adj* hungry.

impatiēns, -entis *adj* unable to endure, impatient.

impatienter *adv* intolerably.

impatientia, -ae *f* want of endurance.

impavidē *adv see* **impavidus**.

impavidus *adj* fearless, undaunted.

impedīmentum, -ī *nt* hindrance, obstacle; (*pl*) baggage, luggage, supply train.

impediō, -īre, -īvī *and* **iī, -ītum** *vt* to hinder, entangle; to encircle; (*fig*) to embarrass, obstruct, prevent.

impedītiō, -ōnis *f* obstruction.

impedītus *adj* (*MIL*) hampered with baggage, in difficulties; (*place*) difficult, impassable; (*mind*) busy, obsessed.

impēgī *perf of* **impingō**.

impellō, -ellere, -ulī, -ulsum *vt* to strike, drive; to set in motion, impel, shoot; to incite, urge on; (*fig*) to overthrow, ruin.

impendeō, -ēre *vi* to overhang; to be imminent, threaten.

impendiō *adv* very much.

impendium, -ī *and* **iī** *nt* expense, outlay; interest on a loan.

impendō, -endere, -endī, -ēnsum *vt* to weigh out, pay out, spend; (*fig*) to devote.

impenetrābilis *adj* impenetrable.

impēnsa, -ae *f* expense, outlay.

impēnsē *adv* very much; earnestly.

impēnsus *ppp of* **impendō** ♦ *adj* (*cost*) high, dear; (*fig*) great, earnest.

imperātor, -ōris *m* commander-in-chief, general; emperor; chief, master.

imperātōrius *adj* of a general; imperial.

imperātum, -ī *nt* order.

imperceptus *adj* unknown.

impercussus *adj* noiseless.

imperditus *adj* not slain.

imperfectus *adj* unfinished, imperfect.

imperfossus *adj* not stabbed.

imperiōsus *adj* powerful, imperial; tyrannical.

imperītē *adv* awkwardly.

imperītia, -ae *f* inexperience.

imperītō, -āre *vt, vi* to rule, command.

imperītus *adj* inexperienced, ignorant.

imperium, -ī *and* **iī** *nt* command, order; mastery, sovereignty, power; military command, supreme authority; empire; (*pl*) those in command, the authorities.

impermissus *adj* unlawful.

imperō, -āre, -āvī, -ātum *vt, vi* to order, command; to requisition, demand; to rule, govern, control; to be emperor.

imperterritus *adj* undaunted.

impertiō, -īre, -īvī *and* **iī, -ītum** *vt* to share, communicate, impart.

imperturbātus *adj* unruffled.

impervius *adj* impassable.

impetibilis *adj* intolerable.

impetis (*gen*), **-e** (*abl*) *m* force; extent.

impetrābilis *adj* attainable; successful.

impetrātiō, -ōnis *f* favour.

impetriō, -īre *vt* to succeed with the auspices.

impetrō, -āre, -āvī, -ātum *vt* to achieve; to obtain, secure (*a request*).

impetus, -ūs *m* attack, onset; charge; rapid motion, rush; (*mind*) impulse, passion.

impexus *adj* unkempt.

impiē *adv* wickedly.

impietās, -ātis *f* impiety, disloyalty, unfilial conduct.

impiger, -rī *adj* active, energetic.

impigrē *adv see adj*.

impigritās, -ātis *f* energy.

impingō, -ingere, -ēgī, -āctum *vt* to dash, force against; to force upon; (*fig*) to bring against, drive.

impiō, -āre *vt* to make sinful.

impius *adj* (*to gods*) impious; (*to parents*) undutiful; (*to country*) disloyal; wicked, unscrupulous.

implācābilis *adj* implacable.

implācābiliter *adv see adj*.

implācātus *adj* unappeased.

implacidus *adj* savage.

impleō, -ēre, -ēvī, -ētum *vt* to fill; to satisfy; (*time, number*) to make up, complete; (*duty*) to discharge, fulfil.

implexus *adj* entwined; involved.

implicātiō, -ōnis *f* entanglement.

implicātus *adj* complicated, confused.

implicitē *adv* intricately.

implicō, -āre, -āvī *and* **uī, -ātum** *and* **itum** *vt* to entwine, enfold, clasp; (*fig*) to entangle, involve; to connect closely, join.

implōrātiō, -ōnis *f* beseeching.

implōrō, -āre, -āvī, -ātum *vt* to invoke, entreat, appeal to.

implūmis *adj* unfledged.

impluō, -ere *vi* to rain upon.

impluvium, -ī *and* **iī** *nt* roof-opening of the Roman atrium; rain basin in the atrium.

impolītē *adv* without ornament.

impolītus adj unpolished, inelegant

impollūtus adj unstained.

impōnō, -ōnere, -osuī, -ositum vt to put in, lay on, place; to embark; (fig) to impose, inflict, assign; to put in charge (*acc*) to impose; (with dat) to impose upon cheat.

importō, -āre, -āvī, -ātum vt to bring in, import; (fig) to bring upon, introduce.

importūnē adv see adj.

importūnitās, -ātis f insolence, ill nature.

importūnus adj unsuitable; troublesome; ill-natured, uncivil, bullying.

importuōsus adj without a harbour

impos, -tis adj not master (of).

impositus, impostus ppp of **impōnō**.

impotēns, -entis adj powerless weak; with no control over; headstrong, violent.

impotenter adv weakly; violently.

impotentia, -ae f poverty; want of self-control, violence.

impraesentiārum adv at present.

imprānsus adj fasting, without breakfast.

imprecor, -ārī vt to invoke.

impressiō, -ōnis f (MIL) thrust, raid; (mind) impression; (speech) emphasis (rhythm) beat.

impressus ppp of **imprimō**.

imprīmīs adv especially.

imprimō, -imere, -essī, -essum vt to press upon, impress, imprint, stamp

improbātiō, -ōnis f blame.

improbē adv badly, wrongly; persistently.

improbitās, -ātis f badness, dishonesty.

improbō, -āre, -āvī, -ātum vt to disapprove, condemn, reject.

improbulus adj a little presumptuous.

improbus adj bad, inferior (in quality); wicked, perverse, cruel; unruly, persistent, rebellious.

imprōcērus adj undersized.

imprōdictus adj not postponed.

imprōmptus adj unready, slow.

improperātus adj lingering.

improsper, -ī adj unsuccessful.

improsperē adv unfortunately.

imprōvidē adv see adj.

imprōvidus adj unforeseeing, thoughtless.

imprōvīsus adj unexpected; ~ō, ~ē ~ō, ex ~ō unexpectedly.

imprūdēns, -entis adj unforeseeing, not expecting; ignorant, unaware.

imprūdenter adv thoughtlessly, unawares.

imprūdentia, -ae f thoughtlessness; ignorance; aimlessness.

impūbēs, -eris and **is** adj youthful; chaste.

impudēns, -entis adj shameless, impudent.

impudenter adv see adj.

impudentia, -ae f impudence.

impudīcitia, -ae f lewdness.

impudīcus adj shameless; immodest.

impugnātiō, -ōnis f assault.

impugnō, -āre, -āvī, -ātum vt to attack; (fig) to oppose, impugn.

impulī perf of **impellō**.

impulsiō, -ōnis pressure; (mind) impulse.

impulsor, -ōris m instigator.

impulsus ppp of **impellō**.

impulsus, -ūs m push, pressure, impulse; (fig) instigation.

impūne adv safely, with impunity.

impūnitās, -ātis f impunity.

impūnītē adv with impunity.

impūnītus adj unpunished.

impūrātus adj vile.

impūrē adv see ad.

impūritās, -ātis f uncleanness.

impūrus adj unclean; infamous, vile.

imputātus adj unpruned.

imputō, -āre, -āvī, -ātum vt to put to one's account; to ascribe, credit, impute.

īmulus adj little tip of.

īmus adj lowest, deepest, bottom of; last.

in prep (with abl) in, on, at; among; in the case of; (time) during; (with acc) into, on to, to, towards; against; (time) for, till; (purpose) for; ~ armīs under arms; ~ equō on horseback; ~ eō esse ut be in the position of; be on the point of; ~ hōrās hourly; ~ modum in the manner of; ~ rem of use; ~ universum in general.

inaccessus adj unapproachable.

inacēscō, -ere vi to turn sour.

Īnachidēs, -ae m Perseus; Epaphus.

Īnachis, -idis f Io.

Īnachius adj of Inachus, Argive, Greek.

Īnachus, -ī m first king of Argos.

inadsuētus adj unaccustomed.

inadūstus adj unsinged.

inaedificō, -āre, -āvī, -ātum vt to build on, erect; to wall up, block up.

inaequābilis adj uneven.

inaequālis adj uneven; unequal; capricious.

inaequāliter adv see adj.

inaequātus adj unequal.

inaequō, -āre vt to level up.

inaestimābilis adj incalculable; invaluable; valueless.

inaestuō, -āre vi to rage in.

inamābilis adj hateful.

inamārēscō, -ere vi to become bitter.

inambitiōsus adj unambitious.

inambulātiō, -ōnis f walking about.

inambulō, -āre vi to walk up and down.

inamoenus adj disagreeable.

inanimus adj lifeless, inanimate.

ināniō, -īre vt to make empty.

inānis adj empty, void; poor, unsubstantial; useless, worthless, vain, idle ♦ nt (PHILOS) space; (fig) vanity.

inānitās, -ātis f empty space; inanity.

Noun declensions and verb conjugations are shown on pp xiii to xxv. The present infinitive ending of a verb shows to which conjugation it belongs: -āre = 1st; -ēre = 2nd; -ere = 3rd and -īre = 4th. Irregular verbs are shown on p xxvi

inaniter adv idly, vainly.
inarātus adj fallow.
inardēscō, -dēscere, -sī vi to be kindled, flare up.
inass- etc see **inads-**.
inattenuātus adj undiminished.
inaudāx, -ācis adj timorous.
inaudiō, -īre vt to hear of, learn.
inaudītus adj unheard of, unusual; without a hearing.
inaugurātō adv after taking the auspices.
inaugurō, -āre vi to take auspices ♦ vt to consecrate, inaugurate.
inaurēs, -ium fpl earrings.
inaurō, -āre, -āvi, -ātum vt to gild; (fig) to enrich.
inauspicātō adv without taking the auspices.
inauspicātus adj done without auspices.
inausus adj unattempted.
incaeduus adj uncut.
incalēscō, -ēscere, -uī vi to grow hot; (fig) to warm, glow.
incalfaciō, -ere vt to heat.
incallidē adv unskilfully.
incallidus adj stupid, simple.
incandēscō, -ēscere, -uī vi to become hot; to turn white.
incānēscō, -ēscere, -uī vi to grow grey.
incantātus adj enchanted.
incānus adj grey.
incassum adv in vain.
incastīgātus adj unrebuked.
incautē adv negligently.
incautus adj careless, heedless; unforeseen, unguarded.
incēdō, -ēdere, -ēssī, -ēssum vi to walk, parade, march; (MIL) to advance; (feelings) to come upon.
incelebrātus adj not made known.
incēnātus adj supperless.
incendiārius, -ī and **iī** m incendiary.
incendium, -ī and **iī** nt fire, conflagration; heat; (fig) fire, vehemence, passion.
incendō, -ere, -ī, incēnsum vt to set fire to, burn; to light, brighten; (fig) to inflame, rouse, incense.
incēnsiō, -ōnis f burning.
incēnsus ppp of **incendō**.
incēnsus adj not registered.
incēpī perf of **incipiō**.
inceptiō, -ōnis f undertaking.
inceptō, -āre vt to begin, attempt.
inceptor, -ōris m originator.
inceptum, -ī nt beginning, undertaking, attempt.
inceptus ppp of **incipiō**.
incērō, -āre vt to cover with wax.
incertō adv not for certain.
incertus adj uncertain, doubtful, unsteady ♦ nt uncertainty.
incessō, -ere, -īvī vt to attack; (fig) to assail.
incessus, -ūs m gait, pace, tramp; invasion; approach.

incestē adv see adj.
incestō, -āre vt to pollute, dishonour.
incestus adj sinful; unchaste, incestuous ♦ nt incest.
incestus, -ūs m incest.
incho- etc see **incoh-**.
incidō, -idere, -idī, -āsum vi to fall upon, fall into; to meet, fall in with, come across; to befall, occur, happen; in mentem ~ occur to one.
incīdō, -dere, -dī, -sum vt to cut open; to cut up; to engrave, inscribe; to interrupt, cut short.
incīle, -is nt ditch.
incīlō, -āre vt to rebuke.
incingō, -gere, -xī, -ctum vt to gird, wreathe; to surround.
incinō, -ere vt to sing, play.
incipiō, -ipere, -ēpī, -eptum vt, vi to begin.
incipissō, -ere vt to begin.
incisē adv in short clauses.
incīsim adv in short clauses.
incīsiō, -ōnis f clause.
incīsum, -ī nt clause.
incīsus ppp of **incīdō**.
incitāmentum, -ī nt incentive.
incitātē adv impetuously.
incitātiō, -ōnis f inciting; rapidity.
incitātus ppp of **incitō** ♦ adj swift, rapid; **equō ~ō** at a gallop.
incitō, -āre, -āvī, -ātum vt to urge on, rush; to rouse, encourage, excite; to inspire; to increase; **sē ~** rush; **currentem ~** ≈ spur a willing horse.
incitus adj swift.
incitus adj immovable; **ad ~ās, ~a redigere** bring to a standstill.
inclāmō, -āre vt, vi to call out, cry out to; to scold, abuse.
inclārēscō, -ēscere, -uī vi to become famous.
inclēmēns, -entis adj severe.
inclēmenter adv harshly.
inclēmentia, -ae f severity.
inclīnātiō, -ōnis f leaning, slope; (fig) tendency, inclination, bias; (CIRCS) change; (voice) modulation.
inclīnātus adj inclined, prone; falling; (voice) deep.
inclīnō, -āre, -āvī, -ātum vt to bend, turn; to turn back; (fig) to incline, direct, transfer; to change ♦ vi to bend, sink; (MIL) to give way; (fig) to change, deteriorate; to incline, tend, turn in favour.
inclitus etc see **inclutus**.
inclūdō, -dere, -sī, -sum vt to shut in, keep in, enclose; to obstruct, block; (fig) to include; (time) to close, end.
inclūsiō, -ōnis f imprisonment.
inclūsus ppp of **inclūdō**.
inclutus adj famous, glorious.
incoctus ppp of **incoquō**.
incoctus adj uncooked, raw.
incōgitābilis adj thoughtless.

incōgitāns, -antis adj thoughtless.
incōgitantia, -ae f thoughtlessness.
incōgitō, -āre vt to contrive.
incognitus adj unknown, unrecognised; (law) untried.
incohātus adj unfinished.
incohō, -āre, -āvī, -ātum vt to begin, start.
incola, -ae f inhabitant, resident.
incolō, -ere, -uī vt to live in, inhabit ♦ vi to live, reside.
incolumis adj safe and sound, unharmed.
incolumitās, -ātis f safety.
incomitātus adj unaccompanied.
incommendātus adj unprotected.
incommodē adv inconveniently, unfortunately.
incommoditās, -ātis f inconvenience, disadvantage.
incommodō, -āre vi to be inconvenient, annoy.
incommodum, -ī nt inconvenience, disadvantage, misfortune.
incommodus adj inconvenient, troublesome.
incommūtābilis adj unchangeable.
incompertus adj unknown.
incompositē adv see adj.
incompositus adj in disorder, irregular.
incōmptus adj undressed, inelegant.
inconcessus adj forbidden.
inconciliō, -āre vt to win over (by guile); to trick, inveigle, embarrass.
inconcinnus adj inartistic, awkward.
inconcussus adj unshaken, stable.
inconditē adv confusedly.
inconditus adj undisciplined, not organised; (language) artless.
inconsīderātē adv see adj.
inconsīderātus adj thoughtless, ill-advised.
inconsōlābilis adj incurable.
inconstāns, -antis adj fickle, inconsistent.
inconstanter adv inconsistently
inconstantia, -ae f fickleness, inconsistency.
inconsultē adv indiscreetly.
inconsultū without consulting.
inconsultus adj indiscreet, ill-advised; unanswered; not consulted.
inconsūmptus adj unconsumed
incontāminātus adj untainted.
incontentus adj untuned.
incontinēns, -entis adj intemperate.
incontinenter adv without self-control.
incontinentia, -ae f lack of self-control.
inconveniēns, -entis adj ill-matched.
incoquō, -quere, -xī, -ctum vt to boil; to dye.
incorrēctus adj unrevised.
incorruptē adv justly.
incorruptus adj unspoiled; uncorrupted, genuine.
incrēbrēscō, incrēbēscō, -ēscere, -uī vi to increase, grow, spread.

incrēdibilis adj incredible, extraordinary.
incrēdibiliter adv see adj.
incrēdulus adj incredulous.
incrēmentum, -ī nt growth, increase; addition; offspring.
increpitō, -āre vt to rebuke; to challenge.
increpō, -āre, -uī, -itum vi to make a noise, sound; (news) to be noised abroad ♦ vt to cause to make a noise; to exclaim against, rebuke.
incrēscō, -scere, -vī vi to grow in, increase.
incrētus adj sifted in.
incruentātus adj unstained with blood.
incruentus adj bloodless, without bloodshed.
incrūstō, -āre vt to encrust.
incubō, -āre, -uī, -itum vi to lie in or on; (fig) to brood over.
incubuī perf of **incubō**; perf of **incumbō**.
inculcō, -āre, -āvī, -ātum vt to force in; to force upon, impress on.
inculpātus adj blameless.
incultē adv uncouthly.
incultus adj uncultivated; (fig) neglected, uneducated, rude.
incultus, -ūs m neglect, squalor.
incumbō, -mbere, -buī, -bitum vi to lean, recline on; to fall upon, throw oneself upon; to oppress, lie heavily upon; (fig) to devote attention to, take pains with; to incline.
incūnābula, -ōrum ntpl swaddling clothes; (fig) cradle, infancy, birthplace, origin.
incūrātus adj neglected.
incūria, -ae f negligence.
incūriōsē adv carelessly.
incūriōsus adj careless, indifferent.
incurrō, -rrere, -rrī and **curri, -rsum** vi to run into, rush, attack; to invade; to meet with, get involved in; (events) to occur, coincide.
incursiō, -ōnis f attack; invasion, raid; collision.
incursō, -āre vt, vi to run into, assault; to frequently invade; (fig) to meet, strike.
incursus, -ūs m assault, striking; (mind) impulse.
incurvō, -āre vt to bend, crook.
incurvus adj bent, crooked.
incūs, -ūdis f anvil.
incūsātiō, -ōnis f blaming.
incūsō, -āre, -āvī, -ātum vt to find fault with, accuse.
incussī perf of **incutiō**.
incussus ppp of **incutiō**.
incussus, -ūs m shock.
incustōdītus adj unguarded, unconcealed.
incūsus adj forged.
incutiō, -tere, -ssī, -ssum vt to strike, dash against; to throw; (fig) to strike into, inspire with.
indāgātiō, -ōnis f search.
indāgātor, -ōris m explorer.

Noun declensions and verb conjugations are shown on pp xiii to xxv. The present infinitive ending of a verb shows to which conjugation it belongs: -āre = 1st; -ēre = 2nd; -ere = 3rd and -īre = 4th. Irregular verbs are shown on p xxvi

indāgātrix, -rīcis _f_ female explorer.
indāgō, -āre _vt_ to track down; (_fig_) to trace, investigate.
indāgō, -inis _f_ (_hunt_) drive, encirclement.
indaudiō _etc see_ **inaudiō.**
inde _adv_ from there, from that, from them; on that side; from then, ever since; after that, then.
indēbitus _adj_ not due.
indēclīnātus _adj_ constant.
indecor, -is _adj_ dishonourable, a disgrace.
indecōrē _adv_ indecently.
indecorō, -āre _vt_ to disgrace.
indecōrus _adj_ unbecoming, unsightly.
indēfēnsus _adj_ undefended.
indēfessus _adj_ unwearied, tireless.
indēflētus _adj_ unwept.
indēiectus _adj_ undemolished.
indēlēbilis _adj_ imperishable.
indēlībātus _adj_ unimpaired.
indemnātus _adj_ unconvicted.
indēplōrātus _adj_ unlamented.
indēprēnsus _adj_ undetected.
indeptus _ppa of_ **indipīscor.**
indēsertus _adj_ unforsaken.
indēstrictus _adj_ unscathed.
indētōnsus _adj_ unshorn.
indēvītātus _adj_ unerring.
index, -icis _m_ forefinger; witness, informer; (_book, art_) title, inscription; (_stone_) touchstone; (_fig_) indication, pointer, sign.
India, -iae _f_ India.
indicātiō, -ōnis _f_ value.
indīcente mē without my telling.
indicium, -ī _and_ **iī** _nt_ information, evidence; reward for information; indication, sign, proof; ~ **profitērī, offerre** ≈ _turn King's evidence_; ~ **postulāre, dare** ask, grant permission to give evidence.
indicō, -āre, -āvī, -ātum _vt_ to point out; to disclose, betray; to give information, give evidence; to put a price on.
indīcō, -īcere, -īxī, -ictum _vt_ to declare, proclaim, appoint.
indictus _ppp of_ **indīcō.**
indictus _adj_ not said, unsung; **causā ~ā** without a hearing.
Indicus _adj see n._
indidem _adv_ from the same place _or_ thing.
indidī _perf of_ **indō.**
indifferēns, -entis _adj_ neither good nor bad.
indigena, -ae _m_ native ♦ _adj_ native.
indigēns, -entis _adj_ needy.
indigentia, -ae _f_ need; craving.
indigeō, -ēre, -uī _vi_ (_with abl_) to need, want, require; to crave.
indiges, -etis _m_ national deity.
indīgestus _adj_ confused.
indignābundus _adj_ enraged.
indignāns, -antis _adj_ indignant.
indignātiō, -ōnis _f_ indignation.
indignē _adv_ unworthily; indignantly.
indignitās, -ātis _f_ unworthiness, enormity;

insulting treatment; indignation.
indignor, -ārī, -ātus _vt_ to be displeased with, be angry at.
indignus _adj_ unworthy, undeserving; shameful, severe; undeserved.
indigus _adj_ in want.
indīligēns, -entis _adj_ careless.
indīligenter _adv see adj._
indīligentia, -ae _f_ carelessness.
indipīscor, -ī, indeptus _vt_ to obtain, get, reach.
indīreptus _adj_ unplundered.
indiscrētus _adj_ closely connected, indiscriminate, indistinguishable.
indisertē _adv_ without eloquence.
indisertus _adj_ not eloquent.
indispositus _adj_ disorderly.
indissolūbilis _adj_ imperishable.
indistinctus _adj_ confused, obscure.
inditus _ppp of_ **indō.**
indīviduus _adj_ indivisible; inseparable ♦ _nt_ atom.
indō, -ere, -idī, -itum _vt_ to put in _or_ on; to introduce; to impart, impose.
indocilis _adj_ difficult to teach, hard to learn; untaught.
indoctē _adv_ unskilfully.
indoctus _adj_ untrained, illiterate, ignorant.
indolentia, -ae _f_ freedom from pain.
indolēs, -is _f_ nature, character, talents.
indolēscō, -ēscere, -uī _vi_ to feel sorry.
indomitus _adj_ untamed, wild; ungovernable.
indormiō, -īre _vi_ to sleep on; to be careless.
indōtātus _adj_ with no dowry; unhonoured; (_fig_) unadorned.
indubitō, -āre _vi_ to begin to doubt.
indubius _adj_ undoubted.
indūcō, -ūcere, -ūxī, -uctum _vt_ to bring in, lead on; to introduce; to overlay, cover over; (_fig_) to move, persuade, seduce; (_book-keeping_) to enter; (_dress_) to put on; (_public show_) to exhibit; (_writing_) to erase; **animum, in animum ~** determine, imagine.
inductiō, -ōnis _f_ leading, bringing on; (_mind_) purpose, intention; (_logic_) induction.
inductus _ppp of_ **indūcō.**
indugredior _etc see_ **ingredior.**
induī _perf of_ **induō.**
indulgēns -entis _pres p of_ **indulgeō** ♦ _adj_ indulgent, kind.
indulgenter _adv_ indulgently.
indulgentia, -ae _f_ indulgence, gentleness.
indulgeō, -gēre, -sī _vi_ (_with dat_) to be kind to, indulge, give way to; to indulge in ♦ _vt_ to concede; **sibi ~** take liberties.
induō, -uere, -uī, -ūtum _vt_ (_dress_) to put on; (_fig_) to assume, entangle.
indup- _etc see_ **imp-.**
indūrēscō, -ēscere, -uī _vi_ to harden.
indūrō, -āre _vt_ to harden.
Indus, -ī _m_ Indian; Ethiopian; mahout.
Indus _adj see n._
industria, -ae _f_ diligence; **dē, ex ~ā** on

purpose.
industriē adv see **industrius.**
industrius adj diligent, painstaking.
indūtiae, -ārum fpl truce, armistice.
indūtus ppp of **induō.**
indūtus, -us m wearing.
induviae, -ārum fpl clothes.
indūxī perf of **indūcō.**
inēbriō, -āre vt to intoxicate; (fig) to saturate.
inedia, -ae f starvation.
inēditus adj unpublished.
inēlegāns, -antis adj tasteless.
inēleganter adv without taste.
inēluctābilis adj inescapable.
inēmorior, -ī vi to die in.
inemptus adj unpurchased.
inēnārrābilis adj indescribable.
inēnōdābilis adj inexplicable.
ineō, -īre, -īvī and **iī, -itum** vi tc go in, come in;
to begin ♦ vt to enter; to begin, enter upon,
form, undertake; **cōnsilium ~** frm a plan;
grātiam ~ win favour; **numerum ~**
enumerate; **ratiōnem ~** calculate, consider,
contrive; **suffrāgium ~** vote; **viam ~** find out a
way.
ineptē adv see adj.
ineptia, -ae f stupidity; (pl) nonsense.
ineptiō, -īre vi to play the fool.
ineptus adj unsuitable; silly, tactless, absurd.
inermis, inermus adj unarmed, defenceless;
harmless.
inerrāns, -antis adj fixed.
inerrō, -āre vi to wander about in.
iners, -tis adj unskilful; inactive, indolent,
timid; insipid.
inertia, -ae f lack of skill; idleness, laziness.
inērudītus adj uneducated.
inēscō, -āre vt to entice, deceive.
inēvectus adj mounted.
inēvītābilis adj inescapable.
inexcītus adj peaceful.
inexcūsābilis adj with no excuse.
inexercitātus adj untrained.
inexhaustus adj unexhausted.
inexōrābilis adj inexorable; (things) severe.
inexperrēctus adj unawakened.
inexpertus adj inexperienced; untried.
inexpiābilis adj inexpiable; implacable.
inexplēbilis adj insatiable.
inexplētus adj incessant.
inexplicābilis adj inexplicable; impracticable,
unending.
inexplōrātō adv without making a
reconnaissance.
inexplōrātus adj unreconnoitred.
inexpugnābilis adj impregnable, safe.
inexspectātus adj unexpected
inexstinctus adj unextinguishe, insatiable,
imperishable.
inexsuperābilis adj insurmountable.

inextrīcābilis adj inextricable.
īnfabrē adv unskilfully.
īnfabricātus adj unfashioned.
īnfacētus adj not witty, crude.
īnfācundus adj ineloquent.
īnfāmia, -ae f disgrace, scandal.
īnfāmis adj infamous, disreputable.
īnfāmō, -āre, -āvī, -ātum vt to disgrace,
bring into disrepute.
īnfandus adj unspeakable, atrocious.
īnfāns, -antis adj mute, speechless; young,
infant; tongue-tied; childish ♦ m/f infant,
child.
īnfantia, -ae f inability to speak; infancy; lack
of eloquence.
īnfatuō, -āre vt to make a fool of.
īnfaustus adj unlucky.
īnfector, -ōris m dyer.
īnfectus ppp of **īnficiō.**
īnfectus adj undone, unfinished; rē ~ā without
achieving one's purpose.
īnfēcunditās, -ātis f infertility.
īnfēcundus adj unfruitful.
īnfēlīcitās, -ātis f misfortune.
īnfēlīciter adv see adj.
īnfēlīcō, -āre vt to make unhappy.
īnfēlīx, -īcis adj unfruitful; unhappy, unlucky.
īnfēnsē adv aggressively.
īnfēnsō, -āre vt to make dangerous, make
hostile.
īnfēnsus adj hostile, dangerous.
īnferciō, -īre vt to cram in.
īnferiae, -ārum fpl offerings to the dead.
īnferior, -ōris compar of **īnferus.**
īnferius compar of **īnfrā.**
īnfernē adv below.
īnfernus adj beneath; of the lower world,
infernal ♦ mpl the shades ♦ ntpl the lower
world.
īnferō, -re, intulī, illātum vt to carry in,
bring to, put on; to move forward; (fig) to
introduce, cause; (book-keeping) to enter;
(logic) to infer; **bellum ~** make war (on);
pedem ~ advance; **sē ~** repair, rush, strut
about; **signa ~** attack, charge.
īnferus (compar ~**ior,** superl **īnfimus**) adj lower,
below ♦ mpl the dead, the lower world ♦
compar lower; later; inferior ♦ superl lowest,
bottom of; meanest, humblest.
īnfervēscō, -vēscere, -buī vi to boil.
īnfestē adv aggressively.
īnfestō, -āre vt to attack.
īnfestus adj unsafe; dangerous, aggressive.
īnficēt- see **īnfacēt-.**
īnficiō, -icere, -ēcī, -ectum vt to dip, dye,
discolour; to taint, infect; (fig) to instruct,
corrupt, poison.
īnfidēlis adj faithless.
īnfidēlitās, -ātis f disloyalty.
īnfidēliter adv treacherously.

infīdus *adj* unsafe, treacherous.

infīgō, -gere, -xī, -xum *vt* to thrust, drive in; (*fig*) to impress, imprint.

infimus *superl of* **inferus.**

infindō, -ere *vt* to cut into, plough.

infīnitās, -ātis *f* boundless extent, infinity.

infīnītē *adv* without end.

infīnītiō, -ōnis *f* infinity.

infīnītus *adj* boundless, endless, infinite; indefinite.

infirmātiō, -ōnis *f* invalidating, refuting.

infirmē *adv* feebly.

infirmitās, -ātis *f* weakness; infirmity, sickness.

infirmō, -āre *vt* to weaken; to invalidate, refute.

infirmus *adj* weak, indisposed; weak-minded; (*things*) trivial.

infit *vi* (*defec*) begins.

infitiālis *adj* negative.

infitiās eō deny.

infitiātiō, -ōnis *f* denial.

infitiātor, -ōris *m* denier (of a debt).

infitior, -ārī, -ātus *vt* to deny, repudiate.

infixus *ppp of* **infīgō.**

inflammātiō, -ōnis *f* (*fig*) exciting.

inflammō, -āre, -āvī, -ātum *vt* to set on fire, light; (*fig*) to inflame, rouse.

inflatē *adv* pompously.

inflātiō, -ōnis *f* flatulence.

inflātus, -ūs *m* blow; inspiration ♦ *adj* blown up, swollen; (*fig*) puffed up, conceited; (*style*) turgid.

inflectō, -ctere, -xī, -xum *vt* to bend, curve; to change; (*voice*) to modulate; (*fig*) to affect, move.

inflētus *adj* unwept.

inflexiō, -ōnis *f* bending.

inflexus *ppp of* **inflectō.**

inflīgō, -gere, -xī, -ctum *vt* to dash against, strike; to inflict.

inflō, -āre, -āvī, -ātum *vt* to blow, inflate; (*fig*) to inspire, puff up.

influō, -ere, -xī, -xum *vi* to flow in; (*fig*) to stream, pour in.

infodiō, -odere, -ōdī, -ossum *vt* to dig in, bury.

infōrmātiō, -ōnis *f* sketch, idea.

infōrmis *adj* shapeless; hideous.

infōrmō, -āre, -āvī, -ātum *vt* to shape, fashion; to sketch; to educate.

infortūnātus *adj* unfortunate.

infortūnium, -ī *and* **iī** *nt* misfortune.

infossus *ppp of* **infodiō.**

infrā (*compar* **inferius**) *adv* underneath, below ♦ *compar* lower down ♦ *prep* (*with acc*) below, beneath, under; later than.

infrāctiō, -ōnis *f* weakening.

infrāctus *ppp of* **infringō.**

infragilis *adj* strong.

infremō, -ere, -uī *vi* to growl.

infrēnātus *ppp of* **infrēnō.**

infrēnātus *adj* without a bridle.

infrendō, -ere *vi* to gnash.

infrēnis, -us *adj* unbridled.

infrēnō, -āre, -āvī, -ātum *vt* to put a bridle on, harness; (*fig*) to curb.

infrequēns, -entis *adj* not crowded, infrequent; badly attended.

infrequentia, -ae *f* small number; emptiness.

infringō, -ingere, -ēgī, -āctum *vt* to break, bruise; (*fig*) to weaken, break down, exhaust.

infrōns, -ondis *adj* leafless.

infūcātus *adj* showy.

infula, -ae *f* woollen band, fillet, badge of honour.

infumus *etc see* **infimus.**

infundō, -undere, -ūdī, -usum *vt* to pour in *or* on; to serve; (*fig*) to spread.

infuscō, -āre *vt* to darken; to spoil, tarnish.

infūsus *ppp of* **infundō.**

ingeminō, -āre *vt* to redouble ♦ *vi* to be redoubled.

ingemīscō, -īscere, -uī *vi* to groan, sigh ♦ *vt* to sigh over.

ingemō, -ere, -uī *vt, vi* to sigh for, mourn.

ingenerō, -āre, -āvī, -ātum *vt* to engender, produce, create.

ingeniātus *adj* with a natural talent.

ingeniōsē *adv* cleverly.

ingeniōsus *adj* talented, clever; (*things*) naturally suited.

ingenitus *ppp of* **ingignō** ♦ *adj* inborn, natural.

ingenium, -ī *and* **iī** *nt* nature; (*disposition*) bent, character; (*intellect*) ability, talent, genius; (*person*) genius.

ingēns, -entis *adj* huge, mighty, great.

ingenuē *adv* liberally, frankly.

ingenuitās, -ātis *f* noble birth, noble character.

ingenuus *adj* native, innate; free-born; noble, frank; delicate.

ingerō, -rere, -ssī, -stum *vt* to carry in; to heap on; to throw, hurl; (*fig*) to press, obtrude.

ingignō, -ignere, -enuī, -enitum *vt* to engender, implant.

inglōrius *adj* inglorious.

ingluviēs, -ēī *f* maw; gluttony.

ingrātē *adv* unwillingly; ungratefully.

ingrātiīs, ingrātīs *adv* against one's will.

ingrātus *adj* disagreeable, unwelcome; ungrateful, thankless.

ingravēscō, -ere *vi* to grow heavy, become worse, increase.

ingravō, -āre *vt* to weigh heavily on; to aggravate.

ingredior, -dī, -ssus *vt, vi* to go in, enter; to walk, march; to enter upon, engage in; to commence, begin to speak.

ingressiō, -ōnis *f* entrance; beginning; pace.

ingressus, -ūs *m* entrance; (*MIL*) inroad; beginning; walking, gait.

ingruō, -ere, -ī *vi* to fall upon, assail.

inguen, -inis *nt* groin.

ingurgitō, -āre *vt* to pour in; **sē ~** gorge

oneself; (fig) to be absorbed in.
ingustātus adj untasted.
inhabilis adj unwieldy, awkward; unfit.
inhabitābilis adj uninhabitable.
inhabitō, -āre vt to inhabit.
inhaereō, -rēre, -sī, -sum vi to stick in, cling
to; to adhere, be closely connected with; to
be always in.
inhaerēscō, -ere vi to take hold, cling fast.
inhālō, -āre vt to breathe on.
inhibeō, -ēre, -uī, -itum vt to check, restrain,
use, practise; ~ rēmīs/nāvem backwater.
inhibitiō, -ōnis f backing water
inhiō, -āre vi to gape ♦ vt to gape at, covet.
inhonestē adv see adj.
inhonestō, -āre vt to dishonour
inhonestus adj dishonourable, inglorious;
ugly.
inhonōrātus adj unhonoured; unrewarded.
inhonōrus adj defaced.
inhorreō, -ēre, -uī vt to stand erect, bristle.
inhorrēscō, -ēscere, -uī vi to bristle up; to
shiver, shudder, tremble.
inhospitālis adj inhospitable.
inhospitālitās, -ātis f inhospitality
inhospitus adj inhospitable.
inhūmānē adv savagely; uncivilly.
inhūmānitās, -ātis f barbarity; discourtesy,
churlishness, meanness.
inhūmāniter adv = inhūmānē
inhūmānus adj savage, brutal; ill-bred,
uncivil, uncultured.
inhumātus adj unburied.
inibi adv there, therein; about to happen.
īniciō, -icere, -iēcī, -iectum vt to throw into,
put on; (fig) to inspire, cause; (speech) to
hint, mention; **manum** ~ take possession.
iniectus, -ūs m putting in, throwing over.
inimīcē adv hostilely.
inimīcitia, -ae f enmity.
inimīcō, -āre vt to make enemies.
inimīcus adj unfriendly, hostile; injurious ♦
m/f enemy; **~issimus** greatest enemy.
inīquē adv unequally, unjustly.
inīquitās, -ātis f unevenness, difficulty;
injustice, unfair demands.
inīquus adj unequal, uneven; adverse,
unfavourable, injurious; unfair, unjust;
excessive; impatient, discontented ♦ m
enemy.
initiō, -āre vt to initiate.
initium, -ī and **iī** nt beginning; (pl) elements,
first principles; holy rites, mysteries.
initus ppp of **ineō**.
initus, -ūs m approach; beginning.
iniūcundē adv see adj.
iniūcunditās, -ātis f unpleasantness.
iniūcundus adj unpleasant.
iniungō, -ungere, -ūnxī, -ūnctum vt to join,
attach; (fig) to impose, inflict.

iniūrātus adj unsworn.
iniūria, -ae f wrong, injury, injustice; insult,
outrage; severity, revenge; unjust
possession; **~ā** unjustly.
iniūriōsē adv wrongfully.
iniūriōsus adj unjust, wrongful; harmful.
iniūrius adj wrong, unjust.
iniūssū without orders (from).
iniūssus adj unbidden.
iniūstē adv see adj.
iniūstitia, -ae f injustice, severity.
iniūstus adj unjust, wrong; excessive, severe.
inl- etc see **ill-**.
inm- etc see **imm-**.
innābilis adj that none may swim.
innāscor, -scī, -tus vi to be born in, grow up
in.
innatō, -āre vt to swim in, float on; to swim,
flow into.
innātus ppa of **innāscor** ♦ adj innate, natural.
innāvigābilis adj unnavigable.
innectō, -ctere, -xuī, -xum vt to tie, fasten
together, entwine; (fig) to connect; to
contrive.
innītor, -tī, -xus and **sus** vi to rest, lean on; to
depend.
innō, -āre vi to swim in, float on, sail on.
innocēns, -entis adj harmless; innocent;
upright, unselfish.
innocenter adv blamelessly.
innocentia, -ae f innocence; integrity,
unselfishness.
innocuē adv innocently.
innocuus adj harmless; innocent; unharmed.
innōtēscō, -ēscere, -uī vi to become known.
innovō, -āre vt to renew; **sē** ~ return.
innoxius adj harmless, safe; innocent;
unharmed.
innuba, -ae adj unmarried.
innūbilus adj cloudless.
innūbō, -bere, -psī vi to marry into.
innumerābilis adj countless.
innumerābilitās, -ātis f countless number.
innumerābiliter adv innumerably.
innumerālis adj numberless.
innumerus adj countless.
innuō, -ere, -īuī vi to give a nod.
innūpta, -ae adj unmarried.
Īnō, -ūs f daughter of Cadmus.
inoblītus adj unforgetful.
inobrutus adj not overwhelmed.
inobservābilis adj unnoticed.
inobservātus adj unobserved.
inoffēnsus adj without hindrance,
uninterrupted.
inofficiōsus adj irresponsible; disobliging.
inolēns, -entis adj odourless.
inolēscō, -scere, -vī vi to grow in.
inōminātus adj inauspicious.
inopia, -ae f want, scarcity, poverty,

helplessness.
inopīnāns, -antis _adj_ unaware.
inopīnātō _adv_ unexpectedly.
inopīnātus _adj_ unexpected; off one's guard.
inopīnus _adj_ unexpected.
inopiōsus _adj_ in want.
inops, -is _adj_ destitute, poor, in need (of);
  helpless, weak; (_speech_) poor in ideas.
inōrātus _adj_ unpleaded.
inōrdinātus _adj_ disordered, irregular.
inōrnātus _adj_ unadorned, plain; uncelebrated.
īnōus _adj see n._
inp - _etc see_ **imp -**.
inquam _vt_ (_defec_) to say; (_emphatic_) I repeat,
  maintain.
inquiēs, -ētis _adj_ restless.
inquiētō, -āre _vt_ to unsettle, make difficult.
inquiētus _adj_ restless, unsettled.
inquilīnus, -ī _m_ inhabitant, tenant.
inquinātē _adv_ filthily.
inquinātus _adj_ filthy, impure.
inquinō, -āre, -āvī, -ātum _vt_ to defile, stain,
  contaminate.
inquīrō, -rere, -sīvī, -sītum _vt_ to search for,
  inquire into; (_law_) to collect evidence.
inquīsītiō, -ōnis _f_ searching, inquiry; (_law_)
  inquisition.
inquīsītor, -ōris _m_ searcher, spy;
  investigator.
inquīsītus _ppp of_ **inquīrō**.
inquīsītus _adj_ not investigated.
inr - _etc see_ **irr -**.
īnsalūtātus _adj_ ungreeted.
īnsānābilis _adj_ incurable.
īnsānē _adv_ madly.
īnsānia, -ae _f_ madness; folly, mania, poetic
  rapture.
īnsāniō, -īre, -īvī, -ītum _vi_ to be mad, rave; to
  rage; to be inspired.
īnsānitās, -ātis _f_ unhealthiness.
īnsānum _adv_ (_slang_) frightfully.
īnsānus _adj_ mad; frantic, furious; outrageous.
īnsatiābilis _adj_ insatiable; never cloying.
īnsatiābiliter _adv see adj._
īnsatietās, -ātis _f_ insatiateness.
īnsaturābilis _adj_ insatiable.
īnsaturābiliter _adv see adj._
īnscendō, -endere, -endī, -ēnsum _vt, vi_ to
  climb up, mount, embark.
īnscēnsiō, -ōnis _f_ going on board.
īnscēnsus _ppp of_ **īnscendō**.
īnsciēns, -entis _adj_ unaware; stupid.
īnscienter _adv_ ignorantly.
īnscientia, -ae _f_ ignorance, inexperience;
  neglect.
īnscītē _adv_ clumsily.
īnscītia, -ae _f_ ignorance, stupidity,
  inattention.
īnscītus _adj_ ignorant, stupid.
īnscius _adj_ unaware, ignorant.
īnscrībō, -bere, -psī, -ptum _vt_ to write on,
  inscribe; to ascribe, assign; (_book_) to entitle;
  (_for sale_) to advertise.

īnscrīptiō, -ōnis _f_ inscribing, title.
īnscrīptus _ppp of_ **īnscrībō**.
īnsculpō, -ere, -sī, -tum _vt_ to carve in,
  engrave on.
īnsectātiō, -ōnis _f_ hot pursuit; (_words_)
  abusing, persecution.
īnsectātor, -ōris _m_ persecutor.
īnsector, -ārī, -ātus; -ō, -āre _vt_ to pursue,
  attack, criticise.
īnsectus _adj_ notched.
īnsēdābiliter _adv_ incessantly.
īnsēdī _perf of_ **īnsīdō**.
īnsenēscō, -ēscere, -uī _vi_ to grow old in.
īnsēnsilis _adj_ imperceptible.
īnsepultus _adj_ unburied.
īnsequēns, -entis _pres p of_ **īnsequor** ♦ _adj_ the
  following.
īnsequor, -quī, -cūtus _vt_ to follow, pursue
  hotly; to proceed; (_time_) to come after, come
  next; (_fig_) to attack, persecute.
īnserō, -erere, -ēvī, -itum _vt_ to graft; (_fig_) to
  implant.
īnserō, -ere, -uī, -tum _vt_ to let in, insert; to
  introduce, mingle, involve.
īnsertō, -āre _vt_ to put in.
īnsertus _ppp of_ **īnserō**.
īnserviō, -īre, -iī, -ītum _vt, vi_ to be a slave (to);
  to be devoted, submissive (to).
īnsessus _ppp of_ **īnsīdō**.
īnsībilō, -āre _vi_ to whistle in.
īnsideō, -ēre _vi_ to sit on _or_ in; to remain fixed
  ♦ _vt_ to hold, occupy.
īnsidiae, -ārum _fpl_ ambush; (_fig_) trap,
  trickery.
īnsidiātor, -ōris _nt_ soldier in ambush; (_fig_)
  waylayer, plotter.
īnsidior, -ārī, -ātus _vi_ to lie in ambush; (_with
  dat_) to lie in wait for, plot against.
īnsidiōsē _adv_ insidiously.
īnsidiōsus _adj_ artful, treacherous.
īnsīdō, -īdere, -ēdī, -ēssum _vi_ to settle on;
  (_fig_) to become fixed, rooted in ♦ _vt_ to
  occupy.
īnsigne, -is _nt_ distinguishing mark, badge,
  decoration; (_pl_) insignia, honours; (_speech_)
  purple passages.
īnsigniō, -īre _vt_ to distinguish.
īnsignis _adj_ distinguished, conspicuous.
īnsignītē _adv_ remarkably.
īnsigniter _adv_ markedly.
īnsilia, -um _npl_ treadle (of a loom).
īnsiliō, -īre, -uī _vi_ to jump into _or_ onto.
īnsimulātiō, -ōnis _f_ accusation.
īnsimulō, -āre, -āvī, -ātum _vt_ to charge,
  accuse, allege (_esp falsely_).
īnsincērus _adj_ adulterated.
īnsinuātiō, -ōnis _f_ ingratiating.
īnsinuō, -āre, -āvī, -ātum _vt_ to bring in,
  introduce stealthily ♦ _vi_ to creep in, worm
  one's way in, penetrate; **sē ~** ingratiate
  oneself; to make one's way into.
īnsipiēns, -entis _adj_ senseless, foolish.
īnsipienter _adv_ foolishly.

īnsipientia, -ae f folly.
īnsistō, -istere, -titī vi to stand on step on; to stand firm, halt, pause; to tread on the heels, press on, pursue; to enter upon, apply oneself to, begin; to persist, continue.
īnsitiō, -ōnis f grafting; grafting time.
īnsitīvus adj grafted; (fig) spurious.
īnsitor, -ōris m grafter.
īnsitus ppp of **īnserō** ♦ adj innate; incorporated.
īnsociābilis adj incompatible.
īnsōlābiliter adv unconsolably.
īnsolēns, -entis adj unusual, unaccustomed; excessive, extravagant, insolent
īnsolenter adv unusually; immoderately, insolently.
īnsolentia, -ae f inexperience, novelty, strangeness; excess, insolerce.
īnsolēscō, -ere vi to become insolent, elated.
īnsolidus adj soft.
īnsolitus adj unaccustomed, unusual.
īnsomnia, -ae f sleeplessness.
īnsomnis adj sleepless.
īnsomnium, -ī and **iī** nt dream.
īnsonō, -āre, -uī vi to resound, sound; to make a noise.
īnsōns, -ontis adj innocent; harmless.
īnsōpītus adj sleepless.
īnspectō, -āre vt to look at.
īnspectus ppp of **īnspiciō.**
īnspērāns, -antis adj not expecting.
īnspērātus adj unexpected; **~ō, ex ~ē** unexpectedly.
īnspergō, -gere, -sī, -sum vt to sprinkle on.
īnspiciō, -icere, -exī, -ectum vt to look into; to examine, inspect; (MIL) to review; (mind) to consider, get to know.
īnspīcō, -āre vt to sharpen.
īnspīrō, -āre, -āvī, -ātum vt, vi to blow on, breathe into.
īnspoliātus adj unpillaged.
īnspūtō, -āre vt to spit on.
īnstābilis adj unsteady, not firm; (fig) inconstant.
īnstāns, -antis pres p of **īnstō** ♦ adj present; urgent, threatening.
īnstanter adv vehemently.
īnstantia, -ae f presence; vehemence.
īnstar nt (indecl) likeness, appearance; as good as, worth.
īnstaurātiō, -ōnis f renewal.
īnstaurātīvus adj renewed.
īnstaurō, -āre, -āvī, -ātum vt to renew, restore; to celebrate; to requite.
īnsternō, -ernere, -rāvī, -rātum vt to spread over, cover.
īnstīgātor, -ōris m instigator.
īnstīgātrīx, -rīcis f female instigator.
īnstīgō, -āre vt to goad, incite, instigate.
īnstillō, -āre vt to drop on, instil.

īnstimulātor, -ōris m instigator.
īnstimulō, -āre vt to urge on.
īnstinctor, -ōris m instigator.
īnstinctus adj incited, inspired.
īnstinctus, -ūs m impulse, inspiration.
īnstipulor, -ārī, -ātus vi to bargain for.
īnstita, -ae f flounce of a lady's tunic.
īnstitī perf of **īnstō.**
īnstitiō, -ōnis f stopping.
īnstitor, -ōris m pedlar.
īnstituō, -uere, -uī, -ūtum v: to set, implant; to set up, establish, build, appoint; to marshal, arrange, organize to teach, educate; to undertake, resolve on.
īnstitūtiō, -ōnis f custom; arrangement; education; (pl) principles of education.
īnstitūtum, -ī nt way of life, tradition, law; stipulation, agreement; purpose; (pl) principles.
īnstō, -āre, -itī vi to stand on or in; to be close, be hard on the heels of, pursue; (events) to approach, impend; (fig) to press on, work hard at; (speech) to insist, urge.
īnstrātus ppp of **īnsternō.**
īnstrēnuus adj languid, slow.
īnstrepō, -ere vi to creak.
īnstructiō, -ōnis f building; setting out.
īnstructius adv in better style.
īnstructor, -ōris m preparer.
īnstructus ppp of **īnstruō** ♦ adj provided, equipped; prepared, versed.
īnstructus, -ūs m equipment
īnstrūmentum, -ī nt tool, instrument; equipment, furniture, stock; (fig) means, provision; dress, embellishment.
īnstruō, -ere, -xī, -ctum vt to erect, build up; (MIL) to marshal, array; to equip, provide, prepare; (fig) to teach, train.
īnsuāsum, -ī nt a dark colour.
īnsuāvis adj disagreeable.
īnsūdō, -āre vi to perspire on.
īnsuēfactus adj accustomed.
īnsuēscō, -scere, -vī, -tum vt to train, accustom ♦ vi to become accustomed.
īnsuētus ppp of **īnsuēscō.**
īnsuētus adj unaccustomed, unused; unusual.
īnsula, -ae f island; block of houses.
īnsulānus, -ī m islander.
īnsulsē adv see adj.
īnsulsitās, -ātis f lack of taste, absurdity.
īnsulsus adj tasteless, absurd, dull.
īnsultō, -āre, vt, vi to jump on, leap in; (fig) to exult, taunt, insult
īnsultūra, -ae f jumping on.
īnsum, inesse, īnfuī vi to be in or on; to belong to.
īnsūmō, -ere, -psī, -ptum vt to spend, devote.
īnsuō, -uere, -uī, -ūtum vt to sew in, sew up in.

Noun declensions and verb conjugations are shown on pp xiii to xxv. The present infinitive ending of a verb shows to which conjugation it belongs: **-āre** = 1st; **-ēre** = 2nd; **-ere** = 3rd and **-īre** = 4th. Irregular verbs are shown on p xxvi

īnsuper *adv* above, on top; besides, over and above; (*prep with abl*) besides.

īnsuperābilis *adj* unconquerable, impassable.

īnsurgō, -gere, -rēxī, -rēctum *vi* to stand up, rise to; to rise, grow, swell; to rise against.

īnsusurrō, -āre *vt, vi* to whisper.

īnsūtus *ppp of* **īnsuō.**

intābēscō, -ēscere, -uī *vi* to melt away, waste away.

intāctilis *adj* intangible.

intāctus *adj* untouched, intact; untried; undefiled, chaste.

intāminātus *adj* unsullied.

intēctus *ppp of* **integō.**

intēctus *adj* uncovered, unclad; frank.

integellus *adj* fairly whole *or* pure.

integer, -rī *adj* whole, complete, unimpaired, intact; sound, fresh, new; (*mind*) unbiassed, free; (*character*) virtuous, pure, upright; (*decision*) undecided, open; in **~rum restituere** restore to a former state; **ab, dē, ex ~rō** afresh; **~rum est mihi** I am at liberty (to).

integō, -egere, -ēxī, -ēctum *vt* to cover over; to protect.

integrāscō, -ere *vi* to begin all over again.

integrātiō, -ōnis *f* renewing.

integrē *adv* entirely; honestly; correctly.

integritās, -ātis *f* completeness, soundness; integrity, honesty; (*language*) correctness.

integrō, -āre *vt* to renew, replenish, repair; (*mind*) to refresh.

integumentum, -ī *nt* cover, covering, shelter.

intellēctus *ppp of* **intellegō.**

intellēctus, -ūs *m* understanding; (*word*) meaning.

intellegēns, -entis *pres p of* **intellegō** ♦ *adj* intelligent, a connoisseur.

intellegenter *adv* intelligently.

intellegentia, -ae *f* discernment, understanding; taste.

intellegō, -egere, -ēxī, -ēctum *vt* to understand, perceive, realize; to be a connoisseur.

intemerātus *adj* pure, undefiled.

intemperāns, -antis *adj* immoderate, extravagant; incontinent.

intemperanter *adv* extravagantly.

intemperantia, -ae *f* excess, extravagance; arrogance.

intemperātē *adv* dissolutely.

intemperātus *adj* excessive.

intemperiae, -ārum *fpl* inclemency; madness.

intemperiēs, -ēī *f* inclemency, storm; (*fig*) fury.

intempestīvē *adv* inopportunely.

intempestīvus *adj* unseasonable, untimely.

intempestus *adj* (*night*) the dead of; unhealthy.

intemptātus *adj* untried.

intendō, -dere, -dī, -tum *vt* to stretch out,

strain, spread; (*weapon*) to aim; (*tent*) to pitch; (*attention, course*) to direct, turn; (*fact*) to increase, exaggerate; (*speech*) to maintain; (*trouble*) to threaten ♦ *vi* to make for, intend; **animō ~** purpose; **sē ~** exert oneself.

intentē *adv* strictly.

intentiō, -ōnis *f* straining, tension; (*mind*) exertion, attention; (*law*) accusation.

intentō, -āre *vt* to stretch out, aim; (*fig*) to threaten with, attack.

intentus *ppp of* **intendō** ♦ *adj* taut; attentive, intent; strict; (*speech*) vigorous.

intentus, -ūs *m* stretching out.

intepeō, -ēre *vi* to be warm.

intepēscō, -ēscere, -uī *vi* to be warmed.

inter *prep* (*with acc*) between, among, during, in the course of; in spite of; **~ haec** meanwhile; **~ manūs** within reach; **~ nōs** confidentially; **~ sē** mutually, one another; **~ sīcāriōs** in the murder court; **~ viam** on the way.

interāmenta, -ōrum *ntpl* ship's timbers.

interaptus *adj* joined together.

interārēscō, -ere *vi* to wither away.

interbibō, -ere *vi* to drink up.

interbītō, -ere *vi* to fall through.

intercalāris *adj* intercalary.

intercalārius *adj* intercalary.

intercalō, -āre *vt* to intercalate.

intercapēdō, -inis *f* interruption, respite.

intercēdō, -ēdere, -essī, -essum *vi* to come between, intervene; to occur; to become surety; to interfere, obstruct; (*tribune*) to protest, veto.

interceptiō, -ōnis *f* taking away.

interceptor, -ōris *m* embezzler.

interceptus *ppp of* **intercipiō.**

intercessiō, -ōnis *f* (*law*) becoming surety; (*tribune*) veto.

intercessor, -ōris *m* mediator, surety; interposer of the veto; obstructor.

intercidō, -ere, -ī *vi* to fall short; to happen in the meantime; to get lost, become obsolete, be forgotten.

intercīdō, -dere, -dī, -sum *vt* to cut through, sever.

intercinō, -ere *vt* to sing between.

intercipiō, -ipere, -ēpi, -eptum *vt* to intercept; to embezzle, steal; to cut off, obstruct.

intercīsē *adv* piecemeal.

intercīsus *ppp of* **intercīdō.**

interclūdō, -dere, -sī, -sum *vt* to cut off, block, shut off, prevent; **animam ~** suffocate.

interclūsiō, -ōnis *f* stoppage.

interclūsus *ppp of* **interclūdō.**

intercolumnium, -ī and iī *nt* space between two pillars.

intercurrō, -ere *vi* to mingle with; to intercede; to hurry in the meantime.

intercursō, -āre *vi* to crisscross; to attack

between the lines.

intercursus, -ūs m intervention.

intercus, -tis adj: **aqua ~** dropsy.

interdīcō, -īcere, -īxī, -ictum vt, vi to forbid, interdict; (praetor) to make a provisional order; **aquā et ignī ~** banish.

interdictiō, -ōnis f prohibiting, banishment.

interdictum, -ī nt prohibition; provisional order (by a praetor).

interdiū adv by day.

interdō, -are vt to make at intervals; to distribute; **nōn ~uim** I wouldn't care.

interductus, -ūs m punctuation.

interdum adv now and then, occasionally.

intereā adv meanwhile, in the meantime; nevertheless.

interēmī perf of **interimō**.

interemptus ppp of **interimō**.

intereō, -īre, -iī, -itum vi to be lost, perish, die.

interequitō, -āre vt, vi to ride between.

interesse infin of **intersum**.

interfātiō, -ōnis f interruption.

interfātur, -ārī, -ātus vi to interrupt.

interfectiō, -ōnis f killing.

interfector, -ōris m murderer.

interfectrīx, -rīcis f murderess.

interfectus ppp of **interficiō**.

interficiō, -icere, -ēcī, -ectum vt to kill, destroy.

interflō, -ierī vi to pass away.

interfluō, -ere, -xī vt, vi to flow between.

interfodiō, -ere vt to pierce.

interfugiō, -ere vi to flee among.

interfuī perf of **intersum**.

interfulgeō, -ēre vi to shine amongst.

interfūsus ppp lying between; marked here and there.

interiaceō, -ēre vi to lie between.

interibi adv in the meantime.

intericiō, -icere, -iēcī, -iectum vi to put amongst or between, interpose, mingle; **annō ~iectō** after a year.

interiectus, -ūs m coming in between; interval.

interiī perf of **intereō**.

interim adv meanwhile, in the meantime; sometimes; all the same.

interimō, -imere, -ēmī, -emptum vt to abolish, destroy, kill.

interior, -ōris adj inner, interior; nearer, on the near side; secret, private; more intimate, more profound.

interitiō, -ōnis f ruin.

interitus, -ūs m destruction, ruin, death.

interiūnctus adj joined together.

interius adv inwardly; too short.

interlābor, -ī vi to glide between.

interlegō, -ere vt to pick here and there.

interlinō, -inere, -ēvī, -itum vt to smear in

parts; to erase here and there.

interloquor, -quī, -cūtus vi to interrupt.

interlūceō, -cēre, -xī vi to shine through, be clearly seen.

interlūnia, -ōrum ntpl new moon.

interluō, -ere vt to wash, flow between.

intermēnstruus adj of the new moon ♦ nt new moon.

interminātus ppa of **interminor** ♦ adj forbidden.

interminātus adj endless.

interminor, -ārī, -ātus vi to threaten; to forbid threateningly.

intermisceō, -scēre, -scuī, -xtum vt to mix, intermingle.

intermissiō, -ōnis f interruption.

intermittō, -ittere, -īsī, -issum vt to break off; to interrupt; to omit, neglect; to allow to elapse ♦ vi to cease, pause.

intermixtus ppp of **intermisceō**.

intermorior, -ī, -tuus vi to die suddenly.

intermortuus adj falling unconscious.

intermundia, -ōrum ntpl space between worlds.

intermūrālis adj between two walls.

internātus adj growing among.

internecīnus adj murderous, of extermination.

interneciō, -ōnis f massacre, extermination.

internecīvus adj = **internecīnus**.

internectō, -ere vt to enclasp.

internōdia, -ōrum ntpl space between joints.

internōscō, -scere, -vī, -tum vt to distinguish between.

internūntia, -iae f messenger, mediator, go-between.

internūntiō, -āre vi to exchange messages.

internūntius, -ī and **iī** m messenger, mediator, go-between.

internus adj internal, civil ♦ ntpl domestic affairs.

interō, -erere, -rīvī, -rītum vt to rub in; (fig) to concoct.

interpellātiō, -ōnis f interruption.

interpellātor, -ōris m interrupter.

interpellō, -āre, -āvī, -ātum vt to interrupt; to disturb, obstruct.

interpolis adj made up.

interpolō, -āre vt to renovate, do up; (writing) to falsify.

interpōnō, -ōnere, -osuī, -ositum vt to put between or amongst, insert; (time) to allow to elapse; (person) to introduce, admit; (pretext etc) to put forward, interpose; **fidem ~** pledge one's word; **sē ~** interfere, become involved.

interpositiō, -ōnis f introduction.

interpositus ppp of **interpōnō**.

interpositus, -ūs m obstruction.

interpres, -tis m/f agent, negotiator;

Noun declensions and verb conjugations are shown on pp xiii to xxv. The present infinitive ending of a verb shows to which conjugation it belongs: **-āre** = 1st; **-ēre** = 2nd; **-ere** = 3rd and **-īre** = 4th. Irregular verbs are shown on p xxvi

interpreter, explainer, translator.
interpretātiō, -ōnis f interpretation, exposition, meaning.
interpretātus *adj* translated.
interpretor, -ārī, -ātus *vt* to interpret, explain, translate, understand.
interprimō, -imere, -essī, -essum *vt* to squeeze.
interpūnctiō, -ōnis f punctuation.
interpūnctus *adj* well-divided ♦ *ntpl* punctuation.
interquiēscō, -scere, -vī *vi* to rest awhile.
interrēgnum, -ī *nt* regency, interregnum; interval between consuls.
interrēx, -ēgis *m* regent; deputy consul.
interritus *adj* undaunted, unafraid.
interrogātiō, -ōnis f question; (*law*) cross-examination; (*logic*) syllogism.
interrogātiuncula, -ae f short argument.
interrogō, -āre, -āvī, -ātum *vt* to ask, put a question; (*law*) to cross-examine, bring to trial.
interrumpō, -umpere, -ūpī, -uptum *vt* to break up, sever; (*fig*) to break off, interrupt.
interruptē *adv* interruptedly.
intersaepiō, -īre, -sī, -tum *vt* to shut off, close.
interscindō, -ndere, -dī, -ssum *vt* to cut off, break down.
interserō, -erere, -ēvī, -itum *vt* to plant at intervals.
interserō, -ere, -uī, -tum *vt* to interpose.
intersitus *ppp of* **interserō**.
interspīrātiō, -ōnis f pause for breath.
interstinguō, -guere, -ctum *vt* to mark, spot; to extinguish.
interstringō, -ere *vt* to strangle.
intersum, -esse, -fuī *vi* to be between; to be amongst, be present at; (*time*) to elapse; **~est** there is a difference; it is of importance, it concerns, it matters; **meā ~est** it is important for me.
intertextus *adj* interwoven.
intertrahō, -here, -xī *vt* to take away.
intertrīmentum, -ī *nt* wastage; loss, damage.
interturbātiō, -ōnis f confusion.
intervallum, -ī *nt* space, distance, interval; (*time*) pause, interval, respite; difference.
intervellō, -ere *vt* to pluck out; to tear apart.
interveniō, -enīre, -ēnī, -entum *vi* to come on the scene, intervene; to interfere (with), interrupt; to happen, occur.
interventor, -ōris *m* intruder.
interventus, -ūs *m* appearance, intervention; occurrence.
intervertō, -tere, -tī, -sum *vt* to embezzle; to rob, cheat.
intervīsō, -ere, -ī, -um *vt* to have a look at, look and see; to visit occasionally.
intervolitō, -āre *vi* to fly about, amongst.
intervomō, -ere *vt* to throw up (amongst).
intervortō *vt see* **intervertō**.
intestābilis *adj* infamous, wicked.

intestātō *adv* without making a will.
intestātus *adj* intestate; not convicted by witnesses.
intestīnus *adj* internal ♦ *nt and ntpl* intestines, entrails.
intexō, -ere, -uī, -tum *vt* to inweave, embroider, interlace.
intibum, -ī *nt* endive.
intimē *adv* most intimately, cordially.
intimus *adj* innermost; deepest, secret; intimate ♦ *m* most intimate friend.
intingō (intinguō), -gere, -xī, -ctum *vt* to dip in.
intolerābilis *adj* unbearable; irresistible.
intolerandus *adj* intolerable.
intolerāns, -antis *adj* impatient; unbearable.
intoleranter *adv* excessively.
intolerantia, -ae f insolence.
intonō, -āre, -uī, -ātum *vi* to thunder, thunder out.
intōnsus *adj* unshorn, unshaven; long-haired, bearded; uncouth.
intorqueō, -quēre, -sī, -tum *vt* to twist, wrap round; to hurl at.
intortus *ppp of* **intorqueō** ♦ *adj* twisted, curled; confused.
intrā *adv* inside, within ♦ *prep* (*with acc*) inside, within; (*time*) within, during; (*amount*) less than, within the limits of.
intrābilis *adj* navigable.
intractābilis *adj* formidable.
intractātus *adj* not broken in; unattempted.
intremīscō, -īscere, -uī *vi* to begin to shake.
intremō, -ere *vi* to tremble.
intrepidē *adv see adj*.
intrepidus *adj* calm, brave; undisturbed.
intrīcō, -āre *vt* to entangle.
intrīnsecus *adv* on the inside.
intrītus *adj* not worn out.
intrīvī *perf of* **interō**.
intrō *adv* inside, in.
intrō, -āre, -āvī, -ātum *vt, vi* to go in, enter; to penetrate.
intrōdūcō, -ūcere, -ūxī, -uctum *vt* to bring in, introduce, escort in; to institute.
intrōductiō, -ōnis f bringing in.
intrōeō, -īre, -iī, -itum *vi* to go into, enter.
intrōferō, -ferre, -tulī, -lātum *vt* to carry inside.
intrōgredior, -dī, -ssus *vi* to step inside.
introitus, -ūs *m* entrance; beginning.
intrōlātus *ppp of* **intrōferō**.
intrōmittō, -ittere, -īsī, -issus *vt* to let in, admit.
intrōrsum, intrōrsus *adv* inwards, inside.
intrōrumpō, -ere *vi* to break into.
intrōspectō, -āre *vt* to look in at.
intrōspiciō, -icere, -exī, -ectum *vt* to look inside; to look at, examine.
intubum, -ī *nt see* **intibum**.
intueor, -ērī, -itus *vt* to look at, watch; to contemplate, consider; to admire.
intumēscō, -ēscere, -uī *vi* to begin to swell,

rise; to increase; to become angry.
intumulātus *adj* unburied.
intuor *etc see* **intueor**.
inturbidus *adj* undisturbed; quiet.
intus *adv* inside, within, in; from within.
intūtus *adj* unsafe; unguarded.
inula, -ae *f* elecampane.
inultus *adj* unavenged; unpunished.
inumbrō, -āre *vt* to shade; to cover.
inundō, -āre, -āvī, -ātum *vt* vi ɔ overflow,
    flood.
inunguō, -unguere, -ūnxī, -ūnctum *vt* to
    anoint.
inurbānē *adv see adj.*
inurbānus *adj* rustic, unmannerly,
    unpolished.
inurgeō, -ēre *vi* to push, butt.
inūrō, -rere, -ssī, -stum *vt* to brand; (*fig*) to
    brand, inflict.
inūsitātē *adv* strangely.
inūsitātus *adj* unusual, extraordinary.
inūstus *ppp of* **inūrō**.
inūtilis *adj* useless; harmful.
inūtilitās, -ātis *f* uselessness, harmfulness.
inūtiliter *adv* unprofitably.
invādō, -dere, -sī, -sum *vt, v* to get in, make
    one's way in; to enter upon; to fall upon,
    attack, invade; to seize, take possession of.
invalēscō, -ēscere, -uī *vi* to grow stronger.
invalidus *adj* weak; inadequate.
invāsī *perf of* **invādō**.
invectiō, -ōnis *f* importing; invective.
invectus *ppp of* **invehō**.
invehō, -here, -xī, -ctum *vt* to carry in, bring
    in; **sē** ~ attack.
invehor, -hī, -ctus *vi* to ride, drive, sail in or
    into, enter; to attack; to inveigh against.
invēndibilis *adj* unsaleable.
inveniō, -enīre, -ēnī, -entum *v* to find, come
    upon; to find out, discover; to invent,
    contrive; to win, get.
inventiō, -ōnis *f* invention; (*RHET*) compiling
    the subject-matter.
inventor, -ōris *m* inventor, discoverer.
inventrīx, -rīcis *f* inventor, discoverer.
inventus *ppp of* **inveniō** ♦ *nt* invention,
    discovery.
invenustus *adj* unattractive; unlucky in love.
inverēcundus *adj* immodest, shameless.
invergō, -ere *vt* to pour upon.
inversiō, -ōnis *f* transposition; irony.
inversus *ppp of* **invertō** ♦ *adj* upside down,
    inside out; perverted.
invertō, -tere, -tī, -sum *vt* to turn over,
    invert; to change, pervert.
invesperāscit, -ere *vi* it is dusk.
investīgātiō, -ōnis *f* search.
investīgātor, -ōris *m* investigator.
investīgō, -āre, -āvī, -ātum *vt* to follow the
    trail of; (*fig*) to track down, find out

inveterāscō, -scere, -vī *vi* to grow old (in); to
    become established, fixed, inveterate; to
    grow obsolete.
inveterātiō, -ōnis *f* chronic illness.
inveterātus *adj* of long standing, inveterate.
invexī *perf of* **invehō**.
invicem *adv* in turns, alternately; mutually,
    each other.
invictus *adj* unbeaten, unconquerable.
invidentia, -ae *f* envy.
invideō, -idēre, -īdī, -īsum *vt, vi* to cast an
    evil eye on; (*with dat*) to envy, grudge; to
    begrudge.
invidia, -ae *f* envy, jealousy, ill-will;
    unpopularity.
invidiōsē *adv* spitefully.
invidiōsus *adj* envious, spiteful; enviable;
    invidious, hateful.
invidus *adj* envious, jealous, hostile.
invigilō, -āre *vi* to be awake over; to watch
    over, be intent on.
inviolābilis *adj* invulnerable; inviolable.
inviolātē *adv* inviolately.
inviolātus *adj* unhurt; inviolable.
invīsitātus *adj* unseen, unknown, strange.
invīsō, -ere, -ī, -um *vi* to go and see, visit,
    have a look at; to inspect.
invīsus *adj* hateful, detested; hostile.
invīsus *adj* unseen.
invītāmentum, -ī *nt* attraction, inducement.
invītātiō, -ōnis *f* invitation; entertainment.
invītātus, -ūs *m* invitation.
invītē *adv* unwillingly.
invītō, -āre, -āvī, -ātum *vt* to invite; to treat,
    entertain; to summon; to attract, induce.
invītus *adj* against one's will, reluctant.
invius *adj* trackless, impassable; inaccessible.
invocātus *ppp of* **invocō**.
invocātus *adj* unbidden, uninvited.
invocō, -āre, -āvī, -ātum *vt* to call upon,
    invoke; to appeal to; to call.
involātus, -ūs *m* flight.
involitō, -āre *vi* to play upon.
involō, -āre *vi* to fly at, pounce on, attack.
involūcre, -is *nt* napkin.
involūcrum, -ī *nt* covering, case.
involūtus *ppp of* **involvō** ♦ *adj* complicated.
involvō, -vere, -vī, -ūtum *vt* to roll on; to
    wrap up, envelop, entangle.
involvolus, -ī *m* caterpillar.
invulnerātus *adj* unwounded.
iō *interj* (*joy*) hurrah!; (*pain*) oh!; (*calling*) ho
    there!
Iōannēs, -is *m* John.
iocātiō, -ōnis *f* joke.
iocor, -ārī, -ātus *vt, vi* to joke, jest.
iocōsē *adv* jestingly.
iocōsus *adj* humorous, playful.
ioculāris *adj* laughable, funny ♦ *ntpl* jokes.
ioculārius *adj* ludicrous.

ioculātor, -ōris m jester.
ioculor, -ārī vi to joke.
ioculus, -ī m a bit of fun.
iocus, -ī m (pl -a, -ōrum nt) joke, jest; extrā ~um joking apart; per ~um for fun.
Iōnes, -um mpl Ionians.
Iōnia, -iae f Ionia, coastal district of Asia Minor.
Iōnium, -ī nt Ionian Sea, W. of Greece.
Iōnius, -icus adj Ionian.
iōta nt (indecl) Greek letter I.
Iovis gen of Iuppiter.
Iphianasse, -ae f Iphigenia.
Iphigenīa, -ae f daughter of Agamemnon (who sacrificed her at Aulis to Diana).
ipse, -a, -um, -īus prep self, himself etc; in person, for one's own part, of one's own accord, by oneself; just, precisely, very; the master, the host.
ipsissimus his very own self; nunc ~um right now.
īra, -ae f anger, rage; object of indignation.
īrācundē adv angrily.
īrācundia, -ae f irascibility, quick temper; rage, resentment.
īrācundus adj irascible, choleric; resentful.
īrāscor, -ī vi to be angry, get furious.
īrātē adv see adj.
īrātus adj angry, furious.
īre infin of eō.
Īris, -dis (acc -m) f messenger of the gods; the rainbow.
īrōnīa, -ae f irony.
irrāsus adj unshaven.
irraucēscō, -cēscere, -sī vi to become hoarse.
irredivīvus adj irreparable.
irreligātus adj not tied.
irreligiōsē adv see adj.
irreligiōsus adj impious.
irremeābilis adj from which there is no returning.
irreparābilis adj irretrievable.
irrepertus adj undiscovered.
irrēpō, -ere, -sī vi to steal into, insinuate oneself into.
irreprehēnsus adj blameless.
irrequiētus adj restless.
irresectus adj unpared.
irresolūtus adj not slackened.
irrētiō, -īre, -iī, -ītum vt to ensnare, entangle.
irretortus adj not turned back.
irreverentia, -ae f disrespect.
irrevocābilis adj irrevocable; implacable.
irrevocātus adj without an encore.
irrīdeō, -dēre, -sī, -sum vi to laugh, joke ♦ vt to laugh at, ridicule.
irrīdiculē adv unwittily.
irrīdiculum, -ī nt laughing stock.
irrigātiō, -ōnis f irrigation.
irrigō, -āre, -āvī, -ātum vt to water, irrigate; to inundate; (fig) to shed over, flood, refresh.
irriguus adj well-watered, swampy; refreshing.
irrīsiō, -ōnis f ridicule, mockery.

irrīsor, -ōris m scoffer.
irrīsus ppp of irrīdeō.
irrīsus, -ūs m derision.
irrītābilis adj excitable.
irrītāmen, -inis nt excitement, provocation.
irrītātiō, -ōnis f incitement, irritation.
irrītō, -āre, -āvī, -ātum vt to provoke, incite, enrage.
irritus adj invalid, null and void; useless, vain, ineffective; (person) unsuccessful; ad ~um cadere come to nothing.
irrogātiō, -ōnis f imposing.
irrogō, -āre vt to propose (a measure) against; to impose.
irrōrō, -āre vt to bedew.
irrumpō, -umpere, -ūpī, -uptum vt, vi to rush in, break in; to intrude, invade.
irruō, -ere, -ī vi to force a way in, rush in, attack; (speech) to make a blunder.
irruptiō, -ōnis f invasion, raid.
irruptus ppp of irrumpō.
irruptus adj unbroken.
is, ea, id pron he, she, it; this, that, the; such; nōn is sum quī I am not the man to; id (with vi) for this reason; id quod what; ad id hitherto; for the purpose; besides; in eō est it has come to this; one is on the point of; it depends on this.
Ismara, -ōrum ntpl, -us, -ī m Mt Ismarus in Thrace.
Ismarius adj Thracian.
Isocratēs, -is m Athenian orator and teacher of rhetoric.
istāc adv that way.
iste, -a, -ud, -īus pron that of yours; (law) your client, the plaintiff, the defendant; (contemptuous) the fellow; that, such.
Isthmius adj, ntpl the Isthmian Games.
Isthmus (-os), -ī m Isthmus of Corinth.
istic, -aec, -uc and oc pron that of yours, that.
istīc adv there; in this, on this occasion.
istinc adv from there; of that.
istiusmodī such, of that kind.
istō, istōc adv to you, there, yonder.
istōrsum adv in that direction.
istūc adv (to) there, to that.
ita adv thus, so; as follows; yes; accordingly; itane? really?; nōn ita not so very; ita ut just as; ita ... ut so, to such an extent that; on condition that; only in so far as; ita ... ut nōn without; ut ... ita just as ... so; although ... nevertheless.
Ītalī, -ōrum mpl Italians.
Ītalia, -iae f Italy.
Ītalicus, -is, -us adj Italian.
itaque conj and so, therefore, accordingly.
item adv likewise, also.
iter, -ineris nt way, journey, march; a day's journey or march; route, road, passage; (fig) way, course; ~ mihi est I have to go to; ~ dare grant a right of way; ~ facere to journey, march, travel; ex, in ~inere on the way, on the march; māgnīs ~ineribus by forced

marches.

iterātiō, -ōnis f repetition.

iterō, -āre, -āvī, -ātum vt to repeat renew; to plough again.

iterum adv again, a second time; ~ atque ~ repeatedly.

Ithaca, -ae, -ē, -ēs f island W of Greece (home of Ulysses).

Ithacēnsis, -us adj Ithacan.

Ithacus, -ī m Ulysses.

itidem adv in the same way, similarly

itiō, -ōnis f going.

itō, -āre vi to go.

itus, -ūs m going, movement, departure.

iuba, -ae f mane; crest.

Iuba, -ae m king of Numidia (supporter of Pompey).

iubar, -is nt brightness, light.

iubātus adj crested.

iubeō, -bēre, -ssī, -ssum vt to order, command, tell; (greeting) to bid (word) to prescribe; (POL) to decree, ratify, appoint.

iūcundē adv agreeably.

iūcunditās, -ātis f delight, enjoyment.

iūcundus adj delightful, pleasing

Iūdaea, -ae f Judaea, Palestine.

Iūdaeus, -ī m Jew.

Iūdaeus, Iūdaicus adj Jewish

iūdex, -icis m judge; (pl) panel of judges; (fig) critic.

iūdicātiō, -ōnis f judicial inquiry; opinion.

iūdicātum, -ī nt judgment, precedent.

iūdicātus, -ūs m office of judge.

iūdiciālis adj judicial, forensic.

iūdiciārius adj judiciary.

iūdicium, -ī and **iī** nt trial; court of justice; sentence; judgment, opinion; discernment, taste, tact; **in ~ vocāre, ~ō arcessere** sue, summon.

iūdicō, -āre, -āvī, -ātum vt to judge, examine, sentence, condemn; to form an opinion of, decide; to declare.

iugālis adj yoked together; nuptial.

iugātiō, -ōnis f training (of a vine)

iūgerum, -ī nt a land measure (240 x 120 feet).

iūgis adj perpetual, never-failing

iūglāns, -andis f walnut tree.

iugō, -āre, -āvī, -ātum vt to couple, marry.

iugōsus adj hilly.

lugulae, -ārum fpl Orion's Belt.

iugulō, -āre, -āvī, -ātum vt to cut the throat of, kill, murder.

iugulus, -ī m, **-um, -ī** nt throat.

iugum, -ī nt (animals) yoke, collar; (a pair) team; (MIL) yoke of subjugation; (mountain) ridge, height, summit; (ASTRO) Libra; (loom) crossbeam; (ship) thwart; (fig) yoke bond.

lugurtha, -ae m king of Numidia (rebel against Rome).

lugurthīnus adj see n.

Iūlēus adj of Iulus; of Caesar; of July.

Iūlius, -ī m Roman family name (esp Caesar); (month) July.

Iūlius, -iānus adj see n.

Iūlus, -ī m son of Aeneas, Ascanius.

iūmentum, -ī nt beast of burden, packhorse.

iunceus adj of rushes; slender.

iuncōsus adj rushy.

iūnctiō, -ōnis f union.

iūnctūra, -ae f joint; combination; relationship.

iūnctus ppp of iungō ♦ adj connected, attached.

iuncus, -ī m rush.

iungō, -gere, iūnxī, iūnctum vt to join together, unite; to yoke, harness; to mate; (river) to span, bridge; (fig) to bring together, connect, associate; (agreement) to make; (words) to compound.

iūnior, -ōris adj younger.

Iūniperus, -ī f juniper.

Iūnius, -ī m Roman family name; (month) June.

Iūnius adj of June.

Iūnō, -ōnis f Roman goddess wife of Jupiter, patroness of women and marriage.

Iūnōnālis adj see n.

Iūnōnicola, -ae m worshipper of Juno.

Iūnōnigena, -ae m Vulcan.

Iūnōnius adj = Iūnōnālis.

Iuppiter, Iovis m Jupiter (king of the gods, god of sky and weather); **~ Stygius** Pluto; **sub Iove** in the open air.

iūrātor, -ōris m sworn judge.

iūrecōnsultus etc see **iūriscōnsultus**.

iūreiūrō, -āre vi to swear.

iūreperītus etc see **iūrisperītus**.

iūrgium, -ī and **iī** nt quarrel, brawl.

iūrgō, -āre vi to quarrel, squabble ♦ vt to scold.

iūridiciālis adj of law, juridical.

iūriscōnsultus, -ī m lawyer.

iūrisdictiō, -ōnis f administration of justice; authority.

iūrisperītus adj versed in the law.

iūrō, -āre, -āvī, -ātum vi, vt to swear, take an oath; to conspire; **in nōmen ~** swear allegiance to; **in verba ~** take a prescribed form of oath; **~ātus** having sworn, under oath.

iūs, iūris nt broth, soup.

iūs, iūris nt law, right, justice; law court; jurisdiction, authority; **~ gentium** international law; **~ pūblicum** constitutional law; **summum ~** the strict letter of the law; **~ dīcere** administer justice; **suī iūris** independent; **iūre** rightly, justly.

iūsiūrandum, iūrisiūrandī nt oath.

iussī perf of **iubeō**.

iussū abl m by order.

iussus ppp of iubeō ♦ nt order, command, prescription.

Noun declensions and verb conjugations are shown on pp xiii to xxv. The present infinitive ending of a verb shows to which conjugation it belongs: -āre = 1st -ēre = 2nd; -ere = 3rd and -īre = 4th. Irregular verbs are shown on p xxvi

iūstē adv duly, rightly.
iūstificus adj just dealing.
iūstitia, -ae f justice, uprightness, fairness.
iūstitium, -ī and **iī** nt cessation of legal business.
iūstus adj just, fair; lawful, right; regular, proper ♦ nt right ♦ ntpl rights; formalities, obsequies.
iūtus ppp of **iuvō**.
iuvenālis adj youthful ♦ ntpl youthful games.
Iuvenālis, -is m Juvenal (Roman satirist).
iuvenāliter adv vigorously, impetuously.
iuvenca, -ae f heifer; girl.
iuvencus, -ī m bullock; young man ♦ adj young.
iuvenēscō, -ēscere, -uī vi to grow up; to grow young again.
iuvenīlis adj youthful.
iuvenīliter adv see adj.
iuvenis adj young ♦ m/f young man or woman (20-45 years), man, warrior.
iuvenor, -ārī vi to behave indiscreetly.
iuventa, -ae f youth.
iuventās, -ātis f youth.
iuventūs, -ūtis f youth, manhood; men, soldiers.
iuvō, -āre, iūvī, iūtum vt to help, be of use to; to please, delight; ~at mē I am glad.
iuxtā adv near by, close; alike, just the same ♦ prep (with acc) close to, hard by; next to; very like, next door to; ~ ac, cum, quam just the same as.
iuxtim adv near; equally.
īvī perf of **eō**.
Ixīōn, -onis m Lapith king (bound to a revolving wheel in Tartarus).
Ixīoneus adj see n.
Ixīonidae, -ārum mpl Centaurs.
Ixīonidēs, -ae m Pirithous.

J, j

J see **I**.

K, k

Kalendae, -ārum fpl Kalends, first day of each month.
Karthāgō see **Carthāgō**.

L, l

labāscō, -ere vi to totter, waver.
lābēcula, -ae f aspersion.
labefaciō, -facere, -fēcī, -factum (pass -fīō, -fierī) vt to shake; (fig) to weaken, ruin.
labefactō, -āre, -āvī, -ātum vt to shake; (fig) to weaken, destroy.
labellum, -ī nt lip.
lābellum, -ī nt small basin.
Laberius, -ī m Roman family name (esp a writer of mimes).
lābēs, -is f sinking, fall; ruin, destruction.
lābēs, -is f spot, blemish; disgrace, stigma; (person) blot.
labia, -iae f lip.
Labiēnus, -ī m Roman surname (esp Caesar's officer who went over to Pompey).
labiōsus adj large-lipped.
labium, -ī and **iī** nt lip.
labō, -āre vi to totter, be unsteady, give way; to waver hesitate, collapse.
lābor, -bī, -psus vi to slide, glide; to sink, fall; to slip away, pass away; (fig) to fade, decline, perish; to be disappointed, make a mistake.
labor (-ōs), -ōris m effort, exertion, labour; work, task; hardship, suffering, distress; (ASTRO) eclipse.
labōrifer, -ī adj sore afflicted.
labōriōsē adv laboriously, with difficulty.
labōriōsus adj troublesome, difficult; industrious.
labōrō, -āre, -āvī, -ātum vi to work, toil, take pains; to suffer, be troubled (with), be in distress; to be anxious, worried ♦ vt to work out, make, produce.
labōs etc see **labor**.
labrum, -ī nt lip; edge, rim; primīs ~īs gustāre acquire a smattering of.
lābrum, -ī nt tub, vat; bath.
lābrusca, -ae f wild vine.
lābruscum, -ī nt wild grape.

labyrintheūs adj labyrinthine.
labyrinthus, -ī m labyrinth, maze (esp that of Cnossos in Crete).
lac, lactis nt milk.
Lacaena, -ae f Spartan woman ♦ adj Spartan.
Lacedaemōn (-ō), -onis (acc -ona) f Sparta.
Lacedaemonius adj Spartan.
lacer, -ī adj torn, mangled, lacerated; tearing.
lacerātiō, -ōnis f tearing.
lacerna, -ae f cloak (worn in cold weather).
lacernātus adj cloaked.
lacerō, -āre, -āvī, -ātum vt to tear, acerate, mangle; (ship) to wreck; (speech) to slander, abuse; (feeling) to torture, distress; (goods, time) to waste, destroy.
lacerta, -ae f lizard; a seafish.
lacertōsus adj brawny.
lacertus, -ī m upper arm, arm; (pl) brawn, muscle.
lacertus, -ī m lizard; a sea fish.
lacessō, -ere, -īvī and **iī, -ītum** vt to strike, provoke, challenge; (fig) to incite, exasperate.
Lachesis, -is f one of the Fates.
lacinia, -ae f flap, corner (of dress)
Lacīnium, -ī nt promontory in S. Italy, with a temple of Juno.
Lacīnius adj see n.
Lacō (-ōn), -ōnis m Spartan; Spartan dog.
Lacōnicus adj Spartan ♦ nt sweating bath.
lacrima, -ae f tear; (plant) gumdrop.
lacrimābilis adj mournful.
lacrimābundus adj bursting into tears.
lacrimō, -āre, -āvī, -ātum vt, vi to weep, weep for.
lacrimōsus adj tearful; lamentable.
lacrimula, -ae f tear, crocodile tear.
lacrum- etc see **lacrim-**.
lactāns, -antis adj giving milk; sucking.
lactātiō, -ōnis f allurement.
lactēns, -entis adj sucking; milky, juicy.
lacteolus adj milk-white.
lactēs, -ium fpl guts, small intestines.
lactēscō, -ere vi to turn to milk.
lacteus adj milky, milk-white.
lactō, -āre vt to dupe, wheedle
lactūca, -ae f lettuce.
lacūna, -ae f hole, pit; pool, pond; (fig) deficiency.
lacūnar, -āris nt panel ceiling.
lacūnō, -āre vt to panel.
lacūnōsus adj sunken.
lacus, -ūs m vat, tank; lake; reservoir, cistern.
laedō, -dere, -sī, -sum vt to hurt, strike, wound; (fig) to offend, annoy, break.
Laelius, -ī m Roman family name (esp the friend of Scipio).
laena, -ae f a lined cloak.
Laērtēs, -ae m father of Ulysses
Laērtiadēs m Ulysses.

Laērtius adj see n.
laesī perf of **laedō**.
laesiō, -ōnis f attack.
Laestrygonēs, -um mpl fabulous cannibals of Campania, founders of Formiae.
Laestrygonius adj see n.
laesus ppp of **laedō**.
laetābilis adj joyful
laetē adv gladly.
laetificō, -āre vt to gladden.
laetificus adj glad, joyful.
laetitia, -ae f joy, delight, exuberance.
laetor, -ārī, -ātus vi to rejoice, be glad.
laetus adj glad, cheerful; delighting (in); pleasing, welcome; (growth) fertile, rich; (style) exuberant.
laevē adv awkwardly.
laevus adj left; stupid; ill-omened, unfortunate; (augury) lucky, favourable ♦ f left hand.
laganum, -ī nt a kind of oilcake.
lagēos, -ī f a Greek vine.
lagoena, -ae f flagon.
lagōis, -idis f a kind of grouse.
lagōna, -ae f flagon.
Lāiadēs, -ae m Oedipus.
Lāius, -ī m father of Oedipus.
lallō, -āre vi to sing a lullaby.
lāma, -ae f bog.
lamberō, -āre vt to tear to pieces.
lambō, -ere, -ī vt to lick, touch; (river) to wash.
lāmenta, -ōrum ntp' lamentation.
lāmentābilis adj mournful, sorrowful.
lāmentārius adj sorrowful.
lāmentātiō, -ōnis f weeping, lamentation.
lāmentor, -ārī, -ātus vi to weep, lament ♦ vt to weep for, bewail.
lamia, -ae f witch.
lāmina (lammina, lāmna), -ae f plate, leaf (of metal, wood); blade; coin.
lampas, -dis f torch; brightness, day.
Lamus, -ī m Laestrygonian king.
lāna, -ae f wool.
lānārius, -ī and **iī** m wool-worker.
lānātus adj woolly.
lancea, -ae f spear, lance.
lancinō, -āre vt to tear up; to squander.
lāneus adj woollen.
languefaciō, -ere vt to make weary.
langueō, -ēre vi to be weary, be weak, droop; to be idle, dull.
languēscō, -ēscere, -uī vi to grow faint, droop.
languidē adv see adj.
languidulus adj languid.
languidus adj faint, languid, sluggish; listless, feeble.
languor, -ōris m faintness, fatigue, weakness; dullness, apathy.
laniātus, -ūs m mangling; (mind) anguish.

Noun declensions and verb conjugations are shown on pp xiii to xxv. The present infinitive ending of a verb shows to which conjugation it belongs: **-āre** = 1st; **-ēre** = 2nd; **-ere** = 3rd and **-īre** = 4th. Irregular verbs are shown on p xxvi

laniēna, -ae *f* butcher's shop.
lānificium, -ī *and* **iī** *nt* wool-working.
lānificus *adj* wool-working.
lāniger, -ī *adj* fleecy ♦ *m/f* ram, sheep.
laniō, -āre, -āvī, -ātum *vt* to tear to pieces, mangle.
lanista, -ae *m* trainer of gladiators, fencing master; (*fig*) agitator.
lānitium, -ī *and* **iī** *nt* woolgrowing.
lanius, -ī *and* **iī** *m* butcher.
lanterna, -ae *f* lamp.
lanternārius, -ī *and* **iī** *m* guide.
lānūgō, -inis *f* down, woolliness.
Lānuvīnus *adj see n.*
Lānuvium, -ī *nt* Latin town on the Appian Way.
lānx, lancis *f* dish, platter; (*balance*) scale.
Lāomedōn, -ontis *m* king of Troy (*father of Priam*).
Lāomedontēus *adj and* **ontiadēs, -ae** *m* son of *Lāomedōn*; (*pl*) Trojans.
Lāomedontius *adj* Trojan.
lapathum, -ī *nt*, **-us, -ī** *f* sorrel.
lapicīda, -ae *m* stonecutter.
lapicīdīnae, -ārum *fpl* quarries.
lapidārius *adj* stone- (*in cpds*).
lapidātiō, -ōnis *f* throwing of stones.
lapidātor, -ōris *m* stone thrower.
lapideus *adj* of stones, stone- (*in cpds*).
lapidō, -āre *vt* to stone ♦ *vi* to rain stones.
lapidōsus *adj* stony; hard as stone.
lapillus, -ī *m* stone, pebble; precious stone, mosaic piece.
lapis, -dis *m* stone; milestone, boundary stone, tombstone; precious stone; marble; auctioneer's stand; (*abuse*) blockhead; **bis ad eundem (offendere)** ≈ *make the same mistake twice*; **Juppiter ~** the Jupiter stone.
Lapithae, -ārum *and* **-um** *mpl* Lapiths (*mythical people of Thessaly*).
Lapithaeus, -ēius *adj see n.*
lappa, -ae *f* goosegrass.
lāpsiō, -ōnis *f* tendency.
lāpsō, -āre *vi* to slip, stumble.
lāpsus *ppa of* **lābor.**
lāpsus, -ūs *m* fall, slide, course, flight; error, failure.
laqueāria, -ium *ntpl* panelled ceiling.
laqueātus *adj* panelled, with a panelled ceiling.
laqueus, -ī *m* noose, snare, halter; (*fig*) trap.
Lār, Laris *m* tutelary deity, household god; hearth, home.
lārdum *etc see* **lāridum.**
largē *adv* plentifully, generously, very much.
largificus *adj* bountiful.
largifluus *adj* copious.
largiloquus *adj* talkative.
largior, -īrī, -ītus *vt* to give freely, lavish; to bestow, confer ♦ *vi* to give largesses.
largitās, -ātis *f* liberality, abundance.
largiter *adv* = **large.**
largītiō, -ōnis *f* giving freely, distributing; bribery.

largītor, -ōris *m* liberal giver, dispenser; spendthrift; briber.
largus *adj* copious, ample; liberal, bountiful.
lāridum, -ī *nt* bacon fat.
Lārissa (Lārīsa), -ae *f* town in Thessaly.
Lārissaeus, -ēnsis *adj see n.*
Lārius, -ī *m* lake Como.
larix, -cis *f* larch.
larva, -ae *f* ghost; mask.
larvātus *adj* bewitched.
lasanum, -ī *nt* pot.
lasārpīcifer, -ī *adj* producing asafoetida.
lascīvia, -ae *f* playfulness; impudence, lewdness.
lascīviō, -īre *vi* to frolic, frisk; to run wild, be irresponsible.
lascīvus *adj* playful, frisky; impudent, lustful.
laserpīcium, -ī *and* **iī** *nt* silphium.
lassitūdō, -inis *f* fatigue, heaviness.
lassō, -āre, *vt* to tire, fatigue.
lassulus *adj* rather weary.
lassus *adj* tired, exhausted.
lātē *adv* widely, extensively; **longē ~que** far and wide, everywhere.
latebra, -ae *f* hiding place, retreat; (*fig*) loophole, pretext.
latebricola, -ae *adj* low-living.
latebrōsē *adv* in hiding.
latebrōsus *adj* secret, full of coverts; porous, secret.
latēns, -entis *pres p of* **lateō** ♦ *adj* hidden, secret.
latenter *adv* in secret.
lateō, -ēre, -uī *vi* to lie hid, lurk, skulk; to be in safety, live a retired life; to be unknown, escape notice.
later, -is *m* brick, tile; **~em lavāre** ≈ *waste one's time.*
laterāmen, -inis *nt* earthenware.
laterculus, -ī *m* small brick, tile; kind of cake.
latericius *adj* of bricks ♦ *nt* brickwork.
lāterna *etc see* **lanterna.**
latēscō, -ere *vi* to hide oneself.
latex, -icis *m* water; any other liquid.
Latiar, -iaris *nt* festival of Jupiter Latiaris.
Latiaris *adj* Latin.
latibulum, -ī *nt* hiding place, den, lair.
lāticlāvius *adj* with a broad purple stripe ♦ *m* senator, patrician.
lātifundium, -ī *and* **iī** *nt* large estate.
Latīnē *adv* in Latin, into Latin; **~ loquī** speak Latin, speak plainly, speak correctly; **~ reddere** translate into Latin.
Latīnitās, -ātis *f* good Latin, Latinity; Latin rights.
Latīnus *adj* Latin ♦ *m* legendary king of the Laurentians.
lātiō, -ōnis *f* bringing; proposing.
latitō, -āre *vi* to hide away, lurk, keep out of the way.
lātitūdō, -inis *f* breadth, width; size; broad pronunciation.
Latium, -ī *nt* district of Italy including Rome; Latin rights.

Latius = Latiaris, Latinus.
Lātōis, -idis f Diana.
Lātōis, , -ius adj see n.
lātom- etc see **lautum-**.
Lātōna, -ae f mother of Apollo and Diana.
Lātōnigenae, -ārum pl Apollo and Diana.
Lātōnius adj, f Diana.
lātor, -ōris m proposer.
Lātōus adj of Latona ♦ m Apollo.
lātrātor, -ōris m barker.
lātrātus, -ūs m barking.
lātrō, -āre vi to bark; to rant, roar ♦ vt to bark at; to clamour for.
latrō, -ōnis m mercenary soldier bandit, brigand; (chess) man.
latrōcinium, -ī and **iī** nt highway robbery, piracy.
latrōcinor, -āri, -ātus vi to serve as a mercenary; to be a brigard or pirate.
latrunculus, -ī m brigand; (chess) man.
lātumiae etc see **lautumiae.**
lātus ppp of **ferō.**
lātus adj broad, wide; extensive, (pronunciation) broad; (style) diffuse.
latus, -eris nt side, flank; lungs body; ~ dare expose oneself; ~ tegere walk beside; ~eris dolor pleurisy; ab ~ere on the flank.
latusculum, -ī nt little side
laudābilis adj praiseworthy.
laudābiliter adv laudably.
laudātiō, -ōnis f commendation, eulogy; panegyric, testimonial.
laudātor, -ōris m, **-rīx, -rīcis** f praiser, eulogizer; speaker of a funeral oration.
laudātus adj excellent.
laudō, -āre, -āvī, -ātum vt to praise, commend, approve; to pronounce a funeral oration over; to quote, name.
laurea, -ae f bay tree; crown of bay; triumph.
laureātus adj crowned with bay (despatches) victorious.
Laurentēs, -um mpl Laurentians (people of ancient Latium).
Laurentius adj see n.
laureola, -ae f triumph.
laureus adj of bay.
lauricomus adj bay-covered.
lauriger, -ī adj crowned with bay.
laurus, -ī f bay tree; bay crown, victory, triumph.
laus, laudis f praise, approval; glory, fame; praiseworthy act, merit, worth.
lautē adv elegantly, splendidly; excellently.
lautia, -ōrum ntpl State banquet.
lautitia, -ae f luxury.
lautumiae, -ārum fpl stone quarry; prison.
lautus ppp of **lavō** ♦ adj neat, elegant, sumptuous; fine, grand, distinguished.
lavābrum, -ī nt bath.
lavātiō, -ōnis f washing, bath; bathing gear.

Lāvīnium, -ī nt town of ancient Latium.
Lāvīnius adj see n.
lavō, -āre, lāvī, lautum (lavātum and **lōtum)** vt to wash, bathe; to wet, soak, wash away.
laxāmentum, -ī nt respite, relaxation.
laxē adv loosely, freely.
laxitās, -ātis f roominess.
laxō, -āre, -āvī, -ātum vt to extend, open out; to undo; to slacken; (fig) to release, relieve; to relax, abate ♦ vi (price) to fall off.
laxus adj wide, loose, roomy; (time) deferred; (fig) free, easy.
lea, -ae f lioness.
leaena, -ae f lioness.
Lēander, -rī m Hero's lover (who swam the Hellespont).
lebēs, -ētis m basin, pan, cauldron.
lectīca, -ae f litter, sedan chair.
lectīcārius, -ī and **iī** m litter-bearer.
lectīcula, -ae f small litter; bier.
lēctiō, -ōnis f selecting; reading, calling the roll.
lectisterniātor, -ōris m arranger of couches.
lectisternium, -ī and **iī** nt religious feast.
lēctitō, -āre vt to read frequently.
lēctiuncula, -ae f light reading.
lēctor, -ōris m reader.
lectulus, -ī m couch, bed.
lectus, -ī m couch, bed; bier.
lēctus ppp of **legō** ♦ adj picked; choice, excellent.
Lēda, -ae and **ē, -ēs** f mother of Castor, Pollux, Helen and Clytemnestra.
Lēdaeus adj see n.
lēgātiō, -ōnis f mission, embassy; members of a mission; (MIL) staff appointment; command of a legion; lībera ~ free commission (to visit provinces); vōtīva ~ free commission for paying a vow in a province.
lēgātor, -ōris m testator.
lēgātum, -ī nt legacy, bequest.
lēgātus, -ī m delegate, ambassador; deputy, lieutenant; commander (of a legion).
lēgifer, -ī adj law-giving.
legiō, -ōnis f legion (up to 6000 men); (pl) troops, army.
legiōnārius adj legionary.
lēgirupa, -ae; -iō, -iōnis m lawbreaker.
lēgitimē adv lawfully, properly.
lēgitimus adj lawful, legal; right, proper.
legiuncula, -ae f small legion.
lēgō, -āre, -āvī, -ātum vt to send, charge, commission; to appoint as deputy or lieutenant; (will) to leave, bequeath.
legō, -ere, lēgī, lēctum vt to gather, pick; to choose, select; (sail) to furl; (places) to traverse, pass, coast along; (view) to scan; (writing) to read, recite; senātum ~ call the

roll of the senate.

lēgulēius, -ī *and* **ī ī** *m* pettifogging lawyer.

legūmen, -inis *nt* pulse, bean.

lembus, -ī *m* pinnace, cutter.

Lemnias *f* Lemnian woman.

Lemnicola, -ae *m* Vulcan.

lēmniscātus *adj* beribboned.

lēmniscus, -ī *m* ribbon (*hanging from a victor's crown*).

Lēmnius *adj see n.*

Lēmnos (-us), -ī *f* Aegean island, abode of Vulcan.

Lemurēs, -um *mpl* ghosts.

lēna, -ae *f* procuress; seductress.

Lēnaeus *adj* Bacchic ♦ *m* Bacchus.

lēnīmen, -inis *nt* solace, comfort.

lēnīmentum, -ī *nt* sop.

lēniō, -īre, -īvī *and* **iī, -ītum** *vt* to soften, soothe, heal, calm.

lēnis *adj* soft, smooth, mild, gentle, calm.

lēnitās, -ātis *f* softness, smoothness, mildness, tenderness.

lēniter *adv* softly, gently; moderately, half-heartedly.

lēnitūdō, -inis *f* smoothness, mildness.

lēnō, -ōnis *m* pander, brothel keeper; go-between.

lēnōcinium, -ī *and* **ī ī** *nt* pandering; allurement; meretricious ornament.

lēnōcinor, -ārī, -ātus *vi* to pay court to; to promote.

lēnōnius *adj* pander's.

lēns, lentis *f* lentil.

lentē *adv* slowly; calmly, coolly.

lentēscō, -ere *vi* to become sticky, soften; to relax.

lentīscifer, -ī *adj* bearing mastic trees.

lentīscus, -ī *f* mastic tree.

lentitūdō, -inis *f* slowness, dullness, apathy.

lentō, -āre *vt* to bend.

lentulus *adj* rather slow.

lentus *adj* sticky, sluggish; pliant; slow, lasting, lingering; (*person*) calm, at ease, indifferent.

lēnunculus, -ī *m* skiff.

leō, -ōnis *m* lion.

Leōnidās, -ae *m* Spartan king who fell at Thermopylae.

leōnīnus *adj* lion's.

Leontīnī, -ōrum *mpl* town in Sicily.

Leontīnus *adj see n.*

lepas, -dis *f* limpet.

lepidē *adv* neatly, charmingly; (*reply*) very well, splendidly.

lepidus *adj* pleasant, charming, neat, witty.

lepōs (lepor), -ōris *m* pleasantness, charm; wit.

lepus, -oris *m* hare.

lepusculus, -ī *m* young hare.

Lerna, -ae *and* **ē, -ēs** *f* marsh near Argos (*where Hercules killed the Hydra*).

Lernaeus *adj* Lernaean.

Lesbias, -iadis *f* Lesbian woman.

Lesbis, Lesbius *adj see n.*

Lesbos (-us), -ī *f* Aegean island (*home of Alcaeus and Sappho*).

Lesbous *f* Lesbian woman.

lētālis *adj* deadly.

Lēthaeus *adj* of Lethe; infernal; soporific.

lēthargicus, -ī *m* lethargic person.

lēthargus, -ī *m* drowsiness.

Lēthē, -ēs *f* river in the lower world, which caused forgetfulness.

lētifer, -ī *adj* fatal.

lētō, -āre *vt* to kill.

lētum, -ī *nt* death; destruction.

Leucadius *adj see n.*

Leucas, -dis *and* **dia, -diae** *f* island off W. Greece.

Leucothea, -ae, -ē, -ēs *f* Ino (*a sea goddess*).

Leuctra, -ōrum *ntpl* battlefield in Boeotia.

Leuctricus *adj see n.*

levāmen, -inis *nt* alleviation, comfort.

levāmentum, -ī *nt* mitigation, consolation.

levātiō, -ōnis *f* relief; diminishing.

lēvī *perf of* **linō.**

leviculus *adj* rather vain.

levidēnsis *adj* slight.

levipēs, -edis *adj* light-footed.

levis *adj* (*weight*) light; (*MIL*) light-armed; (*fig*) easy, gentle; (*importance*) slight, trivial; (*motion*) nimble, fleet; (*character*) fickle, unreliable.

lēvis *adj* smooth; (*youth*) beardless, delicate.

levisomnus *adj* light-sleeping.

levitās, -ātis *f* lightness; nimbleness; fickleness, frivolity.

lēvitās, -ātis *f* smoothness; fluency.

leviter *adv* lightly; slightly; easily.

levō, -āre *vt* to lighten, ease; (*fig*) to alleviate, lessen; to comfort, relieve; to impair; (*danger*) to avert; **sē ~** rise.

lēvō, -āre *vt* to smooth, polish.

lēvor, -ōris *m* smoothness.

lēx, lēgis *f* law, statute; bill; rule, principle; contract, condition; **lēgem ferre** propose a bill; **lēgem perferre** carry a motion; **lēge agere** proceed according to law; **sine lēge** out of control.

lībāmen, -inis *nt* offering, libation.

lībāmentum, -ī *nt* offering, libation.

lībātiō, -ōnis *f* libation.

lībella, -ae *f* small coin, as; level; **ad ~am** exactly; **ex ~ā** sole heir.

libellus, -ī *m* small book; notebook, diary, letter; notice, programme, handbill; petition, complaint; lampoon.

lībēns, -entis *adj* willing, glad.

libenter *adv* willingly, with pleasure.

liber, -rī *m* inner bark (of a tree); book; register.

Līber, -ī *m* Italian god of fertility (*identified with Bacchus*).

līber, -ī *adj* free, open, unrestricted, undisturbed; (*with abl*) free from; (*speech*) frank; (*POL*) free, not slave, democratic.

Lībera, -ae *f* Proserpine; Ariadne
Līberālia, -ālium *ntpl* festival of Liber in March.
līberālis *adj* of freedom, of free citizens, gentlemanly, honourable; generous, liberal; handsome.
līberālitās, -ātis *f* courtesy, kindness; generosity; bounty.
līberāliter *adv* courteously, nobly generously.
līberātiō, -ōnis *f* delivery, freeing; (*law*) acquittal.
līberātor, -ōris *m* liberator, deliverer.
līberē *adv* freely, frankly, boldly
līberī, -ōrum *mpl* children.
līberō, -āre, -āvī, -ātum *vt* to free, set free, release; to exempt; (*law*) to acquit (*slave*) to give freedom to; **fidem ~** keep one's promise; **nōmina ~** cancel debts
līberta, -ae *f* freedwoman.
lībertās, -ātis *f* freedom, liberty status of a freeman; (*POL*) independence; freedom of speech, outspokenness.
lībertīnus *adj* of a freedman, freed **♦** *m* freedman **♦** *f* freedwoman.
lībertus, -ī *m* freedman.
libet (lubet), -ēre, -uit *and* **itum est** *vi* (*impers*) it pleases; **mihi ~ I like; ~t ~** as you please.
libīdinōsē *adv* wilfully.
libīdinōsus *adj* wilful, arbitrary, extravagant; sensual, lustful.
libīdō (lubīdō), -inis *f* desire, passion; wilfulness, caprice; lust.
libita, -ōrum *ntpl* pleasure, fancy
Libitīna, -ae *f* goddess of burials.
lībō, -āre, -āvī, -ātum *vt* to taste, sip, touch; to pour (*a libation*), offer; to extract, take out; to impair.
lībra, -ae *f* pound; balance, pair of scales; **ad ~am** of equal size.
lībrāmentum, -ī *nt* level surface, weight (*to give balance or movement*); (*water*) fall.
lībrāria, -ae *f* head spinner.
lībrāriolus, -ī *m* copyist.
lībrārium, -ī *and* **ī ī** *nt* bookcase.
lībrārius *adj* of books **♦** *m* copyist
lībrātus *adj* level; powerful.
lībrīlis *adj* weighing a pound.
lībritor, -ōris *m* slinger.
lībrō, -āre, -āvī, -ātum *vt* to poise, hold balanced; to swing, hurl.
lībum, -ī *nt* cake.
Liburna, -ae *f* a fast galley, frigate
Liburnī, -ōrum *mpl* people of Illyria.
Liburnus *adj* Liburnian.
Libya, -ae, -ē, -ēs *f* Africa.
Libycus *adj* African.
Libyes, -um *mpl* Libyans, people in N. Africa.
Libyssus, Libystinus, Libystis *c* = **Libycus.**
licēns, -entis *adj* free, bold, unrestricted.
licenter *adv* freely, lawlessly.

licentia, -ae *f* freedom, license; lawlessness, licentiousness.
liceō, -ēre, -uī *i* to be for sale, value at.
liceor, -ērī, -itus *vt* *vi* to bid (at an auction), bid for.
licet, -ēre, -uit *and* **itum est** *vi* (*impers*) it is permitted, it is lawful; (*reply*) all right **♦** *conj* although; **mihi ~** I may.
Licinius, -ī *m* Roman family name (*esp with surname Crassus*).
Licinius *adj* see *n*.
licitātiō, -ōnis *f* bidding (*at a sale*).
licitor, -ārī, *vi* to make a bid.
licitus *adj* lawful.
līcium, -ī *and* **ī ī** *nt* thread.
līctor, -ōris *m* lictor (*an attendant with fasces preceding a magistrate*).
licuī *perf of* **liceō** *perf of* **liquēscō.**
liēn, -ēnis *m* spleen.
ligāmen, -inis *nt* band, bandage.
ligāmentum, -ī *nt* bandage.
Liger, -is *m* river Loire.
lignārius, -ī *and* **ī ī** *m* carpenter.
lignātiō, -ōnis *f* fetching wood.
lignātor, -ōris *m* woodcutter.
ligneolus *adj* wooden.
ligneus *adj* wooden.
lignor, -ārī *vi* to fetch wood.
lignum, -ī *nt* wood, firewood, timber; **in silvam ~a ferre** ≈ *carry coals to Newcastle.*
ligō, -āre, -āvī, -ātum *vt* to tie up, bandage; (*fig*) to unite.
ligō, -ōnis *m* mattock, hoe.
ligula, -ae *f* shoestrap.
Ligur, -ris *m/f* Ligurian.
Liguria, -riae *f* district of N.W. Italy.
ligūriō (ligurriō), -īre *vt* to lick; to eat daintily; (*fig*) to feast on, lust after.
ligūrītiō, -ōnis *f* daintiness.
Ligus, -ris *m/f* Ligurian.
Ligusticus, -stinus *adj* see *n.*
ligustrum, -ī *nt* privet.
līlium, -ī *and* **ī ī** *n*: lily; (*MIL*) spiked pit.
līma, -ae *f* file; (*fig*) revision.
līmātius *adv* more elegantly.
līmātulus *adj* refined.
līmāx, -ācis *f* slug, snail.
limbus, -ī *m* fringe, hem.
līmen, -inis *nt* threshold, lintel; doorway, entrance; house, home; (*fig*) beginning.
līmes, -itis *m* path between fields, boundary; path, track, way; frontier, boundary line.
līmō, -āre, -āvī, -ātum *vt* to file; (*fig*) to polish, refine; to file down, investigate carefully; to take away from.
līmōsus *adj* muddy.
limpidus *adj* clear, limpid.
līmus *adj* sidelong, askance.
līmus, -ī *m* mud, slime, dirt.
līmus, -ī *m* ceremonial apron.

Noun declensions and verb conjugations are shown on pp xiii to xxv. The present infinitive ending of a verb shows to which conjugation it belongs: -**āre** = 1st; -**ēre** = 2nd; -ere = 3rd and -**īre** = 4th. Irregular verbs are shown on p xxvi

līnea, -ae *f* line, string; plumbline; boundary; ad ~am, rectā ~ā vertically; extrēmā ~ā amāre love at a distance.

līneāmentum, -ī *nt* line; feature; outline.

līneus *adj* flaxen, linen.

lingō, -ere *vt* to lick.

lingua, -ae *f* tongue; speech, language; tongue of land; ~ Latīna Latin.

lingula, -ae *f* tongue of land.

līniger, -ī *adj* linen-clad.

linō, -ere, lēvī, litum *vt* to daub, smear; to overlay; (writing) to rub out; (fig) to befoul.

linquō, -ere, līquī *vt* to leave, quit; to give up, let alone; (pass) to faint, swoon; ~itur ut it remains to.

linteātus *adj* canvas.

linteō, -ōnis *m* linen weaver.

linter, -ris *f* boat; trough.

linteum, -ī *nt* linen cloth, canvas; sail.

linteus *adj* linen.

lintriculus, -ī *m* small boat.

līnum, -ī *nt* flax; linen; thread, line, rope; net.

Lipara, -ae, -ē, -ēs *f* island N. of Sicily (now Lipari).

Liparaeus, -ēnsis *adj see n.*

lippiō, -īre *vi* to have sore eyes.

lippitūdō, -inis *f* inflammation of the eyes.

lippus *adj* blear-eyed, with sore eyes; (fig) blind.

liquefaciō, -facere, -fēcī, -factum (pass -fīō) *vt* to melt, dissolve; to decompose; (fig) to enervate.

liquēns, -entis *adj* fluid, clear.

liquēscō, -ere, licuī *vi* to melt; to clear; (fig) to grow soft, waste away.

liquet, -ēre, licuit *vi* (impers) it is clear, it is evident; nōn ~ not proven.

līquī *perf of* linquō.

liquidō *adv* clearly.

liquidus *adj* fluid, liquid, flowing; clear, transparent, pure; (mind) calm, serene ♦ *nt* liquid water.

liquō, -āre *vt* to melt; to strain.

līquor, -ī *vi* to flow; (fig) to waste away.

liquor, -ōris *m* fluidity; liquid, the sea.

Līris, -is *m* river between Latium and Campania.

līs, lītis *f* quarrel, dispute; lawsuit; matter in dispute; lītem aestimāre assess damages.

litātiō, -ōnis *f* favourable sacrifice.

lītera *etc see* littera.

lītigātor, -ōris *m* litigant.

lītigiōsus *adj* quarrelsome, contentious; disputed.

lītigium, -ī *and* iī *nt* quarrel.

lītigō, -āre *vi* to quarrel; to go to law.

litō, -āre, -āvī, -ātum *vi* to offer an acceptable sacrifice, obtain favourable omens; (with dat) to propitiate ♦ *vt* to offer successfully.

lītorālis *adj* of the shore.

lītoreus *adj* of the shore.

littera, -ae *f* letter (of the alphabet).

litterae, -ārum *fpl* writing; letter, dispatch; document, ordinance; literature; learning, scholarship; ~ās discere learn to read and write; homō trium ~ārum thief (of fur); sine ~īs uncultured.

litterārius *adj* of reading and writing.

litterātē *adv* in clear letters; literally.

litterātor, -ōris *m* grammarian.

litterātūra, -ae *f* writing, alphabet.

litterātus *adj* with letters on it, branded; educated, learned.

litterula, -ae *f* small letter; short note; (pl) studies.

litūra, -ae *f* correction, erasure, blot.

litus *ppp of* linō.

lītus, -oris *nt* shore, beach, coast; bank; ~ arāre labour in vain.

lituus, -ī *m* augur's staff; trumpet; (fig) starter.

līvēns, -entis *pres p of* līveō ♦ *adj* bluish, black and blue.

līveō, -ēre *vi* to be black and blue; to envy.

līvēscō, -ere *vi* to turn black and blue.

Līvianus *adj* = Līvius.

līvidulus *adj* a little jealous.

līvidus *adj* bluish, black and blue; envious, malicious.

Līvius, -ī Roman family name (esp the famous historian, Livy.

Līvius *adj see n.*

līvor, -ōris *m* bluish colour; envy, malice.

lixa, -ae *m* sutler, camp-follower.

locātiō, -ōnis *f* leasing; lease, contract.

locātōrius *adj* concerned with leases.

locitō, -āre *vt* to let frequently.

locō, -āre, -āvī, -ātum *vt* to place, put; to give in marriage; to let, lease, hire out; to contract for; (money) to invest.

loculus, -ī *m* little place; (pl) satchel, purse.

locuplēs, -ētis *adj* rich, opulent; reliable, responsible.

locuplētō, -āre *vt* to enrich.

locus, -ī *m* (pl -ī *m and* -a *nt*) place, site, locality, region; (mil) post; (theatre) seat; (book) passage; (speech) topic, subject, argument; (fig) room, occasion; situation, state; rank, position; -ī individual spots; ~a regions, ground; -ī commūnēs general arguments; ~ō (with gen) instead of; in ~ō opportunely; eō ~ī in the position; intereā ~ī meanwhile.

lōcusta, -ae *f* locust.

locūtiō, -ōnis *f* speech; pronunciation.

locūtus *ppa of* loquor.

lōdīx, -īcis *f* blanket.

logica, -ōrum *ntpl* logic.

logos (-us), -ī *m* word; idle talk; witticism.

lōlīg- *etc see* lollīg-.

lolium, -ī *and* iī *nt* darnel.

lollīgō, -inis *f* cuttlefish.

lōmentum, -ī *nt* face cream.

Londinium, -ī *nt* London.

longaevus *adj* aged.

longē *adv* far, far off; (time) long; (compar) by far, very much; ~ esse be far away, of no

avail; ~ **latēque** everywhere.
longinquitās, -ātis f length; distance;
duration.
longinquus adj distant, remote; foreign,
strange; lasting, wearisome; (time) long
deferred.
longitūdō, -inis f length; duration; ~**inem**
lengthwise.
longiusculus adj rather long.
longulē adv rather far.
longulus adj rather long.
longurius, -ī and **iī** m long pole.
longus adj long; vast; (time) long, protracted,
tedious; (hope) far-reaching; ~**a nāvis**
warship; ~**um est** it would be tedious; nē
~**um faciam** ≈ to cut a long story short.
loquācitās, -ātis f talkativeness.
loquāciter adv see adj.
loquāculus adj somewhat talkative.
loquāx, -ācis adj talkative, chattering.
loquella, -ae f language, words.
loquor, -quī, cūtus vt, vi to speak, talk, say; to
talk about, mention; (fig) to indicate; **rēs**
~**quitur ipsa** the facts speak for themselves.
lōrārius, -ī and **iī** m flogger.
lōrātus adj strapped.
lōreus adj of leather strips.
lōrīca, -ae f breastplate; parapet.
lōrīcātus adj mailed.
lōripēs, -edis adj bandylegged.
lōrum, -ī nt strap; whip, lash; leather charm;
(pl) reins.
lōtos (-us), -ī f lotus.
lōtus ppp of **lavō**.
lubēns see **libēns**.
lubentia, -ae f pleasure.
lubet, lubīdō see **libet, libīdō**.
lūbricō, -āre vt to make slippery.
lūbricus adj slippery, slimy; gliding, fleeting;
(fig) dangerous, hazardous.
Lūca bōs f elephant.
Lūcania, -iae f district of S. Italy.
Lūcanica f kind of sausage.
Lūcanus adj Lucanian ♦ m the epic poet Lucan.
lūcar, -āris nt forest tax.
lucellum, -ī nt small gain.
lūceō, -cēre, -xī vi to shine, be light; (impers)
to dawn, be daylight; (fig) to shine, be clear;
meridiē nōn ~**cēre** ≈ (argue) that black is white.
Lūcerēs, -um mpl a Roman patrician tribe.
Lūceria, -iae f town in Apulia.
Lūcerīnus adj see n.
lucerna, -ae f lamp; (fig) ≈ midnight oil.
lūcēscō, -ere vi to begin to shine, get light,
dawn.
lūcidē adv clearly.
lūcidus adj bright, clear; (fig) lucid.
lūcifer, -ī adj light-bringing ♦ m morning star,
Venus; day.
lūcifugus adj shunning the light.

Lūcīlius, -ī m Roman family name (esp the first
Latin satirist).
Lūcīna, -ae f goddess of childbirth.
lūcīscō etc see **lūcēscō**.
Lucmō (Lucumō), -ōnis m Etruscan prince
or priest.
Lucrētia, -iae f wife of Collatinus, ravished by
Tarquin.
Lucrētius, -ī m Roman family name (esp the
philosophic poet).
lucrifuga, -ae m non-profiteer.
Lucrīnēnsis adj see n.
Lucrīnus, -ī m lake near Baiae (famous for
oysters).
lucror, -ārī, -ātus vi to gain, win, acquire.
lucrōsus adj profitable.
lucrum, -ī nt profit, gain; greed; wealth; ~**ī
facere** gain, get the credit of; ~**ō esse** be of
advantage; **in** ~**īs pōnere** count as gain.
luctāmen, -inis nt struggle, exertion.
luctātiō, -ōnis wrestling; fight, contest.
luctātor, -ōris m wrestler.
lūctificus adj baleful.
lūctisonus adj mournful.
luctor, -ārī, -ātus vi to wrestle; to struggle,
fight.
lūctuōsus adj sorrowful, lamentable.
lūctus, -ūs m mourning, lamentation;
mourning (dress).
lūcubrātiō, -ōnis f work by lamplight,
nocturnal study.
lūcubrō, -āre, -āvī, -ātum vi to work by night
♦ vt to compose by night.
lūculentē adv splendidly, right.
lūculenter adv very well.
lūculentus adj bright; (fig) brilliant, excellent,
rich, fine.
Lūcullus, -ī m Roman surname (esp the
conqueror of Mithridates).
lūcus, -ī m grove; wood.
lūdia, -ae f woman gladiator.
lūdibrium, -ī and **iī** nt mockery, derision;
laughing stock; sport, play; ~**iō habēre** make
fun of.
lūdibundus adj playful; safely, easily.
lūdicer, -rī adj playful; theatrical.
lūdicum, -ī nt public show, play; sport.
lūdificātiō, -ōnis f ridicule; tricking.
lūdificātor, -ōris m mocker.
lūdificō, -āre; -or, -ārī, -ātus vt to make a fool
of, ridicule; to delude, thwart.
lūdiō, -ōnis m actor.
lūdius, -ī and **iī** m actor; gladiator.
lūdō, -dere, -sī, -sum vi to play; to sport,
frolic; to dally, make love ♦ vt to play at; to
amuse oneself with; to mimic, imitate; to
ridicule, mock; to delude.
lūdus, -ī m game; sport, play; (pl) public
spectacle, games; school; (fig) child's play;
fun, jest; (love) dalliance; ~**um dare** humour;

~**ōs facere** put on a public show; make fun of.
luella, -ae _f_ atonement.
luēs, -is _f_ plague, pest; misfortune.
Lugdūnēnsis _adj see n._
Lugdūnum, -ī _nt_ town in E. Gaul (_now_ Lyons).
lūgeō, -gēre, -xī _vt, vi_ to mourn; to be in mourning.
lūgubris _adj_ mourning; disastrous; (_sound_) plaintive ♦ _ntpl_ mourning dress.
lumbī, -ōrum _mpl_ loins.
lumbrīcus, -ī _m_ worm.
lūmen, -inis _m_ light; lamp, torch; day; eye; life; (_fig_) ornament, glory; clarity.
lūmināre, -is _nt_ window.
lūminōsus _adj_ brilliant.
lūna, -ae _f_ moon; month; crescent.
lūnāris _adj_ of the moon.
lūnātus _adj_ crescent-shaped.
lūnō, -āre _vt_ to bend into a crescent.
luō, -ere, -ī _vt_ to pay; to atone for; to avert by expiation.
lupa, -ae _f_ she-wolf; prostitute.
lupānar, -āris _nt_ brothel.
lupātus _adj_ toothed ♦ _m and ntpl_ curb.
Lupercal, -ālis _nt_ a grotto sacred to Pan.
Lupercālia, -ālium _ntpl_ festival of Pan in February.
Lupercus, -ī _m_ Pan; priest of Pan.
lupīnum, -ī _nt_ lupin; sham money, counters.
lupīnus _adj_ wolf's.
lupīnus, -ī _m_ lupin; sham money, counters.
lupus, -ī _m_ wolf; (_fish_) pike; toothed bit; grapnel; ~ **in fābulā** ≈ _talk of the devil_.
lūridus _adj_ pale yellow, ghastly pallid.
lūror, -ōris _m_ yellowness.
lūscinia, -ae _f_ nightingale.
luscitiōsus _adj_ purblind.
luscus _adj_ one-eyed.
lūsiō, -ōnis _f_ play.
Lūsitānia, -iae _f_ part of W. Spain (_including what is now_ Portugal).
Lūsitānus _adj see n._
lūsitō, -āre _vi_ to play.
lūsor, -ōris _m_ player; humorous writer.
lūstrālis _adj_ lustral, propitiatory; quinquennial.
lūstrātiō, -ōnis _f_ purification; roving.
lūstrō, -āre, -āvī, -ātum _vt_ to purify; (_motion_) to go round, encircle, traverse; (_MIL_) to review; (_eyes_) to scan, survey; (_mind_) to consider; (_light_) to illuminate.
lūstror, -ārī _vi_ to frequent brothels.
lūstrum, -ī _nt_ den, lair; (_pl_) wild country; (_fig_) brothels; debauchery.
lūstrum, -ī _nt_ purificatory sacrifice; (_time_) five years.
lūsus _ppp of_ **lūdō**.
lūsus, -ūs _m_ play, game, sport; dalliance.
lūteolus _adj_ yellow.
Lutetia, -ae _f_ town in N. Gaul (_now_ Paris).
lūteus _adj_ yellow, orange.
luteus _adj_ of clay; muddy, dirty, (_fig_) vile.
lutitō, -āre _vt_ to throw mud at.

lutulentus _adj_ muddy, filthy; (_fig_) foul.
lūtum, -ī _nt_ dyer's weed; yellow.
lutum, -ī _nt_ mud, mire; clay.
lūx, lūcis _f_ light; daylight; day; life; (_fig_) public view; glory, encouragement, enlightenment; **lūce** in the daytime; **prīmā lūce** at daybreak; **lūce carentēs** the dead.
lūxī _perf of_ **lūceō**; _perf of_ **lūgeō**.
luxor, -ārī _vi_ to live riotously.
luxuria, -ae, -ēs, -ēī _f_ rankness, profusion; extravagance, luxury.
luxuriō, -āre, -or, -ārī _vi_ to grow to excess, be luxuriant; (_fig_) to be exuberant, run riot.
luxuriōsē _adv_ voluptuously.
luxuriōsus _adj_ luxuriant; excessive, extravagant; voluptuous.
luxus, -ūs _m_ excess, debauchery, pomp.
Lyaeus, -ī _m_ Bacchus; wine.
Lycaeus, -ī _m_ mountain in Arcadia (_sacred to Pan_).
Lycāōn, -onis _m_ father of Callisto, the Great Bear.
Lycāonius _adj see n._
Lycēum (Lycīum), -ī _nt_ Aristotle's school at Athens.
lychnūchus, -ī _m_ lampstand.
lychnus, -ī _m_ lamp.
Lycia, -ae _f_ country in S.W. Asia Minor.
Lycius _adj_ Lycian.
Lyctius _adj_ Cretan.
Lycurgus, -ī _m_ Thracian king killed by Bacchus; Spartan lawgiver; Athenian orator.
Lȳdia, -iae _f_ country of Asia Minor.
Lȳdius _adj_ Lydian; Etruscan.
Lȳdus, -ī _m_ Lydian.
lympha, -ae _f_ water.
lymphāticus _adj_ crazy, frantic.
lymphātus _adj_ distracted.
Lynceus, -eī _m_ keen-sighted Argonaut.
lynx, lyncis _m/f_ lynx.
lyra, -ae _f_ lyre; lyric poetry.
lyricus _adj_ of the lyre, lyrical.
Lysiās, -ae _m_ Athenian orator.

_M, m_

Macedō, -onis _m_ Macedonian.
Macedonia _f_ Macedonia.
Macedonicus, -onius _adj see n._
macellum, -ī _nt_ market.
maceō, -ēre _vi_ to be lean.
macer, -rī _adj_ lean, meagre; poor.
māceria, -ae _f_ wall.
mācerō, -āre _vt_ to soften; (_body_) to enervate; (_mind_) to distress.

macēscō, -ere vi to grow thin.
machaera, -ae f sword.
machaerophorus, -ī m soldier armed with a sword.
Machāōn, -onis m legendary Greek surgeon.
Machāonius adj see n.
māchina, -ae f machine, engine; (fig) scheme, trick.
māchināmentum, -ī nt engine.
māchinātiō, -ōnis f mechanism machine; (fig) contrivance.
māchinātor, -ōris m engineer; (fig) contriver.
māchinor, -ārī, -ātus vt to devise; contrive; (fig) to plot, scheme.
maciēs, -ēī f leanness, meagreness; poorness.
macilentus adj thin.
macrēscō, -ere vi to grow thin.
macritūdō, -inis f leanness.
macrocollum, -ī nt large size of paper.
mactābilis adj deadly.
mactātus, -ūs m sacrifice.
macte blessed; well done!
mactō, -āre, -āvī, -ātum vt to sacrifice; to punish, kill.
mactō, -āre vt to glorify.
macula, -ae f spot, stain; (net) mesh (fig) blemish, fault.
maculō, -āre, -āvī, -ātum vt to stain, defile.
maculōsus adj dappled, mottled; stained, polluted.
madefaciō, -facere, -fēcī, -factum (pass -fīō, -fierī) vt to wet, soak.
madeō, -ēre vi to be wet, be drenched; to be boiled soft; (comedy) to be drunk; (fig) to be steeped in.
madēscō, -ere vi to get wet, become moist.
madidus adj wet, soaked; sodden, drunk.
madulsa, -ae m drunkard.
Maeander (-ros), -rī m a winding river of Asia Minor; winding, wandering.
Maecēnās, -ātis m friend of Augustus, patron of poets.
maena, -ae f sprat.
Maenala, -ōrum ntpl mountain range in Arcadia.
Maenalis, -ius adj of Maenalus; Arcadian.
Maenalus (-os), -ī m Maenala.
Maenas, -dis f Bacchante.
Maeniānum nt balcony.
Maenius, -ī m Roman family name; ~ā columna whipping post in the Forum.
Maeonia, -ae f Lydia.
Maeonidēs, -dae m Homer.
Maeonius, -s adj Lydian; Homeric Etruscan.
Maeōticus, -us adj Scythian, Maeotic.
Maeōtis, -dis f Sea of Azov.
maereō, -ēre vi to mourn, be sad.
maeror, -ōris m mourning, sorrow, sadness.
maestiter adv see adj.
maestitia, -ae f sadness, melancholy.
maestus adj sad, sorrowful; gloomy;

mourning.
māgālia, -um ntpl huts.
mage etc see **magis**.
magicus adj magical.
magis (mage) adv more; eō ~ the more, all the more.
magister, -rī m master, chief, director; (school) teacher; (fig) instigator; ~ **equitum** chief of cavalry, second in command to a dictator; ~ **mōrum** censor; ~ **sacrōrum** chief priest.
magisterium, -ī anc ī ī nt presidency, tutorship.
magistra, -ae f mistress, instructress.
magistrātus, -ūs m magistracy, office; magistrate, official.
magnanimitās, -ātis f greatness.
māgnanimus adj great, brave.
Magnēs, -ētis m Magnesian; magnet.
Magnēsia f district of Thessaly.
Magnēsius, -ēsus, -ētis adj see n.
magnidicus adj boastful.
magnificē adv grandly; pompously.
magnificentia, -ae f greatness, grandeur; pomposity.
magnificō, -āre vt to esteem highly.
magnificus (compar -entior superl -entissimus) adj great, grand, splendid; pompous.
magniloquent a, -ae f elevated language; pomposity.
magniloquus adj boastful.
magnitūdō, -iris f greatness, size, large amount; dignity.
magnopere adv greatly, very much.
magnus (compar māior superl māximus) adj great, large, big, tall; (voice) loud; (age) advanced; (value) high, dear; (fig) grand, noble, important; **avunculus** ~ great-uncle; ~**a loquī** boast; ~**ī aestimāre** think highly of; ~**ī esse** be highly esteemed; ~**ō stāre** cost dear; ~**ō opere** very much.
magus, -ī m wise man; magician ♦ adj magic.
Māia, -ae f mother of Mercury.
māiestās, -ātis f greatness, dignity, majesty; treason; ~**ātem laedere, minuere** offend against the sovereignty of; **lēx ~ātis** law against treason.
māior, -ōris compar of **māgnus**; ~ **nātū** older, elder.
māiōrēs, -ōrum mpl ancestors; **in ~us crēdere/ferre** exaggerate.
Māius, -ī m May ♦ adj of May.
māiusculus adj somewhat greater; a little older.
māla, -ae f cheek, jaw.
malacia, -ae f dead calm.
malacus adj soft.
male (compar pēius, superl pessimē) adv badly, wrongly, unfortunately; not; (with words having bad sense) very much; ~ **est animō** I

feel ill; ~ **sānus** insane; ~ **dīcere** abuse, curse; ~ **facere** harm.

maledicē *adv* abusively.

maledictiō, -ōnis *f* abuse.

maledictum, -ī *nt* curse.

maledicus *adj* scurrilous.

malefactum, -ī *nt* wrong.

ɪmaleficē *adv see adj.*

ɪmaleficium, -ī *and* **iī** *nt* misdeed, wrong, mischief.

maleficus *adj* wicked ♦ *m* criminal.

malesuādus *adj* seductive.

malevolēns, -entis *adj* spiteful.

malevolentia, -ae *f* ill-will.

malevolus *adj* ill-disposed, malicious.

mālifer, -ī *adj* apple-growing.

malīgnē *adv* spitefully; grudgingly.

malīgnitās, -ātis *f* malice; stinginess.

malīgnus *adj* unkind, ill-natured, spiteful; stingy; (*soil*) unfruitful; (*fig*) small, scanty.

malitia, -ae *f* badness, malice; roguishness.

malitiōsē *adv see adj.*

malitiōsus *adj* wicked, crafty.

maliv- *etc see* **malev-**.

mālle *infin of* **mālō**.

malleolus, -ī *m* hammer; (*MIL*) fire-brand.

malleus, -ī *m* hammer, mallet, maul.

mālō, -le, -uī *vt* to prefer; would rather.

malobathrum, -ī *nt* an oriental perfume.

māluī *perf of* **mālō**.

mālum, -ī *nt* apple, fruit.

malum, -ī *nt* evil, wrong, harm, misfortune; (*interj*) mischief.

mālus, -ī *f* apple tree.

mālus, -ī *m* mast, pole.

malus (*compar* **pēior** *superl* **pessimus**) *adj* bad, evil, harmful; unlucky; ugly; ī **in** ~**am rem** go to hell!

malva, -ae *f* mallow.

Māmers, -tis *m* Mars.

Māmertīnī, -ōrum *mpl* mercenary troops who occupied Messana.

mamma, -ae *f* breast; teat.

mammilla, -ae *f* breast.

mānābilis *adj* penetrating.

manceps, -ipis *m* purchaser; contractor.

mancipium, -ī *and* **iī** *nt* formal purchase; property; slave.

mancipō, -āre *vt* to sell, deliver up.

mancup- *etc see* **mancip-**.

mancus *adj* crippled.

mandātum, -ī *nt* commission, command; (*law*) contract.

mandātus, -ūs *m* command.

mandō, -āre, -āvī, -ātum *vt* to entrust, commit; to commission, command.

mandō, -ere, -ī, mānsum *vt* to chew, eat, devour.

mandra, -ae *f* drove of cattle.

mandūcus, -ī *m* masked figure of a glutton.

māne *nt* (*indecl*) morning ♦ *adv* in the morning, early.

maneō, -ēre, mānsī, mānsum *vi* to remain;

to stay, stop; to last, abide, continue ♦ *vt* to wait for, await; **in condiciōne** ~ abide by an agreement.

Mānēs, -ium *mpl* ghosts, shades of the dead; the lower world; bodily remains.

mangō, -ōnis *m* dealer.

manicae, -ārum *fpl* sleeves, gloves; handcuffs.

manicātus *adj* with long sleeves.

manicula, -ae *f* little hand.

manifestō, -āre *vt* to disclose.

manifestō *adv* clearly, evidently.

manifestus *adj* clear, obvious; convicted, caught.

manipl- *etc see* **manipul-**.

manipulāris *adj* of a company ♦ *m* private (in the ranks); fellow soldier.

manipulātim *adv* by companies.

manipulus, -ī *m* bundle (*esp of hay*); (*MIL*) company.

Manlius, -iānus *adj see n.*

Manlius, -ī *m* Roman family name (*esp the saviour of the Capitol from the Gauls*); a severe disciplinarian.

mannus, -ī *m* Gallic horse.

mānō, -āre, -āvī, -ātum *vi* to flow, drip, stream; (*fig*) to spread, emanate.

mānsī *perf of* **maneō**.

mānsiō, -ōnis *f* remaining, stay.

mānsitō, -āre *vi* to stay on.

mānsuēfaciō, -facere, -fēcī, -factum (*pass* -**fīō, -fierī**) *vt* to tame.

mānsuēscō, -scere, -vī, -tum *vt* to tame ♦ *vi* to grow tame, grow mild.

mānsuētē *adv see adj.*

mānsuētūdō, -inis *f* tameness; gentleness.

mānsuētus *ppp of* **mānsuēscō** ♦ *adj* tame; mild, gentle.

mānsus *ppp of* **mandō**; *ppp of* **maneō**.

mantēle, -is *nt* napkin, towel.

mantēlum, -ī *nt* cloak.

mantica, -ae *f* knapsack.

manticinor, -ārī, -ātus *vi* to be a prophet.

mantō, -āre *vi* to remain, wait.

Mantua, -ae *f* birthplace of Vergil in N. Italy.

manuālis *adj* for the hand.

manubiae, -ārum *fpl* money from sale of booty.

manūbrium, -ī *and* **iī** *nt* handle, haft.

manuleātus *adj* with long sleeves.

manūmissiō, -ōnis *f* emancipation (of a slave).

manūmittō, -ittere, -īsī, -issum *vt* to emancipate, make free.

manupretium, -ī *and* **iī** *nt* pay, wages, reward.

manus, -ūs *f* hand; corps, band, company; (*elephant*) trunk; (*art*) touch; (*work*) handiwork, handwriting; (*war*) force, valour, hand to hand fighting; (*fig*) power; ~ **extrēma** finishing touch; ~ **ferrea** grappling iron; ~**um dare** give up, yield; ~**ū** artificially; ~**ū mittere** emancipate; **ad** ~**um** at hand; **in** ~**ū** obvious; subject; **in** ~**ūs venīre** come to hand; **in** ~**ibus** well known; at hand; **in** ~**ibus habēre** be

engaged on; fondle; **per ~ūs fcrcibly; per ~ūs trādere** hand down.
mapālia, -um *ntpl* huts.
mappa, -ae *f* napkin, cloth.
Marathōn, -ōnis *f Attic village famous for Persian defeat.*
Marathōnius *adj see n.*
Marcellia, -iōrum *ntpl festival of the Marcelli.*
Marcellus, -ī *m* Roman surname *(esp the captor of Syracuse).*
marceō, -ēre *vi* to droop, be faint.
marcēscō, -ere *vi* to waste away, grow feeble.
Marciānus *adj see n.*
marcidus *adj* withered; enervated.
Marcius, -ī *m* Roman family name *(esp Ancus, fourth king).*
Marcius *adj see n.*
mare, -is *nt* sea; **~ nostrum** Mediterranean; **~ inferum** Tyrrhenian Sea; **~ superum** Adriatic.
Mareōticus *adj* Mareotic; Egyptian.
margarīta, -ae *f* pearl.
marginō, -āre *vt* to put a border *or* kerb on.
margō, -inis *m/f* edge, border, boundary; **~ cēnae** side dishes.
Mariānus *adj see n.*
Marīca, -ae *f nymph of Minturnae.*
marīnus *adj* of the sea.
marītālis *adj* marriage- *(in cpds).*
maritimus *adj* of the sea, marit.me, coastal ♦ *ntpl* coastal area.
marītō, -āre *vt* to marry.
marītus, -i *m* husband ♦ *adj* nuptial.
Marius, -ī *m* Roman family name *(esp the victor over Jugurtha and the Teutons).*
Marius *adj see n.*
marmor, -is *nt* marble; statue, tablet; sea.
marmoreus *adj* of marble; like marble.
Marō, -ōnis *m* surname of Vergil.
marra, -ae *f* kind of hoe.
Mars, Martis *m* God of war, father of Romulus; war, conflict; planet Mars; **aecuō Marte** on equal terms; **suō Marte** by one's own exertions.
Marsī, -ōrum *mpl people of central Italy, famous as fighters.*
Marsicus, -us *adj* Marsian.
marsuppium, -ī *and* **iī** *nt* purse.
Mārtiālis *adj* of Mars.
Mārticola, -ae *m* worshipper of Mars.
Mārtigena, -ae *m* son of Mars.
Mārtius *adj* of Mars; of March; warlike.
mās, maris *m* male, man ♦ *adj* male; manly.
māsculus *adj* male, masculine; manly.
Masinissa, -ae *m* king of Numidia.
massa, -ae *f* lump, mass.
Massicum, -ī *nt* Massic wine.
Massicus, -ī *m* mountain in Campania, famous for vines.

Massilia, -ae *f* Greek colony in Gaul *(now Marseilles).*
Massiliēnsis *adj see n.*
mastīgia, -ae *nt* scoundrel.
mastrūca, -ae *f* sheepskin.
mastrūcātus *adj* wearing sheepskin.
matara, -ae *and* **is, -is** *f* Celtic javelin.
matelliō, -ōnis *m* pot.
māter, -ris *f* mother; **Māgna ~** Cybele.
mātercula, -ae *f* poor mother.
māteria, -ae; -ēs, -ēi *f* matter, substance; wood, timber; *(fig)* subject matter, theme; occasion, opportunity; *(person)* ability, character.
māteriārius, -ī *and* **iī** *m* timber merchant.
māteriātus *adj* timbered.
māteriēs *etc see* **māteria.**
māterior, -ārī *vi* to fetch wood.
māternus *adj* mother's.
mātertera, -ae *f* aunt (maternal).
mathēmaticus, -ī *m* mathematician; astrologer.
mātricīda, -ae *m* matricide.
mātricīdium, -ī *and* **iī** *nt* a mother's murder.
mātrimōnium, -ī *and* **iī** *nt* marriage.
mātrimus *adj* whose mother is still alive.
mātrōna, -ae *f* married woman, matron, lady.
mātrōnālis *adj* a married woman's.
matula, -ae *f* pot.
mātūrē *adv* at the right time; early, promptly.
mātūrēscō, -ēscere, -uī *vi* to ripen.
mātūritās, -ātis *f* ripeness; *(fig)* maturity, perfection, height.
mātūrō, -āre, -āvī, -ātum *vt* to bring to maturity; to hasten, be too hasty with ♦ *vi* to make haste.
mātūrus *adj* ripe, mature; timely, seasonable; early.
Mātūta, -ae *f goddess of dawn.*
mātūtīnus *adj* morning, early.
Mauritānia, -ae *f* Mauretania *(now Morocco).*
Maurus, -ī *m* Moor ♦ *adj* Moorish, African.
Maurūsius *adj see n.*
Māvors, -tis *m* Mars.
Māvortius *adj see n.*
maxilla, -ae *f* jaw.
maximē *adv* most, very much, especially; precisely, just; certainly, yes; **cum ~** just as; **quam ~** as much as possible.
maximitās, -ātis *f* great size.
maximus *super of* **magnus.**
māxum- *etc see* **māxim-.**
māzonomus, -ī *m* dish.
meāpte my own.
meātus, -ūs *m* movement, course.
mēcastor *interj* by Castor!
mēcum with me.
meddix tuticus *m senior Oscan magistrate.*
Mēdēa, -ae *f Colchian wife of Jason, expert in magic.*

Noun declensions and verb conjugations are shown on pp xiii to xxv. The present infinitive ending of a verb shows to which conjugation it belongs: **-āre** = 1st; **-ēre** = 2nd; **-ere** = 3rd and **-īre** = 4th. Irregular verbs are shown on p xxvi

Mēdēis *adj* magical.
medentēs, -entum *mpl* doctors.
medeor, -ērī *vi (with dat)* to heal, remedy.
mediastīnus, -ī *m* drudge.
mēdica, -ae *f* lucern *(kind of clover)*.
medicābilis *adj* curable.
medicāmen, -inis *nt* drug, medicine;
cosmetic; *(fig)* remedy.
medicāmentum, -ī *nt* drug, medicine; potion,
poison; *(fig)* relief; embellishment.
medicātus, -ūs *m* charm.
medicīna, -ae *f* medicine; cure; *(fig)* remedy,
relief.
medicō, -āre, -āvī, -ātum *vt* to cure; to steep,
dye.
medicor, -ārī *vt, vi* to cure.
medicus *adj* healing ♦ *m* doctor.
medietās, -ātis *f* mean.
medimnum, -ī *nt*, **-us, -ī** *m* bushel.
mediocris *adj* middling, moderate, average.
mediocritās, -ātis *f* mean, moderation;
mediocrity.
mediocriter *adv* moderately, not particularly;
calmly.
Mediolānēnsis *adj see n.*
Mediolānum, -ī *nt* town in N. Italy *(now
Milan).*
meditāmentum, -ī *nt* preparation, drill.
meditātiō, -ōnis *f* thinking about;
preparation, practice.
meditātus *adj* studied.
mediterrāneus *adj* inland.
meditor, -ārī, -ātus *vt, vi* to think over,
contemplate, reflect; to practise, study.
medius *adj* middle, the middle of;
intermediate; intervening; middling,
moderate; neutral ♦ *nt* middle; public ♦ *m*
mediator; **~um complectī** clasp round the
waist; **~um sē gerere** be neutral; **~ō** midway;
~ō temporis meanwhile; **in ~um** for the
common good; **in ~um prōferre** publish; **dē
~ō tollere** do away with; **ē ~ō abīre** die,
disappear; **in ~ō esse** be public; **in ~ō positus**
open to all; **in ~ō relinquere** leave undecided.
medius fidius *interj* by Heaven!
medix *etc see* **meddix**.
medulla, -ae *f* marrow, pith.
medullitus *adv* from the heart.
medullula, -ae *f* marrow.
Mēdus, -ī *m* Mede, Persian.
Mēdus *adj see n.*
Medūsa, -ae *f* Gorgon, whose look turned
everything to stone.
Medūsaeus *adj:* **~ equus** Pegasus.
Megalēnsia (Megalēsia), -um *ntpl festival of
Cybele in April.*
Megara, -ae *f*, **-ōrum** *ntpl town in Greece near
the Isthmus.*
Megarēus *and* **icus** *adj* Megarean.
megistānes, -um *mpl* grandees.
mehercle, mehercule, mehercules *interj* by
Hercules!
mēiō, -ere *vi* to make water.

mel, mellis *nt* honey.
melancholicus *adj* melancholy.
melē *pl* melcs.
Meleager (-ros), -rī *m prince of Calydon.*
melicus *adj* musical; lyrical.
melilōtos, -ī *f* kind of clover.
melimēla, -ōrum *ntpl* honey apples.
Mēlīnum, -ī *nt* Melian white.
melior, -ōris *adj* better.
melisphyllum, -ī *nt* balm.
Melita, -ae Malta.
Melitēnsis *adj* Maltese.
melius *nt* melior ♦ *adv* better.
meliusculē *adv* fairly well.
meliusculus *adj* rather better.
mellifer, -ī *cdj* honey-making.
mellītus *adj* honeyed; sweet.
melos, -ī *nt* tune, song.
Melpomenē, -ēs *f* Muse of tragedy.
membrāna, -ae *f* skin, membrane, slough;
parchment.
membrānula, -ae *f* piece of parchment.
membrātim *adv* limb by limb; piecemeal; in
short sentences.
membrum, -ī *nt* limb, member; part, division;
clause.
mēmet *emphatic form of* **mē**.
meminī, -isse *vi (with gen)* to remember,
think of; to mention.
Memnōn, -onis *m Ethiopian king, killed at Troy.*
Memnonius *adj see n.*
memor, -is *adj* mindful, remembering; in
memory (of).
memorābilis *adj* memorable, remarkable.
memorandus *adj* noteworthy.
memorātus, -ūs *m* mention.
memorātus *adj* famed.
memoria, -ae *f* memory, remembrance; time,
lifetime; history; **haec ~** our day; **~ae
prōdere** hand down to posterity; **post
hominum ~am** since the beginning of
history.
memoriola, -ae *f* weak memory.
memoriter *adv* from memory; accurately.
memorō, -āre, -āvī, -ātum *vt* to mention,
say, speak.
Memphis, -is *and* **idos** *f town in middle Egypt.*
Memphītēs *and* **ītis** *and* **īticus** *adj of
Memphis; Egyptian.*
Menander (-ros), -rī *m Greek writer of comedy.*
Menandrēus *adj see n.*
menda, -ae *f* fault.
mendācium, -ī *and* **iī** *nt* lie.
mendāciunculum, -ī *nt* fib.
mendāx, -ācis *adj* lying; deceptive, unreal ♦
m liar.
mendīcitās, -ātis *f* beggary.
mendīcō, -āre, -or, -ārī, *vi* to beg, go begging.
mendīcus *adj* beggarly, poor ♦ *m* beggar.
mendōsē *adv see adj.*
mendōsus *adj* faulty; wrong, mistaken.
mendum, -ī *nt* fault, blunder.
Menelāēus *adj see n.*

Menelāus, -ī m brother of Agamemnon, husband of Helen.

Menoetiadēs, -ae m Patroclus

mēns, mentis f mind, understanding; feelings, heart; idea, plan, purpose; courage; venit in mentem it occurs; mente captus insane; eā mente ut with the intention of.

mēnsa, -ae f table; meal, course; counter, bank; secunda ~ dessert.

mēnsārius, -ī and **iī** m banker.

mēnsiō, -ōnis f (metre) quantity

mēnsis, -is m month.

mēnsor, -ōris m measurer, surveyor.

mēnstruālis adj for a month.

mēnstruus adj monthly; for a month ♦ nt a month's provisions.

mēnsula, -ae f little table.

mēnsūra, -ae f measure, measurement; standard, standing; amount, size, capacity.

mēnsus ppa of **mētior**.

menta, -ae f mint.

Menteus adj see n.

mentiēns, -ientis m fallacy.

mentiō, -ōnis f mention, hint.

mentior, -īrī, -ītus vi to lie, deceive ♦ vt to say falsely; to feign, imitate.

mentītus adj lying, false.

Mentor, -is m artist in metalwork; ornamental cup.

mentum, -ī nt chin.

meō, -āre vi to go, pass.

mephītis, -is f noxious vapour, malaria.

merācus adj pure.

mercābilis adj buyable.

mercātor, -ōris m merchant, dealer.

mercātūra, -ae f commerce; purchase; goods.

mercātus, -ūs m trade, traffic; market, fair.

mercēdula, -ae f poor wages, small rent.

mercēnārius adj hired, mercenary ♦ m servant.

mercēs, -ēdis f pay, wages, fee; bribe; rent; (fig) reward, retribution, cost.

mercimōnium, -ī and **iī** nt wares, goods.

mercor, -ārī, -ātus vt to trade in, purchase.

Mercurius, -ī m messenger of the gods, god of trade, thieves, speech and the lyre; stella ~ī planet Mercury.

Mercuriālis adj see n.

merda, -ae f dung.

merenda, -ae f lunch.

mereō, -ēre, -uī; -eor, -ērī, -itus rt, vi to deserve; to earn, win, acquire (mil) to serve; bene ~ dē do a service to, serve well; ~ equō serve in the cavalry.

meretrīcius adj a harlot's.

meretrīcula, -ae f pretty harlot.

meretrīx, -īcis f harlot.

mergae, -ārum fpl pitchfork.

merges, -itis f sheaf.

mergō, -gere, -sī, -sum vt to dip, immerse,

sink; (fig) to bury, plunge, drown.

mergus, -ī m (bird) diver.

merīdiānus adj midday; southerly.

merīdiātiō, -ōnis f siesta.

merīdiēs, -ēī f midday, noon; south.

merīdiō, -āre, vi to take a siesta.

meritō, -āre vt to learn.

meritō adv deservedly.

meritōrius adj money-earning ♦ ntpl lodgings.

meritum, -ī nt service, kindness, merit; blame.

meritus ppp of **mereō** ♦ adj deserved, just.

merops, -is f bee-eater.

mersī perf of **mergō**.

mersō, -āre vt to immerse, plunge; to overwhelm.

mersus ppp of **mergō**.

merula, -ae f blackbird.

merum, -ī nt wine.

merus adj pure, undiluted; bare, mere.

merx, mercis f goods, wares.

Messalla, -ae m Roman surname (esp ~ Corvīnus Augustan orator, soldier and literary patron).

Messallīna, -īnae f wife of emperor Claudius; wife of Nero.

Messāna, -ae f Sicilian town (now Messina).

messis, -is f harvest.

messor, -ōris m reaper.

messōrius adj a reaper's.

messuī perf of **metō**.

messus ppp of **metō**.

mēta, -ae f pillar at each end of the Circus course; turning point, winning post; (fig) goal, end, limit.

metallum, -ī nt mine, quarry; metal.

mētātor, -ōris m surveyor.

Metaurus, -ī m river in Umbria, famous for the defeat of Hasdrubal.

Metellus, -ī m Roman surname (esp the commander against Jugurtha).

Mēthymna, -ae f town in Lesbos.

Mēthymnaeus adj see n.

mētior, -tīrī, -nsus vt to measure, measure out; to traverse; (fig) to estimate, judge.

metō, -tere, -ssuī, -ssum vt to reap, gather; to mow, cut down.

mētor, -ārī, -ātus vt to measure off, lay out.

metrēta, -ae f liquid measure (about 9 gallons).

metuculōsus adj frightful.

metuō, -uere, -uī, -ūtum vt to fear, be apprehensive.

metus, -ūs m fear, alarm, anxiety.

meus adj my, mine.

mī dat of **ego**; voc and mpl of **meus**.

mīca, -ae f crumb, grain.

micō, -āre, -uī vi to quiver, flicker, beat, flash, sparkle.

Midās, -ae m Phrygian king whose touch turned

everything to gold.
migrātiō, -ōnis *f* removal, change.
migrō, -āre, -āvī, -ātum *vi* to remove, change, pass away ♦ *vt* to transport, transgress.
mīles, -itis *m* soldier, infantryman; army troops.
Mīlēsius *adj see n.*
Mīlētus, -tī *f* town in Asia Minor.
mīlia, -um *ntpl* thousands; ~ **passuum** miles.
mīliārium (milliārium), -ī *and* **iī** *nt* milestone.
mīlitāris *adj* military, a soldier's.
mīlitāriter *adv* in a soldierly fashion.
mīlitia, -ae *f* military service, war; the army; ~**ae** on service; **domī** ~**aeque** at home and abroad.
mīlitō, -āre *vi* to serve, be a soldier.
milium, -ī *and* **iī** *nt* millet.
mīlle, (*pl* ~**ia**) *num* a thousand; ~ **passūs** a mile.
mīllensimus, -ēsimus *adj* thousandth.
mīllia *etc see* **mīlia.**
mīlliārium *etc see* **mīliārium.**
mīlliēns, -ēs *adv* a thousand times.
Milō, -ōnis *m* tribune who killed Clodius and was defended by Cicero.
Milōniānus *adj see n.*
Miltiadēs, -is *m* Athenian general, victor at Marathon.
mīluīnus *adj* resembling a kite; rapacious.
mīluus (mīlvus), -ī *m* kite; gurnard.
mīma, -ae *f* actress.
Mimallonis, -dis *f* Bacchante.
mīmicē *adv see adj.*
mīmicus *adj* farcical.
Mimnermus, -ī *m* Greek elegiac poet.
mīmula, -ae *f* actress.
mīmus, -ī *m* actor; mime, farce.
mina, -ae *f* Greek silver coin.
mināciter *adv see adj.*
minae, -ārum *fpl* threats; (*wall*) pinnacles.
minanter *adv* threateningly.
minātiō, -ōnis *f* threat.
mināx, -ācis *adj* threatening; projecting.
Minerva, -ae *f* goddess of wisdom and arts, esp weaving; (*fig*) talent, genius; working in wool; **sūs** ~**am** ≈ *"teach your grandmother!"*
miniānus *adj* red-leaded.
miniātulus *adj* painted red.
minimē *adv* least, very little; (*reply*) no, not at all.
minimus *adj* least, smallest, very small; youngest.
miniō, -āre, -āvī, -ātum *vt* to colour red.
minister, -rī *m,* ~**ra,** ~**rae** *f* attendant, servant; helper, agent, tool.
ministerium, -ī *and* **iī** *nt* service, office, duty; retinue.
ministrātor, -ōris *m,* ~**rīx,** ~**rīcis** *f* assistant, handmaid.
ministrō, -āre *vt* to serve, supply; to manage.
minitābundus *adj* threatening.
minitor, -ārī, -ō, -āre *vt, vi* to threaten.
minium, -ī *and* **iī** *nt* vermilion, red lead.

Mīnōis, -idis *f* Ariadne.
Mīnōius, -us *adj see n.*
minor, -ārī, -ātus *vt, vi* to threaten; to project.
minor, -ōris *adj* smaller, less, inferior; younger; (*pl*) descendants.
Mīnōs, -is *m* king of Crete, judge in the lower world.
Mīnōtaurus, -ī *m* monster of the Cretan labyrinth, half bull, half man.
Minturnae, -ārum *fpl* town in S. Latium.
Minturnēnsis *adj see n.*
minum- *etc see* **minim-.**
minuō, -uere, -uī, -ūtum *vt* to make smaller, lessen; to chop up; to reduce, weaken ♦ *vi* (*tide*) to ebb.
minus *nt* minor ♦ *adv* less; not, not at all; **quō** ~ (*prevent*) from.
minusculus *adj* smallish.
minūtal, -ālis *nt* mince.
minūtātim *adv* bit by bit.
minūtē *adv* in a petty manner.
minūtus *ppp of* **minuō** ♦ *adj* small; paltry.
mīrābilis *adj* wonderful, extraordinary.
mīrābiliter *adv see adj.*
mīrābundus *adj* astonished.
mīrāculum, -ī *nt* marvel, wonder; amazement.
mīrandus *adj* wonderful.
mīrātiō, -ōnis *f* wonder.
mīrātor, -ōris *m* admirer.
mīrātrix, -īcis *adj* admiring.
mīrē *adv see adj.*
mīrificē *adv see adj.*
mīrificus *adj* wonderful.
mirmillō *see* **murmillō.**
mīror, -ārī, -ātus *vt* to wonder at, be surprised at, admire ♦ *vi* to wonder, be surprised.
mīrus *adj* wonderful, strange; ~**um quam, quantum** extraordinarily.
miscellānea, -ōrum *ntpl* (*food*) hotchpotch.
misceō, -scēre, -scuī, -xtum *vt* to mix, mingle, blend; to join, combine; to confuse, embroil.
misellus *adj* poor little.
Mīsēnēnsis *adj see n.*
Mīsēnum, -ī *nt* promontory and harbour near Naples.
miser, -ī *adj* wretched, poor, pitiful, sorry.
miserābilis *adj* pitiable, sad, plaintive.
miserābiliter *adv see adj.*
miserandus *adj* deplorable.
miserātiō, -ōnis *f* pity, compassion, pathos.
miserē *adv see adj.*
misereō, -ēre, -uī, -eor, -ērī, -itus *vt, vi* (*with gen*) to pity, sympathize with; ~**et mē** I pity, I am sorry.
miserēscō, -ere *vi* to feel pity.
miseria, -ae *f* misery, trouble, distress.
misericordia, -ae *f* pity, sympathy, mercy.
misericors, -dis *adj* sympathetic, merciful.
miseriter *adv* sadly.
miseror, -ārī, -ātus *vt* to deplore; to pity.

mīsī *perf of* **mittō.**
missa, -ae *f* (*ECCL*) mass.
missilis *adj* missile.
missiō, -ōnis *f* sending; release (*MIL*)
  discharge; (*gladiators*) quarter; (*events*) end;
  sine ~ōne to the death.
missitō, -āre *vt* to send repeatedly.
missus *ppp of* **mittō.**
missus, -ūs *m* sending; throwing; **~ sagittae**
  bowshot.
mitella, -ae *f* turban.
mītēscō, -ere *vi* to ripen; to grow mild.
Mithridātēs, -is *m* king of Pontus, defeated by
  Pompey.
Mithridātēus, -icus *adj see n.*
mītigātiō, -ōnis *f* soothing.
mītigō, -āre, -āvī, -ātum *vt* to ripen, soften;
  to calm, pacify.
mītis *adj* ripe, mellow; soft, mild gentle.
mitra, -ae *f* turban.
mittō, -ere, mīsī, missum *vt* to send,
  dispatch; to throw, hurl; to let go, dismiss; to
  emit, utter; (*news*) to send word; (*gift*) to
  bestow; (*event*) to end; (*speech*) to omit, stop;
  sanguinem ~ bleed ; **ad cēnam ~** invite to
  dinner; **missum facere** forgo.
mītulus, -ī *m* mussel.
mixtim *adv* promiscuously.
mixtūra, -ae *f* mingling.
Mnēmosynē, -ēs *f* mother of the Muses.
mnēmosynon, -ī *nt* souvenir.
mōbilis *adj* movable; nimble, fleet; excitable,
  fickle.
mōbilitās, -ātis *f* agility, rapidity; fickleness.
mōbiliter *adv* rapidly.
mōbilitō, -āre *vt* to make rapid.
moderābilis *adj* moderate.
moderāmen, -inis *nt* control; government.
moderanter *adv* with control.
moderātē *adv* with restraint.
moderātim *adv* gradually.
moderātiō, -ōnis *f* control, government;
  moderation; rules.
moderātor, -ōris *m* controller, governor.
moderātrīx, -īcis *f* mistress, controller.
moderātus *adj* restrained, orderly.
moderor, -ārī, -ātus *vt, vi* (*with dat*) to
  restrain, check; (*with acc*) to manage,
  govern, guide.
modestē *adv* with moderation; humbly.
modestia, -ae *f* temperate behaviour,
  discipline; humility.
modestus *adj* sober, restrained; well-
  behaved, disciplined; modest, unassuming.
modiālis *adj* holding a peck.
modicē *adv* moderately; slightly.
modicus *adj* moderate; middling, small, mean.
modificātus *adj* measured.
modius, -ī *and* **iī** *m* corn measure, peck.
modo *adv* only; at all, in any way; (*with imp*)

just; (*time*) just now, a moment ago, in a
  moment ♦ *conj* if only; **nōn ~** not only; **non ~**
  ... **sed** not only ... but also ...; **~ nōn** all but,
  almost; **~ ... ~** sometimes ... sometimes; **~ ...**
  tum at first ... then.
modulātē *adv* melodiously.
modulātor, -ōris *m* musician.
modulātus *adj* played, measured.
modulor, -ārī, - ātus *vt* to modulate, play,
  sing.
modulus, -ī *m* measure.
modus, -ī *m* measure; size; metre, music;
  way, method; limit, end; **ēius ~ī** such; **~ō, in,**
  ~um like.
moecha, -ae *f* adulteress.
moechor, -ārī *vi* to commit adultery.
moechus, -ī *m* adulterer.
moenera *etc see* **mūnus.**
moenia, -um *ntpl* defences, walls; town,
  stronghold.
moeniō *etc see* **mūniō.**
Moesī, -ōrum *mpl* people on lower Danube
  (*now* Bulgaria).
mola, -ae *f* millstone, mill; grains of spelt.
molāris, -is *m* millstone; (*tooth*) molar.
mōlēs, -is *f* mass, bulk, pile; dam, pier,
  massive structure; (*fig*) greatness, weight,
  effort, trouble.
molestē *adv see adj.*
molestia, -ae *f* trouble, annoyance, worry;
  (*style*) affectation.
molestus *adj* irksome, annoying; (*style*)
  laboured.
mōlīmen, -inis *nt* exertion, labour;
  importance.
mōlīmentum, -ī *nt* great effort.
mōlior, -īrī, -ītus *vt* to labour at, work, build;
  to wield, move, heave; to undertake, devise,
  occasion ♦ *vi* to exert oneself, struggle.
mōlītiō, -ōnis *f* laborious work.
mōlītor, -ōris *m* builder.
mollēscō, -ere *vi* to soften, become
  effeminate.
molliculus *adj* tender.
molliō, -īre, -īvī, -ītum *vt* to soften, make
  supple; to mitigate, make easier; to
  demoralize.
mollis *adj* soft, supple; tender, gentle;
  (*character*) sensitive, weak, unmanly; (*poetry*)
  amatory; (*opinion*) changeable; (*slope*) easy.
molliter *adv* softly, gently; calmly;
  voluptuously.
mollitia, -ae, -ēs, -ēī *f* softness, suppleness;
  tenderness, weakness, effeminacy.
mollitūdō, -inis *f* softness; susceptibility.
molō, -ere *vt* to grind.
Molossī, -ōrum *mpl* Molossians, people in
  Epirus.
Molossicus, -us *adj see n.*
Molossis, -idis *f* country of the Molossians.

Molossus, -ī m Molossian hound.
mōly, -os nt a magic herb.
mōmen, -inis nt movement, momentum.
mōmentum, -ī nt movement; change; (time) short space, moment; (fig) cause, influence, importance; **nullīus ~ī** unimportant.
momordī perf of **mordeō**.
Mona, -ae f Isle of Man; Anglesey.
monachus, -ī m monk.
monēdula, -ae f jackdaw.
moneō, -ēre, -uī, -itum vt to remind, advise, warn; to instruct, foretell.
monēris, -is f galley with one bank of oars.
monērula etc see **monēdula**.
monēta, -ae f mint; money; stamp.
monīle, -is nt necklace, collar.
monim- etc see **monum-**.
monitiō, -ōnis f admonishing.
monitor, -ōris m admonisher; prompter; teacher.
monitum, -ī nt warning; prophecy.
monitus, -ūs m admonition; warning.
monogrammus adj shadowy.
monopodium, -ī and **iī** nt table with one leg.
mōns, montis m mountain.
mōnstrātor, -ōris m shower, inventor.
mōnstrātus adj distinguished.
mōnstrē adv see adj.
mōnstrō, -āre, -āvī, -ātum vt to point out, show; to inform, instruct; to appoint; to denounce.
mōnstrum, -ī nt portent, marvel; monster.
mōnstruōsus adj unnatural.
montānus adj mountainous; mountain- (in cpds), highland.
monticola, -ae m highlander.
montivagus adj mountain-roving.
montuōsus, montōsus adj mountainous.
monumentum, -ī nt memorial, monument; record.
Mopsopius adj Athenian.
mora, -ae f delay, pause; hindrance; space of time, sojourn; **~am facere** put off.
mora, -ae f division of the Spartan army.
mōrālis adj moral.
morātor, -ōris m delayer.
mōrātus adj mannered, of a nature; (writing) in character.
morbidus adj unwholesome.
morbus, -ī m illness, disease; distress.
mordāciter adv see adj.
mordāx, -ācis adj biting, sharp, pungent; (fig) snarling, carking.
mordeō, -dēre, momordī, -sum vt to bite; to bite into, grip; (cold) to nip; (words) to sting, hurt, mortify.
mordicus adv with a bite; (fig) doggedly.
mōrēs pl of **mōs**.
morētum, -ī nt salad.
moribundus adj dying, mortal; deadly.
mōrigeror, -ārī, -ātus vi (with dat) to gratify, humour.
mōrigerus adj obliging, obedient.

morior, -ī, -tuus vi to die; to decay, fade.
moritūrus fut p of **morior**.
mōrologus adj foolish.
moror, -ārī, -ātus vi to delay, stay, loiter ♦ vt to detain, retard; to entertain; (with neg) to heed, object; **nihil, nīl ~** have no objection to; to not care for; to withdraw a charge against.
mōrōsē adv see adj.
mōrōsitās, -ātis f peevishness.
mōrōsus adj peevish, difficult.
Morpheus, -eos m god of dreams.
mors, mortis f death; corpse; **mortem sibi cōnscīscere** commit suicide; **mortis poena** capital punishment.
morsiuncula, -ae f little kiss.
morsus ppp of **mordeō** ♦ ntpl little bits.
morsus, -ūs m bite; grip; (fig) sting, vexation.
mortālis adj mortal; transient; man-made ♦ m human being.
mortālitās, -ātis f mortality, death.
mortārium, -ī and **iī** nt mortar.
mortifer, -ī adj fatal.
mortuus ppa of **morior** ♦ adj dead ♦ m dead man.
mōrum, -ī nt blackberry, mulberry.
mōrus, -ī f black mulberry tree.
mōrus adj foolish ♦ m fool.
mōs, mōris m nature, manner; humour, mood; custom, practice, law; (pl) behaviour, character, morals; **~ māiōrum** national tradition; **mōrem gerere** oblige, humour; **mōre, in mōrem** like.
Mosa, -ae m river Meuse.
Mōsēs, -is m Moses.
mōtiō, -ōnis f motion.
mōtō, -āre vt to keep moving.
mōtus ppp of **moveō**.
mōtus, -ūs m movement; dance, gesture; (mind) impulse, emotion; (POL) rising, rebellion; **terrae ~** earthquake.
movēns, -entis pres p of **moveō** ♦ adj movable ♦ ntpl motives.
moveō, -ēre, mōvī, mōtum vt to move, set in motion; to disturb; to change; to dislodge, expel; to occasion, begin; (opinion) to shake; (mind) to affect, influence, provoke ♦ vi to move; **castra ~** strike camp; **sē ~** budge; to dance.
mox adv presently, soon, later on; next.
Mōysēs see **Mōsēs**.
mūcidus adj snivelling; mouldy.
Mūcius, -ī m Roman family name (esp Scaevola, who burned his right hand before Porsena).
mūcrō, -ōnis m point, edge; sword.
mūcus, -ī m mucus.
mūgilis, -is m mullet.
muginor, -ārī vi to hesitate.
mūgiō, -īre vi to bellow, groan.
mūgītus, -ūs m lowing, roaring.
mūla, -ae f she-mule.
mulceō, -cēre, -sī, -sum vt to stroke, caress;

to soothe, alleviate, delight.
Mulciber, -is *and* **ī** *m* Vulcan.
mulcō, -āre, -āvī, -ātum *vt* to beat, ill-treat, damage.
mulctra, -ae *f*, **-ārium, -ārī**, *and* **āriī, -um, -ī** *nt* milkpail.
mulgeō, -ēre, mulsī *vt* to milk.
muliebris *adj* woman's, feminine; effeminate.
muliebriter *adv* like a woman; effeminately.
mulier, -is *f* woman; wife.
mulierārius *adj* woman's.
muliercula, -ae *f* girl.
mulierōsitās, -ātis *f* fondness for women.
mulierōsus *adj* fond of women.
mūlīnus *adj* mulish.
mūliō, -ōnis *m* mule driver.
mūliōnius *adj* mule driver's.
mullus, -ī *m* red mullet.
mulsī *perf of* **mulceō**; *perf of* **mulgeō**.
mulsus *ppp of* **mulceō**.
mulsus *adj* honeyed, sweet ◆ *nt* honey-wine, mead.
multa, -ae *f* penalty, fine; loss.
multangulus *adj* many-angled.
multātīcius *adj* fine- (*in cpds*).
multātiō, -ōnis *f* fining.
multēsimus *adj* very small.
multicavus *adj* many-holed.
multīcia, -ōrum *ntpl* transparent garments.
multifāriam *adv* in many places.
multifidus *adj* divided into many parts.
multiformis *adj* of many forms.
multiforus *adj* many-holed.
multigeneris, -us *adj* of many kinds.
multiiugis, -us *adj* yoked together; complex.
multiloquium, -ī *and* **iī** *nt* talkativeness.
multiloquus *adj* talkative.
multimodīs *adv* variously.
multiplex, -icis *adj* with many folds, tortuous; many-sided, manifold, various; (*comparison*) far greater; (*character*) fickle, sly.
multiplicō, -āre, -āvī, -ātum *vt* to multiply, enlarge.
multipotēns, -entis *adj* very powerful.
multitūdō, -inis *f* great number, multitude, crowd.
multivolus *adj* longing for much.
multō *adv* much, far, by far; (*time*) long.
multō, -āre, -āvī, -ātum *vt* to punish, fine.
multum *adv* much, very, frequently.
multus (*compar* **plūs** *superl* **plūrimus**) *adj* much, many; (*speech*) lengthy, tedious; (*time*) late; ~ā nocte late at night; nē ~a ≈ *to cut a long story short*.
mūlus, -ī *m* mule.
Mulvius *adj* Mulvian (*a Tiber bridge above Rome*).
mundānus, -ī *m* world citizen.
munditia, -ae, -ēs, -ēī *f* cleanness; neatness, elegance.

mundus *adj* clean, neat, elegant; **in ~ō esse** be in readiness.
mundus, -ī *m* toilet gear; universe, world, heavens; mankind.
mūnerigerulus, -ī *m* bringer of presents.
mūnerō, -āre, -or, -ārī *vt* to present, reward.
mūnia, -ōrum *ntpl* official duties.
mūniceps, -ipis *m/f* citizen (*of a municipium*), fellow-citizen.
mūnicipālis *adj* provincial.
mūnicipium, -ī *and* **iī** *nt* provincial town, burgh.
mūnificē *adv see adj.*
mūnificentia, -ae *f* liberality.
mūnificō, -āre *vt* to treat generously.
mūnificus *adj* liberal.
mūnīmen, -inis *nt* defence.
mūnīmentum, -ī *nt* defencework, protection.
mūniō, -īre, -iī, -ītum *vt* to fortify, secure, strengthen; (*road*) to build; (*fig*) to protect.
mūnis *adj* ready to oblige.
mūnītiō, -ōnis *f* building; fortification; (*river*) bridging.
mūnītō, -āre *vt* (*road*) to open up.
mūnītor, -ōris *m* sapper, builder.
mūnus, -eris *nt* service, duty; gift; public show; entertainment; tax; (*funeral*) tribute; (*book*) work.
mūnusculum, -ī *nt* small present.
mūraena, -ae *f* a fish.
mūrālis *adj* wall- (*in cpds*), mural, for fighting from *or* attacking walls.
mūrex, -icis *m* purple-fish; purple dye, purple; jagged rock.
muria, -ae *f* brine.
murmillō, -ōnis *m* kind of gladiator.
murmur, -is *nt* murmur, hum, rumbling, roaring.
murmurillum, -ī *nt* low murmur.
murmurō, -āre *vi* to murmur, rumble; to grumble.
murra, -ae *f* myrrh.
murreus *adj* perfumed; made of the stone called murra.
murrina, -ae *f* myrrh wine.
murrina, -ōrum *ntpl* murrine vases.
murt- *etc see* **myrt-**.
mūrus, -ī *m* wall; dam; defence.
mūs, mūris *m/f* mouse, rat.
Mūsa, -ae *f* goddess inspiring an art; poem; (*pl*) studies.
mūsaeus *adj* poetic, musical.
musca, -ae *f* fly.
mūscipula, -ae *f*, **-um, -ī** *nt* mousetrap.
mūscōsus *adj* mossy.
mūsculus, -ī *m* mouse; muscle; (*MIL*) shed.
mūscus, -ī *m* moss.
mūsicē *adv* very pleasantly.
mūsicus *adj* of music, of poetry ◆ *m* musician ◆ *f* music, culture ◆ *ntpl* music.

Noun declensions and verb conjugations are shown on pp xiii to xxv. The present infinitive ending of a verb shows to which conjugation it belongs: **-āre** = 1st; **-ēre** = 2nd; **-ere** = 3rd and **-īre** = 4th. Irregular verbs are shown on p xxvi

mussitō, -āre vi to say nothing; to mutter ◆ vt to bear in silence.

mussō, -āre vt, vi to say nothing, brood over; to mutter, murmur.

mustāceum, -ī nt, **-us, -ī** m wedding cake.

mūstēla, -ae f weasel.

mustum, -ī nt unfermented wine, must; vintage.

mūtābilis adj changeable, fickle.

mūtābilitās, -ātis f fickleness.

mūtātiō, -ōnis f change, alteration; exchange.

mutilō, -āre, -āvī, -ātum vt to cut off, maim; to diminish.

mutilus adj maimed.

Mutina, -ae f town in N. Italy (now Modena).

Mutinēnsis adj see n.

mūtiō etc see **muttiō**.

mūtō, -āre, -āvī, -ātum vt to shift; to change, alter; to exchange, barter ◆ vi to change; **~āta verba** figurative language.

muttiō, -īre vi to mutter, mumble.

mūtuātiō, -ōnis f borrowing.

mūtuē adv mutually, in turns.

mūtuitō, -āre vt to try to borrow.

mūtuō adv = **mūtuē**.

mūtuor, -ārī, -ātus vt to borrow.

mūtus adj dumb, mute; silent, still.

mūtuum, -ī nt loan.

mūtuus adj borrowed, lent; mutual, reciprocal; **~um dare** lend; **~um sūmere** borrow; **~um facere** return like for like.

Mycēnae, -ārum fpl Agamemnon's capital in S. Greece.

Mycēnaeus, -ēnsis adj, **-is, -idis** f Iphigenia.

Mygdonius adj Phrygian.

myoparō, -ōnis m pirate galley.

myrīca, -ae f tamarisk.

Myrmidones, -um mpl followers of Achilles.

Myrōn, -ōnis m famous Greek sculptor.

myropōla, -ae m perfumer.

myropōlium, -ī and **īī** nt perfumer's shop.

myrothēcium, -ī and **īī** nt perfume-box.

myrrh- etc see **murr-**.

myrtētum, -ī nt myrtlegrove.

myrteus adj myrtle- (in cpds).

Myrtōum mare Sea N.W. of Crete.

myrtum, -ī nt myrtle-berry.

myrtus, -ī and **ūs** f myrtle.

Mȳsia, -iae f country of Asia Minor.

Mȳsius, -us adj see n.

mysta, -ae m priest of mysteries.

mystagōgus, -ī m initiator.

mystērium, -ī and **īī** nt secret religion, mystery; secret.

mysticus adj mystic.

Mytilēnae, -ārum fpl; **-ē, -es** f capital of Lesbos.

Mytilēnaeus adj see n.

Mytilēnēnsis adj see n.

N, n

nablium, -ī and **īī** nt kind of harp.

nactus ppa o **nancīscor**.

nae etc see **nē**.

naenia etc see **nēnia**.

Naeviānus adj see n.

Naevius, -ī n early Latin poet.

naevus, -ī m mole (on the body).

Nāias, -adis and **s, -dis** f water nymph, Naiad.

Nāicus adj see n.

nam conj (explaining) for; (illustrating) for example; (transitional) now; (interrog) but; (enclitic) an emphatic particle.

namque conj for, for indeed, for example.

nancīscor, -i, nactus and **nanctus** vt to obtain, get; to come upon, find.

nānus, -ī m dwarf.

Napaeae, -ārum fpl dell nymphs.

nāpus, -ī m turnip.

Narbō, -ōnis m town in S. Gaul.

Narbōnēnsis adj see n.

narcissus, -ī m narcissus.

nardus, -ī f, **-um, -ī** nt nard, nard oil.

nāris, -is f rostril; (pl) nose; (fig) sagacity, scorn.

nārrābilis cdj to be told.

nārrātiō, -ōnis f narrative.

nārrātor, -ōris m storyteller, historian.

nārrātus, -ūs m narrative.

nārrō, -āre, -āvī, -ātum vt to tell, relate, say; **male ~** bring bad news.

narthēcium, -ī and **īī** nt medicine chest.

nāscor, -scī, -tus vi to be born; to originate, grow, be produced.

Nāsō, -ōnis m surname of Ovid.

nassa, -ae f wicker basket for catching fish; (fig) snare.

nasturtium, -ī and **īī** nt cress.

nāsus, -ī m nose.

nāsūtē adv sarcastically.

nāsūtus adj big-nosed; satirical.

nāta, -ae f daughter.

nātālicius adj of one's birthday, natal ◆ f birthday party.

nātālis adj of birth, natal ◆ m birthday ◆ mpl birth, origin.

nātātiō, -ōnis f swimming.

natātor, -ōris m swimmer.

nātiō, -ōnis f tribe, race; breed, class.

natis, -is f (usu pl) buttocks.

nātīvus adj created; inborn, native, natural.

natō, -āre vi to swim, float; to flow, overflow; (eyes) to swim, fail; (fig) to waver.

nātrīx, -īcis f watersnake.

nātū abl m by birth, in age; **grandis ~, māgnō ~** quite old; **māior ~** older; **māximus ~** oldest.

nātūra, -ae f birth; nature, quality, character; natural order of things; the physical world; (*physics*) element; **rērum ~ Nature.**

nātūrālis *adj* by birth; by nature, natural.

nātūrāliter *adv* by nature.

nātus *ppa of* **nāscor** ♦ *m* son ♦ *adj* born, made (for); old, of age; **prō, ē rē nātā** under the circumstances, as things are; **annōs vīgintī ~ 20 years old.**

nauarchus, -ī *m* captain.

naucī: nōn esse, facere, habēre to be worthless, consider worthless.

nauclēricus *adj* skipper's.

nauclērus, -ī *m* skipper.

naufragium, -ī *and* **iī** *nt* shipwreck, wreck; **~ facere** be shipwrecked.

naufragus *adj* shipwrecked, wrecked; (*sea*) dangerous to shipping ♦ *m* shipwrecked man; (*fig*) ruined man.

naulum, -ī *nt* fare.

naumachia, -ae f mock sea fight.

nausea, -ae f seasickness.

nauseō, -āre *vi* to be sick; (*fig*) to disgust.

nauseola, -ae f squeamishness.

nauta, (nāvita), -ae *m* sailor, mariner.

nauticus *adj* nautical, sailors' ♦ *mpl* seamen.

nāvālis *adj* naval, of ships ♦ *nt* and *ntpl* dockyard; rigging.

nāvicula, -ae f boat.

nāviculāria, -ae f shipping business.

nāviculārius, -ī *and* **iī** *m* ship-owner.

nāvifragus *adj* dangerous.

nāvigābilis *adj* navigable.

nāvigātiō, -ōnis f voyage.

nāviger, -ī *adj* ship-carrying.

nāvigium, -ī *and* **iī** *nt* vessel, ship.

nāvigō, -āre, -āvī, -ātum *vi* to sail, put to sea ♦ *vt* to sail across, navigate.

nāvis, -is f ship; **~ longa** warship; **~ mercātōria** merchantman; **~ onerāria** transport; **~ praetōria** flagship; **~em dēdūcere** launch; **~em solvere** set sail; **~em statuere** heave to; **~em subdūcere** beach; **~ibus atque quadrīgīs** with might and main.

nāvita *etc see* **nauta.**

nāvitās, -ātis f energy.

nāviter *adv* energetically; absolutely.

nāvō, -āre *vt* to perform energetically; **operam ~** be energetic; to come to the assistance (of).

nāvus *adj* energetic.

Naxos, -ī f Aegean island (*famous for wines and the story of Ariadne*).

nē *interj* truly, indeed.

nē *adv* not ♦ *conj* that not, lest; (*fear*) that; (*purpose*) so that ... not, to avoid, to prevent.

-ne *enclitic* (*introducing a question*)

Neāpolis, -is f Naples.

Neāpolītānus *adj see n.*

nebula, -ae f mist, vapour, cloud.

nebulō, -ōnis *m* idler, good-for-nothing.

nebulōsus *adj* misty, cloudy.

nec *etc see* **neque.**

necdum *adv* and not yet.

necessāriē, -ō *adv* of necessity, unavoidably.

necessārius *adj* necessary, inevitable; indispensable; (*kir*) related ♦ *m*/f relative ♦ *ntpl* necessities.

necesse *adj* (*indecl*) necessary, inevitable; needful.

necessitās, -ātis f necessity, compulsion; requirement, want; relationship, connection.

necessitūdō, -inis f necessity, need, want; connection; friendship (*pl*) relatives.

necessum *etc see* **necesse.**

necne *adv* or not.

necnōn *adv* also, besides.

necō, -āre, -āvī, -ātum *vt* to kill, murder.

necopīnāns, -antis *adj* unaware.

necopīnātō *adv see adj.*

necopīnātus *adj* unexpected.

necopīnus *adj* unexpected; unsuspecting.

nectar, -is *nt* nectar (*the drink of the gods*).

nectareus *adj* of nectar.

nectō, -ctere, -xi *and* **xuī, -xum** *vt* to tie, fasten, connect; to weave; (*fig*) to bind, enslave (*esp for debt*); to contrive, frame.

nēcubi *conj* so that nowhere.

nēcunde *conj* so that from nowhere.

nēdum *adv* much less, much more.

nefandus *adj* abominable, impious.

nefāriē *adv see adj.*

nefārius *adj* heinous, criminal.

nefās *nt* (*indecl*) wickedness, sin, wrong ♦ *interj* horror!, shame!

nefāstus *adj* wicked; unlucky; (*days*) closed to public business.

negātiō, -ōnis f denial.

negitō, -āre *vt* to deny, refuse.

neglēctiō, -ōnis f neglect.

neglēctus *ppp of* **neglegō.**

neglēctus, -ūs *m* neglecting.

neglegēns, -entis *pres p of* **neglegō** ♦ *adj* careless, indifferent.

neglegenter *adv* carelessly.

neglegentia, -ae f carelessness, neglect, coldness.

neglegō, -egere, -ēxi, -ēctum *vt* to neglect, not care for; to slight, disregard; to overlook.

negō, -āre, -āvī, -ātum *vt, vi* to say no; to say not, deny; to refuse, decline.

negōtiālis *adj* business- (*in cpds*).

negōtiāns, -antis *m* businessman.

negōtiātiō, -ōnis f banking business.

negōtiātor, -ōris *m* businessman, banker.

negōtiolum, -ī *nt* trivial matter.

negōtior, -ārī, -ātus *vi* to do business, trade.

negōtiōsus *adj* busy.

Noun declensions and verb conjugations are shown on pp xiii to xxv. The present infinitive ending of a verb shows to which conjugation it belongs: -**āre** =1st; -**ēre** = 2nd; -**ere** = 3rd and -**īre** = 4th. Irregular verbs are shown on p xxvi

negōtium, -ī *and* **iī** *nt* business, work; trouble; matter, thing; **quid est ~i?** what is the matter?

Nēlēius *adj see n.*

Nēleus, -eī *m* father of Nestor.

Nēlēus *adj see n.*

Nemea, -ae *f* town in S. Greece, where Hercules killed the lion.

Nemea, -ōrum *ntpl* Nemean Games.

Nemeaeus *adj* Nemean.

nēmō, -inis *m/f* no one, nobody ♦ *adj* no; **~ nōn** everybody; **nōn ~** many; **~ ūnus** not a soul.

nemorālis *adj* sylvan.

nemorēnsis *adj* of the grove.

nemoricultrīx, -īcis *f* forest dweller.

nemorivagus *adj* forest-roving.

nemorōsus *adj* well-wooded; leafy.

nempe *adv* (*confirming*) surely, of course, certainly; (*in questions*) do you mean?

nemus, -ōris *nt* wood, grove.

nēnia, -ae *f* dirge; incantation; song, nursery rhyme.

neō, nēre, nēvī, nētum *vt* to spin; to weave.

Neoptolemus, -ī *m* Pyrrhus (*son of Achilles*).

nepa, -ae *f* scorpion.

nepōs, -ōtis *m* grandson; descendant; spendthrift.

nepōtīnus, -ī *m* little grandson.

neptis, -is *f* granddaughter.

Neptūnius *adj:* **~ hērōs** Theseus.

Neptūnus, -ī *m* Neptune (*god of the sea*); sea.

nēquam *adj* (*indecl*) worthless, bad.

nēquāquam *adv* not at all, by no means.

neque, nec *adv* not ♦ *conj* and not, but not; neither, nor; **~ ... et** not only not ... but also.

nequeō, -īre, -īvī, -ītum *vi* to be unable, cannot.

nēquīquam *adv* fruitlessly, for nothing; without good reason.

nēquior, nēquissimus *compar, superl of* **nēquam.**

nēquiter *adv* worthlessly, wrongly.

nēquitia, -ae, -ēs *f* worthlessness, badness.

Nērēis, -ēidis *f* Nereid, sea nymph.

Nērēius *adj see n.*

Nēreus, -eī *m* a sea god; the sea.

Nēritius *adj* of Neritos; Ithacan.

Nēritos, -ī *m* island near Ithaca.

Nerō, -ōnis *m* Roman surname (*esp the emperor*).

Nerōniānus *adj see n.*

nervōsē *adv* vigorously.

nervōsus *adj* sinewy, vigorous.

nervulī, -ōrum *mpl* energy.

nervus, -ī *m* sinew; string; fetter, prison; (*shield*) leather; (*pl*) strength, vigour, energy.

nesciō, -īre, -īvī *and* **iī, -ītum** *vt* to not know, be ignorant of; to be unable; **~ quis, quid** somebody, something; **~ an** probably.

nescius *adj* ignorant, unaware; unable; unknown.

Nestor, -oris *m* Greek leader at Troy (*famous

for his great age and wisdom*).

neu *etc see* **nēve.**

neuter, -rī *adj* neither; neuter.

neutiquam *adv* by no means, certainly not.

neutrō *adv* neither way.

nēve, neu *conj* and not; neither, nor.

nēvī *perf of* **neō.**

nex, necis *f* murder, death.

nexilis *adj* tied together.

nexum, -ī *nt* personal enslavement.

nexus *ppp of* **nectō.**

nexus, -ūs *m* entwining, grip; (*law*) bond, obligation, (*esp enslavement for debt*).

nī *adv* not ♦ *conj* if not, unless; that not; **quid nī?** why not?

nīcētērium, -ī *and* **iī** *nt* prize.

nictō, -āre *vi* to wink.

nīdāmentum, -ī *nt* nest.

nīdor, -ōris *m* steam, smell.

nīdulus, -ī *m* little nest.

nīdus, -ī *m* nest; (*pl*) nestlings; (*fig*) home.

niger, -rī *adj* black, dark; dismal, ill-omened; (*character*) bad.

nigrāns, -antis *adj* black, dusky.

nigrēscō, -ere *vi* to blacken, grow dark.

nigrō, -āre *vi* to be black.

nigror, -ōris *m* blackness.

nihil, nīl *nt* (*indecl*) nothing ♦ *adv* not; **~ ad nōs** it has nothing to do with us; **~ est** it's no use; **~ est quod** there is no reason why; **~ nisi** nothing but, only; **~ nōn** everything; **nōn ~** something.

nihilum, -ī *nt* nothing; **~ī esse** be worthless; **~ō minus** none the less.

nīl, nīlum *see* **nihil, nihilum.**

Nīliacus *adj* of the Nile; Egyptian.

Nīlus, -ī *m* Nile; conduit.

nimbifer, -ī *adj* stormy.

nimbōsus *adj* stormy.

nimbus, -ī *m* cloud, rain, storm.

nimiō *adv* much, far.

nīmīrum *adv* certainly, of course.

nimis *adv* too much, very much; **nōn ~** not very.

nimium *adv* too, too much; very, very much.

nimius *adj* too great, excessive; very great ♦ *nt* excess.

ningit, ninguit, -ere *vi* it snows.

ninguēs, -ium *fpl* snow.

Nioba, -ae, -ē, -ēs *f* daughter of Tantalus (*changed to a weeping rock*).

Niobēus *adj see n.*

Nīreus, -eī *and* **eos** *m* handsomest of the Greeks at Troy.

Nīsaeus, -ēius *adj see n.*

Nīsēis, -edis *f* Scylla.

nisi *conj* if not, unless; except, but.

nīsus *ppa of* **nītor.**

nīsus, -ūs *m* pressure, effort; striving, soaring.

Nīsus, -ī *m* father of Scylla.

nītēdula, -ae *f* dormouse.

nitēns, -entis *pres p of* **niteō** ♦ *adj* bright;

brilliant, beautiful.
niteō, -ēre *vi* to shine, gleam; to be sleek, be greasy; to thrive, look beautiful.
nitēscō, -ere, nituī *vi* to brighten, shine, glow.
nitidiusculē *adv* rather more finely.
nitidiusculus *adj* a little shinier.
nitidē *adv* magnificently.
nitidus *adj* bright, shining; sleek; blooming; smart, spruce; (*speech*) refined.
nitor, -ōris *m* brightness, sheen, sleekness, beauty; neatness, elegance.
nītor, -tī, -sus *and* **xus** *vi* to rest on, lean on; to press, stand firmly; to press forward, climb; to exert oneself, strive, labour; to depend on.
nitrum, -ī *nt* soda.
nivālis *adj* snowy.
niveus *adj* of snow, snowy, snow-white.
nivōsus *adj* snowy.
nix, nivis *f* snow.
nīxor, -ārī *vi* to rest on; to struggle.
nīxus *ppp of* **nītor**.
nīxus, -ūs *m* pressure; labour.
nō, nāre, nāvī *vi* to swim, float; to sail, fly.
nōbilis *adj* known, noted, famous, notorious; noble, high-born; excellent.
nōbilitās, -ātis *f* fame; noble birth; the nobility; excellence.
nōbilitō, -āre, -āvī, -ātum *vt* to make famous *or* notorious.
nocēns, -entis *pres p of* **noceō** ♦ *adj* harmful; criminal, guilty.
noceō, -ēre, -uī, -itum *vi* (*with dat*) to harm, hurt.
nocīvus *adj* injurious.
noctifer, -ī *m* evening star.
noctilūca, -ae *f* moon.
noctivagus *adj* night-wandering.
noctū *adv* by night.
noctua, -ae *f* owl.
noctuābundus *adj* travelling by night.
nocturnus *adj* night- (*in cpds*), nocturnal.
nōdō, -āre, -āvī, -ātum *vt* to knot, tie.
nōdōsus *adj* knotty.
nōdus, -ī *m* knot; knob; girdle; (*fig*) bond, difficulty.
nōlō, -le, -uī *vt*, *vi* to not wish, be unwilling, refuse; ~ī, ~īte do not.
Nomas, -dis *m/f* nomad; Numidian.
nōmen, -inis *nt* name; title; (*comm*) demand, debt; (*gram*) noun; (*fig*) reputation, fame; account, pretext; ~ **dare profitērī** enlist; ~ **deferre** accuse; ~**ina facere** enter the items of a debt.
nōmenclātor, -ōris *m* slave who told his master the names of people.
nōminātim *adv* by name, one by one.
nōminātiō, -ōnis *f* nomination.
nōminitō, -āre *vt* to usually name.

nōminō, -āre, -āvī, -ātum *vt* to name, call; to mention; to make famous; to nominate; to accuse, denounce.
nomisma, -tis *nt* coin.
nōn *adv* not; no.
Nōnae, -ārum *fpl* Nones (*7th day of March, May, July, October, 5th of other months*).
nōnāgēsimus *adj* ninetieth.
nōnāgiēns, -ēs *adv* ninety times.
nōnāgintā *num* ninety.
nōnānus *adj* of the ninth legion.
nōndum *adv* not yet
nōngentī, -ōrum *num* nine hundred.
nonna, -ae *f* nun.
nōnne *adv* do not?, is not? *etc.*; (*indirect*) whether not.
nōnnullus *adj* some.
nōnnunquam *adv* sometimes.
nōnus *adj* ninth ♦ *f* ninth hour.
nōnusdecimus *adj* nineteenth.
Nōricum, -ī *nt* country between the Danube and the Alps.
Nōricus *adj see* **n.**
nōrma, -ae *f* rule.
nōs *pron* we, us; I, me.
nōscitō, -āre *vt* to know, recognise; to observe, examine.
nōscō, -scere, -vī, -tum *vt* to get to know, learn; to examine; to recognise, allow; (*perf*) to know.
nōsmet *pron* (*emphatic*) *see* **nōs.**
noster, -rī *adj* our, ours; for us; my; (*with names*) my dear, good old ♦ *m* our friend ♦ *mpl* our side, our troops; ~**rī**, ~**rum** of us.
nostrās, -ātis *adj* of our country, native.
nota, -ae *f* mark, sign, note; (*writing*) note, letter; (*pl*) memoranda, shorthand, secret writing; (*books*) critical mark, punctuation; (*wine, etc*) brand, quality; (*gesture*) sign; (*fig*) sign, token; (*censor's*) black mark; (*fig*) stigma, disgrace.
notābilis *adj* remarkable; notorious.
notābiliter *adv* perceptibly.
notārius, -ī *and* **iī** *m* shorthand writer; secretary.
notātiō, -ōnis *f* marking; choice; observation; (*censor*) stigmatizing; (*words*) etymology.
nōtēscō, -ere, nōtuī *vi* to become known.
nothus *adj* bastard; counterfeit.
nōtiō, -ōnis *f* (*law*) cognisance, investigation; (*philos*) idea.
nōtitia, -ae, -ēs, -ēī *f* fame; acquaintance; (*philos*) idea, preconception.
notō, -āre, -āvī, -ātum *vt* to mark, write; to denote; to observe; to brand, stigmatize.
nōtuī *perf of* **nōtēscō.**
nōtus *ppp of* **nōscō** ♦ *adj* known, familiar; notorious ♦ *mpl* acquaintances.
Notus (-os), -ī *m* south wind.
novācula, -ae *f* razor.

novālis, -isf, **-e, -is** nt fallow land; field; crops.
novātrīx, -īcisf renewer.
nove adv unusually.
novellus adj young, fresh, new.
novem num nine.
November, -ris adj of November ♦ m November.
novendecim num nineteen.
novendiālis adj nine days'; on the ninth day.
novēnī, -ōrum adj in nines; nine.
Novēnsilēs, -ium mpl new gods.
noverca, -aef stepmother.
novercālis adj stepmother's.
nōvī perf of **nōscō**.
novīcius adj new.
noviēns, -ēs adv nine times.
novissimē adv lately; last of all.
novissimus adj latest, last, rear.
novitās, -ātisf newness, novelty; strangeness.
novō, -āre, -āvī, -ātum vt to renew, refresh; to change; (words) to coin; **rēs ~** effect a revolution.
novus adj new, young, fresh, recent; strange, unusual; inexperienced; **~ homō** upstart, first of his family to hold curule office; **~ae rēs** revolution; **~ae tabulae** cancellation of debts; **quid ~ī** what news?
nox, noctisf night; darkness, obscurity; **nocte, noctū** by night; **dē nocte** during the night.
noxa, -aef hurt, harm; offence, guilt; punishment.
noxia, -aef harm, damage; guilt, fault.
noxius adj harmful; guilty.
nūbēcula, -aef cloudy look.
nūbēs, -isf cloud; (fig) gloom; veil.
nūbifer, -ī adj cloud-capped; cloudy.
nūbigena, -ae m cloudborn, Centaur.
nūbilis adj marriageable.
nūbilus adj cloudy; gloomy, sad ♦ ntpl clouds.
nūbō, -bere, -psī, -ptum vi (women) to be married.
nucleus, -ī m nut, kernel.
nūdius day since, days ago; **~ tertius** the day before yesterday.
nūdō, -āre, -āvī, -ātum vt to bare, strip, expose; (MIL) to leave exposed; to plunder; (fig) to disclose, betray.
nūdus adj naked, bare; exposed, defenceless; wearing only a tunic; (fig) destitute, poor; mere; unembellished, undisguised; **vestīmenta dētrahere ~ō** ≈ draw blood from a stone.
nūgae, -ārum fpl nonsense, trifles; (person) waster.
nūgātor, -ōris m silly creature, liar.
nūgātōrius adj futile.
nūgāx, -ācis adj frivolous.
nūgor, -ārī, -ātus vi to talk nonsense; to cheat.
nullus, -īus (dat -ī) adj no, none; not, not at all; non-existent, of no account ♦ m/f nobody.

num interrog particle surely not? (indirect) whether, if.
Numa, -ae m second king of Rome.
nūmen, -inis nt nod, will; divine will, power; divinity, god.
numerābilis adj easy to count.
numerātus adj in cash ♦ nt ready money.
numerō, -āre, -āvī, -ātum vt to count, number; (money) to pay out; (fig) to reckon, consider as.
numerō adv just now, quickly, too soon.
numerōsē adv rhythmically.
numerōsus adj populous; rhythmical.
numerus, -ī m number; many, numbers; (MIL) troop; (fig) a cipher; (pl) mathematics; rank, category, regard; rhythm, metre, verse; **in ~ō esse, habērī** be reckoned as; **nullō ~ō** of no account.
Numida adj see n.
Numidae, -ārum mpl Numidians (people of N. Africa).
Numidia, -iaef the country of the Numidians.
Numidicus adj see n.
Numitor, -ōris m king of Alba (grandfather of Romulus).
nummārius adj money- (in cpds), financial; mercenary.
nummātus adj moneyed.
nummulī, -ōrum mpl some money, cash.
nummus, -ī m coin, money, cash; (Roman coin) sestertius; (Greek coin) two-drachma piece.
numnam, numne see num.
numquam adv never; **~ nōn** always; **nōn ~** sometimes.
numquid (question) do you? does he? etc; (indirect) whether.
nunc adv now; at present, nowadays; but as it is; **~ ... ~** at one time ... at another.
nuncupātiō, -ōnisf pronouncing.
nuncupō, -āre, -āvī, -ātum vt to call, name; to pronounce formally.
nūndinae, -ārum fpl market day; market; trade.
nūndinātiō, -ōnisf trading.
nūndinor, -ārī vi to trade, traffic; to flock together ♦ vt to buy.
nūndinum, -ī nt market time; **trīnum ~** 17 days.
nunq- etc see **numq-**.
nūntiātiō, -ōnisf announcing.
nūntiō, -āre, -āvī, -ātum vt to announce, report, tell.
nūntius adj informative, speaking ♦ m messenger; message, news; injunction; notice of divorce ♦ nt message.
nūper adv recently, lately.
nūpsī perf of **nūbō**.
nūpta, -aef bride, wife.
nūptiae, -ārum fpl wedding, marriage.
nūptiālis adj wedding- (in cpds), nuptial.
nurus, -ūsf daughter-in-law; young woman.
nūsquam adv nowhere; in nothing, for nothing.

nūtō, -āre vi to nod; to sway, totter, falter.
nūtrīcius, -ī m tutor.
nūtrīcō, -āre, -or, -ārī vt to nourish, sustain.
nūtrīcula, -ae f nurse.
nūtrīmen, -inis nt nourishment
nūtrīmentum, -ī nt nourishment, support.
nūtriō, -īre, -īvī, -ītum vt to suckle, nourish, rear, nurse.
nūtrīx, -īcis f nurse, foster mother.
nūtus, -ūs m nod; will, command; (physics) gravity.
nux, nucis f nut; nut tree, almond tree.
Nyctēis, -idis f Antiopa.
nympha, -ae, -ē, -ēs f bride; nymph; water.
Nysa, -ae f birthplace of Bacchus.
Nysaeus, -ēis, -ius adj see n.

O, o

ō interj (expressing joy, surprise, pain, etc) oh!; (with voc) O!
ob prep (with acc) in front of; for, on account of, for the sake of; **quam ~ rem** accordingly.
obaerātus adj in debt ♦ m debtor.
obambulō, -āre vi to walk past, prowl about.
obarmō, -āre vt to arm (against).
obarō, -āre vt to plough up.
obc- etc see **occ-**.
obdō, -ere, -idī, -itum vt to shut to expose.
obdormīscō, -īscere, -īvī vi to fall asleep ♦ vt to sleep off.
obdūcō, -ūcere, -ūxī, -uctum v to draw over, cover; to bring up; (drink) to swallow; (time) to pass.
obductō, -āre vt to bring as a rival.
obductus ppp of **obdūcō**.
obdūrēscō, -ēscere, -uī vi to harden to become obdurate.
obdūrō, -āre vi to persist, stand firm.
obdutīcō, -ōnis f veiling.
obeō, -īre, -īvī, and iī, -itum vi to go to, meet; to die; (ASTRO) to set ♦ vt to visit, travel over; to survey, go over; to envelop; (duty) to engage in, perform; (time) to meet; **ciem ~ die;** (law) to appear on the appointed day.
obequitō, -āre vi to ride up to.
oberrō, -āre vi to ramble about; to make a mistake.
obēsus adj fat, plump; coarse.
ōbex, -icis m/f bolt, bar, barrier.
obf- etc see **off-**.
obg- etc see **ogg-**.

obhaerēscō, -rēscere, -sī vi to stick fast.
obiaceō, -ēre vi to lie over against.
obiciō, -icere, -iēcī, -iectum vt to throw to, set before; (defence) to put up, throw against; (fig) to expose, give up; (speech) to taunt, reproach.
obiectātiō, -ōnis f reproach.
obiectō, -āre vt to throw against; to expose, sacrifice; to reproach; (hint) to let on.
obiectus ppp of **obiciō** ♦ adj opposite, in front of; exposed ♦ ntpl accusations.
obiectus, -ūs m putting in the way, interposing.
obīrātus adj angered.
obiter adv on the way; incidentally.
obitus ppp of **obeō**.
obitus, -ūs m death, ruin; (ASTRO) setting; visit.
obiūrgātiō, -ōnis f reprimand.
obiūrgātor, -ōris m reprover.
obiūrgātōrius adj reproachful.
obiūrgitō, -āre vt to keep on reproaching.
obiūrgō, -āre, -āvī, -ātum vt to scold, rebuke; to deter by reproof.
oblanguēscō, -ēscere, -uī vi to become feeble.
oblātrātrīx, -īcis f nagging woman.
oblātus ppp of **offerō**.
oblectāmentum, -ī nt amusement.
oblectātiō, -ōnis f delight.
oblectō, -āre, -āvī, -ātum vt to delight, amuse, entertain; to detain; (time) to spend pleasantly; **sē ~** enjoy oneself.
oblīdō, -dere, -sī, -sum vt to crush, strangle.
obligātiō, -ōnis f pledge.
obligō, -āre, -āvī, -ātum vt to tie up, bandage; to put under an obligation, embarrass; (law) to render liable, make guilty; to mortgage.
oblimō, -āre vt to cover with mud.
oblinō, -inere, -ēvī, -itum vt to smear over; to defile; (fig) to overload.
oblīquē adv sideways; indirectly.
oblīquō, -āre vt to turn aside, veer.
oblīquus adj slanting, downhill; from the side, sideways; (look) askance, envious; (speech) indirect.
oblīsus ppp of **oblīdō**.
oblitēscō, -ere vi to hide away.
oblitterō, -āre, -āvī, -ātum vt to erase, cancel; (fig) to consign to oblivion.
oblitus ppp of **oblinō**.
oblītus ppa of **oblīvīscor**.
oblīviō, -ōnis f oblivion, forgetfulness.
oblīviōsus adj forgetful.
oblīvīscor, -vīscī, -tus vt, vi to forget.
oblīvium, -ī and iī nt forgetfulness, oblivion.
oblocūtor, -ōris m contradicter.
oblongus adj oblong.
obloquor, -quī, -cūtus vi to contradict, interrupt; to abuse; (music) to accompany.

obluctor, -ārī vi to struggle against.
obmōlior, -īrī vt to throw up (*as a defence*).
obmurmurō, -āre vi to roar in answer.
obmūtēscō, -ēscere, -uī vi to become silent; to cease.
obnātus *adj* growing on.
obnītor, -tī, -xus vi to push against, struggle; to stand firm, resist.
obnīxē *adv* resolutely.
obnīxus *ppa of* **obnītor** ♦ *adj* steadfast.
obnoxiē *adv* slavishly.
obnoxiōsus *adj* submissive.
obnoxius *adj* liable, addicted; culpable; submissive, slavish; under obligation, indebted; exposed (to danger).
obnūbō, -bere, -psī, -ptum vt to veil, cover.
obnūntiātiō, -ōnis f announcement of an adverse omen.
obnūntiō, -āre vt to announce an adverse omen.
oboediēns, -entis *pres p of* **oboediō** ♦ *adj* obedient.
oboedienter *adv* readily.
oboedientia, -ae f obedience.
oboediō, -īre vi to listen; to obey, be subject to.
oboleō, -ēre, -uī vt to smell of.
oborior, -īrī, -tus vi to arise, spring up.
obp- *etc see* **opp-**.
obrēpō, -ere, -sī, -tum vt, vi to creep up to, steal upon, surprise; to cheat.
obrētiō, -īre vt to entangle.
obrigēscō, -ēscere, -uī vi to stiffen.
obrogō, -āre, -āvī, -ātum vt to invalidate (by making a new law).
obruō, -ere, -ī, -tum vt to cover over, bury, sink; to overwhelm, overpower ♦ vi to fall to ruin.
obrussa, -ae f test, touchstone.
obrutus *ppp of* **obruō**.
obsaepiō, -īre, -sī, -tum vt to block, close.
obsaturō, -āre vt to sate, glut.
obscaen- *etc see* **obscen-**.
obscēnē *adv* indecently.
obscēnitās, -ātis f indecency.
obscēnus *adj* filthy; indecent; ominous.
obscūrātiō, -ōnis f darkening, disappearance.
obscūrē *adv* secretly.
obscūritās, -ātis f darkness; (*fig*) uncertainty; (*rank*) lowliness.
obscūrō, -āre, -āvī, -ātum vt to darken; to conceal, suppress; (*speech*) to obscure; (*pass*) to become obsolete.
obscūrus *adj* dark, shady, hidden; (*fig*) obscure, indistinct; unknown, ignoble; (*character*) reserved.
obsecrātiō, -ōnis f entreaty; public prayer.
obsecrō, -āre vt to implore, appeal to.
obsecundō, -āre vi to comply with, back up.
obsēdī *perf of* **obsideō**.
obsēp- *etc see* **obsaep-**.
obsequēns, -entis *pres p of* **obsequor** ♦ *adj*

compliant; (*gods*) gracious.
obsequenter *adv* compliantly.
obsequentia, -ae f complaisance.
obsequiōsus *adj* complaisant.
obsequium, -ī and iī nt compliance, indulgence; obedience, allegiance.
obsequor, -quī, -cūtus vi to comply with, yield to, indulge.
obserō, -āre vt to bar, close.
obserō, -erere, -ēvī, -itum vt to sow, plant; to cover thickly.
observāns, -antis *pres p of* **observō** ♦ *adj* attentive, respectful.
observantia, -ae f respect.
observātiō, -ōnis f watching; caution.
observitō, -āre vt to observe carefully.
observō, -āre, -āvī, -ātum vt to watch, watch for; to guard; (*laws*) to keep, comply with; (*person*) to pay respect to.
obses, -idis m/f hostage; guarantee.
obsessiō, -ōnis f blockade.
obsessor, -ōris m frequenter; besieger.
obsessus *ppp of* **obsideō**.
obsideō, -idēre, -ēdī, -essum vt to sit at, frequent; (*MIL*) to blockade, besiege; to block, fill, take up; to guard, watch for ♦ vi to sit.
obsidiō, -ōnis f siege, blockade; (*fig*) imminent danger.
obsidium, -ī and iī nt siege, blockade; hostageship.
obsīdō, -ere vt to besiege, occupy.
obsignātor, -ōris m sealer; witness.
obsignō, -āre, -āvī, -ātum vt to seal up; to sign and seal; (*fig*) to stamp.
obsistō, -istere, -titī, -titum vi to put oneself in the way, resist.
obsitus *ppp of* **obserō**.
obsolefīō, -fierī vi to wear out, become degraded.
obsolēscō, -scere, -vī, -tum vi to wear out, become out of date.
obsolētius *adv* more shabbily.
obsolētus *ppa of* **obsolēscō** ♦ *adj* worn out, shabby; obsolete; (*fig*) ordinary, mean.
obsōnātor, -ōris m caterer.
obsōnātus, -ūs m marketing.
obsōnium, -ī and iī nt food eaten with bread, (*usu fish*).
obsōnō, -āre, -or, -ārī vi to cater, buy provisions; to provide a meal.
obsonō, -āre vi to interrupt.
obsorbeō, -ēre vt to swallow, bolt.
obstantia, -ium ntpl obstructions.
obstetrix, -īcis f midwife.
obstinātiō, -ōnis f determination, stubbornness.
obstinātē *adv* firmly, obstinately.
obstinātus *adj* firm, resolute; stubborn.
obstinō, -āre vi to be determined, persist.
obstipēscō *etc see* **obstupēscō**.
obstīpus *adj* bent, bowed, drawn back.
obstitī *perf of* **obstitō**; *perf of* **obstō**.
obstō, -āre, -itī vi to stand in the way; to

obstruct, prevent.

obstrepō, -ere, -uī, -itum vi to make a noise; to shout against, cry down, molest ♦ vt to drown (in noise); to fill with noise.

obstrictus ppp of **obstringō**.

obstringō, -ingere, -inxī, -ictum vt to bind up, tie round; (fig) to confine, hamper; to lay under an obligation.

obstructiō, -ōnis f barrier.

obstructus ppp of **obstruō**.

obstrūdō (obtrūdō), -dere, -sī, -sum vt to force on to; to gulp down.

obstruō, -ere, -xī, -ctum vt to build up against, block; to shut, hinder.

obstupefaciō, -facere, -fēcī, -factum (pass **-fīō, -fierī**) vt to astound, paralyse.

obstupēscō, -ēscere, -uī vi to be astounded, paralysed.

obstupidus adj stupefied.

obsum, -esse, -fuī vi to be against, harm.

obsuō, -uere, -uī, -ūtum vt to sew on, sew up.

obsurdēscō, -ēscere, -uī vi to grow deaf; to turn a deaf ear.

obsūtus ppp of **obsuō**.

obtegō, -egere, -ēxī, -ēctum vt to cover over; to conceal.

obtemperātiō, -ōnis f obedience.

obtemperō, -āre, -āvī, -ātum vi (with dat) to comply with, obey.

obtendō, -dere, -dī, -tum vt to spread over, stretch over against; to conceal; to make a pretext of.

obtentus ppp of **obtendō**; ppp of **obtineō**.

obtentus, -ūs m screen; pretext.

obterō, -erere, -rīvī, -rītum vt to trample on, crush; to disparage.

obtestātiō, -ōnis f adjuring; supplication.

obtestor, -ārī, -ātus vt to call to witness; to entreat.

obtexō, -ere, -uī vt to overspread.

obticeō, -ēre vi to be silent.

obticēscō, -ēscere, -uī vi to be struck dumb.

obtigī perf of **obtingō**.

obtigō see **obtegō**.

obtineō, -inēre, -inuī, -entum vt to hold, possess; to maintain; to gain, obtain ♦ vi to prevail, continue.

obtingō, -ngere, -gī vi to fall to one's lot; to happen.

obtorpēscō, -ēscere, -uī vi to become numb, lose feeling.

obtorqueō, -quēre, -sī, -tum vt to twist about, wrench.

obtrectātiō, -ōnis f disparagement.

obtrectātor, -ōris m disparager.

obtrectō, -āre vt, vi to detract, disparage.

obtrītus ppp of **obterō**.

obtrūdō etc see **obstrūdō**.

obtruncō, -āre vt to cut down, slaughter.

obtueor, -ērī, -or, -ī vt to gaze at, see clearly.

obtulī perf of **offerō**.

obtundō, -undere, -udī, -ūsum and **-ūnsum** vt to beat, thump; to blunt; (speech) to deafen, annoy.

obturbō, -āre vt to throw into confusion; to bother, distract.

obturgēscō, -ere vi to swell up.

obtūrō, -āre vt to stop up, close.

obtūsus, obtūnsus ppp of **obtundō** ♦ adj blunt; (fig) dulled, blurred, unfeeling.

obtūtus, -ūs m gaze.

obumbrō, -āre vt to shade, darken; (fig) to cloak, screen.

obuncus adj hooked.

obūstus adj burnt, hardened in fire.

obvallātus adj fortified.

obveniō, -enīre, -ēnī, -entum vi to come up; to fall to; to occur.

obversor, -ārī vi to move about before; (visions) to hover.

obversus ppp of **obvertō** ♦ adj turned towards ♦ mpl enemy.

obvertō, -tere, -tī, -sum vt to direct towards, turn against.

obviam adv to meet, against; ~ **ire** to go to meet.

obvius adj in the way, to meet; opposite, against; at hand, accessible; exposed.

obvolvō, -vere, -vī, -ūtum vt to wrap up, muffle up; (fig) to cloak.

occaecō, -āre, -āvī, -ātum vt to blind, obscure, conceal; to benumb.

occallēscō, -ēscere, -uī vi to grow a thick skin; to become hardened.

occanō, -ere vi to sound the attack.

occāsiō, -ōnis f opportunity, convenient time; (MIL) surprise.

occāsiuncula, -ae f opportunity.

occāsus, -ūs m setting; west; downfall, ruin.

occātiō, -ōnis f harrowing.

occātor, -ōris m harrower.

occēdō, -ere vi to go up to.

occentō, -āre vt, vi to serenade; to sing a lampoon.

occēpī perf of **occipiō**.

occepsō archaic fut of **occipiō**.

occeptō, -āre vt to begin.

occidēns, -entis pres p of **occidō** ♦ m west.

occīdiō, -ōnis f massacre; ~**ōne occīdere** annihilate.

occīdō, -dere, -dī, -sum vt to fell; to cut down, kill; to pester.

occidō, -idere, -idī, -āsum vi to fall; to set; to die, perish, be ruined.

occiduus adj setting; western; failing.

occinō, -ere, -uī vi to sing inauspiciously.

occipiō, -ipere, -ēpī, -eptum vt, vi to begin.

occipitium, -ī and **iī** nt back of the head.

occīsiō, -ōnis f massacre.

occīsor, -ōris m killer.

Noun declensions and verb conjugations are shown on pp xiii to xxv. The present infinitive ending of a verb shows to which conjugation it belongs: **-āre** = 1st; **-ēre** = 2nd; **-ere** = 3rd and **-īre** = 4th. Irregular verbs are shown on p xxvi

occīsus *ppp of* **occīdō.**
occlāmitō, -āre *vi* to bawl.
occlūdō, -dere, -sī, -sum *vt* to shut up; to stop.
occō, -āre *vt* to harrow.
occubō, -āre *vi* to lie.
occulcō, -āre *vt* to trample down.
occulō, -ere, -uī, -tum *vt* to cover over, hide.
occultātiō, -ōnis *f* concealment.
occultātor, -ōris *m* hider.
occultē *adv* secretly.
occultō, -āre, -āvī, -ātum *vt* to conceal, secrete.
occultus *ppp of* **occulō** ♦ *adj* hidden, secret; (*person*) reserved, secretive ♦ *nt* secret, hiding.
occumbō, -mbere, -buī, -bitum *vi* to fall, die.
occupātiō, -ōnis *f* taking possession; business; engagement.
occupātus *adj* occupied, busy.
occupō, -āre, -āvī, -ātum *vt* to take possession of, seize; to occupy, take up; to surprise, anticipate; (*money*) to lend, invest.
occurrō, -rere, -rī, -sum *vi* to run up to, meet; to attack; to fall in with; to hurry to; (*fig*) to obviate, counteract; (*words*) to object; (*thought*) to occur, suggest itself.
occursātiō, -ōnis *f* fussy welcome.
occursō, -āre *vi* to run to meet, meet; to oppose; (*thought*) to occur.
occursus, -ūs *m* meeting.
Ōceanītis, -ītidis *f* daughter of Ocean.
Ōceanus, -ī *m* Ocean, a stream encircling the earth; the Atlantic.
ocellus, -ī *m* eye; darling, gem.
ōcior, -ōris *adj* quicker, swifter.
ōcius *adv* more quickly; sooner, rather; quickly.
ocrea, -ae *f* greave.
ocreātus *adj* greaved.
Octāviānus *adj* of Octavius ♦ *m* Octavian (*a surname of Augustus*).
Octāvius, -ī *m* Roman family name (*esp the emperor Augustus; his father*).
octāvum *adv* for the eighth time.
octāvus *adj* eighth ♦ *f* eighth hour.
octāvusdecimus *adj* eighteenth.
octiēns, -ēs *adv* eight times.
octingentēsimus *adj* eight hundredth.
octingentī, -ōrum *num* eight hundred.
octipēs, -edis *adj* eight-footed.
octō *num* eight.
Octōber, -ris *adj* of October ♦ *m* October.
octōgēnī, -ōrum *adj* eighty each.
octōgēsimus *adj* eightieth.
octōgiēns, -ēs *adv* eighty times.
octōgintā *num* eighty.
octōiugis *adj* eight together.
octōnī, -ōrum *adj* eight at a time, eight each.
octōphoros *adj* (*litter*) carried by eight bearers.
octuplicātus *adj* multiplied by eight.

octuplus *adj* eightfold.
octussis, -is *m* eight asses.
oculātus *adj* with eyes; visible; **~ā diē vēndere** sell for cash.
oculus, -ī *m* eye; sight; (*plant*) bud; (*fig*) darling, jewel; **~ōs adicere ad** glance at, covet; **ante ~ōs pōnere** imagine; **ex ~īs** out of sight; **esse in ~īs** be in view; be a favourite.
ōdī, -isse *vt* to hate, dislike.
odiōsē *adv* see *adj*.
odiōsus *adj* odious, unpleasant.
odium, -ī *and* **iī** *nt* hatred, dislike, displeasure; insolence; **~iō esse** be hateful, be disliked.
odor (-ōs), -ōris *m* smell, perfume, stench; (*fig*) inkling, suggestion.
odōrātiō, -ōnis *f* smelling.
odōrātus *adj* fragrant, perfumed.
odōrātus, -ūs *m* sense of smell; smelling.
odōrifer, -ī *adj* fragrant; perfume-producing.
odōrō, -āre *vt* to perfume.
odōror, -ārī, -ātus *vt* to smell, smell out; (*fig*) to search out; to aspire to; to get a smattering of.
odōrus *adj* fragrant; keen-scented.
odōs *etc see* **odor.**
Odrysius *adj* Thracian.
Odyssēa, -ae *f* Odyssey.
Oeagrius *adj* Thracian.
Oebalia, -iae *f* Tarentum.
Oebalidēs, -idae *m* Castor, Pollux.
Oebalis, -idis *f* Helen.
Oebalius *adj* Spartan.
Oebalus, -ī *m* king of Sparta.
Oedipūs, -odis *and* **ī** *m* king of Thebes; solver of riddles.
oenophorum, -ī *nt* wine basket.
Oenopia, -ae *f* Aegina.
Oenotria, -ae *f* S.E. Italy.
Oenotrius *adj* Italian.
oestrus, -ī *m* gadfly; (*fig*) frenzy.
Oeta, -ae, -ē, -ēs *f* mountain range in Thessaly, associated with Hercules.
Oetaeus *adj* see *n*.
ofella, -ae *f* morsel.
offa, -ae *f* pellet, lump; swelling.
offectus *pp of* **officiō.**
offendō, -endere, -endī, -ēnsum *vt* to hit; to hit on, come upon; to offend, blunder; to take offence; to fail, come to grief.
offēnsa, -ae *f* displeasure, enmity; offence, injury.
offēnsiō, -ōnis *f* stumbling; stumbling block; misfortune, indisposition; offence, displeasure.
offēnsiuncula, -ae *f* slight displeasure; slight check.
offēnsō, -āre *vt, vi* to dash against.
offēnsus *ppp of* **offendō** ♦ *adj* offensive; displeased ♦ *nt* offence.
offēnsus, -ūs *m* shock; offence.
offerō, -re, obtulī, oblātum *vt* to present, show; to bring forward, offer; to expose; to cause, inflict; **sē ~** encounter.

offerumenta, -ae *f* present.
officīna, -ae *f* workshop factory.
officiō, -icere, -ēcī, -ectum *vi* to obstruct; to interfere with; to hurt, prejudice.
officiōsē *adv* courteously.
officiōsus *adj* obliging; dutiful.
officium, -ī *and* **iī** *nt* service, attention; ceremonial; duty, sense of duty; official duty, function.
offigō, -ere *vt* to fasten, drive in.
offirmātus *adj* determined.
offirmō, -āre *vt, vi* to persevere in.
offlectō, -ere *vt* to turn about.
offrēnātus *adj* checked.
offūcia, -ae *f* (*cosmetic*) paint; (*fig*) trick.
offulgeō, -gēre, -sī *vi* to shine on.
offundō, -undere, -ūdī, -ūsum *vt* to pour out to; to pour over; to spread; to cover, fill.
offūsus *ppp of* **offundō**.
oggannniō, -īre *vi* to growl at.
oggerō, -ere *vt* to bring, give.
Ōgygius *adj* Theban.
oh *interj* (*expressing surprise, joy, grief*) oh!
ohē *interj* (*expressing surfeit*) stop!, enough!
oi *interj* (*expressing complaint, weeping*) oh!, oh dear!
oiei *interj* (*lamenting*) oh dear!
Oīleus, -eī *m* father of the less famous Ajax.
olea, -ae *f* olive; olive tree.
oleāginus *adj* of the olive tree.
oleārius *adj* oil- (*in cpds*) ♦ *m* oil seller.
oleaster, -rī *m* wild olive.
olēns, -entis *pres p of* **oleō** ♦ *adj* fragrant; stinking, musty.
oleō, -ēre, -uī *vt, vi* to smell, smell of; (*fig*) to betray.
oleum, -ī *nt* olive oil, oil; wrestling school; **~ et operam perdere** waste time and trouble.
olfaciō, -facere, -fēcī, -factum *vt* to smell, scent.
olfactō, -āre *vt* to smell at.
olidus *adj* smelling, rank.
ōlim *adv* once, once upon a time; at the time, at times; for a good while; one day (in the future).
olit- *etc see* **holit-**.
olīva, -ae *f* olive, olive tree; olive branch, olive staff.
olīvētum, -ī *nt* olive grove.
olīvifer, -ī *adj* olive-bearing.
olīvum, -ī *nt* oil; wrestling school; perfume.
olla, -ae *f* pot, jar.
olle, ollus *etc see* **ille**.
olor, -ōris *m* swan.
olōrinus *adj* swan's.
olus *etc see* **holus**.
Olympia, -ae *f* site of the Greek games in Elis.
Olympia, -ōrum *ntpl* Olympic Games.
Olympiacus *adj* = **Olympicus**.
Olympias, -adis *f* Olympiad, period of four

years.
Olympicus, -us *adj* Olympic.
Olympionīcēs, -ae *m* Olympic winner.
Olympus, -ī *m* mountain in N. Greece, abode of the gods; heaven.
omāsum, -ī *nt* tripe; paunch.
ōmen, -inis *nt* omen, sign; solemnity.
ōmentum, -ī *nt* bowels.
ōminor, -ārī, -ātus *vt* to forebode, prophesy.
ōmissus *ppp of* **ōmittō** ♦ *adj* remiss.
ōmittō, -ittere, -īsī, -issum *vt* to let go; to leave off, give up; to disregard, overlook; (*speech*) to pass over, omit.
omnifer, -ī *adj* all-sustaining.
omnigenus *adj* of all kinds.
omnimodīs *adv* wholly.
omnīnō *adv* entirely, altogether, at all; in general; (*concession*) to be sure, yes; (*number*) in all, just; **~ nōn** not at all.
omniparēns, -entis *adj* mother of all.
omnipotēns, -entis *adj* almighty.
omnis *adj* all, every, any; every kind of; the whole of ♦ *nt* the universe ♦ *mpl* everybody ♦ *ntpl* everything.
omnituēns, -entis *adj* all-seeing.
omnivagus *adj* roving everywhere.
omnivolus *adj* willing everything.
onager, -rī *m* wild ass.
onerārius *adj* (*beast*) of burden; (*ship*) transport.
onerō, -āre, -āvī, -ātum *vt* to load, burden; (*fig*) to overload, oppress; to aggravate.
onerōsus *adj* heavy, burdensome, irksome.
onus, -eris *nt* load, burden, cargo; (*fig*) charge, difficulty.
onustus *adj* loaded, burdened; (*fig*) filled.
onyx, -chis *m/f* onyx; onyx box.
opācitās, -ātis *f* shade.
opācō, -āre *vt* to shade.
opācus *adj* shady; dark.
ope *abl of* **ops**.
opella, -ae *f* light work, small service.
opera, -ae *f* exertion, work; service; care, attention; leisure, time; (*person*) workman, hired rough; **~am dare** pay attention; do one's best; **~ae pretium** worth while; **~ā meā** thanks to me.
operārius *adj* working ♦ *m* workman.
operculum, -ī *nt* cover, lid.
operimentum, -ī *nt* covering.
operiō, -īre, -uī, -tum *vt* to cover; to close; (*fig*) to overwhelm, conceal.
operor, -ārī, -ātus *vi* to work, take pains, be occupied.
operōsē *adv* painstakingly.
operōsus *adj* active, industrious; laborious, elaborate.
opertus *ppp of* **operiō** ♦ *adj* covered, hidden ♦ *nt* secret.
opēs *pl of* **ops**.

opicus *adj* barbarous, boorish.
opifer, -ī *adj* helping.
opifex, -icis *m/f* maker; craftsman, artisan.
ōpiliō, -ōnis *m* shepherd.
opīmitās, -ātis *f* abundance.
opīmus *adj* rich, fruitful, fat; copious, sumptuous; (*style*) overloaded; **spolia ~a** *spoils of an enemy commander killed by a Roman general*.
opīnābilis *adj* conjectural.
opīnātiō, -ōnis *f* conjecture.
opīnātor, -ōris *m* conjecturer.
opīnātus, -ūs *m* supposition.
opīniō, -ōnis *f* opinion, conjecture, belief; reputation, esteem; rumour; **contrā, praeter ~ōnem** contrary to expectation.
opīniōsus *adj* dogmatic.
opīnor, -ārī, -ātus *vi* to think, suppose, imagine ♦ *adj* imagined.
opiparē *adv see adj*.
opiparus *adj* rich, sumptuous.
opitulor, -ārī, -ātus *vi* (*with dat*) to help.
oportet, -ēre, -uit *vt* (*impers*) ought, should.
oppēdō, -ere *vi* to insult.
opperior, -īrī, -tus *vt, vi* to wait, wait for.
oppetō, -ere, -īvī, -ītum *vt* to encounter; to die.
oppidānus *adj* provincial ♦ *mpl* townsfolk.
oppidō *adv* quite, completely, exactly.
oppidulum, -ī *nt* small town.
oppidum, -ī *nt* town.
oppignerō, -āre *vt* to pledge.
oppīlō, -āre *vt* to stop up.
oppleō, -ēre, -ēvī, -ētum *vt* to fill, choke up.
oppōnō, -ōnere, -osuī, -ositum *vt* to put against, set before; to expose; to present; (*argument*) to adduce, reply, oppose; (*property*) to pledge, mortgage.
opportūnitās, -ātis *f* suitableness, advantage; good opportunity.
opportūnē *adv* opportunely.
opportūnus *adj* suitable, opportune; useful; exposed.
oppositiō, -ōnis *f* opposing.
oppositus *ppp of* **oppōnō** ♦ *adj* against, opposite.
oppositus, -ūs *m* opposing.
oppsuī *perf of* **oppōnō**.
oppressiō, -ōnis *f* violence; seizure; overthrow.
oppressus *ppp of* **opprimō**.
oppressus, -ūs *m* pressure.
opprimō, -imere, -essī, -essum *vt* to press down, crush; to press together, close; to suppress, overwhelm, overthrow; to surprise, seize.
opprobrium, -ī *and* **iī** *nt* reproach, disgrace, scandal.
opprobrō, -āre *vt* to taunt.
oppugnātiō, -ōnis *f* attack, assault.
oppugnātor, -ōris *m* assailant.
oppugnō, -āre, -āvī, -ātum *vt* to attack, assault.

ops, -opis *f* power, strength; help.
Ops goddess of plenty.
ops- *etc see* **obs-**.
optābilis *adj* desirable.
optātiō, -ōnis *f* wish.
optātus *adj* longed for ♦ *nt* wish; **~ātō** according to one's wish.
optimās, -ātis *adj* aristocratic ♦ *mpl* the nobility.
optimē *adv* best, very well; just in time.
optimus *adj* best, very good; excellent; **~ō iūre** deservedly.
optiō, -ōnis *f* choice ♦ *m* assistant.
optīvus *adj* chosen.
optō, -āre, -āvī, -ātum *vt* to choose; to wish for.
optum- *etc see* **optim-**.
opulēns, -entis *adj* rich.
opulentia, -ae *f* wealth; power.
opulentō, -āre *vt* to enrich.
opulentē, -er *adv* sumptuously.
opulentus *adj* rich, sumptuous, powerful.
opum *fpl* resources, wealth.
opus, -eris *nt* work, workmanship; (*art*) work, building, book; (*MIL*) siege work; (*colloq*) business; (*with* **esse**) need; **virō ~ est** a man is needed; **māgnō ~ere** much, greatly.
opusculum, -ī *nt* little work.
ōra, -ae *f* edge, boundary; coast; country, region; (*NAUT*) hawser.
ōrāculum, -ī *nt* oracle, prophecy.
ōrātē *adv see adj*.
ōrātiō, -ōnis *f* speech, language; a speech, oration; eloquence; prose; emperor's message; **~ōnem habēre** deliver a speech.
ōrātiuncula, -ae *f* short speech.
ōrātor, -ōris *m* speaker, spokesman, orator.
ōrātōrius *adj* oratorical.
ōrātrīx, -īcis *f* suppliant.
ōrātus, -ūs *m* request.
orbātor, -ōris *m* bereaver.
orbiculātus *adj* round.
orbis, -is *m* circle, ring, disc, orbit; world; (*movement*) cycle, rotation; (*style*) rounding off; **~ lacteus** Milky Way; **~ signifer** Zodiac; **~ fortūnae** wheel of Fortune; **~ terrārum** the earth, world; **in ~em cōnsistere** form a circle; **in ~em īre** go the rounds.
orbita, -ae *f* rut, track, path.
orbitās, -ātis *f* childlessness, orphanhood, widowhood.
orbitōsus *adj* full of ruts.
orbō, -āre, -āvī, -ātum *vt* to bereave, orphan, make childless.
orbus *adj* bereaved, orphan, childless; destitute.
orca, -ae *f* vat.
orchas, -dis *f* kind of olive.
orchēstra, -ae *f* senatorial seats (in the theatre).
Orcus, -ī *m* Pluto; the lower world; death.
ōrdinārius *adj* regular.
ōrdinātim *adv* in order, properly.

ōrdinātiō, -ōnis f orderly arrangement.
ōrdinātus adj appointed.
ōrdinō, -āre, -āvī, -ātum vt to arrange,
regulate, set in order.
ōrdior, -dīrī, -sus vt, vi to begin, undertake.
ōrdō, -inis m line, row, series; order
regularity, arrangement; (MIL) rank, line,
company, (pl) captains; (building) course,
layer; (seats) row; (POL) class, order, station;
ex ~ine in order, in one's turn; one after the
other; **extrā ~inem** irregularly, unusually.
Orēas, -dis f mountain nymph.
Orestēs, -is and **ae** m son of Agamemnon, whom
he avenged by killing his mother.
Orestēus adj see n.
orexis, -is f appetite.
organum, -ī nt instrument, organ.
orgia, -ōrum ntpl Bacchic revels; orgies.
orichalcum, -ī nt copper ore, brass.
ōricilla, -ae f lobe.
oriēns, -entis pres p of **orior** ♦ m morning; east.
orīgō, -inis f beginning, source; ancestry,
descent; founder.
Ōrīōn, -onis and **ōnis** m mythical hunter and
constellation.
orior, -īrī, -tus vi to rise; to spring; descend.
oriundus adj descended, sprung.
ōrnāmentum, -ī nt equipment, dress;
ornament, decoration; distinction, pride of.
ōrnātē adv elegantly.
ōrnātus ppp of **ōrnō** ♦ adj equipped, furnished;
embellished, excellent.
ōrnātus, -ūs m preparation; dress,
equipment; embellishment.
ōrnō, -āre, -āvī, -ātum vt to fit out, equip,
dress, prepare; to adorn, embellish, honour.
ornus, -ī f manna ash.
ōrō, -āre, -āvī, -ātum vt to speak; pead; to
beg, entreat; to pray.
Orontēs, -is and **ī** m river of Syria.
Orontēus adj Syrian.
Orpheus, -eī and **eos** (acc **-ea**) m legendary
Thracian singer, who went down to Hades for
Eurydice.
Orphēus, -icus adj see n.
ōrsus ppa of **ōrdior** ♦ ntpl beginning; utterance.
ōrsus, -ūs m beginning.
ortus ppa of **orior** ♦ adj born, descended.
ortus, -ūs m rising; east; origin, source.
Ortygia, -ae and **ē, -ēs** f Delos.
Ortygius adj see n.
oryx, -gis m gazelle.
oryza, -ae f rice.
os, ossis nt bone; (fig) very soul.
ōs, -ōris nt mouth; face; entrance, opening;
effrontery; **ūnō ōre** unanimously; **n ōre esse**
be talked about; **quō ōre redībō** how shall I
have the face to go back?
oscen, -inis m bird of omen.

ōscillum, -ī nt little mask.
ōscitāns, -antis pres p of **ōscitō** ♦ adj listless,
drowsy.
ōscitanter adv half-heartedly.
ōscitō, -āre; -or, -ārī vi to yawn, be drowsy.
ōsculātiō, -ōnis f kissing.
ōsculor, -ārī, -ātus vt to kiss; to make a fuss
of.
ōsculum, -ī nt sweet mouth; kiss.
Oscus adj Oscan.
Osīris, -is and **idis** m Egyptian god, husband of
Isis.
Ossa, -ae f mountain in Thessaly.
osseus adj bony.
ossifraga, -ae f osprey.
ostendō, -dere, -dī, -tum vt to hold out,
show, display; to expose; to disclose, reveal;
(speech) to say, make known.
ostentātiō, -ōnis f display; showing off,
ostentation; pretence.
ostentātor, -ōris m displayer, boaster.
ostentō, -āre vt to hold out, proffer, exhibit;
to show off, boast of; to make known,
indicate.
ostentum, -ī nt portent.
ostentus ppp of **ostendō**.
ostentus, -ūs m display, appearance; proof.
Ōstia, -ae f, **-ōrum** ntpl port at the Tiber mouth.
ōstiārium, -ī and **iī** nt door tax.
ōstiātim adv from door to door.
Ōstiēnsis adj see n.
ōstium, -ī and **iī** nt door; entrance, mouth.
ostrea, -ae f oyster.
ostreōsus adj rich in oysters.
ostreum, -ī nt oyster.
ostrifer, -ī adj oyster-producing.
ostrīnus adj purple.
ostrum, -ī nt purple; purple dress or
coverings.
ōsus, ōsūrus ppa and fut p of **ōdī**.
Othō, -ōnis m author of a law giving theatre seats
to Equites; Roman emperor after Galba.
Othōniānus adj see n.
ōtiolum, -ī nt bit of leisure.
ōtior, -ārī vi to have a holiday, be idle.
ōtiōsē adv leisurely; quietly; fearlessly.
ōtiōsus adj at leisure, free; out of public
affairs; neutral, indifferent; quiet,
unexcited; (things) free, idle ♦ m private
citizen, civilian.
ōtium, -ī and **iī** nt leisure, time (for), idleness,
retirement; peace, quiet.
ovātiō, -ōnis f minor triumph.
ovīle, -is nt sheep fold, goat fold.
ovillus adj of sheep.
ovis, -is f sheep.
ovō, -āre vi to rejoice; to celebrate a minor
triumph.
ōvum, -ī nt egg.

Noun declensions and verb conjugations are shown on pp xiii to xxv. The present infinitive ending of a verb shows
to which conjugation it belongs: **-āre** = 1st; **-ēre** = 2nd; **-ere** = 3rd and **-īre** = 4th. Irregular verbs are shown on p xxvi

P, p

pābulātiō, -ōnis *f* foraging.
pābulātor, -ōris *m* forager.
pābulor, -ārī *vi* to forage.
pābulum, -ī *nt* food, fodder.
pācālis *adj* of peace.
pācātus *adj* peaceful, tranquil ♦ *nt* friendly country.
Pachȳnum, -ī *nt* S.E. point of Sicily (*now* Cape Passaro).
pācifer, -ī *adj* peace-bringing.
pācificātiō, -ōnis *f* peacemaking.
pācificātor, -ōris *m* peacemaker.
pācificātōrius *adj* peacemaking.
pācificō, -āre *vi* to make a peace ♦ *vt* to appease.
pācificus *adj* peacemaking.
pacīscor, -īscī, -tus *vi* to make a bargain, agree ♦ *vt* to stipulate for; to barter.
pācō, -āre, -āvi, -ātum *vt* to pacify, subdue.
pactiō, -ōnis *f* bargain, agreement, contract; collusion; (*words*) formula.
Pactōlus, -ī *m* river of Lydia (*famous for its gold*).
pactor, -ōris *m* negotiator.
pactum, -ī *nt* agreement, contract.
pactus *ppa of* **pacīscor** ♦ *adj* agreed, settled; betrothed.
Pācuvius, -ī *m* Latin tragic poet.
Padus, -ī *m* river Po.
paeān, -ānis *m* healer, epithet of Apollo; hymn of praise, shout of joy; (*metre*) paeon.
paedagōgus, -ī *m* slave who took children to school.
paedor, -ōris *m* filth.
paelex, -icis *f* mistress, concubine.
paelicātus, -ūs *m* concubinage.
Paelignī, -ōrum *mpl* people of central Italy.
Paelignus *adj see n.*
paene *adv* almost, nearly.
paenīnsula, -ae *f* peninsula.
paenitendus *adj* regrettable.
paenitentia, -ae *f* repentance.
paenitet, -ēre, -uit *vt, vi* (*impers*) to repent, regret, be sorry; to be dissatisfied; **an ~et** is it not enough?
paenula, -ae *f* travelling cloak.
paenulātus *adj* wearing a cloak.
paeōn, -ōnis *m* metrical foot of one long and three short syllables.
paeōnius *adj* healing.
Paestānus *adj see n.*
Paestum, -ī *nt* town in S. Italy.
paetulus *adj* with a slight cast in the eye.
paetus *adj* with a cast in the eye.
pāgānus *adj* rural ♦ *m* villager, yokel.

pāgātim *adv* in every village.
pāgella, -ae *f* small page.
pāgina, -ae *f* (*book*) page, leaf.
pāginula, -ae *f* small page.
pāgus, -ī *m* village, country district; canton.
pāla, -ae *f* spade; (*ring*) bezel.
palaestra, -ae *f* wrestling school, gymnasium; exercise, wrestling; (*RHET*) exercise, training.
palaestricē *adv* in gymnastic fashion.
palaestricus *adj* of the wrestling school.
palaestrīta, -ae *m* head of a wrestling school.
palam *adv* openly, publicly, well-known ♦ *prep* (*with abl*) in the presence of.
Palātīnus *adj* Palatine; imperial.
Palātium, -ī *nt* Palatine Hill in Rome; palace.
palātum, -ī *nt* palate; taste, judgment.
palea, -ae *f* chaff.
paleāria, -ium *ntpl* dewlap.
Palēs, -is *f* goddess of shepherds.
Palīlis *adj* of Pales ♦ *ntpl* festival of Pales.
palimpsēstus, -ī *m* palimpsest.
Palinūrus, -ī *m* pilot of Aeneas; promontory in S. Italy.
paliūrus, -ī *m* Christ's thorn.
palla, -ae *f* woman's robe; tragic costume.
Palladium, -dī *nt* image of Pallas.
Palladius *adj* of Pallas.
Pallantēus *adj see n.*
Pallas, -dis *and* **dos** *f* Athene, Minerva; oil; olive tree.
Pallās, -antis *m* ancestor or son of Evander.
pallēns, -entis *pres p of* **palleō** ♦ *adj* pale; greenish.
palleō, -ēre, -uī *vi* to be pale or yellow; to fade; to be anxious.
pallēscō, -escere, -uī *vi* to turn pale, turn yellow.
palliātus *adj* wearing a Greek cloak.
pallidulus *adj* palish.
pallidus *adj* pale, pallid, greenish; in love.
palliolum, -ī *nt* small cloak, cape, hood.
pallium, -ī *and* **iī** *nt* coverlet; Greek cloak.
pallor, -ōris *m* paleness, fading; fear.
palma, -ae *f* (*hand*) palm, hand; (*oar*) blade; (*tree*) palm, date; branch; (*fig*) prize, victory, glory.
palmāris *adj* excellent.
palmārius *adj* prizewinning.
palmātus *adj* palm-embroidered.
palmes, -itis *m* pruned shoot, branch.
palmētum, -ī *nt* palm grove.
palmifer, -ī *adj* palm-bearing.
palmōsus *adj* palm-clad.
palmula, -ae *f* oar blade.
pālor, -ārī, -ātus *vi* to wander about, straggle.
palpātiō, -ōnis *f* flatteries.
palpātor, -ōris *m* flatterer.
palpebra, -ae *f* eyelid.
palpitō, -āre *vi* to throb, writhe.
palpō, -āre; -or, -ārī *vt* to stroke; to coax, flatter.
palpus, -ī *m* coaxing.

paludāmentum, -ī nt military cloak.
paludātus adj in a general's cloak
paludōsus adj marshy.
palumbēs, -is m/f wood pigeon.
pālus, -ī m stake, pale.
palūs, -ūdis f marsh, pool, lake.
palūster, -ris adj marshy.
pampineus adj of vineshoots.
pampinus, -ī m vineshoot.
Pān, -ānos (acc -āna) m Greek god of shepherds,
    hills and woods, esp associated with Arcadia.
panacēa, -ae f a herb supposed to cure all
    diseases.
Panaetius, -ī m Stoic philosopher.
Panchāaeus adj see n.
Panchāaius adj see n.
Panchāia, -iae f part of Arabia.
panchrēstus adj good for everything.
pancratium, -i and **iī** nt all-in boxing and
    wrestling match.
pandiculor, -āre vi to stretch oneself.
Pandīōn, -onis m king of Athens, father of
    Procne and Philomela.
Pandīonius adj see n.
pandō, -ere, -ī, pānsum and **passum** vt to
    spread out, stretch, extend; to open; (fig) to
    disclose, explain.
pandus adj curved, bent.
pangō, -ere, panxī and **pepigī, pāctum** vt to
    drive in, fasten; to make, compose; to agree,
    settle.
pānicula, -ae f tuft.
pānicum, -ī nt Italian millet.
pānis, -is m bread, loaf.
Pāniscus, -ī m little Pan.
panniculus, -ī m rag.
Pannonia, -ae f country on the middle Danube.
Pannonius adj see n.
pannōsus adj ragged.
pannus, -ī m piece of cloth, rag, patch.
Panormus, -ī f town in Sicily (now Palermo).
pānsa adj splayfoot.
pānsus ppp of **pandō**.
panthēra, -ae f panther.
Panthoidēs, -ae m Euphorbus.
Panthūs, -ī m priest of Apollo at Troy.
panticēs, -um mpl bowels; sausages.
panxī perf of **pangō**.
papae interj (expressing wonder) ooh!
pāpas, -ae m tutor.
papāver, -is nt poppy.
papāvereus adj see n.
Paphius adj see n.
Paphos, -ī f town in Cyprus, sacred to Venus.
pāpiliō, -ōnis m butterfly.
papilla, -ae f teat, nipple; breast.
pappus, -ī m woolly seed.
papula, -ae f pimple.
papȳrifer, -ī adj papyrus-bearing.
papȳrum, -ī nt papyrus; paper.

papȳrus, -ī m/f papyrus; paper.
pār, paris adj equal, like; a match for; proper,
    right ♦ m peer, partner, companion ♦ nt pair;
    pār parī respondēre return like for like;
    parēs cum paribus facillimē congregantur ≈
    birds of a feather flock together; **lūdere pār
    impār** play at evens and odds.
parābilis adj easy to get.
parasīta, -ae f woman parasite.
parasītaster, -rī m sorry parasite.
parasīticus adj of a parasite.
parasītus, -ī m parasite, sponger.
parātē adv with preparation; carefully;
    promptly.
parātiō, -ōnis f trying to get.
paratragoedō, -āre vi to talk theatrically.
parātus ppp of **parō** ♦ adj ready; equipped;
    experienced.
parātus, -ūs m preparation, equipment.
Parca, -ae f Fate.
parcē adv frugally; moderately.
parcō, -cere, pepercī, -sum vt, vi (with dat) to
    spare, economize; to refrain from, forgo;
    (with inf) to forbear, stop.
parcus adj sparing, thrifty; niggardly, scanty;
    chary.
pardus, -ī m panther.
pārēns, -entis pres p of **pāreō** ♦ adj obedient ♦
    mpl subjects.
parēns, -entis m/f parent, father, mother;
    ancestor; founder.
parentālis adj parental ♦ ntpl festival in honour
    of dead ancestors and relatives.
parentō, -āre vi to sacrifice in honour of dead
    parents or relatives; to avenge (with the death of
    another).
pāreō, -ēre, -uī, -itum vi to be visible, be
    evident; (with dat) to obey, submit to, comply
    with; **~et** it is proved.
pariēs, -etis m wall.
parietinae, -ārum fpl ruins.
Parīlia, -ium ntpl festival of Pales.
parīlis adj equal.
pariō, -ere, peperī, -tum vt to give birth to;
    to produce, create, cause; to procure.
Paris, -idis m son of Priam (abductor of Helen).
pariter adv equally, alike; at the same time,
    together.
paritō, -āre vt to get ready.
Parius adj see **Paros**.
parma, -ae f shield, buckler.
parmātus adj armed with a buckler.
parmula, -ae f little shield.
Parnāsis, -idis adj Parnassian.
Parnāsius adj = **Parnāsis**.
Parnāsus, -ī m mount Parnassus in central
    Greece, sacred to the Muses.
parō, -āre, -āvī, -ātum vt to prepare, get
    ready, provide; to intend, set about; to
    procure, get, buy; to arrange.

parocha, -ae *f* provision of necessaries (*to officials travelling*).
parochus, -ī *m* purveyor; host.
paropsis, -dis *f* dish.
Paros, -ī *f* Aegean island (*famous for white marble*).
parra, -ae *f* owl.
Parrhasis, -idis, -ius *adj* Arcadian.
parricīda, -ae *m* parricide, assassin; traitor.
parricīdium, -ī *and* **iī** parricide, murder; high treason.
pars, -tis *f* part, share, fraction; party, side; direction; respect, degree; (*with pl verb*) some; (*pl*) stage part, role; duty, function; **māgna ~** the majority; **māgnam ~tem** largely; **in eam ~tem** in that direction, on that side, in that sense; **nullā ~te** not at all; **omnī ~te** entirely; **ex ~te** partly; **ex alterā ~te** on the other hand; **ex māgnā ~te** to a large extent; **prō ~te** to the best of one's ability; **~tēs agere** play a part; **duae ~tēs** two-thirds; **trēs ~tēs** three-fourths; **multīs ~ibus** a great deal.
parsimōnia, -ae *f* thrift, frugality.
parthenicē, -ēs *f* a plant.
Parthenopē, -ēs *f* old name of Naples.
Parthenopēius *adj see n.*
Parthī, -ōrum *mpl* Parthians (*Rome's great enemy in the East*).
Parthicus, -us *adj see n.*
particeps, -ipis *adj* sharing, partaking ♦ *m* partner.
participō, -āre *vt* to share, impart, inform.
particula, -ae *f* particle.
partim *adv* partly, in part; mostly; some ... others.
partiō, -īre, -īvī, -ītum; -ior, -īrī *vt* to share, distribute, divide.
partītē *adv* methodically.
partītiō, -ōnis *f* distribution, division.
parturiō, -īre *vi* to be in labour; (*fig*) to be anxious ♦ *vt* to teem with, be ready to produce; (*mind*) to brood over.
partus *ppp of* **pariō** ♦ *ntpl* possessions.
partus, -ūs *m* birth; young.
parum *adv* too little, not enough; not very, scarcely.
parumper *adv* for a little while.
parvitās, -ātis *f* smallness.
parvulus, parvolus *adj* very small, slight; quite young ♦ *m* child.
parvus (*comp* **minor** *superl* **minimus**) *adj* small, little, slight; (*time*) short; (*age*) young; **~ī esse** be of little value.
Pascha, -ae *f* Easter.
pāscō, -scere, -vī, -stum *vt* to feed, put to graze; to keep, foster; (*fig*) to feast, cherish ♦ *vi* to graze, browse.
pāscuus *adj* for pasture ♦ *nt* pasture.
Pāsiphaē, -ēs *f* wife of Minos (*mother of the Minotaur*).
passer, -is *m* sparrow; (*fish*) plaice; **~ marīnus** ostrich.

passerculus, -ī *m* little sparrow.
passim *adv* here and there, at random; indiscriminately.
passum, -ī *nt* raisin wine.
passus *ppp of* **pandō** ♦ *adj* spread out, dishevelled; dried.
passus *ppa of* **patior**.
passus, -ūs *m* step, pace; footstep; **mille ~ūs** mile; **mīlia ~uum** miles.
pastillus, -ī *m* lozenge.
pāstor, -ōris *m* shepherd.
pāstōrālis *adj* shepherd's, pastoral.
pāstōricius, pāstōrius *adj* shepherd's.
pāstus *ppp of* **pāscō**.
pāstus, -ūs *m* pasture, food.
Patara, -ae *f* town in Lycia (*with oracle of Apollo*).
Pataraeus *and* **eus** *adj see n.*
Patavīnus *adj see n.*
Patavium, -ī *nt* birthplace of Livy (*now Padua*).
patefaciō, -facere, -fēcī, -factum (*pass* **-fīō, -fierī**) *vt* to open, open up; to disclose.
patefactiō, -ōnis *f* disclosing.
patefīō *etc see* **patefaciō**.
patella, -ae *f* small dish, plate.
patēns, -entis *pres p of* **pateō** ♦ *adj* open, accessible, exposed; broad; evident.
patenter *adv* clearly.
pateō, -ēre, -uī *vi* to be open, accessible, exposed; to extend; to be evident, known.
pater, -ris *m* father; (*pl*) forefathers; senators.
patera, -ae *f* dish, saucer, bowl.
paterfamiliās, patrisfamiliās *m* master of the house.
paternus *adj* father's, paternal; native.
patēscō, -ere *vi* to open out; to extend; to become evident.
patibilis *adj* endurable; sensitive.
patibulātus *adj* pilloried.
patibulum, -ī *nt* fork-shaped yoke, pillory.
patiēns, -entis *pres p of* **patior** ♦ *adj* able to endure; patient; unyielding.
patienter *adv* patiently.
patientia, -ae *f* endurance, stamina; forbearance; submissiveness.
patina, -ae *f* dish, pan.
patior, -tī, -ssus *vt* to suffer, experience; to submit to; to allow, put up with; **facile ~** be well pleased with; **aegrē ~** be displeased with.
Patrae, -ārum *fpl* Greek seaport (*now Patras*).
patrātor, -ōris *m* doer.
patrātus *adj:* **pater ~** officiating priest.
Patrēnsis *adj see n.*
patria, -ae *f* native land, native town, home.
patricius *adj* patrician ♦ *m* aristocrat.
patrimōnium, -ī *and* **iī** *nt* inheritance, patrimony.
patrimus *adj* having a father living.
patrissō, -āre *vi* to take after one's father.
patrītus *adj* of one's father's.
patrius *adj* father's; hereditary, native.

patrō, -āre, -āvī, -ātum vt to achieve, execute, complete.
patrōcinium, -ī and iī nt patronage, advocacy, defence.
patrōcinor, -ārī vi (with dat) to defend, support.
patrōna, -ae f patron goddess; protectress, safeguard.
patrōnus, -ī m patron, protector; (law) advocate, counsel.
patruēlis adj cousin's ♦ m cousin.
patruus, -ī m (paternal) uncle ♦ adj uncle's.
patulus adj open; spreading, broad.
paucitās, -ātis f small number, scarcity.
pauculus adj very few.
paucus adj few, little ♦ mpl a few, the select few ♦ ntpl a few words.
paulātim adv little by little, gradually.
paulisper adv for a little while.
Paullus, -ī m = Paulus.
paulō adv a little, somewhat.
paululus adj very little ♦ nt a little bit.
paulum adv = paulō.
paulus adj little.
Paulus, -ī m Roman surname (esp victor of Pydna).
pauper, -is adj poor; meagre ♦ mpl the poor.
pauperculus adj poor.
pauperiēs, -ēī f poverty.
pauperō, -āre vt to impoverish; to rob.
paupertās, -ātis f poverty, moderate means.
pausa, -ae f stop, end.
pauxillātim adv bit by bit.
pauxillulus adj very little.
pauxillus adj little.
pavefactus adj frightened.
paveō, -ēre, pāvī vi to be terrified, quake ♦ vt to dread, be scared of.
pavēscō, -ere vt, vi to become alarmed (at).
pāvī perf of pāscō.
pavidē adv in a panic.
pavidus adj quaking, terrified.
pavīmentātus adj paved.
pavīmentum, -ī nt pavement, floor.
paviō, -īre vt to strike.
pavitō, -āre vi to be very frightened; to shiver.
pāvō, -ōnis m peacock.
pavor, -ōris m terror, panic.
pāx, pācis f peace; (gods) grace; (mind) serenity ♦ interj enough!; pāce tuā by your leave.
peccātum, -ī nt mistake, fault, sin.
peccō, -āre, -āvī, -ātum vi to make a mistake, go wrong, offend.
pecorōsus adj rich in cattle.
pecten, -inis m comb; (fish) scallop; (loom) reed; (lyre) plectrum.
pectō, -ctere, -xī, -xum vt to comb.
pectus, -oris nt breast; heart, feeling; mind,

thought.
pecū nt flock of sheep; (pl) pastures.
pecuārius adj of cattle ♦ m cattle breeder ♦ ntpl herds.
pecūlātor, -ōris m embezzler.
pecūlātus, -ūs m embezzlement.
pecūliāris adj one's own; special.
pecūliātus adj provided with money.
pecūliōsus adj with private property.
pecūlium, -ī and iī nt small savings, private property.
pecūnia, -ae f property; money.
pecūniārius adj of money.
pecūniōsus adj moneyed, well-off.
pecus, -oris nt cattle, herd, flock; animal.
pecus, -udis f sheep, head of cattle, beast.
pedālis adj a foot long.
pedārius adj (senator) without full rights.
pedes, -itis m foot soldier, infantry ♦ adj on foot.
pedester, -ris adj on foot, pedestrian; infantry- (in cmds); on land; (writing) in prose, prosaic.
pedetemptim adv step by step, cautiously.
pedica, -ae f fetter, snare.
pedis, -is m louse.
pedisequa, -ae f handmaid.
pedisequus, -ī m attendant, lackey.
peditātus, -ūs m infantry.
pedum, -ī nt crook.
Pēgaseus and īs and us adj Pegasean.
Pēgasus, -ī m mythical winged horse (associated with the Muses).
pēgma, -tis nt bookcase; stage elevator.
pēierō, -āre vi to perjure oneself.
pēior, -ōris compar of malus.
pēius adv worse.
pelagius adj of the sea.
pelagus, -ī (pl -ē) nt sea, open sea.
pelamys, -dis f young tunny fish.
Pelasgī, -ōrum mpl Greeks.
Pelasgias and is and us adj Grecian.
Pēleus, -eī and eos (acc -ea) m king of Thessaly (father of Achilles).
Peliās, -ae m uncle of Jason.
Pēlias and iacus and ius adj see Pēlion.
Pēlīdēs, -īdae m Achilles; Neoptolemus.
Pēlion, -ī nt mountain in Thessaly.
Pella, -ae, -ē, -ēs f town of Macedonia (birthplace of Alexander).
pellācia, -ae f attraction.
Pellaeus adj of Pella; Alexandrian; Egyptian.
pellāx, -ācis adj seductive.
pellēctiō, -ōnis f reading through.
pellectus ppp of pelliciō.
pellegō etc see perlegō.
pelliciō, -icere. -exī, -ectum vt to entice, inveigle.
pellicula, -ae f skin, fleece.
pelliō, -ōnis m furrier.

Noun declensions and verb conjugations are shown on pp xiii to xxv. The present infinitive ending of a verb shows to which conjugation it belongs: -āre = 1st; -ēre = 2nd; -ere = 3rd and -īre = 4th. Irregular verbs are shown on p xxvi

pellis, -is _f_ skin, hide; leather, felt; tent.
pellītus _adj_ wearing skins, with leather coats.
pellō, -ere, pepulī, pulsum _vt_ to push, knock, drive; to drive off, rout, expel; (_lyre_) to play; (_mind_) to touch, affect; (_feeling_) to banish.
pellūc- _etc see_ **perlūc-**.
Pelopēis _and_ **ēius** _and_ **ēus** _adj see n._
Pelopidae, -idārum _mpl_ house of Pelops.
Pelopōias _adj see n._
Peloponnēsiacus, -ius _adj see n._
Peloponnēsus, -ī _f_ Peloponnese, S. Greece.
Pelops, -is _m_ son of Tantalus (_grandfather of Agamemnon_).
pelōris, -idis _f_ a large mussel.
pelta, -ae _f_ light shield.
peltastae, -ārum _mpl_ peltasts.
peltātus _adj_ armed with the pelta.
Pēlūsiacus _adj see n._
Pēlūsium, -ī _nt_ Eygptian town at the E. mouth of the Nile.
Pēlūsius _adj see n._
pelvis, -is _f_ basin.
penārius _adj_ provision- (_in cpds_).
Penātēs, -ium _mpl_ spirits of the larder, household gods; home.
penātiger, -ī _adj_ carrying his home gods.
pendeō, -ēre, pependī _vi_ to hang; to overhang, hover; to hang down, be flabby; (_fig_) to depend; to gaze, listen attentively; (_mind_) to be in suspense, be undecided.
pendō, -ere, pependī, pēnsum _vt_ to weigh; to pay; (_fig_) to ponder, value ♦ _vi_ to weigh.
pendulus _adj_ hanging; in doubt.
Pēnēēis _and_ **ēius** _and_ **ēus** _adj see n._
Pēnelopē, ēs _and_ **a, -ae** _f_ wife of Ulysses (_famed for her constancy_).
Pēnelopēus _adj see n._
penes _prep_ (_with acc_) in the power or possession of; in the house of, with.
penetrābilis _adj_ penetrable; piercing.
penetrālis _adj_ penetrating; inner, inmost ♦ _ntpl_ inner room, interior, sanctuary; remote parts.
penetrō, -āre, -āvī, -ātum _vt, vi_ to put into, penetrate, enter.
Pēnēus, -ī _m_ chief river of Thessaly.
pēnicillus, -ī _m_ painter's brush, pencil.
pēniculus, -ī _m_ brush; sponge.
pēnis, -is _m_ penis.
penitē _adj_ inwardly.
penitus _adv_ inside, deep within; deeply, from the depths; utterly, thoroughly.
penna, pinna, -ae _f_ feather, wing; flight.
pennātus _adj_ winged.
penniger, -ī _adj_ feathered.
pennipotēns, -entis _adj_ winged.
pennula, -ae _f_ little wing.
pēnsilis _adj_ hanging, pendent.
pēnsiō, -ōnis _f_ payment, instalment.
pēnsitō, -āre _vt_ to pay; to consider.
pēnsō, -āre, -āvī, -ātum _vt_ to weight out; to compensate, repay; to consider, judge.
pēnsum, -ī _nt_ spinner's work; task, duty;

weight, value; **~ī esse** be of importance; **~ī habēre** care at all about.
pēnsus _ppp of_ **pendō**.
pentēris, -is _f_ quinquereme.
Pentheus, -eī _and_ **eos** _m_ king of Thebes (_killed by Bacchantes_).
pēnūria, -ae _f_ want, need.
penus, -ūs _and_ **ī** _m/f_, **-um, -ī, -us, -oris** _nt_ provisions, store of food.
pependī _perf of_ **pendeō**; _perf of_ **pendō**.
pepercī _perf of_ **parcō**.
peperī _perf of_ **pariō**.
pepigī _perf of_ **pangō**.
peplum, -ī _nt_, **-us, -ī** _m_ state robe of Athena.
pepulī _perf of_ **pellō**.
per _prep_ (_with acc: space_) through, all over; (_: time_) throughout, during; (_: means_) by, by means of; (_: cause_) by reason of, for the sake of; **~ īram** in anger; **~ manūs** from hand to hand; **~ mē** as far as I am concerned; **~ vim** forcibly; **~ ego tē deōs ōrō** in Heaven's name I beg you.
pēra, -ae _f_ bag.
perabsurdus _adj_ very absurd.
peraccommodātus _adj_ very convenient.
perācer, -ris _adj_ very sharp.
peracerbus _adj_ very sour.
peracēscō, -ēscere, -uī _vi_ to get vexed.
perāctiō, -ōnis _f_ last act.
perāctus _ppp of_ **peragō**.
peracūtē _adv_ very acutely.
peracūtus _adj_ very sharp, very clear.
peradulēscēns, -entis _adj_ very young.
peraequē _adv_ quite equally, uniformly.
peragitātus _adj_ harried.
peragō, -agere, -ēgī, -āctum _vt_ to carry through, complete; to pass through, pierce; to disturb; (_law_) to prosecute to a conviction; (_words_) to go over, describe.
peragrātiō, -ōnis _f_ travelling.
peragrō, -āre, -āvī, -ātum _vt_ to travel through, traverse.
peramāns, -antis _adj_ very fond.
peramanter _adv_ devotedly.
perambulō, -āre _vt_ to walk through, traverse.
peramoenus _adj_ very pleasant.
peramplus _adj_ very large.
perangustē _adv see adj._
perangustus _adj_ very narrow.
perantīquus _adj_ very old.
perappositus _adj_ very suitable.
perarduus _adj_ very difficult.
perargūtus _adj_ very witty.
perarō, -āre _vt_ to furrow; to write (on wax).
perattentē _adv see adj._
perattentus _adj_ very attentive.
peraudiendus _adj_ to be heard to the end.
perbacchor, -ārī _vt_ to carouse through.
perbeātus _adj_ very happy.
perbellē _adv_ very nicely.
perbene _adv_ very well.
perbenevolus _adj_ very friendly.
perbenignē _adv_ very kindly.

perbibō, -ere, -ī vt to drink up, imbibe.
perbītō, -ere vi to perish.
perblandus adj very charming.
perbonus adj very good.
perbrevis adj very short.
perbreviter adv very briefly.
perca, -ae f perch.
percalefactus adj quite hot.
percalēscō, -ēscere, -uī vi to become quite
hot.
percallēscō, -ēscere, -uī vi to become quite
hardened ♦ vt to become thoroughly versed
in.
percārus adj very dear.
percautus adj very cautious.
percelebrō, -āre vt to talk much of.
perceler, -is adj very quick.
perceleriter adv see adj.
percellō, -ellere, -ulī, -ulsum vt to knock
down, upset; to strike; (fig) to ruin;
overthrow; to discourage, unnerve.
percēnseō, -ēre, -uī vt to count over; (place)
to travel through; (fig) to review
perceptiō, -ōnis f harvesting; understanding,
idea.
perceptus ppp of percipiō.
percieō, -iēre, -iō, -īre vt to rouse, excite.
percipiō, -ipere, -ēpī, -eptum vt to take, get
hold of; to gather in; (senses) to feel; (mind)
to learn, grasp, understand.
percitus ppp of percieō ♦ adj roused, excited;
excitable.
percoctus ppp of percoquō.
percolō, -āre vt to filter through.
percolō, -olere, -oluī, -ultum vt to embellish;
to honour.
percōmis adj very friendly.
percommodē adv very conveniently.
percommodus adj very suitable
percontātiō, -ōnis f asking questions.
percontātor, -ōris m inquisitive person.
percontor, -ārī, -ātus vt to question, inquire.
percontumāx, -ācis adj very obstinate.
percoquō, -quere, -xī, -ctum v to cook
thoroughly, heat, scorch, riper.
percrēbēscō, percrēbrēscō, -ēscere, -uī vi
to be spread abroad.
percrepō, -āre, -uī vi to resound.
perculī perf of percellō.
perculsus ppp of percellō.
percultus ppp of percolō.
percunct- etc see percont-.
percupidus adj very fond.
percupiō, -ere vi to wish very much.
percūriōsus adj very inquisitive.
percūrō, -āre vt to heal complete y.
percurrō, -rrere, -currī and rrī, -rsum vt to
run through, hurry over; (fig) to run over,
look over ♦ vi to run along; to pass.
percursātiō, -ōnis f travelling through.

percursiō, -ōnis f running over.
percursō, -āre vi to rove about.
percursus ppp of percurrō.
percussiō, -ōnis f beating; (fingers) snapping;
(music) time.
percussor, -ōris m assassin.
percussus ppp of percutiō.
percussus, -ūs m striking.
percutiō, -tere, -ssī, -ssum vt to strike, beat;
to strike through, kill; (feeling) to shock,
impress, move; (colloq) to trick.
perdēlīrus adj quite crazy.
perdidī perf of perdō.
perdifficilis adj very difficult.
perdifficiliter adv with great difficulty.
perdignus adj most worthy.
perdīligēns, -entis adj very diligent.
perdīligenter adv see adj.
perdiscō, -scere, -dicī vt to learn by heart.
perdisertē adv very eloquently.
perditē adv desperately; recklessly.
perditor, -ōris m destroyer.
perditus ppp of perdō ♦ adj desperate, ruined;
abandoned, profligate.
perdiū adv for a very long time.
perdiūturnus adj protracted.
perdīves, -itis adj very rich.
perdīx, -īcis m/f partridge.
perdō, -ere, -idī, -itum vt to destroy, ruin; to
squander, waste; to lose; dī tē ~uint curse
you!
perdoceō, -ēre, -uī, -tum vt to teach
thoroughly.
perdolēscō, -ēscere, -uī vi to take it to heart.
perdomō, -āre, -uī, -itum vt to subjugate,
tame completely.
perdormīscō, -ere vi to sleep on.
perdūcō, -ūcere, -ūxī, -uctum vt to bring,
guide to; to induce, seduce; to spread over;
to prolong, continue.
perductō, -āre vt to guide.
perductor, -ōris m guide; pander.
perductus ppp of perdūcō.
perduelliō, -ōnis f treason.
perduellis, -is m enemy.
perduint archaic subj of perdō.
perdūrō, -āre vi to endure, hold out.
peredō, -edere, -ēdī, -ēsum vt to consume,
devour.
peregrē adv away from home, abroad; from
abroad.
peregrīnābundus adj travelling.
peregrīnātiō, -ōnis f living abroad, travel.
peregrīnātor, -ōris m traveller.
peregrīnitās, -ātis f foreign manners.
peregrīnor, -ārī, -ātus vi to be abroad, travel;
to be a stranger.
peregrīnus adj foreign, strange ♦ m
foreigner, alien.
perēlegāns, -antis adj very polished.

perēleganter *adv* in a very polished manner.
perēloquēns, -entis *adj* very eloquent.
perēmī *perf of* **perimō**.
peremnia, -ium *ntpl* auspices taken on crossing a river.
peremptus *ppp of* **perimō**.
perendiē *adv* the day after tomorrow.
perendinus *adj* (the day) after tomorrow.
perennis *adj* perpetual, unfailing.
perennitās, -ātis *f* continuance.
perennō, -āre *vi* to last a long time.
pereō, -īre, -iī, -itum *vi* to be lost, pass away, perish, die; (*fig*) to be wasted, be in love, be undone.
perequitō, -āre *vt, vi* to ride up and down.
pererrō, -āre, -āvī, -ātum *vt* to roam over, cover.
perērudītus *adj* very learned.
perēsus *ppp of* **peredō**.
perexcelsus *adj* very high.
perexiguē *adv* very meagrely.
perexiguus *adj* very small, very short.
perfacētē *adv* very wittily.
perfacētus *adj* very witty.
perfacile *adv* very easily.
perfacilis *adj* very easy; very courteous.
perfamiliāris *adj* very intimate ♦ *m* very close friend.
perfectē *adv* fully.
perfectiō, -ōnis *f* completion, perfection.
perfector, -ōris *m* perfecter.
perfectus *ppp of* **perficiō** ♦ *adj* complete, perfect.
perferō, -ferre, -tulī, -lātum *vt* to carry through, bring, convey; to bear, endure, put up with; (*work*) to finish, bring to completion; (*law*) to get passed; (*message*) to bring news.
perficiō, -icere, -ēcī, -ectum *vt* to carry out, finish, complete; to perfect; to cause, make.
perficus *adj* perfecting.
perfidēlis *adj* very loyal.
perfidia, -ae *f* treachery, dishonesty.
perfidiōsē *adv see adj*.
perfidiōsus *adj* treacherous, dishonest.
perfidus *adj* treacherous, faithless.
perfigō, -gere, -xī, -xum *vt* to pierce.
perflābilis *adj* that can be blown through.
perflāgitiōsus *adj* very wicked.
perflō, -āre *vt* to blow through, blow over.
perfluctuō, -āre *vt* to flood through.
perfluō, -ere, -xī *vi* to run out, leak.
perfodiō, -odere, -ōdī, -ossum *vt* to dig through, excavate, pierce.
perforō, -āre, -āvī, -ātum *vt* to bore through, pierce.
perfortiter *adv* very bravely.
perfossor, -ōris *m*: ~ parietum burglar.
perfossus *ppp of* **perfodiō**.
perfrāctus *ppp of* **perfringō**.
perfrēgī *perf of* **perfringō**.
perfremō, -ere *vi* to snort along.
perfrequēns, -entis *adj* much frequented.
perfricō, -āre, -uī, -tum *and* **ātum** *vt* to rub all

over; **ōs** ~ put on a bold face.
perfrigefaciō, -ere *vt* to make shudder.
perfrigēscō, -gēscere, -xī *vi* to catch a bad cold.
perfrigidus *adj* very cold.
perfringō, -ingere, -ēgī, -āctum *vt* to break through, fracture, wreck; (*fig*) to violate; to affect powerfully.
perfrīxī *perf of* **perfrigēscō**.
perfrūctus *ppa of* **perfruor**.
perfruor, -uī, -ūctus *vi* (*with abl*) to enjoy to the full; to fulfil.
perfuga, -ae *m* deserter.
perfugiō, -ugere, -ūgī *vi* to flee for refuge, desert to.
perfugium, -ī *and* **iī** *nt* refuge, shelter.
perfūnctiō, -ōnis *f* performing.
perfūnctus *ppa of* **perfungor**.
perfundō, -undere, -ūdī, -ūsum *vt* to pour over, drench, besprinkle; to dye; (*fig*) to flood, fill.
perfungor, -gī, perfūnctus *vi* (*with abl*) to perform, discharge; to undergo.
perfurō, -ere *vi* to rage furiously.
perfūsus *ppp of* **perfundō**.
Pergama, -ōrum *ntpl* Troy.
Pergamēnus *adj see n*.
Pergameus *adj* Trojan.
Pergamum, -ī *nt* town in Mysia (*famous for its library*).
pergaudeō, -ēre *vi* to be very glad.
pergō, -gere, -rēxī, -rēctum *vi* to proceed, go on, continue ♦ *vt* to go on with, continue.
pergraecor, -ārī *vi* to have a good time.
pergrandis *adj* very large; very old.
pergraphicus *adj* very artful.
pergrātus *adj* very pleasant.
pergravis *adj* very weighty.
pergraviter *adv* very seriously.
pergula, -ae *f* balcony; school; brothel.
perhibeō, -ēre, -uī, -itum *vt* to assert, call, cite.
perhīlum *adv* very little.
perhonōrificē *adv* very respectfully.
perhonōrificus *adj* very complimentary.
perhorrēscō, -ēscere, -uī *vi* to shiver, tremble violently ♦ *vt* to have a horror of.
perhorridus *adj* quite horrible.
perhūmāniter *adv see adj*.
perhūmānus *adj* very polite.
Periclēs, -is *and* **ī** *m* famous Athenian statesman and orator.
periclitātiō, -ōnis *f* experiment.
periclitor, -ārī, -ātus *vt* to test, try; to risk, endanger ♦ *vi* to attempt, venture; to run a risk, be in danger.
periculōsē *adv see adj*.
periculōsus *adj* dangerous, hazardous.
periculum (periclum), -ī *nt* danger, risk; trial, attempt; (*law*) lawsuit, writ.
peridōneus *adj* very suitable.
periī *perf of* **pereō**.
perillūstris *adj* very notable; highly honoured.

perimbēcillus adj very weak.
perimō, -imere, -ēmī, -emptum vt to destroy, prevent, kill.
perincommodē adv see adj.
perincommodus adj very inconvenient.
perinde adv just as, exactly as.
perindulgēns, -entis adj very tender.
perinfirmus adj very feeble.
peringeniōsus adj very clever.
perinīquus adj very unfair; very discontented.
perinsignis adj very conspicuous.
perinvītus adj very unwilling.
periodus, -ī f sentence, period.
Peripatēticī, -ōrum mpl Peripatetics (followers of Aristotle).
peripetasmata, -um ntpl curtains.
perīrātus adj very angry.
periscelis, -dis f anklet.
peristrōma, -atis nt coverlet.
peristylum, -ī nt colonnade, peristyle.
perītē adv expertly.
perītia, -ae f practical knowledge skill.
perītus adj experienced, skilled, expert.
periūcundē adv see adj.
periūcundus adj very enjoyable.
periūrium, -ī and iī nt perjury.
periūrō see pēierō.
periūrus adj perjured, lying.
perlābor, -bī, -psus vi to glide along or through, move on.
perlaetus adj very glad.
perlāpsus ppa of perlābor.
perlātē adv very extensively.
perlateō, -ēre vi to lie quite hidden.
perlātus ppp of perferō.
perlegō, -egere, -ēgī, -ēctum vt to survey; to read through.
perlevis adj very slight.
perleviter adv see adj.
perlibēns, -entis adj very willing.
perlibenter adv see adj.
perlīberālis adj very genteel.
perlīberāliter adv very liberally.
perlibet, -ēre vi (impers) (I) should very much like.
perliciō etc see polliciō.
perlitō, -āre, -āvī, -ātum vi to sacrifice with auspicious results.
perlongē adv very far.
perlongus adj very long, very tedious.
perlub- etc see perlib-.
perlūceō, -cēre, -xī vi to shine through, be transparent; (fig) to be quite intelligible.
perlūcidulus adj transparent.
perlūcidus adj transparent; very bright.
perlūctuōsus adj very mournful.
perluō, -ere vt to wash thoroughly; (pass) to bathe.
perlūstrō, -āre vt to traverse; (fig) to survey.

permāgnus adj very big, very great.
permānanter adv by flowing through.
permānāscō, -ere vi to penetrate.
permaneō, -anēre, -ānsī, -ānsum vi to last, persist, endure to the end.
permānō, -āre, -āvī, -ātum vi to flow or ooze through, penetrate.
permānsiō, -ōnis f continuing, persisting.
permarīnus adj of seafaring.
permātūrēscō, -ēscere, -uī vi to ripen fully.
permediocris adj very moderate.
permēnsus ppa of permētior.
permeō, -āre vt, vi to pass through, penetrate.
permētior, -tīrī, -nsus vt to measure out; to traverse.
permīrus adj very wonderful.
permisceō, -scēre, -scuī, -xtum vt to mingle, intermingle; to throw into confusion.
permissiō, -ōnis f unconditional surrender; permission.
permissus ppp of permittō.
permissus, -ūs m leave, permission.
permitiālis adj destructive.
permitiēs, -ēī f ruin.
permittō, -ittere, -īsī, -issum vt to let go, let pass; to hurl; to give up, entrust, concede; to allow, permit.
permixtē adv see adj.
permixtiō, -ōnis f mixture; disturbance.
permixtus ppp of permisceō ♦ adj promiscuous, disordered.
permodestus adj very moderate.
permolestē adv with much annoyance.
permolestus adj very troublesome.
permōtiō, -ōnis f excitement; emotion.
permōtus ppp of permoveō.
permoveō, -ovēre, -ōvī, -ōtum vt to stir violently; (fig) to influence, induce; to excite, move deeply.
permulceō, -cēre, -sī, -sum vt to stroke, caress; (fig) to charm, flatter; to soothe, appease.
permulsus ppp of permulceō.
permultus adj very much, very many.
permūniō, -īre, -īvī, -ītum vt to finish fortifying; to fortify strongly.
permūtātiō, -ōnis f change, exchange.
permūtō, -āre, -āvī, -ātum vt to change completely; to exchange; (money) to remit by bill of exchange.
perna, -ae f ham.
pernecessārius adj very necessary; very closely related.
pernecesse adj indispensable.
pernegō, -āre v to deny flatly.
perniciābilis adj ruinous.
perniciēs, -ēī f destruction, ruin, death.
perniciōsē adv see adj.
perniciōsus adj ruinous.

pernīcitās, -ātis f agility, swiftness.
pernīciter adv nimbly.
pernimius adj much too much.
pernīx, -īcis adj nimble, agile, swift.
pernōbilis adj very famous.
pernoctō, -āre vi to stay all night.
pernōscō, -scere, -vī, -tum vt to examine thoroughly; to become fully acquainted with, know thoroughly.
pernōtēscō, -ēscere, -uī vi to become generally known.
pernōtus ppp of **pernōscō**.
pernox, -octis adj all night long.
pernumerō, -āre vt to count up.
pērō, -ōnis m rawhide boot.
perobscūrus adj very obscure.
perodiōsus adj very troublesome.
perofficiōsē adv very attentively.
peroleō, -ēre vi to give off a strong smell.
peropportūnē adv very opportunely.
peropportūnus adj very timely.
peroptātō adv very much to one's wish.
peropus est it is most essential.
perōrātiō, -ōnis f peroration.
perōrnātus adj very ornate.
perōrnō, -āre vt to give great distinction to.
perōrō, -āre, -āvī, -ātum vt to plead at length; (speech) to bring to a close; to conclude.
perōsus adj detesting.
perpācō, -āre vt to quieten completely.
perparcē adv very stingily.
perparvulus adj very tiny.
perparvus adj very small.
perpāstus adj well fed.
perpauculus adj very very few.
perpaucus adj very little, very few.
perpaulum, -ī nt a very little.
perpauper, -is adj very poor.
perpauxillum, -ī nt a very little.
perpellō, -ellere, -ulī, -ulsum vt to urge, force, influence.
perpendiculum, -ī nt plumbline; **ad ~** perpendicularly.
perpendō, -endere, -endī, -ēnsum vt to weigh carefully, judge.
perperam adv wrongly, falsely.
perpes, -etis adj continuous.
perpessiō, -ōnis f suffering, enduring.
perpessus ppa of **perpetior**.
perpetior, -tī, -ssus vt to endure patiently, allow.
perpetrō, -āre, -āvī, -ātum vt to perform, carry out.
perpetuitās, -ātis f continuity, uninterrupted duration.
perpetuō adv without interruption, forever, utterly.
perpetuō, -āre vt to perpetuate, preserve.
perpetuus adj continuous, entire; universal; **in ~um** forever.
perplaceō, -ēre vi to please greatly.
perplexē adv obscurely.

perplexor, -ārī vi to cause confusion.
perplexus adj confused, intricate, obscure.
perplicātus adj interlaced.
perpluō, -ere vi to let the rain through, leak.
perpoliō, -īre, -īvī, -ītum vt to polish thoroughly.
perpolītus adj finished, refined.
perpopulor, -ārī, -ātus vt to ravage completely.
perpōtātiō, -ōnis f drinking bout.
perpōtō, -āre vi to drink continuously ♦ vt to drink off.
perprimō, -ere vt to lie on.
perpugnāx, -ācis adj very pugnacious.
perpulcher, -rī adj very beautiful.
perpulī perf of **perpellō**.
perpūrgō, -āre, -āvī, -ātum vt to make quite clean; to explain.
perpusillus adj very little.
perquam adv very, extremely.
perquīrō, -rere, -sīvī, -sītum vt to search for, inquire after; to examine carefully.
perquīsītius adv more accurately.
perrārō adv very seldom.
perrārus adj very uncommon.
perrecondītus adj very abstruse.
perrēpō, -ere vt to crawl over.
perrēptō, -āre, -āvī, -ātum vt, vi to creep about or through.
perrēxī perf of **pergō**.
perrīdiculē adv see adj.
perrīdiculus adj very laughable.
perrogātiō, -ōnis f passing (of a law).
perrogō, -āre vt to ask one after another.
perrumpō, -umpere, -ūpī, -uptum vt, vi to break through, force a way through; (fig) to break down.
perruptus ppp of **perrumpō**.
Persae, -ārum mpl Persians.
persaepe adv very often.
persalsē adv see adj.
persalsus adj very witty.
persalūtātiō, -ōnis f greeting everyone in turn.
persalūtō, -āre vt to greet in turn.
persānctē adv most solemnly.
persapiēns, -entis adj very wise.
persapienter adv see adj.
perscienter adv very discreetly.
perscindō, -ndere, -dī, -ssum vt to tear apart.
perscītus adj very smart.
perscrībō, -bere, -psī, -ptum vt to write in full; to describe, report; (record) to enter; (money) to make over in writing.
perscrīptiō, -ōnis f entry; assignment.
perscrīptor, -ōris m writer.
perscrīptus ppp of **perscrībō**.
perscrūtor, -ārī, -ātus vt to search, examine thoroughly.
persecō, -āre, -uī, -tum vt to dissect; to do away with.
persector, -ārī vt to investigate.

persecūtiō, -ōnis f (law) prosecution.
persecūtus ppa of persequor.
persedeō, -edēre, -ēdī, -essum vi to remain sitting.
persegnis adj very slow.
Persēius adj see Perseus.
persentiō, -entīre, -ēnsī vt to see clearly; to feel deeply.
persentīscō, -ere vi to begin to see; to begin to feel.
Persephonē, -ēs f Proserpine.
persequor, -quī, -cūtus vt to follow all the way; to pursue, chase, hunt after; to overtake; (pattern) to be a follower of, copy; (enemy) to proceed against, take revenge on; (action) to perform, carry out; (words) to write down, describe.
Persēs, -ae m last king of Macedonia.
Persēs, -ae m Persian.
Perseus, -eī and eos (acc -ea) m son of Danaë (killer of Medusa, rescuer of Andromeda).
Persēus adj see n.
persevērāns, -antis pres p of persevērō ♦ adj persistent.
persevēranter adv see adj.
persevērāntia, -ae f persistence.
persevērō, -āre, -āvī, -ātum vi to persist ♦ vt to persist in.
persevērus adj very strict.
Persicus adj Persian; of Perses.
Persicum nt peach.
persīdō, -īdere, -ēdī, -essum vi to sink down into.
persignō, -āre vt to record.
persimilis adj very like.
persimplex, -icis adj very simple.
Persis, -idis f Persia.
persistō, -istere, -titī vi to persist.
persōlus adj one and only.
persolūtus ppp of persolvō.
persolvō, -vere, -vī, -ūtum vt to pay, pay up; to explain.
persōna, -ae f mask; character, part; person, personality.
persōnātus adj masked; in an assumed character.
personō, -āre, -uī, -itum vi to resound, ring (with); to play ♦ vt to make resound; to cry aloud.
perspectē adv intelligently.
perspectō, -āre vt to have a look through.
perspectus ppp of perspiciō ♦ adj well-known.
perspeculor, -ārī vt to reconnoitre.
perspergō, -gere, -sī, -sum vt to besprinkle.
perspicāx, -ācis adj sharp, shrewd.
perspicientia, -ae f full understanding.
perspiciō, -icere, -exī, -ectum vt to see through; to examine, observe.
perspicuē adv clearly.
perspicuitās, -ātis f clarity.

perspicuus adj transparent; clear, evident.
persternō, -ernere, -rāvī, -rātum vt to pave all over.
perstimulō, -āre vt to rouse violently.
perstitī perf of persistō; perf of perstō.
perstō, -āre, -itī, -ātum vi to stand fast; to last; to continue, persist.
perstrātus ppp of persternō.
perstrepō, -ere vi to make a lot of noise.
perstrictus ppp of perstringō.
perstringō, -ingere, -inxī, -ictum vt to graze, touch lightly; (words) to touch on, belittle, censure; (senses) to dull, deaden.
perstudiōsē adv very eagerly.
perstudiōsus adj very fond.
persuādeō, -dēre, -sī, -sum vi (with dat) to convince, persuade; ~sum habeō, mihi ~sum est I am convinced.
persuāsiō, -ōnis f convincing.
persuāsus, -ūs m persuasion.
persubtīlis adj very fine.
persultō, -āre vt, vi to prance about, frisk over.
pertaedet, -dēre, -sum est vt (impers) to be weary of, be sick of.
pertegō, -egere, -ēxī, -ēctum vt to cover over.
pertemptō, -āre vt to test carefully; to consider well; to pervade, seize.
pertendō, -ere, -ī vi to push on, persist ♦ vt to go on with.
pertenuis adj very small, very slight.
perterebrō, -āre vt to bore through.
pertergeō, -gēre, -sī, -sum vt to wipe over; to touch lightly.
perterrefaciō, -ere vt to scare thoroughly.
perterreō, -ēre, -uī, -itum vt to frighten thoroughly.
perterricrepus adj with a terrifying crash.
perterritus adj terrified.
pertexō, -ere, -uī, -tum vt to accomplish.
pertica, -ae f pole, staff.
pertimefactus adj very frightened.
pertimēscō, -ēscere, -uī vt, vi to be very alarmed, be very afraid of.
pertinācia, -ae f perseverance, stubbornness.
pertināciter adv see adj.
pertināx, -ācis adj very tenacious; unyielding, stubborn.
pertineō, -ēre, -uī vi to extend, reach; to tend, lead to, concern; to apply, pertain, belong; quod ~et ad as far as concerns.
pertingō, -ere vi to extend.
pertolerō, -āre vt to endure to the end.
pertorqueō, -ēre vt to distort.
pertractātē adv in a hackneyed fashion.
pertractātiō, -ōnis f handling.
pertractō, -āre vt to handle, feel all over; (fig) to treat, study.
pertractus ppp of pertrahō.

pertrahō, -here, -xī, -ctum *vt* to drag across, take forcibly; to entice.
pertrect- *etc see* **pertract-**.
pertristis *adj* very sad, very morose.
pertulī *perf of* **perferō**.
pertumultuōsē *adv* very excitedly.
pertundō, -undere, -udī, -ūsum *vt* to perforate.
perturbātē *adv* in confusion.
perturbātiō, -ōnis *f* confusion, disturbance; emotion.
perturbātrīx, -īcis *f* disturber.
perturbātus *ppp of* **perturbō** ♦ *adj* troubled; alarmed.
perturbō, -āre, -āvī, -ātum *vt* to throw into disorder, upset, alarm.
perturpis *adj* scandalous.
pertūsus *ppp of* **pertundō** ♦ *adj* in holes, leaky.
perungō, -ungere, -ūnxī, -ūnctum *vt* to smear all over.
perurbānus *adj* very refined; over-fine.
perūrō, -rere, -ssī, -stum *vt* to burn up, scorch; to inflame, chafe; to freeze, nip.
Perusia, -iae *f* Etruscan town (*now* Perugia).
Perusīnus *adj see n.*
perūstus *ppp of* **perūrō**.
perūtilis *adj* very useful.
pervādō, -dere, -sī, -sum *vt, vi* to pass through, spread through; to penetrate, reach.
pervagātus *adj* widespread, well-known; general.
pervagor, -ārī, -ātus *vi* to range, rove about; to extend, spread ♦ *vt* to pervade.
pervagus *adj* roving.
pervariē *adv* very diversely.
pervastō, -āre, -āvī, -ātum *vt* to devastate.
pervāsus *ppp of* **pervādō**.
pervectus *ppp of* **pervehō**.
pervehō, -here, -xī, -ctum *vt* to carry, convey, bring through; (*pass*) to ride, drive, sail through; to attain.
pervellō, -ere, -ī *vt* to pull, twitch, pinch; to stimulate; to disparage.
perveniō, -enīre, -ēnī, -entum *vi* to come to, arrive, reach; to attain to.
pervēnor, -ārī *vi* to chase through.
perversē *adv* perversely.
perversitās, -ātis *f* perverseness.
perversus (pervorsus) *ppp of* **pervertō** ♦ *adj* awry, squint; wrong, perverse.
pervertō, -tere, -tī, -sum *vt* to overturn, upset; to overthrow, undo; (*speech*) to confute.
pervesperī *adv* very late.
pervestīgātiō, -ōnis *f* thorough search.
pervestīgō, -āre, -āvī, -ātum *vt* to track down; to investigate.
pervetus, -eris *adj* very old.
pervetustus *adj* antiquated.
pervicācia, -ae *f* obstinacy; firmness.
pervicāciter *adv see adj.*
pervicāx, -ācis *adj* obstinate, wilful; dogged.

pervictus *ppp of* **pervincō**.
pervideō, -idēre, -īdī, -īsum *vt* to look over, survey; to consider; to discern.
pervigeō, -ēre, -uī *vi* to continue to flourish.
pervigil, -is *adj* awake, watchful.
pervigilātiō, -ōnis *f* vigil.
pervigilium, -ī *and* **iī** *nt* vigil.
pervigilō, -āre, -āvī, -ātum *vt, vi* to stay awake all night, keep vigil.
pervīlis *adj* very cheap.
pervincō, -incere, -īcī, -ictum *vt, vi* to conquer completely; to outdo, surpass; to prevail upon, effect; (*argument*) to carry a point, maintain, prove.
pervīvō, -ere *vi* to survive.
pervius *adj* passable, accessible.
pervolgō *etc see* **pervulgō**.
pervolitō, -āre *vt, vi* to fly about.
pervolō, -āre, -āvī, -ātum *vt, vi* to fly through *or* over, fly to.
pervolō, -elle, -oluī *vi* to wish very much.
pervolūtō, -āre *vt* (*books*) to read through.
pervolvō, -vere, -vī, -ūtum *vt* to tumble about; (*book*) to read through; (*pass*) to be very busy (with).
pervor- *etc see* **perver-**.
pervulgātus *adj* very common.
pervulgō, -āre, -āvī, -ātum *vt* to make public, impart; to haunt.
pēs, pedis *m* foot; (*length*) foot; (*verse*) foot, metre; (*sailrope*) sheet; **pedem cōnferre** come to close quarters; **pedem referre** go back; **ante pedēs** self-evident; **pedibus** on foot, by land; **pedibus īre in sententiam** take sides; **pedibus aequīs** (NAUT) with the wind right aft; **servus ā pedibus** footman.
pessimē *superl of* **male**.
pessimus *superl of* **malus**.
pessulus, -ī *m* bolt.
pessum *adv* to the ground, to the bottom; ~ **dare** put an end to, ruin, destroy; ~ **īre** sink, perish.
pestifer, -ī *adj* pestilential; baleful, destructive.
pestilēns, -entis *adj* unhealthy; destructive.
pestilentia, -ae *f* plague, pest; unhealthiness.
pestilitās, -ātis *f* plague.
pestis, -is *f* plague, pest; ruin, destruction.
petasātus *adj* wearing the petasus.
petasunculus, -ī *m* small leg of pork.
petasus, -ī *m* broadbrimmed hat.
petessō, -ere *vt* to be eager for.
petītiō, -ōnis *f* thrust, attack; request, application; (*office*) candidature, standing for; (*law*) civil suit, right of claim.
petītor, -ōris *m* candidate; plaintiff.
petītūriō, -īre *vt* to long to be a candidate.
petītus *ppp of* **petō**.
petītus, -ūs *m* falling to.
petō, -ere, -īvī *and* **iī, -ītum** *vt* to aim at, attack; (*place*) to make for, go to; to seek, look for, demand, ask; to go and fetch; (*law*) to sue; (*love*) to court; (*office*) to stand for.

petorritum, -ī nt carriage.
petrō, -ōnis m yokel.
Petrōnius, -ī m arbiter of fashion under Nero.
petulāns, -antis adj pert, impudent lascivious.
petulanter adv see adj.
petulantia, -ae f pertness, impudence.
petulcus adj butting.
pexus ppp of **pectō**.
Phaeāccius and **cus, -x** adj Phaeacian.
Phaeāces, -cum mpl fabulous islanders in the Odyssey.
Phaedra, -ae f stepmother of Hippolytus.
Phaedrus, -ī m pupil of Socrates; writer of Latin fables.
Phaethōn, -ontis m son of the Sun (killed while driving his father's chariot).
Phaethonteus adj see n.
Phaethontiades, -um fpl sisters of Phaethon.
phalangae, -ārum fpl wooden rollers.
phalangītae, -ārum mpl soldiers of a phalanx.
phalanx, -gis f phalanx; troops, battle order.
Phalaris, -dis m tyrant of Agrigentum
phalerae, -ārum fpl medallions badges; (horse) trappings.
phalerātus adj wearing medallions; ornamented.
Phalēreus, -icus adj see n.
Phalērum, -ī nt harbour of Athens.
pharetra, -ae f quiver.
pharetrātus adj wearing a quiver
Pharius adj see n.
pharmaceutria, -ae f sorceress.
pharmacopōla, -ae m quack doctor.
Pharsālicus, -ius adj see n.
Pharsālus (-os), -ī f town in Thessaly (where Caesar defeated Pompey).
Pharus (-os), -ī f island off Alexandria with a famous lighthouse; lighthouse.
phasēlus, -ī m/f French beans; (boat) pinnace.
Phāsiacus adj Colchian.
Phāsiānus, -āna m/f pheasant.
Phāsis, -dis and **dos** m river of Colchis.
Phāsis adj see n.
phasma, -tis nt ghost.
Pherae, -ārum fpl town in Thessaly (home of Admetus).
Pheraeus adj see n.
phiala, -ae f saucer.
Phīdiacus adj see n.
Phīdiās, -ae m famous Athenian sculptor.
philēma, -tis nt kiss.
Philippī, -ōrum mpl town in Macedonia (where Brutus and Cassius were defeated).
Philippēus adj see n.
Philippicae fpl Cicero's speeches against Antony.
Philippicus adj see n.
Philippus, -ī m king of Macedonia; gold coin.
philitia, (phīditia), -ōrum ntpl public meals

at Sparta.
Philō (-ōn), -ōnis m Academic philosopher (teacher of Cicero).
Philoctētēs, -ae m Greek archer who gave Hercules poisoned arrows.
philologia, -ae f study of literature.
philologus adj scholarly, literary.
Philomēla, -ae f sister of Procne; nightingale.
philosophē adv see adj.
philosophia, -ae f philosophy.
philosophor, -ārī, -ātus vi to philosophize.
philosophus, -ī m philosopher ♦ adj philosophical.
philtrum, -ī nt love potion.
philyra, -ae f inner bark of the lime tree.
phīmus, -ī m dice box.
Phlegethōn, -ontis m a river of Hades.
Phlegethontis adj see n.
Phliāsius adj see n.
Phlīūs, -ūntis f town in Peloponnese.
phōca, -ae f seal.
Phōcaicus adj see n.
Phōceus adj see n.
Phōcis, -idis f country of central Greece.
Phōcius adj see n.
Phoebas, -adis f prophetess.
Phoebē, -ēs f Diana, the moon.
Phoebēius, -ēus adj see n.
Phoebigena, -ae m son of Phoebus, Aesculapius.
Phoebus, -ī m Apollo; the sun.
Phoenīcē, -cēs f Phoenicia.
Phoenīces, -cum mpl Phoenicians.
phoenīcopterus, -ī m flamingo.
Phoenīssus adj Phoenician ♦ f Dido.
Phoenīx, -īcis m friend of Achilles.
phoenīx, -īcis m phoenix.
Phorcis, -idos = Phorcȳnis.
Phorcus, -ī m son of Neptune (father of Medusa).
Phorcȳnis, -ȳnidos f Medusa.
Phraātēs, -ae m king of Parthia.
phrenēsis, -is f delirium.
phrenēticus adj mad, delirious.
Phrixēus adj see n.
Phrixus, -ī m Helle's brother (who took the ram with the golden fleece to Colchis).
Phryges, -um mpl Phrygians; Trojans.
Phrygia, -iae f Phrygia (country of Asia Minor); Troy.
Phrygius adj Phrygian, Trojan.
Phthia, -ae f home of Achilles in Thessaly.
Phthiōta, -ōtēs, -ōtae m native of Phthia.
phthisis f consumption.
Phthīus adj see n.
phy interj bah!
phylaca, -ae f prison.
phylarchus, -ī m chieftain.
physica, -ae and **ē, -ēs** f physics.
physicē adv scientifically.

physicus *adj* of physics, natural ♦ *m* natural philosopher ♦ *ntpl* physics.
physiognōmōn, -onis *m* physiognomist.
physiologia, -ae *f* natural philosophy, science.
piābilis *adj* expiable.
piāculāris *adj* atoning ♦ *ntpl* sin offerings.
piāculum, -ī *nt* sin offering; victim; atonement, punishment; sin, guilt.
piāmen, -inis *nt* atonement.
pīca, -ae *f* magpie.
picāria, -ae *f* pitch hut.
picea, -ae *f* pine.
Picēns, -entis *adj* = **Picēnus.**
Picēnum, -ēnī *nt* Picenum.
Picēnus *adj* of Picenum in E. Italy.
piceus *adj* pitch black; of pitch.
pictor, -ōris *m* painter.
pictūra, -ae *f* painting; picture.
pictūrātus *adj* painted; embroidered.
pictus *ppp of* **pingō** ♦ *adj* coloured, tattooed; (*style*) ornate; (*fear*) unreal.
pīcus, -ī *m* woodpecker.
piē *adv* religiously, dutifully.
Pīeris, -dis *f* Muse.
Pīerius *adj* of the Muses, poetic.
pietās, -ātis *f* sense of duty (*to gods, family, country*), piety, filial affection, love, patriotism.
piger, -rī *adj* reluctant, slack, slow; numbing, dull.
piget, -ēre, -uit *vt* (*impers*) to be annoyed, dislike; to regret, repent.
pigmentārius, -ī *and* **iī** *m* dealer in paints.
pigmentum, -ī *nt* paint, cosmetic; (*style*) colouring.
pignerātor, -ōris *m* mortgagee.
pignerō, -āre *vt* to pawn, mortgage.
pigneror, -ārī, -ātus *vt* to claim, accept.
pignus, -oris *and* **eris** *nt* pledge, pawn, security; wager, stake; (*fig*) assurance, token; (*pl*) children, dear ones.
pigritia, -ae, -ēs, -ēī *f* sluggishness, indolence.
pigrō, -āre, -or, -ārī *vi* to be slow, be slack.
pīla, -ae *f* mortar.
pīla, -ae *f* pillar; pier.
pila, -ae *f* ball, ball game.
pīlānus, -ī *m* soldier of the third line.
pīlātus *adj* armed with javelins.
pīlentum, -ī *nt* carriage.
pilleātus *adj* wearing the felt cap.
pilleolus, -ī *m* skullcap.
pilleum, -ī *nt*, **pilleus, -ī** *m* felt cap presented to freed slaves; (*fig*) liberty.
pilōsus *adj* hairy.
pīlum, -ī *nt* javelin.
pīlus, -ī *m* division of triarii; **prīmus ~** chief centurion.
pilus, -ī *m* hair; a whit.
Pimplēa, -ae *and* **is, -idis** *f* Muse.
Pimplēus *adj* of the Muses.
Pindaricus *adj see n.*

Pindarus, -ī *m* Pindar (*Greek lyric poet*).
Pindus, -ī *m* mountain range in Thessaly.
pīnētum, -ī *nt* pine wood.
pīneus *adj* pine- (*in cpds*).
pingō, -ere, pinxī, pictum *vt* to paint, embroider; to colour; (*fig*) to embellish, decorate.
pinguēscō, -ere *vi* to grow fat, become fertile.
pinguis *adj* fat, rich, fertile; (*mind*) gross, dull; (*ease*) comfortable, calm; (*weather*) thick ♦ *nt* grease.
pīnifer, -ī, pīniger, -ī *adj* pine-clad.
pinna, -ae *f* feather; wing, arrow; battlement; (*fish*) fin.
pinnātus *adj* feathered, winged.
pinniger, -ī *adj* winged; finny.
pinnipēs, -edis *adj* wing-footed.
pinnirapus, -ī *m* plume-snatcher.
pinnula, -ae *f* little wing.
pīnotērēs, -ae *m* hermit crab.
pīnsō, -ere *vt* to beat, pound.
pīnus, -ūs *and* **ī** *f* stone pine, Scots fir; ship, torch, wreath.
pinxī *perf of* **pingō.**
piō, -āre *vt* to propitiate, worship; to atone for, avert; to avenge.
piper, -is *nt* pepper.
pīpilō, -āre *vi* to chirp.
Pīraea, -ōrum *ntpl* Piraeus (*port of Athens*).
Pīraeeus *and* **us, -ī** *m* main port of Athens.
Pīraeus *adj see n.*
pīrāta, -ae *m* pirate.
pīrāticus *adj* pirate ♦ *f* piracy.
Pīrēnē, -ēs *f* spring in Corinth.
Pīrēnis, -idis *adj see n.*
Pīrithous, -ī *m* king of the Lapiths.
pirum, -ī *nt* pear.
pirus, -ī *f* pear tree.
Pīsa, -ae *f* Greek town near the Olympic Games site.
Pīsae, -ārum *fpl* town in Etruria (*now* Pisa).
Pīsaeus *adj see n.*
Pīsānus *adj see n.*
piscārius *adj* fish- (*in cpds*), fishing- (*in cpds*).
piscātor, -ōris *m* fisherman.
piscātōrius *adj* fishing- (*in cpds*).
piscātus, -ūs *m* fishing; fish; catch, haul.
pisciculus, -ī *m* little fish.
piscīna, -ae *f* fishpond; swimming pool.
piscīnārius, -ī *and* **iī** *m* person keen on fish ponds.
piscis -is *m* fish; (ASTRO) Pisces.
piscor, -ārī, -ātus *vi* to fish.
piscōsus *adj* full of fish.
pisculentus *adj* full of fish.
Pīsistratidae, -idārum *mpl* sons of Pisistratus.
Pīsistratus, -ī *m* tyrant of Athens.
pistillum, -ī *nt* pestle.
pistor, -ōris *m* miller; baker.
pistrilla, -ae *f* little mortar.
pīstrīnum, -ī *nt* mill, bakery; drudgery.
pistris, -is *and* **īx, -īcis** *f* sea monster, whale;

swift ship.
pithēcium, -ī and **iī** nt little ape.
pītuīta, -ae f phlegm; catarrh, cold in the head.
pītuītōsus adj phlegmatic.
pius adj dutiful, conscientious; godly, holy; filial, affectionate; patriotic; good, upright ♦ mpl the blessed dead.
pix, picis f pitch.
plācābilis adj easily appeased.
plācābilitās, -ātis f readiness to condone.
plācāmen, -inis, plācāmentum, -ī nt peace-offering.
plācātē adv calmly.
plācātiō, -ōnis f propitiating.
plācātus ppp of **plācō** ♦ adj calm, quiet, reconciled.
placenta, -ae f cake.
Placentia, -iae f town in N. Italy (now Piacenza).
Placentīnus adj see n.
placeō, -ēre, -uī, -itum vi (with dat to please, satisfy; ~**et** it seems good, it is agreed, resolved; **mihi ~eō** I am pleased with myself.
placidē adv peacefully, gently.
placidus adj calm, quiet, gentle.
placitum, -ī nt principle, belief.
placitus ppa of **placeō** ♦ adj pleasing, agreed on.
plācō, -āre, -āvī, -ātum vt to calm, appease, reconcile.
plāga, -ae f blow, stroke, wound.
plaga, -ae f region, zone.
plaga, -ae f hunting net, snare, trap.
plagiārius, -ī and **iī** m plunderer, kidnapper.
plāgigerulus adj much flogged.
plāgōsus adj fond of punishing.
plagula, -ae f curtain.
planctus, -ūs m beating the breast, lamentation.
plānē adv plainly, clearly; completely, quite; certainly.
plangō, -gere, -xī, -ctum vt, vi to beat noisily; to beat in grief; to lament loudly, bewail.
plangor, -ōris m beating; loud lamentation.
plānipēs, -edis m ballet dancer.
plānitās, -ātis f perspicuity.
plānitiēs, -ēī, (-a, -ae) f level ground, plain.
planta, -ae f shoot, slip; sole, foot.
plantāria, -ium ntpl slips, young trees.
plānus adj level, flat; plain, clear ♦ **~ē** level ground; **dē ~ō** easily.
planus, -ī m impostor.
platalea, -ae f spoonbill.
platea, -ae f street.
Platō, -ōnis m Plato (founder of the Academic school of philosophy).
Platōnicus adj see n.
plaudō, -dere, -sī, -sum vt to clap, beat, stamp ♦ vi to clap, applaud; to approve, be

pleased with.
plausibilis adj praiseworthy.
plausor, -ōris m applauder.
plaustrum, -ī nt waggon, cart; (ASTRO) Great Bear; ~ **percellere** upset the applecart.
plausus ppp of **plaudō**.
plausus, -ūs m flapping; clapping, applause.
Plautīnus adj see n.
Plautus, -ī m early Latin comic poet.
plēbēcula, -ae f rabble.
plēbēius adj plebeian; common, low.
plēbicola, -ae m friend of the people.
plēbiscītum, -ī nt decree of the people.
plēbs (plēbēs), -is f common people, plebeians; lower classes, masses.
plectō, -ere vt to punish.
plēctrum, -ī nt plectrum; lyre, lyric poetry.
Plēias, -dis f Pleiad; (pl) the Seven Sisters.
plēnē adv fully, entirely.
plēnus adj full, filled; (fig) sated; (age) mature; (amount) complete; (body) stout, plump; (female) pregnant; (matter) solid; (style) copious; (voice) loud; **ad ~um** abundantly.
plērumque adv generally, mostly.
plērusque adj a large part, most; (pl) the majority, the most; very many.
plexus adj plaited, interwoven.
Plīas see **Plēias**.
plicātrīx, -īcis f clothes folder.
plicō, -āre, -āvī and **uī, -ātum** and **itum** vt to fold, coil.
Plīnius, -ī m Roman family name (esp Pliny the Elder, who died in the eruption of Vesuvius); Pliny the Younger, writer of letters.
plōrātus, -ūs m wailing.
plōrō, -āre, -āvī, -ātum vi to wail, lament ♦ vt to weep for, bewail.
plōstellum, -ī nt cart.
ploxenum, -ī nt cart box.
pluit, -ere, -it vi (impers) it is raining.
plūma, -ae f soft feather, down.
plumbeus adj of lead; (fig) heavy, dull, worthless.
plumbum, -ī nt lead; bullet, pipe, ruler; ~ **album** tin.
plūmeus adj down, downy.
plūmipēs, -edis adj feather-footed.
plūmōsus adj feathered.
plūrimus superl of **multus**.
plūs, -ūris compar of **multus** ♦ adv more.
plūsculus adj a little more.
pluteus, -ī m shelter, penthouse; parapet; couch; bookcase.
Plūtō, -ōnis m king of the lower world.
Plūtōnius adj see n.
pluvia, -ae f rain.
pluviālis adj rainy.
pluvius adj rainy, rain- (in cpds).
pōcillum, -ī nt small cup.
pōculum, -ī nt cup; drink, potion.

Noun declensions and verb conjugations are shown on pp xiii to xxv. The present infinitive ending of a verb shows to which conjugation it belongs: **-āre** = 1st; **ē-e** = 2nd; **-ere** = 3rd and **-īre** = 4th. Irregular verbs are shown on p xxvi

podagra, -ae *f* gout.
podagrōsus *adj* gouty.
podium, -ī *and* **iī** *nt* balcony.
poēma, -tis *nt* poem.
poena, -ae *f* penalty, punishment; **poenas dare** to be punished.
Poenī, -ōrum *mpl* Carthaginians.
Poenus, Pūnicus *adj* Punic.
poēsis, -is *f* poetry, poem.
poēta, -ae *m* poet.
poēticē *adv* poetically.
poēticus *adj* poetic ♦ *f* poetry.
poētria, -ae *f* poetess.
pol *interj* by Pollux!, truly.
polenta, -ae *f* pearl barley.
poliō, -īre, -īvī, -ītum *vt* to polish; to improve, put in good order.
polītē *adv* elegantly.
polītīa, -ae *f* Plato's Republic.
polīticus *adj* political.
polītus *adj* polished, refined, cultured.
pollen, -inis *nt* fine flour, meal.
pollēns, -entis *pres p of* **polleō** ♦ *adj* powerful, strong.
pollentia, -ae *f* power.
polleō, -ēre *vi* to be strong, be powerful.
pollex, -icis *m* thumb.
polliceor, -ērī, -itus *vt* to promise, offer.
pollicitātiō, -ōnis *f* promise.
pollicitor, -ārī, -ātus *vt* to promise.
pollicitum, -ī *nt* promise.
Polliō, -ōnis *m* Roman surname (*esp C. Asinius, soldier, statesman and literary patron under Augustus*).
pollis, -inis *m/f see* **pollen**.
pollūcibiliter *adv* sumptuously.
pollūctus *adj* offered up ♦ *nt* offering.
polluō, -uere, -uī, -ūtum *vt* to defile, pollute, dishonour.
Pollūx, -ūcis *m* twin brother of Castor (*famous as a boxer*).
polus, -ī *m* pole, North pole; sky.
Polyhymnia, -ae *f* a Muse.
Polyphēmus, -ī *m* one-eyed Cyclops.
pōlypus, -ī *m* polypus.
pōmārium, -ī *and* **iī** *nt* orchard.
pōmārius, -ī *and* **iī** *m* fruiterer.
pōmerīdiānus *adj* afternoon.
pōmērium, -ī *and* **iī** *nt* free space round the city boundary.
pōmifer, -ī *adj* fruitful.
pōmoerium *see* **pōmērium**.
pōmōsus *adj* full of fruit.
pompa, -ae *f* procession; retinue, train; ostentation.
Pompeiānus *adj see n.*
Pompeī, -ōrum *mpl* Campanian town buried by an eruption of Vesuvius.
Pompeius, -ī *m* Roman family name (*esp Pompey the Great*).
Pompeius, -ānus *adj see n.*
Pompilius, -ī *m* Numa (*second king of Rome*).
Pompilius *adj see n.*

Pomptīnus *adj* Pomptine (*name of marshy district in S. Latium*).
pōmum, -ī *nt* fruit; fruit tree.
pōmus, -ī *f* fruit tree.
ponderō, -āre *vt* to weigh; to consider, reflect on.
ponderōsus *adj* heavy, weighty.
pondō *adv* in weight; pounds.
pondus, -eris *nt* weight; mass, burden; (*fig*) importance, authority; (*character*) firmness; (*pl*) balance.
pōne *adv* behind.
pōnō, -ere, posuī, positum *vt* to put, place, lay, set; to lay down, lay aside; (*fig*) to regard, reckon; (*art*) to make, build; (*camp*) to pitch; (*corpse*) to lay out, bury; (*example*) to take; (*food*) to serve; (*hair*) to arrange; (*hope*) to base, stake; (*hypothesis*) to suppose, assume; (*institution*) to lay down, ordain; (*money*) to invest; (*sea*) to calm; (*theme*) to propose; (*time*) to spend, devote; (*tree*) to plant; (*wager*) to put down ♦ *vi* (*wind*) to abate.
pōns, pontis *m* bridge; drawbridge; (*ship*) gangway, deck.
ponticulus, -ī *m* small bridge.
Ponticus *adj see* **Pontus**.
pontifex, -icis *m* high priest, pontiff.
pontificālis *adj* pontifical.
pontificātus, -ūs *m* high priesthood.
pontificius *adj* pontiff's.
pontō, -ōnis *m* ferryboat.
pontus, -ī *m* sea.
Pontus, -ī *m* Black Sea; kingdom of Mithridates in Asia Minor.
popa, -ae *m* minor priest.
popanum, -ī *nt* sacrificial cake.
popellus, -ī *m* mob.
popīna, -ae *f* eating house, restaurant.
popīnō, -ōnis *m* glutton.
popl- *etc see* **pūbl-**.
poples, -itis *m* knee.
poposcī *perf of* **poscō**.
poppysma, -tis *nt* clicking of the tongue.
populābilis *adj* destroyable.
populābundus *adj* ravaging.
populāris *adj* of, from, for the people; popular, democratic; native ♦ *m* fellow countryman ♦ *mpl* the people's party, the democrats.
populāritās, -ātis *f* courting popular favour.
populāriter *adv* vulgarly; democratically.
populātiō, -ōnis *f* plundering; plunder.
populātor, -ōris *m* ravager.
pōpuleus *adj* poplar- (*in cpds*).
pōpulifer, -ī *adj* rich in poplars.
populor, -ārī, -ātus, -ō, -āre *vt* to ravage, plunder; to destroy, ruin.
populus, -ī *m* people, nation; populace, the public; large crowds; district.
pōpulus, -ī *f* poplar tree.
porca, -ae *f* sow.
porcella, -ae *f*, **-us, -ī** *m* little pig.

porcīna, -ae f pork.
porcīnārius, -ī and **iī** m pork seller.
Porcius, -ī m family name of Cato.
Porcius adj see n.
porculus, -ī m porker.
porcus, -ī m pig, hog.
porgō etc see **porrigō**.
Porphyriōn, -ōnis m a Giant.
porrēctiō, -ōnis f extending.
porrēctus ppp of **porrigō** ♦ adj long,
protracted; dead.
porrēxī perf of **porrigō**.
porriciō, -ere vt to make an offering of; **inter
caesa et porrēcta** ≈ at the eleventh hour.
porrigō, -igere, -ēxī, -ēctum vt to stretch,
spread out, extend; to offer, hold out.
porrīgō, -inis f scurf, dandruff.
porrō adv forward, a long way off; (time) in
future, long ago; (sequence) next, moreover,
in turn.
porrum, -ī nt leek.
Porsena, Porsenna, Porsinna, -ae f king of
Clusium in Etruria.
porta, -ae f gate; entrance, outlet.
portātiō, -ōnis f carrying.
portendō, -dere, -dī, -tum vt to denote,
predict.
portentificus adj marvellous.
portentōsus adj unnatural.
portentum, -ī nt omen, unnatural happening;
monstrosity, monster; (story) marvel.
porthmeus, -eī and **eos** m ferryman.
porticula, -ae f small gallery.
porticus, -ūs m portico, colonnade; (MIL)
gallery; (PHILOS) Stoicism.
portiō, -ōnis f share, instalment; **prō ~ōne**
proportionally.
portitor, -ōris m customs officer.
portitor, -ōris m ferryman.
portō, -āre, -āvī, -ātum vt to carry, convey,
bring.
portōrium, -ī and **iī** nt customs duty, tax.
portula, -ae f small gate.
portuōsus adj well-off for harbours.
portus, -ūs m harbour, port; (fig) safety,
haven.
pōsca, -ae f a vinegar drink.
poscō, -ere, poposcī vt to ask, require,
demand; to call on.
Posīdōnius, -ī m Stoic philosopher (teacher of
Cicero).
positiō, -ōnis f position, climate.
positor, -ōris m builder.
positūra, -ae f position; formation.
positus ppp of **pōnō** ♦ adj situated.
posse infin of **possum**.
possēdī perf of **possideō**; perf of **possīdō**.
possessiō, -ōnis f seizing; occupation;
possession, property.
possessiuncula, -ae f small estate.

possessor, -ōris m occupier, possessor.
possessus ppp of **possideō** and **possīdō**.
possideō, -idēre, -ēdī, -essum vt to hold,
occupy; to have, possess.
possīdō, -īdere, -ēdī, -essum vt to take
possession of.
possum, -sse, -tuī vi to be able, can; to have
power, avail.
post adv (place) behind; (time) after; (sequence)
next ♦ prep (with acc) behind; after, since;
paulō ~ soon after; **~ urbem conditam** since
the foundation of the city.
posteā adv afterwards, thereafter; next, then;
~ quam conj after.
posterior, -ōris adj later, next; inferior, less
important.
posteritās, -ātis f posterity, the future.
posterius adv later.
posterus adj next, following ♦ mpl posterity.
postferō, -re vt to put after, sacrifice.
postgenitī, -ōrum mpl later generations.
posthabeō, -ēre, -uī, -itum vt to put after,
neglect.
posthāc adv hereafter, in future.
postibi adv then, after that.
postīculum, -ī nt small back building.
postīcus adj back- (in cpds), hind- (in cpds) ♦ nt
back door.
postideā adv after that.
postillā adv afterwards.
postis, -is m doorpost, door.
postlīminium, -ī and **iī** nt right of recovery.
postmerīdiānus adj in the afternoon.
postmodo, postmodum adv shortly,
presently.
postpōnō, -ōnere, -osuī, -ositum vt to put
after, disregard.
postputō, -āre vt to consider less important.
postquam conj after, when.
postrēmō adv finally.
postrēmus adj last, rear; lowest, worst.
postrīdiē adv next day, the day after.
postscaenium, -ī and **iī** nt behind the scenes.
postscrībō, -ere vt to write after.
postulātiō, -ōnis f demand, claim; complaint.
postulātum, -ī nt demand, claim.
postulātus, -ūs m claim.
postulō, -āre, -āvī, -ātum vt to demand,
claim; (law) to summon, prosecute; to apply
for a writ (to prosecute).
postumus adj last, last-born.
postus etc see **positus**.
posuī perf of **pōnō**.
pōtātiō, -ōnis f drinking.
pōtātor, -ōris m toper.
pote etc see **potis**.
potēns, -entis adj able, capable; powerful,
strong, potent; master of, ruling over;
successful in carrying out.
potentātus, -ūs m political power.

Noun declensions and verb conjugations are shown on pp xiii to xxv. The present infinitive ending of a verb shows
to which conjugation it belongs: -**āre** = 1st; -**ēre** = 2nd; -**ere** = 3rd and -**īre** = 4th. Irregular verbs are shown on p xxvi

potenter *adv* powerfully; competently.
potentia, -ae *f* power, force, efficacy;
tyranny.
potērium, -ī *and* **iī** *nt* goblet.
potesse *archaic infin of* **possum**.
potestās, -ātis *f* power, ability; control,
sovereignty, authority; opportunity,
permission; (*person*) magistrate; (*things*)
property; **~ātem suī facere** allow access to
oneself.
potin can (you)?, is it possible?
pōtiō, -ōnis *f* drink, draught, philtre.
potiō, -īre *vt* to put into the power of.
potior, -īrī, -ītus *vi* (*with gen and abl*) to take
possession of, get hold of, acquire; to be
master of.
potior, -ōris *adj* better, preferable.
potis *adj* (*indecl*) able; possible.
potissimum *adv* especially.
potissimus *adj* chief, most important.
pōtitō, -āre *vt* to drink much.
potius *adv* rather, more.
pōtō, -āre, -āvī, -ātum *and* **um** *vt* to drink.
pōtor, -ōris *m* drinker.
pōtrīx, -īcis *f* woman tippler.
potuī *perf of* **possum**.
pōtulenta, -ōrum *ntpl* drinks.
pōtus *ppp of* **pōtō** ♦ *adj* drunk.
pōtus, -ūs *m* drink.
prae *adv* in front, before; in comparison ♦ *prep*
(*with abl*) in front of; compared with; (*cause*)
because of, for; **~ sē** openly; **~ sē ferre**
display; **~ manū** to hand.
praeacūtus *adj* pointed.
praealtus *adj* very high, very deep.
praebeō, -ēre, -uī, -itum *vt* to hold out,
proffer; to give, supply; to show, represent;
sē ~ behave, prove.
praebibō, -ere, -ī *vt* to toast.
praebitor, -ōris *m* purveyor.
praecalidus *adj* very hot.
praecānus *adj* prematurely grey.
praecautus *ppp of* **praecaveō**.
praecaveō, -avēre, -āvī, -autum *vt* to guard
against ♦ *vi* to beware, take precautions.
praecēdō, -dere, -ssī, -ssum *vt* to go before;
to surpass ♦ *vi* to lead the way; to excel.
praecellō, -ere *vi* to excel, be distinguished ♦
vt to surpass.
praecelsus *adj* very high.
praecentiō, -ōnis *f* prelude.
praecentō, -āre *vi* to sing an incantation for.
praeceps, -ipitis *adj* head first, headlong;
going down, precipitous; rapid, violent,
hasty; inclined (to); dangerous ♦ *nt* edge of
an abyss, precipice; danger ♦ *adv* headlong;
into danger.
praeceptiō, -ōnis *f* previous notion; precept.
praeceptor, -ōris *m* teacher.
praeceptrīx, -rīcis *f* teacher.
praeceptum, -ī *nt* maxim, precept; order.
praeceptus *ppp of* **praecipiō**.
praecerpō, -ere, -sī, -tum *vt* to gather

prematurely; to forestall.
praecīdō, -dere, -dī, -sum *vt* to cut off,
damage; (*fig*) to cut short, put an end to.
praecinctus *ppp of* **praecingō**.
praecingō, -ingere, -inxī, -inctum *vt* to gird
in front; to surround.
praecinō, -inere, -inuī, -entum *vt* to play
before; to chant a spell ♦ *vt* to predict.
praecipiō, -ipere, -ēpī, -ēptum *vt* to take
beforehand, get in advance; to anticipate; to
teach, admonish, order.
praecipitanter *adv* at full speed.
praecipitem *acc of* **praeceps**.
praecipitō, -āre, -āvī, -ātum *vt* to throw
down, throw away, hasten; (*fig*) to remove,
carry away, ruin ♦ *vi* to rush headlong, fall;
to be hasty.
praecipuē *adv* especially, chiefly.
praecipuus *adj* special; principal,
outstanding.
praecīsē *adv* briefly, absolutely.
praecīsus *ppp of* **praecīdō** ♦ *adj* steep.
praeclārē *adv* very clearly; excellently.
praeclārus *adj* very bright; beautiful,
splendid; distinguished, noble.
praeclūdō, -dere, -sī, -sum *vt* to close, shut
against; to close to, impede.
praecō, -ōnis *m* crier, herald; auctioneer.
praecōgitō, -āre *vt* to premeditate.
praecognitus *adj* foreseen.
praecolō, -olere, -oluī, -ultum *vt* to cultivate
early.
praecompositus *adj* studied.
praecōnium, -ī *and* **iī** *nt* office of a crier;
advertisement; commendation.
praecōnius *adj* of a public crier.
praecōnsūmō, -ere, -ptum *vt* to use up
beforehand.
praecontrectō, -āre *vt* to consider
beforehand.
praecordia, -ōrum *ntpl* midriff; stomach;
breast, heart; mind.
praecorrumpō, -umpere, -ūpī, -uptum *vt* to
bribe beforehand.
praecox, -cis *adj* early, premature.
praecultus *ppp of* **praecolō**.
praecurrentia, -ium *ntpl* antecedents.
praecurrō, -rrere, -currī *and* **rrī, -rsum** *vi* to
hurry on before, precede; to excel ♦ *vt* to
anticipate; to surpass.
praecursiō, -ōnis *f* previous occurrence;
(*RHET*) preparation.
praecursor, -ōris *m* advance guard; scout.
praecutiō, -ere *vt* to brandish before.
praeda, -ae *f* booty, plunder; (*animal*) prey;
(*fig*) gain.
praedābundus *adj* plundering.
praedamnō, -āre *vt* to condemn beforehand.
praedātiō, -ōnis *f* plundering.
praedātor, -ōris *m* plunderer.
praedātōrius *adj* marauding.
praedēlassō, -āre *vt* to weaken beforehand.
praedēstinō, -āre *vt* to predetermine.

praediātor, -ōris m buyer of landed estates.
praediātōrius adj relating to the sale of estates.
praedicābilis adj laudatory.
praedicātiō, -ōnis f proclamation commendation.
praedicātor, -ōris m eulogist.
praedicō, -āre, -āvī, -ātum vt to proclaim, make public; to declare; to praise, boast.
praedīcō, -īcere, -īxī, -ictum vt to mention beforehand, prearrange; to foretell; to warn, command.
praedictiō, -ōnis f foretelling.
praedictum, -ī nt prediction; command; prearrangement.
praedictus ppp of **praedīcō.**
praediolum, -ī nt small estate.
praediscō, -ere vt to learn beforehand.
praedispositus adj arranged beforehand.
praeditus adj endowed, provided.
praedium, -ī and **iī** nt estate.
praedīves, -itis adj very rich.
praedō, -ōnis m robber, pirate.
praedor, -ārī, -ātus vt, vi to plunder, rob; (fig) to profit.
praedūcō, -ūcere, -ūxī, -uctum vt to draw in front.
praedulcis adj very sweet.
praedūrus adj very hard, very tough.
praeēmineō, -ēre vt to surpass.
praeeō, -īre, -īvī and **iī, -itum** vi to lead the way, go first; (formula) to dictate, recite first ♦ vt to precede, outstrip.
praeesse infin of **praesum.**
praefātiō, -ōnis f formula; preface.
praefātus ppa of **praefor.**
praefectūra, -ae f superintendence; governorship; Italian town governed by Roman edicts, prefecture; district, province.
praefectus ppp of **praeficiō** ♦ m overseer, director, governor, commander; ~ **classis** admiral; ~ **legiōnis** colonel; ~ **urbis** cr **urbī** city prefect (of Rome).
praeferō, -ferre, -tulī, -lātum vt to carry in front, hold out; to prefer; to show, display; to anticipate; (pass) to hurry past, outflank.
praeferōx, -ōcis adj very impetuous, very insolent.
praefervidus adj very hot.
praefestīnō, -āre vi to be too hasty; to hurry past.
praefica, -ae f hired mourner.
praeficiō, -icere, -ēcī, -ectum vt to put in charge, give command over.
praefīdēns, -entis adj over-confident.
praefīgō, -gere, -xī, -xum vt to fasten in front, set up before; to tip, point; to transfix.
praefīniō, -īre, -īvī and **iī, -ītum** vt to determine, prescribe.
praefīscinē, -ī adv without offence.

praeflōrō, -āre vt to tarnish.
praefluō, -ere vt, vi to flow past.
praefocō, -āre vt to choke.
praefodiō, -odere, -ōdī vt to dig in front of; to bury beforehand.
praefor, -ārī, -ātus vt, vi to say in advance, preface; to pray beforehand; to predict.
praefrāctē adv resolutely.
praefrāctus ppp of **praefringō** ♦ adj abrupt; stern.
praefrīgidus adj very cold.
praefringō, -ingere, -ēgī, -āctum vt to break off, shiver.
praefuī perf of **praesum.**
praefulciō, -cīre, -sī, -tum vt to prop up; to use as a prop.
praefulgeō, -ulgēre, -ulsī vt to shine conspicuously; to outshine.
praegelidus adj very cold.
praegestiō, -īre vi to be very eager.
praegnāns, -antis adj pregnant; full.
praegracilis adj very slim.
praegrandis adj very large, very great.
praegravis adj very heavy; very wearisome.
praegravō, -āre vt to weigh down; to eclipse.
praegredior, -dī, -ssus vt, vi to go before; to go past; to surpass.
praegressiō, -ōnis f precession, precedence.
praegustātor, -ōris m taster.
praegustō, -āre vt to taste beforehand.
praehibeō, -ēre vt to offer, give.
praeiaceō, -ēre vt to lie in front of.
praeiūdicium, -ī and **iī** nt precedent, example; prejudgment.
praeiūdicō, -āre, -āvī, -ātum vt to prejudge, decide beforehand.
praeiuvō, -āre vt to give previous assistance to.
praelabor, -bī, -psus vt, vi to move past, move along.
praelambō, -ere vt to lick first.
praelātus ppp of **praeferō.**
praelegō, -ere vt to coast along.
praeligō, -āre vt to bind, tie up.
praelongus adj very long, very tall.
praeloquor, -quī, -cūtus vi to speak first.
praelūceō, -cēre, -xī vi to light, shine; to outshine.
praelūstris adj very magnificent.
praemandāta ntpl warrant of arrest.
praemandō, -āre, -āvī, -ātum vt to bespeak.
praemātūrē adv too soon.
praemātūrus adj too early, premature.
praemedicātus adj protected by charms.
praemeditātiō, -ōnis f thinking over the future.
praemeditātus adj premeditated.
praemeditor, -ārī, -ātus vt to think over, practise.
praemetuenter adv anxiously.

Noun declensions and verb conjugations are shown on pp xiii to xxv. The present infinitive ending of a verb shows to which conjugation it belongs: -āre = 1st; -īre = 2nd; -ere = 3rd and -īre = 4th. Irregular verbs are shown on p xxvi

praemetuō, -ere vi to be anxious ♦ vt to fear the future.

praemissus ppp of **praemittō**.

praemittō, -ittere, -īsī, -issum vt to send in advance.

praemium, -ī and **iī** nt prize, reward.

praemolestia, -ae f apprehension.

praemōlior, -īrī vt to prepare thoroughly.

praemoneō, -ēre, -uī, -itum vt to forewarn, foreshadow.

praemonitus, -ūs m premonition.

praemōnstrātor, -ōris m guide.

praemōnstrō, -āre vt to guide; to predict.

praemordeō, -ēre vt to bite off; to pilfer.

praemorior, -ī, -tuus vi to die too soon.

praemūniō, -īre, -īvī, -ītum vt to fortify, strengthen, secure.

praemūnītiō, -ōnis f (RHET) preparation.

praenārrō, -āre vt to tell beforehand.

praenatō, -āre vt to flow past.

Praeneste, -is nt/f Latin town (now Palestrina).

Praenestīnus adj see n.

praeniteō, -ēre, -uī vi to seem more attractive.

praenōmen, -inis nt first name.

praenōscō, -ere vt to foreknow.

praenōtiō, -ōnis f preconceived idea.

praenūbilus adj very gloomy.

praenūntia, -iae f harbinger.

praenūntiō, -āre vt to foretell.

praenūntius, -ī and **iī** m harbinger.

praeoccupō, -āre, -āvī, -ātum vt to take first, anticipate.

praeolit mihi I get a hint of.

praeoptō, -āre, -āvī, -ātum vt to choose rather, prefer.

praepandō, -ere vt to spread out; to expound.

praeparātiō, -ōnis f preparation.

praeparō, -āre, -āvī, -ātum vt to prepare, prepare for; **ex ~ātō** by arrangement.

praepediō, -īre, -īvī, -ītum vt to shackle, tether; to hamper.

praependeō, -ēre vi to hang down in front.

praepes, -etis adj swift, winged; of good omen ♦ f bird.

praepilātus adj tipped with a ball.

praepinguis adj very rich.

praepolleō, -ēre vi to be very powerful, be superior.

praeponderō, -āre vt to outweigh.

praepōnō, -ōnere, -osuī, -ositum vt to put first, place in front; to put in charge, appoint commander; to prefer.

praeportō, -āre vt to carry before.

praepositiō, -ōnis f preference; (GRAM) preposition.

praepositus ppp of **praepōnō** ♦ m overseer, commander.

praepossum, -sse, -tuī vi to gain the upper hand.

praeposterē adv the wrong way round.

praeposterus adj inverted, perverted; absurd.

praepotēns, -entis adj very powerful.

praeproperanter adv too hastily.

praeproperē adv too hastily.

praeproperus adj overhasty, rash.

praepūtium, -ī and **iī** nt foreskin.

praequam adv compared with.

praequestus adj complaining beforehand.

praeradiō, -āre vt to outshine.

praerapidus adj very swift.

praereptus ppp of **praeripiō**.

praerigēscō, -ēscere, -uī vi to become very stiff.

praeripiō, -ipere, -ipuī, -eptum vt to take before, forestall; to carry off prematurely; to frustrate.

praerōdō, -dere, -sum vt to bite the end of, nibble off.

praerogātīva, -ae f tribe or century with the first vote, the first vote; previous election; omen, sure token.

praerogātīvus adj voting first.

praerōsus ppp of **praerōdō**.

praerumpō, -umpere, -ūpī, -uptum vt to break off.

praeruptus ppp of **praerumpō** ♦ adj steep, abrupt; headstrong.

praes, -aedis m surety; property of a surety.

praesaep- etc see **praesēp-**.

praesāgiō, -īre vt to have a presentiment of, forebode.

praesāgītiō, -ōnis f foreboding.

praesāgium, -ī and **iī** nt presentiment; prediction.

praesāgus adj foreboding, prophetic.

praesciō, -īre, -iī vt to know before.

praescīscō, -ere vt to find out beforehand.

praescius adj foreknowing.

praescrībō, -bere, -psī, -ptum vt to write first; to direct, command; to dictate, describe; to put forward as a pretext.

praescrīptiō, -ōnis f preface, heading; order, rule; pretext.

praescrīptum, -ī nt order, rule.

praescrīptus ppp of **praescrībō**.

praesecō, -āre, -uī, -tum and **-ātum** vt to cut off, pare.

praesēns, -entis adj present, in person; (things) immediate, ready, prompt; (mind) resolute; (gods) propitious ♦ ntpl present state of affairs; **in ~ēns** for the present; **~in rē ~entī** on the spot.

praesēnsiō, -ōnis f foreboding; preconception.

praesēnsus ppp of **praesentiō**.

praesentārius adj instant, ready.

praesentia, -ae f presence; effectiveness.

praesentiō, -entīre, -ēnsī, -ēnsum vt to presage, have a foreboding of.

praesēpe, -is nt, **-ēs, -is** f stable, fold, pen; hovel; hive.

praesēpiō, -īre, -sī, -tum vt to barricade.

praesēpis f = **praesēpe**.

praesertim *adv* especially.
praeserviō, -īre *vi* to serve as a slave.
praeses, -idis *m* guardian, protector; chief, ruler.
praesideō, -idēre, -ēdī *vi* to guard, defend; to preside over, direct.
praesidiārius *adj* garrison-.
praesidium, -ī *and* **iī** *nt* defence, protection; support, assistance; guard, garrison, convoy; defended position, entrenchment.
praesignificō, -āre *vt* to foreshadow.
praesignis *adj* conspicuous.
praesonō, -āre, -uī *vi* to sound before.
praespargō, -ere *vt* to strew before
praestābilis *adj* outstanding; preferable.
praestāns, -antis *pres p of* **praestō** ♦ *adj* outstanding, pre-eminent.
praestantia, -ae *f* pre-eminence.
praestes, -itis *adj* presiding, guardian.
praestīgiae, -ārum *fpl* illusion, sleight of hand.
praestīgiātor, -ōris *m*, **-rīx, -rīcis** *f* conjurer, cheat.
praestinō, -āre *vt* to buy.
praestitī *perf of* **praestō**.
praestituō, -uere, -uī, -ūtum *vt* to prearrange, prescribe.
praestitus *ppp of* **praestō**.
praestō *adv* at hand, ready.
praestō, -āre, -itī, -itum *and* **ātum** *vi* to be outstanding, be superior; (*impers*) it is better ♦ *vt* to excel; to be responsible for, answer for; (*duty*) to discharge, perform; (*quality*) to show, prove; (*things*) to give, offer, provide; **sē ~** behave, prove.
praestōlor, -ārī, -ātus *vt, vi* to wait for, expect.
praestrictus *ppp of* **praestringō**.
praestringō, -ingere, -inxī, -ictum *vt* to squeeze; to blunt, dull; (*eyes*) to dazzle.
praestruō, -ere, -xī, -ctum *vt* to block up; to build beforehand.
praesul, -is *m/f* public dancer.
praesultātor, -ōris *m* public dancer.
praesultō, -āre *vi* to dance before.
praesum, -esse, -fuī *vi* (*with dat*) to be at the head of, be in command of; to take the lead; to protect.
praesūmō, -ere, -psī, -ptum *vt* to take first; to anticipate; to take for granted.
praesūtus *adj* sewn over at the point.
praetemptō, -āre *vt* to feel for, grope for; to test in advance.
praetendō, -dere, -dī, -tum *vt* to hold out, put before, spread in front of; to give as an excuse, allege.
praetentō *etc see* **praetemptō**.
praetentus *ppp of* **praetendō** ♦ *adj* lying over against.
praetepeō, -ēre, -uī *vi* to glow before.

praeter *adv* beyond; excepting ♦ *prep* (*with acc*) past, along; except, besides; beyond, more than, in addition to, contrary to.
praeteragō, -ere *vt* to drive past.
praeterbītō, -ere *vt, vi* to pass by.
praeterdūcō, -ere *vt* to lead past.
praettereā *adv* besides; moreover; henceforth.
praetereō, -īre, -iī, -itum *vi* to go past ♦ *vt* to pass, overtake; to escape, escape the notice of; to omit, leave out, forget, neglect; to reject, exclude; to surpass; to transgress.
praeterequitāns, -antis *adj* riding past.
praeterfluō, -ere *vt, vi* to flow past.
praetergredior, -dī, -ssus *vt* to pass, march past; to surpass.
praeterhāc *adv* further, more.
praeteritus *ppp of* **praetereō** ♦ *adj* past, gone by ♦ *ntpl* the past.
praeterlābor, -bī, -psus *vt* to flow past, move past ♦ *vi* to slip away.
praeterlātus *adj* driving, flying past.
praetermeō, -āre *vi* to pass by.
praetermissiō, -ōnis *f* omission, passing over.
praetermittō, -ittere, -īsī, -issum *vt* to let pass; to omit, neglect; to make no mention of; to overlook.
praeterquam *adv* except, besides.
praetervectiō, -ōnis *f* passing by.
praetervehor, -hī, -ctus *vt, vi* to ride past, sail past; to march past; to pass by, pass over.
praetervolō, -āre *vt, vi* to fly past; to escape.
praetexō, -ere, -uī, -tum *vt* to border, fringe; to adorn; to pretend, disguise.
praetextātus *adj* wearing the toga praetexta, under age.
praetextus *ppp of* **praetexō** ♦ *adj* wearing the toga praetexta ♦ *f* toga with a purple border; Roman tragedy ♦ *nt* pretext.
praetextus, -ūs *m* splendour; pretence.
praetimeō, -ēre *vi* to be afraid in advance.
praetinctus *adj* dipped beforehand.
praetor, -ōris *m* chief magistrate, commander; praetor; propraetor; governor.
praetōriānus *adj* of the emperor's bodyguard.
praetōrium, -ī *and* **iī** *nt* general's tent, camp headquarters; governor's residence; council of war; palace, grand building; emperor's bodyguard.
praetōrius *adj* praetor's, praetorian; of a propraetor; of the emperor's bodyguard ♦ *m* ex-praetor; **~ia cohors** bodyguard of general *or* emperor; **porta ~ia** camp gate facing the enemy.
praetorqueō, -ēre *vt* to strangle first.
praetrepidāns, -antis *adj* very impatient.
praetruncō, -āre *vt* to cut off.
praetulī *perf of* **praeferō**.
praetūra, -ae *f* praetorship.

Noun declensions and verb conjugations are shown on pp xiii to xxv. The present infinitive ending of a verb shows to which conjugation it belongs: **-āre** = 1st, **-ēre** = 2nd; **-ere** = 3rd and **-īre** = 4th. Irregular verbs are shown on p xxvi

praeumbrāns, -antis *adj* obscuring.
praeūstus *adj* hardened at the point;
frostbitten.
praeut *adv* compared with.
praevaleō, -ēre, -uī *vi* to be very powerful,
have most influence, prevail.
praevalidus *adj* very strong, very powerful;
too strong.
praevāricātiō, -ōnis *f* collusion.
praevāricātor, -ōris *m* advocate guilty of
collusion.
praevāricor, -ārī, -ātus *vi* (*with dat*) to favour
by collusion.
praevehor, -hī, -ctus *vi* to ride, fly in front,
flow past.
praeveniō, -enīre, -ēnī, -entum *vt, vi* to come
before; to anticipate, prevent.
praeverrō, -ere *vt* to sweep before.
praevertō, -ere, -ī; -or, -ī *vt* to put first;
prefer; to turn to first, attend first to; to
oustrip; to anticipate, frustrate, prepossess.
praevideō, -idēre, -īdī, -īsum *vt* to foresee.
praevitiō, -āre *vt* to taint beforehand.
praevius *adj* leading the way.
praevolō, -āre *vi* to fly in front.
pragmaticus *adj* of affairs ♦ *m* legal expert.
prandeō, -ēre, -ī *vi* to take lunch ♦ *vt* to eat.
prandium, -ī *and* **iī** *nt* lunch.
prānsor, -ōris *m* guest at lunch.
prānsus *adj* having lunched, fed.
prasinus *adj* green.
prātēnsis *adj* meadow.
prātulum, -ī *nt* small meadow.
prātum, -ī *nt* meadow; grass.
prāvē *adv* wrongly, badly.
prāvitās, -ātis *f* irregularity; perverseness,
depravity.
prāvus *adj* crooked, deformed; perverse, bad,
wicked.
Prāxitelēs, -is *m* famous Greek sculptor.
Prāxitelius *adj see n.*
precāriō *adv* by request.
precārius *adj* obtained by entreaty.
precātiō, -ōnis *f* prayer.
precātor, -ōris *m* intercessor.
preces *pl of* **prex.**
preciae, -ārum *fpl* kind of vine.
precor, -ārī, -ātus *vt, vi* to pray, beg, entreat;
to wish (well), curse.
prehendō, -endere, -endī, -ēnsum *vt* to take
hold of, catch; to seize, detain; to surprise;
(*eye*) to take in; (*mind*) to grasp.
prehēnsō *etc see* **prēnsō.**
prehēnsus *ppp of* **prehendō.**
prēlum, -ī *nt* wine press, oil press.
premō, -mere, -ssī, -ssum *vt* to press,
squeeze; to press together, compress; (*eyes*)
to close; (*reins*) to tighten; (*trees*) to prune; to
press upon, lie, sit, stand on, cover, conceal,
surpass; to press hard on, follow closely;
(*coast*) to hug; to press down, lower, burden;
(*fig*) to overcome, rule; (*words*) to disparage;
to press in, sink, stamp, plant; to press back,

repress, check, stop.
prendō *etc see* **prehendō.**
prēnsātiō, -ōnis *f* canvassing.
prēnsō (prehēnsō), -āre, -āvī, -ātum *vt* to
clutch at, take hold of, buttonhole.
prēnsus *ppp of* **prehendō.**
presbyter, -ī *m* (*ECCL*) elder.
pressē *adv* concisely, accurately, simply.
pressī *perf of* **premō.**
pressiō, -ōnis *f* fulcrum.
pressō, -āre *vt* to press.
pressus *ppp of* **premō** ♦ *adj* (*style*) concise,
compressed; (*pace*) slow; (*voice*) subdued.
pressus, -ūs *m* pressure.
prēstēr, -ēris *m* waterspout.
pretiōsē *adv* expensively.
pretiōsus *adj* valuable, expensive;
extravagant.
pretium, -ī *and* **iī** *nt* price, value; worth;
money, fee, reward; **māgnī ~ī, in ~iō**
valuable; **operae ~** worth while.
prex, -ecis *f* request, entreaty; prayer; good
wish; curse.
Priamēis, -ēidis *f* Cassandra.
Priamēius *adj see* **Priamus.**
Priamidēs, -idae *m* son of Priam.
Priamus, -ī *m* king of Troy.
Priāpus, -ī *m* god of fertility and of gardens.
prīdem *adv* long ago, long.
prīdiē *adv* the day before.
prīmaevus *adj* youthful.
prīmānī, -ōrum *mpl* soldiers of the 1st legion.
prīmārius *adj* principal, first-rate.
prīmigenus *adj* original.
prīmipīlāris, -is *m* chief centurion.
prīmipīlus, -ī *m* chief centurion.
prīmitiae, -ārum *fpl* first fruits.
prīmitus *adv* originally.
prīmō *adv* at first; firstly.
prīmōrdium, -ī *and* **iī** *nt* beginning; **~ia rērum**
atoms.
prīmōris *adj* first, foremost, tip of; principal ♦
mpl nobles; (*MIL*) front line.
prīmulum *adv* first.
prīmulus *adj* very first.
prīmum *adv* first, to begin with, in the first
place; for the first time; **cum, ubi, ut ~** as
soon as; **quam ~** as soon as possible; **~ dum** in
the first place.
prīmus *adj* first, foremost, tip of; earliest;
principal, most eminent; **~ veniō** I am the
first to come; **prīma lūx** dawn, daylight; **~ō**
mēnse at the beginning of the month; **~īs**
digitīs with the fingertips; **~ās agere** play the
leading part; **~ās dare** give first place to; in
~īs in the front line; especially.
prīnceps, -ipis *adj* first, in front, chief, most
eminent ♦ *m* leader, chief; first citizen,
emperor; (*MIL*) company, captain, captaincy
♦ *pl* (*MIL*) the second line.
prīncipālis *adj* original; chief; the emperor's.
prīncipātus, -ūs *m* first place; post of
commander-in-chief; emperorship.

prīncipiālis adj from the beginning.
prīncipium, -ī and **iī** nt beginning, origin; first to vote ♦ pl first principles; (MIL) front line; camp headquarters.
prior, -ōris (nt -us) adj former, previous, first; better, preferable ♦ mpl forefathers.
prīscē adv strictly.
prīscus adj former, ancient, old-fashioned.
prīstinus adj former, original; of yesterday.
prius adv previously, before; in former times; ~ **quam** before, sooner than.
prīvātim adv individually, privately at home.
prīvātiō, -ōnis f removal.
prīvātus adj individual, private; n•t in public office ♦ m private citizen.
Prīvernās, -ātis adj see n.
Prīvernum, -ī nt old Latin town.
prīvīgna, -ae f stepdaughter.
prīvīgnus, -ī m stepson; pl stepchildren.
prīvilēgium, -ī and **iī** nt law in favour of or against an individual.
prīvō, -āre, -āvī, -ātum vt to deprive, rob; to free.
prīvus adj single, one each; own, private.
prō adv (with ut and quam) in proportion (as) ♦ prep (with abl) in front of, on the front of; for, on behalf of, instead of, in return for; as, as good as; according to, in proportion to, by virtue of; ~ **eō ac** just as; ~ **eō quod** just because; ~ **eō quantum, ut** in proportion as.
prō interj (expressing wonder or sorrow) O!, alas!
proāgorus, -ī m chief magistrate (in Sicilian towns).
proavītus adj ancestral.
proavus, -ī m great-grandfather, ancestor.
probābilis adj laudable; credible, probable.
probābilitās, -ātis f credibility.
probābiliter adv credibly.
probātiō, -ōnis f approval; testing
probātor, -ōris m approver.
probātus adj tried, excellent; acceptable.
probē adv well, properly; thoroughly, well done!
probitās, -ātis f goodness, honesty.
probō, -āre, -āvī, -ātum vt to approve, approve of; to appraise; to recommend; to prove, show.
probrōsus adj abusive; disgraceful.
probrum, -ī nt abuse, reproach; disgrace; infamy, unchastity.
probus adj good, excellent; honest, upright.
procācitās, -ātis f impudence.
procāciter adv insolently.
procāx, -ācis adj bold, forward, insolent.
prōcēdō, -ēdere, -essī, -essum vi to go forward, advance; to go out, come forth; (time) to go on, continue; (fig) to make progress, get on; (events) to turn out, succeed.
procella, -ae f hurricane, storm; (MIL) charge.

procellōsus adj stormy.
procer, -is m chief, noble, prince.
prōcēritās, -ātis f height; length.
prōcērus adj tall; long.
prōcessiō, -ōnis f advance.
prōcessus, -ūs m advance, progress.
prōcidō, -ere, -ī vi to fall forwards, fall down.
prōcinctus, -ūs m readiness (for action).
prōclāmātor, -ōris m bawler.
prōclāmō, -āre vi to cry out.
prōclīnātus adj tottering.
prōclīnō, -āre vt to bend.
prōclīvē adv downwards; easily.
prōclīvis, -us adj downhill, steep; (mind) prone, willing; (act) easy; in ~ī easy.
prōclīvitās, -ātis f descent; tendency.
prōclīvus etc see **proclīvis.**
Procnē, -ēs f wife of Tereus (changed to a swallow); swallow.
prōcōnsul, -is m proconsul, governor.
prōcōnsulāris adj proconsular.
prōcōnsulātus, -ūs m proconsulship.
prōcrāstinātiō, -ōnis f procrastination.
prōcrāstinō, -āre vt to put off from day to day.
prōcreātiō, -ōnis f begetting.
prōcreātor, -ōris m creator, parent.
prōcreātrix, -īcis f mother.
prōcreō, -āre vt to beget, produce.
prōcrēscō, -ere vi to be produced, grow up.
Procrūstēs, -ae m Attic highwayman (who tortured victims on a bed).
prōcubō, -āre vi to lie on the ground.
prōcūdō, -dere, -dī, -sum vt to forge; to produce.
procul adv at a distance, far, from afar.
prōculcō, -āre vt to trample down.
prōcumbō, -mbere, -buī, -bitum vi to fall forwards, bend over; to sink down, be broken down.
prōcūrātiō, -ōnis f management; (religion) expiation.
prōcūrātor, -ōris m administrator, financial agent; (province) governor.
prōcūrātrix, -īcis f governess.
prōcūrō, -āre, -āvī, -ātum vt to take care of, manage; to expiate ♦ vi to be a procurator.
prōcurrō, -rrere, -currī and **rrī, -rsum** vi to rush forward; to jut out.
prōcursātiō, -ōnis f charge.
prōcursātor, -ōris m skirmisher.
prōcursō, -āre vi to make a sally.
prōcursus, -ūs m charge.
prōcurvus adj curving forwards.
procus, -ī m nobleman.
procus, -ī m wooer, suitor.
Procyōn, -ōnis m Lesser Dog Star.
prōdeambulō, -āre vi to go out for a walk.
prōdeō, -īre, -iī, -itum vi to come out, come forward, appear; to go ahead, advance; to

project.

prōdesse *infin of* **prōsum.**

prōdīcō, -īcere, -īxī, -ictum *vt* to appoint, adjourn.

prōdictātor, -ōris *m* vice-dictator.

prōdigē *adv* extravagantly.

prōdigentia, -ae *f* profusion.

prōdigiāliter *adv* unnaturally.

prōdigiōsus *adj* unnatural, marvellous.

prōdigium, -ī *and* **iī** *nt* portent; unnatural deed; monster.

prōdigō, -igere, -ēgī, -āctum *vt* to squander.

prōdigus *adj* wasteful; lavish, generous.

prōditiō, -ōnis *f* betrayal.

prōditor, -ōris *m* traitor.

prōditus *ppp of* **prōdō.**

prōdō, -ere, -idī, -itum *vt* to bring forth, produce; to make known, publish; to betray, give up; (*tradition*) to hand down.

prōdoceō, -ēre *vt* to preach.

prodromus, -ī *m* forerunner.

prōdūcō, -ūcere, -ūxī, -uctum *vt* to bring forward, bring out; to conduct; to drag in front; to draw out, extend; (*acting*) to perform; (*child*) to beget, bring up; (*fact*) to bring to light; (*innovation*) to introduce; (*rank*) to promote; (*slave*) to put up for sale; (*time*) to prolong, protract, put off; (*tree*) to cultivate; (*vowel*) to lengthen.

prōductē *adv* long.

prōductiō, -ōnis *f* lengthening.

prōductō, -āre *vt* to spin out.

prōductus *ppp of* **prōdūcō** ♦ *adj* lengthened, long.

proēgmenon, -ī *nt* a preferred thing.

proeliātor, -ōris *m* fighter.

proelior, -ārī, -ātus *vi* to fight, join battle.

proelium, -ī *and* **iī** *nt* battle, conflict.

profānō, -āre *vt* to desecrate.

profānus *adj* unholy, common; impious; ill-omened.

profātus *ppa of* **profor.**

profectiō, -ōnis *f* departure; source.

profectō *adv* really, certainly.

profectus *ppa of* **proficīscor.**

prōfectus *ppp of* **prōficiō.**

prōfectus, -ūs *m* growth, progress, profit.

prōferō, -ferre, -tulī, -lātum *vt* to bring forward, forth or out; to extend, enlarge; (*time*) to prolong, defer; (*instance*) to mention, quote; (*knowledge*) to publish, reveal; **pedem ~** proceed; **signa ~** advance.

professiō, -ōnis *f* declaration; public register; profession.

professor, -ōris *m* teacher.

professōrius *adj* authoritative.

professus *ppa of* **profiteor.**

profēstus *adj* not holiday, working.

prōficiō, -icere, -ēcī, -ectum *vi* to make progress, profit; to be of use.

proficīscor, -icīscī, -ectus *vi* to set out, start; to originate, proceed.

profiteor, -itērī, -essus *vt* to declare,

profess; to make an official return of; to promise, volunteer.

prōflīgātor, -ōris *m* spendthrift.

prōflīgātus *adj* dissolute.

prōflīgō, -āre, -āvī, -ātum *vt* to dash to the ground; to destroy, overthrow; to bring almost to an end; to degrade.

prōflō, -āre *vt* to breathe out.

prōfluēns, -entis *pres p of* **prōfluō** ♦ *adj* flowing; fluent ♦ *f* running water.

prōfluenter *adv* easily.

prōfluentia, -ae *f* fluency.

prōfluō, -ere, -xī *vi* to flow on, flow out; (*fig*) to proceed.

prōfluvium, -ī *and* **iī** *nt* flowing.

profor, -ārī, -ātus *vi* to speak, give utterance.

profugiō, -ugere, -ūgī *vi* to flee, escape; to take refuge (with) ♦ *vt* to flee from.

profugus *adj* fugitive; exiled; nomadic.

prōfuī *perf of* **prōsum.**

profundō, -undere, -ūdī, -ūsum *vt* to pour out, shed; to bring forth, produce; to prostrate; to squander; **sē ~** burst forth, rush out.

profundus *adj* deep, vast, high; infernal; (*fig*) profound, immoderate ♦ *nt* depths, abyss.

profūsē *adv* in disorder, extravagantly.

profūsus *ppp of* **profundō** ♦ *adj* lavish; excessive.

prōgener, -ī *m* grandson-in-law.

prōgenerō, -āre *vt* to beget.

prōgeniēs, -ēī *f* descent; offspring, descendants.

prōgenitor, -ōris *m* ancestor.

prōgignō, -ignere, -enuī, -enitum *vt* to beget, produce.

prōgnātus *adj* born, descended ♦ *m* son, descendant.

Prognē *see* **Procnē.**

prognōstica, -ōrum *ntpl* weather signs.

prōgredior, -dī, -ssus *vi* to go forward, advance; to go out.

prōgressiō, -ōnis *f* advancing, increase; (*RHET*) climax.

prōgressus *ppa of* **prōgredior.**

prōgressus, -ūs *m* advance, progress; (*events*) march.

prōh *see* **prō** *interj.*

prohibeō, -ēre, -uī, -itum *vt* to hinder, prevent; to keep away, protect; to forbid.

prohibitiō, -ōnis *f* forbidding.

prōiciō, -icere, -iēcī, -iectum *vt* to throw down, fling forwards; to banish; (*building*) to make project; (*fig*) to discard, renounce; to forsake; (*words*) to blurt out; (*time*) to defer; **sē ~** rush forward, run into danger; to fall prostrate.

prōiectiō, -ōnis *f* forward stretch.

prōiectus *ppp of* **prōiciō** ♦ *adj* projecting, prominent; abject, useless; downcast; addicted (to).

prōiectus, -ūs *m* jutting out.

proinde, proin *adv* consequently, therefore;

just (as).

prōlābor, -bī, -psus vi to slide, move forward; to fall down; (fig) to go on, come to; to slip out; to fail, fall, sink into ruin.

prōlāpsiō, -ōnis f falling.

prōlāpsus ppa of prōlābor.

prōlātiō, -ōnis f extension; postponement; adducing.

prōlātō, -āre vt to extend; to postpone.

prōlātus ppp of prōferō.

prōlectō, -āre vt to entice.

prōlēs, -is f offspring; child; descendants, race.

prōlētārius, -ī and iī m citizen of the lowest class.

prōliciō, -cere, -xī vt to entice.

prōlixē adv fully, copiously, wil ingy.

prōlixus adj long, wide, spreading; (person) obliging; (CIRCS) favourable.

prōlogus, -ī m prologue.

prōloquor, -quī, -cūtus vt to speak out.

prōlubium, -ī and iī nt inclination.

prōlūdō, -dere, -sī, -sum vi to practise.

prōluō, -uere, -uī, -ūtum vt to wash out, wash away.

prōlūsiō, -ōnis f prelude.

prōluviēs, -ēī f flood; excrement.

prōmereō, -ēre, -uī; prōmereor, -ērī, -itus vt to deserve, earn.

prōmeritum, -ī nt desert, merit, guilt.

Promētheus, -eī and eos m demigod who stole fire from the gods.

Promētheūs adj see n.

prōminēns, -entis pres p of prōmineō ♦ adj projecting ♦ nt headland, spur.

prōmineō, -ēre, -uī vi to jut out, overhang; to extend.

prōmiscam, -ē, -uē adv indiscriminately.

prōmiscuus (prōmiscus) adj indiscriminate, in common; ordinary; open to all.

prōmīsī perf of prōmittō.

prōmissiō, -ōnis f promise.

prōmissor, -ōris m promiser.

prōmissum, -ī nt promise.

prōmissus ppp of prōmittō ♦ adj long.

prōmittō, -ittere, -īsī, -issum vt to let grow; to promise, give promise of.

prōmō, -ere, -psī, -ptum vt to bring out, produce; to disclose.

prōmont- etc see prōmunt-.

prōmōtus ppp of prōmoveō ♦ ntal preferable things.

prōmoveō, -ovēre, -ōvī, -ōtum vt to move forward, advance; to enlarge; to postpone; to disclose.

prōmpsī perf of prōmō.

prōmptē adv readily; easily.

prōmptō, -āre vt to distribute.

prōmptū abl m: in ~ at hand, in readiness; obvious, in evidence; easy.

prōmptus ppp of prōmō ♦ adj at hand, ready; prompt, resolute; easy.

prōmulgātiō, -ōnis f promulgating.

prōmulgō, -āre, -āvī, -ātum vt to make public, publish.

prōmulsis, -idis f hors d'oeuvre.

prōmunturium, -ī and iī nt headland, promontory, ridge.

prōmus, -ī m cellarer, butler.

prōmūtuus adj as a loan in advance.

prōnepōs, -ōtis m great-grandson.

pronoea, -ae f providence.

prōnōmen, -inis nt pronoun.

prōnuba, -ae f matron attending a bride.

prōnūntiātiō, -ōnis f declaration; (RHET) delivery; (logic) proposition.

prōnūntiātor, -ōris m narrator.

prōnūntiātum, -ātī nt proposition.

prōnūntiō, -āre, -āvī, -ātum vt to declare publicly, announce; to recite, deliver; to narrate; to nominate.

prōnurus, -ūs f granddaughter-in-law.

prōnus adj leaning forward; headlong, downwards; sloping, sinking; (fig) inclined, disposed, favourable; easy.

prooemium, -ī and iī nt prelude, preface.

propāgātiō, -ōnis f propagating; extension.

propāgātor, -ōris m enlarger.

propāgō, -āre, -āvī, -ātum vt to propagate; to extend; to prolong.

propāgō, -inis f (plant) layer, slip; (men) offspring, posterity.

prōpalam adv openly, known.

prōpatulum, -ī nt open space.

prōpatulus adj open.

prope adv (comp propius, superl proximē) near; nearly ♦ prep (with acc) near, not far from.

propediem adv very soon.

prōpellō, -ellere, -ulī, -ulsum vt to drive, push forward, impel; to drive away, keep off.

propemodum, -o adv almost.

prōpendeō, -endēre, -endī, -ēnsum vi to hang down; to preponderate; to be disposed (to).

prōpēnsē adv willingly.

prōpēnsiō, -ōnis f inclination.

prōpēnsus adj inclining; inclined, well-disposed; important.

properanter adv hastily, quickly.

properantia, -ae f haste.

properātiō, -ōnis f haste.

properātō adv quickly.

properātus adj speedy.

properē adv quickly.

properipēs, -edis adj swiftfooted.

properō, -āre, -āvī, -ātum vt to hasten, do with haste ♦ vi to make haste, hurry.

Propertius, -ī m Latin elegiac poet.

properus adj quick, hurrying.

prōpexus adj combed forward.
propīnō, -āre vt to drink as a toast; to pass on (a cup).
propinquitās, -ātis f nearness; relationship, friendship.
propinquō, -āre vi to approach ♦ vt to hasten.
propinquus adj near, neighbouring; related ♦ m/f relation ♦ nt neighbourhood.
propior, -ōris adj nearer; more closely related, more like; (time) more recent.
propitiō, -āre vt to appease.
propitius adj favourable, gracious.
propius adv nearer, more closely.
propōla, -ae f retailer.
prōpolluō, -ere vt to defile further.
prōpōnō, -ōnere, -osuī, -ositum vt to set forth, display; to publish, declare; to propose, resolve; to imagine; to expose; (logic) to state the first premise; **ante oculōs** ~ picture to oneself.
Propontiacus adj see n.
Propontis, -idis and **idos** f Sea of Marmora.
prōporrō adv furthermore; utterly.
prōportiō, -ōnis f symmetry, analogy.
prōpositiō, -ōnis f purpose; theme; (logic) first premise.
prōpositum, -ī nt plan, purpose; theme; (logic) first premise.
prōpositus ppp of **prōpōnō**.
prōpraetor, -ōris m propraetor, governor; vice-praetor.
propriē adv properly, strictly; particularly.
proprietās, -ātis f peculiarity, property.
proprītim adv properly.
proprius adj one's own, peculiar; personal, characteristic; permanent; (words) literal, regular.
propter adv near by ♦ prep (with acc) near, beside; on account of; by means of.
proptereā adv therefore.
prōpudium, -ī and **iī** nt shameful act; villain.
prōpugnāculum, -ī nt bulwark, tower; defence.
prōpugnātiō, -ōnis f defence.
prōpugnātor, -ōris m defender, champion.
prōpugnō, -āre vi to make a sortie; to fight in defence.
prōpulsātiō, -ōnis f repulse.
prōpulsō, -āre, -āvī, -ātum vt to repel, avert.
prōpulsus ppp of **prōpellō**.
Propylaea, -ōrum ntpl gateway to the Acropolis of Athens.
prō quaestōre m proquaestor.
prōquam conj according as.
prōra, -ae f prow, bows; ship.
prōrēpō, -ere, -sī, -tum vi to crawl out.
prōrēta -ae m man at the prow.
prōreus, -eī m man at the prow.
prōripiō, -ipere, -ipuī, -eptum vt to drag out; to hurry away; **sē** ~ rush out, run away.
prōrogātiō, -ōnis f extension; deferring.
prōrogō, -āre, -āvī, -ātum vt to extend, prolong, continue; to defer.

prōrsum adv forwards; absolutely.
prōrsus adv forwards; absolutely; in short.
prōrumpō, -umpere, -ūpī, -uptum vt to fling out; (pass) to rush forth ♦ vi to break out, burst forth.
prōruō, -ere, -ī, -tum vt to throw down, demolish ♦ vi to rush forth.
prōruptus ppp of **prōrumpō**.
prōsāpia, -ae f lineage.
proscaenium, -ī and **iī** nt stage.
proscindō, -ndere, -dī, -ssum vt to plough up; (fig) to revile.
prōscrībō, -bere, -psī, -ptum vt to publish in writing; to advertise; to confiscate; to proscribe, outlaw.
prōscrīptiō, -ōnis f advertisement; proscription.
prōscrīpturiō, -īre vi to want to have a proscription.
prōscrīptus ppp of **prōscrībō** ♦ m outlaw.
prōsecō, -āre, -uī, -tum vt to cut off (for sacrifice).
prōsēminō, -āre vt to scatter; to propagate.
prōsentiō, -entīre, -ēnsī vt to see beforehand.
prōsequor, -quī, -cūtus vt to attend, escort; to pursue, attack; to honour (with); (words) to proceed with, continue.
Proserpina, -ae f Proserpine (daughter of Ceres and wife of Pluto).
proseucha, -ae f place of prayer.
prōsiliō, -īre, -uī vi to jump up, spring forward; to burst out, spurt.
prōsocer, -ī m wife's grandfather.
prōspectō, -āre vt to look out at, view; to look forward to, await; (place) to look towards.
prōspectus ppp of **prōspiciō**.
prōspectus, -ūs m sight, view, prospect; gaze.
prōspeculor, -ārī vi to look out, reconnoitre ♦ vt to watch for.
prosper, prosperus adj favourable, successful.
prosperē adv see adj.
prosperitās, -ātis f good fortune.
prosperō, -āre vt to make successful, prosper.
prosperus etc see **prosper**.
prōspicientia, -ae f foresight.
prōspiciō, -icere, -exī, -ectum vi to look out, watch; to see to, take precautions ♦ vt to descry, watch for; to foresee; to provide; (place) to command a view of.
prōsternō, -ernere, -rāvī, -rātum vt to throw in front, prostrate; to overthrow, ruin; **sē** ~ fall prostrate; to demean oneself.
prōstibulum, -ī nt prostitute.
prōstituō, -uere, -uī, -ūtum vt to put up for sale, prostitute.
prōstō, -āre, -itī vi to project; to be on sale; to prostitute oneself.
prōstrātus ppp of **prōsternō**.
prōsubigō, -ere vt to dig up.

prōsum, -desse, -fuī vi (with dat) ɔe useful to, benefit.
Prōtagorās, -ae m Greek sophist native of Abdera).
prōtēctus ppp of **prōtegō.**
prōtegō, -egere, -ēxī, -ēctum v ɔcover over, put a projecting roof on; ( ) to shield, protect.
prōtēlō, -āre vt to drive off.
prōtēlum, -ī nt team of oxen; (fig) uccession.
prōtendō, -dere, -dī, -tum vt to ꞊etch out, extend.
prōtentus ppp of **prōtendō.**
prōterō, -erere, -rīvī, -rītum vt to rample down, crush; to overthrow.
prōterreō, -ēre, -uī, -itum vt to ꞊re away.
protervē adv insolently; boldly.
protervitās, -ātis f forwardness, solence.
protervus adj forward, insolent, ꞊ent.
Prōtesilāeus adj see n.
Prōtesilāus, -ī m first Greek killed a ꞊oy.
Prōteus, -eī and **eos** m seagod wit ꞊ower to assume many forms.
prothȳmē adv gladly.
prōtinam adv immediately.
prōtinus adv forward, onward; cꞇ ꞊nuously; right away, forthwith.
prōtollō, -ere vt to stretch out; to쀼 t off.
prōtractus ppp of **prōtrahō.**
prōtrahō, -here, -xī, -ctum vt to ꞊aw on (to); to drag out; to bring to light, reve a..
prōtrītus ppp of **prōterō.**
prōtrūdō, -dere, -sī, -sum vt to ꞊ust forward, push out; to postpone.
prōtulī perf of **prōferō.**
prōturbō, -āre, -āvī, -ātum vt to ꞊ve off; to overthrow.
prout conj according as.
prōvectus ppp of **prōvehō** ♦ adj ad ꞊nced.
prōvehō, -here, -xī, -ctum vt to cꞇ꞊y along, transport; to promote, advance, ꞊ng to; (speech) to prolong; (pass) to dri ꞊, ride, sail on.
prōveniō, -enīre, -ēnī, -entum come out, appear; to arise, grow; to g ꞊, prosper, succeed.
prōventus, -ūs m increase; resul ꞊ ꞊ccess.
prōverbium, -ī and **iī** nt saying, p ꞊ ꞊rb.
prōvidēns, -entis pres p of **prōvideᴏ** ♦ adj prudent.
prōvidenter adv with foresight.
prōvidentia, -ae f foresight, fore ꞊ught.
prōvideō, -idēre, -īdī, -īsum vi tᴏ ꞊e ahead; to take care, make provision ♦ v ꞊ foresee; to look after, provide for; to ob ꞊ ꞊ᴏ.
prōvidus adj foreseeing, cautiou ꞊rudent; provident.
prōvincia, -ae f sphere of action, ꞊ꞇ꞊y, province.
prōvinciālis adj provincial ♦ mpl ꞊ꞇ ꞊/incials.

prōvīsiō, -ōnis f foresight; precaution.
prōvīsō adv with forethought.
prōvīsō, -ere vi to go and see.
prōvīsor, -ōris m foreseer; provider.
prōvīsus ppp of **prōvideō.**
prōvīsus, -ūs m looking forward; foreseeing; providing providence.
prōvīvō, -vere, -xī vi to live on.
prōvocātiō, -ōnis f challenge; appeal.
prōvocātor, -ōris m kind of gladiator.
prōvocō, -āre, -āvī, -ātum vt to challenge, call out; to provoke; to bring about ♦ vi to appeal.
prōvolō, -āre vi to fly out, rush out.
prōvolvō, -vere, -vī, -ūtum vt to roll forward, tumble over; (pass) to fall down, humble oneself, be ruined; sē ~ wallow.
prōvomō, -ere vt to belch forth.
proximē adv next, nearest; (time) just before or after; (with acc) next to, very close to, very like.
proximitās, -ātis f nearness; near relationship; similarity.
proximus adj nearest, next; (time) previous, last, following, next; most akin, most like ♦ m next of kin ♦ nt next door.
proxum etc see **proxim-.**
prūdēns, -entis adj foreseeing, aware; wise, prudent, circumspect; skilled; versed (in).
prūdenter adv prudently; skilfully.
prūdentia, -ae f prudence, discretion; knowledge.
pruīna, -ae f hoar frost.
pruīnōsus adj frosty.
prūna, -ae f live coal.
prūnitius adj of plum tree wood.
prūnum, -ī nt plum.
prūnus, -ī f plum tree.
prūriō, -īre vi to itch.
prytanēum, -ī nt Greek town hall.
prytanis, -is m Greek chief magistrate.
psallō, -ere vi to play the lyre or lute.
psaltērium, -ī and **iī** nt kind of lute.
psaltria, -ae f girl musician.
psecas, -adis f slave who perfumed the lady's hair.
psēphisma, -tis nt decree of the people.
Pseudocatō, -ōnis m sham Cato.
pseudomenos, -ī m sophistical argument.
pseudothyrum, -ī nt back door.
psithius adj psithian (kind of Greek vine).
psittacus, -ī m parrot.
psychomantēum (-īum), -ī nt place of necromancy.
-pte enclitic (to pronouns) self, own.
ptisanārium, -ī and **iī** nt gruel.
Ptolemaeēus, -us adj see n.
Ptolemaeus, -ī m Ptolemy (name of Egyptian kings).
pūbēns, -entis adj full-grown; (plant) juicy.

Noun declensions and verb conjugations are shown on pp xiii to xxv. The present infinitive ending of a verb shows to which conjugation it belongs: -āre = 1st ēre = 2nd; -ere = 3rd and -īre = 4th. Irregular verbs are shown on p xxvi

pūbertās, -ātis/manhood; signs of puberty.
pūbēs (pūber), -eris _adj_ grown up, adult;
(_plant_) downy.
pūbēs, -is/hair at age of puberty; groin;
youth, men, people.
pūbēscō, -ēscere, -uī _vi_ to grow to manhood,
become mature; to become clothed.
pūblicānus _adj_ of public revenue ♦ _m_ tax
farmer.
pūblicātiō, -ōnis/confiscation.
pūblicē _adv_ by _or_ for the State, at the public
expense; all together.
pūblicitus _adv_ at the public expense; in
public.
pūblicō, -āre, -āvī, -ātum _vt_ to confiscate; to
make public.
Pūblicola, -ae _m_ P. Valerius (_an early Roman
consul_).
pūblicum, -ī _nt_ State revenue; State territory;
public.
pūblicus _adj_ of the State, public, common ♦ _m_
public official; **~a causa** criminal trial; **rēs ~a**
the State; **dē ~ō** at the public expense; **in ~ō**
in public.
Publius, -ī _m_ Roman first name.
pudendus _adj_ shameful.
pudēns, -entis _adj_ bashful, modest.
pudenter _adv_ modestly.
pudet, -ēre, -uit _and_ **itum est** _vt_ (_impers_) to
shame, be ashamed.
pudibundus _adj_ modest.
pudīcē _adv see_ **adj**.
pudīcitia, -ae/modesty, chastity.
pudīcus _adj_ modest, chaste.
pudor, -ōris _m_ shame, modesty, sense of
honour; disgrace.
puella, -ae/girl; sweetheart, young wife.
puellāris _adj_ girlish, youthful.
puellula, -ae/little girl.
puellus, -ī _m_ little boy.
puer, -ī _m_ boy, child; son; slave.
puerīlis _adj_ boyish, child's; childish, trivial.
puerīliter _adv_ like a child; childishly.
pueritia, -ae/childhood, youth.
puerperium, -ī _and_ **iī** _nt_ childbirth.
puerperus _adj_ to help childbirth ♦ _f_ woman in
labour.
puertia _etc see_ **pueritia**.
puerulus, -ī _m_ little boy, slave.
pugil, -is _m_ boxer.
pugilātiō, -iōnis/, **-us, -ūs** _m_ boxing.
pugillāris _adj_ that can be held in the hand ♦
mpl, ntpl writing tablets.
pugillātōrius _adj_: **follis ~** punchball.
pugiō, -ōnis _m_ dirk, dagger.
pugiunculus, -ī _m_ small dagger.
pugna, -ae/fight, battle.
pugnācitās, -ātis/fondness for a fight.
pugnāciter _adv_ aggressively.
pugnāculum, -ī _nt_ fortress.
pugnātor, -ōris _m_ fighter.
pugnāx, -ācis _adj_ fond of a fight, aggressive;
obstinate.

pugneus _adj_ with the fist.
pugnō, -āre, -āvī, -ātum _vi_ to fight; to
disagree; to struggle; **sēcum ~** be
inconsistent; **~ātum est** the battle was
fought.
pugnus, -ī _m_ fist.
pulchellus _adj_ pretty little.
pulcher, -rī _adj_ beautiful, handsome; fine,
glorious.
pulchrē _adv_ excellently; well done!
pulchritūdō, -inis/beauty, excellence.
pūlēium, pūlegium, -ī _and_ **iī** _nt_ pennyroyal.
pūlex, -icis _m_ flea.
pullārius, -ī _and_ **iī** _m_ keeper of the sacred
chickens.
pullātus _adj_ dressed in black.
pullulō, -āre _vi_ to sprout.
pullus, -ī _m_ young (of animals), chicken.
pullus _adj_ dark-grey; mournful ♦ _nt_ dark grey
clothes.
pulmentārium, -ārī _and_ **-āriī, -um, -ī** _nt_
relish; food.
pulmō, -ōnis _m_ lung.
pulmōneus _adj_ of the lungs.
pulpa, -ae/fleshy part.
pulpāmentum, -ī _nt_ tit-bits.
pulpitum, -ī _nt_ platform, stage.
puls, pultis/porridge.
pulsātiō, -ōnis/beating.
pulsō, -āre, -āvī, -ātum _vt_ to batter, knock,
strike.
pulsus _ppp of_ **pellō**.
pulsus, -ūs _m_ push, beat, blow; impulse.
pultiphagus, -ī _m_ porridge eater.
pultō, -āre _vt_ to beat, knock at.
pulvereus _adj_ of dust, dusty, fine as dust;
raising dust.
pulverulentus _adj_ dusty; laborious.
pulvillus, -ī _m_ small cushion.
pulvīnar, -āris _nt_ sacred couch; seat of
honour.
pulvīnus, -ī _m_ cushion, pillow.
pulvis, -eris _m_ dust, powder; arena; effort.
pulvisculus, -ī _m_ fine dust.
pūmex, -icis _m_ pumice stone; stone, rock.
pūmiceus _adj_ of soft stone.
pūmicō, -āre _vt_ to smooth with pumice stone.
pūmiliō, -ōnis _m/f_ dwarf, pygmy.
pūnctim _adv_ with the point.
pūnctum, -ī _nt_ point, dot; vote; (_time_) moment;
(_speech_) short section.
pūnctus _ppp of_ **pungō**.
pungō, -ere, pupugī, pūnctum _vt_ to prick,
sting, pierce; (_fig_) to vex.
Pūnicānus _adj_ in the Carthaginian style.
Pūnicē _adv_ in Punic.
pūniceus _adj_ reddish, purple.
Pūnicum, -ī _nt_ pomegranate.
Pūnicus _adj_ Punic, Carthaginian; purple-red.
pūniō (poeniō), -īre; -ior, -īrī _vt_ to punish; to
avenge.
pūnītor, -ōris _m_ avenger.
pūpa, -ae/doll.

pūpilla, -ae f ward; (eye) pupil.
pūpillāris adj of a ward, of an orphan.
pūpillus, -ī m orphan, ward.
puppis, -is f after part of a ship, stern; ship.
pupugī perf of pungō.
pūpula, -ae f (eye) pupil.
pūpulus, -ī m little boy.
pūrē adv cleanly, brightly; plainly, simply, purely, chastely.
pūrgāmen, -inis nt sweepings, dirt; means of expiation.
pūrgāmentum, -ī nt refuse, dirt.
pūrgātiō, -ōnis f purging; justification.
pūrgō, -āre, -āvī, -ātum vt to cleanse, purge, clear away; to exculpate, justify; t● purify.
pūriter adv cleanly, purely.
purpura, -ae f purple-fish, purple; purple cloth; finery, royalty.
purpurātus adj wearing purple ♦ m courtier.
purpureus adj red, purple, black; wearing purple; bright, radiant.
purpurissum, -ī nt kind of rouge.
pūrus adj clear, unadulterated, free from obstruction or admixture; pure, clean; plain, unadorned; (moral) pure, chaste ♦ ●t clear sky.
pūs, pūris nt pus; (fig) malice.
pusillus adj very little; petty, paltry.
pūsiō, -ōnis m little boy.
pūstula, -ae f pimple, blister.
putāmen, -inis nt peeling, shell, husk.
putātiō, -ōnis f pruning.
putātor, -ōris m pruner.
puteal, -ālis nt low wall round a well or sacred place.
puteālis adj well- (in cpds).
pūteō, -ēre vi to stink.
Puteolānus adj see n.
Puteolī, -ōrum mpl town on the Campanian coast.
puter, putris, -ris adj rotten, decaying; crumbling, flabby.
putēscō, -ēscere, -uī vi to become rotten.
puteus, -ī m well; pit.
pūtidē adv see pūtidus.
pūtidiusculus adj somewhat nauseating.
pūtidus adj rotten, stinking; (speech) affected, nauseating.
putō, -āre, -āvī, -ātum vt to think, suppose; to think over; to reckon, count; (money) to settle; (tree) to prune.
pūtor, -ōris m stench.
putrefaciō, -facere, -fēcī, -factum ●t to make rotten; to make crumble.
putrēscō, -ere vi to rot, moulder.
putridus adj rotten, decayed; withered.
putris etc see puter.
putus adj perfectly pure.
putus, -ī m boy.
pycta, -ēs, -ae m boxer.

Pydna, -ae f town in Macedonia.
Pydnaeus adj see n.
pȳga, -ae f buttocks.
Pygmaeus adj Pygmy.
Pyladēs, -ae and is m friend of Orestes.
Pyladēus adj see n.
Pylae, -ārum fpl Thermopylae.
Pylaicus adj see n.
Pylius adj see n.
Pylos, -ī f Pylus (Peloponnesian town, home of Nestor).
pyra, -ae f funeral pyre.
Pȳramaeus adj see Pȳramus.
pȳramis, -idis f pyramid.
Pȳramus, -ī m lover of Thisbe.
Pȳrēnē, -ēs f Pyrenees.
pyrethrum, -ī nt Spanish camomile.
Pyrgēnsis adj see Pyrgī.
Pyrgī, -ōrum mpl ancient town in Etruria.
pyrōpus, -ī m bronze.
Pyrrha, -ae and ē, -ēs f wife of Deucalion.
Pyrrhaeus adj see n.
Pyrrhō, -ōnis m Greek philosopher (founder of the Sceptics).
Pyrrhōnēus adj see n.
Pyrrhus, -ī m son of Achilles; king of Epirus, enemy of Rome.
Pȳthagorās, -ae m Greek philosopher who founded a school in S. Italy.
Pȳthagorēus, -icus adj Pythagorean.
Pȳthius, -icus adj Pythian, Delphic ♦ m Apollo ♦ f priestess of Apollo ♦ ntpl Pythian Games.
Pȳthō, -ūs f Delphi.
Pȳthōn, -ōnis m serpent killed by Apollo.
pȳtisma, -tis nt what is spit out.
pȳtissō, -āre vi to spit out wine.
pyxis, -dis f small box, toilet box.

Q, q

quā adv where, which way; whereby; as far as; partly ... partly.
quācumque adv wherever; anyhow.
quādam: ~ tenus adv only so far.
quadra, -ae f square morsel; table.
quadrāgēnī, -ōrum adj forty each.
quadrāgēsimus adj fortieth ♦ f 2 ½ per cent tax.
quadrāgiēns, -ēs adv forty times.
quadrāgintā num forty.
quadrāns, -antis m quarter; (coin) quarter as.
quadrantārius adj of a quarter.

Noun declensions and verb conjugations are shown on pp xiii to xxv. The present infinitive ending of a verb shows to which conjugation it belongs: -āre = 1st; -ēre = 2nd; -ere = 3rd and -īre = 4th. Irregular verbs are shown on p xxvi

quadrātum, -ī _nt_ square; (_ASTRO_) quadrature.
quadrātus _ppp of_ **quadrō** ♦ _adj_ square; **~ō agmine** in battle order.
quadriduum, -ī _nt_ four days.
quadriennium, -ī _and_ **iī** _nt_ four years.
quadrifāriam _adv_ in four parts.
quadrifidus _adj_ split in four.
quadrīgae, -ārum _fpl_ team of four; chariot.
quadrīgārius, -ī _and_ **iī** _m_ chariot racer.
quadrīgātus _adj_ stamped with a chariot.
quadrigulae, -ārum _fpl_ little four horse team.
quadriiugī, -ōrum _mpl_ team of four.
quadriiugis, -us _adj_ of a team of four.
quadrilībris _adj_ weighing four pounds.
quadrīmulus _adj_ four years old.
quadrīmus _adj_ four years old.
quadringēnārius _adj_ of four hundred each.
quadringēnī, -ōrum _adj_ four hundred each.
quadringentēsimus _adj_ four-hundredth.
quadringentī, -ōrum _num_ four hundred.
quadringentiēns, -ēs _adv_ four hundred times.
quadripertītus _adj_ fourfold.
quadrirēmis, -is _f_ quadrireme.
quadrivium, -ī _and_ **iī** _nt_ crossroads.
quadrō, -āre _vt_ to make square; to complete ♦ _vi_ to square, fit, agree.
quadrum, -ī _nt_ square.
quadrupedāns, -antis _adj_ galloping.
quadrupēs, -edis _adj_ four-footed, on all fours ♦ _m/f_ quadruped.
quadruplātor, -ōris _m_ informer, twister.
quadruplex, -icis _adj_ four-fold.
quadruplum, -ī _nt_ four times as much.
quaeritō, -āre _vt_ to search diligently for; to earn (a living); to keep on asking.
quaerō, -rere, -sīvī _and_ **siī, -sītum** _vt_ to look for, search for; to seek, try to get; to acquire, earn; (_plan_) to think out, work out; (_question_) to ask, make inquiries; (_law_) to investigate; (_with infin_) to try, wish; **quid ~ris?** in short; **sī ~ris/~rimus** to tell the truth.
quaesītiō, -ōnis _f_ inquisition.
quaesītor, -ōris _m_ investigator, judge.
quaesītus _ppp of_ **quaerō** ♦ _adj_ special; far-fetched ♦ _nt_ question ♦ _ntpl_ gains.
quaesīvī _perf of_ **quaerō**.
quaesō, -ere _vt_ to ask, beg.
quaesticulus, -ī _m_ slight profit.
quaestiō, -ōnis _f_ seeking, questioning; investigation, research; criminal trial; court; **servum in ~ōnem ferre** take a slave for questioning by torture; **~ōnēs perpetuae** standing courts.
quaestiuncula, -ae _f_ trifling question.
quaestor, -ōris _m_ quaestor, treasury official.
quaestōrius _adj_ of a quaestor ♦ _m_ ex-quaestor ♦ _nt_ quaestor's tent or residence.
quaestuōsus _adj_ lucrative, productive; money-making; wealthy.
quaestūra, -ae _f_ quaestorship; public money.
quaestus, -ūs _m_ profit, advantage; money-making, occupation; **~uī habēre** make money

out of; **~um facere** make a living.
quālibet _adv_ anywhere; anyhow.
quālis _adj_ (_interrog_) what kind of?; (_relat_) such as, even as.
quāliscumque _adj_ of whatever kind; any, whatever.
quāliscunque _adj_ = **quāliscumque**.
quālitās, -ātis _f_ quality, nature.
quāliter _adv_ just as.
quālubet _adv_ anywhere; anyhow.
quālus, -ī _m_ wicker basket.
quam _adv_ (_interrog, excl_) how?, how much?; (_comparison_) as, than; (_with superl_) as … as possible; (_emphatic_) very; **dīmidium ~ quod** half of what; **quīntō diē ~** four days after.
quamdiū _adv_ how long?; as long as.
quamlibet, quamlubet _adv_ as much as you like, however.
quamobrem _adv_ (_interrog_) why?; (_relat_) why ♦ _conj_ therefore.
quamquam _conj_ although; and yet.
quamvīs _adv_ however, ever so ♦ _conj_ however much, although.
quānam _adv_ what way.
quandō _adv_ (_interrog_) when?; (_relat_) (_with sī, nē, num_) ever ♦ _conj_ when; since.
quandōcumque, quandocunque _adv_ whenever, as often as; some day.
quandōque _adv_ whenever; some day ♦ _conj_ seeing that.
quandō quidem _conj_ seeing that, since.
quanquam _etc see_ **quamquam**.
quantillus _adj_ how little, how much.
quantopere _adv_ how much; (_after_ **tantopere**) as.
quantulus _adj_ how little, how small.
quantuluscumque _adj_ however small, however trifling.
quantum _adv_ how much; as much as; **~cumque** as much as ever; **~libet** however much; **~vīs** as much as you like; although.
quantus _adj_ how great; so great as, such as; **~ī** how dear, how highly; **~ō** (_with compar_) how much; the; **in ~um** as far as.
quantuscumque _adj_ however great, whatever size.
quantuslibet _adj_ as great as you like.
quantus quantus _adj_ however great.
quantusvīs _adj_ however great.
quāpropter _adv_ why; and therefore.
quāquā _adv_ whatever way.
quārē _adv_ how, why; whereby; and therefore.
quartadecumānī, -ōrum _mpl_ men of the fourteenth legion.
quartānus _adj_ every four days ♦ _f_ quartan fever ♦ _mpl_ men of the fourth legion.
quartārius, -ī _and_ **iī** _m_ quarter pint.
quartus _adj_ fourth; **quartum/quartō** for the fourth time.
quartusdecimus _adj_ fourteenth.
quasi _adv_ as if; as it were; (_numbers_) about.
quasillus, -ī _m_, **-um, -ī** _nt_ wool basket.
quassātiō, -ōnis _f_ shaking.

quassō, -āre, -āvī, -ātum vt to shake, toss; to shatter, damage.

quassus ppp of **quatiō** ♦ adj broken.

quatefaciō, -facere, -fēcī vt to shake, give a jolt to.

quātenus adv (interrog) how far?; **ow** long?; (relat) as far as; in so far as, since.

quater adv four times; ~ **deciēs** fourteen times.

quaternī, -ōrum adj four each, in ours.

quatiō, -tere, -ssum vt to shake, disturb, brandish; to strike, shatter; (fig) to agitate, harass.

quattuor num four.

quattuordecim num fourteen.

quattuorvirātus, -ūs m membership of quattuorviri.

quattuorvirī, -ōrum mpl board of four officials.

-que conj and; both ... and; (after neg) but.

quemadmodum adv (interrog) how?; (relat) just as.

queō, -īre, -īvī and **iī, -itum** vi to be able, can.

quercētum, -ī nt oak forest.

querceus adj of oak.

quercus, -ūs f oak; garland of oak leaves; acorn.

querēla, querella, -ae f complaint; plaintive sound.

queribundus adj complaining.

querimōnia, -ae f complaint; elegy.

queritor, -ārī vi to complain much.

quernus adj oak- (in cpds).

queror, -rī, -stus vt, vi to complain; lament; (birds) to sing.

querquetulānus adj of oakwoods.

querulus adj complaining; plaintive, warbling.

questus ppa of **queror**.

questus, -ūs m complaint, lament.

quī, quae, quod pron (interrog) what?, which?; (relat) who, which, that; what; and this, he, etc.; (with **sī, nisi, nē, num**) any.

quī adv (interrog) how?; (relat) with which, whereby; (indef) somehow; (excl) indeed.

quia conj because; ~**nam** why?

quicquam nt see **quisquam**.

quicque nt see **quisque**.

quicquid nt see **quisquis**.

quīcum with whom, with which.

quīcumque, quīcunque pron whoever, whatever, all that; every possible.

quid nt see **quis** ♦ adv why?

quīdam, quaedam, quoddam pron a certain, a sort of, a ....

quiddam nt something.

quidem adv (emphatic) in fact; (qualifying) at any rate; (conceding) it is true; (adding) for instance; **nē** ... ~ not even.

quidlibet nt anything.

quidnam nt see **quisnam**.

quidnī adv why not?

quidpiam nt = **quispiam**.

quidquam nt = **quisquam**.

quidquid nt = **quisquis**.

quiēs, -ētis f rest, peace, quiet; sleep, dream, death; neutrality; lair.

quiēscō, -scere, -vī, -tum vi to rest, keep quiet; to be at peace, keep neutral; to sleep; (with acc and infin) to stand by and see; (with infin) to cease.

quiētē adv peacefully, quietly.

quiētus ppa of **quiēscō** ♦ adj at rest; peaceful, neutral; calm, quiet, asleep.

quīlibet, quaelibet, quodlibet pron any, anyone at all.

quīn adv (interrog) why not?; (correcting) indeed, rather ♦ conj who not; but that, but, without; (preventing) from; (doubting) that.

quīnam, quaenam, quodnam pron which?, what?

Quīnct- etc see **Quīnt-**.

quīncūnx, -ūncis m five-twelfths; number five on a dice; **in ~ūncem dispositī** arranged in oblique lines.

quīndeciēns, -ēs adv fifteen times.

quīndecim num fifteen; ~ **prīmī** fifteen chief magistrates.

quīndecimvirālis adj of the council of fifteen.

quīndecimvirī, -ōrum mpl council of fifteen.

quīngēnī, -ōrum adj five hundred each.

quīngentēsimus adj five-hundredth.

quīngentī, -ōrum num five hundred.

quīngentiēns, -ēs adv five hundred times.

quīnī, -ōrum adj five each; five; ~ **dēnī** fifteen each; ~ **vīcēnī** twenty-five each.

quīnquāgēnī, -ōrum adj fifty each.

quīnquāgēsimus adj fiftieth ♦ f 2 per cent tax.

quīnquāgintā num fifty.

Quīnquātria, -iōrum and **ium** ntpl festival of Minerva.

Quīnquātrūs, -uum fpl festival of Minerva.

quīnque num five.

quīnquennālis adj quinquennial; lasting five years.

quīnquennis adj five years old; quinquennial.

quīnquennium, -ī and **iī** nt five years.

quīnquēpartītus adj fivefold.

quīnqueprīmī, -ōrum mpl five leading men.

quīnquerēmis adj five-banked ♦ f quinquereme.

quīnquevirātus, -ūs m membership of the board of five.

quīnquevirī, -ōrum mpl board of five.

quīnquiēns, -ēs adv five times.

quīnquiplicō, -āre vt to multiply by five.

quīntadecimānī, -ōrum mpl men of the fifteenth legion.

quīntānus adj of the fifth ♦ f street in a camp

between the 5th and 6th maniples ♦ _mpl_ men of the fifth legion.

Quīntiliānus, -ī _m_ Quintilian (_famous teacher of rhetoric in Rome_).

Quīntīlis _adj_ of July.

quīntum, -ō _adv_ for the fifth time.

Quīntus, -ī _m_ Roman first name.

quīntus _adj_ fifth.

quīntusdecimus _adj_ fifteenth.

quippe _adv_ (_affirming_) certainly, of course ♦ _conj_ (_explaining_) for in fact, because, since; ~ **quī** since I, he _etc_.

quippiam _etc see_ **quispiam**.

quippinī _adv_ certainly.

Quirīnālis _adj_ of Romulus; Quirinal (hill).

Quirīnus, -ī _m_ Romulus ♦ _adj_ of Romulus.

Quirīs, -ītis _m_ inhabitant of Cures; Roman citizen; citizen.

quirītātiō, -ōnis _f_ shriek.

Quirītēs _pl_ inhabitants of Cures; Roman citizens.

quirītō, -āre _vi_ to cry out, wail.

quis, quid _pron_ who?, what?; (_indef_) anyone, anything.

quīs _poetic form of_ **quibus**.

quisnam, quaenam, quidnam _pron_ who?, what?

quispiam, quaepiam, quodpiam _and_ **quidpiam** _pron_ some, some one, something.

quisquam, quaequam, quicquam _and_ **quidquam** _pron_ any, anyone, anything; **nec** ~ and no one.

quisque, quaeque, quodque _pron_ each, every, every one; **quidque, quicque** everything; **decimus** ~ every tenth; **optimus** ~ all the best; **primus** ~ the first possible.

quisquiliae, -ārum _fpl_ refuse, rubbish.

quisquis, quaequae, quodquod, quidquid _and_ **quicquid** _pron_ whoever, whatever, all.

quīvīs, quaevīs, quodvīs, quidvīs _pron_ any you please, anyone, anything.

quīvīscumque, quaevīscumque, quodvīscumque _pron_ any whatsoever.

quō _adv_ (_interrog_) where?; whither?; for what purpose?, what for?; (_relat_) where, to which (place), to whom; (_with compar_) the (more); (_with sī_) anywhere ♦ _conj_ (_with subj_) in order that; **nōn** ~ not that.

quoad _adv_ how far?; how long? ♦ _conj_ as far as, as long as; until.

quōcircā _conj_ therefore.

quōcumque _adv_ whithersoever.

quod _conj_ as for, in that, that; because; why; ~ **sī** but if.

quōdam modo _adv_ in a way.

quoi, quōius _old forms of_ **cui, cūius**.

quōlibet _adv_ anywhere, in any direction.

quom _etc see_ **cum** _conj_.

quōminus _conj_ that not; (_preventing_) from.

quōmodo _adv_ (_interrog_) how?; (_relat_) just as; **~cumque** howsoever; **~nam** how?

quōnam _adv_ where, where to?

quondam _adv_ once, formerly; sometimes;

(_fut_) one day.

quōniam _conj_ since, seeing that.

quōpiam _adv_ anywhere.

quōquam _adv_ anywhere.

quoque _adv_ also, too.

quōquō _adv_ to whatever place, wherever.

quōquō modo _adv_ howsoever.

quōquō versus, -um _adv_ in every direction.

quōrsus, quōrsum _adv_ where to?, in what direction?; what for?, to what end?

quot _adj_ how many; as many as, every.

quotannīs _adv_ every year.

quotcumque _adj_ however many.

quotēnī, -ōrum _adj_ how many.

quotīd- _etc see_ **cottīd-**.

quotiēns, -ēs _adv_ how often?; (_relat_) as often as.

quotiēnscumque _adv_ however often.

quotquot _adj_ however many.

quotumus _adj_ which number?, what date?.

quotus _adj_ what number, how many; ~ **quisque** how few; **~a hōra** what time.

quotuscumque _adj_ whatever number, however big.

quōusque _adv_ how long, till when; how far.

quōvīs _adv_ anywhere.

quum _etc see_ **cum** _conj_.

R, r

rabidē _adv_ furiously.

rabidus _adj_ raving, mad; impetuous.

rabiēs, -em, -ēf madness, rage, fury.

rabiō, -ere _vi_ to rave.

rabiōsē _adv_ wildly.

rabiōsulus _adj_ somewhat rabid.

rabiōsus _adj_ furious, mad.

rabula, -ae _m_ wrangling lawyer.

racēmifer, -ī _adj_ clustered.

racēmus, -ī _m_ stalk of a cluster; bunch of grapes; grape.

radiātus _adj_ radiant.

rādīcitus _adv_ by the roots; utterly.

rādīcula, -ae _f_ small root.

radiō, -āre _vt_ to irradiate ♦ _vi_ to radiate, shine.

radius, -i _and_ **iī** _m_ stick, rod; (_light_) beam, ray; (_loom_) shuttle; (MATH) rod for drawing figures, radius of a circle; (_plant_) long olive; (_wheel_) spoke.

rādīx, -īcis _f_ root; radish; (_hill_) foot; (_fig_) foundation, origin.

rādō, -dere, -sī, -sum _vt_ to scrape, shave, scratch; to erase; to touch in passing, graze, pass along.

raeda, -ae _f_ four-wheeled carriage.

raedārius, -ī *and* **iī** *m* driver.
Raetī, -ōrum *mpl* Alpine people between Italy and Germany.
Raetia, -iae *f* country of the Raeti.
Raeticus *and* **ius** *and* **us** *adj see n.*
rāmālia, -ium *ntpl* twigs, brushwood.
rāmentum, -ī *nt* shavings, chips.
rāmeus *adj* of branches.
rāmex, -icis *m* rupture, blood vessels of the lungs.
Ramnēnsēs, Ramnēs, -ium *mpl* one of the original Roman tribes; a century of equites.
rāmōsus *adj* branching.
rāmulus, -ī *m* twig, sprig.
rāmus, -ī *m* branch, bough.
rāna, -ae *f* frog; frogfish.
rancēns, -entis *adj* putrid.
rancidulus *adj* rancid.
rancidus *adj* rank, rancid; disgusting.
rānunculus, -ī *m* tadpole.
rapācida, -ae *m* son of a thief.
rapācitās, -ātis *f* greed.
rapāx, -ācis *adj* greedy, grasping, ravenous.
raphanus, -ī *m* radish.
rapidē *adv* swiftly, hurriedly.
rapiditās, -ātis *f* rapidity.
rapidus *adj* tearing, devouring; swift, rapid; hasty, impetuous.
rapīna, -ae *f* pillage, robbery; booty, prey.
rapiō, -ere, -uī, -tum *vt* to tear, snatch, carry off; to seize, plunder; to hurry, seize quickly.
raptim *adv* hastily, violently.
raptiō, -ōnis *f* abduction.
raptō, -āre, -āvī, -ātum *vt* to seize and carry off, drag away, move quickly; to plunder, lay waste; (*passion*) to agitate.
raptor, -ōris *m* plunderer, robber, ravisher.
raptus *ppp of* **rapiō** ♦ *nt* plunder.
raptus, -ūs *m* carrying off, abduction; plundering.
rāpulum, -ī *nt* small turnip.
rāpum, -ī *nt* turnip.
rārēfaciō, -facere, -fēcī, -factum (*pass* -fīō, -fierī) *vt* to rarefy.
rārēscō, -ere *vi* to become rarefied, grow thin; to open out.
rāritās, -ātis *f* porousness, open texture; thinness, fewness.
rārō, -ē *adv* seldom.
rārus *adj* porous, open in texture; thin, scanty; scattered, straggling, here and there; (*MIL*) in open order; few, infrequent; uncommon, rare.
rāsī *perf of* **rādō**.
rāsilis *adj* smooth, polished.
rāstrum, -ī *nt* hoe, mattock.
rāsus *ppp of* **rādō**.
ratiō, -ōnis *f* 1. (*reckoning of*) account, calculation; list, register; affair, business.

2. (*relation*) respect, consideration; procedure, method, system, way, kind.
3. (*reason*) reasoning, thought; cause, motive; science, knowledge, philosophy; ~ atque ūsus theory and practice; ~ est it is reasonable; **Stōicōrum** ~ Stoicism; ~ōnem dūcere, inīre calculate; ~ōnem habēre take account of, have to do with, consider; ~ōnem reddere give an account of; **cum** ~ōne reasonably; **meae** ~ōnēs my interests; ā ~ōnibus accountant.
ratiōcinātiō, -ōnis *f* reasoning; syllogism.
ratiōcinātīvus *adj* syllogistic.
ratiōcinātor, -ōris *m* accountant.
ratiōcinor, -ārī, -ātus *vt, vi* to calculate; to consider; to argue, infer.
ratiōnālis *adj* rational; syllogistic.
ratis, -is *f* raft; boat.
ratiuncula, -ae *f* small calculation; slight reason; petty syllogism.
ratus *ppa of* **reor** ♦ *adj* fixed, settled, sure; valid; **prō** ~**ā** (**parte**) proportionally; ~**um** dūcere, facere, habēre ratify.
raucisonus *adj* hoarse.
raucus *adj* hoarse; harsh, strident.
raudus, -eris *nt* copper coin.
raudusculum, -ī *nt* bit of money.
Ravenna, -ae *f* port in N.E. Italy.
Ravennās, -ātis *adj see n.*
rāvis, -im *f* hoarseness.
rāvus *adj* grey, tawny.
rea, -ae *f* defendant, culprit.
reāpse *adv* in fact, actually.
Reāte, -is *nt* ancient Sabine town.
Reātīnus *adj see n.*
rebellātiō, -ōnis *f* revolt.
rebellātrīx, -īcis *f* rebellious.
rebelliō, -ōnis *f* revolt.
rebellis *adj* rebellious ♦ *mpl* rebels.
rebellium, -ī *and* **iī** *nt* revolt.
rebellō, -āre *vi* to revolt.
rebītō, -ere *vi* to return.
reboō, -āre *vi* to re-echo ♦ *vt* to make resound.
recalcitrō, -āre *vi* to kick back.
recaleō, -ēre *vi* to be warm again.
recalēscō, -ere *vi* to grow warm again.
recalfaciō, -facere, -fēcī *vt* to warm again.
recalvus *adj* bald in front.
recandēscō, -ēscere, -uī *vi* to whiten (*in response to*); to glow.
recantō, -āre, -āvī, -ātum *vt* to recant; to charm away.
reccidī *perf of* **recidō**.
recēdō, -ēdere, -essī, -essum *vi* to move back, withdraw, depart; (*place*) to recede; (*head*) to be severed.
recellō, -ere *vi* to spring back.
recēns, -entis *adj* fresh, young, recent; (*writer*) modern; (*with ab*) immediately after ♦ *adv* newly, just.

recēnseō, -ēre, -uī, -um *vt* to count; to review.
recēnsiō, -ōnis *f* revision.
recēnsus *ppp of* recēnseō.
recēpī *perf of* recipiō.
receptāculum, -ī *nt* receptacle, reservoir; refuge, shelter.
receptō, -āre *vt* to take back; to admit, harbour; to tug hard at.
receptor, -ōris *m* (male) receiver, shelterer.
receptrīx, -īcis *f* (female) receiver, shelterer.
receptum, -ī *nt* obligation.
receptus *ppp of* recipiō.
receptus, -ūs *m* withdrawal; retreat; return; refuge; ~uī canere sound the retreat.
recessī *perf of* recēdō.
recessim *adv* backwards.
recessus, -ūs *m* retreat, departure; recess, secluded spot; (*tide*) ebb.
recidīvus *adj* resurrected; recurring.
recidō, -idere, -cidī, -āsum *vi* to fall back; to recoil, relapse; (*fig*) to fall, descend.
recīdō, -dere, -dī, -sum *vt* to cut back, cut off.
recingō, -gere, -ctum *vt* to ungird, loose.
recinō, -ere *vt, vi* to re-echo, repeat; to sound a warning.
reciper- *etc see* recuper-.
recipiō, -ipere, -ēpī, -eptum *vt* to take back, retake; to get back, regain, rescue; to accept, admit; (*MIL*) to occupy; (*duty*) to undertake; (*promise*) to pledge, guarantee; sē ~ withdraw, retreat; nōmen ~ receive notice of a prosecution.
reciprocō, -āre *vt* to move to and fro; (*ship*) to bring round to another tack; (*proposition*) to reverse ♦ *vi* (*tide*) to rise and fall.
reciprocus *adj* ebbing.
recīsus *ppp of* recīdō.
recitātiō, -ōnis *f* reading aloud, recital.
recitātor, -ōris *m* reader, reciter.
recitō, -āre, -āvī, -ātum *vt* to read out, recite.
reclāmātiō, -ōnis *f* outcry (*of disapproval*).
reclāmitō, -āre *vi* to cry out against.
reclāmō, -āre *vi* to cry out, protest; to reverberate.
reclīnis *adj* leaning back.
reclīnō, -āre, -āvī, -ātum *vt* to lean back.
reclūdō, -dere, -sī, -sum *vt* to open up; to disclose.
reclūsus *ppp of* reclūdō.
recoctus *ppp of* recoquō.
recōgitō, -āre *vi* to think over, reflect.
recognitiō, -ōnis *f* review.
recognōscō, -ōscere, -ōvī, -itum *vt* to recollect; to examine, review.
recolligō, -igere, -ēgī, -ēctum *vt* to gather up; (*fig*) to recover, reconcile.
recolō, -olere, -oluī, -ultum *vt* to recultivate; to resume; to reflect on, contemplate; to revisit.
recomminīscor, -ī *vi* to recollect.

recompositus *adj* rearranged.
reconciliātiō, -ōnis *f* restoration, reconciliation.
reconciliō, -āre, -āvī, -ātum *vt* to win back again, restore, reconcile.
reconcinnō, -āre *vt* to repair.
reconditus *ppp of* recondō ♦ *adj* hidden, secluded; abstruse, profound; (*disposition*) reserved.
recondō, -ere, -idī, -itum *vt* to store away, stow; to hide away, bury.
recōnflō, -āre *vt* to rekindle.
recoquō, -quere, -xī, -ctum *vt* to cook again, boil again; to forge again, recast; (*fig*) to rejuvenate.
recordātiō, -ōnis *f* recollection.
recordor, -ārī, -ātus *vt, vi* to recall, remember; to ponder over.
recreō, -āre, -āvī, -ātum *vt* to remake, reproduce; to revive, refresh.
recrepō, -āre *vt, vi* to ring, re-echo.
recrēscō, -scere, -vī *vi* to grow again.
recrūdēscō, -ēscere, -uī *vi* (*wound*) to open again; (*war*) to break out again.
rēctā *adv* straight forward, right on.
rēctē *adv* straight; correctly, properly, well; quite; (*inf*) good, all right, no thank you.
rēctiō, -ōnis *f* government.
rēctor, -ōris *m* guide, driver, helmsman; governor, master.
rēctum, -ī *nt* right, virtue.
rēctus *ppp of* regō ♦ *adj* straight; upright, steep; right, correct, proper; (*moral*) good, virtuous.
recubō, -āre *vi* to lie, recline.
recultus *ppp of* recolō.
recumbō, -mbere, -buī *vi* to lie down, recline; to fall, sink down.
recuperātiō, -ōnis *f* recovery.
recuperātor, -ōris *m* recapturer; (*pl*) board of justices who tried civil cases requiring a quick decision, esp cases involving foreigners.
recuperātōrius *adj* of the recuperatores.
recuperō, -āre, -āvī, -ātum *vt* to get back, recover, recapture.
recūrō, -āre *vt* to restore.
recurrō, -ere, -ī *vi* to run back; to return, recur; to revert.
recursō, -āre *vi* to keep coming back, keep recurring.
recursus, -ūs *m* return, retreat.
recurvō, -āre *vt* to bend back, curve.
recurvus *adj* bent, curved.
recūsātiō, -ōnis *f* refusal, declining; (*law*) objection, counterplea.
recūsō, -āre, -āvī, -ātum *vt* to refuse, decline, be reluctant; (*law*) to object, plead in defence.
recussus *adj* reverberating.
redāctus *ppp of* redigō.
redambulō, -āre *vi* to come back.
redamō, -āre *vt* to love in return.
redārdēscō, -ere *vi* to blaze up again.

redarguō, -ere, -ī vt to refute, contradict.
redauspicō, -āre vi to take auspices for going back.
redditus ppp of **reddō**.
reddō, -ere, -idī, -itum vt to give back, return, restore; to give in, response, repay; to give up, deliver, pay; (copy) to represent, reproduce; (speech) to report, repeat, recite, reply; to translate; (with adj) to make; **iūdicium ~** fix the date for a trial; **iūs ~** administer justice.
redēgī perf of **redigō**.
redēmī perf of **redimō**.
redemptiō, -ōnis f ransoming; bribing; (revenue) farming.
redemptō, -āre vt to ransom.
redemptor, -ōris m contractor.
redemptūra, -ae f contracting.
redemptus ppp of **redimō**.
redeō, -īre, -iī, -itum vi to go back, come back, return; (speech) to revert (money) to come in; (circs) to be reduced to, come to.
redhālō, -āre vt to exhale.
redhibeō, -ēre vt to take back.
redigō, -igere, -ēgī, -āctum vt to drive back, bring back; (money) to collect, raise; (to a condition) to reduce, bring; (number) to reduce; **ad irritum ~** make useless.
rediī perf of **redeō**.
redimīculum, -ī nt band.
redimiō, -īre, -iī, -ītum vt to bind, crown, encircle.
redimō, -imere, -ēmī, -emptum vt to buy back; to ransom, redeem; to release, rescue; (good) to procure; (evil) to avert; (fault) to make amends for; (comm) to undertake by contract, hire.
redintegrō, -āre, -āvī, -ātum vt x restore, renew, refresh.
redipīscor, -ī vt to get back.
reditiō, -ōnis f returning.
reditus, -ūs m return, returning; (money) revenue.
redivīvus adj renovated.
redoleō, -ēre, -uī vi to give out a smell ♦ vt to smell of, smack of.
redomitus adj broken in again.
redōnō, -āre vt to restore; to give up.
redūcō, -ūcere, -ūxī, -uctum vt x draw back; to lead back, bring back; to escort home; to marry again; (troops) to withdraw; (fig) to restore; (to a condition) to make into.
reductiō, -ōnis f restoration.
reductor, -ōris m man who brings back.
reductus ppp of **redūcō** ♦ adj secluded, aloof.
reduncus adj curved back.
redundantia, -ae f extravagance.
redundō, -āre, -āvī, -ātum vi to overflow; to abound, be in excess; (fig) to stream.
reduvia, -ae f hangnail.

redux, -cis adj (gods) who brings back; (men) brought back, returned.
refectus ppp of **reficiō**.
refellō, -ere, -ī vt to disprove, rebut.
referciō, -cīre, -sī, -tum vt to stuff, cram, choke full.
referiō, -īre vt to hit back; to reflect.
referō, -ferre, -ttulī, -lātum vt to bring back, carry back; to give back, pay back, repay; to repeat, renew; (authority) to refer to, trace back to; (blame, credit) to ascribe; (likeness) to reproduce, resemble; (memory) to recall; (news) to report, mention; (opinion) to reckon amongst; (record) to enter; (senate) to lay before, move; (speech) to reply, say in answer; **grātiam ~** be grateful, requite; **pedem, gradum ~** return; retreat; **ratiōnēs ~** present an account; **sē ~** return.
rēfert, -ferre, -tulit vi (impers) it is of importance, it matters, it concerns; **meā ~** it matters to me.
refertus ppp of **referciō** ♦ adj crammed, full.
referveō, -ēre vi to boil over.
refervēscō, -ere vi to bubble up.
reficiō, -icere, -ēcī, -ectum vt to repair, restore; (body, mind) to refresh, revive; (money) to get back, get in return; (POL) to re-elect.
refīgō, -gere, -xī, -xum vt to unfasten, take down; (fig) to annul.
refingō, -ere vt to remake.
refīxus ppp of **refīgō**.
reflāgitō, -āre vt to demand back.
reflātus, -ūs m contrary wind.
reflectō, -ctere, -xī, -xum vt to bend back, turn back; (fig) to bring back ♦ vi to give way.
reflexus ppp of **reflectō**.
reflō, -āre, -āvī, -ātum vi to blow contrary ♦ vt to breathe out again.
refluō, -ere vi to flow back, overflow.
refluus adj ebbing.
reformīdō, -āre vt to dread; to shun in fear.
reformō, -āre vt to reshape.
refotus ppp of **refoveō**.
refoveō, -ovēre, -ōvī, -ōtum vt to refresh, revive.
refrāctāriolus adj rather stubborn.
refrāctus ppp of **refringō**.
refrāgor, -ārī, -ātus vi (with dat) to oppose, thwart.
refrēgī perf of **refringō**.
refrēnō, -āre, -uī vt to curb, restrain.
refricō, -āre, -uī, -ātum vt to scratch open; to reopen, renew ♦ vi to break out again.
refrīgerātiō, -ōnis f coolness.
refrīgerō, -āre, -āvī, -ātum vi to cool, cool off; (fig) to flag.
refrīgēscō, -gēscere, -xī vi to grow cold; (fig) to flag, grow stale.

Noun declensions and verb conjugations are shown on pp xiii to xxv. The present infinitive ending of a verb shows to which conjugation it belongs: **-āre** = 1st; **-ēre** = 2nd; **-ere** = 3rd and **-īre** = 4th. Irregular verbs are shown on p xxvi

refringō, -ingere, -ēgī, -āctum *vt* to break open; to break off; (*fig*) to break, check.

refrīxī *perf of* **refrīgēscō**.

refugiō, -ugere, -ūgī *vi* to run back, flee, shrink ♦ *vt* to run away from, shun.

refugium, -ī *and* **iī** *nt* refuge.

refugus *adj* fugitive, receding.

refulgeō, -gēre, -sī *vi* to flash back, reflect light.

refundō, -undere, -ūdī, -ūsum *vt* to pour back, pour out; (*pass*) to overflow.

refūsus *ppp of* **refundō**.

refūtātiō, -ōnis *f* refutation.

refūtātus, -ūs *m* refutation.

refūtō, -āre, -āvī, -ātum *vt* to check, repress; to refute, disprove.

rēgālis *adj* king's, royal, regal.

rēgāliter *adv* magnificently; tyrannically.

regerō, -rere, -ssī, -stum *vt* to carry back, throw back.

rēgia, -ae *f* palace; court; (*camp*) royal tent; (*town*) capital.

rēgiē *adv* regally; imperiously.

rēgificus *adj* magnificent.

regignō, -ere *vt* to reproduce.

Rēgillānus *and* **ēnsis** *adj see* **Rēgillus**.

Rēgillus, -ī *m Sabine town*; lake in Latium (*scene of a Roman victory over the Latins*).

regimen, -inis *nt* guiding, steering; rudder; rule, command, government; ruler.

rēgīna, -ae *f* queen, noblewoman.

Rēginus *adj see* **Rēgium**.

regiō, -ōnis *f* direction, line; boundary line; quarter, region; district, ward, territory; (*fig*) sphere, province; **ē ~ōne** in a straight line; (*with gen*) exactly opposite.

regiōnātim *adv* by districts.

Rēgium, -ī *and* **iī** *nt* town in extreme S. of Italy, (*now* Reggio).

rēgius *adj* king's, kingly, royal; princely, magnificent.

reglūtinō, -āre *vt* to unstick.

rēgnātor, -ōris *m* ruler.

rēgnātrīx, -īcis *adj* imperial.

rēgnō, -āre, -āvī, -ātum *vi* to be king, rule, reign; to be supreme, lord it; (*things*) to prevail, predominate ♦ *vt* to rule over.

rēgnum, -ī *nt* kingship, monarchy; sovereignty, supremacy; despotism; kingdom; domain.

regō, -ere, rēxī, rēctum *vt* to keep straight, guide, steer; to manage, direct; to control, rule, govern; **~ fīnēs** (*law*) mark out the limits.

regredior, -dī, -ssus *vi* to go back, come back, return; (*MIL*) to retire.

regressus *ppa of* **regredior**.

regressus, -ūs *m* return; retreat.

rēgula, -ae *f* rule, ruler; stick, board; (*fig*) rule, pattern, standard.

rēgulus, -ī *m* petty king, chieftain; prince.

Rēgulus, -ī *m Roman consul taken prisoner by the Carthaginians*.

regustō, -āre *vt* to taste again.

rēiciō, -icere, -iēcī, -iectum *vt* to throw back, throw over the shoulder, throw off; to drive back, repel; to cast off, reject; to reject with contempt, scorn; (*jurymen*) to challenge, refuse; (*matter for discussion*) to refer; (*time*) to postpone; **sē ~** fling oneself.

rēiectāneus *adj* to be rejected.

rēiectiō, -ōnis *f* rejection; (*law*) challenging.

rēiectō, -āre *vt* to throw back.

rēiectus *ppp of* **rēiciō**.

relābor, -bī, -psus *vi* to glide back, sink back, fall back.

relanguēscō, -ēscere, -ī *vi* to faint; to weaken.

relātiō, -ōnis *f* (*law*) retorting; (*pl*) magistrate's report; (*RHET*) repetition.

relātor, -ōris *m* proposer of a motion.

relātus, -ūs *m* official report; recital.

relaxātiō, -ōnis *f* easing.

relaxō, -āre, -āvī, -ātum *vt* to loosen, open out; (*fig*) to release, ease, relax, cheer.

relēctus *ppp of* **relegō**.

relēgātiō, -ōnis *f* banishment.

relēgō, -āre, -āvī, -ātum *vt* to send away, send out of the way; to banish; (*fig*) to reject; to refer, ascribe.

relegō, -egere, -ēgī, -ēctum *vt* to gather up; (*place*) to traverse, sail over again; (*speech*) to go over again, reread.

relentēscō, -ere *vi* to slacken off.

relēvī *perf of* **relinō**.

relevō, -āre, -āvī, -ātum *vt* to lift up; to lighten; (*fig*) to relieve, ease, comfort.

relictiō, -ōnis *f* abandoning.

relictus *ppp of* **relinquō**.

relicuus *etc see* **reliquus**.

religātiō, -ōnis *f* tying up.

religiō, -ōnis *f* religious scruple, reverence, awe; religion; superstition; scruples, conscientiousness; holiness, sanctity (*in anything*); object of veneration, sacred place; religious ceremony, observance.

religiōsē *adv* devoutly; scrupulously, conscientiously.

religiōsus *adj* devout, religious; superstitious; involving religious difficulty; scrupulous, conscientious; (*objects*) holy, sacred.

religō, -āre, -āvī, -ātum *vt* to tie up, fasten behind; (*ship*) to make fast, moor; (*fig*) to bind.

relinō, -inere, -ēvī *vt* to unseal.

relinquō, -inquere, -īquī, -ictum *vt* to leave, leave behind; to bequeath; to abandon, forsake; (*argument*) to allow; (*pass*) to remain.

rēliquiae, -ārum *fpl* leavings, remainder, relics.

reliquus *adj* remaining, left; (*time*) subsequent, future; (*debt*) outstanding ♦ *nt* remainder, rest; arrears ♦ *mpl* the rest; **~um est** it remains, the next point is; **~ī facere**

leave behind, leave over, omit; ir -um for the future.
rell- *etc see* **rel-**.
relūceō, -cēre, -xī *vi* to blaze.
relūcēscō, -cēscere, -xī *vi* to become bright again.
reluctor, -ārī, -ātus *vi* to struggle against, resist.
remaneō, -anēre, -ānsī *vi* to remain behind; to remain, continue, endure.
remānō, -āre *vi* to flow back.
remānsiō, -ōnis *f* remaining behind.
remedium, -ī *and* **iī** *nt* cure, remedy medicine.
remēnsus *ppa of* **remētior**.
remeō, -āre *vi* to come back, go back, return.
remētior, -tīrī, -nsus *vt* to measure again; to go back over.
rēmex, -igis *m* rower, oarsman.
Rēmī, -ōrum *mpl* people of Gaul (*in region of what is now* Rheims).
rēmigātiō, -ōnis *f* rowing.
rēmigium, -ī *and* **iī** *nt* rowing; oars, oarsmen.
rēmigō, -āre *vi* to row.
remigrō, -āre *vi* to move back, return (home).
reminīscor, -ī *vt*, *vi* (*usu with gen*) to remember, call to mind.
remisceō, -scēre, -xtum *vt* to mix up, mingle.
remissē *adv* mildly, gently.
remissiō, -ōnis *f* release; (*tension*) slackening, relaxing; (*payment*) remission; (*mind*) slackness, mildness, relaxation; (*illness*) abating.
remissus *ppa of* **remittō** ♦ *adj* slack, negligent; mild, indulgent, cheerful.
remittō, -ittere, -īsī, -issum *vt* to let go back, send back, release; to slacken, loosen, relax; to emit, produce; (*mind*) to relax, relieve; (*notion*) to discard, give up; (*offence, penalty*) to let off, remit; (*right*) to resign, sacrifice; (*sound*) to give back ♦ *vi* to abate.
remixtus *ppa of* **remisceō**.
remōlior, -īrī, -ītus *vt* to heave back
remollēscō, -ere *vi* to become soft again, be softened.
remolliō, -īre *vt* to weaken.
remora, -ae *f* hindrance.
remorāmina, -um *ntpl* hindrances.
remordeō, -dēre, -sum *vt* (*fig*) to worry, torment.
remoror, -ārī, -ātus *vi* to linger, stay behind ♦ *vt* to hinder, delay, defer.
remorsus *ppa of* **remordeō**.
remōtē *adv* far.
remōtiō, -ōnis *f* removing.
remōtus *ppa of* **removeō** ♦ *adj* distant, remote; secluded; (*fig*) far removed, free from.
removeō, -ovēre, -ōvī, -ōtum *vt* to move back, withdraw, set aside; to subtract.

remūgiō, -īre *vi* to bellow in answer, re-echo.
remulceō, -cēre, -sī *vi* to stroke; (*tail*) to droop.
remulcum, -ī *nt* towrope.
remūnerātiō, -ōnis *f* recompense, reward.
remūneror, -ārī, -ātus *vt* to repay, reward.
remurmurō, -āre *vi* to murmur in answer.
rēmus, -ī *m* oar.
Remus, -ī *m* brother of Romulus.
renārrō, -āre *vt* to tell over again.
renāscor -scī, -tus *vi* to be born again; to grow, spring up again.
renātus *ppa of* **renāscor**.
renāvigō, -āre *vi* to sail back
reneō, -ēre *vt* to unspin, undo.
rēnēs, -um *mpl* kidneys.
renīdeō, -ēre *vi* to shine back, be bright; to be cheerful, smile, laugh.
renīdēscō, -ere *vi* to reflect the gleam of.
renītor, -ī *vi* to struggle, resist.
renō, -āre *vi* to swim back.
rēnō, -ōnis *m* fur.
renōdō, -āre *vt* to tie back in a knot.
renovāmen, -inis *nt* new condition.
renovātiō, -ōnis *f* renewal; compound interest.
renovō, -āre, -āvī, -ātum *vt* to renew, restore; to repair, revive, refresh; (*speech*) to repeat; **faenus** ~ to take compound interest.
renumerō, -āre *vt* to pay back.
renūntiātiō, -ōnis *f* report, announcement.
renūntiō, -āre, -āvī, -ātum *vt* to report, bring back word; to announce, make an official statement; (*election*) to declare elected, return; (*duty*) to refuse, call off, renounce.
renūntius, -ī *and* **iī** *m* reporter.
renuō, -ere, -ī *vt*, *vi* to deny, decline, refuse.
renūtō, -āre *vi* to refuse firmly.
reor, rērī, ratus *vi* to think, suppose.
repāgula, -ōrum *ntpl* (*door*) bolts, bars.
repandus *adj* curving back, turned up.
reparābilis *adj* retrievable.
reparcō, -ere *vi* to be sparing with, refrain.
reparō, -āre, -āvī, -ātum *vt* to retrieve, recover; to restore, repair; to purchase; (*mind, body*) to refresh; (*troops*) to recruit.
repastinātiō, -ōnis *f* digging up again.
repellō, -ellere, -pulī, -ulsum *vt* to push back, drive back, repulse; to remove, reject.
rependō, -endere, -endī, -ēnsum *vt* to return by weight; to pay, repay; to requite, compensate.
repēns, -entis *adj* sudden; new.
repēnsus *ppa of* **rependō**.
repentē *adv* suddenly.
repentīnō *adv* suddenly.
repentīnus *adj* sudden, hasty; upstart.
repercō *etc see* **reparcō**.
repercussus, -ūs *m* reflection, echo.

Noun declensions and verb conjugations are shown on pp xiii to xxv. The present infinitive ending of a verb shows to which conjugation it belongs: **-āre** = 1st; **ēre** = 2nd; **-ere** = 3rd and **-īre** = 4th. Irregular verbs are shown on p xxvi

repercutiō, -tere, -ssī, -ssum vt to make rebound, reflect, echo.

reperiō, -īre, repperī, -tum vt to find, find out; to get, procure; to discover, ascertain; to devise, invent.

repertor, -ōris m discoverer, inventor, author.

repertus ppp of **reperiō** ♦ ntpl discoveries.

repetītiō, -ōnis f repetition; (RHET) anaphora.

repetītor, -ōris m reclaimer.

repetītus ppp of **repetō** ♦ adj: **altē/longē** ~ farfetched.

repetō, -ere, -īvī and **iī, -ītum** vt to go back to, revisit; to fetch back, take back; (MIL) to attack again; (action, speech) to resume, repeat; (memory) to recall, think over; (origin) to trace, derive; (right) to claim, demand back; **rēs** ~ demand satisfaction; reclaim one's property; **pecūniae ~undae** extortion.

repetundae, -ārum fpl extortion (by a provincial governor).

repexus adj combed.

repleō, -ēre, -ēvī, -ētum vt to fill up, refill; to replenish, make good, complete; to satiate, fill to overflowing.

replētus adj full.

replicātiō, -ōnis f rolling up.

replicō, -āre vt to roll back, unroll, unfold.

rēpō, -ere, -sī, -tum vi to creep, crawl.

repōnō, -ōnere, -osuī, -ositum vt to put back, replace, restore; to bend back; to put (in the proper place); (performance) to repeat; (something received) to repay; (store) to lay up, put away; (task) to lay aside, put down; (hope) to place, rest; (with prō) substitute; **in numerō, in numerum** ~ count, reckon among.

reportō, -āre, -āvī, -ātum vt to bring back, carry back; (prize) to win, carry off; (words) to report.

reposcō, -ere vt to demand back; to claim, require.

repositus ppp of **repōnō** ♦ adj remote.

repostor, -ōris m restorer.

repostus etc see **repositus**.

repōtia, -ōrum ntpl second drinking.

repperī perf of **reperiō**.

reppulī perf of **repellō**.

repraesentātiō, -ōnis f vivid presentation; (COMM) cash payment.

repraesentō, -āre, -āvī, -ātum vt to exhibit, reproduce; to do at once, hasten; (COMM) to pay cash.

reprehendō, -endere, -endī, -ēnsum vt to hold back, catch, restrain; to hold fast, retain; to blame, rebuke, censure; to refute.

reprehēnsiō, -ōnis f check; blame, reprimand, refutation.

reprehēnsō, -āre vt to keep holding back.

reprehēnsor, -ōris m censurer, critic, reviser.

reprehēnsus ppp of **reprehendō**.

reprendō etc see **reprehendō**.

repressor, -ōris m restrainer.

repressus ppp of **reprimō**.

reprimō, -imere, -essī, -essum vt to keep back, force back; to check, restrain, suppress.

reprōmissiō, -ōnis f counterpromise.

reprōmittō, -ittere, -īsī, -issum vt to promise in return, engage oneself.

rēptō, -āre vi to creep about, crawl along.

repudiātiō, -ōnis f rejection.

repudiō, -āre, -āvī, -ātum vt to reject, refuse, scorn; (wife) to divorce.

repudium, -ī and **iī** nt divorce; repudiation.

repuerāscō, -ere vi to become a child again; to behave like a child.

repugnanter adv reluctantly.

repugnant a, -ium ntpl contradictions.

repugnō, -āre, -āvī, -ātum vi to oppose, resist; to disagree, be inconsistent.

repulsa, -ae f refusal, denial, repulse; (election) rebuff.

repulsō, -āre vi to throb, reverberate.

repulsus ppp of **repellō**.

repulsus, -ūs m (light) reflection; (sound) echoing.

repungō, -ere vt to prod again.

repūrgō, -āre, -āvī, -ātum vt to clear again, cleanse again; to purge away.

reputātiō, -ōnis f pondering over.

reputō, -āre, -āvī, -ātum vt to count back; to think over, consider.

requiēs, -ētis f rest, relaxation, repose.

requiēscō, -scere, -vī, -tum vi to rest, find rest; to cease ♦ vt to stay.

requiētus adj rested, refreshed.

requīritō, -āre vt to keep asking after.

requīrō, -rere, -sīvī and **siī, -sītum** vt to search for, look for; to ask, inquire after; (with ex or ab) to question; to need, want, call for; to miss, look in vain for.

requīsītus ppp of **requīrō**.

rēs, reī f thing, object; circumstance, case, matter, affair; business, transaction; fact, truth, reality; possessions, wealth, money; advantage, interest; (law) case; (MIL) campaign, operations; (POL) politics, power, the State; (writing) subject matter, story, history; ~ **mihi est tēcum** I have to do with you; ~ **dīvīna** sacrifice; ~ **mīlitāris** war; ~ **pūblica** public affairs, politics, the State, republic; ~ **rūstica** agriculture; **rem facere** get rich; **rem gerere** wage war, fight; **ad rem** to the point, to the purpose; **in rem** usefully; **ob rem** to the purpose; **ob eam rem** therefore; **ī in malam rem** go to the devil!; **contrā rem pūblicam** unconstitutionally; **ē rē pūblicā** constitutionally; **rē vērā** in fact, actually; **eā rē** for that reason; **tuā rē, ex tuā rē** to your advantage; **ab rē** unhelpfully; **ē rē (nātā)** as things are; **prō rē** according to circumstances; **rēs adversae** failure, adversity; **rēs dubiae** danger; **rēs gestae**

achievements, career; **rēs novae** revolution; **rēs prosperae, secundae** success, prosperity; **rērum māximus** greatest in the world; **rērum scrīptor** historian.

resacrō *etc see* **resecrō.**

resaeviō, -īre *vi* to rage again.

resalūtō, -āre *vt* to greet in return.

resānēscō, -ēscere, -uī *vi* to heal up again.

resarciō, -cīre, -tum *vt* to patch up, repair.

rescindō, -ndere, -dī, -ssum *vt* to cut back, cut open, break down; to open up (*law, agreement*) to repeal, annul.

rescīscō, -īscere, -īvī *and* **iī, -ītum** *vt* to find out, learn.

rescissus *ppp of* **rescindō.**

rescrībō, -bere, -psī, -ptum *vt* to write back, reply; to rewrite, revise; (*emperors*) to give a decision; (*MIL*) to transfer, re-enlist; (*money*) to place to one's credit, pay back.

rescrīptus *ppp of* **rescrībō** ♦ *nt* imperial rescript.

resecō, -āre, -uī, -tum *vt* to cut back, cut short; to curtail; **ad vīvum ~** cut to the quick.

resecrō, -āre *vt* to pray again; to free from a curse.

resectus *ppp of* **resecō.**

resecūtus *ppa of* **resequor.**

resēdī *perf of* **resideō**; *perf of* **resīdō.**

resēminō, -āre *vt* to reproduce.

resequor, -quī, -cūtus *vt* to answer.

reserō, -āre, -āvī, -ātum *vt* to unbar, unlock; to disclose.

reservō, -āre, -āvī, -ātum *vt* to keep back, reserve; to preserve, save.

reses, -idis *adj* remaining; inactive, idle; calm.

resideō, -idēre, -ēdī *vi* to remain behind; to be idle, be listless; (*fig*) to remain, rest.

resīdō, -īdere, -ēdī *vi* to sit down, sink down, settle; to subside; (*fig*) to abate, calm down.

residuus *adj* remaining, left over; (*money*) outstanding.

resignō, -āre *vt* to unseal, open; (*fig*) to reveal; (*COMM*) to cancel, pay back.

resiliō, -īre, -uī *vi* to spring back; to recoil, rebound, shrink.

resīmus *adj* turned up.

rēsīna, -ae *f* resin.

rēsīnātus *adj* smeared with resin.

resipiō, -ere *vt* to savour of, smack of.

resipīscō, -īscere, -iī *and* **uī** *vi* to come to one's senses.

resistō, -istere, -titī *vi* to stand still, stop, halt; to resist, oppose; to rise again.

resolūtus *ppp of* **resolvō.**

resolvō, -vere, -vī, -ūtum *vt* to unfasten, loosen, open, release; to melt, dissolve; to relax; (*debt*) to pay up; (*difficulty*) to banish, dispel; (*tax*) to abolish; (*words*) to explain.

resonābilis *adj* answering.

resonō, -āre *vi* to resound, re-echo ♦ *vt* to echo the sound of; to make resound.

resonus *adj* echoing.

resorbeō, -ēre *vt* to suck back, swallow again.

respectō, -āre *vt* to look back; to gaze about, watch ♦ *vt* to look back at, look for; to have regard for.

respectus *ppp of* **respiciō.**

respectus, -ūs *m* looking back; refuge; respect, regard.

respergō, -gere, -sī, -sum *vt* to besprinkle, splash.

respersiō, -ōnis *f* sprinkling.

respersus *ppp of* **respergō.**

respiciō, -icere, -exī, -ectum *vt* to look back at, see behind; (*help*) to look to; (*care*) to have regard for, consider, respect ♦ *vi* to look back, look.

respīrāmen, -inis *nt* windpipe.

respīrātiō, -ōnis *f* breathing; exhalation; taking breath, pause.

respīrātus, -ūs *m* inhaling.

respīrō, -āre, -āvī, -ātum *vt, vi* to breathe, blow back; to breathe again, revive; (*things*) to abate.

resplendeō, -ēre *vi* to flash back, shine brightly.

respondeō, -ondēre, -ondī, -ōnsum *vt* to answer, reply; (*lawyer, priest, oracle*) to advise, give a response; (*law court*) to appear; (*pledge*) to promise in return; (*things*) to correspond, agree, match; **pār parī ~** return like for like, give tit for tat.

respōnsiō, -ōnis *f* answering; refutation.

respōnsitō, -āre *vi* to give advice.

respōnsō, -āre *vt, vi* to answer back; to defy.

respōnsor, -ōris *m* answerer.

respōnsum, -ī *nt* answer, reply; response, opinion, oracle.

rēspūblica, reīpūblicae *f* public affairs, politics, the State, republic.

respuō, -ere, -ī *vt* to spit out, eject; to reject, refuse.

restagnō, -āre *vi* to overflow; to be flooded.

restaurō, -āre *vt* to repair, rebuild.

resticula, -ae *f* rope, cord.

restinctiō, -ōnis *f* quenching.

restinctus *ppp of* **restinguō.**

restinguō, -guere, -xī, -ctum *vt* to extinguish, quench; (*fig*) to destroy.

restiō, -ōnis *m* rope maker.

restipulātiō, -ōnis *f* counterobligation.

restipulor, -ārī *vt* to stipulate in return.

restis, -is *f* rope.

restitī *perf of* **resistō**; *perf of* **restō.**

restitō, -āre *vi* to stay behind, hesitate.

restituō, -uere, -uī, -ūtum *vt* to replace, restore; to rebuild, renew; to give back, return; (*to a condition*) to reinstate; (*decision*) to quash, reverse; (*character*) to reform.

Noun declensions and verb conjugations are shown on pp xiii to xxv. The present infinitive ending of a verb shows to which conjugation it belongs: **-āre** = 1st; **-ēre** = 2nd; **-ere** = 3rd and **-īre** = 4th. Irregular verbs are shown on p xxvi

restitūtiō, -ōnis *f* restoration; reinstating.
restitūtor, -ōris *m* restorer.
restitūtus *ppp of* **restituō**.
restō, -āre, -itī *vi* to stand firm; to resist; to remain, be left; to be in store (for); **quod ~at** for the future.
restrictē *adv* sparingly; strictly.
restrictus *ppp of* **restringō** ♦ *adj* tight, short; niggardly; severe.
restringō, -ngere, -nxī, -ctum *vt* to draw back tightly, bind fast; (*teeth*) to bare; (*fig*) to check.
resultō, -āre *vi* to rebound; to re-echo.
resūmō, -ere, -psī, -ptum *vt* to take up again, get back, resume.
resupīnō, -āre *vt* to turn back, throw on one's back.
resupīnus *adj* lying back, face upwards.
resurgō, -gere, -rēxī, -rēctum *vi* to rise again, revive.
resuscitō, -āre *vt* to revive.
retardātiō, -ōnis *f* hindering.
retardō, -āre, -āvī, -ātum *vt* to retard, detain, check.
rēte, -is *nt* net; (*fig*) snare.
retēctus *ppp of* **retegō**.
retegō, -egere, -ēxī, -ēctum *vt* to uncover, open; to reveal.
retemptō, -āre *vt* to try again.
retendō, -endere, -endī, -entum *and* **ēnsum** *vt* to slacken, relax.
retēnsus *ppp of* **retendō**.
retentiō, -ōnis *f* holding back.
retentō *etc see* **retemptō**.
retentō, -āre *vt* to keep back, hold fast.
retentus *ppp of* **retendō**; *ppp of* **retineō**.
retēxī *perf of* **retegō**.
retexō, -ere, -uī, -tum *vt* to unravel; (*fig*) to break up, cancel; to renew.
rētiārius, -ī *and* **iī** *m* net-fighter.
reticentia, -ae *f* saying nothing; pause.
reticeō, -ēre, -uī *vi* to be silent, say nothing ♦ *vt* to keep secret.
rēticulum, -ī *nt* small net, hairnet; network bag.
retināculum, -ī *nt* tether, hawser.
retinēns, -entis *pres p of* **retineō** ♦ *adj* tenacious, observant.
retinentia, -ae *f* memory.
retineō, -inēre, -inuī, -entum *vt* to hold back, detain, restrain; to keep, retain, preserve.
retinniō, -īre *vi* to ring.
retonō, -āre *vi* to thunder in answer.
retorqueō, -quēre, -sī, -tum *vt* to turn back, twist.
retorridus *adj* dried up, wizened.
retortus *ppp of* **retorqueō**.
retractātiō, -ōnis *f* hesitation.
retractō, -āre, -āvī, -ātum *vt* to rehandle, take up again; to reconsider, revise; to withdraw ♦ *vi* to draw back, hesitate.
retractus *ppp of* **retrahō** ♦ *adj* remote.

retrahō, -here, -xī, -ctum *vt* to draw back, drag back; to withdraw, remove.
retrectō *etc see* **retractō**.
retribuō, -uere, -uī, -ūtum *vt* to restore, repay.
retrō *adv* back, backwards, behind; (*time*) back, past.
retrōrsum *adv* backwards, behind; in reverse order.
retrūdō, -dere, -sum *vt* to push back; to withdraw.
rettulī *perf of* **referō**.
retundō, -undere, -udī *and* **tudī, -ūsum** *and* **ūnsum** *vt* to blunt; (*fig*) to check, weaken.
retūnsus, retūsus *ppp of* **retundō** ♦ *adj* blunt, dull.
reus, -ī *m* the accused, defendant; guarantor, debtor, one responsible; culprit, criminal; **vōtī ~** one who has had a prayer granted.
revalēscō, -ēscere, -uī *vi* to recover.
revehō, -here, -xī, -ctum *vt* to carry back, bring back; (*pass*) to ride, drive, sail back.
revellō, -ellere, -ellī, -ulsum (**olsum**) *vt* to pull out, tear off; to remove.
revēlō, -āre *vt* to unveil, uncover.
reveniō, -enīre, -ēnī, -entum *vi* to come back, return.
rēvērā *adv* in fact, actually.
reverendus *adj* venerable, awe-inspiring.
reverēns, -entis *pres p of* **revereor** ♦ *adj* respectful, reverent.
reverenter *adv* respectfully.
reverentia, -ae *f* respect, reverence, awe.
revereor, -ērī, -itus *vt* to stand in awe of; to respect, revere.
reversiō (revorsiō), -ōnis *f* turning back; recurrence.
reversus *ppa of* **revertor**.
revertō, -ere, -ī; revertor, -tī, -sus *vi* to turn back, return; to revert.
revexī *perf of* **revehō**.
revictus *ppp of* **revincō**.
revinciō, -cīre, -xī, -ctum *vt* to tie back, bind fast.
revincō, -incere, -īcī, -ictum *vt* to conquer, repress; (*words*) to refute, convict.
revinctus *ppp of* **revinciō**.
revirēscō, -ēscere, -uī *vi* to grow green again; to be rejuvenated; to grow strong again, flourish again.
revīsō, -ere *vt, vi* to come back to, revisit.
revīvēscō, -vīscō, -vīscere, -xī *vi* to come to life again, revive.
revocābilis *adj* revocable.
revocāmen, -inis *nt* recall.
revocātiō, -ōnis *f* recalling; (*word*) withdrawing.
revocō, -āre, -āvī, -ātum *vt* to call back, recall; (*action*) to revoke; (*former state*) to recover, regain; (*growth*) to check; (*guest*) to invite in return; (*judgment*) to apply, refer; (*law*) to summon again; (*performer*) to encore; (*troops*) to withdraw.

revolō, -āre *vi* to fly back.

revolsus *etc see* **revulsus**.

revolūbilis *adj* that may be rolled back.

revolūtus *ppp of* **revolvō**.

revolvō, -vere, -vī, -ūtum *vt* to roll back, unroll, unwind; (*speech*) to relate, repeat; (*thought*) to think over; (*writing*) to read over; (*pass*) to revolve, return, come round.

revomō, -ere, -uī *vt* to disgorge.

revor- *etc see* **rever-**.

revulsus *ppp of* **revellō**.

rēx, rēgis *m* king; tyrant, despot; leader; patron, rich man.

rēxī *perf of* **regō**.

Rhadamanthus, -ī *m judge in the lower world.*

Rhaetī *etc see* **Raetī**.

Rhamnūs, -ūntis *f town in Attica (famous for its statue of Nemesis).*

Rhamnūsis, -ūsidis *f* Nemesis.

Rhamnūsius *adj see n.*

rhapsōdia, -ae *f a book of Homer.*

Rhea, -ae *f* Cybele.

Rhea Silvia, -ae, -ae *f mother of Romulus and Remus.*

Rhēgium *etc see* **Rēgium**.

Rhēnānus *adj* Rhenish.

rhēnō *etc see* **rēnō**.

Rhēnus, -ī *m* Rhine.

Rhēsus, -ī *m* Thracian king (*killed at Troy*).

rhētor, -oris *m* teacher of rhetoric; orator.

rhētorica, -ae *and* **ē, -ēs** *f* art of oratory, rhetoric.

rhētoricē *adv* rhetorically, in an oratorical manner.

rhētoricī, -ōrum *mpl* teachers of rhetoric.

rhētoricus *adj* rhetorical, on rhetoric.

rhīnocerōs, -ōtis *m* rhinoceros.

rhō *nt* (*indecl*) Greek letter rho.

Rhodanus, -ī *m* Rhone.

Rhodius *adj see* **Rhodopē**.

Rhodopē, -ēs *f mountain range in Thrace.*

Rhodopēius *adj* Thracian.

Rhodos (Rhodus), -ī *f* island of Rhodes.

Rhoetēum, -ī *nt promontory on the Dardanelles* (*near Troy*).

Rhoetēus *adj* Trojan.

rhombus, -ī *m* magician's circle; (*fish*) turbot.

rhomphaea, -ae *f* long barbarian javelin.

rhythmicus, -ī *m* teacher of prose rhythm.

rhythmos (-us), -ī *m* rhythm, symmetry.

rīca, -ae *f* sacrificial veil.

rīcinium, -ī *and* **iī** *nt small cloak with hood.*

rictum, -ī *nt*, **-us, -ūs** *m* open mouth, gaping jaws.

rīdeō, -dēre, -sī, -sum *vi* to laugh, smile ♦ *vt* to laugh at, smile at; to ridicule

rīdibundus *adj* laughing.

rīdiculāria, -ium *ntpl* jokes.

rīdiculē *adv* jokingly; absurdly.

rīdiculus *adj* amusing, funny; ridiculous, silly

♦ *m* jester ♦ *nt* joke.

rigēns, -entis *pres p of* **rigeō** ♦ *adj* stiff, rigid, frozen.

rigeō, -ēre *vi* to be stiff.

rigēscō, -ēscere, -uī *vi* to stiffen, harden; to bristle.

rigidē *adv* rigorously.

rigidus *adj* stiff, rigid, hard; (*fig*) hardy, strict, inflexible.

rigō, -āre *vt* to water, moisten, bedew; to convey (water).

rigor, -ōris *m* stiffness, hardness; numbness, cold; strictness, severity.

riguī *perf of* **rigēscō**.

riguus *adj* irrigating; watered.

rīma, -ae *f* crack, chink.

rīmor, -ārī, -ātus *vt* to tear open; to search for, probe, examine; to find out.

rīmōsus *adj* cracked, leaky.

ringor, -ī *vi* to snarl.

rīpa, -ae *f* river bank; shore.

Rīphaeī, -ōrum *mpl mountain range in N. Scythia.*

Rīphaeus *adj see* **Rīphaeī**.

rīpula, -ae *f* riverbank.

riscus, -ī *m* trunk, chest.

rīsī *perf of* **rīdeō**.

rīsor, -ōris *m* scoffer.

rīsus, -ūs *m* laughter, laugh; laughing stock.

rīte *adv* with the proper formality *or* ritual; duly, properly, rightly; in the usual manner; fortunately.

rītus, -ūs *m* ritual, ceremony; custom, usage; ~ū after the manner of.

rīvālis, -is *m* rival in love.

rīvālitās, -ātis *f* rivalry in love.

rīvulus, -ī *m* brook.

rīvus, -ī *m* stream, brook; ē ~ō flūmina māgna facere ≈ *make a mountain of a molehill.*

rixa, -ae *f* quarrel, brawl, fight.

rixor, -ārī, -ātus *vi* to quarrel, brawl, squabble.

rōbīginōsus *adj* rusty.

rōbīgō, -inis *f* rust; blight, mould, mildew.

rōboreus *adj* of oak.

rōborō, -āre *vt* to strengthen, invigorate.

rōbur, -oris *nt* oak; hard wood; prison, dungeon (*at Rome*); (*fig*) strength, hardness, vigour; best part, élite, flower.

rōbustus *adj* of oak; strong, hard; robust, mature.

rōdō, -dere, -sī, -sum *vt* to gnaw; (*rust*) to corrode; (*words*) to slander.

rogālis *adj* of a pyre.

rogātiō, -ōnis *f* proposal, motion, bill; request; (*RHET*) question.

rogātiuncula, -ae *f* unimportant bill; question.

rogātor, -ōris *m* proposer; polling clerk.

rogātus, -ūs *m* request.

Noun declensions and verb conjugations are shown on pp xiii to xxv. The present infinitive ending of a verb shows to which conjugation it belongs: **-āre** = 1st; **-ēre** = 2nd; **-ere** = 3rd and **-īre** = 4th. Irregular verbs are shown on p xxvi

rogitō, -āre _vt_ to ask for, inquire eagerly.
rogō, -āre, -āvī, -ātum _vt_ to ask, ask for; (_bill_) to propose, move; (_candidate_) to put up for election; **lēgem** ~, **populum** ~ introduce a bill; **magistrātum populum** ~ nominate for election to an office; **militēs sacrāmentō** ~ administer the oath to the troops; **mālō emere quam rogāre** I'd rather buy it than borrow it.
rogus, -ī _m_ funeral pyre.
Rōma, -ae _f_ Rome.
Rōmānus _adj_ Roman.
Rōmuleus, -us _adj_ of Romulus; Roman.
Rōmulidae, -idārum _mpl_ the Romans.
Rōmulus, -ī _m founder and first king of Rome._
rorāriī, -ōrum _mpl_ skirmishers.
rōridus _adj_ dewy.
rōrifer, -ī _adj_ dew-bringing.
rōrō, -āre _vi_ to distil dew; to drip, trickle ♦ _vt_ to bedew, wet.
rōs, rōris _m_ dew; moisture, water; (_plant_) rosemary; ~ **marīnus** rosemary.
rosa, -ae _f_ rose; rose bush.
rosāria, -ōrum _ntpl_ rose garden.
rōscidus _adj_ dewy; wet.
Roscius, -ī _m_: L. ~ Othō _tribune in 67 BC, whose law reserved theatre seats for the equites;_ Q. ~ Gallus _famous actor defended by Cicero;_ Sex. ~ _of Ameria, defended by Cicero._
Roscius, -iānus _adj see n._
rosētum, -ī _nt_ rosebed.
roseus _adj_ rosy; of roses.
rōsī _perf of_ **rōdō.**
rōstrātus _adj_ beaked, curved; **columna ~a** _column commemorating a naval victory._
rōstrum, -ī _nt_ (_bird_) beak, bill; (_animal_) snout, muzzle; (_ship_) beak, end of prow; (_pl_) orators' platform in the Forum.
rōsus _ppp of_ **rōdō.**
rota, -ae _f_ wheel; potter's wheel, torture wheel; car, disc.
rotō, -āre, -āvī, -ātum _vt_ to turn, whirl, roll; (_pass_) to revolve.
rotundē _adv_ elegantly.
rotundō, -āre _vt_ to round off.
rotundus _adj_ round, circular, spherical; (_style_) well-turned, smooth.
rubefaciō, -facere, -fēcī, -factum _vt_ to redden.
rubēns, -entis _pres p of_ **rubeō** ♦ _adj_ red; blushing.
rubeō, -ēre _vi_ to be red; to blush.
ruber, -rī _adj_ red; **mare ~rum** Red Sea; Persian Gulf; **ōceanus** ~ Indian Ocean; **Saxa ~ra** _stone quarries between Rome and Veii._
rubēscō, -ēscere, -uī _vi_ to redden, blush.
rubēta, -ae _f_ toad.
rubēta, -ōrum _ntpl_ bramble bushes.
rubeus _adj_ of bramble.
Rubicō, -ōnis _m stream marking the frontier between Italy and Gaul._
rubicundulus _adj_ reddish.
rubicundus _adj_ red, ruddy.

rūbīg- _etc see_ **rōbīg-.**
rubor, -ōris _m_ redness; blush; bashfulness; shame.
rubrīca, -ae _f_ red earth, red ochre.
rubuī _perf of_ **rubēscō.**
rubus, -ī _m_ bramble bush; bramble, blackberry.
ructō, -āre; -or, -ārī _vt, vi_ to belch.
ructus, -us _m_ belching.
rudēns, -entis _pres p p of_ **rudō** ♦ _m_ rope; (_pl_) rigging.
Rudiae, -iārum _fpl_ town in S. Italy (_birthplace of Ennius_).
rudiārius, -ī _and_ **iī** _m_ retired gladiator.
rudīmentum, -ī _nt_ first attempt, beginning.
Rudīnus _adj see_ **Rudiae.**
rudis _adj_ unwrought, unworked, raw; coarse, rough, badly-made; (_age_) new, young; (_person_) uncultured, unskilled, clumsy; ignorant (of), inexperienced (in).
rudis, -is _f_ stick, rod; foil (_for fighting practice_); (_fig_) discharge.
rudō, -ere, -īvī, -ītum _vi_ to roar, bellow, bray; to creak.
rūdus, -eris _nt_ rubble, rubbish; piece of copper.
rūdus, -eris _nt_ copper coin.
Rūfulī, -ōrum _mpl_ military tribunes (_chosen by the general_).
rūfulus _adj_ red-headed.
rūfus _adj_ red, red-haired.
rūga, -ae _f_ wrinkle, crease.
rūgō, -āre _vi_ to become creased.
rūgōsus _adj_ wrinkled, shrivelled, corrugated.
ruī _perf of_ **ruō.**
ruīna, -ae _f_ fall, downfall; collapse, falling in; debris, ruins; destruction, disaster, ruin (_fig_).
ruīnōsus _adj_ collapsing; ruined.
rumex, -icis _f_ sorrel.
rūmificō, -āre _vt_ to report.
Rūmīna, -ae _f goddess of nursing mothers;_ **fīcus ~ālis** the fig tree of Romulus and Remus (_under which the she-wolf suckled them_).
rūminātiō, -ōnis _f_ chewing the cud; (_fig_) ruminating.
rūminō, -āre _vt, vi_ to chew the cud.
rūmor, -ōris _m_ noise, cheering; rumour, hearsay; public opinion; reputation.
rumpia _etc see_ **rhomphaea.**
rumpō, -ere, rūpī, ruptum _vt_ to break, burst, tear; to break down, burst through; (_activity_) to interrupt; (_agreement_) to violate, annul; (_delay_) to put an end to; (_voice_) to give vent to; (_way_) to force through.
rūmusculī, -ōrum _mpl_ gossip.
rūna, -ae _f_ dart.
runcō, -āre _vt_ to weed.
ruō, -ere, -ī, -tum _vi_ to fall down, tumble; to rush, run, hurry; to come to ruin ♦ _vt_ to dash down, hurl to the ground; to throw up, turn up.
rūpēs, -is _f_ rock, cliff.

rūpī perf of **rumpō.**
ruptor, -ōris m violator.
ruptus ppp of **rumpō.**
rūricola, -ae adj rural, country- (in cpds).
rūrigena, -ae m countryman.
rūrsus, rūrsum (rūsum) adv back, backwards; on the contrary, in return; again.
rūs, rūris nt the country, countryside; estate, farm; **rūs** to the country; **rūrī** in the country; **rūre** from the country.
ruscum, -ī nt butcher's-broom.
russus adj red.
rūsticānus adj country- (in cpds), rustic.
rūsticātiō, -ōnis f country life.
rūsticē adv in a countrified manner, awkwardly.
rūsticitās, -ātis f country manners, rusticity.
rūsticor, -ārī vi to live in the country.
rūsticulus, -ī m yokel.
rūsticus adj country- (in cpds), rural; simple, rough, clownish ♦ m countryman.
rūsum see **rūrsus.**
rūta, -ae f (herb) rue; (fig) unpleasantness.
ruta caesa ntpl minerals and timber on an estate.
rutilō, -āre vt to colour red ♦ vi to glow red.
rutilus adj red, auburn.
rutrum, -ī nt spade, shovel, trowel.
rūtula, -ae f little piece of rue.
Rutulī, -ōrum mpl ancient Latin people.
Rutulus adj Rutulian.
Rutupiae, -iārum fpl seaport in Kent (now Richborough).
Rutupīnus adj see n.
rutus ppp of **ruō.**

S, s

Saba, -ae f town in Arabia Felix.
Sabaeus adj see n.
Sabāzia, -iōrum ntpl festival of Bacchus.
Sabāzius, -ī m Bacchus.
sabbata, -ōrum ntpl Sabbath, Jewish holiday.
Sabellus, -ī m Sabine, Samnite.
Sabellus, -icus adj see n.
Sabīnī, -ōrum mpl Sabines (a people of central Italy).
Sabīnus adj Sabine ♦ f Sabine woman ♦ nt Sabine estate; Sabine wine; **herba ~a** savin (a kind of juniper).
Sabrīna, -ae f river Severn.

saburra, -ae f sand, ballast.
Sacae, -ārum mpl tribe of Scythians.
saccipērium, -ī and **iī** nt purse-pocket.
saccō, -āre vt to strain, filter.
sacculus, -ī m little bag, purse.
saccus, -ī m bag, purse, wallet.
sacellum, -ī nt chapel.
sacer, -rī adj sacred, holy; devoted for sacrifice, forfeited, accursed, criminal, infamous; **Mōns ~** hill to which the Roman plebs seceded; **Via ~ra** street from the Forum to the Capitol.
sacerdōs, -ōtis m/f priest, priestess.
sacerdōtium, -ī and **iī** nt priesthood.
sacrāmentum, -ī nt deposit made by parties to a lawsuit; civil lawsuit, dispute; (MIL) oath of allegiance, engagement.
sacrārium, -ī and **iī** nt shrine, chapel.
sacrātus adj holy, hallowed; **~āta lēx** a law whose violation was punished by devotion to the infernal gods.
sacricola, -ae m/f sacrificing priest or priestess.
sacrifer, -ī adj carrying holy things.
sacrificālis adj sacrificial.
sacrificātiō, -ōnis f sacrificing.
sacrificium, -ī and **iī** nt sacrifice.
sacrificō, -āre vt, vi to sacrifice.
sacrificulus, -ī m sacrificing priest; **rēx ~** high priest.
sacrificus adj sacrificial.
sacrilegium, -ī and **iī** nt sacrilege.
sacrilegus adj sacrilegious; profane, wicked ♦ m templerobber.
sacrō, -āre, -āvī, -ātum vt to consecrate; to doom, curse; to devote, dedicate; to make inviolable; (poetry) to immortalize.
sacrōsanctus adj inviolable, sacrosanct.
sacruficō etc see **sacrificō.**
sacrum, -rī nt holy thing, sacred vessel; shrine; offering, victim; rite; (pl) sacrifice, worship, religion; **~ra facere** sacrifice; **inter ~rum saxumque** ≈ with one's back to the wall; **hērēditās sine ~rīs** a gift with no awkward obligations.
saeclum etc see **saeculum.**
saeculāris adj centenary; (ECCL) secular, pagan.
saeculum, -ī nt generation, lifetime, age; the age, the times; century; **in ~a** (ECCL) for ever.
saepe adv often, frequently.
saepe numerō adv very often.
saepēs, -is f hedge, fence.
saepīmentum, -ī nt enclosure.
saepiō, -īre, -sī, -tum vt to hedge round, fence in, enclose; (fig) to shelter, protect.
saeptus ppp of **saepiō** ♦ nt fence, wall; stake, pale; (sheep) fold; (Rome) voting area in the Campus Martius.
saeta, -ae f hair, bristle.

Noun declensions and verb conjugations are shown on pp xiii to xxv. The present infinitive ending of a verb shows to which conjugation it belongs: **-āre** = 1st; **-ēre** = 2nd; **-ere** = 3rd and **-īre** = 4th. Irregular verbs are shown on p xxvi

saetiger, -ī _adj_ bristly.
saetōsus _adj_ bristly, hairy.
saevē, -iter _adv_ fiercely, cruelly.
saevidicus _adj_ furious.
saeviō, -īre, -iī, -ītum _vi_ to rage, rave.
saevitia, -ae _f_ rage; ferocity, cruelty.
saevus _adj_ raging, fierce; cruel, barbarous.
sāga, -ae _f_ fortune teller.
sagācitās, -ātis _f_ (_dogs_) keen scent; (_mind_) shrewdness.
sagāciter _adv_ keenly; shrewdly.
sagātus _adj_ wearing a soldier's cloak.
sagāx, -ācis _adj_ (_senses_) keen, keen-scented; (_mind_) quick, shrewd.
sagīna, -ae _f_ stuffing, fattening; food, rich food; fatted animal.
sagīnō, -are _vt_ to cram, fatten; to feed, feast.
sāgiō, -īre _vi_ to perceive keenly.
sagitta, -ae _f_ arrow.
sagittārius, -ī _and_ **iī** _m_ archer.
sagittifer, -ī _adj_ armed with arrows.
sagmen, -inis _nt_ tuft of sacred herbs (_used as a mark of inviolability_).
sagulum, -ī _nt_ short military cloak.
sagum, -ī _nt_ military cloak; woollen mantle.
Saguntīnus _adj see_ **Saguntum.**
Saguntum, -ī _nt_, **-us (os), -ī** _f town in E. Spain._
sāgus _adj_ prophetic.
sāl, salis _m_ salt; brine, sea; (_fig_) shrewdness, wit, humour, witticism; good taste.
salacō, -ōnis _m_ swaggerer.
Salamīnius _adj see_ **Salamīs.**
Salamīs, -īnis _f Greek island near Athens; town in Cyprus._
salapūtium, -ī _and_ **iī** _nt_ manikin.
salārius _adj_ salt- (_in cpds_) ♦ _nt_ allowance, salary.
salāx, -ācis _adj_ lustful, salacious.
salebra, -ae _f_ roughness, rut.
Saliāris _adj_ of the Salii; sumptuous.
salictum, -ī _nt_ willow plantation.
salientēs, -ium _fpl_ springs.
salignus _adj_ of willow.
Saliī, -ōrum _mpl priests of Mars._
salillum, -ī _nt_ little saltcellar.
salīnae, -ārum _fpl_ saltworks.
salīnum, -ī _nt_ saltcellar.
saliō, -īre, -uī, -tum _vi_ to leap, spring; to throb.
saliunca, -ae _f_ Celtic nard.
salīva, -ae _f_ saliva, spittle; taste.
salix, -icis _f_ willow.
Sallustiānus _adj see_ **Sallustius.**
Sallustius, -ī _m_ Sallust (_Roman historian_); _his wealthy grand-nephew._
Salmōneus, -eos _m_ son of Aeolus (_punished in Tartarus for imitating lightning_).
Salmōnis, -idis _f his daughter Tyro._
salsāmentum, -ī _nt_ brine, pickle; salted fish.
salsē _adv_ wittily.
salsus _adj_ salted; salt, briny; (_fig_) witty.
saltātiō, -ōnis _f_ dancing, dance.
saltātor, -ōris _m_ dancer.

saltātōrius _adj_ dancing- (_in cpds_).
saltātrīx, -īcis _f_ dancer.
saltātus, -ūs _m_ dance.
saltem _adv_ at least, at all events; **nōn ~** not even.
saltō, -āre _vt, vi_ to dance.
saltuōsus _adj_ wooded.
saltus, -ūs _m_ leap, bound.
saltus, -ūs _m_ woodland pasture, glade; pass, ravine.
salūber _adj see_ **salūbris.**
salūbris _adj_ health-giving, wholesome; healthy, sound.
salūbritās, -ātis _f_ healthiness; health.
salūbriter _adv_ wholesomely; beneficially.
saluī _perf of_ **saliō.**
salum, -ī _nt_ sea, high sea.
salūs, -ūtis _f_ health; welfare, life; safety; good wish, greeting; **~ūtem dīcere** greet; bid farewell.
salūtāris _adj_ wholesome, healthy; beneficial; **~ littera** letter A (_for_ **absolvō** = _acquittal_).
salūtāriter _adv_ beneficially.
salūtātiō, -ōnis _f_ greeting; formal morning visit, levee.
salūtātor, -ōris _m_ morning caller; male courtier.
salūtātrīx, -rīcis _f_ morning caller; female courtier.
salūtifer, -ī _adj_ health-giving.
salūtigerulus _adj_ carrying greetings.
salūtō, -āre, -āvī, -ātum _vt_ to greet, salute, wish well; to call on, pay respects to.
salvē _adv_ well, in good health; all right.
salvē _impv of_ **salveō.**
salveō, -ēre _vi_ to be well, be in good health; **~ē, ~ētō, ~ēte** hail!, good day!, goodbye!; **~ēre iubeō** I bid good day.
salvus, salvos _adj_ safe, alive, intact, well; without violating; all right; **~ sīs** good day to you!; **~a rēs est** all is well; **~ā lēge** without breaking the law.
Samaous _adj see_ **Samē.**
Samarobrīva, -ae _f_ Belgian town (_now Amiens_).
sambūca, -ae _f_ harp.
sambūcistria, -ae _f_ harpist.
Samē, -ēs _f old name of the Greek island Cephallenia._
Samius _adj_ Samian ♦ _ntpl_ Samian pottery.
Samnīs, -ītis _adj_ Samnite.
Samnium, -ī _and_ **iī** _nt_ district of central Italy.
Samos (-us), -ī _f Aegean island off Asia Minor_ (_famous for its pottery and as the birthplace of Pythagoras_).
Samothrāces, -um _mpl_ Samothracians.
Samothrācia, -iae _and_ **a, -ae** _f_ Samothrace (_island in the N. Aegean_).
Samothrācius _adj see n._
sānābilis _adj_ curable.
sānātiō, -ōnis _f_ healing.
sanciō, -īre, -xī, -ctum _vt_ to make sacred or inviolable; to ordain, ratify; to enact a

punishment against.

sanctimōnia, -ae f sanctity; chastity.

sanctiō, -ōnis f decree, penalty for violating a law.

sanctitās, -ātis f sacredness; integrity, chastity.

sanctitūdō, -inis f sacredness.

sanctō adv solemnly, religiously.

sanctor, -ōris m enacter.

sanctus ppp of **sanciō** ♦ adj sacred, inviolable; holy, venerable; pious, virtuous, chaste.

sandaligerula, -ae f sandalbearer

sandalium, -ī and **iī** nt sandal, slipper.

sandapila, -ae f common bier.

sandyx, -ycis f scarlet.

sānē adv sensibly; (intensive) very, doubtless; (ironical) to be sure, of course; (concessive) of course, indeed; (in answer) certainly, surely; (with impv) then, if you please; ~ **quam** very much; **haud** ~ not so very, not quite.

sanguen etc see **sanguis**.

sanguināns, -āntis adj bloodthirsty

sanguinārius adj bloodthirsty.

sanguineus adj bloody, of blood; blood-red.

sanguinolentus adj bloody; blood-red; sanguinary.

sanguis, -inis m blood, bloodshed; descent, family; offspring; (fig) strength, life; **~inem dare** shed one's blood; **~inem mittere** let blood.

saniēs, -em, -ē f diseased blood, matter; venom.

sānitās, -ātis f (body) health, sound condition; (mind) sound sense, sanity; (style) correctness, purity.

sanna, -ae f grimace, mocking.

sanniō, -ōnis m clown.

sānō, -āre, -āvī, -ātum vt to cure, heal; (fig) to remedy, relieve.

Sanquālis avis f osprey.

sānus adj (body) sound, healthy; (mind) sane, sensible; (style) correct; **male ~** mad, inspired; **sānun es?** are you in your senses?

sanxī perf of **sanciō**.

sapa, -ae f new wine.

sapiēns, -entis pres p of **sapiō** ♦ adj wise, discreet ♦ m wise man, philosopher; man of taste.

sapienter adv wisely, sensibly.

sapientia, -ae f wisdom, discernment; philosophy; knowledge.

sapiō, -ere, -īvī and **uī** vi to have a flavour or taste; to have sense, be wise ♦ vt to taste of, smell of, smack of; to understand.

sapor, -ōris m taste, flavour; (food) delicacy; (fig) taste, refinement.

Sapphicus adj see **Sapphō**.

Sapphō, -ūs f famous Greek lyric poetess, native of Lesbos.

sarcina, -ae f bundle, burden; (MIL) pack.

sarcinārius adj baggage- (in cpds).

sarcinātor, -ōris m patcher.

sarcinula, -ae f little pack.

sarciō, -cīre, -sī, -tum vt to patch, mend, repair.

sarcophagus, -ī m sepulchre.

sarculum, -ī nt light hoe.

Sardēs (-is), -ium fpl Sardis (capital of Lydia).

Sardiānus adj see **Sardēs**.

Sardinia, -iniae f island of Sardinia.

sardonyx, -chis f sardonyx.

Sardus, -ous, -iniēnsis adj see **Sardinia**.

sariō, -īre, -īvī and **uī** vt to hoe, weed.

sarīsa, -ae f Macedonian lance.

sarīsophorus, -ī m Macedonian lancer.

Sarmatae, -ārum mpl Sarmatians (a people of S.E. Russia).

Sarmaticus, -is adj see **Sarmatae**.

sarmentum, -ī nt twigs, brushwood.

Sarpēdōn, -onis m king of Lycia.

Sarra, -ae f Tyre.

sarrācum, -ī nt cart.

Sarrānus adj Tyrian.

sarriō etc see **sariō**.

sarsī perf of **sarciō**.

sartāgō, -inis f frying pan.

sartor, -ōris m hoer, weeder.

sartus ppp of **sarciō**.

sat etc see **satis**.

satagō, -ere vi to have one's hands full, be in trouble; to bustle about, fuss.

satelles, -itis m/f attendant, follower; assistant, accomplice.

satiās, -ātis f sufficiency; satiety.

satietās, -ātis f sufficiency; satiety.

satin, satine see **satisne**.

satiō, -āre, -āvī, -ātum vt to satisfy, appease; to fill, saturate; to glut, cloy, disgust.

satiō, -ōnis f sowing, planting; (pl) fields.

satis, sat adj enough, sufficient ♦ adv enough, sufficiently; tolerably, fairly, quite; **~ accipiō** take sufficient bail; **~ agō, agitō** have one's hands full, be harassed; **~ dō** offer sufficient bail; **~ faciō** satisfy: give satisfaction, make amends; (creditor) pay.

satisdatiō, -ōnis f giving security.

satisdō see **satis**.

satisfaciō see **satis**.

satisfactiō, -ōnis f amends, apology.

satisne adv quite, really.

satius compar of **satis**: better, preferable.

sator, -ōris m sower, planter; father; promoter.

satrapēs, -is m satrap (Persian governor).

satur, -ī adj filled, sated; (fig) rich.

satura, -ae f mixed dish; medley; (poem) satire; per **~am** confusingly.

satureia, -ōrum ntpl (plant) savory.

saturitās, -ātis f repletion; fulness, plenty.

Saturnālia, -ium and **iōrum** ntpl festival of

Noun declensions and verb conjugations are shown on pp xiii to xxv. The present infinitive ending of a verb shows to which conjugation it belongs: -āre = 1st; -ēre = 2nd; -ere = 3rd and -īre = 4th. Irregular verbs are shown on p xxvi

Saturn in December.
Saturnia, -iae f Juno.
Saturnīnus, -ī m revolutionary tribune in 103 and 100 B.C.
Saturnius adj see n.
Saturnus, -ī m Saturn (god of sowing, ruler of the Golden Age); the planet Saturn.
saturō, -āre, -āvī, -ātum vt to fill, glut, satisfy; to disgust.
satus ppp of **serō** ♦ m son ♦ f daughter ♦ ntpl crops.
satus, -ūs m sowing, planting; begetting.
satyriscus, -ī m little satyr.
satyrus, -ī m satyr.
sauciātiō, -ōnis f wounding.
sauciō, -āre vt to wound, hurt.
saucius adj wounded, hurt; ill, stricken.
Sauromatae etc see **Sarmatae**.
sāviātiō, -ōnis f kissing.
sāviolum, -ī nt sweet kiss.
sāvior, -ārī vt to kiss.
sāvium, -ī and **iī** nt kiss.
saxātilis adj rock- (in cpds).
saxētum, -ī nt rocky place.
saxeus adj of rock, rocky.
saxificus adj petrifying.
saxōsus adj rocky, stony.
saxulum, -ī nt small rock.
saxum, -ī nt rock, boulder; the Tarpeian Rock.
scaber, -rī adj rough, scurfy; mangy, itchy.
scabiēs, -em, -ē f roughness, scurf; mange, itch.
scabillum, -ī nt stool; a castanet played with the foot.
scabō, -ere, scābī vt to scratch.
Scaea porta, -ae, -ae f the west gate of Troy.
scaena, -ae f stage, stage setting; (fig) limelight, public life; outward appearance, pretext.
scaenālis adj theatrical.
scaenicus adj stage- (in cpds), theatrical ♦ m actor.
Scaevola, -ae m early Roman who burned his hand off before Porsenna; famous jurist of Cicero's day.
scaevus adj on the left; perverse ♦ f omen.
scālae, -ārum fpl steps, ladder, stairs.
scalmus -ī m tholepin.
scalpellum, -ī nt scalpel, lancet.
scalpō, -ere, -sī, -tum vt to carve, engrave; to scratch.
scalprum, -ī nt knife, penknife; chisel.
scalpurriō, -īre vi to scratch.
Scamander, -rī m river of Troy (also called Xanthus).
scammōnea, -ae f (plant) scammony.
scamnum, -ī nt bench, stool; throne.
scandō, -ere vt, vi to climb, mount.
scapha, -ae f boat, skiff.
scaphium, -ī and **iī** nt a boat-shaped cup.
scapulae, -ārum fpl shoulder blades;

shoulders.
scāpus, -ī m shaft; (loom) yarnbeam.
scarus, -ī m (fish) scar.
scatebra, -ae f gushing water.
scateō, -ēre; -ō, -ere vi to bubble up, gush out; (fig) to abound, swarm.
scatūrīginēs, -um fpl springs.
scatūriō, -īre vi to gush out; (fig) to be full of.
scaurus adj large-ankled.
scelerātē adv wickedly.
scelerātus adj desecrated; wicked, infamous, accursed; pernicious.
scelerō, -āre vt to desecrate.
scelerōsus adj vicious, accursed.
scelestē adv wickedly.
scelestus adj wicked, villainous, accursed; unlucky.
scelus, -eris nt wickedness, crime, sin; (person) scoundrel; (event) calamity.
scēn- etc see **scaen-**.
scēptrifer, -ī adj sceptered.
scēptrum, -ī nt staff, sceptre; kingship, power.
scēptūchus, -ī m sceptre-bearer.
scheda etc see **scida**.
schēma, -ae f form, figure, style.
Schoenēis, -ēidis f Atalanta.
Schoenēius adj see **Schoenēis**.
Schoeneus, -eī m father of Atalanta.
schoenobatēs, -ae m rope dancer.
schola, -ae f learned discussion, dissertation; school; sect, followers.
scholasticus adj of a school ♦ m rhetorician.
scida, -ae f sheet of paper.
sciēns, -entis pres p of **sciō** ♦ adj knowing, purposely; versed in, acquainted with.
scienter adv expertly.
scientia, -ae f knowledge, skill.
scīlicet adv evidently, of course; (concessive) no doubt; (ironical) I suppose, of course.
scilla etc see **squilla**.
scindō, -ndere, -dī, -ssum vt to cut open, tear apart, split, break down; to divide, part.
scintilla, -ae f spark.
scintillō, -āre vi to sparkle.
scintillula, -ae f little spark.
sciō, -īre, -īvī, -ītum vt to know; to have skill in; (with infin) to know how to; quod ~iam as far as I know; ~ītō you may be sure.
Scīpiadēs, -ae m Scipio.
scīpiō, -ōnis m staff.
Scīpiō, -ōnis m famous Roman family name (esp the conqueror of Hannibal Africanus); Aemilianus (destroyer of Carthage and patron of literature).
scirpeus adj rush (in cpds) ♦ f wickerwork frame.
scirpiculus, -ī m rush basket.
scirpus, -ī m bulrush.
scīscitor, -ārī, -ātus; -ō, -āre vt to inquire; to question.
scīscō, -scere, -vī, -tum vt to inquire, learn; (POL) to approve, decree, appoint.

scissus ppp of **scindō** ♦ adj split; (voice) harsh.
scītāmenta, -ōrum ntpl dainties.
scītē adv cleverly, tastefully.
scītor, -ārī, -ātus vt, vi to inquire; to consult.
scītulus adj neat, smart.
scītum, -ī nt decree, statute.
scītus ppp of **sciō**; ppp of **scīscō** ♦ adj clever, shrewd, skilled; (words) sensible, witty; (appearance) fine, smart.
scītus, -ūs m decree.
sciūrus, -ī m squirrel.
scīvī perf of **sciō**; perf of **scīscō**.
scobis, -is f sawdust, filings.
scomber, -rī m mackerel.
scōpae, -ārum fpl broom.
Scopās, -ae m famous Greek sculptor.
scopulōsus adj rocky.
scopulus, -ī m rock, crag, promontory; (fig) danger.
scorpiō, -ōnis, -us and **os, -ī** m scorpion; (MIL) a kind of catapult.
scortātor, -ōris m fornicator.
scorteus adj of leather.
scortor, -ārī vi to associate with harlots.
scortum, -ī nt harlot, prostitute.
screātor, -ōris m one who clears his throat noisily.
screātus, -ūs m clearing the throat.
scrība, -ae m clerk, writer.
scrībō, -bere, -psī, -ptum vt to write, draw; to write down, describe; (document) to draw up; (law) to designate; (MIL) to enlist.
scrīnium, -ī and **iī** nt book box, lettercase.
scrīptiō, -ōnis f writing; composition; text.
scrīptitō, -āre, -āvī, -ātum vt to write regularly, compose.
scrīptor, -ōris m writer, author; secretary; rērum ~ historian.
scrīptula, -ōrum ntpl lines of a squared board.
scrīptum, -ī nt writing, book, work; (law) ordinance; **duōdecim ~a** Twelve Lines (a game played on a squared board).
scrīptūra, -ae f writing; composition; document; (POL) tax on public pastures; (will) provision.
scrīptus ppp of **scrībō**.
scrīptus, -ūs m clerkship.
scrīpulum, -ī nt small weight, scruple.
scrobis, -is f ditch, trench; grave.
scrōfa, -ae f breeding sow.
scrōfipāscus, -ī m pig breeder.
scrūpeus adj stony, rough.
scrūpōsus adj rocky, jagged.
scrūpulōsus adj stony, rough; (fig) precise.
scrūpulum etc see **scrīpulum**.
scrūpulus, -ī m small sharp stone; (fig) uneasiness, doubt, scruple.
scrūpus, -ī m sharp stone; (fig) uneasiness.
scrūta, -ōrum ntpl trash.

scrūtor, -ārī, -ātus vt to search, probe into, examine; to find out.
sculpō, -ere, -sī, -tum vt to carve, engrave.
sculpōneae, -ārum fpl clogs.
sculptilis adj carved.
sculptor, -ōris m sculptor.
sculptus ppp of **sculpō**.
scurra, -ae m jester; dandy.
scurrīlis adj jeering.
scurrīlitās, -ātis f scurrility.
scurror, -ārī vi to play the fool.
scūtāle, -is nt sling strap.
scūtātus adj carrying a shield.
scutella, -ae f bowl.
scutica, -ae f whip.
scutra, -ae f flat dish.
scutula, -ae f small dish.
scutula f wooden roller; secret letter.
scutulāta, -ae f a checked garment.
scūtulum, -ī nt small shield.
scūtum, -ī nt shield.
Scylla, -ae f dangerous rock or sea monster (in the Straits of Messina).
Scyllaeus adj see **Scylla**.
scymnus, -ī m cub.
scyphus, -ī m wine cup.
Scyrius, -ias adj see **Scyros**.
Scyros and **us, -ī** f Aegean island near Euboea.
scytala see **scutula**.
Scytha and **ēs, -ae** m Scythian.
Scythia, -iae f Scythia (country N.E. of the Black Sea).
Scythicus adj Scythian.
Scythis, -idis f Scythian woman.
sē pron himself, herself, itself, themselves; one another; **apud ~** at home; in his senses; **inter ~** mutually.
sēbum, -ī nt tallow, suet, grease.
sēcēdō, -ēdere, -essī, -essum vi to withdraw, retire; to revolt, secede.
sēcernō, -ernere, -rēvī, -rētum vt to separate, set apart; to dissociate; to distinguish.
sēcessiō, -ōnis f withdrawal; secession.
sēcessus, -ūs m retirement, solitude; retreat, recess.
sēclūdō, -dere, -sī, -sum vt to shut off, seclude; to separate, remove.
sēclūsus ppp of **sēclūdō** ♦ adj remote.
secō, -āre, -uī, -tum vt to cut; to injure; to divide; (MED) to operate on; (motion) to pass through; (dispute) to decide.
sēcrētiō, -ōnis f separation.
sēcrētō adv apart, in private, in secret.
sēcrētum, -ī nt privacy, secrecy; retreat, remote place; secret, mystery.
sēcrētus ppp of **sēcernō** ♦ adj separate; solitary, remote; secret, private.
secta, -ae f path; method, way of life; (POL) party; (PHILOS) school.

Noun declensions and verb conjugations are shown on pp xiii to xxv. The present infinitive ending of a verb shows to which conjugation it belongs: **-āre** = 1st; **-ēre** = 2nd; **-ere** = 3rd and **-īre** = 4th. Irregular verbs are shown on p xxvi

sectārius *adj* leading.
sectātor, -ōris *m* follower, adherent.
sectilis *adj* cut; for cutting.
sectiō, -ōnis *f* auctioning of confiscated goods.
sector, -ōris *m* cutter; buyer at a public sale.
sector, -ārī, -ātus *vt* to follow regularly, attend; to chase, hunt.
sectūra, -ae *f* digging.
sectus *ppp of* **secō.**
sēcubitus, -ūs *m* lying alone.
sēcubō, -āre, -uī *vi* to sleep by oneself; to live alone.
secuī *perf of* **secō.**
sēcul- *etc see* **saecul-.**
sēcum with himself *etc.*
secundānī, -ōrum *mpl* men of the second legion.
secundārius *adj* second-rate.
secundō *adv* secondly.
secundō, -āre *vt* to favour, make prosper.
secundum *prep* (*place*) behind, along; (*time*) after; (*rank*) next to; (*agreement*) according to, in favour of ♦ *adv* behind.
secundus *adj* following, next, second; inferior; favourable, propitious, fortunate ♦ *fpl* (*play*) subsidiary part; (*fig*) second fiddle ♦ *ntpl* success, good fortune; ~**ō flūmine** downstream; **rēs ~ae** prosperity, success.
secūricula, -ae *f* little axe.
secūrifer, -ī *adj* armed with an axe.
secūriger, -ī *adj* armed with an axe.
secūris, -is *f* axe; (*fig*) death blow; (*POL*) authority, supreme power.
secūritās, -ātis *f* freedom from anxiety, composure; negligence; safety, feeling of security.
secūrus *adj* untroubled, unconcerned; carefree, cheerful; careless.
secus *nt* (*indecl*) sex.
secus *adv* otherwise, differently; badly; **nōn ~** even so.
secūtor, -ōris *m* pursuer.
sed *conj* but; but also, but in fact.
sēdātē *adv* calmly.
sēdātiō, -ōnis *f* calming.
sēdātus *ppp of* **sēdō** ♦ *adj* calm, quiet, composed.
sēdecim *num* sixteen.
sēdecula, -ae *f* low stool.
sedentārius *adj* sitting.
sedeō, -ēre, sēdī, sessum *vi* to sit; (*army*) to be encamped, blockade; (*magistrates*) to be in session; (*clothes*) to suit, fit; (*places*) to be low-lying; (*heavy things*) to settle, subside; (*weapons*) to stick fast; (*inactivity*) to be idle; (*thought*) to be firmly resolved.
sēdēs, -is *f* seat, chair; abode, home; site, ground, foundation.
sēdī *perf of* **sedeō.**
sedīle, -is *nt* seat, chair.
sēditiō, -ōnis *f* insurrection, mutiny.
sēditiōsē *adv* seditiously.

sēditiōsus *adj* mutinous, factious; quarrelsome; troubled.
sēdō, -āre, -āvī, -ātum *vt* to calm, allay, lull.
sēdūcō, -ūcere, -ūxī, -uctum *vt* to take away, withdraw; to divide.
sēductiō, -ōnis *f* taking sides.
sēductus *ppp of* **sēdūcō** ♦ *adj* remote.
sēdulitās, -ātis *f* earnestness, assiduity; officiousness.
sēdulō *adv* busily, diligently; purposely.
sēdulus *adj* busy, diligent, assiduous; officious.
seges, -itis *f* cornfield; crop.
Segesta, -ae *f* town in N.W. Sicily.
Segestānus *adj see* **Segesta.**
segmentātus *adj* flounced.
segmentum, -ī *nt* brocade.
segne, -iter *adv* slowly, lazily.
segnipēs, -edis *adj* slow of foot.
segnis *adj* slow, sluggish, lazy.
segnitia, -ae *and* **ēs, -em, -ē** *f* slowness, sluggishness, sloth.
sēgregō, -āre, -āvī, -ātum *vt* to separate, put apart; to dissociate.
sēiugātus *adj* separated.
sēiugis, -is *m* chariot and six.
sēiūnctim *adv* separately.
sēiūnctiō, -ōnis *f* separation.
sēiūnctus *ppp of* **sēiungō.**
sēiungō, -gere, sēiūnxī, sēiūnctum *vt* to separate, part.
sēlēctiō, -ōnis *f* choice.
sēlēctus *ppp of* **sēligō.**
Seleucus, -ī *m* king of Syria.
sēlībra, -ae *f* half pound.
sēligō, -igere, -ēgī, -ēctum *vt* to choose, select.
sella, -ae *f* seat, chair, stool, sedan chair; ~ **cūrūlis** chair of office for higher magistrates.
sellisternia, -ōrum *ntpl* sacred banquets to goddesses.
sellula, -ae *f* stool; sedan chair.
sellulārius, -ī *and* **iī** *m* mechanic.
sēmanimus *etc see* **sēmianimis.**
semel *adv* once; once for all; first; ever; ~ **atque iterum** again and again; ~ **aut iterum** once or twice.
Semelē, -ēs *f* mother of Bacchus.
Semelēius *adj see* **Semelē.**
sēmen, -inis *nt* seed; (*plant*) seedling, slip; (*men*) race, child; (*physics*) particle; (*fig*) origin, instigator.
sēmentifer, -ī *adj* fruitful.
sēmentis, -is *f* sowing, planting; young corn.
sēmentīvus *adj* of seed time.
sēmermis *etc see* **sēmiermis.**
sēmēstris *adj* half-yearly, for six months.
sēmēsus *adj* half-eaten.
sēmet *pron* self, selves.
sēmiadapertus *adj* half-open.
sēmianimis, -us *adj* half-dead.
sēmiapertus *adj* half-open.
sēmibōs, -ovis *adj* half-ox.

sēmicaper, -rī *adj* half-goat.
sēmicremātus, sēmicremus *adj* half-burned.
sēmicubitālis *adj* half a cubit long
sēmideus *adj* half-divine ♦ *m* demigod.
sēmidoctus *adj* half-taught.
sēmiermis, -us *adj* half-armed.
sēmiēsus *adj* half-eaten.
sēmifactus *adj* half-finished.
sēmifer, -ī *adj* half-beast; half-savage.
sēmigermānus *adj* half-German.
sēmigravis *adj* half-overcome.
sēmigrō, -āre *vi* to go away.
sēmihiāns, -antis *adj* half-opened.
sēmihomō, -inis *m* half-man, half-human.
sēmihōra, -ae *f* half an hour.
sēmilacer, -ī *adj* half-mangled.
sēmilautus *adj* half-washed.
sēmilīber, -ī *adj* half-free.
sēmilixa, -ae *m* not much better than a camp follower.
sēmimarīnus *adj* half in the sea.
sēmimās, -āris *m* hermaphrodite ♦ *adj* castrated.
sēmimortuus *adj* half-dead.
sēminārium, -ī *and* **iī** *nt* nursery, seed plot.
sēminātor, -ōris *m* originator.
sēminecis *adj* half-dead.
sēminium, -ī *and* **iī** *nt* procreation; breed.
sēminō, -āre *vt* to sow; to produce; to beget.
sēminūdus *adj* half-naked; almost unarmed.
sēmipāgānus *adj* half-rustic.
sēmiplēnus *adj* half-full, half-manned.
sēmiputātus *adj* half-pruned.
Semīramis, -is *and* **idis** *f queen of Assyria.*
Semīramius *adj see n.*
sēmirāsus *adj* half-shaven.
sēmireductus *adj* half turned back
sēmirefectus *adj* half-repaired.
sēmirutus *adj* half-demolished, half in ruins.
sēmis, -issis *m (coin)* half an as; (*interest*) ½ per cent per month (*i.e. 6 per cent per annum*); (*area*) half an acre.
sēmisepultus *adj* half-buried.
sēmisomnus *adj* half-asleep.
sēmisupīnus *adj* half lying back.
sēmita, -ae *f* path, way.
sēmitālis *adj* of byways.
sēmitārius *adj* frequenting byways
sēmiūst- *etc see* **sēmūst-.**
sēmivir, -ī *adj* half-man; emasculated; unmanly.
sēmivīvus *adj* half-dead.
sēmodius, -ī *and* **iī** *m* half a peck.
sēmōtus *ppp of* **sēmoveō** ♦ *adj* remote; distinct.
sēmoveō, -ovēre, -ōvī, -ōtum *vt* to put aside, separate.
semper *adv* always, ever, every time.
sempiternus *adj* everlasting, lifelong.

Semprōnius, -ī *m* Roman family name (*esp the Gracchi*).
Semprōnius, -iānus *adj see n.*
sēmūncia, -ae *f* half an ounce; a twenty-fourth.
sēmūnciārius *adj* (*interest*) at the rate of one twenty-fourth.
sēmūstulātus *adj* half-burned.
sēmūstus *adj* half-burned.
senāculum, -ī *nt* open air meeting place (*of the Senate*).
sēnāriolus, -ī *m* little trimeter.
sēnārius, -ī *and* **iī** *m* (iambic) trimeter.
senātor, -ōris *m* senator.
senātōrius *adj* senatorial, in the Senate.
senātus, -ūs *m* Senate; meeting of the Senate.
senātūscōnsultum, -ī *nt* decree of the Senate.
Seneca, -ae *m Stoic philosopher, tutor of Nero.*
senecta, -ae *f* old age.
senectus *adj* old, aged.
senectūs, -ūtis *f* old age; old men.
seneō, -ēre *vi* to be old.
senēscō, -ēscere, -uī *vi* to grow old; (*fig*) to weaken, wane, pine away.
senex *-is* (*compar -ior*) *adj* old (*over 45*) ♦ *m/f* old man, old woman.
sēnī, -ōrum *adj* six each, in sixes; six; ~ **dēnī** sixteen each.
senīlis *adj* of an old person, senile.
sēniō, -ōnis *m* number six on a dice.
senior *compar of* **senex.**
senium, -ī *and* **iī** *nt* weakness of age, decline; affliction; peevishness.
Senonēs, -um *mpl tribe of S. Gaul.*
sēnsī *perf of* **sentiō.**
sēnsifer, -ī *adj* sensory.
sēnsilis *adj* having sensation.
sēnsim *adv* tentatively, gradually.
sēnsus *ppp of* **sentiō** ♦ *ntpl* thoughts.
sēnsus, -ūs *m* (*body*) feeling, sensation, sense; (*intellect*) understanding, judgment, thought; (*emotion*) sentiment, attitude, frame of mind; (*language*) meaning, purport, sentence; **commūnis** ~ universal human feelings, human sympathy, social instinct.
sententia, -ae *f* opinion, judgment; purpose, will; (*law*) verdict, sentence; (*POL*) vote, decision; (*language*) meaning, sentence, maxim, epigram; **meā ~ā** in my opinion; **dē meā ~ā** in accordance with my wishes; **ex meā ~ā** to my liking; **ex animī meī ~ā** to the best of my knowledge and belief; **in ~am pedibus īre** support a motion.
sententiola, -ae *f* phrase.
sententiōsē *adv* pointedly.
sententiōsus *adj* pithy.
senticētum, -ī *nt* thornbrake.
sentīna, -ae *f* bilge water; (*fig*) dregs, scum.
sentiō, -īre, sēnsī, sēnsum *vt* (*senses*) to

feel, see, perceive; (*circs*) to experience, undergo; (*mind*) to observe, understand; (*opinion*) to think, judge; (*law*) to vote, decide.

sentis, -is *m* thorn, brier.

sentīscō, -ere *vt* to begin to perceive.

sentus *adj* thorny; untidy.

senuī *perf of* **senēscō**.

seorsum, seorsus *adv* apart, differently.

sēparābilis *adj* separable.

sēparātim *adv* apart, separately.

sēparātiō, -ōnis *f* separation, severing.

sēparātius *adv* less closely.

sēparātus *adj* separate, different.

sēparō, -āre, -āvī, -ātum *vt* to part, separate, divide; to distinguish.

sepeliō, -elīre, -elīvī *and* **eliī, -ultum** *vt* to bury; (*fig*) to overwhelm, overcome.

sēpia, -ae *f* cuttlefish.

Sēplasia, -ae *f* street in Capua where perfumes were sold.

sēpōnō, -ōnere, -osuī, -ositum *vt* to put aside, pick out; to reserve; to banish; to appropriate; to separate.

sēpositus *ppp of* **sēpōnō** ♦ *adj* remote; distinct, choice.

sēpse *pron* oneself.

septem *num* seven.

September, -ris *m* September ♦ *adj* of September.

septemdecim *etc see* **septendecim**.

septemfluus *adj* with seven streams.

septemgeminus *adj* sevenfold.

septemplex, -icis *adj* sevenfold.

septemtriō *etc see* **septentriōnēs**.

septemvirālis *adj* of the septemviri ♦ *mpl* the septemviri.

septemvirātus, -ūs *m* office of septemvir.

septemvirī, -ōrum *mpl* board of seven officials.

septēnārius, -ī *and* **iī** *m* verse of seven feet.

septendecim *num* seventeen.

septēnī, -ōrum *adj* seven each, in sevens.

septentriō, -ōnis *m*, **-ōnēs, -ōnum** *mpl* Great Bear, Little Bear; north; north wind.

septentriōnālis *adj* northern ♦ *ntpl* northern regions.

septiēns, -ēs *adv* seven times.

septimānī, -ōrum *mpl* men of the seventh legion.

septimum *adv* for the seventh time; ~ decimus seventeenth.

septimus *adj* seventh.

septingentēsimus *adj* seven hundredth.

septingentī, -ōrum *adj* seven hundred.

septuāgēsimus *adj* seventieth.

septuāgintā *adj* seventy.

septuennis *adj* seven years old.

septumus *adj see* **septimus**.

septūnx, -ūncis *m* seven ounces, seven-twelfths.

sepulcrālis *adj* funeral.

sepulcrētum, -ī *nt* cemetery.

sepulcrum, -ī *nt* grave, tomb.

sepultūra, -ae *f* burial, funeral.

sepultus *ppp of* **sepeliō**.

Sequāna, -ae *f* river Seine.

Sequānī, -ōrum *mpl* people of N. Gaul.

sequāx, -ācis *adj* pursuing, following.

sequens, -entis *pres p of* **sequor** ♦ *adj* following, next.

sequester, -rī *and* **ris** *m* trustee; agent, mediator.

sequestrum, -rī *nt* deposit.

sēquius *compar of* **secus**; otherwise; nihilō ~ nonetheless.

sequor, -quī, -cūtus *vt, vi* to follow; to accompany, go with; (*time*) to come after, come next, ensue; (*enemy*) to pursue; (*objective*) to make for, aim at; (*pulling*) to come away easily; (*share, gift*) to go to, come to; (*words*) to come naturally.

sera, -ae *f* door bolt, bar.

Serāpēum, -ēī *nt* temple of Serapis.

Serāpis, -is *and* **idis** *m* chief Egyptian god.

serēnitās, -ātis *f* fair weather.

serēnō, -āre *vt* to clear up, brighten up.

serēnus *adj* fair, clear; (*wind*) fair-weather; (*fig*) cheerful, happy ♦ *nt* clear sky, fair weather.

Sēres, -um *mpl* Chinese.

serēscō, -ere *vi* to dry off.

sēria, -ae *f* tall jar.

sērica, -ōrum *ntpl* silks.

Sēricus *adj* Chinese; silk.

seriēs, -ēī, -ē *f* row, sequence, succession.

sēriō *adv* in earnest, seriously.

sēriola, -ae *f* small jar.

Serīphius *adj see* **Serīphus**.

Serīphus (-os), -ī *f* Aegean island.

sērius *adj* earnest, serious.

sērius *compar of* **sērō**.

sermō, -ōnis *m* conversation, talk; learned discussion, discourse; common talk, rumour; language, style; every day language, prose; (*pl*) Satires (of Horace).

sermōcinor, -ārī *vi* to converse.

sermunculus, -ī *m* gossip, rumour.

serō, -ere, sēvī, -satum *vt* to sow, plant; (*fig*) to produce, sow the seeds of.

serō, -ere, -tum *vt* to sew, join, wreathe; (*fig*) to compose, devise, engage in.

sērō (*compar* **-ius**) *adv* late; too late.

serpēns, -entis *m/f* snake, serpent; (*constellation*) Draco.

serpenticena, -ae *m* offspring of a serpent.

serpentipēs, -edis *adj* serpent-footed.

serperastra, -ōrum *ntpl* splints.

serpō, -ere, -sī, -tum *vi* to creep, crawl; (*fig*) to spread slowly.

serpyllum, -ī *nt* wild thyme.

serra, -ae *f* saw.

serrācum *etc see* **sarrācum**.

serrātus *adj* serrated, notched.

serrula, -ae *f* small saw.

Sertōriānus *adj see* **Sertōrius**.

Sertōrius, -ī m commander under Marius, who held out against Sulla in Spain.
sertus ppp of **serō** ♦ ntpl garlands.
serum, -ī nt whey, serum.
sērum, -ī nt late hour.
sērus adj late; too late; ~**ā nocte** late at night.
serva, -ae f maidservant, slave.
servābilis adj that cannot be saved.
servātor, -ōris m deliverer; watcher.
servātrīx, -īcis f deliverer.
servīlis adj of slaves, servile.
servīliter adv slavishly.
Servīlius, -ī m Roman family name of many consuls.
Servīlius, -ānus adj see n.
serviō, -īre, -īvī and **iī, -ītum** vi to be a slave; (with dat) to serve, be of use to, be good for; (property) to be mortgaged.
servitium, -ī and **iī** nt slavery, servitude; slaves.
servitūdō, -inis f slavery.
servitūs, -ūtis f slavery, service; slaves; (property) liability.
Servius, -ī m sixth king of Rome; famous jurist of Cicero's day.
servō, -āre, -āvī, -ātum vt to save, rescue; to keep, preserve, retain; to store, reserve; to watch, observe, guard; (place) to remain in.
servolus, -ī m young slave.
servos, -ī m see **servus.**
servula, -ae f servant girl.
servulus, -ī m young slave.
servus, -ī m slave, servant ♦ adj slavish, serving; (property) liable to a burden.
sescēnāris adj a year and a half old.
sescēnī, -ōrum adj six hundred each.
sescentēsimus adj six hundredth.
sescentī, -ōrum num six hundred; an indefinitely large number.
sescentiēns, -ēs adv six hundred times.
sēsē etc see **sē.**
seselis, -is f (plant) seseli.
sesqui adv one and a half times.
sesquialter, -ī adj one and a half.
sesquimodius, -ī and **iī** m a peck and a half.
sesquioctāvus adj of nine to eight.
sesquiopus, -eris nt a day and a half's work.
sesquipedālis adj a foot and a half.
sesquipēs, -edis m a foot and a half.
sesquiplāga, -ae f a blow and a half.
sesquiplex, -icis adj one and a half times.
sesquitertius adj of four to three.
sessilis adj for sitting on.
sessiō, -ōnis f sitting; seat; session; loitering.
sessitō, -āre, -āvī vi to sit regularly.
sessiuncula, -ae f small meeting.
sessor, -ōris m spectator; resident.
sēstertium, -ī nt 1000 sesterces; **dēr**a ~**ia** 10,000 sesterces; **centēna mīlia** ~**ium** 100,000 sesterces; **deciēns** ~**ium** 1,000,000 sesterces.

sēstertius, -ī and **iī** m sesterce, a silver coin.
Sestius, -ī m tribune defended by Cicero.
Sestius, -iānus adj of a Sestius.
Sestos (-us), -ī f town on Dardanelles (home of Hero).
Sestus adj see **Sestos.**
sēt- etc see **saet-.**
Sētia, -iae f town in S. Latium (famous for wine).
Sētiaīnus adj see **Sētia.**
sētius compar of **secus.**
seu etc see **sīve.**
sevērē adv sternly, severely.
sevēritās, -ātis f strictness, austerity.
sevērus adj strict, stern; severe, austere; grim, terrible.
sēvī perf of **serō.**
sēvocō, -āre vt to call aside; to withdraw, remove.
sēvum etc see **sēbum.**
sex num six.
sexāgēnārius adj sixty years old.
sexāgēnī, -ōrum adj sixty each.
sexāgēsimus adj sixtieth.
sexāgiēns, -ēs adv sixty times.
sexāgintā num sixty.
sexangulus adj hexagonal.
sexcēn- etc see **sescēn-.**
sexcēnārius adj of six hundred.
sexennis adj six years old, after six years.
sexennium, -ī and **iī** nt six years.
sexiēns, -ēs adv six times.
sexprīmī, -ōrum mpl a provincial town, council.
sextadecimānī, -ōrum mpl men of the sixteenth legion.
sextāns, -antis m a sixth; (coin, weight) a sixth of an as.
sextārius, -ī and **iī** m pint.
Sextīlis, -is m August ♦ adj of August.
sextula, -ae f a sixth of an ounce.
sextum adv for the sixth time.
sextus adj sixth; ~ **decimus** sixteenth.
sexus, -ūs m sex.
sī conj if; if only; to see if; **sī forte** in the hope that; **sī iam** assuming for the moment; **sī minus** if not; **sī quandō** whenever; **sī quidem** if indeed; since; **sī quis** if anyone, whoever; **mīrum sī** surprising that; **quod sī** and if, but if.
sībila, -ōrum ntpl whistle, hissing.
sībilō, -āre vi to hiss, whistle ♦ vt to hiss at.
sībilus, -ī m whistle, hissing.
sībilus adj hissing.
Sibulla, Sibylla, -ae f prophetess, Sibyl.
Sibyllīnus adj see **Sibylla.**
sīc adv so, thus, this way, as follows; as one is, as things are; on this condition; yes.
sīca, -ae f dagger.
Sicānī, -ōrum mpl ancient people of Italy

Noun declensions and verb conjugations are shown on pp xiii to xxv. The present infinitive ending of a verb shows to which conjugation it belongs: **-āre** = 1st; **-ēre** = 2nd; **-ere** = 3rd and **-īre** = 4th. Irregular verbs are shown on p xxvi

(later of Sicily).

Sicānia, -iae f Sicily.

Sicānus, -ius adj Sicanian, Sicilian.

sīcārius, -ī and **iī** m assassin, murderer.

siccē adv (speech) firmly.

siccitās, -ātis f dryness, drought; (body) firmness; (style) dullness.

siccō, -āre, -āvī, -ātum vt to dry; to drain, exhaust; (sore) to heal up.

siccoculus adj dry-eyed.

siccus adj dry; thirsty, sober; (body) firm, healthy; (argument) solid, sound; (style) flat, dull ♦ nt dry land.

Sicilia, -ae f Sicily.

sicilicula, -ae f little sickle.

Siciliēnsis, -s, -dis adj Sicilian.

sīcine is this how?

sīcubi adv if anywhere, wheresoever.

Siculus adj Sicilian.

sīcunde adv if from anywhere.

sīcut, sīcutī adv just as, as in fact; (comparison) like, as; (example) as for instance; (with subj) as if.

Sicyōn, -ōnis f town in N. Peloponnese.

Sicyōnius adj see **Sicyōn.**

sīdereus adj starry; (fig) radiant.

Sidicīnī, -ōrum mpl people of Campania.

Sidicīnus adj see n.

sīdō, -ere, -ī vi to sit down, settle; to sink, subside; to stick fast.

Sīdōn, -ōnis f famous Phoenician town.

Sīdōnis, -ōnidis adj Phoenician ♦ f Europa; Dido.

Sīdōnius adj Sidonian, Phoenician.

sīdus, -eris nt constellation; heavenly body, star; season, climate, weather; destiny; (pl) sky; (fig) fame, glory.

siem archaic subj of **sum.**

Sigambrī etc see **Sugambrī.**

Sīgēum, -ī nt promontory near Troy.

Sīgēus, -ius adj Sigean.

sigilla, -ōrum ntpl little figures; seal.

sigillātus adj decorated with little figures.

signātor, -ōris m witness (to a document).

signifer, -ī adj with constellations; ~ orbis Zodiac ♦ m (MIL) standard-bearer.

significanter adv pointedly, tellingly.

significātiō, -ōnis f indication, signal, token; sign of approval; (RHET) emphasis; (word) meaning.

significō, -āre, -āvī, -ātum vt to indicate, show; to betoken, portend; (word) to mean.

signō, -āre, -āvī, -ātum vt to mark, stamp, print; (document) to seal; (money) to coin, mint; (fig) to impress, designate, note.

signum, -ī nt mark, sign, token; (MIL) standard; signal, password; (art) design, statue; (document) seal; (ASTRO) constellation; ~a cōnferre join battle; ~a cōnstituere halt; ~a convertere wheel about; ~a ferre move camp; attack; ~a inferre attack; ~a prōferre advance; ~a sequī march in order; ab ~īs discēdere leave the ranks; sub ~īs īre march

in order.

Sīla, -ae f forest in extreme S. Italy

sīlānus, -ī m fountain, jet of water.

silēns, -entis pres p of **sileō** ♦ adj still, silent ♦ mpl the dead.

silentium, -ī and **iī** nt stillness, silence; (fig) standstill, inaction.

Sīlēnus, -ī m old and drunken companion of Bacchus.

sileō, -ēre, -uī vi to be still, be silent; to cease ♦ vt to say nothing about.

siler, -is nt willow.

silēscō, -ere vi to calm down, fall silent.

silex, -icis m flint, hard stone; rock.

silicernium, -ī and **iī** nt funeral feast.

silīgō, -inis f winter wheat; fine flour.

siliqua, -ae f pod, husk; (pl) pulse.

sillybus, -ī m label bearing a book's title.

Silurēs, -um mpl British tribe in S. Wales.

silūrus, -ī m sheatfish.

sīlus adj snub-nosed.

silva, -ae f wood, forest; plantation, shrubbery; (plant) flowering stem; (LIT) material.

Silvānus, -ī m god of uncultivated land.

silvēscō, -ere vi to run to wood.

silvestris adj wooded, forest- (in cpds); wild; pastoral.

silvicola, -ae m/f sylvan.

silvicultrīx, -īcis adj living in the woods.

silvifragus adj tree-breaking.

silvōsus adj woody.

sīmia, -ae f ape.

simile, -is nt comparison, parallel.

similis adj like, similar; ~ atque like what; vērī ~ probable.

similiter adv similarly.

similitūdō, -inis f likeness, resemblance; imitation; analogy; monotony; (RHET) simile.

sīmiolus, -ī m monkey.

sīmītū adv at the same time, together.

sīmius, -ī and **iī** m ape.

Simoīs, -entis m river of Troy.

Simōnidēs, -is m Greek lyric poet of Ceos (famous for dirges).

Simōnidēus adj see n.

simplex, -icis adj single, simple; natural, straightforward; (character) frank, sincere.

simplicitās, -ātis f singleness; frankness, innocence.

simpliciter adv simply, naturally; frankly.

simplum, -ī nt simple sum.

simpulum, -ī nt small ladle; **excitāre fluctūs in ~ō ≈ raise a storm in a teacup.**

simpuvium, -ī and **iī** nt libation bowl.

simul adv at the same time, together; at once; likewise, also; both … and; ~ ac atque, ut as soon as ♦ conj as soon as.

simulācrum, -ī nt likeness, image, portrait, statue; phantom, ghost; (writing) symbol; (fig) semblance, shadow.

simulāmen, -inis nt copy.

simulāns, -antis pres p of **simulō** ♦ adj

imitative.
simulātē *adv* deceitfully.
simulātiō, -ōnis *f* pretence, shamming, hypocrisy.
simulātor, -ōris *m* imitator; pretender, hypocrite.
simulatque *conj* as soon as.
simulō, -āre, -āvī, -ātum *vt* to imitate, represent; to impersonate; to pretend, counterfeit.
simultās, -ātis *f* feud, quarrel.
simulus *adj* snub-nosed.
sīmus *adj* snub-nosed.
sīn *conj* but if; ~ **aliter, minus** but if not.
sināpi, -is *nt*, **-is, -is** *f* mustard.
sincērē *adv* honestly.
sincēritās, -ātis *f* integrity.
sincērus *adj* clean, whole, genuine; (*fig*) pure, sound, honest.
sincipitāmentum, -ī *nt* half a head.
sinciput, -itis *nt* half a head; brain.
sine *prep* (*with abl*) without, -less (*in cpds*).
singillātim *adv* singly, one by one.
singulāris *adj* one at a time, single, sole; unique, extraordinary.
singulāriter *adv* separately; extremely.
singulārius *adj* single.
singulī, -ōrum *adj* one each, single one.
singultim *adv* in sobs.
singultō, -āre *vi* to sob, gasp, gurgle ♦ *vt* to gasp out.
singultus, -ūs *m* sob, gasp, death rattle.
singulus *etc see* **singulī**.
sinister, -rī *adj* left; (*fig*) perverse, unfavourable; (*Roman auspices*) lucky; (*Greek auspices*) unlucky.
sinistra, -rae *f* left hand, left-hand side.
sinistrē *adv* badly.
sinistrōrsus, -um *adv* to the left.
sinō, -ere, sīvī, situm *vt* to let, allow; to let be; **nē dī sīrint** God forbid!
Sinōpē, -ēs *f* Greek colony on the Black Sea.
Sinōpēnsis, -eus *adj see* **Sinōpē**.
Sinuessa, -ae *f* town on the borders of Latium and Campania.
Sinuessānus *adj see* **Sinuessa**.
sīnum *etc see* **sīnus**.
sinuō, -āre, -āvī, -ātum *vt* to wind, curve.
sinuōsus *adj* winding, curved.
sinus, -ūs *m* curve, fold; (*fishing*) net; (*GEOG*) bay, gulf, valley; (*hair*) curl; (*ship*) sail; (*toga*) fold, pocket, purse; (*person*) bosom; (*fig*) protection, love, heart, hiding place; **in -ū gaudēre** be secretly glad.
sīnus, -ī *m* large cup.
sīparium, -ī *and* **iī** *nt* act curtain.
sīphō, -ōnis *m* siphon; fire engine.
sīquandō *adv* if ever.
sīquī, sīquis *pron* if any, if anyone, whoever.
sīquidem *adv* if in fact ♦ *conj* since.

sīrempse *adj* the same.
Sīrēn, -ēnis *f* Siren.
sīris, sīrit *perf subj of* **sinō**.
Sīrius, -ī *m* Dog Star ♦ *adj* of Sirius.
sirpe, -is *nt* silphium.
sīrus, -ī *m* corn pit.
sīs (*for* **sī vīs**) *adv* please.
sistō, -ere, stitī, statum *vt* to place, set, plant; (*law*) to produce in court; (*monument*) to set up; (*movement*) to stop, arrest, check ♦ *vi* to stand, rest; (*law*) to appear in court; (*movement*) to stand still, stop, stand firm; **sē ~** appear, present oneself; **tūtum ~** see safe; **vadimōnium ~** duly appear in court; **-ī nōn potest** the situation is desperate.
sistrum, -ī *nt* Egyptian rattle, cymbal.
sisymbrium, -ī *and* **iī** *nt* fragrant herb, perhaps mint.
Sīsyphius *adj*, **-idēs, -idae** *m* Ulysses.
Sīsyphus, -ī *m* criminal condemned in Hades to roll a rock repeatedly up a hill.
sitella, -ae *f* lottery urn.
Sīthonis, -idis *adj* Thracian.
Sīthonius *adj* Thracian.
sitīculōsus *adj* thirsty, dry.
sitiēns, -entis *pres p of* **sitiō** ♦ *adj* thirsty, dry; parching; (*fig*) eager.
sitienter *adv* eagerly.
sitiō, -īre *vi* to be thirsty; to be parched ♦ *vt* to thirst for, covet.
sitis, -is *f* thirst; drought.
sittybus *etc see* **sillybus**.
situla, -ae *f* bucket.
situs *ppp of* **sinō** ♦ *adj* situated, lying; founded; (*fig*) dependent.
situs, -ūs *m* situation, site; structure; neglect, squalor, mould; (*mind*) dullness.
sīve *conj* or if; or; whether ... or.
sīvī *perf of* **sinō**.
smaragdus, -ī *m/f* emerald.
smīlax, -acis *f* bindweed.
Smintheus, -eī *m* Apollo.
Smyrna, -ae *f* Ionian town in Asia Minor.
Smyrnaeus *adj see* **Smyrna**.
sobol- *etc see* **subol-**.
sobriē *adv* temperately; sensibly.
sobrīna, -ae *f* cousin (*on the mother's side*).
sobrīnus, -ī *m* cousin (*on the mother's side*).
sobrius *adj* sober; temperate, moderate; (*mind*) sane, sensible.
soccus, -ī *m* slipper (*esp the sock worn by actors in comedy*); comedy.
socer, -ī *m* father-in-law.
sociābilis *adj* compatible.
sociālis *adj* of allies, confederate; conjugal.
sociāliter *adv* sociably.
sociennus, -ī *m* friend.
societās, -ātis *f* fellowship, association; alliance.
sociō, -āre, -āvī, -ātum *vt* to unite, associate,

share.

sociofraudus, -ī m deceiver of friends.

socius adj associated, allied ♦ m friend, companion; partner, ally.

sōcordia, -ae f indolence, apathy; folly.

sōcordius adv more carelessly, lazily.

sōcors, -dis adj lazy, apathetic; stupid.

Sōcratēs, -is m famous Athenian philosopher.

Sōcraticus adj of Socrates, Socratic ♦ mpl the followers of Socrates.

socrus, -ūs f mother-in-law.

sodālicium, -ī and **iī** nt fellowship; secret society.

sodālicius adj of fellowship.

sodālis, -is m/f companion, friend; member of a society, accomplice.

sodālitās, -ātis f companionship, friendship; society, club; secret society.

sodālitius etc see **sodālicius**.

sodēs adv please.

sōl, sōlis m sun; sunlight, sun's heat; (poetry) day; (myth) Sun god; ~ **oriēns**, ~**is ortus** east; ~ **occidēns**, ~**is occāsus** west.

sōlāciolum, -ī nt a grain of comfort.

sōlācium, -ī and **iī** nt comfort, consolation, relief.

sōlāmen, -inis nt solace, relief.

sōlāris adj of the sun.

sōlārium, -ī and **iī** nt sundial; clock; balcony, terrace.

sōlātium etc see **sōlācium**.

sōlātor, -ōris m consoler.

soldūriī, -ōrum mpl retainers.

soldus etc see **solidus**.

solea, -ae f sandal, shoe; fetter; (fish) sole.

soleārius, -ī and **iī** m sandal maker.

soleātus adj wearing sandals.

soleō, -ēre, -itus vi to be accustomed, be in the habit, usually do; **ut** ~ as usual.

solidē adv for certain.

soliditās, -ātis f solidity.

solidō, -āre vt to make firm, strengthen.

solidus adj solid, firm, dense; whole, complete; (fig) sound, genuine, substantial ♦ nt solid matter, firm ground.

sōliferreum, -ī nt an all-iron javelin.

sōlistimus adj (AUG) most favourable.

sōlitārius adj solitary, lonely.

sōlitūdō, -inis f solitariness, loneliness; destitution; (place) desert.

solitus ppa of **soleō** ♦ adj usual, customary ♦ nt custom; **plūs ~ō** more than usual.

solium, -ī and **iī** nt seat, throne; tub; (fig) rule.

sōlivagus adj going by oneself; single.

sollemne, -is nt religious rite, festival; usage, practice.

sollemnis adj annual, regular; religious, solemn; usual, ordinary.

sollemniter adv solemnly.

sollers, -tis adj skilled, clever, expert; ingenious.

sollerter adv cleverly.

sollertia, -ae f skill, ingenuity.

sollicitātiō, -ōnis f inciting.

sollicitō, -āre, -āvī, -ātum vt to stir up, disturb; to trouble, distress, molest; to rouse, urge, incite, tempt, tamper with.

sollicitūdō, -inis f uneasiness, anxiety.

sollicitus adj agitated, disturbed; (mind) troubled, worried, alarmed; (things) anxious, careful; (cause) disquieting.

solliferreum etc see **sōliferreum**.

sollistimus etc see **sōlistimus**.

soloecismus, -ī m grammatical mistake.

Solōn, -ōnis m famous Athenian lawgiver.

sōlor, -ārī, -ātus vt to comfort, console; to relieve, ease.

sōlstitiālis adj of the summer solstice; midsummer.

sōlstitium, -ī and **iī** nt summer solstice; midsummer, summer heat.

solum, -ī nt ground, floor, bottom; soil, land, country; (foot) sole; (fig) basis; **~ō aequāre** raze to the ground.

sōlum adv only, merely.

sōlus (gen **-īus**, dat **-ī**) see **vicis**; adj only, alone; lonely, forsaken; (place) lonely, deserted.

solūtē adv loosely, freely, carelessly, weakly, fluently.

solūtiō, -ōnis f loosening; payment.

solūtus ppp of **solvō** ♦ adj loose, free; (from distraction) at ease, at leisure, merry; (from obligation) exempt; (from restraint) free, independent, unprejudiced; (moral) lax, weak, insolent; (language) prose, unrhythmical; (speaker) fluent; **ōrātiō ~a**, **verba ~a** prose.

solvō, -vere, -vī, -ūtum vt to loosen, undo; to free, release, acquit, exempt; to dissolve, break up, separate; to relax, slacken, weaken; to cancel, remove, destroy; to solve, explain; to pay, fulfil; (argument) to refute; (discipline) to undermine; (feelings) to get rid of; (hair) to let down; (letter) to open; (sail) to unfurl; (siege) to raise; (troops) to dismiss ♦ vi to set sail; to pay; **nāvem** ~ set sail; **poenās** ~ be punished; **praesēns** ~ pay cash; **rem** ~ pay; **sacrāmentō** ~ discharge; **~vendō esse** be solvent.

Solyma, -ōrum ntpl Jerusalem.

Solymus adj of the Jews.

somniculōsē adv sleepily.

somniculōsus adj sleepy.

somnifer, -ī adj soporific; fatal.

somniō, -āre vt to dream, dream about; to talk nonsense.

somnium, -ī and **iī** nt dream; nonsense, fancy.

somnus, -ī m sleep; sloth.

sonābilis adj noisy.

sonipēs, -edis m steed.

sonitus, -ūs m sound, noise.

sonivius adj noisy.

sonō, -āre, -uī, -itum vi to sound, make a noise ♦ vt to utter, speak, celebrate; to sound like.

sonor, -ōris m sound, noise.

sonōrus adj noisy, loud.
sōns, sontis adj guilty.
sonticus adj critical; important.
sonus, -ī m sound, noise; (fig) tone.
sophistēs, -ae m sophist.
Sophoclēs, -is m famous Greek tragic poet.
Sophoclēus adj of Sophocles, Sophoclean.
sophus adj wise.
sōpiō, -īre, -īvī, -ītum vt to put to sleep; (fig) to calm, lull.
sopor, -ōris m sleep; apathy.
sopōrifer, -ī adj soporific, drowsy.
sopōrō, -āre vt to lull to sleep; to make soporific.
sopōrus adj drowsy.
Sōracte, -is nt mountain in S. Etruria.
sorbeō, -ēre, -uī vt to suck, swallow; (fig) to endure.
sorbillō, -āre vt to sip.
sorbitiō, -ōnis f drink, broth.
sorbum, -ī nt service berry.
sorbus, -ī f service tree.
sordeō, -ēre vi to be dirty, be sordid; to seem shabby; to be of no account.
sordēs, -is f dirt, squalor, shabbiness; mourning; meanness; vulgarity; (people) rabble.
sordēscō, -ere vi to become dirty.
sordidātus adj shabbily dressed, in mourning.
sordidē adv meanly, vulgarly.
sordidulus adj soiled, shabby.
sordidus adj dirty, squalid, shabby; in mourning; poor, mean; base, vile.
sōrex, -icis m shrewmouse.
sōricīnus adj of the shrewmouse.
sōrītēs, -ae m chain syllogism.
soror, -ōris f sister.
sorōricīda, -ae m murderer of a sister.
sorōrius adj of a sister.
sors, sortis f lot; allotted duty; oracle, prophecy; fate, fortune; (money) capital, principal.
sōrsum etc see **seōrsum**.
sortilegus adj prophetic ♦ m soothsayer.
sortior, -īrī, -ītus vi to draw or cast lots ♦ vt to draw lots for, allot, obtain by lot; to distribute, share; to choose; to receive.
sortītiō, -ōnis f drawing lots, choosing by lot.
sortītus ppa of **sortior** ♦ adj assigned, allotted; ~ō by lot.
sortītus, -ūs m drawing lots.
Sosius, -ī m Roman family name (esp two brothers Sosii, famous booksellers in Rome).
sōspes, -itis adj safe and sound, unhurt; favourable, lucky.
sōspita, -ae f saviour.
sōspitālis adj beneficial.
sōspitō, -āre vt to preserve, prosper.
sōtēr, -ēris m saviour.

spādīx, -īcis adj chestnut-brown.
spadō, -ōnis m eunuch.
spargō, -gere, -sī, -sum vt to throw, scatter, sprinkle; to strew, spot, moisten; to disperse, spread abroad.
sparsus ppp of **spargō** ♦ adj freckled.
Sparta, -ae, -ē, -ēs f famous Greek city.
Spartacus, -ī m gladiator who led a revolt against Rome.
Spartānus, -icus adj Spartan.
Spartiātēs, -iātae m Spartan.
spartum, -ī nt Spanish broom.
sparulus, -ī m bream.
sparus, -ī m hunting spear.
spatha, -ae f broadsword.
spatior, -ārī, -ātus vi to walk; to spread.
spatiōsē adv greatly; after a time.
spatiōsus adj roomy, ample, large; (time) prolonged.
spatium, -ī and **iī** nt space, room, extent; (between points) distance; (open space) square, walk, promenade; (race) lap, track, course; (time) period, interval; (opportunity) time, leisure; (metre) quantity.
speciēs, -ēī f seeing, sight; appearance, form, outline; (thing seen) sight; (mind) idea; (in sleep) vision, apparition; (fair show) beauty, splendour; (false show) pretence, pretext; (classification) species; **in ~em** for the sake of appearances; like; **per ~em** under the pretence; **sub ~ē** under the cloak.
specillum, -ī nt probe.
specimen, -inis nt sign, evidence, proof; pattern, ideal.
speciōsē adv handsomely.
speciōsus adj showy, beautiful; specious, plausible.
spectābilis adj visible; notable, remarkable.
spectāclum, spectāculum, -ī nt sight, spectacle; public show, play; theatre, seats.
spectāmen, -inis nt proof.
spectātiō, -ōnis f looking; testing.
spectātor, -ōris m onlooker, observer, spectator; critic.
spectātrīx, -īcis f observer.
spectātus ppp of **spectō** ♦ adj tried, proved, worthy, excellent.
spectiō, -ōnis f the right to take auspices.
spectō, -āre, -āvī, -ātum vt to look at, observe, watch; (place) to face; (aim) to look to, bear in mind, contemplate, tend towards; (judging) to examine, test.
spectrum, -ī nt spectre.
specula, -ae f watchtower, lookout; height.
spēcula, -ae f slight hope.
speculābundus adj on the lookout.
speculāris adj transparent ♦ ntpl window.
speculātor, -ōris m explorer, investigator; (MIL) spy, scout.
speculātōrius adj for spying, scouting ♦ f spy

Noun declensions and verb conjugations are shown on pp xiii to xxv. The present infinitive ending of a verb shows to which conjugation it belongs: **-āre** = 1st **-ēre** = 2nd; **-ere** = 3rd and **-īre** = 4th. Irregular verbs are shown on p xxvi

boat.

speculātrīx, -īcis *f* watcher.

speculor, -ārī, -ātus *vt* to spy out, watch for, observe.

speculum, -ī *nt* mirror.

specus, -ūs *m, nt* cave; hollow, chasm.

spēlaeum, -ī *nt* cave, den.

spēlunca, -ae *f* cave, den.

spērābilis *adj* to be hoped for.

spērāta, -ātae *f* bride.

Spercheïs, -idis *adj see* **Spercheus.**

Spercheus (-os), -ī *m river in Thessaly.*

spernō, -ere, sprēvī, sprētum *vt* to remove, reject, scorn.

spērō, -āre, -āvī, -ātum *vt* to hope, hope for, expect; to trust; to look forward to.

spēs, speī *f* hope, expectation; **praeter spem** unexpectedly; **spē dēiectus** disappointed.

Speusippus, -ī *m successor of Plato in the Academy.*

sphaera, -ae *f* ball, globe, sphere.

Sphinx, -ingis *f fabulous monster near Thebes.*

spīca, -ae *f (grain)* ear; *(plant)* tuft; *(ASTRO)* brightest star in Virgo.

spīceus *adj* of ears of corn.

spīculum, -ī *nt* point, sting; dart, arrow.

spīna, -ae *f* thorn; prickle; fish bone; spine, back; *(pl)* difficulties, subtleties.

spīnētum, -ī *nt* thorn hedge.

spīneus *adj* of thorns.

spīnifer, -ī *adj* prickly.

spīnōsus *adj* thorny, prickly; *(style)* difficult.

spinter, -ēris *nt* elastic bracelet.

spīnus, -ī *f* blackthorn, sloe.

spīra, -ae *f* coil; twisted band.

spīrābilis *adj* breathable, life-giving.

spīrāculum, -ī *nt* vent.

spīrāmentum, -ī *nt* vent, pore; breathing space.

spīritus, -ūs *m* breath, breathing; breeze, air; inspiration; character, spirit, courage, arrogance.

spīrō, -āre, -āvī, -ātum *vi* to breathe, blow; to be alive; to be inspired ♦ *vt* to emit, exhale; *(fig)* to breathe, express.

spissātus *adj* condensed.

spissē *adv* closely; slowly.

spissēscō, -ere *vi* to thicken.

spissus *adj* thick, compact, crowded; slow; *(fig)* difficult.

splendeō, -ēre *vi* to be bright, shine; to be illustrious.

splendēscō, -ere *vi* to become bright.

splendidē *adv* brilliantly, magnificently, nobly.

splendidus *adj* bright, brilliant, glittering; *(sound)* clear; *(dress, house)* magnificent; *(person)* illustrious; *(appearance)* showy.

splendor, -ōris *m* brightness, lustre; magnificence; clearness; nobility.

spoliātiō, -ōnis *f* plundering.

spoliātor, -ōris *m* robber.

spoliātrīx, -īcis *f* robber.

spoliō, -āre, -āvī, -ātum *vt* to strip; to rob, plunder.

spolium, -ī *and* **iī** *nt (beast)* skin; *(enemy)* spoils, booty.

sponda, -ae *f* bed frame; bed, couch.

spondālium, -ī *and* **iī** *nt* hymn accompanied by the flute.

spondeō, -ēre, spopondī, spōnsum *vt* to promise, pledge, vow; *(law)* to go bail for; *(marriage)* to betroth.

spondēus, -ī *m* spondee.

spongia, -ae *f* sponge; coat of mail.

spōnsa, -ae *f* fiancée, bride.

spōnsālia, -ium *ntpl* engagement.

spōnsiō, -ōnis *f* promise, guarantee; *(law)* agreement that the loser in a suit pays the winner a sum; bet.

spōnsor, -ōris *m* guarantor, surety.

spōnsus *ppp of* **spondeō** ♦ *m* fiancé, bridegroom ♦ *nt* agreement, covenant.

spōnsus, -ūs *m* contract, surety.

sponte *f (abl)* voluntarily, of one's own accord; unaided, by oneself; spontaneously.

spopondī *perf of* **spondeō.**

sportella, -ae *f* fruit basket.

sportula, -ae *f* small basket; gift to clients, dole.

sprētiō, -ōnis *f* contempt.

sprētor, -ōris *m* despiser.

sprētus *ppp of* **spernō.**

sprēvī *perf of* **spernō.**

spūma, -ae *f* foam, froth.

spūmēscō, -ere *vi* to become frothy.

spūmeus *adj* foaming, frothy.

spūmifer, -ī *adj* foaming.

spūmiger, -ī *adj* foaming.

spūmō, -āre *vi* to foam, froth.

spūmōsus *adj* foaming.

spuō, -uere, -uī, -ūtum *vi* to spit ♦ *vt* to spit out.

spurcē *adv* obscenely.

spurcidicus *adj* obscene.

spurcificus *adj* obscene.

spurcitia, -ae *and* **ēs, -ēī** *f* filth, smut.

spurcō, -āre *vt* to befoul.

spurcus *adj* filthy, nasty, foul.

spūtātilicus *adj* despicable.

spūtātor, -ōris *m* spitter.

spūtō, -āre *vt* to spit out.

spūtum, -ī *nt* spit, spittle.

squāleō, -ēre, -uī *vi* to be rough, stiff, clotted; to be parched; to be neglected, squalid, filthy; to be in mourning.

squālidē *adv* rudely.

squālidus *adj* rough, scaly; neglected, squalid, filthy; *(speech)* unpolished.

squālor, -ōris *m* roughness; filth, squalor.

squāma, -ae *f* scale; scale armour.

squāmeus *adj* scaly.

squāmifer, -ī *adj* scaly.

squāmiger, -ī *adj* scaly ♦ *mpl* fishes.

squāmōsus *adj* scaly.

squilla, -ae *f* prawn, shrimp.

st *interj* sh!

stabilīmentum, -ī *nt* support.

stabiliō, -īre *vt* to make stable; to establish.

stabilis *adj* firm, steady; (*fig*) steadfast, unfailing.

stabilitās, -ātis *f* firmness, steadiness, reliability.

stabulō, -āre *vt* to house, stable ♦ *vi* to have a stall.

stabulum, -ī *nt* stall, stable, steading; lodging, cottage; brothel.

stacta, -ae *f* myrrh oil.

stadium, -ī *and* **iī** *nt* stade, furlong; racetrack.

Stagīra, -ōrum *ntpl* town in Macedonia (*birthplace of Aristotle*).

Stagīrītēs, -ītae *m* Aristotle.

stagnō, -āre *vi* to form pools; to be inundated ♦ *vt* to flood.

stagnum, -ī *nt* standing water, pool, swamp; waters.

stāmen, -inis *nt* warp; thread; (*instrument*) string; (*priest*) fillet.

stāmineus *adj* full of threads.

stata *adj*: **Stata māter** Vesta.

statārius *adj* standing, stationary, steady; calm ♦ *f* refined comedy ♦ *mpl* actors in this comedy.

statēra, -ae *f* scales.

statim *adv* steadily; at once, immediately; **~ ut** as soon as.

statiō, -ōnis *f* standing still; station, post, residence; (*pl*) sentries; (*NAUT*) anchorage.

Statius, -ī *m* Caecilius (*early writer of comedy*); Papinius (*epic and lyric poet of the Silver Age*).

statīvus *adj* stationary ♦ *ntpl* standing camp.

stator, -ōris *m* attendant, orderly.

Stator, -ōris *m* the Stayer (*epithet of Jupiter*).

statua, -ae *f* statue.

statūmen, -inis *nt* (*ship*) rib.

statuō, -uere, -uī, -ūtum *vt* to set up, place; to bring to a stop; to establish, constitute; to determine, appoint; to decide, settle; to decree, prescribe; (*with infin*) to resolve, propose; (*with acc and infin*) to judge, consider, conclude; (*army*) to draw up; (*monument*) to erect; (*price*) to fix; (*sentence*) to pass; (*tent*) to pitch; (*town*) to build; **condiciōnem ~** dictate (to); **fīnem ~** put an end (to); **iūs ~** lay down a principle; **modum ~** impose restrictions; **apud animum ~** make up one's mind; **dē sē ~** commit suicide; **gravius ~** deal severely with.

statūra, -ae *f* height, stature.

status *ppp of* **sistō** ♦ *adj* appointed, due.

status, -ūs *m* posture, attitude; position; (*social*) standing, status, circumstances; (*POL*) situation, state, form of government; (*nature*) condition; **reī pūblicae ~** the political situation; constitution; **dē ~ū movēre** dislodge.

statūtus *ppp of* **statuō**.

stega, -ae *f* deck.

stēliō *see* **stēlliō**.

stēlla, -ae *f* star; **~ errāns** planet.

stēllāns, -antis *adj* starry.

stēllātus *adj* starred; set in the sky.

stēllifer, -ī *adj* starry.

stēlliger, -ī *adj* starry.

stēlliō, -ōnis *m* newt.

stemma, -tis *nt* pedigree.

stercoreus *adj* filthy.

stercorō, -āre *vt* to manure.

stercus, -oris *nt* dung.

sterilis *adj* barren, sterile; bare, empty; unprofitable, fruitless.

sterilitās, -ātis *f* barrenness.

sternāx, -ācis *adj* bucking.

sternō, -ere, strāvī, strātum *vt* to spread, cover, strew; to smooth, level; to stretch out, extend; to throw to the ground, prostrate; to overthrow; (*bed*) to make; (*horse*) to saddle; (*road*) to pave.

sternūmentum, -ī *nt* sneezing.

sternuō, -ere, -ī *vt, vi* to sneeze.

Steropē, -ēs *f* a Pleiad.

sterquilīnium, -ī *and* **iī, (-um, -ī)** *nt* dung heap.

stertō, -ere, -uī *vi* to snore.

Stēsichorus, -ī *m* Greek lyric poet.

stetī *perf of* **stō**.

Stheneleïus *and* **eis** *and* **ēidis** *adj* see *n*.

Sthenelus, -ī *m* father of Eurystheus; father of Cycnus.

stigma, -tis *nt* brand.

stigmatiās, -ae *m* branded slave.

stilla, -ae *f* drop.

stillicidium, -ī *and* **iī** *nt* dripping water, rainwater from the eaves.

stillō, -āre, -āvī, -ātum *vi* to drip, trickle ♦ *vt* to let fall in drops, distil.

stilus, -ī *m* stake; pen; (*fig*) writing, composition, style; **~um vertere** erase.

stimulātiō, -ōnis *f* incentive.

stimulātrīx, -īcis *f* provocative woman.

stimuleus *adj* smarting.

stimulō, -āre, -āvī, -ātum *vt* to goad; to trouble, torment; to rouse, spur on, excite.

stimulus, -ī *m* goad; (*MIL*) stake; (*pain*) sting, pang; (*incentive*) spur, stimulus.

stinguō, -ere *vt* to extinguish.

stīpātiō, -ōnis *f* crowd, retinue.

stīpātor, -ōris *m* attendant; (*pl*) retinue, bodyguard.

stīpendiārius *adj* tributary, liable to a money tax; (*MIL*) receiving pay ♦ *mpl* tributary peoples.

stīpendium, -ī *and* **iī** *nt* tax, tribute; soldier's pay; military service, campaign; **~ merēre, merērī** serve; **~ ēmerērī** complete one's period of service.

Noun declensions and verb conjugations are shown on pp xiii to xxv. The present infinitive ending of a verb shows to which conjugation it belongs: -āre = 1st; -ēre = 2nd; -ere = 3rd and -īre = 4th. Irregular verbs are shown on p xxvi

stīpes, -itis m log, trunk; tree; (*insult*) blockhead.

stīpō, -āre, -āvī, -ātum vt to press, pack together; to cram, stuff full; to crowd round, accompany in a body.

stips, stipis f donation, contribution.

stipula, -ae f stalk, blade, stubble; reed.

stipulātiō, -ōnis f promise, bargain.

stipulātiuncula, -ae f slight stipulation.

stipulātus adj promised.

stipulor, -ārī vt, vi to demand a formal promise, bargain, stipulate.

stīria, -ae f icicle.

stirpēs etc see **stirps.**

stirpitus adj thoroughly.

stirps, -is f lower trunk and roots, stock; plant, shoot; family, lineage, progeny; origin; **ab ~e** utterly.

stīva, -ae f plough handle.

stlattārius adj seaborne.

stō, stāre, stetī, statum vi to stand; to remain in position, stand firm; to be conspicuous; (*fig*) to persist, continue; (*battle*) to go on; (*hair*) to stand on end; (NAUT) to ride at anchor; (*play*) to be successful; (*price*) to cost; (*with* **ab, cum, prō**) to be on the side of, support; (*with* **in**) to rest, depend on; (*with* **per**) to be the fault of; **stat sententia** one's mind is made up; **per Āfrānium stetit quōminus dīmicārētur** thanks to Afranius there was no battle.

Stōicē adv like a Stoic.

Stōicus adj Stoic ♦ m Stoic philosopher ♦ ntpl Stoicism.

stola, -ae f long robe (*esp worn by matrons*).

stolidē adv stupidly.

stolidus adj dull, stupid.

stomachor, -ārī, -ātus vi to be vexed, be annoyed.

stomachōsē adv see adj.

stomachōsus adj angry, irritable.

stomachus, -ī m gullet; stomach; taste, liking; dislike, irritation, chagrin.

stōrea (storia), -ae f rush mat, rope mat.

strabō, -ōnis m squinter.

strāgēs, -is f heap, confused mass; havoc, massacre.

strāgulus adj covering ♦ nt bedspread, rug.

strāmen, -inis nt straw, litter.

strāmentum, -ī nt straw, thatch; straw bed; covering, rug.

strāmineus adj straw-thatched.

strangulō, -āre, -āvī, -ātum vt to throttle, choke.

strangūria, -ae f difficult discharge of urine.

stratēgēma, -tis nt a piece of generalship, stratagem.

stratēgus, -ī m commander, president.

stratiōticus adj military.

strātum, -ī nt coverlet, blanket; bed, couch; horsecloth, saddle; pavement.

strātus ppp of **sternō** ♦ adj prostrate.

strāvī perf of **sternō.**

strēnuē adv energetically, quickly.

strēnuitās, -ātis f energy, briskness.

strēnuus adj brisk, energetic, busy; restless.

strepitō, -āre vi to make a noise, rattle, rustle.

strepitus, -ūs m din, clatter, crashing, rumbling; sound.

strepō, -ere, -uī vi to make a noise, clang, roar, rumble, rustle etc ♦ vt to bawl out.

striāta, -ae f scallop.

strictim adv superficially, cursorily.

strictūra, -ae f mass of metal.

strictus ppp of **stringō** ♦ adj close, tight.

strīdeō, -ēre, -ī; -ō, -ere, -ī vi to creak, hiss, shriek, whistle.

strīdor, -ōris m creaking, hissing, grating.

strīdulus adj creaking, hissing, whistling.

strigilis f scraper, strigil.

strigō, -āre vi to stop, jib.

strigōsus adj thin, scraggy; (*style*) insipid.

stringō, -ngere, -nxī, -ctum vt to draw together, draw tight; to touch, graze; to cut off, prune, trim; (*sword*) to draw; (*mind*) to affect, pain.

stringor, -ōris m twinge.

strix, -igis f screech owl.

stropha, -ae f trick.

Strophades, -um fpl islands off S Greece.

strophiārius, -ī and **iī** m maker of breastbands.

strophium, -ī and **iī** nt breastband; headband.

structor, -ōris m mason, carpenter; (*at table*) server, carver.

structūra, -ae f construction, works.

structus ppp of **struō.**

struēs, -is f heap, pile.

struix, -icis f heap, pile.

strūma, -ae f tumour.

strūmōsus adj scrofulous.

struō, -ere, -xī, -ctum vt to pile up; to build, erect; to arrange in order; to make, prepare; to cause, contrive, plot.

strūtheus adj sparrow- (*in cpds*).

strūthiocamēlus, -ī m ostrich.

Strȳmōn, -onis m river between Macedonia and Thrace (*now* Struma).

Strȳmonius adj Strymonian, Thracian.

studeō, -ēre, -uī vi (*usu with dat*) to be keen, be diligent, apply oneself to; to study; (*person*) to be a supporter of.

studiōsē adv eagerly, diligently.

studiōsus adj (*usu with gen*) keen on, fond of, partial to; studious ♦ m student.

studium, -ī and **iī** nt enthusiasm, application, inclination; fondness, affection; party spirit, partisanship; study, literary work.

stultē adv foolishly.

stultiloquentia, -ae f foolish talk.

stultiloquium, -ī and **iī** nt foolish talk.

stultitia, -ae f folly, silliness.

stultividus adj simple-sighted.

stultus adj foolish, silly ♦ m fool.

stupefaciō, -facere, -fēcī, -factum (pass
-fīō, -fierī) vt to stun, astound.
stupeō, -ēre, -uī vi to be stunned; te
astonished; to be brought to a standstill ♦ vt
to marvel at.
stupēscō, -ere vi to become amazed.
stūpeus etc see **stuppeus.**
stupiditās, -ātis f senselessness.
stupidus adj senseless, astoundec; dull,
stupid.
stupor, -ōris m numbness, bewilcerment;
dullness, stupidity.
stuppa, -ae f tow.
stuppeus adj of tow.
stuprō, -āre, -āvī, -ātum vt to defile; to
ravish.
stuprum, -ī nt debauchery, unchastity.
sturnus, -ī m starling.
Stygius adj of the lower world, Stygian.
stylus etc see **stilus.**
Stymphalicus, (-ius, -is) adj Stymphalian.
Stymphalum, -ī nt, **Stymphalus, -ī** m
district of Arcadia (famous for birds of prey
killed by Hercules).
Styx, -ygis and **ygos** f river of Hades.
Styxius adj see n.
suādēla, -ae f persuasion.
suādeō, -dēre, -sī, -sum vi (with dat) to
advise, urge, recommend.
suāsiō, -ōnis f speaking in favour (of a
proposal); persuasive type of oratory.
suāsor, -ōris m adviser; advocate.
suāsus ppp of **suādeō.**
suāsus, -ūs m advice.
suāveolēns, -entis adj fragrant.
suāviātiō etc see **sāviātiō.**
suāvidicus adj charming.
suāviloquēns, -entis adj charming.
suāviloquentia, -ae f charm of speech.
suāvior etc see **sāvior.**
suāvis adj sweet, pleasant, delightful.
suāvitās, -ātis f sweetness, pleasantness,
charm.
suāviter adv see **suāvis.**
suāvium etc see **sāvium.**
sub prep 1. with abl (place) under, beneath; (hills,
walls) at the foot of, close to; (time) during,
at; (order) next to; (rule) under, in the reign
of. 2. with acc (place) under, along under; (hills,
walls) up to, to; (time) up to, just before, just
after; ~ **ictum venīre** come within range; ~
manum to hand.
subabsurdē adv see adj.
subabsurdus adj somewhat absurd.
subaccūsō, -āre vt to find some fault with.
subāctiō, -ōnis f working (the soil).
subāctus ppp of **subigō.**
subadroganter adv a little conceitedly.
subagrestis adj rather boorish.
subalāris adj carried under the arms.

subamārus adj rather bitter.
subaquilus adj brownish.
subauscultō, -āre vt, vi to listen secretly,
eavesdrop.
subbasilicānus, -ī m lounger.
subblandior, -īrī vi (with dat) to flirt with.
subc- etc see **succ-.**
subdidī perf of **subdō.**
subdifficilis adj rather difficult.
subdiffīdō, -ere vi to be a little doubtful.
subditīcius adj sham.
subdītīvus adj sham.
subditus ppp of **subdō** ♦ adj spurious.
subdō, -ere, -idī, -itum vt to put under,
plunge into; to subdue; to substitute, forge.
subdoceō, -ēre vt to teach as an assistant.
subdolē adv slily.
subdolus adj sly, crafty, underhand.
subdubitō, -āre vi to be a little undecided.
subdūcō, -ūcere, -ūxī, -uctum vt to pull up,
raise; to withdraw, remove; to take away
secretly, steal; (account) to balance; (ship) to
haul up, beach; **sē ~** steal away, disappear.
subductiō, -ōnis f (ship) hauling up; (thought)
reckoning.
subductus ppp of **subdūcō.**
subedō, -ēsse, -ēdī vt to wear away
underneath.
subēgī perf of **subigō.**
subeō, -īre, -iī, -itum vi to go under, go in; to
come up to, climb, advance; to come
immediately after; to come to the
assistance; to come as a substitute, succeed;
to come secretly, steal in; to come to mind,
suggest itself ♦ vt to enter, plunge into; to
climb; to approach, attack; to take the place
of; to steal into; to submit to, undergo,
suffer; (mind) to occur to.
sūber, -is nt cork tree; cork.
subesse infin of **subsum.**
subf- etc see **suff-.**
subg- etc see **sugg-.**
subhorridus adj somewhat uncouth.
subiaceō, -ēre, -uī vi to lie under, be close
(to); to be connected (with).
subiciō, -icere, -iēcī, -iectum vt to put under,
bring under; to bring up, throw up; to bring
near; to submit, subject, expose; to
subordinate, deal with under; to append, add
on, answer; to adduce, suggest; to
substitute; to forge; to suborn; **sē ~** grow up.
subiectē adv submissively.
subiectiō, -ōnis f laying under; forging.
subiectō, -āre vt to lay under, put to; to throw
up.
subiector, -ōris m forger.
subiectus ppp of **subiciō** ♦ adj neighbouring,
bordering; subject, exposed.
subigitātiō, -ōnis f lewdness.
subigitō, -āre vt to behave improperly to.

Noun declensions and verb conjugations are shown on pp xiii to xxv. The present infinitive ending of a verb shows
to which conjugation it belongs: **-āre** = 1st **-ēre** = 2nd; **-ere** = 3rd and **-īre** = 4th. Irregular verbs are shown on p xxvi

subigō, -igere, -ēgī, -āctum _vt_ to bring up to; to impel, compel; to subdue, conquer; (_animal_) to tame, break in; (_blade_) to sharpen; (_boat_) to row, propel; (_cooking_) to knead; (_earth_) to turn up, dig; (_mind_) to train.

subiī _perf of_ **subeō**.

subimpudēns, -entis _adj_ rather impertinent.

subinānis _adj_ rather empty.

subinde _adv_ immediately after; repeatedly.

subinsūlsus _adj_ rather insipid.

subinvideō, -ēre _vi_ to be a little envious of.

subinvīsus _adj_ somewhat odious.

subinvītō, -āre _vt_ to invite vaguely.

subīrāscor, -scī, -tus _vi_ to be rather angry.

subīrātus _adj_ rather angry.

subitārius _adj_ sudden, emergency (_in cpds_).

subitō _adv_ suddenly.

subitus _ppp of_ **subeō** ♦ _adj_ sudden, unexpected; (_man_) rash; (_troops_) hastily raised ♦ _nt_ surprise, emergency.

subiūnctus _ppp adj_ **subiungō**.

subiungō, -ungere, -ūnxī, -ūnctum _vt_ to harness; to add, affix; to subordinate, subdue.

sublābor, -bī, -psus _vi_ to sink down; to glide away.

sublāpsus _ppa of_ **sublābor**.

sublātē _adv_ loftily.

sublātiō, -ōnis _f_ elevation.

sublātus _ppp of_ **tollō** ♦ _adj_ elated.

sublectō, -āre _vt_ to coax.

sublēctus _ppp of_ **sublegō**.

sublegō, -egere, -ēgī, -ēctum _vt_ to gather up; to substitute; (_child_) to kidnap; (_talk_) to overhear.

sublestus _adj_ slight.

sublevātiō, -ōnis _f_ alleviation.

sublevō, -āre, -āvī, -ātum _vt_ to lift up, hold up; to support, encourage; to lighten, alleviate.

sublica, -ae _f_ pile, palisade.

sublicius _adj_ on piles.

subligāculum, -ī, subligar, -āris _nt_ loincloth.

subligō, -āre _vt_ to fasten on.

sublīmē _adv_ aloft, in the air.

sublīmis _adj_ high, raised high, lifted up; (_character_) eminent, aspiring; (_language_) lofty, elevated.

sublīmitās, -ātis _f_ loftiness.

sublīmus _etc see_ **sublīmis**.

sublingiō, -ōnis _m_ scullion.

sublinō, -inere, -ēvī, -itum _vt_: **ōs ~** to fool, bamboozle.

sublitus _ppp of_ **sublinō**.

sublūceō, -ēre _vi_ to glimmer.

subluō, -ere _vt_ (_river_) to flow past the foot of.

sublūstris _adj_ faintly luminous.

sublūtus _ppp of_ **subluō**.

subm- _etc see_ **summ-**.

subnātus _adj_ growing up underneath.

subnectō, -ctere, -xuī, -xum _vt_ to tie under, fasten to.

subnegō, -āre _vt_ to half refuse.

subnexus _ppp of_ **subnectō**.

subniger, -rī _adj_ darkish.

subnīxus _and_ **sus** _adj_ supported, resting (on); relying (on).

subnuba, -ae _f_ rival.

subnūbilus _adj_ overcast.

subō, -āre _vi_ to be in heat.

subobscēnus _adj_ rather indecent.

subobscūrus _adj_ somewhat obscure.

subodiōsus _adj_ rather odious.

suboffendō, -ere _vi_ to give some offence.

subolēs, -is _f_ offspring, children.

subolēscō, -ere _vi_ to grow up.

subolet, -ēre _vi_ (_impers_) there is a faint scent; **~ mihi** I detect, have an inkling.

suborior, -īrī _vi_ to spring up in succession.

subōrnō, -āre, -āvī, -ātum _vt_ to fit out, equip; to instigate secretly, suborn.

subortus, -ūs _m_ rising up repeatedly.

subp- _etc see_ **supp-**.

subrancidus _adj_ slightly tainted.

subraucus _adj_ rather hoarse.

subrēctus _ppp of_ **subrigō**.

subrēmigō, -āre _vi_ to paddle under (water).

subrēpō, -ere, -sī, -tum _vi_ to creep along, steal up to.

subreptus _ppp of_ **subripiō**.

subrīdeō, -dēre, -sī _vi_ to smile.

subrīdiculē _adv_ rather funnily.

subrigō, -igere, -ēxī, -ēctum _vt_ to lift, raise.

subringor, -ī _vi_ to make a wry face, be rather vexed.

subripiō, -ipere, -ipuī _and_ **upuī, -eptum** _vt_ to take away secretly, steal.

subrogō, -āre _vt_ to propose as successor.

subrōstrānī, -ōrum _mpl_ idlers.

subrubeō, -ēre _vi_ to blush slightly.

subrūfus _adj_ ginger-haired.

subruō, -ere, -ī, -tum _vt_ to undermine, demolish.

subrūsticus _adj_ rather countrified.

subrutus _ppp of_ **subruō**.

subscrībō, -bere, -psī, -ptum _vt_ to write underneath; (_document_) to sign, subscribe; (_censor_) to set down; (_law_) to add to an indictment, prosecute; (_fig_) to record; (_with dat_) to assent to, approve.

subscrīptiō, -ōnis _f_ inscription underneath; signature; (_censor_) noting down; (_law_) subscription (to an indictment); register.

subscrīptor, -ōris _m_ subscriber (to an indictment).

subscrīptus _ppp of_ **subscrībō**.

subsecīvus _etc see_ **subsicīvus**.

subsecō, -āre, -uī, -ctum _vt_ to cut off, clip.

subsēdī _perf of_ **subsīdō**.

subsellium, -ī _and_ **iī** _nt_ bench, seat; (_law_) the bench, the court.

subsentiō, -entīre, -ēnsī _vt_ to have an inkling of.

subsequor, -quī, -cūtus _vt, vi_ to follow closely; to support; to imitate.

subserviō, -īre _vi_ to be a slave; (_fig_) to comply

(with).
subsicīvus *adj* left over; (*time*) spare; (*work*) overtime.
subsidiārius *adj* in reserve ♦ *mpl* reserves.
subsidium, -ī *and* **iī** *nt* reserve ranks, reserve troops; relief, aid, assistance.
subsīdō, -īdere, -ēdī, -essum *vi* to sit down, crouch, squat; to sink down, settle, subside; (*ambush*) to lie in wait; (*residence*) to stay, settle ♦ *vt* to lie in wait for.
subsignānus *adj* special reserve (troops).
subsignō, -āre *vt* to register; to guarantee.
subsiliō, -īre, -uī *vi* to leap up.
subsistō, -istere, -titī *vi* to stand still, make a stand; to stop, halt; to remain, continue, hold out; (*with dat*) to resist ♦ *vt* to withstand.
subsortior, -īrī, -ītus *vt* to choose as a substitute by lot.
subsortītiō, -ōnis *f* choosing of substitutes by lot.
substantia, -ae *f* means, wealth.
substernō, -ernere, -rāvī, -rātum *vt* to scatter under, spread under; (*fig*) to put at one's service.
substitī *perf of* **subsistō**.
substituō, -uere, -uī, -ūtum *vt* to put next; to substitute; (*idea*) to present, imagine.
substitūtus *ppp of* **substituō**.
substō, -āre *vi* to hold out.
substrātus *ppp of* **substernō**.
substrictus *ppp of* **substringō** ♦ *adj* narrow, tight.
substringō, -ngere, -nxī, -ctum *vt* to bind up; to draw close; to check.
substructiō, -ōnis *f* foundation.
substruō, -ere, -xī, -ctum *vt* to lay, pave.
subsultō, -āre *vi* to jump up.
subsum, -esse *vi* to be underneath; to be close to, be at hand; (*fig*) to underlie, be latent in.
subsūtus *adj* fringed at the bottom.
subtēmen, -inis *nt* woof; thread.
subter *adv* below, underneath ♦ *prep* (*with acc and abl*) beneath; close up to.
subterdūcō, -cere, -xī *vt* to withdraw secretly.
subterfugiō, -ugere, -ūgī *vt* to escape from, evade.
subterlābor, -ī *vt, vi* to flow past under; to slip away.
subterrāneus *adj* underground.
subtexō, -ere, -uī, -tum *vt* to weave in; to veil, obscure.
subtīlis *adj* slender, fine; (*senses*) delicate, nice; (*judgment*) discriminating, precise; (*style*) plain, direct.
subtīlitās, -ātis *f* fineness; (*judgment*) acuteness, exactness; (*style*) plainness, directness.
subtīliter *adv* finely; accurately; simply.

subtimeō, -ēre *vt* to be a little afraid of.
subtractus *ppp of* **subtrahō**.
subtrahō, -here, -xī, -ctum *vt* to draw away from underneath; to take away secretly; to withdraw, remove.
subtristis *adj* rather sad.
subturpiculus *adj* a little bit mean.
subturpis *adj* rather mean.
subtus *adv* below, underneath.
subtūsus *adj* slightly bruised.
subūcula, -ae *f* shirt, vest.
sūbula, -ae *f* awl.
subulcus, -ī *m* swineherd.
Subūra, -ae *f* a disreputable quarter of Rome.
Subūrānus *adj see* **Subūra**.
suburbānitās, -ātis *f* nearness to Rome.
suburbānus *adj* near Rome ♦ *nt* villa near Rome ♦ *mpl* inhabitants of the towns near Rome.
suburbium, -ī *and* **iī** *nt* suburb.
suburgeō, -ēre *vt* to drive close (to).
subvectiō, -ōnis *f* transport.
subvectō, -āre *vt* to carry up regularly.
subvectus *ppp of* **subvehō**.
subvectus, -ūs *m* transport.
subvehō, -here, -xī, -ctum *vt* to carry up, transport upstream.
subveniō, -enīre, -ēnī, -entum *vi* (*with dat*) to come to the assistance of, relieve, reinforce.
subventō, -āre *vi* (*with dat*) to come quickly to help.
subvereor, -ērī *vi* to be a little afraid.
subversor, -ōris *m* subverter.
subversus *ppp of* **subvertō**.
subvertō, -tere, -tī, -sum *vt* to turn upside down, upset; to overthrow, subvert.
subvexī *perf of* **subvehō**.
subvexus *adj* sloping upwards.
subvolō, -āre *vi* to fly upwards.
subvolvō, -ere *vt* to roll uphill.
subvortō *etc see* **subvertō**.
succavus *adj* hollow underneath.
succēdō, -ēdere, -essī, -essum *vt, vi* (*with dat*) to go under, pass into, take on; (*with dat, acc, in*) to go up, climb; (*with dat, acc, ad, sub*) to march on, advance to; (*with dat, in*) to come to take the place of, relieve; (*with dat, in, ad*) to follow after, succeed, succeed to; (*result*) to turn out, be successful.
succendō, -endere, -endī, -ēnsum *vt* to set fire to, kindle; (*fig*) to fire, inflame.
succēnseō *etc see* **suscēnseō**.
succēnsus *ppp of* **succendō**.
succenturiātus *adj* in reserve.
succenturiō, -ōnis *m* under-centurion.
successī *perf of* **succēdō**.
successiō, -ōnis *f* succession.
successor, -ōris *m* successor.
successus *ppp of* **succēdō**.

Noun declensions and verb conjugations are shown on pp xiii to xxv. The present infinitive ending of a verb shows to which conjugation it belongs: **-āre** = 1st; **-ēre** = 2nd; **-ere** = 3rd and **-īre** = 4th. Irregular verbs are shown on p xxvi

successus, -ūs *m* advance uphill; result, success.
succīdia, -ae *f* leg *or* side of meat, flitch.
succīdō, -dere, -dī, -sum *vt* to cut off, mow down.
succidō, -ere, -ī *vi* to sink, give way.
succiduus *adj* sinking, failing.
succinctus *ppp of* **succingō.**
succingō, -gere, -xī, -ctum *vt* to gird up, tuck up; to equip, arm.
succingulum, -ī *nt* girdle.
succinō, -ere *vi* to chime in.
succīsus *ppp of* **succīdō.**
succlāmātiō, -ōnis *f* shouting, barracking.
succlāmō, -āre, -āvī, -ātum *vt* to shout after, interrupt with shouting.
succontumēliōsē *adv* somewhat insolently.
succrēscō, -ere *vi* to grow up (from *or* to).
succrispus *adj* rather curly.
succumbō, -mbere, -buī, -bitum *vi* to fall, sink under; to submit, surrender.
succurrō, -rere, -rī, -sum *vi* to come quickly up; to run to the help of, succour; (*idea*) to occur.
succus *etc see* **sūcus.**
succussus, -ūs *m* shaking.
succustōs, -ōdis *m* assistant keeper.
succutiō, -tere, -ssī, -ssum *vt* to toss up.
sūcidus *adj* juicy, fresh, plump.
sūcinum, -ī *nt* amber.
sūctus *ppp of* **sūgō.**
sucula, -ae *f* winch, windlass.
sucula, -ae *f* piglet; (*pl*) the Hyads.
sūcus, -ī *m* juice, sap; medicine, potion; taste, flavour; (*fig*) strength, vigour, life.
sūdārium, -ī *and* **iī** *nt* handkerchief.
sūdātōrius *adj* for sweating ♦ *nt* sweating bath.
sudis, -is *f* stake, pile, pike, spike.
sūdō, -āre, -āvī, -ātum *vi* to sweat, perspire; to be drenched with; to work hard ♦ *vt* to exude.
sūdor, -ōris *m* sweat, perspiration; moisture; hard work, exertion.
sudus *adj* cloudless, clear ♦ *nt* fine weather.
sueō, -ēre *vi* to be accustomed.
suēscō, -scere, -vī, -tum *vi* to be accustomed ♦ *vt* to accustom.
Suessa, -ae *f* town in Latium.
Suessiōnēs, -um *mpl* people of Gaul (*now* Soissons*).
suētus *ppp of* **suēscō** ♦ *adj* accustomed; usual.
Suēvī, -ōrum *mpl* people of N.E. Germany.
sūfes, -etis *m* chief magistrate of Carthage.
suffarcinātus *adj* stuffed full.
suffectus *ppp of* **sufficiō** ♦ *adj* (*consul*) appointed to fill a vacancy during the regular term of office.
sufferō, -re *vt* to support, undergo, endure.
suffes *etc see* **sūfes.**
sufficiō, -icere, -ēcī, -ectum *vt* to dye, tinge; to supply, provide; to appoint in place (of another), substitute ♦ *vi* to be adequate, suffice.

suffīgō, -gere, -xī, -xum *vt* to fasten underneath, nail on.
suffimen, -inis, suffimentum, -ī *nt* incense.
suffiō, -īre *vt* to fumigate, perfume.
suffixus *ppp of* **suffīgō.**
sufflāmen, -inis *nt* brake.
sufflō, -āre *vt* to blow up; to puff up.
suffocō, -āre *vt* to choke, stifle.
suffodiō, -odere, -ōdī, -ossum *vt* to stab; to dig under, undermine.
suffossus *ppp of* **suffodiō.**
suffrāgātiō, -ōnis *f* voting for, support.
suffrāgātor, -ōris *m* voter, supporter.
suffrāgātōrius *adj* supporting a candidate.
suffrāgium, -ī *and* **iī** *nt* vote, ballot; right of suffrage; (*fig*) judgment, approval; ~ **ferre** vote.
suffrāgor, -ārī, -ātus *vi* to vote for; to support, favour.
suffringō, -ere *vt* to break.
suffugiō, -ugere, -ūgī *vt* to run for shelter ♦ *vt* to elude.
suffugium, -ī *and* **iī** *nt* shelter, refuge.
suffulciō, -cīre, -sī, -tum *vt* to prop up, support.
suffundō, -undere, -ūdī, -ūsum *vt* to pour in; to suffuse, fill; to tinge, colour, blush; to overspread.
suffūror, -ārī *vi* to filch.
suffuscus *adj* darkish.
suffūsus *ppp of* **suffundō.**
Sugambrī, -ōrum *mpl* people of N.W. Germany.
suggerō, -rere, -ssī, -stum *vt* to bring up to, supply; to add on, put next.
suggestum, -ī *nt* platform.
suggestus *ppp of* **suggerō.**
suggestus, -ūs *m* platform, stage.
suggrandis *adj* rather large.
suggredicr, -dī, -ssus *vi* to come up close, approach ♦ *vt* to attack.
sūgillātiō, -ōnis *f* affronting.
sūgillātus *adj* bruised; insulted.
sūgō, -gere, -xī, -ctum *vt* to suck.
suī *gen of* **sē.**
suī *perf of* **suō.**
suillus *adj* of pigs.
sulcō, -āre *vt* to furrow, plough.
sulcus, -ī *m* furrow; trench; track.
sulfur *etc see* **sulpur.**
Sulla, -ae *m* famous Roman dictator.
Sullānus *adj* see n.
sullāturiō, -īre *vi* to hanker after being a Sulla.
Sulmō, -ōnis *m* town in E. Italy (*birthplace of Ovid*).
Sulmōnēnsis *adj* see n.
sultis *adv* please.
sum, esse, fuī *vi* to be, exist; ~ **ab** belong to; ~ **ad** be designed for; ~ **ex** consist of; **est, sunt** there is, are; **est mihi** I have; **mihi tēcum nīl est** I have nothing to do with you; **est quod** something; there is a reason for; **est ubi**

sometimes; **est ut** it is possible that; **est** (*with gen*) to belong to, be the duty of, **be** characteristic of; (*with infin*) it is possible, it is permissible; **sunt qui** some; **fuit Ilium** Troy is no more.

sümen, -inis *nt* udder, teat; sow.

summa, -ae *f* main part, chief point, main issue; gist, summary; sum, amount, the whole; supreme power; ~ **rērum** the general interest, the whole responsibility; ~ **summārum** the universe; **ad ~am** in short, in fact; in conclusion; **in ~ā** in all; **after** all.

Summānus, -i *m* god of nocturnal thunderbolts.

summās, -ātis *adj* high-born, eminent.

summātim *adv* cursorily, summarily.

summātus, -ūs *m* sovereignty.

summē *adv* in the highest degree, extremely.

summergō, -gere, -sī, -sum *vt* to plunge under, sink.

summersus *ppp of* **summergō**.

sumministrō, -āre, -āvī, -ātum *vt* to provide, furnish.

summissē *adv* softly; humbly, modestly.

summissiō, -ōnis *f* lowering.

summissus *ppp of* **summittō** ♦ *adj* low; (*voice*) low, calm; (*character*) mean, grovelling, submissive, humble.

summittō, -ittere, -īsī, -issum *vt* (*growth*) to send up, raise, rear; to despatch, supply; to let down, lower, reduce, moderate; to supersede; to send secretly; **animum** ~ submit; **sē** ~ condescend.

summoleste *adv* with some annoyance.

summolestus *adj* a little annoying.

summoneō, -ēre, -uī *vt* to drop a hint to.

summōrōsus *adj* rather peevish.

summōtor, -ōris *m* clearer.

summōtus *ppp of* **summoveō**.

summoveō, -ovēre, -ōvī, -ōtum *vt* to move away, drive off; to clear away (*to make room*); to withdraw, remove, banish; (*fig*) to dispel.

summum, -i *nt* top, surface.

summum *adv* at the most.

summus *adj* highest, the top of, the surface of; last, the end of; (*fig*) utmost, greatest, most important; (*person*) distinguished, excellent ♦ *m* head of the table.

summūtō, -āre *vt* to substitute.

sūmō, -ere, -psī, -ptum *vt* to take, take up; to assume, arrogate; (*action*) to undertake; (*argument*) to assume, take for granted; (*dress*) to put on; (*punishment*) to exact; (*for a purpose*) to use, spend.

sūmptiō, -ōnis *f* assumption.

sūmptuārius *adj* sumptuary.

sūmptuōsē *adv see adj*.

sūmptuōsus *adj* expensive, lavish, extravagant.

sūmptus *ppp of* **sūmō**.

sūmptus, -ūs *m* expense, cost.

Sūnium, -i *and* **ii** *nt S.E. promontory of Attica*.

suō, suere, suī, sūtum *vt* to sew, stitch, join together.

suōmet, suōpte *emphatic abl of* **suus**.

suovetaurīlia, -ium *ntpl* sacrifice of a pig, sheep and bull.

supellex, -ectilis *f* furniture, goods, outfit.

super *etc adj see* **superus**.

super *adv* above, on the top; besides, moreover; left, remaining ♦ *prep* (*with abl*) upon, above; concerning; besides; (*time*) at; (*with acc*) over, above, on; beyond; besides, over and above.

superā *etc see* **suprā**.

superābilis *adj* surmountable, conquerable.

superaddō, -ere, -itum *vt* to add over and above.

superāns, -antis *pres p of* **superō** ♦ *adj* predominant.

superātor, -ōris *m* conqueror.

superbē *adv* arrogantly, despotically.

superbia, -ae *f* arrogance, insolence, tyranny; pride, lofty spirit.

superbiloquentia, -ae *f* arrogant speech.

superbiō, -īre *vi* to be arrogant, take a pride in; to be superb.

superbus *adj* arrogant, insolent, overbearing; fastidious; superb, magnificent.

supercilium, -i *and* **ii** *nt* eyebrow; (*hill*) brow, ridge; (*fig*) arrogance.

superēmineō, -ēre *vt* to overtop.

superesse *infin of* **supersum**.

superficiēs, -ēi *f* surface; (*law*) a building (*esp on another's land*).

superfiō, -ierī *vi* to be left over.

superfixus *adj* fixed on top.

superfluō, -ere *vi* to overflow.

superfui *perf of* **supersum**.

superfundō, -undere, -ūdī, -ūsum *vt, vi* to pour over, shower; (*pass*) to overflow, spread out.

superfūsus *ppp of* **superfundō**.

supergredior, -dī, -ssus *vt* to surpass.

superiaciō, -iacere, -iēcī, -iectum *and* **iactum** *vt* to throw over, overspread; to overtop; (*fig*) to exaggerate.

superiectus *ppp of* **superiaciō**.

superimmineō, -ēre *vi* to overhang.

superimpendēns, -entis *adj* overhanging.

superimpōnō, -ōnere, -osuī, -ositum *vt* to place on top.

superimpositus *ppp of* **superimpōnō**.

superincidēns, -entis *adj* falling from above.

superincubāns, -antis *adj* lying upon.

superincumbō, -ere *vi* to fling oneself down upon.

superingerō, -ere *vt* to pour down.

superiniciō, -icere, -iēcī, -iectum *vt* to throw upon, put on top.

superiniectus *ppp of* **superinicō.**
superīnsternō, -ere *vt* to lay over.
superior, -ōris *adj* higher, upper; (*time, order*) preceding, previous, former; (*age*) older; (*battle*) victorious, stronger; (*quality*) superior, greater.
superlātiō, -ōnis *f* exaggeration.
superlātus *adj* exaggerated.
supernē *adv* at the top, from above.
supernus *adj* upper; celestial.
superō, -āre, -āvī, -ātum *vi* to rise above, overtop; to have the upper hand; to be in excess, be abundant; to be left over, survive ♦ *vt* to pass over, surmount, go beyond; to surpass, outdo; (*MIL*) to overcome, conquer; (*NAUT*) to sail past, double.
superobruō, -ere *vt* to overwhelm.
superpendēns, -entis *adj* overhanging.
superpōnō, -ōnere, -osuī, -ositum *vt* to place upon; to put in charge of.
superpositus *ppp of* **superpōnō.**
superscandō, -ere *vt* to climb over.
supersedeō, -edēre, -ēdī, -essum *vi* to forbear, desist from.
superstes, -itis *adj* standing over; surviving.
superstitiō, -ōnis *f* awful fear, superstition.
superstitiōsē *adv* superstitiously; scrupulously.
superstitiōsus *adj* superstitious; prophetic.
superstō, -āre *vt, vi* to stand over, stand on.
superstrātus *adj* spread over.
superstruō, -ere, -xī, -ctum *vt* to build on top.
supersum, -esse, -fuī *vi* to be left, remain; to survive; to be in abundance, be sufficient; to be in excess.
supertegō, -ere *vt* to cover over.
superurgēns, -entis *adj* pressing from above.
superus (*compar* -**ior,** *superl* **suprēmus, summus**) *adj* upper, above ♦ *mpl* the gods above; the living ♦ *ntpl* the heavenly bodies; higher places; **mare ~um** Adriatic Sea.
supervacāneus *adj* extra, superfluous.
supervacuus *adj* superfluous, pointless.
supervādō, -ere *vt* to climb over, surmount.
supervehor, -hī, -ctus *vt* to ride past, sail past.
superveniō, -enīre, -ēnī, -entum *vt* to overtake, come on top of ♦ *vi* to come on the scene, arrive unexpectedly.
superventus, -ūs *m* arrival.
supervolitō, -āre *vt* to fly over.
supervolō, -āre *vt, vi* to fly over.
supīnō, -āre, -āvī, -ātum *vt* to upturn, lay on its back.
supīnus *adj* lying back, face up; sloping, on a slope; backwards; (*mind*) indolent, careless.
suppāctus *ppp of* **suppingō.**
suppaenitet, -ēre *vt impers* to be a little sorry.
suppalpor, -ārī *vi* to coax gently.
suppār, -aris *adj* nearly equal.
supparasītor, -ārī *vi* to flatter gently.

supparus, -ī *m,* **supparum, -ī** *nt* woman's linen garment; topsail.
suppeditātiō, -ōnis *f* abundance.
suppeditō, -āre, -āvī, -ātum *vi* to be at hand, be in full supply, be sufficient; to be rich in ♦ *vt* to supply, furnish.
suppēdō, -ere *vi* to break wind quietly.
suppetiae, -ārum *fpl* assistance.
suppetior, -ārī, -ātus *vi* to come to the assistance of.
suppetō, -ere, -īvī, *and* **iī, -ītum** *vi* to be available, be in store; to be equal to, suffice for.
suppīlō, -āre *vt* to steal.
suppingō, -ingere, -āctum *vt* to fasten underneath.
supplantō, -āre *vt* to trip up.
supplēmentum, -ī *nt* full complement; reinforcements.
suppleō, -ēre *vt* to fill up, make good, make up to the full complement.
supplex, -icis *adj* suppliant, in entreaty.
supplicātiō, -ōnis *f* day of prayer, public thanksgiving.
suppliciter *adv* in supplication.
supplicium, -ī *and* **iī** *nt* prayer, entreaty; sacrifice; punishment, execution, suffering; ~**iō afficere** execute.
supplicō, -āre, -āvī, -ātum *vi* (*with dat*) to entreat, pray to, worship.
supplōdō, -dere, -sī *vt* to stamp.
supplōsiō, -ōnis *f* stamping.
suppōnō, -ōnere, -osuī, -ositum *vt* to put under, apply; to subject; to add on; to substitute, falsify.
supportō, -āre *vt* to bring up, transport.
supposicius *adj* spurious.
suppositiō, -ōnis *f* substitution.
suppositus *ppp of* **suppōnō.**
supposuī *perf of* **suppōnō.**
suppressiō, -ōnis *f* embezzlement.
suppressus *ppp of* **supprimō** ♦ *adj* (*voice*) low.
supprimō, -imere, -essī, -essum *vt* to sink; to restrain, detain, put a stop to; to keep secret, suppress.
supprōmus, -ī *m* underbutler.
suppudet, -ēre *vt* (*impers*) to be a little ashamed.
suppūrō, -āre *vi* to fester.
suppus *adj* head downwards.
supputō, -āre *vt* to count up.
suprā *adv* above, up on top; (*time*) earlier, previously; (*amount*) more; ~ **quam** beyond what ♦ *prep* (*with acc*) over, above; beyond; (*time*) before; (*amount*) more than, over.
suprāscandō, -ere *vt* to surmount.
suprēmum *adv* for the last time.
suprēmus *adj* highest; last, latest; greatest; supreme ♦ *ntpl* moment of death; funeral rites; testament.
sūra, -ae *f* calf (of the leg).
sūrculus, -ī *m* twig, shoot; graft, slip.
surdaster, -rī *adj* rather deaf.

surditās, -ātis f deafness.
surdus adj deaf; silent.
surēna, -ae m grand vizier (of the Parthians).
surgō, -ere, surrēxī, surrēctum *i to rise,
  get up, stand up; to arise, spring up, grow.
surpere etc = surripere etc.
surr- etc see subr-.
surrēxī perf of surgō.
surruptīcius adj stolen.
surrupuī perf of subripiō.
sūrsum, sūrsus adv upwards, up, high up; ~
  deōrsum up and down.
sūs, suis m/f pig, boar, hog, sow.
Sūsa, -ōrum ntpl ancient Persian capital.
suscēnseō, -ēre, -uī vi to be angry, be
  irritated.
susceptiō, -ōnis f undertaking.
susceptus ppp of suscipiō.
suscipiō, -ipere, -ēpī, -eptum vt to take up,
  undertake; to receive, catch; (child) to
  acknowledge; to beget; to take under one's
  protection.
suscitō, -āre, -āvī, -ātum vt to lift, raise; to
  stir, rouse, awaken; to encourage, excite.
suspectō, -āre vt, vi to look up at, watch; to
  suspect, mistrust.
suspectus ppp of suspiciō ♦ adj suspected,
  suspicious.
suspectus, -ūs m looking up; esteem.
suspendium, -ī and iī nt hanging.
suspendō, -endere, -endī, -ēnsum vt to
  hang, hang up; (death) to hang; (building) to
  support; (mind) to keep in suspense;
  (movement) to check, interrupt; (pass) to
  depend.
suspēnsus ppp of suspendō ♦ adj raised,
  hanging, poised; with a light touch; (fig) in
  suspense, uncertain, anxious; dependent; ~ō
  gradū on tiptoe.
suspicāx, -ācis adj suspicious.
suspiciō, -icere, -exī, -ectum vt to look up at,
  look up to; to admire, respect; to mistrust.
suspiciō, -ōnis f mistrust, suspicion.
suspiciōsē adv suspiciously.
suspiciōsus adj suspicious.
suspicor, -ārī, -ātus vt to suspect; to surmise,
  suppose.
suspīrātus, -ūs m sigh.
suspīritus, -ūs m deep breath, difficult
  breathing; sigh.
suspīrium, -ī and iī nt deep breath, sigh.
suspīrō, -āre, -āvī, -ātum vi to sigh ♦ vt to
  sigh for; to exclaim with a sigh.
susque dēque adv up and down.
sustentāculum, -ī nt prop.
sustentātiō, -ōnis f forbearance.
sustentō, -āre, -āvī, -ātum vt to hold up,
  support; (fig) to uphold, uplift; (food, means)
  to sustain, support; (enemy) to check, hold;
  (trouble) to suffer; (event) to hold back,

postpone.
sustineō, -inēre, -inuī, -entum vt to hold up,
  support; to check, control; (fig) to uphold,
  maintain; (food, means) to sustain, support;
  (trouble) to bear, suffer, withstand; (event) to
  put off.
sustollō, -ere vt to lift up, raise; to destroy.
sustulī perf of tollō.
susurrātor, -ōris m whisperer.
susurrō, -āre vt, vi to murmur, buzz, whisper.
susurrus, -ūs m murmuring, whispering.
susurrus adj whispering.
sūtēla, -ae f trick.
sūtilis adj sewn.
sūtor, -ōris m shoemaker; ~ nē suprā
  crepidam ≈ let the cobbler stick to his last.
sūtōrius adj shoemaker's; ex-cobbler.
sūtrīnus adj shoemaker's.
sūtūra, -ae f seam.
sūtus ppp of suō.
suus adj his, her, its, their; one's own, proper,
  due, right ♦ mpl one's own troops, friends,
  followers etc ♦ nt one's own property.
Sybaris, -is f town in S. Italy (noted for its
  debauchery).
Sybarīta, -ītae m Sybarite.
Sychaeus, -ī m husband of Dido.
sycophanta, -ae m slanderer, cheat,
  sycophant.
sycophantia, -ae f deceit.
sycophantiōsē adv deceitfully.
sycophantor, -ārī, vi to cheat.
Syēnē, -ēs f town in S. Egypt (now Assuan).
syllaba, -ae f syllable.
syllabātim adv syllable by syllable.
symbola, -ae f contribution.
symbolus, -ī m token, symbol.
symphōnia, -ae f concord, harmony.
symphōniacus adj choir (in cpds).
Symplēgades, -um fpl clashing rocks in the
  Black Sea.
synedrus, -ī m senator (in Macedonia).
Synephēbī, -ōrum mpl Youths Together
  (comedy by Caecilius).
syngrapha, -ae f promissory note.
syngraphus, -ī m written contract; passport,
  pass.
Synnada, -ōrum ntpl town in Phrygia (famous
  for marble).
Synnadēnsis adj see n.
synodūs, -ontis m bream.
synthesis, -is f dinner service; suit of clothes;
  dressinggown.
Syphāx, -ācis m king of Numidia.
Syrācūsae, -ārum fpl Syracuse.
Syrācūsānus, Syrācūsānius, Syrācosius
  adj Syracusan.
Syria, -iae f country at the E. end of the
  Mediterranean.
Syrius, -us and iacus, -iscus adj Syrian.

syrma, -ae *f* robe with a train; (*fig*) tragedy.
Syrtis, -is *f Gulf of Sidra in N. Africa*; sandbank.

T, t

tabella, -ae *f* small board, sill; writing tablet, voting tablet, votive tablet; picture; (*pl*) writing, records, dispatches.
tabellārius *adj* about voting ♦ *m* courier.
tābeō, -ēre *vi* to waste away; to be wet.
taberna, -ae *f* cottage; shop; inn; (*circus*) stalls.
tabernāculum, -ī *nt* tent; ~ **capere** choose a site (for auspices).
tabernāriī, -ōrum *mpl* shopkeepers.
tābēs, -is *f* wasting away, decaying, melting; putrefaction; plague, disease.
tābēscō, -ēscere, -uī *vi* to waste away, melt, decay; (*fig*) to pine, languish.
tābidulus *adj* consuming.
tābidus *adj* melting, decaying; pining; corrupting, infectious.
tābificus *adj* melting, wasting.
tabula, -ae *f* board, plank; writing tablet; votive tablet; map; picture; auction; (*pl*) account books, records, lists, will; ~ **Sullae** Sulla's proscriptions; **XII ~ae** Twelve Tables of Roman laws; **~ae novae** cancellation of debts.
tabulārium, -ī and iī *nt* archives.
tabulātiō, -ōnis *f* flooring, storey.
tabulātum, -ī *nt* flooring, storey; (*trees*) layer, row.
tābum, -ī *nt* decaying matter; disease, plague.
taceō, -ēre, -uī, -itum *vi* to be silent, say nothing; to be still, be hushed ♦ *vt* to say nothing about, not speak of.
tacitē *adv* silently; secretly.
taciturnitās, -ātis *f* silence, taciturnity.
taciturnus *adj* silent, quiet.
tacitus *ppp of* **taceō** ♦ *adj* silent, mute, quiet; secret, unmentioned; tacit, implied; **per ~um** quietly.
Tacitus, -ī *m famous Roman historian.*
tāctilis *adj* tangible.
tāctiō, -ōnis *f* touching; sense of touch.
tāctus *ppp of* **tangō.**
tāctus, -ūs *m* touch, handling, sense of touch; influence.
taeda, -ae *f* pitch pine, pinewood; torch; plank; (*fig*) wedding.
taedet, -ēre, -uit and taesum est *vt* (*impers*) to be weary (of), loathe.
taedifer, -ī *adj* torch-bearing.
taedium, -ī and iī *nt* weariness, loathing.

Taenaridēs, -idae *m Spartan* (*esp Hyacinthus*).
Taenarius, -is *adj* of Taenarus; Spartan.
Taenarum (-on), -ī *nt*, **Taenarus (-os), -ī** *m/f* town and promontory in S. Greece (*now* Matapan); the lower world.
taenia, -ae *f* hairband, ribbon.
taesum est *perf of* **taedet.**
taeter, -rī *adj* foul, hideous, repulsive.
taetrē *adv* hideously.
taetricus *see* **tetricus.**
tagāx, -ācis *adj* light-fingered.
Tagus, -ī *m* river of Lusitania (*now* Tagus).
tālāris *adj* reaching to the ankles ♦ *ntpl* winged sandals; a garment reaching to the ankles.
tālārius *adj* of dice.
Talāsius, -ī *and* **iī** *m* god of weddings; wedding cry.
tālea, -ae *f* rod, stake.
talentum, -ī *nt* talent, *a Greek weight about 25.4kg*; a large sum of money (*esp the Attic talent of 60 minae*).
tāliō, -ōnis *f* retaliation in kind.
tālis *adj* such; the following.
talpa, -ae *f* mole.
tālus, -ī *m* ankle; heel; (*pl*) knuckle bones, oblong dice.
tam *adv* so, so much, so very.
tamdiū *adv* so long, as long.
tamen *adv* however, nevertheless, all the same.
Tāmesis, -is *and* **a, -ae** *m* Thames.
tametsī *conj* although.
tamquam *adv* as, just as, just like ♦ *conj* as if.
Tanagra, -ae *f town in Boeotia.*
Tanais, -is *m* river in Sarmatia (*now* Don).
Tanaquil, -ilis *f wife of the elder Tarquin.*
tandem *adv* at last, at length, finally; (*question*) just.
tangō, -ere, tetigī, tāctum *vt* to touch, handle; (*food*) to taste; (*with force*) to hit, strike; (*with liquid*) to sprinkle; (*mind*) to affect, move; (*place*) to reach; to border on; (*task*) to take in hand; (*by trick*) to take in, fool; (*in words*) to touch on, mention; **dē caelō tāctus** struck by lightning.
tanquam *see* **tamquam.**
Tantaleus *adj*, **-idēs, -idae** *m* Pelops, Atreus, Thyestes *or* Agamemnon.
Tantalis, -idis *f* Niobe *or* Hermione.
Tantalus, -ī *m* father of Pelops (*condemned to hunger and thirst in Tartarus, or to the threat of an overhanging rock*).
tantillus *adj* so little, so small.
tantisper *adv* so long, just for a moment.
tantopere *adv* so much.
tantulus *adj* so little, so small.
tantum *adv* so much, so, as; only, merely; ~ **modo** only; ~ **nōn** all but, almost; ~ **quod** only just.
tantummodo *adv* only.
tantundem *adv* just as much, just so much.
tantus *adj* so great; so little ♦ *nt* so much; so little; **~ī esse** be worth so much, be so dear,

be so important; **~ō** so much, so far; (*with
compar*) so much the; **~ō opere** so much; in
~um to such an extent; **tria ~a three** times as
much.
tantusdem *adj* just so great.
tapēta, -ae *m*, **-ia, -ium** *ntpl* carpet, tapestry,
hangings.
Taprobanē, -ēs *f* Ceylon.
tardē *adv* slowly, tardily.
tardēscō, -ere *vi* to become slow, falter.
tardipēs, -edis *adj* limping.
tarditās, -ātis *f* slowness, tardiness; (*mind*)
dullness.
tardiusculus *adj* rather slow.
tardō, -āre, -āvī, -ātum *vt* to retard, impede
♦ *vi* to delay, go slow.
tardus *adj* slow, tardy, late; (*mind*) dull;
(*speech*) deliberate.
Tarentīnus *adj* Tarentine.
Tarentum, -ī *nt* town in S. Italy (*now*
Taranto).
tarmes, -itis *m* woodworm.
Tarpēius *adj* Tarpeian; **mōns ~** *the* Tarpeian
Rock on the Capitoline Hill from which criminals
were thrown.
tarpezīta, -ae *m* banker.
Tarquiniēnsis *adj* of Tarquinii.
Tarquinī ī, -iōrum *mpl* ancient town in Etruria.
Tarquinius *adj* of Tarquin.
Tarquinius, -ī *m* Tarquin (*esp Priscus, the fifth
king of Rome, and Superbus, the last king*).
Tarracīna, -ae *f*, **-ae, -ārum** *fpl* town in Latium.
Tarracō, -ōnis *f* town in Spain (*now
Tarragona*).
Tarracōnēnsis *adj see n.*
Tarsēnsis *adj see n.*
Tarsus, -ī *f* capital of Cilicia.
Tartareus *adj* infernal.
Tartarus (-os), -ī *m*, **-a, -ōrum** *ntpl* Tartarus,
the lower world (*esp the part reserved for
criminals*).
tat *interj* hallo there!
Tatius, -ī *m* Sabine king (*who ruled jointly with
Romulus*).
Tatius *adj see n.*
Taum, -ī *nt* Firth of Tay.
taureus *adj* bull's ♦ *f* whip of bull's hide.
Taurī, -ōrum *mpl* Thracians of the Crimea.
Tauricus *adj see n.*
tauriformis *adj* bull-shaped.
Taurīnī, -ōrum *mpl* people of N. Italy (*now*
Turin).
taurīnus *adj* bull's.
Tauromenītānus *adj see n.*
Tauromenium, -ī *and* **ī ī** *nt* town in E Sicily.
taurus, -ī *m* bull.
Taurus, -ī *m* mountain range in S.E. Asia Minor.
taxātiō, -ōnis *f* valuing.
taxeus *adj* of yews.
taxillus, -ī *m* small dice.

taxō, -āre *vt* to value, estimate.
taxus, -ī *f* yew.
Tāygeta, -ōrum *ntpl*, **Tāygetus, -ī** *m* mountain
range in S. Greece.
Tāygetē, -ēs *f* a Pleiad.
tē *acc and abl of* **tū.**
-te *suffix for* **tū.**
Teānēnsis *adj see n.*
Teānum, -ī *nt* town in Apulia; town in Campania.
techina, -ae *f* trick.
Tecmessa, -ae *f* wife of Ajax.
tēctor, -ōris *m* plasterer.
tēctōriolum, -ī *nt* a little plaster.
tēctōrium, -ī *and* **ī ī** *nt* plaster, stucco.
tēctōrius *adj* of a plasterer.
tēctum, -ī *nt* roof, ceiling, canopy; house,
dwelling, shelter.
tēctus *ppp of* **tegō** ♦ *adj* hidden; secret,
reserved, close.
tēcum with you.
Tegea, -ae *f* town in Arcadia.
Tegeaeus *adj* Arcadian ♦ *m* the god Pan ♦ *f*
Atalanta.
Tegeātae, -ātārum *mpl* Tegeans.
teges, -etis *f* mat.
tegillum, -ī *nt* hood, cowl.
tegimen, -inis *nt* covering.
tegimentum, -ī *nt* covering.
tegm- *etc see* **tegim-.**
tegō, -ere, tēxī, -tēctum *vt* to cover; to hide,
conceal; to protect, defend; to bury; **latus ~**
walk by the side of.
tēgula, -ae *f* tile; (*pl*) tiled roof.
tegum- *etc see* **tegim.**
Tēius *adj* of Teos.
tēla, -ae *f* web; warp; yarnbeam, loom; (*fig*)
plan.
Telamōn, -ōnis *m* father of Ajax.
Tēlegonus, -ī *m* son of Ulysses and Circe.
Tēlemachus, -ī *m* son of Ulysses and Penelope.
Tēlephus, -ī *m* king of Mysia (*wounded by
Achilles' spear*).
tellūs, -ūris *f* the earth; earth, ground; land,
country.
tēlum, -ī *nt* weapon, missile; javelin, sword;
(*fig*) shaft, dart.
temerārius *adj* accidental; rash, thoughtless.
temerē *adv* by chance, at random; rashly,
thoughtlessly; **nōn ~** not for nothing; not
easily; hardly ever.
temeritās, -ātis *f* chance; rashness,
thoughtlessness.
temerō, -āre, -āvī, -ātum *vt* to desecrate,
disgrace.
tēmētum, -ī *nt* wine, alcohol.
temnō, -ere *vt* to slight, despise.
tēmō, -ōnis *m* beam (of plough or carriage);
cart; (ASTRO) the Plough.
Tempē *ntpl* famous valley in Thessaly.
temperāmentum, -ī *nt* moderation,

Noun declensions and verb conjugations are shown on pp xiii to xxv. The present infinitive ending of a verb shows
to which conjugation it belongs: **-āre** = 1st; **-ēre** = 2nd; **-ere** = 3rd and **-īre** = 4th. Irregular verbs are shown on p xxvi

compromise.

temperāns, -antis _pres p of_ **temperō** ♦ _adj_
moderate, temperate.

temperanter _adv_ with moderation.

temperantia, -ae _f_ moderation, self-control.

temperātē _adv_ with moderation.

temperātiō, -ōnis _f_ proper mixture,
composition, constitution; organizing
power.

temperātor, -ōris _m_ organizer.

temperātus _ppp of_ **temperō** ♦ _adj_ moderate,
sober.

temperī _adv_ in time, at the right time.

temperiēs, -ēī _f_ due proportion; temperature,
mildness.

temperō, -āre, -āvī, -ātum _vt_ to mix in due
proportion, blend, temper; to regulate,
moderate, tune; to govern, rule ♦ _vi_ to be
moderate, forbear, abstain; (_with dat_) to
spare, be lenient to.

tempestās, -ātis _f_ time, season, period;
weather; storm; (_fig_) storm, shower.

tempestīvē _adv_ at the right time,
appropriately.

tempestīvitās , -ātis _f_ seasonableness.

tempestīvus _adj_ timely, seasonable,
appropriate; ripe, mature; early.

templum, -ī _nt_ space marked off for taking
auspices; open space, region, quarter;
sanctuary; temple.

temporārius _adj_ for the time, temporary.

temptābundus _adj_ making repeated
attempts.

temptāmentum, -ī _nt_ trial, attempt, proof.

temptāmina, -um _ntpl_ attempts, essays.

temptātiō, -ōnis _f_ trial, proof; attack.

temptātor, -ōris _m_ assailant.

temptō, -āre, -āvī, -ātum _vt_ to feel, test by
touching; to make an attempt on, attack; to
try, essay, attempt; to try to influence,
tamper with, tempt, incite; **vēnās ~** feel the
pulse.

tempus, -oris _nt_ time; right time,
opportunity; danger, emergency,
circumstance; (_head_) temple; (_verse_) unit of
metre; (_verb_) tense; **~ore** at the right time, in
time; **ad ~us** at the right time; for the
moment; **ante ~us** too soon; **ex ~ore** on the
spur of the moment; to suit the
circumstances; **in ~ore** in time; **in ~us**
temporarily; **per ~us** just in time; **prō ~ore** to
suit the occasion.

tēmulentus _adj_ intoxicated.

tenācitās, -ātis _f_ firm grip; stinginess.

tenāciter _adv_ tightly, firmly.

tenāx, -ācis _adj_ gripping, tenacious; sticky;
(_fig_) firm, persistent; stubborn; stingy.

tendicula, -ae _f_ little snare.

tendō, -ere, tetendī, tentum _and_ **tēnsum** _vt_
to stretch, spread; to strain; (_arrow_) to aim,
shoot; (_bow_) to bend; (_course_) to direct; (_lyre_)
to tune; (_tent_) to pitch; (_time_) to prolong;
(_trap_) to lay ♦ _vi_ to encamp; to go, proceed; to

aim, tend; (_with infin_) to endeavour, exert
oneself.

tenebrae, -ārum _fpl_ darkness, night;
unconsciousness, death, blindness; (_place_)
dungeon, haunt, the lower world; (_fig_)
ignorance, obscurity.

tenebricōsus _adj_ gloomy.

tenebrōsus _adj_ dark, gloomy.

Tenedius _adj see n._

Tenedos (-us), -ī _f_ Aegean island near Troy.

tenellulus _adj_ dainty little.

teneō, -ēre, -uī _vt_ to hold, keep; to possess,
occupy, be master of; to attain, acquire;
(_argument_) to maintain, insist; (_category_) to
comprise; (_goal_) to make for; (_interest_) to
fascinate; (_law_) to bind, be binding on; (_mind_)
to grasp, understand, remember; (_move-
ment_) to hold back, restrain ♦ _vi_ to hold on,
last, persist; (_rumour_) to prevail; **cursum ~**
keep on one's course; **sē ~** remain; to
refrain.

tener, -ī _adj_ tender, delicate; young, weak;
effeminate; (_poet_) erotic.

tenerāscō, -ere _vi_ to grow weak.

tenerē _adv_ softly.

teneritās, -ātis _f_ weakness.

tenor, -ōris _m_ steady course; **ūnō ~ōre**
without a break, uniformly.

tēnsa, -ae _f_ carriage bearing the images of the
gods in procession.

tēnsus _ppp of_ **tendō** ♦ _adj_ strained.

tentā- _etc see_ **temptā-**.

tentīgō, -inis _f_ lust.

tentō _etc see_ **temptō**.

tentōrium, -ī _and_ **iī** _nt_ tent.

tentus _ppp of_ **tendō**.

tenuiculus _adj_ paltry.

tenuis _adj_ thin, fine; small, shallow; (_air_)
rarefied; (_water_) clear; (_condition_) poor,
mean, insignificant; (_style_) refined, direct,
precise.

tenuitās, -ātis _f_ thinness, fineness; poverty,
insignificance; (_style_) precision.

tenuiter _adv_ thinly; poorly; with precision;
superficially.

tenuō, -āre, -āvī, -ātum _vt_ to make thin,
attenuate, rarefy; to lessen, reduce.

tenus _prep_ (_with gen or abl_) as far as, up to,
down to; **verbō ~** in name, nominally.

Teos, -ī _f_ town on coast of Asia Minor
(_birthplace of Anacreon_).

tepefaciō, -facere, -fēcī, -factum _vt_ to
warm.

tepeō, -ēre _vi_ to be warm, be lukewarm; (_fig_)
to be in love.

tepēscō, -ēscere, -uī _vi_ to grow warm; to
become lukewarm, cool off.

tepidus _adj_ warm, lukewarm.

tepor, -ōris _m_ warmth; coolness.

ter _adv_ three times, thrice.

terdeciēns _and_ **ēs** _adv_ thirteen times.

terebinthus, -ī _f_ turpentine tree.

terebra, -ae _f_ gimlet.

terebrō, -āre vt to bore.
terēdō, -inis f grub.
Terentia, -iae f Cicero's wife.
Terentius, -ī m Roman family name (esp the comic poet Terence).
Terentius, -iānus adj see n.
teres, -etis adj rounded (esp cylindrical), smooth, shapely; (fig) polished, elegant.
Tēreus, -eī and **eos** m king of Thrace (husband of Procne, father of Itys).
tergeminus adj threefold, triple.
tergeō, -gēre, -sī, -sum vt to wipe off, scour, clean; to rub up, burnish.
tergīnum, -ī nt rawhide.
tergiversātiō, -ōnis f refusal, subterfuge.
tergiversor, -ārī, -ātus vi to hedge, boggle, be evasive.
tergō etc see **tergeō**.
tergum, -ī nt back; rear; (land) ridge; (water) surface; (meat) chine; (skin) hide, leather, anything made of leather; **~a vertere** take to flight; **ā ~ō** behind, in the rear.
tergus, -oris see **tergum**.
termes, -itis m branch.
Terminālia, -ium ntpl Festival of the god of Boundaries.
terminātiō, -ōnis f decision; (words) clausula.
terminō, -āre, -āvī, -ātum vt to set bounds to, limit; to define, determine; to end.
terminus, -ī m boundary line, limit, bound; god of boundaries.
ternī, -ōrum adj three each; three.
terō, -ere, -trīvī, -trītum vt to rub, crush, grind; to smooth, sharpen; to wear away, use up; (road) to frequent; (time) to waste; (word) to make commonplace.
Terpsichorē, -ēs f Muse of dancing
terra, -ae f dry land, earth, ground, soil; land, country; **orbis ~ārum** the world; **ubi ~ārum** where in the world.
terrēnus adj of earth; terrestrial, land- (in cpds) ♦ nt land.
terreō, -ēre, -uī, -itum vt to frighten, terrify; to scare away; to deter.
terrestris adj earthly, on earth, land- (in cpds).
terribilis adj terrifying, dreadful.
terricula, -ōrum ntpl scare, bogy.
terrificō, -āre vt to terrify.
terrificus adj alarming, formidable.
terrigena, -ae m earth-born.
terriloquus adj alarming.
territō, -āre vt to frighten, intimidate.
territōrium, -ī and **iī** nt territory.
territus adj terrified.
terror, -ōris m fright, alarm, terror; a terror.
tersī perf of **tergeō**.
tersus ppp of **tergeō** ♦ adj clean; neat, terse.
tertiadecimānī, -ōrum mpl men of the thirteenth legion.
tertiānus adj recurring every second day ♦ f a

fever ♦ mpl men of the third legion.
tertiō adv for the third time; thirdly.
tertium adv for the third time.
tertius adj third; **~ decimus (decumus)** thirteenth.
terūncius, -ī and **iī** m quarter-as; a fourth; (fig) farthing.
tesqua (tesca), -ōrum ntpl waste ground, desert.
tessella, -ae f cube of mosaic stone.
tessera, -ae f cube, dice; (MIL) password; token (for mutual recognition of friends); ticket (for doles).
tesserārius, -ī and **iī** m officer of the watch.
testa, -ae f brick, tile; (earthenware) pot, jug, sherd; (fish) shell, shellfish.
testāmentārius adj testamentary ♦ m forger of wills.
testāmentum, -ī nt will, testament.
testātiō, -ōnis f calling to witness.
testātus ppa of **testor** ♦ adj public.
testiculus, -ī m testicle.
testificātiō, -ōnis f giving evidence, evidence.
testificor, -ārī, -ātus vt to give evidence, vouch for; to make public, bring to light; to call to witness.
testimōnium, -ī and **iī** nt evidence, testimony, proof.
testis, -is m/f witness; eyewitness.
testis, -is m testicle.
testor, -ārī, -ātus vt to give evidence, testify; to prove, vouch for; to call to witness, appeal to ♦ vi to make a will.
testū (abl -ū) nt earthenware lid, pot.
testūdineus adj of tortoiseshell, tortoise- (in cpds).
testūdō, -inis f tortoise; tortoiseshell; lyre, lute; (MIL) shelter for besiegers, covering of shields; (building) vault.
testum, -ī nt earthenware lid, pot.
tēte emphatic acc of **tū**.
tetendī perf of **tendō**.
tēter etc see **taeter**.
Tēthys, -os f sea goddess; the sea.
tetigī perf of **tangō**.
tetrachmum, tetradrachmum, -ī nt four drachmas.
tetraō, -ōnis m blackcock, grouse or capercailzie.
tetrarchēs, -ae m tetrarch, ruler.
tetrarchia, -ae f tetrarchy.
tetricus adj gloomy, sour.
tetulī archaic perf of **ferō**.
Teucer, -rī m son of Telamon of Salamis; son-in-law of Dardanus.
Teucrī, -rōrum mpl Trojans.
Teucria, -riae f Troy.
Teutonī, -ōrum and **es, -um** mpl Teutons (a German people).

Noun declensions and verb conjugations are shown on pp xiii to xxv. The present infinitive ending of a verb shows to which conjugation it belongs: **-āre** = 1st; **-ēre** = 2nd; **-ere** = 3rd and **-īre** = 4th. Irregular verbs are shown on p xxvi

Teutonicus *adj* Teutonic, German.
texī *perf of* **tegō**.
texō, -ere, -uī, -tum *vt* to weave; to plait; to build, make; (*fig*) to compose, contrive.
textilis *adj* woven ♦ *nt* fabric.
textor, -ōris *m* weaver.
textrīnum, -ī *nt* weaving; shipyard.
textūra, -ae *f* web, fabric.
textus *ppp of* **texō** ♦ *nt* web, fabric.
textus, -ūs *m* texture.
texuī *perf of* **texō**.
Thāis, -idis *f* an Athenian courtesan.
thalamus, -ī *m* room, bedroom; marriage bed; marriage.
thalassicus *adj* sea-green.
thalassinus *adj* sea-green.
Thalēs, -is *and* **ētis** *m* early Greek philosopher (*one of the seven wise men*).
Thalia, -ae *f* Muse of comedy.
thallus, -ī *m* green bough.
Thamyrās, -ae *m* blinded Thracian poet.
Thapsitānus *adj see* **Thapsus**.
Thapsus (-os), -ī *f* town in N. Africa (*scene of Caesar's victory*).
Thasius *adj see* **Thasus**.
Thasus (-os), -ī *f* Greek island in N. Aegean.
Thaumantias, -dis *f* Iris.
theātrālis *adj* of the theatre, in the theatre.
theātrum, -ī *nt* theatre; audience; (*fig*) theatre, stage.
Thēbae, -ārum *fpl* Thebes (*capital of Boeotia*); town in Upper Egypt.
Thēbais, -aidis *f* Theban woman; epic poem by Statius.
Thēbānus *adj* Theban.
thēca, -ae *f* case, envelope.
Themis, -dis *f* goddess of justice.
Themistoclēs, -ī *and* **is** *m* famous Athenian statesman.
Themistoclēus *adj see* **Themistoclēs**.
thēnsaurārius *adj* of treasure.
thēnsaurus *see* **thēsaurus**.
theologus, -ī *m* theologian.
Theophrastus, -ī *m* Greek philosopher (*successor to Aristotle*).
Theopompēus, -īnus *adj see n.*
Theopompus, -ī *m* Greek historian.
thermae, -ārum *fpl* warm baths.
Thermōdōn, -ontis *m* river of Pontus (*where the Amazons lived*).
Thermōdontēus, -ontiacus *adj* Amazonian.
thermopōlium *nt* restaurant serving warm drinks.
thermopotō, -āre *vt* to refresh with warm drinks.
Thermopylae, -ārum *fpl* famous Greek pass defended by Leonidas.
thēsaurus, -ī *m* treasure, store; storehouse, treasury.
Thēseus, -eī *and* **eos** *m* Greek hero (*king of Athens*).
Thēsēus, -ēius *adj*, **-īdēs, -īdae** *m* Hippolytus; (*pl*) Athenians.

Thespiae, -ārum *fpl* Boeotian town near Helicon.
Thespiēnsis *and* **as, -adis** *adj* Thespian.
Thespis, -is *m* traditional founder of Greek tragedy.
Thessalia, -iae *f* Thessaly (*district of N. Greece*).
Thessalicus, -us *and* **is, -idis** *adj* Thessalian.
Thetis, -idis *and* **idos** *f* sea nymph (*mother of Achilles*); the sea.
thiasus, -ī *m* Bacchic dance.
Thoantēus *adj see n.*
Thoās, -antis *m* king of Crimea (*killed by Orestes*); king of Lemnos (*father of Hypsipyle*).
tholus, -ī *m* rotunda.
thōrāx, -ācis *m* breastplate.
Thrāca, -ae, (-ē, -ēs), (-ia, -iae) *f* Thrace.
Thracius, (Thrēicius) *adj* Thracian.
Thrasea, -ae *m* Stoic philosopher under Nero.
Thrasymachus, -ī *m* Greek sophist.
Thrāx, -ācis *m* Thracian; kind of gladiator.
Thrēssa, -ae, (Thrēissa, -ae) *f* Thracian woman.
Thrēx, -ēcis *m* kind of gladiator.
Thūcydidēs, -is *m* famous Greek historian.
Thūcydidius *adj* Thucydidean.
Thūlē, -ēs *f* island in the extreme N. (*perhaps Shetland*).
thunnus *see* **thynnus**.
thūr, -is *nt* = **tūs, tūris**.
Thūriī, -iōrum *mpl* town in S. Italy.
Thūrīnus *adj see n.*
thūs *see* **tūs**.
thȳa (thȳia), -ae *f* citrus tree.
Thybris, -is *and* **idis** *m* river Tiber.
Thyestēs, -ae *m* brother of Atreus (*whose son's flesh he served up to him to eat*).
Thyestēus *adj*, **-iadēs, -iadae** *m* Aegisthus.
Thyias (Thȳas), -adis *f* Bacchante.
Thȳlē *see* **Thūlē**.
thymbra, -ae *f* savory.
thymum, -ī *nt* garden thyme.
Thȳnia, -iae *f* Bithynia.
thynnus, -ī *m* tunnyfish.
Thȳnus, (-iacus), (-ias) *adj* Bithynian.
Thyōneus, -eī *m* Bacchus.
thyrsus, -ī *m* Bacchic wand.
tiāra, -ae *f*, **-ās, -ae** *m* turban.
Tiberiānus *adj see n.*
Tiberīnus, -īnis *adj*, **-īnus, -īnī** *m* Tiber.
Tiberis (Tibris), -is *m* river Tiber.
Tiberius, -ī *m* Roman praenomen (*esp the second emperor*).
tibi *dat of* **tū**.
tibia, -ae *f* shinbone; pipe, flute.
tībīcen, -inis *m* flute player; pillar.
tībīcina, -ae *f* flute player.
tībīcinium, -ī *and* **iī** *nt* flute playing.
Tibullus, -ī *m* Latin elegiac poet.
Tībur, -is *nt* town on the river Anio (*now Tivoli*).
Tīburs, -tis, (-tīnus), (-nus) *adj* Tiburtine.
Tīcīnus, -ī *m* tributary of the river Po.

Tigellīnus, -ī m favourite of Nero.
tigillum, -ī nt small log, small beam.
tignārius adj working in wood; **faber ~** carpenter.
tignum, -ī nt timber, trunk, log.
Tigrānēs, -is m king of Armenia.
tigris, -is and **idis** f tiger.
tīlia, -ae f lime tree.
Tīmaeus, -ī m Sicilian historian; Pythagorean philosopher; a dialogue of Plato.
timefactus adj frightened.
timeō, -ēre, -uī vt, vi to fear, be afraid.
timidē adv timidly.
timiditās, -ātis f timidity, cowardice.
timidus adj timid, cowardly.
timor, -ōris m fear, alarm; a terror.
tinctilis adj dipped in.
tinctus ppp of **tingō**.
tinea, -ae f moth, bookworm.
tingō, -gere, -xī, -ctum vt to dip, soak; to dye, colour; (fig) to imbue.
tinnīmentum, -ī nt ringing noise.
tinniō, -īre vt, vi to ring, tinkle.
tinnītus, -ūs m ringing, jingle.
tinnulus adj ringing, jingling.
tintinnābulum, -ī nt bell.
tintinō, -āre vi to ring.
tīnus, -ī m a shrub, laurustinus.
tinxī perf of **tingō**.
Tīphys, -os m helmsman of the Argo.
tippula, -ae f water spider.
Tīresiās, -ae m blind soothsayer of Thebes.
Tīridātēs, -ae m king of Armenia.
tīrō, -ōnis m recruit, beginner.
Tīrō, -ōnis m Cicero's freedman secretary.
tīrōcinium, -ī and **ī** nt first campaign; recruits; (fig) first attempt, inexperience.
Tīrōniānus adj see **Tīrō**.
tīrunculus, -ī m young beginner.
Tīryns, -this f ancient town in S.E. Greece (home of Hercules).
Tīrynthius adj of Tiryns, of Hercules ♦ m Hercules.
tis archaic gen of **tū**.
Tīsiphonē, -ēs f a Fury.
Tīsiphonēus adj guilty.
Tītān, -ānis, (-ānus, -ānī) m Titan (an ancient race of gods); the sun.
Tītānius, (-āniacus), (-ānis) adj see r.
Tīthōnius adj see n.
Tīthōnus, -ī m consort of Aurora (granted immortality without youth).
tītillātiō, -ōnis f tickling.
tītillō, -āre vt to tickle.
titubanter adv falteringly.
titubātiō, -ōnis f staggering.
titubō, -āre vi to stagger, totter; to stammer; to waver, falter.
titulus, -ī m inscription, label, notice; title of honour; fame; pretext.

Tityos, -ī m giant punished in Tartarus.
Tmōlus, -ī m mountain in Lydia.
toculiō, -ōnis m usurer.
tōfus, -ī m tufa.
toga, -ae f toga (dress of the Roman citizen); (fig) peace; ~ **candida** dress of election candidates; ~ **picta** ceremonial dress of a victor in triumph; ~ **praetexta** purple-edged toga of magistrates and children; ~ **pūra**, **virīlis** plain toga of manhood.
togātus adj wearing the toga ♦ m Roman citizen; client ♦ f drama on a Roman theme.
togula, -ae f small toga.
tolerābilis adj bearable, tolerable; patient.
tolerābiliter adv patiently.
tolerāns, -antis pres p of **tolerō** ♦ adj patient.
toleranter adv patiently.
tolerantia, -ae f endurance.
tolerātiō, -ōnis f enduring.
tolerātus adj tolerable.
tolerō, -āre, -āvī, -ātum vt to bear, endure; to support, sustain.
tollēnō, -ōnis m crane, derrick, lift.
tollō, -ere, sustulī, sublātum vt to lift, raise; to take away, remove; to do away with, abolish, destroy; (anchor) to weigh; (child) to acknowledge, bring up; (mind) to elevate, excite, cheer; (passenger) to take on board; **signa ~** decamp.
Tolōsa, -ae f Toulouse.
Tolōsānus adj see **Tolōsa**.
tolūtim adv at a trot.
tomāculum, -ī nt sausage.
tōmentum, -ī nt stuffing, padding.
Tomis, -is f town on the Black Sea (to which Ovid was exiled).
Tomītānus adj see **Tomis**.
Tonāns, -antis m Thunderer (epithet of Jupiter).
tondeō, -ēre, totondī, tōnsum vt to shear, clip, shave; to crop, reap, mow; to graze, browse on; (fig) to fleece, rob.
tonitrālis adj thunderous.
tonitrus, -ūs m, **-ua, -uōrum** ntpl thunder.
tonō, -āre, -uī vi to thunder ♦ vt to thunder out.
tōnsa, -ae f oar.
tōnsillae, -ārum fpl tonsils.
tōnsor, -ōris m barber.
tōnsōrius adj for shaving.
tōnstrīcula, -ae f barber girl.
tōnstrīna, -ae f barber's shop.
tōnstrīx, -īcis f woman barber.
tōnsūra, -ae f shearing, clipping.
tōnsus ppp of **tondeō**.
tōnsus, -ūs m coiffure.
tōphus see **tōfus**.
topiārius adj of ornamental gardening ♦ m topiarist ♦ f topiary
topicē, -ēs f the art of finding topics.

toral, -ālis *nt* valance.
torcular, -āris *and* **um, -ī** *nt* press.
toreuma, -tis *nt* embossed work, relief.
tormentum, -ī *nt* windlass, torsion catapult, artillery; shot; rack, torture; (*fig*) torment, anguish.
tormina, -um *ntpl* colic.
torminōsus *adj* subject to colic.
tornō, -āre, -āvī, -ātum *vt* to turn (in a lathe), round off.
tornus, -ī *m* lathe.
torōsus *adj* muscular.
torpēdō, -inis *f* numbness, lethargy; (*fish*) electric ray.
torpeō, -ēre *vi* to be stiff, be numb; to be stupefied.
torpēscō, -ēscere, -uī *vi* to grow stiff, numb, listless.
torpidus *adj* benumbed.
torpor, -ōris *m* numbness, torpor, listlessness.
torquātus *adj* wearing a neckchain.
Torquātus, -ī *m surname of Manlius.*
torqueō, -quēre, -sī, -tum *vt* to turn, twist, bend, wind; (*missile*) to whirl, hurl, brandish; (*body*) to rack, torture; (*mind*) to torment.
torquēs *and* **is, -is** *m/f* neckchain, necklace, collar.
torrēns, -entis *pres p of* **torreō** ♦ *adj* scorching, hot; rushing, rapid ♦ *m* torment.
torreō, -ēre, -uī, tostum *vt* to parch, scorch, roast.
torrēscō, -ere *vi* to become parched.
torridus *adj* parched, dried up; frostbitten.
torris, -is *m* brand, firebrand.
torsī *perf of* **torqueō**.
tortē *adv* awry.
tortilis *adj* twisted, winding.
tortor, -ārī *vi* to writhe.
tortor, -ōris *m* torturer, executioner.
tortuōsus *adj* winding; (*fig*) complicated.
tortus *ppp of* **torqueō** ♦ *adj* crooked; complicated.
tortus, -ūs *m* twisting, writhing.
torulus, -ī *m* tuft (of hair).
torus, -ī *m* knot, bulge; muscle, brawn; couch, bed; (*earth*) bank, mound; (*language*) ornament.
torvitās, -ātis *f* wildness, grimness.
torvus *adj* wild, grim, fierce.
tostus *ppp of* **torreō**.
tot *adj* (*indecl*) so many, as many.
totidem *adj* (*indecl*) just as many, the same number of.
totiēns, totiēs *adv* so often, as often.
totondī *perf of* **tondeō**.
tōtus (*gen* **-īus**, *dat* **-ī**) *adj* entire, the whole, all; entirely, completely taken up with; **ex ~ō** totally; **in ~ō** on the whole.
toxicum, -ī *nt* poison.
trabālis *adj* for beams; **clāvus ~** large nail.
trabea, -ae *f* ceremonial robe.
trabeātus *adj* wearing a ceremonial robe.

trabs, -abis *f* beam, timber; tree; ship; roof.
Trāchīn, -īnis *f* town in Thessaly (*where Hercules cremated himself*).
Trāchīnius *adj see* **Trāchīn**.
tractābilis *adj* manageable, tractable.
tractātiō, -ōnis *f* handling, treatment.
tractātus, -ūs *m* handling.
tractim *adv* slowly, little by little.
tractō, -āre, -āvī, -ātum *vt* to maul; to handle, deal with, manage; (*activity*) to conduct, perform; (*person*) to treat; (*subject*) to discuss, consider.
tractus *ppp of* **trahō** ♦ *adj* fluent.
tractus, -ūs *m* dragging, pulling, drawing; train, track; (*place*) extent, region, district; (*movement*) course; (*time*) lapse; (*word*) drawling.
trādidī *perf of* **trādō**.
trāditiō, -ōnis *f* surrender; handing down.
trāditor, -ōris *m* traitor.
trāditus *ppp of* **trādō**.
trādō, -ere, -idī, -itum *vt* to hand over, deliver, surrender; to commit, entrust; to betray; to bequeath, hand down; (*narrative*) to relate, record; (*teaching*) to propound; **sē ~** surrender, devote oneself.
trādūcō (trānsdūcō), -ūcere, -ūxī, -uctum *vt* to bring across, lead over, transport across; to transfer; to parade, make an exhibition of (in public); (*time*) to pass, spend.
trāductiō, -ōnis *f* transference; (*time*) passage; (*word*) metonymy.
trāductor, -ōris *m* transferrer.
trāductus *ppp of* **trādūcō**.
trādux, -ucis *m* vine layer.
tragicē *adv* dramatically.
tragicocomoedia, -ae *f* tragicomedy.
tragicus *adj* of tragedy, tragic; in the tragic manner, lofty; terrible, tragic ♦ *m* writer of tragedy.
tragoedia, -ae *f* tragedy; (*fig*) bombast.
tragoedus, -ī *m* tragic actor.
trāgula, -ae *f* kind of javelin.
trahea, -ae *f* sledge.
trahō, -here, -xī, -ctum *vt* to draw, drag, pull, take with one; to pull out, lengthen; to draw together, contract; to carry off, plunder; (*liquid*) to drink, draw; (*money*) to squander; (*wool*) to spin; (*fig*) to attract; (*appearance*) to take on; (*consequence*) to derive, get; (*praise, blame*) to ascribe, refer; (*thought*) to ponder; (*time*) to spin out.
trāiciō, -icere, -iēcī, -iectum *vt* to throw across, shoot across; (*troops*) to get across, transport; (*with weapon*) to pierce, stab; (*river, etc*) to cross; (*fig*) to transfer ♦ *vi* to cross.
trāiectiō, -ōnis *f* crossing, passage; (*fig*) transferring; (*RHET*) exaggeration; (*words*) transposition.
trāiectus *ppp of* **trāiciō**.
trāiectus, -ūs *m* crossing, passage.

trālāt- *etc see* trānslāt-.
Trallēs, -ium *fpl town in Lydia.*
Talliānus *adj see n.*
trālūceō *etc see* trānslūceō.
trāma, -ae *f* woof, web.
trāmes, -itis *m* footpath, path.
trāmittō *etc see* trānsmittō.
trānatō *etc see* trānsnatō.
trānō, -āre, -āvī, -ātum *vt, vi* to swim across; (*air*) to fly through.
tranquillē *adv* quietly.
tranquillitās, -ātis *f* quietness, calm; (*fig*) peace, quiet.
tranquillō, -āre *vt* to calm.
tranquillus *adj* quiet, calm ♦ *nt* calm sea.
trāns *prep* (*with acc*) across, over, beyond.
trānsabeō, -īre, -iī *vt* to pierce.
trānsāctor, -ōris *m* manager.
trānsāctus *ppp of* trānsigō.
trānsadigō, -ere *vt* to drive through, pierce.
Trānsalpīnus *adj* Transalpine.
trānscendō (trānsscendō), -endere, -endī, -ēnsum *vt, vi* to pass over, surmount; to overstep, surpass, transgress.
trānscrībō (transscrībō), -bere, psī, -ptum *vt* to copy out; (*fig*) to make over, transfer.
trānscurrō, -rere, -rī, -sum *vt, vi* to run across, run past, traverse.
trānscursus, -ūs *m* running through; (*speech*) cursory remark.
trānsd- *etc see* trād-.
trānsēgī *perf of* trānsigō.
trānsenna, -ae *f* net, snare; trellis, latticework.
trānseō, -īre, -iī, -itum *vt, vi* to pass over, cross over; to pass along *or* through; to pass by; to outstrip, surpass, overstep (*change*) to turn into; (*speech*) to mention briefly, leave out, pass on; (*time*) to pass, pass away.
trānsferō, -ferre, -tulī, -lātum *vt* to bring across, transport, transfer; (*change*) to transform; (*language*) to translate, (*RHET*) to use figuratively; (*time*) to postpone; (*writing*) to copy.
trānsfīgō, -gere, -xī, -xum *vt* to pierce; to thrust through.
trānsfīxus *ppp of* trānsfīgō.
trānsfodiō, -odere, -ōdī, -ossum *vt* to run through, stab.
trānsfōrmis *adj* changed in shape.
trānsfōrmō, -āre *vt* to change in shape.
trānsfossus *ppp of* trānsfodiō.
trānsfuga, -ae *m/f* deserter.
trānsfugiō, -ugere, -ūgī *vi* to desert, come over.
trānsfugium, -ī *and* iī *nt* desertion.
trānsfundō, -undere, -ūdī, -ūsum -t to decant, transfuse.
trānsfūsiō, -ōnis *f* transmigration.

trānsfūsus *ppp of* trānsfundō.
trānsgredior, -dī, -ssus *vt, vi* to step across, cross over, cross; to pass on; to exceed.
trānsgressiō, -ōnis *f* passage; (*words*) transposition.
trānsgressus *ppa of* trānsgredior.
trānsgressus, -ūs *m* crossing.
trānsiciō *etc see* trāiciō.
trānsigō, -igere, -ēgī, -āctum *vt* to carry through, complete, finish; (*difference*) to settle; (*time*) to pass, spend; (*with* cum) to put an end to; (*with weapon*) to stab.
trānsiī *perf of* trānseō.
trānsiliō, trānssiliō, -īre, -uī *vi* to jump across ♦ *vt* to leap over; (*fig*) to skip, disregard; to exceed.
trānsitiō, -ōnis *f* passage; desertion; (*disease*) infection.
trānsitō, -āre *vi* to pass through.
trānsitus *ppp of* trānseō.
trānsitus, -ūs *m* passing over, passage; desertion; passing by; transition.
trānslātīcius, trālātīcius *adj* traditional, customary, common.
trānslātiō, trālātiō, -ōnis *f* transporting, transferring; (*language*) metaphor.
trānslātīvus *adj* transferable.
trānslātor, -ōris *m* transferrer.
trānslātus *ppp of* trānsferō.
trānslegō, -ere *vt* to read through.
trānslūceō, -ēre *vi* to be reflected; to shine through.
trānsmarīnus *adj* overseas.
trānsmeō, -āre *vi* to cross.
trānsmigrō, -āre *vi* to emigrate.
trānsmissiō, -ōnis *f* crossing.
trānsmissus *ppp of* trānsmittō.
trānsmissus, -ūs *m* crossing.
trānsmittō, -ittere, -īsī, -issum *vt* to send across, put across; to let pass through; to transfer, entrust, devote; to give up, pass over; (*place*) to cross over, go through, pass ♦ *vi* to cross.
trānsmontānus *adj* beyond the mountains.
trānsmoveō, -ovēre, -ōvī, -ōtum *vt* to move, transfer.
trānsmūtō, -āre *vt* to shift.
trānsnatō, trānatō, -āre *vi* to swim across ♦ *vt* to swim.
trānsnō *etc see* trānō.
Trānspadānus *adj* north of the Po.
trānspectus, -ūs *m* view.
trānspiciō, -ere *vt* to look through.
trānspōnō, -ōnere, -osuī, -ositum *vt* to transfer.
trānsportō, -āre *vt* to carry across, transport, remove.
trānspositus *ppp of* trānspōnō.
Trānsrhēnānus *adj* east of the Rhine.
trānss- *etc see* trāns-.

Noun declensions and verb conjugations are shown on pp xiii to xxv. The present infinitive ending of a verb shows to which conjugation it belongs: -āre = 1st -ēre = 2nd; -ere = 3rd and -īre = 4th. Irregular verbs are shown on p xxvi

Trānstiberīnus *adj* across the Tiber.
trānstineō, -ēre *vi* to get through.
trānstrum, -ī *nt* thwart.
trānstulī *perf of* **trānsferō.**
trānsultō, -āre *vi* to jump across.
trānsūtus *adj* pierced.
trānsvectiō, -ōnis *f* crossing.
trānsvectus *ppp of* **trānsvehō.**
trānsvehō, -here, -xi, -ctum *vt* to carry across, transport.
trānsvehor, -hī, -ctus *vi* to cross, pass over; (*parade*) to ride past; (*time*) to elapse.
trānsverberō, -āre *vt* to pierce through, wound.
trānsversus (trāversus) *adj* lying across, crosswise, transverse; **digitum ~um** a finger's breadth; **dē ~ō** unexpectedly; **ex ~ō** sideways.
trānsvolitō, -āre *vt* to fly through.
trānsvolō, -āre *vt, vi* to fly across, fly through; to move rapidly across; to fly past, disregard.
trānsvorsus *etc see* **trānsversus.**
trapētus, -ī *m* olive mill, oil mill.
trapezīta *etc see* **tarpezīta.**
Trapezūs, -ūntis *f* Black Sea town (*now* Trebizond).
Trasumennus (Trasimēnus), -ī *m* lake in Etruria (*where Hannibal defeated the Romans*).
trāv- *see* **trānsv-.**
trāvectiō *etc see* **trānsvectiō.**
traxī *perf of* **trahō.**
trecēnī, -ōrum *adj* three hundred each.
trecentēsimus *adj* three-hundredth.
trecentī, -ōrum *num* three hundred.
trecentiēns, -ēs *adv* three hundred times.
trechedīpna, -ōrum *ntpl* dinner shoes (*of parasites*).
tredecim *num* thirteen.
tremebundus *adj* trembling.
tremefaciō, -facere, -fēcī, -factum *vt* to shake.
tremendus *adj* formidable, terrible.
tremēscō (tremīscō), -ere *vi* to begin to shake ♦ *vt* to be afraid of.
tremō, -ere, -uī *vi* to tremble, quake, quiver ♦ *vt* to tremble at, dread.
tremor, -ōris *m* shaking, quiver, tremor; earthquake.
tremulus *adj* trembling, shivering.
trepidanter *adv* with agitation.
trepidātiō, -ōnis *f* agitation, alarm, consternation.
trepidē *adv* hastily, in confusion.
trepidō, -āre, -āvī, -ātum *vi* to be agitated, bustle about, hurry; to be alarmed; to flicker, quiver ♦ *vt* to start at.
trepidus *adj* restless, anxious, alarmed; alarming, perilous.
trēs, trium *num* three.
trēssis, -is *m* three asses.
trēsvirī, triumvirōrum *mpl* three commissioners, triumvirs.

Trēverī, -ōrum *mpl* people of E. Gaul (*about what is now* Trèves).
Trēvericus *adj see n.*
triangulum, -ī *nt* triangle.
triangulus *adj* triangular.
triāriī, -ōrum *mpl* the third line (*in Roman battle order*), the reserves.
tribuārius *adj* of the tribes.
tribūlis, -is *m* fellow tribesman.
tribulum, -ī *nt* threshing sledge.
tribulus, -ī *m* star thistle.
tribūnal, -ālis *nt* platform; judgment seat; camp platform, cenotaph.
tribūnātus, -ūs *m* tribuneship, rank of tribune.
tribūnicius *adj* of a tribune ♦ *m* ex-tribune.
tribūnus, -ī *m* tribune; **~ plēbis** tribune of the people, a magistrate who defended the rights of the plebeians; **~ mīlitum** *or* **mīlitāris** military tribune, an officer under the legatus; **~ī aerāriī** paymasters.
tribuō, -uere, -uī, -ūtum *vt* to assign, allot; to give, bestow, pay; to concede, allow; to ascribe, attribute; (*subject*) to divide; (*time*) to devote.
tribus, -ūs *m* tribe.
tribūtārius *adj*: **~ae tabellae** letters of credit.
tribūtim *adv* by tribes.
tribūtiō, -ōnis *f* distribution.
tribūtum, -ī *nt* contribution, tribute, tax.
tribūtus *ppp of* **tribuō.**
tribūtus *adj* arranged by tribes.
trīcae, -ārum *fpl* nonsense; tricks, vexations.
trīcēnī, -ōrum *adj* thirty each, in thirties.
triceps, -ipitis *adj* three-headed.
trīcēsimus *adj* thirtieth.
trichila, -ae *f* arbour, summerhouse.
triciēns, -ēs *adv* thirty times.
trīclīnium, -ī *and* **iī** *nt* dining couch; dining room.
trīcō, -ōnis *m* mischief-maker.
trīcor, -ārī *vi* to make mischief, play tricks.
tricorpor, -is *adj* three-bodied.
tricuspis, -idis *adj* three-pointed.
tridēns, -entis *adj* three-pronged ♦ *m* trident.
tridentifer, -ī *adj* trident-wielding.
tridentiger, -i *adj* trident-wielding.
triduum, -ī *nt* three days.
triennia, -ium *ntpl* a triennial festival.
triennium, -ī *and* **iī** *nt* three years.
triēns, -entis *m* a third; (*coin*) a third of an as; (*measure*) a third of a pint.
trientābulum, -ī *nt* land given by the State as a third of a debt.
trientius *adj* sold for a third.
triērarchus, -ī *m* captain of a trireme.
triēris, -is *f* trireme.
trietēricus *adj* triennial ♦ *ntpl* festival of Bacchus.
trietēris, -idis *f* three years; a triennial festival.
trifāriam *adv* in three parts, in three places.
trifaux, -aucis *adj* three-throated.

trifidus adj three-forked.
triformis adj triple.
trifūr, -ūris m archthief.
trifurcifer, -ī m hardened criminal.
trigeminus adj threefold, triple ♦ mpl triplets.
trigintā num thirty.
trigōn, -ōnis m a ball game.
trilībris adj three-pound.
trilinguis adj three-tongued.
trilīx, -īcis adj three-ply, three-stranded.
trimēstris adj of three months.
trimetrus, -ī m trimeter.
trīmus adj three years old.
Trīnacria, -iae f Sicily.
Trīnacrius, -is, -idis adj Sicilian.
trīnī, -ōrum adj three each, in threes; triple.
Trinobantēs, -um mpl British tribe in East Anglia.
trinōdis adj three-knotted.
triōbolus, -ī m half-a-drachma.
Triōnēs, -um mpl the Plough; the Little Bear.
tripartītō adv in or into three parts.
tripartītus, tripertītus adj divided into three parts.
tripectorus adj three-bodied.
tripedālis adj three-foot.
tripert- etc see **tripart-**.
tripēs, -edis adj three-legged.
triplex, -icis adj triple, threefold ♦ ā three times as much ♦ mpl three-leaved writing tablet.
triplus adj triple.
Triptolemus, -ī m inventor of agriculture, judge in Hades.
tripudiō, -āre vi to dance.
tripudium, -ī and **iī** nt ceremonial dance, dance; a favourable omen (when the sacred chickens ate greedily).
tripūs, -odis f tripod; the Delphic oracle.
triquetrus adj triangular; Sicilian.
trirēmis adj with three banks of oars ♦ f trireme.
trīs etc see **trēs**.
triscurria, -ōrum ntpl sheer fooling.
tristē adv sadly; severely.
tristī = **trīvistī**.
tristiculus adj rather sad.
tristificus adj ominous.
tristimōnia, -ae f sadness.
tristis adj sad, glum, melancholy; gloomy, sombre, dismal; (taste) bitter; (smell) offensive; (temper) severe, sullen, ill-humoured.
tristitia, -ae f sadness, sorrow, melancholy; moroseness, severity.
tristitiēs, -ēī f sorrow.
trisulcus adj three-forked.
tritavus, -ī m great-great-great-grandfather.
trīticeus adj of wheat, wheaten.
trīticum, -ī nt wheat.

Trītōn, -ōnis m sea god (son of Neptune); African lake (where Minerva was born).
Trītōnius, -ōniacus, -ōnis adj of Lake Triton, of Minerva ♦ f Minerva.
trītūra, -ae f threshing.
trītus ppp of **terō** ♦ adj well-worn; (judgment) expert; (language) commonplace, trite.
trītus, -ūs m rubbing, friction.
triumphālis adj triumphal ♦ ntpl insignia of a triumph.
triumphō, -āre, -āvī, -ātum vi to celebrate a triumph; to triumph, exult ♦ vt to triumph over, win by conquest.
triumphus, -ī m triumphal procession, victory parade; triumph, victory.
triumvir, -ī m commissioner, triumvir; mayor (of a provincial town).
triumvirālis adj triumviral.
triumvirātus, -ūs m office of triumvir, triumvirate.
triumvirī, -ōrum mpl three commissioners, triumvirs.
trivenēfica, -ae f old witch.
trīvī perf of **terō**.
Trivia, -ae f Diana.
triviālis adj common, popular.
trivium, -ī and **iī** nt crossroads; public street.
trivius adj of the crossroads.
Trōas, -adis f the district of Troy, Troad; Trojan woman ♦ adj Trojan.
trochaeus, -ī m trochee; tribrach.
trochlea, -ae f block and tackle.
trochus, -ī m hoop.
Trōglodytae, -ārum mpl cave dwellers of Ethiopia.
Trōia, -ae f Troy.
Trōilus, -ī m son of Priam.
Trōiugena, -ae m/f Trojan; Roman.
Trōius and **ānus** and **cus** adj Trojan.
tropaeum, -ī nt victory memorial, trophy; victory; memorial, token.
Trōs, -ōis m king of Phrygia; Trojan.
trucīdātiō, -ōnis f butchery.
trucīdō, -āre, -āvī, -ātum vt to slaughter, massacre.
truculentē adv see **truculentus**.
truculentia, -ae f ferocity, inclemency.
truculentus adj ferocious, grim, wild.
trudis, -is f pike.
trūdō, -dere, -sī, -sum vt to push, thrust, drive; (buds) to put forth.
trulla, -ae f ladle, scoop; washbasin.
truncō, -āre, -āvī, -ātum vt to lop off, maim, mutilate.
truncus, -ī m (tree) trunk, bole; (human) trunk, body; (abuse) blockhead ♦ adj maimed, broken, stripped (of); defective.
trūsī perf of **trūdō**.
trūsitō, -āre vt to keep pushing.
trūsus ppp of **trūdō**.

Noun declensions and verb conjugations are shown on pp xiii to xxv. The present infinitive ending of a verb shows to which conjugation it belongs: **-āre** = 1st; **-ēre** = 2nd; **-ere** = 3rd and **-īre** = 4th. Irregular verbs are shown on p xxvi

trutina, -ae *f* balance, scales.
trux, -ucis *adj* savage, grim, wild.
trȳgōnus, -ī *m* stingray.
tū *pron* you, thou.
tuātim *adv* in your usual fashion.
tuba, -ae *f* trumpet, war trumpet.
tūber, -is *nt* swelling, lump; (*food*) truffle.
tuber, -is *f* kind of apple tree.
tubicen, -inis *m* trumpeter.
tubilūstria, -ōrum *ntpl* festival of trumpets.
tuburcinor, -ārī *vi* to gobble up, guzzle.
tubus, -ī *m* pipe.
tuditō, -āre *vt* to strike repeatedly.
tueor, -ērī, -itus *and* **tūtus** *vt* to see, watch, look; to guard, protect, keep.
tugurium, -ī *and* **iī** *nt* hut, cottage.
tuitiō, -ōnis *f* defence.
tuitus *ppa of* **tueor.**
tulī *perf of* **ferō.**
Tulliānum, -ī *nt* State dungeon of Rome.
Tulliānus *adj see* **Tullius.**
Tulliola, -ae *f* little Tullia (*Cicero's daughter*).
Tullius, -ī *and* **iī** *m* Roman family name (*esp the sixth king*); the orator Cicero.
Tullus, -ī *m* third king of Rome.
tum *adv* (*time*) then, at that time; (*sequence*) then, next ♦ *conj* moreover, besides; ~ ... ~ at one time ... at another; ~ ... **cum** at the time when, whenever; **cum** ... ~ not only ... but; ~ **dēmum** only then; ~ **ipsum** even then; ~ **māximē** just then; ~ **vērō** then more than ever.
tumefaciō, -facere, -fēcī, -factum *vt* to make swell; (*fig*) to puff up.
tumeō, -ēre *vi* to swell, be swollen; (*emotion*) to be excited; (*pride*) to be puffed up; (*language*) to be turgid.
tumēscō, -ēscere, -uī *vi* to begin to swell, swell up.
tumidus *adj* swollen, swelling; (*emotion*) excited, enraged; (*pride*) puffed up; (*language*) bombastic.
tumor, -ōris *m* swelling, bulge; hillock; (*fig*) commotion, excitement.
tumulō, -āre *vt* to bury.
tumulōsus *adj* hilly.
tumultuārius *adj* hasty; (*troops*) emergency.
tumultuātiō, -ōnis *f* commotion.
tumultuō, -āre; -or, -ārī *vi* to make a commotion, be in an uproar.
tumultuōsē *adv see* **tumultuōsus.**
tumultuōsus *adj* uproarious, excited, turbulent.
tumultus, -ūs *m* commotion, uproar, disturbance; (*MIL*) rising, revolt, civil war; (*weather*) storm; (*mind*) disorder.
tumulus, -ī *m* mound, hill; burial mound, barrow.
tunc *adv* (*time*) then, at that time; (*sequence*) then, next; ~ **dēmum** only then; ~ **quoque** then too; even so.
tundō, -ere, tutudī, tūnsum *and* **tūsum** *vt* to beat, thump, hammer; (*grain*) to pound;

(*speech*) to din, importune.
Tūnēs, -ētis *m* Tunis.
tunica, -ae *f* tunic; (*fig*) skin, husk.
tunicātus *adj* wearing a tunic.
tunicula, -ae *f* little tunic.
tūnsus *ppp of* **tundō.**
tuor *etc see* **tueor.**
turba, -ae *f* disorder, riot, disturbance; brawl, quarrel; crowd, mob, troop, number.
turbāmenta, -ōrum *ntpl* propaganda.
turbātē *adv* in confusion.
turbātiō, -ōnis *f* confusion.
turbātor, -ōris *m* agitator.
turbātus *ppp of* **turbō** ♦ *adj* troubled, disorderly.
turbellae, -ārum *fpl* stir, row.
turben *etc see* **turbō.**
turbidē *adv* in disorder.
turbidus *adj* confused, wild, boisterous; (*water*) troubled, muddy; (*fig*) disorderly, troubled, alarmed, dangerous.
turbineus *adj* conical.
turbō, -āre, -āvī, -ātum *vt* to disturb, throw into confusion; (*water*) to trouble, make muddy.
turbō, -inis *m* whirl, spiral, rotation; reel, whorl, spindle; (*toy*) top; (*wind*) tornado, whirlwind; (*fig*) storm.
turbulentē *and* **er** *adv* wildly.
turbulentus *adj* agitated, confused, boisterous, stormy; troublemaking, seditious.
turdus, -ī *m* thrush.
tūreus *adj* of incense.
turgeō, -gēre, -sī *vi* to swell, be swollen; (*speech*) to be bombastic.
turgēscō, -ere *vi* to swell up, begin to swell; (*fig*) to become enraged.
turgidulus *adj* poor swollen.
turgidus *adj* swollen, distended; bombastic.
tūribulum, -ī *nt* censer.
tūricremus *adj* incense-burning.
tūrifer, -ī *adj* incense-producing.
tūrilegus *adj* incense-gathering.
turma, -ae *f* troop, squadron (*of cavalry*); crowd.
turmālis *adj* of a troop; equestrian.
turmātim *adv* troop by troop.
Turnus, -ī *m* Rutulian king (*chief opponent of Aeneas*).
turpiculus *adj* ugly little; slightly indecent.
turpificātus *adj* debased.
turpilucricupidus *adj* fond of filthy lucre.
turpis *adj* ugly, deformed, unsightly; base, disgraceful ♦ *nt* disgrace.
turpiter *adv* repulsively; shamefully.
turpitūdō, -inis *f* deformity; disgrace, infamy.
turpō, -āre *vt* to disfigure, soil.
turriger, -ī *adj* turreted.
turris, -is *f* tower, turret; siege tower; (*elephant*) howdah; (*fig*) mansion.
turrītus *adj* turreted; castellated; towering.

U, u

tursī perf of **turgeō.**
turtur, -is m turtledove.
tūs, tūris nt incense, frankincense
Tusculānēnsis adj at Tusculum.
Tusculānum, -ānī nt villa at Tusculum (esp
Cicero's).
Tusculānus adj Tusculan.
tūsculum, -ī nt a little incense.
Tusculum, -ī nt Latin town near Rome.
Tusculus adj Tusculan.
Tuscus adj Etruscan.
tussiō, -īre vi to cough, have a cough.
tussis, -is f cough.
tūsus ppp of **tundō.**
tūtāmen, -inis nt defence.
tūtāmentum, -ī nt protection.
tūte emphatic form of **tū.**
tūtē adv safely, in safety.
tūtēla, -ae f keeping, charge, protection; (of
minors) guardianship, wardship; person)
watcher, guardian; ward, charge
tūtemet emphatic form of **tū.**
tūtor, -ārī, -ātus, -ō, -āre vt to watch, guard,
protect; to guard against.
tūtor, -ōris m protector; (law) guardian.
tutudī perf of **tundō.**
tūtus ppp of **tueō** ♦ adj safe, secure; cautious ♦
nt safety.
tuus adj your, yours, thy, thine; your own,
your proper; of you.
Tydeus, -eī and **eos** m father of Diomede.
Tydīdēs, -īdae m Diomede.
tympanotrība, -ae m timbrel player.
tympanum (typanum), -ī nt drum, timbrel
(esp of the priests of Cybele); (mechanism)
wheel.
Tyndareus, -eī m king of Sparta (husband of
Leda).
Tyndaridae, -idārum mpl Castor and Pollux.
Tyndaris, -idis f Helen; Clytemnestra.
Typhoeus, -eos m giant under Etna.
Typhōius, -is adj see n.
typus, -ī m figure.
tyrannicē adv see **tyrannicus.**
tyrannicīda, -ae m tyrannicide.
tyrannicus adj tyrannical.
tyrannis, -idis f despotism, tyranny.
tyrannoctonus, -ī m tyrannicide.
tyrannus, -ī m ruler, king; despot, tyrant.
Tyrās, -ae m river Dniester.
Tyrius adj Tyrian, Phoenician, Carthaginian;
purple.
tyrotarichos, -ī m dish of salt fish and cheese.
Tyrrhēnia, -iae f Etruria.
Tyrrhēnus adj Etruscan, Tyrrhenian.
Tyrtaeus, -ī m Spartan war poet.
Tyrus (-os), -ī f Tyre (famous Phoenician
seaport).

ūber, -is nt breast, teat; (fig) richness.
ūber, -is adj fertile, plentiful, rich (in);
(language) full, copious.
ūberius (superl -rime) compar adj more fully,
more copiously.
ūbertās, -ātis f richness, plenty, fertility.
ūbertim adv copiously.
ubī adv (interrog) where; (relat) where, in
which, with whom; when
ubīcumque adv wherever; everywhere.
Ubiī, -ōrum mpl German tribe on the lower
Rhine.
ubīnam adv where (in fact)?
ubīquāque adv everywhere.
ubīque adv everywhere, anywhere.
ubiubī adv wherever
ubīvīs adv anywhere.
ūdus adj wet, damp.
ulcerō, -āre vt to make sore, wound.
ulcerōsus adj full of sores; wounded.
ulcīscor, -ī, ultus vt to take vengeance on,
punish; to take vengeance for, avenge.
ulcus, -eris nt sore, ulcer; ~ **tangere** touch on a
delicate subject.
ūlīgō, -inis f moisture, marshiness.
Ulixēs, -is m Ulysses, Odysseus (king of Ithaca,
hero of Homer's Odyssey).
ullus (gen -īus, dat -ī) adj any.
ulmeus adj of elm.
ulmus, -ī f elm; (pl) elm rods.
ulna, -ae f elbow; arm; (measure) ell.
ulterior, -ōris compar adj farther, beyond,
more remote.
ulterius compar of **ultrā.**
ultimus superl adj farthest, most remote, the
end of; (time) earliest, latest, last; (degree)
extreme, greatest, lowest ♦ ntpl the end;
~um to the last time; **ad ~um** finally.
ultiō, -ōnis f vengeance, revenge.
ultor, -ōris m avenger, punisher.
ultrō adv beyond, farther, besides ♦ prep (with
acc) beyond, on the far side of; (time) past;
(degree) over and above.
ultrīx, -īcis adj avenging.
ultrō adv on the other side, away; besides; of
one's own accord, unasked, voluntarily.
ultrō tribūta ntpl State expenditure for public
works.
ultus ppa of **ulcīscor.**
ulula, -ae f screech owl.
ululātus, -ūs m wailing, shrieking, yells,
whoops.

Noun declensions and verb conjugations are shown on pp xiii to xxv. The present infinitive ending of a verb shows
to which conjugation it belongs: -**āre** = 1st; -**ēre** = 2nd; -**ere** = 3rd and -**īre** = 4th. Irregular verbs are shown on p xxvi

ululō, -āre, -āvī, -ātum vi to shriek, yell, howl
♦ vt to cry out to.
ulva, -ae f sedge.
umbella, -ae f parasol.
Umber, -rī adj Umbrian ♦ m Umbrian dog.
umbilīcus, -ī m navel; (fig) centre; (book) roller end; (sea) cockle or pebble.
umbō, -ōnis m boss (of a shield); shield; elbow.
umbra, -ae f shadow, shade; (dead) ghost; (diner) uninvited guest; (fish) grayling; (painting) shade; (place) shelter, school, study; (unreality) semblance, mere shadow.
umbrāculum, -ī nt arbour; school; parasol.
umbrāticola, -ae m lounger.
umbrāticus adj fond of idling; in retirement.
umbrātilis adj in retirement, private, academic.
Umbria, -riae f Umbria (district of central Italy).
umbrifer, -ī adj shady.
umbrō, -āre vt to shade.
umbrōsus adj shady.
ūmectō, -āre vt to wet, water.
ūmectus adj damp, wet.
ūmeō, -ēre vi to be damp, be wet.
umerus, -ī m upper arm, shoulder.
ūmēscō, -ere vi to become damp, get wet.
ūmidē adv with damp.
ūmidulus adj dampish.
ūmidus adj wet, damp, dank, moist.
ūmor, -ōris m liquid, fluid, moisture.
umquam, unquam adv ever, at any time.
ūnā adv together.
ūnanimāns, -antis adj in full agreement.
ūnanimitās, -ātis f concord.
ūnanimus adj of one accord, harmonious.
ūncia, -ae f a twelfth; (weight) ounce; (length) inch.
ūnciārius adj of a twelfth; (interest) 8⅓ per cent.
ūnciātim adv little by little.
uncīnātus adj barbed.
ūnciola, -ae f a mere twelfth.
ūnctiō, -ōnis f anointing.
ūnctitō, -āre vt to anoint regularly.
ūnctiusculus adj rather too unctuous.
ūnctor, -ōris m anointer.
ūnctūra, -ae f anointing (of the dead).
ūnctus ppp of **ungō** ♦ adj oiled; greasy, resinous; (fig) rich, sumptuous ♦ nt sumptuous dinner.
uncus, -ī m hook, grappling-iron.
uncus adj hooked, crooked, barbed.
unda, -ae f wave, water; (fig) stream, surge.
unde adv from where, whence; from whom, from which; ~ **petitur** the defendant; ~ **unde** from wherever; somehow or other.
ūndeciēns and **ēs** adv eleven times.
ūndecim num eleven.
ūndecimus adj eleventh.
undecumque adv from wherever.
ūndēnī, -ōrum adj eleven each, eleven.
ūndēnōnāgintā num eighty-nine.
ūndeoctōgintā num seventy-nine.

ūndēquadrāgintā num thirty-nine.
ūndēquīnquāgēsimus adj forty-ninth.
ūndēquīnquāgintā num forty-nine.
ūndēsexāgintā num fifty-nine.
ūndētrīcēsimus adj twenty-ninth.
ūndēvīcēsimānī, -ōrum mpl men of the nineteenth legion.
ūndēvīcēsimus adj nineteenth.
ūndēvīgintī num nineteen.
undique adv from every side, on all sides, everywhere; completely.
undisonus adj sea-roaring.
undō, -āre vi to surge; (fig) to roll, undulate.
undōsus adj billowy.
ūnetvīcēsimānī, -ōrum mpl men of the twenty-first legion.
ūnetvīcēsimus adj twenty-first.
ungō (unguō), -gere, ūnxī, ūnctum vt to anoint, smear, grease.
unguen, -inis nt fat, grease, ointment.
unguentārius, -ī and **iī** m perfumer.
unguentātus adj perfumed.
unguentum, -ī nt ointment, perfume.
unguiculus, -ī m fingernail.
unguis, -is m nail (of finger or toe); claw, talon, hoof; **ad ~em** with perfect finish; **trānsversum ~em** a hair's breadth; **dē tenerō ~ī** from earliest childhood.
ungula, -ae f hoof, talon, claw.
unguō etc see **ungō**.
ūnicē adv solely, extraordinarily.
ūnicolor, -ōris adj all one colour.
ūnicus adj one and only, sole; unparalleled, unique.
ūnifōrmis adj simple.
ūnigena, -ae adj only-begotten; of the same parentage.
ūnimanus adj with only one hand.
ūniō, -ōnis m a single large pearl.
ūniter adv together in one.
ūniversālis adj general.
ūniversē adv in general.
ūniversitās, -ātis f the whole; the universe.
ūniversus adj all taken together, entire, general ♦ mpl the community as a whole ♦ nt the universe; **in ~um** in general.
unquam etc see **umquam**.
ūnus num one ♦ adj sole, single, only; one and the same; the outstanding one; an individual; ~ **et alter** one or two; ~ **quisque** every single one; **nēmō ~** not a single one; **ad ~um** to a man.
ūnxī perf of **ungō**.
ūpiliō, -ōnis m shepherd.
upupa, -ae f hoopoe; crowbar.
Urania, -ae and **ē, -ēs** f Muse of astronomy.
urbānē adv politely; wittily, elegantly.
urbānitās, -ātis f city life; refinement, politeness; wit.
urbānus adj town (in cpds), city (in cpds); refined, polite; witty, humorous; impertinent ♦ m townsman.
urbicapus, -ī m taker of cities.

urbs, urbis f city; Rome.
urceolus, -ī m jug.
urceus, -ī m pitcher, ewer.
ūrēdō, -inis f blight.
urgeō, -gēre, -sī vt, vi to force on, push
forward; to press hard on, pursue closely; to
crowd, hem in; to burden, oppress;
(argument) to press, urge; (work, etc) to urge
on, ply hard, follow up.
ūrīna, -ae f urine.
ūrīnātor, -ōris m diver.
urna, -ae f water jar, urn; voting urn, lottery
urn, cinerary urn, money jar.
urnula, -ae f small urn.
ūrō, -ere, ūssi, ūstum vt to burn; to scorch,
parch; (cold) to nip; (MED) to cauterize;
(rubbing) to chafe, hurt; (passion) to fire,
inflame; (vexation) to annoy, oppress.
ursa, -ae f she-bear, bear; (ASTRO) Great Bear,
Lesser Bear.
ursī perf of **urgeō.**
ursīnus adj bear's.
ursus, -ī m bear.
urtīca, -ae f nettle.
ūrus, -ī m wild ox.
Usipetēs, -etum, (-iī, -iōrum) mpl German
tribe on the Rhine.
ūsitātē adv in the usual manner.
ūsitātus adj usual, familiar.
uspiam adv anywhere, somewhere
usquam adv anywhere; in any way at all.
usque adv all the way (to, from), right on,
right up to; (time) all the time, as long as,
continuously; (degree) even, as much as; ~
quāque everywhere; every moment, on
every occasion.
ūssī perf of **ūrō.**
ūstor, -ōris m cremator.
ūstulō, -āre vt to burn.
ūstus ppp of **ūrō.**
ūsūcapiō, -apere, -ēpī, -aptum vt to acquire
ownership of, take over.
ūsūcapiō, -ōnis f ownership by use or
possession.
ūsūra, -ae f use, enjoyment; interest, usury.
ūsūrārius adj for use and enjoyment; paying
interest.
ūsurpātiō, -ōnis f making use (of).
ūsurpō, -āre, -āvī, -ātum vt to make use of,
employ, exercise; (law) to take possession
of, enter upon; (senses) to perceive, make
contact with; (word) to call by, speak of.
ūsus ppa of **ūtor.**
ūsus, -ūs m use, enjoyment, practice;
experience, skill; usage, custom;
intercourse, familiarity; usefulness, benefit,
advantage; need, necessity; ~ est, ~ venit
there is need (of); ~uī esse, ex ~ū esse be of
use, be of service; ~ū venīre happen; ~ et
frūctus use and enjoyment, usufruct.

ut, utī adv how; (relat) as; (explaining)
considering how, according as; (place)
where; ~ in ōrātōre for an orator ♦ conj 1. with
indic: (manner) as; (concessive) while, though;
(time) when, as soon as. 2. with subj:
(expressing the idea of a verb) that, to;
(purpose) so that, to; (causal) seeing that;
(concessive) granted that, although; (result)
that, so that; (fear) that not; ~ ... ita while ...
nevertheless; ~ nōn without; ~ quī seeing
that I, he, etc; ~ quisque māximē the more.
utcumque (utcunque) adv however;
whenever; one way or another.
ūtēnsilis adj of use ♦ ntpl necessaries.
ūter, -ris m bag, skin, bottle.
uter (gen -rīus, dat -rī), **-ra, -rum** pron which (of
two), the one that; one or the other.
utercumque, utracumque, utrumcumque
pron whichever of two).
uterlibet, utralibet, utrumlibet pron
whichever (of the two) you please, either
one.
uterque, utraque, utrumque pron each (of
two), either, both.
uterum, -ī nt, **uterus, -ī** m womb; child; belly.
utervīs, utravīs, utrumvīs pron whichever
(of two) you please; either.
ūtī infin of **ūtor.**
utī etc see **ut.**
ūtibilis adj useful, serviceable.
Utica, -ae f town near Carthage (where Cato
committed suicide).
Uticēnsis adj see n.
ūtilis adj useful, expedient, profitable; fit (for).
ūtilitās, -ātis f usefulness, expediency,
advantage.
ūtiliter adv usefully, advantageously.
utinam adv I wish!, would that!, if only!
utique adv at least, by all means, especially.
ūtor, ūtī, ūsus vi (with abl) to use, employ; to
possess, enjoy; to practise, experience;
(person) to be on intimate terms with, find;
ūtendum rogāre borrow.
utpote adv inasmuch as, as being.
ūtrārius, -ī and **iī** m watercarrier.
ūtriculārius, -ī and **iī** m bagpiper.
utrimque (utrinque) adv on both sides, on
either side.
utrō adv in which direction.
utrobīque see **utrubīque.**
utrōque adv in both directions, both ways.
utrubī adv on which side.
utrubīque adv on both sides, on either side.
utrum adv whether.
utut adv however.
ūva, -ae f grape, bunch of grapes; vine;
cluster.
ūvēscō, -ere vi to become wet.
ūvidulus adj moist.
ūvidus adj wet, damp; drunken.

uxor, -ōris *f* wife.
uxorcula, -ae *f* little wife.
uxōrius *adj* of a wife; fond of his wife.

V, v

vacāns, -antis *pres p of* **vacō** ♦ *adj* unoccupied; (*woman*) single.
vacātiō, -ōnis *f* freedom, exemption; exemption from military service; payment for exemption from service.
vacca, -ae *f* cow.
vaccīnium, -ī *and* **iī** *nt* hyacinth.
vaccula, -ae *f* heifer.
vacēfiō, -ierī *vi* to become empty.
vacillō, -āre *vi* to stagger, totter; to waver, be unreliable.
vacīvē *adv* at leisure.
vacīvitās, -ātis *f* want.
vacīvus *adj* empty, free.
vacō, -āre, -āvī, -ātum *vi* to be empty, vacant, unoccupied; to be free, aloof (from); to have time for, devote one's time to; ~**at** there is time.
vacuātus *adj* empty.
vacuēfaciō, -facere, -fēcī, -factum *vt* to empty, clear.
vacuitās, -ātis *f* freedom, exemption; vacancy.
vacuus *adj* empty, void, wanting; vacant; free (from); clear; disengaged, at leisure; (*value*) worthless; (*woman*) single ♦ *nt* void, space.
vadimōnium, -ī *and* **iī** *nt* bail, security; ~ **sistere** appear in court; ~ **dēserere** default.
vādō, -ere *vi* to go, go on, make one's way.
vador, -ārī, -ātus *vt* to bind over by bail.
vadōsus *adj* shallow.
vadum, -ī *nt* shoal, shallow, ford; water, sea; bottom.
vae *interj* woe!, alas!
vafer, -rī *adj* crafty, subtle.
vafrē *adv* artfully.
vagē *adv* far afield.
vāgīna, -ae *f* sheath, scabbard; (*grain*) husk.
vāgiō, -īre *vi* to cry.
vāgītus, -ūs *m* crying, bleating.
vagor, -ārī, -ātus *vi* to wander, rove, go far afield; (*fig*) to spread.
vāgor, -ōris *m* cry.
vagus *adj* wandering, unsettled; (*fig*) fickle, wavering, vague.
vah *interj* (*expressing surprise, joy, anger*) oh!, ah!
valdē *adv* greatly, intensely; very.
valē, valēte *interj* goodbye, farewell.

valēns, -entis *pres p of* **valeō** ♦ *adj* strong, powerful, vigorous; well, healthy.
valenter *adv* strongly.
valentulus *adj* strong.
valeō, -ēre, -uī, -itum *vi* to be strong; to be able, have the power (to); to be well, fit, healthy; (*fig*) to be powerful, effective, valid; (*force*) to prevail; (*money*) to be worth; (*word*) to mean; ~ **apud** have influence over, carry weight with; ~**ēre iubeō** say goodbye to; ~**ē dīcō** say goodbye; ~**eās** away with you!
valēscō, -ere *vi* to grow strong, thrive.
valētūdinārium, -ī *and* **iī** *nt* hospital.
valētūdō, -inis *f* state of health, health; illness.
valgus *adj* bow-legged.
validē *adv* powerfully, very.
validus *adj* strong, powerful, able; sound, healthy; effective.
vallāris *adj* (*decoration*) for scaling a rampart.
vallēs, vallis, -is *f* valley.
vallō, -āre, -āvī, -ātum *vt* to palisade, entrench, fortify.
vallum, -ī *nt* rampart, palisade, entrenchment.
vallus, -ī *m* stake; palisade, rampart; (*comb*) tooth.
valvae, -ārum *fpl* folding door.
vānēscō, -ere *vi* to disappear, pass away.
vānidicus, -ī *m* liar.
vāniloquentia, -ae *f* idle talk.
vāniloquus *adj* untruthful; boastful.
vānitās, -ātis *f* emptiness; falsehood, worthlessness, fickleness; vanity.
vānitūdō, -inis *f* falsehood.
vannus, -ī *f* winnowing fan.
vānus *adj* empty; idle, useless, groundless; false, untruthful, unreliable; conceited.
vapidus *adj* spoilt, corrupt.
vapor, -ōris *m* steam, vapour; heat.
vapōrārium, -ī *and* **iī** *nt* steam pipe.
vapōrō, -āre *vt* to steam, fumigate, heat ♦ *vi* to burn.
vappa, -ae *f* wine that has gone flat; (*person*) good-for-nothing.
vāpulō, -āre *vi* to be flogged, beaten; to be defeated.
variantia, -ae *f* diversity.
variātiō, -ōnis *f* difference.
vāricō, -āre *vi* to straddle.
vāricōsus *adj* varicose.
vāricus *adj* with feet wide apart.
variē *adv* diversely, with varying success.
varietās, -ātis *f* difference, diversity.
variō, -āre, -āvī, -ātum *vt* to diversify, variegate; to make different, change, vary ♦ *vi* to change colour; to differ, vary.
varius *adj* coloured, spotted, variegated; diverse, changeable, various; (*ability*) versatile; (*character*) fickle.
Varius, -ī *m* epic poet (*friend of Vergil and Horace*).
varix, -icis *f* varicose vein.

Varrō, -ōnis m consul defeated at Cannae; antiquarian writer of Cicero's day.

Varrōniānus adj see **Varrō**.

vārus adj knock-kneed; crooked; contrary.

vas, vadis m surety, bail.

vās, vāsis (pl **vāsa, -ōrum**) nt vessel, dish; utensil, implement; (MIL) baggage.

vāsārium, -ī and **iī** nt furnishing allowance (of a governor).

vāsculārius, -ī and **iī** m metalworker.

vāsculum, -ī nt small dish.

vastātiō, -ōnis f ravaging.

vastātor, -ōris m ravager.

vastē adv (size) enormously; (speech) coarsely.

vastificus adj ravaging.

vastitās, -ātis f desolation, desert devastation, destruction.

vastitiēs, -ēī f ruin.

vastō, -āre, -āvī, -ātum vt to make desolate, denude; to lay waste, ravage.

vastus adj empty, desolate, uncultivated; ravaged, devastated; (appearance) uncouth, rude; (size) enormous, vast.

vāsum etc see **vās**.

vātēs, -is m/f prophet, prophetess; poet, bard.

Vāticānus adj Vatican (hill on right bank of Tiber).

vāticinātiō, -ōnis f prophesying, prediction.

vāticinātor, -ōris m prophet.

vāticinor, -ārī, -ātus vt, vi to prophesy; to celebrate in verse; to rave, rant.

vāticinus adj prophetic.

-ve conj or; either ... or.

vēcordia, -ae f senselessness; insanity.

vēcors, -dis adj senseless, foolish, mad.

vectīgal, -ālis nt tax; honorarium (to a magistrate); income.

vectiō, -ōnis f transport.

vectis, -is m lever, crowbar; (door) bolt, bar.

Vectis, -is f Isle of Wight.

vectō, -āre vt to carry; (pass) to ride.

vector, -ōris m carrier; passenger, rider.

vectōrius adj transport (in cpds).

vectūra, -ae f transport; (payment) carriage, fare.

vectus ppp of **vehō**.

Vediovis, -is = **Vēiovis**.

vegetus adj lively, sprightly.

vēgrandis adj small.

vehemēns, -entis adj impetuous, violent; powerful, strong.

vehementer adv violently, eagerly; powerfully, very much.

vehementia, -ae f vehemence.

vehiculum, -ī nt carriage, cart; (sea) vessel.

vehō, -here, -xī, -ctum vt to carry, convey; (pass) to ride, sail, drive.

Vēiēns, -entis, (-entānus), (-us) adj see **Vēiī**.

Vēiī, -ōrum mpl ancient town in S. Etruria.

Vēiovis, -is m ancient Roman god (anti-Jupiter).

vel conj or, or perhaps; or rather; or else; either ... or ♦ adv even, if you like; perhaps; for instance; ~ māximus the very greatest.

Vēlābrum, -ī nt low ground between Capitol and Palatine hills.

vēlāmen, -inis nt covering, garment.

vēlāmentum, -ī nt curtain; (pl) draped olive branches carried by suppliants.

vēlārium, -ī and **iī** nt awning.

vēlātī, -ōrum mpl supernumerary troops.

vēles, -itis m light-armed soldier, skirmisher.

vēlifer, -ī adj carrying sail.

vēlificātiō, -ōnis f sailing.

vēlificō, -āre vi to sail ♦ vt to sail through.

vēlificor, -ārī vi to sail; (with dat) to make an effort to obtain.

Velīnus, -ī m a Sabine lake.

vēlitāris adj of the light-armed troops.

vēlitātiō, -ōnis f skirmishing.

vēlitēs pl of **vēles**.

vēlitor, -ārī vi to skirmish.

vēlivolus adj sail-winged.

velle infin of **volō**.

vellicō, -āre vt to pinch, pluck, twitch; (speech) to taunt, disparage.

vellō, -ere, vellī and **vulsī, vulsum** vt to pluck, pull, pick; to pull out, tear up.

vellus, -eris nt fleece, pelt; wool; fleecy clouds.

vēlō, -āre, -āvī, -ātum vt to cover up, clothe, veil; (fig) to conceal.

vēlōcitās, -ātis f speed, rapidity.

vēlōciter adv rapidly.

vēlōx, -ōcis adj fast, quick, rapid.

vēlum, -ī nt sail; curtain, awning; rēmis ~īsque with might and main; ~a dare set sail.

velut, velutī adv as, just as; for instance; just as if.

vēmēns etc see **vehemēns**.

vēna, -ae f vein, artery; vein of metal; water course; (fig) innermost nature of feelings, talent, strength; ~ās temptāre feel the pulse; ~ās tenēre have one's finger on the pulse (of).

vēnābulum, -ī nt hunting spear.

Venāfrānus adj see n.

Venāfrum, -ī nt Samnite town famous for olive oil.

vēnālicius adj for sale ♦ m slave dealer.

vēnālis adj for sale; bribable ♦ m slave offered for sale.

vēnāticus adj hunting (in cpds).

vēnātiō, -ōnis f hunting; a hunt; public show of fighting wild beasts; game.

vēnātor, -ōris m hunter.

vēnātōrius adj hunter's.

vēnātrīx, -īcis f huntress.

vēnātūra, -ae f hunting.

vēnātus, -ūs m hunting.

vēndibilis adj saleable; (fig) popular.

vēnditātiō, -ōnis f showing off, advertising.
vēnditātor, -ōris m braggart.
vēnditiō, -ōnis f sale.
vēnditō, -āre vt to try to sell; to praise up, advertise; **sē ~ ingratiate** oneself (with).
vēnditor, -ōris m seller.
vēndō (pass **vēneō**), **-ere, -idī, -itum** vt to sell; to betray; to praise up.
venēficium, -ī and **iī** nt poisoning; sorcery.
venēficus adj poisonous; magic ♦ m sorcerer ♦ f sorceress.
venēnātus adj poisonous; magic.
venēnifer, -ī adj poisonous.
venēnō, -āre vt to poison.
venēnum, -ī nt drug, potion; dye; poison; magic charm; (fig) mischief; charm.
vēneō, -īre, -iī, -itum vi to be sold.
venerābilis adj honoured, venerable.
venerābundus adj reverent.
venerātiō, -ōnis f respect, reverence.
venerātor, -ōris m reverencer.
Venereus, Venerius adj of Venus ♦ m highest throw at dice.
veneror, -ārī, -ātus vt to worship, revere, pray to; to honour, respect; to ask for, entreat.
Venetia, -iae f district of the Veneti.
Veneticus adj see n.
Venetus adj Venetian; (colour) blue.
vēnī perf of **veniō**.
venia, -ae f indulgence, favour, kindness; permission, leave; pardon, forgiveness; **bonā tuā ~ā** by your leave; **bonā ~ā audīre** give a fair hearing.
vēniī perf of **vēneō**.
veniō, -īre, vēnī, ventum vi to come; (fig) to fall into, incur, go as far as; **in amīcitiam ~** make friends (with); **in spem ~** entertain hopes.
vēnor, -ārī, -ātus vt, vi to hunt, chase.
venter, -ris m stomach, belly; womb, unborn child.
ventilātor, -ōris m juggler.
ventilō, -āre vt to fan, wave, agitate.
ventiō, -ōnis f coming.
ventitō, -āre vi to keep coming, come regularly.
ventōsus adj windy; like the wind; fickle; conceited.
ventriculus, -ī m belly; (heart) ventricle.
ventriōsus adj pot-bellied.
ventulus, -ī m breeze.
ventus, -ī m wind.
vēnūcula, -ae f kind of grape.
vēnum, vēnō for sale.
vēnumdō (vēnundō), -āre, -edī, -atum vt to sell, put up for sale.
venus, -eris f charm, beauty; love, mating.
Venus, -eris f goddess of love; planet Venus; highest throw at dice.
Venusia, -iae f town in Apulia (birthplace of Horace).
Venusīnus adj see **Venusia**.

venustās, -ātis f charm, beauty.
venustē adv charmingly.
venustulus adj charming little.
venustus adj charming, attractive, beautiful.
vēpallidus adj very pale.
veprēcula, -ae f little brier bush.
veprēs, -is m thornbush, bramblebush.
vēr, vēris nt spring; ~ **sacrum** offerings of firstlings.
vērātrum, -ī nt hellebore.
vērāx, -ācis adj truthful.
verbēna, -ae f vervain; (pl) sacred boughs carried by heralds or priests.
verber, -is nt lash, scourge; (missile) strap; (pl) flogging, strokes.
verberābilis adj deserving a flogging.
verberātiō, -ōnis f punishment.
verbereus adj deserving a flogging.
verberō, -āre, -āvī, -ātum vt to flog, beat, lash.
verberō, -ōnis m scoundrel.
verbōsē adv verbosely.
verbōsus adj wordy.
verbum, -ī nt word; saying, expression; (GRAM) verb; (pl) language, talk; ~ **ē (dē, prō) ~ō** literally; **ad ~um** word for word; ~**ī causa** (grātiā) for instance; ~**ō** orally; briefly; ~**a dare** cheat, fool; ~**a facere** talk; **meīs ~īs** in my name.
vērē adv really, truly, correctly.
verēcundē adv see adj.
verēcundia, -ae f modesty, shyness; reverence, dread; shame.
verēcundor, -ārī vi to be bashful, feel shy.
verēcundus adj modest, shy, bashful.
verendus adj venerable.
vereor, -ērī, -itus vt, vi to fear, be afraid; to revere, respect.
verētrum, -ī nt the private parts.
Vergiliae, -ārum fpl the Pleiads.
Vergilius, -ī m Vergil, Virgil (famous epic poet).
vergō, -ere vt to turn, incline ♦ vi to turn, incline, decline; (place) to face.
vēridicus adj truthful.
vērī similis adj probable.
vērī similitūdō, -inis f probability.
vēritās, -ātis f truth, truthfulness; reality, real life; (character) integrity; (language) etymology.
veritus ppa of **vereor**.
vermiculātus adj inlaid with wavy lines, mosaic.
vermiculus, -ī m grub.
vermina, -um ntpl stomach pains.
vermis, -is m worm.
verna, -ae f slave born in his master's home.
vernāculus adj of home-born slaves; native.
vernīlis adj slavish; (remark) smart.
vernīliter adv slavishly.
vernō, -āre vi to bloom, be spring-like; to be young.
vernula, -ae f young home-born slave; native.

vērnus adj of spring.
vērō adv in fact, assuredly; (confirming) certainly, yes; (climax) indeed; (adversative) but in fact; **minimē ~** certainly not.
Vērōna, -ae f town in N. Italy (birthplace of Catullus).
Vērōnēnsis adj see **Vērōna**.
verpus, -ī m circumcised man.
verrēs, -is m boar.
Verrēs, -is m praetor prosecuted by Cicero.
verrīnus adj boar's, pork (in cpds).
Verrius and **īnus** adj see n.
verrō, -rere, -rī, -sum vt to sweep, scour; to sweep away, carry off.
verrūca, -ae f wart; (fig) slight blemish.
verrūcōsus adj warty.
verruncō, -āre vi to turn out successfully.
versābundus adj rotating.
versātilis adj revolving; versatile.
versicolor, -ōris adj of changing or various colours.
versiculus, -ī m short line; (pl) unpretentious verses.
versificātor, -ōris m versifier.
versipellis adj of changed appearance; crafty ♦ m werewolf.
versō, -āre, -āvī, -ātum vt to keep turning, wind, twist; (fig) to upset, disturb, ruin; (mind) to ponder, consider.
versor, -ārī, -ātus vi to live, be, be situated; to be engaged (in), be busy (with).
versum adv turned, in the direction.
versūra, -ae f borrowing to pay a debt; loan.
versus ppp of **vertō** ♦ adv turned, in the direction.
versus, -ūs m line, row; verse; (dance) step.
versūtē adv craftily.
versūtiae, -ārum fpl tricks.
versūtiloquus adj sly.
versūtus adj clever; crafty, deceitful.
vertex, -icis m whirlpool, eddy; whirlwind; crown of the head, head; top, summit; (sky) pole.
verticōsus adj eddying, swirling.
vertīgō, -inis f turning round; dizziness.
vertō, -tere, -tī, -sum vt to turn; to turn over, invert; to turn round; to turn into, change, exchange; (cause) to ascribe, impute; (language) to translate; (war) to overthrow, destroy; (pass) to be (in), be engaged (in) ♦ vi to turn; to change; to turn out; **in fugam ~** put to flight; **terga ~** flee; **solum ~** emigrate; **vitiō ~** blame; **annō ~tente** in the course of a year.
Vertumnus, -ī m god of seasons.
verū, -ūs nt spit; javelin.
vērum adv truly, yes; but actually; but, yet; **~ tamen** nevertheless.
vērum, -ī nt truth, reality; right; **~ī similis** probable.
vērus adj true, real, actual; truthful, right,

reasonable.
verūtum, -ī nt javelin.
verūtus adj armed with the javelin.
vervēx, -ēcis m wether.
vēsānia, -ae f madness.
vēsāniēns, -entis adj raging.
vēsānus adj mad, insane; furious, raging.
vescor, -ī vi (with abl) to feed, eat; to enjoy.
vescus adj little, feeble; corroding.
vēsīca, -ae f bladder; purse; football.
vēsīcula, -ae f small bladder, blister.
vespa, -ae f wasp.
Vespasiānus, -ī n Roman emperor.
vesper, -is and **ī** m evening; supper; evening star; west; **~e, ~** in the evening.
vespera, -ae f evening.
vesperāscō, -ere vi to become evening, get late.
vespertīliō, -ōnis m bat.
vespertīnus adj evening (in cpds), in the evening; western.
vesperūgō, -inis f evening star.
Vesta, -ae f Roman goddess of the hearth.
Vestālis adj Vestal ♦ f virgin priestess of Vesta.
vester, -rī adj your, yours.
vestibulum, -ī nt forecourt, entrance.
vestīgium, -ī and **ī** nt footstep, footprint, track; (fig) trace, sign, vestige; (time) moment, instant; **ē ~iō** instantly.
vestīgō, -āre, -āvī, -ātum vt to track, trace, search for, discover.
vestīmentum, -ī nt clothes.
vestiō, -īre, -iī, -ītum vt to clothe, dress; to cover, adorn.
vestipica, -ae f wardrobe woman.
vestis, -is f clothes, dress; coverlet, tapestry, blanket; (snake) slough; **~em mūtāre** change one's clothes; go into mourning.
vestispica etc see **vestipica**.
vestītus, -ūs m clothes, dress; covering; **mūtāre ~um** go into mourning; **redīre ad suum ~um** come out of mourning.
Vesuvius, -ī m the volcano Vesuvius.
veterānus adj veteran.
veterāscō, -scere, -vī vi to grow old.
veterātor, -ōris m expert, old hand; sly fox.
veterātōriē adv see **veterātōrius**.
veterātōrius adj crafty.
veterīnus adj of burden ♦ f and ntpl beasts of burden.
veternōsus adj lethargic, drowsy.
veternus, -ī m lethargy, drowsiness.
vetitus ppp of **vetō** ♦ nt prohibition.
vetō, -āre, -uī, -itum vt to forbid, prohibit, oppose; (tribune) to protest.
vetulus adj little old, poor old.
vetus, -eris adj old, former ♦ mpl the ancients ♦ fpl the old shops (in the Forum) ♦ ntpl antiquity, tradition.
vetustās, -ātis f age, long standing; antiquity;

great age, future age.

vetustus *adj* old, ancient; old-fashioned.

vexāmen, -inis *nt* shaking.

vexātiō, -ōnis *f* shaking; trouble, distress.

vexātor, -ōris *m* troubler, opponent.

vexī *perf of* **vehō.**

vexillārius, -ī *and* **iī** *m* standard-bearer, ensign; (*pl*) special reserve of veterans.

vexillum, -ī *nt* standard, flag; company, troop; ~ **prōpōnere** hoist the signal for battle.

vexō, -āre, -āvī, -ātum *vt* to shake, toss, trouble, distress, injure, attack.

via, -ae *f* road, street, way; journey, march; passage; (*fig*) way, method, fashion; the right way; ~**ā** properly; **inter ~ās** on the way.

viālis *adj* of the highways.

viārius *adj* for the upkeep of roads.

viāticātus *adj* provided with travelling money.

viāticus *adj* for a journey ♦ *nt* travelling allowance; (*MIL*) prizemoney, savings.

viātor, -ōris *m* traveller; (*law*) summoner.

vībīx, -īcis *f* weal.

vibrō, -āre, -āvī, -ātum *vt* to wave, shake, brandish, hurl, launch ♦ *vi* to shake, quiver, vibrate; to shimmer, sparkle.

vīburnum, -ī *nt* wayfaring-tree *or* guelder rose.

vīcānus *adj* village (*in cpds*) ♦ *mpl* villagers.

Vica Pota, -ae, -ae *f* goddess of victory.

vicārius *adj* substituted ♦ *m* substitute, proxy; underslave.

vīcātim *adv* from street to street; in villages.

vice (*with gen*) on account of; like.

vicem in turn; (*with gen*) instead of; on account of; like; **tuam** ~ on your account.

vīcēnārius *adj* of twenty.

vīcēnī, -ōrum *adj* twenty each, in twenties.

vicēs *pl of* **vicis.**

vīcēsimānī, -ōrum *mpl* men of the twentieth legion.

vīcēsimārius *adj* derived from the 5 per cent tax.

vīcēsimus *adj* twentieth ♦ *f* a 5 per cent tax.

vīcī *perf of* **vincō.**

vicia, -ae *f* vetch.

viciēns *and* **ēs** *adv* twenty times.

vīcīnālis *adj* neighbouring.

vīcīnia, -ae *f* neighbourhood, nearness.

vīcīnitās, -ātis *f* neighbourhood, nearness.

vīcīnus *adj* neighbouring, nearby; similar, kindred ♦ *m/f* neighbour ♦ *nt* neighbourhood.

vicis *gen* (*acc* **-em**, *abl* **-e**) *f* interchange, alternation, succession; recompense, retaliation; fortune, changing conditions; duty, function, place; **in ~em** in turn, mutually.

vicissim *adv* in turn, again.

vicissitūdō, -inis *f* interchange, alternation.

victima, -ae *f* victim, sacrifice.

victimārius, -ī *and* **iī** *m* assistant at sacrifices.

victitō, -āre *vi* to live, subsist.

victor, -ōris *m* conqueror, victor, winner ♦ *adj*

victorious.

victōria, -ae *f* victory.

victōriātus, -ūs *m* silver coin stamped with Victory.

Victōriola, -ae *f* little statue of Victory.

victrīx, -īcis *f* conqueror ♦ *adj* victorious.

victus *ppp of* **vincō.**

vīctus, -ūs *m* sustenance, livelihood; way of life.

vīculus, -ī *m* hamlet.

vīcus, -ī *m* (*city*) quarter, street; (*country*) village, estate.

vidēlicet *adv* clearly, evidently; (*ironical*) of course; (*explaining*) namely.

videō, -ēre, vīdī, vīsum *vt* to see, look at; (*mind*) to observe, be aware, know; to consider, think over; to see to, look out for; to live to see; (*pass*) to seem, appear; to seem right, be thought proper; **mē ~ē** rely on me; **vīderit** let him see to it; **mihi ~eor esse** I think I am; **sī (tibi) vidētur** if you like.

viduāta *adj* widowed.

viduitās, -ātis *f* bereavement, want; widowhood.

vīdulus, -ī *m* trunk, box.

viduō, -āre *vt* to bereave.

viduus *adj* bereft, bereaved; unmarried; (*with abl*) without ♦ *f* widow; spinster.

Vienna, -ae *f* town in Gaul on the Rhone.

viētus *adj* shrivelled.

vigeō, -ēre, -uī *vi* to thrive, flourish.

vigēscō, -ere *vi* to begin to flourish, become lively.

vīgēsimus *etc see* **vīcēsimus.**

vigil, -is *adj* awake, watching, alert ♦ *m* watchman, sentinel; (*pl*) the watch, police.

vigilāns, -antis *pres p of* **vigilō** ♦ *adj* watchful.

vigilanter *adv* vigilantly.

vigilantia, -ae *f* wakefulness; vigilance.

vigilāx, -ācis *adj* watchful.

vigilia, -ae *f* lying awake, sleeplessness; keeping watch, guard; a watch, the watch, sentries; vigil; vigilance.

vigilō, -āre, -āvī, -ātum *vi* to remain awake; to keep watch; to be vigilant ♦ *vt* to spend awake, make while awake at night.

vīgintī *num* twenty.

vīgintīvirātus, -ūs *m* membership of a board of twenty.

vīgintīvirī, -ōrum *mpl* a board or commission of twenty men.

vigor, -ōris *m* energy, vigour.

vīlica, -ae *f* wife of a steward.

vīlicō, -āre *vi* to be an overseer.

vīlicus, -ī *m* overseer, manager of an estate, steward.

vīlis *adj* cheap; worthless, poor, mean, common.

vīlitās, -ātis *f* cheapness, low price; worthlessness.

vīliter *adv* cheaply.

vīlla, -ae *f* country house, villa.

vīllic- *etc see* **vīlic-.**

villōsus adj hairy, shaggy.
vīllula, -ae f small villa.
vīllum, -ī nt a drop of wine.
villus, -ī m hair, fleece; (*cloth*) nap.
vīmen, -inis nt osier; basket.
vīmentum, -ī nt osier.
Vīminālis adj Viminal (*hill of Rome*).
vīmineus adj of osiers, wicker.
vīnāceus adj grape (*in cpds*).
Vīnālia, -ium ntpl Wine festival.
vīnārius adj of wine, wine (*in cpds*) ♦ m vintner
  ♦ nt wine flask.
vincibilis adj easily won.
vinciō, -cīre, -xī, -ctum vt to bind, fetter; to
  encircle; (*fig*) to confine, restrain, envelop,
  attach.
vinclum nt see **vinculum**.
vincō, -ere, vīcī, victum vt to conquer,
  defeat, subdue; to win, prevail, be
  successful; (*fig*) to surpass, excel; (*argument*)
  to convince, refute, prove conclusively;
  (*life*) to outlive.
vinctus ppp of **vinciō**.
vinculum, -ī nt bond, fetter, chain; pl) prison.
vīndēmia, -ae f vintage grape harvest.
vīndēmiātor, -ōris m vintager.
vīndēmiola, -ae f small vintage.
Vīndēmitor, -ōris m the Vintager (*a star in
  Virgo*).
vindex, -icis m champion, protector;
  liberator; avenger ♦ adj avenging.
vindicātiō, -ōnis f punishment of offences.
vindiciae, -ārum fpl legal claim; ~ās ab
  lībertāte in servitūtem dare condemn a free
  person to slavery.
vindicō, -āre, -āvī, -ātum vt to lay claim to;
  to claim, appropriate; to liberate, protect,
  champion; to avenge, punish; **in lībertātem ~**
  emancipate.
vindicta, -ae f rod used in manumitting a
  slave; defence, deliverance; revenge,
  punishment.
vīnea, -ae f vineyard; vine; (*MIL*) penthouse
  (for besiegers).
vīnētum, -ī nt vineyard.
vīnitor, -ōris m vine-dresser.
vinnulus adj delightful.
vīnolentia, -ae f wine drinking.
vīnolentus adj drunk.
vīnōsus adj fond of wine, drunken.
vīnum, -ī nt wine.
vinxī perf of **vinciō**.
viola, -ae f violet; stock.
violābilis adj vulnerable.
violāceus adj violet.
violārium, -ī and **iī** nt violet bed.
violārius, -ī and **iī** m dyer of violet.
violātiō, -ōnis f desecration.
violātor, -ōris m violator, desecrator.
violēns, -entis adj raging, vehement.

violenter adv violently furiously.
violentia, -ae f violence, impetuosity.
violentus adj violent, impetuous, boisterous.
violō, -āre, -āvī, -ātum vt to do violence to,
  outrage, violate; (*agreement*) to break.
vīpera, -ae f viper, adder, snake.
vīpereus adj snake's, serpent's.
vīperīnus adj snake's, serpent's.
vir, virī m man; grown man; brave man, hero;
  husband; (*MIL*) footsoldier.
virāgō, -inis f heroine, warrior maid.
virecta, -ōrum ntpl grassy sward.
vireō, -ēre, -uī vi to be green; (*fig*) to be fresh,
  flourish.
virēs pl of **vīs**.
virēscō, -ere vi to grow green.
virga, -ae f twig; graft; rod, staff, walking
  stick, wand; (*colour*) stripe.
virgātor, -ōris m flogger.
virgātus adj made of osiers; striped.
virgētum, -ī nt thicket of osiers.
virgeus adj of brushwood.
virgidēmia, -ae f crop of flogging.
virginālis adj maidenly, of maids.
virginārius adj of maids.
virgineus adj maidenly, virgin, of virgins.
virginitās, -ātis f maidenhood.
virgō, -inis f maid, virgin; young woman, girl;
  constellation Virgo; a Roman aqueduct.
virgula, -ae f wand.
virgulta, -ōrum ntpl thicket, shrubbery;
  cuttings, slips.
virguncula, -ae f little girl.
viridāns, -antis adj green.
viridārium, -ī and **iī** nt plantation, garden.
viridis adj green; fresh, young, youthful ♦ ntpl
  greenery.
viriditās, -ātis f verdure, greenness;
  freshness.
viridor, -ārī vi to become green.
virīlis adj male, masculine; man's, adult;
  manly, brave, bold; ~ **pars** one's individual
  part or duty; **prō ~ī parte, portiōne** to the best
  of one's ability.
virīlitās, -ātis f manhood.
virīliter adv manfully.
virītim adv individually, separately.
vīrōsus adj slimy; rank.
virtūs, -ūtis f manhood, full powers; strength,
  courage, ability, worth; (*MIL*) valour,
  prowess, heroism; (*moral*) virtue; (*things*)
  excellence, worth.
vīrus, -ī nt slime; poison; offensive smell; salt
  taste.
vīs (*acc* **vim**, *abl* **vī**, *pl* **vīrēs**) f power, force,
  strength; violence, assault; quantity,
  amount; (*mind*) energy, vigour; (*word*)
  meaning, import; (*pl*) strength; (*MIL*) troops;
  per vim forcibly; **dē vī damnārī** be convicted

of assault; **prō vīribus** with all one's might.

vīs *2nd pers of* **volō.**

viscātus *adj* limed.

viscerātiō, -ōnis *f* public distribution of meat.

viscō, -āre *vt* to make sticky.

viscum, -ī *nt* mistletoe; bird lime.

viscus, -eris (*usu pl* **-era, -erum**) *nt* internal organs; flesh; womb, child; (*fig*) heart, bowels.

vīsendus *adj* worth seeing.

vīsiō, -ōnis *f* apparition; idea.

vīsitō, -āre *vt* to see often; to visit.

vīsō, -ere, -ī, -um *vt* to look at, survey; to see to; to go and see, visit.

Visurgis, -is *m* river Weser.

vīsus *ppp of* **videō** ♦ *nt* vision.

vīsus, -ūs *m* sight, the faculty of seeing; a sight, vision.

vīta, -ae *f* life, livelihood; way of life; career, biography.

vītābilis *adj* undesirable.

vītābundus *adj* avoiding, taking evasive action.

vītālis *adj* of life, vital ♦ *nt* subsistence ♦ *ntpl* vitals.

vītāliter *adv* with life.

vītātiō, -ōnis *f* avoidance.

Vitellius, -ī *m* Roman emperor in AD 69.

Vitellius, -iānus *adj see n.*

vitellus, -ī *m* little calf; (*egg*) yolk.

vīteus *adj* of the vine.

vīticula, -ae *f* little vine.

vītigenus *adj* produced from the vine.

vitilēna, -ae *f* procuress.

vitiō, -āre, -āvī, -ātum *vt* to spoil, corrupt, violate; to falsify.

vitiōsē *adv* badly, defectively.

vitiōsitās, -ātis *f* vice.

vitiōsus *adj* faulty, corrupt; wicked, depraved; ~ **cōnsul** *a consul whose election had a religious flaw in it.*

vītis, -is *f* vine; vine branch; centurion's staff, centurionship.

vītisator, -ōris *m* vine planter.

vitium, -ī *and* **iī** *nt* fault, flaw, defect; (*moral*) failing, offence, vice; (*religion*) flaw in the auspices.

vītō, -āre, -āvī, -ātum *vt* to avoid, evade, shun.

vītor, -ōris *m* basket maker, cooper.

vitreus *adj* of glass; glassy ♦ *ntpl* glassware.

vītricus, -ī *m* stepfather.

vitrum, -ī *nt* glass; woad.

vitta, -ae *f* headband, sacrificial fillet.

vittātus *adj* wearing a fillet.

vitula, -ae *f* (*of cow*) calf.

vitulīnus *adj* of veal ♦ *f* veal.

vītulor, -ārī *vi* to hold a celebration.

vitulus, -ī *m* calf; foal; ~ **marīnus** seal.

vituperābilis *adj* blameworthy.

vituperātiō, -ōnis *f* blame, censure; scandalous conduct.

vituperātor, -ōris *m* critic.

vituperō, -āre *vt* to find fault with, disparage; (*omen*) to spoil.

vīvārium, -ī *and* **iī** *nt* fishpond, game preserve.

vīvātus *adj* animated.

vīvāx, -ācis *adj* long-lived; lasting; (*sulphur*) inflammable.

vīvēscō, -ere *vi* to grow, become active.

vīvidus *adj* full of life; (*art*) true to life, vivid; (*mind*) lively.

vīvirādīx, -īcis *f* a rooted cutting, layer.

vīvīscō *etc see* **vīvēscō.**

vīvō, -vere, -xī, -ctum *vi* to live, be alive; to enjoy life; (*fame*) to last, be remembered; (*with abl*) to live on; ~**ve** farewell!; ~**xērunt** they are dead.

vīvus *adj* alive, living; (*light*) burning; (*rock*) natural; (*water*) running; ~**ō videntīque** before his very eyes; **mē** ~**ō** as long as I live, in my lifetime; **ad** ~**um resecāre** cut to the quick; **dē** ~**ō dētrahere** take out of capital.

vix *adv* with difficulty, hardly, scarcely.

vixdum *adv* hardly, as yet.

vīxī *perf of* **vīvō.**

vocābulum, -ī *nt* name, designation; (*GRAM*) noun.

vōcālis *adj* speaking, singing, tuneful ♦ *f* vowel.

vocāmen, -inis *nt* name.

vocātiō, -ōnis *f* invitation; (*law*) summons.

vocātus, -ūs *m* summons, call.

vōciferātiō, -ōnis *f* loud cry, outcry.

vōciferor, -ārī *vt* to cry out loud, shout.

vocitō, -āre, -āvī, -ātum *vt* to usually call; to shout.

vocīvus *etc see* **vacīvus.**

vocō, -āre, -āvī, -ātum *vt* to call, summon; to call, name; (*gods*) to call upon; (*guest*) to invite; (*MIL*) to challenge; (*fig*) to bring (*into some condition or plight*); ~ **dē** name after; ~**in dubium** ~ call in question; **in iūdicium** ~ call to account.

vōcula, -ae *f* weak voice; soft tone; gossip.

volaema *ntpl* kind of large pear.

Volaterrae, -ārum *fpl* old Etruscan town (*now* Volterra).

Volaterrānus *adj see n.*

volāticus *adj* winged; fleeting, inconstant.

volātilis *adj* winged; swift; fleeting.

volātus, -ūs *m* flight.

Volcānius *adj see n.*

Volcānus, -ī *m* Vulcan (*god of fire*); fire.

volēns, -entis *pres p of* **volō** ♦ *adj* willing, glad, favourable; **mihi** ~**entī est** it is acceptable to me.

volg- *etc see* **vulg-.**

volitō, -āre *vi* to fly about, flutter; to hurry, move quickly; (*fig*) to hover, soar; to get excited.

voln- *etc see* **vuln-.**

volō, -āre, -āvī, -ātum *vi* to fly; to speed.

volō, velle, voluī *vt* to wish, want; to be

willing; to will, purpose, determine; (*opinion*) to hold, maintain; (*word, action*) to mean; ~ **dīcere** I mean; **bene** ~ like; **male** ~ dislike; **ōrātum tē** ~ I beg you; **paucīs tē** ~ a word with you!; **numquid vīs?** (*before leaving*) is there anything else?; **quid sibi vult? what** does he mean?; **what is he driving at?**; **velim faciās** please do it; **vellem fēcissēs** I wish you had done it.

volōnēs, -um *mpl* volunteers.

volpēs *etc see* **vulpēs.**

Volscī, -ōrum *mpl people in S. Latium.*

Volscus *adj* Volscian.

volsella, -ae *f* tweezers.

volsus *ppp of* **vellō.**

volt, voltis *older forms of* **vult, vultis.**

Voltumna, -ae *f patron goddess of Etruria.*

voltus *etc see* **vultus.**

volūbilis *adj* spinning, revolving; (*fortune*) fickle; (*speech*) fluent.

volubilitās, -ātis *f* whirling motion; roundness; fluency; inconstancy.

volūbiliter *adv* fluently.

volucer, -ris *adj* winged; flying, swift; fleeting.

volucris, -is *f* bird; insect.

volūmen, -inis *nt* roll, book; coil, eddy, fold.

voluntārius *adj* voluntary ♦ *mpl* volunteers.

voluntās, -ātis *f* will, wish, inclination; attitude, goodwill; last will, testament; **suā ~āte** of one's own accord; **ad ~ātem** with the consent (of).

volup *adv* agreeably, to one's satisfaction.

voluptābilis *adj* agreeable.

voluptās, -ātis *f* pleasure, enjoyment; (*pl*) entertainments, sports.

voluptuārius *adj* pleasureable, agreeable; voluptuous.

volūtābrum, -ī *nt* wallowing place.

volūtātiō, -ōnis *f* wallowing.

volūtō, -āre *vt* to roll about, turn over; (*mind*) to occupy, engross; (*thought*) to ponder, think over; (*pass*) to wallow, flounder.

volūtus *ppp of* **volvō.**

volva, -ae *f* womb; (*dish*) sow's womb.

volvō, -vere, -vī, -ūtum *vt* to roll, turn round; to roll along; (*air*) to breathe; (*book*) to open; (*circle*) to form; (*thought*) to ponder, reflect on; (*time*) to roll on; (*trouble*) to undergo; (*pass*) to roll, revolve ♦ *vi* to revolve, elapse.

vōmer, -eris *m* ploughshare.

vomica, -ae *f* sore, ulcer, abscess, boil.

vōmis *etc see* **vōmer.**

vomitiō, -ōnis *f* vomiting.

vomitus, -ūs *m* vomiting, vomit.

vomō, -ere, -uī, -itum *vt* to vomit, throw up; to emit, discharge.

vorāgō, -inis *f* abyss, chasm, depth.

vorāx, -ācis *adj* greedy, ravenous; consuming.

vorō, -āre, -āvī, -ātum *vt* to swallow, devour; (*sea*) to swallow up; (*reading*) to devour.

vors-, vort- *etc see* **vers-, vert-** *etc.*

vōs *pron* you.

Vosegus, -ī *m* Vosges mountains.

voster *etc see* **vester.**

vōtīvus *adj* votive, promised in a vow.

votō *etc see* **vetō.**

vōtum, -ī *nt* vow, prayer; votive offering; wish, longing; **~ī damnārī** have one's prayer granted.

vōtus *ppp of* **voveō.**

voveō, -ēre, vōvī, vōtum *vt* to vow, promise solemnly; to dedicate; to wish.

vōx, vōcis *f* voice; sound, cry, call; word, saying, expression; accent; **unā vōce** unanimously.

Vulcānus *see* **Volcānus.**

vulgāris *adj* common, general.

vulgāriter *adv* in the common fashion.

vulgātor, -ōris *m* betrayer.

vulgātus *adj* common; generally known, notorious.

vulgivagus *adj* roving; inconstant.

vulgō *adv* publicly, commonly, usually, everywhere.

vulgō, -āre, -āvī, -ātum *vt* to make common, spread; to publish, divulge, broadcast; to prostitute; to level down.

vulgus, -ī *nt* (*occ m*) the mass of the people, the public; crowd, herd; rabble, populace.

vulnerātiō, -ōnis *f* wounding, injury.

vulnerō, -āre, -āvī, -ātum *vt* to wound, hurt; to damage.

vulnificus *adj* wounding, dangerous.

vulnus, -eris *nt* wound, injury; (*things*) damage, hole; (*fig*) blow, misfortune, pain.

vulpēcula, -ae *f* little fox.

vulpēs, -is *f* fox; (*fig*) cunning.

vulsī *perf of* **vellō.**

vulsus *ppp of* **vellō.**

vulticulus, -ī *m* a mere look (from).

vultum *etc see* **vultus.**

vultuōsus *adj* affected.

vultur, -is *m* vulture.

vulturius, -ī and iī *m* vulture, bird of prey; (*dice*) an unlucky throw.

Vulturnus, -ī *m* river in Campania.

vultus, -ūs *m* look, expression (*esp* in the eyes); face; (*things*) appearance.

vulva *etc see* **volva.**

Noun declensions and verb conjugations are shown on pp xiii to xxv. The present infinitive ending of a verb shows to which conjugation it belongs: **-āre** = 1st; **-ēre** = 2nd; **-ere** = 3rd and **-īre** = 4th. Irregular verbs are shown on p xxvi

X, x

Xanthippē, -ēs f wife of Socrates.
Xanthus, -ī m river of Troy (*identified with Scamander*); *river of Lycia.*
xenium, -ī and **iī** nt present.

Xenocratēs, -is m disciple of Plato.
Xenophanēs, -is m early Greek philosopher.
Xenophōn, -ontis m famous Greek historian.
Xenophontēus adj see n.
xērampelinae, -ārum fpl dark-coloured clothes.
Xerxēs, -is m Persian king defeated at Salamis.
xiphiās, -ae m swordfish.
xystum, -ī nt, **xystus, -ī** m open colonnade, walk, avenue.

Z, z

Zacynthius adj see n.
Zacynthus (-os), -ī f island off W. Greece (*now* Zante).
Zama, -ae f town in Numidia (*where Scipio defeated Hannibal*).
Zamēnsis adj see n.
zāmia, -ae f harm.
Zanclaeus and **ēius** adj see n.
Zanclē, -ēs f old name of Messana.
zēlotypus adj jealous.

Zēnō and **ōn, -ōnis** m founder of Stoicism; a philosopher of Elea; an Epicurean teacher of Cicero.
Zephyrītis, -idis f Arsinoe (*queen of Egypt*).
Zephyrus, -ī m west wind, zephyr; wind.
Zēthus, -ī m brother of Amphion.
Zeuxis, -is and **idis** m famous Greek painter.
zmaragdus etc see **smaragdus**.
Zmyrna etc see **Smyrna**.
zōdiacus, -ī m zodiac.
zōna, -ae f belt, girdle; (GEOG) zone; (ASTRO) Orion's Belt.
zōnārius adj of belts; **sector** ~ cutpurse ♦ m belt maker.
zōnula, -ae f little belt.
zōthēca, -ae f private room.
zōthēcula, -ae f cubicle.

ROMAN LIFE AND CULTURE

KEY EVENTS IN ROMAN HISTORY

B.C.

753	Foundation of Rome. Romulus became first king.
600-510	Rome ruled by Etruscan kings.
510	Expulsion of Tarquin and republic established.
507	Consecration of Temple of Jupiter on Capitol.
451	Code of Twelve Tables laid basis of Roman law.
390	Gauls sacked Rome.
367	Lex Liciniae Sextiae; plebeians allowed to be consul.
354	Treaty with Samnites.
343-341	First Samnite war; Romans occupied northern Campania.
340-338	Latin War; separate treaties made with Latins.
327-304	Second Samnite war; Rome increased influence in southern Italy.
321	Samnites defeated Romans at Caudine Forks; truce.
312	Appian Way, first Roman road, built.
298-290	Third Samnite war; Rome now all-powerful in southern Italy.
287	Hortensian Law; People's Assembly became a law-making body.
282-272	Wars with Tarentum and King Pyrrhus of Epirus.
270	Whole peninsula under Roman power.
264-241	First Punic war; Rome defended Greek cities in Sicily.
260	Fleet built; first naval victory at Mylae against Carthaginians.
241	Roman victory over Carthage secured Sicily, source of corn supply.
226	River Ebro treaty; Carthage should not cross into northern Spain.
218-201	Second Punic war against Hannibal.
216	Rome defeated at Battle of Cannae.
214-205	First Macedonian war with Philip V.
202	Scipio defeated Hannibal at Zama.
201	Peace concluded with Carthage; Rome now controlled the western Mediterranean.
200-196	Second Macedonian war; freedom of Greece proclaimed.
172-168	Third Macedonian war; Perseus crushed at Pydna.
148	Macedonia became a Roman province.
146	Carthage destroyed; Corinth destroyed.
133	Tiberius Gracchus became tribune; his assassination caused class conflict.
123-122	Gaius Gracchus carried out political/economic reforms.
121	Gaius was killed.
111-105	Marius and Sulla conducted war against Jugurtha of Numidia.
91-89	Social war between Rome and allies.
89-85	War with Mithridates VI of Pontus.
83-82	Civil war between Sulla and Marius; Sulla captured Rome.
81-79	Sulla, dictator, restored constitution, introduced reforms.
78	Death of Sulla.

77-72	Pompey fought Sertorius in Spain.
73-71	Spartacus' slave revolt.
70	Pompey and Crassus joint consuls; tribunes restored.
67	End of war against Mithridates; pirates controlled by Pompey.
63	Cicero suppressed Catiline's conspiracy.
60	First Triumvirate (Caesar, Pompey, Crassus) was formed.
58-51	Caesar conquered Gaul.
53	Battle of Carrhae; Rome defeated by Parthians; Crassus killed.
49	Caesar crossed Rubicon; civil war with Pompey began.
48	Pompey defeated by Caesar at Pharsalus; Caesar became dictator.
44	Caesar assassinated; Antony sought revenge against conspirators.
43	Second Triumvirate (Antony, Octavian, Lepidus).
42	Battle of Philippi; Triumvirate defeated Brutus and Cassius.
41-40	Antony and Octavian divided territory.
33-32	Rupture between Antony and Octavian.
31	Battle of Actium; Octavian defeated Antony and Cleopatra at sea.
27	Octavian returned powers to Senate; received name Augustus.
18	Julian laws promoted morality, condemned adultery, regulated divorce.
12	Augustus became Pontifex Maximus, head of state religion.
2	Augustus became 'pater patriae', father of his country; apex of his power.

A.D.

4	Tiberius adopted as Augustus' heir.
6	Annexation of Judaea.
9	Varus' three legions destroyed in Germany.
14	Death of Augustus.
14-37	Tiberius emperor; efficient administrator but unpopular.
14-16	Germanicus' successful campaign in Germany.
19	Germanicus died mysteriously; funeral at Antioch.
21-22	Sefanus organized Praetorian Guard.
26-31	Sefanus powerful in Rome; executed in 31.
37-41	Caligula emperor; cruel and tyrannical, was murdered by a tribune.
41-54	Claudius emperor; conquered Britain; showed political judgement.
57-68	Nero emperor; great fire (64); Christians persecuted.
68-69	Year of four emperors - Galba, Otho, Vitellius, Vespasian.
69-79	Vespasian began Flavian dynasty. Colosseum built.
70	Titus, Vespasian's son, captured Jerusalem, destroyed the Temple.
79-81	Titus emperor. Vesuvius erupted (79), Pompeii destroyed.
81-96	Domitian emperor. Border built in Germany; period ended in terror.
96-98	Nerva emperor after Domitian's assassination.
98-117	Trajan emperor - conqueror of Dacia and Parthian empire.
117-138	Hadrian, cultured traveller, soldier and administrator of empire.
122	Hadrian's Wall built between Solway and Tyne.
138-161	Antoninus Pius emperor; orderly, peaceful rule.
141-143	Antonine's Wall built between Forth and Clyde.
161-180	Marcus Aurelius emperor; Commodus, his son, shared power (177-180).

162	War with Parthia.
175-180	War against Germans on the Danube.
180-192	Commodus emperor.
193-211	Septimius Severus became emperor after crisis; died in Britain. Authorized special benefits for army.
211-217	Deterioration under criminal rule of Caracalla.
212	All free men of the empire became citizens.
284-305	Diocletian and Maximian co-emperors, empire divided into 12 dioceses. Prices imposed throughout empire.
303	Christians persecuted by Diocletian.
312	Constantine's victory at Milvian Bridge gave him Rome.
313	Edict of Milan ended persecution of Christians.
324	Constantine became sole emperor.
325	Council of Nicaea made Christianity religion of the empire.
330	Constantine made Byzantium seat of government; renamed it Constantinople.
337	Constantine died a Christian, trying to reorganize the empire.
379-395	Emperor Theodosius kept empire formally intact.
410	Alaric and Goths captured and destroyed Rome.

GOVERNMENT AND ADMINISTRATION

Republic

There was no written constitution. The Republic evolved from the struggle between the Senate and the People - Senatus Populusque Romanus - SPQR.

The Senate (Senatus)
This was the governing body, largely in the hands of the nobles (nobiles) or patricians (patricii).

- it prepared proposals to bring before the people
- it passed decrees (senatus consulta)
- it dealt with emergencies
- it controlled finances and building contracts
- it appointed magistrates to provinces
- it directed foreign relations
- it supervised state religion

The People (Populus)
The resolutions of the people, plebiscita, could have the force of law, but the Senate was allowed greater control. There were four assemblies:

- comitia curiata — formal duties
- comitia centuriata — elected magistrates
- comitia tributa — elected lesser magistrates
- concilium plebis — passed plebiscita

The Knights (Equites)
A third element, or class, emerged (originally from Rome's cavalry) to engage in trade and finance. These businessmen acquired more political influence and became wealthy. By the time of Cicero, they could enter the Senate. Cicero tried to reconcile the three classes, **senatores**, **equites** and **plebs** by his **concordia ordinum** (harmony of the classes).

Magistrates (Magistratus)
A magistrate was an official elected annually by the people. Offices were held in a strict order - **cursus honorum**. After ten years' military service, a young man could begin on the lowest rung of the ladder as follows:

Age	Office	Number	Duties
28	**Quaestor**	(8)	• administered finance maintained public records
30	**Aedile**	(4)	• maintained roads, water supply organized games and festivals
33(39)	**Praetor**	(6)	• civil judge could introduce laws
39(43)	**Consul**	(2)	• commanded army conducted elections presided over Senate carried out its decrees

Other magistrates:

Tribune	(10)	• defended plebs' rights
(tribunus plebis)		had right of veto
Censor	(2)	• conducted census (every 5 years)
		conducted purification
		revised roll of senators
Dictator	(1)	• ruled in crisis (maximum of 6 months)
		conducted military and domestic
		matters

Imperium (supreme power) was held by consuls and praetors and dictators.
Potestas (power to enforce laws) was held by all magistrates.
Lictores (lictors *or* officials) carried **fasces** (bundles of rods) in front of consuls, praetors and dictators as a sign of their authority.

ORGANIZATION OF THE ARMY

Empire

At the time of Augustus there were 28 **legions** (later 25), each legion consisting of approximately 5000 infantrymen, trained for close combat. It was organized as follows:

Legio	Legion	5000 men
10 Cohortes	Cohorts	500 men
6 Centuriae	Centuries	80/100 men

Officers

Legatus	legionary commander
6 **Tribuni Militum**	tribunes
60 **Centuriones**	centurions (from ranks), in charge of centuries

Recruitment	Citizens
Length of service	20/25 years
Duties	Offensive in important battles, repelling invasion *etc*
Pay	250/300 denarii per day
On retirement	Land or cash bounty

Additional **auxiliary forces** were recruited to help the legions. Particularly necessary were cavalry, drawn from all parts of the Empire, slingers, bowmen, etc. Infantrymen were often recruited locally and formed cohorts of about 500 men.

Auxilia	Auxiliaries	
Ala	Cavalry unit	500 men approx.
16 Turmae	turmae	32 men
Cohors	Infantry unit	500 men

Officers	
Decurio	Decurion (cavalry officer)
Recruitment	Non-citizens
Length of service	25 years
Duties	Frontier skirmishes, occupation, assisting legions

| Pay | 100 denarii per day |
| On retirement | Citizenship for self/family |

The **Praetorian Guard** was the Emperor's special bodyguard. Three cohorts were based in Rome, six more in nearby towns.

| **Praetorium** | Praetorian Guard | 4500 men |
| **9 Cohortes** | cohorts | 500 men |

Officers
| **2 Praefecti Praetorio** | praetorian prefects |

Recruitment	Citizens (Italy)
Length of service	16 years
Duties	Preserving emperor's power and safety
Pay	1000 denarii per day
On retirement	5000 denarii

FAMILY TREE

tritavus m **tritavia**
(great-great-great-great-grandfather) | (great-great-great-great-grandmother)

atavus m **atavia**
(great-great-great-grandfather) | (great-great-great-grandmother)

abavus m **abavia**
(great-great-grandfather) | (great-great-grandmother)

proavus m **proavia**
(great-grandfather) | (great-grandmother)

avus m **avia**
(grandfather) | (grandmother)

pater m **māter**
(father) | (mother)

noverca m **pater** m **māter** m **vītricus**
(stepmother) | (father) | (mother) | (stepfather)

Father's side (paternal):

patruus māximus	(great-great-granduncle)
patruus māior	(great-granduncle)
patruus māgnus	(grand-uncle)
patruus	(uncle)
amita māxima	(great-great-grandaunt)
amita māior	(great-grandaunt)
amita māgna	(grand-aunt)
amita	(aunt)

Mother's side (maternal):

avunculus māximus	(great-great-granduncle)
avunculus māior	(great-granduncle)
avunculus māgnus	(grand-uncle)
avunculus	(uncle)
mātertera māxima	(great-great-grandaunt)
mātertera māior	(great-grandaunt)
mātertera māgna	(grand-aunt)
mātertera	(aunt)

In-laws:

prōsocer m **prōsocrus**
(grandfather-in-law) | (grandmother-in-law)

socer m **socrus**
(father-in-law) | (mother-in-law)

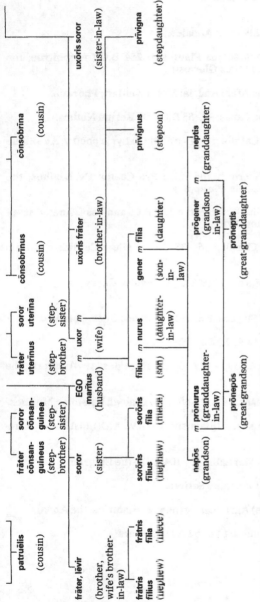

Note: This is the Family Tree of the man designated **EGO** in the fourth generation from the end.

MAJOR WRITERS

ENNIUS (Quintus Ennius: b 239 B.C.) **Annales.**

PLAUTUS (Titus Maccus *or* Maccius Plautus: b 254 B.C.) **Amphitruo**; the **Aulularia**; the **Menaechmi** and **Miles Gloriosus.**

TERENCE (Publius Terentius Afer) **Andria; Mother-in-law; Phormio.**

LUCRETIUS (Titus Lucretius Carus: 94 - 55 B.C.) **De Rerum Natura.**

CATULLUS (Gaius Valerius Catullus: c.84 - c.54 B.C.) Lyric poetry; **Ave atque vale.**

CICERO (Marcus Tullius Cicero: b 106 B.C.) **Pro Caelio; De Legibus;** the **Tusculan Disputations; De Officiis; Philippics.**

JULIUS CAESAR (Gaius Iulius Caesar: b c.102 B.C. and assassinated in 44 B.C.) **Bellum Gallicum; Bellum Civile.**

SALLUST (Gaius Sallustius Crispus: 86 - 35 B.C.) **Bellum Catilinae; Bellum Iugurthinum.**

VIRGIL (Publius Vergilius Maro: 70 - 19 B.C.) **Eclogues; Georgics;** the **Aeneid.**

HORACE (Quintus Horatius Flaccus: b 65 A.D.) **Satires; Odes; Epistles.**

LIVY (Titus Livius: 59 B.C. - 17 A.D.) **Ab Urbe Condita.**

OVID (Publius Ovidius Naso: 43 B.C. - 17 A.D.) the **Heroides, Ars Amatoria;** the **Metamorphoses; Tristia.**

SENECA (Lucius Annaeus Seneca: 4 B.C. - 65 A.D.) **Dialogi; Epistolae Morales.**

QUINTILIAN (Marcus Fabius Quintilianus: c.35 - c.95 A.D.) **Institutio Oratorio.**

MARTIAL (Marcus Valerius Martialis: 40 - 104 A.D.) the **Epigrams.**

JUVENAL (Decimus Iunius Iuvenalis) **Satires.**

TACITUS (Cornelius Tacitus) **Agricola; Germania; Histories;** the **Annals.**

PLINY (Gaius Plinius Secundus: b 61 *or* 62 A.D.) **Letters.**

GEOGRAPHICAL NAMES

The following list of geographical names and their adjectives includes both ancient and medieval Latin forms. The former are printed in Roman type, the latter in Italics. Medieval place names tend to have a variety of Latin forms, but only one has been selected in each case; occasionally both the ancient and the medieval forms have been given. Modern names which have a ready-made Latin form (e.g. America) have been omitted, and many names not included in this selection can be easily Latinized on the analogy of those which do appear.

Aachen	Aquīsgrānum nt	adj Aquīsgrānēnsis
Aberdeen	Aberdōnia f	adj Aberdōnēnsis
Abergavenny	Gobannium nt	
Aberystwith	Aberīstyvium nt	
Adige, River	Athesis m	
Adriatic	Mare superum nt	adj Hadriāticus
Aegean	Mare Aegaeum nt	adj Aegaeus
Afghanistan	Ariāna f	adj Ariānus
Africa	Libya f,	adj Libycus,
	Africa f	Africānus
Agrigento	Agrigentum nt	adj Agrigentīnus
Aisne, River	Axona m	
Aix-en-Provence	Aquae Sextiae fpl	adj Aquēnsis
Aix-la-Chapelle	Aquīsgrānum nt	adj Aquisgrānēnsis
Aix-Les-Bains	Aquae Grātiānae fpl	
Ajaccio	Adiacium nt	adj Adiacēnsis
Aldborough	Isurium (nt)	
	Brigantum	
Alexandria	Alexandrēa,	
	Alexandrīa f	adj Alexandrīnus
Algiers	Algerium nt	adj Algerīnus
Alps	Alpēs fpl	adj Alpīnus
Alsace	Alsatia f	
Amalfi	Amalphis f	adj Amalphītānus
Ambleside	Galava f	
Amiens	Ambiānum nt	adj Ambiānēnsis
Amsterdam	Amstelodamum nt	adj Amstelodamēnsis
Ancaster	Causennae fpl	
Angers	Andegāvum nt	adj Andegāvēnsis
Anglesey	Mona f	
Aniene, River	Aniō m	adj Aniēnus
Anjou	Andegāvēnsis ager m	
Ankara	Ancyra f	adj Ancyrānus
Antibes	Antipolis f	adj Antipolītānus
Antioch	Antiochīa f	adj Antiochēnus
Antwerp	Antwerpium nt	adj Antwerpiēnsis
Anzio	Antium nt	adj Antiās, Antiānus
Aosta	Augusta Praetōria f	
Apennines	Mōns Apennīnus m	

Aragon	Aragōnia f	
Archangel	Archangelopolis f	
Ardennes	Arduenna f	
Arezzo	Ārētium nt	adj Ārētīnus
Argenteuil	Argentōlium nt	
Argyll	Argadia f	
Arles	Arelās f	adj Arelātēnsis
Armagh	Armācha f	adj Armāchānus
Arno, River	Arnus m	adj Arniēnsis
Arras	Atrebatēs mpl	adj Atrebatēnsis
Artois	Atrebatēs mpl	
Assisi	Assīsium nt	adj Assīsiēnsis
Athens	Athēnae fpl	adj Athēniēnsis
Atlantic	Mare Atlanticum nt	
Augsburg	Augusta (f) Vindelicōrum	adj Augustānus
Autun	Augustodūnum nt	adj Augustodūnēnsis
Auvergne	Arvernī mpl	adj Arvernus
Aventine	Aventīnus m	
Avignon	Aveniō f	adj Aveniōnēnsis
Avon, River	Auvona m	
Babylon	Babylōn f	adj Babylōnius
Baden-Baden	Aquae Aurēliae fpl	
Balearic Islands	Baliārēs Insulae fpl	adj Baliāricus
Balkh	Bactra ntpl	adj Bactriānus
Baltic	Balticum Mare nt	
Bangor	Bangertium nt	adj Bangertiēnsis
Barcelona	Barcinō f	adj Barcinōnēnsis
Bari	Bārium nt	adj Bārēnsis
Basle	Basilēa f	adj Basilēēnsis
Basques	Vasconēs mpl	adj Vasconicus
Bath	Aquae (fpl) Sulis	
Bayeux	Augustodūrum nt	
Bayreuth	Barūthum nt	
Beauvais	Bellovacī mpl	adj Bellovacēnsis
Beirut	Bērȳtus f	adj Bērȳtius
Belgium	Belgae mpl	adj Belgicus
Bergen	Bergae fpl	
Berlin	Berolīnum nt	adj Berolīnēnsis
Berne	Vērona f	
Berwick	Barvīcum nt	
Besançon	Vesontiō m	adj Bisuntīnus
Black Sea	Pontus (Euxīnus) m	adj Ponticus
Bobbio	Bobbium nt	adj Bobbiēnsis
Bohemia	Boiohaemī mpl	
Bologna	Bonōnia f	adj Bonōniēnsis
Bonn	Bonna f	
Bordeaux	Burdigala f	adj Burdigalēnsis
Boulogne	Bonōnia f	adj Bononiēnsis
Bourges	Avāricum nt	adj Avāricēnsis
Brabant	Brabantia f	
Braganza	Brigantia f	adj Brigantiēnsis

Brancaster	Brancdūnum *nt*	
Brandenburg	Brandenburgia *f*	*adj* Brandenburgēnsis
Bremen	Brēma *f*	*adj* Brēmēnsis
Breslau	Bratislavia *f*	*adj* Bratislaviēnsis
Brindisi	Brundisium *nt*	*adj* Brundisīnus
Bristol	Bristolium *nt*	*adj* Bristoliēnsis
Britain	Britannia *f*	*adj* Britannicus
Brittany	Armoricae *fpl*	
Bruges	Brugae *fpl*	*adj* Brugēnsis
Brunswick	Brunsvicum *nt*	*adj* Brunsvīcēnsis
Brussels	Bruxellae *fpl*	*adj* Bruxellēnsis
Bucharest	Bucarestum *nt*	*adj* Bucarestiēnsis
Burgos	Burgī *mpl*	*adj* Burgitānus
Burgundy	Burgundiōnēs *mpl*	
Cadiz	Gādēs *fpl*	*adj* Gāditānus
Caen	Cadomum *nt*	*adj* Cadomēnsis
Caerleon	Isca *f*	
Caermarthen	Maridūnum *nt*	
Caernarvon	Segontium *nt*	
Caerwent	Venta (*f*) Silurum	
Cagliari	Caralis *f*	*adj* Caralītānus
Cairo	Cairus *f*	
Calais	Calētum *nt*	*adj* Calētanus
Cambrai	Camerācum *nt*	*adj* Camerācēnsis
Cambridge	Cantabrigia *f*	*adj* Cantabrigiēnsis
Campagna	Campānia *f*	*adj* Campānus
Cannes	Canoē *f*	
Canterbury	Durovernum *nt*,	*adj* Cantuāriēnsis
	Cantuāria *f*	
Capri	Capreae *fpl*	*adj* Capreēnsis
Cardigan	Ceretica *f*	
Carlisle	Luguvallium *nt*	
Cartagena	Carthāgō Nova *f*	
Carthage	Carthāgō *f*	*adj* Carthāginiēnsis
Caspian Sea	Mare Caspium *nt*	
Cevennes	Gebenna *f*	*adj* Gebennicus
Ceylon	Tāprobanē *f*	
Champagne	Campānia *f*	*adj* Campānicus
Chartres	Carnūtēs *mpl*	*adj* Carnōtēnus
Chelmsford	Caesaromagus *m*	
Cherbourg	Caesaris burgus *m*	
Chester	Deva *f*	
Chichester	Rēgnum *nt*	
China	Sērēs *mpl*	*adj* Sēricus
Cirencester	Corinium (*nt*)	
	Dobunōrum	
Clairvaux	Clāra Vallis *f*	*adj* Clāravallēnsis
Clermont	Nemossus *f*	
Cluny	Clīniacum *nt*	*adj* Clīniacēnsis
Clyde, *River*	Clōta *f*	
Colchester	Camulodūnum *nt*	
Cologne	Colōnia Agrippīna *f*	*adj* Colōniēnsis

Como, *Lake*	Lārius *m*	*adj* Lārius
Constance, *Lake*	Lacus Brigantīnus *m*	
Copenhagen	Hafnia *f*	
Corbridge	Corstopitum *nt*	
Cordoba	Corduba *f*	*adj* Cordubēnsis
Corfu	Corcȳra *f*	*adj* Corcȳraeus
Corinth	Corinthus *f*	*adj* Corinthius
Cork	Corcagia *f*	*adj* Corcagiēnsis
Cornwall	Cornubia *f*	
Cracow	Cracovia *f*	*adj* Cracoviēnsis
Crete	Crēta *f*	*adj* Crētēnsis, Crēticus
Cumberland	Cumbria *f*	
Cyprus	Cyprus *f*	*adj* Cyprius
Cyrene	Cȳrēnae *fpl*	*adj* Cȳrēnaicus
Damascus	Damascus *f*	*adj* Damascēnus
Danube, *River*	*(lower)* Ister *m*,	
	(upper) Dānuvius *m*	
Dardanelles	Hellēspontus *m*	*adj* Hellēspontius
Dee, *River*	Deva *f*	
Denmark	Dānia *f*	*adj* Dānicus
Derby	Derventiō *m*	
Devon	Devōnia *f*	
Dijon	Diviō *f*	*adj* Diviōnēnsis
Dneiper, *River*	Borysthenēs *m*	
Dneister, *River*	Danaster *m*	
Don, *River* (Russian)	Tanais *m*	
Doncaster	Dānum *nt*	
Dorchester	Durnovāria *f*	
Douro, *River*	Durius *m*	
Dover	Dubrī *mpl*	
Dover, *Straits of*	Fretum Gallicum *nt*	
Dresden	Dresda *f*	*adj* Dresdēnsis
Dublin	Dublīnum *nt*	*adj* Dublīnēnsis
Dumbarton	Britannodūnum *nt*	
Dundee	Taodūnum *nt*	
Dunstable	Durocobrīvae *fpl*	
Durham	Dunelmum *nt*	*adj* Dunelmēnsis
Ebro, *River*	Hibērus *m*	
Eden, *River*	Itūna *f*	
Edinburgh	Edinburgum *nt*	*adj* Edinburgēnsis
Egypt	Aegyptus *f*	*adj* Aegyptius
Elba	Ilva *f*	
Elbe, *River*	Albis *m*	
England	Anglia *f*	*adj* Anglicus
Etna	Aetna *f*	*adj* Aetnaeus
Europe	Eurōpa	*adj* Eurōpaeus
Exeter	Isca *(f)* Dumnoniōrum	
Fiesole	Faesulae *fpl*	*adj* Faesulānus
Flanders	Menapiī *mpl*	
Florence	Flōrentia *f*	*adj* Flōrentīnus
Fontainebleau	Bellofontānum *nt*	
Forth, *River*	Bodotria *f*	

France	Gallia *f*	*adj* Gallicus
Frankfurt	Francofurtum *nt*	
Frejus	Forum (*nt*) Iūliī	*adj* Foroiūliēnsis
Friesland	Frīsiī *mpl*	*adj* Frīsius
Gallipoli	Callipolis *f*	*adj* Callipolitānus
Galloway	Gallovidia *f*	
Ganges	Gangēs *m*	*adj* Gangēticus
Garda, *Lake*	Bēnācus *m*	
Garonne, *River*	Garumna *f*	
Gaul	Gallia *f*	*adj* Gallicus
Gdansk	Gedānum *m*	
Geneva	Genāva *f*	*adj* Genāvēnsis
Geneva, *Lake*	Lemannus lacus *m*	
Genoa	Genua *f*	*adj* Genuēnsis
Germany	Germānia *f*	*adj* Germānicus
Ghent	Gandavum *nt*	*adj* Gandavēnsis
Gibraltar	Calpē *f*	*adj* Calpētānus
Gibraltar, *Straits of*	Fretum Gāditānum *nt*	
Glasgow	Glasgua *f*	*adj* Glasguēnsis
Gloucester	Glēvum *nt*	
Gothenburg	Gothoburgum *nt*	
Graz	Graecium *nt*	
Greece	Graecia *f*	*adj* Graecus
Greenwich	Grenovicum *nt*	
Grenoble	Grātiānopolis *f*	
Groningen	Groninga *f*	
Guadalquivir, *River*	Baetis *m*	
Guadiana, *River*	Anas *m*	
Guernsey	Sarnia *f*	
Hague, *The*	Haga (*f*) Comitis	
Halle	Halla *f*	*adj* Hallēnsis
Hamadān	Ecbatana *ntpl*	
Hamburg	Hamburgum *nt*	*adj* Hamburgēnsis
Hanover	Hannovera *f*	
Harwich	Harvicum *nt*	
Havre	Grātiae Portus *m*	
Hebrides	Ebūdae Insulae *fpl*	
Hexham	Axelodūnum *nt*	
Holland	Batāvī *mpl*	*adj* Batāvus
Ibiza	Ebusus *f*	*adj* Ebusitānus
Ilkley	Olicāna *f*	
Inn, *River*	Aenus *m*	
Ipswich	Gippevicum *nt*	
Ireland	Hibernia *f*	*adj* Hibernicus
Isar, *River*	Isara *f*	
Istanbul	Bȳzantium *nt*	*adj* Bȳzantīnus
Italy	Italia *f*	*adj* Italicus
Jersey	Caesarea *f*	
Jerusalem	Hierosolyma *ntpl*	*adj* Hierosolymītānus
Jutland	Chersonnēsus Cimbrica *f*	
Karlsbad	Aquae Carolīnae *fpl*	

Kent	Cantium _nt_	
Kiel	Chilonium _nt_	
Koblenz	Cōnfluentēs _mpl_	
Lancaster	Lancastria _f_	
Lanchester	Longovicium _nt_	
Land's End	Bolerium Prōmunturium _nt_	
Lausanne	Lausōnium _nt_	_adj_ Lausōniēnsis
Lebanon	Libanus _m_	
Leeds	Ledesia _f_	
Leicester	Ratae (_fpl_) Coritānōrum	
Leiden	Lugdūnum (_nt_) Batāvōrum	
Leipsig	Lipsia _f_	_adj_ Lipsiēnsis
Lērida	Ilerda _f_	_adj_ Ilerdēnsis
Lichfield	Etocētum _nt_	
Limoges	Augustorītum _nt_	
Lincoln	Lindum _nt_	
Lisbon	Olisīpō _m_	_adj_ Olisīpōnēnsis
Lizard Point	Damnonium Prōmunturium _nt_	
Loire, _River_	Liger _m_	_adj_ Ligericus
Lombardy	Langobardia _f_	
London	Londinium _nt_	_adj_ Londiniēnsis
Lorraine	Lōthāringia _f_	
Lucerne	Lūceria _f_	_adj_ Lūcernēnsis
Lund	Londinium (_nt_) Gothōrum	
Lyons	Lugdūnum _nt_	_adj_ Lugdūnēnsis
Madrid	Matrītum _nt_	_adj_ Matrītēnsis
Maggiore, _Lake_	Verbannus _m_	
Main, _River_	Moenus _m_	
Mainz	Mogontiacum _nt_	
Majorca	Baliāris Māior _f_	
Malta	Melita _f_	
Man, _Isle of_	Monapia _f_	
Manchester	Mancunium _nt_	
Marmara, _Sea of_	Propontis _f_	
Marne, _River_	Māterna _f_	
Marseilles	Massilia _f_	_adj_ Massiliēnsis
Matapan	Taenarum _nt_	_adj_ Taenarius
Mediterranean	Mare internum _nt_	
Melun	Melodūnum _nt_	
Mērida	Ēmerita _f_	_adj_ Ēmeritēnsis
Messina	Messāna _f_	_adj_ Messānius
Metz	Dīvodūrum _nt_	
Meuse, _River_	Mosa _f_	
Milan	Mediōlānum _nt_	_adj_ Mediōlānēnsis
Minorca	Baliāris Minor _f_	
Modena	Mutina _f_	_adj_ Mutinēnsis
Mons	Montēs _mpl_	
Monte Cassino	Casīnum _nt_	_adj_ Casīnās
Moray	Moravia _f_	

Morocco	Maurētānia f	adj Maurus
Moscow	Moscovia f	
Moselle, River	Mosella f	
Munich	Monacum nt	adj Monacēnsis
Nantes	Namnētēs mpl	
Naples	Neāpolis f	adj Neāpolītānus
Neckar, River	Nīcer m	
Newcastle	Pōns (m) Aeliī, Novum Castrum nt	adj Novocastrēnsis
Nice	Nīcaea f	adj Nicaeēnsis
Nile, River	Nīlus m	adj Nīlōticus
Nîmes	Nemausus f	adj Nemausēnsis
Norway	Norvēgia f	adj Norvēgiānus
Norwich	Nordovīcum nt	
Oder, River	Viadrus m	
Oporto	Portus Calēnsis m	
Orange	Arausiō f	
Orkneys	Orcadēs fpl	
Orléans	Aurēliānum nt	adj Aurēliānēnsis
Oudenarde	Aldenarda f	
Oxford	Oxonia f	adj Oxoniēnsis
Padua	Patavium nt	adj Patavīnus
Palermo	Panormus m	adj Panormitānus
Paris	Lutetia f, Parīsiī mpl	adj Parīsiēnsis
Patras	Patrae pl	adj Patrēnsis
Persian Gulf	Mare Rubrum nt	
Piacenza	Placentia f	adj Placentīnus
Po, River	Padus	adj Padānus
Poitiers	Limōrum nt	
Poland	Polōnia f	
Portsmouth	Māgnus Portus m	
Portugal	Lūsitānia f	
Pozzuoli	Puteolī mpl	adj Puteolānus
Prague	Prāga f	adj Prāgēnsis
Provence	Prōvincia f	
Pyrenees	Pyrēnaeī montēs mpl	
Red Sea	Sinus Arābicus m	
Rheims	Dūrocortorum nt	
Rhine, River	Rhēnus m	adj Rhēnānus
Rhodes	Rhodos f	adj Rhodius
Rhône, River	Rhodanus m	
Richborough	Rutupiae fpl	adj Rutupīnus
Rimini	Arīminum	adj Arīminēnsis
Rochester	Dūrobrīvae fpl	
Rome	Rōma f	adj Rōmānus
Rotterdam	Roterodamum nt	adj Roterodamēnsis
Rouen	Rothomagus f	adj Rothomagēnsis
Saar, River	Sangona f	
Salisbury	Sarisbēria f	
Salzburg	Iuvāvum nt	adj Salisburgēnsis
Saône, River	Arar m	

Savoy	Sabaudia f	
Scheldt, River	Scaldis m	
Schleswig	Slesvīcum nt	
Scilly Isles	Cassiterides fpl	
Scotland	Calēdonia f	adj Calēdonius
Seine, River	Sēquana f	
Severn, River	Sabrīna f	
Seville	Hīspalis f	adj Hispalēnsis
Shrewsbury	Salōpia f	
Sicily	Sicilia f	adj Siculus
Sidra, Gulf of	Syrtis (māior) f	
Silchester	Callēva (f) Atrebatum	
Soissons	Augusta (f) Suessiōnum	
Solway Firth	Itūna (f) aestuārium	
Somme, River	Samara f	
Spain	Hispānia f	adj Hispānus
St. Albans	Verulamium nt	
St. Andrews	Andreopolis f	
St. Bernard	(Great) Mōns Pennīnus m,	
	(Little) Alpis Grāia f	
St. Gallen	Sangallēnse coenobium nt	adj Sangallēnsis
St. Gotthard	Alpēs summae fpl	
St. Moritz	Agaunum nt	adj Agaunēnsis
Strasbourg	Argentorātus f	adj Argentorātēnsis
Swabia	Suēvia f	adj Suēvicus
Sweden	Suēcia f	adj Suēcicus
Switzerland	Helvētia f	adj Helvēticus
Syracuse	Syrācūsae fpl	adj Syrācūsānus
Tangier	Tingī f	adj Tingitānus
Taranto	Tarentum nt	adj Tarentīnus
Tarragona	Tarracō f	adj Tarracōnēnsis
Tay, River	Taus m	
Thames, River	Tamesis m	
Thebes	Thēbae fpl	adj Thēbānus
Tiber, River	Tiberis m	adj Tiberīnus
Tivoli	Tībur nt	adj Tīburtīnus
Toledo	Tolētum nt	adj Tolētānus
Toulon	Tolōna f	adj Tolōnēnsis
Toulouse	Tolōsa f	adj Tolōsānus
Tours	Caesarodūnum nt	
Trèves, Trier	Augusta (f) Treverōrum	
Trieste	Tergeste nt	adj Tergestīnus
Tripoli	Tripolis f	adj Tripolitānus
Tunis	Tūnēs f	adj Tūnētānus
Turin	Augusta (f) Taurīnōrum	adj Taurīnus
Tuscany	Etrūria f	adj Etrūscus
Tyrrhenian Sea	Mare īnferum nt	
Utrecht	Ultrāiectum nt	adj Ultrāiectēnsis
Vardar, River	Axius m	
Venice	Venetī mpl, Venetiae fpl	adj Venetus
Verdun	Virodūnum nt	adj Virodūnēnsis

Versailles	Versăliae fpl	adj Versăliēnsis
Vichy	Aquae (fpl) Sōlis	
Vienna	Vindobona f	adj Vindobenēnsis
Vosges	Vosegus m	
Wales	Cambria f	
Wallsend	Segedūnum nt	
Warsaw	Varsavia f	adj Varsaviēnsis
Wash, The	Metaris (m) aestuārium	
Wear, River	Vedra f	
Weser, River	Visurgis m	
Westminster	Westmonastērium nt	adj Westmonastēriēnsis
Wiesbaden	Mattiacum nt	adj Mattiacus
Wight, Isle of	Vectis f	
Winchester	Venta (f) Belgārum	
Worcester	Vigornia f	
Worms	Vormatia f	
Wroxeter	Viroconium nt	
York	Eburācum nt	adj Eburācēnsis
Zuider Zee	Flēvō m	
Zurich	Turicum nt	adj Tigurīnus

NUMERALS

	Cardinal		Ordinal	
1	ūnus	I	prīmus	1st
2	duo	II	secundus, alter	2nd
3	trēs	III	tertius	3rd
4	quattuor	IV	quārtus	4th
5	quīnque	V	quīntus	5th
6	sex	VI	sextus	6th
7	septem	VII	septimus	7th
8	octō	VIII	octāvus	8th
9	novem	IX	nōnus	9th
10	decem	X	decimus	10th
11	undecim	XI	undecimus	11th
12	duodecim	XII	duodecimus	12th
13	tredecim	XIII	tertius decimus	13th
14	quattuordecim	XIV	quārtus decimus	14th
15	quīndecim	XV	quīntus decimus	15th
16	sēdecim	XVI	sextus decimus	16th
17	septendecim	XVII	septimus decimus	17th
18	duodēvīgintī	XVIII	duodēvīcēsimus	18th
19	ūndēvīgintī	XIX	ūndēvīcēsimus	19th
20	vīgintī	XX	vīcēsimus	20th
21	vīgintī ūnus	XXI	vīcēsimus prīmus	21st
28	duodētrīgintā	XXVIII	duodētrīcēsimus	28th
29	ūndētrīgintā	XXIX	ūndētrīcēsimus	29th
30	trīgintā	XXX	trīcēsimus	30th
40	quadrāgintā	XL	quadrāgēsimus	40th
50	quīnquāgintā	L	quīnquāgēsimus	50th
60	sexāgintā	LX	sexāgēsimus	60th
70	septuāgintā	LXX	septuāgēsimus	70th
80	octōgintā	LXXX	octōgēsimus	80th
90	nōnāgintā	XC	nōnāgēsimus	90th
100	centum	C	centēsimus	100th
101	centum et ūnus	CI	centēsimus prīmus	101st
122	centum vīgintī duo	CXXII	centēsimus vīcēsimus alter	122nd
200	ducentī	CC	ducentēsimus	200th
300	trecentī	CCC	trecentēsimus	300th
400	quadringentī	CCCC	quadringentēsimus	400th
500	quīngentī	D	quīngentēsimus	500th
600	sēscentī	DC	sēscentēsimus	600th
700	septingentī	DCC	septingentēsimus	700th
800	octingentī	DCCC	octingentēsimus	800th
900	nōngentī	DCCCC	nōngentēsimus	900th
1000	mīlle	M	mīllēsimus	1000th
1001	mīlle et ūnus	MI	mīllēsimus prīmus	1001st
1102	mīlle centum duo	MCII	mīllēsimus centēsimus alter	1102nd
3000	tria mīlia	MMM	ter mīllēsimus	3000th
5000	quīnque mīlia	IↃↃ	quīnquiēs mīllēsimus	5000th
10,000	decem mīlia	CCIↃↃ	deciēs mīllēsimus	10,000th
100,000	centum mīlia	CCCIↃↃↃ	centiēs mīllēsimus	100,000th
1,000,000	deciēs centēna mīlia	CCCCIↃↃↃↃ	deciēs centiēs mīllēsimus	1,000,000th

NUMERALS

	Distributive		Adverb	
1	singulī	I	semel	1st
2	bīnī	II	bis	2nd
3	ternī (trīnī)	III	ter	3rd
4	quaternī	IV	quater	4th
5	quīnī	V	quīnquiēs	5th
6	sēnī	VI	sexiēs	6th
7	septēnī	VII	septiēs	7th
8	octōnī	VIII	octiēs	8th
9	novēnī	IX	noviēs	9th
10	dēnī	X	deciēs	10th
11	undēnī	XI	undeciēs	11th
12	duodēnī	XII	duodeciēs	12th
13	ternī dēnī	XIII	ter deciēs	13th
14	quaternī dēnī	XIV	quattuordeciēs	14th
15	quīnī dēnī	XV	quīndeciēs	15th
16	sēnī dēnī	XVI	sēdeciēs	16th
17	septēnī dēnī	XVII	septiēs deciēs	17th
18	duodēvīcēnī	XVIII	duodēvīciēs	18th
19	ūndēvīcēnī	XIX	ūndēvīciēs	19th
20	vīcēnī	XX	vīciēs	20th
21	vīcēnī singulī	XXI	semel et vīciēs	21st
28	duodētrīcēnī	XXVIII	duodētrīciēs	28th
29	ūndētrīcēnī	XXIX	ūndētrīciēs	29th
30	trīcēnī	XXX	trīciēs	30th
40	quadrāgēnī	XL	quadrāgiēs	40th
50	quīnquāgēnī	L	quīnquāgiēs	50th
60	sexāgēnī	LX	sexāgiēs	60th
70	septuāgēnī	LXX	septuāgiēs	70th
80	octōgēnī	LXXX	octōgiēs	80th
90	nōnagēnī	XC	nōnāgiēs	90th
100	centēnī	C	centiēs	100th
101	centēnī singulī	CI	semel et centiēs	101st
122	centēnī vīcēnī bīnī	CXXII	centiēs vīciēs bis	122nd
200	ducēnī	CC	ducentiēs	200th
300	trecēnī	CCC	trecentiēs	300th
400	quadringēnī	CCCC	quadringentiēs	400th
500	quīngēnī	D	quīngentiēs	500th
600	sexcēnī	DC	sexcentiēs	600th
700	septingēnī	DCC	septingentiēs	700th
800	octingēnī	DCCC	octingentiēs	800th
900	nōngēnī	DCCCC	nōngentiēs	900th
1000	singula mīlia	M	mīlliēs	1000th
1001	singula mīlia singulī	MI	semel et mīlliēs	1001st
1102	singula mīlia centēnī bīnī	MCII	mīlliēs centiēs bis	1102nd
3000	trīna mīlia	MMM	ter mīlliēs	3000th
5000	quīna mīlia	IↃↃ	quīnquiēs mīlliēs	5000th
10,000	dēna mīlia	CCIↃↃ	deciēs mīlliēs	10,000th
100,000	centēna mīlia	CCCIↃↃↃ	centiēs mīlliēs	100,000th
1,000,000	deciēs centēna mīlia	CCCCIↃↃↃↃ	mīlliēs mīlliēs	1,000,000th

DATES

MONTHS

Three days of the month have special names:

Kalendae the 1st.

Nōnae the 5th of most months, but the 7th of March, May, July and October.

> "In March, July, October May,
> The Nones are on the 7th day."

Idūs the 13th of most months, but the 15th of March, May, July and October.

If the date is one of these three days, it is expressed in the ablative, with the adjective of the month in agreement, *e.g.*

1st January, **Kalendīs Iānuāriīs**, usually abbreviated **Kal. Ian.**

The day immediately before any of these three is expressed by **prīdiē** with the accusative, *e.g.*

4th February, **prīdiē Nōnās Februāriās**, usually abbreviated **prid. Non. Feb.**

All other dates are expressed as so many days before the next named day, and in reckoning the interval both the date and the named day are counted, *e.g.* the 11th is the 5th day before the 15th.

The formula is all in the accusative, begining with the words **ante diem**, *e.g.* 11th March, **ante diem quīntum Idūs Martiās**, usually abbreviated **a.d. V Id. Mar.**

The following selection of dates for April and May should be a sufficient guide to the dates of any month in the year:—

APRIL		MAY
Kal. Apr.	1	Kal. Mai.
a.d IV Non. Apr.	2	a.d. VI Non. Mai.
a.d. III Non. Apr.	3	a.d. V Non. Mai.
prid. Non. Apr.	4	a.d. IV Non. Mai.
Non. Apr.	5	a.d. III Non. Mai.
a.d. VIII Id. Apr.	6	prid. Non. Mai.
a.d. VII Id. Apr.	7	Non. Mai.
a.d. VI Id. Apr.	8	a.d. VIII Id. Mai.
a.d. V Id. Apr.	9	a.d. VII Id. Mai.
a.d. IV Id. Apr.	10	a.d. VI Id. Mai.
a.d. III Id. Apr.	11	a.d. V Id. Mai.
prid. Id. Apr.	12	a.d. IV Id. Mai.
Id. Apr.	13	a.d. III Id. Mai.
a.d. XVIII Kal. Mai.	14	prid. Id. Mai.
a.d. XVII Kal. Mai.	15	Id. Mai.
a.d. XVI Kal. Mai.	16	a.d. XVII Kal. Iun.

a.d. XV Kal. Mai.	17	a.d. XVI Kal. Iun.
a.d. XII Kal. Mai.	20	a.d. XIII Kal. Iun.
a.d. VII Kal. Mai.	25	a.d. VIII Kal. Iun.
prid. Kal. Mai.	30	a.d. III Kal. Iun.
—	31	prid. Kal. Iun.

YEARS

A year is denoted either by giving the names of the consuls or by reckoning the number of years from the traditional date of the foundation of Rome, 753 B.C. (A date B.C. should be subtracted from 754, a date A.D. should be added to 753.)

E.g. "In the year 218 B.C.," *either* P. Cornelio Scipione Ti. Sempronio Longo coss. *or* a. u. c. DXXXVI.

MEASURES

Length

12 ūnciae = 1 pēs
5 pedēs = 1 passus
125 passūs = 1 stadium
8 stadia = mīlle passūs

The Roman mile was about 1.48 km.

Area

100 pedēs quadrātī = 1 scrīpulum
144 scrīpula = 1 āctus quadrātus
2 āctūs quadrātī = 1 iugerum
2 iugera = 1 hērēdium
100 hērēdia = 1 centuria

The **iugerum** was about 2529.28 square metres.

Capacity

	4 cochleāria	=	1 cyathus
	12 cyathī	=	1 sextārius
(*liquid*)	6 sextāriī	=	1 congius
	8 congiī	=	1 amphora
	20 amphorae	=	1 culleus
(*dry*)	8 sextāriī	=	1 sēmodius
	2 sēmodiī	=	1 modius

The **sextārius** was about half a litre, the **modius** about 9 litres.

Weight

4 scrīpula = 1 sextula
6 sextulae = 1 ūncia
12 ūnciae = 1 lībra

The Roman lb. was about 326 gr, and the **ūncia** was therefore about 27 gr. The twelfths of the **lībra** have the following names, which are also used to denote fractions generally, *e.g.* **hērēs ex triente**, heir to a third of an estate.

$\frac{1}{12}$ ūncia	$\frac{5}{12}$ quīncūnx	$\frac{3}{4}$ dōdrāns
$\frac{1}{6}$ sextāns	$\frac{1}{2}$ sēmis	$\frac{5}{6}$ dextāns
$\frac{1}{4}$ quadrāns	$\frac{7}{12}$ septūnx	$\frac{11}{12}$ deūnx
$\frac{1}{3}$ triēns	$\frac{2}{3}$ bēs	

MONEY

Roman

2½ assēs = 1 sēstertius (*or* nummus)
4 sēstertii = 1 dēnārius
25 dēnārii = 1 aureus

The sesterce is represented by a symbol for 2½, properly **II S(ēmis)**, usually standardized in the form HS. The *ntpl* **sēstertia** with the distributive numeral denotes thousands of sesterces, and the numeral adverb with the *gen pl* **sēstertium** (understanding **centena milia**) means hundred thousands, *e.g.*

10,000 sesterces = dēna sēstertia   = HS X̄
1,000,000   ”   = deciēs sēstertium = HS IX̄I

Greek

100 drachumae = 1 mina
60 minae   = 1 talentum

LATIN VERSE

QUANTITY

Both vowels and syllables in Latin may be described as long or short. A long vowel or syllable is one on which the voice dwells for a longer time than on a short one, in much the same way as a minim is long compared with a crotchet in musical notation.

A syllable is long if the vowel in it is either long in itself or followed by two or more consonants. The letter z counts as a double consonant, the letter h not at all, and the following pairs of consonants occurring in the same word after a short vowel do not necessarily make the syllable long:

br, cr, dr, fr, gr, pr, tr; fl, gl, pl.

A syllable is short if its vowel is a short one and not followed by two or more consonants (except for the groups noted in the preceding paragraph).

Examples: In **dūcō** both the vowels are long ("by nature") and therefore the two syllables are long.

In **deus** both the vowels are short, neither is followed by more than one consonant, and therefore the two syllables are short; but if a word beginning with a consonant follows, then the syllable -**us** will become long.

In **adsunt** both the vowels are short, but they are both followed by two consonants, and the two syllables are therefore "long by position".

This long or short characteristic of Latin vowels and syllables is called "quantity." To determine the quantities of vowels no general rules can be given, and some of them are now not known for certain. The vowel quantities of words will have to be learned when the words are learned, or else looked up when the need arises. In final syllables, however, there is a certain regularity to be found, and the following table shows the commonest of these:

ENDING

	Long	Short
-a	1st decl abl sing	1st decl nom and voc sing
	1st conj impv sing	all nom and acc ntpl
	numerals and most adverbs	**ita, quia**
-e	5th decl abl sing	all other noun and verb endings
	2nd conj impv sing	
	most adverbs	**bene, male**
	Greek nouns	enclitics

-i	*all endings, except*	**quasi, nisi:** *and sometimes* **mihi, tibi, sibi, ibi, ubi**
-o	*all endings, except*	*sometimes iambic words, esp* **cito, duo, ego, homo, modo, puto, rogo, scio**
-u	*all endings*	
-as	*all endings, except*	*Greek nouns*
-es	*all endings, except*	*3rd decl nom sing with short* **-e-** *in stem* **es** (be) *and compounds* **penes**
-is	*1st and 2nd decl dat and abl pl 3rd decl acc pl 4th conj 2nd pers sing* **vīs, sīs, velīs**	*all others*
-os	*all endings, except*	*2nd decl nom sing* **os** (bone) **compos, impos**
-us	*3rd decl nom sing with long* **-u-** *in stem 4th decl gen sing and nom and acc pl*	*all others*

METRES

Latin Verse is a pattern of long and short syllables, grouped together in "feet" or in lyric lines.

FEET

The commonest Feet employed in Latin metres are:

Anapaest	(short—short—long)	˘ ˘ —
Dactyl	(long—short—short)	— ˘ ˘
Iambus	(short—long)	˘ —
Proceleusmatic	(short—short—short—short)	˘ ˘ ˘ ˘
Spondee	(long—long)	— —
Tribrach	(short—short—short)	˘ ˘ ˘
Trochee	(long—short)	— ˘

CAESURA AND DIAERESIS

The longer lines usually have a regular break near the middle, occurring either in the middle of a foot (**Caesura**) or at the end of a foot (**Diaeresis**). This break need not imply a pause in the sense of the words, but merely the end of a word, provided that it does not go too closely with the word following, as in the case of a preposition before a noun. See examples on pages 4–9 where the caesura is marked †, and the diaeresis //.

ELISION

A vowel or a vowel followed by **m** at the end of a word ("open vowel") is regularly elided before a vowel at the beginning of the next word in the same line. In reciting, the elided syllable should not be dropped entirely, but slurred into the following vowel. An open vowel at the end of a line does not elide before a vowel at the beginning of the next line.

FINAL SYLLABLES

Where the metre requires the final syllable in a line to be long, this syllable may in fact be a short one. This position in the line is commonly called a **syllaba anceps**, and marked down as being either long or short. It is perhaps better to regard this syllable, when the vowel is short, as long by position, since metrical length is a matter of duration, and the end of a line calls naturally for a slight pause in reading, even if the sense runs on to the next line. In the metrical schemes which follow, a long final syllable should be understood in this sense: it may in itself be a short one.

Latin metres fall into three fairly distinct categories, associated with three different genres of verse: 1. *Dactylic*
2. *Iambic and Trochaic*
3. *Lyric*

DACTYLIC VERSE

The Dactylic metres are the **Hexameter** and the **Pentameter**. The Hexameter is the medium of epic, didactic and pastoral poetry, of satires and epistles, and other examples of occasional verse. In conjunction with the Pentameter it forms the **Elegiac Couplet**, the metre most commonly used for love poetry, occasional pieces, and the epigram.

Dactylic Hexameter

The first four feet may be either **dactyls** or **spondees**, the 5th is regularly a dactyl, the 6th always a spondee. In Virgil and later poets the last word is either disyllabic or trisyllabic. A **Caesura** normally occurs in either the 3rd or the 4th foot, and pastoral poetry often has the "**Bucolic Diaeresis**" at the end of the 4th foot. In Virgilian and later usage there is a tendency for words and feet to overlap in the first four feet and to coincide in the last two. Similarly in the first part of the line the metrical ictus and the normal accent of the spoken word tend to fall on different syllables, whereas they regularly coincide in the last two feet.

Example:

Clāss(em) āp|tent tăcĭ|tī' sŏcĭ|ōsqu(e) ād | lītŏră| tōrquēnt

(*Virgil, Aen.* 4, 289)

Occasional lines will be found in the poets, which deliberately violate the above rules for the sake of obtaining some special effect,

pēr cō|nūbĭă| nōstrā,' pēr| īncēp|tōs hўmĕ|nāeōs

(*Aen.* 4, 316)

The above echoes Greek hexameter, where the final word is Greek and has four syllables, and the caesura comes between the two short syllables of the dactyl in the 3rd foot:

cūm sŏcĭ|īs nā|tōquĕ' pĕ|nātĭbŭs| ēt māg|nīs dīs

(*Aen.* 3, 12)

Note the solemn, archaic touch, suggesting a line of Ennius, where the 5th foot is a spondee, and the last word is monosyllabic.

pārtŭri̇|ent m̄ōn|tēs,† nā|scētŭr| rĭdĭcŭ|lŭs mūs

(Hor, A. P. 139)

The monosyllabic ending, above, creates a comic effect.

Dactylic Pentameter

This line has two equal parts of 2½ feet each. The two feet in the first part may be either **dactyls** or **spondees**, those in the second part are always dactylic. The two half-feet are long (though the final syllable may be a short one), and there is always a diaeresis between the two parts of the line. In Ovid and later poets the last word in the line is regularly disyllabic.

Example:

Aēnē|ān ăni̇|mō // nōxquĕ dĭ|ēsquĕ rĕ|fērt

(Ovid, Her. 7, 26)

SCANSION

The following procedure may assist beginners to scan a normal hexameter or pentameter correctly:—

1. Mark off elisions.
2. Mark the first syllable long, and (Hexameter) the last five dactyl and spondee, or (Pentameter) the last seven syllables, two dactyls and a long syllable.
3. Mark all diphthongs long.
4. Mark all syllables that are long by position, omitting any doubtful cases.
5. Mark any other syllables known to be long.
6. Mark any syllables known to be short.
7. Fill in the few (if any) remaining syllables, and identify the principal caesura.
8. Read the line aloud.

IAMBIC AND TROCHAIC VERSE

The Iambic and Trochaic metres occur mainly in dramatic verse, but some are found elsewhere, as in the lyrics of Catullus and Horace. The principal Iambic metres are the **Senarius**, the **Septenarius**, and the **Octonarius**; the principal Trochaic metres are the **Septenarius** and **Octonarius**.

Iambic Senarius

Basically this line consists of six iambic feet, but in practice such a line is very rare.

Example:

Phăsēl|lŭs ĭl|lĕ quēm| vĭ dē|tĭs, hōs|pĭ tēs

(*Cat.* 4, 1)

In drama the last foot is always iambic, and the 5th regularly a spondee. The **spondee** is also very common in the first four feet, the **dactyl** and the **tribrach** are frequent, occasionally the **anapaest** is found, and, more rarely, the **proceleusmatic**. There is usually a **caesura** in either the third or the fourth foot.

Example:

Ĭn hāc| hă bĭ tās|sĕ plătĕ|ā dĭc|tŭmst Chrȳ|sĭdēm

(*Ter, And.* 796)

Iambic Septenarius

This line consists of seven and a half feet, basically iambic, but allowing the same variations as in the Senarius. The 4th foot is regularly an Iambus, and is usually followed by a diaeresis: this is an aid to identifying the line.

Example:

N(am) ĭdcĭr|c(o) āccēr|sōr nūp|tĭ ās| quŏd m(i) ād|părā|rĭ sēn|sĭt

(*Ter, And.* 690)

Iambic Octonarius

This line has eight iambic feet, with the same variations as in the other iambic lines. The 4th and 8th feet are regularly iambic, and a diaeresis follows the 4th foot.

Example:

Cūrā|bĭ tūr.| sēd pătĕr| ădēst.| căvĕt(e) ēs|sĕ trĭs|tĕm sēn|tĭ āt

(*Ter, And.* 403)

Trochaic Septenarius

Apart from drama, this line is common in popular verses, and comes into its own in later Latin poetry. It consists of seven and a half **trochees**, but in practice only the seventh foot is regularly trochaic, while the others may be **spondee, dactyl, tribrach,** or (more rarely) **anapaest.** There is usually a **diaeresis** after the 4th foot.

Example:

Crās ă|mēt quī| nūnqu:am) ă|māvĭt,| quīqu(e) ă| māvĭt| crās ă|mēt

(*Pervigilium Veneris*)

Trochaic Octonarius

This is a line of eight trochees, allowing the same variations as above. There is a diaeresis after the 4th foot.

Example:

Prōin tū| sōllĭcĭ|tūdĭn|(em) īstām| fālsām| quāe t(e) ēx|crŭcĭăt| mĭttās

(*Ter, Heaut.* 177)

LYRIC VERSE

In most lyric metres the line is not to be subdivided into feet, but is itself the unit of scansion, and has a fixed number of syllables. The commonest, which are those used by Catullus and Horace, are the **Hendecasyllabic**, the **Asclepiads**, the **Glyconic** and the **Pherecratic**, which occur either singly or in combinations to form either couplets or stanzas of four lines. Beside these groupings there are the **Alcaic** and **Sapphic** stanzas. Elisions occur much more rarely than in the other metres.

Hendecasyllabic

This is Catullus's favourite line. It consists of eleven syllables in the following pattern:

$$- - - \;\; \breve{}\breve{}\; \breve{}\; - \; \breve{}\; - -$$

Either the first or the second syllable may occasionally be short, and there is usually a caesura after the 5th syllable.

Example:

Vīvāmūs, mĕă Lēsbĭ(a), ātqu(e) ămēmūs

(*Cat.* 5, 1)

Asclepiads

There are two Asclepiad lines, of which the **Lesser** is by far the commoner. It has twelve syllables, in the following pattern with a caesura after the 6th syllable:

– – – ⏑ – ‖ – ⏑ – ⏑ – –

Māecēnās, ătăvīs⁺ ēdĭtĕ rēgĭbūs

(Hor, Od. I, 1, 1)

The **Greater Asclepiad** is formed by adding a **choriambus** – ⏑ ⏑ – after the 6th syllable with a **diaeresis** both before and after it.

Example:

Nūllām, Vārĕ, săcrā vītĕ prĭus sēvĕrĭs ārbŏrēm

(Hor, Od. I, 18, 1)

Glyconic

The **Glyconic** occurs by itself in Catullus, but more usually it is found in combination with the **Lesser Asclepiad** or the **Pherecratic**. It consists of eight syllables (– – – ⏑ ⏑ – ⏑ –), so that it is like a Lesser Asclepiad minus the **choriambus**. It has no regular caesura.

Example:

Dōnēc grātŭs ĕrām tĭbī

(Hor. Od. III, 9, 1)

Pherecratic

The **Pherecratic** is a Glyconic minus the second last (short) syllable. It is found only in combination with other lines.

Example:

Sūspēndĭssĕ pŏtēntī

(Hor, Od. I, 5, 11)

Alcaic Stanza

The **Alcaic stanza** has four lines, of which the first two have the same pattern
— — ⌣ — — — ⌣ ⌣ — ⌣ —. In these there is a regular **caesura** after the 5th syllable. The
third line is — — ⌣ — — — ⌣ — and the 4th — ⌣ ⌣ — ⌣ ⌣ — ⌣ — —. Neither of the last two
lines has a regular break in it

Example:

Nūnc ēs bībēndūm,[†] nūnc pĕdĕ lībĕrō
pūlsāndă tēllūs,[†] nūnc Sălĭārĭbūs
ōrnārĕ pūlvīnār dĕōrūm
tēmpŭs ĕrāt dăpĭbūs, sŏdālēs.

(*Hor, Od. I.* 37, 1-4)

Sapphic Stanza

The **Sapphic stanza** also has four lines, of which the first three are the same:
— ⌣ — — — ⌣ ⌣ — ⌣ — —. As in the Alcaic there is a **caesura** after the 5th syllable. The
last line is a short **Adonic** — ⌣ ⌣ — —

Example:

Īntĕgēr vītāe[†] scĕlĕrīsquĕ pūrūs
nōn ĕgēt Māurīs[†] iăcŭlīs nĕqu(e) ārcū
nēc vĕnēnātīs[†] grăvĭdā săgīttīs,
Fūscĕ, phărētrā.

(*Hor, Od. I.* 22, 1-4)

LATIN PHRASES USED IN ENGLISH

What follows is a list of some of the Latin phrases used in English today.

ab initio   from the beginning.

ab ovo   (lit: from the egg) from the beginning.

absit omen   (lit: may the (evil) omen be absent) may the presentiment not become real or take place.

ab urbe condita   (used in dates) from the foundation of the city (*i.e. from the foundation of Rome in 753 B.C.*).

A.D.   abbr for **anno Domini**.

ad hoc   (lit: for this) for a particular purpose only: **an ad hoc committee; an ad hoc decision.**

ad hominem   (lit: according to the person) 1 directed against a person rather than against his or her arguments. 2 based on or appealing to emotion rather than reason.

ad infinitum   without end; endlessly; to infinity.

ad interim   for the meantime; for the present: **ad interim measures.**

ad-lib   (abbr for **ad libitum**) ♦ *adj* improvised; impromptu ♦ *adv* without restraint; freely; as one pleases ♦ *vb* to improvise and deliver without preparation.

ad libitum   (lit: according to pleasure) as one pleases.

ad majorem Dei gloriam   for the greater glory of God (*the Jesuit motto*).

ad nauseam   (lit: to (the point of) nausea) to a disgusting extent.

ad rem   (lit: to the matter) to the point; without digression: **to reply ad rem; an ad rem discussion.**

advocatus diaboli   devil's advocate.

ad valorem   (lit: according to value) in proportion to the estimated value of the goods taxed.

aet.   (abbr for **aetatis**) at the age of.

Agnus Dei   Lamb of God.

alma mater   (lit: nurturing mother) one's former university, college or school.

alter ego   (lit: other self) 1 a second self. 2 a very close and intimate friend.

a.m.   abbr for **ante meridiem**.

AMDG   abbr for **ad majorem Dei gloriam**.

amor patriae   love of one's country; patriotism.

an.   (abbr for **anno**) in the year.

anno Domini   in the year of our Lord.

anno urbis conditae   in the year of the foundation of the city (*i.e. of Rome in 753 B.C., used in dates*)

anno regni   in the year of the reign (of).

annus mirabilis	(lit: wonderful year) a year of wonders.
antebellum	(lit: before the war) of or during the period before a war, especially the American Civil War.
ante meridiem	before noon.
ante-mortem	before death (*esp in legal or medical contexts*).
a.p.	(abbr for **ante prandium**) before a meal (*in prescriptions*).
apparatus criticus	(lit: critical apparatus) textual notes (*list of variant readings, etc., relating to a document, especially in a scholarly edition of a text*).
aq.	abbr for **aqua**.
aqua vitae	(lit: water of life) brandy.
a.r.	abbr for **anno regni**.
arbiter elegantiae *or* **elegantiarum**	judge in a matter of taste.
arcus senilis	(lit: senile bow) opaque circle around the cornea of the eye (*often seen in elderly people*).
argumentum ad hominem	(lit: argument according to the person: Logic) **1** fallacious argument that attacks not an opponent's beliefs but his motives or character. **2** argument that shows an opponent's statement to be inconsistent with his other beliefs.
ars longa vita brevis	art is long, life is short.
AUC	abbr for: **1 ab urbe condita**. **2 anno urbis conditae**.
aut vincere aut mori	death or victory.
aurora australis	the southern lights.
aurora borealis	the northern lights.
ave	**1** hail! **2** farewell!
ave atque vale	hail and farewell!
Ave Maria	Hail Mary.
beatae memoriae	of blessed memory.
Beata Virgo	the Blessed Virgin.
Beata Virgo Maria	the Blessed Virgin Mary.
b.i.d	(abbr for **bis in die**) twice a day (*in prescriptions*).
bis dat, qui cito dat	the person who gives promptly gives twice.
BV	abbr for **Beata Virgo**.
c, ca	abbr for **circa**.
camera obscura	(lit: dark chamber) camera obscura.
carpe diem	(lit: seize the day) enjoy the pleasures of the moment, without concern for the future.
casus belli	(lit: occasion of war) **1** an event or act used to justify a war. **2** the immediate cause of a quarrel.
caveat emptor	let the buyer beware.
cetera desunt	the rest is missing.

ceteris paribus	other things being equal.
circa	around.
Codex Juris Canonici	(lit: book of canon law) the official code of canon law (*in the Roman Catholic Church*).
cogito, ergo sum	I think, therefore I am (*the basis of Descartes' philosophy*).
compos mentis	of sound mind; sane.
coram populo	in the presence of the people; openly.
corpus delicti	(lit: the body of the crime: *LAW*) the body of facts that constitute an offence.
Corpus Juris Canonici	(lit: body of canon law) the official compilation of canon law (*in the Roman Catholic Church*).
Corpus Juris Civilis	(lit: body of civil law) the body of Roman or civil law.
corrigenda	things to be corrected.
corpus vile	(lit: worthless body) person or thing fit only to be the object of an experiment.
culpa	1 (*LAW*) an act of neglect. 2 (*gen*) a fault; sin; guilt.
cum grano salis	with a grain of salt; not too literally.
cum laude	(*chiefly US*) with praise (*the lowest of three designations for above-average achievement in examinations*).
curriculum vitae	(lit: the course of one's life) curriculum vitae.
de facto	*adv* in fact ♦ *adj* existing in fact.
de gustibus non est disputandum	there is no arguing about tastes.
de jure	according to law; by right; legally.
de mortuis nil nisi bonum	say nothing but good of the dead.
de novo	anew.
Deo gratias	thanks be to God.
Deo Optimo Maximo	to God, the best, the Greatest.
Deo volente	God willing.
de profundis	out of the depths of misery or dejection.
deus ex machina	(lit: the god from the machine) 1 (*in ancient Greek and Roman drama*) a god introduced into a play to resolve the plot. 2 any unlikely or artificial device serving this purpose.
Dies Irae	(lit: the day of wrath) 1 a famous Latin hymn of the 13th century, describing the Last Judgment. It is used in the Mass for the dead. 2 a musical setting of this hymn, usually part of a setting of the Requiem.
disjecta membra	the scattered remains.
DOM	abbr for **Deo Optimo Maximo**.
dramatis personae	(lit: the persons of the drama) the list of characters in a drama.

Ecce Homo — behold the man (*the words of Pontius Pilate to Christ's accusers* [*John 19:5*]).

editio princeps — (lit: the first edition) the first printed edition of a work.

e.g., eg — abbr for **exempli gratia**.

emeritus — retired from office.

e pluribus unum — one out of many (*motto of USA*).

ER — 1 (abbr for **Elizabeth Regina**) Queen Elizabeth; 2 (abbr for **Eduardus Rex**) King Edward.

errare est humanum — to err is human.

erratum (*pl* **errata**) — error.

et seq. — (abbr for **et sequens**) and the following.

et seqq. — (abbr for **et sequentia**) and those that follow.

ex — (lit: out of, from) 1 (*FINANCE*) not participating in; excluding; without: **ex bonus; ex dividend; ex rights.** 2 (*COMMERCE*) without charge to the buyer until removed from: **ex quay; ex ship; ex works.**

ex cathedra — (lit: from the chair) 1 with authority. 2 defined by the pope as infallibly true, to be accepted by all Roman Catholics.

exeat — (lit: let him or her go out) formal leave of absence.

exempli gratia — for example.

exeunt — they go out (*used as a stage direction*).

exeunt omnes — they all go out (*used as a stage direction*).

exit — he or she goes out (*used as a stage direction*).

ex libris — (lit: from the books (of)) from the collection or library of.

ex officio — by right of position or office.

ex parte — (*LAW*) on behalf of one side or party only (*of an application in a judicial proceeding*): **an ex parte injunction.**

ex post facto — having retrospective effect: **an ex post facto law.**

ex silentio — (lit: from silence) based on a lack of evidence to the contrary (*of a theory, assumption etc*).

extempore — (lit: instantaneously) without planning or preparation; impromptu.

ex voto — *adv, adj* in accordance with a vow ♦ *n* offering made in fulfilment of a vow.

facile princeps — (lit: easily first) an obvious leader.

fecit (*abbr* **fec**) — (he or she) made it (*used formerly on works of art next to the artist's name*).

felo de se — suicide.

festina lente — more haste, less speed.

fiat lux — let there be light.

Fidei Defensor — defender of the faith.

fidus Achates	(lit: faithful Achates) faithful friend or companion (*the name of the faithful companion of Aeneas in Virgil's Aeneid*).
floruit	(he or she) flourished (*used to indicate the period when a historical figure, whose birth and death dates are unknown, was most active*).
fons et origo	the source and origin.
genius loci	(lit: genius of the place) 1 the guardian spirit of a place. 2 the special atmosphere of a particular place.
Gloria in Excelsis Deo	(lit: glory to God in the highest) 1 the Greater Doxology, beginning in Latin with these words. 2 a musical setting of this.
Gloria Patri	(lit: glory to the father) 1 the Lesser Doxology, beginning in Latin with these words. 2 a musical setting of this.
hinc illae lacrimae	hence those tears.
HJ	(abbr for hic jacet) here lies (*on gravestones*).
HJS	(abbr for hic jacet sepultus) here lies buried (*on gravestones*).
horrible dictu	horrible to relate.
ibid.	abbr for ibidem.
ibidem	in the same place (*in annotations, bibliographies, etc., when referring to a book, article, chapter, or page previously cited*).
id est	that is (to say); in other words.
idem	the same (*used to refer to an article, chapter, etc., previously cited*).
i.e.	abbr for id est.
ign.	abbr for ignotus.
ignoratio elenchi	(lit: an ignorance of proof: *Logic*) 1 a purported refutation of a proposition that does not in fact prove it false but merely establishes a related but strictly irrelevant proposition. 2 the fallacy of arguing in this way.
ignotum per ignotius	(lit: the unknown by means of the more unknown) an explanation that is obscurer than the thing to be explained.
ignotus	unknown.
ignis fatuus	will o' the wisp.
Imp.	1 (abbr for **Imperator**) Emperor; 2 (abbr for **Imperatrix**) Empress.
in absentia	in one's absence; in the absence of: he was condemned **in absentia**.
in aeternum	forever; eternally.
in articulo mortis	at the point of death.

in camera	(lit: in the chamber) in private.
in extenso	at full length.
in extremis	(lit: in the furthest reaches) 1 in extremity; in dire straits. 2 at the point of death.
infra	below.
infra dig	(abbr for **infra dignitatem**) beneath one's dignity.
in loco parentis	in place of a parent (*said of a person acting in a parental capacity*).
in medias res	(lit: into the midst of things) in or into the middle of events or a narrative.
in memoriam	in memory of; as a memorial to (*used in obituaries, epitaphs etc*).
in perpetuum	for ever.
in personam	(lit: against the person) directed against a specific person or persons (*LAW: of a judicial act*).
in propria persona	in person; personally.
in rem	(lit: against the matter) directed against property rather than against a specific person (*LAW: of a judicial act*).
in rerum natura	in the nature of things.
INRI	(lit: Jesus of Nazareth, King of the Jews) abbr for **Iesus Nazarenus Rex Iudaeorum** (*the inscription placed over Christ's head during the Crucifixion*).
in situ	(lit: in position) in the natural, original, or appropriate position.
inter alia	among other things.
inter alios	among other people.
inter vivos	(*LAW*) between living people: **an inter vivos gift**.
in toto	totally; entirely; completely.
in utero	within the womb.
in vacuo	in a vacuum.
in vino veritas	in wine there is truth.
in vitro	(lit: in glass) made to occur outside the body of the organism in an artificial environment (*of biological processes or reactions*): **in vitro fertilization**.
in vivo	(lit: in a living (thing)) occurring or carried out in the living organism (*of biological processes or experiments*).
ipse dixit	(lit: he himself said it) an arbitrary and unsupported assertion.
ipsissima verba	the very words.
ipso facto	by the fact itself.
i.q.	(lit: the same as) abbr for **idem quod**.
lapsus linguae	a slip of the tongue.
lc	(abbr for **(in) loco citato**) in the place cited.

lex loci	the law of the place.
lex non scripta	the unwritten law; common law.
lex scripta	the written law; statute law.
lex talionis	the law of revenge or retaliation.
loc. cit.	(abbr for (in) **loco citato**) in the place cited (*in textual annotation*).
magna cum laude	(chiefly US) with great praise (*the second of three designations for above-average achievement in examinations*).
magnum opus	a great work of art or literature (*especially the greatest single work of an artist*).
mala fide	undertaken in bad faith.
mare clausum	(lit: closed sea: *LAW*) a sea coming under the jurisdiction of one nation and closed to all others.
mare liberum	(lit: free sea: *LAW*) a sea open to navigation by shipping of all nations.
mare nostrum	(lit: our sea) the Mediterranean.
mater	mother (*often used facetiously*).
mater dolorosa	(lit: sorrowful mother) the Virgin Mary sorrowing for the dead Christ (*especially as depicted in art*).
materfamilias	(lit: mother of family) the mother of a family or the female head of a family.
materia medica	(lit: medical matter) **1** the branch of medical science concerned with the study of drugs used in the treatment of disease. **2** the drugs used in the treatment of disease.
mea culpa	(lit: my fault) an acknowledgement of guilt.
memento mori	(lit: remember you must die) an object, such as a skull, intended to remind people of the inevitability of death.
mens sana in corpore sano	a healthy mind in a healthy body.
mens rea	(lit: guilty mind: *LAW*) a criminal intention or knowledge that an act is wrong.
miles gloriosus	a braggart soldier (*especially as a stock figure in comedy*).
mirabile dictu	wonderful to relate.
mittimus	(lit: we send) a warrant of commitment to prison or a command to a jailer directing him to hold someone in prison.
modus operandi	procedure; method of operating; manner of working.
modus ponens	(lit: mood that affirms) the principle that whenever a conditional statement and its antecedent are given to be true its consequent may be validly inferred.

modus tollens	(lit: mood that denies) the principle that whenever a conditional statement and the negation of its consequent are given to be true, the negation of its antecedent may be validly inferred.
modus vivendi	(lit: way of living) a working arrangement between conflicting interests; practical compromise.
motu proprio	(lit: of his own accord) an administrative papal bull.
multum in parvo	much in a small space.
mutatis mutandis	with the necessary changes.
NB, N.B., nb, n.b.	(abbr for **nota bene**) note well.
nem. con.	(abbr for **nemine contradicente**) no-one contradicting; unanimously.
nemo me impune lacessit	no-one provokes me with impunity.
ne plus ultra	(lit: not more beyond) the extreme or perfect point or state.
nihil	nil; nothing.
nihil obstat	there is no obstacle.
nil desperandum	(lit: nothing to be despaired of) never despair.
nisi prius	(lit: unless previously) 1 *in England* (a) a direction that a case be brought up to Westminster for trial before a single judge and jury. (b) the writ giving this direction. 2 *in the US* a court where civil actions are tried by a single judge sitting with a jury as distinguished from an appellate court.
nolens volens	whether willing or unwilling.
noli me tangere	(lit: do not touch me) a warning against interfering with or against touching a person or thing.
nolle prosequi	(lit: do not pursue) an entry made on the court record when the plaintiff in a civil suit or prosecutor in a criminal prosecution undertakes not to continue the action or prosecution.
nolo contendere	(lit: I do not wish to contend) a plea made by a defendant to a criminal charge having the same effect in those proceedings as a plea of guilty but not precluding him from denying the charge in a subsequent action.
non compos mentis	(lit: not in control of one's mind) mentally incapable of managing one's own affairs; of unsound mind; insane.
non prosequitur	(lit: he does not proceed) a judgment in favour of a defendant when the plaintiff failed to take the necessary steps in an action within the time allowed.
non sequitur	(lit: it does not follow) 1 (*gen*) a statement having little or no relevance to what preceded it. 2 (*Logic*) a conclusion that does not follow from the premises.
nulli secundus	second to none.

numen	(lit: divine power) 1 (*especially in ancient Roman religion*) a deity or spirit presiding over a thing or place. 2 a guiding principle, force, or spirit.
Nunc Dimittis	(lit: now let depart) 1 the Canticle of Simeon (*Luke 2:29-32*). 2 a musical setting of this.
ob.	1 abbr for obiit. 2 (abbr for obiter) incidentally; in passing.
obiit	he or she died (*on gravestones*).
obiter dictum	(lit: something said in passing) 1 (*LAW*) an observation by a judge on some point of law not directly in issue in the case before him and thus neither requiring his decision nor serving as a precedent, but nevertheless of persuasive authority. 2 any comment, remark, or observation made in passing.
obscurum per obscurius	(lit: the obscure by means of the more obscure) an explanation that is obscurer than the thing to be explained.
omnium-gatherum	(often facetious) a miscellaneous collection; assortment.
onus probandi	(*LAW*) the burden of proof.
op. cit.	(abbr of opere citato) in the work cited.
opus anglicanum	(lit: English work) fine embroidery (*especially of church vestments*).
ora pro nobis	pray for us.
O tempora! O mores!	oh the times! oh the customs!
p.a.	abbr of per annum.
pace	by leave of; with due deference to (*used to acknowledge politely someone who disagrees with the speaker or writer*).
pari passu	with equal speed or progress; equably (*often used to refer to the right of creditors to receive assets from the same source without one taking precedence*).
passim	here and there; throughout (*used to indicate that what is referred to occurs frequently in the work cited*).
paterfamilias	(lit: father of the family) 1 the male head of a household. 2 the head of a household having authority over its members.
pax vobiscum	peace be with you.
peccavi	(lit: I have sinned) a confession of guilt.
peculium	(lit: property) property that a father or master allowed his child or slave to hold as his own.
per annum	every year; year by year.
per ardua ad astra	through difficulties to the stars (*motto of the RAF*).
per capita	(lit: according to heads) of or for each person.
per contra	on the contrary.

per diem	(lit: for the day) **1** every day; by the day. **2** an allowance for daily expenses, usually those incurred while working.
per mensem	every month; by the month.
per pro	(abbr for **per procurationem**) by delegation to; through the agency of (*used when signing documents on behalf of someone else*).
persona grata	an acceptable person (*especially a diplomat acceptable to the government of the country to which he is sent*).
persona non grata	unacceptable or unwelcome person.
petitio principii	(lit: an assumption at the beginning: *Logic*) a form of fallacious reasoning in which the conclusion has been assumed in the premises; begging the question.
pia mater	(lit: pious mother) the innermost of the three membranes that cover the brain and spinal cord.
pinxit	(he or she) painted this (*used formerly on works of art next to the artist's name*).
p.m., P.M., pm, PM	abbr. for **1** post meridiem **2** postmortem.
post-bellum	(lit: after war) of or during the period after a war, especially the American Civil War.
post hoc	(lit: after this: *Logic*) the fallacy of assuming that temporal succession is evidence of causal relation.
post hoc, ergo propter hoc	after this, therefore because of this (*a fallacy of reasoning*).
post meridiem	after noon.
postmortem	(lit: after death) *n* **1** dissection and examination of a dead body to determine the cause of death. **2** analysis or study of a recently completed event ♦ *adj* occurring after death.
pp	abbr for **1** per pro. **2** post prandium after a meal (*in prescriptions*).
PPS	(lit: after postscript; abbr for **post postscriptum**) additional postscript.
pr	(abbr for: **per rectum**) through the rectum (*in prescriptions*).
prima facie	at a first view.
primum mobile	(lit: first moving (thing)) prime mover.
primus inter pares	first among equals.
prn	(abbr for **pro re nata**) as the situation demands, as needed (*in prescriptions*).
pro forma	(lit: for form's sake) **1** prescribing a set form or procedure. **2** performed in a set manner.
pro patria	for one's country.
pro rata	in proportion.
pro tempore	for the time being.
proxime accessit	(lit: he or she came next) the runner-up.

q.e.	(abbr for **quod est**) which is.
QED	abbr for **quod erat demonstrandum**.
QEF	abbr for **quod erat faciendum**.
quid pro quo	(lit something for something) **1** a reciprocal exchange. **2** something given in compensation, especially an advantage or object given in exchange for another.
quis custodiet ipsos custodes?	who will guard the guards?
q.l.	(abbr for **quantum libet**) as much as you please (*in prescriptions*).
qm	(abbr for **quaque mane**) every morning (*in prescriptions*).
qn	(abbr for **quaque nocte**) every night (*in prescriptions*).
quod erat demonstrandum	which was to be proved.
quod erat faciendum	which was to be done.
quot homines, tot sententiæ	there are as many opinions as there are people.
quo vadis?	whither goest thou?
qqv	(abbr for **quae vide**) which (*words, items etc*) see (*denoting a cross reference to more than one item*).
qs	(abbr for **quantum sufficit**) as much as will suffice (*in prescriptions*).
qv	(abbr for **quod vide**) which (*word, item etc*) see (*denoting a cross reference*).
rara avis	(lit rare bird) an unusual, uncommon or exceptional person or thing.
reductio ad absurdum	(lit reduction to the absurd) **1** a method of disproving a proposition by showing that its inevitable consequences would be absurd. **2** a method of indirectly proving a proposition by assuming its negation to be true and showing that this leads to an absurdity. **3** application of a principle or a proposed principle to an instance in which it is absurd.
requiescat	(lit may he or she rest) a prayer for the repose of the souls of the dead.
requiescat in pace	may he or she rest in peace.
res gestae	(lit things done) **1** things done or accomplished; achievements. **2** (*LAW*) incidental facts and circumstances that are admissible in evidence because they introduce or explain the matter in issue.
res ipsa loquitur	(*LAW*) the thing or matter speaks for itself.
res judicata	(*LAW*) a matter already adjudicated upon that cannot be raised again.
res publica	(lit the public thing) the state, republic, or commonwealth.

resurgam	I shall rise again.
RI	1 (abbr for **Regina et Imperatrix**) Queen and Empress. 2 (abbr for **Rex et Imperator**) King and Emperor.
rigor mortis	(lit: rigidity of death) the stiffness of joints and muscular rigidity of a dead body.
RIP	abbr for **requiescat** or **requiescant in pace**.
risus sardonicus	(lit: sardonic laugh) fixed contraction of the facial muscles resulting in a peculiar distorted grin, caused especially by tetanus.
sanctum sanctorum	(lit: holy of holies) 1 (*Bible*) the holy of holies. 2 (*often facetious*) an especially private place.
sartor resartus	the tailor patched.
schola cantorum	(lit: school of singers) a choir or choir school maintained by a church.
scire facias	(lit: cause (him) to know) 1 (*LAW, rare*) a judicial writ founded upon some record, such as a judgement, letters patent, etc., requiring the person against whom it is brought to show cause why the record should not be enforced or annulled. 2 a proceeding begun by the issue of such a writ.
semper fidelis	always faithful.
semper idem	always the same.
seq.	(abbr for **sequens**) the following (one).
seqq.	(abbr for **sequentia**) the following (ones).
seriatim	in order.
sic	thus (*often used to call attention to some quoted mistake*).
sic itur ad astra	such is the way to the stars.
sic transit gloria mundi	so passes the glory of the world.
si monumentum requiris, circumspice	if you seek (his) monument, look around you (*inscription on the architect Sir Christopher Wren's tomb in St Paul's Cathedral*).
sine die	without a day.
sine prole	(*LAW*) without issue.
sine qua non	(lit: without which not) an indispensable condition or requirement.
sl	(abbr for **sine loco**) without place (*of publication*).
sp	abbr for **sine prole**.
spiritus asper	rough breathing.
spiritus lenis	smooth breathing.
SPQR	(abbr for **Senatus Populusque Romanus**) the Senate and People of Rome.
sq.	(abbr for **sequens**) the following (one).
sqq.	(abbr for **sequentia**) the following (ones).

Stabat Mater	(lit: the mother was standing) 1 a Latin hymn, probably of the 13th century, commemorating the sorrows of the Virgin Mary at the crucifixion and used in the Mass and various other services. 2 a musical setting of this hymn.
status quo	(lit: the state in which) the existing state of affairs.
stet	let it stand.
sub judice	before a court of law or a judge; under judicial consideration.
sub rosa	(lit: under the rose) secretly.
sub voce	under the word.
sui generis	(lit: of its own kind) unique.
sui juris	(lit: of one's own right) (*LAW*) of full age and not under disability; legally competent to manage one's own affairs; independent.
summa cum laude	(*chiefly U.S.*) with the utmost praise (*the highest of three designations for above-average achievement in examinations. In Britain it is sometimes used to designate a first-class honours degree*).
summum bonum	the principle of goodness in which all moral values are included or from which they are derived; highest or supreme good.
suo jure	(*chiefly LAW*) in one's own right.
suo loco	(*chiefly LAW*) in a person or thing's own or rightful place.
supra	above.
sursum corda	lift up your hearts (to God).
SV	abbr for **sub voce**.
tabula rasa	(lit: a scraped tablet) 1 the mind in its uninformed original state. 2 an opportunity for a fresh start; clean slate.
taedium vitae	(lit: weariness of life) the feeling that life is boring and dull.
Te Deum	(lit: Thee, God) 1 an ancient Latin hymn in rhythmic prose, sung or recited at matins in the Roman Catholic Church and in English translation at morning prayer in the Church of England and used by both churches as an expression of thanksgiving on special occasions. 2 a musical setting of this hymn. 3 a service of thanksgiving in which the recital of this hymn forms a central part.
te igitur	(lit: Thee, therefore: *Roman Catholic Church*) the first prayer of the canon of the Mass.
tempore	in the time of.
tempus fugit	time flies.
terminus ad quem	(lit: the end to which) the aim or terminal point.
terminus a quo	(lit: the end from which) the starting point; beginning.

terra firma	the solid earth; firm ground.
terra incognita	an unexplored or unknown land, region or area for study.
tertium quid	a third something.
t.i.d.	(abbr for **ter in die**) three times a day (*in prescriptions*).
tu quoque	you likewise (*a retort made by a person accused of a crime implying that the accuser is also guilty of the same crime*).
uberrima fides	utmost good faith.
ubique	everywhere.
ubi supra	where (mentioned or cited) above.
ultima Thule	(lit: the most distant Thule) 1 the utmost boundary or limit. 2 a remote goal or aim.
ultra vires	beyond one's powers.
una voce	with one voice.
urbi et orbi	(*Roman Catholic Church*) to the city and the world (*a phrase qualifying the solemn papal blessing*).
ut dict.	(abbr for **ut dictum**) as directed.
ut infra	as below.
ut supra	as above.
v.	abbr for 1 **verso**. 2 **versus**. 3 **vide**.
vade in pace	go in peace.
vade mecum	(lit: go with me) a handbook or other aid carried on the person for immediate use when needed.
væe victis	woe to the conquered!
vale	farewell!
veni, vidi, vici	I came, I saw, I conquered.
venire facias	(lit: you must make come: LAW) a writ directing a sheriff to summon suitable persons to form a jury.
verbatim et litteratim	word for word and letter for letter.
verb. sap.	(abbr for **verbum sapienti sat est**) a word is enough to the wise.
verso	1 the back of a sheet of printed paper. 2 the side of a coin opposite to the obverse; reverse.
versus	1 against; in opposition to. 2 as opposed to; in contrast with.
via	by way of.
via media	a middle course.
vice	in the place of; instead of; as a substitute for.
vice versa	the other way round.
vide	see.
videlicet	namely; to wit.

vi et armis (lit: by force and arms) a kind of trespass accompanied by force and violence.

VIR (abbr for **Victoria Imperatrix Regina**) Victoria, Empress and Queen.

virginibus puerisque for maidens and youths.

vis inertiæ the power of inertia.

viva voce (lit: with living voice) *adv*, *adj* by word of mouth ♦ *n* an oral examination.

viz. abbr for **videlicet**.

vl (abbr for **varia lecto**) variant reading.

vollente Deo God willing.

vox populi the voice of the people; popular or public opinion.

vox populi, vox Dei the voice of the people is the voice of God.

VR (abbr for **Victoria Regina**) Queen Queen Victoria.

VRI (abbr for **Victoria Regina et Imperatrix**) Victoria, Queen and Empress.

English-Latin

A, a

a, an *art* not translated; (*a certain*) quīdam; **twice a day** bis in diē; **four acres a man** quaterna in singulōs iūgera.
aback *adv*: **taken ~** dēprehēnsus.
abaft *adv* in puppī ♦ *prep* post, pōne.
abandon *vt* relinquere; (*wilfully*) dērelinquere, dēserere; (*to danger*) ōbicere; (*to pleasure*) dēdere; (*plan*) abicere; **~ hope** spem abicere.
abandoned *adj* perditus.
abase *vt* dēprimere; **~ oneself** sē prōsternere.
abash *vt* perturbāre; rubōrem incutere (*dat*).
abate *vt* minuere, imminuere; (*a portion*) remittere ♦ *vi* (*fever*) dēcēdere; (*passion*) dēfervēscere; (*price*) laxāre; (*storm*) cadere.
abatement *n* remissiō *f*, dēminūtiō *f*.
abbess *n* abbātissa *f*.
abbey *n* abbātia *f*.
abbot *n* abbās *m*.
abbreviate *vt* imminuere.
abbreviation *n* (*writing*) nota *f*.
abdicate *vt* sē abdicāre (*abl*).
abdication *n* abdicātiō *f*.
abduct *vt* abripere.
abduction *n* raptus *m*.
aberration *n* error *m*.
abet *vt* adiuvāre, adesse (*dat*), favēre (*dat*).
abettor *n* adiūtor *m*, minister *m*, fautor *m*, socius *m*.
abeyance *n*: **in ~** intermissus; **be in ~** iacēre.
abhor *vt* ōdisse, invīsum habēre.
abhorrence *n* odium *nt*.
abhorrent *adj*: **~ to** aliēnus ab.
abide *vi* (*dwell*) habitāre; (*tarry*) commorārī; (*last*) dūrāre; **~ by** *vt fus* stāre (*abl*), perstāre in (*abl*).
abiding *adj* perpetuus, diūturnus.
ability *n* (*to do*) facultās *f*, potestās *f*; (*physical*) vīrēs *fpl*; (*mental*) ingenium *nt*; **to the best of my ~** prō meā parte, prō virīlī parte
abject *adj* abiectus, contemptus; (*downcast*) dēmissus.
abjectly *adv* humiliter, dēmissē.
abjure *vt* ēiūrāre.
ablative *n* ablātīvus *m*.
ablaze *adj* flāgrāns, ardēns.
able *adj* perītus, doctus; **be ~** posse, valēre.
able-bodied *adj* rōbustus.
ablution *n* lavātiō *f*.
ably *adv* perītē, doctē.
abnegation *n* abstinentia *f*.

abnormal *adj* inūsitātus; (*excess*) immodicus.
abnormally *adv* inūsitātē, praeter mōrem.
aboard *adv* in nāvī; **go ~** nāvem cōnscendere; **put ~** impōnere.
abode *n* domicilium *nt*, sēdes *f*.
abolish *vt* tollere, ē mediō tollere, abolēre; (*law*) abrogāre.
abolition *n* dissolūtiō *f*; (*law*) abrogātiō *f*.
abominable *adj* dētestābilis, nefārius.
abominably *adv* nefāriē, foedē.
abominate *vt* dētestārī.
abomination *n* odium *nt*; (*thing*) nefas *nt*.
aboriginal *adj* prīscus.
aborigines *n* aborīginēs *mpl*.
abortion *n* abortus *m*.
abortive *adj* abortīvus; (*fig*) inritus; **be ~ ad** inritum redigī.
abound *vi* abundāre, superesse; **~ in** abundāre (*abl*), adfluere (*abl*).
abounding *adj* abundāns, adfluēns; cōpiōsus ab.
about *adv* (*place*) usu expressed by cpd verbs; (*number*) circiter, ferē, fermē ♦ *prep* (*place*) circā, circum (*acc*); (*number*) circā, ad (*acc*); (*time*) sub (*acc*); (*concerning*) dē (*abl*); **~ to die** moritūrus; **I am ~ to go in** eō est ut eam.
above *adv* suprā; **from ~** dēsuper; **over and ~** īnsuper ♦ *prep* suprā (*acc*); (*motion*) super (*acc*); (*rest*) super (*abl*); **be ~** (*conduct*) indignārī.
abreast *adv* (*ships*) aequātīs prōrīs; **walk ~ of** latus tegere (*dat*).
abridge *vt* contrahere, compendī facere.
abridgement *n* epitomē *f*.
abroad *adv* peregrē; (*out of doors*) forīs; **be ~** peregrīnārī; **from ~** peregrē.
abrogate *vt* dissolvere; (*law*) abrogāre.
abrupt *adj* subitus, repentīnus; (*speech*) concīsus.
abscess *n* vomica *f*.
abscond *vi* aufugere.
absence *n* absentia *f*; **in my ~** mē absente; **leave of ~** commeātus *m*.
absent *adj* absēns; **be ~** abesse; **~ oneself** *vi* deesse, nōn adesse.
absent-minded *adj* immemor, parum attentus.
absolute *adj* absolūtus, perfectus; (*not limited*) īnfīnītus; (*not relative*) simplex; **~ power** rēgnum *nt*, dominātus *m*; **~ ruler** rēx.
absolutely *adv* absolūtē, omnīnō.
absolution *n* venia *f*.

absolve vt absolvere, exsolvere; (from
punishment) condōnāre.
absorb vt bibere, absorbēre; (fig) distringere;
I am ~ed in tōtus sum in (abl).
absorbent adj bibulus.
abstain vi abstinēre, sē abstinēre; (from
violence) temperāre.
abstemious adj sobrius.
abstinence n abstinentia f, continentia f.
abstinent adj abstinēns, sobrius.
abstract adj mente perceptus, cōgitātiōne
comprehēnsus ♦ n epitomē f ♦ vt abstrahere,
dēmere.
abstraction n (idea) nōtiō f; (inattention)
animus parum attentus.
abstruse adj reconditus, obscūrus, abstrūsus.
absurd adj ineptus, absurdus.
absurdity n ineptiae fpl, insulsitās f.
absurdly adv ineptē, absurdē.
abundance n cōpia f, abundantia f; there is ~
of abundē est (gen).
abundant adj cōpiōsus, abundāns, largus; be
~ abundāre.
abundantly adv abundē, abundanter, adfātim.
abuse vt abūtī (abl); (words) maledīcere (dat)
♦ n probra ntpl, maledicta ntpl, convīcium nt,
contumēlia f.
abusive adj maledicus, contumēliōsus.
abut vi adiacēre; ~ting on cōnfīnis (dat),
fīnitimus (dat).
abysmal adj profundus.
abyss n profundum nt, vorāgō f; (water) gurges
m; (fig) barathrum nt.
academic adj scholasticus; (style) umbrātilis;
(sect) Acadēmicus.
academy n schola f; (Plato's) Acadēmīa f.
accede vi adsentīrī; ~ to accipere.
accelerate vt, vi adcelerāre, festīnāre;
(process) mātūrāre.
accent n vōx f; (intonation) sonus m; (mark)
apex m ♦ vt (syllable) acuere; (word) sonum
admovēre (dat).
accentuate vt exprimere.
accept vt accipere.
acceptable adj acceptus, grātus, probābilis;
be ~ placēre.
acceptation n significātiō f.
access n aditus m; (addition) accessiō f; (illness)
impetus m.
accessary n socius m, particeps m.
accessible adj (person) adfābilis, facilis; be ~
(place) patēre; (person) facilem sē praebēre.
accession n (addition) accessiō f; (king's)
initium rēgnī.
accident n cāsus m, calamitās f.
accidental adj fortuītus.
accidentally adv cāsū, fortuītō.
acclaim vt adclāmāre.
acclamation n clāmor m, studium nt.
acclimatize vt aliēnō caelō adsuēfacere.
accommodate vt accommodāre, aptāre;
(lodging) hospitium parāre (dat); ~ oneself to
mōrigerārī (dat).

accommodating adj facilis.
accommodation n hospitium nt.
accompany vt comitārī; (courtesy) prōsequī;
(to Forum) dēdūcere; (music) concinere (dat).
accomplice n socius m, particeps m, cōnscius
m.
accomplish vt efficere, perficere, patrāre.
accomplished adj doctus, perītus.
accomplishment n effectus m, perfectiō f,
fīnis m; ~s pl artēs fpl.
accord vi inter sē congruere, cōnsentīre ♦ vt
dare, praebēre, praestāre ♦ n cōnsēnsus m,
concordia f; (music) concentus m; of one's
own ~ suā sponte, ultrō; with one ~ unā vōce.
accordance n: in ~ with ex, ē (abl), secundum
(acc).
according adv: ~ to ex, ē (abl), secundum (acc);
(proportion) prō (abl); ~ as prōut.
accordingly adv itaque, igitur, ergō.
accost vt appellāre, adloquī, compellāre.
account n ratiō f; (story) nārrātiō f, expositiō f;
on ~ of ob (acc); propter (acc), causā (gen); be
of no ~ (person) nihilī aestimārī, nēquam
esse; on that ~ idcircō ideō; on your ~ tuā
grātiā, tuō nōmine; give an ~ ratiōnem
reddere; present an ~ ratiōnem referre; take
~ of ratiōnem habēre (gen); put down to my
~ mihī expēnsum ferre; the ~s balance ratiō
cōnstat/convenit.
account vi: ~ for ratiōnēs reddere, adferre
(cūr); that ~s for it haec causa est; (prov) hinc
illae lacrimae.
accountant n ā ratiōnibus, ratiōcinātor m.
accountable adj reus; I am ~ for mihi ratiō
reddenda est (gen).
account book n tabulae fpl; cōdex acceptī et
expēnsī.
accoutred adj īnstructus, ōrnātus.
accoutrements n ōrnāmenta ntpl, arma ntpl.
accredited adj pūblicā auctōritāte missus.
accretion n accessiō f.
accrue vi (addition) cēdere; (advantage)
redundāre.
accumulate vt cumulāre, congerere,
coacervāre ♦ vi crēscere, cumulārī.
accumulation n cumulus m, acervus m.
accuracy n cūra f; (writing) subtīlitās f.
accurate adj (work) exāctus, subtīlis; (worker)
dīligēns.
accurately adv subtīliter, ad amussim,
dīligenter.
accursed adj sacer; (fig) exsecrātus,
scelestus.
accusation n (act) accūsātiō f; (charge) crīmen
nt; (unfair) īnsimulātiō f; (false) calumnia f;
bring an ~ against accūsāre; (to a magistrate)
nōmen dēferre (gen).
accusative n (case) accūsātīvus m.
accuse vt accūsāre, crīminārī, reum facere;
(falsely) īnsimulāre; the ~d reus; (said by
prosecutor) iste.
accuser n accūsātor m; (civil suit) petītor m;
(informer) dēlātor m.

accustom *vt* adsuēfacere; ~ **oneself** adsuēscere, consuēscere.
accustomed *adj* adsuētus; **be** ~ solēre; **become** ~ adsuēscere, consuēscere.
ace *n* ūniō *f*; **I was within an** ~ **of going** minimum āfuit quin īrem.
acerbity *n* acerbitās *f*.
ache *n* dolor *m* ♦ *vi* dolēre.
achieve *vt* cōnficere, patrāre; (*win*) cōnsequī, adsequī.
achievement *n* factum *nt*, rēs gesta.
acid *adj* acidus.
acknowledge *vt* (*fact*) agnōscere; (*fault*) fatērī, cōnfitērī; (*child*) tollere; (*service*) grātias agere prō (*abl*); **I have to** ~ **your letter of 1st March** accēpī litterās tuās Kal. Mart. datās.
acknowledgement *n* cōnfessiō *f*; grātia *f*.
acme *n* fastīgium *nt*, flōs *m*.
aconite *n* aconītum *nt*.
acorn *n* glāns *f*.
acoustics *n* rēs audītōria *f*.
acquaint *vt* certiōrem facere, docēre; ~ **oneself with** cognōscere; ~**ed with** gnārus (*gen*), perītus (*gen*).
acquaintance *n* (*with fact*) cognitiō *f*, scientia *f*; (*with person*) familiāritās *f*, ūsus *m*; (*person*) nōtus *m*, familiāris *m*.
acquiesce *vi* (*assent*) adquiēscere; (*submit*) aequō animō patī.
acquiescence *n*: **with your** ~ tē nōn adversante, pāce tuā.
acquire *vt* adquīrere, adipīscī, cōnsequī; nancīscī.
acquirements *n* artēs *fpl*.
acquisition *n* (*act*) comparātiō *f*, quaestus *m*; (*thing*) quaesītum *nt*.
acquisitive *adj* quaestuōsus.
acquit *vt* absolvere; ~ **oneself** sē praestāre, officiō fungī.
acquittal *n* absolūtiō *f*.
acre *n* iūgerum *nt*.
acrid *adj* asper, ācer.
acrimonious *adj* acerbus, truculentus.
acrimony *n* acerbitās *f*.
acrobat *n* fūnambulus *m*.
acropolis *n* arx *f*.
across *adv* trānsversus ♦ *prep* trāns (*acc*).
act *n* factum *nt*, facinus *nt*; (*play*) āctus *m*; (*POL*) āctum *nt*, senātus cōnsultum *nt*, dēcrētum *nt*; **I was in the** ~ **of saying** in eō erat ut dīcerem; **caught in the** ~ dēprehēnsus ♦ *vi* facere, agere; (*conduct*) sē gerere; (*stage*) histriōnem esse, partēs agere; (*pretence*) simulāre ♦ *vt*: ~ **a part** partēs agere, persōnam sustinēre; ~ **the part of** age~e; ~ **as** esse, munere fungī (*gen*); ~ **upon** (*instructions*) exsequī.
action *n* (*doing*) āctiō *f*; (*deed*) factum *nt*, facinus *nt*; (*legal*) āctiō *f*, līs *f*; (*MIL*) proelium *nt*; (*of play*) āctiō *f*; (*of speaker*) gestus *m*; **bring an** ~ **against** lītem intendere, āctiōnem īnstituere (*dat*); **be in** ~ agere, rem gerere;

active *adj* impiger, strēnuus, sēdulus, nāvus.
actively *adv* impigrē, strēnuē, nāviter.
activity *n* (*motion*) mōtus *m*; (*energy*) industria *f*, sēdulitās *f*.
actor *n* histriō *m*; (*in comedy*) cōmoedus *m*; (*in tragedy*) tragoedus *m*.
actress *n* mīma *f*.
actual *adj* vērus, ipse.
actually *adv* rē vērā.
actuate *vt* movēre, incitāre.
acumen *n* acūmen *nt*, ingenī aciēs, argūtiae *fpl*.
acute *adj* acūtus, ācer; (*pain*) ācer; (*speech*) argūtus, subtīlis.
acutely *adv* acūtē, ācriter, argūtē.
acuteness *n* (*mind*) acūmen *nt*, aciēs *f*, subtīlitas *f*.
adage *n* prōverbium *nt*.
adamant *n* adamās *m* ♦ *adj* obstinātus.
adamantine *adj* adamantinus.
adapt *vt* accommodāre.
adaptable *adj* flexibilis, facile accommodandus.
adaptation *n* accommodātiō *f*.
add *vt* addere, adicere, adiungere; **be ~ed** accēdere.
adder *n* vīpera *f*.
addicted *adj* dēditus.
addition *n* adiūnctiō *f*, accessiō *f*; additāmentum *nt*, incrēmentum *nt*; **in** ~ īnsuper, praetereā; **in** ~ **to** praeter (*acc*).
additional *adj* novus, adiūnctus.
addled *adj* (*egg*) irritus; (*brain*) inānis.
address *vt* compellāre, alloquī; (*crowd*) cōntiōnem habēre apud (*acc*); (*letter*) īnscrībere; ~ **oneself** (*to action*) accingī ♦ *n* adloquium *nt*; (*public*) cōntiō *f*; (*letter*) īnscrīptiō *f*.
adduce *vt* (*argument*) adferre; (*witness*) prōdūcere.
adept *adj* perītus.
adequate *adj* idōneus, dignus, pār; **be** ~ sufficere.
adequately *adv* satis, ut pār est.
adhere *vi* haerēre, adhaerēre; ~ **to** inhaerēre (*dat*), inhaerēscere in (*abl*); (*agreement*) manēre, stāre in (*abl*).
adherent *n* adsectātor *m*; (*of party*) fautor *m*; (*of person*) cliēns *m*.
adhesive *adj* tenax.
adieu *interj* valē, valēte; **bid** ~ **to** valēre iubēre.
adjacent *adj* fīnitimus, vīcīnus; **be** ~ **to** adiacēre (*dat*).
adjoin *vi* adiacēre (*dat*).
adjoining *adj* fīnitimus, adiūnctus; proximus.
adjourn *vt* (*short time*) differre; (*longer time*) prōferre; (*case*) ampliāre ♦ *vi* rem differre, prōferre.
adjournment *n* dīlātiō *f*, prōlātiō *f*.
adjudge *vt* addīcere, adiūdicāre.
adjudicate *vi* dēcernere.

adjudicator *n* arbiter *m*.
adjunct *n* appendix *f*, accessiō *f*.
adjure *vt* obtestārī, obsecrāre.
adjust *vt* (*adapt*) accommodāre; (*put in order*) compōnere.
adjutant *n* (*MIL*) optiō *m*; (*civil*) adiūtor *m*.
administer *vt* administrāre, gerere; (*justice*) reddere; (*oath to*) iūreiūrandō adigere; (*medicine*) dare, adhibēre.
administration *n* administrātiō *f*.
administrator *n* administrātor *m*, prōcūrātor *m*.
admirable *adj* admīrābilis, ēgregius.
admirably *adv* ēgregiē.
admiral *n* praefectus classis; ~'s **ship** nāvis praetōria.
admiralty *n* praefectī classium.
admiration *n* admīrātiō *f*, laus *f*.
admire *vt* admīrārī; mirārī.
admirer *n* laudātor *m*; amātor *m*.
admissible *adj* aequus.
admission *n* (*entrance*) aditus *m*; (*of guilt etc*) cōnfessiō *f*.
admit *vt* (*let in*) admittere, recipere, accipere; (*to membership*) adscīscere; (*argument*) concēdere; (*fault*) fatērī; ~ **of** patī, recipere.
admittedly *adv* sānē.
admonish *vt* admonēre, commonēre, hortārī.
admonition *n* admonitiō *f*.
ado *n* negōtium *nt*; **make much ~ about nothing** fluctūs in simpulō excitāre; **without more ~** prōtinus, sine morā.
adolescence *n* prīma adulēscentia *f*.
adolescent *adj* adulēscēns ♦ *n* adulēscentulus *m*.
adopt *vt* (*person*) adoptāre; (*custom*) adscīscere; ~ **a plan** consilium capere.
adoption *n* (*person*) adoptiō *f*; (*custom*) adsūmptiō *f*; **by ~** adoptīvus.
adoptive *adj* adoptīvus.
adorable *adj* amābilis, venustus.
adorably *adv* venustē.
adoration *n* (*of gods*) cultus *m*; (*of kings*) venerātiō *f*; (*love*) amor *m*.
adore *vt* (*worship*) venerārī; (*love*) adamāre.
adorn *vt* ōrnāre, exōrnāre, decorāre.
adornment *n* ōrnāmentum *nt*, decus *nt*; ōrnātus *m*.
adrift *adj* fluctuāns; **be ~** fluctuāre.
adroit *adj* sollers, callidus.
adroitly *adv* callidē, scītē.
adroitness *n* sollertia *f*, calliditās *f*.
adulation *n* adūlātiō *f*, adsentātiō *f*.
adulatory *adj* blandus.
adult *adj* adultus.
adulterate *vt* corrumpere, adulterāre.
adulterer *n* adulter *m*.
adulteress *n* adultera *f*.
adulterous *adj* incestus.
adultery *n* adulterium *nt*; **commit ~** adulterāre.
adults *npl* pūberēs *mpl*.
adumbrate *vt* adumbrāre.
advance *vt* prōmovēre; (*a cause*) fovēre; (*money*) crēdere; (*opinion*) dīcere; (*to honours*) prōvehere; (*time*) mātūrāre ♦ *vi* prōcēdere, prōgredī, adventāre; (*MIL*) signa prōferre, pedem īnferre; (*progress*) prōficere; (*walk*) incēdere; ~ **to the attack** signa īnferre ♦ *n* prōgressus *m*, prōcessus *m*; (*attack*) impetus *m*; (*money*) mūtuae pecūniae; **in ~** mātūrius; **fix in ~** praefīnīre; **get in ~** praecipere.
advanced *adj* prōvectus; **well ~** (*task*) adfectus.
advancement *n* (*POL*) honōs *m*.
advantage *n* (*benefit*) commodum *nt*, bonum *nt*, ūsus *m*; (*of place or time*) opportūnitās *f*; (*profit*) fructus *m*; (*superiority*) praestantia *f*; **it is an ~** bono est; **be of ~ to** prōdesse (*dat*), ūsuī esse (*dat*); **to your ~** in rem tuam; **it is to your ~** tibi expedit, tuā interest; **take ~ of** (*CIRCS*) ūtī; (*person*) dēcipere, fallere; **have an ~ over** praestāre (*dat*); **be seen to ~** māximē placēre.
advantageous *adj* ūtilis, opportūnus.
advantageously *adv* ūtiliter, opportūnē.
advent *n* adventus *m*.
adventitious *adj* fortuītus.
adventure *n* (*exploit*) facinus memorābile *nt*; (*hazard*) perīculum *nt*.
adventurer *n* vir audāx *m*; (*social*) parasītus *m*.
adventurous *adj* audāx.
adversary *n* adversārius *m*, hostis *m*.
adverse *adj* adversus, contrārius, inimīcus.
adversely *adv* contrāriē, inimīcē, male.
adversity *n* rēs adversae *fpl*, calamitās *f*.
advert *vi*: ~ **to** attingere.
advertise *vt* prōscrībere; vēnditāre.
advertisement *n* prōscrīptiō *f*, libellus *m*.
advice *n* cōnsilium *nt*; (*POL*) auctōritās *f*; (*legal*) respōnsum *nt*; **ask ~ of** cōnsulere; **on the ~ of** Sulla auctōre Sullā.
advisable *adj* ūtilis, operae pretium.
advise *vt* monēre, suādēre (*dat*), cēnsēre (*dat*); ~ **against** dissuādēre.
advisedly *adv* cōnsultō.
adviser *n* auctor *m*, suāsor *m*.
advocacy *n* patrōcinium *nt*.
advocate *n* patrōnus *m*, causidicus *m*; (*supporter*) auctor *m*; **be an ~** causam dīcere ♦ *vt* suādēre, cēnsēre.
adze *n* ascia *f*.
aedile *n* aedīlis *m*.
aedile's *adj* aedīlicius.
aedileship *n* aedīlitās *f*.
aegis *n* aegis *f*; (*fig*) praesidium *nt*.
Aeneid *n* Aenēis *f*.
aerial *adj* āerius.
aesthetic *adj* pulchritūdinis amāns, artificiōsus.
afar *adv* procul; **from ~** procul.
affability *n* cōmitās *f*, facilitās *f*, bonitās *f*.
affable *adj* cōmis, facilis, commodus.
affably *adv* cōmiter.
affair *n* negōtium *nt*, rēs *f*.
affect *vt* afficere, movēre, commovēre;

(*concern*) attingere; (*pretence*) simulāre.
affectation n simulātiō f; (*RHET*) adfectātiō f; (*in
diction*) īnsolentia f; quaesīta *ntpl*.
affected *adj* (*style*) molestus, pūtidus.
affectedly *adv* pūtidē.
affecting *adj* miserābilis.
affection n amor m, cāritās f, studium nt;
(*family*) pietās f.
affectionate *adj* amāns, pius.
affectionately *adv* amanter, piē.
affiance *vt* spondēre.
affidavit n testimōnium nt.
affinity n affīnitās f, cognātiō f.
affirm *vt* adfirmāre, adsevērāre.
affirmation n adfirmātiō f.
affirmative *adj*: **I reply in the** ~ āiō.
affix *vt* adfīgere, adiungere.
afflict *vt* adflīctāre, angere, vexāre; affligere.
affliction n miseria f, dolor m, rēs adversae *fpl*.
affluence n cōpia f, opēs *fpl*.
affluent *adj* dīves, opulentus, locuplēs.
afford *vt* praebēre, dare; **I cannot** ~ rēs mihi
nōn suppetit ad.
affray n rixa f, pugna f.
affright *vt* terrēre ♦ n terror m, pavor m.
affront *vt* offendere, contumēliam dīcere (*dat*)
♦ n iniūria f, contumēlia f.
afield *adv* forīs; **far** ~ peregrē.
afloat *adj* natāns; **be** ~ natāre.
afoot *adv* pedibus; **be** ~ gerī.
aforesaid *adj* suprā dictus.
afraid *adj* timidus; **be** ~ **of** timēre, metuere;
verērī.
afresh *adv* dēnuō, dē integrō.
Africa n Africa f.
aft *adv* in puppī, puppim versus.
after *adj* posterior ♦ *adv* post (*acc*), posteā; **the
day** ~ postrīdiē ♦ *conj* postquam; **the day** ~
postrīdiē quam ♦ *prep* post (*acc*); (*in rank*)
secundum (*acc*); (*in imitation*) ad (*acc*, dē
(*abl*); ~ **all** tamen, dēnique; ~ **reading the
book** librō lēctō; **one thing** ~ **another** aliud
ex aliō; **immediately** ~ statim ab.
aftermath n ēventus m.
afternoon n: **in the** ~ post merīdiem ♦ *adj*
postmerīdiānus.
afterthought n posterior cōgitātiō f.
afterwards *adv* post, posteā, deinde.
again *adv* rūrsus, iterum; ~ **and** ~ etiam atque
etiam, identidem; **once** ~ dēnuō; (*new point in
a speech*) quid?
against *prep* contrā (*acc*), adversus (*acc*), in
(*acc*); ~ **the stream** adversō flūmine; ~ **one's**
will invitus.
agape *adj* hiāns.
age n (*life*) aetās f; (*epoch*) aetās f, saeculum nt;
old ~ senectūs f; **he is of** ~ suī iūris est; **he is
eight years of** ~ octō annōs nātus est, nōnum
annum agit; **of the same** ~ aequālis.
aged *adj* senex, aetāte prōvectus; (*things*)
antīquus.
agency n opera f; **through the** ~ **of** per (*acc*).
agent n āctor m, prōcūrātor m; (*in crime*)

minister m.
aggrandize *vt* augēre, amplificāre.
aggrandizement n amplificātiō f.
aggravate *vt* (*wound*) exulcerāre; (*distress*)
augēre; **become** ~**d** ingravēscere.
aggravating *adj* molestus.
aggregate n summa f.
aggression n incursiō f, iniūria f.
aggressive *adj* ferōx.
aggressiveness n ferōcitās f.
aggressor n oppugnātor m.
aggrieved *adj* īrātus; **be** ~ indignārī.
aghast *adj* attonitus, stupefactus; **stand** ~
obstupēscere.
agile *adj* pernix, vēlōx.
agility n pernīcitās f.
agitate *vt* agitāre; (*mind*) commovēre,
perturbāre.
agitation n commōtiō f, perturbātiō f,
trepidātiō f; (*POL*) tumultus m.
agitator n turbātor m, concitātor m.
aglow *adj* fervidus ♦ *adv*: **be** ~ fervēre.
ago *adv* abhinc (*acc*); **three days** ~ abhinc trēs
diēs; **long** ~ antīquitus, iamprīdem,
iamdūdum; **a short time** ~ dūdum.
agog *adj* sollicitus, ērēctus.
agonize *vt* cruciāre, torquēre.
agonizing *adj* horribilis.
agony n cruciātus m, dolor m.
agrarian *adj* agrārius; ~ **party** agrāriī *mpl*.
agree *vi* (*together*) cōnsentīre, congruere;
(*with*) adsentīrī (*dat*), sentīre cum; (*bargain*)
pacīscī; (*facts*) cōnstāre, convenīre; (*food*)
facilem esse ad concoquendum; ~ **upon**
cōnstituere, compōnere; **it is agreed** constat
(*inter omnes*).
agreeable *adj* grātus, commodus, acceptus.
agreeableness n dulcēdō f, iūcunditās f.
agreeably *adv* iūcundē.
agreement n (*together*) cōnsēnsus m,
concordia f; (*with*) adsēnsus m; (*pact*) pactiō f,
conventum nt, foedus nt; **according to** ~
compāctō, ex compositō; **be in** ~ cōnsentīre,
congruere.
agricultural *adj* rūsticus, agrestis.
agriculture n rēs rūstica f, agrī cultūra f.
aground *adv*: **be** ~ sīdere; **run** ~ in lītus ēicī,
offendere.
ague n horror m, febris f.
ahead *adv* ante; **go** ~ anteīre, praeīre; **go-** ~ *adj*
impiger; **ships in line** ~ agmen nāvium.
aid *vt* adiuvāre, succurrere (*dat*), subvenīre
(*dat*) ♦ n auxilium nt, subsidium nt.
aide-de-camp n optiō m.
ail *vt* dolēre ♦ *vi* aegrōtāre, labōrāre, languēre.
ailing *adj* aeger, īnfirmus.
ailment n morbus m, valētūdō f.
aim *vt* intendere; ~ **at** petere; (*fig*) adfectāre,
spectāre, sequī; (*with verb*) id agere ut ♦ n
fīnis m, prōpositum nt.
aimless *adj* inānis, vānus.
aimlessly *adv* sine ratiōne.
aimlessness n vānitās f.

air n āёr m; (breeze) aura f; (look) vultus m, speciēs f; (tune) modus m; **in the open** ~ sub dīvō; ~s fastus m; **give oneself ~s** sē iactāre.
airily adv hilarē.
airy adj (of air) āerius; (light) tenuis; (place) apertus; (manner) hilaris.
aisle n āla f.
ajar adj sēmiapertus.
akin adj cōnsanguineus, cognātus.
alacrity n alacritās f.
alarm n terror m, formīdō f, trepidātiō f; (sound) clāmor m; **sound an** ~ ad arma conclāmāre; **give the** ~ increpāre; **be in a state of** ~ trepidāre ◆ vt terrēre, perterrēre, perturbāre.
alarming adj formīdolōsus.
alas interj heu.
albeit conj etsī, etiamsī.
alcove n zōthēca f.
alder n alnus f.
alderman n decuriō m.
ale n cervīsia f.
alehouse n caupōna f, taberna f.
alert adj prōmptus, alacer, vegetus.
alertness n alacritās f.
alien adj externus; ~ **to** abhorrēns ab ◆ n peregrīnus m.
alienate vt aliēnāre, abaliēnāre, āvertere, āvocāre.
alienation n aliēnātiō f.
alight vi (from horse) dēscendere, dēsilīre; (bird) īnsīdere.
alight adj: **be** ~ ārdēre; **set** ~ accendere.
alike adj pār, similis ◆ adv aequē, pariter.
alive adj vīvus; **be** ~ vīvere.
all adj omnis; (together) ūniversus, cūnctus; (whole) tōtus; ~ **but** paene; ~ **for** studiōsus (gen); ~ **in** cōnfectus; ~ **of** tōtus; ~ **over with** āctum dē (abl); ~ **the best men** optimus quisque; ~ **the more** eō plūs, tantō plūs; **at** ~ ullō modō, quid; **it is** ~ **up with** actum est de (abl); **not at** ~ haudquāquam ◆ n fortūnae fpl.
allay vt sēdāre, mītigāre, lēnīre.
allegation n adfirmātiō f; (charge) īnsimulātiō f.
allege vt adfirmāre, praetendere; (in excuse) excūsāre.
allegiance n fidēs f; **owe** ~ **to** in fidē esse (gen); **swear** ~ **to** in verba iūrāre (gen).
allegory n allēgoria f, immūtāta ōrātiō f.
alleviate vt mītigāre, adlevāre, sublevāre.
alleviation n levātiō f, levāmentum nt.
alley n (garden) xystus m; (town) angiportus m.
alliance n societās f, foedus nt.
allied adj foederātus, socius; (friends) coniūnctus.
alligator n crocodīlus m.
allocate vt adsignāre, impertīre.
allot vt adsignāre, distribuere; **be ~ted** obtingere.
allotment n (land) adsignātiō f.
allow vt sinere, permittere (dat), concēdere (dat), patī; (admit) fatērī, concēdere;

(approve) comprobāre; **it is ~ed** licet (dat + infin); ~ **for** vt fus ratiōnem habēre (gen).
allowance n venia f, indulgentia f; (pay) stīpendium nt; (food) cibāria ntpl; (for travel) viāticum nt; **make** ~ **for** indulgēre (dat), ignōscere (dat), excusāre.
alloy n admixtum nt.
all right adj rēctē; **it is** ~ bene est.
allude vi: ~ **to** dēsignāre, attingere, significāre.
allure vt adlicere, pellicere.
allurement n blanditia f, blandīmentum nt, illecebra f.
alluring adj blandus.
alluringly adv blandē.
allusion n mentiō f, indicium nt.
alluvial adj: ~ **land** adluviō f.
ally n socius m ◆ vt sociāre, coniungere.
almanac n fāstī mpl.
almighty adj omnipotēns.
almond n (nut) amygdalum nt; (tree) amygdala f.
almost adv paene, ferē, fermē, propemodum.
alms n stipem (no nom) f.
aloe n aloē f.
aloft adj sublīmis ◆ adv sublīmē.
alone adj sōlus, sōlitārius, ūnus ◆ adv sōlum.
along prep secundum (acc), praeter (acc) ◆ adv porrō; **all** ~ iamdūdum, ab initiō; ~ **with** unā cum (abl).
alongside adv: **bring** ~ adpellere; **come** ~ ad crepīdinem accēdere.
aloof adv procul; **stand** ~ sē removēre ◆ adj sēmōtus.
aloofness n sōlitūdō f, sēcessus m.
aloud adv clārē, māgnā vōce.
alphabet n elementa ntpl.
Alps n Alpēs fpl.
already adv iam.
also adv etiam, et, quoque; īdem.
altar n āra f.
alter vt mūtāre, commūtāre; (order) invertere.
alteration n mūtātiō f, commūtātiō f.
altercation n altercātiō f, iūrgium nt.
alternate adj alternus ◆ vt variāre.
alternately adv invicem.
alternation n vicem (no nom) f, vicissitūdō f.
alternative adj alter, alius ◆ n optiō f.
although conj quamquam (indic), etsī/etiamsī (+ cond clause); quamvīs (+ subj).
altitude n altitūdō f.
altogether adv omnīnō; (emphasis) plānē, prōrsus.
altruism n beneficentia f.
alum n alūmen nt.
always adv semper.
amalgamate vt miscēre, coniungere.
amalgamation n coniūnctiō f, temperātiō f.
amanuensis n librārius m.
amass vt cumulāre, coacervāre.
amateur n idiōta m.
amatory adj amātōrius.
amaze vt obstupefacere; attonāre; **be ~d**

obstupēscere.
amazement n stupor m; **in ~** attonitus, stupefactus.
ambassador n lēgātus m.
amber n sūcinum nt.
ambidextrous adj utrīusque manūs compos.
ambiguity n ambiguitās f; (RHET) amphibolia f.
ambiguous adj ambiguus, anceps, dubius.
ambiguously adv ambiguē.
ambition n glōria f, laudis studium.
ambitious adj glōriae cupidus, laudis avidus.
amble vi ambulāre.
ambrosia n ambrosia f.
ambrosial adj ambrosius.
ambuscade n īnsidiae fpl.
ambush n īnsidiae fpl ♦ vt īnsidiārī (cat).
ameliorate vt corrigere, meliōrem reddere.
amelioration n prōfectus m.
amenable adj facilis, docilis.
amend vt corrigere, ēmendāre.
amendment n ēmendātiō f.
amends n (apology) satisfactiō f; **make ~ for** expiāre; **make ~ to** satisfacere (dat)
amenity n (scenery) amoenitās f; (comfort) commodum nt.
amethyst n amethystus f.
amiability n benignitās f, suāvitās f.
amiable adj benignus, suāvis.
amiably adv benignē, suāviter.
amicable adj amīcus, cōmis.
amicably adv amīcē, cōmiter.
amid, amidst prep inter (acc).
amiss adv perperam, secus, incommodē; **take ~** aegrē ferre.
amity n amīcitia f.
ammunition n tēla ntpl.
amnesty n venia f.
among, amongst prep inter (acc), apud (acc).
amorous adj amātōrius, amāns.
amorously adv cum amōre.
amount vi: **~ to** efficere; (fig) esse ♦ n summa f.
amours n amōrēs mpl.
amphibious adj anceps.
amphitheatre n amphitheātrum nt.
ample adj amplus, satis.
amplification n amplificātiō f.
amplify vt amplificāre.
amplitude n amplitūdō f, cōpia f.
amputate vt secāre, amputāre.
amuck adv: **run ~** bacchārī.
amulet n amulētum nt.
amuse vt dēlectāre, oblectāre.
amusement n oblectāmentum nt, dēlectātiō f; **for ~** animī causā.
amusing adj rīdiculus, facētus.
an indef art see **a**.
anaemic adj exsanguis.
analogous adj similis.
analogy n prōportiō f, comparātiō f.
analyse vt excutere, perscrūtārī.
analysis n explicātiō f.
anapaest n anapaestus m.

anarchical adj sēditiōsus.
anarchy n reī pūblicae perturbātiō, lēgēs nullae fpl, licentia f.
anathema n exsecrātiō f; (object) pestis f.
ancestor n proavus m; **~s** pl māiōrēs mpl.
ancestral adj patrius.
ancestry n genus nt, orīgō f.
anchor n ancora f; **lie at ~** in ancorīs stāre; **weigh ~** ancoram tollere ♦ vi ancoram iacere.
anchorage n statiō f.
ancient adj antīquus, prīscus, vetustus; **~ history, ~ world** antīquitās f; **from/in ~ times** antīquitus; **the ~s** veterēs.
and conj et, atque, ac, -que; **~ . . .** not nec, neque; **~ so** itaque.
anecdote n fābella f.
anent prep dē (abl).
anew adv dēnuō, ab integrō.
angel n angelus m.
angelic adj angelicus; (fig) dīvīnus, eximius.
anger n īra f ♦ vt inrītāre.
angle n angulus m ♦ vi hāmō piscārī.
angler n piscātor m.
Anglesey n Mona f.
angrily adv īrātē.
angry adj īrātus; **be ~** īrāscī (dat).
anguish n cruciātus m, dolor m; (mind) angor m.
angular adj angulātus.
animal n animal nt; (domestic) pecus f; (wild) fera f.
animate vt animāre.
animated adj excitātus, vegetus.
animation n ārdor m, alacritās f.
animosity n invidia f, inimīcitia f.
ankle n tālus m.
annalist n annālium scrīptor m.
annals n annālēs mpl.
annex vt addere.
annexation n adiectiō f.
annihilate vt dēlēre, exstinguere, perimere.
annihilation n exstinctiō f, interneciō f.
anniversary n diēs anniversārius; (public) sollemne nt.
annotate vt adnotāre.
annotation n adnotātiō f.
announce vt nūntiāre; (officially) dēnūntiāre, prōnūntiāre; (election result) renūntiāre.
announcement n (official) dēnūntiātiō f; (news) nūntius m.
announcer n nūntius m.
annoy vt inrītāre, vexāre; **be ~ed with** aegrē ferre.
annoyance n molestia f, vexātiō f; (felt) dolor m.
annoying adj molestus.
annual adj annuus, anniversārius.
annually adv quotannīs.
annuity n annua ntpl.
annul vt abrogāre, dissolvere, tollere.
annulment n abrogātiō f.
anoint vt ungere, illinere.

anomalous adj novus.
anomaly n novitās f.
anon adv mox.
anonymous adj incertī auctōris.
anonymously adv sine nōmine.
another adj alius; (second) alter; **of** ~ aliēnus;
one after ~ alius ex aliō; **one** ~ inter sē, alius
alium; **in** ~ **place** alibī; **to** ~ **place** aliō; **in** ~
way aliter; **at** ~ **time** aliās.
answer vt respondēre (dat); (by letter)
rescrībere (dat); (agree) respondēre,
congruere; ~ **a charge** crīmen dēfendere; ~
for vt fus (surety) praestāre; (account)
ratiōnem referre; (substitute) īnstar esse
(gen) ◆ n respōnsum nt; (to a charge) dēfēnsiō
f; ~ **to the name of** vocārī; **give an** ~
respondēre.
answerable adj reus; **I am** ~ **for** ... ratiō mihī
reddenda est ... (gen).
ant n formīca f.
antagonism n simultās f, inimīcitia f.
antagonist n adversārius m, hostis m.
antarctic adj antarcticus.
antecedent adj antecēdēns, prior.
antediluvian adj prīscus, horridus,
Deucaliōnēus.
antelope n dorcas f.
anterior adj prior.
anteroom n vestibulum nt.
anthology n excerpta ntpl; **make an** ~
excerpere.
anthropology n rēs hūmānae fpl.
anticipate vt (expect) exspectāre; (forestall)
antevenīre, occupāre, (in thought) animō
praecipere.
anticipation n exspectātiō f, spēs f;
praesūmptiō f.
antics n gestus m, ineptiae fpl.
anticyclo..e n serēnitās f.
antidote n remedium nt, medicāmen nt.
antipathy n fastīdium nt, odium nt; (things)
repugnantia f.
antiphonal adj alternus.
antiphony n alterna ntpl.
antipodes n contrāria pars terrae.
antiquarian adj historicus.
antiquary n antīquārius m.
antiquated adj prīscus, obsolētus.
antique adj antīquus, prīscus.
antiquity n antīquitās f, vetustās f, veterēs
mpl.
antithesis n contentiō f, contrārium nt.
antlers n cornua ntpl.
anvil n incūs f.
anxiety n sollicitūdō f, metus m, cūra f;
anxietās f.
anxious adj sollicitus, anxius; avidus;
cupidus.
any adj ullus; (interrog) ecquī; (after sī, nisī,
num, nē) quī; (indef) quīvīs, quīlibet; **hardly** ~
nullus ferē; ~ **further** longius; ~ **longer** (of
time) diutius.
anybody pron aliquis; (indef) quīvīs, quīlibet;

(after sī, nisī, num, nē) quis; (interrog) ecquis,
numquis; (after neg) quisquam; **hardly** ~
nēmō ferē.
anyhow adv ullō modō, quōquō modō.
anyone pron see **anybody**.
anything pron aliquid; quidvīs, quidlibet;
(interrog) ecquid, numquid; (after neg)
quicquam; (after sī, nisī, num, nē) quid;
hardly ~ nihil ferē.
anywhere adv usquam, ubīvīs.
apace adv citō, celeriter.
apart adv seōrsum, sēparātim ◆ adj dīversus;
be six feet ~ sex pedēs distāre; **set** ~
sēpōnere; **stand** ~ distāre; **joking** ~ remōtō
iocō; ~ **from** praeter (acc).
apartment n cubiculum nt, conclāve nt.
apathetic adj lentus, languidus, ignāvus.
apathy n lentitūdō f, languor m, ignāvia f.
ape n sīmia f ◆ vt imitārī.
aperture r hiātus m, forāmen nt, rīma f.
apex n fastīgium nt.
aphorism n sententia f.
apiary n alveārium nt.
apiece adv in singulōs; **two** ~ bīnī.
aplomb n cōnfīdentia f.
apocryphal adj commentīcius.
apologet c adj cōnfitēns, veniam petēns.
apologize vi veniam petere, sē excūsāre.
apology r excūsātiō f.
apoplectic adj apoplēcticus.
apoplexy n apoplēxis f.
apostle n apostolus m.
apothecary n medicāmentārius m.
appal vt perterrēre, cōnsternere.
appalling adj dīrus.
apparatus n īnstrūmenta ntpl, ōrnāmenta ntpl.
apparel n vestis f, vestīmenta ntpl.
apparent adj manifestus, apertus, ēvidēns.
apparently adv speciē, ut vidētur.
apparition n vīsum nt, speciēs f.
appeal vi (to magistrate) appellāre; (to people)
prōvocāre ad; (to gods) invocāre, testārī; (to
senses) placēre (dat) ◆ n appellātiō f,
prōvocātiō f, testātiō f.
appear vi (in sight) appārēre; (in court) sistī; (in
public) prōdīre; (at a place) adesse, advenīre;
(seem) vidērī.
appearance n (coming) adventus m; (look)
aspectus m, faciēs f; (semblance) speciēs f;
(thing) vīsum nt; **for the sake of** ~ **s** in
speciem; (formula) dicis causā; **make one's** ~
prōcēdere, prōdīre.
appeasable adj plācābilis.
appease vt plācāre, lēnīre, mītigāre, sēdāre.
appeasement n plācātiō f; (of enemy)
pācificātiō f.
appellant n appellātor m.
appellation n nōmen nt.
append vt adiungere, subicere.
appendage n appendix f, adiūnctum nt.
appertain vi pertinēre.
appetite n adpetītus m; (for food) fāmēs f.
applaud vt plaudere; (fig) laudāre.

applause n plausus m; (fig) adsēnsiō f, adprobātiō f.

apple n pōmum nt; mālum nt; ~ **tree** n mālus f; ~ **of my eye** ocellus meus; **upset the ~ cart** plaustrum percellere.

appliance n māchina f, īnstrūmentum nt.

applicable adj aptus, commodus; **be ~** pertinēre.

applicant n petītor m.

application n (work) industria f; (mental) intentiō f; (asking) petītiō f; (MED) fōmentum nt.

apply vt adhibēre, admovēre; (use) ūtī (abl); ~ **oneself to** sē adplicāre, incumbere in (acc) ♦ vi pertinēre; (to a person) adīre (acc); (for office) petere.

appoint vt (magistrate) creāre, facere, cōnstituere; (commander) praeficere; (guardian, heir) īnstituere; (time) dīcere, statuere; (for a purpose) dēstināre; to office) creāre.

appointment n cōnstitūtum nt; (duty) mandātum nt; (office) magistrātus m; **have an ~ with** cōnstitūtum habēre cum; **keep an ~** ad cōnstitūtum venīre.

apportion vt dispertīre, dīvīdere; (land) adsignāre.

apposite adj aptus, appositus.

appraisal n aestimātiō f.

appraise vt aestimāre.

appreciable adj haud exiguus.

appreciate vt aestimāre.

appreciation n aestimātiō f.

apprehend vt (person) comprehendere; (idea) intellegere, mente comprehendere; (fear) metuere, timēre.

apprehension n comprehensiō f; metus m, formīdō f.

apprehensive adj anxius, sollicitus; ~ **of** metuere.

apprentice n discipulus m, tīrō m.

apprenticeship n tīrōcinium nt.

apprise vt docēre, certiōrem facere.

approach vt appropinquāre ad (acc), accēdere ad; (person) adīre ♦ vi (time) adprop nquāre; (season) appetere ♦ n (act) accessus m, aditus m; (time) adpropinquātiō f; (way) aditus m; **make ~es to** adīre ad, ambīre, petere.

approachable adj (place) patēns; (person) facilis.

approbation n adprobātiō f, adsēnsiō f.

appropriate adj aptus, idōneus, proprius ♦ vt adscīscere, adsūmere.

appropriately adv aptē, commodē.

approval n adprobātiō f, adsēnsus m, favor m.

approve vt, vi adprobāre, comprobāre, adsentīrī (dat); (law) scīscere.

approved adj probātus, spectātus.

approximate adj propinquus ♦ vi: ~ **to** accēdere ad.

approximately adv prope, propemodum; (number) ad (acc).

appurtenances n īnstrūmenta ntpl, apparātus

m.

apricot n armēniacum nt; ~ **tree** n armēniaca f.

April n mēnsis Aprīlis m; **of ~** Aprīlis.

apron n operīmentum nt.

apropos of prep quod attinet ad.

apse n apsis f.

apt adj aptus, idōneus; (pupil) docilis, prōmptus; ~ **to** prōnus, prōclīvis ad; **be ~ to** solēre.

aptitude n ingenium nt, facultās f.

aptly adv aptē.

aquarium n piscīna f.

aquatic adj aquātilis.

aqueduct n aquae ductus m.

aquiline adj (nose) aduncus.

arable land n arvum nt.

arbiter n arbiter m.

arbitrarily adv ad libīdinem, licenter.

arbitrary adj libīdinōsus (act); (ruler) superbus.

arbitrate vi dīiūdicāre, disceptāre.

arbitration n arbitrium nt, dīiūdicātiō f.

arbitrator n arbiter m, disceptātor m.

arbour n umbrāculum nt.

arbutus n arbutus f.

arc n arcus m.

arcade n porticus f.

arch n fornix m, arcus m ♦ vt arcuāre ♦ adj lascīvus, vafer.

archaeologist n antīquitātis investīgātor m.

archaeology n antīquitātis investīgātiō f.

archaic adj prīscus.

archaism n verbum obsolētum nt.

archbishop n archiepiscopus m.

arched adj fornicātus.

archer n sagittārius m.

archery n sagittāriōrum ars f.

architect n architectus m.

architecture n architectūra f.

architrave n epistylium nt.

archives n tabulae (pūblicae) fpl.

arctic adj arcticus, septentriōnālis ♦ n septentriōnēs mpl.

ardent adj ārdēns, fervidus, vehemēns.

ardently adv ārdenter, ācriter, vehementer.

ardour n ārdor m, fervor m.

arduous adj difficilis, arduus.

area n regiō f; (MATH) superficiēs f.

arena n harēna f.

argonaut n argonauta m.

argosy n onerāria f.

argue vi (discuss) disserere, disceptāre; (dispute) ambigere; disputāre; (reason) argūmentārī ♦ vt (prove) arguere.

argument n (discussion) contrōversia f, disputātiō f; (reason) ratiō f; (proof, theme) argūmentum nt.

argumentation n argūmentātiō f.

argumentative adj lītigiōsus.

aria n canticum nt.

arid adj āridus, siccus.

aright adv rectē, vērē.

arise vi orīrī, coorīrī, exsistere; ~ **from** nāscī ex, proficīscī ab.

aristocracy n optimātēs mpl, nōbilēs mpl; (govt) optimātium dominātus m.
aristocrat n optimās m.
aristocratic adj patricius, generōsus.
arithmetic n numerī mpl, arithmētica ntpl.
ark n arca f.
arm n bracchium nt; (upper) lacertus m; (sea) sinus m; (weapon) tēlum nt ♦ vt armāre ♦ vi arma capere.
armament n bellī apparātus m; cōpiae fpl.
armed adj (men) armātus; light-~ troops levis armātūra f, vēlitēs mpl.
armistice n indutiae fpl.
armlet n armilla f.
armour n arma ntpl; (kind of) armātūra f.
armourer n (armōrum) faber m.
armoury n armāmentārium nt.
armpit n āla f.
arms npl (MIL) arma ntpl; by force of ~ vī et armīs; under ~ in armīs.
army n exercitus m; (in battle) aciēs f; (on march) agmen nt.
aroma n odor m.
aromatic adj frāgrāns.
around adv circum (acc), circā (acc) ♦ prep circum (acc).
arouse vt suscitāre, ērigere, excitāre.
arraign vt accūsāre.
arrange vt (in order) compōnere, ōrdināre, dīgerere, dispōnere; (agree) pacīscī; ~ a truce indūtias compōnere.
arrangement n ōrdō m, collocātiō f, dispositiō f; pactum nt, cōnstitūtum nt.
arrant adj summus.
array n vestis f, habitus m; (MIL) aciēs f ♦ vt vestīre, exōrnāre; (MIL) īnstruere.
arrears n residuae pecūniae fpl, reliqua ntpl.
arrest vt comprehendere, adripere; (attention) in sē convertere; (movement) morārī, tardāre ♦ n comprehēnsiō f.
arrival n adventus m.
arrive vi advenīre (ad + acc), pervenīre (ad + acc).
arrogance n superbia f, adrogantia f, fastus m.
arrogant adj superbus, adrogāns.
arrogantly adv superbē, adroganter.
arrogate vt adrogāre.
arrow n sagitta f.
arsenal n armāmentārium nt.
arson n incēnsiōnis crīmen nt.
art n ars f, artificium nt; fine ~s ingenuae artēs.
artery n artēria f.
artful adj callidus, vafer, astūtus.
artfully adv callidē, astūtē.
artfulness n astūtia f, dolus m.
artichoke n cinara f.
article n rēs f, merx f; (clause) caput nt; (term) condiciō f.
articulate adj explānātus, distinctus ♦ vi explānāre, exprimere.
articulately adv explānātē, clārē.
articulation n prōnūntiātiō f.
artifice n ars f, artificium nt, dolus m.

artificer n artifex m, opifex m, faber m.
artificial adj (work) artificiōsus; (appearance) fūcātus.
artificially adv arte, manū.
artillery n tormenta ntpl.
artisan n faber m, opifex m.
artist n artifex m; pictor m.
artistic adj artificiōsus, ēlegāns.
artistically adv artificiōsē, ēleganter.
artless adj (work) inconditus; (person) simplex.
artlessly adv incondītē; simpliciter, sine dolō.
artlessness n simplicitās f.
as adv (before adj, adv) tam; (after aequus, īdem, similis) ac, atque; (correlative) quam, quālis, quantus ♦ conj (compar) ut (+ indic), sīcut, velut, quemadmodum; (cause) cum (+ indic), quōniam, quippe quī; (time) dum, ut ♦ relat pron quī, quae, quod (+ subj); ~ being utpote; ~ follows ita; ~ for quod attinet ad; ~ if quasī, tamquam si, velut; (= while) usu expressed by pres part; ~ it were ut ita dīcam; ~ yet adhūc; ~ soon ~ simul ac/atque (+ perf indic); ~ ... as possible quam (+ superl).
as n (coin) as m.
ascend vt, vi ascendere.
ascendancy n praestantia f, auctōritās f.
ascendant adj surgēns, potēns; be in the ~ praestāre.
ascent n ascēnsus m; (slope) clīvus m.
ascertain vt comperīre, cognōscere.
ascetic adj nimis abstinēns, austērus.
asceticism n dūritia f.
ascribe vt adscrībere, attribuere, adsignāre.
ash n (tree) fraxinus f ♦ adj fraxineus.
ashamed adj: I am ~ pudet mē; ~ of pudet (+ acc of person, + gen of thing).
ashen adj pallidus.
ashes n cinis m.
ashore adv (motion) in lītus; (rest) in lītore; go ~ ēgredī.
Asia n Asia f.
aside adv sēparatim, sē- (in cpd).
ask vt (question) rogāre, quaerere; (request) petere, poscere; (beg, entreat) orāre; ~ for vt fus petere; rogāre; scīscitārī; percontārī.
askance adv oblīquē; look ~ at līmīs oculīs aspicere, invidēre (dat).
askew adv prāvē.
aslant adv oblīquē.
asleep adj sōpītus; be ~ dormīre; fall ~ obdormīre, somnum inīre.
asp n aspis f.
asparagus n asparagus m.
aspect n (place) aspectus m; (person) vultus m; (CIRCS) status m; have a southern ~ ad merīdiem spectāre; there is another ~ to the matter aliter sē rēs habet.
aspen n pōpulus f.
asperity n acerbitās f.
asperse vt maledīcere (dat), calumniārī.
aspersion n calumnia f; cast ~s on calumniārī, īnfamiā aspergere.
asphalt n bitūmen nt.

asphyxia n strangulātiō f.
asphyxiate vt strangulāre.
aspirant n petītor m.
aspirate n (GRAM) aspīrātiō f.
aspiration n spēs f; (POL) ambitiō f.
aspire vi: ~ **to** adfectāre, petere, spērāre.
ass n asinus m, asellus m; (fig) stultus
assail vt oppugnāre, adorīrī, aggredī
assailable adj expugnābilis.
assailant n oppugnātor m.
assassin n sīcārius m, percussor m.
assassinate vt interficere, occīdere, iugulāre.
assassination n caedēs f, parricidium nt.
assault vt oppugnāre, adorīrī, aggredī;
(speech) invehī in (acc) ♦ n impetus n,
oppugnātiō f; (personal) vīs f.
assay vt (metal) spectāre; temptāre, cōnārī.
assemble vt convocāre, congregāre, cōgere ♦
vi convenīre, congregārī.
assembly n coetus m, conventus m; (plebs)
concilium nt; (Roman people) comitia ntpl;
(troops) cōntiō f; (things) congeriēs f.
assent vi adsentīrī, adnuere ♦ n adsēnsus m.
assert vt adfirmāre, adsevērāre, dīcere.
assertion n adfirmātiō f, adsevērātiō 7, dictum
nt, sententia f.
assess vt cēnsēre, aestimāre; ~ **damages**
lītem aestimāre.
assessment n cēnsus m, aestimātiō f.
assessor n cēnsor m; (assistant) cōnsessor m.
assets n bona ntpl.
assiduity n dīligentia f, sēdulitās f, industria f.
assiduous adj dīligēns, sēdulus, industrius.
assign vt tribuere, attribuere; (land)
adsignāre; (in writing) perscrībere; (task)
dēlēgāre; (reason) adferre.
assignation n cōnstitūtum nt.
assignment n adsignātiō f, perscrīptiō f; (task)
mūnus nt, pēnsum nt.
assimilate vt aequāre; (food) concoquere;
(knowledge) concipere.
assist vt adiuvāre, succurrere (dat), adesse
(dat).
assistance n auxilium nt, opem (no nom) f;
come to the ~ of subvenīre (dat); **be of ~ to**
auxiliō esse (dat).
assistant n adiūtor m, minister m.
assize n conventus m; **hold ~s** conventūs
agere.
associate vt cōnsociāre, coniungere ♦ vi rem
inter sē cōnsociāre; ~ **with** familiāriter ūtī
(abl) ♦ n socius m, sodālis m.
association n societās f; (club) sodālitās f.
assort vt dīgerere, dispōnere ♦ vi congruere.
assortment n (of goods) variae mercēs fpl.
assuage vt lēnīre, mītigare, sēdāre.
assume vt (for oneself) adsūmere, adrogāre;
(hypothesis) pōnere; (office) inīre.
assumption n (hypothesis) sūmptiō f, positum
nt.
assurance n (given) fidēs f, pignus nt; (belt)
fīdūcia f; (boldness) cōnfīdentia f.
assure vt cōnfirmāre, prōmittere (dat).

assured adj (person) fīdēns; (fact) explōrātus,
certus.
assuredly adv certō, certē, prcfectō, sānē.
astern adv ā puppī; (movement) retrō; ~ **of**
post.
asthma n anhēlitus m.
astonish vt obstupefacere; attonāre.
astonished adj attonitus, stupefactus; **be ~ed**
at admīrārī.
astonishing adj mīrificus, mīrus.
astonishment n stupor m, admīrātiō f.
astound vt obstupefacere.
astray adj vagus; **go ~** errāre, aberrāre,
deerrāre.
astride adj vāricus.
astrologer n Chaldaeus m, mathēmaticus m.
astrology n Chaldaeōrum dīvīnātiō f.
astronomer n astrologus m.
astronomy n astrologia f.
astute adj callidus, vafer.
astuteness n calliditās f.
asunder adv sēparātim, dis- (in cpd).
asylum n asylum nt.
at prep in (abl), ad (acc); (time) usu expressed by
abl; (towns, small islands) loc; ~ **the house of**
apud (acc); ~ **all events** saltem; see also **dawn,
hand, house** etc.
atheism n deōs esse negāre.
atheist n atheos m; **be an ~** deōs esse negāre.
Athenian adj Atheniensis.
Athens n Athenae fpl; **at/from ~** Athenis; **to ~**
Athenas.
athirst adj sitiens; (fig) avidus.
athlete n athlēta m.
athletic adj rōbustus, lacertōsus.
athletics n athlētica ntpl.
athwart prep trāns (acc).
atlas n orbis terrārum dēscrīptiō f.
atmosphere n āēr m.
atom n atomus f, corpus indīviduum nt.
atone vi: ~ **for** expiāre.
atonement n expiātiō f, piāculum nt.
atrocious adj immānis, nefārius, scelestus.
atrociously adv nefāriē, scelestē.
atrociousness n immānitās f.
atrocity n nefas nt, scelus nt, flāgitium nt.
atrophy n marcēscere.
attach vt adiungere, adfīgere, illigāre; (word)
subicere; ~**ed to** amāns (gen).
attachment n vinculum nt; amor m, studium
nt.
attack vt oppugnāre, adorīrī, aggredī;
impetum facere in (acc); (speech) īnsequī,
invehī in (acc); (disease) ingruere in (acc) ♦ n
impetus m, oppugnātiō f, incursus m.
attacker n oppugnātor m.
attain vt adsequī, adipīscī, cōnsequī; ~ **to**
pervenīre ad.
attainable adj impetrābilis, in prōmptū.
attainder n: **bill of ~** prīvilēgium nt.
attainment n adeptiō f.
attainments npl doctrīna f, ērudītiō f.
attaint vt māiestātis condemnāre.

attempt vt cōnārī, temptāre; (with effort)
mōlīrī ♦ n cōnātus m, inceptum nt; (risk)
perīculum nt; **first ~s** rudīmenta ntpl.

attend vt (meeting) adesse (dat), interesse
(dat); (person) prōsequī, comitārī; (master)
appārēre (dat); (invalid) cūrāre ♦ vi animum
advertere, animum attendere; **~ to** (task)
adcūrāre; **~ upon** prōsequī, adsectārī; **~ the
lectures of** audīre; **not ~** aliud agere; **~ first to**
praevertere (dat); **well ~ed** frequēns; **thinly
~ed** īnfrequēns.

attendance n (courtesy) adsectātiō f; (MED)
cūrātiō f; (service) apparitiō f; **constant ~**
adsiduitās f; **full ~** frequentia f; **poor ~**
īnfrequentia f; **dance ~ on** haerēre (dat).

attendant n famulus m, minister m; (on
candidate) sectātor m; (on nobleman)
adsectātor m; (on magistrate) apparitor m.

attention n animadversiō f, animī attentiō f;
(to work) cūra f; (respect) observantia f;
attract ~ digitō mōnstrārī; **call ~ to** indicāre;
pay ~ to animadvertere, observāre;
ratiōnem habēre (gen); **~ !** hōc age!

attentive adj intentus; (to work) dīligēns.

attentively adv intentē, dīligenter.

attenuate vt attenuāre.

attest vt cōnfirmāre, testārī.

attestation n testificātiō f.

attestor n testis m.

attic n cēnāculum nt.

attire vt vestīre ♦ n vestis f, habitus m.

attitude n (body) gestus m, status m, habitus
m; (mind) ratiō f.

attorney n āctor m; advocātus m.

attract vt trahere, attrahere, adlicere.

attraction n vīs attrahendī; illecebra f,
invītāmentum nt.

attractive adj suāvis, venustus, lepidus.

attractively adv suāviter, vēnustē, lepidē.

attractiveness n venustās f, lepōs m.

attribute vt tribuere, attribuere, adsignāre ♦
n proprium nt.

attrition n attrītus m.

attune vt modulārī.

auburn adj flāvus.

auction n auctiō f; (public) hasta f; **hold an ~**
auctiōnem facere; **sell by ~** sub hastā
vēndere.

auctioneer n praecō m.

audacious adj audāx; protervus.

audaciously adv audācter, protervē.

audacity n audācia f, temeritās f.

audible adj: **be ~** exaudīrī posse.

audibly adv clārā vōce.

audience n audītōrēs mpl; (interview) aditus m;
give an ~ to admittere.

audit vt īnspicere ♦ n ratiōnum īnspectiō f.

auditorium n cavea f.

auditory adj audītōrius.

auger n terebra f.

augment vt augēre, adaugēre ♦ vi crēscere,
augērī.

augmentation n incrēmentum nt.

augur n augur m; **~'s staff** lituus m ♦ vi
augurārī; (fig) portendere.

augural adj augurālis.

augurship n augurātus m.

augury n augurium nt, auspicium nt; ōmen nt;
take ~ies augurārī; **after taking ~ies**
augurātō.

august adj augustus.

August n mēnsis Augustus, Sextīlis; **of ~**
Sextīlis.

aunt n (paternal) amita f; (maternal) mātertera
f.

auspices n auspicium nt; **take ~** auspicārī;
after taking ~ auspicātō; **without taking ~**
inauspicātō.

auspicious adj faustus, fēlīx.

auspiciously adv fēlīciter, prosperē.

austere adj austērus, sevērus, dūrus.

austerely adv sevērē.

austerity n sevēritās f, dūritia f.

authentic adj vērus, certus.

authenticate vt recognōscere.

authenticity n auctōritās f, fidēs f.

author n auctor m, inventor m; scrīptor m.

authoress n auctor f.

authoritative adj fīdus; imperiōsus.

authority n auctōritās f, potestās f, iūs nt; (MIL)
imperium nt; (LIT) auctor m, scrīptor m;
enforce ~ iūs suum exsequī; **have great ~**
multum pollēre; **on Caesar's ~** auctōre
Caesare; **an ~ on** perītus (gen).

authorize vt potestātem facere (dat),
mandāre; (law) sancīre.

autobiography n dē vītā suā scrīptus liber m.

autocracy n imperium singulāre nt, tyrannis f.

autocrat n tyrannus m, dominus m.

autocratic adj imperiōsus.

autograph n manus f, chīrographum nt.

automatic adj necessārius.

automatically adv necessāriō.

autonomous adj līber.

autonomy n lībertās f.

Autumn n auctumnus m.

autumnal adj auctumnālis.

auxiliaries npl auxilia ntpl, auxiliāriī mpl.

auxiliary adj auxiliāris ♦ n adiūtor m; **~ forces**
auxilia ntpl; novae copiae fpl.

avail vi valēre ♦ vt prōdesse (dat); **~ oneself of**
ūtī (abl) ♦ n ūsus m; **of no ~** frustrā.

available adj ad manum, in prōmptū.

avalanche n montis ruīna f.

avarice n avāritia f, cupīditās f.

avaricious adj avārus, cupidus.

avariciously adv avārē.

avenge vt ulcīscī (+ abl), vindicāre.

avenger n ultor m, vindex m.

avenue n xystus m; (fig) aditus m, iānua f.

aver vt adfirmāre, adsevērāre.

average n medium nt; **on the ~** ferē.

averse adj āversus (ab); **be ~ to** abhorrēre ab.

aversion n odium nt, fastīdium nt.

avert vt arcēre, dēpellere; (by prayer)
dēprecārī.

aviary n aviārium nt.
avid adj avidus.
avidity n aviditās f.
avidly adv avidē.
avoid vt vītāre, fugere, dēclīnāre; (battle) dētrectāre.
avoidance n fuga f, dēclīnātiō f.
avow vt fatērī, cōnfitērī.
avowal n cōnfessiō f.
avowed adj apertus.
avowedly adv apertē, palam.
await vt exspectāre; (future) manēre
awake vt suscitāre, exsuscitare ♦ vi expergīscī ♦ adj vigil.
awaken vt exsuscitāre.
award vt tribuere; (law) adiūdicāre ♦ n (decision) arbitrium nt, iūdicium nt; (thing) praemium nt.
aware adj gnārus ♦ adj conscius (gen); **be ~** scīre; **become ~ of** percipere.
away adv ā-, ab- (in cpd); **be ~** abesse ab (abl); **far ~** procul, longē; **make ~ with** dē mediō tollere.
awe n formīdō f, reverentia f, rēligiō; **stand in ~ of** verērī; (gods) venerārī.
awe-struck adj stupidus.
awful adj terribilis, formīdolōsus, dīrus.
awfully adv formīdolōsē.
awhile adv aliquamdiū, aliquantisper, parumper.
awkward adj incallidus, inconcinnus (to handle) inhabilis; (fig) molestus.
awkwardly adv incallidē, imperītē.
awkwardness n imperītia f, īnscītia ⌐
awl n sūbula f.
awning n vēlum nt.
awry adj prāvus, dissidēns.
axe n secūris f.
axiom n prōnūntiātum nt, sententia f.
axiomatic adj ēvidēns, manifestus.
axis n axis m.
axle n axis m.
aye adv semper; **for ~** in aeternum.
azure adj caeruleus.

B, b

baa vi bālāre ♦ n bālātus m.
babble vi garrīre, blaterāre.
babbler n garrulus m.
babbling adj garrulus.
babe n īnfāns m/f.
babel n dissonae vōcēs fpl.
baboon n sīmia f.
baby n īnfāns m/f.
Bacchanalian adj Bacchicus.
Bacchante n Baccha f.

bachelor n caelebs m; (degree) baccalaureus m.
back n tergum nt; (animal) dorsum nt; (head) occipitium nt; **at one's ~** ā tergō; **behind one's ~** (fig) clam (acc); **put one's ~ up** stomachum movēre (dat); **turn one's ~ on** sē āvertere ab ♦ adj āversus, postīcus ♦ adv retrō, retrōrsum, re- (in cpds) ♦ vt obsecundāre (dat), adesse (dat); **~ water** inhibēre rēmīs, inhibēre nāvem ♦ vi: **~ out of** dētrectāre, dēfugere.
backbite vt obtrectāre (dat), maledīcere (dat).
backbone n spīna f.
backdoor n postīcum nt.
backer n fautor m.
background n recessus m, umbra f.
backing n fidēs f, favor m.
backslide vi dēscīscere.
backward adj āversus; (slow) tardus; (late) sērus.
backwardness n tardītās f, pigritia f.
backwards adv retrō, retrōrsum.
bacon n lārdum nt.
bad adj malus, prāvus, improbus, turpis; **go ~** corrumpī; **be ~ for** obesse (dat), nocēre (dat).
badge n īnsigne nt, īnfula f.
badger n mēles f ♦ vt sollicitāre.
badly adv male, prāvē, improbē, turpiter.
badness n prāvitās f, nēquitia f, improbitās f.
baffle vt ēlūdere, fallere, frustrārī.
bag n saccus m, folliculus m; **hand~** mantica f.
bagatelle n nūgae fpl, floccus m.
baggage n impedīmenta ntpl, vāsa ntpl, sarcinae fpl; **~ train** impedīmenta ntpl; **without ~** expedītus.
bail n vadimōnium nt; (person) vas m; **become ~ for** spondēre prō (abl); **accept ~ for** vadārī; **keep one's ~** vadimōnium obīre ♦ vt spondēre prō (abl).
bailiff n (POL) apparitor m; (private) vīlicus m.
bait n esca f, illecebra f ♦ vt lacessere.
bake vt coquere, torrēre.
bakehouse n pistrīna f.
baker n pistor m.
bakery n pistrīna f.
balance n (scales) lībra f, trutina f; (equilibrium) lībrāmentum nt; (money) reliqua ntpl ♦ vt lībrāre; (fig) compēnsāre; **the account ~s** ratiō cōnstat.
balance sheet n ratiō acceptī et expēnsī.
balcony n podium nt, Maeniānum nt.
bald adj calvus; (style) āridus, iēiūnus.
baldness n calvitium nt; (style) iēiūnitās f.
bale n fascis m; **~ out** vt exhaurīre.
baleful adj fūnestus, perniciōsus, tristis.
balk n tignum nt ♦ vt frustrārī, dēcipere.
ball n globus m; (play) pila f; (wool) glomus nt; (dance) saltātiō f.
ballad n carmen nt.
ballast n saburra f.
ballet n saltātiō f.
ballot n suffrāgium nt.
ballot box urna f.
balm n unguentum nt; (fig) sōlātium nt.
balmy adj lēnis, suāvis.

balsam n balsamum nt.
balustrade n cancellī mpl.
bamboozle vt cōnfundere.
ban vt interdīcere (dat), vetāre ♦ n interdictum nt.
banal adj trītus.
banana n ariēna f; (tree) pāla f.
band n vinculum nt, redimīculum nt; (head) īnfula f; (men) caterva f, manus f, grex f ♦ vi: ~ **together** cōnsociārī.
bandage n fascia f, īnfula f ♦ vt obligāre, adligāre.
bandbox n: **out of a** ~ (fig) dē capsulā.
bandeau n redimīculum nt.
bandit n latrō m.
bandy vt iactāre; ~ **words** altercārī ♦ adj vārus.
bane n venēnum nt, pestis f, perniciēs f.
baneful adj perniciōsus, pestifer.
bang vt pulsāre ♦ n fragor m.
bangle n armilla f.
banish vt pellere, expellere, ēicere; (law) aquā et ignī interdīcere (dat); (temporarily) relēgāre; (feeling) abstergēre.
banishment n (act) aquae et ignis interdictiō f; relēgātiō f; (state) exsilium nt, fuga f.
bank n (earth) agger m; (river) rīpa f; (money) argentāria f.
banker n argentārius m; (public) mēnsārius m.
bankrupt adj: **be** ~ solvendō nōn esse; **declare oneself** ~ bonam cōpiam ēiūrāre; **go** ~ dēcoquere ♦ n dēcoctor m.
banner n vexillum nt.
banquet n cēna f, epulae fpl; convīvium nt; (religious) daps f ♦ vi epulārī.
banter n cavillātiō f ♦ vi cavillārī.
baptism n baptisma nt.
baptize vt baptizāre.
bar n (door) sera f; (gate) claustrum nt; (metal) later m; (wood) asser m; (lever) vectis m; (obstacle) impedīmentum nt; (law-court) cancellī mpl; (barristers) advocātī mpl; (profession) forum nt; **of the** ~ forēnsis; **practise at the** ~ causās agere.
bar vt (door) obserāre; (way) obstāre (dat), interclūdere, prohibēre; (exception) excipere, exclūdere.
barb n acūleus m, dēns m, hāmus m.
barbarian n barbarus m ♦ adj barbarus.
barbarism n barbaria f.
barbarity n saevitia f, ferōcia f, immānitās f, inhūmānitās f.
barbarous adj barbarus, saevus, immānis, inhūmānus.
barbarously adv barbarē, inhūmānē.
barbed adj hāmātus.
barber n tōnsor m; ~**'s shop** tōnstrīna f.
bard n vātēs m/f; (Gallic) bardus m.
bare adj nūdus; (mere) merus; **lay** ~ nūdāre, aperīre, dētegere ♦ vt nūdāre.
barefaced adj impudēns.
barefoot adj nūdis pedibus.
bare-headed adj capite aperto.
barely adv vix.

bargain n pactum nt, foedus nt; **make a** ~ pacīscī; **make a bad** ~ male emere; **into the** ~ grātiīs ♦ vi pacīscī.
barge n linter f.
bark n cortex m; (dog) lātrātus m; (ship) nāvis f, ratis f ♦ vi lātrāre.
barking n latratus m.
barley n hordeum nt; **of** ~ hordeāceus.
barn n horreum nt.
barrack vt obstrepere (dat).
barracks n castra ntpl.
barrel n cūpa f; ligneum vās nt.
barren adj sterilis.
barrenness n sterilitās f.
barricade n claustrum nt, mūnīmentum nt ♦ vt obsaepīre, obstruere; ~ **off** intersaepīre.
barrier n impedīmentum nt; (racecourse) carcer nt.
barrister n advocātus m, patrōnus m, causidicus m.
barrow n ferculum nt; (mound) tumulus m.
barter vt mūtāre ♦ vi mercēs mūtāre ♦ n mūtātiō f, commercium nt.
base adj turpis, vīlis; (birth) humilis, ignōbilis; (coin) adulterīnus.
base n fundāmentum nt; (statue) basis f; (hill) rādīcēs fpl; (MIL) castra ntpl.
baseless adj falsus, inānis.
basely adv turpiter.
basement n basis f; (storey) īmum tabulātum nt.
baseness n turpitūdō f.
bashful adj pudīcus, verēcundus.
bashfulness n pudor m, verēcundia f.
basic adj prīmus.
basin n alveolus m, pelvis f; **wash**~ aquālis m.
basis n fundāmentum nt.
bask vi aprīcārī.
basket n corbis f, fiscus m; (for bread) canistrum nt; (for wool) quasillum nt.
basking n aprīcātiō f.
bas-relief n toreuma nt.
bass adj (voice) gravis.
bastard adj nothus.
bastion n prōpugnāculum nt.
bat n vespertīliō m; (games) clāva f.
batch n numerus m.
Bath n Aquae Sulis fpl.
bath n balneum nt; (utensil) lābrum nt, lavātiō f; **Turkish** ~ Lacōnicum nt; **cold** ~ frīgidārium nt; **hot** ~ calidārium nt; ~ **superintendent** balneātor m ♦ vt lavāre.
bathe vt lavāre ♦ vi lavārī, perluī.
bathroom n balneāria ntpl.
baths n (public ~) balneae fpl.
batman n cālō m.
baton n virga f, scīpiō m.
battalion n cohors f.
batter vt quassāre, pulsāre, verberāre.
battering ram n ariēs m.
battery n (assault) vīs f.
battle n pugna f, proelium nt, certāmen nt; **a** ~ **was fought** pugnatum est; **pitched** ~ iūstum

proelium; **line of** ~ aciēs f; **drawn** ~ ɛnceps
proelium. ◆ vi pugnāre, contendere; ~ **order**
aciēs f.
battle-axe n bipennis f.
battlefield, battle-line n aciēs f.
battlement n pinna f.
bawl vt vōciferārī, clāmitāre.
bay n (sea) sinus m; (tree) laurus f, laurea f; **of** ~
laureus; **at** ~ interclūsus ◆ adj (colour) spādīx
◆ vi (dog) lātrāre.
be vi esse; (CIRCS) versārī; (condition) sē habēre;
~ **at** adesse (dat); ~ **amongst** interesse (dat); ~
in inesse (dat); **consul-to-**~ cōnsul
dēsignātus; **how are you?** quid agis?; **so** ~ **it**
estō; see also **absent, here** etc.
beach n lītus nt, acta f ◆ vt (ship) subdūcere.
beacon n ignis m.
bead n pilula f.
beadle n apparitor m.
beak n rōstrum nt.
beaked adj rōstrātus.
beaker n cantharus m, scyphus m.
beam n (wood) trabs f, tignum nt; (balance)
iugum nt; (light) radius m; (ship) latus nt; **on
the** ~ ā latere ◆ vi fulgēre; (person) ɛdrīdēre.
beaming adj hilaris.
bean n faba f.
bear n ursus m, ursa f; **Great B~** septentriōnēs
mpl, Arctos f; **Little B~** septentriō minor m,
Cynosūra f; **~'s** ursīnus ◆ vt (carry) ferre,
portāre; (endure) ferre, tolerāre, patī;
(produce) ferre, fundere; (child) parere; ~
down upon appropinquāre; ~ **off** ferre; ~ **out**
vt arguere; ~ **up** vi: ~ **up under** obsistere (dat),
sustinēre; ~ **upon** innītī (dat); (refer)
pertinēre ad; **I have lost my ~s** ubi sim
nesciō.
bearable adj tolerābilis.
beard n barba f ◆ vt ultrō lacessere.
bearded adj barbātus.
beardless adj imberbis.
bearer n bāiulus m; (letter) tabellārius m; (litter)
lectīcārius m; (news) nūntius m.
bearing n (person) gestus m, vultus m;
(direction) regiō f; **have no ~ on** nihīl
pertinēre ad; **I have lost my ~s** ubi sim
nesciō.
beast n bestia f; (large) bēlua f; (wild) fera f;
(domestic) pecus f.
beastliness n foeditās f, stuprum nt.
beastly adj foedus.
beast of burden n iūmentum nt.
beat n ictus m; (heart) palpitātiō f; (music)
percussiō f; (oars, pulse) pulsus m.
beat vt ferīre, percutere, pulsāre; (the body in
grief) plangere; (punish) caedere; (whip)
verberāre; (conquer) vincere, superāre ◆ vi
palpitāre, micāre; ~ **back** repellere; ~ **in**
perfringere; ~ **out** excutere; (metal)
extundere; ~ **a retreat** receptui canere; ~
about the bush circuitiōne ūtī; **be ~en**
vāpulāre; **dead** ~ cōnfectus.

beating n verbera ntpl; (defeat) clādes f;
(time) percussiō f; **get a** ~ vāpulāre.
beatitude n beātitūdō f, fēlīcitās f.
beau n nitidus homō m; (lover) amāns m.
beauteous adj pulcher, fōrmōsus.
beautiful adj pulcher, fōrmōsus; (looks)
decōrus; (scenery) amoenus.
beautifully adv pulchrē.
beautify vt exōrnāre, decorāre.
beauty n fōrma f, pulchritūdō f, amoenitās f.
beaver n castor m, fiber m; (helmet) buccula f.
becalmed adj ventō dēstitūtus.
because conj quod, quia, quōniam (+ indic),
quippe quī; ~ **of** propter (acc).
beck n nūtus m.
beckon vt innuere, vocāre.
become vi fierī; **what will** ~ **of me?** quid me
fīet? ◆ vt decēre, convenīre in (acc).
becoming adj decēns, decōrus.
becomingly adv decōrē, convenienter.
bed n cubīle nt, lectus m, lectulus m; **go to** ~
cubitum īre; **make a** ~ lectum sternere; **be
~ridden** lectō tenērī; **camp** ~ grabātus m;
(flower) pulvīnus m; **marriage** ~ lectus
geniālis m; **river~** alveus m.
bedaub vt illinere, oblinere.
bedclothes n strāgula ntpl.
bedding n strāgula ntpl.
bedeck vt ōrnāre, exōrnāre.
bedew vt inrōrāre.
bedim vt obscūrāre.
bedpost n fulcrum nt.
bedraggled adj sordidus, madidus.
bedroom n cubiculum nt.
bedstead n sponda f.
bee n apis f; **queen** ~ rēx m.
beech n fāgus f ◆ adj fāginus.
beef n būbula f.
beehive n alvus f.
beekeeper n apiārius m.
beer n cervīsia f, fermentum nt.
beet n bēta f.
beetle n (insect) scarabaeus m; (implement)
fistūca f.
beetling adj imminēns, mināx.
befall vi, vt accidere, ēvenīre (dat); (good)
contingere (dat).
befit vt decēre, convenīre in (acc).
before adv ante, anteā, antehāc ◆ prep ante
(acc); (place) prō (abl); (presence) apud (acc),
cōram (abl) ◆ conj antequam, priusquam.
beforehand adv ante, anteā; prae (in cpd).
befoul vt inquināre, foedāre.
befriend vt favēre (dat), adiuvāre; (in trouble)
adesse (dat).
beg vt ōrāre, obsecrāre, precārī, poscere ab,
petere ab; ~ **for** petere ◆ vi mendīcāre.
beget vt gignere, prōcreāre, generāre.
begetter n generātor m, creātor m.
beggar m mendīcus m.
beggarly adj mendīcus, indigēns.
beggary n mendīcitās f, indigentia f.
begin vi, vt incipere, coepisse; (speech)

exōrdīrī; (*plan*) īnstituere, incohāre; (*time*)
inīre; ~ **with** incipere ab.
beginning *n* initium *nt*, prīncipium *nt*,
exōrdium *nt*, inceptiō *f*; (*learning*) rudīmenta
ntpl, elementa *ntpl*; (*origin*) orīgō *f*, fōns *m*; **at**
the ~ of spring ineunte vēre.
begone *interj* apage, tē āmovē.
begotten *adj* genitus, nātus.
begrudge *vt* invidēre (*dat*).
beguile *vt* dēcipere, fallere.
behalf *n*: **on ~ of** prō (*abl*); **on my ~** meō
nōmine.
behave *vi* sē gerere, sē praebēre (*with adj*);
well ~d bene mōrātus.
behaviour *n* mōrēs *mpl*.
behead *vt* dētruncāre, secūrī percutere.
behest *n* iūssum *nt*.
behind *adv* pōne, post, ā tergō ♦ *prep* post (*acc*),
pōne (*acc*).
behindhand *adv* sērō; **be ~** parum prōficere.
behold *vt* aspicere, cōnspicere, intuērī ♦ *interj*
ecce, ēn.
beholden *adj* obnoxius, obstrictus, obligātus.
behoof *n* ūsus *m*.
behove *vt* oportēre.
being *n* (*life*) animātiō *f*; (*nature*) nātūra *f*;
(*person*) homō *m/f*.
bejewelled *adj* gemmeus, gemmātus.
belabour *vt* verberāre, caedere.
belated *adj* sērus.
belch *vi* ructāre, ēructāre.
beldam *n* anus *f*.
beleaguer *vt* obsidēre, circumsedēre.
belie *vt* abhorrēre ab, repugnāre.
belief *n* fidēs *f*, opīniō *f*; (*opinion*) sententia *f*; **to**
the best of my ~ ex animī meī sententiā; **past**
~ incrēdibilis.
believe *vt*, *vi* (*thing*) crēdere; (*person*) crēdere
(*dat*); (*suppose*) crēdere, putāre, arbitrārī,
opīnārī; **~ in gods** deōs esse crēdere; **make ~**
simulāre.
believer *n* deōrum cultor *m*; Christiānus *m*.
belike *adv* fortasse.
belittle *vt* obtrectāre.
bell *n* tintinnābulum *nt*; (*public*) campāna *f*.
belle *n* fōrmōsa *f*, pulchra *f*.
belles-lettres *n* litterae *fpl*.
bellicose *adj* ferōx.
belligerent *adj* bellī particeps.
bellow *vi* rūdere, mūgīre ♦ *n* mūgītus *m*.
bellows *n* follis *m*.
belly *n* abdōmen *nt*, venter *m*; (*sail*) sinus *m* ♦ *vi*
tumēre.
belong *vi* esse (*gen*), proprium esse (*gen*),
inesse (*dat*); (*concern*) attinēre, pertinēre.
belongings *n* bona *ntpl*.
beloved *adj* cārus, dīlectus, grātus.
below *adv* īnfrā, subter ♦ *adj* īnferus ♦ *prep*
īnfrā (*acc*), sub (*abl, acc*).
belt *n* zōna *f*; (*sword*) balteus *m*.
bemoan *vt* dēplōrāre, lāmentārī.
bemused *adj* stupefactus, stupidus.
bench *n* subsellium *nt*; (*rowing*) trānstrum *nt*;

(*law*) iūdicēs *mpl*; **seat on the ~** iūdicātus *m*.
bend *vt* flectere, curvāre, inclīnāre; (*bow*)
intendere; (*course*) tendere, flectere; (*mind*)
intendere ♦ *vi* sē īnflectere; (*person*) sē
dēmittere; **~ back** reflectere; **~ down** *vi*
dēflectere; sē dēmittere ♦ *n* flexus *m*,
ānfrāctus *m*.
beneath *adv* subter ♦ *prep* sub (*acc or abl*).
benediction *n* bonae precēs *fpl*.
benedictory *adj* faustus.
benefaction *n* beneficium *nt*, dōnum *nt*.
benefactor *n* patrōnus *m*; **be a ~** bene merērī
(*dē*).
beneficence *n* beneficentia *f*, līberālitās *f*.
beneficent *adj* beneficus.
beneficial *adj* ūtilis, salūbris.
benefit *n* beneficium *nt*; (*derived*) fructus *m*;
have the ~ of fruī (*abl*) ♦ *vt* prōdesse (*dat*),
usuī esse (*dat*).
benevolence *n* benevolentia *f*, benignitās *f*.
benevolent *adj* benevolus, benignus.
benevolently *adv* benevolē, benignē.
benighted *adj* nocte oppressus; (*fig*) ignārus,
indoctus.
benign *adj* benignus, cōmis.
bent *n* (*mind*) inclīnātiō *f*, ingenium *nt* ♦ *adj*
curvus, flexus; (*mind*) attentus; **be ~ on**
studēre (*dat*).
benumb *vt* stupefacere.
benumbed *adj* stupefactus, torpidus; **be ~**
torpēre.
bequeath *vt* lēgāre.
bequest *n* lēgātum *nt*.
bereave *vt* orbāre, prīvāre.
bereavement *n* damnum *nt*.
bereft *adj* orbus, orbātus, prīvātus.
berry *n* bāca *f*.
berth *n* statiō *f*; **give a wide ~ to** dēvītāre.
beryl *n* bēryllus *m*.
beseech *vt* implōrāre, ōrāre, obsecrāre.
beset *vt* obsidēre, circumsedēre.
beside *prep* ad (*acc*), apud (*acc*); (*close*) iuxtā
(*acc*); **~ the point** nihil ad rem; **be ~ oneself**
nōn esse apud sē.
besides *adv* praetereā, accēdit quod; (*in*
addition) īnsuper ♦ *prep* praeter (*acc*).
besiege *vt* obsidēre, circumsedēre.
besieger *n* obsessor *m*.
besmear *vt* illinere.
besmirch *vt* maculāre.
besom *n* scōpae *fpl*.
besotted *adj* stupidus.
bespatter *vt* aspergere.
bespeak *vt* (*order*) imperāre; (*denote*)
significāre.
besprinkle *vt* aspergere.
best *adj* optimus; **the ~ part** māior pars ♦ *n* flōs
m, rōbur *nt*; **do one's ~** prō virīlī parte agere;
do one's ~ to operam dare ut; **have the ~ of it**
vincere; **make the ~ of (a situation)** aequō
animō accipere; **to the ~ of one's ability** prō
virīlī parte; **to the ~ of my knowledge** quod
sciam ♦ *adv* optimē.

bestial adj foedus.
bestir vt movēre; ~ **oneself** expergīscī.
bestow vt dōnāre, tribuere, dare, cōnferre.
bestride vt (horse) sedēre in (abl).
bet n pignus nt ♦ vt oppōnere ♦ vi pignore contendere.
betake vt cōnferre, recipere; ~ o.s. sē cōnferre.
bethink vt: ~ **oneself** sē colligere; ~ **oneself of** respicere.
betide vi accidere, ēvenīre.
betoken vt significāre; (foretell) portendere.
betray vt prōdere, trādere; (feelings) arguere; **without ~ing one's trust** salvā fidē.
betrayal n prōditiō f.
betrayer n prōditor m; (informer) index m.
betroth vt spondēre, dēspondēre.
betrothal n spōnsālia ntpl.
better adj melior; **it is ~ to** praestat (infin); **get the ~ of** vincere, superāre; **I am ~** (in health) melius est mihī; **I had ~ go** praestat īre; **get ~** convalēscere; **think ~ of** sententiam mūtāre dē ♦ adv melius ♦ vt corrigere; ~ **oneself** prōficere.
betterment n prōfectus m.
between prep inter (acc).
beverage n pōtiō f.
bevy n manus f, grex f.
bewail vt dēflēre, lāmentārī, dēplōrāre.
beware vt cavēre.
bewilder vt cōnfundere, perturbāre.
bewildered adj attonitus.
bewilderment n perturbātiō f, admīrātiō f.
bewitch vt fascināre; (fig) dēlēnīre.
beyond adv ultrā, suprā ♦ prep ultrā (acc), extrā (acc); (motion) trāns (acc); (amount) ultrā, suprā (acc); **go/pass ~** excēdere, ēgredī.
bezel n pāla f.
bias n inclīnātiō f; (party) favor m ♦ vt inclīnāre.
biassed adj prōpēnsior.
bibber n pōtor m, pōtātor m.
Bible n litterae sacrae fpl.
bibulous adj bibulus.
bicephalous adj biceps.
bicker vi altercārī, iūrgāre.
bid vt iubēre; (guest) vocāre, invītāre ♦ vi (at auction) licērī; ~ **for** licērī; ~ **good day** salvēre iubēre; **he ~s fair to make progress** spēs est eum prōfecturum esse.
biddable adj docilis.
bidding n iussum nt; (auction) licitātiō f.
bide vt manēre, opperīrī.
biennial adj biennālis.
bier n ferculum nt.
bifurcate vi sē scindere.
bifurcation n (road) trivium nt.
big adj māgnus, grandis, amplus; (with child) gravida; **very ~** permāgnus; **talk ~** glōriārī.
bight n sinus m.
bigness n māgnitūdō f, amplitūdō f.
bigot n nimis obstinātus fautor m.

bigoted adj contumāx.
bigotry n contumācia f, nimia obstinātio f.
bile n bīlis f, fel nt.
bilgewater n sentīna f.
bilk vt fraudāre.
bill n (bird) rōstrum nt; (implement) falx f; (law) rogātiō f, lēx f; (money) syngrapha f; (notice) libellus m, titulus m; **introduce a ~** populum rogāre, lēgem ferre; **carry a ~** lēgem perferre.
billet n hospitium nt ♦ vt in hospitia dīvidere.
billhook n falx f.
billow n fluctus m.
billowy adj undōsus.
billy goat n caper m.
bin n lacus m.
bind vt adligāre, dēligāre, vincīre; (by oath) adigere; (by obligation) obligāre, obstringere; (wound) obligāre; ~ **fast** dēvincīre; ~ **together** conligāre; ~ **over** vt vadārī.
binding n compāgēs f ♦ adj (law) ratus; **it is ~ on** oportet.
bindweed n convolvulus m.
biographer n vītae nārrātor m.
biography n vīta f.
bipartite adj bipartītus.
biped n bipēs m.
birch n bētula f; (flogging) virgae ulmeae fpl.
bird n avis f; ~**s of a feather** parēs cum paribus facillimē congerantur; **kill two ~s with one stone** ūnō saltū duōs aprōs capere, dē eādem fidēliā duōs parietēs dealbāre; ~**'s-eye view of** dēspectus in (acc).
birdcatcher n auceps m.
birdlime n viscum nt.
birth n (act) partus m; (origin) genus nt; **low ~** ignōbilitās f; **high ~** nōbilitās f; **by ~** nātū, ortū.
birthday n nātālis m.
birthday party n nātālicia ntpl.
birthplace n locus nātālis m; (fig) incūnābula ntpl.
birthright n patrimōnium nt.
bisect vt dīvidere.
bishop n epīscopus m.
bison n ūrus m.
bit n pars f; (food) frustum nt; (broken off) fragmentum nt; (horse) frēnum nt; ~ **by ~** minūtātim; **a ~** adv aliquantulum; **a ~ sad** tristior.
bitch n canis f.
bite vt mordēre; (frost) ūrere ♦ n morsus m; **with a ~** mordicus.
biting adj mordāx.
bitter adj (taste) acerbus, amārus; (words) asper.
bitterly adv acerbē, asperē.
bittern n būtiō m, ardea f.
bitterness n acerbitās f.
bitumen n bitūmen nt.
bivouac n excubiae fpl ♦ vi excubāre.
bizarre adj īnsolēns.

blab *vt, vi* garrīre, effūtīre.

black *adj (dull)* āter; *(glossy)* niger; *(dirt)* sordidus; *(eye)* līvidus; *(looks)* trux; ~ **and blue** līvidus; ♦ *n* ātrum *nt*, nigrum *nt*; **dressed in** ~ ātrātus; *(in mourning)* sordidātus.

blackberry *n* mōrum *nt*.

blackbird *n* merula *f*.

blacken *vt* nigrāre, nigrum reddere; *(character)* īnfāmāre, obtrectāre *(dat)*.

blackguard *n* scelestus, scelerātus *m*.

blacking *n* ātrāmentum *nt*.

blacklist *n* prōscrīptiō *f*.

black magic *n* magicae artēs *fpl*.

blackmail *n* minae *fpl*. ♦ *vt* minīs cōgere.

black mark *n* nota *f*.

blacksmith *n* faber *m*.

bladder *n* vēsīca *f*.

blade *n (grass)* herba *f*; *(oar)* palma *f*; *(sword)* lāmina *f*.

blame *vt* reprehendere, culpāre; **I am to** ~ reus sum ♦ *n* reprehēnsiō *f*, culpa *f*.

blameless *adj* innocēns.

blamelessly *adv* innocenter.

blamelessness *n* innocentia *f*, integritās *f*.

blameworthy *adj* accūsābilis, nocēns.

blanch *vi* exalbēscere, pallēscere.

bland *adj* mītis, lēnis.

blandishment *n* blanditiae *fpl*.

blank *adj* vacuus, pūrus; *(look)* stolidus.

blanket *n* lōdīx *f*; **wet** ~ nimium sevērus.

blare *vi* canere, strīdere ♦ *n* clangor *m*, strīdor *m*.

blarney *n* lēnōcinium *nt*.

blaspheme *vi* maledīcere.

blasphemous *adj* maledicus, impius.

blasphemy *n* maledicta *ntpl*, impiētās *f*.

blast *n* flātus *m*, īnflātus *m* ♦ *vt* disicere, discutere; *(crops)* rōbīgine adficere.

blatant *adj* raucus.

blaze *n* flamma *f*, ignis *m*, fulgor *m* ♦ *vi* flāgrāre, ārdēre, fulgēre; ~ **up** exārdēscere ♦ *vt*: ~ **abroad** pervulgāre.

blazon *vt* promulgāre.

bleach *vt* candidum reddere.

bleak *adj* dēsertus, tristis, inamoenus.

bleary-eyed *adj* lippus.

bleat *vi* bālāre ♦ *n* bālātus *m*.

bleed *vi* sanguinem fundere ♦ *vt* sanguinem mittere *(dat)*; **my heart ~s** animus mihī dolet.

bleeding *adj* crūdus, sanguineus ♦ *n* sanguinis missiō *f*.

blemish *n* macula *f*, vitium *nt* ♦ *vt* maculāre, foedāre.

blend *vt* miscēre, immiscēre, admiscēre ♦ *n* coniūnctiō *f*.

bless *vt* beāre; laudāre; *(ECCL)* benedīcere; ~ **with** augēre *(abl)*; ~ **my soul!** ita mē dī ament!

blessed *adj* beātus, fortūnātus; *(emperors)* dīvus.

blessing *n (thing)* commodum *nt*, bonum *nt*; *(ECCL)* benedictiō *f*.

blight *n* rōbīgō *f*, ūrēdō *f* ♦ *vt* rōbīgine adficere; *(fig)* nocēre *(dat)*.

blind *adj* caecus; *(in one eye)* luscus; *(fig)* ignārus, stultus; *(alley)* nōn pervius; *(forces)* necessārius; **turn a** ~ **eye to** cōnīvēre in *(abl)* ♦ *vt* excaecāre, caecāre; *(fig)* occaecāre; *(with light)* praestringere.

blindfold *adj* capite obvolūtō.

blindly *adv* temerē.

blindness *n* caecitās *f*; *(fig)* temeritās *f*, īnsipientia *f*.

blink *vi* nictāre.

bliss *n* fēlīcitās *f*, laetitia *f*.

blissful *adj* fēlīx, beātus, laetus.

blissfully *adv* fēlīciter, beātē.

blister *n* pustula *f*.

blithe *adj* hilaris, laetus.

blithely *adv* hilare, laetē.

blizzard *n* hiems *f*.

bloated *adj* tumidus, turgidus.

blob *n* gutta *f*, particula *f*.

block *n (wood)* stīpes *m*, caudex *m*; *(stone)* massa *f*; *(houses)* īnsula *f*; ~ **letter** quadrāta littera; **stumbling** ~ offēnsiō *f*.

block *vt* claudere, obstruere, interclūdere; ~ **the way** obstāre.

blockade *n* obsidiō *f*; **raise a** ~ obsidiōnem solvere ♦ *vt* obsidēre, interclūdere.

blockhead *n* caudex *m*, bārō *m*, truncus *m*.

blockhouse *n* castellum *nt*.

blond *adj* flāvus.

blood *n* sanguis *m*; *(shed)* cruor *m*; *(murder)* caedēs *f*; *(kin)* genus *nt*; **let** ~ sanguinem mittere; **staunch** ~ sanguinem supprimere; **bad** ~ simultās *f*; **in cold** ~ cōnsultō; **own flesh and** ~ cōnsanguineus.

bloodless *adj* exsanguis; *(victory)* incruentus.

bloodshed *n* caedēs *f*.

bloodshot *adj* sanguineus.

bloodstained *adj* cruentus.

bloodsucker *n* hirūdō *f*.

bloodthirsty *adj* sanguinārius.

blood vessel *n* vēna *f*.

bloody *adj* cruentus.

bloom *n* flōs *m*; **in** ~ flōrēns ♦ *vi* flōrēre, flōrēscere, vigēre.

blossom *n* flōs *m* ♦ *vi* efflōrēscere, flōrēre.

blot *n* macula *f*; *(erasure)* litūra *f* ♦ *vt* maculāre; ~ **out** dēlēre, oblitterāre.

blotch *n* macula *f*.

blotched *adj* maculōsus.

blow *vt, vi (wind)* flāre; *(breath)* adflāre, anhēlāre; *(instrument)* canere; *(flower)* efflōrēscere; *(nose)* ēmungere; ~ **out** *vi* exstinguere; ~ **over** *vi (storm)* cadere; *(fig)* abīre; ~ **up** *vt* īnflāre; *(destroy)* disturbāre ♦ *n* ictus *m*; *(on the cheek)* alapa *f*; *(fig)* plāga *f*; *(misfortune)* calamitās *f*; **aim a** ~ **at** petere; **come to** ~**s** ad manūs venīre.

blowy *adj* ventōsus.

bludgeon *n* fustis *m*.

blue *adj* caeruleus; **black and** ~ līvidus; **true** ~ fīdissimus; ~ **blood** nōbilitās *f*.

bluff *n* rūpēs *f*, prōmunturium *nt* ♦ *adj*

inurbānus ♦ vt fallere, dēcipere, verba dare (dat), impōnere (dat).
blunder vi errāre, offendere ♦ n error m, errātum nt; (in writing) mendum nt.
blunt adj hebes; (manners) horridus, rūsticus, inurbānus; be ~ hebēre ♦ vt hebetāre, obtundere, retundere.
bluntly adv līberius, plānē et apertē.
blur n macula f ♦ vt obscūrāre.
blurt vt: ~ out ēmittere.
blush vi rubēre, ērubēscere ♦ n rubor m.
bluster vi dēclāmitāre, lātrāre.
boa n boa f.
Boadicea n Boudicca f.
boar n verrēs m; (wild) aper m.
board n tabula f; (table) mēnsa f; (food) vīctus m; (committee) concilium nt; (judicial) quaestiō f; (of ten men) decemvirī mpl; (gaming) abacus m, alveus m; on ~ in nāvī; go on ~ in nāvem cōnscendere; go by the ~ intercidere, perīre; above ~ sine fraude ♦ vt (building) contabulāre; (ship) cōnscendere; (person) vīctum praebēre (dat) ♦ vi: ~ with dēvertere ad.
boarder n hospes m.
boast vi glōriārī, sē iactāre; ~ of glōriārī dē (abl) ♦ n glōria f, glōriātiō f, iactātiō ⌐.
boastful adj glōriōsus.
boastfully adv glōriōsē.
boasting n glōriātiō f ♦ adj glōriōsus.
boat n linter f, scapha f, cymba f; (ship) nāvis f; be in the same ~ (fig) in eādem nāvī esse.
boatman n nauta m.
boatswain n hortātor m.
bobbin n fūsus m.
bode vt portendere, praesāgīre.
bodiless adj sine corpore.
bodily adj corporeus.
bodkin n acus f.
body n corpus nt; (dead) cadāver nt; (small) corpusculum nt; (person) homō m/f; (cf people) globus m, numerus m; (of troops) manus f, caterva f; (of cavalry) turma f; (of officials) collēgium nt; (heavenly) astrum nt; in a ~ ūniversī, frequentēs.
bodyguard n custōs m, stīpātōrēs mpl; (emperor's) praetōriānī mpl.
bog n palūs f.
bogey n mōnstrum nt.
boggle vi tergiversārī, haesitāre.
boggy adj palūster.
bogus adj falsus, fictus.
Bohemian adj līberior, solūtior, lībīdinōsus.
boil vt coquere; (liquid) fervefacere; ~ down dēcoquere ♦ vi fervēre, effervēscere; (sea) exaestuāre; (passion) exārdēscere, aestuāre; ~ over effervēscere ♦ n (MED) fūrunculus m.
boiler n cortīna f.
boiling adj (hot) fervēns.
boisterous adj (person) turbulentus, vehemēns; (sea) turbidus, agitātus; (weather) procellōsus, violentus.
boisterously adv turbidē, turbulentē.

boisterousness n tumultus m, violentia f.
bold adj audāx, fortis, intrepidus; (impudent) impudēns, protervus; (language) līber; (headland) prōminēns; make ~ audēre.
boldly adv audācter, fortiter, intrepidē; impudenter.
boldness n audācia f, cōnfīdentia f; impudentia f, petulantia f; (speech) lībertās f.
bolster n pulvīnus m ♦ vt: ~ up sustinēre, cōnfirmāre.
bolt n (door) claustrum nt, pessulus m, sera f; (missile) tēlum nt, sagitta f; (lightning) fulmen nt; make a ~ for it sē prōripere, aufugere; a ~ from the blue rēs subita, rēs inopīnāta ♦ vi (door) obserāre, obdere.
bombard vt tormentīs verberāre; (fig) lacessere.
bombast n ampullae fpl.
bombastic adj tumidus, īnflātus; be ~ ampullārī.
bond n vinculum nt, catēna f, compes f; (of union) cōpula f, iugum nt, nōdus m; (document) syngrapha f; (agreement) foedus nt ♦ adj servus, addictus.
bondage n servitūs f, famulātus m.
bone n os nt; (fish) spīna f ♦ vt exossāre.
boneless adj exos.
bonfire n ignis festus m.
bonhomie n festīvitās f.
bon mot n dictum nt, sententia f.
bonny adj pulcher, bellus.
bony adj osseus.
boo vt explōdere.
book n liber m; (small) libellus m; (scroll) volūmen nt; (modern form) cōdex m; ~s (COMM) rationēs fpl, tabulae fpl; bring to ~ in iūdicium vocāre.
bookbinder n glūtinātor m.
bookcase n librārium nt, pēgma nt.
bookish adj litterārum studiōsus.
book-keeper n āctuārius m.
bookseller n librārius m, bibliopōla m.
bookshop n bibliothēca f, librāria taberna f.
bookworm n tinea f.
boom n (spar) longurius m; (harbour) ōbex m/f ♦ vi resonāre.
boon n bonum nt, beneficium nt, dōnum nt ♦ adj festīvus; ~ companion sodālis m, compōtor m.
boor n agrestis m, rūsticus m.
boorish adj agrestis, rūsticus, inurbānus.
boorishly adv rūsticē.
boost vt efferre; (wares) vēnditāre.
boot n calceus m; (MIL) caliga f; (rustic) pērō m; (tragic) cothurnus m ♦ vi prōdesse; to ~ īnsuper, praetereā.
booted adj calceātus, caligātus.
booth n taberna f.
bootless adj inūtilis, vānus.
bootlessly adv frustrā.
booty n praeda f, spolia ntpl.
border n ōra f, margō f; (country) fīnis m; (dress) limbus m ♦ vt praetexere, margināre;

fīnīre ♦ *vi:* ~ **on** adiacēre (*dat*), imminēre
(*dat*), attingere; (*fig*) fīnitimum esse (*dat*).
bordering *adj* fīnitimus.
bore *vt* perforāre, perterebrāre; (*person*)
obtundere, fatīgāre; ~ **out** exterebrāre ♦ *n*
terebra *f*; (*hole*) forāmen *nt*; (*person*) homō
importūnus *m*, ineptus *m*.
boredom *n* lassitūdō *f*.
borer *n* terebra *f*.
born *adj* nātus; **be** ~ nāscī.
borough *n* mūnicipium *nt*.
borrow *vt* mūtuārī.
borrowed *adj* mūtuus; (*fig*) aliēnus.
borrowing *n* mūtuātiō *f*; (*to pay a debt*)
versūra *f*.
bosky *adj* nemorōsus.
bosom *n* sinus *m*; (*fig*) gremium *nt*; ~ **friend**
familiāris *m/f*, sodālis *m*; **be a** ~ **friend of** ab
latere esse (*gen*).
boss *n* bulla *f*; (*shield*) umbō *m*.
botanist *n* herbārius *m*.
botany *n* herbāria *f*.
botch *vt* male sarcīre, male gerere.
both *pron* ambō, uterque (*gen* **utriusque,** *each
of two*) ♦ *adv:* ~ ... **and** et ... et, cum ... tum.
bother *n* negōtium *nt* ♦ *vt* vexāre, molestus
esse (*dat*) ♦ *vi* operam dare.
bothersome *adj* molestus.
bottle *n* lagoena *f*, amphora *f* ♦ *vt* (*wine*)
diffundere.
bottom *n* fundus *m*; (*ground*) solum *nt*; (*ship*)
carīna *f*; **the** ~ **of** īmus; **be at the** ~ **of** (*cause*)
auctōrem esse; **go to the** ~ pessum īre,
perīre; **send to the** ~ pessum dare; **from the** ~
funditus, ab īnfimō.
bottomless *adj* profundus, fundō carēns.
bottommost *adj* īnfimus.
bough *n* rāmus *m*.
boulder *n* saxum *nt*.
boulevard *n* platea *f*.
bounce *vi* salīre, resultāre.
bound *n* fīnis *m*, modus *m*, terminus *m*; (*leap*)
saltus *m*; **set** ~**s to** modum facere (*dat*) ♦ *vt*
fīnīre, dēfīnīre, termināre ♦ *vi* salīre,
saltāre ♦ *adj* adligātus, obligātus, obstrictus;
be ~ **to** (*duty*) dēbēre; **it is** ~ **to happen**
necesse est ēveniat; **be** ~ **for** tendere in (*acc*);
be storm~ tempestāte tenērī.
boundaries *npl* fīnēs *mpl*.
boundary *n* fīnis *m*; (*of fields*) terminus *m*;
(*fortified*) līmes *m*; ~ **stone** terminus *m*.
boundless *adj* immēnsus, īnfīnītus.
boundlessness *n* īnfīnitās *f*, immēnsum *nt*.
bounteous *adj see* **bountiful**.
bounteously *adv* largē, līberāliter, cōpiōsē.
bountiful *adj* largus, mūnificus, benignus.
bounty *n* largitās *f*, līberālitās *f*; (*store*) cōpia *f*.
bouquet *n* corollārium *nt*; (*of wine*) flōs *m*.
bourn *n* fīnis *m*.
bout *n* certāmen *nt*; (*drinking*) cōmissātiō *f*.
bovine *adj* būbulus; (*fig*) stolidus.
bow *n* arcus *m*; (*ship*) prōra *f*; (*courtesy*)
salūtātiō *f*; **have two strings to one's** ~

duplicī spē ūtī; **rain**~ arcus *m* ♦ *vi* flectere,
inclīnāre ♦ *vi* caput dēmittere.
bowels *n* alvus *f*; (*fig*) viscera *ntpl*.
bower *n* umbrāculum *nt*, trichila *f*.
bowl *n* (*cooking*) catīnus *m*; (*drinking*) calix *m*;
(*mixing wine*) crātēra *f*; (*ball*) pila *f* ♦ *vt*
volvere; ~ **over** prōruere.
bow-legged *adj* valgus.
bowler *n* (*game*) dator *m*.
bowstring *n* nervus *m*.
box *n* arca *f*, capsa *f*; (*for clothes*) cista *f*; (*for
medicine*) pyxis *f*; (*for perfume*) alabaster *m*;
(*tree*) buxus *f*; (*wood*) buxum *nt*; (*blow on ears*)
alapa *f* ♦ *vt* inclūdere; ~ **the ears of** alapam
dūcere (*dat*), colaphōs īnfringere (*dat*) ♦ *vi*
(*fight*) pugnīs certāre.
boxer *n* pugil *m*.
boxing *n* pugilātiō *f*.
boxing glove *n* caestus *m*.
boy *n* puer *m*; **become a** ~ **again** repuerāscere.
boycott *vt* repudiāre.
boyhood *n* pueritia *f*; **from** ~ ā puerō.
boyish *adj* puerīlis.
boyishly *adv* puerīliter.
brace *n* (*building*) fībula *f*; (*strap*) fascia *f*; (*pair*)
pār *nt* ♦ *vt* adligāre; (*strengthen*) firmāre.
bracelet *n* armilla *f*.
bracing *adj* (*air*) salūbris.
bracken *n* filix *f*.
bracket *n* uncus *m*.
brackish *adj* amārus.
bradawl *n* terebra *f*.
brag *vi* glōriārī, sē iactāre.
braggart *n* glōriōsus *m*.
braid *vt* nectere.
brain *n* cerebrum *nt*; ingenium *nt*.
brainless *adj* sōcors, stultus.
brainy *adj* ingeniōsus.
brake *n* (*wood*) dūmētum *nt*; (*on wheel*)
sufflāmen *nt*.
bramble *n* rubus *m*.
bran *n* furfur *m*.
branch *n* rāmus *m*; (*kind*) genus *nt* ♦ *vi:* ~ **out**
rāmōs porrigere.
branching *adj* rāmōsus.
brand *n* (*fire*) torris *m*, fax *f*; (*mark*) nota *f*;
(*sword*) ēnsis *m*; (*variety*) genus *nt* ♦ *vt* (*mark*)
inūrere; (*stigma*) notāre; ~ **new** recēns.
brandish *vt* vibrāre.
brass *n* orichalcum *nt*.
bravado *n* ferōcitās *f*; **out of** ~ per speciem
ferōcitātis.
brave *adj* fortis, ācer ♦ *vt* adīre, patī.
bravely *adv* fortiter, ācriter.
bravery *n* fortitūdō *f*, virtūs *f*.
bravo *interj* bene, euge, macte.
brawl *n* rixa *f*, iūrgium *nt* ♦ *vi* rixārī.
brawn *n* lacertī *mpl*.
brawny *adj* lacertōsus, rōbūstus.
bray *vi* rūdere.
brazen *adj* aēneus; (*fig*) impudēns.
brazier *n* foculus *m*.
breach *n* (*in wall*) ruīna *f*; (*of friendship*)

dissēnsiō f ♦ vt perfringere; ~ of trust mala fidēs; commit a ~ of promise prōmissīs nōn stāre.
breach of the peace n iūrgium nt, tumultus m.
bread n pānis m.
breadth n lātitūdō f; in ~ in lātitūdinem (acc).
break vt frangere, perfringere; ~ down vt īnfringere, dīrüere; ~ in vt (animal) domāre; ~ into pieces dīrumpere; ~ off vt abrumpere, dēfringere; (action) dīrimere; ~ open effringere, solvere; ~ through vt fus interrumpere; ~ up vt dissolvere, interrumpere; ~ one's word fidem fallere, violāre; without ~ing the law salvīs lēgibus ♦ vi rumpī, frangī; (day) illūcēscere; (strength) dēficere; ~ off vi dēsinere; ~ into intrāre; ~ out vi ērumpere; (sore) recrūdēscere; (trouble) exārdēscere; ~ up vi dīlābī, dissolvī; (meeting) dīmittī; ~ through vi inrumpere; ~ with dissidēre ab ♦ n intermissiō f, intervallum nt.
breakable adj fragilis.
breakage n frāctum nt.
breakdown n (activity) mora f; (health) dēbilitās f.
breaker n fluctus m.
breakfast n iēntāculum nt, prandium nt ♦ vi ientāre, prandēre.
breakwater n mōlēs f.
bream n sparulus m.
breast n pectus nt; (woman's) mamma f; make a clean ~ of cōnfitērī.
breastplate n lōrīca f.
breastwork n lōrīca f, pluteus m.
breath n spīritus m, anima f; (bad) hālitus m; (quick) anhēlitus m; (of wind) aura f, adflātus m; below one's ~ mussitāns; catch one's ~ obstipēscere; hold one's ~ animam comprimere, continēre; take a ~ spīritum dūcere; take one's ~ away exanimāre; waste one's ~ operam perdere; out of ~ exanimātus.
breathable adj spīrābilis.
breathe vt, vi spīrāre, respīrāre; (quickly) anhēlāre; ~ again respīrāre; ~ in vt, vi spīritum dūcere; ~ out vt, vi exspīrāre, exhālāre; ~ upon īnspīrāre (dat), adflāre (dat); ~ one's last animam agere, efflāre.
breathing n hālitus m, respīrātiō f.
breathing space n respīrātiō f.
breathless adj exanimātus.
breeches n brācae fpl.
breed n genus nt ♦ vt generāre, prōcreāre; (raise) ēducāre, alere; (fig) adferre, efficere; well-bred generōsus.
breeder n (animal) mātrix f; (man) generātor m; (fig) nūtrix f.
breeding n (act) fētūra f; (manners) mōrēs mpl; good ~ hūmānitās f.
breeze n aura f, flātus m.
breezy adj ventōsus; (manner) hilaris.
brevity n brevitās f.
brew vt coquere ♦ vi (fig) parārī, imminēre.

bribe vt corrumpere ♦ vi largīrī ♦ n pecūnia f, mercēs f.
briber n corruptor m, largītor m.
bribery n ambitus m, largītiō f.
brick n later m ♦ adj latericius.
brickwork n latericium nt.
bridal adj nūptiālis; (bed) geniālis ♦ n nūptiae fpl.
bride n nūpta f.
bridegroom m marītus m.
bridge n pōns m ♦ vt pontem impōnere (dat).
bridle n frēnum nt ♦ vt frēnāre, īnfrēnāre.
brief adj brevis; to be ~ nē longum sit, nē multa.
briefly adv breviter, paucīs verbīs.
briefness n brevitās f.
brier n veprēs m, sentis m.
brig n liburna f.
brigade n legiō f; (cavalry) turma f.
brigadier n lēgātus m.
brigand n latrō m, praedō m.
brigandage n latrōcinium nt.
bright adj clārus, lūculentus; (sky) serēnus; (intellect) ingeniōsus; (manner) hilaris, laetus; be ~ lūcēre, splendēre.
brighten vt illūstrāre; laetificāre ♦ vi lūcēscere; (person) hilarem fierī.
brightly adv clārē.
brightness n fulgor m, candor m; (sky) serēnitās f.
brilliance n splendor m, fulgor m; (style) nitor m, lūmen nt, īnsignia ntpl.
brilliant adj clārus, illūstris, splendidus; (fig) īnsignis, praeclārus, lūculentus.
brilliantly adv splendidē, praeclārē, lūculentē.
brim n lābrum nt, margō f; fill to the ~ explēre.
brimstone n sulfur nt.
brindled adj varius.
brine n salsāmentum nt.
bring vt ferre; (person) dūcere; (charge) intendere; (to a place) adferre, addūcere, advehere, dēferre; (to a destination) perdūcere; (to a worse state) redigere; ~ about vt efficere; ~ before dēferre ad, referre ad; ~ back vt (thing) referre; (person) redūcere; ~ down vt dēdūcere, dēferre; ~ forth (from store) dēprōmere; (child) parere; (crops) ferre, ēdere; ~ forward vt (for discussion) iactāre, iacere; (reason) adferre; ~ home (bride) dēdūcere; (in triumph) dēportāre; ~ home to pervincere; ~ in vt invehere, indūcere, intrōdūcere; (import) importāre; (revenue) reddere; ~ off vt (success) reportāre; ~ on īnferre, importāre; (stage) indūcere; ~ out vt efferre; (book) ēdere; (play) dare; (talent) ēlicere; ~ over perdūcere, trādūcere; ~ to bear adferre; ~ to light nūdāre, dētegere; ~ to pass perficere, peragere; ~ to shore ad litus appellere; ~ together contrahere, cōgere; (enemies) conciliāre; ~ up (child) ēducāre, tollere; (troops) admovēre; (topic) prōferre; ~ upon oneself sibī cōnscīscere, sibī contrahere.

brink n ōra f, margō f.
briny adj salsus.
brisk adj alacer, vegetus, ācer.
briskly adv ācriter.
briskness n alacritās f.
bristle n sēta f ♦ vi horrēre, horrēscere.
bristly adj horridus, hirsūtus.
Britain n Brittania f.
Britons n Brittani mpl.
brittle adj fragilis.
broach vt (topic) in medium prōferre.
broad adj lātus; (accent) lātus; (joke) inurbānus; (daylight) multus.
broadcast vt dissēmināre.
broaden vt dīlātāre.
broadly adv lātē.
broadsword n gladius m.
brocade n Attalica ntpl.
brochure n libellus m.
brogue n pērō m.
broil n rixa f, iūrgium nt ♦ vt torrēre.
broiling adj torridus.
broken adj frāctus; (fig) cōnfectus; (speech) īnfrāctus.
broken-hearted adj dolōre cōnfectus.
broker n īnstitor m.
bronze n aes nt ♦ adj aēneus, aerātus.
brooch n fībula f.
brood n fētus m; (fig) gēns f ♦ vi incubāre (dat); (fig) incubāre (dat), fovēre; ~ over meditārī.
brook n rīvus m ♦ vt ferre, patī.
brooklet n rīvulus m.
broom n (plant) genista f; (brush) scōpae fpl.
broth n iūs nt.
brother n frāter m; (full) germānus m; ~ and sister marītus mpl.
brotherhood n frāternitās f.
brother-in-law n lēvir m, uxōris frāter m, sorōris marītus m.
brotherly adj frāternus.
brow n frōns f; (eye) supercilium nt; (hill) dorsum nt.
browbeat vt obiūrgāre, exagitāre.
brown adj fulvus, spādīx; (skin) adūstus.
browse vi pāscī, dēpāscī.
bruise vt atterere, frangere, contundere ♦ n vulnus nt.
bruit vt pervulgāre.
brunt n vīs f; bear the ~ of exhaurīre.
brush n pēniculus m; (artist's) pēnicillus m; (quarrel) rixa f ♦ vt verrere, dētergēre; (teeth) dēfricāre; ~ aside vt aspernārī, neglegere; ~ up vt (fig) excolere.
brushwood n virgulta ntpl; (for cutting) sarmenta ntpl.
brusque adj parum cōmis.
brutal adj atrōx, saevus, inhūmānus.
brutality n atrōcitās f, saevitia f.
brutally adv atrōciter, inhūmānē.
brute n bēlua f, bestia f.
brutish adj stolidus.
bubble n bulla f ♦ vi bullāre; ~ over effervēscere; ~ up scatēre.

buccaneer n praedō m, pīrāta m.
buck n cervus m ♦ vi exsultāre.
bucket n situla f, fidēlia f.
buckle n fībula f ♦ vt fībulā nectere; ~ to accingī.
buckler n parma f.
buckram n carbasus m.
bucolic adj agrestis.
bucolics n būcolica ntpl.
bud n gemma f, flōsculus m ♦ vi gemmāre.
budge vi movērī, cēdere.
budget n pūblicae pecūniae ratiō f ♦ vi: ~ for prōvidēre (dat).
buff adj lūteus.
buffalo n ūrus m.
buffet n (blow) alapa f; (fig) plāga f; (sideboard) abacus m ♦ vt iactāre, tundere.
buffoon n scurra m, balatrō m.
buffoonery n scurrilitās f.
bug n cīmex m.
bugbear n terricula ntpl, terror m.
bugle n būcina f.
bugler n būcinātor m.
build vt aedificāre, struere; (bridge) facere; (road) mūnīre; ~ on vt (add) adstruere; (hopes) pōnere; ~ on sand in aquā fundāmenta pōnere; ~ up vt exstruere; (to block) inaedificāre; (knowledge) īnstruere; ~ castles in the air spem inānem pāscere ♦ n statūra f.
builder n aedificātor m, structor m.
building n (act) aedificātiō f; (structure) aedificium nt.
bulb n bulbus m.
bulge vi tumēre, tumēscere, prōminēre ♦ vi tuberculum nt; (of land) locus prōminēns m.
bulk n māgnitūdō f, amplitūdō f; (mass) mōlēs f; (most) plērīque, māior pars.
bulky adj amplus, grandis.
bull n taurus m; ~'s taurīnus; take the ~ by the horns rem fortiter adgredī.
bulldog n Molossus m.
bullet n glāns f.
bulletin n libellus m.
bullion n aurum īnfectum nt, argentum īnfectum nt.
bullock n iuvencus m.
bully n obiūrgātor m, patruus m ♦ vt obiūrgāre, exagitāre.
bulrush n scirpus m.
bulwark n prōpugnāculum nt; (fig) arx f.
bump n (swelling) tuber nt, tuberculum nt; (knock) ictus m ♦ vi: ~ against offendere.
bumper n plēnum pōculum nt ♦ adj plēnus, māximus.
bumpkin n rūsticus m.
bumptious adj adrogāns.
bunch n fasciculus m; (of berries) racēmus m.
bundle n fascis m; (of hay) manipulus m ♦ vt obligāre.
bung n obtūrāmentum nt ♦ vt obtūrāre.
bungle vt male gerere.
bunk n lectus m, lectulus m.

buoy n cortex m ♦ vt sublevāre.
buoyancy n levitās f.
buoyant adj levis; (fig) hilaris.
bur n lappa f.
burden n onus nt; **beast of** ~ iūmentum nt ♦ vt onerāre; **be a** ~ oneri esse.
burdensome adj gravis, molestus.
bureau n scrīnium nt.
burgeon vi gemmāre.
burgess n mūniceps m.
burgh n mūnicipium nt.
burgher n mūniceps m.
burglar n fūr m.
burglary n fūrtum nt.
burial n fūnes nt, humātiō f, sepultūra f.
burin n caelum nt.
burlesque n imitātiō f ♦ vt per iocum imitārī.
burly adj crassus.
burn vt incendere, ūrere; (to ashes) cremāre ♦ vi ārdēre, flāgrāre; ~ **up** ambūrere, combūrere, exūrere; **be ~ed down** dēflāgrāre; ~ **out** vi exstinguī; ~ **the midnight oil** lūcubrāre ♦ n (MED) ambūstum nt.
burning adj igneus.
burnish vt polīre.
burrow n cuniculus m ♦ vi dēfodere.
burst vt rumpere, dīrumpere ♦ vi rumpī, dīrumpī; ~ **in** inrumpere; ~ **into tears** in lacrimās effundī; ~ **open** refringere; ~ **out** ērumpere, prōrumpere; ~ **out laughing** cachinnum tollere; ~ **through** perrumpere per (acc); ~ **upon** offerrī (dat), invādere ♦ n ēruptiō f; (noise) fragor m; ~ **of applause** clāmōrēs mpl; **with a** ~ **of speed** citātō gradū, citātō equō.
bury vt sepelīre, humare; (ceremony) efferre; (hiding) condere; (things) dēfodere; (fig) obruere; ~ **the hatchet** amīcitiam reconciliāre.
bush n frutex m; dūmus m; **beat about the** ~ circuitiōne ūtī.
bushel n medimnus m.
bushy adj fruticōsus; (thick) dēnsus; (hair) hirsūtus.
busily adv strēnuē, impigrē.
business n negōtium nt; (occupation) ars f, quaestus m; (public life) forum nt; (matter) rēs f; **it is your** ~ tuum est; **make it one's** ~ **to** id agere ut; **you have no** ~ **to** nōn tē decet (infin); **mind one's own** ~ suum negōtium agere; ~ **days** diēs fāstī mpl.
businessman negōtiātor m.
buskin n cothurnus m.
bust n imāgō f.
bustle vi trepidāre, festīnāre; ~ **about** discurrere.
busy adj negōtiōsus, occupātus; (active) operōsus, impiger, strēnuus; ~ **in** occupātus (abl); ~ **on** intentus (dat); **keep** ~ vt exercēre; ~ **oneself with** pertractāre, studēre (dat).
busybody n: **be a** ~ alienīs negōtīs sē immiscēre.
but conj sed, at; (2nd place) autem, tamen ♦ adv

modo ♦ prep praeter (acc); **nothing** ~ nihil nisī; ~ **that,** ~ **what** quīn; **not** ~ **what** nihilōminus.
butcher n lanius m ♦ vt trucīdāre.
butcher's shop n laniēna f.
butchery n strāgēs f, occīdiō f.
butler n prōmus m.
butt n (cask) cadus m; (of ridicule) lūdibrium nt ♦ vi arietāre; ~ **in** interpellāre.
butter n būtyrum nt.
butterfly n pāpiliō m.
buttock n clūnis m/f.
button n bulla f.
buttonhole vt (fig) dētinēre, prēnsāre.
buttress n antērides jpl ♦ vt fulcīre.
buxom adj nitidus.
buy vt emere; ~ **provisions** obsonāre; ~ **back** vt redimere; ~ **off** vt redimere; ~ **up** vt coemere.
buyer n emptor m; (at auctions) manceps m.
buzz n strīdor m, susurrus m ♦ vi strīdere, susurrāre.
buzzard n būteō m.
by prep (near) ad (acc), apud (acc); prope (acc); (along) secundum (acc); (past) praeter (acc); (agent) a, ab (abl); (instrument) abl; (time) ante (acc); (oath) per (acc) ♦ adv prope, iuxtā; ~ **and** ~ mox; **be** ~ adesse, adstāre; ~ **force of arms** vī et armās; ~ **land and sea** terrī marique.
bygone adj praeteritus.
bystander n arbiter m; pl circumstantēs mpl.
byway n dēverticulum nt, trāmes m, sēmita f.
byword n prōverbium nt.

C, c

cabal n factiō f.
cabbage n brassica f, caulis m.
cabin n casa f; (ship) cubiculum nt.
cabinet n armārium nt.
cable n fūnis m; (anchor) ancorāle nt.
cache n thēsaurus m.
cachet n nota f.
cackle vi strepere n ♦ strepitus m, clangor m.
cacophonous adj dissonus.
cacophony n vōcēs dissonae fpl.
cadaverous adj cadāverōsus.
cadence n clausula numerōsa f, numerus m.
cadet n (son) nātū minor; (MIL) contubernālis m.
cage n cavea f ♦ vt inclūdere.
caitiff n ignāvus m.
cajole vt blandīrī, dēlēnīre.
cake n placenta f.
calamitous adj exitiōsus, calamitōsus.

calamity n calamitās f, malum nt; (MIL) clādēs f.
calculate vt ratiōnem dūcere, inīre.
calculation n ratiō f.
calculator n ratiōcinātor m.
calendar n fāstī mpl.
calends n Kalendae fpl.
calf n (animal) vitulus m, vitula f; (leg) sūra f.
calibre n (fig) ingenium nt, auctōritās f.
call vt vocāre; (name) appellāre, nōmināre; (aloud) clāmāre; (to a place) advocāre, convocāre; ~ **aside** sēvocāre; ~ **down** (curse) dētestārī; ~ **for** vt fus postulāre, requīrere; ~ **forth** ēvocāre, excīre, ēlicere; ~ **in** vt advocāre; ~ **together** convocāre; ~ **on** vt fus (for help) implōrāre; (visit) salūtāre; ~ **off** vt āvocāre, revocāre; ~ **out** vi exclāmāre; ~ **up** vt (dead) excitāre, ēlicere; (MIL) ēvocāre ♦ n vōx f, clāmor m; (summons) invītātiō f; (visit) salūtātiō f.
caller n salūtātor m.
calling n ars f, quaestus m.
callous adj dūrus; **become** ~ obdūrēscere.
callow adj rudis.
calm adj tranquillus, placidus; (mind) aequus ♦ vi: ~ **down** (fig) dēfervēscere ♦ vt sēdāre, tranquillāre ♦ n tranquillitās f; **dead** ~ (at sea) malacia f.
calmly adv tranquillē, placidē; aequō animō.
calumniate vt obtrectāre, crīminārī; (falsely) calumniārī.
calumniator n obtrectātor m.
calumny n opprobria ntpl, obtrectātiō f.
calve vi parere.
cambric n linteum nt.
camel n camēlus m.
camouflage n dissimulātiō f ♦ vt dissimulāre.
camp n castra ntpl; **summer** ~ aestīva ntpl; **winter** ~ hīberna ntpl; **in** ~ sub pellibus; **pitch** ~ castra pōnere; **strike** ~ castra movēre ♦ adj castrēnsis ♦ vi tendere.
campaign n stīpendium nt, bellum nt; (rapid) expedītiō f ♦ vi bellum gerere, stīpendium merēre.
campaigner n mīles m; **old** ~ veterānus m; (fig) veterātor m.
campbed n grabātus m.
camp followers n lixae mpl.
can n hirnea f.
can vi posse (+ infin); (know how) scīre.
canaille n vulgus nt, plebs f.
canal n fossa nāvigābilis f, eurīpus m.
cancel vt indūcere, abrogāre.
cancellation n (writing) litūra f; (law) abrogātiō f.
cancer n cancer m; (fig) carcinōma nt, ulcus nt.
cancerous adj (fig) ulcerōsus.
candelabrum n candēlābrum nt.
candid adj ingenuus, apertus, līber, simplex.
candidate n petītor m; **be a** ~ **for** petere.
candidature n petītiō f.
candidly adv ingenuē.
candle n candēla f.
candlestick n candēlābrum nt.

candour n ingenuitās f, simplicitās f, lībertās f.
cane n (reed) harundō f; (for walking, punishing) virga f ♦ vt verberāre.
canine adj canīnus.
canister n capsula f.
canker n (plants) rōbigō f; (fig) aerūgō f, carcinōma nt ♦ vt corrumpere.
Cannae n Cannae fpl.
cannibal n anthrōpophagus m.
cannon n tormentum nt.
cannot nōn posse, nequīre; **I** ~ **help but** ... facere nōn possum quīn ... (subj), nōn possum nōn ... (infin).
canny adj prūdens, prōvidus, cautus, circumspectus.
canoe n linter f.
canon n nōrma f, rēgula f; (ECCL) canonicus m.
canopy n aulaeum nt.
cant n fūcus m, fūcāta verba ntpl ♦ vt oblīquāre.
cantankerous adj importūnus.
cantankerousness n importūnitās f.
canter n lēnis cursus m ♦ vi lēniter currere.
canticle n canticum nt.
canto n carmen nt.
canton n pāgus m.
canvas n carbasus m, linteum nt ♦ adj carbaseus; **under** ~ sub pellibus.
canvass vi ambīre ♦ vt prēnsāre, circumīre.
canvassing n ambitus m, ambitiō f.
cap n pilleus m; (priest's) galērus m, apex m.
capability n facultās f, potestās f.
capable adj capāx, doctus, perītus.
capably adv bene, doctē.
capacious adj capāx, amplus.
capacity n capācitās f, amplitūdō f; (mind) ingenium nt.
caparison n ephippium nt.
cape n (GEOG) prōmunturium nt; (dress) chlamys f.
caper vi saltāre; (animal) lascīvīre ♦ n saltus m.
capering n lascivia f.
capital adj (chief) praecipuus, prīnceps; (excellent) ēgregius; (law) capitālis; **convict of a** ~ **offence** capitis damnāre ♦ n (town) caput nt; (money) sors f; (class) negōtiātorēs mpl; **make** ~ **out of** ūtī (abl).
capitalist n faenerātor m.
capital punishment n capitis supplicum nt.
capitation tax n capitum exāctiō f.
Capitol n Capitolium nt.
capitulate vi sē dēdere; **troops who have ~d** dēditīciī mpl.
capitulation n dēditiō f.
capon n capō m.
caprice n libīdō f, incōnstantia f.
capricious adj incōnstāns, levis.
capriciously adv incōnstanter, leviter.
capriciousness n incōnstantia f, libīdō f.
capsize vt ēvertere ♦ vi ēvertī.
captain m dux m, praefectus m, prīnceps m;

(*MIL*) centuriō *m*; (*naval*) nāvarchus *m*; (*of merchant ship*) magister *m* ♦ *vt* praeesse (*dat*), dūcere.
captaincy *n* centuriātus *m*.
caption *n* caput *nt*.
captious *adj* mōrōsus; (*question*) capciōsus.
captiously *adv* mōrōsē.
captiousness *n* mōrōsitās *f*.
captivate *vt* capere, dēlēnīre, adlicere.
captive *n* captīvus *m*.
captivity *n* captīvitās *f*, vincula *ntpl*.
captor *n* (*by storm*) expugnātor *m*; vietor *m*.
capture *n* (*by storm*) expugnātiō *f* ♦ *vr* capere.
car *n* currus *m*.
caravan *n* commeātus *m*.
carbuncle *n* (*MED*) fūrunculus *m*; (*stone*) acaustus *m*.
carcass *n* cadāver *nt*.
card *n* charta *f*; (*ticket*) tessera *f*; (*wool*) pecten *nt* ♦ *vt* pectere.
cardamom *n* amōmum *nt*.
cardinal *adj* praecipuus; ~ **point** cardō *m* ♦ *n* (*ECCL*) cardinālis.
care *n* cūra *f*; (*anxiety*) sollicitūdō *f*; (*attention*) dīligentia *f*; (*charge*) custōdia *f*; **take** ~ cavēre; **take** ~ **of** cūrāre ♦ *vi* cūrāre; ~ **for** *vt* *fus* (*look after*) cūrāre; (*like*) amāre; **I don't** ~ nīl moror; **I couldn't care less about**... floccī nōn faciō..., pendō; **I don't** ~ **about** mittō, nihil moror; **for all I** ~ per mē.
career *n* curriculum *nt*; (*POL*) cursus honōrum; (*completed*) rēs gestae *fpl* ♦ *vi* ruere volāre.
carefree *adj* sēcūrus.
careful *adj* (*cautious*) cautus; (*attentive*) dīligēns, attentus; (*work*) accūrātus.
carefully *adv* cautē; dīligenter, attentē; accūrātē.
careless *adj* incautus, neglegēns.
carelessly *adv* incautē, neglegenter.
carelessness *n* incūria *f*, neglegentia *f*.
caress *vt* fovēre, blandīrī ♦ *n* blandīmentum *nt*, amplexus *m*.
cargo *n* onus *nt*.
caricature *n* (*picture*) gryllus *m*; (*fig*) imāgō dētorta *f* ♦ *vt* dētorquēre.
carmine *n* coccum *nt* ♦ *adj* coccineus.
carnage *n* strāgēs *f*, caedēs *f*.
carnal *adj* corporeus; (*pleasure*) libīdinōsus.
carnival *n* fēriae *fpl*.
carol *n* carmen *nt* ♦ *vi* cantāre.
carouse *vi* perpōtāre, cōmissārī ♦ *n* cōmissātiō *f*.
carp *vi* obtrectāre; ~ **at** carpere, rōdere.
carpenter *n* faber *m*, lignārius *m*.
carpet *n* tapēte *nt*.
carriage *n* (*conveying*) vectūra *f*; (*vehicle*) vehiculum *nt*; (*for journeys*) raeda *f*, petorritum *nt*; (*for town*) carpentum *nt*, pīlentum *nt*; (*deportment*) gestus *m*, incessus *m*; ~ **and pair** bīgae *fpl*; ~ **and four** quadrīgae *fpl*.
carrier *n* vector *m*; (*porter*) bāiulus *m*; ~ **etter** ~ tabellārius *m*.

carrion *n* cadāver *nt*.
carrot *n* carōta *f*.
carry *vt* portāre, vehere, ferre, gerere; (*law*) perferre; (*by assault*) expugnāre; ~ **away** auferre, āvehere; (*by force*) rapere; (*with emotion*) efferre; ~ **all before one** ēvincere; ~ **along** (*building*) dūcere; ~ **back** reportāre; revehere, referre; ~ **down** dēportāre, dēvehere; ~ **in** invehere, intrōferre; ~ **off** auferre, asportāre, āvehere; (*by force*) abripere, ēripere; (*prize*) ferre, reportāre; (*success*) bene gerere; ~ **on** *vt* gerere; (*profession*) exercēre; ~ **out** *vi* efferre, ēgerere, ēvehere; (*task*) exsequī; ~ **out an undertaking** rem suscipere; ~ **over** trānsportāre, trānsferre; ~ **the day** vincere; ~ **one's point** pervincere; ~ **through** perferre; ~ **to** adferre, advehere; ~ **up** subvehere ♦ *vi* (*sound*) audīrī; ~ **on** *vi* pergere; (*flirt*) lascīvīre.
cart *n* plaustrum *nt*; carrus *nt*; **put the** ~ **before the horse** praeposterum dīcere ♦ *vt* plaustrō vehere.
Carthage *n* Carthāgo, Carthāginis *f*.
Carthaginian *adj* Carthāginiēnsis; Pūnicus; **the** ~**s** Poenī *mpl*.
carthorse *n* iūmentum *nt*.
carve *vt* sculpere; (*on surface*) caelāre; (*meat*) secāre; ~ **out** exsculpere.
carver *n* caelātor *m*.
carving *n* caelātūra *f*.
cascade *n* cataracta *m*.
case *n* (*instance*) exemplum *nt*, rēs *f*; (*legal*) āctiō *f*, līs *f*, causa *f*; (*plight*) tempus *nt*; (*GRAM*) cāsus *m*; (*receptacle*) thēca *f*, involucrum *nt*; **in** ~ sī; (*to prevent*) nē; **in any** ~ utut est rēs; **in that** ~ ergō; **such is the** ~ sic sē rēs habet; **civil** ~ causa prīvāta; **criminal** ~ causa pūblica; **win a** ~ causam, lītem obtinēre; **lose a** ~ causam, lītem āmittere.
casement *n* fenestra *f*.
cash *n* nummī *mpl*; (*ready*) numerātum *nt*, praesēns pecūnia *f*; **pay** ~ ex arcā absolvere, repraesentāre.
cash box *n* arca *f*.
cashier *n* dispēnsātor *m* ♦ *vt* (*MIL*) exauctōrāre.
cash payment *n* repraesentātiō *f*.
cask *n* cūpa *f*.
casket *n* arcula *f*, pyxis *f*.
casque *n* galea *f*, cassis *f*.
cast *vt* iacere; (*account*) inīre; (*eyes*) conicere; (*lots*) conicere; (*covering*) exuere; (*metal*) fundere; ~ **ashore** ēicere; ~ **away** prōicere; ~ **down** dēicere; (*humble*) abicere; ~ **in one's teeth** exprobrāre; ~ **lots** sortīrī; ~ **off** *vi* abicere, exuere; ~ **out** prōicere, ēicere, pellere ♦ *n* iactus *m*; (*moulding*) typus *m*, fōrma *f*; **with a** ~ **in the eye** paetus *m*.
castanet *n* crotalum *nt*.
castaway *n* ēiectus *m*.
caste *n* ōrdō *m*.
castigate *vt* animadvertere, castīgāre.
castigation *n* animadversiō *f*, castīgātiō *f*.

castle n arx f, castellum nt.
castrate vt castrāre.
casual adj fortuītus; (person) neglegēns.
casually adv temerē.
casualty n înfortūnium nt; pl: **casualties** occīsī mpl.
casuist n sophistēs m.
cat n fēlēs f.
cataclysm n dīluvium nt, ruīna f.
catalogue n index m.
catapult n catapulta f, ballista f.
cataract n cataracta f.
catarrh n gravēdō f; **liable to** ~ gravēdinōsus.
catastrophe n calamitās f, ruīna f.
catastrophic adj calamitōsus, exitiōsus.
catch vt capere, dēprehendere, excipere; (disease) contrahere, nancīscī; (fire) concipere, comprehendere; (meaning) intellegere; ~ **at** captāre; ~ **out** vi dēprehendere; ~ **up with** adsequī; ~ **birds** aucupārī; ~ **fish** piscārī ♦ n bolus m.
categorical adj (statement) plānus.
categorically adv sine exceptiōne.
category n numerus m, genus nt.
cater vi obsōnāre.
cateran n praedātor m.
caterer n obsōnātor m.
caterpillar n ērūca f.
caterwaul vi ululāre.
catgut n chorda f.
catharsis n pūrgātiō f.
cathedral n aedēs f.
catholic adj generālis.
catkin n iūlus m.
cattle n (collectively) pecus nt; (singly) pecus f; (for plough) armenta ntpl.
cattle breeder n pecuārius m.
cattle market n forum boārium nt.
cattle thief n abāctor m.
cauldron n cortīna f.
cause n causa f; (person) auctor m; (law) causa f; (party) partēs fpl; **give** ~ **for** māteriam dare (gen); **make common** ~ **with** facere cum, stāre ab; **plead a** ~ causam dīcere; **in the** ~ **of** prō (abl); **without** ~ iniūriā ♦ vt efficere ut (+ subj), facere, facessere (with ut); cūrāre (with gerundive); (feelings) movēre, inicere, ciēre.
causeless adj vānus, sine causā.
causeway n agger m.
caustic adj (fig) mordāx.
cauterize vt adūrere.
caution n (wariness) cautiō f, prūdentia f; (warning) monitum nt ♦ vt monēre, admonēre.
cautious adj cautus, prōvidus, prūdens.
cautiously adv cautē, prūdenter.
cavalcade n pompa f.
cavalier n eques m ♦ adj adrogāns.
cavalierly adv adroganter.
cavalry n equitēs mpl, equitātus m ♦ adj equester; **troop of** ~ turma f.
cavalryman n eques m.

cave n spēlunca f, caverna f; antrum nt; ~ **in** vi concidere, conlābī.
cavern n spēlunca f, caverna f.
cavil vi cavillārī; ~ **at** carpere, cavillārī ♦ n captiō f, cavillātiō f.
cavity n caverna f, cavum nt.
cavort vi saltāre.
caw vi cornīcārī.
cease vi dēsinere, dēsistere.
ceaseless adj adsiduus, perpetuus.
ceaselessly adv adsiduē, perpetuō.
cedar n cedrus f ♦ adj cedrinus.
cede vt cēdere, concēdere.
ceiling n tēctum nt; (panelled) lacūnar nt, laqueārium nt.
celebrate vt (rite) celebrāre, agitāre; (in crowds) frequentāre; (person, theme) laudāre, celebrāre, dīcere.
celebrated adj praeclārus, illūstris, nōtus; **the** ~ **ille.**
celebration n celebrātiō f; (rite) sollemne nt.
celebrity n celebritās f, fāma f; (person) vir illūstris.
celerity n celeritās f, vēlōcitās f.
celery n apium nt.
celestial adj caelestis; dīvīnus.
celibacy n caelibātus m.
celibate n caelebs m.
cell n cella f.
cellar n cella f.
cement n ferrūmen nt ♦ vt coagmentāre.
cemetery n sepulchrētum nt.
cenotaph n tumulus honōrārius, tumulus inānis m.
censer n tūribulum nt, acerra f.
censor n cēnsor m ♦ vt cēnsēre.
censorious adj cēnsōrius, obtrectātor.
censorship n cēnsūra f.
censure n reprehēnsiō f, animadversiō f; (censor's) nota f ♦ vt reprehendere, animadvertere, increpāre; notāre.
census n cēnsus m.
cent n: **one per** ~ centēsima f; **12 per** ~ **per annum** centēsima f (ie monthly).
centaur n centaurus m.
centaury n (plant) centaurēum nt.
centenarian n centum annōs nātus m, nāta f.
centenary n centēsimus annus m.
centesimal adj centēsimus.
central adj medius.
centralize vt in ūnum locum cōnferre; (power) ad ūnum dēferre.
centre n centrum nt, media pars f; **the** ~ **of** medius.
centuple adj centuplex.
centurion n centuriō m.
century n (MIL) centuria f; (time) saeculum nt.
ceramic adj fictilis.
cereal n frūmentum nt.
ceremonial adj sollemnis ♦ n rītus m.
ceremonious adj (rite) sollemnis; (person) officiōsus.
ceremoniously adv sollemniter; officiōsē.

ceremony n caerimōnia f, rītus m; (*politeness*) officium nt; (*pomp*) apparātus m; **master of ceremonies** dēsignātor m.

cerise n coccum nt ♦ adj coccineus.

certain adj (*sure*) certus; (*future*) explōrātus; a ~ quīdam, quaedam, quoddam; **be** ~ (*know*) prō certō scīre/habēre.

certainly adv certē, certō, sine dubiō; (*yes*) ita, māximē; (*concessive*) quidem.

certainty n (*thing*) certum nt; (*belief*) fidēs f; **for a** ~ prō certō, explōrātē; **regard as a** ~ prō explōrātō habēre.

certificate n testimōnium nt.

certify vt (*writing*) recognōscere; (*fact*) adfirmāre, testificārī.

cessation n fīnis m; (*from labour*) quiēs f; (*temporary*) intermissiō f; (*of hostilities*) indutiae fpl.

chafe vt ūrere; (*fig*) inrītāre ♦ vi stomachārī.

chaff n palea f ♦ vt lūdere.

chaffinch n fringilla f.

chagrin n dolor m, stomachus m ♦ vt stomachum facere (*dat*), sollicitāre.

chain n catēna f; (*for neck*) torquis m; (*sequence*) seriēs f; ~s pl vincula ntpl ♦ vt vincīre.

chair n sella f; (*of office*) sella curūlis f; (*sedan*) sella gestātōria f, lectīca f; (*teacher's*) cathedra f.

chairman n (*at meeting*) magister m; (*of debate*) disceptātor m.

chalet n casa f.

chalice n calix m.

chalk n crēta f.

chalky adj crētōsus.

challenge n prōvocātiō f ♦ vt prōvocāre, lacessere; (*statement*) in dubium vocāre; (*fig*) invītāre, dēposcere.

challenger n prōvocātor m.

chamber n conclāve nt; (*bed*) cubiculum nt; (*bridal*) thalamus m; (*parliament*) cūria f.

chamberlain n cubiculārius m.

chambermaid n serva f, ancilla f.

chameleon n chamaeleōn f.

chamois n rūpicapra f.

champ vt mandere.

champion n prōpugnātor m, patrōnus m; (*winner*) victor m ♦ vt favēre (*dat*), adesse (*dat*).

chance n fors f, fortūna f, cāsus m; (*opportunity*) occāsiō f; potestās f, facultās f; (*prospect*) spēs f; **game of** ~ ālea f; **by** ~ cāsū, fortuītō; **have an eye to the main** ~ forō ūtī; **on the** ~ **of** sī forte ♦ adj fortuītus ♦ vi accidere, ēvenīre; **it chanced that**... accidit ut... (+ subj); ~ **upon** vt fus incidere in, invenīre ♦ vt periclitārī.

chancel n absis f.

chancellor n cancellārius m.

chancy adj dubius, perīculōsus.

chandelier n candēlābrum nt.

chandler n candēlārum propōla m.

change n mūtātiō f, commūtātiō f, permūtātiō

f; (*POL*) rēs novae fpl; (*alternation*) vicēs fpl, vicissitūdō f; (*money*) nummī minōrēs mpl ♦ vt mūtāre, commūtāre, permūtāre ♦ vi mūtārī; ~ **hands** abaliēnarī; ~ **places** ōrdinem permūtāre, inter sē loca permūtāre.

changeable adj incōnstāns, mūtābilis.

changeableness n incōnstantia f, mūtābilitās f.

changeful adj varius.

changeless adj cōnstāns, immūtābilis.

changeling adj subditus m.

channel n canālis m; (*sea*) fretum nt; (*irrigation*) rīvus m; (*groove*) sulcus m.

chant vt cantāre, canere ♦ n cantus m.

chaos n chaos nt; (*fig*) perturbātiō f.

chaotic adj perturbātus.

chap n rīma f; (*man*) homō m.

chapel n sacellum nt, aedicula f.

chaplain n diāconus m.

chaplet n corōna f, sertum nt.

chaps n (*animal*) mālae fpl.

chapter n caput nt.

char vt ambūrere.

character n (*inborn*) indolēs f, ingenium nt, nātūra f; (*moral*) mōrēs mpl; (*reputation*) existimātiō f; (*kind*) genus nt; (*mark*) signum nt, littera f; (*THEAT*) persōna f, partēs fpl; **sustain a** ~ **persōnam gerere; I know his** ~ sciō quālis sit.

characteristic adj proprius ♦ n proprium nt.

characteristically adv suō mōre.

characterize vt dēscrībere; proprium esse (*gen*).

charcoal n carbō m.

charge n (*law*) accūsātiō f, crīmen nt; (*MIL*) impetus m, dēcursus m; (*cost*) impēnsa f; (*task*) mandātum nt, onus nt; (*trust*) cūra f, tūtēla f; **bring a** ~ **against** lītem intendere (*dat*); **entertain a** ~ **against** nōmen recipere (*gen*); **give in** ~ in custōdiam trādere; **put in** ~ **of** praeficere (*acc, dat*); **be in** ~ **of** praesse (*dat*) ♦ vt (*law*) accūsāre; (*falsely*) īnsimulāre; (*MIL*) incurrere in (*acc*), signa īnferre in (*acc*), impetum facere in (*acc*); (*duty*) mandāre; (*cost*) ferre, īnferre; (*empty space*) complēre; (*trust*) committere; (*speech*) hortārī; ~ **to the account of** expēnsum ferre (*dat*).

chargeable adj obnoxius.

charger n (*dish*) lānx f; (*horse*) equus m.

charily adv cautē, parcē.

chariot n currus m; (*races*) quadrīgae fpl; (*war*) essedum nt.

charioteer n aurīga m; (*war*) essedārius m.

charitable adj benevolus, benignus.

charitably adv benevolē, benignē.

charity n amor m, benignitās f, līberālitās f.

charlatan n planus m.

charm n (*spell*) carmen nt; (*amulet*) bulla f; (*fig*) blanditiae fpl, dulcēdō f, illecebra f; (*beauty*) venus f, lepōs m ♦ vt (*magic*) fascināre; (*delight*) dēlectāre, dēlēnīre.

charming adj venustus, lepidus; (*speech*) blandus; (*scenery*) amoenus.

charmingly *adv* venustē, blandē.
chart *n* tabula *f.*
charter *n* diplōma *nt* ♦ *vt* condūcere.
chary *adj* (*cautious*) cautus; (*sparing*) parcus.
chase *vt* fugāre; (*hunt*) vēnārī; (*pursue*)
persequī, īnsequī; (*engrave*) caelāre; ~ **away**
pellere, abigere ♦ *n* vēnātus *m*, vēnātiō *f*;
(*pursuit*) īnsectātiō *f.*
chaser *n* (*in metal*) caelātor *m.*
chasm *n* hiātus *m.*
chaste *adj* castus, pudīcus; (*style*) pūrus.
chasten *vt* castīgāre, corrigere.
chastener *n* castīgātor *m*, corrēctor *m.*
chastise *vt* castīgāre, animadvertere.
chastisement *n* castīgātiō *f*, poena *f.*
chastity *n* castitās *f*, pudīcitia *f.*
chat *vi* colloquī, sermōcinārī ♦ *n* sermō *m*,
colloquium *nt.*
chatelaine *n* domina *f.*
chattels *n* bona *ntpl*, rēs mancipī.
chatter *vi* garrīre; (*teeth*) crepitāre ♦ *n*
garrulitās *f*, loquācitās *f.*
chatterbox *n* lingulāca *m/f.*
chatterer *n* garrulus *m*, loquāx *m.*
chattering *adj* garrulus, loquāx ♦ *n* garrulitās
f, loquācitās *f*; (*teeth*) crepitus *m.*
cheap *adj* vīlis; **hold** ~ parvī aestimāre; **buy** ~
bene emere.
cheapen *vt* pretium minuere (*gen*).
cheaply *adv* vīliter, parvō pretiō.
cheapness *n* vīlitās *f.*
cheat *vt* dēcipere, fraudāre, dēfraudāre,
frustrārī ♦ *n* fraudātor *m.*
check *vt* cohibēre, coercēre; (*movement*)
impedīre, inhibēre; (*rebuke*) reprehendere;
(*test*) probāre ♦ *n* impedīmentum *nt*, mora *f*;
(MIL) offēnsiō *f*; (*rebuke*) reprehēnsiō *f*; (*test*)
probātiō *f*; (*ticket*) tessera *f.*
checkmate *n* incitae calcēs *fpl* ♦ *vt* ad incitās
redigere.
cheek *n* gena *f*; (*impudence*) ōs *nt*; ~ **s** *pl* mālae
fpl; **how have you the** ~ **to say?** quō ōre dīcis?
cheekbone *n* maxilla *f.*
cheeky *adj* impudēns.
cheep *vi* pīpilāre.
cheer *vt* hilarāre, exhilarāre; hortārī; (*in
sorrow*) cōnsōlārī ♦ *vi* clāmāre, adclāmāre; ~
up! bonō animō es! ♦ *n* (*shout*) clāmor *m*,
plausus *m*; (*food*) hospitium *nt*; (*mind*) animus
m.
cheerful *adj* alacer, hilaris, laetus.
cheerfully *adv* hilare, laetē.
cheerfulness *n* hilaritās *f.*
cheerily *adv* hilare.
cheerless *adj* tristis, maestus.
cheerlessly *adv* triste.
cheery *adj* hilaris.
cheese *n* cāseus *m.*
chef *n* coquus *m.*
cheque *n* perscrīptiō *f*, syngrapha *f.*
chequer *vt* variāre.
chequered *adj* varius; (*mosaic*) tessellātus.
cherish *vt* fovēre, colere.

cherry *n* (*fruit*) cerasum *nt*; (*tree*) cerasus *f.*
chess *n* latrunculī *mpl.*
chessboard *n* abacus *m.*
chest *n* (*box*) arca *f*, arcula *f*; (*body*) pectus *nt*; ~
of drawers armārium *nt.*
chestnut *n* castanea *f* ♦ *adj* (*colour*) spādīx.
chevalier *n* eques *m.*
chevaux-de-frise *n* ēricius *m.*
chew *vt* mandere.
chic *adj* expolītus, concinnus.
chicanery *n* (*law*) calumnia *f*; (*fig*) dolus *m.*
chick *n* pullus *m.*
chicken *n* pullus *m*; **don't count your ~s before
they're hatched** adhūc tua messis in herbā
est.
chicken-hearted *adj* timidus, ignāvus.
chick-pea *n* cicer *nt.*
chide *vt* reprehendere, increpāre, obiūrgāre.
chief *n* prīnceps *m*, dux *m* ♦ *adj* praecipuus,
prīmus; ~ **point** caput *nt.*
chief command *n* summa imperiī.
chiefly *adv* in prīmīs, praesertim, potissimum.
chieftain *n* prīnceps *m*, rēgulus *m.*
chilblain *n* perniō *m.*
child *n* īnfāns *m/f*; puer *m*, puerulus *m*, puella *f*;
fīlius *m*, fīlia *f*; ~ **'s play** lūdus *m.*
childbed *n* puerperium *nt.*
childbirth *n* partus *m.*
childhood *n* pueritia *f*; **from** ~ ā puerō.
childish *adj* puerīlis.
childishly *adv* puerīliter.
childless *adj* orbus.
childlessness *n* orbitās *f.*
childlike *adj* puerīlis.
children *npl* līberī *mpl.*
chill *n* frīgus *nt* ♦ *adj* frīgidus ♦ *vt* refrīgerāre.
chilly *adj* frīgidus, frīgidior.
chime *vi* sonāre, canere; ~ **in** interpellāre; (*fig*)
cōnsonāre ♦ *n* sonus *m.*
chimera *n* chimaera *f*; (*fig*) somnium *nt.*
chimerical *adj* commentīcius.
chimney *n* camīnus *m.*
chin *n* mentum *nt.*
china *n* fictilia *ntpl.*
chink *n* rīma *f*; (*sound*) tinnītus *m* ♦ *vi* crepāre,
tinnīre.
chip *n* assula *f*, fragmentum *nt* ♦ *vt* dolāre.
chirp *vi* pīpilāre.
chirpy *adj* hilaris.
chisel *n* scalprum *nt*, scalpellum *nt* ♦ *vt*
sculpere.
chit *n* (*child*) pūsiō *m*, puerulus *m.*
chitchat *n* sermunculī *mpl.*
chitterlings *n* hillae *fpl.*
chivalrous *adj* generōsus.
chivalry *n* virtūs *f*; (*men*) iuventūs *f*; (*class*)
equitēs *mpl.*
chive *n* caepe *nt.*
chock *n* cuneus *m.*
chock-full *adj* refertus.
choice *n* dēlēctus *m*, ēlēctiō *f*; (*of alternatives*)
optiō *f* ♦ *adj* lēctus, eximius, exquīsītus.
choiceness *n* ēlegantia *f*, praestantia *f.*

choir n chorus m.
choke vt suffocāre; (emotion) reprimere; (passage) obstruere.
choler n bīlis f; (anger) īra f, stomachus m.
choleric adj īrācundus.
choose vt legere, ēligere, dēligere; (alternative) optāre; (for office) dēsignāre; (with infin) velle, mālle.
chop vt concīdere; ~ **off** praecīdere ♦ n (meat) offa f.
chopper n secūris f.
choppy adj (sea) asper.
choral adj symphōniacus.
chord n (string) nervus m, chorda f.
chortle vi cachinnāre.
chorus n (singers) chorus m; (song) concentus m, symphōnia f; **in** ~ ūnā vōce.
christen vt baptizāre.
Christian adj Christiānus.
Christianity n Christiānismus m.
chronic adj inveterātus; **become** ~ inveterāscere.
chronicle n annālēs mpl, ācta pūblica ntpl ♦ vt in annālēs referre.
chronicler n annālium scrīptor m.
chronological adj: **in** ~ **order** servātō temporum ōrdine; **make a** ~ **error** temporibus errāre.
chronology n temporum ratiō f, temporum ōrdō m.
chronometer n hōrologium nt.
chubby adj pinguis.
chuck vt conicere; ~ **out** extrūdere.
chuckle vi rīdēre ♦ n rīsus m.
chum n sodālis m.
church n ecclēsia f.
churl n rūsticus m.
churlish adj difficilis, importūnus; avārus.
churlishly adv rūsticē, avārē.
churlishness n mōrōsitās f, avāritia f.
chute n (motion) lāpsus m; (place) dēclīve nt.
cicada n cicāda f.
cincture n cingulum nt.
cinder n cinis m.
cipher n numerus m, nihil nt; (code) notae fpl; **in** ~ per notās.
circle n orbis m, circulus m, gȳrus m; **form a** ~ in orbem cōnsistere ♦ vi sē circumagere, circumīre.
circlet n īnfula f.
circuit n ambitus m, circuitus m; (assizes) conventus m.
circuitous adj longus; **a** ~ **route** circuitus m; (speech) ambāgēs fpl.
circular adj rotundus.
circulate vt (news) pervulgāre ♦ vi circumagī; (news) circumferrī, percrēbrēscere.
circulation n ambitus m; **be in** ~ in manibus esse; **go out of** ~ obsolēscere.
circumcise vt circumcīdere.
circumference n ambitus m.
circumlocution n ambāgēs fpl, circuitiō f.
circumnavigate vt circumvehī.

circumscribe vt circumscrībere; (restrict) coercēre, fīnīre.
circumspect adj cautus, prūdēns.
circumspection n cautiō f, prūdentia f, circumspectiō f.
circumspectly adv cautē, prūdenter.
circumstance n rēs f; ~**s** rērum status m; (wealth) rēs f; **as** ~**s arise** ē rē nātā; **under the** ~**s** cum haec ita sint, essent; **under no** ~**s** nēquāquam.
circumstantial adj adventīcius; (detailed) accūrātus; ~ **evidence** coniectūra f.
circumstantially adv accūrātē, subtīliter.
circumvallation n circummūnītiō f.
circumvent vt circumvenīre, fallere.
circus n circus m.
cistern n lacus m, cisterna f.
citadel n arx f
citation n (law) vocātiō f; (mention) commemorātiō f.
cite vt in iūs vocāre; (quote) commemorāre, prōferre.
citizen n cīvis m/f; (of provincial town) mūniceps m; **fellow** ~ cīvis m/f; **Roman** ~**s** Quirītēs mpl ♦ adj cīvīlis, cīvicus.
citizenship n cīvitās f; **deprived of** ~ **capite** dēminūtus; **loss of** ~ **capitis** dēminūtiō f.
citron n (fruit) citrum nt; (tree) citrus f.
city n urbs f, oppidum nt.
civic adj cīvīlis, cīvicus.
civil adj (of citizens) cīvīlis; (war) cīvīlis, intestīnus, domesticus; (manners) urbānus, cōmis, officiōsus; (lawsuit) prīvātus.
civilian n togātus m.
civility n urbānitās f, cōmitās f; (act) officium nt.
civilization n exculta hominum vīta f, cultus atque hūmānitās.
civilize vt excolere, expolīre, ad hūmānum cultum dēdūcere.
civil war n bellum cīvīle, bellum domesticum, bellum intestīnum.
clad adj vestītus.
claim vt (for oneself) adrogāre, adserere; (something due) poscere, postulāre, vindicāre; (at law) petere; (statement) adfirmāre ♦ n postulātiō f, postulātum nt; (at law) petītiō f, vindiciae fpl.
claimant n petītor m.
clam n chāma f.
clamber vi scandere.
clammy adj ūmidus, lentus.
clamorous adj vōciferāns.
clamour n strepitus m, clāmōrēs mpl ♦ vi: ~ **against** obstrepere (dat).
clamp n cōnfībula f.
clan n gēns f.
clandestine adj fūrtīvus.
clandestinely adv clam, fūrtim.
clang n clangor m, crepitus m ♦ vi increpāre.
clangour n clangor m.
clank n crepitus m ♦ vi crepitāre.
clansman n gentīlis m.

clap vi plaudere, applaudere; ~ **eyes on** cōnspicere; ~ **in prison** in vincula conicere ♦ n plausus m; (thunder) fragor m.

clapper n plausor m.

claptrap n iactātiō f.

claque n plausōrēs mpl, operae fpl.

clarify vt pūrgāre; (knowledge) illūstrāre ♦ vi liquēre.

clarinet n tībia f.

clarion n lituus m, cornū nt.

clarity n perspicuitās f.

clash n concursus m; (sound) strepitus m, crepitus m; (fig) discrepantia f ♦ vi concurrere; (sound) increpāre; (fig) discrepāre ♦ vt conflīgere.

clasp n fībula f; (embrace) amplexus m ♦ vt implicāre; amplectī, complectī; ~ **together** interiungere.

class n (POL) ōrdō m, classis f; (kind) genus nt; (school) classis f ♦ vt dēscrībere; ~ **as in** numerō (gen pl) referre, repōnere, habēre.

classic n scrīptor classicus m.

classical adj classicus; ~ **literature** litterae Graecae et Rōmānae.

classics npl scrīptōrēs Graecī et Rōmānī.

classify vt dēscrībere, in ōrdinem redigere.

class-mate n condiscipulus m.

clatter n crepitus m ♦ vi increpāre.

clause n (GRAM) incīsum nt, membrum nt; (law) caput nt; (will) ēlogium nt; **in short ~s** incīsim.

claw n unguis m, ungula f ♦ vt (unguibus) lacerāre.

clay n argilla f; **made of ~** fictilis.

clayey adj argillāceus.

claymore n gladius m.

clean adj mundus; (fig) pūrus, castus; ~ **slate** novae tabulae fpl; **make a ~ sweep of** omnia tollere; **show a ~ pair of heels** sē in pedēs conicere; **my hands are ~** innocēns sum ♦ adv prōrsus, tōtus ♦ vt pūrgāre.

cleanliness n munditia f.

cleanly adj mundus, nitidus ♦ adv mundē, pūrē.

cleanse vt pūrgāre, abluere, dētergēre.

clear adj clārus; (liquid) limpidus; (space) apertus, pūrus; (sound) clārus; (weather) serēnus; (fact) manifestus, perspicuus; (language) illūstris, dīlūcidus; (conscience) rēctus, innocēns; **it is ~** liquet; ~ **of** līber (abl), expers (gen); **be ~ about** rēctē intellegere; **keep ~ of** ēvītāre; **the coast is ~** arbitrī absunt ♦ vt (of obstacles) expedīre, pūrgāre; (of a charge) absolvere; (self) pūrgāre; (profit) lucrārī; ~ **away** āmovēre, tollere; ~ **off** vt (debt) solvere, exsolvere ♦ vi facessere; ~ **out** ēluere, dētergēre; ~ **up** vt (difficulty) illūstrāre, ēnōdāre, explicāre ♦ vi (weather) disserēnāscere.

clearance n pūrgātiō f; (space) intervallum nt.

clearing n (in forest) lūcus m.

clearly adv clārē; manifestē, apertē, perspicuē; (with clause) vidēlicet.

clearness n clāritās f; (weather) serēnitās f;

(mind) acūmen nt; (style) perspicuitās f.

clear-sighted adj sagāx, perspicāx.

cleavage n discidium nt.

cleave vt (out) findere, discindere ♦ vi (cling): ~ **to** haerēre (dat), adhaerēre (dat).

cleaver n dolabra f.

cleft n rīma f, hiātus m ♦ adj fissus, discissus.

clemency n clēmentia f, indulgentia f; **with ~** clēmenter.

clement adj clēmēns, misericors.

clench vt (nail) retundere; (hand) comprimere.

clerk n scrība m; (of court) lēctor m.

clever adj callidus, ingeniōsus, doctus, astūtus.

cleverly adv doctē, callidē, ingeniōsē.

cleverness n calliditās f, sollertia f.

clew n glomus nt.

cliché n verbum trītum nt.

client n cliēns m/f; (lawyer's) cōnsultor m; **body of ~s** clientēla f.

clientele n clientēla f.

cliff n rūpēs f, scopulus m.

climate n caelum nt.

climax n (RHET) gradātiō f; (fig) culmen nt.

climb vt, vi scandere, ascendere; ~ **down** dēscendere ♦ n ascēnsus m.

climber n scandēns m.

clime n caelum nt, plāga f.

clinch vt cōnfirmāre.

cling vi adhaerēre; ~ **together** cohaerere.

clink vi tinnīre ♦ n tinnītus m.

clip vt tondēre; praecīdere.

clippers n forfex f.

clique n factiō f.

cloak n (rain) lacerna f; (travel) paenula f; (MIL) sagum nt; palūdāmentum nt; (Greek) pallium nt; (fig) involūcrum nt; (pretext) speciēs f ♦ vt tegere, dissimulāre.

clock n hōrologium nt; (sun) sōlārium nt; (water) clepsydra f; **ten o'~** quarta hōra.

clockwise adv dextrōvorsum, dextrōrsum.

clod n glaeba f.

clog n (shoe) sculpōnea f; (fig) impedīmentum nt ♦ vt impedīre.

cloister n porticus f.

cloistered adj (fig) umbrātilis.

close adj (shut) clausus; (tight) artus; (narrow) angustus; (near) propinquus; (compact) refertus, dēnsus; (stingy) parcus; (secret) obscūrus; (weather) crassus; ~ **together** dēnsus, refertus; **at ~ quarters** comminus; **be ~ at hand** īnstāre; **keep ~ to** adhaerēre; ~ **to** prope (acc), iuxtā (acc) ♦ adv prope, iuxtā ♦ n angiportus m.

close vt claudere, operīre; (finish) perficere, fīnīre, conclūdere, termināre; (ranks) dēnsāre ♦ vi claudī; conclūdī, terminārī; (time) exīre; (wound) coīre; (speech) perōrāre; ~ **with** (fight) manum cōnserere, signa cōnferre; (deal) pacīscī; (offer) accipere ♦ n fīnis m, terminus m; (action) exitus m; (sentence) conclūsiō f; **at the ~ of summer** aestāte exeunte.

closely adv prope; (attending) attentē;

(*associating*) coniūnctē; **follow** ~ īnstāre (*dat*).
closeness n propinquitās f; (*weather*) gravitās
   f, crassitūdō f; (*with money*) parsimōnia f;
   (*friends*) coniūnctiō f; (*manner*) caut ō f.
closet n cubiculum nt, cella f ♦ vt inclūdere.
clot n (*blood*) concrētus sanguis m ♦ vi
   concrēscere.
cloth n textile nt; (*piece*) pannus m; (*linen*)
   linteum nt; (*covering*) strāgulum nt.
clothe vt vestīre.
clothes n vestis f, vestītus m, vestīmenta ntpl.
clothier n vestiārius m.
clothing n vestis f, vestītus m, vestīmenta ntpl.
clotted adj concrētus.
cloud n nūbēs f; (*storm*) nimbus m; (*dust*)
   globus m; (*disfavour*) invidia f ♦ vt nūbibus
   obdūcere; (*fig*) obscūrāre.
clouded adj obnūbilus.
cloudiness n nūbilum nt.
cloudless adj pūrus, serēnus.
cloudy adj obnūbilus.
clout n pannus m.
clover n trifolium nt.
cloven adj (*hoof*) bifidus.
clown n (*boor*) rūsticus m; (*comic*) scurra m.
clownish adj rūsticus, inurbānus.
clownishness n rūsticitās f.
cloy vt satiāre.
cloying adj pūtidus.
club n (*stick*) fustis m, clāva f; (*society*)
   sodālitās f; ~ **together** vi in commūne
   cōnsulere, pecūniās cōnferre.
club-footed adj scaurus.
cluck vi singultīre ♦ n singultus m.
clue n indicium nt, vestīgium nt.
clump n massa f; (*earth*) glaeba f; (*trees*)
   arbustum nt; (*willows*) salictum nt.
clumsily adv ineptē, inēleganter; inconditē,
   īnfabrē.
clumsiness n īnscītia f.
clumsy adj (*person*) inconcinnus, ineptus;
   (*thing*) inhabilis; (*work*) inconditus
cluster n cumulus m; (*grapes*) racēmus m;
   (*people*) corōna f ♦ vi congregārī.
clutch vt prehendere, adripere; ~ **at** captāre
   nt, comprehēnsiō f; **from one's ~es** ē
   manibus; **in one's ~es** in potestāte.
clutter n turba f ♦ vt impedīre, obstruere.
coach n currus m, raeda f, pīlentum nt; (*trainer*)
   magister m ♦ vt ēdocēre, praecipere (*dat*).
coachman n aurīga m, raedārius m.
coagulate vt cōgere ♦ vi concrēscere.
coagulation n concrētiō f.
coal n carbō m; **carry ~s to Newcastle** in silvam
   ligna ferre.
coalesce vi coīre, coalēscere.
coalition n coitiō f, cōnspīrātiō f.
coarse adj (*quality*) crassus; (*manners*)
   rūsticus, inurbānus; (*speech*) īnfacētus.
coarsely adv inurbānē, inēleganter.
coarseness n crassitūdō f; rūsticitās f.
coast n lītus nt, ōra maritima f ♦ vi: ~ **along**
   legere, praetervehī.

coastal adj lītorālis, maritimus.
coastline n lītus nt.
coat n pallium nt; (*animals*) pellis f ♦ vt
   indūcere, inlinere.
coating n corium nt.
coax vt blandīrī, dēlēnīre.
coaxing adj blandus ♦ n blanditiae fpl.
cob n (*horse*) mannus m; (*swan*) cygnus m.
cobble n lapis m ♦ vt sarcīre.
cobbler n sūtor m.
cobweb n arāneum nt.
cock n gallus m, gallus gallīnāceus m; (*other
   birds*) mās m; (*tap*) epitonium nt; (*hay*)
   acervus m.
cockatrice n basiliscus m.
cockchafer n scarabaeus m.
cockcrow n gallī cantus m ♦ vt ērigere.
cockerel n pullus m.
cockroach n blatta f.
cocksure adj cōnfīdēns.
cod n callarias m.
coddle vt indulgēre (*dat*), permulcēre.
code n fōrmula f; (*secret*) notae fpl.
codicil n cōdicillī mpl.
codify vt in ōrdinem redigere.
coequal adj aequālis.
coerce vt cōgere.
coercion n vīs f.
coffer n arca f, cista f; (*public*) fiscus m.
coffin n arca f.
cog n dēns m.
cogency n vīs f, pondus nt.
cogent adj gravis, validus.
cogitate vi cōgitāre, meditārī.
cogitation n cōgitātiō f; meditātiō f.
cognate adj cognātus.
cognition n cognitiō f.
cognizance n cognitiō f; **take ~ of** cognōscere.
cognizant adj gnārus.
cohabit vi cōnsuēscere.
cohabitation n cōnsuētūdō f.
coheir n cohērēs m/f.
cohere vi cohaerēre; (*statement*) congruere.
coherence n coniūnctiō f; (*fig*) convenientia f.
coherent adj congruēns.
cohesion n coagmentātiō f.
cohesive adj tenāx.
cohort n cohors f.
coil n spīra f ♦ vt glomerāre.
coin n nummus m ♦ vt cūdere; (*fig*) fingere.
coinage n monēta f; (*fig*) fictum nt.
coincide vi concurrere; (*opinion*) cōnsentīre.
coincidence n concursus m; cōnsēnsus m; **by a**
   ~ cāsū.
coincidental adj fortuītus.
coiner n (*of money*) signātor m.
col n iugum nt.
colander n cōlum nt.
cold adj frīgidus; (*icy*) gelidus; **very ~**
   perfrīgidus; **be, feel ~** algēre, frīgēre; **get ~**
   algēscere, frīgēscere ♦ n frīgus nt; (*felt*)
   algor m; (*malady*) gravēdō f; **catch ~**
   algēscere, frīgus colligere; **catch a ~**

gravēdinem contrahere; **have a ~** gravēdine
labōrāre.
coldish _adj_ frīgidulus, frīgidior.
coldly _adv (manner)_ sine studiō.
coldness _n_ frīgus _nt_, algor _m_.
cold water _n_ frīgida _f._
colic _n_ tormina _ntpl._
collar _n_ collāre _nt._
collarbone _n_ iugulum _nt._
collate _vt_ cōnferre, comparāre.
collateral _adj_ adiūnctus; _(evidence)_
cōnsentāneus.
collation _n_ collātiō _f; (meal)_ prandium _nt_,
merenda _f._
colleague _n_ collēga _m._
collect _vt_ colligere, cōgere, congerere;
(persons) congregāre, convocāre; _(taxes)_
exigere; _(something due)_ recipere; **~ oneself**
animum colligere; **cool and ~ed** aequō animō
♦ _vi_ convenīre, congregārī.
collection _n (persons)_ coetus _m_, conventus _m_;
(things) congeriēs _f; (money)_ exāctiō _f._
collective _adj_ commūnis.
collectively _adv_ commūniter.
collector _n (of taxes)_ exāctor _m._
college _n_ collēgium _nt._
collide _vi_ concurrere, cōnflīctārī.
collier _n_ carbōnārius _m._
collision _n_ concursus _m._
collocation _n_ collocātiō _f._
collop _n_ offa _f._
colloquial _adj_ cottīdiānus.
colloquy _n_ sermō _m_, colloquium _nt._
collude _vi_ praevāricārī.
collusion _n_ praevāricātiō _f._
collusive _adj_ praevāricātor.
colonel _n_ lēgātus _m._
colonial _adj_ colōnicus ♦ _n_ colōnus _m._
colonist _n_ colōnus _m._
colonization _n_ dēductiō _f._
colonize _vt_ colōniam dēdūcere, cōnstituere in
(acc).
colonnade _n_ porticus _f._
colony _n_ colōnia _f._
colossal _adj_ ingēns, vastus.
colossus _n_ colossus _m._
colour _n_ color _m; (paint)_ pigmentum _nt;_
(artificial) fūcus _m; (complexion)_ color _m;_
(pretext) speciēs _f;_ **take on a ~** colōrem
dūcere; **under ~ of** per speciem _(gen);_ **local ~**
māteria dē regiōne sūmpta ♦ _vt_ colōrāre;
(dye) īnficere, fūcāre; _(fig)_ praetendere _(dat)_
♦ _vi_ rubēre, ērubēscere.
colourable _adj_ speciōsus.
coloured _adj (naturally)_ colōrātus; _(artificially)_
fūcātus.
colourful _adj_ fūcōsus, varius.
colouring _n_ pigmentum _nt; (dye)_ fūcus _m._
colourless _adj_ perlūcidus; _(person)_ pallidus;
(fig) īnsulsus.
colours _n (MIL)_ signum _nt_, vexillum _nt; (POL)_
partēs _fpl;_ **sail under false ~** aliēnō nōmine
ūtī; **with flying ~** māximā cum gloriā.
colour sergeant _n_ signifer _m._

colt _n_ equuleus _m_, equulus _m._
coltsfoot _n_ farfarus _m._
column _n_ columna _f; (MIL)_ agmen _nt._
coma _n_ sopor _m._
comb _n_ pecten _m; (bird)_ crista _f; (loom)_ pecten
m; (honey) favus _m_ ♦ _vt_ pectere.
combat _n_ pugna _f_, proelium _nt_, certāmen _nt_ ♦
_vi_ pugnāre, dīmicāre, certāre ♦ _vt_ pugnāre
cum _(abl)_, obsistere _(dat)._
combatant _n_ pugnātor _m_ ♦ _adj_ pugnāns; **non ~**
imbellis.
combative _adj_ ferōx, pugnāx.
combination _n_ coniūnctiō _f_, cōnfūsiō _f;_
(persons) cōnspīrātiō _f; (illegal)_ coniūrātiō _f._
combine _vt_ coniungere, iungere ♦ _vi_ coīre,
coniungī ♦ _n_ societās _f._
combustible _adj_ ignī obnoxius.
combustion _n_ dēflāgrātiō _f_, incendium _nt._
come _vi_ venīre, advenīre; _(after a journey)_
dēvenīre; _(interj)_ age!; **how ~s it that...?;** quī
fit ut...?; **~ across** _vi_ invenīre, offendere; **~**
after sequī, excipere, succēdere _(dat);_ **~**
again revenīre, redīre; **~ away** _vi_ abscēdere;
(when pulled) sequī; **~ back** _vi_ revenīre,
redīre; regredī; **~ between** intervenīre,
intercēdere; **~ down** _vi_ dēvenīre,
dēscendere; _(from the past)_ trādī, prōdī; **~**
forward _vi_ prōcēdere, prōdīre; **~ from** _vi_
(origin) dēfluere; **~ in** _vi_ inīre, introīre;
ingredī; _(revenue)_ redīre; **~ near** accēdere ad
(acc), appropinquāre _(dat);_ **~ nearer and**
nearer adventāre; **~ of** _vi (family)_ ortum esse
ab, ex _(abl);_ **~ off** _vi_ ēvādere, discēdere; **~ on**
_vi_ prōcēdere; _(progress)_ prōficere; _(interj)_
age, agite; **~ on the scene** intervenīre,
supervenīre, adesse; **~ out** _vi_ exīre, ēgredī;
(hair, teeth) cadere; _(flower)_ flōrēscere; _(book)_
ēdī; **~ over** _vi_ trānsīre; _(feeling)_ subīre,
occupāre; **~ to** _vi_ advenīre ad, in _(acc);_
(person) adīre; _(amount)_ efficere; **~ to the**
help of subvenīre _(dat);_ succurrere _(dat);_ **~ to**
nought ad nihilum recidere; **~ to pass**
ēvenīre, fierī; **~ together** convenīre, coīre; **~**
up _vi_ subīre, succēdere; _(growth)_ prōvenīre;
~ upon _vt fus_ invenīre; **he is coming to** animus
eī redit.
comedian _n (actor)_ cōmoedus _m; (writer)_
cōmicus _m._
comedienne _n_ mīma _f._
comedy _n_ cōmoedia _f._
comeliness _n_ decor _m_, decōrum _nt._
comely _adj_ decōrus, pulcher.
comestibles _n_ vīctus _m._
comet _n_ comētēs _m._
comfort _vt_ sōlārī, cōnsōlārī, adlevāre ♦ _n_
sōlācium _nt_, cōnsōlātiō _f._
comfortable _adj_ commodus; **make oneself ~**
corpus cūrāre.
comfortably _adv_ commodē.
comforter _n_ cōnsōlātor _m._
comfortless _adj_ incommodus; **be ~** sōlātiō
carēre.
comforts _npl_ commoda _ntpl._
comic _adj_ cōmicus; facētus ♦ _n_ scurra _m._

comical adj facētus, rīdiculus.
coming adj futūrus ◆ n adventus m.
comity n cōmitās f.
command vt iubēre (+ acc and infin), imperāre (dat and ut +subj); dūcere; (feelings) regere; (resources) fruī (abl); (view) prōspectāre ◆ n (MIL) imperium nt; (sphere) prōvincia f; (order) imperium nt, iussum nt, mandātum nt; **be in ~ (of)** praeesse (dat); **put in ~ of** praeficere (dat); **~ of language** fācundia f.
commandant n praefectus m.
commandeer vt pūblicāre.
commander n dux m, praefectus m.
commander in chief n imperātor m.
commandment n mandātum nt.
commemorate vt celebrāre, memoriae trādere.
commemoration n celebrātiō f.
commence vt incipere, exōrdīrī, initium facere (gen).
commencement n initium nt, exōrdium nt, prīncipium nt.
commend vt laudāre; (recommend) commendāre; (entrust) mandāre; **~ oneself** sē probāre.
commendable adj laudābilis, probābilis.
commendation n laus f, commendātiō f.
commendatory adj commendātīcius.
commensurable adj pār.
commensurate adj congruēns, conveniēns.
comment vi dīcere, scrībere; **~ on** interpretārī; (with notes) adnotāre ◆ n dictum nt, sententia f.
commentary n commentāriī mpl.
commentator n interpres m.
commerce n mercātūra f, commercium nt; **engage in ~** mercātūrās facere, negōtiārī.
commercial dealings n commercium nt.
commercial traveller n īnstitor m.
commination n minae fpl.
comminatory adj mināx.
commingle vt intermiscēre.
commiserate vt miserērī (gen).
commiseration n misericordia f; (RHET) commiserātiō f.
commissariat n rēs frūmentāria f, commeātus m; (staff) frūmentāriī mpl.
commissary n lēgātus m; reī frūmentāriae praefectus m.
commission n (charge) mandātum nt; (persons) triumvirī mpl, decemvirī mpl, etc; (abroad) lēgātiō f; **get a ~** (MIL) tribūnum fierī; **standing ~** (law) quaestiō perpetua f ◆ vt mandāre, adlēgāre.
commissioner n lēgātus m; **three ~s** triumvirī mpl; **ten ~s** decemvirī mpl.
commit vt (charge) committere, mandāre; (crime) admittere; (to prison) conicere; (to an undertaking) obligāre, obstringere; **~ to memory** memoriae trādere; **~ an error** errāre; **~ a theft** fūrtum facere; see also **suicide**.
commitment n mūnus nt, officium nt.

committee n dēlēctī mpl.
commodious adj capāx.
commodity n merx f, rēs f.
commodore n praefectus classis m.
common adj (for all) commūnis; (ordinary) vulgāris, cottīdiānus; (repeated) frequēns, crēber; (inferior) nēquam ◆ n compāscuus ager m, prātum nt; **~ man** homō plēbēius m; **~ soldier** gregārius mīles m.
commonalty n plēbs f.
commoner n homō plēbēius m.
common law n mōs māiōrum m.
commonly adv ferē, vulgō.
common people n plēbs f, vulgus nt.
commonplace n trītum prōverbium nt; (RHET) locus commūnis m ◆ adj vulgāris, trītus.
commons n plēbs f; (food) diāria ntpl.
common sense n prūdentia f.
commonwealth n cīvitās f, rēs pūblica f.
commotion n perturbātiō f, tumultus m; **cause a ~** tumultuārī.
communal adj commūnis.
commune n pāgus m ◆ vi colloquī, sermōnēs cōnferre.
communicate vt commūnicāre; (information) nūntiāre, patefacere ◆ vi: **~ with** commūnicāre (dat), commercium habēre (gen), agere cum (abl).
communication n (dealings) commercium nt; (information) litterae fpl, nūntius m; (passage) commeātus m; **cut off the ~s of** interclūdere.
communicative adj loquāx.
communion n societās f.
communiqué n litterae fpl, praedicātiō f.
communism n bonōrum aequātiō f.
community n cīvitās f, commūne nt; (participation) commūniō f.
commutation n mūtātiō f.
commute vt mūtāre, commūtāre.
compact n foedus nt, conventum nt ◆ adj dēnsus ◆ vt dēnsāre.
companion n socius m, comes m/f; (intimate) sodālis m; (at school) condiscipulus m; (in army) commīlitō m, contubernālis m.
companionable adj facilis, commodus.
companionship n sodālitās f, cōnsuētūdō f; (MIL) contubernium nt.
company n societās f, cōnsuētūdō f; (gathering) coetus m, conventus m; (guests) cēnantēs mpl; (commercial) societās f; (magistrates) collēgium nt; (MIL) manipulus m; (THEAT) grex m, caterva f; **~ of ten** decuria f.
comparable adj comparābilis, similis.
comparative adj māgnus, sī cum aliīs cōnfertur.
comparatively adv ut in tālī tempore, ut in eā regiōne, ut est captus hominum; **~ few** perpaucī, nullus ferē.
compare vt comparāre, cōnferre; **~d with ad** (acc).
comparison n comparātiō f, collātiō f; (RHET) similitūdō f; **in ~ with** prō (abl).
compartment n cella f, pars f.

compass n ambitus m, spatium nt, modus m; **pair of ~es** circinus m ♦ vt circumdare, cingere; (*attain*) cōnsequī.
compassion n misericordia f.
compassionate adj misericors, clēmēns.
compassionately adv clēmenter.
compatibility n convenientia f.
compatible adj congruēns, conveniēns; **be ~** congruere.
compatibly adv congruenter, convenienter.
compatriot n cīvis m, populāris m.
compeer n pār m; aequālis m.
compel vt cōgere.
compendious adj brevis.
compendiously adv summātim.
compendium n epitomē f.
compensate vt compēnsāre, satisfacere (*dat*).
compensation n compēnsātiō f; pretium nt, poena f.
compete vi certāre, contendere.
competence n facultās f; (*law*) iūs nt; (*money*) quod sufficit.
competent adj perītus, satis doctus, capāx; (*witness*) locuplēs; **it is ~** licet.
competition n certāmen nt, contentiō f.
competitor n competītor m, aemulus m.
compilation n collectānea ntpl, liber m.
compile vt compōnere.
compiler n scrīptor m.
complacency n amor suī m.
complacent adj suī contentus.
complain vi querī, conquerī; **~ of** (*person*) nōmen dēferre (*gen*).
complainant n accūsātor m, petītor m.
complaint n questus m, querimōnia f; (*law*) crīmen nt; (*MED*) morbus m, valētūdō f.
complaisance n cōmitās f, obsequium nt, indulgentia f.
complaisant adj cōmis, officiōsus, facilis.
complement n complēmentum nt; numerus suus m; **make up the ~ of** complēre.
complete vt (*amount, time*) complēre, explēre; (*work*) cōnficere, perficere, absolvere, peragere ♦ adj perfectus, absolūtus, integer; (*victory*) iūstus; (*amount*) explētus.
completely adv funditus, omnīnō, absolūtē, plānē; penitus.
completeness n integritās f; (*perfection*) perfectiō f.
completion n (*process*) absolūtiō f, cōnfectiō f; (*end*) fīnis m; **bring to ~** absolvere.
complex adj implicātus, multiplex.
complexion n color m.
complexity n implicātiō f.
compliance n accommodātiō f, obsequium nt, obtemperātiō f.
compliant adj obsequēns, facilis.
complicate vt implicāre, impedīre.
complicated adj implicātus, involūtus, impedītus.
complication n implicātiō f.
complicity n cōnscientia f.

compliment n blandīmentum nt, honōs m ♦ vt blandīrī, laudāre; **~ on** grātulārī (*dat*) dē (*abl*).
complimentary adj honōrificus, blandus.
compliments npl (*as greeting*) salūs f.
comply vi obsequī (*dat*), obtemperāre (*dat*); mōrem gerere (*dat*), mōrigerārī (*dat*).
component n elementum nt, pars f.
comport vt gerere.
compose vt (*art*) compōnere, condere, pangere; (*whole*) efficere, cōnflāre; (*quarrel*) compōnere, dīrimere; (*disturbance*) sēdāre; **be ~d of** cōnsistere ex (*abl*), cōnstāre ex (*abl*).
composed adj tranquillus, placidus.
composer n auctor m, scrīptor m.
composite adj multiplex.
composition n (*process*) compositiō f, scrīptūra f; (*product*) opus nt, poēma nt, carmen nt; (*quality*) structūra f.
composure n sēcūritās f, aequus animus m; (*face*) tranquillitās f.
compound vt miscēre; (*words*) duplicāre; iungere ♦ vi (*agree*) pacīscī ♦ adj compositus ♦ n (*word*) iūnctum verbum nt; (*area*) saeptum nt.
compound interest n anatocismus m.
comprehend vt intellegere, comprehendere; (*include*) continēre, complectī.
comprehensible adj perspicuus.
comprehension n intellegentia f, comprehēnsiō f.
comprehensive adj capāx; **be ~** lātē patēre, multa complectī.
compress vt comprimere, coartāre ♦ n fōmentum nt.
compression n compressus m.
comprise vt continēre, complectī, comprehendere.
compromise n (*by one side*) accommodātiō f; (*by both sides*) comprōmissum nt ♦ vi comprōmittere ♦ vt implicāre, in suspiciōnem vocāre; **be ~d** in suspiciōnem venīre.
comptroller n moderātor m.
compulsion n necessitās f, vīs f; **under ~** coāctus.
compulsory adj necesse, lēge imperātus; **use ~ measures** vim adhibēre.
compunction n paenitentia f.
computation n ratiō f.
compute vt computāre, ratiōnem dūcere.
comrade n socius m, contubernālis m.
comradeship n contubernium nt.
concatenation n seriēs f.
concave adj concavus.
conceal vt cēlāre, abdere, abscondere; (*fact*) dissimulāre.
concealment n occultātiō f; (*place*) latebrae fpl; (*of facts*) dissimulātiō f; **in ~** abditus, occultus; **be in ~** latēre, latitāre; **go into ~** dēlitēscere.
concede vt concēdere.
conceit n (*idea*) nōtiō f; (*wit*) facētiae fpl; (*pride*)

superbia *f*, adrogantia *f*, vānitās *f*.
conceited *adj* glōriōsus, adrogāns.
conceitedness *n* adrogantia *f*, vānitās *f*.
conceive *vt* concipere, comprehendere,
intellegere.
concentrate *vt* (*in one place*) cōgere,
congregāre; (*attention*) intendere, cēfīgere.
concentrated *adj* dēnsus.
concentration *n* animī intentiō *f*.
concept *n* nōtiō *f*.
conception *n* conceptus *m*; (*mind*)
intellegentia *f*, īnfōrmātiō *f*; (*idea*) nōtiō *f*,
cōgitātiō *f*, cōnsilium *nt*.
concern *vt* (*refer*) attinēre ad (*acc*), interesse
(*gen*); (*worry*) sollicitāre; **it ~s me** meā rēfert,
meā interest; **as far as I am ~ed** per mē ♦ *n*
rēs *f*, negōtium *nt*; (*importance*) mōmentum
nt; (*worry*) sollicitūdō *f*, cūra *f*; (*regret*) dolor
m.
concerned *adj* sollicitus, anxius; **be ~ about** molestē ferre.
concerning *prep* dē (*abl*).
concernment *n* sollicitūdō *f*.
concert *n* (*music*) concentus *m*; (*agreement*)
cōnsēnsus *m*; **in ~** ex compositō, ūnc animō ♦
vt compōnere; (*plan*) inīre.
concession *n* concessiō *f*; **by the ~ of** concessū
(*gen*); **make a ~** concēdere, tribuere
conciliate *vt* conciliāre.
conciliation *n* conciliātiō *f*.
conciliator *n* arbiter *m*.
conciliatory *adj* pācificus.
concise *adj* brevis; (*style*) dēnsus.
concisely *adv* breviter.
conciseness *n* brevitās *f*.
conclave *n* sēcrētus cōnsessus *m*.
conclude *vt* (*end*) termināre, fīnīre, cōnficere;
(*settle*) facere, compōnere, pangere; (*infer*)
īnferre, colligere.
conclusion *n* (*end*) fīnis *m*; (*of action*) exitus *m*;
(*of speech*) perōrātiō *f*; (*inference*) coniectūra
f; (*decision*) placitum *nt*, sententia *f*; **in ~**
dēnique; **try ~s with** contendere cum.
conclusive *adj* certus, manifestus, gravis.
conclusively *adv* sine dubiō.
concoct *vt* coquere; (*fig*) cōnflāre.
concoction *n* (*fig*) māchinātiō *f*.
concomitant *adj* adiūnctus.
concord *n* concordia *f*; (*music*) harmonia *f*.
concordant *adj* concors.
concordat *n* pactum *nt*, foedus *nt*.
concourse *n* frequentia *f*, celebrātiō *f*;
(*moving*) concursus *m*.
concrete *adj* concrētus; **in the ~** rē.
concretion *n* concrētiō *f*.
concubine *n* concubīna *f*.
concupiscence *n* libīdō *f*.
concur *vi* (*time*) concurrere; (*opinion*)
cōnsentīre, adsentīre.
concurrence *n* (*time*) concursus *m*; (*opinion*)
cōnsēnsus *m*.
concurrent *adj* (*time*) aequālis; (*opinion*)
cōnsentāneus; **be ~** concurrere, cōnsentīre.

concurrently *adv* simul, ūnā.
concussion *n* ictus *m*.
condemn *vt* damnāre, condemnāre;
(*disapprove*) improbāre; **~ to death** capitis
damnāre; **~ for treason** dē māiestāte
damnāre.
condemnation *n* damnātiō *f*; condemnātiō *f*.
condemnatory *adj* damnātōrius.
condense *vt* dēnsāre; (*words*) premere.
condescend *vi* dēscendere, sē submittere.
condescending *adj* cōmis.
condescension *n* cōmitās *f*.
condiment *n* condīmentum *nt*.
condition *n* (*of body*) habitus *m*; (*external*)
status *m*, condiciō *f*, rēs *f*; (*in society*) locus *m*,
fortūna *f*; (*of agreement*) condiciō *f*, lēx *f*; **~s of
sale** mancipī lēx *f*; **on ~ that** eā condicione ut
(*subj*); **in ~** (*animals*) nitidus ♦ *vt* fōrmāre,
regere.
conditional *adj*: **the assistance is ~ on** eā
condiciōne succurritur ut (*subj*).
conditionally *adv* sub condiciōne.
conditioned *adj* (*character*) mōrātus.
condole *vi*: **~ with** cōnsōlārī.
condolence *n* cōnsōlātiō *f*.
condonation *n* venia *f*.
condone *vt* condōnāre, ignōscere (*dat*).
conduce *vi* condūcere (ad), prōficere (ad).
conducive *adj* ūtilis, accommodātus.
conduct *vt* dūcere; (*escort*) dēdūcere; (*to a
place*) addūcere, perdūcere; (*business*)
gerere, administrāre; (*self*) gerere ♦ *n*
mōrēs *mpl*; (*past*) vīta *f*, facta *ntpl*; (*business*)
administrātiō *f*; **safe ~** praesidium *nt*.
conductor *m* dux *m*, ductor *m*.
conduit *n* canālis *m*, aquae ductus *m*.
cone *n* cōnus *m*.
coney *n* cunīculus *m*.
confabulate *vi* colloquī.
confection *n* cuppēdō *f*.
confectioner *n* cuppēdinārius *m*.
confectionery *n* dulcia *ntpl*.
confederacy *n* foederātae cīvitātēs *fpl*,
societās *f*.
confederate *adj* foederātus ♦ *n* socius *m* ♦ *vi*
coniūrāre, foedus facere.
confederation *n* societās *f*.
confer *vt* cōnferre, tribuere ♦ *vi* colloquī,
sermōnem cōnferre; **~ about** agere dē (*abl*).
conference *n* colloquium *nt*, congressus *m*.
conferment *n* dōnātiō *f*.
confess *vt* fatērī, cōnfitērī.
confessedly *adv* manifestō.
confession *n* cōnfessiō *f*.
confidant *n* cōnscius *m*.
confide *vi* fīdere (*dat*), cōnfīdere (*dat*) ♦ *vt*
crēdere, committere
confidence *n* fidēs *f*, fīdūcia *f*; **have ~ in** fīdere
(*dat*), cōnfīdere (*dat*); **inspire ~ in** fidem
facere (*dat*); **tell in ~** tūtīs auribus dēpōnere.
confident *adj* fīdēns; **~ in** frētus (*abl*); **be ~ that**
certō scīre, prō certō habēre.
confidential *adj* arcānus, intimus.

confidentially adv inter nōs.
confidently adv fīdenter.
confiding adj crēdulus.
configuration n figūra f, fōrma f.
confine vt (prison) inclūdere, in vincula conicere; (limit) termināre, circumscrībere; (restrain) coercēre, cohibēre; (to bed) dētinēre; **be ~d** (women) parturīre.
confinement n custōdia f, vincula ntpl, inclūsiō f; (women) puerperium nt.
confines n fīnēs mpl.
confirm vt (strength) corrōborāre, firmāre; (decision) sancīre, ratum facere; (fact) adfirmāre, comprobāre.
confirmation n cōnfirmātiō f, adfirmātiō f.
confirmed adj ratus.
confiscate vt pūblicāre.
confiscation n pūblicātiō f.
conflagration n incendium nt, dēflāgrātiō f.
conflict n (physical) concursus m; (hostile) certāmen nt, proelium nt; (verbal) contentiō f, contrōversia f; (contradiction) repugnantia f, discrepantia f ♦ vi inter sē repugnāre.
conflicting adj contrārius.
confluence n cōnfluēns m.
confluent adj cōnfluēns.
conform vt accommodāre ♦ vi sē cōnfōrmāre (ad), obsequī (dat), mōrem gerere (dat).
conformable adj accommodātus, conveniēns.
conformably adv convenienter.
conformation n structūra f, confōrmātiō f.
conformity n convenientia f, cōnsēnsus m.
confound vt (mix) cōnfundere, permiscēre; (amaze) obstupefacere; (thwart) frustrārī; (suppress) opprimere, obruere; **~ you!** dī tē perduint.
confounded adj miser, sacer, nefandus.
confoundedly adv mīrum quantum nefāriē.
confraternity n frāternitās f.
confront vt sē oppōnere (dat), obviam īre (dat), sē cōram offerre.
confuse vt permiscēre, perturbāre.
confused adj perturbātus.
confusedly adv perturbātē, prōmiscuē.
confusion n perturbātiō f; (shame) rubor m.
confutation n refūtātiō f.
confute vt refūtāre, redarguere, convincere.
congé n commeātus m.
congeal vt congelāre, dūrāre ♦ vi concrēscere.
congealed adj concrētus.
congenial adj concors, congruēns, iūcundus.
congeniality n concordia f, mōrum similitūdō f.
congenital adj nātīvus.
conger n conger m.
congested adj refertus, dēnsus; (with people) frequentissimus.
congestion n congeriēs f; frequentia f.
conglomerate vt glomerāre.
conglomeration n congeriēs f, cumulus m.
congratulate vt grātulārī (dat).
congratulation n grātulātiō f.

congratulatory adj grātulābundus.
congregate vt congregāre, cōgere ♦ vi convenīre, congregārī.
congregation n conventus m, coetus m.
congress n conventus m, cōnsessus m, concilium nt; senātus m.
congruence n convenientia f.
congruent adj conveniēns, congruēns.
congruently adv convenienter, congruenter.
congruous adj see **congruent**.
conical adj turbinātus.
coniferous adj cōnifer.
conjectural adj opīnābilis.
conjecturally adv coniectūrā.
conjecture n coniectūra f ♦ vt conicere, augurārī.
conjoin vt coniungere.
conjoint adj coniūnctus.
conjointly adv coniūnctē, ūnā.
conjugal adj coniugālis.
conjugate vt dēclīnāre.
conjugation n (GRAM) dēclīnātiō f.
conjunct adj coniūnctus.
conjunction n coniūnctiō f, concursus m.
conjure vt (entreat) obtestārī, obsecrāre; (spirits) ēlicere, ciēre ♦ vi praestigiīs ūtī.
conjurer n praestigiātor m.
conjuring n praestigiae fpl.
connate adj innātus, nātūrā īnsitus.
connect vt iungere, coniungere, cōpulāre, connectere.
connected adj coniūnctus; (unbroken) continēns; (by marriage) adfīnis; **be ~ed with** contingere; **be closely ~ed with** inhaerēre (dat), cohaerēre cum (abl).
connectedly adv coniūnctē, continenter.
connection n coniūnctiō f, contextus m, seriēs f; (kin) necessitūdō f; (by marriage) adfīnitās f; **~ between ... and ...** ratiō (gen) ... cum ... (abl); **I have no ~ with you** nīl mihī tēcum est.
connivance n venia f, dissimulātiō f.
connive vi conīvēre in (abl), dissimulāre.
connoisseur n intellegēns m.
connotation n vīs f, significātiō f.
connote vt significāre.
connubial adj coniugālis.
conquer vt vincere, superāre.
conquerable adj superābilis, expugnābilis.
conqueror n victor m.
conquest n victōria f; (town) expugnātiō f; (prize) praemium nt, praeda f; **the ~ of Greece** Graecia capta.
conscience n cōnscientia f; **guilty ~ mala** cōnscientia; **have a clear ~** nullīus culpae sibi cōnscium esse; **have no ~** nullam rēligiōnem habēre.
conscientious adj probus, rēligiōsus.
conscientiously adv bonā fidē, rēligiōsē.
conscientiousness n fidēs f, rēligiō f.
conscious adj sibī cōnscius; (aware) gnārus; (physically) mentis compos; **be ~** sentīre.
consciously adv sciēns.
consciousness n animus m; (of action)

cōnscientia f; **he lost ~** animus eum relīquit.
conscript n tīrō m ◆ vt cōnscrībere.
conscription n dēlēctus m; (of wea th·
pūblicātiō f.
consecrate vt dēdicāre, cōnsecrāre; (self)
dēvovēre.
consecrated adj sacer.
consecration n dēdicātiō f, cōnsecrātiō f;
(self) dēvōtiō f.
consecutive adj dēinceps, continuus.
consecutively adv dēinceps, ōrdine.
consensus n cōnsēnsus m.
consent vi adsentīre (dat), adnuere (ınfin);
(together) cōnsentīre ◆ n (one side) adsēnsus
m; (all) cōnsēnsus m; **by common ~** omnium
cōnsēnsū.
consequence n ēventus m, exitus m; (logic)
conclūsiō f; (importance) mōmentum nt,
auctōritās f; **it is of ~ interest; what will be
the ~ of?** quō ēvādet?
consequent adj cōnsequēns.
consequential adj cōnsentāneus; (person)
adrogāns.
consequently adv itaque, igitur, proptereā.
conservation n cōnservātiō f.
conservative adj reī pūblicae cōnservandae
studiōsus; (estimate) mediōcris; **~ party**
optimātēs mpl.
conservator n custōs m, cōnservātor m.
conserve vt cōnservāre, servāre.
consider vt cōnsīderāre, contemplārī; (reflect)
sēcum volūtāre, meditari, dēlībe·āre,
cōgitāre; (deem) habēre, dūcere; (respect)
respicere, observāre.
considerable adj aliquantus, nōnnūllus;
(person) illūstris.
considerably adv aliquantum; (with compar)
aliquantō, multō.
considerate adj hūmānus, benignus.
considerately adv hūmānē, benignē.
consideration n cōnsīderātiō f, contemplātiō
f, dēlīberātiō f; (respect) respectus m, ratiō f;
(importance) mōmentum nt; (reason) ratiō f;
(pay) pretium nt; **for a ~** mercēde, datā
mercēde; **in ~ of** propter (acc), prō (abl); **on
no ~** nēquāquam; **with ~** cōnsultō; **without ~**
temerē; **take into ~** ad cōnsilium cōferre;
show ~ for respectum habēre (gen).
considered adj (reasons) exquīsītus.
considering prep prō (abl), propter (acc) ◆ conj
ut, quōniam.
consign vt mandāre, committere.
consist vi cōnstāre; **~ in** cōnstāre ex (abl),
continērī (abl), positum esse in (abl); **~ with**
congruere (dat), convenīre (dat).
consistence n firmitās f.
consistency n cōnstantia f.
consistent adj cōnstāns; (with) cōnsentāneus,
cōngruens; (of movement) aequāb lis; **be ~**
cohaerēre.
consistently adv constanter.
consolable adj cōnsōlābilis.
consolation n cōnsōlātiō f; (thing) sōlācium nt.

consolatory adj cōnsōlātōrius.
console vt cōnsōlārī.
consoler n cōnsōlātor m.
consolidate vt (liquid) cōgere; (strength)
corrōborāre; (gains) obtinēre ◆ vi
concrēscere.
consolidation n concrētiō f; cōnfirmātiō f.
consonance n concentus m.
consonant adj cōnsonus, haud absonus ◆ n
cōnsonāns f.
consort n cōnsors m/f, socius m; (married)
coniunx m/f ◆ vi: **~ with** familiāriter ūtī (abl),
coniūnctissimē vīvere cum (abl).
conspectus n summārium nt.
conspicuous adj ēminēns, īnsignis,
manifestus; **be ~** ēminēre.
conspicuously adv manifestō, palam, ante
oculōs.
conspiracy n coniūrātiō f.
conspirator n coniūrātus m.
conspire vi coniūrāre; (for good) cōnspīrāre.
constable n lictor m.
constancy n cōnstantia f, firmitās f; **with ~**
cōnstanter.
constant adj cōnstāns; (faithful) fīdus, fidēlis;
(continuous) adsiduus.
constantly adv adsiduē, saepe, crēbrō.
constellation n sīdus nt.
consternation n trepidātiō f, pavor m; **throw
into ~** perterrēre, cōnsternere.
constituency n suffrāgātōrēs mpl.
constituent adj: **~ part** elementum nt ◆ n
(voter) suffrāgātor m.
constitute vt creāre, cōnstituere; esse.
constitution n nātūra f, status m; (body)
habitus m; (POL) cīvitātis fōrma f, reī pūblicae
status m, lēgēs fpl.
constitutional adj lēgitimus, iūstus.
constitutionally adv ē rē pūblicā.
constrain vt cōgere.
constraint n vīs f; **under ~** coāctus; **without ~**
suā sponte.
constrict vt comprimere, cōnstringere.
constriction n contractiō f.
construct vt aedificāre, exstruere.
construction n aedificātiō f; (method)
structūra f; (meaning) interpretātiō f; **put a
wrong ~ on** in malam partem interpretārī.
construe vt interpretārī.
consul n cōnsul m; **~ elect** cōnsul dēsignātus;
ex ~ cōnsulāris m.
consular adj cōnsulāris.
consulship n cōnsulātus m; **stand for the ~**
cōnsulātum petere; **hold the ~** cōnsulātum
gerere; **in my ~** mē cōnsule.
consult vt cōnsulere; **~ the interests of**
cōnsulere (dat) ◆ vi dēlīberāre, cōnsiliārī.
consultation n (asking) cōnsultātiō f;
(discussion) dēlīberātiō f.
consume vt cōnsūmere, absūmere; (food)
edere.
consumer n cōnsūmptor m.
consummate adj summus, perfectus ◆ vt

perficere, absolvere.
consummation _n_ absolūtiō _f_; fīnis _m_, ēventus _m_.
consumption _n_ cōnsūmptiō _f_; (_disease_) tābēs _f_, phthisis _f_.
consumptive _adj_ pulmōnārius.
contact _n_ tāctus _m_, contāgiō _f_; **come in ~ with** contingere.
contagion _n_ contāgiō _f_.
contagious _adj_ tābificus; **be ~** contāgiīs vulgārī.
contain _vt_ capere, continēre; (_self_) cohibēre.
container _n_ vās _nt_.
contaminate _vt_ contāmināre, īnficere.
contamination _n_ contāgiō _f_, lābēs _f_.
contemplate _vt_ contemplārī, intuērī; (_action_) in animō habēre; (_prospect_) spectāre.
contemplation _n_ contemplātiō _f_; (_thought_) cōgitātiō _f_.
contemplative _adj_ cōgitāns, meditāns; **in a ~ mood** cōgitātiōnī dēditus.
contemporaneous _adj_ aequālis.
contemporaneously _adv_ simul.
contemporary _adj_ aequālis.
contempt _n_ contemptiō _f_; **be an object of ~** contemptuī esse; **treat with ~** contemptum habēre, conculcāre.
contemptible _adj_ contemnendus, abiectus, vīlis.
contemptuous _adj_ fastīdiōsus.
contemptuously _adv_ contemptim, fastīdiōsē.
contend _vi_ certāre, contendere; (_in battle_) dīmicāre, pugnāre; (_in words_) adfirmāre, adsevērāre.
contending _adj_ contrārius.
content _adj_ contentus ♦ _n_ aequus animus _m_ ♦ _vt_ placēre (_dat_), satisfacere (_dat_); **be ~ed** satis habēre.
contentedly _adv_ aequō animō.
contention _n_ certāmen _nt_; contrōversia _f_; (_opinion_) sententia _f_.
contentious _adj_ pugnāx, lītigiōsus.
contentiously _adv_ pugnāciter.
contentiousness _n_ contrōversiae studium _nt_.
contentment _n_ aequus animus _m_.
contents _n_ quod inest, quae insunt; (_of speech_) argūmentum _nt_.
conterminous _adj_ adfīnis.
contest _n_ certāmen _nt_, contentiō _f_ ♦ _vt_ (_law_) lēge agere dē (_abl_); (_office_) petere; (_dispute_) repugnāre (_dat_), resistere (_dat_).
contestable _adj_ contrōversus.
contestant _n_ petītor _m_, aemulus _m_.
context _n_ contextus _m_.
contiguity _n_ vīcīnia _f_, propinquitās _f_.
contiguous _adj_ vīcīnus, adiacēns; **be ~ to** adiacēre (_dat_), contingere.
continence _n_ continentia _f_, abstinentia _f_.
continent _adj_ continēns, abstinēns ♦ _n_ continēns _f_.
continently _adv_ continenter, abstinenter.
contingency _n_ cāsus _m_, rēs _f_.
contingent _adj_ fortuītus ♦ _n_ (_MIL_) numerus _m_.

continual _adj_ adsiduus, perpetuus.
continually _adv_ adsiduē, semper.
continuance _n_ perpetuitās _f_, adsiduitās _f_.
continuation _n_ continuātiō _f_; (_of a command_) prōrogātiō _f_; (_of a story_) reliqua pars _f_.
continue _vt_ continuāre; (_time_) prōdūcere; (_command_) prōrogāre ♦ _vi_ (_action_) pergere; (_time_) manēre; (_endurance_) perstāre, dūrāre; **~ to** _imperf indic_.
continuity _n_ continuātiō _f_; (_of speech_) perpetuitās _f_.
continuous _adj_ continuus, continēns, perpetuus.
continuously _adv_ perpetuō, continenter.
contort _vt_ contorquēre, dētorquēre.
contortion _n_ distortiō _f_.
contour _n_ fōrma _f_.
contraband _adj_ interdictus, vetitus.
contract _n_ pactum _nt_, mandātum _nt_, conventum _nt_; (_POL_) foedus _nt_; **trial for a breach of ~** mandātī iūdicium _nt_ ♦ _vt_ (_narrow_) contrahere, addūcere; (_short_) dēminuere; (_illness_) contrahere; (_agreement_) pacīscī; (_for work_) locāre; (_to do work_) condūcere ♦ _vi_ pacīscī.
contraction _n_ contractiō _f_; (_word_) compendium _nt_.
contractor _n_ redemptor _m_, conductor _m_.
contradict _vt_ (_person_) contrādīcere (_dat_), refrāgārī (_dat_); (_statement_) īnfitiās īre (_dat_); (_self_) repugnāre (_dat_).
contradiction _n_ repugnantia _f_, īnfitiae _fpl_.
contradictory _adj_ repugnāns, contrārius; **be ~** inter sē repugnāre.
contradistinction _n_ oppositiō _f_.
contraption _n_ māchina _f_.
contrariety _n_ repugnantia _f_.
contrariwise _adv_ ē contrāriō.
contrary _adj_ contrārius, adversus; (_person_) difficilis, mōrōsus; **~ to** contrā (_acc_), praeter (_acc_); **~ to expectations** praeter opiniōnem ♦ _n_ contrārium _nt_; **on the ~** ē contrāriō, contrā; (_retort_) immo.
contrast _n_ discrepantia _f_ ♦ _vt_ comparāre, oppōnere ♦ _vi_ discrepāre.
contravene _vt_ (_law_) violāre; (_statement_) contrādīcere (_dat_).
contravention _n_ violātiō _f_.
contribute _vt_ cōnferre, adferre, contribuere. ♦ _vi_: **~ towards** cōnferre ad (_acc_), adiuvāre; **~ to the cost** impēnsās cōnferre.
contribution _n_ conlātiō _f_; (_money_) stipem (_no nom_) _f_.
contributor _n_ quī cōnfert.
contributory _adj_ adiūnctus.
contrite _adj_ paenitēns.
contrition _n_ paenitentia _f_.
contrivance _n_ māchinātiō _f_, excōgitātiō _f_; (_thing_) māchina _f_; (_idea_) cōnsilium _nt_; (_deceit_) dolus _m_.
contrive _vt_ māchinārī, excōgitāre, struere; (_to do_) efficere ut.
contriver _n_ māchinātor _m_, artifex _m_, auctor _m_.

control n (*restraint*) frēnum nt; (*power*)
  moderātiō f, potestās f, imperium nt; **have ~**
  of praeesse (*dat*); **out of ~** impotēns ♦ *vt*
  moderārī (*dat*), imperāre (*dat*).
controller n moderātor m.
controversial adj concertātōrius.
controversy n contrōversia f, disceptātiō f.
controvert vt redarguere, impugnāre, in
  dubium vocāre.
contumacious adj contumāx, pervicāx.
contumaciously adv contumāciter,
  pervicāciter.
contumacy n contumācia f, pervicācia f.
contusion n sūgillātiō f.
conundrum n aenigma nt.
convalesce vi convalēscere.
convalescence n melior valētūdō f.
convalescent adj convalēscēns.
convene vt convocāre.
convenience n opportūnitās f, commoditās f;
  (*thing*) commodum nt; **at your ~** commodō
  tuō.
convenient adj idōneus, commodus,
  opportūnus; **be ~** convenīre; **very ~**
  percommodus.
conveniently adv opportūnē, commodē.
convention n (*meeting*) conventus m;
  (*agreement*) conventum nt; (*custom*) mōs m,
  iūsta ntpl.
conventional adj iūstus, solitus.
conventionality n mōs m, cōnsuētūdō f.
converge vi in medium vergere, in eundem
  locum tendere.
conversant adj perītus, doctus, exercitātus;
  be ~ with versārī in (*abl*).
conversation n sermō m, colloquium nt.
converse n sermō m, colloquium nt; (*opposite*)
  contrārium nt ♦ vi colloquī, sermōnem
  cōnferre ♦ adj contrārius.
conversely adv ē contrāriō, contrā.
conversion n mūtātiō f; (*moral*) mōrum
  ēmendātiō f.
convert vt mūtāre, convertere; (*to an opinion*)
  dēdūcere ♦ n discipulus m.
convertible adj commūtābilis.
convex adj convexus.
convexity n convexum nt.
convey vt vehere, portāre, convehere;
  (*property*) abaliēnāre; (*knowledge*)
  commūnicāre; (*meaning*) significāre; **~**
  across trānsmittere, trādūcere,
  trānsvehere; **~ away** auferre, āvehere; **~**
  down dēvehere, dēportāre; **~ into**
  importāre, invehere; **~ to** advehere, adferre;
  ~ up subvehere.
conveyance n vehiculum nt; (*property*)
  abaliēnātiō f.
convict vt (*prove guilty*) convincere; (*sentence*)
  damnāre ♦ n reus m.
conviction n (*law*) damnātiō f; (*argument*)
  persuāsiō f; (*belief*) fidēs f; **carry ~** fidem
  facere; **have a ~** persuāsum habēre.
convince vt persuādēre (*dat*); **I am firmly ~d**

mihi persuāsum habeō.
convincing adj (*argument*) gravis; (*evidence*)
  manifestus.
convincingly adv manifestō.
convivial adj convīvalis, festīvus.
conviviality n festīvitās f.
convocation n conventus m.
convoke vt convocāre.
convolution n spīra f.
convoy n praesidium nt ♦ vt prōsequī.
convulse vt agitāre; **be ~d with laughter** sē in
  cachinnōs effundere.
convulsion n (*MED*) convulsiō f; (*PCL*) tumultus
  m.
convulsive adj spasticus.
coo vi gemere.
cook vt coquere ♦ n coquus m.
cookery n ars coquīnāria f.
cool adj frīgidus; (*conduct*) impudens; (*mind*)
  impavidus, lentus ♦ n frīgus nt ♦ vt
  refrīgerāre; (*passion*) restinguere, sēdāre ♦
  vi refrīgēscere, refrīgerārī, dēfervēscere.
coolly adv aequō animō; impudenter.
coolness n frīgus nt; (*mind*) aequus animus m;
  impudentia f.
coop n hara f; (*barrel*) cūpa f ♦ vt inclūdere.
co-operate vi operam cōnferre; **~ with**
  adiuvāre, socius esse (*gen*).
co-operation n cōnsociātiō f; auxilium nt,
  opera f.
co-operative adj (*person*) officiōsus.
co-operator n socius m.
co-opt vt cooptāre.
coot n fulica f.
copartner n socius m.
copartnership n societās f.
cope vi: **~ with** contendere cum (*abl*); **able to ~**
  with pār (*dat*); **unable to ~ with** impār (*dat*).
copier n librārius m.
coping n fastīgium nt.
copious adj cōpiōsus, largus, plēnus,
  abundāns.
copiously adv cōpiōsē, abundanter.
copiousness n cōpia f, ūbertās f.
copper n aes nt ♦ adj aēneus.
coppersmith n faber aerārius m.
coppice, copse n dūmētum nt, virgultum
  nt.
copy n exemplar nt ♦ vt imitārī; (*writing*)
  exscrībere, trānscrībere.
copyist n librārius m.
coracle n linter f.
coral n cūrālium nt.
cord n fūniculus m.
cordage n fūnēs mpl.
cordial adj cōmis, festīvus, amīcus; (*greetings*)
  multus.
cordiality n cōmitās f, studium nt.
cordially adv cōmiter, libenter, ex animō.
cordon n corōna f.
core n (*fig*) nucleus m.
cork n sūber nt; (*bark*) cortex m.
corn n frūmentum nt ♦ adj frūmentārius; (*on*

the foot) clāvus m; **price of** ~ annōnaf.
corndealer n frūmentārius m.
cornfield n seges f.
cornel n (tree) cornus f.
corner n angulus m.
cornet n cornū nt.
cornice n corōnaf.
coronet n diadēma nt.
corporal adj corporeus.
corporal punishment n verbera ntpl.
corporation n collēgium nt; (civic)
    magistrātūs mpl.
corporeal adj corporeus.
corps n manusf.
corpse n cadāver nt.
corpulence n obēsum corpus nt.
corpulent adj obēsus, pinguis.
corpuscle n corpusculum nt.
corral n praesēpe nt.
correct vt corrigere, ēmendāre; (person)
    castīgāre ♦ adj vērus; (language) integer;
    (style) ēmendātus.
correction n ēmendātiō f; (moral) corrēctiō f;
    (punishment) castīgātiō f.
correctly adv bene, vērē.
correctness n (fact) vēritās f; (language)
    integritās f; (moral) probitāsf.
corrector n ēmendātor m, corrēctor m.
correspond vi (agree) respondēre (dat),
    congruere (dat); (by letter) inter sē scrībere.
correspondence n similitūdō f; epistulae fpl.
correspondent n epistulārum scrīptor m.
corresponding adj pār.
correspondingly adv pariter.
corridor n porticusf.
corrigible adj ēmendābilis.
corroborate vt cōnfirmāre.
corroboration n cōnfirmātiō f.
corrode vt ērōdere, edere.
corrosive adj edāx.
corrugate vt rūgare.
corrugated adj rūgōsus.
corrupt vt corrumpere, dēprāvāre; (text)
    vitiāre ♦ adj corruptus, vitiātus; (person)
    prāvus, vēnālis; (text) vitiātus.
corrupter n corruptor m.
corruptible adj (matter) dissolūbilis; (person)
    vēnālis.
corruption n (of matter) corruptiō f; (moral)
    corruptēlaf, dēprāvātiō f; (bribery) ambitus
    m.
corsair n pīrāta m.
cortège n pompaf.
coruscate vi fulgēre.
coruscation n fulgor m.
Corybant n Corybas m.
Corybantic adj Corybantius.
cosmetic n medicāmen nt.
cosmic adj mundānus.
cosmopolitan adj mundānus.
cosmos n mundus m.
cost vt emī, stāre (dat); **it ~ me dear** māgnō
    mihi stetit, male ēmī; **it ~ me a talent** talentō

mihi stetit, talentō ēmī; **it ~ me my freedom**
    lībertātem perdidī ♦ n pretium nt, impēnsa f;
    ~ of living annōna f; **to your ~** incommodō tuō,
    dētrīmentō tuō; **at the ~ of one's reputation**
    violātā fāmā, nōn salvā existimātiōne; **I sell**
    at ~ price quantī ēmī vēndō.
costliness n sūmptus m; cāritās f.
costly adj cārus; (furnishings) lautus,
    sūmptuōsus.
costume n habitus m.
cosy adj commodus.
cot n lectulus m.
cote n columbārium nt.
cottage n casa f, tugurium nt.
cottager n rūsticus m.
cotton n (tree) gossympinus f; (cloth) xylinum
    nt.
couch n lectus m ♦ vi recumbere ♦ vt (lance)
    intendere; (words) exprimere, reddere.
cough n tussis f ♦ vi tussīre.
council n concilium nt; (small) cōnsilium nt.
councillor n (town) dēcuriō m.
counsel n (debate) cōnsultātiō f; (advice)
    cōnsilium nt; (law) advocātus m, patrōnus m;
    take ~ cōnsiliārī, dēlīberāre; **take ~ of**
    cōnsulere ♦ vt suādēre (dat), monēre.
counsellor n cōnsiliārius m.
count vt numerāre, computāre; **~ as** dūcere,
    habēre; **~ amongst** pōnere in (abl); **~ up** vt
    ēnumerāre; **~ upon** cōnfīdere (dat); **be ~ed**
    among in numerō esse (gen) ♦ vi aestimārī,
    habērī ♦ n ratiō f; (in indictment) caput nt;
    (title) comes m.
countenance n faciēs f, vultus m, ōs nt; (fig)
    favor m; **put out of ~** conturbāre ♦ vt favēre
    (dat), indulgēre (dat).
counter n (for counting) calculus m; (for play)
    tessera f; (shop) mēnsa f ♦ adj contrārius ♦
    adv contrā, obviam ♦ vt obsistere (dat),
    respondēre (dat).
counteract vt obsistere (dat), adversārī (dat);
    (malady) medērī (dat).
counterattack n in vicem oppugnāre,
    adgredī.
counterattraction n altera illecebra f.
counterbalance vt compēnsāre, exaequāre.
counterclockwise adv sinistrōrsus.
counterfeit adj falsus, fūcātus, adsimulātus,
    fictus ♦ vt fingere, simulāre, imitārī.
countermand vt renūntiāre.
counterpane n lōdīx f, strāgulum nt.
counterpart n pār m/fnt.
counterpoise n aequum pondus nt ♦ vt
    compēnsāre, exaequāre.
countersign n (MIL) tessera f.
counting table n abacus m.
countless adj innumerābilis.
countrified adj agrestis, rūsticus.
country n (region) regiō f, terra f; (territory)
    fīnēs mpl; (native) patria f; (not town) rūs nt;
    (open) agrī mpl; **of our ~** nostrās; **live in the ~**
    rūsticārī; **living in the ~** rūsticātiō f.

country house n vīlla f.
countryman n agricola m; **fellow** ~ populāris m, cīvis m.
countryside n agrī mpl, rus nt.
couple n pār nt; a ~ of duo ♦ vt cōpulare, coniungere.
couplet n distichon nt.
courage n fortitūdō f, animus m; (mil) virtūs f; **have the** ~ **to** audēre; **lose** ~ animōs dēmittere; **take** ~ bonō animō esse.
courageous adj fortis, ācer; audāx.
courageously adv fortiter, ācriter.
courier n tabellārius m.
course n (movement) cursus m; (route) iter nt; (sequence) seriēs f; (career) dēcursus; (for races) stadium nt, circus m; (of dinner) ferculum nt; (of stones) ōrdō m; (of water) lāpsus m; **of** ~ certē, sānē, scīlicet; **as a matter of** ~ continuō; **in due** ~ mox; **in the** ~ **of** inter (acc), in (abl); **keep on one's** ~ cursum tenēre; **be driven off one's** ~dēicī; **second** ~ secunda mēnsa.
court n (space) ārea f; (of house) ātrium nt; (of king) aula f; (suite) cohors f, comitēs mpl; (law) iūdicium nt, iūdicēs mpl; **pay** ~ **to** ambīre, īnservīre (dat); **hold a** ~ forum agere; **bring into** ~ in iūs vocāre ♦ vt colere, ambīre; (danger) sē offerre (dat); (woman) petere.
courteous adj cōmis, urbānus, hūmānus.
courteously adv cōmiter, urbānē.
courtesan n meretrīx f.
courtesy n (quality) cōmitās f, hūmānitās f; (act) officium nt.
courtier n aulicus m; ~**s** pl aula f.
courtly adj officiōsus.
cousin n cōnsobrīnus m, cōnsobrīna f.
cove n sinus m.
covenant n foedus nt, pactum nt ♦ vi pacīscī.
cover vt tegere, operīre; (hide) vēlāre; (march) claudere; ~ **over** obdūcere; ~ **up** vi obtegere ♦ n integumentum nt, operculum nt; (shelter) latebrae fpl, suffugium nt; (pretence) speciēs f; **under** ~ **of** sub (abl), sub speciē (gen); **take** ~ dēlitēscere.
covering n integumentum nt, involucrum nt, operculum nt; (of couch) strāgulum nt.
coverlet n lōdīx f.
covert adj occultus; (language) oblīquus ♦ n latebra f, perfugium nt; (thicket) dūmētum nt.
covertly adv occultē, sēcrētō.
covet vt concupīscere, expetere.
covetous adj avidus, cupidus.
covetously adv avidē, cupidē.
covetousness n aviditās f, cupiditās f.
covey n grex f.
cow n vacca f ♦ vt terrēre.
coward n ignāvus m.
cowardice n ignāvia f.
cowardly adj ignāvus.
cower vi subsīdere.
cowherd m bubulcus m.
cowl n cucullus m.
coxswain n rēctor m.

coy adj pudens, verēcundus.
coyly adv pudenter, modestē.
coyness n pudor m, verēcundia f.
cozen vt fallere, dēcipere.
crab n cancer m.
crabbed adj mōrōsus, difficilis.
crack n (chink) rīma f; (sound) crepitus m ♦ vt findere, frangere; (whip) crepitāre (abl) ♦ vi (open) fatīscere; (sound) crepāre, crepitāre.
crackle vi crepitāre.
crackling n crepitus m.
cradle n cūnae fpl; (fig) incūnābula ntpl.
craft n ars f; (deceit) dolus m; (boat) nāvigium nt.
craftily adv callidē, sollerter; dolōsē.
craftsman n artifex m, faber m.
craftsmanship n ars f, artificium nt.
crafty adj callidus, sollers; dolōsus.
crag n rūpēs f, scopulus m.
cram vt farcīre, refercīre; (with food) sagīnāre.
cramp n convulsiō f; (tool) cōnfībula f ♦ vt coercēre, coartāre.
crane n (bird) grus f; (machine) māchina f, trochlea f.
crank n uncus m; (person) ineptus m.
crannied adj rīmōsus.
cranny n rīma f.
crash n (fall) ruīna f; (noise) fragor m ♦ vi ruere; strepere.
crass adj crassus; ~ **stupidity** mera stultitia.
crate n crātēs fpl.
crater n crātēr m.
cravat n fōcale nt.
crave vt (desire) concupīscere, adpetere, exoptāre; (request) ōrāre, obsecrāre.
craven adj ignāvus.
craving n cupīdō f, dēsīderium nt, adpetītiō f.
crawl vi (animal) serpere; (person) rēpere.
crayfish n commarus m.
craze n libīdō f ♦ vt mentem aliēnāre.
craziness n dēmentia f.
crazy adj dēmēns, fatuus.
creak vi crepāre.
creaking n crepitus m.
cream n spūma lactis f; (fig) flōs m.
crease n rūga f ♦ vt rūgāre.
create vt creāre, facere, gignere.
creation n (process) fabricātiō f; (result) opus nt; (human) hominēs mpl.
creative adj (nature) creātrīx; (mind) inventor, inventrīx.
creator n creātor m, auctor m, opifex m.
creature n animal nt; (person) homō m/f.
credence n fidēs f.
credentials n litterae commendātīciae fpl; (fig) auctōritās f.
credibility n fidēs f; (source) auctōritās f.
credible adj crēdibilis; (witness) locuplēs.
credit n (belief) fidēs f; (repute) existimātiō f; (character) auctōritās f, grātia f; (comm) fidēs f; **be a** ~ **to** decus esse (gen); **it is to your** ~ tibī laudī est; **give** ~ **for** laudem tribuere (gen);

have ~ fidē stāre ♦ *vt* crēdere (*dat*); (*with money*) acceptum referre (*dat*).
creditable *adj* honestus, laudābilis.
creditably *adv* honestē, cum laude.
creditor *n* crēditor *m*.
credulity *n* crēdulitās *f*.
credulous *adj* crēdulus.
creed *n* dogma *nt*.
creek *n* sinus *m*.
creel *n* vīdulus *m*.
creep *vi* (*animal*) serpere; (*person*) rēpere; (*flesh*) horrēre.
cremate *vt* cremāre.
crescent *n* lūna *f*.
crescent-shaped *adj* lūnātus.
cress *n* nasturtium *nt*.
crest *n* crista *f*.
crested *adj* cristātus.
crestfallen *adj* dēmissus.
crevasse *n* hiātus *m*.
crevice *n* rīma *f*.
crew *n* nautae *mpl*, rēmigēs *mpl*, grex *f*, turba *f*.
crib *n* (*cot*) lectulus *m*; (*manger*) praesēpe *nt*.
cricket *n* gryllus *m*.
crier *n* praecō *m*.
crime *n* scelus *nt*, facinus *nt*, flāgitium *nt*.
criminal *adj* scelestus, facinorōsus, flāgitiōsus ♦ *n* reus *m*.
criminality *n* scelus *nt*.
criminally *adv* scelestē, flāgitiōsē.
crimson *n* coccum *nt* ♦ *adj* coccineus.
cringe *vi* adūlārī, adsentārī.
crinkle *n* rūga *f*.
cripple *vt* dēbilitāre, mūtilāre; (*fig*) frangere ♦ *adj* claudus.
crisis *n* discrīmen *nt*.
crisp *adj* fragilis; (*manner*) alacer; (*hair*) crispus.
crisscross *adj* in quīncūncem dispositus.
criterion *n* index *m*, indicium *nt*; **take as a ~** referre ad (*acc*).
critic *n* iūdex *m*; (*literary*) criticus, grammaticus *m*; (*adverse*) castīgātor *m*.
critical *adj* (*mind*) accūrātus, ēlegāns; (*blame*) cēnsōrius, sevērus; (*danger*) perīculōsus, dubius; **~ moment** discrīmen *nt*.
critically *adv* accūrātē, ēleganter; sevērē; cum perīculō.
criticism *n* iūdicium *nt*; (*adverse*) reprehēnsiō *f*.
criticize *vt* iūdicāre; reprehendere, castīgāre.
croak *vi* (*raven*) crōcīre; (*frog*) coaxāre.
croaking *n* cantus *m* ♦ *adj* raucus.
crock *n* olla *f*.
crockery *n* fictilia *ntpl*.
crocodile *n* crocodīlus *m*; **weep ~ tears** lacrimās cōnfingere.
crocus *n* crocus *m*.
croft *n* agellus *m*.
crone *n* anus *f*.
crony *n* sodālis *m*.
crook *n* pedum *nt* ♦ *vt* incurvāre.
crooked *adj* incurvus, aduncus; (*deformed*)

prāvus; (*winding*) flexuōsus; (*morally*) perversus.
crookedly *adv* perversē, prāvē.
crookedness *n* prāvitās *f*.
croon *vt*, *vi* cantāre.
crop *n* (*grain*) seges *f*, messis *f*; (*tree*) fructus *m*; (*bird*) ingluviēs *f* ♦ *vt* (*reap*) metere; (*graze*) carpere, tondēre; **~ up** *vi* intervenīre.
cross *n* (*mark*) decussis *m*; (*torture*) crux *f* ♦ *adj* trānsversus, oblīquus; (*person*) acerbus, īrātus ♦ *vt* trānsīre; (*water*) trāicere; (*mountain*) trānscendere; superāre; (*enemy*) obstāre (*dat*), frustrārī; **~ out** *vt* (*writing*) expungere ♦ *vi* trānsīre; **~ over** (*on foot*) trānsgredī; (*by sea*) trānsmittere.
crossbar *n* iugum *nt*.
crossbow *n* scorpiō *m*.
cross-examination *n* interrogātiō *f*.
cross-examine *vt* interrogāre, percontārī.
crossing *n* trānsitus *m*; (*on water*) trāiectus *m*.
cross purpose *n*: **be at ~s** dīversa spectāre.
cross-question *vt* interrogāre.
crossroads *n* quadrivium *nt*.
crosswise *adv* ex trānsversō; **divide ~** decussāre.
crotchety *adj* mōrōsus, difficilis.
crouch *vi* subsīdere, sē submittere.
crow *n* cornīx *f*; **as the ~ flies** rēctā regiōne ♦ *vi* cantāre; (*fig*) exsultāre, gestīre.
crowbar *n* vectis *m*.
crowd *n* turba *f*, concursus *m*, frequentia *f*; (*small*) grex *m*; multitūdō *f*; **in ~s** gregātim ♦ *vi* frequentāre, celebrāre ♦ *vt* (*place*) complēre; (*person*) stīpāre.
crowded *adj* frequēns.
crown *n* corōna *f*; (*royal*) diadēma *nt*; (*of head*) vertex *m*; (*fig*) apex *m*, flōs *m*; **the ~ of** summus ♦ *vt* corōnāre; (*fig*) cumulāre, fastīgium impōnere (*dat*).
crucial *adj* gravissimus, māximī mōmentī; **~ moment** discrīmen *nt*.
crucifixion *n* crucis supplicium *nt*.
crucify *vt* crucī suffīgere.
crude *adj* crūdus; (*style*) dūrus, inconcinnus.
crudely *adv* dūrē, asperē.
crudity *n* asperitās *f*.
cruel *adj* crūdēlis, saevus, atrōx.
cruelly *adv* crūdēliter, atrōciter.
cruelty *n* crūdēlitās *f*, saevitia *f*, atrōcitās *f*.
cruise *n* nāvigātiō *f* ♦ *vi* nāvigāre.
cruiser *n* speculātōria nāvis *f*.
crumb *n* mīca *f*.
crumble *vi* corruere, putrem fierī ♦ *vt* putrefacere, friāre.
crumbling *adj* putris.
crumple *vt* rūgāre.
crunch *vt* dentibus frangere.
crupper *n* postilēna *f*.
crush *vt* frangere, contundere, obterere; (*fig*) afflīgere, opprimere, obruere ♦ *n* turba *f*, frequentia *f*.
crust *n* crusta *f*; (*bread*) frustum *nt*.

crusty adj (fig) stomachōsus.
crutch n baculum nt.
cry vt, vi clāmāre, clāmitāre; (weep) flēre; (infant) vāgīre; ~ **down** dētrectāre; ~ **out** exclāmāre, vōciferārī; ~ **out aga nst** adclāmāre, reclāmāre; ~ **up** laudāre, vēnditāre ♦ n clāmor m, vōx f; (cf flc's) vāgītus m; (of grief) plōrātus m.
cryptic adj arcānus.
crystal n crystallum nt ♦ adj crystallinus.
cub n catulus m.
cube n cubus m.
cubit n cubitum nt.
cuckoo n coccyx m.
cucumber n cucumis m.
cud n: **chew the** ~ rūminārī.
cudgel n fustis m ♦ vt verberāre.
cue n signum nt, indicium nt.
cuff n (blow) alapa f.
cuirass n lōrīca f.
culinary adj coquīnārius.
cull vt legere, carpere, dēlībāre.
culminate vi ad summum fastīgium renīre.
culmination n fastīgium nt.
culpability n culpa f, noxa f.
culpable adj nocēns.
culprit n reus m.
cultivate vt (land) colere, subigere; (mind) excolere; (interest) fovēre, studēre (dat).
cultivation n cultus m, cultūra f.
cultivator n cultor m, agricola m.
cultural adj hūmānior.
culture n hūmānitās f, bonae artēs fpl.
cultured adj doctus, litterātus.
culvert n cloāca f.
cumber vt impedīre, obesse (dat); (load) onerāre.
cumbersome adj molestus, gravis.
cumulative adj alius ex aliō; **be** ~ cumulārī.
cuneiform adj cuneātus.
cunning adj callidus, astūtus ♦ n ars f, astūtia f, calliditās f.
cunningly adv callidē, astūtē.
cup n pōculum nt; **drink the** ~ **of** (fig) exanclāre, exhaurīre; **in one's** ~**s** ēbrius, pōtus.
cupboard n armārium nt.
Cupid n Cupīdō m, Amor m.
cupidity n avāritia f.
cupola n tholus m.
cupping glass n cucurbita f.
cur n canis m.
curable adj sānābilis.
curative adj salūbris.
curator n custōs m.
curb vt frēnāre, īnfrēnāre; (fig) coercēre, cohibēre ♦ n frēnum nt.
curdle vt cōgere ♦ vi concrēscere.
curds n concrētum lac nt.
cure vt sānāre, medērī (dat) ♦ n remedium nt; (process) sānātiō f.
curio n dēliciae fpl.
curiosity n studium nt; (thing) mīrāculum nt.
curious adj (inquisitive) cūriōsus, cupidus;

(artistic) ēlabōrātus; (strange) mīrus, novus.
curiously adv cūriōsē; summā arte; mīrum in modum.
curl n (natural) cirrus m; (artificial) cincinnus m ♦ vt (hair) crispāre ♦ vi (smoke) volvī.
curling irons n calamistrī mpl.
curly adj crispus.
currency n (coin) monēta f; (use) ūsus m; **gain** ~ (rumour) percrēbrēscere.
current adj vulgātus, ūsitātus; (time) hīc ♦ n flūmen nt; **with the** ~ secundō flūmine; **against the** ~ adversō flūmine.
currently adv vulgō.
curriculum n īnstitūtiō f.
curry vt (favour) aucupārī.
curse n exsecrātiō f, maledictum nt; (formula) exsecrābile carmen nt; (fig) pestis f; ~**s** (interj) malum! ♦ vt exsecrārī, maledīcere (dat).
cursed adj exsecrātus, sacer; scelestus.
cursorily adv breviter, strictim.
cursory adj brevis.
curt adj brevis.
curtail vt minuere, contrahere.
curtailment n dēminūtiō f, contractiō f.
curtain n aulaeum nt ♦ vt vēlāre.
curule adj curūlis.
curve n flexus m, arcus m ♦ vt flectere, incurvāre, arcuāre.
cushion n pulvīnus m.
custodian n custōs m.
custody n custōdia f, tūtēla f; (prison) carcer m; **hold in** ~ custōdīre.
custom n mōs m, cōnsuētūdō f; (national) īnstitūtum nt; ~**s** pl portōria ntpl.
customarily adv plērumque, dē mōre, vulgō.
customary adj solitus, ūsitātus; (rite) sollemnis; **it is** ~ mōs est.
customer n emptor m.
customs officer n portitor m.
cut vt secāre, caedere, scindere; (corn) metere; (branch) amputāre; (acquaintance) āversārī; (hair) dētondēre; ~ **away** abscindere, resecāre; ~ **down** rescindere, caedere, succīdere; ~ **into** incīdere; ~ **off** vt abscīdere, praecīdere; (exclude) exclūdere; (intercept) interclūdere, intercipere; (head) abscindere; ~ **out** vt excīdere, exsecāre; (omit) ōmittere; ~ **out for** aptus ad, nātus ad (acc); ~ **round** circumcīdere; ~ **short** praecīdere; (speech) incīdere, interrumpere; ~ **through** intercīdere; ~ **up** vt concīdere ♦ n vulnus nt.
cutlass n gladius m.
cutlery n cultrī mpl.
cutter n sector m; (boat) lembus m.
cutthroat n sīcārius m.
cutting n (plant) propāgō f ♦ adj acūtus; (fig) acerbus, mordāx.
cuttlefish n sēpia f.
cyclamen n baccar nt.
cycle n orbis m.
cyclone n turbō f.

cylinder n cylindrus m.
cymbal n cymbalum nt.
cynic n (PHILOS) cynicus m.
cynical adj mordāx, acerbus.
cynically adv mordāciter, acerbē.
cynicism n acerbitās f.
cynosure n cynosūra f.
cypress n cypressus f.

$$D, d$$

dabble vi: ~ **in** gustāre, leviter attingere.
dactyl n dactylus m.
dactylic adj dactylicus.
dagger n sīca f, pugiō f.
daily adj diūrnus, cottīdiānus ♦ adv cottīdiē, in diēs.
daintily adv molliter, concinnē; fastīdiōsē.
daintiness n munditia f, concinnitās f; (squeamish) fastīdium nt.
dainty adj mundus, concinnus, mollis; fastīdiōsus ♦ npl: **dainties** cuppēdia ntpl.
dais n suggestus m.
daisy n bellis f.
dale n vallis f.
dalliance n lascīvia f.
dally vi lūdere; morārī.
dam n mōlēs f, agger m; (animal) māter f ♦ vt obstruere, exaggerāre.
damage n damnum nt, dētrīmentum nt, malum nt; (inflicted) iniūria f; (law) damnum nt; **assess ~s** lītem aestimāre ♦ vt laedere, nocēre (dat); (by evidence) laedere; (reputation) violāre.
damageable adj fragilis.
dame n mātrōna f, domina f.
damn vt damnāre, exsecrārī.
damnable adj dētestābilis, improbus.
damnably adv improbē.
damnation n malum nt.
damp adj ūmidus ♦ n ūmor m ♦ vt madefacere; (enthusiasm) restinguere, dēmittere.
damsel n puella f, virgō f.
damson n Damascēnum nt.
dance vi saltāre ♦ n saltātiō f; (religious) tripudium nt.
dancer n saltātor m, saltātrīx f.
dandruff n porrīgō f.
dandy n dēlicātus m.
danger n perīculum nt, discrīmen nt.
dangerous adj perīculōsus, dubius; (in attack) īnfestus.
dangerously adv perīculōsē.
dangle vt suspendere ♦ vi pendēre.

dank adj ūmidus.
dapper adj concinnus, nitidus.
dapple vt variāre, distinguere.
dappled adj maculōsus, distinctus.
dare vt audēre; (challenge) prōvocāre; **I ~ say** haud sciō an.
daring n audācia f ♦ adj audāx.
daringly adv audācter.
dark adj obscūrus, opācus; (colour) fuscus, āter; (fig) obscūrus; **it is getting ~** advesperāscit; **keep ~** silēre ♦ n tenebrae fpl; (mist) cālīgō f; **keep in the ~** cēlāre.
darken vt obscūrāre, occaecāre.
darkish adj subobscūrus.
darkling adj obscūrus.
darkness n tenebrae fpl; (mist) cālīgō f.
darksome adj obscūrus.
darling adj cārus, dīlēctus ♦ n dēliciae fpl, voluptās f.
darn vt resarcīre.
darnel n lolium nt.
dart n tēlum nt; iaculum nt ♦ vi ēmicāre, sē conicere ♦ vt iaculārī, iacere.
dash vt adflīgere; (hope) frangere; ~ **against** illīdere, incutere; ~ **down** dēturbāre; ~ **out** ēlīdere; ~ **to pieces** discutere; ~ **to the ground** prōsternere ♦ vi currere, sē incitāre, ruere ♦ n impetus m; (quality) ferōcia f.
dashing adj ferōx, animōsus.
dastardly adj ignāvus.
date n (fruit) palmula f; (time) tempus nt, diēs m; **out of** ~ obsolētus; **become out of** ~ exolēscere; **to** ~ adhūc; **be up to** ~ praesentī mōre ūtī ♦ vt (letter) diem adscrībere; (past event) repetere ♦ vi initium capere.
dative n datīvus m.
daub vt inlinere.
daughter n fīlia f; (little) fīliola f.
daughter-in-law n nurus f.
daunt vt terrēre, perterrēre.
dauntless adj impavidus, intrepidus.
dauntlessly adv impavidē, intrepidē.
dawdle vi cessāre, cunctārī.
dawdler n cunctātor m.
dawn n aurōra f, dīlūculum nt; (fig) orīgō f; prima lux f; **at** ~ prīmā lūce ♦ vi dīlūcēscere; **day ~s** diēs illūcēscit; **it ~s upon me** mente concipiō.
day n diēs m/f; (period) aetās f; ~ **about** alternīs diēbus; ~ **by** ~ in diēs; cotīdiē; **by** ~ adj diūrnus ♦ adv interdiū; **during the** ~ interdiū; **every** ~ cotīdiē; **from** ~ **to** ~ in diēs, diem dē diē; **late in the** ~ multō diē; **next** ~ postrīdiē; **one** ~/**some** ~ ōlim; **the** ~ **after** adv postrīdiē ♦ conj postrīdiē quam; **the** ~ **after tomorrow** perendiē; **the** ~ **before** adv prīdiē ♦ conj prīdiē quam; **the** ~ **before yesterday** nūdius tertius; **the present** ~ haec aetās; **time of** ~ hōra; **twice a** ~ bis (in) diē; ~**s of old** praeteritum tempus; ~**s to come** posteritās; **better** ~**s** rēs prosperae; **evil** ~**s** rēs adversae; **three** ~**s** trīduum nt; **two** ~**s** biduum nt; **win**

the ~ vincere.
daybook n adversāria ntpl.
daybreak n aurōra f, prīma lūx f.
daylight n diēs m; (become) ~ illūcēscere.
daystar n lūcifer m.
daytime n diēs m; in the ~ interdiū.
daze vt obstupefacere ♦ n stupor m.
dazzle vt praestringere.
dazzling adj splendidus, nitēns.
deacon n diāconus m.
deaconess n diāconissa f.
dead adj mortuus; (in battle) occīsus; (LIT) frīgidus; (place) iners, sōlitarius; (senses) hebes; ~ of night nox intempesta f; be ~ to nōn sentīre; in ~ earnest sēriō ac vērō; rise from the ~ revīvīscere ♦ adv prōrsus, omnīnō.
dead beat adj cōnfectus.
dead body n cadāver m.
dead calm n malacia f.
dead certainty n rēs certissima.
deaden vt (senses) hebetāre, obtundere; (pain) restinguere.
deadlock n incitae fpl; reach a ~ ad incitās redigī.
dead loss n mera iactūra.
deadly adj fūnestus, exitiōsus, exitiābilis; (enmity) implācābilis; (pain) acerbissimus.
dead weight n mōlēs f.
deaf adj surdus; become ~ obsurdēscere; be ~ to nōn audīre, obdūrēscere contrā.
deafen vt (with noise) obtundere.
deafness n surditās f.
deal n (amount) cōpia f; a good ~ aliquantum nt, bona pars f; (wood) abiēs f ♦ adj abiegnus ♦ vt (blow) dare, īnflīgere; (share) dīvidere, partīrī ♦ vi agere, negōtiārī; ~ with ~t fus (person) agere cum (abl); (matter) tractāre.
dealer n (wholesale) negōtiātor m, mercātor m; (retail) caupō m.
dealings n commercium nt, negōtium nt, rēs f.
dean n decānus m.
dear adj (love) cārus, grātus; (cost) cārus, pretiōsus; my ~ Quintus mī Quīnte; (beginning of letter from Marcus) Marcus Quintō salūtem; ~ me! (sorrow) hei!; (surprise) ehem!; buy ~ male emere; sell ~ bene vēndere.
dearly adv (love) valdē, ārdenter; (value) magnī.
dearness n cāritās f.
dearth n inopia f, pēnūria f.
death n mors f; (natural) obitus m; (violent) nex f, interitus m; condemn to ~ capitis damnāre; put to ~ interficere; give the ~ blow to interimere.
deathbed n: on one's ~ moriēns, moribundus.
deathless adj immortālis.
deathly adj pallidus.
debar vt prohibēre, exclūdere.
debase vt dēprāvāre, corrumpere; (coin) adulterāre; (self) prōsternere, dēmittere.
debasement n dēdecus nt; (coin) adulterium

nt.
debatable adj ambiguus, dubius.
debate vt disputāre, disceptāre ♦ n contrōversia f, disceptātiō f, altercātiō f.
debater n disputātor m.
debauch vt corrumpere, pellicere ♦ n cōmissātiō f.
debauched adj perditus, prāvus.
debauchee n cōmissātor m.
debaucher n corruptor m.
debauchery n luxuria f, stuprum nt.
debilitate vt dēbilitāre.
debility n īnfirmitās f.
debit n expēnsum nt ♦ vt in expēnsum referre.
debonair adj urbānus, cōmis.
debouch vi exīre.
debris n rūdus nt.
debt n aes aliēnum nt; (booked) nōmen nt; (fig) dēbitum nt; be in ~ in aere aliēnō esse; pay off ~ aes aliēnum persolvere; run up ~ aes aliēnum contrahere; collect ~s nōmina exigere; abolition of ~s novae tabulae fpl.
debtor n dēbitor m.
decade n decem annī mpl.
decadence n occāsus m.
decadent adj dēgener, dēterior.
decamp vi (MIL) castra movēre; (fig) discēdere, aufugere.
decant vt dēfundere, diffundere.
decanter n lagoena f.
decapitate vt dētruncāre.
decay vi dīlābī, perīre, putrēscere; (fig) tābēscere, senēscere ♦ n ruīna f, lāpsus m; (fig) occāsus m, dēfectiō f.
deceased adj mortuus.
deceit n fraus f, fallācia f, dolus m.
deceitful adj fallāx, fraudulentus, dolōsus.
deceitfully adv fallāciter, dolōsē.
deceive vt dēcipere, fallere, circumvenīre, fraudāre.
deceiver n fraudātor m.
December n mēnsis December m; of ~ December.
decemvir n decemvir m; of the ~s decemvirālis.
decemvirate n decemvirātus m.
decency n honestum nt, decōrum nt, pudor m.
decent adj honestus, pudēns.
decently adv honestē, pudenter.
deception n fraus f, fallācia f.
deceptive adj fallāx, fraudulentus.
decide vt, vi (dispute) dīiūdicāre, dēcernere, dīrimere; ~ to do statuere, cōnstituere (infin); I have ~d mihi certum est; ~ the issue dēcernere.
decided adj certus, firmus.
decidedly adv certē, plānē.
deciduous adj cadūcus.
decimate vt decimum quemque occīdere.
decipher vt expedīre, ēnōdāre.
decision n (of judge) iūdicium nt; (of council) dēcrētum nt; (of senate) auctōritās f; (of referee) arbitrium nt; (personal) sententia f;

(quality) cōnstantia f.
decisive adj certus; ~ **moment** discrīmen nt.
decisively adv sine dubiō. ♦
deck vt ōrnāre, exōrnāre ♦ n
(ship) pōns m; **with a ~** cōnstrātus.
decked adj ōrnātus; (ship) cōnstrātus.
declaim vt, vi dēclāmāre, prōnūntiāre.
declamation n dēclāmātiō f.
declamatory adj dēclāmātōrius.
declaration n adfirmātiō f, adsevērātiō f;
(formal) prōfessiō f; (of war) dēnūntiātiō f.
declare vt affirmāre, adsevērāre; (secret)
aperīre, expōnere; (proclamation)
dēnūntiāre, ēdīcere; (property in census)
dēdicāre; (war) indīcere.
declension n dēclīnātiō f.
declination n dēclīnātiō f.
decline n (slope) dēclīve nt, dēiectus m; (of age)
senium nt; (of power) dēfectiō f; (of nation)
occāsus m ♦ vi inclīnāre, occidere; (fig)
ruere, dēlābī, dēgenerāre ♦ vt dētrectāre,
recūsare; (GRAM) dēclīnāre.
decode vt expedīre, ēnōdāre.
decompose vt dissolvere ♦ vi putrēscere.
decomposed adj putridus.
decomposition n dissolūtiō f.
decorate vt ōrnāre, decorāre.
decoration n ōrnāmentum nt; (medal) īnsigne
nt.
decorous adj pudēns, modestus, decōrus.
decorously adv pudenter, modestē.
decorum n pudor m, honestum nt.
decoy n illecebra f ♦ vt adlicere, inescāre.
decrease n dēminūtiō f, dēcessiō f ♦ vt
dēminuere, extenuāre ♦ vi dēcrēscere.
decree n (of magistrate) dēcrētum nt, ēdictum
nt; (of senate) cōnsultum nt, auctōritās f; (of
people) scītum nt ♦ vt ēdīcere, dēcernere;
(people) scīscere, iubēre; **the senate ~s**
placet senātuī.
decrepit adj īnfirmus, dēbilis, dēcrepitus.
decrepitude n īnfirmitās f, dēbilitās f.
decry vt obtrectāre, reprehendere.
decurion n decuriō m.
dedicate vt dēdicāre, cōnsecrāre; (life)
dēvovēre.
dedication n dēdicātiō f; dēvōtiō f.
dedicatory adj commendātīcius.
deduce vt colligere, conclūdere.
deduct vt dēmere, dētrahere.
deduction n (inference) conclūsiō f,
cōnsequēns nt; (subtraction) dēductiō f,
dēminūtiō f.
deed n, factum nt, facinus nt; gestum nt; (legal)
tabulae fpl; **~s** pl rēs gestae fpl.
deem vt dūcere, cēnsēre, habēre.
deep adj altus, profundus; (discussion)
abstrūsus; (sleep) artus; (sound) gravis;
(width) lātus; **three ~** (MIL) ternī in
lātitūdinem ♦ n altum m.
deepen vt dēfodere, altiōrem reddere; (fig)
augēre ♦ vi altiōrem fierī; (fig) crēscere.
deepest adj īmus.

deeply adv altē, graviter; (inside) penitus; **very**
~ valdē, vehementer.
deep-seated adj (fig) inveterātus.
deer n cervus m, cerva f; (fallow) dāma f.
deface vt dēfōrmāre, foedāre.
defaced adj dēfōrmis.
defacement n dēfōrmitās f.
defalcation n peculātus m.
defamation n calumnia f, opprobrium nt.
defamatory adj contumēliōsus, probrōsus.
defame vt īnfāmāre, obtrectāre, calumniārī.
default vi dēesse; (money) nōn solvere ♦ n
dēfectiō f, culpa f; **let judgment go by ~**
vadimōnium dēserere, nōn respondēre.
defaulter n reus m.
defeat vt vincere, superāre; (completely)
dēvincere; (plan) frustrārī, disicere ♦ n
clādēs f; (at election) repulsa f, offēnsiō f; (of
plan) frustrātiō f.
defeatism n patientia f.
defeatist n imbellis m.
defect n vitium nt.
defection n dēfectiō f, sēditiō f.
defective adj mancus, vitiōsus.
defence n praesidium nt, tūtēla f; patrōcinium
nt; (speech) dēfēnsiō f; **speak in ~** dēfendere.
defenceless adj inermis, indēfēnsus; **leave ~**
nūdāre.
defences npl mūnīmenta ntpl, mūnītiōnēs fpl.
defend vt dēfendere, tuērī, custōdīre.
defendant n reus m.
defender n dēfēnsor m, prōpugnātor m; (law)
patrōnus m.
defensible adj iūstus.
defensive adj dēfēnsiōnis causā; **be on the ~**
sē dēfendere.
defensively adv dēfendendō.
defer vt cifferre, prōlātāre ♦ vi mōrem gerere
(dat); **I ~ to you in this** hōc tibī tribuō.
deference n obsequium nt, observantia f;
show ~ to observāre, īnservīre (dat).
deferential adj observāns, officiōsus.
deferment n dīlatiō f, prōlātiō f.
defiance n ferōcia f, minae fpl.
defiant adj ferōx, mināx.
defiantly adv ferōciter, mināciter.
deficiency n vitium nt; (lack) pēnūria f, inopia
f.
deficient adj vitiōsus, inops; **be ~** dēesse,
dēficere.
deficit n lacūna f.
defile n faucēs fpl, angustiae fpl ♦ vt inquināre,
contāmināre.
defilement n sordēs f, foeditās f.
define vt (limits) fīnīre, dēfīnīre, termināre;
(meaning) explicāre.
definite adj certus, dēfīnītus.
definitely adv dēfīnītē; prōrsus.
definition n dēfīnītiō f, explicātiō f.
definitive adj dēfīnītīvus.
deflate vt laxāre.
deflect vt dēdūcere, dēclīnāre ♦ vi dēflectere,
dēgredī.

deflection n dēclīnātiō f, flexus m.
deform vt dēfōrmāre.
deformed adj dēfōrmis, distortus.
deformity n dēfōrmitās f, prāvitās f.
defraud vt fraudāre, dēfraudāre.
defrauder n fraudātor m.
defray vt solvere, suppeditāre.
deft adj habilis.
deftly adv habiliter.
defunct adj mortuus.
defy vt contemnere, spernere, adversārī (dat);
(challenge) prōvocāre, lacessere.
degeneracy n dēprāvātiō f.
degenerate adj dēgener ♦ vi dēgenerāre,
dēscīscere.
degradation n īnfāmia f, ignōminia f, nota f.
degrade vt notāre, abicere; (from office)
movēre.
degrading adj turpis, indignus.
degree n gradus; (social) locus m; in some ~
aliquā ex parte; by ~s gradātim, sēnsim.
deification n apotheōsis f.
deified adj (emperor) dīvus.
deify vt cōnsecrāre, inter deōs referre.
deign vi dignārī.
deity n deus m.
dejected adj adflīctus, dēmissus.
dejectedly adv animō dēmissō.
dejection n maestitia f.
delay vt dēmorārī, dētinēre, retardāre ♦ vi
cunctārī, cessāre ♦ n mora f, cunctātiō f.
delayer n morātor m, cunctātor m.
delectable adj iūcundus, amoenus.
delegate vt lēgāre, mandāre, committere ♦ n
lēgātus m.
delegation n lēgātiō f, lēgātī mpl.
delete vt dēlēre.
deleterious adj perniciōsus, noxius.
deletion n (writing) litūra f.
deliberate vi dēlīberāre, cōnsulere ♦ adj (act)
cōnsīderātus; (intention) certus; (manner)
cōnsīderātus; (speech) lentus.
deliberately adv dē industriā.
deliberation n dēlīberātiō f.
deliberative adj dēlīberātīvus.
delicacy n (judgment) subtīlitās f, ēlegantia f;
(manners) mollitia f, luxus m; (health)
valētūdō f; (food) cuppēdia ntpl.
delicate adj mollis; (health) īnfīrmus; (shape)
gracilis; (feelings) hūmānus.
delicately adv molliter; hūmānē.
delicious adj suāvis, lautus.
delight n voluptās f, gaudium nt, dēlectātiō f ♦
vt dēlectāre, oblectāre, iuvāre ♦ vi gaudēre,
dēlectārī.
delightful adj iūcundus, dulcis, festīvus;
(scenery) amoenus.
delightfully adv iūcundē, suāviter.
delimitation n dēfīnītiō f.
delineate vt dēscrībere, dēpingere.
delineation n dēscrīptiō f.
delinquency n culpa f, dēlictum nt, noxa f.
delinquent n nocēns m/f, reus m.

delirious adj dēlīrus, āmēns, furiōsus; be ~
furere, dēlīrāre.
delirium n furor m, āmentia f.
deliver vt (from) līberāre, exsolvere, ēripere;
(blow) intendere; (message) referre; (speech)
habēre; ~ to dēferre, trādere, dare; ~ up
dēdere, trādere; be ~ed of parere.
deliverance n līberātiō f.
deliverer n līberātor m.
delivery n (of things due) trāditiō f; (of speech)
āctiō f, prōnūntiātiō f; (of child) partus m.
dell n convallis f.
Delphi n Delphī mpl.
delude vt dēcipere, frustrārī, dēlūdere.
deluge n ēluviō f ♦ vt inundāre.
delusion n error m, fraus f.
delusive adj fallāx, inānis.
delve vt fodere.
demagogue n plēbicola m.
demand vt poscere, postulāre, imperāre;
(urgently) flāgitāre, poscere; (thing due)
exigere; (answer) quaerere; ~ back repetere
♦ n postulātiō f, postulātum nt.
demarcation n līmes m.
demean vt (self) dēmittere.
demeanour n gestus m, mōs m, habitus m.
demented adj dēmēns, furiōsus.
demerit n culpa f, vitium nt.
demesne n fundus m.
demigod n hērōs m.
demise n obitus m ♦ vt lēgāre.
democracy n cīvitās populāris f.
democrat n homō populāris m/f.
democratic adj populāris.
demolish vt dēmōlīrī, dīruere, dēstruere;
(argument) discutere.
demolition n ruīna f, ēversiō f.
demon n daemōn m.
demonstrate vt (show) mōnstrāre, ostendere,
indicāre; (prove) dēmōnstrāre.
demonstration n exemplum nt; (proof)
dēmōnstrātiō f.
demonstrative adj (manner) vehemēns; (RHET)
dēmōnstrātīvus.
demoralization n corruptiō f, dēprāvātiō f.
demoralize vt corrumpere, dēprāvāre,
labefactāre.
demote vt locō movēre.
demur vi gravārī, recūsāre ♦ n mora f,
dubitātiō f.
demure adj modestus, verēcundus.
demurely adv modestē, verēcundē.
demureness n modestia f, verēcundia f,
pudor m.
demurrer n (law) exceptiō f.
den n latibulum nt, latebra f; (of vice) lustrum
nt.
denarius n dēnārius m.
denial n īnfitiātiō f, negātiō f.
denigrate vt obtrectāre, calumniārī.
denizen n incola m/f.
denominate vt nōmināre, appellāre.
denomination n nōmen nt; (religious) secta f.

denote *vt* notāre, significāre.
denouement *n* exitus *m*.
denounce *vt* dēferre, incūsāre.
denouncer *n* dēlātor *m*.
dense *adj* dēnsus; (*crowd*) frequēns; (*person*) stolidus.
density *n* crassitūdō *f*; (*crowd*) frequentia *f*.
dent *n* nota *f*.
dentate *adj* dentātus.
denture *n* dentēs *mpl*.
denudation *n* spoliātiō *f*.
denude *vt* spoliāre, nūdāre.
denunciation *n* (*report*) indicium *nt*, dēlātiō *f*; (*threat*) minae *fpl*.
deny *vt* īnfitiārī, īnfitiās īre, negāre, abnuere; (*on oath*) abiūrāre; ~ **oneself** genium dēfraudāre.
depart *vi* discēdere (*abl*), abīre, exīre, ēgredī.
department *n* (*district*) regiō *f*, pars *f*; (*duty*) prōvincia *f*, mūnus *nt*.
departure *n* discessus *m*, abitus *m*, dīgressus *m*, exitus *m*; (*change*) mūtātiō *f*; (*death*) obitus *m*.
depend *vi* pendēre; (*be dependent*) pendēre ex (*abl*), nītī (*abl*); (*rely*) fīdere, cōnfīdere; **~ing on** frētus (*abl*).
dependable *adj* fīdus.
dependant *n* cliēns *m/f*.
dependence *n* clientēla *f*; (*reliance*) fīdūcia *f*.
dependency *n* prōvincia *f*.
dependent *adj* subiectus, obnoxius.
depict *vt* dēscrībere, dēpingere; (*to the life*) expingere.
deplete *vt* dēminuere.
depletion *n* dēminūtiō *f*.
deplorable *adj* turpis, nefandus, pessimus.
deplorably *adv* turpiter, pessimē, miserē.
deplore *vt* dēplōrāre, dēfiēre, conquerī.
deploy *vt* explicāre; instruere, dispōnere.
depopulate *vt* vastāre, nūdāre.
depopulation *n* vastātiō *f*, sōlitūdō *f*.
deport *vt* (*banish*) dēportāre; (*self*) gerere.
deportation *n* exsilium *nt*.
deportment *n* gestus *m*, habitus *m*.
depose *vt* dēmovēre, dēpellere; (*evidence*) testārī.
deposit *n* fīdūcia *f*, dēpositum *nt* ♦ *vt* dēpōnere, mandāre.
depositary *n* sequester *m*.
deposition *n* (*law*) testimōnium *nt*, indicium *nt*.
depository *n* apothēca *f*.
depot *n* (*for arms*) armāmentārium *nt*; (*for trade*) emporium *nt*.
deprave *vt* dēprāvāre, corrumpere.
depraved *adj* prāvus.
depravity *n* dēprāvātiō *f*, turpitūdō *f*.
deprecate *vt* abōminārī, dēprecārī.
deprecation *n* dēprecātiō *f*.
depreciate *vt* obtrectāre, dētrectāre.
depreciation *n* obtrectātiō *f*; (*price*) vīlitās *f*.
depredation *n* praedātiō *f*, dīreptiō *f*.
depress *vt* dēprimere; (*mind*) adflīgere,

frangere; **be ~ed** iacēre, animum dēspondēre.
depressing *adj* maestus, tristis.
depression *n* (*place*) cavum *nt*; (*mind*) tristitia *f*, sollicitūdō *f*.
deprivation *n* prīvātiō *f*, spoliātiō *f*.
deprive *vt* prīvāre, spoliāre.
depth *n* altitūdō *f*; (*place*) profundum *nt*, gurges *m*.
deputation *n* lēgātiō *f*, lēgātī *mpl*.
depute *vt* lēgāre, mandāre.
deputy *n* lēgātus *m*; (*substitute*) vicārius *m*.
derange *vt* conturbāre.
deranged *adj* īnsānus, mente captus.
derangement *n* perturbātiō *f*; (*mind*) īnsānia *f*, dēmentia *f*.
derelict *adj* dēsertus.
dereliction *n* (*of duty*) neglegentia *f*.
deride *vt* dērīdēre, inlūdere.
derision *n* rīsus *m*, irrīsiō *f*.
derisive *adj* mordāx.
derivation *n* orīgō *f*.
derive *vt* dūcere, trahere; (*advantage*) capere, parāre; (*pleasure*) dēcerpere, percipere; **be ~d** dēfluere.
derogate *vi* dērogāre, dētrahere; **~ from** imminuere, obtrectāre.
derogation *n* imminūtiō *f*, obtrectātiō *f*.
derogatory *adj* indignus; **~ remarks** obtrectātiō *f*.
derrick *n* trochlea *f*.
descant *vt* disserere ♦ *n* cantus *m*.
descend *vi* dēscendere; (*water*) dēlābī; (*from heaven*) dēlābī; (*by inheritance*) pervenīre, prōdī; (*morally*) dēlābī, sē dēmittere; **be ~ed from** orīrī ex (*abl*).
descendant *n* prōgeniēs *f*; **~s** *pl* minōrēs *mpl*, posterī *mpl*.
descent *n* dēscensus *m*; (*slope*) clīvus *m*, dēiectus *m*; (*birth*) genus *nt*; (*hostile*) dēcursus *m*, incursiō *f*; **make a ~ upon** inrumpere in (*acc*), incursāre in (*acc*).
describe *vt* dēscrībere; (*tell*) nārrāre; (*portray*) dēpingere, exprimere.
description *n* dēscrīptiō *f*; (*tale*) nārrātiō *f*; (*kind*) genus *nt*.
descry *vt* cernere, cōnspicere, prōspectāre.
desecrate *vt* prōfānāre, exaugurāre.
desecration *n* exaugurātiō *f*, violātiō *f*.
desert *vt* dēserere, dērelinquere, dēstituere ♦ *vi* dēscīscere, dēficere ♦ *adj* dēsertus, sōlitārius ♦ *n* (*place*) sōlitūdō *f*, loca dēserta *ntpl*; (*merit*) meritum *nt*.
deserted *adj* dēsertus.
deserter *n* dēsertor *m*; (*MIL*) trānsfuga *m*.
desertion *n* dēfectiō *f*, trānsfugium *nt*.
deserve *vt* merērī; dignus esse quī (+ *subj*); **~ well of** bene merērī dē (*abl*).
deserved *adj* meritus.
deservedly *adv* meritō.
deserving *adj* dignus.
desiccate *vt* siccāre.
design *n* (*drawing*) adumbrātiō *f*; (*plan*)

designate–devolve

cōnsilium *nt*, **prōpositum** *nt*; **by** ~ **cōnsultō** ♦ *vt* adumbrāre; in animō habēre.
designate *vt* dēsignāre, mōnstrāre; (*as heir*) scrībere; (*as official*) dēsignāre ♦ *adj* dēsignātus.
designation *n* nōmen *nt*, titulus *m*.
designedly *adv* dē industriā, cōnsultō.
designer *n* auctor *m*, inventor *m*.
designing *adj* vafer, dolōsus.
desirable *adj* optābilis, expetendus, grātus.
desire *n* cupīditās *f*; studium *nt*; (*uncontrolled*) libīdō *f*; (*natural*) adpetītiō *f* ♦ *vt* cupere; (*much*) exoptāre, expetere; (*command*) iubēre.
desirous *adj* cupidus, avidus, studiōsus.
desist *vi* dēsistere.
desk *n* scrīnium *nt*.
desolate *adj* dēsertus, sōlitārius; (*place*) vastus ♦ *vt* vastāre.
desolation *n* sōlitūdō *f*, vastitās *f*; (*process*) vastātiō *f*.
despair *vi* dēspērāre dē (*abl*), animum dēspondēre ♦ *n* dēspērātiō *f*.
despairingly *adv* dēspēranter.
despatch *see* **dispatch**.
desperado *n* homō dēspērātus *m*.
desperate *adj* (*hopeless*) dēspērātus; (*wicked*) perditus; (*dangerous*) perīculōsus.
desperately *adv* dēspēranter.
desperation *n* dēspērātiō *f*.
despicable *adj* dēspectus, abiectus, turpis.
despicably *adv* turpiter.
despise *vt* contemnere, dēspicere, spernere.
despiser *n* contemptor *m*.
despite *n* malevolentia *f*, odium *nt*.
despoil *vt* spoliāre, nūdāre.
despoiler *n* spoliātor *m*, praedātor *m*.
despond *vi* animum dēspondēre, dēspērāre.
despondency *n* dēspērātiō *f*.
despondent *adj* abiectus, adflīctus, dēmissus; **be** ~ animum dēspondēre.
despondently *adv* animō dēmissō.
despot *n* dominus *m*, rēx *m*.
despotic *adj* imperiōsus, superbus.
despotically *adv* superbē.
despotism *n* dominātiō *f*, superbia *f*, rēgnum *nt*.
dessert *n* secunda mēnsa *f*.
destination *n* fīnis *m*.
destine *vt* dēstināre, dēsignāre; **~d to be** futūrus.
destiny *n* fātum *nt*; **of** ~ fātālis.
destitute *adj* inops, pauper, prīvātus ~ **of** expers (*gen*).
destitution *n* inopia *f*, egestās *f*.
destroy *vt* dēlēre, ēvertere, dīrimere, perdere.
destroyer *n* ēversor *m*.
destructible *adj* fragilis.
destruction *n* exitium *nt*, ēversiō *f*, excidium *nt*.
destructive *adj* exitiābilis, perniciōsus.
destructively *adv* perniciōsē.

desuetude *n* dēsuētūdō *f*.
desultorily *adv* carptim.
desultory *adj* varius, incōnstāns.
detach *vt* abiungere, sēiungere, āmovēre, sēparāre.
detachment *n* (*MIL*) manus *f*, cohors *f*; (*mind*) integer animus *m*, līber animus.
detail *n*: **~s** *pl* singula *ntpl*; **in** ~ singillātim ♦ *vt* exsequī.
detain *vt* dēmorārī, dētinēre, distinēre, morārī.
detect *vt* dēprehendere, patefacere.
detection *n* dēprehēnsiō *f*.
detective *n* inquīsītor *m*.
detention *n* retentiō *f*; (*prison*) vincula *ntpl*.
deter *vt* dēterrēre, absterrēre, impedīre.
deteriorate *vi* dēgenerāre.
deterioration *n* dēprāvātiō *f*, lāpsus *m*.
determinate *adj* certus, fīnītus.
determination *n* obstinātiō *f*, cōnstantia *f*; (*intention*) prōpositum *nt*, sententia *f*.
determine *vt* (*fix*) fīnīre; (*decide*) statuere, cōnstituere.
determined *adj* obstinātus; (*thing*) certus; **I am ~ to** mihī certum est (*infin*).
determinedly *adv* cōnstanter.
deterrent *n*: **act as a ~ to** dēterrēre.
detest *vt* ōdisse, dētestārī.
detestable *adj* dētestābilis, odiōsus.
detestation *n* odium *nt*, invidia *f*.
dethrone *vt* rēgnō dēpellere.
detour *n* circuitus *m*; **make a ~** iter flectere; (*MIL*) agmen circumdūcere.
detract *vi*: **~ from** dērogāre, dētrahere.
detraction *n* obtrectātiō *f*.
detractor *n* obtrectātor *m*, invidus *m*.
detriment *n* damnum *nt*, dētrīmentum *nt*.
detrimental *adj* damnōsus; **be ~ to** dētrīmentō esse (*dat*).
devastate *vt* vastāre, populārī.
devastation *n* vastātiō *f*, populātiō *f*; (*state*) vastitās *f*.
develop *vt* ēvolvere, explicāre; (*person*) ēducāre, alere ♦ *vi* crēscere; ~ **into** ēvādere in (*acc*).
development *n* explicātiō *f*; (*of men*) ēducātiō *f*; (*of resources*) cultus *m*; (*of events*) exitus *m*.
deviate *vi* dēcēdere dē viā, aberrāre, dēclīnāre; (*speech*) dēgredī.
deviation *n* dēclīnātiō *f*; (*from truth*) error *m*; (*in speech*) dīgressus *m*.
device *n* (*plan*) cōnsilium *nt*; (*machine*) māchina *f*; (*emblem*) īnsigne *nt*.
devil *n* diabolus *m*; **go to the ~** abī in malam crucem!; **talk of the ~** lupus in fābulā!
devilish *adj* scelestus, impius.
devil-may-care *adj* praeceps, lascīvus.
devilment *n* malitia *f*.
devilry *n* magicae artēs *fpl*.
devious *adj* dēvius, errābundus.
devise *vt* excōgitāre, commentārī, fingere.
devoid *adj* vacuus, expers; **be ~ of** carēre (*abl*).
devolve *vi* obtingere, obvenīre ♦ *vt* dēferre,

committere.
devote vt dēdicāre; (*attention*) dēdere,
trādere; (*life*) dēvovēre.
devoted adj dēditus, studiōsus; (*victim*)
dēvōtus, sacer; **be ~ to** studēre (*dat*),
incumbere (*dat*).
devotee n cultor m.
devotion n amor m, studium nt; rēligiō f.
devour vt dēvorāre, cōnsūmere; (*fig*) haurīre.
devout adj pius, rēligiōsus.
devoutly adv piē, rēligiōsē.
dew n rōs m.
dewy adj rōscidus.
dexterity n ars f, sollertia f.
dexterous adj sollers, habilis.
dexterously adv sollerter, habiliter.
diabolical adj scelestus, nefārius.
diadem n diadēma nt.
diagnose vt discernere, diiūdicāre.
diagnosis n iūdicium nt.
diagonal adj oblīquus.
diagram n fōrma f.
dial n sōlārium nt.
dialect n dialectus f, sermō m.
dialectic n ars disserendī f, dialecticē f ♦ adj
dialecticus.
dialectician n dialecticus m.
dialogue n dialogus m, colloquium nt.
diameter n diametros f.
diamond n adamās m.
diaphanous adj perlūcidus.
diaphragm n praecordia ntpl.
diary n ephēmeris f.
diatribe n convīcium nt.
dice n tālus m, tessera f; **game of ~** ālea f.
dictate vt dictāre ♦ n praeceptum nt; **~s of**
nature nātūrae iūdicia ntpl.
dictation n dictāta ntpl; (*fig*) arbitrium nt.
dictator n dictātor m; **~'s** dictātōrius.
dictatorial adj imperiōsus, superbus.
dictatorship n dictātūra f.
diction n (*enunciation*) ēlocūtiō f; (*words*) ōrātiō
f.
dictionary n verbōrum thēsaurus m.
die n signum nt; **the ~ is cast** iacta ālea est ♦ vi
morī, perīre, obīre; (*in battle*) cadere,
occumbere; **~ off** dēmorī; **~ out** ēmorī; **be**
dying to exoptāre.
diet n (*food*) diaeta f; (*meeting*) conventus m.
differ vi differe, discrepāre, dissentīre.
difference n discrepantia f, dissimilitūdō f; (*of*
opinion) dissēnsiō f; **there is a ~** interest.
different adj dīversus, varius, dissimilis; **~**
from alius ... ac; **in ~ directions** dīversī; **they**
say **~ things** alius aliud dīcit.
differentiate vt discernere.
differently adv dīversē, variē, alius aliter; **~**
from aliter ... ac.
difficult adj difficilis, arduus; **very ~**
perdifficilis, perarduus.
difficulty n difficultās f, labor m, negōtium nt;
with ~ difficulter, aegrē, vix; **be in ~**
labōrāre.

diffidence n diffīdentia f; (*shyness*) pudor m;
with ~ modestē.
diffident adj diffīdēns; (*shy*) modestus,
verēcundus.
diffidently adv modestē.
diffuse vt ciffundere, dispergere; **be ~d**
diffluere ♦ adj fūsus, diffūsus, cōpiōsus.
diffusely adv diffūsē, cōpiōsē.
diffuseness n cōpia f.
dig vt fodere; dūcere; (*nudge*) fodicāre; **~ up** vt
effodere, ēruere.
digest vt coquere, concoquere ♦ n
summārium nt.
digestion n concoctiō f; **with a bad ~** crūdus.
digger n fossor m.
dignified adj gravis, augustus.
dignify vt honōrāre, honestāre.
dignity n gravitās f, māiestās f, amplitūdō f.
digress vi dēvertere, dīgredī, dēclīnāre.
digression n dēclīnātiō f, dīgressus m.
dike n (*ditch*) fossa f; (*mound*) agger m.
dilapidated adj ruīnōsus.
dilapidation n ruīna f.
dilate vt dīlātāre; (*speech*) plūra dīcere.
dilatorily adv tardē, cunctanter.
dilatoriness n mora f, cunctātiō f.
dilatory adj tardus, lentus, segnis.
dilemma n nōdus m, angustiae fpl; **be in a ~**
haerēre; **be on the horns of a ~** auribus
tenēre lupum.
diligence n dīligentia f, industria f, cūra f.
diligent adj dīligēns, industrius, sēdulus.
diligently adv dīligenter, sēdulō.
dill n anēthum nt.
dilly-dally vi cessāre.
dilute vt dīluere, temperāre.
dim adj obscūrus; (*fig*) hebes ♦ vt obscūrāre;
hebetāre.
dimension n modus m; **~s** pl amplitūdō f,
māgnitūdō f.
diminish vt minuere, imminuere, extenuāre,
īnfringere ♦ vi dēcrēscere.
diminution n imminūtiō f, dēminūtiō f.
diminutive adj parvulus, exiguus ♦ n (*word*)
dēminūtum nt.
diminutiveness n exiguitās f.
dimly adv obscūrē.
dimness n tenebrae fpl, cālīgō f.
dimple n gelasīnus m.
din n fragor m, strepitus m; **make a ~** strepere
♦ vt obtundere.
dine vi cēnāre.
diner n convīva m.
dinghy n scapha f.
dingy adj sordidus; (*colour*) fuscus.
dining room n cēnātiō f.
dinner n cēna f.
dinner party convīvium nt.
dint n ictus m; **by ~ of** per (*acc*).
dip vt imbuere, mergere ♦ vi mergī; **~ into**
(*study*) perstringere.
diploma n diplōma nt.
diplomacy n (*embassy*) lēgātiō f; (*tact*)

iūdicium nt, sagācitās f.
diplomat n lēgātus m.
diplomatic adj sagāx, circumspect us.
diptych n tabellae fpl.
dire adj dīrus, horridus.
direct vt regere, dīrigere; (attention) attendere, admovēre, advertere; (course) tendere; (business) administrāre, moderārī; (letter) īnscrībere; (order) imperāre (dat), iubēre; (to a place) viam mōnstrāre (dat); (weapon) intendere ♦ adj rēctus, dīrēctus; (person) simplex; (language) apertus ♦ adv rēctā.
direction n (of going) cursus m, iter nt; (of looking) pars f, regiō f; (control) administrātiō f, regimen nt; (order) praeceptum rt; iussum nt; in the ~ of Rome Rōmam versus; in all ~s passim, undique; in both ~s utrōque.
directly adv (place) rēctā; (time) prōtinus, continuō, statim; (language) apertē ♦ conj simulac.
directness n (fig) simplicitās f.
director n dux m, gubernātor m, moderātor m.
dirge n nēnia f.
dirk n pūgiō m.
dirt n sordēs f; (mud) lūtum nt.
dirty adj sordidus, foedus; (speech) inquinātus ♦ vt foedāre, inquināre.
disability n vitium nt.
disable vt dēbilitāre, imminuere.
disabled adj mutilus, dēbilis.
disabuse vt errōrem dēmere (dat).
disaccustom vt dēsuēfacere.
disadvantage n incommodum nt, dētrīmentum nt; it is a ~ dētrīmentō est.
disadvantageous adj incommodus, inīquus.
disadvantageously adv incommodē.
disaffected adj aliēnātus, sēditiōsus.
disaffection n aliēnātiō f, sēditiō f.
disagree vi discrepāre, dissentīre, dissidēre.
disagreeable adj molestus, incommodus, iniūcundus.
disagreeably adv molestē, incommodē.
disagreement n discordia f, dissēnsiō f, discrepantia f.
disallow vt improbāre, abnuere, vetāre.
disappear vi dēperīre, perīre, abīre, diffugere, ēvānēscere.
disappearance n dēcessiō f, fuga f.
disappoint vt dēcipere, spē dēicere, frustrārī; be ~ed in a hope ā spē dēcidere, dē spē dēicī.
disappointment n frustrātiō f, malum nt.
disapprobation n reprehēnsiō f, improbātiō f.
disapproval n improbātiō f.
disapprove vt, vi improbāre, reprehendere.
disarm vt exarmāre, dearmāre; (fig) mītigāre.
disarrange vt turbāre, cōnfundere.
disarranged adj incompositus.
disarrangement n turbātiō f.
disarray n perturbātiō f ♦ vt perturbāre.
disaster n calamitās f, cāsus m; (MIL) clādēs f.
disastrous adj īnfēlīx, exitiōsus, calamitōsus.
disavow vt diffitērī, īnfitiārī.

disavowal n īnfitiātiō f.
disband vt dīmittere.
disbelief n diffīdentia f, suspiciō f.
disbelieve vt diffīdere (dat).
disburden vt exonerāre.
disburse vt ērogāre, expendere.
disbursement n impēnsa f.
disc n orbis m.
discard vt mittere, pōnere, prōicere.
discern vt cōnspicere, dīspicere, cernere; (fig) intellegere.
discernment n iūdicium nt, intellegentia f, sagācitās f.
discharge vt (load) exonerāre; (debt) exsolvere; (duty) fungī (abl), exsequī; (officer) exauctōrāre; (troops) missōs facere, dīmittere; (weapon) iacere, iaculārī; (prisoner) absolvere; (from body) ēdere, reddere ♦ vi (river) effundī, īnfluere ♦ n (bodily) dēfluxiō f; (MIL) missiō f, dīmissiō f; (of a duty) perfūnctiō f.
disciple n discipulus m.
discipline n (MIL) modestia f; (punishment) castīgātiō f; (study) disciplīna f ♦ vt coercēre, castīgāre.
disciplined adj modestus.
disclaim vt renūntiāre, repudiāre, rēicere.
disclaimer n repudiātiō f.
disclose vt aperīre, patefacere, indicāre.
disclosure n indicium nt.
discoloration n dēcolōrātiō f.
discolour vt dēcolōrāre.
discoloured adj dēcolor.
discomfit vt vincere, conturbāre, dēprehendere.
discomfiture n clādēs f; (POL) repulsa f.
discomfort n molestia f, incommodum nt.
disconcert vt conturbāre, percellere.
disconcerting adj molestus.
disconnect vt abiungere, sēiungere.
disconnected adj dissolūtus, abruptus.
disconnectedly adv dissolūtē.
disconsolate adj maestus, dēmissus.
disconsolately adv animō dēmissō.
discontent n offēnsiō f, fastīdium nt, taedium nt.
discontented adj invidus, fastīdiōsus, parum contentus.
discontentedly adv invītus, inīquō animō.
discontinuance n intermissiō f.
discontinue vt intermittere ♦ vi dēsistere, dēsinere.
discord n discordia f; (music) dissonum nt.
discordance n discrepantia f, dissēnsiō f.
discordant adj discors, discrepāns; (music) dissonus, absonus.
discount vt dētrahere; (fig) praetermittere ♦ n dēcessiō f; be at a ~ iacēre.
discountenance vt improbāre.
discourage vt dēhortārī, dēterrēre; be ~d animum dēmittere, animō dēficere.
discouragement n animī abiectiō f; (cause) incommodum nt.

discourse n sermō m; (_lecture_) ōrātiō f ♦ vi conloquī, disserere, disputāre.
discourteous adj inurbānus, asper, inhūmānus.
discourteously adv inhūmānē, rūsticē.
discourtesy n inhūmānitās f, acerbitās f.
discover vt (_find_) invenīre, reperīre; (_detect_) dēprehendere; (_reveal_) aperīre, patefacere; (_learn_) cognōscere.
discoverer n inventor m.
discovery n inventum nt.
discredit vt notāre, fidem imminuere (_gen_) ♦ n invidia f, lābēs f; **be in ~** iacēre.
discreditable adj inhonestus, turpis.
discreditably adv inhonestē, turpiter.
discreet adj prūdēns, sagāx, cautus.
discreetly adv prūdenter, sagāciter, cautē.
discrepancy n discrepantia f, dissēnsiō f.
discretion n prūdentia f; (_tact_) iūdicium nt; (_power_) arbitrium nt, arbitrātus m; **at your ~** arbitrātū tuō; **surrender at ~** in dēditiōnem venīre, sine ullā pactiōne sē tradere; **years of ~** adulta aetās f.
discretionary adj līber.
discriminate vt, vi discernere, internōscere, distinguere.
discriminating adj perspicāx, sagāx.
discrimination n discrīmen nt, iūdicium nt.
discursive adj vagus, loquāx; **be ~** excurrere.
discuss vt agere, disputāre, disceptāre dē (_abl_); **~ terms of peace** dē pāce agere.
discussion n disceptātiō f, disputātiō f.
disdain vt contemnere, aspernārī, fastīdīre ♦ n contemptiō f, fastīdium nt.
disdainful adj fastīdiōsus, superbus.
disdainfully adv fastīdiōsē, superbē.
disease n morbus m; pestilentia f.
diseased adj aeger, aegrōtus.
disembark vi ē nave ēgredī ♦ vt mīlitēs ē nāve expōnere.
disembarkation n ēgressus m.
disembodied adj sine corpore.
disembowel vt exenterāre.
disencumber vt exonerāre.
disengage vt expedīre, līberāre; (_mind_) abstrahere, abdūcere.
disengaged adj vacuus, ōtiōsus.
disentangle vt expedīre, explicāre, exsolvere.
disfavour n invidia f.
disfigure vt dēfōrmāre, foedāre.
disfigured adj dēfōrmis.
disfigurement n dēfōrmātiō f.
disfranchise vt cīvitātem adimere (_dat_).
disfranchised adj capite dēminūtus.
disfranchisement n capitis dēminūtiō f.
disgorge vt ēvomere.
disgrace n dēdecus nt, ignōminia f, īnfāmia f ♦ vt dēdecorāre, dēdecorī esse (_dat_).
disgraceful adj ignōminiōsus, flāgitiōsus, turpis; **~ thing** flāgitium nt.
disgracefully adv turpiter, flāgitiōsē.
disgruntled adj mōrōsus, invidus.

disguise n integumentum nt; (_fig_) speciēs f, simulātiō f; **in ~ mūtātā veste** ♦ vt obtegere, involvere; (_fact_) dissimulāre; **~ oneself** vestem mūtāre.
disgust vt displicēre (_dat_), fastīdium movēre (_dat_); **be ~ed stomachārī; I am ~ed** mē taedet, mē piget ♦ n fastīdium nt, taedium nt.
disgusting adj taeter, foedus, dēfōrmis.
disgustingly adv foedē.
dish n lanx f; (_course_) ferculum nt.
dishearten vt percellere; **be ~ed** animō dēficere, animum dēmittere.
dishevelled adj solūtus, passus.
dishonest adj perfidus, inīquus, improbus.
dishonestly adv improbē, dolō malō.
dishonesty n mala fidēs f, perfidia f, fraus f.
dishonour n dēdecus nt, ignōminia f, turpitūdō f ♦ vt dēdecorāre.
dishonourable adj ignōminiōsus, indecōrus, turpis.
dishonourably adv turpiter, inhonestē.
disillusion vt errōrem adimere (_dat_).
disinclination n odium nt.
disinclined adj invītus, āversus.
disinfect vt pūrgāre.
disingenuous adj dolōsus, fallāx.
disingenuously adv dolōsē.
disinherit vt abdicāre, exhērēdāre.
disinherited adj exhērēs.
disintegrate vt dissolvere ♦ vi dīlābī, dissolvī.
disinter vt effodere, ēruere.
disinterested adj grātuītus, favōris expers.
disinterestedly adv sine favōre.
disinterestedness n innocentia f, integritās f.
disjoin vt sēiungere.
disjointed adj parum cohaerēns.
disk n orbis m.
dislike n odium nt, offēnsiō f, invidia f ♦ vt ōdisse; **I ~ mihi** displicet, mē piget (_gen_).
dislocate vt extorquēre.
dislocated adj luxus.
dislodge vt dēmovēre, dēicere, dēpellere, dētrūdere.
disloyal adj īnfīdus, īnfidēlis; (_to gods, kin, country_) impius.
disloyally adv īnfidēliter.
disloyalty n perfidia f, īnfidēlitās f; impietās f.
dismal adj fūnestus, maestus.
dismally adv miserē.
dismantle vt nūdāre; (_building_) dīruere.
dismay n pavor m, formīdō f ♦ vt terrēre, perturbāre.
dismember vt discerpere.
dismiss vt dīmittere; (_troops_) missōs facere; (_from service_) exauctōrāre; (_fear_) mittere, pōnere.
dismissal n missiō f, dīmissiō f.
dismount vi dēgredī, (ex equō) dēscendere.
disobedience n contumācia f.
disobedient adj contumāx.
disobediently adv contrā iūssa.
disobey vt nōn pārēre (_dat_), aspernārī.

disoblige vt displicēre (dat), offendere.
disobliging adj inofficiōsus, difficilis.
disobligingly adv contrā officium.
disorder n turba f, cōnfūsiō f; (MED) morbus m; (POL) mōtus m, tumultus m ♦ vt turbāre, miscēre, sollicitāre.
disorderly adj immodestus, inōrdinātus, incompositus; (POL) turbulentus, sēditiōsus; **in a ~ manner** nullō ōrdine, temerē.
disorganize vt dissolvere, perturbāre.
disown vt (statement) īnfitiārī; (thing) abnuere, repudiāre; (heir) abdicāre.
disparage vt obtrectāre, dētrectāre.
disparagement n obtrectātiō f, probrum nt.
disparager n obtrectātor m, dētrectātor m.
disparate adj dispār.
disparity n discrepantia f, dissimilitūdō f.
dispassionate adj studiī expers.
dispassionately adv sine īrā et studiō.
dispatch vt mittere, dīmittere; (finish) absolvere, perficere; (kill) interficere ♦ n (letter) litterae fpl; (speed) celeritās f.
dispel vt dispellere, discutere.
dispensation n (distribution) partītiō f; (exemption) venia f; (of heaven) sors f; **by divine ~** dīvīnitus.
dispense vt dispertīrī, dīvidere ♦ vi: **~ with** ōmittere, praetermittere, repudiāre.
dispersal n dīmissiō f, diffugium n.
disperse vt dispergere, dissipāre, disicere ♦ vi diffugere, dīlābī.
dispirited adj dēmissō animō; **be ~ an** mō dēficere, animum dēmittere.
displace vt locō movēre.
display n ostentātiō f, iactātiō f; **for ~** per speciem ♦ vt exhibēre, ostendere, praestāre, sē ferre.
displease vt displicēre (dat), offendere; **be ~d** aegrē ferre, stomachārī, indignārī.
displeasing adj ingrātus, odiōsus.
displeasure n invidia f, offēnsiō f, odium nt.
disport vt: **~ oneself** lūdere.
disposal n (sale) vēnditiō f; (power) arbitrium nt.
dispose vt (troops) dispōnere; (mind) inclīnāre, addūcere ♦ vi: **~ of** abaliēnāre, vēndere; (get rid) tollere; (argument) refellere.
disposed adj adfectus, inclīnātus, prōnus; **well ~** benevolus, bonō animō.
disposition n animus m, adfectiō f, ingenium nt, nātūra f; (of troops) dispositiō f.
dispossess vt dētrūdere, spoliāre.
disproportion n inconcinnitās f.
disproportionate adj impār, incōncinnus.
disproportionately adv inaequāliter.
disprove vt refūtāre, redarguere, refellere.
disputable adj dubius, ambiguus.
disputation n disputātiō f.
dispute n altercātiō f, contrōversia f; (violent) iūrgium nt; **beyond ~** certissimus ♦ vi altercārī, certāre, rixārī ♦ vt negāre; **in**

dubium vocāre.
disqualification n impedīmentum nt.
disqualify vt impedīre.
disquiet n sollicitūdō f ♦ vt sollicitāre.
disquisition n disputātiō f.
disregard n neglegentia f, contemptiō f ♦ vt neglegere, contemnere, ōmittere.
disrepair n vitium nt; **in ~** male sartus.
disreputable adj inhonestus, īnfāmis.
disrepute n īnfāmia f.
disrespect n neglegentia f, contumācia f.
disrespectful adj contumāx, īnsolēns.
disrespectfully adv īnsolenter.
disrobe vt nūdāre, vestem exuere (dat) ♦ vi vestem exuere.
disrupt vt dīrumpere, dīvellere.
disruption n discidium nt.
dissatisfaction n molestia f, aegritūdō f, dolor m.
dissatisfied adj parum contentus; **I am ~ with** ... mē taedet (gen) ....
dissect vt incīdere; (fig) investīgāre.
dissemble vt, vi dissimulāre; mentīrī.
dissembler n simulātor m.
disseminate vt dīvulgāre, dissēmināre.
dissension n discordia f, dissēnsiō f; (violent) iūrgium nt.
dissent vi dissentīre, dissidēre ♦ n dissēnsiō f.
dissertation n disputātiō f.
disservice n iniūria f, incommodum nt.
dissimilar adj dispār, dissimilis.
dissimilarity n discrepantia f, dissimilitūdō f.
dissident adj discors.
dissimulation n dissimulātiō f.
dissipate vt dissipāre, diffundere, disperdere.
dissipated adj dissolūtus, lascīvus, luxuriōsus.
dissipation n dissipātiō f; (vice) luxuria f, licentia f.
dissociate vt dissociāre, sēiungere.
dissociation n sēparātiō f, discidium nt.
dissoluble adj dissolūbilis.
dissolute adj dissolūtus, perditus, libīdinōsus.
dissolutely adv libīdinōsē, luxuriōsē.
dissoluteness n luxuria f.
dissolution n dissolūtiō f, discidium nt.
dissolve vt dissolvere; (ice) liquefacere; (meeting) dīmittere; (contract) dīrimere ♦ vi liquēscere; (fig) solvī.
dissonance n dissonum nt.
dissonant adj dissonus.
dissuade vt dissuādēre (dat), dēhortārī.
dissuasion n dissuāsiō f.
distaff n colus f.
distance n intervallum nt, spatium nt; (long way) longinquitās f; **at a ~** (far) longē; (within sight) procul; (fight) ēminus; **at a ~ of** ... spatiō (gen) ...; **within striking ~** intrā iactum tēlī.
distant adj longinquus; (measure) distāns; (person) parum familiāris; **be ~** abesse (abl).

distaste n fastīdium nt.
distasteful adj molestus, iniūcundus.
distemper n morbus m.
distend vt distendere.
distil vt, vi stillāre.
distinct adj (different) dīversus; (separate)
distinctus; (clear) clārus, argūtus; (marked)
distinctus; (sure) certus; (well-drawn)
expressus.
distinction n discrīmen nt; (dissimilarity)
discrepantia f; (public status) amplitūdō f;
(honour) honōs m, decus nt; (mark) īnsigne nt;
there is a ~ interest; **without ~** prōmiscuē.
distinctive adj proprius, īnsignītus.
distinctively adv propriē, īnsignītē.
distinctly adv clārē, distinctē, certē,
expressē.
distinguish vt distinguere, internōscere,
dīiūdicāre, discernere; (honour) decorāre,
ōrnāre; **~ oneself** ēminēre.
distinguished adj īnsignis, praeclārus,
ēgregius, amplissimus.
distort vt dētorquēre; (fig) dēprāvāre.
distorted adj distortus.
distortion n distortiō f; dēprāvātiō f.
distract vt distrahere, distinēre, āvocāre;
(mind) aliēnāre.
distracted adj āmēns, īnsānus.
distraction n (state) indīligentia f; (cause)
invītāmentum nt; (madness) furor m,
dēmentia f; **to ~** efflīctim.
distraught adj āmēns, dēmēns.
distress n labor m, dolor m, aegrimōnia f,
aerumna f; **be in ~** labōrāre ♦ vt adflīgere,
sollicitāre.
distressed adj adflīctus, sollicitus; **be ~ at rem**
aegrē ferre.
distressing adj tristis, miser, acerbus.
distribute vt distribuere, dīvidere, dispertīre.
distribution n partītiō f, distribūtiō f.
district n regiō f, pars f.
distrust n diffīdentia f ♦ vt diffīdere (dat), nōn
crēdere (dat).
distrustful adj diffīdēns.
distrustfully adv diffīdenter.
disturb vt perturbāre, conturbāre;
commovēre; (mind) sollicitāre.
disturbance n turba f, perturbātiō f; (POL)
mōtus m, tumultus m.
disturber n turbātor m.
disunion n discordia f, discidium nt.
disunite vt dissociāre, sēiungere.
disuse n dēsuētūdō f; **fall into ~** obsolēscere.
disused adj dēsuētus, obsolētus.
disyllabic adj disyllabus.
ditch n fossa f, scrobis m.
dithyrambic adj dithyrambicus.
dittany n dictamnum nt.
ditty n carmen nt, cantilēna f.
diurnal adj diūrnus.
divan n lectus m, lectulus m.
dive vi dēmergī.
diver n ūrīnātor m.

diverge vi dēvertere, dīgredī; (road) sē
scindere; (opinions) discrepāre.
divergence n dīgressiō f; discrepantia f.
divers adj complūrēs.
diverse adj varius, dīversus.
diversify vt variāre.
diversion n (of water) dērīvātiō f; (of thought)
āvocātiō f; (to amuse) oblectāmentum nt;
create a ~ (MIL) hostēs dīstringere; **for a ~**
animī causā.
diversity n varietās f, discrepantia f.
divert vt dēflectere, āvertere; (attention)
āvocāre, abstrahere; (water) dērīvāre; (to
amuse) oblectāre, placēre (dat).
diverting adj iūcundus; (remark) facētus.
divest vt exuere, nūdāre; **~ oneself of** (fig)
pōnere, mittere.
divide vt dīvidere; (troops) dīdūcere; **~ among**
partīrī, distribuere; **~ from** sēparāre ab,
sēiungere ab; **~ out** dispertīrī, dīvidere ♦ vi
discēdere, sē scindere; (senate) in
sententiam īre; **be ~d** (opinions) discrepāre.
divination n dīvīnātiō f; (from birds) augurium
nt; (from entrails) haruspicium nt.
divine adj dīvīnus ♦ vt dīvīnāre, augurārī,
hariolārī; **by ~ intervention** dīvīnitus.
divinely adv dīvīnē.
diviner n dīvīnus m, augur m, haruspex m.
divinity n (status) dīvīnitās f; (god) deus m, dea
f.
divisible adj dīviduus.
division n (process) dīvīsiō f, partītiō f;
(variance) discordia f, dissēnsiō f; (section)
pars f; (grade) classis f; (of army) legiō f; (of
time) discrīmen nt; (in senate) discessiō f.
divorce n dīvortium nt, repudium nt ♦ vt (wife)
nūntium mittere (dat); (things) dīvellere,
sēparāre.
divulge vt aperīre, patefacere, ēvulgāre,
ēdere.
dizziness n vertīgō f.
dizzy adj vertīginōsus; (fig) attonitus.
do vt facere, agere; (duty) fungī (abl); (wrong)
admittere; **~ away with** vt fus tollere; (kill)
interimere; **~ one's best to** id agere ut (subj);
~ without repudiāre; **~ not** . . . nolī/nolīte (+
infin); **how ~ you ~?** quid agis?; **I have nothing
to ~ with you** mihī tēcum nihil est
commercī; **it has nothing to ~ with me** nihil
est ad mē; **that will ~** iam satis est; **be done**
fierī; **have done with** dēfungī (abl).
docile adj docilis.
docility n docilitās f.
dock n (ships) nāvāle nt; (law) cancellī mpl ♦ vt
praecīdere.
dockyard n nāvālia ntpl.
doctor n medicus m; (UNIV) doctor m ♦ vt
cūrāre.
doctrine n dogma nt, dēcrētum nt; (system)
ratiō f.
document n litterae fpl, tabula f.
dodge vt dēclīnāre, ēvādere ♦ n dolus m.
doe n cerva f.

doer *n* āctor *m*, auctor *m*.
doff *vt* exuere.
dog *n* canis *m/f*; ~ **star** Canīcula *f*; ~'s canīnus ♦ *vt* īnsequī, īnstāre (*dat*).
dogged *adj* pertināx.
doggedly *adv* pertināciter.
dogma *n* dogma *nt*, praeceptum *nt*.
dogmatic *adj* adrogāns.
dogmatically *adv* adroganter.
doing *n* factum *nt*.
dole *n* sportula *f* ♦ *vt*: ~ **out** dispertīrī dīvidere.
doleful *adj* lūgubris, flēbilis, maestus.
dolefully *adv* flēbiliter.
dolefulness *n* maestitia *f*, miseria *f*.
doll *n* pūpa *f*.
dolorous *adj* lūgubris, maestus.
dolour *n* maestitia *f*, dolor *m*.
dolphin *n* delphīnus *m*.
dolt *n* stīpes *m*, caudex *m*.
domain *n* ager *m*; (*king's*) rēgnum *nt*
dome *n* tholus *m*, testūdō *f*.
domestic *adj* domesticus, familiāris; (*animal*) mānsuētus ♦ *n* famulus *m*, servus *m* famula *f*, ancilla *f*; ~s *pl* familia *f*.
domesticate *vt* mānsuēfacere.
domesticated *adj* mānsuētus.
domesticity *n* larēs suī *mpl*.
domicile *n* domicilium *nt*, domus *f*.
dominant *adj* superior, praepotēns.
dominate *vt* dominārī in (*acc*), imperāre (*dat*); (*view*) dēspectāre.
domination *n* dominātiō *f*, dominātus *m*.
domineer *vi* dominārī, rēgnāre.
dominion *n* imperium *nt*, rēgnum *nt*.
don *vt* induere ♦ *n* scholasticus *m*.
donate *vt* dōnāre.
donation *n* dōnum *nt*.
donkey *n* asellus *m*.
donor *n* dōnātor *m*.
doom *n* fātum *nt* ♦ *vt* damnāre.
door *n* (*front*) iānua *f*; (*back*) postīcum *nt*; (*double*) forēs *fpl*; **folding** ~s valvae *fpl*; **out of** ~s forīs; (*to*) forās; **next** ~ **to** iuxtā (*acc*).
doorkeeper *n* iānitor *m*.
doorpost *n* postis *m*.
doorway *n* ōstium *nt*.
dormant *adj* sōpītus; **lie** ~ iacēre.
dormitory *n* cubiculum *nt*.
dormouse *n* glīs *m*.
dose *n* pōculum *nt*.
dot *n* pūnctum *nt*.
dotage *n* senium *nt*.
dotard *n* senex dēlīrus *m*.
dote *vi* dēsipere; ~ **upon** dēamāre.
doting *adj* dēsipiēns, peramāns.
dotingly *adv* perditē.
double *adj* duplex; (*amount*) duplus; (*meaning*) ambiguus ♦ *n* duplum *nt* ♦ *vt* duplicāre; (*promontory*) superāre; (*fold*) complicāre ♦ *vi* duplicārī; (*MIL*) currere.
double-dealer *n* fraudātor *m*.
double-dealing *adj* fallāx, dolōsus ♦ *n* fraus

f, dolus *m*.
doublet *n* tunica *f*.
doubly *adv* bis, dupliciter.
doubt *n* dubium *nt*; (*hesitancy*) dubitātiō *f*; (*distrust*) suspiciō *f*; **give one the benefit of the** ~ innocentem habēre; **no** ~ sānē; **I do not** ~ **that** ... non dubito quīn ... (+ *subj*); **there is no** ~ **that** nōn dubium est quīn (*subj*) ♦ *vt* dubitāre; (*distrust*) diffīdere (*dat*), suspicārī.
doubtful *adj* dubius, incertus; (*result*) anceps; (*word*) ambiguus.
doubtfully *adv* dubiē; (*hesitation*) dubitanter.
doubtless *adv* scīlicet, nīmīrum.
doughty *adj* fortis, strēnuus.
dove *n* columba *f*.
dovecote *n* columbārium *nt*.
dowdy *adj* inconcinnus.
dower *n* dōs *f* ♦ *vt* dōtāre.
dowerless *adj* indōtātus.
down *n* plūmae *fpl*, lānūgō *f*; (*thistle*) pappus *m*.
down *adv* deōrsum; **be** ~ iacēre; ~ **with!** perea(n)t; **up and** ~ sūrsum deōrsum ♦ *prep* dē (*abl*); ~ **from** dē (*abl*).
downcast *adj* dēmissus, maestus.
downfall *n* ruīna *f*; (*fig*) occāsus *m*.
downhearted *adj* dēmissus, frāctus animī.
downhill *adj* dēclīvis; (*fig*) prōclīvis ♦ *adv* in praeceps.
downpour *n* imber *m*.
downright *adj* dīrectus; (*intensive*) merus.
downstream *adv* secundō flūmine.
downtrodden *adj* subiectus, oppressus.
downward *adj* dēclīvis, prōclīvis.
downwards *adv* deōrsum.
downy *adj* plūmeus.
dowry *n* dōs *f*.
doyen *n* pater *m*.
doze *vi* dormītāre.
dozen *n* duodecim.
drab *adj* sordidior.
drachma *n* drachma *f*.
draft *n* (*writing*) exemplum *nt*; (*MIL*) dīlēctus *m*; (*money*) syngrapha *f*; (*literary*) silva *f* ♦ *vt* scrībere; (*MIL*) mittere.
drag *vt* trahere ♦ *vi* (*time*) trahī; ~ **on** *vi* (*war*) prōdūcere ♦ *n* harpagō *m*; (*fig*) impedīmentum *nt*.
dragnet *n* ēverriculum *nt*.
dragon *n* drācō *m*.
dragoon *n* eques *m*.
drain *n* cloāca *f* ♦ *vt* (*water*) dērīvāre; (*land*) siccāre; (*drink*) exhaurīre; (*resources*) exhaurīre.
drainage *n* dērīvātiō *f*.
drake *n* anas *m*.
drama *n* fābula *f*; **the** ~ scaena *f*.
dramatic *adj* scaenicus.
dramatist *n* fābulārum scrīptor *m*.
dramatize *vt* ad scaenam compōnere.
drape *vt* vēlāre.
drapery *n* vestīmenta *ntpl*.
drastic *adj* vehemēns, efficāx.
draught *n* (*air*) aura *f*; (*drink*) haustus *m*; (*net*)

bolus *m*.

draughts *n* latrunculī *mpl*.

draw *vt* dūcere, trahere; (*bow*) addūcere; (*inference*) colligere; (*picture*) scrībere, pingere; (*sword*) stringere, dēstringere; (*tooth*) eximere; (*water*) haurīre; ~ **aside** sēdūcere; ~ **away** āvocāre; ~ **back** *vt* retrahere ♦ *vi* recēdere; ~ **near** adpropinquāre; ~ **off** dētrahere; (*water*) dērīvāre; ~ **out** *vi* ēdūcere; (*lengthen*) prōdūcere; ~ **over** obdūcere; ~ **taut** addūcere; ~ **together** contrahere; ~ **up** *vt* (*MIL*) īnstruere; (*document*) scrībere.

drawback *n* scrūpulus *m*; **this was the only** ~ hōc ūnum dēfuit.

drawing *n* dēscrīptiō *f*; (*art*) graphicē *f*.

drawing room *n* sellāria *f*.

drawings *npl* līneāmenta *ntpl*.

drawl *vi* lentē dīcere.

drawling *adj* lentus in dīcendō.

dray *n* plaustrum *nt*.

dread *n* formīdō *f*, pavor *m*, horror *m* ♦ *adj* dīrus ♦ *vt* expavēscere, extimēscere, formīdāre.

dreadful *adj* terribilis, horribilis, formīdolōsus, dīrus.

dreadfully *adv* vehementer, atrōciter.

dream *n* somnium *nt* ♦ *vt*, *vi* somniāre.

dreamy *adj* somniculōsus.

dreariness *n* (*place*) vastitās *f*; (*mind*) tristitia *f*.

dreary *adj* (*place*) vastus; (*person*) tristis.

dregs *n* faex *f*; (*of oil*) amurca *f*; **drain to the** ~ exhaurīre.

drench *vt* perfundere.

dress *n* vestis *f*, vestītus *m*, vestīmenta *ntpl*; (*style*) habitus *m* ♦ *vt* vestīre; (*wound*) cūrāre; (*tree*) amputāre ♦ *vi* induī; ~ **up** *vi* vestum induere.

dressing *n* (*MED*) fōmentum *nt*.

drift *n* (*motion*) mōtus *m*; (*snow*) agger *m*; (*language*) vīs *f*; **I see the** ~ **of your speech** videō quōrsum ōrātiō tua tendat ♦ *vi* fluitāre; (*fig*) lābī, ferrī.

drill *n* terebra *f*; (*MIL*) exercitātiō *f* ♦ *vt* (*hole*) terebrāre; (*MIL*) exercēre; (*pupil*) īnstruere.

drink *vt*, *vi* bibere, pōtāre; ~ **a health** propīnāre, Graecō mōre bibere; ~ **deep of** exhaurīre; ~ **in** haurīre; ~ **up** ēpōtāre ♦ *n* pōtiō *f*.

drinkable *adj* pōtulentus.

drinker *n* pōtor *m*.

drinking bout *n* pōtātiō *f*.

drip *vi* stillāre, dēstillāre.

drive *vt* agere; (*force*) cōgere; ~ **away** abigere; (*fig*) pellere, prōpulsāre; ~ **back** repellere; ~ **home** dēfīgere; ~ **in/into** īnfīgere in (*acc*); (*flock*) cōgere in (*acc*); ~ **off** dēpellere; ~ **out** exigere, expellere, exturbāre; ~ **through** trānsfīgere ♦ *vi* vehī; ~ **away** āvehī; ~ **back** revehī; ~ **in** invehī; ~ **on** *vt* impellere; ~ **round** circumvehī; ~ **past** praetervehī; **what are you driving at?** quōrsum tua spectat ōrātiō?

♦ *n* gestātiō *f*.

drivel *vi* dēlīrāre.

drivelling *adj* dēlīrus, ineptus ♦ *n* ineptiae *fpl*.

driver *n* aurīga *m*; rēctor *m*.

drizzle *vi* rōrāre.

droll *adj* facētus, ioculāris.

drollery *n* facētiae *fpl*.

dromedary *n* dromas *m*.

drone *n* (*bee*) fūcus *m*; (*sound*) bombus *m* ♦ *vi* fremere.

droop *vi* dēmittī; (*flower*) languēscere; (*mind*) animum dēmittere.

drooping *adj* languidus.

drop *n* gutta *f* ♦ *vi* cadere; (*liquid*) stillāre ♦ *vt* mittere; (*anchor*) iacere; (*hint*) ēmittere; (*liquid*) īnstillāre; (*work*) dēsistere ab (*abl*) ♦ *vi*: ~ **behind** cessāre; ~ **in** *vi* vīsere, supervenīre; ~ **out** excidere.

dross *n* scōria *f*; (*fig*) faex *f*.

drought *n* siccitās *f*.

drouth *n* sitis *f*.

drove *n* grex *f*.

drover *n* bubulcus *m*.

drown *vt* mergere, obruere; (*noise*) obscūrāre ♦ *vi* aquā perīre.

drowse *vi* dormītāre.

drowsily *adv* somniculōsē.

drowsiness *n* sopor *m*.

drowsy *adj* sēmisomnus, somniculōsus.

drub *vt* pulsāre, verberāre.

drudge *n* mediastīnus *m* ♦ *vi* labōrāre.

drudgery *n* labor *m*.

drug *n* medicāmentum *nt* ♦ *vt* medicāre.

Druids *n* Druidae, Druidēs *mpl*.

drum *n* tympanum *nt*; (*container*) urna *f*.

drummer *n* tympanista *m*.

drunk *adj* pōtus, ēbrius, tēmulentus.

drunkard *n* ēbriōsus *m*.

drunken *adj* ēbriōsus, tēmulentus.

drunkenness *n* ēbrietās *f*.

dry *adj* siccus, āridus; (*thirst*) sitiēns; (*speech*) āridus, frīgidus; (*joke*) facētus; **be** ~ **ārēre** ♦ *vt* siccāre ♦ *vi* ārēscere; ~ **up** exārēscere.

dryad *n* dryas *f*.

dry rot *n* rōbīgō *f*.

dual *adj* duplex.

duality *n* duplex nātūra *f*.

dubiety *n* dubium *nt*.

dubious *adj* dubius, incertus; (*meaning*) ambiguus.

dubiously *adv* dubiē; ambiguē.

duck *n* anas *f* ♦ *vt* dēmergere ♦ *vi* dēmergī, sē dēmittere.

duckling *n* anaticula *f*.

duct *n* ductus *m*.

dudgeon *n* dolor *m*, stomachus *m*.

due *adj* dēbitus, meritus, iūstus; **be** ~ **dēbērī**; **it is** ~ **to me that . . . not** per mē stat quōminus (+ *subj*); **be** ~ **to** orīrī ex, fierī (*abl*) ♦ *n* iūs *nt*, dēbitum *nt*; (*tax*) vectīgal *nt*; (*harbour*) portōrium *nt*; **give every man his** ~ **suum** cuīque tribuere ♦ *adv* rēctā; ~ **to** ob (+ *acc*); propter (+ *acc*).

duel n certāmen nt.
dug n über nt.
duke n dux m.
dulcet adj dulcis.
dull adj hebes; (weather) subnūbilus, (language) frīgidus; (mind) tardus; **be ~** hebēre; **become ~** hebēscere ♦ vt hebetāre, obtundere, retundere.
dullard n stolidus m.
dulness n (mind) tarditās f, stultitia f.
duly adv rītē, ut pār est.
dumb adj mūtus; **be struck ~** obmūtēscere.
dun n flāgitātor m ♦ vt flāgitāre ♦ adj fuscus.
dunce n bārō m.
dune n tumulus m.
dung n fimus m.
dungeon n carcer m, rōbur nt.
dupe vt dēlūdere, fallere ♦ n crēdulus m.
duplicate n exemplar nt ♦ vt duplicāre.
duplicity n fraus f, perfidia f.
durability n firmitās f, firmitūdō f.
durable adj firmus, perpetuus.
durably adv firmē.
duration n spatium nt; (long) diūturnitās f.
duresse n vīs f.
during prep inter (acc), per (acc).
dusk n crepusculum nt, vesper m; **at ~ primā** nocte, primīs tenebrīs.
dusky adj fuscus.
dust n pulvis m; **throw ~ in the eyes of** tenebrās offundere (dat) ♦ vt dētergēre.
dusty adj pulverulentus.
dutiful adj pius, officiōsus.
dutifully adv piē, officiōsē.
dutifulness n pietās f.
duty n (moral) officium nt; (task) mūnus nt; (tax) vectīgal nt; **be on ~** (MIL) statiōnem agere, excubāre; **do one's ~** officiō fungī; **do ~ for** (pers) in locum sufficī (gen); (thing) adhibērī prō (abl); **it is my ~** dēbeō, mē oportet, meum est; **it is the ~ of a commander** ducis est; **sense of ~** pietās f.
duty call n salūtātiō f.
duty-free adj immūnis.
dwarf n nānus m.
dwell vi habitāre; **~ in** incolere; **~ upon** (theme) commorārī in (abl).
dweller n incola m.
dwelling n domus f, domicilium nt; (place) sēdēs f.
dwindle vi dēcrēscere, extenuārī.
dye n fūcus m, color m ♦ vt īnficere, fūcāre.
dyer n īnfector m.
dying adj moribundus, moriēns.
dynasty n domus (rēgia) f.
dyspepsia n crūditās f.

E, e

each adj & pron quisque; (of two) uterque; **~ other** inter sē; **one ~** singulī; **~ year** quotannīs.
eager adj avidus, cupidus, alācer; **~ for** avidus (+ gen).
eagerly adv avidē, cupidē, ācriter.
eagerness n cupīdō f, ārdor m, studium nt; alacritās f.
eagle n aquila f.
ear n auris f; (of corn) spīca f; **give ~** aurem praebēre, auscultāre; **go in at one ~ and out at the other** surdīs auribus nārrārī; **prick up one's ~s** aurēs ērigere; **with long ~s** aurītus.
earl n comes m.
earlier adv ante; anteā.
early adj (in season) mātūrus; (in day) mātūtīnus; (at beginning) prīmus; (in history) antīquus ♦ adv (in day) māne; (before time) mātūrē, temperī; **~ in life** ab ineunte aetāte.
earn vt merērī, cōnsequī; **~ a living** vīctum quaerere, quaestum facere.
earnest adj (serious) sērius; (eager) ācer, sēdulus ♦ n pignus nt; (money) arrabō m; **in ~** sēdulō, ēnīxē.
earnestly adv sēriō, graviter, sēdulō.
earnestness n gravitās f, studium nt.
earnings n quaestus m.
earring n elenchus m.
earth n (planet) tellūs f; (inhabited) orbis terrārum m; (land) terra f; (soil) solum nt, humus f; (fox's) latibulum nt; **where on ~?** ubī gentium?; **of the ~** terrestris.
earthen adj (ware) fictilis; (mound) terrēnus.
earthenware n fictilia ntpl ♦ adj fictilis.
earthly adj terrestris.
earthquake n terrae mōtus m.
earthwork n agger m
earthy adj terrēnus.
ease n facilitās f; (leisure) ōtium nt; **at ~** ōtiōsus; (in mind) sēcūrus; **ill at ~** sollicitus ♦ vt laxāre, relevāre; (pain) mītigāre.
easily adv facile; (gladly) libenter; (at leisure) ōtiōsē; **not ~** nōn temerē.
easiness n facilitās f.
east n Oriēns m, sōlis ortus m; **~ wind** eurus m.
Easter n Pascha f.
easterly, eastern adj orientālis.
eastward adv ad orientem.
easy adj facilis; (manner) adfābilis, facilis; (mind) sēcūrus; (speech) expedītus; (discipline) remissus. **~ circumstances** dīvitiae fpl, abundantia f.
eat vt edere; cōnsūmere; vescī (abl); **~ away** rōdere; **~ up** exedere.
eatable adj esculentus.
eating n cibus m.

eaves n suggrunda f.
eavesdropper n sermōnis auceps m.
ebb n dēcessus m, recessus m; **at ~tide**
  minuente aestū; **be at a low ~** (fig) iacēre ♦ vi
  recēdere.
ebony n ebenus f.
ebullient adj fervēns.
ebullition n fervor m.
eccentric adj īnsolēns.
eccentricity n īnsolentia f.
echo n imāgō f ♦ vt, vi resonāre.
eclipse n dēfectus m, dēfectiō f ♦ vt obscūrāre;
  be ~d dēficere, labōrāre.
eclogue n ecloga f.
economic adj quaestuōsus, sine iactūrā.
economical adj (person) frūgī, parcus.
economically adv nullā iactūrā factā.
economics n reī familiāris dispēnsātiō f.
economize vi parcere.
economy n frūgālitās f.
ecstasy n alacritās f, furor m.
ecstatic adj gaudiō ēlātus.
eddy n vertex m ♦ vi volūtārī.
edge n ōra f, margō f; (of dish) labrum nt; (of
  blade) aciēs f; **take the ~ off** obtundere; **on ~**
  (fig) suspēnsō animō ♦ vt (garment)
  praetexere; (blade) acuere ♦ vi: **~ in sē**
  īnsinuāre.
edging n limbus m.
edible adj esculentus.
edict n ēdictum nt, dēcrētum nt.
edification n ērudītiō f.
edifice n aedificium nt.
edify vt ērudīre.
edit vt recognōscere, recēnsēre.
edition n ēditiō f.
educate vt ērudīre, īnfōrmāre; **~ in** īnstituere
  ad (acc).
education n doctrīna f; (process) īnstitūtiō f.
eel n anguilla f.
eerie adj mōnstruōsus.
efface vt dēlēre, tollere.
effect n (result) ēventus m; (impression) vīs f,
  effectus m; (show) iactātiō f; **~s** pl bona ntpl;
  for ~ iactātiōnis causā; **in ~** rē vērā; **to this ~**
  in hanc sententiam; **without ~** inritus ♦ vt
  efficere, facere, patrāre.
effective adj valēns, validus; (RHET) gravis,
  ōrnātus.
effectively adv validē, graviter, ōrnātē.
effectiveness n vīs f.
effectual adj efficāx, idōneus.
effectually adv efficāciter.
effectuate vt efficere, cōnsequī.
effeminacy n mollitiēs f.
effeminate adj mollis, effēminātus.
effeminately adv molliter, effēminātē.
effervesce vi effervēscere.
effete adj effētus.
efficacious adj efficāx.
efficaciously adv efficāciter.
efficacy n vīs f.
efficiency n virtūs f, perītia f.

efficient adj capāx, perītus; (logic) efficiēns.
efficiently adv perītē, bene.
effigy n simulācrum nt, effigiēs f.
effloresce vi flōrēscere.
efflorescence n (fig) flōs m.
effluvium n hālitus m.
effort n opera f, cōnātus m; (of mind) intentiō f;
  make an ~ ēnītī.
effrontery n audācia f, impudentia f.
effusive adj officiōsus.
egg n ōvum nt; **lay an ~** ōvum parere ♦ vt
  impellere, īnstīgāre.
egoism n amor suī m.
egoist n suī amāns m.
egotism n iactātiō f.
egotist n glōriōsus m.
egregious adj singulāris.
egress n exitus m.
eight num octō; **~ each** octōnī; **~ times** octiēns.
eighteen num duodēvīgintī.
eighteenth adj duodēvīcēsimus.
eighth adj octāvus.
eight hundred num octingentī.
eight hundredth adj octingentēsimus.
eightieth adj octōgēsimus.
eighty num octōgintā; **~ each** octōgēnī; **~ times**
  octōgiēns.
either pron alteruter, uterlibet, utervīs ♦ conj
  aut, vel; **~ ... or** aut ... aut; vel ... vel.
ejaculation n clāmor m.
eject vt ēicere, expellere.
ejection n expulsiō f.
eke vt: **eke out** parcendō prōdūcere.
elaborate vt ēlabōrāre ♦ adj ēlabōrātus,
  exquīsītus.
elaborately adv summō labōre, exquīsītē.
elan n ferōcia f.
elapse vi abīre, intercēdere; **allow to ~**
  intermittere; **a year has ~d since** annus est
  cum (indic).
elated adj ēlātus; **be ~** efferrī.
elation n laetitia f.
elbow n cubitum nt.
elder adj nātū māior, senior ♦ n (tree)
  sambūcus f.
elderly adj aetāte prōvectus.
elders npl patrēs mpl.
eldest adj nātū māximus.
elecampane n inula f.
elect vt ēligere, dēligere; (magistrate) creāre;
  (colleague) cooptāre ♦ adj dēsignātus;
  (special) lēctus.
election n (POL) comitia ntpl.
electioneering n ambitiō f.
elector n suffrāgātor m.
elegance n ēlegantia f, lepōs m, munditia f,
  concinnitās f.
elegant adj ēlegāns, concinnus, nitidus.
elegantly adv ēleganter, concinnē.
elegiac adj: **~ verse** elegī mpl, versūs alternī
  mpl.
elegy n elegīa f.
element n elementum nt; **~s** pl initia ntpl,

prīncipia *ntpl*; **out of one's** ~ peregrīnus.
elementary *adj* prīmus.
elephant *n* elephantus *m*, elephas *m*.
elevate *vt* efferre, ērigere.
elevated *adj* ēditus, altus.
elevation *n* altitūdō *f*; (*style*) ēlātiō *f*.
eleven *num* ūndecim; ~ **each** ūndēnī; ~ **times**
ūndeciēns.
eleventh *adj* ūndecimus.
elf *n* deus *m*.
elicit *vt* ēlicere; (*with effort*) ēruere.
elide *vt* ēlīdere.
eligible *adj* idōneus, aptus.
eliminate *vt* tollere, āmovēre.
elite *n* flōs *m*, rōbur *nt*.
elk *n* alcēs *f*.
ell *n* ulna *f*.
ellipse *n* (*RHET*) dētractiō *f*; (*oval*) ōvum *nt*.
elm *n* ulmus *f* ♦ *adj* ulmeus.
elocution *n* prōnūntiātiō *f*.
elongate *vt* prōdūcere.
elope *vi* aufugere.
eloquence *n* ēloquentia *f*; (*natural*) fācundia *f*,
dīcendī vīs *f*.
eloquent *adj* ēloquēns; (*natural*) fācundus;
(*fluent*) disertus.
eloquently *adv* fācundē, disertē.
else *adv* aliōquī, aliter ♦ *adj* alius; **or** ~ aliōquī;
who ~ quis alius.
elsewhere *adv* alibī; ~ **to** aliō.
elucidate *vt* ēnōdāre, illūstrāre.
elucidation *n* ēnōdātiō *f*, explicātiō *f*.
elude *vt* ēvītāre, frustrārī, fallere.
elusive *adj* fallāx.
emaciated *adj* macer.
emaciation *n* maciēs *f*.
emanate *vi* mānāre; (*fig*) ēmānāre, orīrī.
emanation *n* exhālātiō *f*.
emancipate *vt* ēmancipāre, manū mittere,
līberāre.
emancipation *n* lībertās *f*.
emasculate *vt* ēnervāre, dēlumbāre.
embalm *vt* condīre.
embankment *n* agger *m*, mōlēs *f*.
embargo *n* interdictum *nt*.
embark *vi* cōnscendere, nāvem cōnscendere;
~ **upon** (*fig*) ingredī ♦ *vt* impōnere.
embarkation *n* cōnscēnsiō *f*.
embarrass *vt* (*by confusing*) perturbāre; (*by
obstructing*) impedīre; (*by revealing*)
dēprehendere; **be** ~**ed** haerēre.
embarrassing *adj* incommodus,
intempestīvus.
embarrassment *n* (*in speech*) haesitātiō *f*; (*in
mind*) sollicitūdō *f*; (*in business*) angustiae *fpl*,
difficultās *f*; (*cause*) molestia *f*,
impedīmentum *nt*.
embassy *n* lēgātiō *f*.
embedded *adj* dēfixus.
embellish *vt* adōrnāre, exōrnāre, decorāre.
embellishment *n* decus *nt*, exōrnātiō *f*,
ōrnāmentum *nt*.
embers *n* cinis *m*, favilla *f*.

embezzle *vt* peculārī, dēpeculārī.
embezzlement *n* peculātus *m*.
embezzler *n* peculātor *m*.
embitter *vt* exacerbāre.
emblazon *vt* īnsignīre.
emblem *n* īnsigne *nt*.
embodiment *n* exemplar *nt*.
embody *vt* repraesentāre; (*MIL*) cōnscrībere.
embolden *vt* cōnfirmāre; ~ **the hearts of**
animōs cōnfirmāre.
emboss *vt* imprimere, caelāre.
embrace *vt* amplectī, complectī; (*items*)
continēre, comprehendere; (*party*) sequī;
(*opportunity*) adripere ♦ *nt* amplexus *m*,
complexus *m*.
embroider *vt* acū pingere.
embroidery *n* vestis picta *f*.
embroil *vt* miscēre, implicāre.
emend *vt* ēmendāre, corrigere.
emendation *n* ēmendātiō *f*, corrēctiō *f*.
emerald *n* smaragdus *m*.
emerge *vi* ēmergere, exsistere; ēgredī.
emergency *n* tempus *nt*, discrīmen *nt* ♦ *adj*
subitārius.
emigrate *vi* migrāre, ēmigrāre.
emigration *n* migrātiō *f*.
eminence *n* (*ground*) tumulus *m*, locus ēditus
m; (*rank*) praestantia *f*, amplitūdō *f*.
eminent *adj* ēgregius, ēminēns, īnsignis,
amplus.
eminently *adv* ēgregiē, prae cēterīs, in
prīmīs.
emissary *n* lēgātus *m*
emit *vt* ēmittere.
emolument *n* lucrum *nt*, ēmolumentum *nt*.
emotion *n* animī mōtus *m*, commōtiō *f*,
adfectus *m*.
emotional *adj* (*person*) mōbilis; (*speech*)
flexanimus.
emperor *n* prīnceps *m*, imperātor *m*.
emphasis *n* pondus *nt*; (*words*) impressiō *f*.
emphasize *vt* exprimere.
emphatic *adj* gravis.
emphatically *adv* adsevēranter, vehementer.
empire *n* imperium *nt*.
employ *vt* ūtī (*abl*); (*for purpose*) adhibēre;
(*person*) exercēre.
employed *adj* occupātus.
employees *npl* operae *fpl*.
employer *n* redemptor *m*.
employment *n* (*act*) ūsus *m*; (*work*) quaestus
m.
empower *vt* permittere (*dat*), potestātem
facere (*dat*).
emptiness *n* inānitās *f*.
empty *adj* inānis, vacuus; (*fig*) vānus, inritus ♦
vt exhaurīre, exinānīre ♦ *vi* (*river*) īnfluere.
emulate *vt* aemulārī.
emulation *n* aemulātiō *f*.
emulous *adj* aemulus.
emulously *adv* certātim.
enable *vt* potestātem facere (*dat*); efficere
ut(*subj*).

enact vt dēcernere, ēdīcere, scīscere; (part) agere.

enactment n dēcrētum nt, lēx f.

enamoured adj amāns; **be ~ of** dēamāre.

encamp vi castra pōnere, tendere.

encampment n castra ntpl.

encase vt inclūdere.

enchant vt fascināre; (fig) dēlectāre.

enchantment n fascinātiō f; blandīmentum nt.

enchantress n sāga f.

encircle vt cingere, circumdare, amplectī.

enclose vt inclūdere, saepīre.

enclosure n saeptum nt, māceria f.

encompass vt cingere, circumdare, amplectī.

encounter vt obviam īre (dat), occurrere (dat); (in battle) concurrere cum (abl), congredī cum ♦ n occursus m, concursus m.

encourage vt cōnfirmāre, (co)hortārī, sublevāre, favēre (dat).

encouragement n hortātiō f, favor m, auxilium nt.

encroach vi invādere; **~ upon** occupāre; (fig) imminuere.

encrust vt incrustāre.

encumber vt impedīre, onerāre.

encumbrance n impedīmentum nt, onus nt.

end n fīnis m; (aim) prōpositum nt; (of action) ēventus m, exitus m; (of speech) perōrātiō f; **~ to** ~ continuī; **at a loose** ~ vacuus, ōtiōsus; **for two days on** ~ biduum continenter; **in the** ~ dēnique; **the** ~ **of** extrēmus; (time) exāctus; **put an** ~ **to** fīnem facere (dat), fīnem impōnere (dat); **to the** ~ **that** eō cōnsiliō ut (subj); **to what** ~? quō?, quōrsum? ♦ vt fīnīre, cōnficere; (mutual dealings) dīrimere ♦ vi dēsinere; (event) ēvādere; (sentence) cadere; (speech) perōrāre; (time) exīre; **~ up as** ēvādere; **~ with** dēsinere in (acc).

endanger vt perīclitārī, in discrīmen addūcere.

endear vt dēvincīre.

endearing adj blandus.

endearment n blanditiae fpl.

endeavour vt cōnārī, ēnītī ♦ n cōnātus m.

ending n fīnis m, exitus m.

endive n intubum nt.

endless adj īnfīnītus; (time) aeternus, perpetuus.

endlessly adv sine fīne, īnfīnītē.

endorse vt ratum facere.

endow vt dōnāre, īnstruere.

endowed adj praeditus (+ abl).

endowment n dōnum nt.

endurance n patientia f.

endure vi dūrāre, permanēre ♦ vt ferre, tolerāre, patī.

enemy n (public) hostis m, hostēs mpl; (private) inimīcus m; **greatest** ~ inimīcissimus m; **~ territory** hosticum nt.

energetic adj impiger, nāvus, strēnuus; (style) nervōsus.

energetically adv impigrē, nāviter, strēnuē.

energy n impigritās f, vigor m, incitātiō f; (mind) contentiō f; (style) nervī mpl.

enervate vt ēnervāre, ēmollīre.

enervation n languor m.

enfeeble vt īnfirmāre, dēbilitāre.

enfold vt involvere, complectī.

enforce vt (law) exsequī; (argument) cōnfirmāre.

enfranchise vt cīvitāte dōnāre; (slave) manū mittere.

engage vt (affection) dēvincīre; (attention) distinēre, occupāre; (enemy) manum cōnserere cum (abl); (hire) condūcere; (promise) spondēre, recipere; **~ the enemy** proelium cum hostibus committere; **be ~d in** versārī in (abl) ♦ vi: **~ in** ingredī, suscipere.

engagement n (comm) occupātiō f; (mil) pugna f, certāmen nt; (agreement) spōnsiō f; **keep an** ~ fidem praestāre; **break an** ~ fidem fallere; **I have an** ~ **at your house** prōmīsī ad tē.

engaging adj blandus.

engender vt ingenerāre, ingignere.

engine n māchina f.

engineer n māchinātor m ♦ vt mōlīrī.

engraft vt īnserere.

engrave vt īnsculpere, incīdere, caelāre.

engraver n sculptor m, caelātor m.

engraving n sculptūra f, caelātūra f.

engross vt dīstringere, occupāre; **~ed in** tōtus in (abl).

engulf vt dēvorāre, obruere.

enhance vt amplificāre, augēre, exaggerāre.

enigma n aenigma nt, ambāgēs fpl.

enigmatic adj ambiguus, obscūrus.

enigmatically adv per ambāgēs, ambiguē.

enjoin vt imperāre (dat), iniungere (dat).

enjoy vt fruī (abl); (advantage) ūtī (abl); (pleasure) percipere, dēcerpere; **~ oneself** dēlectārī, geniō indulgēre.

enjoyable adj iūcundus.

enjoyment n fructus m; dēlectātiō f, voluptās f.

enlarge vt augēre, amplificāre, dīlātāre; (territory) prōpāgāre; **~ upon** amplificāre.

enlargement n amplificātiō f, prōlātiō f.

enlighten vt inlūstrāre; docēre, ērudīre.

enlightenment n ērudītiō f, hūmānitās f.

enlist vt scrībere, cōnscrībere; (sympathy) conciliāre ♦ vi nōmen dare.

enliven vt excitāre.

enmesh vt impedīre, implicāre.

enmity n inimīcitia f, simultās f.

ennoble vt honestāre, excolere.

ennui n taedium nt.

enormity n immānitās f; (deed) scelus nt, nefās nt.

enormous adj immānis, ingēns.

enormously adv immēnsum.

enough adj satis (indecl gen) ♦ adv satis; **more than** ~ satis superque; **I have had** ~ **of** ... mē taedet (gen) ....

enquire vi quaerere, percontārī; **~ into**

cognōscere, inquīrere in (acc).
enquiry n percontātiō f; (legal) quaestiō f.
enrage vt inrītāre, incendere.
enrapture vt dēlectāre.
enrich vt dītāre, locuplētāre; ~ **with** augēre (abl).
enrol vt adscrībere, conscrībere ♦ vi nōmen dare.
enshrine vt dēdicāre; (fig) sacrāre.
enshroud vt involvere.
ensign n signum nt, īnsigne nt; (officer) signifer m.
enslave vt in servitūtem redigere.
enslavement n servitūs f.
ensnare vt dēcipere, inlaqueāre, inrētīre.
ensue vi īnsequī.
ensure vt praestāre; ~ **that** efficere ut (subj).
entail vt adferre.
entangle vt impedīre, implicāre, inrētīre.
entanglement n implicātiō f.
enter vi inīre, ingredī, intrāre; (riding) invehī; ~ **into** introīre in (acc); ~ **upon** inīre, ingredī ♦ vt (place) intrare; (account) ferre, indūcere; (mind) subīre.
enterprise n inceptum nt; (character) prōmptus animus m.
enterprising adj prōmptus, strēnuus.
entertain vt (guest) invītāre, excipere; (state of mind) habēre, concipere; (to amuse) oblectāre.
entertainer n acroāma nt.
entertainment n hospitium nt; oblectāmentum nt; acroāma nt.
enthral vt capere.
enthusiasm n studium nt, fervor m; ~ **for** studium nt (+ gen).
enthusiastic adj studiōsus, fervidus.
enthusiastically adv summō studiō.
entice vt inlicere, ēlicere, invītāre.
enticement n illecebra f, lēnōcinium nt.
entire adj integer, tōtus, ūniversus.
entirely adv omnīnō, funditus, penitus.
entitle vt (book) īnscrībere; **be ~d to** merērī, dignum esse quī (subj), iūs habēre (gen).
entity n rēs f.
entomb vt humāre, sepelīre.
entrails n intestīna ntpl, exta ntpl.
entrance n aditus m, introitus m; (act) ingressiō f; (of house) vestibulum nt; (of harbour) ōstium nt.
entrance vt fascināre, cōnsōpīre, capere.
entreat vt implōrāre, obsecrāre; (successfully) exōrāre.
entreaty n precēs fpl.
entrenchment n mūnītiō f.
entrust vt committere, crēdere, mandāre; (for keeping) dēpōnere.
entry n introitus m, aditus m; **make an ~** (book) in tabulās referre.
entwine vt implicāre, involvere.
enumerate vt numerāre, dīnumerāre.
enunciate vt ēdīcere; (word) exprimere.
envelop vt implicāre, involvere.

envelope n involucrum nt.
enviable adj beātus.
envious adj invidus, invidiōsus.
enviously adv invidiōsē.
environment n vīcīnia f; **our ~** ea in quibus versāmur.
envoy n lēgātus m.
envy n invidia f ♦ vt invidēre (dat).
enwrap vt involvere.
ephemeral adj brevis.
ephor n ephorus m.
epic adj epicus ♦ **n epos** nt.
epicure n dēlicātus m.
epigram n sententia f; (poem) epigramma nt.
epilepsy n morbus comitiālis m.
epilogue n epilogus m.
episode n ēventum nt.
epistle n epistula f, litterae fpl.
epitaph n epigramma nt, titulus m.
epithet n adsūmptum nt.
epitome n epitomē f.
epoch n saeculum nt.
equable adj aequālis; (temper) aequus.
equal adj aequus, pār; **be ~ to** aequāre; (task) sufficere (dat) ♦ **n** pār m/f ♦ vt aequāre, adaequāre.
equality n aequālitās f.
equalize vt adaequāre, exaequāre.
equally adv aequē, pariter.
equanimity n aequus animus m.
equate vt aequāre.
equator n aequinoctiālis circulus m.
equestrian adj equester.
equidistant adj: **be ~** aequō spatiō abesse, idem distāre.
equilibrium n lībrāmentum nt.
equine adj equīnus.
equinoctial adj aequinoctiālis.
equinox n aequinoctium nt.
equip vt armāre, īnstruere, ōrnāre.
equipment n arma ntpl, īnstrūmenta ntpl, adparātus m.
equipoise n lībrāmentum nt.
equitable adj aequus, iūstus.
equitably adv iūstē, aequē.
equity n aequum nt, aequitās f.
equivalent adj pār, īdem īnstar (gen).
equivocal adj anceps, ambiguus.
equivocally adv ambiguē.
equivocate vi tergiversārī.
era n saeculum nt.
eradicate vt ēvellere, exstirpāre.
erase vt dēlēre, indūcere.
erasure n litūra f.
ere conj priusquam.
erect vt ērigere; (building) exstruere; (statue) pōnere ♦ adj ērēctus.
erection n (process) exstructiō f; (product) aedificium nt.
erode vt rōdere.
erotic adj amātōrius.
err vi errāre, peccāre.
errand n mandātum nt.

errant *adj* vagus.
erratic *adj* incōnstāns.
erroneous *adj* falsus.
erroneously *adv* falsō, perperam.
error *n* error *m*; (*moral*) peccātum *nt*; (*writing*) mendum *nt*.
erudite *adj* doctus.
erudition *n* doctrīna *f*, ērudītiō *f*.
erupt *vi* ērumpere.
eruption *n* ēruptiō *f*.
escapade *n* ausum *nt*.
escape *vi* effugere, ēvādere ♦ *vt* fugere, ēvītāre; (*memory*) excidere ex (*abl*); ~ **the notice of** fallere, praeterīre ♦ *n* effugium *nt*, fuga *f*; **way of** ~ effugium *nt*.
eschew *vt* vītāre.
escort *n* praesidium *nt*; (*private*) dēductor *m* ♦ *vt* comitārī, prōsequī; (*out of respect*) dēdūcere.
especial *adj* praecipuus.
especially *adv* praecipuē, praesertim, māximē, in prīmīs.
espionage *n* inquīsītiō *f*.
espouse *vt* (*wife*) dūcere; (*cause*) fovēre.
espy *vt* cōnspicere, cōnspicārī.
essay *n* cōnātus *m*; (*test*) perīculum *nt*; (*literary*) libellus *m* ♦ *vt* cōnārī, incipere.
essence *n* vīs *f*, nātūra *f*.
essential *adj* necesse, necessārius.
essentially *adv* necessāriō.
establish *vt* īnstituere, condere; (*firmly*) stabilīre.
established *adj* firmus, certus; **be** ~ cōnstāre; **become** ~ (*custom*) inveterāscere.
establishment *n* (*act*) cōnstitūtiō *f*; (*domestic*) familia *f*.
estate *n* fundus *m*, rūs *nt*; (*in money*) rēs *f*; (*rank*) ōrdō *m*.
esteem *vt* aestimāre, respicere ♦ *n* grātia *f*, opīniō *f*.
estimable *adj* optimus.
estimate *vt* aestimāre, ratiōnem inīre (*gen*) ♦ *n* aestimātiō *f*, iūdicium *nt*.
estimation *n* opīniō *f*, sententia *f*.
estrange *vt* aliēnāre, abaliēnāre.
estrangement *n* aliēnātiō *f*, discidium *nt*.
estuary *n* aestuārium *nt*.
eternal *adj* aeternus, perennis.
eternally *adv* semper, aeternum.
eternity *n* aeternitās *f*.
etesian winds *n* etēsiae *fpl*.
ether *n* (*sky*) aethēr *m*.
ethereal *adj* aetherius, caelestis.
ethic, ethical *adj* mōrālis.
ethics *n* mōrēs *mpl*, officia *ntpl*.
Etruscan *n* Etruscus *m* ♦ *adj like* **bonus.**
etymology *n* verbōrum notātiō *f*.
eulogist *n* laudātor *m*.
eulogize *vt* laudāre, conlaudāre.
eulogy *n* laudātiō *f*.
eunuch *n* eunūchus *m*.
euphony *n* sonus *m*.
evacuate *vt* (*place*) exinānīre; (*people*)

dēdūcere.
evacuation *n* discessiō *f*.
evade *vt* dēclināre, dēvītāre, ēlūdere.
evaporate *vt* exhālāre ♦ *vi* exhālārī.
evaporation *n* exhālātiō *f*.
evasion *n* tergiversātiō *f*.
evasive *adj* ambiguus.
eve *n* vesper *m*; (*before festival*) pervigilium *nt*; **on the** ~ **of** prīdiē (*gen*).
even *adj* aequus, aequālis; (*number*) pār ♦ *adv* et, etiam; (*tentative*) vel; ~ **if** etsī, etiamsī; **tametsī;** ~ **more** etiam magis; ~ **so** nihilōminus; ~ **yet** etiamnum; **not** ~ ... nē quidem ♦ *vt* aequāre.
evening *n* vesper *m* ♦ *adj* vespertīnus; ~ **is drawing on** invesperāscit; **in the** ~ vesperī.
evening star *n* Vesper *m*, Hesperus *m*.
evenly *adv* aequāliter, aequābiliter.
evenness *n* aequālitās *f*, aequābilitās *f*.
event *n* ēventum *nt*; (*outcome*) ēventus *m*.
eventide *n* vespertīnum tempus *nt*.
eventuality *n* cāsus *m*.
eventually *adv* mox, aliquandō, tandem.
ever *adv* unquam; (*after* sī, nisī, num, nē) quandō; (*always*) semper; (*after interrog*) -nam, tandem; ~ **so** nimium, nimium quantum; **best** ~ omnium optimus; **for** ~ in aeternum.
everlasting *adj* aeternus, perpetuus, immortālis.
evermore *adv* semper, in aeternum.
every *adj* quisque, omnis; ~ **four years** quintō quōque annō; ~ **now and then** interdum; **in** ~ **direction** passim; undique; ~ **other day** alternis diebus; ~ **day** cottīdiē ♦ *adj* cottīdiānus.
everybody *pron* quisque, omnēs *mpl*; ~ **agrees** inter omnēs constat; ~ **knows** nēmō est quīn sciat.
everyday *adj* cottīdiānus.
everyone *pron see* **everybody.**
everything omnia *ntpl*; **your health is** ~ **to me** meā māximē interest tē valēre.
everywhere *adv* ubīque, passim.
evict *vt* dēicere, dētrūdere.
eviction *n* dēiectiō *f*.
evidence *n* testimōnium *nt*, indicium *nt*; (*person*) testis *m/f*; (*proof*) argūmentum *nt*; **on the** ~ **of** fidē (*gen*); **collect** ~ **against** inquīrere in (*acc*); **turn King's** ~ indicium profitērī.
evident *adj* manifestus, ēvidēns, clārus; **it is** ~ appāret.
evidently *adv* manifestō, clārē.
evil *adj* malus, improbus, scelerātus.
evildoer *n* scelerātus *m*, maleficus *m*.
evil eye *n* fascinum *nt*, malum *nt*, improbitās *f*.
evil-minded *adj* malevolus.
evince *vt* praestāre.
evoke *vt* ēvocāre, ēlicere.
evolution *n* seriēs *f*, prōgressus *m*; (*MIL*) dēcursus *m*, dēcursiō *f*.
evolve *vt* explicāre, ēvolvere ♦ *vi* crēscere.
ewe *n* ovis *f*.
ewer *n* hydria *f*.
exacerbate *vt* exacerbāre, exasperāre.

exact vt exigere ♦ adj accūrātus; (person) dīligēns; (number) exāctus.
exaction n exāctiō f.
exactly adv accūrātē; (reply) ita prōrsus; ~ as perinde que.
exactness n cūra f, dīligentia f.
exaggerate vt augēre, in māius extollere.
exalt vt efferre, extollere; laudāre.
exaltation n ēlātiō f.
examination n inquīsītiō f, scrūtātiō f; (of witness) interrogātiō f; (test) probātiō f.
examine vt investīgāre, scrūtārī; īnspicere; (witness) interrogāre; (case) quaerere dē (abl); (candidate) probāre.
examiner n scrūtātor m.
example n exemplum nt, documentum nt; for ~ exemplī grātiā; **make an ~ of** animadvertere in (acc); **I am an ~** exemplō sum.
exasperate vt exacerbāre, inrītāre.
exasperation n inrītātiō f.
excavate vt fodere.
excavation n fossiō f.
excavator n fossor m.
exceed vt excēdere, superāre.
exceedingly adv nimis, valdē, nimium quantum.
excel vt praestāre (dat), exsuperāre ♦ vi excellere.
excellence n praestantia f, virtūs f.
excellent adj ēgregius, praestāns, optimus.
excellently adv ēgregiē, praeclārē.
except vt excipere ♦ prep praeter (acc) ♦ adv nisī ♦ conj praeterquam, nisī quod.
exception n exceptiō f; **make an ~ of** excipere; **take ~ to** gravārī quod; **with the ~ of** praeter (acc).
exceptional adj ēgregius, eximius.
exceptionally adv ēgregiē, eximiē.
excerpt vt excerpere ♦ n excerptum n.
excess n immoderātiō f, intemperantia f ♦ adj supervacāneus; **be in ~** superesse.
excessive adj immoderātus, immodestus, nimius.
excessively adv immodicē, nimis.
exchange vt mūtāre, permūtāre ♦ n permūtātiō f; (of currencies) collybus m.
exchequer n aerārium nt; (emperor's) fiscus m.
excise n vectīgālia ntpl ♦ vt excīdere.
excision n excīsiō f.
excitable adj mōbilis.
excite vt excitāre, concitāre; (to action) incitāre, incendere; (to hope) ērigere; exacuere; (emotion) movēre, commovēre.
excitement n commōtiō f.
exclaim vt exclāmāre; ~ **against** adclāmāre (dat).
exclamation n clāmor m, exclāmātiō f.
exclude vt exclūdere.
exclusion n exclūsiō f.
exclusive adj proprius.
exclusively adv sōlum.
excogitate vt excōgitāre.
excrescence n tūber nt.

excruciating adj acerbissimus.
exculpate vt pūrgāre, absolvere.
excursion n iter nt; (MIL) excursiō f.
excuse n excūsātiō f; (false) speciēs f ♦ vt excūsāre, ignōscere (dat); (something due) remittere; **plead in ~** excūsāre; **put forward as an ~** praetendere.
execrable adj dētestābilis, sacer, nefārius.
execrate vt dētestārī, exsecrārī.
execration n dētestātiō f, exsecrātiō f.
execute vt efficere, patrāre, exsequī; suppliciō afficere; (behead) secūrī percutere.
execution n effectus m; (penalty) supplicium nt, mors f.
executioner n carnifex m.
exemplar n exemplum nt.
exempt adj immūnis, līber ♦ vt līberāre.
exemption n (from tax) immūnitās f; (from service) vacātiō f.
exercise n exercitātiō f, ūsus m; (school) dictāta ntpl ♦ vt exercēre, ūtī (abl); (mind) acuere.
exert vt extendere, intendere, ūtī (abl); ~ **oneself** mōlīrī, ēnītī, sē intendere.
exertion n mōlīmentum nt; (mind) intentiō f.
exhalation n exhālātiō f, vapor m.
exhale vt exhālāre, exspīrāre.
exhaust vt exhaurīre; (tire) dēfatīgāre, cōnficere.
exhaustion n dēfatīgātiō f.
exhaustive adj plēnus.
exhibit vt exhibēre, ostendere, expōnere; (on stage) ēdere.
exhibition n expositiō f, ostentātiō f.
exhilarate vt exhilarāre.
exhort vt hortārī, cohortārī.
exhortation n hortātiō f, hortāmen nt.
exhume vt ēruere.
exigency n necessitās f.
exile n exsilium nt, fuga f; (temporary) relēgātiō f; (person) exsul m; **live in ~** exsulāre ♦ vt in exsilium pellere, dēportāre; (temporarily) relēgāre.
exist vi esse.
existence n vīta f.
exit n exitus m, ēgressus m.
exodus n discessus m.
exonerate vt absolvere.
exorbitant adj nimius, immoderātus.
exotic adj peregrīnus.
expand vt extendere, dīlātāre.
expanse n spatium nt, lātitūdō f.
expatiate vi: ~ **upon** amplificāre.
expatriate vt extermināre ♦ n extorris m.
expect vt exspectāre, spērāre.
expectancy, expectation n spēs f, exspectātiō f; opīniō f.
expediency n ūtile nt, ūtilitās f.
expedient adj ūtilis, commodus; **it is ~** expedit ♦ n modus m, ratiō f.
expediently adv commodē.
expedite vt mātūrāre.

expedition n (*MIL*) expedītiō f.
expeditious adj prōmptus, celer.
expeditiously adv celeriter.
expel vt pellere, expellere, ēicere.
expend vt impendere, expendere.
expenditure n impēnsae fpl, sūmptus m.
expense n impēnsae fpl, impendia ntpl; **at my ~**
meō sūmptū; **at the public ~** dē pūblicō.
expensive adj cārus, pretiōsus; (*furnishings*)
lautus.
expensively adv sūmptuōsē, māgnō pretiō.
experience n ūsus m, experientia f ♦ vt
experīrī, patī.
experienced adj perītus, expertus (+ *gen*).
experiment n experīmentum nt ♦ vi: **~ with**
experīrī.
expert adj perītus, sciēns.
expertly adv perītē, scienter.
expertness n perītia f.
expiate vt expiāre, lūere.
expiatio n (*act*) expiātiō f; (*penalty*) piāculum
nt.
expiatory adj piāculāris.
expiration n (*breath*) exspīrātiō f; (*time*) exitus
m.
expire vi exspīrāre; (*die*) animam agere,
animam efflāre; (*time*) exīre.
expiry n exitus m, fīnis m.
explain vt explicāre, expōnere, explānāre,
interpretārī; (*lucidly*) ēnōdāre; (*in detail*)
ēdisserere.
explanation n explicātiō f, ēnōdātiō f,
interpretātiō f.
explicit adj expressus, apertus.
explicitly adv apertē.
explode vt discutere ♦ vi dīrumpī.
exploit n factum nt, ausum nt; **~s** pl rēs gestae
fpl ♦ vt ūtī (*abl*), fruī (*abl*).
explore vt, vi explōrāre, scrūtārī.
explorer n explōrātor m.
explosion n fragor m.
exponent n interpres m, auctor m.
export vt exportāre ♦ n exportātiō f.
exportation n exportātiō f.
expose vt dētegere, dēnūdāre, patefacere;
(*child*) expōnere; (*to danger*) obicere; (*MIL*)
nūdare; (*for sale*) prōpōnere; **~ o.s.** se
obicere.
exposed adj apertus, obnoxius.
exposition n explicātiō f, interpretātiō f.
expostulate vi expostulāre, conquerī.
expostulation n expostulātiō f.
exposure n (*of child*) expositiō f; (*of guilt*)
dēprehēnsiō f; (*to hardship*) patientia f.
expound vt expōnere, interpretārī.
expounder n interpres m.
express vt (*in words*) exprimere, dēclārāre,
ēloquī; (*in art*) effingere ♦ adj expressus;
(*speed*) celerrimus.
expression n significātiō f; (*word*) vōx f,
verbum nt; (*face*) vultus m.
expressive adj significāns; **~ of** index (*gen*); **be**
very ~ māximam vim habēre.

expressively adv significanter.
expressiveness n vīs f.
expressly adv plānē.
expulsion n expulsiō f, ēiectiō f.
expurgate vt pūrgāre.
exquisite adj ēlegāns, exquīsītus, eximius;
(*judgment*) subtīlis.
exquisitely adv ēleganter, exquīsītē.
ex-service adj ēmeritus.
extant adj superstes; **be ~** exstāre.
extempore adv ex tempore, subitō ♦ adj
extemporālis.
extemporize vi subita dīcere.
extend vt extendere, dīlātāre; (*hand*)
porrigere; (*line*) dūcere; (*office*) prōrogāre;
(*territory*) propāgāre ♦ vi patēre, porrigī; **~**
into incurrere in (*acc*).
extension n prōductiō f, prōlātiō f; (*of office*)
prōrogātiō f; (*of territory*) propāgātiō f; (*extra*)
incrēmentum nt.
extensive adj effūsus, amplus, lātus.
extensively adv lātē.
extent n spatium nt, amplitūdō f; **to a large ~**
māgnā ex parte; **to some ~** aliquā ex parte;
to this ~ hāctenus; **to such an ~** adeō.
extenuate vt levāre, mītigāre.
exterior adj externus, exterior ♦ n speciēs f.
exterminate vt occīdiōne occīdere,
interimere.
extermination n occīdiō f, interneciō f.
external adj externus.
externally adv extrīnsecus.
extinct adj mortuus; (*custom*) obsolētus.
extinction n exstinctiō f, interitus m.
extinguish vt exstinguere, restinguere.
extinguisher n exstinctor m.
extirpate vt exstirpāre, excīdere.
extol vt laudāre, laudibus efferre.
extort vt extorquēre, exprimere.
extortion n (*offence*) rēs repetundae fpl.
extortionate adj inīquus, rapāx.
extra adv īnsuper, praetereā ♦ adj additus.
extract vt excerpere, extrahere ♦ n: **make ~s**
excerpere.
extraction n ēvulsiō f; (*descent*) genus nt.
extraneous adj adventīcius, aliēnus.
extraordinarily adv mīrificē, eximiē.
extraordinary adj extraōrdinārius; (*strange*)
mīrus, novus; (*outstanding*) eximius,
īnsignis.
extravagance n intemperantia f; (*language*)
immoderātiō f, luxuria f; (*spending*) sūmptus
m.
extravagant adj immoderātus, immodestus;
(*spending*) sūmptuōsus, prōdigus.
extreme adj extrēmus, ultimus.
extremely adv valdē, vehementer.
extremity n extrēmum nt, fīnis m; (*distress*)
angustiae fpl; **the ~ of** extrēmus.
extricate vt expedīre, absolvere; **~ oneself**
ēmergere.
exuberance n ūbertās f, luxuria f.
exuberant adj ūber, laetus, luxuriōsus.

exuberantly adv ūbertim.
exude vt exsūdāre ♦ vi mānāre.
exult vi exsultārī, laetārī, gestīre.
exultant adj laetus.
exultantly adv laetē.
exultation n laetitia f.
eye n oculus m; (needle) forāmen nt; cast ~s on oculōs conicere in (acc); have an ~ to spectāre; in your ~s iūdice tē; keep one's ~s on oculōs dēfigere in (abl); lose an ~ alterō oculō capī; see ~ to ~ cōnsentīre; set ~s on cōnspicere; shut one's ~s to cōnīvēre in (abl); take one's ~s off oculōs dēicere ab (abl); up to the ~s in tōtus in (abl); with a cast in the ~ paetus; with sore ~s lippus; sore ~s lippitūdō f; with one's own ~s cōram; with one's ~s open sciēns ♦ vt intuērī, aspicere.
eyeball n pūpula f.
eyebrow n supercilium nt.
eyelash n palpebrae pilus m.
eyelid n palpebra f.
eyeshot n oculōrum coniectus m.
eyesight n aciēs f, oculī mpl.
eyesore n turpe nt; it is an ~ to me oculī meī dolent.
eye tooth n dēns canīnus m.
eyewash n sycophantia f.
eyewitness n arbiter m; be an ~ of interesse (dat).

F, f

fable n fābula f, apologus m.
fabled adj fābulōsus.
fabric n (built) structūra f; (woven) textile nt.
fabricate vt fabricārī; (fig) comminīscī, fingere.
fabricated adj commentīcius.
fabrication n (process) fabricātiō f; (thing) commentum nt.
fabricator n auctor m.
fabulous adj commentīcius, fictus.
fabulously adv incrēdibiliter.
facade n frōns f.
face n faciēs f, ōs nt; (aspect) aspectus m; (impudence) ōs nt; ~ to ~ cōram; how shall I have the ~ to go back? quō ōre redībō?; on the ~ of it ad speciem, prīmō aspectū; put a bold ~ on fortēm sē praebēre; save ~ factum pūrgāre; set one's ~ against adversārī (dat) ♦ vt spectāre ad (acc); (danger) obviam īre (dat), sē oppōnere (dat) ♦ vi (place) spectāre, vergere; ~ about (MIL) signa convertere.
facetious adj facētus, salsus.

facetiously adv facētē, salsē.
facetiousness n facētiae fpl, salēs mpl.
facile adj facilis.
facilitate vt expedīre.
facilities npl opportūnitēs f.
facility n facilitās f.
facing adj adversus ♦ prep exadversus (acc).
facsimile n exemplār nt.
fact n rēs f, vērum nt; as a matter of ~ enimvērō; the ~ that quod; in ~ rē vērā ♦ conj etenim; (climax) dēnique.
faction n factiō f.
factious adj factiōsus, sēditiōsus.
factiously adv sēditiōsē.
factor n prōcūrātor m.
factory n officīna f.
faculty n facultās f, vīs f.
fad n libīdō f.
fade vi dēflōrēscere, marcēscere.
faded adj marcidus.
faggot n sarmentum nt.
fail vi dēficere, dēesse; (fig) cadere, dēcidere; (in business) forō cēdere; ~ to nōn posse; ~ to come nōn venīre ♦ vi dēficere, dēstituere.
failing n culpa f, vitium nt.
failure n (of supply) dēfectiō f; (in action) offēnsiō f; (at election) repulsa f.
fain adv libenter.
faint adj (body) languidus, dēfessus; (impression) hebes, levis; (courage) timidus; (colour) pallidus; be ~ languēre; hebēre ♦ vi intermorī, animō linquī; I feel ~ animō male est.
faint-hearted adj animo dēmissus; timidus.
faintly adv languidē; leviter.
faintness n dēfectiō f, languor m; levitās f.
fair adj (appearance) pulcher, fōrmōsus; (hair) flāvus; (skin) candidus; (weather) serēnus; (wind) secundus; (copy) pūrus; (dealings) aequus; (speech) speciōsus, blandus; (ability) mediocris; (reputation) bonus ♦ n nūndinae fpl; ~ and square sine fūcō ac fallāciīs.
fairly adv iūre, iūstē; mediocriter.
fairness n aequitās f.
fair play n aequum et bonum nt.
fairy n nympha f.
faith n fidēs f; in good ~ bonā fidē.
faithful adj fidēlis, fīdus.
faithfully adv fidēliter.
faithfulness n fidēlitās f.
faithless adj īnfidēlis, īnfīdus, perfidus.
faithlessly adv īnfidēliter.
faithlessness n īnfidēlitās f.
fake vt simulāre.
falchion n falx f.
falcon n falcō m.
fall vi cadere; (gently) lābī; (morally) prōlābī; (dead) concidere, occidere; (fortress) expugnārī, capī; ~ at accidere; ~ away dēficere, dēscīscere; ~ back cēdere; (MIL) pedem referre; ~ between intercidere; ~ behind cessāre; ~ by the way intercidere; ~ down dēcidere, dēlābī; (building) ruere,

corruere; ~ **due** cadere; ~ **flat** sē
prōsternere; (*speech*) frīgēre; ~ **forward**
prōlābī; ~ **foul of** incurrere in (*acc*); ~
headlong sē praecipitāre; ~ **in, into** incidere;
~ **in with** occurrere (*dat*); ~ **off** dēcidere; (*fig*)
dēscīscere; ~ **on** incumbere in (*acc*), incidere
in (*acc*); ~ **out** excidere; (*event*) ēvenīre;
(*hair*) dēfluere; ~ **short of** deesse ad; ~ **to** (*by
lot*) obtingere, obvenīre (*dat*); ~ **to the
ground** (*case*) iacēre; ~ **upon** invādere,
ingruere in (*acc*); (*one's neck*) in collum
invādere ♦ *n* cāsus *m*; (*building*) ruīna *f*;
(*moral*) lāpsus *m*; (*season*) autumnus *m*; **the ~
of Capua** Capua capta.
fallacious *adj* captiōsus, fallāx.
fallaciously *adv* fallāciter.
fallacy *n* captiō *f*.
fallible *adj*: **be ~** errāre solēre.
fallow *adj* (*land*) novālis ♦ *n* novāle *nt*; **lie ~**
cessāre.
false *adj* falsus, fictus.
falsehood *n* falsum *nt*, mendācium *nt*; **tell a ~**
mentīrī.
falsely *adv* falsō.
falsify *vt* vitiāre, interlinere.
falter *vi* (*speech*) haesitāre; (*gait*) titubāre.
faltering *adj* (*speech*) īnfrāctus; (*gait*) titubāns
♦ *n* haesitātiō *f*.
fame *n* fāma *f*, glōria *f*, nōmen *nt*.
famed *adj* illūstris, praeclārus.
familiar *adj* (*friend*) intimus; (*fact*) nōtus;
(*manner*) cōmis; ~ **spirit** genius *m*; **be ~ with**
nōvisse; **be on ~ terms with** familiāriter ūtī
(*abl*).
familiarity *n* ūsus *m*, cōnsuētūdō *f*.
familiarize *vt* adsuēfacere.
familiarly *adv* familiāriter.
family *n* domus *f*, gēns *f* ♦ *adj* domesticus,
familiāris; ~ **property** rēs familiāris *f*.
famine *n* famēs *f*.
famished *adj* famēlicus.
famous *adj* illūstris, praeclārus, nōbilis; **make
~** nōbilitāre; **the ~** ille.
fan *n* flābellum *nt*; (*winnowing*) vannus *f* ♦ *vt*
ventilāre; ~ **the flames of** (*fig*) īnflammāre.
fanatic *n* (*religious*) fānāticus *m*.
fanciful *adj* (*person*) incōnstāns; (*idea*)
commentīcius.
fancy *n* (*faculty*) mēns *f*; (*idea*) opīnātiō *f*;
(*caprice*) libīdō *f*; **take a ~ to** amāre incipere;
~ **oneself** se amāre ♦ *vt* animō fingere,
imāginārī, sibi prōpōnere; ~ **you thinking . . . !**
tē crēdere . . . ! ♦ *adj* dēlicātus.
fancy-free *adj* sēcūrus, vacuus.
fang *n* dēns *m*.
fantastic *adj* commentīcius, mōnstruōsus.
fantasy *n* imāginātiō *f*; (*contemptuous*)
somnium *nt*.
far *adj* longinquus ♦ *adv* longē, procul; (*with
compar*) multō; **be ~ from** longē abesse ab; **be
not ~ from doing** haud multum abest quin
(+*subj*); **by ~** longē; **how ~?** quātenus?,
quoūsque?; **so ~** hāctenus, eātenus; (*limited*)

quādam tenus; **thus ~** hāctenus; ~ **and wide**
lātē; ~ **be it from me to say** equidem dīcere
nōlim; ~ **from thinking . . .** I adeō nōn crēdō . . .
ut; **as ~ as** *prep* tenus (*abl*) ♦ *adv* ūsque ♦ *conj*
quātenus; (*know*) quod.
farce *n* mīmus *m*.
farcical *adj* rīdiculus.
fare *vi* sē habēre, agere ♦ *n* vectūra *f*; (*boat*)
naulum *nt*; (*food*) cibus *m*.
farewell *interj* valē, valēte; **say ~ to** valēre
iubēre.
far-fetched *adj* quaesītus, arcessītus, altē
repetītus.
farm *n* fundus *m*, praedium *nt* ♦ *vt* (*soil*) colere;
(*taxes*) redimere; ~ **out** locāre.
farmer *n* agricola *m*; (*of taxes*) pūblicānus *m*.
farming *n* agrīcultūra *f*.
farrow *vt* parere ♦ *n* fētus *m*.
far-sighted *adj* prōvidus, prūdēns.
farther *adv* longius, ultrā ♦ *adj* ulterior.
farthest *adj* ultimus, extrēmus ♦ *adv*
longissimē.
fasces *n* fascēs *mpl*.
fascinate *vt* dēlēnīre, capere.
fascination *n* dulcēdō *f*, dēlēnīmenta *ntpl*,
lēnōcinia *ntpl*.
fashion *n* mōs *m*, ūsus *m*; (*manner*) modus *m*,
ratiō *f*; (*shape*) fōrma *f* ♦ *vt* fingere, fōrmāre;
after the ~ of rītū (*gen*); **come into ~** in
mōrem venīre; **go out of ~** obsolēscere.
fashionable *adj* ēlegāns; **it is ~** mōris est.
fashionably *adv* ēleganter.
fast *adj* (*firm*) firmus; (*quick*) celer; **make ~**
dēligāre ♦ *adv* firmē; celeriter; **be ~ asleep**
artē dormīre ♦ *vi* iēiūnus esse, cibō
abstinēre ♦ *n* iēiūnium *nt*.
fasten *vt* fīgere, ligāre; ~ **down** dēfīgere; ~ **on**
inligāre; ~ **to** adligāre; ~ **together** conligāre,
cōnfīgere.
fastening *n* iūnctūra *f*.
fastidious *adj* dēlicātus, ēlegāns.
fastidiously *adv* fastīdiōsē.
fastidiousness *n* fastīdium *nt*.
fasting *n* iēiūnium *nt*, inedia *f* ♦ *adj* iēiūnus.
fastness *n* arx *f*, castellum *nt*.
fat *adj* pinguis, opīmus, obēsus; **grow ~**
pinguēscere ♦ *n* adeps *m/f*.
fatal *adj* (*deadly*) fūnestus, exitiābilis; (*fated*)
fātālis.
fatality *n* fātum *nt*, cāsus *m*.
fatally *adv*: **be ~ wounded** vulnere perīre.
fate *n* fātum *nt*, fortūna *f*, sors *f*.
fated *adj* fātālis.
fateful *adj* fātālis; fūnestus.
Fates *npl* (*goddesses*) Parcae *fpl*.
father *n* pater *m*; (*fig*) auctor *m* ♦ *vt* gignere; ~
upon addīcere, tribuere.
father-in-law *n* socer *m*.
fatherland *n* patria *f*.
fatherless *adj* orbus.
fatherly *adj* paternus.
fathom *n* sex pedēs *mpl* ♦ *vt* (*fig*) exputāre.
fathomless *adj* profundus.

fatigue r. fatīgātio f, dēfatīgātiō f ♦ vt fatīgāre, dēfatīgāre.
fatness n pinguitūdō f.
fatten vt sagīnāre.
fatty adj pinguis.
fatuity n īnsulsitās f, ineptiae fpl.
fatuous adj fatuus, īnsulsus, ineptus.
fault n culpa f, vitium nt; (written) mendum nt; **count as a ~** vitiō vertere; **find ~ with** incūsāre; **it is not your ~ that ...** nōn per tē stat quōminus (subj).
faultily adv vitiōsē, mendōsē.
faultiness n vitium nt.
faultless adj ēmendātus, integer.
faultlessly adv ēmendātē.
faulty adj vitiōsus, mendōsus.
faun n faunus m.
fauna n animālia ntpl.
favour n grātia f, favor m; (done) beneficium nt; **win ~ with** grātiam inīre apud; **by your ~** bonā veniā tuā ♦ vt favēre (dat), indulgēre (dat).
favourable adj faustus, prosperus, secundus.
favourably adv faustē, fēlīciter, benignē.
favourite adj dīlectus, grātissimus ♦ r dēliciae fpl.
favouritism n indulgentia f, studium nt.
fawn n hinnuleus m ♦ adj (colour) gilvus ♦ vi: **~ upon** adūlārī.
fawning adj blandus ♦ n adūlātiō f.
fear n timor m, metus m, formīdō f ♦ vt timēre, metuere, formīdāre, verērī; **fearing that** veritus ne (+ imperf subj).
fearful adj timidus; horrendus, terribilis, formīdolōsus.
fearfully cdv timidē; formīdolōsē.
fearless adj impavidus, intrepidus.
fearlessly adv impavidē, intrepidē.
fearlessness n fīdentia f, audācia f.
fearsome adj formīdolōsus.
feasible adj: **it is ~** fierī potest.
feast n epulae fpl; (private) convīvium n ; (public) epulum nt; (religious) daps f; (festival) festus diēs m ♦ vi epulārī, convīvārī; (fig) pāscī ♦ vt: **~ one's eyes on** oculōs pāscere (abl).
feat n factum nt, facinus nt.
feather n penna f; (downy) plūma f; **birds of a ~ flock together** parēs cum paribus facillimē congregantur.
feathered adj pennātus.
feathery adj plūmeus.
feature n līneāmentum nt; (fig) propri.m nt.
February n mēnsis Februārius m; **of ~** Februārius.
federal adj sociālis, foederātus.
federate vi societātem facere.
federated adj foederātus.
federation n societās f, foederātae cīvitātēs fpl.
fee n honōs m, mercēs f.
feeble adj imbēcillus, īnfirmus, dēbilis.
feebleness n imbēcillitās f, īnfirmitās f.
feebly adv īnfirmē.

feed vt alere, pāscere ♦ vi pāscī; **~ on** vescī (abl) ♦ n pābulum nt.
feel vt sentīre; (with hand) tractāre, tangere; (emotion) capere, adficī (abl); (opinion) cēnsēre, sentīre; **~ one's way** pedetemptim prōgredī ♦ vi sentīre; **I ~ glad** gaudeō; **~ sure** pro certō habēre.
feeling n sēnsus m, tāctus m; (mind) animus m, adfectus m; (pity) misericordia f; **good ~** voluntās f; **bad ~** invidia f.
feign vt simulāre, fingere.
feignedly adv simulātē, fictē.
feint n simulātiō f.
felicitate vt grātulārī (dat).
felicitation n grātulātiō f.
felicitous adj fēlīx, aptus.
felicity n fēlīcitās f.
feline adj fēlīnus.
fell vt (tree) succīdere; (enemy) sternere, caedere ♦ adj dīrus, crūdēlis, atrōx ♦ n mōns m; (skin) pellis f.
fellow n socius m, aequālis m; (contemptuous) homō m.
fellow citizen n cīvis m/f.
fellow countryman n cīvis m/f, populāris m/f.
fellow feeling n misericordia f.
fellowship n societās f, sodālitās f.
fellow slave n cōnservus m;
fellow soldier n commīlitō m.
fellow student n condiscipulus m.
felon n nocēns m.
felonious adj scelestus, scelerātus.
felony n scelus nt, noxa f.
felt n coāctum nt.
female adj muliebris ♦ n fēmina f.
feminine adj muliebris.
fen n palūs f.
fence n saepēs f; **sit on the ~** quiēscere, medium sē gerere ♦ vt saepīre; **~ off** intersaepīre ♦ vi bātuere, rudibus lūdere.
fencing n rudium lūdus m; **~ master** lānista m.
fend vt arcēre ♦ vi prōvidēre.
fennel n ferula f.
fenny adj palūster.
ferment n fermentum nt; (fig) aestus m ♦ vt fermentāre; (fig) excitāre, accendere ♦ vi fervēre.
fermentation n fervor m.
fern n filix f.
ferocious adj ferōx, saevus, truculentus.
ferociously adv truculentē.
ferocity n ferōcitās f, saevitia f.
ferret n viverra m ♦ vt: **~ out** rīmārī, ēruere.
ferry n trāiectus m; (boat) cymba f, pontō m ♦ vt trānsvehere.
ferryman n portitor m.
fertile adj fertīlis, fēcundus.
fertility n fertīlitās f, fēcunditās f.
fertilize vt fēcundāre, laetificāre.
fervent adj fervidus, ārdēns.
fervently adv ārdenter.
fervid adj fervidus.
fervour n ārdor m, fervor m.

festal _adj_ festus.
fester _vi_ exulcerārī.
festival _n_ diēs festus _m_, sollemne _nt_.
festive _adj_ (_time_) festus; (_person_) festīvus.
festivity _n_ hilaritās _f_; (_event_) sollemne _nt_.
festoon _n_ sertum _nt_ ♦ _vt_ corōnāre.
fetch _vt_ arcessere, addūcere; (_price_) vēnīre (_gen_); ~ **out** dēprōmere; ~ **water** aquārī.
fetching _adj_ lepidus, blandus.
fetid _adj_ foetidus, pūtidus.
fetter _n_ compēs _f_, vinculum _nt_ ♦ _vt_ compedēs inicere (_dat_), vincīre; (_fig_) impedīre.
fettle _n_ habitus _m_, animus _m_.
feud _n_ simultās _f_, inimīcitia _f_.
fever _n_ febris _f_.
feverish _adj_ febrīculōsus; (_fig_) sollicitus.
few _adj_ paucī; **very** ~ perpaucī; **how ~?** quotus quisque?
fewness _n_ paucitās _f_.
fiancé _n_ spōnsus _m_.
fiasco _n_ calamitās _f_; **be a** ~ frīgēre.
fiat _n_ ēdictum _nt_.
fibre _n_ fibra _f_.
fickle _adj_ incōnstāns, levis, mōbilis.
fickleness _n_ incōnstantia _f_, levitās _f_, mōbilitās _f_.
fiction _n_ fābula _f_, commentum _nt_.
fictitious _adj_ fictus, falsus, commentīcius; (_character_) persōnātus.
fictitiously _adv_ fictē.
fidelity _n_ fidēlitās _f_, fidēs _f_.
fidget _vi_ sollicitārī.
field _n_ ager _m_; (_ploughed_) arvum _nt_; (_of grain_) seges _f_; (_MIL_) campus _m_, aciēs _f_; (_scope_) campus _m_, locus _m_; **in the** ~ (_MIL_) mīlitiae; **hold the** ~ vincere, praevalēre; ~ **of vision** cōnspectus _m_.
fiend _n_ diabolus _m_.
fiendish _adj_ nefārius, improbus.
fierce _adj_ saevus, ācer, atrōx; (_look_) torvus.
fiercely _adv_ ācriter, atrōciter, saevē.
fierceness _n_ saevitia _f_, atrōcitās _f_.
fieriness _n_ ārdor _m_, fervor _m_.
fiery _adj_ igneus, flammeus; (_fig_) ārdēns, fervidus.
fife _n_ tībia _f_.
fifteen _num_ quīndecim; ~ **each** quīndēnī; ~ **times** quīndeciēns.
fifteenth _adj_ quīntus decimus.
fifth _adj_ quīntus ♦ _n_ quīnta pars _f_.
fiftieth _adj_ quīnquāgēsimus.
fifty _num_ quīnquāgintā.
fig _n_ fīcus _f_; (_tree_) fīcus _f_; **of** ~ fīculnus; **not care a** ~ **for** floccī nōn facere.
fight _n_ pugna _f_, proelium _nt_ ♦ _vi_ pugnāre, dīmicāre; ~ **it out** dēcernere, dēcertāre; ~ **to the end** dēpugnāre ♦ _vt_ (_battle_) committere; (_enemy_) pugnāre cum (_abl_).
fighter _n_ pugnātor _m_.
fighting _n_ dīmicātiō _f_.
figment _n_ commentum _nt_.
figurative _adj_ trānslātus; **in** ~ **language** trānslātīs per similitūdinem verbīs; **use ~ly**

trānsferre.
figure _n_ figūra _f_, fōrma _f_; (_in art_) signum _nt_; (_of speech_) figūra _f_, trānslātiō _f_; (_pl, on pottery_) sigilla _ntpl_ ♦ _vt_ figūrāre, fōrmāre; (_art_) fingere, effingere; ~ **to oneself** sibi prōpōnere.
figured _adj_ sigillātus.
figurehead _n_ (_of ship_) īnsigne _nt_.
filament _n_ fibra _f_.
filch _vt_ fūrārī, surripere.
file _n_ (_tool_) līma _f_; (_line_) ōrdō _m_, agmen _nt_; (_of papers_) fasciculus _m_; ~**s** _pl_ tabulae _fpl_; **in single** ~ simplicī ōrdine; **the rank and** ~ gregāriī mīlitēs ♦ _vt_ līmāre.
filial _adj_ pius.
filigree _n_ ciatrēta _ntpl_.
fill _vt_ implēre, explēre, complēre; (_office_) fungī (_abl_); ~ **up** supplēre.
fillet _n_ īnfula _f_, vitta _f_ ♦ _vt_ (_fish_) exossāre.
fillip _n_ stimulus _m_.
filly _n_ equula _f_.
film _n_ membrāna _f_.
filter _n_ cōlum _nt_ ♦ _vt_ dēliquāre ♦ _vi_ percōlārī.
filth _n_ sordēs _f_, caenum _nt_.
filthily _adv_ foedē, inquinātē.
filthiness _n_ foeditās _f_, impūritās _f_.
filthy _adj_ foedus, impūrus; (_speech_) inquinātus.
fin _n_ pinna _f_.
final _adj_ ultimus, postrēmus, extrēmus.
finally _adv_ dēnique, tandem, postrēmō.
finance _n_ rēs nummāria _f_; (_state_) vectīgālia _ntpl_.
financial _adj_ aerārius.
financier _n_ faenerātor _m_.
finch _n_ fringilla _f_.
find _vt_ invenīre, reperīre; (_supplies_) parāre; (_verdict_) iūdicāre; (_pleasure_) capere; ~ **fault with** incūsāre; ~ **guilty** damnāre; ~ **out** comperīre, cognōscere.
finder _n_ inventor _m_.
finding _n_ iūdicium _nt_, sententia _f_.
fine _n_ (_law_) multa _f_, damnum _nt_; **in** ~ dēnique ♦ _vt_ multāre ♦ _adj_ (_thin_) tenuis, subtīlis; (_refined_) ēlegāns, mundus, decōrus; (_beautiful_) pulcher, venustus; (_showy_) speciōsus; (_of weather_) serēnus.
finely _adv_ pulchrē, ēleganter, subtīliter.
fineness _n_ tenuitās _f_; ēlegantia _f_; pulchritūdō _f_; speciēs _f_; serēnitās _f_.
finery _n_ ōrnātus _m_, munditiae _fpl_.
finesse _n_ astūtia _f_, ars _f_, argūtiae _fpl_.
finger _n_ digitus _m_; **a ~'s breadth** trānsversus digitus; **not lift a** ~ (_in effort_) nē manum quidem vertere ♦ _vt_ pertractāre.
fingertips _npl_ extrēmī digitī.
finish _n_ fīnis _m_; (_art_) perfectiō _f_ ♦ _vt_ fīnīre, perficere, cōnficere; (_with art_) perficere, expolīre ♦ _vi_ dēsinere; ~ **off** transigere, peragere, absolvere.
finishing post _n_ mēta _f_.
finishing touch _n_ manus extrēma.
finite _adj_ circumscrīptus.

fir n abiēs f; **of ~** abiēgnus.
fire n ignis m; (conflagration) incendium nt; (in hearth) focus m; (fig) ārdor m, calor m, impetus m; **be on ~** ārdēre, flagrāre catch ~ flammam concipere, ignem comprehendere; **set on ~** accendere, incendere ♦ vt incendere; (fig) īnflammāre; (missile) iaculārī.
firebrand n fax f.
fire brigade n vigilēs mpl.
fireplace n focus m.
fireside n focus m.
firewood n lignum nt.
firm n societās f ♦ adj firmus, stabilis; (mind) cōnstāns; **stand ~** perstāre.
firmament n caelum nt.
firmly adv firmē, cōnstanter.
firmness n firmitās f, firmitūdō f; cōnstantia f.
first adj prīmus, prīnceps; (of two) prior ♦ adv prīmum; **at ~** prīmō, prīncipiō; **at ~ hand** ipse, ab ipsō; **come in ~** vincere; **give ~ aid to** ad tempus medērī (dat); **I was the ~ to see** prīmus vīdī.
first-class adj classicus.
first fruits npl prīmitiae fpl.
firstly adv prīmum.
first-rate adj eximius, lūculentus.
firth n aestuārium nt, fretum nt.
fiscal adj vectīgālis, aerārius.
fish n piscis m ♦ vi piscārī; (fig) expiscārī.
fisher, fisherman n piscātor m.
fishing n piscātus m ♦ adj piscātōrius.
fishing-rod n harundō f.
fish market n forum piscārium nt.
fishmonger n piscārius m.
fish pond n piscīna f.
fissile adj fissilis.
fissure n rīma f.
fist n pugnus m.
fit n (MED) convulsiō f; (of anger, illness) impetus m; **by ~s and starts** temerē, carptim ♦ vt aptāre, accommodāre; (dress) sedēre (dat); ~ **out** armāre, īnstruere ♦ adj aptus, idōneus, dignus; **I see ~ to** mihi vidētur; ~ **for** aptus ad (+ acc).
fitful adj dubius, incōnstāns.
fitfully adv incōnstanter.
fitly adv dignē, aptē.
fitness n convenientia f.
fitting n adparātus m, īnstrūmentum nt ♦ adj idōneus, dignus; **it is ~** convenit, decet.
fittingly adv dignē, convenienter.
five num quīnque; ~ **each** quīnī; ~ **times** quīnquiēns; ~ **years** quīnquennium nt lūstrum nt; ~ **sixths** quīnque partēs.
five hundred num quīngentī; ~ **each** quīngēnī; ~ **times** quīngentiēns.
five hundredth adj quīngentēsimus.
fix vt fīgere; (time) dīcere, cōnstituere; (decision) statuere ♦ n angustiae fpl; **put in a ~** dēprehendere.
fixed adj fixus; (attention) intentus; (decision) certus; (star) inerrāns; **be firmly ~ in** īnsidēre

(dat).
fixedly adv intentē.
fixity n stabilitās f; (of purpose) cōnstantia f.
fixtures npl adfīxa ntpl.
flabbergast vt obstupefacere.
flabbiness n mollitia f.
flabby adj flaccidus, mollis.
flag n vexillum nt; ~ **officer** praefectus classis m ♦ vi flaccēre, flaccēscere, languēscere.
flagellate vt verberāre.
flagon n lagoena f.
flagrant adj manifestus; flāgitiōsus.
flagrantly adv flāgitiōsē.
flagship n nāvis imperātōria f.
flail n fūstis m.
flair n iūdicium nt.
flake n squāma f; ~s pl (snow) nix f.
flame n flamma f ♦ vi flagrāre, exārdēscere.
flaming adj flammeus.
flamingo n phoenīcopterus m.
flank n latus nt; cornū nt; **on the ~** ab latere, ad latus ♦ vt latus tegere (gen).
flap n flābellum nt; (dress) lacinia f ♦ vt plaudere (abl).
flare n flamma f, fulgor m ♦ vi exārdēscere, flagrāre.
flash n fulgor m; (lightning) fulgur nt; (time) mōmentum nt ♦ vi fulgēre; (motion) micāre.
flashy adj speciōsus.
flask n ampulla f.
flat adj plānus; (ground) aequus; (on back) supīnus; (on face) prōnus; (music) gravis; (style) āridus, frīgidus; **fall ~** (fig) frīgēre ♦ n (land) plānitiēs f; (sea) vadum nt; (house) tabulātum nt.
flatly adv prōrsus.
flatness n plānitiēs f.
flatten vt aequāre, complānāre.
flatter vt adūlārī (dat), adsentārī (dat), blandīrī (dat).
flatterer n adsentātor m.
flattering adj blandus.
flatteringly adv blandē.
flattery n adūlātiō f, adsentātiō f, blanditiae fpl.
flatulence n īnflātiō f.
flatulent adj īnflātus.
flaunt vt iactāre ♦ vi iactāre, glōriārī.
flaunting n iactātiō f ♦ adj glōriōsus.
flauntingly adv glōriōsē.
flautist n tībīcen m.
flavour n gustātus m, sapor m ♦ vt imbuere, condīre.
flavouring n condītiō f.
flavourless adj īnsulsus.
flaw n vitium nt.
flawless adj ēmendātus.
flax n līnum nt.
flaxen adj flāvus.
flay vt dēglūbere.
flea n pūlex m.
fleck n macula f ♦ vt variāre.
fledged adj pennātus.
flee vi fugere, effugere; (for refuge) cōnfugere.

fleece n vellus nt ♦ vt tondēre; (fig) spoliāre.
fleecy adj lāneus.
fleet n classis f ♦ adj vēlōx, celer.
fleeting adj fugāx.
fleetness n vēlōcitās f, celeritās f.
flesh n cārō f; (fig) corpus nt; **in the ~** vīvus;
   one's own ~ and blood cōnsanguineus; **put
   on ~** pinguēscere.
fleshiness n corpus nt.
fleshliness n libīdō f.
fleshly adj libīdinōsus.
fleshy adj pinguis.
flexibility n lentitia f.
flexible adj flexibilis, lentus.
flicker vi coruscāre.
flickering adj tremulus.
flight n (flying) volātus m; (fleeing) fuga f;
   (steps) scāla f; **put to ~** fugāre, **in fugam
   conicere; take to ~** sē in fugam dare, terga
   vertere.
flightiness n mōbilitās f.
flighty adj mōbilis, incōnstāns.
flimsy adj tenuis, pertenuis.
flinch vi recēdere.
fling vt iacere, conicere; (missile) intorquēre; **~
   away** abicere, prōicere; **~ open** patefacere; **~
   in one's teeth** obicere (dat); **~ to the ground**
   prōsternere ♦ vi sē incitāre ♦ n iactus m.
flint n silex m.
flinty adj siliceus.
flippancy n lascīvia f.
flippant adj lascīvus, protervus.
flippantly adv petulanter.
flirt vi lūdere, lascīvīre ♦ n lascīvus m, lascīva
   f.
flit vi volitāre.
flitch n succīdia f.
float vi innāre, fluitāre; (in air) volitāre; **~
   down** dēfluere.
flock n grex m; (wool) floccus m ♦ vi
   concurrere, congregārī, cōnfluere; **~ in**
   adfluere.
flog vt verberāre, virgīs caedere.
flogging n verbera ntpl.
flood n (deluge) ēluviō f; (river) torrēns m; (tide)
   accessus m; (fig) flūmen nt ♦ vt inundāre.
floodgate n cataracta f.
floor n solum nt; (paved) pavīmentum nt;
   (storey) tabulātum nt; (threshing) ārea f ♦ vt
   contabulāre; **be ~ed** (in argument) iacēre.
flora n herbae fpl.
floral adj flōreus.
florid adj flōridus.
flotilla n classicula f.
flounce vi sē conicere ♦ n īnstita f.
flounder vi volutāre; (in speech) haesitāre.
flour n fārīna f.
flourish vi flōrēre, vigēre ♦ vt vibrāre,
   iactāre ♦ n (RHET) calamistrī mpl; (music)
   clangor m.
flout vt aspernārī, inlūdere (dat).
flow vi fluere, mānāre; (tide) accēdere; **~ back**
   recēdere; **~ between** interfluere; **~ down**

dēfluere; **~ into** īnfluere in (acc); **~ out**
   prōfluere, ēmānāre; **~ past** praeterfluere; **~
   through** permānāre; **~ together** cōnfluere; **~
   towards** adfluere ♦ n flūmen nt, cursus m;
   (tide) accessus m; (words) flūmen nt.
flower n flōs m, flōsculus m ♦ vi flōrēre,
   flōrēscere.
floweret n flōsculus m.
flowery adj flōridus.
flowing adj prōfluēns; **~ with** abundāns (abl).
flowingly adv prōfluenter.
flown adj īnflātus.
fluctuate vi aestuāre, fluctuāre.
fluctuating adj incōnstāns, incertus.
fluctuation n aestus m, dubitātiō f.
fluency n fācundia f, verbōrum cōpia f.
fluent adj disertus, prōfluēns.
fluently adv disertē, prōfluenter.
fluid adj liquidus ♦ n liquor m.
fluidity n liquor m.
fluke n (anchor) dēns m; (luck) fortuītum nt.
flurry n trepidātiō f ♦ vt sollicitāre, turbāre.
flush n rubor m; **in the first ~ of victory** victōriā
   ēlātus ♦ vi ērubēscere ♦ adj (full) abundāns;
   (level) aequus.
fluster n trepidātiō f ♦ vt turbāre, sollicitāre.
flute n tībia f; **play the ~** tībiā canere.
fluted adj striātus.
flutter n tremor m; (fig) trepidātiō f ♦ vi (heart)
   palpitāre; (mind) trepidāre; (bird) volitāre.
fluvial adj fluviātilis.
flux n fluxus m; **be in a state of ~** fluere.
fly n musca f ♦ vi volāre; (flee) fugere; **~ apart**
   dissilīre; **~ at** involāre in (acc); **~ away**
   āvolāre; **~ from** fugere; **~ in the face of**
   obviam īre (dat); **~ out** ēvolāre; **~ to** advolāre
   ad (acc); **~ up** ēvolāre, subvolāre; **let ~ at**
   immittere in (acc).
flying adj volucer, volātilis; (time) fugāx.
foal n equuleus m, equulus m ♦ vt parere.
foam n spūma f ♦ vi spūmāre; (with rage)
   saevīre.
foaming adj spūmeus.
focus vt (mind) intendere.
fodder n pābulum nt.
foe n hostis m; (private) inimīcus m.
fog n cālīgō f, nebula f.
foggy adj cālīginōsus, nebulōsus.
foible n vitium nt.
foil n (metal) lāmina f; (sword) rudis f ♦ vt
   ēlūdere, ad inritum redigere.
foist vt inculcāre, interpōnere.
fold n sinus m; (sheep) ovīle nt ♦ vt plicāre,
   complicāre; (hands) comprimere; (sheep)
   inclūdere; **~ back** replicāre; **~ over** plicāre; **~
   together** complicāre; **~ up** involvere in
   (abl).
folding doors npl valvae fpl.
foliage n frondēs fpl.
folk n hominēs mpl ♦ adj patrius.
follow vt sequī; (calling) facere; (candidate)
   adsectārī; (enemy) īnsequī; (example)
   imitārī; (instructions) pārēre (dat);

(predecessor) succēdere (dat); (road)
pergere; (speaker) intellegere; ~ **closely**
īnsequī; ~ **hard on the heels of** īnsequī,
īnsistere (dat), īnstāre (dat); ~ **out** exsequī; ~
to the grave exsequī; ~ **up** subsequī
īnsistere (dat) ♦ vi (time) īnsequī; (irference)
sequī; **as ~s** ita, in hunc modum.

follower n comes m; (of candidate) adsectātor
m; (of model) imitātor m; (of teacher) audītor
m.

following adj tālis; īnsequēns, proximus,
posterus; **on the ~ day** postrīdiē, postero diē,
proximo diē ♦ n adsectātōrēs mpl.

folly n stultitia f, dēmentia f, īnsipientia f.

foment vt fovēre; (fig) augēre.

fond adj amāns, studiōsus; ineptus; **be ~ of**
amāre.

fondle vt fovēre, mulcēre.

fondly adv amanter; ineptē.

food n cibus m; (fig) pābulum nt.

fool n stultus m, ineptus m; (jester) scurra m;
make a ~ of ludibriō habēre; **play the ~**
dēsipere ♦ vt dēcipere, lūdere; ~ **away**
disperdere ♦ vi dēsipere.

foolery n ineptiae fpl, nūgae fpl.

foolhardy adj temerārius.

foolish adj stultus, ineptus, īnsipiēns.

foolishly adv stultē, ineptē.

foolishness n stultitia f, īnsipientia .

foot n pēs m; (MIL) peditātus m; **a ~ long** pedālis;
on ~ pedes; **set ~ on** īnsistere (dat); **set on ~**
īnstituere; **the ~ of** īmus ♦ vt (bill) so vere.

football n follis m.

footing n locus m, status m; **keep one's ~**
īnsistere; **on an equal ~** ex aequō.

footman n pedisequus m.

footpad n grassātor m.

footpath n sēmita f, trāmes m.

footprint n vestīgium nt.

foot soldier n pedes m.

footstep n vestīgium nt; **follow in the ~s of**
vestīgiīs ingredī (gen).

foppish adj dēlicātus.

for prep (advantage) dat; (duration) acc; (after
noun) gen; (price) abl; (behalf) prō (abl); (cause)
propter (acc), causā (gen); (after neg) prae
(abl); (feelings) erga (acc); (lieu) prō (abl);
(purpose) ad, in (acc); (time fixed) in (acc) ♦
conj namque; nam (1st word), enim (2nd
word); (with pron) quippe quī; ~ **a long time**
diū; ~ **some time** aliquamdiū.

forage n pābulum nt ♦ vi pābulārī, frūmentārī.

forager n pābulātor m, frūmentātor n

foraging n pābulātiō f, frūmentātiō f.

forasmuch as conj quōniam.

foray n incursiō f.

forbear vi parcere (dat), supersedēre infin).

forbearance n venia f, indulgentia f.

forbears n māiōrēs mpl.

forbid vt vetāre (+ acc and infin), interdīcere
(dat and quominus and subj); **Heaven ~!** dī
meliōra!

forbidding adj tristis.

force n vīs f; (band of men) manus m; **by ~ of**
arms vī et armis ♦ vt cōgere, impellere;
(way) rumpere, mōlīrī; (growth) festīnāre; ~
an engagement hostes proeliārī cogere; ~
down dētrūdere; ~ **out** extrūdere, expellere,
exturbāre; ~ **upon** inculcāre; ~ **a way in**
intrōrumpere, inrumpere.

forced adj (march) māgnus; (style) quaesītus; ~
march māgnum iter.

forceful adj validus.

forceps n forceps m/f.

forces npl (MIL) cōpiae fpl.

forcible adj validus; (fig) gravis.

forcibly adv vī, violenter; (fig) graviter.

ford n vadum nt ♦ vt vadō trānsīre.

fore adj prior; **to the ~** praestō ♦ adv: ~ **and aft**
in longitūdinem.

forearm n bracchium nt ♦ vt: **be ~ed**
praecavēre.

forebode vt ōminārī, portendere; prasentīre.

foreboding n praesēnsiō f, ōmen nt.

forecast n praedictiō f ♦ vt praedīcere,
prōvidēre.

forecourt n vestibulum nt.

forefathers n māiōrēs mpl.

forefinger n index m.

foreground n ēminentia ntpl.

forehead n frōns f.

foreign adj peregrīnus, externus; (goods)
adventīcius; ~ **to** aliēnus ab; ~ **ways**
peregrīnitās f.

foreigner n peregrīnus m, advena m.

foreknow vt praenōscere.

foreknowledge n prōvidentia f.

foreland n prōmunturium nt.

foremost adj prīmus, prīnceps.

forenoon n antemerīdiānum tempus nt.

forensic adj forēnsis.

forerunner n praenūntius m.

foresee vt praevidēre.

foreshadow vt praemonēre.

foresight n prōvidentia f.

forest n silva f.

forestall vt occupāre, antevenīre.

forester n silvicola m.

foretaste vt praegustāre

foretell vt praedīcere, vāticinārī.

forethought n prōvidentia f.

forewarn vt praemonēre

foreword n praefātiō f.

forfeit n multa f, damnum nt ♦ vt āmittere,
perdere, multārī (abl), (bail) dēserere.

forfeiture n damnum nt.

forgather vi congregārī, convenīre.

forge n fornāx f ♦ vt fabricārī, excūdere;
(document) subicere; (will) suppōnere;
(signature) imitārī; (money) adulterīnōs
nummōs percutere.

forged adj falsus, adulterīnus, commentīcius.

forger n (of will) subiector m.

forgery n falsum nt, commentum nt.

forget vt oblīvīscī (gen); (thing learnt)
dēdiscere; **be forgotten** memoriā cadere, ex

animō effluere.
forgetful _adj_ immemor; (_by habit_) oblīviōsus.
forgetfulness _n_ oblīviō _f_.
forgive _vt_ ignōscere (_dat_), veniam dare (_dat_).
forgiveness _n_ venia _f_.
forgo _vt_ dīmittere, renūntiāre; (_rights_) dēcēdere dē iūre.
fork _n_ furca _f_; (_small_) furcula _f_; (_road_) trivium _nt_.
forlorn _adj_ inops, dēstitūtus, exspēs.
form _n_ fōrma _f_, figūra _f_; (_of procedure_) fōrmula _f_; (_condition_) vigor _m_; (_etiquette_) mōs _m_; (_seat_) scamnum _nt_; (_school_) schola _f_; (_hare's_) latibulum _nt_ ♦ _vt_ fōrmāre, fingere, efficere; (_MIL_) īnstruere; (_plan_) inīre, capere.
formal _adj_ iūstus; (_rite_) sollemnis.
formality _n_ iūsta _ntpl_, rītus _m_; **as a ~** dicis causā; **with due ~** rītē.
formally _adv_ rītē.
formation _n_ fōrma _f_, figūra _f_; (_process_) cōnfōrmātiō _f_; **in ~** (_MIL_) īnstructus.
former _adj_ prior, prīstinus, vetus; **the ~** ille.
formerly _adv_ anteā, ōlim, quondam.
formidable _adj_ formīdolōsus.
formidably _adv_ formīdolōsē.
formula _n_ fōrmula _f_; (_dictated_) praefātiō _f_.
formulate _vt_ compōnere.
forsake _vt_ dērelinquere, dēstituere, dēserere.
forswear _vt_ pēierāre, abiūrāre.
fort _n_ castellum _nt_.
forth _adv_ forās; (_time_) posthāc.
forthwith _adv_ extemplō, statim, prōtinus.
fortieth _adj_ quadrāgēsimus.
fortification _n_ (_process_) mūnītiō _f_; (_place_) mūnīmentum _nt_, arx _f_.
fortify _vt_ mūnīre, ēmūnīre, commūnīre; (_fig_) cōnfirmāre.
fortitude _n_ fortitūdō _f_.
fortnight _n_ quīndecim diēs _mpl_.
fortnightly _adv_ quīntō decimō quōque diē.
fortress _n_ arx _f_, castellum _nt_.
fortuitous _adj_ fortuītus.
fortuitously _adv_ fortuītō, cāsū.
fortunate _adj_ fēlīx, fortūnātus.
fortunately _adv_ fēlīciter, bene.
fortune _n_ fortūna _f_, fors _f_; (_wealth_) rēs _f_, dīvitiae _fpl_; **good ~** fēlīcitās _f_, secundae rēs _fpl_; **bad ~** adversae rēs _fpl_; **make one's ~** rem facere, rem quaerere; **tell ~s** hariolārī.
fortune-hunter _n_ captātor _m_.
fortune-teller _n_ hariolus _m_, sāga _f_.
forty _num_ quadrāgintā; **~ each** quadrāgēnī; **~ times** quadrāgiēns.
forum _n_ forum _nt_.
forward _adj_ (_person_) protervus, audāx; (_fruit_) praecox ♦ _adv_ porrō, ante; **bring ~** prōferre; **come ~** prōdīre ♦ _vt_ (_letter_) perferre; (_cause_) adiuvāre, favēre (_dat_).
forwardness _n_ audācia _f_, alacritās _f_.
forwards _adv_ porrō, prōrsus; **backwards and ~** rursum prōrsum, hūc illūc.
fosse _n_ fossa _f_.
foster _vt_ alere, nūtrīre; (_fig_) fovēre.

foster child _n_ alumnus _m_, alumna _f_.
foster father _n_ altor _m_, ēducātor _m_.
foster mother _n_ altrīx _f_, nūtrīx _f_.
foul _adj_ foedus; (_speech_) inquinātus; **fall ~ of** inruere in (_acc_).
foully _adv_ foedē, inquinātē.
foul-mouthed _adj_ maledicus.
foulness _n_ foedītās _f_.
found _vt_ condere, fundāre, īnstituere; (_metal_) fundere.
foundation _n_ fundāmenta _ntpl_.
founder _n_ fundātor _m_, conditor _m_ ♦ _vi_ submergī, naufragium facere.
foundling _n_ expositīcia _f_.
fount _n_ fōns _m_.
fountain _n_ fōns _m_.
fountainhead _n_ fōns _m_, orīgō _f_.
four _num_ quattuor (_indecl_); **~ each** quaternī; **~ times** quater; **~ days** quadriduum _nt_; **~ years** quadriennium _nt_.
fourfold _adj_ quadruplex ♦ _adv_ quadrifāriam.
four hundred _num_ quadringentī; **~ each** quadringēnī; **~ times** quadringentiēns.
four hundredth _adj_ quadringentēsimus.
fourteen _num_ quattuordecim; **~ each** quaternī dēnī; **~ times** quater deciēns.
fourteenth _adj_ quartus decimus.
fourth _adj_ quartus ♦ _n_ quadrāns _m_; **three ~s** dōdrāns _m_, trēs partēs _fpl_.
fowl _n_ avis _f_; gallīna _f_.
fowler _n_ auceps _m_.
fox _n_ vulpes _f_; **~'s** vulpīnus.
foxy _adj_ astūtus, vafer.
fracas _n_ rīxa _f_.
fraction _n_ pars _f_.
fractious _adj_ difficilis.
fracture _n_ frāctum os _nt_ ♦ _vt_ frangere.
fragile _adj_ fragilis.
fragility _n_ fragilitās _f_.
fragment _n_ fragmentum _nt_.
fragrance _n_ odor _m_.
fragrant _adj_ suāvis.
fragrantly _adv_ suāviter.
frail _adj_ fragilis, īnfirmus, dēbilis.
frailty _n_ dēbilitās _f_; (_moral_) error _m_.
frame _vt_ fabricārī, fingere, effingere; (_document_) compōnere ♦ _n_ fōrma _f_; (_of mind_) adfectiō _f_, habitus _m_; **in a ~ of mind** animātus.
framer _n_ fabricātor _m_, opifex _m_; (_of law_) lātor _m_.
framework _n_ compāgēs _f_.
franchise _n_ suffrāgium _nt_, cīvitās _f_.
frank _adj_ ingenuus, apertus; (_speech_) līber.
frankincense _n_ tūs _nt_.
frankly _adv_ ingenuē, apertē, līberē.
frankness _n_ ingenuitās _f_; (_speech_) lībertās _f_.
frantic _adj_ furēns, furiōsus, dēlīrus.
frantically _adv_ furenter.
fraternal _adj_ frāternus.
fraternally _adv_ frāternē.
fraternity _n_ frāternitās _f_; (_society_) sodālitās _f_; (_guild_) collēgium _nt_.
fraternize _vi_ amīcitiam iungere.
fratricide _n_ frātricīda _m_; (_act_) frātris

parricīdium *nt.*
fraud *n* fraus *f*, dolus *m*, falsum *nt*; (*criminal*) dolus malus *m*.
fraudulence *n* fraus *f*.
fraudulent *adj* fraudulentus, dolōsus.
fraudulently *adv* dolōsē, dolō malō.
fraught *adj* plēnus.
fray *n* pugna *f*, rīxa *f* ♦ *vt* terere.
freak *n* mōnstrum *nt*; (*caprice*) libīdō *f*
freckle *n* lentīgō *f.*
freckly *adj* lentīginōsus.
free *adj* līber; (*disengaged*) vacuus; (*generous*) līberālis; (*from cost*) grātuītus; (*from duty*) immūnis; (*from encumbrance*) expedītus; **be ~ from** vacāre (*abl*); **I am still ~ to integrum est mihī** (*infin*); **set ~** absolvere, līberāre; (*slave*) manū mittere ♦ *adv* grātīs, grātuītō ♦ *vt* līberāre, expedīre, exsolvere.
freebooter *n* praedō *m.*
freeborn *adj* ingenuus.
freedman *n* lībertus *m.*
freedom *n* lībertās *f*; (*from duty*) immūnitās *f.*
freehold *n* praedium līberum *nt* ♦ *adj* immūnis.
freely *adv* līberē; (*lavishly*) cōpiōsē, largē; (*frankly*) apertē; (*voluntarily*) ultrō, suā sponte.
freeman *n* cīvis *m.*
free will *n* voluntās *f*; **of one's own ~** suā sponte.
freeze *vt* gelāre, glaciāre ♦ *vi* concrēscere.
freezing *adj* gelidus; **it is ~** gelat.
freight *n* vectūra *f*; (*cargo*) onus *nt* ♦ *vt* onerāre.
freighter *n* nāvis onerāria *f.*
frenzied *adj* furēns, furiōsus, fānāticus.
frenzy *n* furor *m*, īnsania *f.*
frequency *n* adsiduitās *f.*
frequent *adj* frequēns, crēber ♦ *vt* frequentāre, commeāre in (*acc*).
frequently *adv* saepe, saepenumerō, frequenter.
fresh *adj* (*new*) recēns, novus; (*vigorous*) integer; (*water*) dulcis; (*wind*) ācer.
freshen *vt* renovāre ♦ *vi* (*wind*) incrēbrēscere.
freshly *adv* recenter.
freshman *n* tīrō *m.*
freshness *n* novitās *f*, viriditās *f.*
fret *vi* maerēre, angī ♦ *vt* sollicitāre.
fretful *adj* mōrōsus, querulus.
fretfulness *n* mōrōsitās *f.*
fretted *adj* laqueātus.
friable *adj* puter.
friction *n* trītus *m.*
friend *n* amīcus *m*, familiāris *m/f*, hospes *m*, sodālis *m*; **make ~s with** sē cōnferre ad amīcitiam (*gen*).
friendless *adj* sine amīcīs.
friendliness *n* cōmitās *f*, officium *nt.*
friendly *adj* cōmis, facilis, benīgnus; **on ~ terms** familiāriter.
friendship *n* amīcitia *f*, familiāritās *f.*

frigate *n* liburna *f.*
fright *n* horror *m*, pavor *m*, terror *m*; **take ~** extimēscere, expavēscere.
frighten *vt* terrēre, exterrēre, perterrēre; **~ away** absterrēre; **~ off** dēterrēre; **~ the life out of** exanimāre.
frightful *adj* horribilis, immānis; (*look*) taeter.
frightfully *adv* foedē.
frigid *adj* frīgidus.
frigidity *n* frīgus *nt.*
frill *n* fimbriae *fpl*; (*RHET*) calamistrī *mpl.*
fringe *n* fimbriae *fpl.*
frisk *vi* lascīvīre, exsultāre.
frisky *adj* lascīvus.
fritter *vt*: **~ away** dissipāre; (*time*) extrahere.
frivolity *n* levitās *f.*
frivolous *adj* levis, inānis.
frivolously *adv* ināniter.
fro *adv*: **to and ~** hūc illūc.
frock *n* stola *f.*
frog *n* rāna *f.*
frolic *n* lūdus *m* ♦ *vi* lūdere, lascīvīre.
frolicsome *adj* lascīvus, hilaris.
from *prep* ab (*abl*), ā (*before consonants*); (*out*) ē, ex (*abl*); (*cause*) propter (*acc*); (*prevention*) quōminus, quīn; **~ all directions** undique.
front *n* frōns *f*; **in ~** ā fronte, adversus; **in ~ of** prō (+ *abl*).
frontier *n* līmes *m*, cōnfīnia *ntpl*; **~s** fīnes *mpl.*
front line *n* prīma aciēs.
frost *n* gelū *nt.*
frostbitten *adj*: **be ~** vī frīgoris ambūrī.
frosty *adj* gelidus, glaciālis.
froth *n* spūma *f* ♦ *vi* spūmās agere.
frothy *adj* spūmeus.
froward *adj* contumāx.
frown *n* frontis contractiō *f* ♦ *vi* frontem contrahere.
frozen *adj* glaciēlis.
fructify *vt* fēcundāre.
frugal *adj* parcus, frūgī.
frugality *n* frūgālitās *f*, parsimōnia *f.*
frugally *adv* parcē, frūgāliter.
fruit *n* frūctus *m* (*tree*) māla *ntpl*; (*berry*) bāca *f*; (*fig*) frūctus *m*; **~s** *pl* (*of earth*) frūgēs *fpl.*
fruiterer *n* pōmārius *m.*
fruitful *adj* fēcundus, frūctuōsus.
fruitfully *adv* ferāciter.
fruitfulness *n* fēcunditās *f*, ūbertās *f.*
fruition *n* frūctus *m.*
fruitless *adj* inūtilis, vānus.
fruitlessly *adv* nēquīquam, frustrā.
fruit tree *n* pōmum *nt.*
frustrate *vt* frustrārī, ad inritum redigere.
frustration *n* frustrātiō *f.*
fry *vt* frīgere.
frying pan *n* sartāgō *f*; **out of the ~ into the fire** incidit in Scyllam quī vult vītāre Charybdim.
fuel *n* fōmes *m.*
fugitive *adj* fugitīvus ♦ *n* fugitīvus *m*, trānsfuga *m*; (*from abroad*) extorris *m.*
fulfil *vt* (*duty*) explēre, implēre; (*promise*)

praestāre; (*order*) exsequī, perficere.
fulfilment *n* absolūtiō *f*.
full *adj* plēnus (*+ abl*), refertus, explētus; (*entire*) integer; (*amount*) solidus; (*brother*) germānus; (*measure*) iūstus; (*meeting*) frequēns; (*style*) cōpiōsus; **at ~ length** porrēctus; **at ~ speed** citātō gradū, citātō equō.
fuller *n* fullō *m*.
full-grown *adj* adultus.
full moon *n* lūna plēna.
fullness *n* (*style*) cōpia *f*; (*time*) mātūritās *f*.
fully *adv* plēnē, penitus, funditus.
fulminate *vi* intonāre.
fulsome *adj* fastīdiōsus, pūtidus.
fumble *vi* haesitāre.
fume *n* fūmus *m*, hālitus *m* ♦ *vi* stomachārī.
fumigate *vt* suffīre.
fun *n* iocus *m*, lūdus *m*; **for ~** animī causā; **make ~ of** inlūdere, dēlūdere, lūdibriō habēre.
function *n* officium *nt*, mūnus *nt*.
fund *n* cōpia *f*.
fundamental *adj* prīmus ♦ *n* prīncipium *nt*, elementum *nt*.
funds *npl* sors *f*, pecūniae *fpl*.
funeral *n* fūnus *nt*, exsequiae *fpl* ♦ *adj* fūnebris.
funeral pile *n* rogus *m*.
funeral pyre *n* rogus *m*.
funeral rites *npl* exsequiae *fpl*, Inferiae *fpl*.
funereal *adj* fūnebria, lūgubris.
funnel *n* Infundibulum *nt*.
funny *adj* ioculāris, rīdiculus.
fur *n* pellis *m*.
furbelow *n* Instita *f*.
furbish *vt* expolīre; **~ up** interpolāre.
Furies *npl* Furiae *fpl*.
furious *adj* saevus, vehemēns, perīrātus.
furiously *adv* furenter, saevē, vehementer.
furl *vt* (*sail*) legere.
furlong *n* stadium *nt*.
furlough *n* commeātus *m*.
furnace *n* fornāx *f*.
furnish *vt* praebēre, suppeditāre; (*equip*) Instruere, ōrnāre.
furniture *n* supellex *f*.
furrow *n* sulcus *m* ♦ *vt* sulcāre.
furry *adj* villōsus.
further *adj* ulterior ♦ *adv* ultrā, porrō; amplius ♦ *vt* adiuvāre, cōnsulere (*dat*).
furtherance *n* prōgressus *m*; (*means*) Instrūmentum *nt*.
furthermore *adv* praetereā, porrō.
furthest *adj* ultimus ♦ *adv* longissimē.
furtive *adj* fūrtīvus, clandestīnus.
furtively *adv* clam, fūrtim.
fury *n* furor *m*, saevitia *f*; īra *f*.
fuse *vt* fundere; (*together*) coniungere.
fusion *n* coniūnctiō *f*.
fuss *n* importūnitās *f*, querimōnia *f* ♦ *vi* conquerī, sollicitārī.
fussy *adj* importūnus, incommodus.
fusty *adj* mūcidus.
futile *adj* inānis, inūtilis, futtilis.

futility *n* vānitās *f*, futtilitās *f*.
future *adj* futūrus, posterus ♦ *n* posterum *nt*, reliquum *nt*; **in ~** posthāc; **for the ~** in posterum.
futurity *n* posterum tempus *nt*, posteritās *f*.

G, g

gabble *vi* garrīre.
gable *n* fastīgium *nt*.
gadfly *n* tabānus *m*.
gag *vt* ōs praeligāre (*dat*), ōs obvolvere (*dat*).
gage *n* pignus *nt*.
gaiety *n* laetitia *f*, hilaritās *f*, festīvitās *f*.
gaily *adv* hilare, festīve.
gain *n* lucrum *nt*, quaestus *m* ♦ *vt* comparāre; adipīscī; (*profit*) lucrārī; (*thing*) parāre, cōnsequī, capere; (*case*) vincere; (*place*) pervenīre ad; (*possession of*) potīrī (*gen*); (*victory*) reportāre; **~ over** conciliāre; **~ ground** incrēbrēscere; **~ possession of** potior (*+ abl*); **~ the upper hand** rem obtinēre.
gainful *adj* quaestuōsus.
gainsay *vt* contrādīcere (*dat*).
gait *n* incessus *m*, ingressiō *f*.
gaiters *n* ocreae *fpl*.
gala *n* diēs festus *m*.
galaxy *n* circulus lacteus *m*.
gale *n* ventus *m*.
gall *n* fel *nt*, bīlis *m* ♦ *vt* ūrere.
gallant *adj* fortis, audāx; (*courteous*) officiōsus.
gallantly *adv* fortiter; officiōsē.
gallantry *n* virtūs *f*; urbānitās *f*.
gall bladder *n* fel *nt*.
gallery *n* porticus *f*.
galley *n* nāvis āctuāria *f*; (*cook's*) culīna *f*.
galling *adj* amārus, mordāx.
gallon *n* congius *m*.
gallop *n* cursus *m*; **at the ~** citātō equō, admissō equō ♦ *vi* admissō equō currere.
gallows *n* Infēlīx arbor *m*, furca *f*.
gallows bird *n* furcifer *m*.
galore *adv* adfatim.
gamble *n* ālea *f* ♦ *vi* āleā lūdere.
gambler *n* āleātor *m*.
gambling *n* ālea *f*.
gambol *n* lūsus *m* ♦ *vi* lūdere, lascīvīre, exsultāre.
game *n* lūdus *m*; (*with dice*) ālea *f*; (*hunt*) praeda *f*; **play the ~** rēctē facere; **public ~s** lūdī *mpl*; **Olympic ~s** Olympia *npl*; **the ~'s up** āctum est ♦ *adj* animōsus.
gamester *n* āleātor *m*.
gammon *n* perna *f*.
gander *n* ānser *m*.

gang n grex m, caterva f.
gangster n grassātor m.
gangway n forus m.
gaol n carcer m.
gaoler n custōs m.
gap n hiātus m, lacūna f.
gape vi hiāre, inhiāre; (opening) dēhiscere.
garb n habitus m, amictus m ♦ vt amicīre.
garbage n quisquiliae fpl.
garden r hortus m; (public) hortī mpl.
gardener n hortulānus m; (ornamenta') topiārius m.
gardening n hortī cultūra f; (ornamertal) topiāria f.
gargle vi gargarissāre.
garish adj speciōsus, fūcātus.
garland n sertum nt, corōna f ♦ vt corōnāre.
garlic n ālium nt.
garment n vestis f, vestīmentum nt.
garnish vt ōrnāre, decorāre.
garret n cēnāculum nt.
garrison n praesidium nt, dēfēnsōrēs mpl ♦ vt praesidiō mūnīre, praesidium collocāre in (abl).
garrotte vt laqueō gulam frangere (dat).
garrulity n garrulitās f.
garrulous adj garrulus, loquāx.
gas n vapor m.
gash n vulnus nt ♦ vt caedere, lacerāre.
gasp n anhēlitus m, singultus m ♦ vi anhēlāre.
gastronomy n gula f.
gate n porta f.
gather vt colligere, cōgere; (fruit) legere; (inference) colligere, conicere ♦ vi congregārī.
gathering n conventus m, coetus m.
gauche adj inconcinnus, illepidus.
gaudily adv splendidē, speciōsē.
gaudy adj speciōsus, fūcātus, lautus.
gauge n modulus m ♦ vt mētīrī.
Gaul n Gallia f; (person) Gallus m.
gaunt adj macer.
gauntlet n manica f.
gauze n Coa ntpl.
gay adj hilaris, festīvus, laetus.
gaze vi intuērī; ~ at intuērī, adspectāre, contemplārī.
gazelle n oryx m.
gazette n ācta diūrna ntpl, ācta pūblica ntpl.
gear n īnstrūmenta ntpl; (ship's) armāmenta ntpl.
gelding n cantērius m.
gelid adj gelidus.
gem n gemma f.
gender n genus nt.
genealogical adj dē stirpe.
genealogical table n stemma nt.
genealogist n geneālogus m.
genealogy n geneālogia f.
general adj generālis, ūniversus; (usual) vulgāris, commūnis; in ~ omnīnō ♦ n dux m, imperātor m; ~'s tent praetorium nt.
generalissimo n imperātor m.

generality n vulgus nt, plērīque mpl.
generalize vi ūnīversē loquī.
generally adv ferē, plērumque; (discuss) īnfīnītē.
generalship n ductus m.
generate vt gignere, generāre.
generation n aetās f, saeculum nt.
generic adj generālis.
generically adv genere.
generosity n līberālitās f, largitās f.
generous adj līberālis, largus, benīgnus.
generously adv līberāliter, largē, benīgnē.
genesis n orīgō f, prīncipium nt.
genial adj cōmis, hilaris.
geniality n cōmitās f, hilaritās f.
genially adv cōmiter, hilare.
genitive n genitīvus m.
genius n (deity) genius m; (talent) ingenium nt, indolēs f; of ~ ingeniōsus.
genre n genus nt.
genteel adj urbānus, polītus.
gentility n urbānitās f, ēlegantia f.
gentle adj (birth) ingenuus; (manner) hūmānus, indulgēns, mītis; (slope) lēnis, mollis; (thing) placidus, lēnis.
gentleman n vir m, ingenuus m, vir honestus m.
gentlemanly adj ingenuus, līberālis, honestus.
gentleness n hūmānitās f, indulgentia f, lēnitās f.
gentlewoman n ingenua f, mulier honesta f.
gently adv lēniter, molliter, placidē.
gentry n ingenuī mpl, optimātēs mpl; (contempt) hominēs mpl.
genuine adj vērus, germānus, sincērus.
genuinely adv germānē, sincērē.
genuineness n fidēs f.
geographical adj geōgraphicus; ~ position situs m.
geography n geōgraphia f.
geometrical adj geōmetricus.
geometry n geōmetria f.
Georgics n Geōrgica ntpl.
germ n germen nt, sēmen nt.
germane adj adfīnis.
germinate vi gemmāre.
gesticulate vi sē iactāre, gestū ūtī.
gesticulation n gestus m.
gesture n gestus m, mōtus m.
get vt adipīscī, nancīscī, parāre; (malady) contrahere; (request) impetrāre; (return) capere; (reward) ferre; ~ sth done cūrāre (with gerundive); ~ sb to do persuādēre (dat), addūcere; ~ by heart ēdiscere; ~ in repōnere; ~ the better of superāre; go and ~ accessere ♦ vi fierī; ~ about (rumour) palam fierī, percrēbrēscere; ~ away effugere; ~ at (intent) spectāre; ~ behind cessāre; ~ off absolvī; ~ on prōficere; ~ out effugere, ēvādere; ~ out of hand lascīvīre; ~ out of the way dē viā dēcēdere; ~ ready parāre; ~ rid of abicere, tollere; ~ to pervenīre ad;

~ to know cognōscere; **~ together**
congregārī; **~ up** exsurgere.
get-up n ōrnātus m.
ghastliness n pallor m.
ghastly adj pallidus; (sight) taeter.
ghost n larva f, īdōlon nt; **~s** pl mānēs mpl; **give
up the ~** animam agere, efflāre.
giant n Gigas m.
gibberish n barbaricus sermō m.
gibbet n furca f.
gibe vi inrīdēre.
giddiness n vertīgō f.
giddy adj vertīginōsus; (fig) levis.
gift n dōnum nt; (small) mūnusculum nt; **~s** pl
(mind) ingenium nt.
gifted adj ingeniōsus.
gig n cisium nt.
gigantic adj ingēns, immānis.
gild vt inaurāre.
gill n (measure) quartārius m; (fish) branchia f.
gilt adj aurātus.
gimlet n terebra f.
gin n pedica f, laqueus m.
ginger n zingiberī nt.
gingerly adv pedetemptim.
giraffe n camēlopardālis f.
gird vt circumdāre; **~ on** accingere; **~ oneself**
cingī; **~ up** succingere.
girder n tignum nt.
girdle n cingulus m ♦ vt cingere.
girl n puella f, virgō f.
girlhood n aetās puellāris f.
girlish adj puellāris.
girth n ambitus m, amplitūdō f.
gist n firmāmentum nt.
give vt dare, dōnāre, tribuere; (thing due)
reddere; **~ away** largīrī; (bride) in
matrimōnium collocāre; (secret) prōdere; **~
back** reddere, restituere; **~ birth (to)** pārēre;
~ in (name) profitērī; **~ off** ēmittere; **~ out**
(orders) ēdere; (sound) ēmittere; **~ thanks**
gratias agere; **~ up** dēdere, trādere; (hope of)
dēspērāre; (rights) dēcēdere dē, renūntiāre;
~ way cēdere; (MIL) inclīnāre ♦ vi labāre; **~ in**
sē victum fatērī; (MIL) manūs dare; **~ out** (fail)
dēficere; (pretend) ferre; **~ up** dēsistere; **~
way** cēdere.
giver n dator m.
glacial adj glaciālis.
glad adj laetus, alacer, hilaris; **be ~** gaudēre.
gladden vt exhilarāre, oblectāre.
glade n saltus m.
gladiator n gladiātor m.
gladiatorial adj gladiātōrius; **present a ~ show**
gladiātōrēs dare.
gladly adv laetē, libenter.
gladness n laetitia f, alacritās f, gaudium nt.
glamorous adj venustus.
glamour n venustās f.
glance n aspectus m ♦ vi oculōs conicere; **~ at**
aspicere; (fig) attingere, perstringere; **~ off**
stringere.

glare n fulgor m ♦ vi fulgēre; **~ at torvīs oculīs
intuērī.**
glaring adj (look) torvus; (fault) manifestus; **be
~** ante pedēs positum esse.
glass n vitrum nt; (mirror) speculum nt.
glassy adj vitreus.
glaze vt vitrō obdūcere.
gleam n fulgor m, lūx f ♦ vi fulgēre, lūcēre.
gleaming adj splendidus, nitidus.
glean vi spīcās legere.
gleaning n spīcilegium nt.
glebe n fundus m.
glee n hilaritās f, gaudium nt.
gleeful adj hilaris, festīvus, laetus.
gleefully adv hilare, laetē.
glen n vallis f.
glib adj prōfluēns, fācundus.
glibly adv prōfluenter.
glide n lāpsus m ♦ vi lābī; **~ away** ēlābī.
glimmer vi sublūcēre ♦ n: **a ~ of hope** spēcula
f.
glimpse n aspectus m ♦ vt cōnspicārī.
glint vi renīdēre.
glisten vi fulgēre, nitēre.
glitter vi micāre.
gloaming n crepusculum nt.
gloat vi: **~ over** inhiāre, animō haurīre, oculōs
pāscere (abl).
globe n globus m, sphaera f; (inhabited) orbis
terrārum m.
globular adj globōsus.
globule n globulus m, pilula f.
gloom n tenebrae fpl; tristitia f.
gloomy adj tenebricōsus; tristis, dēmissus.
glorify vt illūstrāre, extollere, laudāre.
glorious adj illūstris, praeclārus, splendidus.
gloriously adv praeclārē, splendidē.
glory n laus f, glōria f, decus nt ♦ vi glōriārī, sē
iactāre.
gloss n nitor m ♦ vt: **~ over** (fig) dissimulāre.
glossy adj nitidus.
glove n manica f.
glow n (light) lūmen nt; (heat) ārdor m;
(passion) calor m ♦ vi lūcēre, ārdēre, calēre,
candēre.
glowing adj candēns, ārdēns, calidus.
glue n glūten nt ♦ vt glūtināre.
glum adj tristis, maestus.
glut vt explēre, saturāre ♦ n satietās f,
abundantia f.
glutton n gāneō m, helluō m.
gluttonous adj edāx, vorāx, avidus.
gluttony n gula f, edācitās f.
gnarled adj nōdōsus.
gnash vt, vi frendere; **~ one's teeth** dentibus
frendere.
gnat n culex m.
gnaw vt rōdere; **~ away** ērōdere.
gnawing adj mordāx.
go vi īre, vādere; (depart) abīre, discēdere;
(event) ēvādere; (mechanism) movērī; **~
about** incipere, adgredī; **~ after** īnsequī; **~
away** abīre, discēdere; **~ back** redīre,

regredī; ~ **before** anteīre, praeīre; ~ by
praeterīre; (*rule*) sequī, ūtī (*abl*); ~ **down**
dēscendere; (*storm*) cadere; (*star*) occidere;
~ **for** petere; ~ **forward** prōgredī; ~ **in** intrāre,
ingredī; ~ **in for** (*profession*) facere,
exercēre; ~ **off** abīre; ~ **on** pergere; (*event*)
agī; ~ **out** exīre, ēgredī; (*fire*) extinguī; ~ **over**
trānsīre; (*to enemy*) dēscīscere; (*preparation*)
meditarī; (*reading*) legere; (*work done*)
retractāre; ~ **round** circumīre, ambīre; ~
through percurrere; penetrāre; (*suffer*)
perferre; ~ **to** adīre, petere; ~ **up** ascendere;
~ **to the help of** subvenīre (+ *dat*); ~ **to meet**
obviam īre; ~ **with** comitārī; ~ **without**
carēre (*abl*), sē abstinēre (*abl*) ♦ n vīs f,
ācrimōnia f.
goad n stimulus m ♦ vt irrītāre; pungere; (*fig*)
stimulāre.
go-ahead adj impiger.
goal n fīnis m, mēta f.
goat n caper m, capra f.
gobble vt dēvorāre.
go-between n internūntius m, internūntia f;
(*bribery*) sequester m.
goblet n pōculum nt, scyphus m.
god n deus m.
goddess n dea f.
godhead n dīvīnitās f, nūmen nt.
godless adj impius.
godlike adj dīvīnus.
godliness n pietās f, rēligiō f.
godly adj pius.
godsend n quasi caelō dēmissus.
going n itiō f; (*way*) iter nt; (*departure*)
profectiō f, discessus m.
goitre n strūma nt.
gold n aurum m ♦ adj aureus.
golden adj aureus; (*hair*) flāvus.
gold leaf n bractea f.
goldmine n aurāria f.
goldsmith n aurārius m, aurifex m.
good adj bonus, probus; (*fit*) idōneus, aptus;
(*considerable*) magnus; ~ **day!** salvē, salvēte!;
~ **looks** fōrma f, pulchritūdō f; ~ **nature**
facilitās f, cōmitās f ♦ n bonum nt,
commodum nt; **do** ~ **to** prōdesse (*dat*); **make** ~
supplēre, praestāre; **seem** ~ vidērī; ♦ interj
bene.
goodbye interj valē, valēte; **say** ~ **to** valēre
iubēre.
good-for-nothing adj nēquam.
good-humoured adj cōmis.
good-looking adj pulcher.
goodly adj pulcher; (*size*) amplus.
good nature n facilitās f, cōmitās f.
good-natured adj facilis, benīgnus.
benevolus.
goodness n bonitās f; (*character*) virtūs f,
probitās f, pietās f.
goods npl bona ntpl; (*for sale*) merx f.
good-tempered adj mītis, lēnis.
goodwill n benevolentia f, favor m, grātia f.
goose n ānser m/f.

goose flesh n horror m.
gore n cruor m ♦ vt cornibus cōnfodere.
gorge n faucēs fpl, gula f; (GEOG) angustiae fpl ♦
vt: ~ **oneself** sē ingurgitāre.
gorgeous adj lautus, splendidus.
gorgeously adv lautē, splendidē.
gorgeousness n lautitia f.
gormandize vi helluārī.
gory adj cruentus.
gospel n ēvangelium nt.
gossip n (*talk*) sermunculus m, rūmusculus m,
fāma f; (*person*) lingulāca f ♦ vi garrīre.
gouge vt ēruere.
gourd n cucurbita f.
gourmand n helluō m, gāneō m.
gout n podagra f, articulāris morbus m.
gouty adj arthrīticus.
govern vt (*subjects*) regere; (*state*)
administrāre, gubernāre; (*emotion*)
moderārī (*dat*), cohibēre.
governess n ēducātrīx f.
government n gubernātiō f, administrātiō f;
(*men*) magistrātūs mpl.
governor n gubernātor m, moderātor m;
(*province*) prōcōnsul m, prōcūrātor m.
gown n (*men*) toga f; (*women*) stola f.
grab vt adripere, corripere.
grace n grātia f, lepōs m, decor m; (*favour*)
grātia f, venia f; (*of gods*) pāx f; **be in the good**
~**s of** in grātiā esse apud (*acc*); **with a bad** ~
invītus ♦ vt decorāre, ōrnāre.
graceful adj decōrus, venustus, lepidus.
gracefully adv venustē, lepidē.
graceless adj il epidus, impudēns.
gracious adj benīgnus, prōpitius, misericors.
graciously adv benīgnē, līberāliter.
graciousness n benīgnitās f, līberālitās f.
gradation n gradus m.
grade n gradus m.
gradient n clīvus m.
gradual adj lēnis.
gradually adv gradātim, sēnsim, paulātim.
graft n surculus m; (PCL) ambitus m ♦ vt
īnserere.
grafting n īnsitiō f.
grain n frūmentum nt; (*seed*) grānum nt;
against the ~ invītā Minervā.
grammar n grammatica f.
grammarian n grammaticus m.
granary n horreum m.
grand adj (*person*) amplus, illūstris, ēgregius;
(*way of life*) lautus, māgnificus; (*language*)
grandis, sublīmis.
granddaughter n neptis f; **great** ~ prōneptis f.
grandeur n māiestās f, māgnificentia f; (*style*)
granditās f.
grandfather n avus m; **great** ~ proavus m;
great-great-~ abavus m; **of a** ~ avītus.
grandiloquence n māgniloquentia f.
grandiloquent adj grandiloquus, tumidus.
grandiose adj māgnificus.
grandmother n avia f; **great** ~ proavia f.
grandson n nepōs m; **great** ~ prōnepōs m.

grant *vt* dare, concēdere, tribuere; (*admit*) fatērī ♦ *n* concessiō *f*.

grape *n* ūva *f*.

graphic *adj* expressus; **give a ~ account of** ante oculōs ponere, oculīs subicere.

grapnel *n* manus ferrea *f*, harpagō *f*.

grapple *vi* luctārī.⁷

grappling iron *n* manus ferrea *f*.

grasp *vt* prēnsāre, comprehendere; (*with mind*) complectī, adsequī, percipere, intellegere; **~ at** captāre, adpetere ♦ *n* manus *f*, comprehēnsiō *f*; (*mind*) captus *m*.

grasping *adj* avārus, rapāx.

grass *n* herba *f*.

grasshopper *n* gryllus *m*.

grassy *adj* herbōsus; herbidus.

grate *n* focus *m* ♦ *vt* atterere; **~ upon** offendere.

grateful *adj* grātus; **feel ~** grātiam habēre.

gratefully *adv* grātē.

gratification *n* voluptās *f*.

gratify *vt* mōrem gerere (*dat*), mōrigerārī (*dat*), grātificārī (*dat*).

gratifying *adj* iūcundus.

gratis *adv* grātuītō, grātīs.

gratitude *n* grātia *f*; **show ~** grātiam referre.

gratuitous *adj* grātuītus.

gratuitously *adv* grātuītō.

gratuity *n* stips *f*; (*MIL*) dōnātīvum *nt*.

grave *n* sepulchrum *nt* ♦ *adj* gravis, austērus ♦ *vt* scalpere.

gravel *n* glārea *f*.

gravely *adv* graviter, sevērē.

gravitate *vi* vergere.

gravity *n* (*person*) sevēritās *f*, tristitia *f*; (*CIRCS*) gravitās *f*, mōmentum *nt*; (*physics*) nūtus *m*; **by force of ~** nūtū suō.

gray *adj* rāvus; (*hair*) cānus.

graze *vi* pāscī ♦ *vt* (*cattle*) pāscere; (*by touch*) stringere.

grazing *n* pāstus *m*.

grease *n* arvīna *f* ♦ *vt* ungere.

greasy *adj* pinguis, ūnctus.

great *adj* māgnus, grandis, ingēns, amplus; (*fame*) īnsignis, praeclārus; **as ~ as ...** tantus ... quantus; **~ deal** plūrimum; **~ many** plūrimī; **how ~** quantus; **very ~** permāgnus.

greatcoat *n* lacerna *f*.

greatest *adj* māximus.

greatly *adv* multum, māgnopere.

greave *n* ocrea *f*.

greed *n* avāritia *f*.

greedily *adv* avārē, cupidē.

greedy *adj* avārus, cupidus; avidus.

Greek *adj* Graecus.

green *adj* viridis; (*unripe*) crūdus; **be ~** virēre.

greenness *n* viriditās *f*.

greens *n* olus *nt*.

greet *vt* salūtāre.

greeting *n* salūs *f*, salūtātiō *f*.

grey *adj* rāvus; (*hair*) cānus.

greyhound *n* vertagus *m*.

grief *n* dolor *m*, maeror *m*, lūctus *m*; **come to ~** perīre.

grievance *n* querimōnia *f*; iniūria *f*.

grieve *vi* dolēre, maerēre, lūgēre.

grievous *adj* tristis, lūctuōsus; molestus, gravis, acerbus.

grievously *adv* graviter, valdē.

grim *adj* trux, truculentus; atrōx.

grimace *n* ōris dēprāvātiō *f*; **make a ~** ōs dūcere.

grime *n* sordēs *f*, lutum *nt*.

grimy *adj* sordidus, lutulentus.

grin *n* rīsus *m* ♦ *vi* adrīdēre.

grind *vt* contundere; (*corn*) molere; (*blade*) acuere; **~ down** (*fig*) opprimere.

grindstone *n* cōs *f*.

grip *vt* comprehendere, arripere ♦ *n* comprehēnsiō *f*; **come to ~s with** in complexum venīre (*gen*).

gripe *n* tormina *ntpl*.

grisly *adj* horridus, dīrus.

grist *n* (*fig*) ēmolumentum *nt*.

grit *n* harēna *f*.

groan *n* gemitus *m* ♦ *vi* gemere, ingemere.

groin *n* inguen *nt*.

groom *n* agāsō *m*.

groove *n* canālis *m*, stria *f*.

grope *vi* praetentāre.

gross *adj* crassus, pinguis; (*morally*) turpis, foedus.

grossly *adv* foedē, turpiter; (*very*) valdē.

grossness *n* crassitūdō *f*; turpitūdō *f*.

grotto *n* spēlunca *f*, antrum *nt*.

ground *n* (*bottom*) solum *nt*; (*earth*) terra *f*, humus *f*; (*cause*) ratiō *f*, causa *f*; (*sediment*) faex *f*; **on the ~** humī; **on the ~s that** quod (+ *subj*); **to the ~** humum; **gain ~** prōficere; (*rumour*) incrēbrēscere; **lose ~** cēdere; (*MIL*) inclīnāre ♦ *vt* īnstituere ♦ *vi* (*ship*) sīdere.

grounding *n* īnstitūtiō *f*.

groundless *adj* vānus, inānis.

groundlessly *adv* frustrā, temerē.

grounds *n* faex *f*; (*property*) praedium *nt*; (*reason*) causa *f*; **I have good ~ for doing** nōn sine causā faciō, iūstīs dē causīs faciō.

groundwork *n* fundāmentum *nt*.

group *n* globus *m*, circulus *m* ♦ *vt* dispōnere.

grouse *n* (*bird*) tetraō *m*; (*complaint*) querēla *f* ♦ *vi* querī.

grove *n* nemus *nt*, lūcus *m*.

grovel *vi* serpere, sē prōsternere, sē advolvere.

grovelling *adj* humilis, abiectus.

grow *vi* crēscere, glīscere; (*spread*) percrēbrēscere; (*become*) fierī; **~ old** (con)senēscere; **~ up** adolēscere, pūbēscere; **let ~** (*hair*) prōmittere ♦ *vt* (*crops*) colere; (*beard*) dēmittere.

growl *n* fremitus *m* ♦ *vi* fremere.

grown-up *adj* adultus, grandis.

growth *n* incrēmentum *nt*, auctus *m*.

grub *n* vermiculus *m*.

grudge *n* invidia *f* ♦ *vt* invidēre (*dat*); (*thing*) gravārī.

grudgingly *adv* invītus, gravātē.

gruesome adj taeter.
gruff adj acerbus, asper.
grumble vi querī, mussāre ♦ n querēla f.
grumpy adj mōrōsus, querulus.
grunt n grunnītus m ♦ vi grunnīre.
guarantee n (money) spōnsiō f; (promise) fidēs
  f; (person) praes m ♦ vt spondēre, praestāre.
guarantor n spōnsor m.
guard n custōdia f, praesidium nt; (person)
  custōs m; **on** ~ in statiōne; **be on one's** ~
  cavēre; **keep** ~ statiōnem agere; **off one's** ~
  imprūdēns, inopīnāns; **be taken off one's** ~
  dē gradū dēicī ♦ vt custōdīre, dēfendere;
  (keep) cōnservāre; ~ **against** cavēre.
guarded adj cautus.
guardedly adv cautē.
guardhouse n custōdia f.
guardian n custōs m; (of minors) tūtor m.
guardianship n custōdia f, tūtēla f.
guardian spirit n genius m.
gudgeon n gōbius m.
guerdon n praemium nt, mercēs f.
guess n coniectūra f ♦ vt dīvīnāre, conicere.
guest n hospes m, hospita f; (at dinner) convīva
  m; **uninvited** ~ umbra f; ~**'s** hospitālis.
guffaw n cachinnus m ♦ vi cachinnāre.
guidance n moderātiō f; **under the** ~ **of God**
  dūcente deō.
guide n dux m, ductor m; (in policy) auctor m ♦
  vt dūcere; (steer) regere; (control) moderārī.
guild n collēgium nt.
guile n dolus m, fraus f.
guileful adj dolōsus, fraudulentus.
guilefully adv dolosē.
guileless adj simplex, innocēns.
guilelessly adv sine fraude.
guilt n culpa f, scelus nt.
guiltless adj innocēns, īnsōns.
guiltlessly adv integrē.
guilty adj nocēns, sōns; **find** ~ damnāre.
guise n speciēs f.
guitar n fidēs fpl; **play the** ~ fidibus canere.
gulf n sinus m; (chasm) hiātus m.
gull n mergus m ♦ vt dēcipere.
gullet n gula f, guttur nt.
gullible adj crēdulus.
gulp vt dēvorāre, haurīre.
gum n gummī nt; (mouth) gingīva f.
gumption n prūdentia f.
gurgle vi singultāre.
gush vi sē prōfundere, ēmicāre ♦ n
  scatūrīginēs fpl.
gust n flāmen nt, impetus m.
gusto n studium nt.
gusty adj ventōsus.
gut n intestīnum nt ♦ vt exenterāre; (fig)
  extergēre.
gutter n canālis m.
guzzle vi sē ingurgitāre.
gymnasium n gymnasium nt, palaestra f;
  head of a ~ gymnasiarchus m.
gymnastic adj gymnicus; ~**s** pl palaestra f.
gyrate vi volvī.

H, h

habit n mōs m, cōnsuētūdō f; (dress) habitus m,
  vestītus m; **be in the** ~ **of** solēre.
habitable adj habitābilis.
habitation n domus f, domicilium nt; (place)
  sēdēs f.
habitual adj ūsitātus.
habitually adv ex mōre, persaepe.
habituate vt adsuēfacere, īnsuēscere.
hack vt caedere concīdere ♦ n (horse)
  caballus m.
hackneyed adj trītus.
Hades n īnferī mpl.
haft n manubrium nt.
hag n anus f.
haggard adj ferus.
haggle vi altercārī.
hail n grandō f ♦ vi: **it** ~**s** grandinat ♦ vt
  salūtāre, adclāmāre ♦ interj avē, avēte; salvē,
  salvēte; **I** ~ **from Rome** Rōma mihi patria est.
hair n capillus m, crīnis m; (single) pīlus m;
  (animals) sēta f, villus nt; **deviate a** ~**'s**
  breadth from trānsversum digitum
  discēdere ab; **split** ~**s** cavillārī.
hairdresser n tōnsor m.
hairless adj (head) calvus; (body) glaber.
hairpin n crīnāle nt.
hairsplitting adj captiōsus ♦ n cavillātiō f.
hairy adj pilōsus.
halberd n bipennis f.
halcyon n alcēdō f; ~ **days** alcēdōnia ntpl.
hale adj validus, rōbustus ♦ vt trahere, rapere.
half n dīmidium nt, dīmidia pars f ♦ adj
  dīmidius, dīmidiātus; ~ **as much again**
  sesquī; **well begun is** ~ **done** dīmidium factī
  quī coepit habet.
half-asleep adj sēmisomnus.
half-baked adj (fig) rudis.
half-dead adj sēmianimis, sēmivīvus.
half-full adj sēmiplēnus.
half-hearted adj incūriōsus, sōcors.
half-heartedly adv sine studiō.
half-hour n sēmihōra f.
half-moon n lūna dīmidiāta f.
half-open adj sēmiapertus.
half pound n sēlībra f.
half-way adj medius; ~ **up the hill** in mediō
  colle.
half-yearly adj sēmestris.
hall n ātrium nt; (public) exedra f.
hallo interj heus.

hallow *vt* sacrāre.
hallucination *n* error *m*, somnium *nt*.
halo *n* corōna *f*.
halt *vi* īnsistere, cōnsistere ♦ *vt* sistere ♦ *n*: **come to a ~** cōnsistere, agmen cōnstituere ♦ *adj* claudus.
halter *n* capistrum *nt*; (*fig*) laqueus *m*.
halve *vt* bipartīre.
ham *n* perna *f*.
hamlet *n* vīcus *m*.
hammer *n* malleus *m* ♦ *vt* tundere; **~ out** excūdere.
hamper *n* corbis *f* ♦ *vt* impedīre; (*with debt*) obstringere.
hamstring *vt* poplitem succīdere (*dat*).
hand *n* manus *f*; **left ~** laeva *f*, sinistra *f*; **right ~** dextra *f*; **an old ~** veterātor *m*; **at ~** praestō, ad manum; **be at ~** adesse; **at first ~** ipse; **at second ~** ab aliō; **on the one ~ ... on the other** et ... et, quidem ... at; **near at ~** in expedītō, inibī; **the matter in ~** quod nunc īnstat, quae in manibus sunt; **get out of ~** lascīvīre; **have a ~ in** interesse (*dat*); **have one's ~s full** satis agere; **lay ~s on** manum adferre, inicere (*dat*); **live from ~ to mouth** ad hōram vīvere; **pass from ~ to ~** per manūs trādere; **take in ~** suscipere; **~s** *pl* (*workmen*) operae *fpl* ♦ *vt* trādere, porrigere; **~ down** trādere, prōdere; **~ over** dēferre, reddere.
handbill *n* libellus *m*.
handbook *n* ars *f*.
handcuffs *n* manicae *fpl*.
handful *n* manipulus *m*.
handicap *n* impedīmentum *nt*.
handicraft *n* artificium *nt*, ars operōsa *f*.
handily *adv* habiliter.
handiness *n* habilitās *f*; commoditās *f*.
handiwork *n* opus *nt*, manus *f*.
handkerchief *n* sūdārium *nt*.
handle *n* (*cup*) ānsa *f*; (*knife*) manubrium *nt*; (*fig*) ānsa *f*, occāsiō *f* ♦ *vt* tractāre.
handling *n* tractātiō *f*.
handmaid *n* famula *f*.
handsome *adj* fōrmōsus, pulcher; (*gift*) līberālis.
handsomely *adv* pulchrē; līberāliter.
handsomeness *n* pulchritūdō *f*, fōrma *f*.
hand-to-hand *adv*: **fight ~** manum cōnserere, comminus pugnāre.
handwriting *n* manus *f*.
handy *adj* (*to use*) habilis; (*near*) praestō.
hang *vt* suspendere; (*head*) dēmittere; (*wall*) vestīre ♦ *vi* pendēre; **~ back** gravārī, dubitāre; **~ down** dēpendēre; **~ on to** haerēre (*dat*); **~ over** imminēre (*dat*), impendēre (*dat*); **go and be ~ed** abī in malam crucem!
hanger-on *n* cliēns *m/f*, assecla *m/f*.
hanging *n* (*death*) suspendium *nt*; **~s** *pl* aulaea *ntpl* ♦ *adj* pendulus.
hangman *n* carnifex *m*.
hanker *vi*: **~ after** appetere, exoptāre.
hap *n* fors *f*.
haphazard *adj* fortuītus.

hapless *adj* miser, īnfēlīx.
haply *adv* fortasse.
happen *vi* accidere, ēvenīre, contingere; (*become*) fierī; **as usually ~s** ut fit; **~ upon** incidere in (*acc*); **it ~s that** accidit ut (*+subj*).
happily *adv* fēlīciter, beātē, bene.
happiness *n* fēlīcitās *f*.
happy *adj* fēlīx, beātus; laetus; (*in some respect*) fortūnātus.
harangue *n* cōntiō *f* ♦ *vt* cōntiōnārī apud (+ *acc*), hortārī.
harass *vt* vexāre, lacessere, exagitāre, sollicitāre.
harassing *adj* molestus.
harbinger *n* praenūntius *m*.
harbour *n* portus *m* ♦ *vt* recipere.
harbour dues *n* portōria *ntpl*.
hard *adj* dūrus; (*CIRCS*) asper, inīquus; (*task*) difficilis, arduus; **~ of hearing** surdaster; **grow ~** dūrēscere ♦ *adv* sēdulō, valdē; **~ by** prope, iuxtā; **I am ~ put to it to do** aegerrimē faciō.
hard cash *n* praesēns pecūnia *f*.
harden *vt* dūrāre ♦ *vi* dūrēscere; (*fig*) obdūrēscere; **become ~ed** obdūrēscere.
hard-fought *adj* atrōx.
hard-hearted *adj* crūdēlis, dūrus, inhūmānus.
hardihood *n* audācia *f*.
hardily *adv* sevērē.
hardiness *n* rōbur *nt*; dūritia *f*.
hardly *adv* vix, aegrē; (*severely*) dūriter, acerbē; **~ any** nullus ferē.
hardness *n* dūritia *f*; (*fig*) asperitās *f*, inīquitās *f*; (*difficulty*) difficultās *f*; **~ of hearing** surditās *f*.
hard-pressed *adj*: **be ~** labōrāre.
hardship *n* labor *m*, malum *nt*, iniūria *f*.
hard-working *adj* industrius, nāvus, sēdulus.
hardy *adj* dūrus, rōbustus, sevērus.
hare *n* lepus *m*.
hark *interj* auscultā, auscultāte ♦ *vi*: **~ back to** repetere.
harm *n* iniūria *f*, damnum *nt*, malum *nt*, dētrīmentum *nt*; **come to ~** dētrīmentum capere, accipere ♦ *vt* laedere, nocēre (*dat*).
harmful *adj* damnōsus, noxius.
harmfully *adv* male.
harmless *adj* innocēns.
harmlessly *adv* innocenter; (*escape*) salvus, incolumis, inviolātus.
harmonious *adj* cōnsonus, canōrus; (*fig*) concors; (*things*) congruēns.
harmoniously *adv* modulātē; concorditer; convenienter.
harmonize *vi* concinere, cōnsentīre, congruere.
harmony *n* concentus *m*; (*fig*) concordia *f*, cōnsēnsus *m*.
harness *n* arma *ntpl* ♦ *vt* īnfrēnāre, iungere.
harp *n* fidēs *fpl*; **play the ~** fidibus canere ♦ *vi*: **~ on** (*fig*) cantāre, dictitāre; **be always ~ing on the same thing** cantilēnam eandem canere.

harpist n fidicen m, fidicina f.
harpoon n iaculum nt.
harpy n Harpyia f.
harrow n rāstrum nt ♦ vt occāre.
harrower n occātor m.
harrowing adj horrendus.
harry vt vexāre, dīripere.
harsh adj dūrus, acerbus, asper; (person) inclēmēns, sevērus.
harshly adv acerbē, asperē; sevērē.
harshness n acerbitās f, asperitās f; crūdēlitās f.
hart n cervus m.
harvest n messis f ♦ vt metere, dēmetere.
harvester n messor m.
hash n farrāgō f ♦ vt comminuere.
haste n festīnātiō f, properātiō f; in ~ festīnanter; **in hot** ~ incitātus; **make** ~ festīnāre.
hasten vt mātūrāre, adcelerāre ♦ vi festīnāre, properāre, mātūrāre.
hastily adv properē, raptim; temerē, incōnsulte; īrācundē.
hastiness n temeritās f; (temper) īrācundia f.
hasty adj properus, celer; (action) incōnsultus, temerārius; (temper) īrācundus, ācer; **over** ~ praeproperus.
hat n petasus m.
hatch vt exclūdere, parere.
hatchet n dolābra f.
hate n odium nt, invidia f ♦ vt ōdisse.
hated adj: **to be** ~ **(by sb)** odiō esse (+ dat).
hateful adj odiōsus, invīsus.
hatefully adv odiōsē.
hatred n odium nt.
haughtily adv adroganter, superbē, insolenter.
haughtiness n fastus m, adrogantia f, superbia f.
haughty adj adrogāns, superbus, īnsolēns.
haul vt trahere ♦ n bolus m.
haulage n vectūra f.
haulm n culmus m.
haunch n femur nt.
haunt vt frequentāre ♦ n locus m; (animals) lustrum nt.
have vt habēre, tenēre; (get done) cūrāre (gerundive); **I** ~ **a house** est mihī domus; **I** ~ **to go** mihī abeundum est; ~ **it out with** rem dēcernere cum; ~ **on** gerere, gestāre, induī; **I had better go** melius est īre, praestat īre; **I had rather** mālim, māllem.
haven n portus m; (fig) perfugium nt.
havoc n exitium nt, vastātiō f, ruīna f.
hawk n accipiter m ♦ vt (wares) circumferre.
hawker n īnstitor m.
hay n faenum nt; **make** ~ **while the sun shines** forō ūtī.
hazard n perīculum nt, discrīmen nt, ālea f ♦ vt perīclitārī, in āleam dare.
hazardous adj perīculōsus.
haze n nebula f.
hazel n corylus f.
hazy adj nebulōsus; (fig) incertus.

he pron hic, ille, is.
head n caput nt; (person) dux m, prīnceps m; (composition) caput nt; (mind) animus m, ingenium nt; ~ **over heels** cernuus; **off one's** ~ dēmēns; **be at the** ~ **of** dūcere, praeesse (dat); **come to a** ~ caput facere; (fig) in discrīmen addūcī; **give one his** ~ indulgēre (dat), habēnās immittere (dat); **keep one's** ~ praesentī animō ūtī; **lose one's** ~ suī compotem nōn esse; **shake one's** ~ abnuere ♦ vt dūcere, praeesse (dat); ~ **off** intercipere ♦ vi (in a direction) tendere.
headache n capitis dolor m.
headfirst adj praeceps.
heading n caput nt.
headland n prōmunturium nt.
headlong adj praeceps ♦ adv in praeceps; **rush** ~ sē praecipitāre.
headquarters n (MIL) praetōrium nt.
headship n prīncipātus m.
headsman n carnifex m.
headstrong adj impotēns, pervicāx.
headway n prōfectus m.
heady adj incōnsultus; (wine) vehemēns.
heal vt sānāre, medērī (dat) ♦ vi sānēscere; ~ **over** obdūcī.
healer n medicus m.
healing adj salūbris.
health n valētūdō f, salūs f; **state of** ~ valētūdō f; **ill** ~ valētūdō; **be in good** ~ valēre; **drink the** ~ **of** propīnāre (dat).
healthful adj salūbris.
healthiness n sānitās f.
healthy adj sānus, integer; (conditions) salūber.
heap n acervus m, cumulus m; **in** ~**s** acervātim ♦ vt acervāre; ~ **together** congerere; ~ **up** adcumulāre, coacervāre, congerere.
hear vt audīre; (case) cognōscere; ~ **clearly** exaudīre; ~ **in secret** inaudīre.
hearer n audītor m.
hearing n (sense) audītus m; (act) audītiō f; (of case) cognitiō f; **get a** ~ sibī audientiam facere; **hard of** ~ surdaster; **without a** ~ indictā causā.
hearken vi auscultāre.
hearsay n fāma f, rūmor m.
heart n cor nt; (emotion) animus m, pectus nt; (courage) animus m; (interior) viscera ntpl; **by** ~ memoriā, memoriter; **learn by** ~ ēdiscere; **the** ~ **of the matter** rēs ipsa; **lose** ~ animum dēspondēre; **take to** ~ graviter ferre.
heartache n dolor m, angor m.
heartbroken adj animī frāctus, aeger; **be** ~ animō labōrāre.
heartburning n invidia f.
heartfelt adj sincērus.
hearth n focus m; ~ **and home** ārae et focī.
heartily adv vehementer, valdē.
heartiness n studium nt, vigor m.
heartless adj dūrus, inhūmānus, crūdēlis.
heartlessly adv inhūmānē.
heartlessness n inhūmānitās f, crūdēlitās f.
hearty adj studiōsus, vehemēns; (health)

rōbustus; (*feeling*) sincērus.
heat *n* ārdor *m*, calor *m*; (*emotion*) ārdor *m*,
aestus *m*; (*race*) missus *m* ♦ *vt* calefacere,
fervefacere; (*fig*) accendere; **become ~ed**
incalēscere.
heatedly *adv* ferventer, ārdenter.
heath *n* inculta loca *ntpl*.
heathcock *n* attagēn *m*.
heathen *n* pāgānus *m*.
heather *n* erīcē *f*.
heave *vt* tollere; (*missile*) conicere; (*sigh*)
dūcere ♦ *vi* tumēre, fluctuāre.
heaven *n* caelum *nt*, dī *mpl*; ~ **forbid!** dī
meliōra; **from ~** dīvīnitus; **in ~'s name** prō
deum fidem!; **be in seventh ~** digitō caelum
attingere.
heavenly *adj* caelestis, dīvīnus.
heavily *adv* graviter.
heaviness *n* gravitās *f*, pondus *nt*; (*of spirit*)
maestitia *f*.
heavy *adj* gravis; (*air*) crassus; (*spirit*)
maestus; (*shower*) māgnus, dēnsus.
heckle *vt* interpellāre.
heckler *n* interpellātor *m*.
hectic *adj* violēns, ācer, fervidus.
hector *vt* obstrepere (*dat*).
hedge *n* saepēs *f* ♦ *vt* saepīre; **~ off**
intersaepīre ♦ *vi* tergiversārī.
hedgehog *n* echīnus *m*, ēricius *m*.
heed *vt* cūrāre, respicere ♦ *n* cūra *f*, opera *f*;
pay ~ animum attendere; **take ~** cavēre.
heedful *adj* attentus, cautus, dīligēns.
heedfully *adv* attentē, cautē.
heedfulness *n* cūra *f*, dīligentia *f*.
heedless *adj* incautus, immemor, neglegēns.
heedlessly *adv* incautē, neglegenter, temerē.
heedlessness *n* neglegentia *f*.
heel *n* calx *f*; **take to one's ~s** sē in pedēs
conicere ♦ *vi* sē inclīnāre.
hegemony *n* prīncipātus *m*.
heifer *n* būcula *f*.
height *n* altitūdō *f*; (*person*) prōcēritās *f*; (*hill*)
collis *m*, iugum *nt*; (*fig*) fastīgium *nt*; **the ~ of**
summus.
heighten *vt* augēre, exaggerāre.
heinous *adj* atrōx, nefārius.
heinously *adv* atrōciter, nefāriē.
heinousness *n* atrōcitās *f*.
heir *n* hērēs *m*; **sole ~** hērēs ex asse.
heiress *n* hērēs *f*.
heirship *n* hērēditās *f*.
hell *n* Tartarus *m*, Īnfernī *mpl*.
hellish *adj* Īnfernus, scelestus.
helm *n* gubernāculum *nt*, clāvus *m*.
helmet *n* galea *f*.
helmsman *n* gubernātor *m*.
helots *n* Hīlōtae *mpl*.
help *n* auxilium *nt*, subsidium *nt*; **I am a ~**
auxiliō sum ♦ *vt* iuvāre (+ *acc*), auxiliārī,
subvenīre (*dat*), succurrere (*dat*) ♦ *vi*
prōdesse; **I cannot ~** facere nōn possum quīn
(*subj*); **it can't be ~ed** fierī nōn potest aliter;
so ~ me God ita me dī ament.

helper *n* adiūtor *m*, adiūtrix *f*.
helpful *adj* ūtilis; **be ~ to** auxiliō esse (*dat*).
helpless *adj* inops.
helplessness *n* inopia *f*.
hem *n* ōra *f*, limbus *m* ♦ *vt*: ~ **in** interclūdere,
circumsedēre.
hemlock *n* cicūta *f*.
hemp *n* cannabis *f*.
hen *n* gallīna *f*.
hence *adv* hinc; (*consequence*) igitur, ideō.
henceforth, henceforward *adv* dehinc,
posthāc, ex hōc tempore.
her *adj* suus, ēius.
herald *n* praecō *m*; (*POL*) fētiālis *m* ♦ *vt*
praenūntiāre.
herb *n* herba *f*, olus *nt*.
herbage *n* herbae *fpl*.
herd *n* pecus *nt*; grex *f*, armentum *nt* ♦ *vi*
congregārī.
herdsman *n* pāstor *m*.
here *adv* hīc; **be ~** adesse; ~ **and there** passim;
here ... there alibī ... alibī; **from ~** hinc; ~ **is**
... ecce (*acc*) ....
hereabouts *adv* hīc ferē.
hereafter *adv* posthāc, posteā.
hereat *adv* hīc.
hereby *adv* ex hōc, hinc.
hereditary *adj* hērēditārius, patrius.
heredity *n* genus *nt*.
herein *adv* hīc.
hereinafter *adv* īnfrā.
hereof *adv* ēius reī.
hereupon *adv* hīc, quō factō.
herewith *adv* cum hōc, ūnā.
heritable *adj* hērēditārius.
heritage *n* hērēditās *f*.
hermaphrodite *n* androgynus *m*.
hermit *n* homō sōlitārius *m*.
hero *n* vir fortissimus *m*; (*demigod*) hērōs *m*.
heroic *adj* fortissimus, māgnanimus; (*epic*)
hērōicus; (*verse*) hērōus.
heroically *adv* fortissimē, audācissimē.
heroism *n* virtūs *f*, fortitūdō *f*.
heron *n* ardea *f*.
hers *pron* suus, ēius.
herself *pron* ipsa *f*; (*reflexive*) sē.
hesitancy *n* dubitātiō *f*.
hesitant *adj* incertus, dubius.
hesitate *vi* dubitāre, haesitāre.
hesitating *adj* dubius.
hesitatingly *adv* cunctanter.
hesitation *n* dubitātiō *f*; **with ~** dubitanter.
heterogeneous *adj* dīversus, aliēnigenus.
hew *vt* dolāre, caedere; ~ **down** excīdere,
interscindere.
hexameter *n* hexameter *m*.
heyday *n* flōs *m*.
hiatus *n* hiātus *m*.
hiccup *n* singultus *m* ♦ *vi* singultīre.
hide *vt* cēlāre, abdere, abscondere, occultāre;
~ **away** abstrūdere; ~ **from** cēlāre (*acc*) ♦ *vi*
sē abdere, latēre; ~ **away** dēlitēscere ♦ *n*
pellis *f*, corium *nt*.

hideous adj foedus, dēfōrmis, turpis.
hideously adv foedē.
hideousness n foeditās f, dēfōrmitās f.
hiding n (place) latebra f.
hierarchy n ōrdinēs mpl.
high adj altus, excelsus; (ground) ēditus; (pitch) acūtus; (rank) amplus; (price) cārus; (tide) māximus; (wind) māgnus; ~ **living** luxuria f; ~ **treason** māiestās f; ~ **and mighty** superbus; **on** ~ sublīmis ♦ adv altē.
highborn adj nōbilis, generōsus.
high-class adj (goods) lautus.
high-flown adj īnflātus, tumidus.
high-handed adj superbus, īnsolēns.
high-handedly adv superbē, licenter
high-handedness n licentia f, superbia f.
highland adj montānus.
highlander n montānus m.
highlands npl montāna ntpl.
highly adv (value) māgnī; (intensity) valdē.
highly-strung adj trepidus.
high-minded adj generōsus.
high-spirited adj ferōx, animōsus.
highway n via f.
highwayman n grassātor m, latrō m.
hilarious adj festīvus, hilaris.
hilariously adv festīvē, hilare.
hilarity n festīvitās f, hilaritās f.
hill n collis m, mōns m; (slope) clīvus m.
hillock n tumulus m.
hilly adj montuōsus, clīvōsus.
hilt n manubrium nt, capulus m.
himself pron ipse; (reflexive) sē.
hind n cerva f.
hinder vt impedīre, obstāre (dat), morārī.
hindmost adj postrēmus; (in column) novissimus.
hindrance n impedīmentum nt, mora f.
hinge n cardō f.
hint n indicium nt, suspiciō f; **throw out a** ~ inicere ♦ vt subicere, significāre.
hip n coxendīx f.
hippodrome n spatium nt.
hire vt condūcere; ~ **out** locāre ♦ n conductiō f, locātiō f; (wages) mercēs f.
hired adj mercennārius, conductus.
hireling n mercennārius m.
hirsute adj hirsūtus.
his adj suus, ēius.
hiss vi sībilāre ♦ vt: ~ **off stage** explōdere, exsībilāre ♦ n sībilus m.
historian n historicus m, rērum scrīptor m.
historical adj historicus.
history n historia f; **the** ~ **of Rome** rēs Rōmānae fpl; **since the beginning of** ~ post hominum memoriam; **ancient** ~ antīquitās f.
histrionic adj scaenicus.
hit n ictus m, plāga f; **a** ~! (in duel) habet! ♦ vt ferīre, icere, percutere; ~ **against** offendere; ~ **upon** invenīre.
hitch n mora f ♦ vt implicāre; ~ **up** succingere.
hither adv hūc; ~ **and thither** hūc illūc ♦ adj citerior.

hitherto adv adhūc, hāctenus, hūcusque.
hive n alveārium nt.
hoar adj cānus ♦ n pruīna f.
hoard n thēsaurus m, acervus m ♦ vt condere, recondere.
hoarfrost n pruīna f.
hoarse adj raucus, fuscus.
hoarsely adv raucā vōce.
hoary adj cānus.
hoax n fraus f, fallācia f, lūdus m ♦ vt dēcipere, fallere.
hobble vi claudicāre.
hobby n studium nt.
hob-nob vi familiāriter ūtī (abl).
hocus-pocus n trīcae fpl.
hoe n sarculum nt ♦ vt sarrīre.
hog n sūs m, porcus m; ~**'s** porcīnus.
hogshead n dōlium nt.
hoist vt tollere; (sail) vēla dare.
hold n (grasp) comprehēnsiō f; (power) potestās f; (ship) alveus m; **gain a** ~ **over** obstringere, sibi dēvincīre; **get** ~ **of** potīrī (abl); **keep** ~ **of** retinēre; **lose** ~ **of** ōmittere; **take** ~ **of** prehendere, comprehendere ♦ vt tenēre, habēre; (possession) obtinēre; possidēre; (office) gerere, fungī (abl); (capacity) capere; (meeting) habēre; ~ **a meeting** concilium habēre; ~ **one's own with** parem esse (dat); ~ **over** differre, prōlātāre; ~ **water** (fig) stāre ♦ vi manēre, dūrāre; (opinion) dūcere, existimāre, adfirmāre; ~ **back** vt retinēre, inhibēre ♦ vi gravārī, dubitāre; ~ **cheap** parvī facere; ~ **fast** vt retinēre, amplectī ♦ vi haerēre; ~ **good** valēre; ~ **out** vt porrigere, extendere; (hope) ostendere ♦ vi dūrāre, perstāre; ~ **together** cohaerēre; ~ **up** tollere; (falling) sustinēre; (movement) obstāre (dat), morārī; ~ **with** adsentīre (dat).
holdfast n fībula f.
holding n (land) agellus m.
hole n forāmen nt cavum nt; **make a** ~ **in** pertundere, perforāre.
holiday n ōtium nt; festus diēs m; **on** ~ fēriātus; ~**s** pl fēriae fpl.
holily adv sanctē.
holiness n sanctitās f.
hollow adj cavus, concavus; (fig) inānis, vānus ♦ n cavum nt, caverna f ♦ vt excavāre.
hollowness n (fig) vānitās f.
holly n aquifolium nt.
holy adj sanctus.
homage n observantia f, venerātiō f; **pay** ~ **to** venerārī, colere.
home n domus f; (own, country) patria f; **at** ~ domī; **from** ~ domō ♦ adj domesticus ♦ adv domum.
homeless adj profugus.
homely adj simplex, rūsticus; (speech) plēbēius.
homestead n fundus m.
homewards adv domum.
homicide n (act) homicīdium nt, caedēs f;

(_person_) homicīda _m_.
homily _n_ sermō _m_.
homogeneous _adj_ aequābilis.
homologous _adj_ cōnsimilis.
hone _n_ cōs _f_ ♦ _vt_ acuere.
honest _adj_ probus, frūgī, integer.
honestly _adv_ probē, integrē.
honesty _n_ probitās _f_, fidēs _f_.
honey _n_ mel _nt_.
honeycomb _n_ favus _m_.
honeyed _adj_ mellītus, mulsus.
honorarium _n_ stips _f_.
honorary _adj_ honōrārius.
honour _n_ honōs _m_; (_repute_) honestās _f_;
   existimātiō _f_; (_chastity_) pudor _m_; (_trust_) fidēs _f_;
   (_rank_) dignitās _f_; (_award_) decus _nt_, īnsigne _nt_;
   (_respect_) observantia _f_ ♦ _vt_ honōrāre,
   decorāre; (_respect_) observāre, colere; **do ~ to**
   honestāre.
honourable _adj_ honestus, probus; (_rank_)
   illūstris, praeclārus.
honourably _adv_ honestē.
hood _n_ cucullus _m_.
hoodwink _vt_ verba dare (_dat_).
hoof _n_ ungula _f_.
hook _n_ uncus _m_, hāmus _m_ ♦ _vt_ hāmō capere.
hooked _adj_ aduncus, hāmātus.
hoop _n_ circulus _m_; (_toy_) trochus _m_.
hoot _vi_ obstrepere; **~ off** (_stage_) explōdere.
hop _n_ saltus _m_; **catch on the ~** in ipsō articulō
   opprimere ♦ _vi_ salīre.
hope _n_ spēs _f_; **in the ~ that** sī forte; **give up ~**
   spem dēpōnere, dēspērāre; **past ~**
   dēspērātus; **entertain ~s** spem habēre ♦ _vt_
   spērāre.
hopeful _adj_ bonae speī; **be ~** aliquam spem
   habēre.
hopefully _adv_ nōn sine spē.
hopeless _adj_ dēspērātus.
hopelessly _adv_ dēspēranter.
hopelessness _n_ dēspērātiō _f_.
horde _n_ multitūdō _f_.
horizon _n_ fīniēns _m_.
horizontal _adj_ aequus, lībrātus.
horizontally _adv_ ad lībram.
horn _n_ cornū _nt_; (_shepherd's_) būcina _f_.
horned _adj_ corniger.
hornet _n_ crabrō _m_; **stir up a ~'s nest** crabrōnēs
   inrītāre.
horny _adj_ corneus.
horoscope _n_ sīdus nātālicium _nt_.
horrible _adj_ horrendus, horribilis, dīrus,
   foedus.
horribly _adv_ foedē.
horrid _adj_ horribilis.
horrify _vt_ terrēre, perterrēre.
horror _n_ horror _m_, terror _m_; odium _nt_.
horse _n_ equus _m_; (_cavalry_) equitēs _mpl_; **flog a**
   dead ~ asellum currere docēre; **spur a**
   willing ~ currentem incitāre; **~'s** equīnus.
horseback _n_: **ride on ~back** in equō vehī; **fight**
   on ~back ex equō pugnāre.
horseman _n_ eques _m_.

horseradish _n_ armoracia _f_.
horse soldier _n_ eques _m_.
horticulture _n_ hortōrum cultus _m_.
hospitable _adj_ hospitālis.
hospitably _adv_ hospitāliter.
hospital _n_ valētūdinārium _nt_.
hospitality _n_ hospitālitās _f_, hospitium _nt_.
host _n_ hospes _m_; (_inn_) caupō _m_; (_number_)
   multitūdō _f_; (MIL) exercitus _m_.
hostage _n_ obses _m/f_.
hostelry _n_ taberna _f_, dēversōrium _nt_.
hostile _adj_ hostīlis, īnfēnsus, inimīcus;
   īnfestus; **in a ~ manner** īnfensē, hostīliter,
   inimīcē.
hostility _n_ inimīcitia _f_; **hostilities** _pl_ bellum _nt_.
hot _adj_ calidus, fervidus, aestuōsus; (_boiling_)
   fervēns; (_fig_) ārdēns; **be ~** calēre, fervēre,
   ārdēre; **get ~** calēscere.
hotch-potch _n_ farrāgō _f_.
hotel _n_ dēversōrium _nt_.
hot-headed _adj_ ārdēns, temerārius, praeceps.
hotly _adv_ ārdenter, ācriter.
hot-tempered _adj_ īrācundus.
hot water _n_ calida _f_.
hound _n_ canis _m_ ♦ _vt_ īnstāre (_dat_).
hour _n_ hōra _f_.
hourly _adv_ in hōrās.
house _n_ domus _f_, aedēs _fpl_; (_country_) vīlla _f_;
   (_family_) domus _f_, gēns _f_; **at the ~ of** apud (_acc_);
   full ~ frequēns senātus, frequēns theātrum
   ♦ _vt_ hospitiō accipere, recipere; (_things_)
   condere.
household _n_ familia _f_, domus _f_ ♦ _adj_
   familiāris, domesticus.
householder _n_ paterfamiliās _m_, dominus _m_.
housekeeping _n_ reī familiāris cūra _f_.
housemaid _n_ ancilla _f_.
housetop _n_ fastīgium _nt_.
housewife _n_ māterfamiliās _f_, domina _f_.
housing _n_ hospitium _nt_; (_horse_) ōrnāmenta
   ntpl.
hovel _n_ gurgustium _nt_.
hover _vi_ pendēre; (_fig_) impendēre.
how _adv_ (_interrog_) quemadmodum; quōmodō,
   quō pactō; (_excl_) quam; **~ great/big/large**
   quantus; **~ long** (_time_) quamdiū; **~ many** quot;
   ~ much quantum; **~ often** quotiēns.
howbeit _adv_ tamen.
however _adv_ tamen; autem, nihilōminus;
   utcumque, quōquō modō; **~ much** quamvīs,
   quantumvīs; **~ great** quantuscumque.
howl _n_ ululātus _m_ ♦ _vi_ ululāre; (_wind_) fremere.
howsoever _adv_ utcumque.
hub _n_ axis _m_.
hubbub _n_ tumultus _m_.
huckster _n_ īnstitor _m_, propōla _m_.
huddle _n_ turba _f_ ♦ _vi_ congregārī.
hue _n_ color _m_; **~ and cry** clāmor _m_.
huff _n_ offēnsiō _f_ ♦ _vt_ offendere.
hug _n_ complexus _m_ ♦ _vt_ complectī.
huge _adj_ ingēns, immānis, immēnsus, vastus.
hugely _adv_ vehementer.
hugeness _n_ immānitās _f_.

hulk n alveus m.
hull n alveus m.
hum n murmur nt, fremitus m ♦ vi
murmurāre, fremere.
human adj hūmānus.
human being n homō m/f.
humane adj hūmānus, misericors.
humanely adv hūmānē, hūmāniter.
humanism n litterae fpl.
humanist n homō litterātus m.
humanity n hūmānitās f; misericordia f.
humanize vt excolere.
humanly adv hūmānitus.
human nature n hūmānitās f.
humble adj humilis, modestus ♦ vt dēprimere;
(oneself) summittere.
humbleness n humilitās f.
humbly adv summissē, modestē.
humbug n trīcae fpl.
humdrum adj vulgāris; (style) pedester.
humid adj ūmidus, madidus; **be ~** madēre.
humidity n ūmor m.
humiliate vt dēprimere, dēdecorāre
humiliation n dēdecus nt.
humility n modestia f, animus summissus m.
humorist n homō facētus m.
humorous adj facētus, ioculāris, rīdiculus.
humorously adv facētē.
humour n facētiae fpl; (disposition) ingenium
nt; (mood) libīdō f; **be in a bad ~** sibī
displicēre ♦ vt indulgēre (dat), mōrem
gerere (dat), mōrigerārī (dat).
hump n gibbus m.
hunchback n gibber m.
hundred num centum; **~ each** centēnī **~ times**
centiēns.
hundredth adj centēsimus.
hundredweight n centumpondium nt.
hunger n famēs f ♦ vi ēsurīre.
hungrily adv avidē.
hungry adj ēsuriēns, iēiūnus, avidus; **be ~**
ēsurīre.
hunt n vēnātiō f, vēnātus m ♦ vt vēnārī,
indāgāre, exagitāre.
hunter n vēnātor m.
hunting n vēnātiō f; (fig) aucupium nt.
hunting spear n vēnābulum nt.
huntress n vēnātrix f.
huntsman n vēnātor m.
hurdle n crātēs f; (obstacle) obex m/f.
hurl vt conicere, ingerere, iaculārī, iācere.
hurly-burly n turba f, tumultus m.
hurrah interj euax, iō.
hurricane n procella f.
hurried adj praeproperus, praeceps, trepidus.
hurriedly adv properātō, cursim, festīnanter.
hurry vt adcelerāre, mātūrāre ♦ vi festīnāre,
properāre; **~ along** vt rapere; **~ away** vi
discēdere, properāre; **~ about** vi discurrere;
~ on vt mātūrāre; **~ up** vi properāre ♦ n
festīnātiō f; **in a ~** festīnanter, raptim.
hurt n iniūria f, damnum nt; vulnus nt ♦ vt
laedere, nocēre (dat); **it ~s** dolet.

hurtful adj nocēns, damnōsus.
hurtfully adv nocenter, damnōsē.
hurtle vi volāre; sē praecipitāre.
husband n vir m, marītus m ♦ vt parcere (dat).
husbandry n agrī cultūra f; (economy)
parsimōnia f.
hush n silentium nt ♦ vt silentium facere (dat),
lēnīre ♦ vi tacēre, silēre; **~ up** comprimere,
cēlāre ♦ interj st!
hushed adj tacitus.
husk n folliculus m, siliqua f ♦ vt dēglūbāre.
husky adj fuscus, raucus.
hustle vt trūdere, īnstāre (dat).
hut n casa f, tugurium nt.
hutch n cavea f.
hyacinth n hyacinthus m.
hybrid n hibrida m/f.
hydra n hydra f.
hyena n hyaena f.
hygiene n salūbritās f.
hygienic adj salūbris.
hymeneal adj nūptiālis.
hymn n carmen nt ♦ vt canere.
hyperbole n superlātiō f.
hypercritical adj Aristarchus m.
hypocaust n hypocaustum nt.
hypocrisy n simulātiō f, dissimulātiō f.
hypocrite n simulātor m, dissimulātor m.
hypocritical adj simulātus, fictus.
hypothesis n positum nt, sūmptiō f,
coniectūra f.
hypothetical adj sūmptus.

I, i

I pron ego.
iambic adj iambēus.
iambus n iambus m.
ice n glaciēs f.
icicle n stīria f.
icon n simulacrum nt.
icy adj glaciālis, gelidus.
idea n nōtiō f, nōtitia f, imāgō f; (Platonic) fōrma
f; (expressed) sententia f; **conceive the ~ of**
īnfōrmāre; **with the ~ that** eō cōnsiliō ut (+
subj).
ideal adj animō comprehēnsus; (perfect)
perfectus, optimus ♦ n: specimen nt, speciēs
f, exemplar nt.
identical adj īdem, cōnsimilis.
identify vt agnōscere.
identity n: **establish the ~ of** cognōscere quis
sit.
Ides n Īdūs fpl.
idiocy n animī imbēcillitās f.

idiom n proprium nt, sermō m.
idiomatic adj proprius.
idiomatically adv sermōne suō, sermōne
propriō.
idiosyncrasy n proprium nt, libīdō f.
idiot n excors m.
idiotic adj fatuus, stultus.
idiotically adv stultē, ineptē.
idle adj ignāvus, dēses, iners; (unoccupied)
ōtiōsus, vacuus; (useless) inānis, vānus; be ~
cessāre, dēsidēre; **lie** ~ (money) iacēre ♦ vi
cessāre.
idleness n ignāvia f, dēsidia f, inertia f; ōtium
nt.
idler n cessātor m.
idly adv ignāvē; ōtiōsē; frustrā, nēquīquam.
idol n simulacrum nt; (person) dēliciae fpl.
idolater n falsōrum deōrum cultor m.
idolatry n falsōrum deōrum cultus m.
idolize vt venerārī.
idyll n carmen Theocritēum nt.
if conj sī; (interrog) num, utrum; ~ **anyone** sī
quis; ~ **ever** sī quandō; ~ **not** nisī; ~ **only** dum,
dummodo; ~ ... **or** sīve ... sīve; **as** ~ quasi,
velut; **but** ~ sīn, quodsī; **even** ~ etiamsī.
igneous adj igneus.
ignite vt accendere, incendere ♦ vi ignem
concipere.
ignoble adj (birth) ignōbilis; (repute)
illīberālis, turpis.
ignominious adj ignōminiōsus, īnfāmis,
turpis.
ignominiously adv turpiter.
ignominy n ignōminia f, īnfāmia f, dēdecus nt.
ignoramus n idiōta m, indoctus m.
ignorance n īnscītia f, ignōrātiō f.
ignorant adj ignārus, indoctus; (of something)
īnscītus, rudis; (unaware) īnscius; **be** ~ **of**
nescīre, ignōrāre.
ingorantly adv īnscienter, īnscītē, indoctē.
ignore vt praetermittere.
ilex n īlex f.
Iliad n Ilias f.
ill adj aeger, aegrōtus, invalidus; (evil) malus;
be ~ aegrōtāre; **fall** ~ in morbum incidere; ~
at ease sollicitus ♦ adv male, improbē ♦ n
malum nt, incommodum nt, aerumna f,
damnum nt.
ill-advised adj incōnsultus.
ill-bred adj agrestis, inurbānus.
ill-disposed adj malevolus, invidus.
illegal adj illicitus, vetitus.
illegally adv contrā lēgēs.
ill-fated adj īnfēlīx.
ill-favoured adj turpis.
ill-gotten adj male partus.
ill-health n valētūdō f.
illicit adj vetitus.
illimitable adj īnfīnītus.
illiteracy n litterārum īnscītia f.
illiterate adj illitterātus, inērudītus.
ill-natured adj malevolus, malignus.
illness n morbus m, valētūdō f.

illogical adj absurdus.
ill-omened adj dīrus, īnfaustus.
ill-starred adj īnfēlīx.
ill-tempered adj īrācundus, amārus,
stomachōsus.
ill-timed adj immātūrus, intempestīvus.
ill-treat vt malefacere (dat).
illuminate vt illūmināre, illūstrāre.
illumination n lūmina ntpl.
illusion n error m, somnium nt.
illusive, illusory adj fallāx.
illustrate vt illūstrāre; (with instances)
exemplō cōnfirmāre.
illustration n exemplum nt.
illustrious adj illūstris, īnsignis, praeclārus.
illustriously adv praeclārē.
ill will n invidia f.
image n imāgō f, effigiēs f; (idol) simulacrum
nt; (verbal) figūra f, similitūdō f.
imagery n figūrae fpl.
imaginary adj commentīcius, fictus.
imagination n cōgitātiō f, opīnātiō f.
imaginative adj ingeniōsus.
imagine vt animō fingere, animum indūcere,
ante oculōs pōnere; (think) opīnārī, arbitrārī.
imbecile adj animō imbēcillus, fatuus, mente
captus.
imbecility n animī imbēcillitās f.
imbibe vt adbibere; (fig) imbuī (abl).
imbrue vt īnficere.
imbue vt imbuere, īnficere, tingere.
imitable adj imitābilis.
imitate vt imitārī.
imitation n imitātiō f; (copy) imāgō f.
imitator n imitātor m, imitātrix f, aemulātor
m.
immaculate adj integer, ēmendātus.
immaculately adv integrē, sine vitiō.
immaterial adj indifferēns.
immature adj immātūrus.
immeasurable adj immēnsus, īnfīnītus.
immediate adj īnstāns, praesēns; (neighbour)
proximus.
immediately adv statim, extemplō,
cōnfestim.
immemorial adj antīquissimus; **from time** ~
post hominum memoriam.
immense adj immēnsus, immānis, ingēns,
vastus.
immersely adv vehementer.
immersity n immēnsum nt, māgnitūdō f.
immerse vt immergere, mergere.
immigrant n advena m.
immigrate vi migrāre.
imminent adj īnstāns, praesēns; **be** ~
imminēre, impendēre.
immobile adj fīxus, immōbilis.
immoderate adj immoderātus, immodestus.
immoderately adv immoderātē, immodestē.
immodest adj impudīcus, inverēcundus.
immoate vt immolāre.
immoral adj prāvus, corruptus, turpis.
immorality n corruptī mōrēs mpl, turpitūdō f.

immorally adv prāvē, turpiter.
immortal adj immortālis, aeternus.
immortality n immortālitās f.
immortalize vt in astra tollere.
immortally adv aeternum.
immovable adj fīxus, immōbilis.
immune adj immūnis, vacuus.
immunity n immūnitās f, vacātiō f.
immure vt inclūdere.
immutability n immūtābilitās f.
immutable adj immūtābilis.
imp n puer improbus m.
impact n ictus m, incussus m.
impair vt imminuere, corrumpere.
impale vt induere, īnfīgere.
impalpable adj tenuissimus.
impart vt impertīre, commūnicāre; (courage) addere.
impartial adj aequus, medius.
impartiality n aequābilitās f.
impartially adv sine favōre.
impassable adj invius; (mountains) inexsuperābilis; (fig) inexplicābilis.
impasse n mora f, incitae fpl.
impassioned adj ārdēns, fervidus.
impassive adj rigidus, sēnsū carēns.
impatience n aviditās f; (of anything) impatientia f.
impatient adj trepidus, avidus; impatiēns.
impatiently adv aegrē.
impeach vt diem dīcere (dat), accūsāre.
impeachment n accūsātiō f, crīmen n.
impeccable adj ēmendātus.
impecunious adj pauper.
impede vt impedīre, obstāre (dat).
impediment n impedīmentum nt.
impel vt impellere, incitāre.
impend vi impendēre, imminēre, īnstāre.
impenetrable adj impenetrābilis; (country) invius, impervius.
impenitent adj: I am ~ nīl mē paenitet.
imperative adj necessārius.
imperceptible adj tenuissimus, obscūrus.
imperceptibly adv sēnsim.
imperfect adj imperfectus, vitiōsus.
imperfection n vitium nt.
imperfectly adv vitiōsē.
imperial adj imperātōrius, rēgius.
imperil vt in discrīmen addūcere, labefactāre.
imperious adj imperiōsus, superbus.
imperiously adv superbē.
imperishable adj immortālis, aeternus.
impersonate vt partēs agere (gen).
impertinence n importūnitās f, protervitās f.
impertinent adj importūnus, protervus, ineptus.
impertinently adv importūnē, ineptē, protervē.
imperturbable adj immōtus, gravis.
impervious adj impervius, impenetrābilis.
impetuosity n ārdor m, violentia f, vīs f.
impetuous adj violēns, fervidus, effrēnātus.
impetuously adv effrēnātē.

impetus n impetus m.
impiety n impietās f.
impinge vi incidere.
impious adj impius, profānus; it is ~ nefas est.
impiously adv impiē.
impish adj improbus.
implacable adj implācābilis, inexōrābilis, dūrus.
implacably adv dūrē.
implant vt īnserere, ingignere.
implement n īnstrūmentum nt ♦ vt implēre, exsequī.
implicate vt implicāre, impedīre.
implication n indicium nt.
implicit adj tacitus; absolūtus.
implicitly adv absconditē; (trust) omnīnō, summā fidē.
implore vt implōrāre, obsecrāre.
imply vt significāre, continēre; be ~ied inesse.
impolite adj inurbānus, illepidus.
impolitely adv inurbānē.
impolitic adj incōnsultus, imprūdēns.
imponderable adj levissimus.
import vt importāre, invehere; (mean) velle ♦ n significātiō f.
importance n gravitās f, mōmentum nt; (rank) dignitās f, amplitūdō f, auctōritās f; it is of great ~ to me meā māgnī rēfert.
important adj gravis, magnī mōmentī; it is ~ interest (+ gen) rēfert; more ~, most ~ antīquior, antīquissimus.
importation n invectiō f.
imports npl importātīcia ntpl.
importunate adj molestus.
importune vt flāgitāre, īnstāre (dat).
impose vt impōnere; (by order) indīcere, iniungere; ~ upon illūdere, fraudāre, abūtī (abl).
imposing adj māgnificus, lautus.
imposition n fraus f; (tax) tribūtum nt.
impossible adj: it is ~ fierī nōn potest.
impost n tribūtum nt, vectīgal nt.
impostor n planus m, fraudātor m.
imposture n fraus f, fallācia f.
impotence n īnfirmitās f.
impotent adj īnfirmus, dēbilis; (with rage) impotēns.
impotently adv frustrā; (rage) impotenter.
impound vt inclūdere; (confiscate) pūblicāre.
impoverish vt in inopiam redigere.
impracticable adj: be ~ fierī nōn posse.
imprecate vt exsecrārī.
imprecation n exsecrātiō f.
impregnable adj inexpugnābilis.
impregnate vt imbuere, īnficere.
impress vt imprimere; (on mind) īnfīgere; (person) permovēre; (MIL) invītum scrībere.
impression n (copy) exemplar nt; (mark) signum nt; (feeling) impulsiō f; (belief) opīnātiō f; make an ~ of exprimere; make an ~ on commovēre; have the ~ opīnārī.
impressionable adj crēdulus.
impressive adj gravis.

impressively adv graviter.
impressiveness n gravitās f.
imprint n impressiō f, signum nt ♦ vt imprimere; (on mind) īnfīgere, inūrere.
imprison vt inclūdere, in vincula conicere.
imprisonment n custōdia f, vincula ntpl.
improbable adj incrēdibilis, haud vērīsimilis.
impromptu adv ex tempore.
improper adj indecōrus, ineptus.
improperly adv prāvē, perperam.
impropriety n culpa f, offēnsa f.
improve vt ēmendāre, corrigere; (mind) excolere ♦ vi prōficere, meliōrem fierī.
improvement n ēmendātiō f, prōfectus m.
improvident adj imprōvidus; (with money) prōdigus.
improvidently adv imprōvidē; prōdigē.
improvise vt ex tempore compōnere, excōgitāre.
imprudence n imprūdentia f.
imprudent adj imprūdēns.
imprudently adv imprūdenter.
impudence n impudentia f, audācia f.
impudent adj impudēns, audāx.
impudently adv impudenter, protervē.
impugn vt impugnāre, in dubium vocāre.
impulse n impetus m, impulsus m.
impulsive adj praeceps, violentus.
impulsively adv impetū quōdam animī.
impulsiveness n impetus m, violentia f.
impunity n impūnitās f; with ~ impūne.
impure adj impūrus, incestus, inquinātus.
impurely adv impūrē, incestē, inquinātē.
impurity n impūritās f, sordēs fpl.
imputation n crīmen nt.
impute vt attribuere, adsignāre; ~ as a fault vitiō vertere.
in prep in (abl); (with motion) in (acc); (authors) apud (acc); (time) abl; ~ doing this dum hoc faciō; ~ my youth adulēscēns; ~ that quod ♦ adv (rest) intrā; (motion) intrō.
inaccessible adj inaccessus.
inaccuracy n neglegentia f, incūria f; (error) mendum nt.
inaccurate adj parum dīligēns, neglegēns.
inaccurately adv neglegenter.
inaction n inertia f.
inactive adj iners, quiētus; be ~ cessāre.
inactivity n inertia f, ōtium nt.
inadequate adj impār, parum idōneus.
inadequately adv parum.
inadvertency n imprūdentia f.
inadvertent adj imprūdēns.
inadvertently adv imprūdenter.
inane adj inānis, vānus; ineptus, stultus.
inanely adv ineptē.
inanimate adj inanimus.
inanity n ineptiae fpl, stultitia f.
inapplicable adj: be ~ nōn valēre.
inappropriate adj aliēnus, parum aptus.
inarticulate adj īnfāns.
inartistic adj sine arte, dūrus, inēlegāns.
inasmuch as conj quōniam, cum (subj).

inattention n incūria f, neglegentia f.
inattentive adj neglegēns.
inattentively adv neglegenter.
inaudible adj: be ~ audīrī nōn posse.
inaugurate vt inaugurāre, cōnsecrāre.
inauguration n cōnsecrātiō f.
inauspicious adj īnfaustus, īnfēlix.
inauspiciously adv malīs ōminibus.
inborn adj innātus.
incalculable adj inaestimābilis.
incantation n carmen nt.
incapable adj inhabilis, indocilis; be ~ nōn posse.
incapacitate vt dēbilitāre.
incapacity n inertia f, īnscītia f.
incarcerate vt inclūdere, in vincula conicere.
incarnate adj hūmānā speciē indūtus.
incautious adj incautus, temerārius.
incautiously adv incautē.
incendiary adj incendiārius.
incense n tūs nt ♦ vt inrītāre, stomachum movēre (dat); be ~d stomachārī.
incentive n incitāmentum nt, stimulus m.
inception n initium nt, exōrdium nt.
incessant adj adsiduus.
incessantly adv adsiduē.
incest n incestus m.
inch n digitus m, ūncia f.
incident n ēventum nt, cāsus m, rēs f.
incidental adj fortuītus.
incidentally adv cāsū.
incipient adj prīmus.
incisive adj ācer.
incite vt īnstīgāre, impellere, hortārī, incitāre.
incitement n invītāmentum nt, stimulus m.
inciter n īnstimulātor m.
incivility n importūnitās f, inhūmānitās f.
inclemency n (weather) intemperiēs f.
inclement adj asper, tristis.
inclination n inclīnātiō f, animus m, libīdō f; (slope) clīvus m.
incline vt inclīnāre; (person) indūcere ♦ vi inclīnāre, incumbere; ~ towards sē adclīnāre ♦ n adclīvitās f, clīvus m.
inclined adj inclīnātus, prōpēnsus; I am ~ to think haud sciō an.
include vt inclūdere, continēre, complectī.
incognito adv clam.
incoherent adj interruptus; be ~ nōn cohaerēre.
income n frūctus m, mercēs f.
incommensurate adj dispār.
incommode vt molestiam adferre (dat).
incomparable adj singulāris, eximius.
incompatibility n discrepantia f, repugnantia f.
incompatible adj īnsociābilis, repugnāns; be ~ with dissidēre ab, repugnāre (dat).
incompetence n inertia f, īnscītia f.
incompetent adj iners, īnscītus.
incomplete adj imperfectus.
incomprehensible adj incrēdibilis.

inconceivable adj incrēdibilis.
inconclusive adj inānis.
incongruous adj absonus, aliēnus.
inconsiderable adj exiguus.
inconsiderate adj imprōvidus, incōnsultus.
inconsistency n discrepantia f, incōnstantia f.
inconsistent adj incōnstāns; **be ~** discrepāre;
    be ~ with abhorrēre ab, repugnāre (dat).
inconsistently adv incōnstanter.
inconsolable adj nōn cōnsōlābilis.
inconspicuous adj obscūrus; **be ~** latēre.
inconstancy n incōnstantia f, levitās f.
inconstant adj incōnstāns, levis, mōbilis.
inconstantly adv incōnstanter.
incontestable adj certus.
incontinence n incontinentia f.
incontinent adj intemperāns.
inconvenience n incommodum nt ♦ vt
    incommodāre.
inconvenient adj incommodus.
inconveniently adv incommodē.
incorporate vt īnserere, adiungere.
incorrect adj falsus; **be ~** nōn cōnstāre.
incorrectly adv falsō, perperam.
incorrigible adj improbus, perditus.
incorruptibility n integritās f.
incorruptible adj incorruptus.
increase n incrēmentum nt, additāmentum nt,
    auctus m ♦ vt augēre, amplificāre ♦ vi
    crēscere, incrēscere.
increasingly adv magis magisque.
incredible adj incrēdibilis.
incredibly adv incrēdibiliter.
incredulous adj incrēdulus.
increment n incrēmentum nt.
incriminate vt crīminārī.
inculcate vt inculcāre, īnfīgere.
incumbent adj: **it is ~ on** oportet.
incur vt subīre; (guilt) admittere.
incurable adj īnsānābilis.
incursion n incursiō f.
indebted adj obnoxius; **be ~** dēbēre.
indecency n obscēnitās f.
indecent adj obscēnus, impudīcus.
indecently adv obscēnē.
indecision n dubitātiō f.
indecisive adj anceps, dubius; **the battle is ~**
    ancipitī Marte pugnātur.
indecisively adv incertō ēventū.
indecorous adj indecōrus.
indeed adv profectō, sānē; (concessive)
    quidem; (interrog) itane vērō?; (reply) certē,
    vērō; (with pron) dēmum; (with adj, adv conj)
    adeō.
indefatigable adj impiger.
indefensible adj: **be ~** dēfendī nōn posse;
    (belief) tenērī nōn posse; (offence) excūsārī
    nōn posse.
indefinite adj incertus, ambiguus, īnfīnītus.
indefinitely adv ambiguē; (time) in incertum.
indelicate adj pūtidus, indecōrus.
independence n lībertās f.
independent adj līber, suī iūris.

indescribable adj inēnārrābilis.
indestructible adj perennis.
indeterminate adj incertus.
index n index m.
indicate vt indicāre, significāre.
indication n indicium nt, signum nt.
indict vt diem dīcere (dat), accūsāre, nōmen
    dēferre (gen).
indictment n accūsātiō f.
indifference n neglegentia f, languor m.
indifferent adj (manner) neglegēns, frīgidus,
    sēcūrus; (quality) mediocris.
indifferently adv neglegenter; mediocriter;
    (without distinction) promiscuē, sine
    discrīmine.
indigence n indigentia f, egestās f.
indigenous adj indigena.
indigent adj indigēns, egēnus.
indigestible adj crūdus.
indigestion n crūditās f.
indignant adj indignābundus, īrātus; **be ~**
    indignārī.
indignantly adv īrātē.
indignation n indignātiō f, dolor m.
indignity n contumēlia f, indignitās f.
indigo n Indicum nt.
indirect adj oblīquus.
indirectly adv oblīquē, per ambāgēs.
indirectness n ambāgēs fpl.
indiscipline n lascīvia f, licentia f.
indiscreet adj incōnsultus, imprūdēns.
indiscreetly adv incōnsultē, imprūdenter.
indiscretion n imprūdentia f; (act) culpa f.
indiscriminate adj prōmiscuus.
indiscriminately adv prōmiscuē, sine
    discrīmine.
indispensable adj necesse, necessārius.
indisposed adj īnfirmus, aegrōtus, (will)
    āversus, aliēnātus; **be ~** aegrōtāre;
    abhorrēre, aliēnārī.
indisposition n īnfirmitās f, valētūdō f.
indisputable adj certus, manifestus.
indisputably adv certē, sine dubiō.
indissoluble adj indissolūbilis.
indistinct adj obscūrus, obtūsus; (speaker)
    balbus.
indistinctly adv obscūrē; **pronounce ~**
    opprimere; **speak ~** balbutīre.
individual adj proprius ♦ n homō m/f, prīvātus
    m; **~s** pl singulī mpl.
individuality n proprium nt.
individually adv singulātim, prīvātim.
indivisible adj indīviduus.
indolence n dēsidia f, ignāvia f, inertia f.
indolent adj dēses, ignāvus, iners.
indolently adv ignāvē.
indomitable adj indomitus.
indoor adj umbrātilis.
indoors adv intus; (motion) intrā.
indubitable adj certus.
indubitably adv sine dubiō.
induce vt indūcere, addūcere, persuādēre
    (dat).

inducement _n_ illecebra _f_, praemium _nt_.
induction _n_ (_logic_) inductiō _f_.
indulge _vt_ indulgēre (_dat_).
indulgence _n_ indulgentia _f_, venia _f_; (_favour_)
  grātia _f_.
indulgent _adj_ indulgēns, lēnis.
indulgently _adv_ indulgenter.
industrious _adj_ industrius, impiger, dīligēns.
industriously _adv_ industriē.
industry _n_ industria _f_, dīligentia _f_, labor _m_.
inebriated _adj_ ēbrius.
inebriation _n_ ēbrietās _f_.
ineffable _adj_ eximius.
ineffective _adj_ inūtilis, invalidus.
ineffectively _adv_ ināniter.
ineffectual _adj_ inritus.
inefficient _adj_ īnscītus, parum strēnuus.
inelegant _adj_ inēlegāns, inconcinnus.
inelegantly _adv_ inēleganter.
inept _adj_ ineptus.
ineptly _adv_ ineptē.
inequality _n_ dissimilitūdō _f_, inīquitās _f_.
inert _adj_ iners, sōcors, immōbilis.
inertia _n_ inertia _f_.
inertly _adv_ tardē, lentē.
inestimable _adj_ inaestimābilis.
inevitable _adj_ necessārius.
inevitably _adv_ necessāriō.
inexact _adj_ parum subtīlis.
inexhaustible _adj_ perennis.
inexorable _adj_ inexōrābilis.
inexpediency _n_ inūtilitās _f_, incommodum _nt_.
inexpedient _adj_ inūtilis; **it is ~** nōn expedit.
inexpensive _adj_ vīlis.
inexperience _n_ imperītia _f_, īnscītia _f_.
inexperienced _adj_ imperītus, rudis, īnscītus.
inexpert _adj_ imperītus.
inexpiable _adj_ inexpiābilis.
inexplicable _adj_ inexplicābilis, inēnōdābilis.
inexpressible _adj_ inēnārrābilis.
inextricable _adj_ inexplicābilis.
infallible _adj_ certus, errōris expers.
infamous _adj_ īnfāmis, flāgitiōsus.
infamously _adv_ flāgitiōsē.
infamy _n_ īnfāmia _f_, flāgitium _nt_, dēdecus _nt_.
infancy _n_ īnfantia _f_; (_fig_) incūnābula _ntpl_.
infant _n_ īnfāns _m/f_.
infantile _adj_ puerīlis.
infantry _n_ peditēs _mpl_, peditātus _m_.
infantryman _n_ pedes _m_.
infatuate _vt_ īnfatuāre.
infatuated _adj_ dēmēns.
infatuation _n_ dēmentia _f_.
infect _vt_ īnficere.
infection _n_ contāgiō _f_.
infer _vt_ īnferre, colligere.
inference _n_ conclūsiō _f_.
inferior _adj_ (_position_) īnferior; (_quality_)
  dēterior.
infernal _adj_ īnfernus.
infest _vt_ frequentāre.
infidel _adj_ impius.
infidelity _n_ perfidia _f_, īnfidēlitās _f_.

infiltrate _vi_ sē īnsinuāre.
infinite _adj_ īnfīnītus, immēnsus.
infinitely _adv_ longē, immēnsum.
infinitesimal _adj_ minimus.
infinity _n_ īnfīnitās _f_.
infirm _adj_ īnfirmus, invalidus.
infirmary _n_ valētūdinārium _nt_.
infirmity _n_ morbus _m_.
inflame _vt_ accendere, incendere, īnflammāre.
  be ~d exārdēscere.
inflammation _n_ (_MED_) īnflātiō _f_.
inflate _vt_ īnflāre.
inflated _adj_ (_fig_) īnflātus, tumidus.
inflexible _adj_ rigidus.
inflexion _n_ (_GRAM_) flexūra _f_; (_voice_) flexiō _f_.
inflict _vt_ īnflīgere, incutere; (_burden_)
  impōnere; (_penalty_) sūmere; **be ~ed with**
  labōrāre ex.
infliction _n_ poena _f_; malum _nt_.
influence _n_ (_physical_) impulsiō _f_, mōmentum
  _nt_; (_moral_) auctōritās _f_; (_partial_) grātia _f_; **have**
  ~ valēre; **have great ~ with** plūrimum posse
  apud; **under the ~ of** īnstinctus (_abl_) ♦ _vt_
  impellere, movēre, addūcere.
influential _adj_ gravis, potēns; grātiōsus.
influenza _n_ gravēdō _f_.
inform _vt_ docēre, certiōrem facere; **~ against**
  nōmen dēferre (_gen_).
informant _n_ index _m_, auctor _m_.
information _n_ indicium _nt_, nūntius _m_.
informer _n_ index _m_, dēlātor _m_; **turn ~** indicium
  profitērī.
infrequent _adj_ rārus.
infrequently _adv_ rārō.
infringe _vt_ violāre, imminuere.
infringement _n_ violātiō _f_.
infuriate _vt_ efferāre.
infuriated _adj_ furibundus.
infuse _vt_ īnfundere; (_fig_) inicere.
ingenious _adj_ ingeniōsus, callidus; (_thing_)
  artificiōsus.
ingeniously _adv_ callidē, summā arte.
ingenuity _n_ ars _f_, artificium _nt_, acūmen _nt_.
ingenuous _adj_ ingenuus, simplex.
ingenuously _adv_ ingenuē, simpliciter.
ingenuousness _n_ ingenuitās _f_.
ingle _n_ focus _m_.
inglorious _adj_ inglōrius, ignōbilis, inhonestus.
ingloriously _adv_ sine glōriā, inhonestē.
ingot _n_ later _m_.
ingrained _adj_ īnsitus.
ingratiate _vt_: **~ oneself with** grātiam inīre ab,
  sē īnsinuāre in familiāritātem (_gen_); **~**
  oneself into sē īnsinuāre in (_acc_).
ingratitude _n_ ingrātus animus _m_.
ingredient _n_ pars _f_.
inhabit _vt_ incolere, habitāre in (_abl_).
inhabitable _adj_ habitābilis.
inhabitant _n_ incola _m/f_.
inhale _vt_ haurīre.
inharmonious _adj_ dissonus.
inherent _adj_ īnsitus; **be ~ in** inhaerēre (_dat_),
  inesse (_dat_).

inherently *adv* nātūrā.
inherit *vt* excipere.
inheritance *n* hērēditās *f*, patrimōnium *nt*;
    divide an ~ herctum ciēre; **come into an ~**
    hērēditātem adīre.
inheritor *n* hērēs *m/f*.
inhibit *vt* prohibēre, inhibēre.
inhospitable *adj* inhospitālis.
inhuman *adj* inhūmānus, immānis, crūdēlis.
inhumanity *n* inhūmānitās *f*, crūdēlitās *f*.
inhumanly *adv* inhūmānē, crūdēliter.
inimical *adj* inimīcus.
inimitable *adj* singulāris, eximius.
iniquitous *adj* inīquus, improbus, nefārius.
iniquity *n* scelus *nt*, flāgitium *nt*.
initial *adj* prīmus.
initiate *vt* initiāre; (*with knowledge*) imbuere.
initiative *n* initium *nt*; **take the ~** initium
    capere, facere; occupāre (*inf*).
inject *vt* inicere.
injudicious *adj* incōnsultus, imprūdēns.
injunction *n* iussum *nt*, praeceptum *nt*.
injure *vt* laedere, nocēre (*dat*).
injurious *adj* damnōsus, nocēns.
injury *n* iniūria *f*, damnum *nt*; (*bodily*) vulnus
    nt.
injustice *n* iniūria *f*, inīquitās *f*.
ink *n* ātrāmentum *nt*.
inkling *n* audītiō *f*, suspiciō *f*.
inland *adj* mediterrāneus; **further ~** interior.
inlay *vt* īnserere.
inlet *n* sinus *m*, aestuārium *nt*.
inly *adv* penitus.
inmate *n* inquilīnus *m*.
inmost *adj* intimus.
inn *n* dēversōrium *nt*; caupōna *f*, taberna *f*.
innate *adj* innātus, īnsitus.
inner *adj* interior.
innermost *adj* intimus.
innkeeper *n* caupō *m*.
innocence *n* innocentia *f*.
innocent *adj* innocēns, īnsōns; (*character*)
    integer, castus.
innocently *adv* innocenter, integrē, castē.
innocuous *adj* innoxius.
innovate *vt* novāre.
innovation *n* novum *nt*, nova rēs *f*.
innovator *n* novārum rērum auctor *m*.
innuendo *n* verbum inversum *nt*.
innumerable *adj* innumerābilis.
inoffensive *adj* innocēns.
inoffensively *adv* innocenter.
inopportune *adj* intempestīvus.
inopportunely *adv* intempestīvē.
inordinate *adj* immodicus, immoderātus.
inordinately *adv* immoderātē.
inquest *n* quaestiō *f*; **hold an ~ on** quaerere dē.
inquire *vi* exquīrere, rogāre; **~ into** inquīrere
    in (*acc*), investigāre.
inquiry *n* quaestiō *f*, investīgātiō *f*; (*asking*)
    interrogātiō *f*; **make ~** exquīrere; **make ~ies
    about** inquīrere in (*acc*); **hold an ~ on**
    quaerere dē, quaestiōnem īnstituere dē.

inquisition *n* inquīsītiō *f*.
inquisitive *adj* cūriōsus.
inquisitiveness *n* cūriōsitās *f*.
inquisitor *n* inquīsītor *m*.
inroad *n* incursiō *f*, impressiō *f*; **make an ~**
    incursāre.
insane *adj* īnsānus, mente captus; **be ~**
    īnsānīre.
insanity *n* īnsānia *f*, dēmentia *f*.
insatiable *adj* īnsatiābilis, inexplēbilis,
    īnsaturābilis.
insatiably *adv* īnsaturābiliter.
inscribe *vt* īnscrībere.
inscription *n* epigramma *nt*; (*written*)
    īnscrīptiō *f*.
inscrutable *adj* obscūrus.
insect *n* bestiola *f*.
insecure *adj* īnstabilis, intūtus.
insecurity *n* perīcula *ntpl*.
insensate *adj* ineptus, stultus.
insensible *adj* torpidus; (*fig*) dūrus.
insensitive *adj* dūrus.
inseparable *adj* coniūnctus; **be the ~**
    companion of ab latere esse (*gen*).
inseparably *adv* coniūnctē.
insert *vt* īnserere, immittere, interpōnere.
insertion *n* interpositiō *f*.
inshore *adv* prope lītus.
inside *adv* intus; (*motion*) intrō ♦ *adj* interior ♦
    n pars *f* interior ♦ *prep* intrā (*acc*); **get right ~**
    sē īnsinuāre in (*acc*); **turn ~ out** excutere; **on
    the ~** interior.
insidious *adj* īnsidiōsus, subdolus.
insidiously *adv* īnsidiōsē.
insight *n* intellegentia *f*, cognitiō *f*.
insignia *n* īnsignia *ntpl*.
insignificance *n* levitās *f*.
insignificant *adj* levis, exiguus, nullīus
    mōmentī; (*position*) humilis.
insincere *adj* simulātus, fūcōsus.
insincerely *adv* simulātē.
insincerity *n* simulātiō *f*, fraus *f*.
insinuate *vt* īnsinuāre; (*hint*) significāre ♦ *vi*
    sē īnsinuāre.
insinuating *adj* blandus.
insinuation *n* ambigua verba *ntpl*.
insipid *adj* īnsulsus, frīgidus.
insipidity *n* īnsulsitās *f*.
insist *vi* īnstāre; **~ on** postulāre.
insistence *n* pertinācia *f*.
insistent *adj* pertināx.
insolence *n* īnsolentia *f*, contumācia *f*,
    superbia *f*.
insolent *adj* īnsolēns, contumāx, superbus.
insolently *adv* īnsolenter.
insoluble *adj* inexplicābilis.
insolvency *n* reī familiāris naufragium *nt*.
insolvent *adj*: **be ~** solvendō nōn esse.
inspect *vt* īnspicere; (*MIL*) recēnsēre.
inspection *n* cognitiō *f*; (*MIL*) recēnsiō *f*.
inspector *n* cūrātor *m*.
inspiration *n* adflātus *m*, īnstinctus *m*.
inspire *vt* īnstinguere, incendere.

instability *n* mōbilitās *f.*
install *vt* inaugurāre.
instalment *n* pēnsiō *f.*
instance *n* exemplum *nt;* **for ~** exemplī causā, grātiā; **at the ~** admonitū; **at my ~** mē auctōre ♦ *vt* memorāre.
instant *adj* īnstāns, praesēns ♦ *n* temporis pūnctum *nt,* mōmentum *nt.*
instantaneous *adj* praesēns.
instantaneously *adv* continuō, īlicō.
instantly *adv* īlicō, extemplō.
instead of *prep* prō (*abl*), locō (*gen*); (*with verb*) nōn . . . sed.
instigate *vt* īnstigāre, impellere.
instigation *n* impulsus *m,* stimulus *m;* auctōritās *f;* **at my ~** mē auctōre.
instigator *n* īnstimulātor *m,* auctor *m.*
instil *vt* imbuere, adspīrāre, inicere.
instinct *n* nātūra *f,* ingenium *nt,* sēnsus *m.*
instinctive *adj* nātūrālis.
instinctively *adv* nātūrā, ingeniō suō.
institute *vt* īnstituere, inaugurāre.
institution *n* īnstitūtum *nt;* societās *f.*
instruct *vt* docēre, īnstituere, īnstruere; ērudīre; (*order*) praecipere (*dat*).
instruction *n* doctrīna *f,* disciplīna *f;* praeceptum *nt;* **give ~s** dēnūntiāre, praecipere.
instructor *n* doctor *m,* praeceptor *m.*
instructress *n* magistra *f.*
instrument *n* īnstrūmentum *nt;* (*music*) fidēs *fpl;* (*legal*) tabulae *fpl.*
instrumental *adj* ūtilis.
instrumentalist *n* fidicen *m,* fidicina *f.*
instrumentality *n* opera *f.*
insubordinate *adj* turbulentus, sēditiōsus.
insubordination *n* intemperantia *f,* licentia *f.*
insufferable *adj* intolerandus, intolerābilis.
insufficiency *n* inopia *f.*
insufficient *adj* minor; **be ~** nōn sufficere.
insufficiently *adv* parum.
insulate *vt* sēgregāre.
insult *n* iniūria *f,* contumēlia *f,* probrum *nt* ♦ *vt* maledīcere (*dat*), contumēliam impōnere (*dat*).
insulting *adj* contumēliōsus.
insultingly *adv* contumēliōsē.
insuperable *adj* inexsuperābilis.
insupportable *adj* intolerandus, intolerābilis.
insurance *n* cautiō *f.*
insure *vi* cavēre.
insurgent *n* rebellis *m.*
insurmountable *adj* inexsuperābilis.
insurrection *n* mōtus *m,* sēditiō *f.*
intact *adj* integer, intāctus, incolumis.
integrity *n* integritās *f,* innocentia *f,* fidēs *f.*
intellect *n* ingenium *nt,* mēns *f,* animus *m.*
intellectual *adj* ingeniōsus.
intelligence *n* intellegentia *f,* acūmen *nt;* (*MIL*) nūntius *m.*
intelligent *adj* ingeniōsus, sapiēns, argūtus.
intelligently *adv* ingeniōsē, sapienter, satis acūtē.

intelligible *adj* perspicuus, apertus.
intemperance *n* intemperantia *f,* licentia *f.*
intemperate *adj* intemperāns, intemperātus.
intemperately *adv* intemperanter.
intend *vt* (*with inf*) in animō habēre, velle; (*with object*) dēstināre.
intense *adj* ācer, nimius.
intensely *adv* valdē, nimium.
intensify *vt* augēre, amplificāre; **be ~ied** ingravēscere.
intensity *n* vīs *f.*
intensive *adj* ācer, multus, adsiduus.
intensively *adv* summō studiō.
intent *adj* ērēctus, intentus; **be ~ on** animum intendere in (*acc*) ♦ *n* cōnsilium *nt;* **with ~** cōnsultō.
intention *n* cōnsilium *nt,* prōpositum *nt;* **it is my ~** mihī in animō est; **with the ~ of** eā mente, eō cōnsiliō ut (*subj*).
intentionally *adv* cōnsultō, dē industriā.
inter *vt* humāre.
intercalary *adj* intercalāris.
intercalate *vt* intercalāre.
intercede *vi* intercēdere, dēprecārī.
intercept *vt* excipere, intercipere; (*cut off*) interclūdere.
intercession *n* dēprecātiō *f;* (*tribune's*) intercessiō *f.*
intercessor *n* dēprecātor *m.*
interchange *vt* permūtāre ♦ *n* permūtātiō *f,* vicissitūdō *f.*
intercourse *n* commercium *nt,* ūsus *m,* cōnsuetūdō *f.*
interdict *n* interdictum *nt* ♦ *vt* interdīcere (*dat*), vetāre.
interest *n* (*advantage*) commodum *nt;* (*study*) studium *nt;* (*money*) faenus *nt,* ūsūra *f;* **compound ~** anatocismus *m;* **rate of ~** faenus *nt;* **~ at 12 per cent (per annum)** centēsimae *fpl;* **it is ~** interest; **it is in my ~** meā interest; **consult the ~s of** cōnsulere (*dat*); **take an ~ in** animum intendere (*dat*) ♦ *vt* dēlectāre, capere; (*audience*) tenēre; **~ oneself in** studēre (*dat*).
interested *adj* attentus; (*for gain*) ambitiōsus.
interesting *adj* iūcundus, novus.
interfere *vi* intervenīre; (*with*) sē interpōnere (*dat*), sē admiscēre ad; (*hinder*) officere (*dat*).
interference *n* interventus *m,* intercessiō *f.*
interim *n:* **in the ~** interim, intereā.
interior *adj* interior ♦ *n* pars interior *f;* (*country*) interiōra *ntpl.*
interject *vt* exclāmāre.
interjection *n* interiectiō *f.*
interlace *vt* intexere.
interlard *vt* variāre.
interlock *vt* implicāre.
interloper *n* interpellātor *m.*
interlude *n* embolium *nt.*
intermarriage *n* cōnūbium *nt.*
intermediary *adj* medius ♦ *n* internūntius *m.*
intermediate *adj* medius.
interment *n* humātiō *f.*

interminable adj sempiternus, longus.
intermingle vt intermiscēre ♦ vi sē immiscēre.
intermission n intercapēdō f, intermissiō f.
intermittent adj interruptus.
intermittently adv interdum.
intern vt inclūdere.
internal adj internus; (POL) domesticus.
internally adv intus, domī.
international adj: ~ **law** iūs gentium.
internecine adj internecīvus.
interplay n vicēs fpl.
interpolate vt interpolāre.
interpose vt interpōnere ♦ vi intercēdere.
interposition n intercessiō f.
interpret vt interpretārī.
interpretation n interpretātiō f.
interpreter n interpres m/f.
interrogate vt interrogāre, percontārī.
interrogation n interrogātiō f, percontātiō f.
interrupt vt (action) intercipere; (speaker) interpellāre; (talk) dirimere; (continuity) intermittere.
interrupter n interpellātor m.
interruption n interpellātiō f; intermissiō f.
intersect vt dīvidere, secāre.
intersperse vt distinguere.
interstice n rīma f.
intertwine vt intexere, implicāre.
interval n intervallum nt, spatium nt; **after an** ~ spatiō interpositō; **after an ~ of a year** annō interiectō; **at ~s** interdum; **at frequent ~s** identidem; **leave an** ~ intermittere.
intervene vt intercēdere, intervenīre.
intervention n intercēssiō f, interventus m; **by the ~ of** intercursū (gen).
interview n colloquium nt, aditus m ♦ vt convenīre.
interweave vt implicāre, intexere.
intestate adj intestātus ♦ adv intestātō.
intestine adj intestīnus; (POL) domesticus ♦ npl intestīna ntpl; (victim's) exta ntpl.
intimacy n familiāritās f.
intimate adj familiāris; **be an ~ friend of** ab latere esse (gen); **a very ~ friend** perfamiliāris m/f ♦ vt dēnūntiāre.
intimately adv familiāriter.
intimation n dēnūntiātiō f; (hint) indicium nt.
intimidate vt minārī (dat), terrōrem inicere (dat).
intimidation n metus m, minae fpl.
into prep in (acc), intrā (acc).
intolerable adj intolerandus, intolerābilis.
intolerably adv intoleranter.
intolerance n impatientia f.
intolerant adj impatiēns, intolerāns.
intonation n sonus m, flexiō f.
intone vt cantāre.
intoxicate vt ēbrium reddere.
intoxicated adj ēbrius.
intoxication n ēbrietās f.
intractable adj indocilis, difficilis.
intransigent adj obstinātus.

intrepid adj intrepidus, impavidus.
intrepidity n audācia f, fortitūdō f.
intricacy n implicātiō f.
intricate adj implicātus, involūtus.
intricately adv implicitē.
intrigue n factiō f, artēs fpl, fallācia f ♦ vi māchinārī, fallāciīs ūtī.
intriguing adj factiōsus; blandus.
intrinsic adj vērus, innātus.
intrinsically adv per sē.
introduce vt indūcere, īnferre, importāre; (acquaintance) commendāre; (custom) īnstituere.
introduction n exōrdium nt, prooemium nt; (of person) commendātiō f; **letter of ~** litterae commendātīciae fpl.
intrude vi sē interpōnere, intervenīre.
intruder n interpellātor m, advena m; (fig) aliēnus m.
intrusion n interpellātiō f.
intuition n sēnsus m, cognitiō f.
inundate vt inundāre.
inundation n ēluviō f.
inure vt dūrāre, adsuēfacere.
invade vt invādere.
invalid adj aeger, dēbilis; (null) inritus.
invalidate vt īnfirmāre.
invaluable adj inaestimābilis.
invariable adj cōnstāns, immūtābilis.
invariably adv semper.
invasion n incursiō f.
invective n convīcium nt.
inveigh vi: ~ **against** invehī in (acc), īnsectārī.
inveigle vt illicere, pellicere.
invent vt fingere, comminīscī, invenīre.
invention n inventum nt; (faculty) inventiō f.
inventor n inventor m, auctor m.
inverse adj inversus.
inversely adv inversō ōrdine.
invert vt invertere.
invest vt (in office) inaugurāre; (MIL) obsidēre, circumsedēre; (money) locāre.
investigate vt investīgāre, indāgāre; (case) cognōscere.
investigation n investīgātiō f, indāgātiō f; (case) cognitiō f.
investment n (MIL) obsessiō f; (money) locāta pecūnia f.
inveterate adj inveterātus, vetus; **become ~** inveterāscere.
invidious adj invidiōsus.
invidiously adv invidiōsē.
invigorate vt recreāre, reficere.
invincible adj invictus.
inviolable adj inviolātus; (person) sacrōsanctus.
inviolably adv inviolātē.
inviolate adj integer.
invisible adj caecus; **be ~** vidērī nōn posse.
invitation n invītātiō f; **at the ~ of** invītātū (gen).
invite vt invītāre, vocāre.
inviting adj suāvis, blandus.

invitingly *adv* blandē, suāviter.
invocation *n* testātiō *f.*
invoke *vt* invocāre, testārī.
involuntarily *adv* īnscienter, invītus.
involuntary *adj* coāctus.
involve *vt* implicāre, involvere; **be ~d in** inligārī (*abl*).
invulnerable *adj* inviolābilis; **be ~** vulnerārī nōn posse.
inward *adj* interior.
inwardly *adv* intus.
inwards *adv* intrōrsus.
inweave *vt* intexere.
inwrought *adj* intextus.
irascibility *n* īrācundia *f.*
irascible *adj* īrācundus.
irate *adj* īrātus.
ire *n* īra *f.*
iris *n* hyacinthus *m.*
irk *vt* incommodāre; **I am ~ed** mē piget.
irksome *adj* molestus.
irksomeness *n* molestia *f.*
iron *n* ferrum *nt*; **of ~** ferreus ♦ *adj* ferreus.
ironical *adj* inversus.
ironically *adv* inversīs verbīs.
iron mine *n* ferrāria *f.*
ironmonger *n* negōtiātor ferrārius *m.*
ironmongery *n* ferrāmenta *ntpl.*
iron ore *n* ferrum īnfectum *nt.*
iron-tipped *adj* ferrātus.
irony *n* illūsiō *f*, verbōrum inversiō *f*, dissimulātiō *f.*
irradiate *vt* illūstrāre.
irrational *adj* absurdus, ratiōnis expers; (*animal*) brūtus.
irrationally *adv* absurdē, sine ratiōne.
irreconcilable *adj* repugnāns, īnsociābilis.
irrefutable *adj* certus, invictus.
irregular *adj* incompositus; (*ground*) inaequālis; (*meeting*) extraōrdinārius; (*troops*) tumultuārius.
irregularity *n* inaequālitās *f*; (*conduct*) prāvitās *f*, licentia *f*; (*election*) vitium *nt.*
irregularly *adv* nullō ōrdine; (*elected*) vitiō.
irrelevant *adj* aliēnus.
irreligion *n* impietās *f.*
irreligious *adj* impius.
irremediable *adj* īnsānābilis.
irreparable *adj* irrevocābilis.
irreproachable *adj* integer, innocēns.
irresistible *adj* invictus.
irresolute *adj* dubius, anceps.
irresolutely *adv* dubitanter.
irresolution *n* dubitātiō *f.*
irresponsibility *n* licentia *f.*
irresponsible *adj* lascīvus, levis.
irretrievable *adj* irrevocābilis.
irreverence *n* impietās *f.*
irreverent *adj* impius.
irreverently *adv* impiē.
irrevocable *adj* irrevocābilis.
irrigate *vt* inrigāre.
irrigation *n* inrigātiō *f.*

irritability *n* īrācundia *f.*
irritable *adj* īrācundus.
irritate *vt* inrītāre, stomachum movēre (*dat*).
irritation *n* īrācundia *f*, stomachus *m.*
island *n* īnsula *f.*
islander *n* īnsulānus *m.*
isle *n* īnsula *f.*
isolate *vt* sēgregāre, sēparāre.
isolation *n* sōlitūdō *f.*
issue *n* (*result*) ēventus *m*, exitus *m*; (*children*) prōlēs *f*; (*question*) rēs *f*; (*book*) ēditiō *f*; **decide the ~** dēcernere, dēcertāre; **the point at ~** quā dē rē agitur ♦ *vt* distribuere; (*book*) ēdere; (*announcement*) prōmulgāre; (*coin*) ērogāre ♦ *vi* ēgredī, ēmānāre; (*result*) ēvādere, ēvenīre.
isthmus *n* isthmus *m.*
it *pron* hōc. id.
itch *n* (*disease*) scabiēs *f*; (*fig*) cacoēthes *nt* ♦ *vi* prūrīre.
item *n* nōmen *nt*, rēs *f.*
iterate *vt* iterāre.
itinerant *adj* vāgus, circumforāneus.
itinerary *n* iter *nt.*
its *adj* suus, ēius.
itself *pron* ipse, ipsa, ipsum.
ivory *n* ebur *nt* ♦ *adj* eburneus.
ivy *n* hedera *f.*

J, j

jabber *vi* blaterāre.
jackdaw *n* grāculus *m.*
jaded *adj* dēfessus, fatīgātus.
jagged *adj* serrātus.
jail *n* carcer *m.*
jailer *n* custōs *m*, carcerārius *m.*
jam *vt* comprimere; (*way*) obstruere.
jamb *n* postis *m.*
jangle *vi* crepitāre; rixārī.
janitor *n* iānitor *m.*
January *n* mēnsis Iānuārius *m*; **of ~** Iānuārius.
jar *n* urna *f*; (*for wine*) amphora *f*; (*for water*) hydria *f*; (*sound*) offēnsa *f*; (*quarrel*) rixa *f* ♦ *vi* offendere.
jasper *n* iaspis *f.*
jaundice *n* morbus arquātus.
jaundiced *adj* ictericus.
jaunt *n*: **take a ~** excurrere.
jauntily *adv* hilare, festīvē.
jauntiness *n* hilaritās *f.*
jaunty *adj* hilaris, festīvus.
javelin *n* iaculum *nt*, pīlum *nt*; **throw the ~** iaculārī.
jaw *n* māla *f*; **~s** *pl* faucēs *fpl.*

jay n grāculus m.
jealous adj invidus; **be ~ of** invidēre (dat).
jealousy n invidia f.
jeer n irrīsiō f ♦ vi irrīdēre; **~ at** illūdēre.
jejune adj iēiūnus, exīlis.
jeopardize vt in perīculum addūcere.
jeopardy n perīculum nt.
jerk n subitus mōtus m.
jest n iocus m.
jester n scurra m.
jet n (mineral) gagātēs m; (of water) saltus m ♦ vi salīre.
jetsam n ēiectāmenta ntpl.
jettison vt ēicere.
jetty n mōlēs f.
Jew n Iūdaeus.
jewel n gemma f.
Jewish adj Iūdaicus.
jig n tripudium nt.
jilt vt repudiāre.
jingle n nēnia f ♦ vi crepitāre, tinnīre.
job n opus nt.
jocose adj see **jocular**.
jocular adj facētus, ioculāris.
jocularity n facētiae fpl.
jocularly adv facētē, per iocum.
jocund adj hilaris, festīvus.
jog vt fodicāre; (fig) stimulāre ♦ vi ambulāre.
join vt iungere, coniungere, cōpulāre ♦ vi coniungī, sē coniungere; **~ in** interesse (dat), sē immiscēre (dat); **~ battle with** proelium committere (+ abl).
joiner n faber m.
joint adj commūnis ♦ n commissūra f (of body) articulus m, nōdus m; **~ by ~** articulātim.
jointed adj geniculātus.
joint-heir n cohērēs m/f.
jointly adv ūnā, coniūnctē.
joist n tignum nt.
joke n iocus m ♦ vi iocārī, lūdere.
joking n iocus m; **~ apart** remōtō iocō.
jokingly adv per iocum.
jollity n hilaritās f, festīvitās f.
jolly adj hilaris, festīvus.
jolt vt iactāre.
jolting n iactātiō f.
jostle vt agitāre, offendere.
jot n minimum nt; **not a ~** nihil; **not care a ~** nōn floccī facere.
journal n ācta diūrna ntpl.
journey n iter nt.
journeyman n opifex m.
Jove n Iuppiter m.
jovial adj hilaris.
joviality n hilaritās f.
jovially adv hilare.
jowl n māla f; **cheek by ~** iuxtā.
joy n gaudium nt, laetitia f, alacritās f.
joyful adj laetus, hilaris.
joyfully adv laetē, hilare.
joyfulness n gaudium nt, laetitia f.
joyless adj tristis, maestus.

joyous adj see **joyful.**
joyously adv see **joyfully.**
jubilant adj laetus, gaudiō exsultāns.
judge n iūdex m, arbiter m ♦ vt iūdicāre; (think) exīstimāre, cēnsēre; **~ between** diiūdicāre.
judgeship n iūdicātus m.
judgment n iūdicium nt, arbitrium nt; (opinion) sententia f; (punishment) poena f; (wisdom) iūdicium nt; **in my ~** meō animō, meō arbitrātū; **pass ~ on** statuere dē; **sit in ~** iūdicium exercēre.
judgment seat n tribūnal nt.
judicature n iūrisdictiō f; (men) iūdicēs mpl.
judicial adj iūdiciālis; (law) iūdiciārius.
judiciary n iūdicēs mpl.
judicious adj prūdēns, cōnsīderātus.
judiciously adv prūdenter.
jug n hydria f, urceus m.
juggler n praestīgiātor m.
juggling n praestīgiae fpl.
juice n liquor m, sūcus m.
juicy adj sūcī plēnus.
July n mēnsis Quīnctīlis, Iūlius m; **of ~** Quīnctīlis, Iūlius.
jumble n congeriēs f ♦ vt cōnfundere.
jump n saltus m ♦ vi salīre; **~ across** transilīre; **~ at** (opportunity) captāre, adripere, amplectī; **~ down** dēsilīre; **~ on to** īnsilīre in (acc).
junction n coniūnctiō f.
juncture n tempus nt.
June n mēnsis Iūnius; **of ~** Iūnius.
junior adj iūnior, nātū minor.
juniper n iūniperus f.
Juno n Iūnō, Iūnōnis f.
Jupiter n Iuppiter, Iovis m.
juridical adj iūdiciārius.
jurisconsult n iūriscōnsultus m.
jurisdiction n iūrisdictiō f, diciō f; **exercise ~** iūs dīcere.
jurisprudence n iūrisprūdentia f.
jurist n iūriscōnsultus m.
juror n iūdex m.
jury n iūdicēs mpl.
just adj iūstus, aequus ♦ adv (exactly) prōrsus; (only) modo; (time) commodum, modo; (with adv) dēmum, dēnique; (with pron) adeō dēmum, ipse; **~ as** (comparison) aequē ac, perinde ac, quemadmodum; sīcut; **~ before** (time) cum māximē, sub (acc); **~ now** modo, nunc; **~ so** ita prōrsus, sānē; **only ~** vix.
justice n iūstitia f, aequitās f, iūs nt; (person) praetor m; **administer ~** iūs reddere.
justiciary n praetor m.
justifiable adj iūstus.
justifiably adv iūre.
justification n pūrgātiō f, excūsātiō f.
justify vt excūsāre, pūrgāre.
justly adv iūstē, aequē; iūre, meritō.
jut vi prōminēre, excurrere.
jutting adj prōiectus.
juvenile adj iuvenīlis, puerīlis.

K, k

keel *n* carīna *f*.

keen *adj* ācer; (*mind*) acūtus, argūtus; (*sense*) sagāx; (*pain*) acerbus; **I am ~ on** studeō.

keenly *adv* ācriter, sagāciter, acūtē, acerbē.

keenness *n* (*scent*) sagācitās *f*; (*sight*) aciēs *f*; (*pain*) acerbitās *f*; (*eagerness*) studium *nt*, ārdor *m*.

keep *vt* servāre, tenēre, habēre; (*celebrate*) agere, celebrāre; (*guard*) custōdīre; (*obey*) observāre; (*preserve*) cōnservāre; (*rear*) alere, pāscere; (*store*) condere; **~ apart** distinēre; **~ away** arcēre; **~ back** dētinēre, reservāre; **~ down** comprimere; (*exuberance*) dēpāscere; **~ in** cohibēre, claudere; **~ in with** grātiam sequī (*gen*); **~ off** arcēre, dēfendere; **~ one's word** fidem praestāre; **~ one's hands off** manūs abstinēre; **~ house** domī sē retinēre; **~ secret** cēlāre; **~ together** continēre; **~ up** sustinēre, cōnservāre; **~ up with** subsequī; **~ waiting** dēmorārī ◆ *vi* dūrāre, manēre ◆ *n* arx *f*.

keeper *n* custōs *m*.

keeping *n* custōdia *f*; **in ~ with** prō (*abl*); **be in ~ with** convenīre (*dat*).

keg *n* cadus *m*.

ken *n* cōnspectus *m*.

kennel *n* stabulum *nt*.

kerb *n* crepīdō *f*.

kernel *n* grānum *nt*, nucleus *m*.

kettle *n* lebēs *f*.

key *n* clāvis *f*; (*fig*) claustra *ntpl*, iānua *f*; **~ position** cardō *m*.

kick *vi* calcitrāre ◆ *vt* calce ferīre.

kid *n* haedus *m*.

kidnap *vt* surripere.

kidnapper *n* plagiārius *m*.

kidney *n* rēn *m*.

kidney bean *n* phasēlus *m*.

kid's *adj* haedīnus.

kill *vt* interficere, interimere; (*in battle*) occīdere; (*murder*) necāre, iugulāre; (*time*) perdere.

killer *n* interfector *m*.

kiln *n* fornāx *f*.

kin *n* cognātī *mpl*, propinqui *mpl*; **next of ~** proximī *mpl*.

kind *adj* bonus, benīgnus, benevolus ◆ *n* genus *nt*; **of such a ~** tālis; **what ~ of** quālis ◆ *adj* cōmis.

kindle *vt* incendere, succendere, īnflammāre.

kindliness *n* cōmitās *f*, hūmānitās *f*.

kindling *n* (*fuel*) fōmes *m*.

kindly *adv* benīgnē.

kindness *n* benīgnitās *f*, benevolentia *f*; (*act*) beneficium *nt*, officium *nt*, grātia *f*.

kindred *n* necessitūdō *f*, cognātiō *f*; propinquī *mpl*, cognātī *mpl* ◆ *adj* cognātus, adfīnis.

king *n* rēx *m*.

kingdom *n* rēgnum *nt*.

kingfisher *n* alcēdō *f*.

kingly *adj* rēgius, rēgālis.

kingship *n* rēgnum *nt*.

kink *n* vitium *nt*.

kinsfolk *n* cognātī *mpl*, necessāriī *mpl*.

kinsman *n* cognātus *m*, propinquus *m*, necessārius *m*.

kinswoman *n* cognāta *f*, propinqua *f*, necessāria *f*.

kismet *n* fātum *nt*.

kiss *n* ōsculum *nt* ◆ *vt* ōsculārī.

kit *n* (*MIL*) sarcina *f*.

kitchen *n* culīna *f*.

kitchen garden *n* hortus *m*.

kite *n* mīluus *m*.

kite's *adj* mīluīnus.

knack *n* calliditās *f*, artificium *nt*; **have the ~ of** callēre.

knapsack *n* sarcina *f*.

knave *n* veterātor *m*.

knavish *adj* improbus.

knavishly *adv* improbē.

knead *vt* depsere, subigere.

knee *n* genū *nt*.

kneel *vi* genibus nītī.

knife *n* culter *m*; (*surgeon's*) scalprum *nt*.

knight *n* eques *m* ◆ *vt* in ōrdinem equestrem recipere.

knighthood *n* ōrdō equester *m*.

knightly *adj* equester.

knit *vt* texere; (*brow*) contrahere.

knob *n* bulla *f*.

knock *vt* ferīre, percutere; **~ at** pulsāre; **~ against** offendere; **~ down** dēicere, adflīgere; (*at auction*) addīcere; **~ off** dēcutere; (*work*) dēsistere ab; **~ out** ēlīdere, excutere; (*unconscious*) exanimāre; (*fig*) dēvincere; **~ up** suscitāre ◆ *n* pulsus *m*, ictus *m*.

knock-kneed *adj* vārus.

knoll *n* tumulus *m*.

knot *n* nōdus *m* ◆ *vt* nectere.

knotty *adj* nōdōsus; **~ point** nōdus *m*.

know *vt* scīre; (*person*) nōvisse; **~ all about** explōrātum habēre; **~ again** agnōscere; **~ how to** scīre; **not ~** ignōrāre, nescīre; **let me ~** fac sciam, fac mē certiōrem; **get to ~** cognōscere ◆ *n* **in the ~** cōnscius.

knowing *adj* prūdēns, callidus.

knowingly *adv* cōnsultō, sciēns.

knowledge *n* scientia *f*, doctrīna *f*; (*practical*) experientia *f*; (*of something*) cognitiō *f*.

knowledgeable *adj* gnārus, doctus.

known *adj* nōtus; **make ~** dēclārāre.

knuckle *n* articulus *m*.

knuckle bone *n* tālus *m*.

kotow *vi* adulārī.

kudos *n* glōria *f*, laus *f*.

L, l

label n titulus m ♦ vt titulō īnscrībere.
laboratory n officīna f.
laborious adj labōriōsus, operōsus.
laboriously adv operōsē.
laboriousness n labor m.
labour n labor m, opera f; (work done) opus nt; (work allotted) pēnsum nt; (workmen) operae fpl; **be in ~** parturīre ♦ vi labōrāre, ēnītī; **~ at** ēlabōrāre; **~ under a delusion** errōre fallī.
laboured adj adfectātus.
labourer n operārius m; **~s** pl operae fpl.
labyrinth n labyrinthus m.
lace n texta rēticulāta ntpl; (shoe) ligula f ♦ vt nectere.
lacerate vt lacerāre.
laceration n lacerātiō f.
lack n inopia f, dēfectiō f ♦ vt egēre (abl), carēre (abl).
lackey n pedisequus m.
laconic adj brevis.
laconically adv ūnō verbō, paucīs verbīs.
lacuna n lacūna f.
lad n puer m.
ladder n scāla f.
lade vt onerāre.
laden adj onustus, onerātus.
lading n onus nt.
ladle n trulla f.
lady n domina f, mātrōna f, mulier f.
ladylike adj līberālis, honestus.
lag vi cessāre.
lagoon n stagnum nt.
lair n latibulum nt.
lake n lacus m.
lamb n agnus m; (flesh) agnīna f; **ewe ~** agna f.
lame adj claudus; (argument) inānis; **be ~** claudicāre.
lameness n claudicātiō f.
lament n lāmentātiō f, lāmentum nt ♦ vt lūgēre, lāmentārī; (regret) dēplōrāre.
lamentable adj lāmentābilis, miserābilis.
lamentably adv miserābiliter.
lamentation n lāmentātiō f.
lamp n lucerna f, lychnus m.
lampoon n satura f ♦ vt carmine dēstringere.
lance n hasta f, lancea f.
lancer n hastātus m.
lancet n scalpellum nt.
land n terra f; (country) terra f, regiō f; (territory) fīnēs mpl; (native) patria f; (property) praedium nt, ager m; (soil) solum nt ♦ vt expōnere ♦ vi ē nāve ēgredī ♦ adj terrēnus, terrestris.
landfall n adpulsus m.
landing place n ēgressus m.

landlady n caupōna f.
landlord n dominus m; (inn) caupō m.
landmark n lapis m; **be a ~** ēminēre.
landscape n agrōrum prōspectus m.
landslide n terrae lābēs f, lāpsus m.
landwards adv terram versus.
lane n (country) sēmita f; (town) angiportus m.
language n lingua f; (style) ōrātiō f, sermō m; (diction) verba ntpl; **bad ~** maledicta ntpl.
languid adj languidus, remissus.
languidly adv languidē.
languish vi languēre, languēscere; (with disease) tābēscere.
languor n languor m.
lank, lanky adj exīlis, gracilis.
lantern n lanterna f, lucerna f.
lap n gremium nt, sinus m ♦ vt lambere; (cover) involvere.
lapse n (time) lāpsus m; (mistake) errātum nt; **after the ~ of a year** interiectō annō ♦ vi lābī; (agreement) inritum fierī; (property) revertī.
larceny n fūrtum nt.
larch n larix f ♦ adj larignus.
lard n adeps m/f.
larder n cella penāria f.
large adj māgnus, grandis, amplus; **at ~** solūtus; **very ~** permāgnus; **as ~ as ...** tantus ... quantus.
largely adv plērumque.
largess n largitiō f; (MIL) dōnātīvum nt; (civil) congiārium nt; **give ~** largīrī.
lark n alauda f.
lascivious adj libīdinōsus.
lasciviously adv libīdinōsē.
lasciviousness n libīdō f.
lash n flagellum nt, lōrum nt; (eye) cilium nt ♦ vt verberāre; (tie) adligāre; (with words) castīgāre.
lashing n verbera ntpl.
lass n puella f.
lassitude n languor m.
last adj ultimus, postrēmus, suprēmus; (in line) novissimus; (preceding) proximus; **at ~** tandem, dēmum, dēnique; **for the ~ time** postrēmum ♦ n fōrma f; **let the cobbler stick to his ~** nē sūtor suprā crepidam ♦ vi dūrāre, permanēre.
lasting adj diūtinus, diūturnus.
lastly adv postrēmō, dēnique.
latch n pessulus m.
latchet n corrigia f.
late adj sērus; (date) recēns; (dead) dēmortuus; (emperor) dīvus; **~ at night** multā nocte; **till ~ in the day** ad multum diem ♦ adv sērō; **too ~** sērō; **too ~ to** sērius quam quī (subj); **of ~** nūper.
lately adv nūper.
latent adj occultus, latitāns.
later adj posterior ♦ adv posteā, posthāc, mox.
latest adj novissimus.
lath n tigillum nt.
lathe n tornus m.
lather n spūma f.

Latin *adj* Latīnus; **speak ~** Latīnē loquī; **understand ~** Latīnē scīre; **translate into ~** Latīnē reddere; **in Latin** latinē.
Latinity *n* Latīnitās *f*.
latitude *n* (*GEOG*) caelum *nt*; (*scope*) lībertās *f*.
latter *adj* posterior; **the ~** hīc.
latterly *adv* nūper.
lattice *n* trānsenna *f*.
laud *n* laus *f* ♦ *vt* laudāre.
laudable *adj* laudābilis, laude dignus.
laudatory *adj* honōrificus.
laugh *n* rīsus *m*; (*loud*) cachinnus *m* ♦ *vi* rīdēre, cachinnāre; **~ at** (*joke*) rīdēre; (*person*) dērīdēre; **~ up one's sleeve** in sinū gaudēre.
laughable *adj* rīdiculus.
laughing stock *n* lūdibrium *nt*.
laughter *n* rīsus *m*.
launch *vt* (*missile*) contorquēre; (*ship*) dēdūcere; **~ an attack** impetum dare ♦ *vi*: **~ out into** ingredī in (*acc*) ♦ *n* celōx *f*, lembus *m*.
laureate *adj* laureātus.
laurel *n* laurus *m* ♦ *adj* laureus.
lave *vt* lavāre.
lavish *adj* prōdigus, largus ♦ *vt* largīrī, profundere.
lavishly *adv* prōdigē, effūsē.
lavishness *n* largitās *f*.
law *n* lēx *f*; (*system*) iūs *nt*; (*divine*) fās *nt*; **civil ~** iūs cīvīle; **constitutional ~** iūs pūblicum; **international ~** iūs gentium; **go to ~** lēge agere, lītigāre; **break the ~** lēges violāre; **pass a ~** (*magistrate*) lēgem perferre; (*people*) lēgem iubēre.
law-abiding *adj* bene mōrātus.
law court *n* iūdicium *nt*; (*building*) basilica *f*.
lawful *adj* lēgitimus; (*morally*) fās.
lawfully *adv* lēgitimē, lēge.
lawgiver *n* lēgum scrīptor *m*.
lawless *adj* exlēx.
lawlessly *adv* licenter.
lawlessness *n* licentia *f*.
lawn *n* prātulum *nt*.
law-suit *n* līs *f*, āctiō *f*.
lawyer *n* iūriscōnsultus *m*, causidicus *m*.
lax *adj* dissolūtus, remissus.
laxity *n* dissolūtiō *f*.
lay *vt* pōnere, locāre; (*ambush*) collocāre, tendere; (*disorder*) sēdāre; (*egg*) parere; (*foundation*) iacere; (*hands*) inicere; (*plan*) capere, inīre; (*trap*) tendere; (*wager*) facere; **~ aside** pōnere; (*in store*) repōnere; **~ by** repōnere; **~ down** dēpōnere; (*rule*) statuere; **~ hold of** prehendere, adripere; **~ in** condere; **~ a motion before** referre ad; **~ on** impōnere; **~ open** patefacere; (*to attack*) nūdāre; **~ out** (*money*) impendere, ērogāre; (*camp*) mētārī; **~ siege to** obsidēre; **~ to heart** in pectus dēmittere; **~ up** recondere; **~ upon** iniungere, impōnere; **~ violent hands on** vim adferre, adhibēre (*dat*); **whatever they could ~ hands on** quod cuīque in manum vēnisset; **~ waste** vastāre ♦ *n* carmen *nt*, melos *nt*.

lay *adj* (*ECCL*) lāicus.
layer *n* corium *nt*; (*stones*) ōrdō *m*; (*plant*) propāgō *f*.
layout *n* dēsignātiō *f*.
laze *vi* ōtiārī.
lazily *adv* ignāvē, ōtiōsē.
laziness *n* ignāvia *f*, dēsidia *f*, pigritia *f*.
lazy *adj* ignāvus, dēsidiōsus, piger.
lea *n* prātum *nt*.
lead *vt* dūcere; (*life*) agere; (*wall*) perdūcere; (*water*) dērīvāre; **~ across** tradūcere; **~ around** circumdūcere; **~ astray** in errōrem indūcere; **~ away** abdūcere; **~ back** redūcere; **~ down** dēdūcere; **~ in** intrōdūcere; **~ on** addūcere; **~ out** ēdūcere; **~ over** tradūcere; **~ the way** dūcere, praeīre; **~ up to** tendere ad, spectare ad; **the road ~s ...** via fert ....
lead *n* plumbum *nt* ♦ *adj* plumbeus.
leaden *adj* (*colour*) līvidus.
leader *n* dux *m*, ductor *m*.
leadership *n* ductus *m*.
leading *adj* prīmus, prīnceps, praecipuus.
leaf *n*, *pl* **leaves** *n* folium *nt*, frōns *f*; (*paper*) scheda *f*; **put forth leaves** frondēscere.
leaflet *n* libellus *m*.
leafy *adj* frondōsus.
league *n* foedus *nt*, societās *f*; (*distance*) tria mīlia passuum ♦ *vi* coniūrāre, foedus facere.
leagued *adj* foederātus.
leak *n* rīma *f* ♦ *vi* mānāre, rimās agere.
leaky *adj* rīmōsus.
lean *adj* macer, exīlis, gracilis ♦ *vi* nītī; **~ back** sē reclīnāre; **~ on** innītī in (*abl*), incumbere (*dat*); **~ over** inclīnāre.
leaning *n* prōpēnsiō *f* ♦ *adj* inclīnātus.
leanness *n* gracilitās *f*, maciēs *f*.
leap *n* saltus *m* ♦ *vi* salīre; (*for joy*) exsultāre; **~ down** dēsilīre; **~ on to** īnsilīre in (*acc*).
leap year *n* annus bissextilis *m*.
learn *vt* discere; (*news*) accipere, audīre; (*by heart*) ēdiscere; (*discover*) cognoscēre.
learned *adj* doctus, ērudītus, litterātus.
learnedly *adv* doctē.
learner *n* tīrō *m*, discipulus *m*.
learning *n* doctrīna *f*, ērudītiō *f*, litterae *fpl*.
lease *n* (*taken*) conductiō *f*; (*given*) locātiō *f* ♦ *vt* condūcere; locāre.
leash *n* cōpula *f*.
least *adj* minimus ♦ *adv* minimē; **at ~** saltem; **to say the ~** ut levissimē dīcam; **not in the ~** haudquāquam.
leather *n* corium *nt*, alūta *f*.
leathery *adj* lentus.
leave *n* (*of absence*) commeātus *m*; (*permission*) potestās *f*, venia *f*; **ask ~** veniam petere; **give ~** potestātem facere; **obtain ~** impetrāre; **by your ~** pace tuā, bonā tuā veniā ♦ *vt* relinquere, dēserere; (*legacy*) lēgāre; **~ alone** nōn tangere, manum abstinēre ab; **~ behind** relinquere; **~ in the lurch** dēstituere, dērelinquere; **~ off** dēsinere, dēsistere ab;

(*temporarily*) intermittere; (*garment*) pōnere;
~ **out** praetermittere, ōmittere ♦ vi
discēdere ab (+ *abl*), abīre.
leaven n fermentum nt.
leavings n rēliquiae fpl.
lecherous adj salāx.
lecture n acroāsis f, audītiō f ♦ vi docēre,
scholam habēre.
lecturer n doctor m.
lecture room n audītōrium nt.
ledge n līmen nt.
ledger n cōdex acceptī et expēnsī.
lee n pars ā ventō tūta.
leech n hirūdō f.
leek n porrum nt.
leer vi līmīs oculīs intuērī.
lees n faex f; (*of oil*) amurca f.
left adj sinister, laevus ♦ n sinistra f, laeva f; **on
the** ~ ā laevā, ad laevam, ā sinistrā.
leg n crūs nt; (*of table*) pēs m.
legacy n lēgātum nt; ~ **hunter** captātor m.
legal adj lēgitimus.
legalize vt sancīre.
legally adv secundum lēgēs, lēge.
legate n lēgātus m.
legation n lēgātiō f.
legend n fābula f; (*inscription*) titulus m.
legendary adj fābulōsus.
legerdemain n praestīgiae fpl.
legging n ocrea f.
legible adj clārus.
legion n legiō f; **men of the 10th** ~ decumānī
mpl.
legionary n legiōnārius m.
legislate vi lēgēs scrībere, lēgēs facere.
legislation n lēgēs fpl, lēgēs scrībendae.
legislator n lēgum scrīptor m.
legitimate adj lēgitimus.
legitimately adv lēgitimē.
leisure n ōtium nt; **at** ~ ōtiōsus, vacuus; **have** ~
for vacāre (*dat*).
leisured adj ōtiōsus.
leisurely adj lentus.
lend vt commodāre, mūtuum dare; (*at interest*)
faenerārī; (*ear*) aures praebēre, admovēre; ~
a ready ear aurēs patefacere; ~ **assistance**
opem ferre.
length n longitūdō f; (*time*) diūturnitās f; **at** ~
tandem, dēmum, dēnique; (*speech*) cōpiōsē.
lengthen vt extendere; (*time*) prōtrahere;
(*sound*) prōdūcere.
lengthwise adv in longitūdinem.
lengthy adj longus, prōlixus.
leniency n clēmentia f.
lenient adj clēmēns, mītis.
leniently adv clēmenter.
lentil n lēns f.
leonine adj leōnīnus.
leopard n pardus m.
less adj minor ♦ adv minus; ~ **than** (*num*) intrā
(*acc*); **much** ~, **still** ~ nēdum.
lessee n conductor m.
lessen vt minuere, imminuere, dēminuere ♦

vi dēcrēscere.
lesson n documentum nt; **be a** ~ **to** documento
esse (*dat*); ~**s** pl dictāta ntpl; **give** ~**s** scholās
habēre; **give** ~**s in** docēre.
lessor n locātor m.
lest conj nē (+ *subj*).
let vt (*allow*) sinere; (*lease*) locāre; (*imper*) fac;
~ **alone** ōmittere; (*mention*) nē dīcam; ~
blood sanguinem mittere; ~ **down**
dēmittere; ~ **fall** ā manibus mittere; (*word*)
ēmittere; ~ **fly** ēmittere; ~ **go** mittere,
āmittere; (*ship*) solvere; ~ **in** admittere; ~
loose solvere; ~ **off** absolvere, ignōscere
(*dat*); ~ **oneself** go geniō indulgēre; ~ **out**
ēmittere; ~ **slip** āmittere, ōmittere.
lethal adj mortifer.
lethargic adj veternōsus.
lethargy n veternus m.
letter n epistula f, litterae fpl; (*of alphabet*)
littera f; **the** ~ **of the law** scrīptum nt; **to the** ~
ad praescrīptum; **by** ~ per litterās; ~**s**
(*learning*) litterae fpl; **man of** ~**s** scrīptor m.
lettered adj litterātus.
lettuce n lactūca f.
levee n salūtātiō f.
level adj aequus, plānus ♦ n plānitiēs f;
(*instrument*) lībra f; **do one's** ~ **best** prō virīlī
parte agere; **put on a** ~ **with** exaequāre cum
♦ vt aequāre, adaequāre, inaequāre; (*to the
ground*) solō aequāre, sternere; (*weapon*)
intendere.
level-headed adj prūdēns.
levelled adj (*weapon*) īnfestus.
lever n vectis m.
levity n levitās f; (*fun*) iocī mpl, facētiae fpl.
levy vt (*troops*) scrībere; (*tax*) exigere ♦ n
dīlectus m.
lewd adj impudīcus.
lewdness n impudīcitia f.
liable adj obnoxius; **render** ~ obligāre.
liaison n cōnsuētūdō f.
liar n mendāx m.
libel n probrum nt, calumnia f ♦ vt calumniārī.
libellous adj probrōsus, fāmōsus.
liberal adj līberālis; (*in giving*) largus,
benīgnus; ~ **education** bonae artēs fpl.
liberality n līberālitās f, largitās f.
liberally adv līberāliter, largē, benīgnē.
liberate vt līberāre; (*slave*) manū mittere.
liberation n līberātiō f.
liberator n līberātor m.
libertine n lībīdinōsus m.
liberty n lībertās f; (*excess*) licentia f; **I am at** ~
to mihī licet (*inf*); **I am still at** ~ **to** integrum
est mihī (*inf*); **take a** ~ **with** licentius ūtī (*abl*),
familiārius sē gerere in (*acc*).
libidinous adj lībīdinōsus.
librarian n librārius m.
library n bibliothēca f.
licence n (*permission*) potestās f; (*excess*)
licentia f.
license vt potestātem dare (*dat*).
licentious adj dissolūtus.

licentiousness n libīdō f, licentia f.
lick vt lambere; mulcēre.
lictor n lictor m.
lid n operculum nt.
lie n mendācium nt; **give the ~ to** redarguere; **tell a ~** mentīrī ♦ vi mentīrī; (*lie down*) iacēre; (*place*) situm esse; (*consist*) continērī; **as far as in me ~s** quantum in mē est; **~ at anchor** stāre; **~ between** interiacēre; **~ down** cubāre, discumbere; **~ heavy on** premere; **~ hid** latēre; **~ in wait** īnsidiārī; **~ low** dissimulāre; **~ on** incumbere (*dat*); **~ open** patēre; hiāre.
lien n nexus m.
lieu n: **in ~ of** locō (*gen*).
lieutenant n decuriō m; legātus m.
life n vīta f; (*in danger*) salūs f, caput nt; (*biography*) vīta f; (*breath*) anima f; (*RHET*) sanguis m; (*time*) aetās f; **come to ~ again** revīvīscere; **draw to the ~** exprimere; **for ~** aetātem; **matter of ~ and death** capitāle nt; **prime of ~** flōs aetātis; **way of ~** mōrēs mpl.
lifeblood n sanguis m.
life-giving adj almus, vītalis.
lifeguard n custōs m; (*emperor's*) praetōriānus m.
lifeless adj exanimis; (*style*) exsanguis.
lifelike adj expressus.
lifelong adj perpetuus.
lifetime n aetās f.
lift vt tollere, sublevāre; **~ up** efferre, attollere.
light n lūx f, lūmen nt; (*painting*) lūmen nt; **bring to ~** in lūcem prōferre; **see in a favourable ~** in meliōrem partem interpretārī; **throw ~ on** lūmen adhibēre (*dat*) ♦ vt accendere, incendere; (*illuminate*) illūstrāre, illūmināre; **be lit up** collūcēre ♦ vi: **~ upon** invenīre, offendere ♦ adj illūstris; (*movement*) agilis; (*weight*) levis; **grow ~** illūcēscere, dīlūcēscere; **make ~ of** parvī pendere.
light-armed adj expedītus.
lighten vi fulgurāre ♦ vt levāre.
lighter n linter f.
light-fingered adj tagāx.
light-footed adj celer, pernīx.
light-headed adj levis, volāticus.
light-hearted adj hilaris, laetus.
lightly adv leviter; pernīciter.
lightness n levitās f.
lightning n fulgur nt; (*striking*) fulmen nt; **be hit by ~** dē caelō percutī; **of ~** fulgurālis.
like adj similis, pār; **~ this** ad hunc modum ♦ adv similiter, sīcut, rītū (*gen*) ♦ vt amāre; **I ~** mihī placet, mē iuvat; **I ~ to** libet (*inf*); **I don't ~** nīl moror, mihī displicet; **look ~** similem esse, referre.
likelihood n vērī similitūdō f.
likely adj vērī similis ♦ adv sānē.
liken vt comparāre, aequiperāre.
likeness n īmāgō f, īnstar nt, similitūdō f.
likewise adv item; (*also*) etiam.
liking n libīdō f, grātia f; **to one's ~** ex sententiā.
lily n līlium nt.
limb n membrum nt, artus m.
lime n calx f; (*tree*) tilia f.
limelight n celebritās f; **enjoy the ~** mōnstrārī digitō.
limestone n calx f.
limit n fīnis m, terminus m, modus m; **mark the ~s of** dētermināre ♦ vt fīnīre, dēfīnīre, termināre; (*restrict*) circumscrībere.
limitation n modus m.
limp adj mollis, flaccidus ♦ vi claudicāre.
limpid adj limpidus.
linden n tilia f.
line n līnea f; (*battle*) aciēs f; (*limit*) modus m; (*outline*) līneāmentum nt; (*writing*) versus m; **in a straight ~** ē regiōne; **~ of march** agmen nt; **read between the ~s** dissimulātā dispicere; **ship of the ~** nāvis longa; **write a ~** pauca scrībere ♦ vt (*street*) saepīre.
lineage n genus nt, stirps f.
lineal adj (*descent*) gentīlis.
lineaments n līneāmenta ntpl, ōris ductūs mpl.
linen n linteum nt ♦ adj linteus.
liner n nāvis f.
linger vi cunctārī, cessāre, dēmorārī.
lingering adj tardus ♦ n cunctātiō f.
linguist n: **be a ~** complūrēs linguās callēre.
link n ānulus m; (*fig*) nexus m, vinculum nt ♦ vt coniungere.
lintel n līmen superum nt.
lion n leō m; **~'s** leōnīnus; **~'s share** māior pars.
lioness n leaena f.
lip n labrum nt; **be on everyone's ~s** in ōre omnium hominum esse, per omnium ōra ferrī.
lip service n: **pay ~ to** verbō tenus obsequī (*dat*).
liquefy vt liquefacere.
liquid adj liquidus ♦ n liquor m.
liquidate vt persolvere.
liquor n liquor m; vīnum nt.
lisp vi balbūtīre.
lisping adj blaesus.
lissom adj agilis.
list n index m, tabula f; (*ship*) inclīnātiō f ♦ vt scrībere ♦ vi (*lean*) sē inclīnāre; (*listen*) auscultāre; (*wish*) cupere.
listen vi auscultāre; **~ to** auscultāre, audīre.
listener n audītor m, auscultātor m.
listless adj languidus.
listlessness n languor m.
literally adv ad verbum.
literary adj (*man*) litterātus; **~ pursuits** litterae fpl, studia ntpl.
literature n litterae fpl.
lithe adj mollis, agilis.
litigant n lītigātor m.
litigate vi lītigāre.
litigation n līs f.
litigious adj lītigiōsus.
litter n (*carriage*) lectīca f; (*brood*) fētus m; (*straw*) strāmentum nt; (*mess*) strāgēs f ♦ vt

sternere; (*young*) parere.

little *adj* parvus, exiguus; (*time*) brevis; **very ~**
perexiguus, minimus; **~ boy** puerulus *m* ♦ *n*
paulum *nt*, aliquantulum *nt*; **for a ~** paulisper,
parumper; **~ or nothing** vix quicquam ♦ *adv*
paulum, nōnnihil; (*with comp*) paulō **~ by ~**
paulātim, sēnsim, gradātim; **think ~of** parvī
aestimāre; **too ~** parum (+ *gen*).

littleness *n* exiguitās *f*.

littoral *n* lītus *nt*.

live *vi* vīvere, vītam agere; (*dwell*) habitāre; **~
down** (*reproach*) ēluere; **~ on** (*food*) vescī
(*abl*) ♦ *adj* vīvus.

livelihood *n* vīctus *m*.

liveliness *n* alacritās *f*, hilaritās *f*.

livelong *adj* tōtus.

lively *adj* alacer, hilaris.

liven *vt* exhilarāre.

liver *n* iecur *nt*.

livery *n* vestis famulāris *f*.

livid *adj* līvidus; **be ~** līvēre.

living *adj* vīvus ♦ *n* vīctus *m*; (*earning*)
quaestus *m*.

lizard *n* lacerta *f*.

lo *interj* ecce.

load *n* onus *nt* ♦ *vt* onerāre.

loaf *n* pānis *m* ♦ *vi* grassārī.

loafer *n* grassātor *m*.

loam *n* lutum *nt*.

loan *n* mūtuum *nt*, mūtua pecūnia *f*.

loathe *vt* fastīdīre, ōdisse.

loathing *n* fastīdium *nt*.

loathsome *adj* odiōsus, taeter.

lobby *n* vestibulum *nt*.

lobe *n* fibra *f*.

lobster *n* astacus *m*.

local *adj* indigena, locī.

locality *n* locus *m*.

locate *vt* reperīre; **be ~d** situm esse.

location *n* situs *m*.

loch *n* lacus *m*.

lock *n* (*door*) sera *f*; (*hair*) coma *f* ♦ *vt* obserāre.

locomotion *n* mōtus *m*.

locust *n* locusta *f*.

lodge *n* casa *f* ♦ *vi* dēversārī ♦ *vt* īnfīgere;
(*complaint*) dēferre.

lodger *n* inquilīnus *m*.

lodging *n* hospitium *nt*, dēversōrium *nt*.

loft *n* cēnāculum *nt*.

loftiness *n* altitūdō *f*, sublīmitās *f*.

lofty *adj* excelsus, sublīmis.

log *n* stīpes *m*; (*fuel*) lignum *nt*.

loggerhead *n*: **be at ~s** rixārī.

logic *n* dialecticē *f*.

logical *adj* dialecticus, ratiōne frētus.

logically *adv* ex ratiōne.

logician *n* dialecticus *m*.

loin *n* lumbus *m*.

loiter *vi* grassārī, cessāre.

loiterer *n* grassātor *m*, cessātor *m*.

loll *vi* recumbere.

lone *adj* sōlus, sōlitārius.

loneliness *n* sōlitūdō *f*.

lonely, lonesome *adj* sōlitārius.

long *adj* longus; (*hair*) prōmissus; (*syllable*)
prōductus; (*time*) longus, diūturnus; **in the ~
run** aliquandō; **for a ~ time** diū; **to make a ~
story short** nē longum sit, nē longum faciam
♦ *adv* diū; **~ ago** iamprīdem, iamdūdum; **as ~
as** *conj* dum; **before ~** mox; **for ~** diū; **how ~**
quamdiū, quōusque; **I have ~ been wishing**
iam prīdem cupiō; **not ~ after** haud multō
post; **any ~er** (*time*) diūtius; (*distance*)
longius; **no ~er** nōn iam ♦ *vi*: **~ for** dēsīderāre,
exoptāre, expetere; **~ to** gestīre.

longevity *n* vīvācitās *f*.

longing *n* dēsīderium *nt*, cupīdō *f* ♦ *adj* avidus.

longingly *adv* avidē.

longitudinally *adv* in longitūdinem.

long-lived *adj* vīvāx.

long-suffering *adj* patiēns.

long-winded *adj* verbōsus, longus.

longwise *adv* in longitūdinem.

look *n* aspectus *m*; (*expression*) vultus *m* ♦ *vi*
aspicere; (*seem*) vidērī, speciem praebēre; **~
about** circumspicere; **~ after** prōvidēre (*dat*),
cūrāre; **~ at** spectāre ad (+ *acc*), aspicere,
intuērī; (*with mind*) contemplārī; **~ back**
respicere; **~ down on** dēspectāre; (*fig*)
dēspicere; **~ for** quaerere, petere; **~ forward
to** exspectāre; **~ here** heus tu, ehodum; **~ into**
īnspicere, intrōspicere; **~ out** prōspicere;
(*beware*) cavēre; **~ round** circumspicere; **~
through** perspicere; **~ to** ratiōnem habēre
(*gen*); (*leader*) spem pōnere in (*abl*); **~
towards** spectāre ad; **~ up** suspicere; **~ up to**
suspicere; **~ upon** habēre.

looker-on *n* arbiter *m*.

lookout *n* (*place*) specula *f*; (*man*) vigil *m*,
excubiae *fpl*.

looks *npl* speciēs *f*; **good ~** fōrma *f*,
pulchritūdō *f*.

loom *n* tēla *f* ♦ *vi* in cōnspectum sē dare.

loop *n* orbis *m*, sinus *m*.

loophole *n* fenestra *f*.

loose *adj* laxus, solūtus, remissus; (*morally*)
dissolūtus; **let ~ on** immittere in (*acc*) ♦ *vt*
(*undo*) solvere; (*slacken*) laxāre.

loosely *adv* solūtē, remissē.

loosen *vt* (re)solvere; (*structure*) labefacere.

looseness *n* dissolūtiō *f*, dissolūtī mōrēs *mpl*.

loot *n* praeda *f*, rapīna *f*.

lop *vt* amputāre.

lopsided *adj* inaequālis.

loquacious *adj* loquāx.

loquacity *n* loquācitās *f*.

lord *n* dominus *m* ♦ *vi*: **~ it** dominārī.

lordliness *n* superbia *f*.

lordly *adj* superbus; (*rank*) nōbilis.

lordship *n* dominātiō *f*, imperium *nt*.

lore *n* litterae *fpl*, doctrīna *f*.

lose *vt* āmittere, perdere; **~ an eye** alterō oculō
capī; **~ heart** animum dēspondēre; **~ one's
way** deerrāre ♦ *vi* (*in contest*) vincī.

loss *n* damnum *nt*, dētrīmentum *nt*; **be at a ~**
haerēre, haesitāre; **suffer ~** damnum

accipere, facere; **~es** (*in battle*) caesī *mpl*.
lost *adj* āmissus, absēns; **be ~** perīre, interīre;
give up for ~ dēplōrāre.
lot *n* sors *f*; **be assigned by ~** sorte obvenīre;
draw a ~ sortem dūcere; **draw ~s for** sortīrī;
a ~ of multus, plūrimus.
loth *adj* invītus.
lottery *n* sortēs *fpl*; (*fig*) ālea *f*.
lotus *n* lōtos *f*.
loud *adj* clārus, māgnus.
loudly *adv* māgnā vōce.
loudness *n* māgna vōx *f*.
lounge *vi* ōtiārī.
louse *n* pedis *m/f*.
lout *n* agrestis *m*.
lovable *adj* amābilis.
love *n* amor *m*; **be hopelessly in ~** dēperīre; **fall
in ~ with** adamāre ♦ *vt* amāre, dīligere; **I ~ to**
mē iuvat (*inf*).
love affair *n* amor *m*.
loveless *adj* amōre carēns.
loveliness *n* grātia *f*, venustās *f*.
lovely *adj* pulcher, amābilis, venustus.
love poem *n* carmen amātōrium *nt*.
lover *n* amāns *m*, amātor *m*.
lovesick *adj* amōre aeger.
loving *adj* amāns.
lovingly *adv* amanter.
low *adj* humilis; (*birth*) ignōbilis; (*price*) vīlis;
(*sound*) gravis; (*spirits*) dēmissus; (*voice*)
dēmissus; **at ~ water** aestūs dēcessū; **be ~**
iacēre; **lay ~** interficere ♦ *vi* mūgīre.
lower *adj* īnferior; **the ~ world** īnferī *mpl*; **of
the ~ world** īnfernus ♦ *adv* īnferius ♦ *vt*
dēmittere, dēprimere ♦ *vi* (*cloud*) obscūrārī,
minārī.
lowering *adj* mināx.
lowest *adj* īnfimus, īmus.
lowing *n* mūgītus *m*.
lowland *adj* campestris.
lowlands *n* campī *mpl*.
lowliness *n* humilitās *f*.
lowly *adj* humilis, obscūrus.
low-lying *adj* dēmisssus; **be ~** sedēre.
lowness *n* humilitās *f*; (*spirit*) tristitia *f*.
loyal *adj* fidēlis, fīdus; (*citizen*) bonus.
loyally *adv* fidēliter.
loyalty *n* fidēs *f*, fidēlitās *f*.
lubricate *vt* ungere.
lucid *adj* clārus, perspicuus.
lucidity *n* perspicuitās *f*.
lucidly *adv* clārē, perspicuē.
luck *n* fortūna *f*, fors *f*; **good ~** fēlicitās *f*; **bad ~**
īnfortūnium *nt*.
luckily *adv* fēlīciter, faustē, prosperē.
luckless *adj* īnfēlīx.
lucky *adj* fēlīx, fortūnātus; (*omen*) faustus.
lucrative *adj* quaestuōsus.
lucre *n* lucrum *nt*, quaestus *m*.
lucubration *n* lūcubrātiō *f*.
ludicrous *adj* rīdiculus.
ludicrously *adv* rīdiculē.
lug *vt* trahere.

luggage *n* impedīmenta *ntpl*, sarcina *f*.
lugubrious *adj* lūgubris, maestus.
lukewarm *adj* tepidus; (*fig*) segnis, neglegēns;
be ~ tepēre.
lukewarmly *adv* segniter, neglegenter.
lukewarmness *n* tepor *m*; (*fig*) neglegentia *f*,
incūria *f*
lull *vt* sōpīre; (*storm*) sēdāre ♦ *n* intermissiō *f*.
lumber *n* scrūta *ntpl*.
luminary *n* lūmen *nt*, astrum *nt*.
luminous *adj* lūcidus, illūstris.
lump *n* massa *f*; (*on body*) tuber *nt*.
lumpish *adj* hebes, crassus, stolidus.
lunacy *n* īnsānia *f*.
lunar *adj* lūnāris.
lunatic *n* īnsānus *m*.
lunch *n* prandium *nt* ♦ *vi* prandēre.
lung *n* pulmō *m*; *pl* (*RHET*) latera *ntpl*.
lunge *n* ictus *m* ♦ *vi* prōsilīre.
lurch *n*: **leave in the ~** dērelinquere, dēstituere
♦ *vi* titubāre.
lure *n* esca *f* ♦ *vt* allicere, illicere, ēlicere.
lurid *adj* lūridus.
lurk *vi* latēre, latitāre, dēlitēscere.
luscious *adj* praedulcis.
lush *adj* luxuriōsus.
lust *n* libīdō *f* ♦ *vi* libīdine flagrāre,
concupīscere.
lustful *adj* libīdinōsus.
lustily *adv* validē, strēnuē.
lustiness *n* vigor *m*, nervī *mpl*.
lustration *n* lūstrum *nt*.
lustre *n* fulgor *m*, splendor *m*.
lustrous *adj* illūstris.
lusty *adj* validus, lacertōsus.
lute *n* cithara *f*, fidēs *fpl*.
lute player *n* citharista *m*, citharistria *f*,
fidicen *m*, fidicina *f*.
luxuriance *n* luxuria *f*.
luxuriant *adj* luxuriōsus.
luxuriate *vi* luxuriārī.
luxuries *pl* lautitiae *fpl*.
luxurious *adj* luxuriōsus, sūmptuōsus, lautus.
luxuriously *adv* sūmptuōsē, lautē.
luxury *n* luxuria *f*, luxus *m*.
lynx *n* lynx *m/f*; **~-eyed** lyncēus.
lyre *n* lyra *f*, fidēs *fpl*; **play the ~** fidibus canere.
lyric *adj* lyricus ♦ *n* carmen *nt*.
lyrist *n* fidicen *m*, fidicina *f*.

M, m

mace *n* scīpiō *m*.
machination *n* dolus *m*.
machine *n* māchina *f*.

mackerel n scomber m.
mad adj īnsānus, furiōsus, vēcors, dēmēns; **be**
~ īnsānīre, furere.
madam n domina f.
madden vt furiāre, mentem aliēnāre (dat).
madly adv insānē, furiōsē, dēmenter.
madness n īnsānia f, furor m, dēmentia f;
(animals) rabiēs f.
maelstrom n vertex m.
magazine n horreum nt, apothēca f.
maggot n vermiculus m.
magic adj magicus ♦ n magicae artēs fpl.
magician n magus m, veneficus m.
magistracy n magistrātus m.
magistrate n magistrātus m.
magnanimity n māgnanimitās f, līberalitās f.
magnanimous adj generōsus, līberālis,
māgnanimus.
magnet n magnēs m.
magnificence n māgnificentia f, adparātus m.
magnificent adj māgnificus, amplus
splendidus.
magnificently adv māgnificē, amplē
splendidē.
magnify vt amplificāre, exaggerāre.
magnitude n māgnitūdō f.
magpie n pīca f.
maid n virgō f; (servant) ancilla f.
maiden n virgō f.
maidenhood n virginitās f.
maidenly adj virginālis.
mail n (armour) lōrīca f; (letters) epistulae fpl.
maim vt mutilāre.
maimed adj mancus.
main adj prīnceps, prīmus; ~ **point** caput nt
♦ n (sea) altum nt, pelagus nt; **with might and**
~ manibus pedibusque, omnibus nervīs.
mainland n continēns f.
mainly adv praecipuē, plērumque.
maintain vt (keep) tenēre, servāre; (keep up)
sustinēre; (keep alive) alere, sustentāre;
(argue) adfirmāre, dēfendere.
maintenance n (food) alimentum nt.
majestic adj augustus, māgnificus.
majestically adv augustē.
majesty n māiestās f.
major adj māior.
majority n māior pars f, plērīque; **have**
attained one's ~ suī iūris esse.
make vt facere, fingere; (appointment) creāre;
(bed) sternere; (cope) superāre; (compulsion)
cōgere; (consequence) efficere; (craft)
fabricārī; (harbour) capere; (living) quaerere;
(sum) efficere; (with adj) reddere; (with verb)
cōgere; ~ **away with** tollere, interimere; ~
good supplēre, resarcīre; ~ **light of** parvī
facere; ~ **one's way** iter facere; ~ **much of**
māgnī aestimāre, multum tribuere (dat); ~
for petere; ~ **out** arguere; ~ **over** dēlēgāre,
trānsferre; ~ **ready** parāre; ~ **a speech**
orātiōnem habēre; ~ **a truce** indutiās
compōnere; ~ **war on** bellum inferre; ~ **up**
(loss) supplēre; (total) efficere; (story)

fingere; **be made** fierī.
make-believe n simulātiō f.
maker n fabricātor m, auctor m.
make-up n medicāmina ntpl.
maladministration n (charge) repetundae fpl.
malady n morbus m.
malcontent adj novārum rērum cupidus.
male adj mās, māsculus.
malefactor n nocēns m, reus m.
malevolence n malevolentia f.
malevolent adj malevolus, malignus.
malevolently adv malignē.
malformation n dēprāvātiō f.
malice n invidia f, malevolentia f; **bear** ~
towards invidēre (dat).
malicious adj invidiōsus, malevolus,
malignus.
maliciously adv malignē.
malign adj malignus, invidiōsus ♦ vt
obtrectāre.
malignant adj malevolus.
maligner n obtrectātor m.
malignity n malevolentia f.
malleable adj ductilis.
mallet n malleus m.
mallow n malva f.
malpractices n dēlicta ntpl.
maltreat vt laedere, vexāre.
malversation n pecūlātus m.
man n (human being) homō m/f; (male) vir m;
(MIL) mīles m; (chess) latrunculus m; **to a** ~
omnēs ad ūnum; ~ **who** is qui; **old** ~ senex m;
young ~ adulēscēns m; ~ **of war** nāvis longa f
♦ vt (ship) complēre; (walls) praesidiō
firmāre.
manacle n manicae fpl ♦ vt manicās inicere
(dat).
manage vt efficere, gerere, gubernāre,
administrāre; (horse) moderārī; (with verb)
posse.
manageable adj tractābilis, habilis.
management n administrātiō f, cūra f;
(finance) dispēnsātiō f.
manager n administrātor m, moderātor m;
dispēnsātor m.
mandate n mandātum nt.
mane n iuba f.
manful adj virīlis, fortis.
manfully adv virīliter, fortiter.
manger n praesēpe nt.
mangle vt dīlaniāre, lacerāre.
mangy adj scaber.
manhood n pūbertās f, toga virīlis f.
mania n īnsānia f.
maniac n furiōsus m.
manifest adj manifestus, apertus, clārus ♦ vt
dēclārāre, aperīre.
manifestation n speciēs f.
manifestly adv manifestō, apertē.
manifesto n ēdictum nt.
manifold adj multiplex, varius.
manikin n homunciō m, homunculus m.
manipulate vt tractāre.

manipulation n tractātiō f.
mankind n hominēs mpl, genus hūmānum nt.
manliness n virtūs f.
manly adj fortis, virīlis.
manner n modus m, ratiō f; (custom) mōs m,
ūsus m; ~s pl mōrēs mpl; **after the ~ of** rītū,
mōre (gen); **good ~s** hūmānitās f, modestia f.
mannered adj mōrātus.
mannerism n mōs m.
mannerly adj bene mōrātus, urbānus.
manoeuvre n (MIL) dēcursus m, dēcursiō f; (fig)
dolus m ♦ vi dēcurrere; (fig) māchinārī.
manor n praedium nt.
mansion n domus f.
manslaughter n homicīdium nt.
mantle n pallium nt; (women's) palla f.
manual adj: ~ **labour** opera f ♦ n libellus m, ars
f.
manufacture n fabrica f ♦ vt fabricārī.
manumission n manūmissiō f.
manumit vt manū mittere, ēmancipāre.
manure n fimus m, stercus nt ♦ vt stercorāre.
manuscript n liber m, cōdex m.
many adj multī; **as ~ as** tot ... quot; **how ~?**
quot?; **so ~** tot; **in ~ places** multifāriam; **a**
good ~ complūrēs; **too ~** nimis multī; **the ~**
vulgus nt; **very ~** permultī, plūrimī.
map n tabula f ♦ vt: ~ **out** dēscrībere,
dēsignāre.
maple n acer nt ♦ adj acernus.
mar vt corrumpere, dēfōrmāre.
marauder n praedātor m, dēpopulātor m.
marble n marmor nt ♦ adj marmoreus.
March n mēnsis Martius m; **of ~** Martius.
march n iter nt; **line of ~** agmen nt; **by forced**
~**es** māgnīs itineribus; **on the ~** ex itinere, in
itinere; **quick ~** plēnō gradū; **a regular day's ~**
iter iūstum nt ♦ vi contendere, iter facere,
incēdere, īre; ~ **out** exīre; ~ **on** signa
prōferre, prōgredī ♦ vt dūcere; ~ **out**
ēdūcere; ~ **in** intrōdūcere.
mare n equa f.
margin n margō f; (fig) discrīmen nt.
marigold n caltha f.
marine adj marīnus ♦ n mīles classicus m.
mariner n nauta m.
marital adj marītus.
maritime adj maritimus.
marjoram n amāracus m.
mark n nota f; (of distinction) īnsigne nt; (target)
scopos m; (trace) vestīgium nt; **beside the ~**
nihil ad rem; **it is the ~ of a wise man to**
sapientis est (inf); **be wide of the ~** errāre ♦
vt notāre, dēsignāre; (observe)
animadvertere, animum attendere; ~ **out**
(site) mētārī, dēsignāre; (for purpose)
dēnotāre.
marked adj īnsignis, manifestus.
markedly adv manifestō.
marker n index m.
market n macellum nt; ~ **day** nūndinae fpl; ~
town emporium nt; **cattle ~** forum boārium
nt; **fish ~** forum piscārium nt.

marketable adj vēndibilis.
marketplace n forum nt.
market prices npl annōna f.
market town n emporium nt.
marking n macula f.
maroon vt dērelinquere.
marriage n mātrimōnium nt, coniugium nt;
(ceremony) nūptiae fpl; **give in ~** collocāre; ~
bed lectus geniālis m.
marriageable adj nūbilis.
marrow n medulla f.
marry vt (a wife) dūcere, in mātrimōnium
dūcere; (a husband) nūbere (dat).
marsh n palūs f.
marshal n imperātor m ♦ vt īnstruere.
marshy adj palūster.
mart n forum nt.
marten n mēlēs f.
martial adj bellicōsus, ferōx.
martyr n dēvōtus m; (ECCL) martyr m/f.
marvel n mīrāculum nt, portentum nt ♦ vi
mīrārī; ~ **at** admīrārī.
marvellous adj mīrus, mīrificus, mīrābilis.
marvellously adv mīrē, mīrum quantum.
masculine adj mās, virīlis.
mash n farrāgō f ♦ vt commiscēre,
contundere.
mask n persōna f ♦ vt persōnam induere (dat);
(fig) dissimulāre.
mason n structor m.
masonry n lapidēs mpl, caementum nt.
masquerade n simulātiō f ♦ vi vestem
mūtāre; ~ **as** speciem sibi induere (gen),
persōnam ferre (gen).
mass n mōlēs f; (of small things) congeriēs f; (of
people) multitūdō f; (ECCL) missa f; **the ~es**
vulgus nt, plēbs f ♦ vt congerere, coacervāre.
massacre n strāgēs f, caedēs f, interneciō f ♦
vt trucīdāre.
massive adj ingēns, solidus.
massiveness n mōlēs f, soliditās f.
mast n mālus m.
master n dominus m; (school) magister m; **be ~**
of dominārī in (abl); (skill) perītum esse
(gen); **become ~ of** potīrī (abl); **be one's own**
~ suī iūris esse; **not ~ of** impotēns (gen); **a**
past ~ veterātor m ♦ vt dēvincere; (skill)
ēdiscere; (passion) continēre.
masterful adj imperiōsus.
masterly adj doctus, perītus.
masterpiece n praeclārum opus nt.
mastery n dominātiō f, imperium nt,
arbitrium nt.
masticate vt mandere.
mastiff n Molossus m.
mat n storea f.
match n (person) pār m/f; (marriage) nūptiae fpl;
(contest) certāmen nt; **a ~ for** pār (dat); **no ~**
for impār (dat) ♦ vt exaequāre, adaequāre ♦
vi congruere.
matchless adj singulāris, ūnicus.
mate n socius m; (married) coniunx m/f ♦ vi
coniungī.

material adj corporeus; (significant) haud levis ♦ n māteriēs f; (literary) silva f.
materialize vi ēvenīre.
materially adv māgnopere.
maternal adj māternus.
mathematical adj mathēmaticus.
mathematician n mathēmaticus m, geōmetrēs m.
mathematics n ars mathēmatica f, numerī mpl.
matin adj mātūtīnus.
matricide n (act) mātricīdium nt; (person) mātricīda m.
matrimony n mātrimōnium nt.
matrix n fōrma f.
matron n mātrōna f.
matter n māteria f, corpus nt; (affair) rēs f; (MED) pūs nt; **what is the ~ with you?** quid tibī est? vi: **it ~s** interest, rēfert.
matting n storea f.
mattock n dolābra f.
mattress n culcita f.
mature adj mātūrus; (age) adultus ♦ vi mātūrēscere.
maturity n mātūritās f; (age) adulta aetās f.
maul n fistūca f ♦ vt contundere, dīlan āre.
maw n ingluviēs f.
mawkish adj pūtidus.
mawkishly adv pūtidē.
maxim n dictum nt, praeceptum nt, sententia f.
maximum adj quam māximus, quam plūrimus.
May n mēnsis Māius m; **of ~** Māius.
may vi posse; **I ~** licet mihī.
mayor n praefectus m.
maze n labyrinthus m.
mead n (drink) mulsum nt; (land) prātum nt.
meagre adj exīlis, iēiūnus.
meagrely adv exīliter, iēiūnē.
meagreness n exīlitās f.
meal n (flour) farīna f; (repast) cibus m.
mealy-mouthed adj blandiloquus.
mean adj humilis, abiectus; (birth) ignōbilis; (average) medius, mediocris ♦ n modus m, mediocritās f ♦ vt dīcere, significāre; (word) valēre; (intent) velle, in animō habēre.
meander vi sinuōsō cursū fluere.
meaning n significātiō f, vīs f, sententia f; **what is the ~ of?** quid sibī vult?, quōrsum spectat?.
meanly adv abiectē, humiliter.
meanness n humilitās f; (conduct) illīberālitās f, avāritia f.
means n īnstrūmentum nt; (of doing) facultās f; (wealth) opēs fpl; **by ~ of** per (acc); **by all ~** māximē; **by no ~** nullō modō, haudquāquam; **of small ~** pauper.
meantime, meanwhile adv intereā, interim.
measles n boa f.
measure n modus m, mēnsūra f; (rhythm) numerī mpl; (plan) cōnsilium nt; (law) rogātiō f, lēx f; **beyond ~** nimium; **in some ~** aliquā ex parte; **take ~s** cōnsulere; **take the ~ of** quālis

sit cognōscere; **without ~** immoderātē ♦ vt mētīrī; **~ out** dīmētīrī; (land) mētārī.
measured adj moderātus.
measureless adj īnfīnītus, immēnsus.
measurement n mēnsūra f.
meat n carō f.
mechanic n opifex m, faber m.
mechanical adj mēchanicus.
mechanical device māchinātiō f.
mechanics n māchinālis scientia f.
mechanism n māchinātiō f.
medal n īnsigne nt.
meddle vi sē interpōnere.
meddlesome adj cūriōsus.
Medes n Mīdī mpl.
mediate vi intercēdere; **~ between** compōnere, conciliāre.
mediator n intercessor m, dēprecātor m.
medical adj medicus.
medicate vt medicāre.
medicinal adj medicus, salūbris.
medicine n (art) medicīna f; (drug) medicāmentum nt.
medicine chest n narthēcium nt.
mediocre adj mediocris.
mediocrity n mediocritās f.
meditate vi meditārī, cōgitāre, sēcum volūtāre.
meditation n cōgitātiō f, meditātiō f.
medium n internūntius m; (means) modus m ♦ adj mediocris.
medley n farrāgō f.
meek adj mītis, placidus.
meekly adv summissō animō.
meet adj idōneus, aptus ♦ n conventus m ♦ vi convenīre ♦ vt obviam īre (dat), occurrere (dat); (fig) obīre; **~ with** invenīre, excipere.
meeting n cōnsilium nt, conventus m.
melancholic adj melancholicus.
melancholy n ātra bīlis f; tristitia f, maestitia f ♦ adj tristis, maestus.
mêlée n turba f, concursus m.
mellow adj mītis; (wine) lēnis; **become ~** mītēscere. **make ~** mītigāre.
mellowness n mātūritās f.
melodious adj canōrus, numerōsus.
melodiously adv numerōsē.
melody n melos nt, modī mpl.
melt vt liquefacere, dissolvere; (fig) movēre ♦ vi liquēscere, dissolvī; (fig) commovērī; **~ away** dēliquēscere.
member n membrum nt; (person) socius m.
membrane n membrāna f.
memento n monumentum nt.
memoir n commentārius m.
memorable adj memorābilis, commemorābilis.
memorandum n hypomnēma nt.
memorial n monumentum nt.
memorize vt ēdiscere.
memory n memoria f; **from ~** memoriter.
menace n minae fpl ♦ vt minārī, minitārī; (things) imminēre (dat).

menacing adj mināx.
menacingly adv mināciter.
menage n familia f.
mend vt sarcīre, reficere ♦ vi meliōrem fierī;
_ (health)_ convalēscere.
mendacious adj mendāx.
mendacity n mendācium nt.
mendicant n mendīcus m.
mendicity n mendīcitās f.
menial adj servīlis, famulāris ♦ n servus m,
famulus m.
menstrual adj mēnstruus.
mensuration n mētiendī ratiō f.
mental adj cōgitātiōnis, mentis.
mentality n animī adfectus m, mēns f.
mentally adv cōgitātiōne, mente.
mention n mentiō f ♦ vt memorāre,
mentiōnem facere _(gen)_; _(casually)_ inicere;
(briefly) attingere; **omit to** ~ praetermittere.
mentor n auctor m, praeceptor m.
mercantile adj mercātōrius.
mercenary adj mercennārius, vēnālis ♦ n
mercennārius mīles m.
merchandise n mercēs fpl.
merchant n mercātor m.
merchantman n nāvis onerāria f.
merchant ship n nāvis onerāria f.
merciful adj misericors, clēmens.
mercifully adv clēmenter.
merciless adj immisericors, inclēmens,
inhūmānus.
mercilessly adv inhūmānē.
mercurial adj hilaris.
mercy n misericordia f, clēmentia f, venia f; **at
the** ~ **of** obnoxius _(dat)_, in manū _(gen)_.
mere n lacus m ♦ adj merus, ipse.
merely adv sōlum, tantum, dumtaxat.
meretricious adj meretricius; ~ **attractions**
lēnōcinia ntpl.
merge vt cōnfundere ♦ vi cōnfundī.
meridian n merīdiēs m ♦ adj merīdiānus.
merit n meritum nt, virtūs f ♦ vt merērī.
meritorious adj laudābilis.
meritoriously adv optimē.
mermaid n nympha f.
merrily adv hilare, festīvē.
merriment n hilaritās f, festīvitās f.
merry adj hilaris, festīvus; **make** ~ lūdere.
merrymaking n lūdus m, festīvitās f.
mesh n macula f.
mess n _(dirt)_ sordēs f, squālor m; _(trouble)_
turba f; _(food)_ cibus m; _(MIL)_ contubernālēs
mpl.
message n nūntius m.
messenger n nūntius m.
messmate n contubernālis m.
metal n metallum nt ♦ adj ferreus, aereus.
metamorphose vt mūtāre, trānsfōrmāre.
metamorphosis n mūtātiō f.
metaphor n trānslātiō f.
metaphorical adj trānslātus.
metaphorically adv per trānslātiōnem.
metaphysics n dialectica ntpl.

mete vt mētīrī.
meteor n fax caelestis f.
meteorology n prognōstica ntpl.
methinks vi: ~ **I am** mihī videor esse.
method n ratiō f, modus m.
methodical adj dispositus; _(person)_ dīligēns.
methodically adv dispositē.
meticulous adj accūrātus.
meticulously adv accūrātē.
meticulousness n cūra f.
metonymy n immūtātiō f.
metre n numerī mpl, modī mpl.
metropolis n urbs f.
mettle n ferōcitās f, virtūs f.
mettlesome adj ferōx, animōsus.
mew n _(bird)_ larus m; ~**s** pl stabula ntpl ♦ vi
vāgīre.
miasma n hālitus m.
mid adj medius ♦ prep inter _(acc)_.
midday n merīdiēs m ♦ adj merīdiānus.
middle adj medius ♦ n medium nt; **in the** ~
medius, in mediō; ~ **of** medius.
middling adj mediocris.
midge n culex m.
midget n pūmiliō m/f.
midland adj mediterrāneus.
midnight n media nox f.
midriff n praecordia ntpl.
midst n medium nt; **in the** ~ medius; **in the** ~ **of**
inter _(acc)_; **through the** ~ **of** per medium.
midsummer n sōlstitium nt ♦ adj sōlstitiālis.
midway adv medius.
midwife n obstetrix f.
midwinter n brūma f ♦ adj brūmālis.
mien n aspectus m, vultus m.
might n vīs f, potentia f; **with** ~ **and main**
omnibus nervīs, manibus pedibusque.
mightily adv valdē, magnopere.
mighty adj ingēns, validus.
migrate vi abīre, migrāre.
migration n peregrīnātiō f.
migratory adj advena.
mild adj mītis, lēnis, clēmēns.
mildew n rōbīgō f.
mildly adv lēniter, clēmenter.
mildness n clēmentia f, mānsuētūdō f;
(weather) caelī indulgentia f.
mile n mīlle passūs mpl; ~**s** pl mīlia passuum.
milestone n lapis m, mīliārium nt.
militant adj ferōx.
military adj mīlitāris ♦ n mīlitēs mpl.
military service n mīlitia f.
militate vi: ~ **against** repugnāre _(dat)_, facere
contrā _(acc)_.
militia n mīlitēs mpl.
milk n lac nt ♦ vt mulgēre.
milk pail n mulctra f.
milky adj lacteus.
mill n pistrīnum nt.
milled adj _(coin)_ serrātus.
millennium n mīlle annī mpl.
miller n pistor m.
millet n mīlium nt.

million *num* deciēs centēna mīlia *ntpl*.
millionaire *n* rēx *m*.
millstone *n* mola *f*, molāris *m*.
mime *n* mīmus *m*.
mimic *n* imitātor *m*, imitātrīx *f* ♦ *vt* imitārī.
mimicry *n* imitātiō *f*.
minatory *adj* mināx.
mince *vt* concīdere; **not ~ words** plānē
apertēque dīcere ♦ *n* minūtal *nt*.
mind *n* mēns *f*, animus *m*, ingenium *nt*;
(*opinion*) sententia *f*; (*memory*) memoria *f*; **be
in one's right ~** mentis suae esse; **be of the
same ~** eadem sentīre; **be out of one's ~**
īnsānīre; **bear in ~** meminisse (*gen*),
memorem esse (*gen*); **call to ~** memoriā
repetere, recordārī; **have a ~ to** libet; **have in
~** in animō habēre; **put one's ~ to** animum
applicāre ad (+ *acc*); **make up one's ~**
animum indūcere, animō obstināre,
statuere; **put in ~ of** admonēre (*gen*); **speak
one's ~** sententiam suam aperīre; **to one's ~**
ex sententiā ♦ *vt* cūrāre, attendere; **~ one's
own business** suum negōtium agere ♦ *vi*
gravārī; **I don't ~** nīl moror; **never ~** mitte.
minded *adj* animātus.
mindful *adj* memor.
mine *n* metallum *nt*; (*MIL*) cuniculus *m*; (*fig*)
thēsaurus *m* ♦ *vi* fodere; (*MIL*) cuniculum
agere ♦ *pron* meus.
miner *n* fossor *m*.
mineral *n* metallum *nt*.
mingle *vt* miscēre, commiscēre ♦ *vi* sē
immiscēre.
miniature *n* minima pictūra *f*.
minimize *vt* dētrectāre.
minimum *n* minimum *nt* ♦ *adj* quam minimus.
minion *n* cliēns *m/f*; dēlicātus *m*.
minister *n* administer *m* ♦ *vi* ministrāre,
servīre.
ministry *n* mūnus *nt*, officium *nt*.
minor *adj* minor ♦ *n* pupillus *m*, pupilla *f*.
minority *n* minor pars *f*; **in one's ~** nōndum suī
iūris.
Minotaur *n* Mīnōtaurus *m*.
minstrel *n* fidicen *m*.
minstrelsy *n* cantus *m*.
mint *n* (*plant*) menta *f*; (*money*) Monēta *f* ♦ *vt*
cūdere.
minute *n* temporis mōmentum *nt*.
minute *adj* minūtus, exiguus, subtīlis.
minutely *adv* subtīliter.
minuteness *n* exiguitās *f*, subtīlitas *f*.
minutiae *n* singula *ntpl*.
minx *n* lascīva *f*.
miracle *n* mīrāculum *nt*, mōnstrum *nt*.
miraculous *adj* mīrus, mīrābilis.
miraculously *adv* dīvīnitus.
mirage *n* falsa speciēs *f*.
mire *n* lutum *nt*.
mirror *n* speculum *nt* ♦ *vt* reddere.
mirth *n* hilaritās *f*, laetitia *f*.
mirthful *adj* hilaris, laetus.
mirthfully *adv* hilare, laetē.

miry *adj* lutulentus.
misadventure *n* īnfortūnium *nt*, cāsus *m*.
misapply *vt* abūtī (*abl*); (*words*) invertere.
misapprehend *vt* male intellegere.
misapprehension *n* error *m*.
misappropriate *vt* intervertere.
misbegotten *adj* nothus.
misbehave *vi* male sē gerere.
miscalculate *vi* errāre, fallī.
miscalculation *n* error *m*.
miscall *vt* maledīcere (*dat*).
miscarriage *n* abortus *m*; (*fig*) error *m*.
miscarry *vi* aborīrī; (*fig*) cadere, inritum esse.
miscellaneous *adj* prōmiscuus, varius.
miscellany *n* farrāgō *f*.
mischance *n* īnfortūnium *nt*.
mischief *n* malum *nt*, facinus *nt*, maleficium *nt*;
(*children*) lascīvia *f*.
mischievous *adj* improbus, maleficus;
lascīvus.
misconceive *vt* male intellegere.
misconception *n* error *m*.
misconduct *n* dēlictum *nt*, culpa *f*.
misconstruction *n* prāva interpretātiō *f*.
misconstrue *vt* male interpretārī.
miscreant *n* scelerātus *m*.
misdeed *n* maleficium *nt*, dēlictum *nt*.
misdemeanour *n* peccātum *nt*, culpa *f*.
miser *n* avārus *m*.
miserable *adj* miser, īnfēlīx; **make oneself ~**
sē cruciāre.
miserably *adv* miserē.
miserliness *n* avāritia *f*.
miserly *adj* avārus.
misery *n* miseria *f*, aerumna *f*.
misfortune *n* malum *nt*, īnfortūnium *nt*,
incommodum *nt*, rēs adversae *fpl*.
misgiving *n* suspiciō *f*, cūra *f*; **have ~s** parum
cōnfīdere.
misgovern *vt* male regere.
misgovernment *n* prāva administrātiō *f*.
misguide *vt* fallere, dēcipere.
misguided *adj* dēmēns.
mishap *n* īnfortūnium *nt*.
misinform *vt* falsa docēre.
misinterpret *vt* male interpretārī.
misinterpretation *n* prāva interpretātiō *f*.
misjudge *vt* male iūdicāre.
mislay *vt* āmittere.
mislead *vt* dēcipere, indūcere, auferre.
mismanage *vt* male gerere.
misnomer *n* falsum nōmen *nt*.
misogyny *n* mulierum odium *nt*.
misplace *vt* in aliēnō locō collocāre.
misplaced *adj* (*fig*) vānus.
misprint *n* mendum *nt*.
mispronounce *vt* prāvē appellāre.
misquote *vt* perperam prōferre.
misrepresent *vt* dētorquēre, invertere;
(*person*) calumniārī.
misrepresentation *n* calumnia *f*.
misrule *n* prāva administrātiō *f*.
miss *vt* (*aim*) aberrāre (*abl*); (*loss*) requīrere,

dēsīderāre; (*notice*) praetermittere ♦ *n* error *m*; (*girl*) virgō *f*.
misshapen *adj* distortus, dēfōrmis.
missile *n* tēlum *nt*.
missing *adj* absēns; **be** ~ dēesse, dēsīderārī.
mission *n* lēgātiō *f*.
missive *n* litterae *fpl*.
misspend *vt* perdere, dissipāre.
misstatement *n* falsum *nt*, mendācium *nt*.
mist *n* nebula *f*, cālīgō *f*.
mistake *n* error *m*; (*writing*) mendum *nt*; **full of**
~**s** mendōsus ♦ *vt*: ~ **for** habēre prō (*abl*); **be**
~**n** errāre, fallī.
mistletoe *n* viscum *nt*.
mistranslate *vt* prāvē reddere.
mistress *n* domina *f*; (*school*) magistra *f*;
(*lover*) amīca *f*.
mistrust *n* diffīdentia *f*, suspiciō *f* ♦ *vt*
diffīdere (*dat*).
mistrustful *adj* diffīdēns.
mistrustfully *adv* diffīdenter.
misty *adj* nebulōsus.
misunderstand *vt* male intellegere ♦ *vi*
errāre.
misunderstanding *n* error *m*; (*quarrel*)
discidium *nt*.
misuse *n* malus ūsus *m* ♦ *vt* abūtī (*abl*).
mite *n* parvulus *m*; (*insect*) vermiculus *m*.
mitigate *vt* mītigāre, lēnīre.
mitigation *n* mītigātiō *f*.
mix *vt* miscēre; ~ **in** admiscēre; ~ **together**
commiscēre; **get** ~**ed up with** admiscērī
cum, sē interpōnere (*dat*).
mixed *adj* prōmiscuus.
mixture *n* (*act*) temperātiō *f*; (*state*) dīversitās
f.
mnemonic *n* artificium memoriae *nt*.
moan *n* gemitus *m* ♦ *vi* gemere.
moat *n* fossa *f*.
mob *n* vulgus *nt*, turba *f* ♦ *vt* circumfundī in
(*acc*).
mobile *adj* mōbilis, agilis.
mobility *n* mōbilitās *f*, agilitās *f*.
mobilize *vt* (*MIL*) ēvocāre.
mock *vt* irrīdēre, lūdibriō habēre, lūdificārī;
(*ape*) imitārī; ~ **at** inlūdere ♦ *n* lūdibrium *nt* ♦
adj simulātus, fictus.
mocker *n* dērīsor *m*.
mockery *n* lūdibrium *nt*, irrīsus *m*.
mode *n* modus *m*, ratiō *f*.
model *n* exemplar *nt*, exemplum *nt* ♦ *vt*
fingere.
modeller *n* fictor *m*.
moderate *adj* (*size*) modicus; (*conduct*)
moderātus ♦ *vt* temperāre; (*emotion*)
temperāre (*dat*) ♦ *vi* mītigārī.
moderately *adv* modicē, moderātē,
mediocriter.
moderation *n* moderātiō *f*, modus *m*; (*mean*)
mediocritās *f*.
moderator *n* praefectus *m*.
modern *adj* recēns.
modernity *n* haec aetās *f*.

modest *adj* pudīcus, verēcundus.
modestly *adv* verēcundē, pudenter.
modesty *n* pudor *m*, verēcundia *f*.
modicum *n* paullulum *nt*, aliquantulum *nt*.
modification *n* mūtātiō *f*.
modify *vt* immūtāre; (*law*) derogāre aliquid
dē.
modulate *vt* (*voice*) īnflectere.
modulation *n* flexiō *f*, inclīnātiō *f*.
moiety *n* dīmidia pars *f*.
moist *adj* ūmidus.
moisten *vt* ūmectāre, rigāre.
moisture *n* ūmor *m*.
molar *n* genuīnus *m*.
mole *n* (*animal*) talpa *f*; (*on skin*) naevus *m*;
(*pier*) mōlēs *f*.
molecule *n* corpusculum *nt*.
molehill *n*: **make a mountain out of a** ~ ē rīvō
flūmina māgna facere, arcem facere ē
cloācā.
molest *vt* sollicitāre, vexāre.
molestation *n* vexātiō *f*.
mollify *vt* mollīre, lēnīre.
molten *adj* liquefactus.
moment *n* temporis mōmentum *nt*, temporis
pūnctum *nt*; **for a** ~ parumper; **in a** ~ iam;
without a ~**'s delay** nūllā interpositā morā;
be of great ~ māgnō mōmentō esse; **it is of** ~
interest.
momentary *adj* brevis.
momentous *adj* gravis, māgnī mōmentī.
momentum *n* impetus *m*.
monarch *n* rēx *m*, tyrannus *m*.
monarchical *adj* rēgius.
monarchy *n* rēgnum *nt*.
monastery *n* monastērium *nt*.
monetary *adj* pecūniārius.
money *n* pecūnia *f*; (*cash*) nummī *mpl*; **for** ~
mercēde; **ready** ~ nummī, praesēns pecūnia;
make ~ rem facere, quaestum facere.
moneybag *n* fiscus *m*.
moneyed *adj* nummātus, pecūniōsus.
moneylender *n* faenerātor *m*.
moneymaking *n* quaestus *m*.
mongoose *n* ichneumōn *m*.
mongrel *n* hibrida *m*.
monitor *n* admonitor *m*.
monk *n* monachus *m*.
monkey *n* sīmia *f*.
monograph *n* libellus *m*.
monologue *n* ōrātiō *f*.
monopolize *vt* absorbēre, sibī vindicāre.
monopoly *n* arbitrium *nt*.
monosyllabic *adj* monosyllabus.
monosyllable *n* monosyllabum *nt*.
monotonous *adj* aequābilis.
monotony *n* taedium *nt*.
monster *n* mōnstrum *nt*, portentum *nt*, bēlua *f*.
monstrosity *n* mōnstrum *nt*.
monstrous *adj* immānis, mōnstruōsus;
improbus.
month *n* mēnsis *m*.
monthly *adj* mēnstruus.

monument n monumentum nt.
monumental adj ingēns.
mood n adfectiō f, adfectus m, animus m;
 (GRAM) modus m; **I am in the ~ for** libet (inf).
moody adj mōrōsus, tristis.
moon n lūna f; **new ~** interlūnium nt.
moonlight n: **by ~** ad lūnam.
moonshine n somnia ntpl.
moonstruck adj lūnāticus.
moor vt religāre ♦ n tesqua ntpl.
moorings n ancorae fpl.
moot n conventus m; **it is a ~ point** discrepat ♦
 vt iactāre.
mop n pēniculus m ♦ vt dētergēre.
mope vi maerēre.
moral adj honestus, probus; (opposed to
 physical) animī; (PHILOS) mōrālis ♦ n
 documentum nt.
morale n animus m; **~ is low** iacet animus.
morality n bonī mōrēs mpl, virtūs f.
moralize vi dē officiīs disserere.
morally adv honestē.
morals npl mōrēs mpl.
morass n palūs f.
moratorium n mora f.
morbid adj aeger.
mordant adj mordāx.
more adj plūs, pluris (in sg + gen, in pl + adj) ♦
 adv plūs, magis, amplius; (extra) ultrā; **~ than**
 amplius quam; **~ than three feet** amplius trēs
 pedēs; **~ and ~** magis magisque; **never ~**
 immo; **~ or less** ferē; **no ~** (time) nōn diūtius,
 nunquam posteā.
moreover adv tamen, autem, praetereā.
moribund adj moribundus.
morning n māne nt; **early in the ~** bene māne;
 this ~ hodiē māne; **good ~** salvē ♦ adj
 mātūtīnus.
morning call n salūtātiō f.
morning watch n (NAUT) tertia vigilia f.
moron n sōcors m.
morose adj acerbus, tristis.
moroseness n acerbitās f, tristitia f.
morrow n posterus diēs m; **on the ~** posterō
 diē, postrīdiē.
morsel n offa f.
mortal adj mortālis, hūmānus; (wound) mortifer ♦ n mortālis m/f, homō m/f; **poor ~**
 homunculus m.
mortality n mortālitās f; (death) mors f; **the ~
 was high** plūrimī periērunt.
mortally adv: **be ~ wounded** mortiferum
 vulnus accipere.
mortar n mortārium nt.
mortgage n pignus nt, fīdūcia f ♦ vt obligāre.
mortification n dolor m, angor m.
mortified adj: **be ~ at** aegrē ferre.
mortify vt mordēre, vexāre; (lust) coercēre ♦
 vi putrēscere.
mortise vt immittere.
mosaic n emblēma nt, lapillī mpl ♦ adj
 tessellātus.
mosquito n culex m.

mosquito net n cōnōpēum nt.
moss n muscus m.
mossy adj muscōsus.
most adj plūrimus, plērusque; **for the ~ part**
 māximam partem ♦ adv māximē, plūrimum.
mostly adv plērumque, ferē.
mote n corpusculum nt.
moth n tinea f.
mother n māter f; **of a ~** māternus.
mother-in-law n socrus f.
motherless adj mātre orbus.
motherly adj māternus.
mother tongue n patrius sermō m.
mother wit n Minerva f.
motif n argūmentum nt.
motion n mōtus m; (for law) rogātiō f; (in
 debate) sententia f; **propose a ~** ferre; **set in ~**
 movēre ♦ vt innuere.
motionless adj immōbilis.
motive n causa f, ratiō f; **I know your ~ in
 asking** sciō cūr rogēs.
motley adj versicolor, varius.
mottled adj maculōsus.
motto n sententia f.
mould n fōrma f; (soil) humus f; (fungus)
 mūcor m ♦ vt fingere, fōrmāre.
moulder vi putrēscere ♦ n fictor m.
mouldering adj puter.
mouldiness n situs m.
mouldy adj mūcidus.
moult vi pennas exuere.
mound n agger m, tumulus m.
mount n mōns m; (horse) equus m ♦ vt
 scandere, cōnscendere, ascendere ♦ vi
 ascendere; **~ up** ēscendere.
mountain n mōns m.
mountaineer n montānus m.
mountainous adj montuōsus.
mourn vi maerēre, lūgēre ♦ vt dēflēre,
 lūgēre.
mourner n plōrātor m; (hired) praefica f.
mournful adj (cause) lūctuōsus, acerbus;
 (sound) lūgubris, maestus.
mournfully adv maestē.
mourning n maeror m, lūctus m; (dress)
 sordēs fpl; **in ~** fūnestus; **be in ~** lūgēre; **put
 on ~** vestem mūtāre, sordēs suscipere;
 wearing ~ ātrātus.
mouse n mūs m.
mousetrap n mūscipulum nt.
mouth n ōs nt; (river) ōstium nt.
mouthful n bucca f.
mouthpiece n interpres m.
movable adj mōbilis ♦ npl: **~s** rēs fpl, supellex
 f.
move vt movēre; (emotion) commovēre; **~
 backwards and forwards** reciprocāre; **~ out
 of the way** dēmovēre; **~ up** admovēre ♦ vi
 movērī; (residence) dēmigrāre; (proposal)
 ferre, cēnsēre; **~ into** immigrāre in (acc); **~
 on** prōgredī.
movement n mōtus m; (process) cursus m;
 (society) societās f.

mover n auctor m.
moving adj flēbilis, flexanimus.
mow vt secāre, dēmetere.
mower n faenisex m.
much adj multus ♦ adv multum; (with compar) multō; **as ~ as** tantum quantum; **so ~** tantum; (with verbs) adeo; **~ less** nēdum; **too ~** nimis ♦ n multum nt.
muck n stercus nt.
mud n lutum nt.
muddle n turba f ♦ vt turbāre.
muffle vt involvere; **~ up** obvolvere.
muffled adj surdus.
mug n pōculum nt.
mulberry n mōrum nt; (tree) mōrus f.
mule n mūlus m.
muleteer n mūliō m.
mulish adj obstinātus.
mullet n mullus m.
multifarious adj multiplex, varius.
multiform adj multifōrmis.
multiply vt multiplicāre ♦ vi crēscere.
multitude n multitūdō f.
multitudinous adj crēberrimus.
mumble vt (words) opprimere ♦ vi murmurāre.
munch vt mandūcāre.
mundane adj terrestris.
municipal adj mūnicipālis.
municipality n mūnicipium nt.
munificence n largitās f.
munificent adj largus, mūnificus.
munificently adv mūnificē.
munitions n bellī adparātus m.
mural adj mūrālis.
murder n parricīdium nt, caedēs f; **charge with ~** inter sīcāriōs accūsāre; **trial for ~** quaestiō inter sīcāriōs ♦ vt interficere, iūgulāre, necāre.
murderer n sīcārius m, homicīda m, parricīda m, percussor m.
murderess n interfectrīx f.
murderous adj cruentus.
murky adj tenebrōsus.
murmur n murmur nt; (angry) fremitus m ♦ vi murmurāre; fremere.
murmuring n admurmurātiō f.
muscle n torus m.
muscular adj lacertōsus.
muse vi meditārī ♦ n Mūsa f.
mushroom n fungus m, bōlētus m.
music n (art) mūsica f; (sound) cantus m, modī mpl.
musical adj (person) mūsicus; (sound) canōrus.
musician n mūsicus m; (strings) fidicen m; (wind) tībīcen m.
muslin n sindōn f.
must n (wine) mustum nt ♦ vi dēbēre; **I ~ go** mē oportet īre, mihī eundum est.
mustard n sināpi nt.
muster vt convocāre, cōgere; (review) recēnsēre ♦ vi convenīre, coīre ♦ n

conventus m; (review) recēnsiō f.
muster roll n album nt.
mustiness n situs m.
musty adj mūcidus.
mutability n incōnstantia f.
mutable adj incōnstāns, mūtābilis.
mute adj mūtus.
mutilate vt mūtilāre, truncāre.
mutilated adj mūtilus, truncus.
mutilation n lacerātiō f.
mutineer n sēditiōsus m.
mutinous adj sēditiōsus.
mutiny n sēditiō f ♦ vi sēditiōnem facere.
mutter vi mussitāre.
mutton n carō ovilla f.
mutual adj mūtuus.
mutually adv mūtuō, inter sē.
muzzle n ōs nt, rōstrum nt; (guard) fiscella f ♦ vt fiscellā capistrāre.
my adj meus.
myriad n decem mīlia; (any large no.) sēscentī.
myrmidon n satelles m.
myrrh n murra f.
myrtle n myrtus f ♦ adj myrteus.
myrtle grove n myrtētum nt.
myself pron ipse, egomet; (reflexive) mē.
mysterious adj arcānus, occultus.
mysteriously adv occultē.
mystery n arcānum nt; (rites) mystēria ntpl; (fig) latebra f.
mystic adj mysticus.
mystical adj mysticus.
mystification n fraus f, ambāgēs fpl.
mystify vt fraudāre, cōnfundere.
myth n fābula f.
mythical adj fābulōsus.
mythology n fābulae fpl.

_N, n_

nabob n rēx m.
nadir n fundus m.
nag n caballus m ♦ vt obiūrgītāre.
naiad n nāias f.
nail n clāvus m; (finger) unguis m; **hit the ~ on the head** rem acū tangere ♦ vt clāvīs adfīgere.
naive adj simplex.
naively adv simpliciter.
naiveté n simplicitās f.
naked adj nūdus.
nakedly adv apertē.
name n nōmen nt; (repute) existimātiō f; (term) vocābulum nt; **by ~** nōmine; **have a bad ~** male audīre; **have a good ~** bene audīre; **in**

the ~ of verbīs (gen); (oath) per ♦ vi
appellāre, vocāre, nōmināre; (appoint)
dīcere.
nameless adj nōminis expers, sine nōmine.
namely adv nempe, dīcō.
namesake n gentīlis m/f.
nanny goat n capra f.
nap n brevis somnus m; (cloth) villus nt.
napkin n linteum nt.
narcissus n narcissus m.
narcotic adj somnifer.
nard n nardus f.
narrate vt nārrāre, ēnārrāre.
narration n nārrātiō f.
narrative n fābula f.
narrator n nārrātor m.
narrow adj angustus ♦ vt coartāre ♦ vi
coartārī.
narrowly adv aegrē, vix.
narrowness n angustiae fpl.
narrows n angustiae fpl.
nasal adj nārium.
nascent adj nāscēns.
nastily adv foedē.
nastiness n foeditās f.
nasty adj foedus, taeter, impūrus.
natal adj nātālis.
nation n populus m; (foreign) gēns f.
national adj pūblicus, cīvīlis; (affairs)
domesticus.
nationality n cīvitās f.
native adj indigena; (speech) patrius ♦ n incola
m, indigena m/f.
native land n patria f.
nativity n ortus m.
natural adj nātūrālis; (innate) nātīvus,
genuīnus, īnsitus.
naturalization n cīvitās f.
naturalize vt cīvitāte dōnāre.
naturalized adj (person) cīvitāte dōnātus;
(thing) īnsitus.
naturally adv nātūrāliter, secundum nātūram;
(of course) scīlicet, certē.
nature n nātūra f; rērum nātūra f; (character)
indolēs f, ingenium nt; (species) genus nt;
course of ~ nātūra f; **I know the ~ of** sciō
quālis sit.
naught n nihil nt; **set at ~** parvī facere.
naughty adj improbus.
nausea n nausea f; (fig) fastīdium nt.
nauseate vt fastīdium movēre (dat); **be ~d**
with fastīdīre.
nauseous adj taeter.
nautical adj nauticus, maritimus.
naval adj nāvālis.
navel n umbilīcus m.
navigable adj nāvigābilis.
navigate vt, vi nāvigāre.
navigation n rēs nautica f; (sailing) nāvigātiō f.
navigator n nauta m, gubernātor m.
navy n classis f, cōpiae nāvālēs fpl.
nay adv nōn; **~ more** immo.
near adv prope ♦ adj propinquus ♦ prep prope

(acc), ad (acc); **lie ~** adiacēre (dat) ♦ vt
adpropinquāre (dat).
nearby adj iuxtā.
nearer adj propior.
nearest adj proximus.
nearly adv paene, prope, fermē.
neat adj nitidus, mundus, concinnus; (wine)
pūrus.
neatly adv mundē, concinnē.
neatness n munditia f.
nebulous adj nebulōsus; (fig) incertus.
necessaries n rēs ad vīvendum necessāriae
fpl.
necessarily adv necessāriō, necesse.
necessary adj necessārius, necesse; **it is ~**
oportet (+ acc and infin or gerundive of vt).
necessitate vt cōgere (infin), efficere ut (subj).
necessitous adj egēnus, pauper.
necessity n necessitās f; (thing) rēs necessāria
f; (want) paupertās f, egestās f.
neck n collum nt.
neckcloth n fōcāle nt.
necklace n monīle nt, torquis m.
nectar n nectar nt.
need n (necessity) necessitās f; (want) egestās f,
inopia f, indigentia f; there **is ~ of** opus est
(abl); **there is no ~ to** nihil est quod, cūr (subj)
♦ vt egēre (abl), carēre, indigēre (abl); **I ~**
opus est mihī (abl).
needful adj necessārius.
needle n acus f.
needless adj vānus, inūtilis.
needlessly adv frustrā, sine causā.
needs adv necesse ♦ npl necessitātēs fpl.
needy adj egēns, inops, pauper.
nefarious adj nefārius, scelestus.
negation n negātiō f, īnfitiātiō f.
negative adj negāns ♦ n negātiō f; **answer in**
the ~ negāre ♦ vt vetāre, contrādīcere (dat).
neglect n neglegentia f, incūria f; (of duty)
dērelictiō f ♦ vt neglegere, ōmittere.
neglectful adj neglegēns, immemor.
negligence n neglegentia f, incūria f.
negligent adj neglegēns, indīligēns.
negligently adv neglegenter, indīligenter.
negligible adj levissimus, minimī mōmentī.
negotiate vi agere dē ♦ vt (deal) peragere;
(difficulty) superāre.
negotiation n āctiō f, pactum nt.
negotiator n lēgātus m, conciliātor m.
negro n Aethiops m.
neigh vi hinnīre.
neighbour n vīcīnus m, fīnitimus m.
neighbourhood n vīcīnia f, vīcīnitās f.
neighbouring adj vīcīnus, fīnitimus,
propinquus.
neighbourly adj hūmānus, amīcus.
neighing n hinnītus m.
neither adv neque, nec; nēve, neu ♦ pron
neuter ♦ adj neuter, neutra, neutrum (like
alter); **~ ... nor** nec/neque ... nec/neque.
neophyte n tīrō m.
nephew n frātris fīlius m, sorōris fīlius m.

Nereid *n* Nērēis *f.*
nerve *n* nervus *m*; (*fig*) audācia *f*; **~s** *pl* pavor *m*,
  trepidātiō *f*; **have the ~ to** audēre ♦ *vt*
  cōnfirmāre.
nervous *adj* diffīdēns, sollicitus, trepidus.
nervously *adv* trepidē.
nervousness *n* sollicitūdō *f*, diffīdentia *f.*
nest *n* nīdus *m* ♦ *vi* nīdificāre.
nestle *vi* recubāre.
nestling *n* pullus *m.*
net *n* rēte *nt* ♦ *vt* inrētīre.
nether *adj* īnferior.
nethermost *adj* īnfimus, īmus.
netting *n* rēticulum *nt.*
nettle *n* urtīca *f* ♦ *vt* inrītāre, ūrere.
neuter *adj* neuter.
neutral *adj* medius; **be ~** neutrī partī sē
  adiungere, medium sē gerere.
neutralize *vt* compēnsāre.
never *adv* nunquam.
nevertheless *adv* nihilōminus, at tamen.
new *adj* novus, integer, recēns.
newcomer *n* advena *m/f.*
newfangled *adj* novus, inaudītus.
newly *adv* nūper, modo.
newness *n* novitās *f.*
news *n* nūntius *m*; **what ~?** quid novī?; **~ was
  brought that** nūntiātum est (*+ acc and infin*).
newspaper *n* ācta diūrna/pūblica *ntpl.*
newt *n* lacerta *f.*
next *adj* proximus; (*time*) īnsequēns ♦ *adv*
  dēinde, dēinceps; **~ day** postrīdiē; **~ to** iuxtā;
  come ~ to excipere.
nibble *vi* rōdere.
nice *adj* bellus, dulcis; (*exact*) accūrātus;
  (*particular*) fastīdiōsus.
nicely *adv* bellē, probē.
nicety *n* subtīlitās *f.*
niche *n* aedicula *f.*
nick *n*: **in the ~ of** time in ipsō articulō
  temporis.
nickname *n* cognōmen *nt.*
niece *n* frātris fīlia *f*, sorōris fīlia *f.*
niggardliness *n* illīberālitās *f*, avāritia *f.*
niggardly *adj* illīberālis, parcus, avārus.
nigh *adv* prope.
night *n* nox *f*; **by ~** noctū; **all ~** pernox; **spend
  the ~** pernoctāre; **be awake all ~** pervigilāre
  ♦ *adj* nocturnus.
night bird *n* noctua *f.*
nightfall *n* prīmae tenebrae *fpl*; **at ~** sub
  noctem.
nightingale *n* luscinia *f.*
nightly *adj* nocturnus ♦ *adv* noctū.
nightmare *n* incubus *m.*
night work *n* lūcubrātiō *f.*
nimble *adj* agilis, pernīx.
nimbleness *n* agilitās *f*, pernīcitās *f*; (*mind*)
  argūtiae *fpl.*
nimbly *adv* pernīciter.
nine *num* novem; **~ each** novēnī; **~ times**
  noviēns; **~ days'** novendiālis.
nine hundred *num* nōngentī.
nine hundredth *adj* nōngentēsimus.

nineteen *num* ūndēvigintī; **~ each** ūndēvīcēnī;
  ~ times deciēns et noviēns.
nineteenth *adj* ūndēvīcēsimus.
ninetieth *adj* nōnāgēsimus.
ninety *num* nōnāgintā; **~ each** nōnāgēnī; **~
  times** nōnāgiēns.
ninth *adj* nōnus.
nip *vt* vellicāre; (*frost*) ūrere.
nippers *n* forceps *m.*
nipple *n* papilla *f.*
no *adv* nōn; (*correcting*) immo; **say ~** negāre ♦
  adj nullus.
nobility *n* nōbilitās *f*; (*persons*) optimātēs *mpl*,
  nōbilēs *mpl.*
noble *adj* nōbilis; (*birth*) generōsus;
  (*appearance*) decōrus.
nobleman *n* prīnceps *m*, optimās *m.*
nobly *adv* nōbiliter, praeclārē.
nobody *n* nēmō *m.*
nocturnal *adj* nocturnus.
nod *n* nūtus *m* ♦ *vi* nūtāre; (*sign*) adnuere;
  (*sleep*) dormītāre.
noddle *n* caput *nt.*
node *n* nōdus *m.*
noise *n* strepitus *m*, sonitus *m*; (*loud*) fragor *m*;
  make a ~ increpāre, strepere ♦ *vt*: **~ abroad**
  ēvulgāre; **be ~d abroad** percrēbrēscere.
noiseless *adj* tacitus.
noiselessly *adv* tacitē.
noisily *adv* cum strepitū.
noisome *adj* taeter, gravis.
noisy *adj* clāmōsus.
nomadic *adj* vagus.
nomenclature *n* vocābula *ntpl.*
nominally *adv* nōmine, verbō.
nominate *vt* nōmināre, dīcere; (*in writing*)
  scrībere.
nomination *n* nōminātiō *f.*
nominative *adj* nōminātīvus.
nominee *n* nōminātus *m.*
nonappearance *n* absentia *f.*
nonce *n*: **for the ~** semel.
nonchalance *n* aequus animus *m.*
nonchalantly *adv* aequō animō.
noncombatant *adj* imbellis.
noncommittal *adj* circumspectus.
nondescript *adj* īnsolitus.
none *adj* nullus ♦ *pron* nēmō *m.*
nonentity *n* nihil *nt*, nullus *m.*
nones *n* Nōnae *fpl.*
nonexistent *adj* quī nōn est.
nonplus *vt* ad incitās redigere.
nonresistance *n* patientia *f.*
nonsense *n* nūgae *fpl*, ineptiae *fpl.*
nonsensical *adj* ineptus, absurdus.
nook *n* angulus *m.*
noon *n* merīdiēs *m* ♦ *adj* merīdiānus.
no one *pron* nēmō *m* (*for gen/abl use* **nullus**).
noose *n* laqueus *m.*
nor *adv* neque, nec; nēve, neu.
norm *n* nōrma *f.*
normal *adj* solitus.
normally *adv* plērumque.

north n septentriōnēs mpl ♦ adj septentriōnālis.
northeast adv inter septentriōnēs et orientem.
northerly adj septentriōnālis.
northern adj septentriōnālis.
North Pole n arctos f.
northwards adv ad septentriōnēs versus.
northwest adv inter septentriōnēs et occidentem ♦ adj: ~ **wind** Cōrus m.
north wind n aquilō m.
nose n nāsus m, nārēs fpl; **blow the ~** ēmungere; **lead by the ~** labiīs ductāre ♦ vi scrūtārī.
nostril n nāris f.
not adv nōn, haud; ~ **at all** haudquāquam; ~ **as if** nōn quod, nōn quō; ~ **but what** nōn quīn; ~ **even** nē... quidem; ~ **so very** nōn ita ~ **that** nōn quō; **and** ~ neque; **does** ~, **did** ~ (interrog) nonne; **if**... ~ nisi; **that** ~ (purpose) nē; (fear) nē nōn; ~ **long after** haud multō post; ~ **only** ... **but also** non modo/solum... sed etiam; ~ **yet** nōndum.
notability n vir praeclārus m.
notable adj īnsignis, īnsignītus, memōrābilis.
notably adv īnsignītē.
notary n scrība m.
notation n notae fpl.
notch n incīsūra f ♦ vt incīdere.
note n (mark) nota f; (comment) adnotātiō f; (letter) litterulae fpl; (sound) vōx f; **make a ~ of** in commentāriōs referre ♦ vt notāre; (observe) animadvertere.
notebook n pugillārēs mpl.
noted adj īnsignis, praeclārus, nōtus.
noteworthy adj memōrābilis.
nothing n nihil, nīl nt; ~ **but** merus, nīl nisi; **come to ~** in inritum cadere; **for ~** frustrā; (gift) grātīs, grātuītō; **good for ~** nēquam; **think ~ of** nihilī facere.
notice n (official) prōscrīptiō f; (private) libellus m; **attract ~** cōnspicī; **escape ~** latēre; **escape the ~ of** fallere; **give ~ of** dēnūntiāre; **take ~ of** animadvertere ♦ vt animadvertere, cōnspicere.
noticeable adj cōnspicuus, īnsignis.
noticeably adv īnsignītē.
notification n dēnūntiātiō f.
notify vt (event) dēnūntiāre, indicāre; (person) renūntiāre (dat), certiōrem facere.
notion n nōtiō f, īnfōrmātiō f; suspiciō f.
notoriety n īnfāmia f.
notorious adj fāmōsus, īnfāmis; (thing) manifestus.
notoriously adv manifestō.
notwithstanding adv nihilōminus, tamen ♦ prep: ~ **the danger** in tantō discrīmine.
nought n nihil, nīl nt.
noun n nōmen nt.
nourish vt alere, nūtrīre.
nourisher n altor m, altrīx f.
nourishment n cibus m, alimenta ntpl.
novel adj novus, inaudītus ♦ n fābella f.
novelty n rēs nova f; novitās f, īnsolentia f.

November n mēnsis November m; **of ~** November.
novice n tīrō m.
now adv nunc; (past) iam; ~ **and then** interdum; **just ~** nunc; (lately) dūdum, modo; ~ ... ~ modo ... modo ♦ conj at, autem.
nowadays adv nunc, hodiē.
nowhere adv nusquam.
nowise adv nullō modō, haudquāquam.
noxious adj nocēns, noxius.
nuance n color m.
nucleus n sēmen nt.
nude adj nūdus.
nudge vt fodicāre.
nudity n nūdātum corpus nt.
nugget n massa f.
nuisance n malum nt, incommodum nt.
null adj inritus.
nullify vt inritum facere; (law) abrogāre.
numb adj torpēns, torpidus; **be ~** torpēre; **become ~** torpēscere.
number n numerus m; **a ~ of** complūrēs, aliquot; **a great ~** multitūdō f, frequentia f; **a small ~** īnfrequentia f; **in large ~s** frequentēs ♦ vt numerāre, ēnumerāre.
numberless adj innumerābilis.
numbness n torpor m.
numerous adj frequēns, crēber, plūrimī.
nun n monacha f.
nuptial adj nūptiālis.
nuptials n nūptiae fpl.
nurse n nūtrix f ♦ vt (child) nūtrīre; (sick) cūrāre; (fig) fovēre.
nursery n (children) cubiculum nt; (plants) sēminārium nt.
nursling n alumnus m, alumna f.
nurture n ēducātiō f.
nut n nux f.
nutrition n alimenta ntpl.
nutritious adj salūbris.
nutshell n putāmen nt.
nut tree n nux f.
nymph n nympha f.

O, o

O interj ō!
oaf n agrestis m.
oak n quercus f; (evergreen) īlex f; (timber) rōbur nt ♦ adj quernus, īlignus, rōboreus; ~ **forest** quercētum nt.
oakum n stuppa f.
oar n rēmus m.
oarsman n rēmex m.
oaten adj avēnāceus.
oath n iūsiūrandum nt; (MIL) sacrāmentum nt;

(*imprecation*) exsecrātiō *f*; **false ~** periūrium
nt; **take an ~** iūrāre; **take an ~ of allegiance to**
in verba iūrāre (*gen*).
oats *n* avēna *f*.
obduracy *n* obstinātus animus *m*.
obdurate *adj* obstinātus, pervicāx.
obdurately *adv* obstinātē.
obedience *n* oboedientia *f*, obsequium *nt*.
obedient *adj* oboediēns, obsequēns; **be ~ to**
pārēre (*dat*), obtemperāre (*dat*), obsequī
(*dat*).
obediently *adv* oboedienter.
obeisance *n* obsequium *nt*; **make ~ to** adōrāre.
obelisk *n* obeliscus *m*.
obese *adj* obēsus, pinguis.
obesity *n* obēsitās *f*, pinguitūdō *f*.
obey *vt* pārēre (*dat*), obtemperāre (*dat*),
oboedīre (*dat*); **~ orders** dictō pārēre.
obituary *n* mortēs *fpl*.
object *n* rēs *f*; (*aim*) fīnis *m*, prōpositum *nt*; **be**
an ~ of hate odiō esse; **with what ~** quō
cōnsiliō ♦ *vi* recūsāre, gravārī; **but, it is ~ed**
at enim; **~ to** improbāre.
objection *n* recūsātiō *f*, mora *f*; **I have no ~** nīl
moror.
objectionable *adj* invīsus, iniūcundus.
objective *adj* externus ♦ *n* prōpositum *nt*, fīnis
m.
objurgate *vt* obiūrgāre, culpāre.
oblation *n* dōnum *nt*.
obligation *n* (*legal*) dēbitum *nt*; (*moral*)
officium *nt*; **lay under an ~** obligāre,
obstringere.
obligatory *adj* dēbitus, necessārius.
oblige *vt* (*force*) cōgere; (*contract*) obligāre,
obstringere; (*compliance*) mōrem gerere
(*dat*), mōrigerārī (*dat*); **I am ~d to** (*action*)
dēbeō (*inf*); (*person*) amāre, grātiam habēre
(*dat*).
obliging *adj* cōmis, officiōsus.
obligingly *adv* cōmiter, officiōsē.
oblique *adj* oblīquus.
obliquely *adv* oblīquē.
obliquity *n* (*moral*) prāvitās *f*.
obliterate *vt* dēlēre, oblitterāre.
obliteration *n* litūra *f*.
oblivion *n* oblīviō *f*.
oblivious *adj* oblīviōsus, immemor.
oblong *adj* oblongus.
obloquy *n* vītuperātiō *f*, opprobrium *nt*.
obnoxious *adj* invīsus.
obscene *adj* obscaenus, impūrus.
obscenity *n* obscaenitās *f*, impūritās *f*.
obscure *adj* obscūrus, caecus ♦ *vt* obscūrāre,
officere (*dat*).
obscurely *adv* obscūrē; (*speech*) per ambāgēs.
obscurity *n* obscūritās *f*; (*speech*) ambāgēs *fpl*.
obsequies *n* exsequiae *fpl*.
obsequious *adj* officiōsus, ambitiōsus.
obsequiously *adv* officiōsē.
obsequiousness *n* adsentātiō *f*.
observance *n* observantia *f*; (*rite*) rītus *m*.
observant *adj* attentus, dīligēns.

observation *n* observātiō *f*, animadversiō *f*;
(*remark*) dictum *nt*.
observe *vt* animadvertere, contemplārī; (*see*)
cernere, cōnspicere; (*remark*) dīcere; (*adhere*
to) cōnservāre, observāre.
observer *n* spectātor *m*, contemplātor *m*.
obsess *vt* occupāre; **I am ~ed by** tōtus sum in
(*abl*).
obsession *n* studium *nt*.
obsolescent *adj*: **be ~** obsolēscere.
obsolete *adj* obsolētus; **become ~** exolēscere.
obstacle *n* impedīmentum *nt*, mora *f*.
obstinacy *n* pertinācia *f*, obstinātus animus *m*.
obstinate *adj* pertināx, obstinātus.
obstinately *adv* obstinātō animō.
obstreperous *adj* clāmōsus, ferus.
obstruct *vt* impedīre, obstruere, obstāre (*dat*);
(*POL*) intercēdere (*dat*); (*fig*) officere (*dat*).
obstruction *n* impedīmentum *nt*; (*POL*)
intercessiō *f*.
obstruct *onist* *n* intercessor *m*.
obtain *vt* adipīscī, nancīscī, cōnsequī;
comparāre; (*by request*) impetrāre ♦ *vi*
tenēre, obtinēre.
obtrude *vi* sē inculcāre ♦ *vt* ingerere.
obtrusive *adj* importūnus, molestus.
obtuse *adj* hebes, stolidus.
obtusely *adv* stolidē.
obtuseness *n* stupor *m*.
obverse *adj* obversus.
obviate *vt* tollere, praevertere.
obvious *adj* ēvidēns, manifestus, apertus; **it is**
**~ appāret.
obviously *adv* ēvidenter, apertē, manifestō.
occasion *n* occāsiō *f*, locus *m*; (*reason*) causa *f*
♦ *vt* movēre, facessere, auctōrem esse (*gen*).
occasional *adj* fortuītus.
occasionally *adv* interdum, nōnnunquam.
occidental *adj* occidentālis.
occult *adj* arcānus.
occupancy *n* possessiō *f*.
occupant *n* habitātor *m*, possessor *m*.
occupation *n* quaestus *m*, occupātiō *f*.
occupier *n* possessor *m*.
occupy *vt* possidēre; (*MIL*) occupāre; (*space*)
complēre; (*attention*) distinēre, occupāre.
occur *vi* ēvenīre, accidere; (*to mind*)
occurrere, in mentem venīre.
occurrence *n* ēventum *nt*; rēs *f*.
ocean *n* mare *nt*, ōceanus *m*.
October *n* mēnsis Octōber *m*; **of ~** Octōber.
ocular *adj* oculōrum; **give ~ proof of** ante
oculōs pōnere, videntī dēmōnstrāre.
odd *adj* (*number*) impār; (*moment*) subsecīvus;
(*appearance*) novus, īnsolitus.
oddity *n* novitās *f*; (*person*) homō rīdiculus *m*.
oddly *adv* mīrum in modum.
odds *n* praestantia *f*; **be at ~ with** dissidēre
cum; **the ~ are against us** imparēs sumus; **the**
~ are in our favour superiōrēs sumus.
ode *n* carmen *nt*.
odious *adj* invīsus, odiōsus.
odium *n* invidia *f*.

odorous *adj* odōrātus.
odour *n* odor *m.*
of *prep gen;* (*origin*) ex, dē; (*cause*) *abl;* **a l ~ us**
   nōs omnēs; **the city ~** Rome urbs Rōma.
off *adv* procul; (*prefix*) ab-; **~ and on** interdum;
   ~ with you aufer tē; **come ~** ēvādere; **well ~**
   beātus; **well ~ for** abundāns (*abl*).
offal *n* quisquiliae *fpl.*
offence *n* offēnsiō *f;* (*legal*) dēlictum *nt;*
   commit an ~ dēlinquere.
offend *vt* laedere, offendere; **be ~ed** aegrē
   ferre ♦ *vi* dēlinquere; **~ against** peccāre in
   (*acc*), violāre.
offender *n* reus *m.*
offensive *adj* odiōsus; (*smell*) gravis;
   (*language*) contumēliōsus; **take the ~** bellum
   īnferre.
offensively *adv* odiōsē; graviter.
offer *vt* offerre, dare, praebēre; (*hand*)
   porrigere; (*violence*) adferre; (*honour*)
   dēferre; (*with verb*) profitērī, pollicērī ♦ *n*
   condiciō *f;* **~ for sale** venditāre.
offering *n* dōnum *nt;* (*to the dead*) īnferiae *fpl.*
off-hand *adj* neglegēns, incūriōsus.
office *n* (*POL*) magistrātus *m,* mūnus *nt,* honōs
   m; (*kindness*) officium *nt;* (*place*) mēnsa *f.*
officer *n* praefectus *m;* lēgātus *m.*
official *adj* pūblicus ♦ *n* adiūtor *m,* minister *m.*
officially *adv* pūblicē.
officiate *vi* operārī, officiō fungī.
officious *adj* molestus.
officiously *adv* molestē.
officiousness *n* occursātiō *f.*
offing *n:* **in the ~** procul.
offset *vt* compēnsāre.
offspring *n* prōgeniēs *f,* līberī *mpl;* (*animal*)
   fētus *m.*
often *adv* saepe, saepenumerō; **as ~ as**
   quotiēns; **totiēs . . . quotiēs; how ~?**
   quotiēns?; **so ~** totiēns; **very ~** persaepe.
ogle *vi:* **~ at** līmīs oculīs intuērī.
ogre *n* mōnstrum *nt.*
oh *interj* (*joy, surprise*) ōh!; (*sorrow*) prō!
oil *n* oleum *nt* ♦ *vt* ungere.
oily *adj* oleōsus.
ointment *n* unguentum *nt.*
old *adj* (*person*) senex; (*thing*) vetus; (*ancient*)
   antīquus, prīscus; **~ age** senectūs *f;* **be ten
   years ~** decem annōs habēre; **ten years ~**
   decem annōs nātus; **two years ~** bīmus; **good
   ~** antīquus; **good ~ days** antīquitās *f;* **grow ~**
   senēscere; **of ~** quondam.
olden *adj* prīscus, prīstinus.
older *adj* nātū māior, senior.
oldest *adj* nātū māximus.
old-fashioned *adj* antīquus, obsolētus.
old man *n* senex *m.*
oldness *n* vetustās *f.*
old woman *n* anus *f.*
oligarchy *n* paucōrum dominātiō *f,*
   optimātium factiō *f.*
olive *n* olea *f;* **~ orchard** olīvētum *nt.*

Olympiad *n* Olympias *f.*
Olympic *adj* Olympicus; **win an ~ victory**
   Olympia vincere.
Olympic Games *n* Olympia *ntpl.*
omen *n* ōmen *nt,* auspicium *nt;* **announce a bad
   ~** obnūntiāre; **obtain favourable ~s** litāre.
ominous *adj* īnfaustus, mināx.
omission *n* praetermissiō *f,* neglegentia *f.*
omit *vt* ōmittere, praetermittere.
omnipotence *n* īnfīnīta potestās *f.*
omnipotent *adj* omnipotēns.
on *prep* (*place*) in (*abl*), in- (*prefix*); (*time*) *abl;*
   (*coast of*) ad (*acc*); (*subject*) dē (*abl*); (*side*) ab
   (*abl*) ♦ *adv* porrō, usque; **and so ~** ac
   deinceps; **~ hearing the news** nūntiō acceptō;
   ~ equal terms (*in battle*) aequō Marte; **~ the
   following day** posterō/proximō diē;
   postrīdiē; **~ this side of** citrā (+ *acc*).
once *adv* semel; (*past*) ōlim, quondam; **at ~**
   extemplō, statim; (*together*) simul; **for ~**
   aliquandō; **~ and for all** semel; **~ more** dēnuō,
   iterum; **~ upon a time** ōlim, quondam.
one *num* ūnus ♦ *pron* quīdam; (*of two*) alter,
   altera, alterum; **~ and the same** ūnus; **~
   another** inter sē, alius alium; **~ or the other**
   alteruter; **~ day** ōlim; **~ each** singulī; **~ would
   have thought** crēderēs; **be ~ of** in numerō
   esse (*gen*); **be at ~** idem sentīre; **it is all ~**
   nihil interest; **the ~** alter, hic; **this is the ~**
   hōc illud est.
one-eyed *adj* luscus.
oneness *n* ūnitās *f.*
onerous *adj* gravis.
oneself *pron* ipse; (*reflexive*) sē.
one-sided *adj* inaequālis, inīquus.
onion *n* caepe *nt.*
onlooker *n* spectātor *m.*
only *adj* ūnus, sōlus; (*son*) ūnicus ♦ *adv* sōlum,
   tantum, modo; (*with clause*) nōn nisi, nīl nisi,
   nihil aliud quam; (*time*) dēmum; **if ~** sī modo;
   (*wish*) utinam.
onrush *n* incursus *m.*
onset *n* impetus *m.*
onslaught *n* incursus *m;* **make an ~ on** (*words*)
   invehī in (*acc*).
onto *prep* in (+ *acc*).
onus *n* officium *nt.*
onward, onwards *adv* porrō.
onyx *n* onyx *m.*
ooze *vi* mānāre, stillāre.
opaque *adj* haud perlūcidus.
open *adj* apertus; (*wide*) patēns, hiāns;
   (*ground*) pūrus, apertus; (*question*) integer;
   lie ~ patēre; **stand ~** hiāre; **throw ~**
   adaperīre, patefacere; **it is ~ to me to** mihī
   integrum est (*inf*); **while the question is still ~**
   rē integrā ♦ *vt* aperīre, patefacere; (*book*)
   ēvolvere; (*letter*) resolvere; (*speech*)
   exōrdīrī; (*with ceremony*) inaugurāre; (*will*)
   resignāre ♦ *vi* aperīrī, hiscere; (*sore*)
   recrūdēscere; **~ out** extendere, pandere; **~
   up** (*country*) aperīre.
open air *n:* **in the ~** sub dīvō.

open-handed *adj* largus, mūnificus.
open-handedness *n* largitās *f*.
open-hearted *adj* ingenuus.
opening *n* forāmen *nt*, hiātus *m*; (*ceremony*)
cōnsecrātiō *f*; (*opportunity*) occāsiō *f*, ānsa *f*
♦ *adj* prīmus.
openly *adv* palam, apertē.
open-mouthed *adj*: **stand ~ at** inhiāre.
operate *vi* rem gerere ♦ *vt* movēre.
operation *n* opus *nt*, āctiō *f*; (*MED*) sectiō *f*.
operative *adj* efficāx.
ophthalmia *n* lippitūdō *f*.
opiate *adj* somnifer.
opine *vi* opīnārī, existimāre.
opinion *n* sententia *f*; (*of person*) existimātiō *f*;
public ~ fāma *f*; **in my ~** meō iūdiciō, meō
animō.
opponent *n* adversārius *m*, hostis *m*.
opportune *adj* opportūnus, tempestīvus.
opportunely *adv* opportūnē.
opportunity *n* occāsiō *f*; (*to act*) facultās *f*;
potestās *f*.
oppose *vt* (*barrier*) obicere; (*contrast*)
oppōnere ♦ *vi* adversārī (*dat*), resistere (*dat*),
obstāre (*dat*); **be ~d to** adversārī (*dat*);
(*opinion*) dīversum esse ab.
opposite *adj* (*facing*) adversus; (*contrary*)
contrārius, dīversus ♦ *prep* contrā (*acc*),
adversus (*acc*); **directly ~ ē** regiōne (*gen*)
♦ *adv* ex adversō.
opposition *n* repugnantia *f*; (*party*) factiō
adversa *f*.
oppress *vt* opprimere, adflīgere; (*burden*)
premere, onerāre.
oppression *n* iniūria *f*, servitūs *f*.
oppressive *adj* gravis, inīquus; **become more
~** ingravēscere.
oppressor *n* tyrannus *m*.
opprobrious *adj* turpis.
opprobriously *adv* turpiter.
opprobrium *n* dēdecus *nt*, ignōminia *f*.
optical *adj* oculōrum.
optical illusion *n* oculōrum lūdibrium *nt*.
optimism *n* spēs *f*.
option *n* optiō *f*, arbitrium *nt*; **I have no ~** nōn
est arbitriī meī.
optional *adj*: **it is ~ for you** optiō tua est.
opulence *n* opēs *fpl*, cōpia *f*.
opulent *adj* dīves, cōpiōsus.
or *conj* aut, vel, -ve; (*after* **utrum**) an; **~ else**
aliōquīn; **~ not** (*direct*) annōn; (*indirect*)
necne.
oracle *n* ōrāculum *nt*.
oracular *adj* fātidicus; (*fig*) obscūrus.
oral *adj*: **give an ~ message** vōce nūntiāre.
orally *adv* vōce, verbīs.
oration *n* ōrātiō *f*.
orator *n* ōrātor *m*.
oratorical *adj* ōrātōrius.
oratory *n* ēloquentia *f*, rhētoricē *f*; (*for prayer*)
sacellum *nt*; **of ~** dīcendī, ōrātōrius.
orb *n* orbis *m*.
orbit *n* orbis *m*, ambitus *m*.
orchard *n* pōmārium *nt*.

ordain *vt* ēdīcere, sancīre.
ordeal *n* labor *m*.
order *n* (*arrangement*) ōrdō *m*; (*class*) ōrdō *m*;
(*battle*) aciēs *f*; (*command*) iussum *nt*,
imperium *nt*; (*money*) perscrīptiō *f*; **in ~**
dispositus; (*succession*) deinceps; **in ~ that/to**
ut (+ *subj*); **in ~ that not** nē (+ *subj*); **put in ~**
dispōnere, ōrdināre; **by ~ of** iussū (*gen*); **out
of ~** incompositus; **without ~s from** iniussū
(*gen*) ♦ *vt* (*arrange*) dispōnere, ōrdināre;
(*command*) iubēre (+ *acc and infin*), imperāre
(*dat and ut/nē +subj*).
orderly *adj* ōrdinātus; (*conduct*) modestus ♦ *n*
accēnsus *m*.
ordinance *n* ēdictum *nt*, institūtum *nt*.
ordinarily *adv* plērumque, ferē.
ordinary *adj* ūsitātus, solitus, cottīdiānus.
ordnance *n* tormenta *ntpl*.
ordure *n* stercus *m*.
ore *n* aes *nt*; **iron ~** ferrum īnfectum *nt*.
Oread *n* (*MYTH*) Oreas *f*.
organ *n* (*bodily*) membrum *nt*; (*musical*)
organum *nt*, hydraulus *m*.
organic *adj* nātūrālis.
organically *adv* nātūrā.
organization *n* ōrdinātiō *f*, structūra *f*.
organize *vt* ōrdināre, īnstituere, adparāre.
orgies *n* orgia *ntpl*.
orgy *n* cōmissātiō *f*.
orient *n* oriēns *m*.
oriental *adj* Asiāticus.
orifice *n* ōstium *nt*.
origin *n* orīgō *f*, prīncipium *nt*; (*source*) fōns *m*;
(*birth*) genus *nt*.
original *adj* prīmus, prīstinus; (*LIT*) proprius
♦ *n* exemplar *nt*.
originally *adv* prīncipiō, antīquitus.
originate *vt* īnstituere, auctōrem esse (*gen*)
♦ *vi* exorīrī; **~ in** innāscī in (*abl*), initium
dūcere ab.
originator *n* auctor *m*.
orisons *n* precēs *fpl*.
ornament *n* ōrnāmentum *nt*; (*fig*) decus *nt* ♦ *vt*
ōrnāre, decorāre; **I am ~** ornamentō sum.
ornamental *adj* decōrus; **be ~** decorī esse.
ornamentally *adv* ōrnātē.
ornate *adj* ōrnātus.
ornately *adv* ōrnātē.
orphan *n* orbus *m*, orba *f*.
orphaned *adj* orbātus.
orthodox *adj* antīquus.
orthography *n* orthographia *f*.
oscillate *vi* reciprocāre.
osculate *vt* ōsculārī.
osier *n* vīmen *nt* ♦ *adj* vīmineus.
osprey *n* haliaeetos *m*.
ostensible *adj* speciōsus.
ostensibly *adv* per speciem.
ostentation *n* iactātiō *f*, ostentātiō *f*.
ostentatious *adj* glōriōsus, ambitiōsus.
ostentatiously *adv* glōriōsē.
ostler *n* agāsō *m*.
ostrich *n* strūthiocamēlus *m*.

other adj alius; (of two) alter; **one or the ~** alteruter; **every ~ year** tertiō quōque annō; **on the ~ side of** ultrā (+ acc); **of ~s** aliēnus.

otherwise adv aliter; (if not) aliōquī.

otter n lutra f.

ought vi dēbēre (+ infin or gerundive or vt); **I ~ mē** oportet; **I ~ to have said** dēbuī dīcere.

ounce n ūncia f; **two ~s** sextāns m; **three ~s** quadrāns m; **four ~s** triēns m; **five ~s** quīncūnx m; **six ~s** sēmis m; **seven ~s** septūnx m; **eight ~s** bēs m; **nine ~s** dōdrāns m; **ten ~s** dextāns m; **eleven ~s** deūnx m.

our adj noster.

ourselves pron ipsī; (reflexive) nōs.

oust vt extrūdere, ēicere.

out adv (rest) forīs; (motion) forās; **~ of** dē, ē/ex (abl); (cause) propter (acc); (beyond) extrā, ultrā (acc); **be ~** (book) in manibus esse; (calculation) errāre; (fire) exstinctum esse; (secret) palam esse.

outbreak n initium nt, ēruptiō f.

outburst n ēruptiō f.

outcast n profugus m.

outcome n ēventus m, exitus m.

outcry n clāmor m, adclāmātiō f; **raise an ~ against** obstrepere (dat).

outdistance vt praevertere.

outdo vt superāre.

outdoor adj sub dīvō.

outer adj exterior.

outermost adj extrēmus.

outfit n īnstrūmenta ntpl; vestīmenta ntpl.

outflank vt circumīre.

outgrow vt excēdere ex.

outing n excursiō f.

outlandish adj barbarus.

outlaw n prōscrīptus m ♦ vt prōscrībere, aquā et ignī interdīcere (dat).

outlawry n aquae et ignis interdictiō f.

outlay n impēnsa f, sūmptus m.

outlet n ēmissārium nt, exitus m.

outline n ductus m, adumbrātiō f ♦ vt adumbrāre.

outlive vt superesse (dat).

outlook n prōspectus m.

outlying adj longinquus, exterior.

outnumber vt numerō superiōrēs esse, multitūdine superāre.

out-of-doors adv forīs.

outpost n statiō f.

outpouring n effūsiō f.

output n fructus m.

outrage n flāgitium nt, iniūria f ♦ vt laedere, violāre.

outrageous adj flāgitiōsus, indignus.

outrageously adv flāgitiōsē.

outrider n praecursor m.

outright adv penitus, prōrsus; semel.

outrun vt praevertere.

outset n initium nt.

outshine vt praelūcēre (dat).

outside adj externus ♦ adv extrā, forīs; (motion to) forās; **~ in** inversus; **from ~**

extrīnsecus ♦ n exterior pars f; (show) speciēs f; **at the ~** summum, ad summum; **on the ~** extrīnsecus ♦ prep extrā (acc).

outsider n aliēnus m; (POL) novus homō m.

outskirts n suburbānus ager m; **on the ~** suburbānus.

outspoken adj līber.

outspokenness n lībertās f.

outspread adj patulus.

outstanding adj ēgregius, īnsignis, singulāris; (debt) residuus.

outstep vt excēdere.

outstretched adj passus, porrēctus, extentus.

outstrip vt praevertere.

outvote vt suffrāgiīs superāre.

outward adj externus; **~ form** speciēs f ♦ adv domō, forās.

outweigh vt praeponderāre.

outwit vt dēcipere, circumvenīre.

outwork n prōpugnāculum nt, bracchium nt.

outworn adj exolētus.

oval adj ōvātus ♦ n ōvum nt.

ovation n (triumph) ovātiō f; **receive an ~ cum** laudibus excipī.

oven n furnus m, fornāx f.

over prep (above) super (abl), suprā (acc); (across) super (acc); (extent) per (acc); (time) inter (acc); **~ and above** super (acc), praeter (acc); **all ~** per; **~ against** adversus (acc) ♦ adv suprā; (excess) nimis; (done) cōnfectus; **~ again** dēnuō; **~ and above** īnsuper; **~ and ~** identidem; **be left ~** superesse, restāre; **it is all ~ with** āctum est dē.

overall adj tōtus ♦ adv ubīque, passim.

overawe vt formīdinem inicere (dat).

overbalance vi titubāre.

overbearing adj superbus.

overboard adv ē nāvī, in mare; **throw ~** excutere, iactāre.

overbold adj importūnus.

overburden vt praegravāre.

overcast adj nūbilus.

overcoat n paenula f, lacerna f.

overcome vt superāre, vincere.

overconfidence n cōnfīdentia f.

overconfident adj cōnfīdēns.

overdo vt modum excēdere in (abl).

overdone adj (style) pūtidus.

overdraw vt (style) exaggerāre.

overdue adj (money) residuus.

overestimate vt māiōris aestimāre.

overflow n ēluviō f ♦ vi abundāre, redundāre ♦ vt inundāre.

overgrown adj obsitus; **be ~** luxuriāre.

overhang vt, vi impendēre, imminēre (dat).

overhaul vt reficere.

overhead adv īnsuper.

overhear vt excipere, auscultāre.

overjoyed adj nimiō gaudiō ēlātus.

overladen adj praegravātus.

overland adv terrā.

overlap vt implicāre.

overlay vt indūcere.

overload *vt* (*fig*) obruere.
overlook *vt* (*place*) dēspectāre, imminēre
(*dat*); (*knowledge*) ignōrāre; (*notice*)
neglegere, praetermittere; (*fault*) ignōscere
(*dat*).
overlord *n* dominus *m*.
overmaster *vt* dēvincere.
overmuch *adv* nimis, plūs aequō.
overnight *adj* nocturnus ♦ *adv* noctū.
overpower *vt* superāre, domāre, obruere,
opprimere.
overpraise *vt* in māius extollere.
overrate *vt* māiōris aestimāre.
overreach *vt* circumvenīre.
overriding *adj* praecipuus.
overrule *vt* rescindere.
overrun *vt* pervagārī; (*fig*) obsidēre.
oversea *adj* trānsmarīnus.
oversee *vt* praeesse (*dat*).
overseer *n* cūrātor *m*, custōs *m*.
overset *vt* ēvertere.
overshadow *vt* officere (*dat*).
overshoot *vt* excēdere.
oversight *n* neglegentia *f*.
overspread *vt* offendere (*dat*), obdūcere.
overstep *vt* excēdere.
overt *adj* apertus.
overtake *vt* cōnsequī; (*surprise*) opprimere,
dēprehendere.
overtax *vt* (*fig*) abūtī (*abl*).
overthrow *vt* ēvertere; (*destroy*) prōflīgāre,
dēbellāre ♦ *n* ēversiō *f*, ruīna *f*.
overtly *adv* palam.
overtop *vt* superāre.
overture *n* exōrdium *nt*; **make ~s to** temptāre,
agere cum, lēgātōs mittere ad.
overturn *vt* ēvertere.
overweening *adj* superbus, adrogāns,
īnsolēns.
overwhelm *vt* obruere, dēmergere,
opprimere.
overwhelming *adj* īnsignis,
vehementissimus.
overwhelmingly *adv* mīrum quantum.
overwork *vi* plūs aequō labōrāre ♦ *vt*
cōnficere ♦ *n* immodicus labor *m*.
overwrought *adj* (*emotion*) ēlātus; (*style*)
ēlabōrātus.
owe *vt* dēbēre.
owing *adj*: **be ~** dēbērī; **~ to** (*person*) per;
(*cause*) ob/propter (*acc*).
owl *n* būbō *m*; ulula *f*.
own *adj* proprius; **my ~** meus; **have of one's ~**
domī habēre; **hold one's ~** parem esse ♦ *vt*
possidēre, habēre; (*admit*) fatērī, cōnfitērī.
owner *n* dominus *m*, possessor *m*.
ownership *n* possessiō *f*, mancipium *nt*.
ox *n* bōs *m*.
ox herd *n* bubulcus *m*.
oyster *n* ostrea *f*.

P, p

pace *n* passus *m*; (*speed*) gradus *m*; **keep ~
gradum cōnferre** ♦ *vi* incēdere; **~ up and
down** spatiārī, inambulāre.
pacific *adj* pācificus; (*quiet*) placidus.
pacification *n* pācificātiō *f*.
pacifist *n* imbellis *m*.
pacify *vt* (*anger*) plācāre; (*rising*) sēdāre.
pack *n* (*MIL*) sarcina *f*; (*animals*) grex *m*; (*people*)
turba *f* ♦ *vt* (*kit*) colligere; (*crowd*) stīpāre; **~
together** coartāre; **~ up** colligere,
compōnere ♦ *vi* vāsa colligere; **send ~ing**
missum facere ♦ *adj* (*animal*) clītellārius.
package *n* fasciculus *m*, sarcina *f*.
packet *n* fasciculus *m*; (*ship*) nāvis āctuāria *f*.
packhorse *n* iūmentum *nt*.
packsaddle *n* clītellae *fpl*.
pact *n* foedus *nt*, pactum *nt*.
pad *n* pulvillus *m*.
padding *n* tōmentum *nt*.
paddle *n* rēmus *m* ♦ *vi* rēmigāre.
paddock *n* saeptum *nt*.
paean *n* paeān *m*.
pagan *adj* pāgānus.
page *n* (*book*) pāgina *f*; (*boy*) puer *m*.
pageant *n* pompa *f*, spectāculum *nt*.
pageantry *n* adparātus *m*.
pail *n* situla *f*.
pain *n* dolor *m*; **be in ~** dolēre ♦ *vt* dolōre
adficere.
painful *adj* acerbus; (*work*) labōriōsus.
painfully *adv* acerbē, labōriōsē.
painless *adj* dolōris expers.
painlessly *adv* sine dolōre.
painlessness *n* indolentia *f*.
pains *npl* opera *f*; **take ~** operam dare; **take ~
with** (*art*) ēlabōrāre.
painstaking *adj* dīligēns, operōsus.
painstakingly *adv* dīligenter, summā cūrā.
paint *n* pigmentum *nt*; (*cosmetic*) fūcus *m* ♦ *vt*
pingere; (*red*) fūcāre; (*in words*) dēpingere;
(*portrait*) dēpingere.
paintbrush *n* pēnicillus *m*.
painter *n* pictor *m*.
painting *n* pictūra *f*.
pair *n* pār *nt* ♦ *vt* coniungere, compōnere.
palace *n* rēgia *f*.
palatable *adj* suāvis, iūcundus.
palate *n* palātum *nt*.
palatial *adj* rēgius.
palaver *n* colloquium *nt*, sermunculī *mpl*.
pale *n* pālus *m*, vallus *m*; **beyond the ~**
extrāneus ♦ *adj* pallidus; **look ~** pallēre;
grow ~ pallēscere; **~ brown** subfuscus; **~
green** subviridis ♦ *vi* pallēscere.
paleness *n* pallor *m*.

palimpsest n palimpsēstus m.
paling n saepēs f.
palisade n (MIL) vallum nt.
palish adj pallidulus.
pall n (funeral) pallium nt ♦ vi taedēre.
pallet n grabātus m.
palliasse n strāmentum nt.
palliate vt extenuāre, excūsāre.
palliation n excūsātiō f.
palliative n lēnīmentum nt.
pallid adj pallidus.
pallor n pallor m.
palm n (hand) palma f; (tree) palma f ♦ vt: ~ off impōnere.
palmy adj flōrēns.
palpable adj tractābilis; (fig) manifestus.
palpably adv manifestō, propalam.
palpitate vi palpitāre, micāre.
palpitation n palpitātiō f.
palsied adj membrīs captus.
palsy n paralysis f.
paltry adj vīlis, frīvolus.
pamper vt indulgēre (dat).
pampered adj dēlicātus.
pamphlet n libellus m.
pan n patina f, patella f; (frying) sartāgō f; (of balance) lanx f.
pancake n laganum nt.
pander n lēnō m ♦ vi: ~ to lēnōcinārī (dat).
panegyric n laudātiō f.
panegyrist n laudātor m.
panel n (wall) abacus m; (ceiling) lacūnār nt; (judges) decuria f.
panelled adj laqueātus.
pang n dolor m.
panic n pavor m ♦ vi trepidāre.
panic-stricken adj pavidus.
panniers n clītellae fpl.
panoply n arma ntpl.
panorama n prōspectus m.
panpipe n fistula f.
pant vi anhēlāre.
panther n panthēra f.
panting n anhēlitus m.
pantomime n mīmus m.
pantry n cella penāria f.
pap n mamma f.
paper n charta f.
papyrus n papyrus f.
par n: on a ~ with pār (dat).
parable n parabolē f.
parade n pompa f; (show) adparātus m ♦ vt trādūcere, iactāre ♦ vi pompam dūcere, incēdere.
paradox n verba sēcum repugnantia; ~es pl paradoxa ntpl.
paragon n exemplar nt, specimen nt.
paragraph n caput nt.
parallel adj parallēlus; (fig) cōnsimilis.
paralyse vt dēbilitāre; (with fear) percellere; be ~d torpēre.
paralysis n dēbilitās f; (fig) torpēdō f.
paramount adj prīnceps, summus.

paramour n adulter m.
parapet n lōrīca f.
paraphernalia n adparātus m.
paraphrase vt vertere.
parasite n parasītus m.
parasol n umbella f.
parboiled adj subcrūdus.
parcel n fasciculus m ♦ vt: ~ out distribuere, dispertīre.
parch vt torrēre.
parched adj torridus, āridus; be ~ ārēre.
parchment n membrāna f.
pardon n venia f ♦ vt ignōscere (dat); (offence) condōnāre.
pardonable adj ignōscendus.
pare vt dēglūbere; (nails) resecāre.
parent n parēns m/f, genitor m, genetrīx f.
parentage n stirps f, genus nt.
parental adj patrius.
parenthesis n interclūsiō f.
parings n praesegmina ntpl.
parish n (ECCL) paroecia f.
parity n aequālitās f.
park n hortī mpl.
parlance n sermō m.
parley n colloquium nt ♦ vi colloquī, agere.
parliament n senātus m; house of ~ cūria f.
parliamentary adj senātōrius.
parlour n exedrium nt.
parlous adj difficilis, perīculōsus.
parochial adj mūnicipālis.
parody n carmen ioculāre nt ♦ vt calumniārī.
parole n fidēs f.
paronomasia n agnōminātiō f.
paroxysm n accessus m.
parricide n (doer) parricīda m; (deed) parricīdium nt.
parrot n psittacus m.
parry vt ēlūdere, prōpulsāre.
parsimonious adj parcus.
parsimoniously adv parcē.
parsimony n parsimōnia f, frūgālitās f.
part n pars f; (play) partēs fpl, persōna f; (duty) officium nt; ~s loca ntpl; (ability) ingenium nt; for my ~ equidem; for the most ~ māximam partem; on the ~ of ab; act the ~ of persōnam sustinēre, partēs agere; have no ~ in expers esse (gen); in ~ partim; it is the ~ of a wise man sapientis est; play one's ~ officiō satisfacere; take ~ in interesse (dat), particeps esse (gen); take in good ~ in bonam partem accipere; take someone's ~ adesse alicuī, dēfendere aliquem; from all ~s undique; in foreign ~s peregrē; in two ~s bifāriam; (MIL) bipartītō; in three ~s trifāriam; (MIL) tripartītō; of ~s ingeniōsus ♦ vt dīvidere, sēparāre, dirimere; ~ company dīversōs discēdere ♦ vi dīgredī, discēdere; (things) dissilīre; ~ with renūntiāre.
partake vi interesse, particeps esse; ~ of gustāre.
partial adj (biased) inīquus, studiōsus; (incomplete) mancus; be ~ to favēre (dat),

studēre (*dat*); **win a ~ victory** aliquā ex parte vincere.
partiality *n* favor *m*, studium *nt*.
partially *adv* partim, aliquā ex parte.
participant *n* particeps *m/f*.
participate *vi* interesse, particeps esse.
participation *n* societās *f*.
particle *n* particula *f*.
parti-coloured *adj* versicolor, varius.
particular *adj* (*own*) proprius; (*special*) praecipuus; (*exact*) dīligēns, accūrātus; (*fastidious*) fastīdiōsus; **a ~ person** quīdam ♦ *n* rēs *f*; **with full ~s** subtīliter; **give all the ~s** omnia exsequī; **in ~** praesertim.
particularity *n* subtīlitās *f*.
particularize *vt* singula exsequī.
particularly *adv* praecipuē, praesertim, in prīmīs, māximē.
parting *n* dīgressus *m*, discessus *m* ♦ *adj* ultimus.
partisan *n* fautor *m*, studiōsus *m*.
partisanship *n* studium *nt*.
partition *n* (*act*) partītiō *f*; (*wall*) pariēs *m*; (*compartment*) loculāmentum *nt* ♦ *vt* dīvidere.
partly *adv* partim, ex parte.
partner *n* socius *m*; (*in office*) collēga *f*.
partnership *n* societās *f*; **form a ~** societātem inīre.
partridge *n* perdīx *m/f*.
parturition *n* partus *m*.
party *n* (*POL*) factiō *f*, partēs *fpl*; (*entertainment*) convīvium *nt*; (*MIL*) manus *f*; (*individual*) homō *m/f*; (*associate*) socius *m*, cōnscius *m*.
party spirit *n* studium *nt*.
parvenu *n* novus homō *m*.
pass *n* (*hill*) saltus *m*; (*narrow*) angustiae *fpl*, faucēs *fpl*; (*crisis*) discrīmen *nt*; (*document*) diplōma *nt*; (*fighting*) petītiō *f*; **things have come to such a ~** in eum locum ventum est, adeō rēs rediit ♦ *vi* īre, praeterīre; (*time*) trānsīre; (*property*) pervenīre; **~ away** abīre; (*die*) morī, perīre; (*fig*) dēfluere; **~ by** praeterīre; **~ for** habērī prō (*abl*); **~ off** abīre; **~ on** pergere; **~ over** trānsīre; **come to ~** fierī, ēvenīre; **let ~** intermittere, praetermittere ♦ *vt* praeterīre; (*riding*) praetervehī; (*by hand*) trādere; (*law*) iubēre; (*limit*) excēdere; (*sentence*) interpōnere, dīcere; (*test*) satisfacere (*dat*); (*time*) dēgere, agere; **~ accounts** ratiōnēs ratās habēre; **~ the day** diem cōnsūmere; **~ a law** lēgem ferre; **~ a decree** dēcernere; **~ off** ferre; **~ over** praeterīre, mittere; (*fault*) ignōscere (*dat*); **~ round** trādere; **~ through** trānsīre.
passable *adj* (*place*) pervius; (*standard*) mediocris.
passably *adv* mediocriter.
passage *n* iter *nt*, cursus *m*; (*land*) trānsitus *m*; (*sea*) trānsmissiō *f*; (*book*) locus *m*; **of ~** (*bird*) advena.
passenger *n* vector *m*.
passer-by *n* praeteriēns *m*.

passing *n* obitus *m* ♦ *adj* admodum.
passion *n* animī mōtus *m*, permōtiō *f*, ārdor *m*; (*anger*) īra *f*; (*lust*) libīdō *f*.
passionate *adj* ārdēns, impotēns, ācer; īrācundus.
passionately *adv* vehementer, ārdenter; īrācundē; **be ~ in love** amōre ārdēre.
passive *adj* iners.
passiveness *n* inertia *f*, patientia *f*.
passport *n* diplōma *nt*.
password *n* tessera *f*.
past *adj* praeteritus; (*recent*) proximus ♦ *n* praeterita *ntpl* ♦ *prep* praeter (*acc*); (*beyond*) ultrā (*acc*).
paste *n* glūten *nt* ♦ *vt* glūtināre.
pastime *n* lūdus *m*, oblectāmentum *nt*.
pastoral *adj* pastōrālis; (*poem*) būcolicus.
pastry *n* crustum *nt*.
pasture *n* pāstus *m*, pāscuum *nt* ♦ *vt* pāscere.
pat *vt* dēmulcēre ♦ *adj* opportūnus.
patch *n* pannus *m* ♦ *vt* resarcīre.
patchwork *n* centō *m*.
pate *n* caput *nt*.
patent *adj* apertus, manifestus ♦ *n* prīvilēgium *nt*.
patently *adv* manifestō.
paternal *adj* paternus.
path *n* sēmita *f*, trāmes *m*.
pathetic *adj* miserābilis.
pathetically *adv* miserābiliter.
pathfinder *n* explorātor *m*.
pathless *adj* āvius.
pathos *n* misericordia *f*; (*RHET*) dolor *m*.
pathway *n* sēmita *f*.
patience *n* patientia *f*.
patient *adj* patiēns ♦ *n* aeger *m*.
patiently *adv* patienter, aequō animō.
patois *n* sermō *m*.
patrician *adj* patricius ♦ *n* patricius *m*.
patrimony *n* patrimōnium *nt*.
patriot *n* amāns patriae *m*.
patriotic *adj* pius, amāns patriae.
patriotically *adv* prō patriā.
patriotism *n* amor patriae *m*.
patrol *n* excubiae *fpl* ♦ *vi* circumīre.
patron *n* patrōnus *m*, fautor *m*.
patronage *n* patrōcinium *nt*.
patroness *n* patrōna *f*, fautrīx *f*.
patronize *vt* favēre (*dat*), fovēre.
patronymic *n* nōmen *nt*.
patter *vi* crepitāre ♦ *n* crepitus *m*.
pattern *n* exemplar *nt*, exemplum *nt*, nōrma *f*; (*ideal*) specimen *nt*; (*design*) figūra *f*.
paucity *n* paucitās *f*.
paunch *n* abdōmen *nt*, venter *m*.
pauper *n* pauper *m*.
pause *n* mora *f*, intervallum *nt* ♦ *vi* īnsistere, intermittere.
pave *vt* sternere; **~ the way** (*fig*) viam mūnīre.
pavement *n* pavīmentum *nt*.
pavilion *n* tentōrium *nt*.
paw *n* pēs *m* ♦ *vt* pede pulsāre.
pawn *n* (*chess*) latrunculus *m*; (*COMM*) pignus *nt*,

fīdūcia f ♦ vt oppignerāre.
pawnbroker n pignerātor m.
pay n mercēs f; (MIL) stīpendium nt; (workman)
manupretium nt ♦ vt solvere, pendere; (debt)
exsolvere; (in full) persolvere; (honour)
persolvere; (MIL) stīpendium numerāre (dat);
(penalty) dare, luere; ~ **down** numerāre; ~ **for**
condūcere; ~ **off** dissolvere, exsolvere; ~ **out**
expendere; (publicly) ērogāre; ~ **up**
dēpendere; ~ **a compliment to** laudāre; ~
respects to salūtāre ♦ vi respondēre; **it ~s**
expedit.
payable adj solvendus.
paymaster n (MIL) tribūnus aerārius n.
payment n solūtiō f; (money) pēnsiō f.
pea n pīsum n; **like as two ~s** tam sim lis quam
lac lactī est.
peace n pāx f; ~ **and quiet** ōtium nt; **breach of**
the ~ vīs f; **establish ~** pācem concil āre; **hold**
one's ~ reticēre; **sue for ~** pācem petere.
peaceable adj imbellis, placidus.
peaceably adv placidē.
peaceful adj tranquillus, placidus, pācātus.
peacefully adv tranquillē.
peacemaker n pācificus m.
peace-offering n piāculum nt.
peach n Persicum nt.
peacock n pāvō m.
peak n apex m, vertex m.
peal n (bell) sonitus m; (thunder) frago~ m ♦ vi
sonāre.
pear n pirum nt; (tree) pirus f.
pearl n margarīta f.
pearly adj gemmeus; (colour) candidus.
peasant n agricola m, colōnus m.
peasantry n agricolae mpl.
pebble n calculus m.
pebbly adj lapidōsus.
peccadillo n culpa f.
peck n (measure) modius m ♦ vt vellicāre.
peculate vi pecūlārī.
peculation n pecūlātus m.
peculiar adj (to one) proprius; (strange)
singulāris.
peculiarity n proprietās f, nota f.
peculiarly adv praecipuē, praesertim.
pecuniary adj pecūniārius.
pedagogue n magister m.
pedant n scholasticus m.
pedantic adj nimis dīligenter.
pedantically adv dīligentior.
pedantry n nimia dīligentia f.
peddle vt circumferre.
pedestal n basis f.
pedestrian adj pedester ♦ n pedes m.
pedigree n stirps f, stemma nt ♦ adj generōsus.
pediment n fastīgium nt.
pedlar n īnstitor m, circumforāneus m.
peel n cortex m ♦ vt glūbere.
peep vi dīspicere ♦ n aspectus m; **at ~ of day**
prīmā lūce.
peer vi: ~ **at** intuērī ♦ n pār m; (rank) patricius
m.

peerless adj ūnicus, ēgregius.
peevish adj stomachōsus, mōrōsus.
peevishly adv stomachōsē, mōrōsē.
peevishness n stomachus m, mōrōsitās f.
peg n clāvus m; **put a round ~ in a square hole**
bovī clītellās impōnere ♦ vt clāvīs dēfīgere.
pelf n lucrum nt.
pellet n globulus m.
pell-mell adv prōmiscuē, turbātē.
pellucid adj perlūcidus.
pelt n pellis f ♦ vt petere ♦ vi violenter cadere.
pen n calamus m, stilus m; (cattle) saeptum nt ♦
vt scrībere.
penal adj poenālis.
penalize vt poenā adficere, multāre.
penalty n poena f, damnum nt; (fine) multa f;
pay the ~ poenās dare.
penance n supplicium nt.
pencil n graphis f.
pending adj sub iūdice ♦ prep inter (acc).
penetrable adj pervius.
penetrate vt penetrāre.
penetrating adj ācer, acūtus; (mind)
perspicāx.
penetration n (mind) acūmen nt.
peninsula n paenīnsula f.
penitence n paenitentia f.
penitent adj: **I am ~** mē paenitet.
penknife n scalpellum nt.
penmanship n scrīptiō f, manus f.
pennant n vexillum nt.
penny n dēnārius m.
pension n annua ntpl.
pensioner n ēmeritus m.
pensive adj attentus.
pensiveness n cōgitātiō f.
pent adj inclūsus.
penthouse n (MIL) vīnea f.
penurious adj parcus, avārus, tenāx.
penuriousness n parsimōnia f, tenācitās f.
penury n egestās f, inopia f.
people n hominēs mpl; (nation) populus m, gēns
f; **common ~** plēbs f ♦ vt frequentāre.
peopled adj frequēns.
pepper n piper nt.
peradventure adv fortasse.
perambulate vi spatiārī, inambulāre.
perceive vt sentīre, percipere, intellegere.
perceptible adj: **be ~** sentīrī posse, audīrī
posse.
perception n sēnsus m.
perch n (bird's) pertica f; (fish) perca f ♦ vi
īnsidēre.
perchance adv fortasse, forsitan (subj).
percolate vi permānāre.
percussion n ictus m.
perdition n exitium nt.
peregrinate vi peregrīnārī.
peregrination n peregrīnātiō f.
peremptorily adv praecīsē, prō imperiō.
peremptory adj imperiōsus.
perennial adj perennis.
perfect adj perfectus, absolūtus; (entire)

integer; (*faultless*) ēmendātus ♦ *vt* perficere, absolvere.
perfection *n* perfectiō *f*, absolūtiō *f*.
perfectly *adv* perfectē, ēmendātē; (*quite*) plānē.
perfidious *adj* perfidus, perfidiōsus.
perfidiously *adv* perfidiōsē.
perfidy *n* perfidia *f*.
perforate *vt* perforāre, terebrāre.
perforation *n* forāmen *nt*.
perforce *adv* per vim, necessāriō.
perform *vt* perficere, peragere; (*duty*) exsequī, fungī (*abl*); (*play*) agere.
performance *n* (*process*) exsecūtiō *f*, fūnctiō *f*; (*deed*) factum *nt*; (*stage*) fābula *f*.
performer *n* āctor *m*; (*music*) tībīcen *m*, fidicen *m*; (*stage*) histriō *m*.
perfume *n* odor *m*, unguentum *nt* ♦ *vt* odōrāre.
perfumer *n* unguentārius *m*.
perfumery *n* unguenta *ntpl*.
perfunctorily *adv* neglegenter.
perfunctory *adj* neglegēns.
perhaps *adv* fortasse, forsitan (*subj*), nesciō an (*subj*); (*tentative*) vel; (*interrog*) an.
peril *n* perīculum *m*, discrīmen *nt*.
perilous *adj* perīculōsus.
perilously *adv* perīculōsē.
perimeter *n* ambitus *m*.
period *n* tempus *nt*, spatium *nt*; (*history*) aetās *f*; (*end*) terminus *m*; (*sentence*) complexiō *f*, ambitus *m*.
periodic *adj* (*style*) circumscrīptus.
periodical *adj* status.
periodically *adv* certīs temporibus, identidem.
peripatetic *adj* vagus; (*sect*) peripatēticus.
periphery *n* ambitus *m*.
periphrasis *n* circuitus *m*.
perish *vi* perīre, interīre.
perishable *adj* cadūcus, fragilis, mortālis.
peristyle *n* peristȳlium *nt*.
perjure *vi*: ~ o.s. pēierāre.
perjured *adj* periūrus.
perjurer *n* periūrus *m*.
perjury *n* periūrium *nt*; **commit** ~ pēierāre.
permanence *n* cōnstantia *f*, stabilitās *f*.
permanent *adj* stabilis, diūturnus, perpetuus.
permanently *adv* perpetuō.
permeable *adj* penetrābilis.
permeate *vt* penetrāre ♦ *vi* permānāre.
permissible *adj* licitus, concessus; **it is** ~ licet.
permission *n* potestās *f*; **ask** ~ veniam petere; **give** ~ veniam dare, potestātem facere; **by** ~ **of** permissū (*gen*); **with your kind** ~ bonā tuā veniā; **without your** ~ tē invītō.
permit *vt* sinere, permittere (*dat*); **I am ~ted** licet mihī.
pernicious *adj* perniciōsus, exitiōsus.
perorate *vi* perōrāre.
peroration *n* perōrātiō *f*, epilogus *m*.
perpendicular *adj* dīrēctus.
perpendicularly *adv* ad perpendiculum, ad līneam.

perpetrate *vt* facere, admittere.
perpetual *adj* perpetuus, perennis, sempiternus.
perpetua lly *adv* perpetuō.
perpetuate *vt* continuāre, perpetuāre.
perpetuity *n* perpetuitās *f*.
perplex *vt* sollicitāre, cōnfundere.
perplexing *adj* ambiguus, perplexus.
perplexity *n* haesitātiō *f*.
perquisite *n* pecūlium *nt*.
persecute *vt* īnsectārī, exagitāre; persequi.
persecution *n* īnsectātiō *f*.
persecutor *n* īnsectātor *m*.
perseverance *n* peseverantia *f*, cōnstantia *f*.
persevere *vi* perseverāre, perstāre; ~ **in** tenēre.
Persian *n* Persa *m*.
persist *vt* īnstāre, perstāre, perseverāre.
persistence, persistency *n* pertinācia *f*, perseverantia *f*.
persistent *adj* pertināx.
persistently *adv* pertināciter, perseveranter.
person *n* homō *m/f*; (*counted*) caput *nt*; (*character*) persōna *f*; (*body*) corpus *nt*; **in** ~ ipse praesēns.
personage *n* vir *m*.
personal *adj* prīvātus, suus.
personality *n* nātūra *f*; (*person*) vir ēgregius *m*.
personally *adv* ipse, cōram.
personal property *n* pecūlium *nt*.
personate *vt* persōnam gerere (*gen*).
personification *n* prosōpopoeia *f*.
personify *vt* hūmānam nātūram tribuere (*dat*).
personnel *n* membra *ntpl*, sociī *mpl*.
perspective *n* scaenographia *f*.
perspicacious *adj* perspicāx, acūtus.
perspicacity *n* perspicācitās *f*, acūmen *nt*.
perspicuity *n* perspicuitās *f*.
perspicuous *adj* perspicuus.
perspiration *n* sūdor *m*.
perspire *vi* sūdāre.
persuade *vt* persuādēre (*dat*); (*by entreaty*) exōrāre.
persuasion *n* persuāsiō *f*.
persuasive *adj* blandus.
persuasively *adv* blandē.
pert *adj* procāx, protervus.
pertain *vi* pertinēre, attinēre.
pertinacious *adj* pertināx.
pertinaciously *adv* pertināciter.
pertinacity *n* pertinācia *f*.
pertinent *adj* appositus; **be** ~ ad rem pertinēre.
pertinently *adv* appositē.
pertly *adv* procāciter, protervē.
perturb *vt* perturbāre.
perturbation *n* animī perturbātiō *f*, trepidātiō *f*.
peruke *n* capillāmentum *nt*.
perusal *n* perlēctiō *f*.
peruse *vt* perlegere; (*book*) ēvolvere.

pervade vt permānāre per, complēre
  (emotion) perfundere.
pervasive adj crēber.
perverse adj perversus, prāvus.
perversely adv perversē.
perversion n dēprāvātiō f.
perversity n perversitās f.
pervert vt dēprāvāre; (words) dētorquēre;
  (person) corrumpere.
perverter n corruptor m.
pessimism n dēspērātiō f.
pest n pestis f.
pester vt sollicitāre.
pestilence n pestilentia f, pestis f.
pestilential adj pestilēns, nocēns.
pestle n pistillum nt.
pet n dēliciae fpl ♦ vt in dēliciīs habēre,
  dēlēnīre.
petard n: **be hoist with his own ~** suō sibī
  gladiō iugulārī.
petition n precēs fpl; (POL) libellus m ♦ vt
  ōrāre.
petrify vt (fig) dēfīgere; **be petrified** stupēre,
  obstupēscere.
pettifogger n lēgulēius m.
pettiness n levitās f.
pettish adj stomachōsus.
petty adj levis, minūtus.
petulance n protervitās f.
petulant adj protervus, petulāns.
petulantly adv petulanter.
pew n subsellium nt.
phalanx n phalanx f.
phantasy n commentīcia ntpl.
phantom n simulacrum nt, īdōlon nt.
phases npi vicēs fpl.
pheasant n phāsiānus m.
phenomenal adj eximius, singulāris.
phenomenon n rēs f, novum nt, spectāculum
  nt.
philander vi lascīvīre.
philanthropic adj hūmānus, beneficus.
philanthropically adv hūmānē.
philanthropy n hūmānitās f, beneficia ntpl.
Philippic n Philippica f.
philologist n grammaticus m.
philology n grammatica ntpl.
philosopher n philosophus m, sapiēns m.
philosophical adj philosophus; (temperament)
  aequābilis.
philosophize vi philosophārī.
philosophy n philosophia f, sapientia f.
philtre n philtrum nt.
phlegm n pituīta f; (temper) lentitūdō f.
phlegmatic adj lentus.
phoenix n phoenīx m.
phrase n locūtiō f; (GRAM) incīsum nt.
phraseology n verba ntpl, ōrātiō f.
physic n medicāmentum nt; **~s** pl physica ntpl.
physical adj physicus; (of body) corporis.
physician n medicus m.
physicist n physicus m.
physique n corpus nt, vīrēs fpl.

piazza n forum nt.
pick n (tool) dolabra f; (best part) lēctī mpl, flōs
  m ♦ vt (choose) legere, dēligere; (pluck)
  carpere; **~ out** ēligere, excerpere; **~ up**
  colligere.
pickaxe n dolabra f.
picked adj ēlēctus, dēlēctus.
picket n (MIL) statiō f.
pickle n muria f ♦ vt condīre.
picture n pictūra f, tabula f ♦ vt dēpingere; (to
  oneself) ante oculōs pōnere.
picturesque adj (scenery) amoenus.
pie n crustum nt.
piebald adj bicolor, varius.
piece n pars f; (broken off) fragmentum nt;
  (food) frustum nt; (coin) nummus m; (play)
  fābula f; **break in ~s** comminuere; **fall to ~s**
  dīlābī; **take to ~s** dissolvere; **tear in ~s**
  dīlaniāre.
piecemeal adv membrātim, minūtātim.
pied adj maculōsus.
pier n mōlēs f.
pierce vt perfodere, trānsfīgere; (bore)
  perforāre; (fig) pungere.
piercing adj acūtus.
piety n pietās f, religiō f.
pig n porcus m, sūs m/f; **buy a ~ in a poke** spem
  pretiō emere; **~'s** suillus.
pigeon n columba f; **wood ~** palumbēs f.
pig-headed adj pervicāx.
pigment n pigmentum nt.
pigsty n hara f.
pike n dolō m, hasta f.
pikeman n hastātus m.
pile n acervus m, cumulus m; (funeral) rogus m;
  (building) mōlēs f; (post) sublica f ♦ vt
  cumulāre, congerere; **~ up** exstruere,
  adcumulāre, coacervāre.
pile-driver n fistūca f.
pilfer vt fūrārī, surripere.
pilferer n fūr m, fūrunculus m.
pilgrim n peregrīnātor m.
pilgrimage n peregrīnātiō f.
pill n pilula f.
pillage n rapīna f, dēpopulātiō f, expīlātiō f ♦ vt
  dīripere, dēpopulārī, expīlāre.
pillager n expīlātor m, praedātor m.
pillar n columen nt, columna f.
pillory n furca f.
pillow n pulvīnus nt, culcita f.
pilot n gubernātor m, ductor m ♦ vt regere,
  gubernāre.
pimp n lēnō m.
pimple n pustula f.
pin n acus f ♦ vt adfīgere.
pincers n forceps m/f.
pinch vt pervellere, vellicāre; (shoe) ūrere;
  (for room) coartāre.
pine n pīnus f ♦ vi tābēscere; **~ away**
  intābēscere; **~ for** dēsīderāre.
pinion n penna f.
pink adj rubicundus.
pinnace n lembus m.

pinnacle n fastīgium nt.
pint n sextārius m.
pioneer n antecursor m.
pious adj pius, religiōsus.
piously adv piē, religiōsē.
pip n grānum nt.
pipe n (music) fistula f, tībia f; (water) canālis m ♦ vi fistulā canere.
piper n tībīcen m.
pipkin n olla f.
piquancy n sāl m, vīs f.
piquant adj salsus, argūtus.
pique n offēnsio f, dolor m ♦ vt offendere.
piracy n latrōcinium nt.
pirate n pīrāta m praedō m.
piratical adj pīrāticus.
piscatorial adj piscātōrius.
piston n embolus m.
pit n fovea f, fossa f; (THEAT) cavea f.
pitch n pix f; (sound) sonus m ♦ vt (camp) pōnere; (tent) tendere; (missile) conicere.
pitch-black adj piceus.
pitched battle n proelium iustum nt.
pitcher n hydria f.
pitchfork n furca f.
pitch pine n picea f.
piteous adj miserābilis, flēbilis.
piteously adv miserābiliter.
pitfall n fovea f.
pith n medulla f.
pithy adj (style) dēnsus; ~ **saying** sententia f.
pitiable adj miserandus.
pitiful adj miser, miserābilis; misericors.
pitifully adv miserē, miserābiliter.
pitiless adj immisericors, immītis.
pitilessly adv crūdēliter.
pittance n (food) dēmēnsum nt; (money) stips f.
pity n misericordia f; **take ~ on** miserērī (+acc of person, gen of things); **it is a ~ that** male accidit quod ♦ vt miserērī (gen); **I ~ mē** miseret (gen).
pivot n cardō m.
placability n plācābilitās f.
placable adj plācābilis.
placard n libellus m.
placate vt plācāre.
place n locus m; **in another ~** alibī; **in the first ~** prīmum; **in ~ of** locō (gen), pro (+ abl); **to this ~** hūc; **out of ~** intempestīvus; **give ~ to** cēdere (dat); **take ~** fierī, accidere; **take the ~ of** in locum (gen) succēdere ♦ vt pōnere, locāre, collocāre; **~ beside** adpōnere; **~ over** (in charge) praepōnere; **~ round** circumdare; **~ upon** impōnere.
placid adj placidus, tranquillus, quiētus.
placidity n tranquillitās f, sedātus animus m.
placidly adv placidē, quiētē.
plagiarism n fūrtum nt.
plagiarize vt fūrārī.
plague n pestilentia f, pestis f.
plain adj (lucid) clārus, perspicuus; (unadorned) subtīlis, simplex; (frank) sincērus; (ugly) invenustus ♦ n campus m,

plānitiēs f; **of the ~** campester.
plainly adv perspicuē; simpliciter, sincērē.
plainness n perspicuitās f; simplicitās f.
plaint n querella f.
plaintiff n petītor m.
plaintive adj flēbilis, queribundus.
plaintively adv flēbiliter.
plait vt implicāre, nectere.
plan n cōnsilium nt; (of a work) fōrma f, dēsignātiō f; (of living) ratiō f; (intent) prōpositum nt; (drawing) dēscrīptiō f ♦ vt (a work) dēsignāre, dēscrībere; (intent) cōgitāre, meditārī; cōnsilium capere or inīre; (with verb) in animō habēre (inf).
plane n (surface) plānitiēs f; (tree) platanus f; (tool) runcīna f ♦ adj aequus, plānus ♦ vt runcīnāre.
planet n stēlla errāns f.
plank n tabula f.
plant n herba f, planta f ♦ vt (tree) serere; (field) cōnserere; (colony) dēdūcere; (feet) pōnere; ~ **firmly** īnfīgere.
plantation n arbustum nt.
planter n sator m, colōnus m.
plaque n tabula f.
plaster n albārium nt, tectōrium nt; (MED) emplastrum nt; ~ **of Paris** gypsum nt ♦ vt dealbāre.
plasterer n albārius m.
plastic adj ductilis, fūsilis.
plate n (dish) catillus m; (silver) argentum nt; (layer) lāmina f ♦ vt indūcere.
platform n suggestus m; rōstrum nt, tribūnal nt.
platitude n trīta sententia f.
platter n patella f, lanx f.
plaudit n plausus m.
plausibility n vērīsimilitūdō f.
plausible adj speciōsus, vērī similis.
play n lūdus m; (THEAT) fābula f; (voice) inclīnātiō f; (scope) campus m; (hands) gestus m; ~ **on words** agnōminātiō f; **fair ~** aequum et bonum ♦ vi lūdere; (fountain) scatēre ♦ vt (music) canere; (instrument) canere (abl); (game) lūdere (abl); (part) agere; ~ **the part of** agere; ~ **a trick on** lūdificārī, impōnere (dat).
playbill n ēdictum nt.
player n lūsor m; (at dice) āleātor m; (on flute) tībīcen m; (on lyre) fidicen m; (on stage) histriō m.
playful adj lascīvus; (words) facētus.
playfully adv per lūdum, per iocum.
playfulness n lascīvia f; facētiae fpl.
playground n ārea f.
playmate n collūsor m.
playwright n fābulārum scrīptor m.
plea n causa f; (in defence) dēfēnsiō f, excūsātiō f.
plead vi causam agere, causam ōrāre, causam dīcere; (in excuse) dēprecārī, excūsāre; ~ **with** obsecrāre.
pleader n āctor m, causidicus m.
pleasant adj iūcundus, dulcis, grātus; (place)

amoenus.
pleasantly *adv* iūcundē, suāviter.
pleasantry *n* facētiae *fpl*, iocus *m*.
please *vt* placēre (*dat*), dēlectāre; **try to ~**
īnservīre (*dat*); **just as you ~** quod
commodum est; **if you ~** sīs; **~d with**
contentus (*abl*); **be ~d with oneself** s.bī
placēre ♦ *adv* amābō.
pleasing *adj* grātus, iūcundus, amoenus; **be ~**
to cordī esse (*dat*).
pleasurable *adj* iūcundus.
pleasure *n* voluptās *f*; (*decision*) arbitrium *nt*; **it**
is my ~ libet; **derive ~** voluptātem capere
♦ *vt* grātificārī (*dat*).
pleasure grounds *n* hortī *mpl*.
pleasure-loving *adj* dēlicātus.
plebeian *adj* plēbēius ♦ *n*: **the ~s** plēbs *f*.
plebiscite *n* suffrāgium *nt*.
plectrum *n* plēctrum *nt*.
pledge *n* pignus *nt* ♦ *vt* obligāre; **~ oneself**
prōmittere, spondēre; **~ one's word** fidem
obligāre, fidem interpōnere.
Pleiads *n* Plēiadēs *fpl*.
plenary *adj* īnfīnītus.
plenipotentiary *n* lēgātus *m*.
plenitude *n* cōpia *f*, mātūritās *f*.
plentiful *adj* cōpiōsus, largus.
plentifully *adv* cōpiōsē, largē.
plenty *n* cōpia *f*, abundantia *f*; (*enough*) satis.
pleonasm *n* redundantia *f*.
pleurisy *n* lateris dolor *m*.
pliable *adj* flexibilis, mollis, lentus.
pliant *adj* flexibilis, mollis, lentus.
pliers *n* forceps *m/f*.
plight *n* habitus *m*, discrīmen *nt* ♦ *vt* spondēre.
plod *vi* labōrāre, operam īnsūmere.
plot *n* coniūrātiō *f*, īnsidiae *fpl*; (*land*) agellus *m*;
(*play*) argūmentum *nt* ♦ *vi* coniūrāre, mōlīrī.
plotter *n* coniūrātus *m*.
plough *n* arātrum *nt* ♦ *vt* arāre; (*sea*) sulcāre; **~**
up exarāre.
ploughing *n* arātiō *f*.
ploughman *n* arātor *m*.
ploughshare *n* vōmer *m*.
pluck *n* fortitūdō *f* ♦ *vt* carpere, legere; **~ out**
ēvellere; **~ up courage** animum recipere,
animō adesse.
plucky *adj* fortis.
plug *n* obtūrāmentum *nt* ♦ *vt* obtūrāre.
plum *n* prūnum *nt*; (*tree*) prūnus *f*.
plumage *n* plūmae *fpl*.
plumb *n* perpendiculum *nt* ♦ *adj* dīrēctus ♦ *adv*
ad perpendiculum ♦ *vt* (*building*) ad
perpendiculum exigere; (*depth*) scrūtārī.
plumber *n* artifex plumbārius *m*.
plumb line *n* līnea *f*, perpendiculum *nt*.
plume *n* crista *f* ♦ *vt*: **~ oneself on** iactāre, prae
sē ferre.
plummet *n* perpendiculum *nt*.
plump *adj* pinguis.
plumpness *n* nitor *m*.
plunder *n* (*act*) rapīna *f*; (*booty*) praeda *f* ♦ *vi*
praedārī ♦ *vt* dīripere, expīlāre.

plunderer *n* praedātor *m*, spoliātor *m*.
plundering *n* rapīna *f* ♦ *adj* praedābundus.
plunge *vt* mergere, dēmergere; (*weapon*)
dēmittere ♦ *vi* mergī, sē dēmergere.
plural *adj* plūrālis.
plurality *n* multitūdō *f*, plūrēs *pl*.
ply *vt* exercēre.
poach *vt* surripere.
pocket *n* sinus *m*.
pocket money *n* pecūlium *nt*.
pod *n* siliqua *f*.
poem *n* poēma *nt*, carmen *nt*.
poesy *n* poēsis *f*.
poet *n* poēta *m*.
poetess *n* poētria *f*.
poetic *adj* poēticus.
poetical *adj* = **poetic**.
poetically *adv* poēticē.
poetry *n* (*art*) poētica *f*; (*poems*) poēmata *ntpl*,
carmina *ntpl*.
poignancy *n* acerbitās *f*.
poignant *adj* acerbus, acūtus.
poignantly *adv* acerbē, acūtē.
point *n* (*dot*) pūnctum *nt*; (*place*) locus *m*;
(*item*) caput *nt*; (*sharp end*) aciēs *f*; (*of sword*)
mucrō *m*; (*of epigram*) acūleī *mpl*; **~ of honour**
officium *nt*; **beside the ~** ab rē; **to the ~** ad
rem; **from this ~** hinc; **to that ~** eō; **up to this**
~ hāctenus, adhūc; **without ~** īnsulsus; **in ~ of**
fact nempe; **make a ~ of doing** consultō
facere; **on the ~ of death** moritūrus; **on**
the ~ of happening inibī; **I was on the ~ of**
saying in eō erat ut dīcerem; **matters have**
reached such a ~ eō rēs recidit; **come to the**
~ ad rem redīre; **the ~ at issue is** illud
quaeritur; **the main ~** cardō *m*, caput *nt*;
turning ~ articulus temporis *m* ♦ *vt* acuere,
exacuere; (*aim*) intendere; (*punctuate*)
distinguere; **~ out** indicāre, dēmōnstrāre,
ostendere.
point-blank *adj* simplex ♦ *adv* praecīsē.
pointed *adj* acūtus; (*criticism*) acūleātus; (*wit*)
salsus.
pointedly *adv* apertē, dīlūcidē.
pointer *n* index *m*.
pointless *adj* īnsulsus, frīgidus.
pointlessly *adv* īnsulsē.
point of view *n* iūdicium *nt*, sententia *f*.
poise *n* lībrāmen *nt*; (*fig*) urbānitās *f* ♦ *vt*
lībrāre.
poison *n* venēnum *nt* ♦ *vt* venēnō necāre; (*fig*)
īnficere.
poisoned *adj* venēnātus.
poisoner *n* venēficus *m*.
poisoning *n* venēficium *nt*.
poisonous *adj* noxius.
poke *vt* trūdere, fodicāre.
polar *adj* septentriōnālis.
pole *n* asser *m*, contus *m*; (ASTRO) polus *m*.
poleaxe *n* bipennis *f*.
polemic *n* contrōversia *f*.
police *n* lictōrēs *mpl*; (*night*) vigilēs *mpl*.
policy *n* ratiō *f*, cōnsilium *nt*; **honesty is the**

best ~ ea māximē condūcunt quae sunt rēctissima.
polish n (appearance) nitor m; (character) urbānitās f; (LIT) līma f ◆ vt polīre; (fig) expolīre.
polished adj polītus, mundus; (person) excultus, urbānus; (style) līmātus.
polite adj urbānus, hūmānus, cōmis.
politely adv urbānē, cōmiter.
politeness n urbānitās f, hūmānitās f, cōmitās f.
politic adj prūdēns, circumspectus.
political adj cīvīlis, pūblicus; ~ life rēs pūblica f.
politician n magistrātus m.
politics n rēs pūblica f; **take up** ~ ad rem pūblicam accēdere.
polity n reī pūblicae fōrma f.
poll n caput nt; (voting) comitia ntpl ◆ vi suffrāgia inīre.
poll tax n tribūtum nt in singula capita impositum.
pollute vt inquināre, contāmināre.
pollution n corruptēla f.
poltroon n ignāvus m.
pomegranate n mālum Pūnicum nt.
pomp n adparātus m.
pomposity n māgnificentia f, glōria f.
pompous adj māgnificus, glōriōsus.
pompously adv māgnificē, glōriōsē.
pompousness n māgnificentia f.
pond n stagnum nt, lacūna f.
ponder vi sēcum reputāre ◆ vt animō volūtāre, in mente agitāre.
ponderous adj gravis, ponderōsus.
ponderously adv graviter.
poniard n pugiō m.
pontiff n pontifex m.
pontifical adj pontificālis, pontificius.
pontoon n pontō m.
pony n mannus m.
pooh-pooh vt dērīdēre.
pool n lacūna f, stagnum nt ◆ vt cōnferre.
poop n puppis f.
poor adj pauper, inops; (meagre) exīlis; (inferior) improbus; (pitiable) miser; ~ **little** misellus.
poorly adj aeger, aegrōtus ◆ adv parum, tenuiter.
pop n crepitus m ◆ vi ēmicāre.
pope n pāpa m.
poplar n pōpulus f.
poppy n papāver nt.
populace n vulgus nt, plēbs f.
popular adj grātus, grātiōsus; (party) populāris.
popularity n populī favor m, studium nt.
popularly adv vulgō.
populate vt frequentāre.
population n populus m, cīvēs mpl.
populous adj frequēns.
porcelain n fictilia ntpl.
porch n vestibulum nt.

porcupine n hystrīx f.
pore n forāmen nt ◆ vi: ~ **over** scrūtārī, incumbere in (acc).
pork n porcīna f.
porous adj rārus.
porridge n puls f.
port n portus m ◆ adj (side) laevus, sinister.
portage n vectūra f.
portal n porta f.
portcullis n cataracta f.
portend vt portendere.
portent n mōnstrum nt, portentum nt.
portento us adj mōnstruōsus.
porter n iānitor m; (carrier) bāiulus m.
portico n porticus f.
portion n pars f; (marriage) dōs f; (lot) sors f.
portliness n amplitūdō f.
portly adj amplus, opīmus.
portrait n imāgō f, effigiēs f.
portray vt dēpingere, exprimere, effingere.
pose n status m, habitus m ◆ vt pōnere ◆ vi habitum sūmere.
poser n nōdus m.
posit vt pōnere.
position n (GEOG) situs m (body) status m, gestus m; (rank) dignitās f; (office) honōs m; (MIL) locus m; **be in a** ~ **to** habēre (inf); **take up a** ~ (MIL) locum capere.
positive adj certus; **be** ~ **about** adfirmāre.
positively adv certō, adfirmātē, rē vērā.
posse n manus f.
possess vt possidēre, habēre; (take) occupāre, potīrī (abl).
possession n possessiō f; ~**s** pl bona ntpl, fortūnae fpl; **take** ~ **of** potīrī (abl), occupāre, manum inicere (dat); (inheritance) obīre; (emotion) invādere, incēdere (dat); **gain** ~ **of** potior (+ abl).
possessor n possessor m, dominus m.
possibility n facultās f; **there is a** ~ fierī potest.
possible adj: **it is** ~ fierī potest; **as big as** ~ quam māximus.
possibly adv fortasse.
post n pālus m; (MIL) statiō f; (office) mūnus nt; (courier) tabellārius m; **leave one's** ~ locō cēdere, signa relinquere ◆ vt (troops) locāre, collocāre; (at intervals) dispōnere; (letter) dare, tabellāriō dare; (entry) in cōdicem referre; **be** ~**ed** (MIL) in statiōne esse.
postage n vectūra f.
poster n libellus m.
posterior adj posterior.
posterity n posterī mpl; (time) posteritās f.
postern n postīcum nt.
posthaste adv summā celeritāte.
posthumous adj postumus.
posthumously adv (born) patre mortuō; (published) auctōre mortuō.
postpone vt differre, prōferre.
postponement n dīlātiō f.
postscr pt n: **add a** ~ adscrībere, subicere.
postulate vt sūmere ◆ n sūmptiō f.
posture n gestus m, status m.

pot n olla f, matella f.
pot-bellied adj ventriōsus.
potency n vīs f.
potent adj efficāx, valēns.
potentate n dynastēs m, tyrannus m.
potential adj futūrus.
potentiality n facultās f.
potentially adv ut fierī posse vidētur; ~ **an emperor** capāx imperiī.
potently adv efficienter.
potion n pōtiō f.
pot-pourri n farrāgō f.
potsherd n testa f.
pottage n iūs nt.
potter n figulus m; ~'s figulāris.
pottery n fictilia ntpl.
pouch n pēra f, sacculus m.
poultice n fōmentum nt, emplastrum nt.
poultry n gallīnae fpl.
pounce vi involāre, īnsilīre.
pound n lībra f; **five ~s** (weight) **of gold** aurī quīnque pondo ♦ vt conterere; pulsāre.
pour vt fundere; ~ **forth** effundere; ~ **in** īnfundere; ~ **on** superfundere; ~ **out** effundere ♦ vi fundī, fluere; ~ **down** ruere, sē praecipitāre.
pouring adj (rain) effūsus.
poverty n paupertās f, egestās f, incpia f; (style) iēiūnitās f.
powder n pulvis m.
powdery adj pulvereus.
power n potestās f; (strength) vīrēs fpl; (excessive) potentia f; (supreme) imperium nt; (divine) nūmen nt; (legal) auctōritās f; (of father) manus f; **as far as is in my ~** quantum in mē est; **have great ~** multum valēre, posse; **have of ~ attorney** cognitōrem esse; **it is still in my ~ to** integrum est mihī (inf).
powerful adj validus, potēns.
powerfully adv valdē.
powerless adj impotēns, imbēcillus; **be ~** nihil valēre.
powerlessness n imbēcillitas f.
practicable adj in apertō; **be ~** fierī posse.
practical adj (person) habilis.
practical joke n lūdus m.
practical knowledge n ūsus m.
practically adv ferē, paene.
practice n ūsus m, exercitātiō f; (RHET) meditātiō f; (habit) consuētūdō f, mōs m; **corrupt ~s** malae artēs.
practise vt (occupation) exercēre, facere; (custom) factitāre; (RHET) meditārī ♦ vi (MED) medicīnam exercēre; (law) causās agere.
practised adj exercitātus, perītus.
practitioner n (MED) medicus m.
praetor n praetor nt; ~'s praetōrius.
praetorian adj praetōrius.
praetorian guards npl praetōriānī mpl.
praetorship n praetūra f.
praise n laus f ♦ vt laudāre.
praiser n laudātor m.
praiseworthy adj laudābilis, laude dignus.

prance vi exsultāre.
prank n lūdus m.
prate vi garrīre.
prating adj garrulus.
pray vi deōs precārī, deōs venerārī ♦ vt precārī, ōrāre; ~ **for** petere, precārī; ~ **to** adōrāre.
prayer(s) n precēs fpl.
prayerful adj supplex.
preach vt, vi docēre, praedicāre.
preacher n ōrātor m.
preamble n exōrdium nt.
prearranged adj cōnstitūtus.
precarious adj dubius, perīculōsus.
precariousness n discrīmen nt.
precaution n cautiō f, prōvidentia f; **take ~s** cavēre, praecavēre.
precede vt praeīre (dat), anteīre (dat), antecēdere.
precedence n prīmārius locus m; **give ~ to** cēdere (dat); **take ~** (thing) antīquius esse; (person) prīmās agere.
precedent n exemplum nt; (law) praeiūdicium nt; **breach of ~** īnsolentia f; **in defiance of ~** īnsolenter.
preceding adj prior, superior.
precept n praeceptum nt.
preceptor n doctor m, magister m.
precinct n terminus m, templum nt.
precious adj cārus; pretiōsus; (style) pūtidus.
precious stone n gemma f.
precipice n locus praeceps m, rūpēs f.
precipitancy n festīnātiō f.
precipitate vt praecipitāre ♦ adj praeceps; praeproperus.
precipitation n festīnātiō f.
precipitous adj dēruptus, praeceps, praeruptus.
precise adj certus, subtīlis; (person) accūrātus.
precisely adv dēmum.
precision n cūra f.
preclude vt exclūdere, prohibēre.
precocious adj praecox.
precocity n festīnāta mātūritās f.
preconceive vt praecipere; **~d idea** praeiūdicāta opīniō f.
preconception n praeceptiō f.
preconcerted adj ex compositō factus.
precursor n praenūntius m.
predatory adj praedātōrius.
predecessor n dēcessor m; **my ~** cuī succēdō.
predestination n fātum nt, necessitās f.
predestine vt dēvovēre.
predetermine vt praefīnīre.
predicament n angustiae fpl, discrīmen nt.
predicate n attribūtum nt.
predict vt praedīcere, augurārī.
prediction n praedictiō f.
predilection n amor m, studium nt.
predispose vt inclīnāre, praeparāre.
predisposition n inclīnātiō f.
predominance n potentia f, praestantia f.

predominant _adj_ praepotēns, praecipuus.
predominantly _adv_ plērumque.
predominate _vi_ pollēre, dominārī.
pre-eminence _n_ praestantia _f._
pre-eminent _adj_ ēgregius, praecipuus, excellēns.
pre-eminently _adv_ ēgregiē, praecipuē, excellenter.
preface _n_ prooemium _nt_, praefātiō _f_ ♦ _vi_ praefārī.
prefect _n_ praefectus _m._
prefecture _n_ praefectūra _f._
prefer _vt_ (_charge_) dēferre; (_to office_) anteferre; (_choice_) antepōnere (_acc and dat_), posthabēre (_dat and acc_); (_with verb_) mālle.
preferable _adj_ potior.
preferably _adv_ potius.
preference _n_ favor _m_; **give ~ to** antepōnere, praeoptāre; **in ~ to** potius quam.
preferment _n_ honōs _m_, dignitās _f._
prefix _vt_ praetendere ♦ _n_ praepositiō _f._
pregnancy _n_ graviditās _f._
pregnant _adj_ gravida.
prejudge _vt_ praeiūdicāre.
prejudice _n_ praeiūdicāta opīniō _f_; (_harmful_) invidia _f_, incommodum _nt_; **without ~** cum bonā veniā ♦ _vt_ obesse (_dat_); **be ~d against** invidēre (_dat_), male opīnārī dē (_abl_).
prejudicial _adj_ damnōsus; **be ~ to** obesse (_dat_), nocēre (_dat_), officere (_dat_), dētrīmentō esse (_dat_).
preliminaries _npl_ praecurrentia _ntpl._
preliminary _adj_ prīmus ♦ _n_ prōlūsiō _f._
prelude _n_ prooemium _nt._
premature _adj_ immātūrus; (_birth_) abortīvus.
prematurely _adv_ ante tempus.
premeditate _vt_ praecōgitāre, praemeditārī.
premeditated _adj_ praemeditātus.
premier _adj_ prīnceps, praecipuus.
premise _n_ (_major_) prōpositiō _f_; (_minor_) adsūmptiō _f_; **~s** _pl_ aedēs _fpl_, domus _f._
premium _n_ praemium _nt_; **be at a ~** male emī.
premonition _n_ monitus _m._
preoccupation _n_ sollicitūdō _f._
preoccupied _adj_ sollicitus, districtus.
preordain _vt_ praefīnīre.
preparation _n_ (_process_) adparātiō _f_, comparātiō _f_; (_product_) adparātus _m_; (_of speech_) meditātiō _f_; **make ~s for** īnstruere, exōrnāre, comparāre.
prepare _vt_ parāre, adparāre, comparāre; (_speech_) meditārī; (_with verb_) parāre; **~d for** parātus ad (+ _acc_).
preponderance _n_ praestantia _f._
preponderate _vi_ praepollēre, vincere.
preposition _n_ praepositiō _f._
prepossess _vt_ commendāre (_dat and acc_), praeoccupāre.
prepossessing _adj_ suāvis, iūcundus.
prepossession _n_ favor _m._
preposterous _adj_ absurdus.
prerogative _n_ iūs _nt._
presage _n_ ōmen _nt_ ♦ _vt_ ōminārī,

portendere.
prescience _n_ prōvidentia _f._
prescient _adj_ prōvidus.
prescribe _vt_ imperāre; (_MED_) praescrībere; (_limit_) fīnīre.
prescript _on_ _n_ (_MED_) compositiō _f_; (_right_) ūsus _m._
presence _n_ praesentia _f_; (_appearance_) aspectus _m_; **~ of mind** praesēns animus _m_; **in the ~ of** cōram (_abl_); apud (_abl_); **in my ~** mē praesente.
present _adj_ praesēns, īnstāns; **be ~** adesse; **be ~ at** interesse (_dat_) ♦ _n_ praesēns tempus _nt_; (_gift_) dōnum _nt_; **at ~** in praesentī, nunc; **for the ~** in praesēns ♦ _vt_ dōnāre, offerre; (_on stage_) indūcere; (_in court_) sistere; **~ itself** occurrere.
presentable _adj_ spectābilis.
presentation _n_ dōnātiō _f._
presentiment _n_ augurium _nt._
presently _adv_ mox.
preservation _n_ cōnservātiō _f._
preserve _vt_ cōnservāre, tuērī; (_food_) condīre.
preside _vi_ praesidēre (_dat_).
presidency _n_ praefectūra _f._
president _n_ praefectus _m._
press _n_ prēlum _nt_ ♦ _vt_ premere; (_crowd_) stīpāre; (_urge_) īnstāre (_dat_); **~ for** flāgitāre; **~ hard** (_pursuit_) īnsequī, īnstāre (_dat_), īnsistere (_dat_); **~ out** exprimere; **~ together** comprimere.
pressing _adj_ īnstāns, gravis.
pressure _n_ pressiō _f_, nīsus _m._
prestige _n_ auctōritās _f_, opīniō _f._
presumably _adv_ sānē.
presume _vt_ sūmere, conicere ♦ _vi_ audēre, confīdere; **I ~** opīnor, crēdō.
presumption _n_ coniectūra _f_; (_arrogance_) adrogantia _f_, licentia _f._
presumptuous _adj_ adrogāns, audāx.
presumptuously _adv_ adroganter, audacter.
presuppose _vt_ praesūmere.
pretence _n_ simulātiō _f_, speciēs _f_; **under ~ of** per speciem (_gen_); **under false ~s** dolō malō.
pretend _vt_ simulāre, fingere; **~ that . . . not** dissimulāre.
pretender _n_ captātor _m._
pretension _n_ postulātum _nt_; **make ~s to** adfectāre, sibī adrogāre.
pretentious _adj_ adrogāns, glōriōsus.
pretext _n_ speciēs _f_; **under ~ of** per speciem (_gen_); **on the ~ that** quod + _subj._
prettily _adv_ pulchrē, bellē.
prettiness _n_ pulchritūdō _f_, lepōs _m._
pretty _adj_ formōsus, pulcher, bellus ♦ _adv_ admodum, satis.
prevail _vi_ vincere; (_custom_) tenēre, obtinēre; **~ upon** persuādēre (_dat_); (_by entreaty_) exōrāre.
prevailing _adj_ vulgātus.
prevalent _adj_ vulgātus; **be ~** obtinēre; **become ~** incrēbrēscere.
prevaricate _vi_ tergiversārī.

prevarication n tergiversātiō f.
prevaricator n veterātor m.
prevent vt impedīre (+ **quōminus/quīn** and subj), prohibēre (+ acc and infin).
prevention n impedītiō f.
previous adj prior, superior.
previously adv anteā, antehāc.
prevision n prōvidentia f.
prey n praeda f ♦ vi: ~ **upon** īnsectārī; (fig) vexāre, carpere.
price n pretium nt; (of corn) annōna f; **at a high** ~ māgnī; **at a low** ~ parvī ♦ vt pretium cōnstituere (gen).
priceless adj inaestimābilis.
prick vt pungere; (goad) stimulāre; ~ **up the ears** aurēs adrigere.
prickle n acūleus m.
prickly adj aculeātus, horridus.
pride n superbia f, fastus m; (boasting) glōria f; (object) decus nt; (best part) flōs m ♦ vt: ~ **oneself on** iactāre, prae sē ferre.
priest n sacerdōs m; (especial) flāmen m; **high** ~ pontifex m, antistēs m.
priestess n sacerdōs f; **high** ~ antistita f.
priesthood n sacerdōtium nt, flāminium nt.
prig n homō fastīdiōsus m.
priggish adj fastīdiōsus.
prim adj modestior.
primarily adv prīncipiō, praecipuē.
primary adj prīmus, praecipuus.
prime adj prīmus, ēgregius; ~ **mover** auctor m ♦ n flōs m; **in one's** ~ flōrēns ♦ vt īnstruere, ērudīre.
primeval adj prīscus.
primitive adj prīstinus, incultus.
primordial adj prīscus.
prince n rēgulus m; rēgis fīlius m; prīnceps m.
princely adj rēgālis.
princess n rēgis fīlia f.
principal adj praecipuus, prīnceps, māximus ♦ n (person) prīnceps m/f; (money) sors f.
principally adv in prīmīs, māximē, māximam partem.
principle n prīncipium nt; (rule) fōrmula f, ratiō f; (character) fidēs f; ~**s** pl īnstitūta ntpl, disciplīna f; **first** ~**s** elementa ntpl, initia ntpl.
print n nota f, signum nt; (foot) vestīgium nt ♦ vt imprimere.
prior adj prior, potior.
priority n: **give** ~ **to** praevertere (dat).
prise vt sublevāre; ~ **open** vectī refringere.
prison n carcer m, vincula ntpl; **put in** ~ in vincula conicere.
prisoner n reus m; (for debt) nexus m; (of war) captīvus m; ~ **at the bar** reus m, rea f; **take** ~ capere.
pristine adj prīscus, prīstinus, vetus.
privacy n sēcrētum nt.
private adj (individual) prīvātus; (home) domesticus; (secluded) sēcrētus ♦ n (mil) gregārius mīles m.
privately adv clam, sēcrētō.
private property n rēs familiāris f.
privation n inopia f, egestās f.

privet n ligustrum nt.
privilege n iūs nt, immūnitās f.
privileged adj immūnis.
privy adj sēcrētus; ~ **to** cōnscius (gen).
prize n praemium nt; (captured) praeda f; ~ **money** manubiae fpl ♦ vt māgnī aestimāre.
pro-Athenian adj rērum Athēniēnsium studiōsus.
probability n vērī similitūdō f.
probable adj vērī similis; **more** ~ vērō propior.
probably adv fortasse.
probation n probātiō f.
probationer n tīrō m.
probe vt īnspicere, scrūtārī.
probity n honestās f, integritās f.
problem n quaestiō f; **the** ~ **is** illud quaeritur.
problematical adj dubius, anceps.
procedure n ratiō f, modus m; (law) fōrmula f.
proceed vi pergere, prōcedere, prōgredī; (narrative) īnsequi; ~ **against** persequī, lītem intendere (dat); ~ **from** orīrī, proficīscī ex.
proceedings n ācta ntpl.
proceeds n frūctus m, reditus m.
process n ratiō f; (law) āctiō f; **in the** ~ **of time** post aliquod tempus.
procession n pompa f; (fig) agmen nt.
proclaim vt ēdīcere, prōnūntiāre, praedicāre, dēclārāre; ~ **war upon** bellum indīcere + dat.
proclamation n ēdictum nt.
proclivity n prōpēnsiō f.
proconsul n prōcōnsul m.
proconsular adj prōcōnsulāris.
proconsulship n prōcōnsulātus m.
procrastinate vt differre, prōferre ♦ vi cunctārī.
procrastination n prōcrāstinātiō f, mora f.
procreate vt generāre, prōcreāre.
procreation n prōcreātiō f.
procreator n generātor m.
procumbent adj prōnus.
procurator n prōcūrātor m.
procure vt parāre, adipīscī, adquīrere; (by request) impetrāre.
procurer n lēnō m.
prod vt stimulāre.
prodigal adj prōdigus ♦ n nepōs m.
prodigality n effūsiō f.
prodigally adv effūsē.
prodigious adj ingēns, immānis.
prodigy n prōdigium nt, portentum nt; (fig) mīrāculum nt.
produce vt ēdere; (young) parere; (crops) ferre; (play) dare, docēre; (line) prōdūcere; (in court) sistere; (into view) prōferre; (from store) prōmere, dēprōmere ♦ n frūctus m; (of earth) frūgēs fpl; (in money) reditus m.
product n opus nt; ~ **of** frūctus (gen).
production n opus nt.
productive adj fēcundus, ferāx, frūctuōsus.
productivity n fēcunditās f, ūbertās f.
profanation n violātiō f.
profane adj profānus, impius ♦ vt violāre, polluere.

profanely _adv_ impiē.
profanity _n_ impietās _f._
profess _vt_ profitērī, prae sē ferre; ~ **to be** profitērī sē.
profession _n_ professiō _f;_ (_occupation_) ars _f,_ haeresis _f._
professor _n_ doctor _m._
proffer _vt_ offerre, pollicērī.
proficiency _n_ prōgressus _m,_ perītia _f;_ **attain** ~ prōficere.
proficient _adj_ perītus.
profile _n_ ōris līneāmenta _ntpl;_ (_portrait_) oblīqua imāgō _f._
profit _n_ lucrum _nt,_ ēmolumentum _nt,_ fructus _m;_ **make a** ~ **out of** quaestuī habēre ♦ _vt_ prōdesse (_dat_) ♦ _vi:_ ~ **by** fruī (_abl_), ūtī (_abl_); (_opportunity_) arripere.
profitable _adj_ fructuōsus, ūtilis.
profitably _adv_ ūtiliter.
profligacy _n_ flāgitium _nt,_ perditī mōrēs _mpl._
profligate _adj_ perditus, dissolūtus ♦ _n_ nepōs _m._
profound _adj_ altus; (_discussion_) abstrūsus.
profoundly _adv_ penitus.
profundity _n_ altitūdō _f._
profuse _adj_ prōdigus, effūsus.
profusely _adv_ effūsē.
profusion _n_ abundantia _f,_ adfluentia _f;_ **in** ~ abundē.
progenitor _n_ auctor _m._
progeny _n_ prōgeniēs _f,_ prōlēs _f._
prognostic _n_ signum _nt._
prognosticate _vt_ ōminārī, augurārī, praedīcere.
prognostication _n_ ōmen _nt,_ praedictiō _f._
programme _n_ libellus _m._
progress _n_ prōgressus _m;_ **make** ~ prōficere ♦ _vi_ prōgredī.
progression _n_ prōgressus _m._
progressively _adv_ gradātim.
prohibit _vt_ vetāre, interdīcere (_dat_).
prohibition _n_ interdictum _nt._
project _n_ prōpositum _nt_ ♦ _vi_ ēminēre, exstāre; (_land_) excurrere ♦ _vt_ prōicere.
projectile _n_ tēlum _nt._
projecting _adj_ ēminēns.
projection _n_ ēminentia _f._
proletarian _adj_ plēbēius.
proletariat _n_ plēbs _f._
prolific _adj_ fēcundus.
prolix _adj_ verbōsus, longus.
prolixity _n_ redundantia _f._
prologue _n_ prologus _m._
prolong _vt_ dūcere, prōdūcere; (_office_) prōrogāre.
prolongation _n_ (_time_) propāgātiō _f;_ (_office_) prōrogātiō _f._
promenade _n_ ambulātiō _f_ ♦ _vi_ inambulāre, spatiārī.
prominence _n_ ēminentia _f._
prominent _adj_ ēminēns, īnsignis; **be** ~ ēminēre.
promiscuous _adj_ prōmiscuus.

promiscuously _adv_ prōmiscuē.
promise _n_ prōmissum _nt;_ **break a** ~ fidem fallere; **keep a** ~ fidem praestāre; **make a** ~ fidem dare; **a youth of great** ~ summae speī adulēscēns ♦ _vt_ prōmittere, pollicērī; (_in marriage_) dēspondēre; ~ **in return** reprōmittere ♦ _vi:_ ~ **well** bonam spem ostendere.
promising _adj_ bonae speī.
promissory note _n_ syngrapha _f._
promontory _n_ prōmunturium _nt._
promote _vt_ favēre (_dat_); (_growth_) alere; (_in rank_) prōdūcere.
promoter _n_ auctor _m,_ fautor _m._
promotion _n_ dignitās _f._
prompt _adj_ alacer, prōmptus ♦ _vt_ incitāre, commovēre; (_speaker_) subicere.
prompter _n_ monitor _m._
promptitude _n_ alacritās _f,_ celeritās _f._
promptly _adv_ extemplō, citō.
promulgate _vt_ prōmulgāre, palam facere.
promulgation _n_ prōmulgātiō _f._
prone _adj_ prōnus; (_mind_) inclīnātus.
prong _n_ dēns _m._
pronounce _vt_ ēloquī, appellāre; (_oath_) interpōnere; (_sentence_) dīcere, prōnūntiāre.
pronounced _adj_ manifestus, īnsignis.
pronouncement _n_ ōrātiō _f,_ adfirmātiō _f._
pronunciation _n_ appellātiō _f._
proof _n_ documentum _nt,_ argūmentum _nt;_ (_test_) probātiō _f_ ♦ _adj_ immōtus, impenetrābilis.
prop _n_ adminiculum _nt,_ firmāmentum _nt_ ♦ _vt_ fulcīre.
propaganda _n_ documenta _ntpl._
propagate _vt_ propāgāre.
propagation _n_ propāgātiō _f._
propel _vt_ incitāre, prōpellere.
propensity _n_ inclīnātiō _f._
proper _adj_ idōneus, decēns, decōrus; rēctus; **it is** ~ decet.
properly _adv_ decōrē; rēctē.
property _n_ rēs _f,_ rēs mancipī, bona _ntpl;_ (_estate_) praedium _nt;_ (_attribute_) proprium _nt;_ (_slave's_) pecūlium _nt._
prophecy _n_ vāticinium _nt,_ praedictiō _f._
prophesy _vt_ vāticinārī, praedīcere.
prophet _n_ vātēs _m,_ fātidicus _m._
prophetess _n_ vātēs _f._
prophetic _adj_ dīvīnus, fātidicus.
prophetically _adv_ dīvīnitus.
propinquity _n_ (_place_) vīcīnitās _f;_ (_kin_) propinquitās _f._
propitiate _vt_ plācāre.
propitiation _n_ plācātiō _f,_ litātiō _f._
propitious _adj_ fēlīx, faustus; (_god_) praesēns.
proportion _n_ mēnsūra _f;_ **in** ~ prō portiōne, prō ratā parte; **in** ~ **to** prō (_abl_).
proportionately _adv_ prō portiōne, prō ratā parte.
proposal _n_ condiciō _f._
propose _vt_ prōpōnere; (_motion_) ferre, rogāre; (_penalty_) inrogāre; (_candidate_) rogāre

magistrātum.
proposer n auctor m, lātor m.
proposition n (offer) condiciō f; (plan)
cōnsilium nt, prōpositum nt; (logic)
prōnūntiātum nt.
propound vt expōnere, in medium prōferre.
propraetor n prōpraetor m.
proprietor n dominus m.
propriety n decōrum nt; (conduct) mcdestia f;
with ~ decenter.
propulsion n impulsus m.
prorogation n prōrogātiō f.
prorogue vt prōrogāre.
prosaic adj pedester.
proscribe vt prōscrībere.
proscription n prōscrīptiō f.
prose n ōrātiō f, ōrātiō solūta f.
prosecute vt (task) exsequī, gerere; (at law)
accūsāre, lītem intendere (dat).
prosecution n exsecūtiō f; (at law) accūsātiō f;
(party) accūsātor m.
prosecutor n accūsātor m.
prosody n numerī mpl.
prospect n prōspectus m; (fig) spēs f ♦ vi
explōrāre.
prospective adj futūrus, spērātus.
prosper vi flōrēre, bonā fortūnā ūtī ♦ vt
fortūnāre.
prosperity n fortūna f, rēs secundae jpl,
fēlīcitās f.
prosperous adj fēlix, fortūnātus, secundus.
prosperously adv prosperē.
prostrate adj prōstrātus, adflīctus; lie ~ iacēre
♦ vt prōsternere, dēicere; ~ oneself
prōcumbere, sē prōicere.
prostration n frāctus animus m.
prosy adj longus.
protagonist n prīmārum partium āctor m.
protect vt tuērī, dēfendere, custōdīre,
prōtegere.
protection n tūtēla f, praesidium nt; (law)
patrōcinium nt; (POL) fidēs f; put oneself under
the ~ of in fidem venīre (gen); take under
one's ~ in fidem recipere.
protector n patrōnus m, dēfēnsor m, custōs m.
protectress n patrōna f.
protégé n cliēns m.
protest n obtestātiō f; (POL) intercessiō f ♦ vi
obtestārī, reclāmāre; (POL) intercēdere.
protestation n adsevērātiō f.
prototype n archetypum nt.
protract vt dūcere, prōdūcere.
protrude vi prōminēre.
protruding adj exsertus.
protuberance n ēminentia f, tūber nt.
protuberant adj ēminēns, turgidus.
proud adj superbus, adrogāns, īnsolēns; be ~
superbīre; be ~ of iactāre.
proudly adv superbē.
prove vt dēmōnstrāre, arguere, probāre; (test)
experīrī ♦ vi (person) sē praebēre; (event)
ēvādere; ~ oneself sē praebēre, sē praestāre;
not ~n nōn liquet.

proved adj expertus.
provenance n orīgō f.
provender n pābulum nt.
proverb n prōverbium nt.
proverbial adj trītus; become ~ in prōverbium
venīre.
provide vt parāre, praebēre; ~ for prōvidēre
(dat); the law ~s lēx iubet; ~ against
praecavēre.
provided that conj dum, dummodo (+ subj).
providence n prōvidentia f; Deus m.
provident adj prōvidus, cautus.
providential adj dīvīnus; secundus.
providentially adv dīvīnitus.
providently adv cautē.
providing conj dum, dummodo.
province n prōvincia f.
provincial adj prōvinciālis; (contemptuous)
oppidānus, mūnicipālis.
provision n parātus m; make ~ for prōvidēre
(dat); make ~ cavēre.
provisionally adv ad tempus.
provisions n cibus m, commeātus m, rēs
frūmentāria f.
proviso n condiciō f; with this ~ hāc lēge.
provocation n inrītāmentum nt, offēnsiō f.
provocative adj (language) molestus,
invidiōsus.
provoke vt inrītāre, lacessere; (to action)
excitāre.
provoking adj odiōsus, molestus.
provost n praefectus m.
prow n prōra f.
prowess n virtūs f.
prowl vi grassārī, vagārī.
proximate adj proximus.
proximity n propinquitās f, vīcīnia f.
proxy n vicārius m.
prude n fastīdiōsa f.
prudence n prūdentia f.
prudent adj prūdēns, cautus, sagāx.
prudently adv prūdenter, cautē.
prudery n fastīdiōsa quaedam pudīcitia f.
prudish adj fastīdiōsus.
prune vt amputāre.
pruner n putātor m.
pruning hook n falx f.
pry vi inquīrere; ~ into scrūtārī.
pseudonym n falsum nōmen nt.
psychology n animī ratiō f.
Ptolemy n Ptolemaeus m.
puberty n pūbertās f.
public adj pūblicus; (speech) forēnsis; ~ life rēs
pūblica f, forum nt; in ~ forīs; appear in ~ in
medium prōdīre; make ~ in mediō pōnere,
forās perferre; make a ~ case of in medium
vocāre; act for the ~ good in medium
cōnsulere; be a ~ figure in lūce versārī,
digitō mōnstrārī ♦ n vulgus nt, hominēs mpl.
publican n (taxes) pūblicānus m; (inn) caupō m.
publication n ēditiō f, prōmulgātiō f; (book)
liber m.
publicity n lūx f, celebritās f.

publicly _adv_ palam; (_by the state_) pūblicē.
public opinion _n_ fāma _f._
publish _vt_ vulgāre, dīvulgāre; (_book_) ēdere.
pucker _vt_ corrūgāre.
puerile _adj_ puerīlis.
puerility _n_ ineptiae _fpl._
puff _n_ aura _f_ ♦ _vt_ īnflāre ♦ _vi_ anhēlāre.
puffed up _adj_ īnflātus, tumidus.
pugilism _n_ pugilātus _m._
pugilist _n_ pugil _m._
pugnacious _adj_ pugnāx.
pugnacity _n_ ferōcitās _f._
puissance _n_ potentia _f_, vīrēs _fpl._
puissant _adj_ potēns.
pull _n_ tractus _m_; (_of gravity_) contentiō _f_ ♦ _vt_
trahere, tractāre; ~ **apart** distrahere; ~ **at**
vellicāre; ~ **away** āvellere; ~ **back** retrahere;
~ **down** dēripere, dētrahere; (_building_)
dēmōlīrī; ~ **off** āvellere; ~ **out** ēvellere,
extrahere; ~ **through** _vi_ pervincere; (_illness_)
convalēscere; ~ **up** (_plant_) ēruere;
(_movement_) coercēre; ~ **to pieces** dīlaniāre.
pullet _n_ pullus gallīnāceus _m._
pulley _n_ trochlea _f._
pulmonary _adj_ pulmōneus.
pulp _n_ carō _f._
pulpit _n_ suggestus _m._
pulsate _vi_ palpitāre, micāre.
pulse _n_ (_plant_) legūmen _nt_; (_of blood_) vēnae _fpl_;
feel the ~ vēnās temptāre.
pulverize _vt_ contundere.
pumice stone _n_ pūmex _m._
pummel _vt_ verberāre.
pump _n_ antlia _f_ ♦ _vt_ haurīre; ~ **out** exhaurīre.
pumpkin _n_ cucurbita _f._
pun _n_ agnōminātiō _f._
punch _n_ ictus _m_ ♦ _vt_ pertundere, percutere.
punctilious _adj_ riligiōsus.
punctiliousness _n_ riligiō _f._
punctual _adj_ accūrātus, dīligēns.
punctuality _n_ dīligentia _f._
punctually _adv_ ad hōram, ad tempus.
punctuate _vt_ distinguere.
punctuation _n_ interpūnctiō _f._
puncture _n_ pūnctiō _f_ ♦ _vt_ pungere.
pundit _n_ scholasticus _m._
pungency _n_ ācrimōnia _f_; (_in debate_) acūleī _mpl._
pungent _adj_ ācer, mordāx.
punish _vt_ pūnīre, animadvertere in (_acc_);
poenam sūmere dē (+ _abl_); **be ~ed** poenās
dare.
punishable _adj_ poenā dignus.
punisher _n_ vindex _m_, ultor _m._
punishment _n_ poena _f_, supplicium _nt_;
(_censors'_) animadversiō _f_; **capital** ~ capitis
supplicium _nt_; **corporal** ~ verbera _ntpl_; **inflict**
~ **on** poenā adficere, poenam capere dē (_abl_),
supplicium sūmere dē (_abl_); **submit to** ~
poenam subīre; **undergo** ~ poenās dare,
pendere, solvere.
punitive _adj_ ulcīscendī causā.
punt _n_ pontō _m._
puny _adj_ pusillus.

pup _n_ catulus _m_ ♦ _vi_ parere.
pupil _n_ discipulus _m_, discipula _f_; (_eye_) aciēs _f_,
pūpula _f._
pupillage _n_ tūtēla _f._
puppet _n_ pūpa _f._
puppy _n_ catulus _m._
purblind _adj_ luscus.
purchase _n_ emptiō _f_; (_formal_) mancipium _nt_ ♦
_vt_ emere.
purchaser _n_ emptor _m_; (_at auction_) manceps _m._
pure _adj_ pūrus, integer; (_morally_) castus;
(_mere_) merus.
purely _adv_ pūrē, integrē; (_solely_) sōlum, nīl
nisi; (_quite_) omnīnō, plānē.
purgation _n_ pūrgātiō _f._
purge _vt_ pūrgāre, expūrgāre.
purification _n_ lūstrātiō _f_, pūrgātiō _f._
purify _vt_ pūrgāre, expūrgāre.
purist _n_ fastīdiōsus _m._
purity _n_ integritās _f_, castitās _f._
purloin _vt_ surripere, fūrārī.
purple _n_ purpura _f_ ♦ _adj_ purpureus.
purport _n_ sententia _f_; (_of words_) vīs _f_; **what is
the ~ of?** quō spectat?, quid vult? ♦ _vt_ velle
spectāre ad.
purpose _n_ prōpositum _nt_, cōnsilium _nt_, mēns _f_;
for that ~ eō; **for the ~ of** ad (_acc_), ut (_subj_), eā
mente ut, eō cōnsiliō ut (_subj_); **on** ~ cōnsultō,
dē industriā; **to the** ~ ad rem; **to what** ~?
quō?, quōrsum?; **to no** ~ frustrā, nēquīquam;
without achieving one's ~ rē īnfectā ♦ _vt_ in
animō habēre, velle.
purposeful _adj_ intentus.
purposeless _adj_ inānis.
purposely _adv_ cōnsultō, dē industriā.
purr _n_ murmur _nt_ ♦ _vi_ murmurāre.
purse _n_ marsupium _nt_, crumēna _f_; **privy** ~
fiscus _m_ ♦ _vt_ adstringere.
pursuance _n_ exsecūtiō _f_; **in** ~ **of** secundum
(_acc_).
pursue _vt_ īnsequī, īnsectārī, persequī;
(_closely_) īnstāre (_dat_), īnsistere (_dat_); (_aim_)
petere; (_course_) īnsistere.
pursuer _n_ īnsequēns _m_; (_law_) accūsātor _m._
pursuit _n_ īnsectātiō _f_; (_hunt_) vēnātiō _f_;
(_ambition_) studium _nt._
purvey _vt_ parāre; (_food_) obsōnāre.
purveyance _n_ prōcūrātiō _f._
purveyor _n_ obsōnātor _m._
purview _n_ prōvincia _f._
pus _n_ pūs _nt._
push _n_ pulsus _m_, impetus _m_ ♦ _vt_ impellere,
trūdere, urgēre; ~ **away** āmovēre; ~ **back**
repellere; ~ **down** dēprimere, dētrūdere; ~
forward prōpellere; ~ **in** intrūdere; ~ **on**
incitāre; ~ **through** perrumpere.
pushing _adj_ cōnfīdēns.
pusillanimity _n_ ignāvia _f_, timor _m._
pusillanimous _adj_ ignāvus, timidus.
pustule _n_ pustula _f._
put _vt_ (_in a state_) dare; (_in a position_) pōnere; (_in
words_) reddere; (_argument_) pōnere; (_spur_)
subdere; (_to some use_) adhibēre; ~ **an end to**

fīnem facere (*dat*); ~ **a question to**
interrogāre; ~ **against** adpōnere; ~ **among**
intericere; ~ **aside** sēpōnere; ~ **away** pōnere,
dēmovēre; (*store*) repōnere; ~ **back**
repōnere; repellere; ~ **beside** adpōnere; ~
between interpōnere; ~ **by** condere; ~ **down**
dēpōnere; (*revolt*) opprimere; ~ **forth**
extendere; (*growth*) mittere; ~ **forward**
ostentāre; (*plea*) adferre; ~ **in** immittere,
īnserere; (*ship*) adpellere; ~ **off** differre; ~ **on**
impōnere; (*clothes*) induere; (*play*) dare; ~
out ēicere; (*eye*) effodere; (*fire*) exstinguere;
(*money*) pōnere; (*tongue*) exserere; ~ **out of**
the way dēmovēre; ~ **out to sea** in altum
ēvehi, solvere; ~ **over** superimpōnere; ~ **to**
adpōnere; (*flight*) dare in (*acc*), fugāre,
prōfligāre; in fugam conicere; (*sea*) solvere;
~ **together** cōnferre; ~ **under** subicere; ~ **up**
(*for sale*) prōpōnere; (*lodge*) dēvertere,
dēversārī apud; ~ **up with** ferre, patī ~ **upon**
impōnere.
putrefaction *n* pūtor *m*.
putrefy *vi* putrēscere.
putrid *adj* putridus.
puzzle *n* nōdus *m* ♦ *vt* impedīre, sollicitāre; **be**
~**d** haerēre.
puzzling *adj* ambiguus, perplexus.
pygmy *n* pygmaeus *m*.
pyramid *n* pȳramis *f*.
pyramidal *adj* pȳramidātus.
pyre *n* rogus *m*.
Pyrenees *npl* Pyrenaeī (montēs) *mpl*.
python *n* pȳthōn *m*.

$$Q, q$$

quack *n* (*doctor*) circulātor *m* ♦ *vi* tetrinnīre.
quadrangle *n* ārea *f*.
quadruped *n* quadrupēs *m/f*.
quadruple *adj* quadruplex.
quaestor *n* quaestor *m*; ~**'s** quaestōrius.
quaestorship *n* quaestūra *f*.
quaff *vt* ēpōtāre, haurīre.
quagmire *n* palūs *f*.
quail *n* (*bird*) coturnīx *f* ♦ *vi* pāvēscere,
trepidāre.
quaint *adj* novus, īnsolitus.
quaintness *n* īnsolentia *f*.
quake *vi* horrēre, horrēscere ♦ *n* (*earth*) mōtus
m.
quaking *n* horror *m*, tremor *m* ♦ *adj* tremulus.
qualification *n* condiciō *f*; (*limitation*) exceptiō
f.
qualified *adj* (*for*) aptus, idōneus, dignus; (*in*)
perītus, doctus.

qualify *vi* prōficere ♦ *vt* temperāre, mītigāre.
qualities *npl* ingenium *nt*.
quality *n* nātūra *f*, vīs *f*; indolēs *f*; (*rank*) locus
m, genus *nt*; **I know the** ~ **of** sciō quālis sit.
qualm *n* riligiō *f*, scrūpulus *m*.
quandary *n* angustiae *fpl*; **be in a** ~ haerēre.
quantity *n* cōpia *f*, numerus *m*; (*metre*) vōcum
mēnsiō *f*; **a large** ~ multum *nt*, plūrimum *nt*; **a**
small ~ aliquantulum *nt*.
quarrel *n* dissēnsiō *f*, contrōversia *f*; (*violent*)
rixa *f*, iūrgium *nt* ♦ *vi* rixārī, altercārī.
quarrelsome *adj* pugnāx, lītigiōsus.
quarry *n* lapicīdinae *fpl*, metallum *nt*; (*prey*)
praeda *f* ♦ *vt* excīdere.
quart *n* duō sextāriī *mpl*.
quartan *n* (*fever*) quartāna *f*.
quarter *n* quarta pars *f*, quadrāns *m*; (*sector*)
regiō *f*; (*direction*) pars *f*, regiō *f*; (*respite*)
missiō *f*; ~**s** castra *ntpl*; (*billet*) hospitium *nt*;
come to close ~**s** manum cōnserere; (*armies*)
signa cōnferre; **winter** ~**s** hīberna *ntpl* ♦ *vt*
quadrifidam dīvidere; (*troops*) in hospitia
dīvidere.
quarterdeck *n* puppis *f*.
quarterly *adj* trimestris ♦ *adv* quartō quōque
mēnse.
quartermaster *n* (*navy*) gubernātor *m*; (*army*)
castrōrum praefectus *m*.
quarterstaff *n* rudis *f*.
quash *vt* comprimere; (*decision*) rescindere.
quatrain *n* tetrastichon *nt*.
quaver *n* tremor *m* ♦ *vi* tremere.
quavering *adj* tremebundus.
quay *n* crepīdō *f*.
queasy *adj* fastīdiōsus.
queen *n* rēgīna *f*; (*bee*) rēx *m*.
queer *adj* īnsolēns, rīdiculus.
quell *vt* opprimere, domāre, dēbellāre.
quench *vt* exstinguere, restinguere; (*thirst*)
sēdāre, explēre.
querulous *adj* querulus, queribundus.
query *n* interrogātiō *f* ♦ *vt* in dubium vocāre ♦
vi rogāre.
quest *n* investīgātiō *f*; **go in** ~ **of** investīgāre,
anquīrere.
question *n* interrogātiō *f*; (*at issue*) quaestiō *f*,
rēs *f*; (*in doubt*) dubium *nt*; **ask a** ~ rogāre,
quaerere, scīscitārī, percontārī; **call in** ~ in
dubium vocāre, addubitāre; **out of the** ~
indignus; **be out of the** ~ improbārī, fierī nōn
posse; **the** ~ **is** illud quaeritur; **there is no** ~
that nōn dubium est quīn (*subj*); **without** ~
sine dubiō ♦ *vt* interrogāre; (*closely*)
percontārī; (*doubt*) in dubium vocāre ♦ *vi*
dubitāre.
questionable *adj* incertus, dubius.
questioner *n* percontātor *m*.
questioning *n* interrogātiō *f*.
queue *n* agmen *nt*.
quibble *n* captiō *f* ♦ *vi* cavillārī.
quibbler *n* cavillātor *m*.
quibbling *adj* captiōsus.
quick *adj* (*speed*) celer, vēlōx, citus; (*to act*)

alacer, impiger; (_to perceive_) sagāx; (_with hands_) facilis; (_living_) vīvus; **be ~** properāre, festīnāre; **cut to the ~** ad vīvum resecāre; (_fig_) mordēre.
quicken _vt_ adcelerāre; (_with life_) animāre.
quickening _adj_ vītālis.
quickly _adv_ celeriter, citō; (_haste_) properē; (_mind_) acūtē; **as ~ as possible** quam celerrimē.
quickness _n_ celeritās _f_, vēlōcitās _f_; (_to act_) alacritās _f_; (_to perceive_) sagācitās _f_, sollertia _f_.
quicksand _n_ syrtis _f_.
quick-tempered _adj_ īrācundus.
quick-witted _adj_ acūtus, sagāx, perspicāx.
quiescence _n_ inertia _f_, ōtium _nt_.
quiescent _adj_ iners, ōtiōsus.
quiet _adj_ tranquillus, quiētus, placidus; (_silent_) tacitus; **be ~** quiēscere; silēre ♦ _n_ quiēs _f_, tranquillitās _f_; silentium _nt_; (_peace_) pāx _f_ ♦ _vt_ pācāre, compōnere.
quietly _adv_ tranquillē, quiētē; tacitē, per silentium; aequō animō.
quietness _n_ tranquillitās _f_; silentium _nt_.
quill _n_ penna _f_.
quince _n_ cydōnium _nt_.
quinquennial _adj_ quinquennālis.
quinquereme _n_ quinquerēmis _f_.
quintessence _n_ flōs _m_, vīs _f_.
quip _n_ sāl _m_, facētiae _fpl_.
quirk _n_ captiuncula _f_; **~s** _pl_ trīcae _fpl_.
quit _vt_ relinquere ♦ _adj_ līber, solūtus.
quite _adv_ admodum, plānē, prōrsus; **not ~** minus, parum; (_time_) nōndum.
quits _n_ parēs _mpl_.
quiver _n_ pharetra _f_ ♦ _vi_ tremere, contremere.
quivering _adj_ tremebundus, tremulus.
quoit _n_ discus _m_.
quota _n_ pars _f_, rata pars _f_.
quotation _n_ (_act_) commemorātiō _f_; (_passage_) locus _m_.
quote _vt_ prōferre, commemorāre.
quoth _vt_ inquit.

R, r

rabbit _n_ cunīculus _m_.
rabble _n_ turba _f_; (_class_) vulgus _nt_, plēbēcula _f_.
rabid _adj_ rabidus.
rabidly _adv_ rabidē.
race _n_ (_descent_) genus _nt_, stirps _f_; (_people_) gēns _f_, nōmen _nt_; (_contest_) certāmen _nt_; (_fig_) cursus _m_, curriculum _nt_; (_water_) flūmen _nt_; **run a ~** cursū certāre; **run the ~** (_fig_) spatium dēcurrere ♦ _vi_ certāre, contendere.
racecourse _n_ (_foot_) stadium _nt_; (_horse_)

spatium _nt_.
racer _n_ cursor _m_.
racial _adj_ gentīlis.
rack _n_ (_torture_) tormentum _nt_; (_shelf_) pluteus _m_; **be on the ~** (_fig_) cruciāri ♦ _vt_ torquēre, cruciāre; **~ off** (_wine_) diffundere.
racket _n_ (_noise_) strepitus _m_.
racy _adj_ (_style_) salsus.
radiance _n_ splendor _m_, fulgor _m_.
radiant _adj_ splendidus, nitidus.
radiantly _adv_ splendidē.
radiate _vi_ fulgēre; (_direction_) dīversōs tendere ♦ _vt_ ēmittere.
radical _adj_ īnsitus, innātus; (_thorough_) tōtus ♦ _n_ novārum rērum cupidus _m_.
radically _adv_ omnīnō, penitus, funditus.
radish _n_ rādīx _f_.
radius _n_ radius _m_.
raffish _adj_ dissolūtus.
raffle _n_ ālea _f_ ♦ _vt_ āleā vēndere.
raft _n_ ratis _f_.
rafter _n_ trabs _f_, tignum _nt_.
rag _n_ pannus _m_.
rage _n_ īra _f_, furor _m_; **be all the ~** in ōre omnium esse; **spend one's ~** exsaevīre ♦ _vi_ furere, saevīre; (_furiously_) dēbacchārī.
ragged _adj_ pannōsus.
raid _n_ excursiō _f_, incursiō _f_, impressiō _f_; **make a ~** excurrere ♦ _vt_ incursiōnem facere in (_acc_).
rail _n_ longurius _m_ ♦ _vt_ saepīre ♦ _vi_: **~ at** maledīcere (_dat_), convīcia facere (_dat_).
railing _n_ saepēs _f_, cancellī _mpl_.
raillery _n_ cavillātiō _f_.
raiment _n_ vestis _f_.
rain _n_ pluvia _f_, imber _m_ ♦ _vi_ pluere; **it is raining** pluit.
rainbow _n_ arcus _m_.
rainstorm _n_ imber _m_.
rainy _adj_ pluvius.
raise _vt_ tollere, ēlevāre; (_army_) cōgere, cōnscrībere; (_children_) ēducāre; (_cry_) tollere; (_from dead_) excitāre; (_laugh_) movēre; (_money_) cōnflāre; (_price_) augēre; (_siege_) exsolvere; (_structure_) exstruere; (_to higher rank_) ēvehere; **~ up** ērigere, sublevāre.
raisin _n_ astaphis _f_.
rajah _n_ dynastēs _m_.
rake _n_ rastrum _nt_; (_person_) nepōs _m_ ♦ _vt_ rādere; **~ in** conrādere; **~ up** (_fig_) ēruere.
rakish _adj_ dissolūtus.
rally _n_ conventus _m_ ♦ _vt_ (_troops_) in ōrdinem revocāre; (_with words_) hortārī; (_banter_) cavillārī ♦ _vi_ sē colligere.
ram _n_ ariēs _m_; (_battering_) ariēs _m_ ♦ _vt_: **~ down** fistūcāre; **~ home** (_fact_) inculcāre.
ramble _n_ errātiō _f_ ♦ _vi_ vagārī, errāre.
rambling _adj_ vagus; (_plant_) errāticus; (_speech_) fluēns.
ramification _n_ rāmus _m_.
rammer _n_ fistūca _f_.
rampage _vi_ saevīre.
rampant _adj_ ferōx.

rampart n agger m, vallum nt.
ranch n lātifundium nt.
rancid adj pūtidus.
rancour n odium nt, acerbitās f, invidia f.
random adj fortuītus; **at ~** temerē.
range n ōrdō m, seriēs f; (mountain) iugum nt;
   (of weapon) iactus m; **within ~** intrā ːēlī
   iactum; **come within ~** sub ictum venīre ♦ vt
   ōrdināre ♦ vi ēvagārī, pervagārī; (in speech)
   excurrere.
rank n (line) ōrdō m; (class) ōrdō m; (position)
   locus m, dignitās f; **~ and file** gregārī mīlitēs
   mpl; **keep the ~s** ōrdinēs observāre; **the ~s**
   (MIL) aciēs, acieī f; **leave the ~s** ōrdine ēgredī,
   ab signīs discēdere; **reduce to the ~s** in
   ōrdinem redigere ♦ vt numerāre ♦ ~i in
   numerō habērī.
rank adj luxuriōsus; (smell) gravis, foetidus.
rankle vi exulcerāre.
rankness n luxuriēs f.
ransack vt dīripere, spoliāre.
ransom n redemptiō f, pretium nt ♦ vt
   redimere.
rant vi latrāre.
ranter n rabula m, latrātor m.
rap n ictus m ♦ vt ferīre.
rapacious adj rapāx, avidus.
rapaciously adv avidē.
rapacity n rapācitās f, aviditās f.
rape n raptus m.
rapid adj rapidus, vēlōx, citus, incitātus.
rapidity n celeritās f, vēlōcitās f, incitātiō f.
rapidly adv rapidē, vēlōciter, citō.
rapine n rapīna f.
rapt adj intentus.
rapture n laetitia f, alacritās f.
rare adj rārus; (occurrence) īnfrequēns;
   (quality) singulāris.
rarefy vt extenuāre.
rarely adv rārō.
rarity n rāritās f; (thing) rēs īnsolita f.
rascal n furcifer m, scelestus m.
rascally adj improbus.
rash adj temerārius, audāx, incōnsultus;
   praeceps.
rashly adv temerē, incōnsultē.
rashness n temeritās f, audācia f.
rat n mūs m/f.
rate n (cost) pretium nt; (standard) nōrma f;
   (tax) vectīgal nt; (speed) celeritās f; **at any ~**
   (concessive) utique, saltem; (adversative)
   quamquam, tamen ♦ vt (value) aestimāre;
   (scold) increpāre, obiūrgāre.
rather adv potius, satius; (somewhat)
   aliquantum; (with comp) aliquantō; (with
   verbs) mālō; (correcting) immo; **~ sad** tristior;
   I would ~ mālō; **I ~ think** haud sciō an; **~ than**
   magis quam, potius quam.
ratification n (formal) sanctiō f.
ratify vt ratum facere, sancīre; (law) iubēre.
rating n taxātiō f, aestimātiō f; (navy) nauta m;
   (scolding) obiūrgātiō f.
ratiocinate vi ratiōcinārī.

ratiocination n ratiōcinātiō f.
ration n dēmēnsum nt.
rational adj animō praeditus; **be ~** sapere.
rationality n ratiō f.
rationally adv ratiōne.
rations npl cibāria ntpl, diāria ntpl.
rattle n crepitus m; (toy) crotalum nt ♦ vi
   crepitāre, increpāre.
raucous adj raucus.
ravage vt dēpopulārī, vāstāre, dīripere.
rave vi furere, īnsānīre; (fig) bacchārī,
   saevīre.
raven n cornīx f.
ravenous adj rapāx, vorāx.
ravenously adv avidē.
ravine n faucēs fpl, hiātus m.
raving adj furiōsus, īnsānus ♦ n furor m.
ravish vt rapere; (joy) efferre.
raw adj crūdus; (person) rudis, agrestis.
ray n radius m; **the first ~ of hope appeared**
   prīma spēs adfulsit.
raze vt excīdere, solō aequāre.
razor n novācula f.
reach n (space) spatium nt; (mind) captus m;
   (weapon) ictus m; **out of ~ of** extrā (acc);
   within ~ ad manum ♦ vt advenīre ad (+ acc);
   attingere; (space) pertinēre ad; (journey)
   pervenīre ad.
react vi adficī; **~ to** ferre.
reaction n: **what was his ~ to?** quō animō
   tulit?
read vt legere; (a book) ēvolvere; (aloud)
   recitāre; **~ over** perlegere.
reader n lēctor m.
readily adv facile, libenter, ultrō.
readiness n facilitās f; **in ~** ad manum, in
   prōmptū, in expedītō.
reading n lēctiō f.
readjust vt dēnuō accommodāre.
ready adj parātus, prōmptus; (manner) facilis;
   (money) praesēns; **get, make ~** parāre,
   expedīre, adōrnāre.
reaffirm vt iterum adfirmāre.
real adj vērus, germānus.
real estate n fundus m, solum nt.
realism n vēritās f.
realistic adj vērī similis.
reality n rēs f, rēs ipsa f, vērum nt; **in ~** rēvērā.
realize vt intellegere, animadvertere; (aim)
   efficere, peragere; (money) redigere.
really adv vērē, rēvērā, profectō; **~?** itane
   vērō?
realm n rēgnum nt.
reap vt metere; **~ the reward of** fructum
   percipere ex.
reaper n messor m.
reappear vi revenīre.
rear vt alere, ēducāre; (structure) exstruere ♦
   vi sē ērigere ♦ n tergum nt; (MIL) novissima
   aciēs f, novissimum agmen nt; **in the ~** ā
   tergō; **bring up the ~** agmen claudere, agmen
   cōgere ♦ adj postrēmus, novissimus.
rearguard n novissimum agmen nt,

novissimī *mpl*.
rearrange *vt* ōrdinem mūtāre (*gen*).
reason *n* (*faculty*) mēns *f*, animus *m*, ratiō *f*;
(*sanity*) sānitās *f*; (*argument*) ratiō *f*; (*cause*)
causa *f*; (*moderation*) modus *m*; **by ~ of**
propter (*acc*); **for this ~** idcircō, ideō,
proptereā; **in ~** aequus, modicus; **with good**
~ iūre; **without ~** temerē, sine causā; **without**
good ~ frustrā, iniūriā; **give a ~ for** ratiōnem
adferre (*gen*); **I know the ~ for** sciō cūr,
quamobrem (*subj*); **there is no ~ for** nōn est
cūr, nihil est quod (*subj*); **lose one's ~**
īnsānīre ♦ *vi* ratiōcinārī, disserere.
reasonable *adj* aequus, iūstus; (*person*)
modestus; (*amount*) modicus.
reasonably *adv* ratiōne, iūstē; modicē.
reasoning *n* ratiō *f*, ratiōcinātiō *f*.
reassemble *vt* colligere, cōgere.
reassert *vt* iterāre.
reassume *vt* recipere.
reassure *vt* firmāre, cōnfirmāre.
rebate *vt* dēdūcere.
rebel *n* rebellis *m* ♦ *adj* sēditiōsus ♦ *vi*
rebelliōnem facere, rebellāre, dēscīscere.
rebellion *n* sēditiō *f*, mōtus *m*.
rebellious *adj* sēditiōsus.
rebound *vi* resilīre.
rebuff *n* repulsa *f* ♦ *vt* repellere, āversārī.
rebuild *vt* renovāre, restaurāre.
rebuke *n* reprehēnsiō *f*, obiūrgātiō *f* ♦ *vt*
reprehendere, obiūrgāre, increpāre.
rebut *vt* refūtāre, redarguere.
recalcitrant *adj* invītus.
recall *n* revocātiō *f*, reditus *m* ♦ *vt* revocāre;
(*from exile*) redūcere; (*to mind*) reminīscī
(*gen*), recordārī (*gen*).
recant *vt* retractāre.
recantation *n* receptus *m*.
recapitulate *vt* repetere, summātim dīcere.
recapitulation *n* ēnumerātiō *f*.
recapture *vt* recipere.
recast *vt* reficere, retractāre.
recede *vi* recēdere.
receipt *n* (*act*) acceptiō *f*; (*money*) acceptum *nt*;
(*written*) apocha *f*.
receive *vt* accipere, capere; (*in turn*) excipere.
receiver *n* receptor *m*.
recent *adj* recēns.
recently *adv* nūper, recēns.
receptacle *n* receptāculum *nt*.
reception *n* aditus *m*, hospitium *nt*.
receptive *adj* docilis.
recess *n* recessus *m*, angulus *m*; (*holiday*)
fēriae *fpl*.
recharge *vt* replēre.
recipe *n* compositiō *f*.
recipient *n* quī accipit.
reciprocal *adj* mūtuus.
reciprocally *adv* mūtuō, inter sē.
reciprocate *vt* referre, reddere.
reciprocity *n* mūtuum *nt*.
recital *n* nārrātiō *f*, ēnumerātiō *f*; (*LIT*) recitātiō
f.

recitation *n* recitātiō *f*.
recite *vt* recitāre; (*details*) ēnumerāre.
reciter *n* recitātor *m*.
reck *vt* ratiōnem habēre (*gen*).
reckless *adj* temerārius, incautus, praeceps.
recklessly *adv* incautē, temerē.
recklessness *n* temeritās *f*, neglegentia *f*.
reckon *vt* (*count*) computāre, numerāre;
(*think*) cēnsēre, dūcere; (*estimate*) aestimāre;
~ on cōnfīdere (*dat*); **~ up** dīnumerāre; (*cost*)
aestimāre; **~ with** contendere cum.
reckoning *n* ratiō *f*.
reclaim *vt* repetere; (*from error*) revocāre.
recline *vi* recumbere; (*at table*) accumbere;
(*plur*) discumbere.
recluse *n* homō sōlitārius *m*.
recognition *n* cognitiō *f*.
recognizance *n* vadimōnium *nt*.
recognize *vt* agnōscere; (*approve*) accipere;
(*admit*) fatērī.
recoil *vi* resilīre; **~ from** refugere; **~ upon**
recidere in (*acc*).
recollect *vt* reminīscī (*gen*).
recollection *n* memoria *f*, recordātiō *f*.
recommence *vt* renovāre, redintegrāre.
recommend *vt* commendāre; (*advise*)
suādēre (*dat*).
recommendation *n* commendātiō *f*; (*advice*)
cōnsilium *nt*; **letter of ~** litterae
commendātīciae.
recompense *vt* remūnerārī, grātiam referre
(*dat*) ♦ *n* praemium *nt*, remūnerātiō *f*.
reconcile *vt* compōnere, reconciliāre; **be ~d in**
grātiam redīre.
reconciliation *n* reconciliātiō *f*, grātia *f*.
recondite *adj* reconditus, abstrūsus.
recondition *vt* reficere.
reconnaissance *n* explōrātiō *f*.
reconnoitre *vt*, *vi* explōrāre; **without**
reconnoitring inexplōrātō.
reconquer *vt* recipere.
reconsider *vt* reputāre, retractāre.
reconstruct *vt* restituere, renovāre.
reconstruction *n* renovātiō *f*.
record *n* monumentum *nt*; (*LIT*) commentārius
m; **~s** *pl* tabulae *fpl*, fāstī *mpl*, ācta *ntpl*; **break**
the ~ priōrēs omnēs superāre ♦ *vt* in
commentārium referre; (*history*)
perscrībere, nārrāre.
recount *vt* nārrāre, commemorāre.
recourse *n*: **have ~ to** (*for safety*) cōnfugere ad;
(*as expedient*) dēcurrere ad.
recover *vt* recipere, recuperāre; (*loss*)
reparāre; **~ oneself** sē colligere; **~ one's**
senses ad sānitātem revertī ♦ *vi*
convalēscere.
recovery *n* recuperātiō *f*; (*from illness*) salūs *f*.
recreate *vt* recreāre.
recreation *n* requiēs *f*, remissiō *f*, lūdus *m*.
recriminate *vi* in vicem accūsāre.
recrimination *n* mūtua accūsātiō *f*.
recruit *n* tīrō *m* ♦ *vt* (*MIL*) cōnscrībere;
(*strength*) reficere.

recruiting officer n conquīsītor m.
rectify vt corrigere, ēmendāre.
rectitude n probitās f.
recumbent adj supīnus.
recuperate vi convalēscere.
recur vi recurrere, redīre.
recurrence n reditus m, reversiō f.
recurrent adj adsiduus.
red adj ruber.
redden vi ērubēscere ♦ vt rutilāre.
reddish adj subrūfus.
redeem vt redimere, līberāre.
redeemer n līberātor m.
redemption n redemptiō f.
red-haired adj rūfus.
red-handed adj: **catch ~ in** manifestō scelere dēprehendere.
red-hot adj fervēns.
red lead n minium nt.
redness n rubor m.
redolent adj: **be ~ of** redolēre.
redouble vt ingemināre.
redoubt n prōpugnāculum nt.
redoubtable adj īnfestus, formīdolōsus.
redound vi redundāre; **it ~s to my credit** mihī honōrī est.
redress n remedium nt; **demand ~** rēs repetere ♦ vt restituere.
reduce vt minuere, attenuāre; (to a condition) redigere, dēdūcere; (MIL) expugnāre; **~ to the ranks in** ōrdinem cōgere.
reduction n imminūtiō f; (MIL) expugnātiō f.
redundancy n redundantia f.
redundant adj redundāns; **be ~** redundāre.
reduplication n geminātiō f.
re-echo vt reddere, referre ♦ vi resonāre.
reed n harundō f.
reedy adj harundineus.
reef n saxa ntpl ♦ vt (sail) subnectere.
reek n fūmus m ♦ vi fūmāre.
reel vi vacillāre, titubāre.
re-enlist vt rescrībere.
re-establish vt restituere.
refashion vt reficere.
refer vt (person) dēlēgāre; (matter) rēicere, remittere ♦ vi: **~ to** spectāre ad; (in speech) attingere, perstringere.
referee n arbiter m.
reference n ratiō f; (in book) locus m.
refine vt excolere, expolīre; (metal) excoquere.
refined adj hūmānus, urbānus, polītus.
refinement n hūmānitās f, cultus m, ēlegantia f.
refit vt reficere.
reflect vt reddere, repercutere ♦ vi meditārī; **~ upon** cōnsīderāre, sēcum reputāre; (blame) reprehendere.
reflection n (of light) repercussus m; (image) imāgō f; (thought) meditātiō f, cōgitātiō f; (blame) reprehēnsiō f; **cast ~s on** maculīs aspergere, vitiō vertere; **with due ~** cōnsīderātē; **without ~** incōnsultē.

reflux n recessus m.
reform n ēmendātiō f ♦ vt (lines) restituere; (error) corrigere, ēmendāre, meliōrem facere ♦ vi sē corrigere.
reformation n corrēctiō f.
reformer n corrēctor m, ēmendātor m.
refract vt īnfringere.
refractory adj contumāx.
refrain vi temperāre, abstinēre (dat), supersedēre (inf).
refresh vt recreāre, renovāre, reficere; (mind) integrāre.
refreshed adj requiētus.
refreshing adj dulcis, iūcundus.
refreshment n cibus m.
refuge n perfugium nt; (secret) latebra f; **take ~ with** perfugere ad (acc); **take ~ in** confugere.
refugee n profugus m.
refulgence n splendor m.
refulgent adj splendidus.
refund vt reddere.
refusal n recūsātiō f, dētrectātiō f.
refuse n pūrgāmenta ntpl; (fig) faex f ♦ vt (request) dēnegāre; (offer) dētrectāre, recūsāre; (with verb) nōlle.
refutation n refūtātiō f, reprehēnsiō f.
refute vt refellere, redarguere, revincere.
regain vt recipere.
regal adj rēgius, rēgālis.
regale vt excipere, dēlectāre; **~ oneself** epulārī.
regalia n īnsignia ntpl.
regally adv rēgāliter.
regard n respectus m, ratiō f; (esteem) grātia f; **with ~ to** ad (acc), quod attinet ad ♦ vt (look) intuērī, spectāre; (deem) habēre, dūcere; **send ~s to** salūtem dīcere (dat).
regarding prep dē (abl).
regardless adj neglegēns, immemor.
regency n interrēgnum nt.
regent n interrēx m.
regicide n (person) rēgis interfector m; (act) rēgis caedēs f.
regime n administrātiō f.
regimen n vīctus m.
regiment n legiō f.
region n regiō f, tractus m.
register n tabulae fpl, album nt ♦ vt in tabulās referre, perscrībere; (emotion) ostendere, sūmere.
registrar n tabulārius m.
registry n tabulārium nt.
regret n dolor m; (for past) dēsīderium nt; (for fault) paenitentia f ♦ vt dolēre; **I ~ mē** paenitet, mē piget (gen).
regretful adj maestus.
regretfully adv dolenter.
regrettable adj īnfēlīx, īnfortūnātus.
regular adj (consistent) cōnstāns; (orderly) ōrdinātus; (habitual) solitus, adsiduus; (proper) iūstus, rēctus.
regularity n moderātiō f, ōrdō m; (consistency) cōnstantia f.

regularly _adv_ ōrdine; cōnstanter; iūstē, rēctē.
regulate _vt_ ōrdināre, dīrigere; (_control_)
moderārī.
regulation _n_ lēx _f_, dēcrētum _nt_.
rehabilitate _vt_ restituere.
rehearsal _n_ meditātiō _f_.
rehearse _vt_ meditārī.
reign _n_ rēgnum _nt_; (_emperor's_) prīncipātus _m_;
in the ~ of Numa rēgnante Numā ♦ _vi_
rēgnāre; (_fig_) dominārī.
reimburse _vt_ rependere.
rein _n_ habēna _f_; **give full ~ to** habēnās
immittere ♦ _vt_ īnfrēnāre.
reindeer _n_ rēnō _m_.
reinforce _vt_ firmāre, cōnfirmāre.
reinforcement _n_ subsidium _nt_; ~s _pl_ novae
cōpiae _fpl_.
reinstate _vt_ restituere, redūcere.
reinstatement _n_ restitūtiō _f_, reductiō _f_; (_to_
legal privileges) postlīminium _nt_.
reinvigorate _vt_ recreāre.
reiterate _vt_ dictitāre, iterāre.
reiteration _n_ iterātiō _f_.
reject _vt_ rēicere; (_with scorn_) respuere,
aspernārī, repudiāre.
rejection _n_ rēiectiō _f_, repulsa _f_.
rejoice _vi_ gaudēre, laetārī ♦ _vt_ dēlectāre.
rejoicing _n_ gaudium _nt_.
rejoin _vt_ redīre ad ♦ _vi_ respondēre.
rejoinder _n_ respōnsum _nt_.
rejuvenate _vt_: **be ~d** repuerāscere.
rekindle _vt_ suscitāre.
relapse _vi_ recidere.
relate _vt_ (_tell_) nārrāre, commemorāre,
expōnere; (_compare_) cōnferre ♦ _vi_
pertinēre.
related _adj_ propinquus; (_by birth_) cognātus; (_by_
marriage) adfīnis; (_fig_) fīnitimus.
relation _n_ (_tale_) nārrātiō _f_; (_connection_) ratiō _f_;
(_kin_) necessārius _m_, cognātus _m_, adfīnis _m_.
relationship _n_ necessitūdō _f_; (_by birth_)
cognātiō _f_; (_by marriage_) adfīnitās _f_;
(_connection_) vīcīnitās _f_.
relative _adj_ cum cēterīs comparātus ♦ _n_
propinquus _m_, cognātus _m_, adfīnis _m_,
necessārius _m_.
relatively _adv_ ex comparātiōne.
relax _vt_ laxāre, remittere ♦ _vi_ languēscere.
relaxation _n_ remissiō _f_, requiēs _f_, lūdus _m_.
relay _n_: **~s of horses** dispositī equī _mpl_.
release _vt_ solvere, exsolvere, līberāre,
expedīre; (_law_) absolvere ♦ _n_ missiō _f_,
līberātiō _f_.
relegate _vt_ relēgāre.
relent _vi_ concēdere, plācārī, flectī.
relentless _adj_ immisericors, inexōrābilis;
(_things_) improbus.
relevant _adj_ ad rem.
reliability _n_ fīdūcia _f_.
reliable _adj_ fīdus.
reliance _n_ fīdūcia _f_, fidēs _f_.
reliant _adj_ frētus.
relic _n_ rēliquiae _fpl_.

relief _n_ levātiō _f_, levāmen _nt_, adlevāmentum _nt_;
(_aid_) subsidium _nt_; (_turn of duty_) vicēs _fpl_; (_art_)
ēminentia _f_; (_sculpture_) toreuma _nt_; **bas ~**
anaglypta _ntpl_; **in ~** ēminēns, expressus;
throw into ~ exprimere, distinguere.
relieve _vt_ levāre, sublevāre; (_aid_) subvenīre
(_dat_); (_duty_) succēdere (_dat_), excipere; (_art_)
distinguere.
religion _n_ religiō _f_, deōrum cultus _m_.
religious _adj_ religiōsus, pius; **~ feeling** religiō
_f_.
religiously _adv_ religiōsē.
relinquish _vt_ relinquere; (_office_) sē abdicāre
(_abl_).
relish _n_ sapor _m_; (_sauce_) condīmentum _nt_; (_zest_)
studium _nt_ ♦ _vt_ dēlectārī (_abl_).
reluctance _n_: **with ~** invītus.
reluctant _adj_ invītus.
reluctantly _adv_ invītus, gravātē.
rely _vi_ fīdere (_dat_), cōnfīdere (_dat_).
relying _adj_ frētus (_abl_).
remain _vi_ manēre, morārī; (_left over_) restāre,
superesse.
remainder _n_ reliquum _nt_.
remaining _adj_ reliquus; **the ~** cēterī _pl_.
remains _n_ rēliquiae _fpl_.
remand _vt_ (_law_) ampliāre.
remark _n_ dictum _nt_ ♦ _vt_ dīcere; (_note_)
observāre.
remarkable _adj_ īnsignis, ēgregius,
memorābilis.
remarkably _adv_ īnsignītē, ēgregiē.
remediable _adj_ sānābilis.
remedy _n_ remedium _nt_ ♦ _vt_ medērī (_dat_),
sānāre.
remember _vt_ meminisse (_gen_); (_recall_)
recordārī (_gen_), reminīscī (_gen_).
remembrance _n_ memoria _f_, recordātiō _f_.
remind _vt_ admonēre, commonefacere.
reminder _n_ admonitiō _f_, admonitum _nt_.
reminiscence _n_ recordātiō _f_.
remiss _adj_ dissolūtus, neglegēns.
remission _n_ venia _f_.
remissness _n_ neglegentia _f_.
remit _vt_ remittere; (_fault_) ignōscere (_dat_);
(_debt_) dōnāre; (_punishment_) condōnāre;
(_question_) referre.
remittance _n_ pecūnia _f_.
remnant _n_ fragmentum _nt_; ~s _pl_ rēliquiae _fpl_.
remonstrance _n_ obtestātiō _f_, obiūrgātiō _f_.
remonstrate _vi_ reclāmāre; **~ with** obiūrgāre;
~ about expostulāre.
remorse _n_ paenitentia _f_, cōnscientia _f_.
remorseless _adj_ immisericors.
remote _adj_ remōtus, reconditus.
remotely _adv_ procul.
remoteness _n_ longinquitās _f_.
removal _n_ āmōtiō _f_; (_going_) migrātiō _f_.
remove _vt_ āmovēre, dēmere, eximere,
removēre; (_out of the way_) dēmovēre ♦ _vi_
migrāre, dēmigrāre.
remunerate _vt_ remūnērārī.
remuneration _n_ mercēs _f_, praemium _nt_.

rend vt scindere, dīvellere.
render vt reddere; (*music*) interpretārī; (*translation*) vertere; (*thanks*) referre.
rendering n interpretātiō f.
rendez-vous n cōnstitūtum nt.
renegade n dēsertor m.
renew vt renovāre, integrāre, īnstaurāre, redintegrāre.
renewal n renovātiō f; (*ceremony*) īnstaurātiō f.
renounce vt renūntiāre, mittere, repudiāre.
renovate vt renovāre, reficere.
renown n fāma f, glōria f.
renowned adj praeclārus, īnsignis, rctus.
rent n (*tear*) fissum nt; (*pay*) mercēs f ♦ vt (*hire*) condūcere; (*lease*) locāre.
renunciation n cessiō f, repudiātiō f.
repair vt reficere, sarcīre ♦ vi sē recipere ♦ n: **keep in good ~** tuērī; **in bad ~** ruīnōsus.
reparable adj ēmendābilis.
reparation n satisfactiō f.
repartee n facētiae fpl, salēs mpl.
repast n cēna f, cibus m.
repay vt remūnerārī, grātiam referre (*dat*); (*money*) repōnere.
repayment n solūtiō f.
repeal vt abrogāre ♦ n abrogātiō f.
repeat vt iterāre; (*lesson*) reddere; (*ceremony*) īnstaurāre; (*performance*) referre.
repeatedly adv identidem, etiam atque etiam.
repel vt repellere, dēfendere.
repellent adj iniūcundus.
repent vi: **I ~** mē paenitet (+ *gen of thing*).
repentance n paenitentia f.
repentant adj paenitēns.
repercussion n ēventus m.
repertory n thēsaurus m.
repetition n iterātiō f.
repine vi conquerī.
replace vt repōnere, restituere; **~ by** substituere.
replacement n supplēmentum nt.
replenish vt replēre, supplēre.
replete adj plēnus.
repletion n satietās f.
replica n apographon nt.
reply vi respondēre ♦ n respōnsum nt.
report n (*talk*) fāma f, rūmor m; (*repute*) opīniō f; (*account*) renūntiātiō f, litterae fpl; (*noise*) fragor m; **make a ~** renūntiāre ♦ vt referre, dēferre, renūntiāre.
repose n quiēs f, requiēs f ♦ vt repōnere, pōnere ♦ vi quiēscere.
repository n horreum nt.
reprehend vt reprehendere, culpāre.
reprehensible adj accūsābilis, improbus.
reprehension n reprehēnsiō f, culpa f.
represent vt dēscrībere, effingere, exprimere, imitārī; (*character*) partēs agere (*gen*), persōnam gerere (*gen*); (*case*) prōpōnere; (*substitute for*) vicārium esse (*gen*).
representation n imāgō f, imitātiō f; **make ~s to** admonēre.

representative n lēgātus m.
repress vt reprimere, cohibēre.
repression n coercitiō f.
reprieve n mora f, venia f ♦ vt veniam dare (*dat*).
reprimand vt reprehendere, increpāre ♦ n reprehēnsiō f.
reprisals n ultiō f.
reproach vt exprobāre, obicere (*dat*) ♦ n exprobrātiō f, probrum nt; (*cause*) opprobrium nt.
reproachful adj contumēliōsus.
reprobate adj perditus.
reproduce vt propāgāre; (*likeness*) referre.
reproduction n prōcreātiō f; (*likeness*) imāgō f.
reproductive adj genitālis.
reproof n reprehēnsiō f, obiūrgātiō f.
reprove vt reprehendere, increpāre, obiūrgāre.
reptile n serpēns f.
republic n lībera rēspūblica f, cīvitās populāris f.
republican adj populāris.
repudiate vt repudiāre.
repudiation n repudiātiō f.
repugnance n fastīdium nt, odium nt.
repugnant adj invīsus, adversus.
repulse n dēpulsiō f; (*at election*) repulsa f ♦ vt repellere, āversārī, prōpulsāre.
repulsion n repugnantia f.
repulsive adj odiōsus, foedus.
reputable adj honestus.
reputation n fāma f, existimātiō f; (*for something*) opīniō f (*gen*); **have a ~** nōmen habēre.
repute n fāma f, existimātiō f; **bad ~** īnfāmia f.
reputed adj: **I am ~ to be** dīcor esse.
request n rogātiō f, postulātum nt; **obtain a ~** impetrāre ♦ vt rogāre, petere; (*urgently*) dēposcere.
require vt (*demand*) imperāre, postulāre; (*need*) egēre (*abl*); (*call for*) requīrere.
requirement n postulātum nt, necessārium nt.
requisite adj necessārius.
requisition n postulātiō f ♦ vt imperāre.
requital n grātia f, vicēs fpl.
requite vt grātiam referre (*dat*), remūnerārī.
rescind vt rescindere, abrogāre.
rescript n rescrīptum nt.
rescue vt ēripere, expedīre, servāre ♦ n salūs f; **come to the ~ of** subvenīre (*dat*).
research n investīgātiō f.
resemblance n similitūdō f, imāgō f, īnstar nt.
resemble vt similem esse (*dat*), referre.
resent vt aegrē ferre, indignārī.
resentful adj īrācundus.
resentment n dolor m, indignātiō f.
reservation n (*proviso*) exceptiō f.
reserve vt servāre; (*store*) recondere; (*in a deal*) excipere ♦ nt (*mil*) subsidium nt; (*disposition*) pudor m, reticentia f; (*caution*) cautiō f; **in ~** in succenturiātus; **without ~**

palam.
reserved *adj* (*place*) adsignātus; (*disposition*)
taciturnus, tēctus.
reservedly *adv* circumspectē.
reserves *npl* subsidia *ntpl*.
reservoir *n* lacus *m*.
reside *vi* habitāre; ~ **in** incolere.
residence *n* domicilium *nt*, domus *f*.
resident *n* incola *m/f*.
residual *adj* reliquus.
residue, residuum *n* reliqua pars *f*.
resign *vt* cēdere; (*office*) abdicāre mē, tē *etc* dē
(+ *abl*); ~ **oneself** acquiēscere ♦ *vi* sē
abdicāre.
resignation *n* abdicātiō *f*; (*state of mind*)
patientia *f*, aequus animus *m*.
resigned *adj* patiēns; **be ~ to** aequō animō
ferre.
resilience *n* mollitia *f*.
resilient *adj* mollis.
resist *vt* resistere (*dat*), adversārī (*dat*),
repugnāre (*dat*).
resistance *n* repugnantia *f*; **offer ~** obsistere
(*dat*).
resistless *adj* invictus.
resolute *adj* fortis, cōnstāns.
resolutely *adv* fortiter, cōnstanter.
resolution *n* (*conduct*) fortitūdō *f*, cōnstantia *f*;
(*decision*) dēcrētum *nt*, sententia *f*; (*into parts*)
sēcrētiō *f*.
resolve *n* fortitūdō *f*, cōnstantia *f* ♦ *vt*
dēcernere, cōnstituere; (*into parts*)
dissolvere; **the senate ~s** placet senātuī.
resonance *n* sonus *m*.
resonant *adj* canōrus.
resort *n* locus celeber *m*; **last ~** ultimum
auxilium *nt* ♦ *vi* frequentāre, ventitāre; (*have
recourse*) dēcurrere, dēscendere, cōnfugere.
resound *vi* resonāre, personāre.
resource *n* subsidium *nt*; (*means*) modus *m*; **~s**
pl opēs *fpl*, cōpiae *fpl*.
resourceful *adj* versūtus, callidus.
resourcefulness *n* calliditās *f*, versūtus
animus *m*.
respect *n* (*esteem*) honōs *m*, observantia *f*;
(*reference*) ratiō *f*; **out of ~** honōris causā; **pay
one's ~s to** salūtāre; **show ~ for** observāre; **in
every ~** ex omnī parte, in omnī genere; **in ~ of**
ad (*acc*), ab (*abl*) ♦ *vt* honōrāre, observāre,
verērī.
respectability *n* honestās *f*.
respectable *adj* honestus, līberālis, frūgī.
respectably *adv* honēstē.
respectful *adj* observāns.
respectfully *adv* reverenter.
respectfulness *n* observantia *f*.
respective *adj* suus (*with* quisque).
respectively *adv* alius ... alius.
respiration *n* respīrātiō *f*, spīritus *m*.
respire *vi* respīrāre.
respite *n* requiēs *f*, intercapēdō *f*, intermissiō
f.
resplendence *n* splendor *m*.

resplendent *adj* splendidus, illūstris.
resplendently *adv* splendidē.
respond *vi* respondēre.
response *n* respōnsum *nt*.
responsibility *n* auctōritās *f*, cūra *f*.
responsible *adj* reus; (*witness*) locuplēs; **be ~
for** praestāre.
responsive *adj* (*pupil*) docilis; (*character*)
facilis.
rest *n* quiēs *f*, ōtium *nt*; (*after toil*) requiēs *f*;
(*remainder*) reliqua pars *f*; **be at ~**
requiēscere; **set at ~** tranquillāre; **the ~ of**
reliquī ♦ *vi* requiēscere, acquiēscere; **~ on**
nītī (*abl*), innītī in (*abl*) ♦ *vt* (*hope*) pōnere in
(*abl*).
rest *n* cēterī *mpl*.
resting place *n* cubīle *nt*, sēdēs *f*.
restitution *n* satisfactiō *f*; **make ~** restituere;
demand ~ rēs repetere.
restive *adj* contumāx.
restless *adj* inquiētus, sollicitus; **be ~**
fluctuārī.
restlessness *n* sollicitūdō *f*.
restoration *n* renovātiō *f*; (*of king*) reductiō *f*.
restore *vt* reddere, restituere; (*to health*)
recreāre; (*to power*) redūcere; (*damage*)
reficere, redintegrāre.
restorer *n* restitūtor *m*.
restrain *vt* coercēre, comprimere, cohibēre.
restraint *n* moderātiō *f*, temperantia *f*, frēnī
mpl; **with ~** abstinenter.
restrict *vt* continēre, circumscrībere.
restricted *adj* artus; **~ to** proprius (*gen*).
restriction *n* modus *m*, fīnis *m*; (*limitation*)
exceptiō *f*.
result *n* ēventus *m*, ēventum *nt*, exitus *m*; **the ~
is that** quō fit ut ♦ *vi* ēvenīre, ēvādere.
resultant *adj* cōnsequēns.
resume *vt* repetere.
resuscitate *vt* excitāre, suscitāre.
retail *vt* dīvendere, vēndere.
retailer *n* caupō *m*.
retain *vt* retinēre, tenēre, cōnservāre.
retainer *n* satelles *m*.
retake *vt* recipere.
retaliate *vi* ulcīscī.
retaliation *n* ultiō *f*.
retard *vt* retardāre, remorārī.
retention *n* cōnservātiō *f*.
retentive *adj* tenāx.
reticence *n* taciturnitās *f*.
reticent *adj* taciturnus.
reticulated *adj* rēticulātus.
retinue *n* satellitēs *mpl*, comitātus *m*.
retire *vi* recēdere, abscēdere; (*from office*)
abīre; (*from province*) dēcēdere; (*MIL*) pedem
referre, sē recipere.
retired *adj* ēmeritus; (*place*) remōtus.
retirement *n* (*act*) recessus *m*, dēcessus *m*;
(*state*) sōlitūdō *f*, ōtium *nt*; **life of ~** vīta
prīvāta.
retiring *adj* modestus, verēcundus.
retort *vt* respondēre, referre ♦ *n*

respōnsum nt.
retouch vt retractāre.
retrace vt repetere, iterāre.
retract vt revocāre, renūntiāre.
retreat n (MIL) receptus m; (place) recessus m, sēcessus m; sound the ~ receptuī canere ♦ vi sē recipere, pedem referre; regredī.
retrench vt minuere, recīdere.
retrenchment n parsimōnia f.
retribution n poena f.
retributive adj ultor, ultrīx.
retrieve vt reparāre, recipere.
retrograde adj (fig) dēterior.
retrogression n regressus m.
retrospect n: in ~ respicientī.
retrospective adj: be ~ retrōrsum sē referre.
retrospectively adv retrō.
return n reditus m; (pay) remūnerātiō f; (profit) fructus m, pretium nt; (statement) professiō f; make a ~ of profitērī; in ~ for prō (+ abl); in ~ in vicem, vicissim ♦ vt reddere, restituere, referre ♦ vi redīre, revenīre, revertī; (from province) dēcēdere.
reunion n convīvium nt.
reunite vt reconciliāre.
reveal vt aperīre, patefacere.
revel n cōmissātiō f, bacchātiō f; ~s pl orgia ntpl ♦ vi cōmissārī, bacchārī; ~ in luxuriārī.
revelation n patefactiō f.
reveller n cōmissātor m.
revelry n cōmissātiō f.
revenge n ultiō f; take ~ on vindicāre in (acc) ♦ vt ulcīscī.
revengeful adj ulcīscendī cupidus.
revenue n fructus m, reditus m, vectīgālia ntpl.
reverberate vi resonāre.
reverberation n repercussus m.
revere vt venerārī, colere.
reverence n venerātiō f; (feeling) religiō f; reverentia f.
reverent adj religiōsus, pius.
reverently adv religiōsē.
reverie n meditātiō f, somnium nt.
reversal n abrogātiō f.
reverse adj contrārius ♦ n contrārium nt; (MIL) clādēs f ♦ vt invertere; (decision) rescindere.
reversion n reditus m.
revert vi redīre, revertī.
review n recognitiō f, recēnsiō f ♦ vt (MIL) recēnsēre.
revile vt maledīcere (dat).
revise vt recognōscere, corrigere; (LIT) līmāre.
revision n ēmendātiō f; (LIT) līma f.
revisit vt revīsere.
revival n renovātiō f.
revive vt recreāre, excitāre ♦ vi revīvīscere, renāscī.
revocation n revocātiō f.
revoke vt renūntiāre, īnfectum reddere.
revolt n sēditiō f, dēfectiō f ♦ vi dēficere, rebellāre.
revolting adj taeter, obscēnus.
revolution n (movement) conversiō f; (change)

rēs novae fpl; (revolt) mōtus m; effect a ~ rēs novāre.
revolutionary adj sēditiōsus, novārum rērum cupidus.
revolve vi volvī, versārī, convertī ♦ vt (in mind) volūtāre.
revulsion n mūtātiō f.
reward n praemium nt, mercēs f ♦ vt remūnerārī, compēnsāre.
rhapsody n carmen nt; (epic) rhapsōdia f.
rhetoric n rhētorica f; of ~ rhētoricus; exercise in ~ dēclāmātiō f; practise ~ dēclāmāre; teacher of ~ rhētōr m.
rhetorical adj rhētoricus, dēclāmātōrius.
rhetorically adv rhētoricē.
rhetorician n rhētōr m, dēclāmātor m.
rhinoceros n rhīnocerōs m.
rhyme n homoeoteleuton nt; without ~ or reason temerē.
rhythm n numerus m, modus m.
rhythmical adj numerōsus.
rib n costa f.
ribald adj obscēnus.
ribaldry n obscēnitās f.
ribbon n īnfula f.
rice n oryza f.
rich adj dīves, locuplēs; opulentus; (fertile) ūber, opīmus; (food) pinguis.
riches n dīvitiae fpl, opēs fpl.
richly adv opulentē, largē, lautē.
richness n ūbertās f, cōpia f.
rid vt līberāre; get ~ of dēpōnere, dēmovēre, exuere.
riddle n aenigma nt; (sieve) cribrum nt ♦ vt (with wounds) cōnfodere.
ride vi equitāre, vehī; ~ a horse in equō vehī; ~ at anchor stāre; ~ away abequitāre, āvehī; ~ back revehī; ~ between interequitāre; ~ down dēvehī; ~ into invehī; ~ off āvehī; ~ out ēvehī; ~ past praetervehī; ~ round circumvehī (dat), circumequitāre; ~ up and down perequitāre; ~ up to adequitāre ad, advehī ad.
rider n eques m.
ridge n iugum nt.
ridicule n lūdibrium nt, irrīsus m ♦ vt irrīdēre, illūdere, lūdibriō habēre.
ridiculous adj rīdiculus, dērīdiculus.
ridiculously adv rīdiculē.
riding n equitātiō f.
rife adj frequēns.
riff-raff n faex populī f.
rifle vi expīlāre, spoliāre.
rift n rīma f.
rig vt (ship) armāre, ōrnāre ♦ n habitus m.
rigging n rudentēs mpl.
right adj rēctus; (just) aequus, iūstus; (true) rēctus, vērus; (proper) lēgitimus, fās; (hand) dexter; it is ~ decet (+ acc and infin); it is not ~ dēdecet (+ acc and infin); you are ~ vēra dīcis; if I am ~ nisi fallor; in the ~ place in locō; at the ~ time ad tempus; at ~ angles ad parēs angulōs; on the ~ ā dextrā ♦ adv rēctē, bene,

probē; (*justifiably*) iūre; ~ **up to** usque ad
(*+ acc*); ~ **on** rēctā ◆ *n* (*legal*) iūs *nt*; (*moral*) fās
nt ◆ *vt* (*replace*) restituere; (*correct*)
corrigere; (*avenge*) ulcīscī.
righteous *adj* iūstus, sanctus, pius.
righteously *adv* iūstē, sanctē, piē.
righteousness *n* sanctitās *f*, pietās *f*.
rightful *adj* iūstus, lēgitimus.
rightfully *adv* iūstē, lēgitimē.
right hand *n* dextra *f*.
right-hand *adj* dexter; ~ **man** comes *m*.
rightly *adv* rēctē, bene; iūre.
right-minded *adj* sānus.
rigid *adj* rigidus.
rigidity *n* rigor *m*; (*strictness*) sevēritās *f*.
rigidly *adv* rigidē, sevērē.
rigmarole *n* ambāgēs *fpl*.
rigorous *adj* dūrus; (*strict*) sevērus.
rigorously *adv* dūriter, sevērē.
rigour *n* dūritia *f*; sevēritās *f*.
rile *vt* inrītāre, stomachum movēre (*dat*).
rill *n* rīvulus *m*.
rim *n* labrum *nt*.
rime *n* pruīna *f*.
rind *n* cortex *m*.
ring *n* ānulus *m*; (*circle*) orbis *m*; (*of people*)
corōna *f*; (*motion*) gȳrus *m* ◆ *vt* circumdare;
(*bell*) movēre ◆ *vi* tinnīre, sonāre.
ringing *n* tinnītus *m* ◆ *adj* canōrus.
ringleader *n* caput *nt*, dux *m*.
ringlet *n* cincinnus *m*.
rinse *vt* colluere.
riot *n* tumultus *m*, rixa *f*; **run** ~ exsultāre,
luxuriārī, tumultuārī, turbās efficere; (*revel*)
bacchārī.
rioter *n* cōmissātor *m*.
riotous *adj* tumultuōsus, sēditiōsus;
(*debauched*) dissolūtus; ~ **living** cōmissātiō *f*,
luxuria *f*.
riotously *adv* tumultuōsē; luxuriōsē.
rip *vt* scindere.
ripe *adj* mātūrus; **of** ~ **judgment** animī
mātūrus.
ripen *vt* mātūrāre ◆ *vi* mātūrēscere.
ripeness *n* mātūritās *f*.
ripple *n* unda *f* ◆ *vi* trepidāre.
rise *vi* orīrī, surgere; (*hill*) ascendere; (*wind*)
cōnsurgere; (*passion*) tumēscere; (*voice*)
tollī; (*in size*) crēscere; (*in rank*) ascendere;
(*in revolt*) coorīrī, arma capere; ~ **and fall**
(*tide*) reciprocāre; ~ **above** superāre; ~ **again**
resurgere; ~ **in** (*river*) orīrī ex (*abl*); ~ **out**
ēmergere; ~ **up** exsurgere ◆ *n* ascēnsus *m*;
(*slope*) clīvus *m*; (*increase*) incrēmentum *nt*;
(*start*) ortus *m*; **give** ~ **to** parere.
rising *n* (*sun*) ortus *m*; (*revolt*) mōtus *m* ◆ *adj*
(*ground*) ēditus.
risk *n* perīculum *nt*; **run a** ~ perīculum subīre,
ingredī ◆ *vt* perīclitārī, in āleam dare.
risky *adj* perīculōsus.
rite *n* rītus *m*.
ritual *n* caerimōnia *f*.
rival *adj* aemulus ◆ *n* aemulus *m*, rīvālis *m* ◆ *vt*

aemulārī.
rivalry *n* aemulātiō *f*.
river *n* flūmen *nt*, fluvius *m* ◆ *adj* fluviātilis.
riverbed *n* alveus *m*.
riverside *n* rīpa *f*.
rivet *n* clāvus *m* ◆ *vt* (*attention*) dēfīgere.
rivulet *n* rīvulus *m*, rīvus *m*.
road *n* via *f*, iter *nt*; **on the** ~ in itinere, ex
itinere; **off the** ~ dēvius; **make a** ~ viam
mūnīre.
roadstead *n* statiō *f*.
roam *vi* errāre, vagārī; ~ **at large** ēvagārī.
roar *n* fremitus *m* ◆ *vi* fremere.
roast *vt* torrēre ◆ *adj* āssus ◆ *n* āssum *nt*.
rob *vt* spoliāre, exspoliāre, expīlāre; (*of hope*)
dēicere dē.
robber *n* latrō *m*, fūr *m*; (*highway*) grassātor *m*.
robbery *n* latrōcinium *nt*.
robe *n* vestis *f*; (*woman's*) stola *f*; (*of state*)
trabea *f* ◆ *vt* vestīre.
robust *adj* rōbustus, fortis.
robustness *n* rōbur *nt*, firmitās *f*.
rock *n* saxum *nt*; (*steep*) rūpēs *f*, scopulus *m* ◆ *vt*
agitāre ◆ *vi* agitārī, vacillāre.
rocky *adj* saxōsus, scopulōsus.
rod *n* virga *f*; (*fishing*) harundō *f*.
roe *n* (*deer*) capreolus *m*, caprea *f*; (*fish*) ōva *ntpl*.
rogue *n* veterātor *m*.
roguery *n* nēquitia *f*, scelus *nt*.
roguish *adj* improbus, malus.
role *n* partēs *fpl*.
roll *n* (*book*) volūmen *nt*; (*movement*) gȳrus *m*;
(*register*) album *nt*; **call the** ~ **of** legere;
answer the ~ **call** ad nōmen respondēre ◆ *vt*
volvere ◆ *vi* volvī, volūtārī; ~ **down** *vt*
dēvolvere ◆ *vi* dēfluere; ~ **over** *vt* prōvolvere
◆ *vi* prōlābī; ~ **up** *vt* convolvere.
roller *n* (*AGR*) cylindrus *m*; (*for moving*)
phalangae *fpl*; (*in book*) umbilīcus *m*.
rollicking *adj* hilaris.
rolling *adj* volūbilis.
Roman *adj* Rōmānus ◆ *n*: **the** ~**s** Rōmānī *mpl*.
romance *n* fābula *f*; amor *m*.
romantic *adj* fābulōsus; amātōrius.
Rome *n* Rōma *f*; **at** ~ Rōmae; **from** ~ Rōmā; **to** ~
Rōmam.
romp *vi* lūdere.
roof *n* tēctum *nt*; (*of mouth*) palātum *nt* ◆ *vt*
tegere, integere.
rook *n* corvus *m*.
room *n* conclāve *nt*; camera *f*; (*small*) cella *f*;
(*bed*) cubiculum *nt*; (*dining*) cēnāculum *nt*;
(*dressing*) apodytērium *nt*; (*space*) locus *m*;
make ~ **for** locum dare (*dat*), cēdere (*dat*).
roominess *n* laxitās *f*.
roomy *adj* capāx.
roost *vi* stabulārī.
rooster *n* gallus gallīnāceus *m*.
root *n* rādīx *f*; **take** ~ coalēscere ◆ *vt*: ~ **out**
ērādīcāre.
rooted *adj* (*fig*) dēfixus; **deeply** ~ (*custom*)
inveterātus; **be** ~ **in** īnsidēre (*dat*); **become**
deeply ~ inveterāscere.

rope n fūnis m; (thin) restis f; (ship's) rudēns m; **know the ~s** perītum esse.
rose n rosa f.
rosemary n rōs marīnus m.
rostrum n rōstra ntpl, suggestus m.
rosy adj roseus, purpureus.
rot n tābēs f ♦ vi putrēscere, pūtēscere ♦ vt putrefacere.
rotate vi volvī, sē convertere.
rotation n conversiō f; (succession) ōrdō m, vicissitūdō f; **in ~** ōrdine; **move in ~** in orbem īre.
rote n: **by ~** memoriter.
rotten adj putridus.
rotund adj rotundus.
rotundity n rotunditās f.
rouge n fūcus m ♦ vt fūcāre.
rough adj asper; (art) incultus, rudis; (manners) agrestis, inurbānus; (stone) impolītus; (treatment) dūrus, sevērus (weather) atrōx, procellōsus ♦ vi: **~ it** dūram vītam vīvere.
rough-and-ready adj fortuītus.
rough draft n (LIT) silva f.
roughen vt asperāre, exasperāre.
rough-hew vt dolāre.
roughly adv asperē, dūriter; (with numbers) circiter.
roughness n asperitās f.
round adj rotundus; (spherical) globōsus; (cylindrical) teres ♦ n (circle) orbis m; (motion) gȳrus m; (series) ambitus m; **go the ~s** (MIL) vigiliās circumīre ♦ vt (cape) superāre; **~ off** rotundāre; (sentence) concludere; **~ up** compellere ♦ adv circum, circā; **go ~** ambīre ♦ prep circum (acc), circā (acc).
roundabout adj: **~ story** ambāgēs fpl; **~ route** circuitus m, ānfrāctus m.
roundly adv (speak) apertē, līberē.
rouse vt excīre, excitāre; (courage) adrigere.
rousing adj vehemēns.
rout n fuga f; (crowd) turba f ♦ vt fugāre, fundere; **in fugam conicere**; prōfligāre.
route n cursus m, iter nt.
routine n ūsus m, ōrdō m.
rove vi errāre, vagārī.
rover n vagus m; (sea) pīrāta m.
row n (line) ōrdō m; (noise) turba f, rixa f ♦ vi (boat) rēmigāre ♦ vt rēmīs incitāre.
rowdy adj turbulentus.
rower n rēmex m.
rowing n rēmigium m.
royal adj rēgius, rēgālis.
royally adv rēgiē, rēgāliter.
royalty n (power) rēgnum nt; (persons) rēgēs mpl, domus rēgia f.
rub vt fricāre, terere; **~ away** conterere; **~ hard** dēfricāre; **~ off** dētergēre; **~ out** dēlēre; **~ up** expolīre.
rubbing n trītus m.
rubbish n quisquiliae fpl; (talk) nūgae fpl.
rubble n rūdus nt.
rubicund adj rubicundus.

rudder n gubernāculum nt, clāvus m.
ruddy adj rubicundus, rutilus.
rude adj (uncivilized) barbarus, dūrus, inurbānus; (insolent) asper, importūnus.
rudely adv horridē, rusticē; petulanter.
rudeness n barbariēs f; petulantia f, importūnitās f.
rudiment n elementum nt, initium nt.
rudimentary adj prīmus, incohātus.
rue n (herb) rūta f ♦ vt: **I ~** mē paenitet (gen).
rueful adj maestus.
ruffian n grassātor m.
ruffle vt agitāre; (temper) sollicitāre, commovēre.
rug n strāgulum nt.
rugged adj horridus, asper.
ruggedness n asperitās f.
ruin n ruīna f; (fig) exitium nt, perniciēs f; **go to ~** pessum īre, dīlābī ♦ vt perdere, dēperdere, pessum dare; (moral) corrumpere, dēprāvāre; **be ~ed** perīre.
ruined adj ruīnōsus.
ruinous adj exitiōsus, damnōsus.
rule n (instrument) rēgula f, amussis f; (principle) nōrma f, lēx f, praeceptum nt; (government) dominātiō f, imperium nt; **ten-foot ~** decempeda f; **as a ~** ferē; **lay down ~s** praecipere; **make it a ~ to** īnstituere (inf); **~ of thumb** ūsus m ♦ vt regere, moderārī ♦ vi rēgnāre, dominārī; (judge) ēdīcere; (custom) obtinēre; **~ over** imperāre (dat).
ruler n (instrument) rēgula f; (person) dominus m, rēctor m.
ruling n ēdictum nt.
rumble vi mūgīre.
rumbling n mūgītus m.
ruminate vi rūminārī.
rummage vi: **~ through** rīmārī.
rumour n fāma f, rūmor m.
rump n clūnis f.
run vi currere; (fluid) fluere, mānāre; (road) ferre; (time) lābī ♦ n cursus m; **~ about** discurrere, cursāre; **~ across** incidere in (acc); **~ after** sectārī; **~ aground** offendere; **~ away** aufugere, terga vertere; (from) fugere, dēfugere; **~ down** dēcurrere, dēfluere ♦ vt (in words) obtrectāre; **~ high** (fig) glīscere; **~ into** incurrere in (acc), īnfluere in (acc); **~ off with** abripere, abdūcere; **~ on** pergere; **~ out** (land) excurrere; (time) exīre; (supplies) dēficere; **~ over** vt (with car) obterere; (details) percurrere; **~ riot** luxuriārī; **~ through** (course) dēcurrere; (money) disperdere; **~ short** dēficere; **~ up to** adcurrere ad; **~ up against** incurrere in (acc); **~ wild** lascīvīre ♦ vt gerere, administrāre.
runaway adj fugitīvus.
rung n gradus m.
runner n cursor m.
running n cursus m ♦ adj (water) vīvus.
rupture n (fig) dissidium nt ♦ vt dīrumpere.
rural adj rūsticus, agrestis.

ruse n fraus f, dolus m.
rush n (plant) cārex f, iuncus m; (movement)
impetus m ♦ vi currere, sē incitāre, ruere; ~
forward sē prōripere; prōruere; ~ in inruere,
incurrere; ~ out ēvolāre, sē effundere ♦ adj
iunceus.
russet adj flāvus.
rust n (iron) ferrūgō f; (copper) aerūgō f ♦ vi
rōbīginem trahere.
rustic adj rūsticus, agrestis.
rusticate vi rūsticārī ♦ vt relēgāre.
rusticity n mōrēs rūsticī mpl.
rustle vi increpāre, crepitāre ♦ n crepitus m.
rusty adj rōbīginōsus.
rut n orbita f.
ruthless adj inexōrābilis, crūdēlis.
ruthlessly adv crūdēliter.
rye n secāle nt.

S, s

sabbath n sabbata ntpl.
sable adj āter, niger.
sabre n acīnacēs m.
sacerdotal adj sacerdōtālis.
sack n saccus m; (MIL) dīreptiō f ♦ vt dīripere,
expīlāre; spoliāre.
sackcloth n cilicium nt.
sacred adj sacer, sanctus.
sacredly adv sanctē.
sacredness n sanctitās f.
sacrifice n sacrificium nt, sacrum nt; (act)
immolātiō f; (victim) hostia f; (fig) iactūra f ♦
vt immolāre, sacrificāre, mactāre; (fig)
dēvovēre, addīcere ♦ vi sacra facere; (give
up) prōicere.
sacrificer n immolātor m.
sacrilege n sacrilegium nt.
sacrilegious adj sacrilegus.
sacristan n aedituus m.
sacrosanct adj sacrōsanctus.
sad adj maestus, tristis; (thing) tristis.
sadden vt dolōre adficere.
saddle n strātum nt ♦ vt sternere; (fig)
impōnere.
saddlebags n clītellae fpl.
sadly adv maestē.
sadness n tristitia f, maestitia f.
safe adj tūtus; (out of danger) incolumis,
salvus; (to trust) fīdus. ~ and sound salvus ♦
n armārium nt.
safe-conduct n fidēs pūblica f.
safeguard n cautiō f, prōpugnāculum nt ♦ vt
dēfendere.
safely adv tūtō, impūne.
safety n salūs f, incolumitās f;

seek ~ in flight salutem fugā petere.
saffron n crocus m ♦ adj croceus.
sag vi dēmittī.
sagacious adj prūdēns, sagāx, acūtus.
sagaciously adv prūdenter, sagāciter.
sagacity n prūdentia f, sagācitās f.
sage n sapiēns m; (herb) salvia f ♦ adj sapiēns.
sagely adv sapienter.
sail n vēlum nt; **set** ~ vēla dare, nāvem solvere;
shorten ~ vēla contrahere ♦ vi nāvigāre; ~
past legere, praetervehī.
sailing n nāvigātiō f.
sailor n nauta m.
sail yard n antenna f.
saint n vir sanctus m.
sainted adj beātus.
saintly adj sanctus.
sake n: for the ~ of grātiā (gen), causā (gen),
propter (acc); (behalf) prō (abl).
salacious adj salāx.
salad n morētum nt.
salamander n salamandra f.
salary n mercēs f.
sale n vēnditiō f; (formal) mancipium nt;
(auction) hasta f; **for** ~ vēnālis; **be for** ~
prōstāre; **offer for** ~ vēnum dare.
saleable adj vēndibilis.
salient adj ēminēns; ~ **points** capita ntpl.
saline adj salsus.
saliva n salīva f.
sallow adj pallidus.
sally n ēruptiō f; (wit) facētiae fpl ♦ vi
ērumpere, excurrere.
salmon n salmō m.
salon n ātrium nt.
salt n sal m ♦ adj salsus.
saltcellar n salīnum nt.
saltpetre n nitrum nt.
salt-pits n salīnae fpl.
salty adj salsus.
salubrious adj salūbris.
salubriously adv salūbriter.
salubriousness n salūbritās f.
salutary adj salūtāris, ūtilis.
salutation n salūs f.
salute vt salūtāre.
salvage vt servāre, ēripere.
salvation n salūs f.
salve n unguentum nt.
salver n scutella f.
same adj īdem; ~ **as** īdem ac; **all the** ~
nihilōminus; **one and the** ~ ūnus et īdem;
from the ~ **place** indidem; **in the** ~ **place**
ibīdem; **to the** ~ **place** eōdem; **at the** ~ **time**
simul, eōdem tempore; (adversative) tamen;
it is all the ~ **to me** meā nōn interest.
Samnites n Samnītēs, Samnītium mpl.
samp e n exemplum nt, specimen nt ♦ vt
gustāre.
sanctify vt cōnsecrāre.
sanctimony n falsa rēligiō f.
sanction n comprobātiō f, auctōritās f ♦ vt
ratum facere.

sanctity n sanctitās f.
sanctuary n fānum nt, dēlubrum nt; (*for men*) asȳlum nt.
sand n harēna f.
sandal n (*outdoors*) crepida f; (*indoors*) solea f.
sandalled adj crepidātus, soleātus.
sandpit n harēnāria f.
sandstone n tōfus m.
sandy adj harēnōsus; (*colour*) flāvus.
sane adj sānus.
sangfroid n aequus animus m.
sanguinary adj cruentus.
sanguine adj laetus.
sanitary adj salūbris.
sanity n mēns sāna f.
sap n sūcus m ♦ vt subruere.
sapience n sapientia f.
sapient adj sapiēns.
sapling n surculus m.
sapper n cunīculārius m.
sapphire n sapphīrus f.
sarcasm n aculeī mpl, dicācitās f.
sarcastic adj dicāx, acūleātus.
sardonic adj amārus.
sash n cingulum nt.
satchel n loculus m.
sate vt explēre, satiāre.
satellite n satelles m.
satiate vt explēre, satiāre, saturāre.
satiety n satietās f.
satire n satura f; (*pl, of Horace*) sermōnēs mpl.
satirical adj acerbus.
satirist n saturārum scrīptor m.
satirize vt perstringere, notāre.
satisfaction n (*act*) explētiō f; (*feeling*) voluptās f; (*penalty*) poena f; **demand** ~ **rēs** repetere.
satisfactorily adv ex sententiā.
satisfactory adj idōneus, grātus.
satisfied adj: **be** ~ satis habēre, contentum esse.
satisfy vt satisfacere (*dat*); (*desire*) explēre.
satrap n satrapēs m.
saturate vt imbuere.
satyr n satyrus m.
sauce n condīmentum nt; (*fish*) garum nt.
saucer n patella f.
saucily adv petulanter.
saucy adj petulāns.
saunter vi ambulāre.
sausage n tomāculum nt, hīllae fpl.
savage adj ferus, efferātus; (*cruel*) atrōx, inhūmānus; saevus.
savagely adv ferōciter, inhūmānē.
savagery n ferōcitās f, inhūmānitās f.
savant n vir doctus m.
save vt servāre; ~ **up** reservāre ♦ prep praeter (*acc*).
saving adj parcus; ~ **clause** exceptiō f ♦ r compendium nt; ~**s** pl peculium nt.
saviour n līberātor m.
savory n thymbra f.
savour n sapor m; (*of cooking*) nīdor m ♦ vi

sapere; ~ **of** olēre, redolēre.
savoury adj condītus.
saw n (*tool*) serra f; (*saying*) prōverbium nt ♦ vt serrā secāre.
sawdust n scobis f.
say vt dīcere; ~ **that** . . . **not** negāre; ~ **no** negāre; **he** ~**s** (*quoting*) inquit; **he** ~**s yes** āit; **they** ~ ferunt (+ acc and infin).
saying n dictum nt.
scab n (*disease*) scabiēs f; (*over wound*) crusta f.
scabbard n vāgīna f.
scabby adj scaber.
scaffold, scaffolding n fala f.
scald vt ūrere.
scale n (*balance*) lanx f; (*fish, etc*) squāma f; (*gradation*) gradūs mpl; (*music*) diagramma nt ♦ vt scālīs ascendere.
scallop n pecten m.
scalp n capitis cutis f.
scalpel n scalpellum nt.
scamp n verberō m.
scamper vi currere.
scan vt contemplārī; (*verse*) mētīrī.
scandal n īnfāmia f, opprobrium nt; (*talk*) calumnia f.
scandalize vt offendere.
scandalous adj flāgitiōsus, turpis.
scansion n syllabārum ēnārrātiō f.
scant adj exiguus, parvus.
scantily adv exiguē, tenuiter.
scantiness n exiguitās f.
scanty adj exiguus, tenuis, exīlis; (*number*) paucus.
scapegoat n piāculum nt.
scar n cicātrīx f.
scarce adj rārus; **make oneself** ~ sē āmovēre, dē mediō recēdere ♦ adv vix, aegrē.
scarcely adv vix, aegrē; ~ **anyone** nēmō ferē.
scarcity n inopia f, angustiae fpl.
scare n formīdō f ♦ vt terrēre; ~ **away** absterrēre.
scarecrow n formīdō f.
scarf n fōcāle nt.
scarlet n coccum nt ♦ adj coccinus.
scarp n rūpēs f.
scathe n damnum nt.
scatter vt spargere; dispergere, dissipāre; (*violently*) disicere ♦ vi diffugere.
scatterbrained adj dēsipiēns.
scattered adj rārus.
scene n spectāculum nt; (*place*) theātrum nt.
scenery n locī faciēs f, speciēs f; (*beautiful*) amoenitās f.
scent n odor m; (*sense*) odōrātus m; **keen** ~ sagācitās f ♦ vt odōrārī. (*perfume*) odōribus perfundere.
scented adj odōrātus.
sceptic n Pyrrhōnēus m.
sceptical adj incrēdulus.
sceptre n scēptrum nt.
schedule n tabulae fpl, ratiō f.
scheme n cōnsilium nt, ratiō f ♦ vt māchinārī,

mōlīrī.
schemer *n* māchinātor *m*.
schism *n* discidium *nt*, sēcessiō *f*.
scholar *n* vir doctus *m*, litterātus *m*; (*pupil*) discipulus *m*.
scholarly *adj* doctus, litterātus.
scholarship *n* litterae *fpl*, doctrīna *f*.
scholastic *adj* umbrātilis.
school *n* (*elementary*) lūdus *m*; (*advanced*) schola *f*; (*high*) gymnasium *nt*; (*sect*) secta *f*, domus *f* ♦ *vt* īnstituere.
schoolboy *n* discipulus *m*.
schoolmaster *n* magister *m*.
schoolmistress *n* magistra *f*.
science *n* doctrīna *f*, disciplīna *f*, ars *f*.
scimitar *n* acīnacēs *m*.
scintillate *vi* scintillāre.
scion *n* prōgeniēs *f*.
Scipio *n* Scīpiō, Scipiōnis *m*.
scissors *n* forfex *f*.
scoff *vi* irrīdēre; ~ **at** dērīdēre.
scoffer *n* irrīsor *m*.
scold *vt* increpāre, obiūrgāre.
scolding *n* obiūrgātiō *f*.
scoop *n* trulla *f* ♦ *vt*: ~ **out** excavāre.
scope *n* (*aim*) fīnis *m*; (*room*) locus *m*, campus *m*; **ample** ~ laxus locus.
scorch *vt* exūrere, torrēre.
scorched *adj* torridus.
score *n* (*mark*) nota *f*; (*total*) summa *f*; (*reckoning*) ratiō *f*; (*number*) vīgintī ♦ *vt* notāre ♦ *vi* vincere.
scorn *n* contemptiō *f* ♦ *vt* contemnere, spernere.
scorner *n* contemptor *m*.
scornful *adj* fastīdiōsus.
scornfully *adv* contemptim.
scorpion *n* scorpiō *m*, nepa *f*.
scot-free *adj* immūnis, impūnītus.
scoundrel *n* furcifer *m*.
scour *vt* (*clean*) tergēre; (*range*) percurrere.
scourge *n* flagellum *nt*; (*fig*) pestis *f* ♦ *vt* verberāre, virgīs caedere.
scout *n* explōrātor *m*, speculātor *m* ♦ *vi* explōrāre, speculārī ♦ *vt* spernere, repudiāre.
scowl *n* frontis contractiō *f* ♦ *vi* frontem contrahere.
scraggy *adj* strigōsus.
scramble *vi*: ~ **for** certātim captāre; ~ **up** scandere.
scrap *n* frūstum *nt*.
scrape *vt* rādere, scabere; ~ **off** abrādere.
scraper *n* strigilis *f*.
scratch *vt* rādere; (*head*) perfricāre; ~ **out** exsculpere, ērādere.
scream *n* clāmor *m*, ululātus *m* ♦ *vi* clāmāre, ululāre.
screech *n* ululātus *m* ♦ *vi* ululāre.
screen *n* obex *m/f*; (*from sun*) umbra *f*; (*fig*) vēlāmentum *nt* ♦ *vt* tegere.
screw *n* clāvus *m*; (*of winepress*) cochlea *f*.
scribble *vt* properē scrībere.

scribe *n* scrība *m*.
script *n* scrīptum *nt*; (*handwriting*) manus *f*.
scroll *n* volūmen *nt*.
scrub *vt* dētergēre, dēfricāre.
scruple *n* rēligiō *f*, scrūpulus *m*.
scrupulous *adj* rēligiōsus; (*careful*) dīligēns.
scrupulously *adv* rēligiōsē, dīligenter.
scrupulousness *n* rēligiō *f*; dīligentia *f*.
scrutinize *vt* scrūtārī, intrōspicere in (*acc*), excutere.
scrutiny *n* scrūtātiō *f*.
scud *vi* volāre.
scuffle *n* rixa *f*.
scull *n* calvāria *f*; (*oar*) rēmus *m*.
scullery *n* culīna *f*.
sculptor *n* fictor *m*, sculptor *m*.
sculpture *n* ars fingendī *f*; (*product*) statuae *fpl* ♦ *vt* sculpere.
scum *n* spūma *f*.
scurf *n* porrīgō *f*.
scurrility *n* maledicta *ntpl*.
scurrilous *adj* maledicus.
scurvy *adj* (*fig*) turpis, improbus.
scythe *n* falx *f*.
sea *n* mare *nt*; aequor *nt*; **open** ~ altum *nt*; **put to** ~ solvere; **be at** ~ nāvigāre; (*fig*) in errōre versārī ♦ *adj* marīnus; (*coast*) maritimus.
seaboard *n* lītus *nt*.
seafaring *adj* maritimus, nauticus.
seafight *n* nāvāle proelium *nt*.
seagull *n* larus *m*.
seal *n* (*animal*) phōca *f*; (*stamp*) signum *nt* ♦ *vt* signāre; ~ **up** obsignāre.
seam *n* sūtūra *f*.
seaman *n* nauta *m*.
seamanship *n* scientia et ūsus nauticārum rērum.
seaport *n* portus *m*.
sear *vt* adūrere, torrēre.
search *n* investigātiō *f* ♦ *vi* investīgāre, explōrāre ♦ *vt* excutere, scrūtārī; **in** ~ **of** causā (+ *gen*); ~ **for** quaerere, exquīrere, investīgāre; ~ **into** inquīrere, anquīrere; ~ **out** explōrāre, indāgāre.
searcher *n* inquīsītor *m*.
searching *adj* acūtus, dīligēns.
seashore *n* lītus *nt*.
seasick *adj*: **be** ~ nauseāre.
seasickness *n* nausea *f*.
seaside *n* mare *nt*.
season *n* annī tempus *nt*, tempestās *f*; (*right time*) tempus *nt*, opportūnitās *f*; **in** ~ tempestīvē ♦ *vt* condīre.
seasonable *adj* tempestīvus.
seasonably *adv* tempestīvē.
seasoned *adj* (*food*) condītus; (*wood*) dūrātus.
seasoning *n* condīmentum *nt*.
seat *n* sēdēs *f*; (*chair*) sedīle *nt*; (*home*) domus *f*, domicilium *nt*; **keep one's** ~ (*riding*) in equō haerēre ♦ *vt* collocāre; ~ **oneself** īnsidēre.
seated *adj*: **be** ~ sedēre.
seaweed *n* alga *f*.
seaworthy *adj* ad nāvigandum ūtilis.

secede vi sēcēdere.
secession n sēcessiō f.
seclude vt sēclūdere, abstrūdere.
secluded adj sēcrētus, remōtus.
seclusion n sōlitūdō f, sēcrētum nt.
second adj secundus, alter; **a ~ time** iterum ♦ n temporis pūnctum nt; (*person*) fautor m; **~ sight** hariolātiō f ♦ vt favēre (*dat*), adesse (*dat*).
secondary adj īnferior, dēterior.
seconder n fautor m.
second-hand adj aliēnus, trītus.
secondly adv deinde.
secrecy n sēcrētum nt, silentium nt.
secret adj secretus; occultus, arcānus; (*stealth*) fūrtīvus ♦ n arcānum nt; **keep ~** dissimulāre, cēlāre; **in ~** clam; **be ~** latēre.
secretary n scrība m, ab epistolīs, ā manū.
secrete vt cēlāre, abdere.
secretive adj tēctus.
secretly adv clam, occultē, sēcrētō.
sect n secta f, schola f, domus f.
section n pars f.
sector n regiō f.
secular adj profānus.
secure adj tūtus ♦ vt (*MIL*) firmāre, ēmūnīre; (*fasten*) religāre; (*obtain*) parāre, nancīscī.
securely adj tūtō.
security n salūs f, impūnitās f; (*money*) cautiō f, pignus nt, spōnsiō f; **sense of ~** sēcūritās f; **give good ~** satis dare; **on good ~** (*loan*) nōminibus rēctis cautus; **stand ~ for** praedem esse prō (*abl*).
sedan n lectīca f.
sedate adj placidus, temperātus, gravis.
sedately adv placidē.
sedateness n gravitās f.
sedge n ulva f.
sediment n faex f.
sedition n sēditiō f, mōtus m.
seditious adj sēditiōsus.
seditiously adv sēditiōsē.
seduce vt illicere, pellicere.
seducer n corruptor m.
seduction n corruptēla f.
seductive adj blandus.
seductively adv blandē.
sedulity n dīligentia f.
sedulous adj dīligēns, sēdulus.
sedulously adv dīligenter, sēdulō.
see vt vidēre, cernere; (*suddenly*) cōnspicārī; (*performance*) spectāre; (*with mind*) intellegere; **go and ~** vīsere, invīsere; **~ to** vidēre, cōnsulere (*dat*); curare (+ acc and gerundive); **~ through** dīspicere; **~ that you are** vidē ut sīs, fac sīs; **~ that you are not** vidē nē sīs, cavē sīs.
seed n sēmen nt; (*in a plant*) grānum nt; (*in fruit*) acinum nt; (*fig*) stirps f, prōgeniēs f.
seedling n surculus m.
seed-time n sēmentis f.
seeing that conj quōniam, siquidem.
seek vt petere, quaerere.

seeker n indāgātor m.
seem vi vidērī.
seeming adj speciōsus ♦ n speciēs f.
seemingly adv ut vidētur.
seemly adj decēns, decōrus; **it is ~** decet.
seep vi mānāre, percōlārī.
seer n vātēs m/f.
seethe vi fervēre.
segregate vt sēcernere, sēgregāre.
segregation n sēparātiō f.
seize vt rapere, corripere, adripere, prehendere; (*MIL*) occupāre; (*illness*) adficere; (*emotion*) invādere, occupāre.
seizure n ēreptiō f, occupātiō f.
seldom adv rārō.
select vt ēligere, excerpere, dēligere ♦ adj lēctus, ēlēctus.
selection n ēlēctiō f, dēlēctus m; (*LIT*) ecloga f.
self n ipse; (*reflexive*) sē; **a second ~** alter īdem.
self-centred adj glōriōsus.
self-confidence n cōnfīdentia f, fidūcia f.
self-confident adj cōnfīdēns.
self-conscious adj pudibundus.
self-control n temperantia f.
self-denial n abstinentia f.
self-evident adj manifestus; **it is ~** ante pedēs positum est.
self-governing adj līber.
self-government n lībertās f.
self-important adj adrogāns.
self-interest n ambitiō f.
selfish adj inhūmānus, avārus; **be ~** suā causā facere.
selfishly adv inhūmānē, avārē.
selfishness n inhūmānitās f, incontinentia f, avāritia f.
self-made adj (*man*) novus.
self-possessed adj aequō animō.
self-possession n aequus animus m.
self-reliant adj cōnfīdēns.
self-respect n pudor m.
self-restraint n modestia f.
self-sacrifice n dēvōtiō f.
selfsame adj ūnus et īdem.
sell vt vēndere; (*in lots*) dīvēndere; **be sold** vēnīre.
seller n vēnditor m.
selvage n limbus m.
semblance n speciēs f, imāgō f.
semicircle n hēmicyclium nt.
senate n senātus m; **hold a meeting of the ~** senātum habēre; **decree of the ~** senātus cōnsultum nt.
senate house n cūria f.
senator n senātor m; (*provincial*) decuriō m; **~s** pl patrēs mpl.
senatorial adj senātōrius.
send vt mittere; **~ across** trānsmittere; **~ ahead** praemittere; **~ away** dīmittere; **~ back** remittere; **~ for** arcessere; (*doctor*) adhibēre; **~ forth** ēmittere; **~ forward** praemittere; **~ in** immittere, intrōmittere; **~ out** ēmittere; (*in different directions*)

dīmittere; ~ **out of the way** ablēgāre; ~ **up**
submittere.
senile *adj* senīlis.
senility *n* senium *nt*.
senior *adj* nātū māior; (*thing*) prior.
sensation *n* sēnsus *m*; (*event*) rēs nova *f*; **lose** ~
obtorpēscere; **create a** ~ hominēs
obstupefacere.
sensational *adj* novus, prōdigiōsus.
sense *n* (*faculty*) sēnsus *m*; (*wisdom*) prūdentia
f; (*meaning*) vis *f*, sententia *f*; **common** ~
prūdentia *f*; **be in one's** ~**s** apud sē esse,
mentis suae esse; **out of one's** ~**s** dēmēns;
recover one's ~**s** resipīscere; **what is the** ~ **of**
quid sibī vult? ♦ *vt* sentīre.
senseless *adj* absurdus, ineptus, īnsipiēns.
senselessly *adv* īnsipienter.
senselessness *n* īnsipientia *f*.
sensibility *n* sēnsus *m*.
sensible *adj* prūdēns, sapiēns.
sensibly *adv* prūdenter, sapienter.
sensitive *adj* mollis, inrītābilis, patibilis.
sensitiveness *n* mollitia *f*.
sensual *adj* libīdinōsus.
sensuality *n* libīdō *f*, voluptās *f*.
sensually *adv* libīdinōsē.
sentence *n* (*judge*) iūdicium *nt*, sententia *f*;
(*GRAM*) sententia *f*; **pass** ~ iūdicāre; **execute** ~
lēge agere ♦ *vt* damnāre; ~ **to death** capitis
damnāre.
sententious *adj* sententiōsus.
sententiously *adv* sententiōsē.
sentient *adj* patibilis.
sentiment *n* (*feeling*) sēnsus *m*; (*opinion*)
sententia *f*; (*emotion*) mollitia *f*.
sentimental *adj* mollis, flēbilis.
sentimentality *n* mollitia *f*.
sentimentally *adv* molliter.
sentries *npl* statiōnēs *fpl*, excubiae *fpl*.
sentry *n* custōs *m*, vigil *m*; **be on** ~ **duty in**
statiōne esse.
separable *adj* dīviduus, sēparābilis.
separate *vt* sēparāre, dīvidere, disiungere;
(*forcibly*) dīrimere, dīvellere ♦ *vi* dīgredī ♦
adj sēparātus, sēcrētus.
separately *adv* sēparātim, seōrsum.
separation *n* sēparātiō *f*; (*violent*) discidium
nt.
September *n* mēnsis September *m*; **of** ~
September.
sepulchral *adj* fūnebris.
sepulchre *n* sepulcrum *nt*.
sepulture *n* sepultūra *f*.
sequel *n* exitus *m*, quae sequuntur.
sequence *n* seriēs *f*, ōrdō *m*.
sequestered *adj* sēcrētus.
serenade *vt* occentāre.
serene *adj* tranquillus, sēcūrus.
serenely *adv* tranquillē.
serenity *n* sēcūritās *f*.
serf *n* servus *m*.
serfdom *n* servitūs *f*.
sergeant *n* signifer *m*.

series *n* seriēs *f*, ōrdō *m*.
serious *adj* gravis, sērius, sevērus.
seriously *adv* graviter, sēriō, sevērē.
seriousness *n* gravitās *f*.
sermon *n* ōrātiō *f*.
serpent *n* serpēns *f*.
serpentine *adj* tortuōsus.
serrated *adj* serrātus.
serried *adj* cōnfertus.
servant *n* (*domestic*) famulus *m*, famula *f*;
(*public*) minister *m*, ministra *f*; **family** ~**s**
familia *f*.
servant maid *n* ancilla *f*.
serve *vt* servīre (*dat*); (*food*) ministrāre,
adpōnere; (*interest*) condūcere (*dat*) ♦ *vi* (*MIL*)
stīpendia merēre, mīlitāre; (*suffice*)
sufficere; ~ **as** esse prō (*abl*); ~ **in the cavalry**
equō merēre; ~ **in the infantry** pedibus
merēre; **having** ~**d one's time** ēmeritus; ~ **a**
sentence poenam subīre; ~ **well** bene merērī
dē (*abl*).
service *n* (*status*) servitium *nt*, famulātus *m*;
(*work*) ministerium *nt*; (*help*) opera *f*; (*by an*
equal) meritum *nt*, beneficium *nt*; (*MIL*) mīlitia
f, stīpendia *ntpl*; **be of** ~ **to** prōdesse (*dat*),
bene merērī dē; **I am at your** ~ adsum tibī;
complete one's ~ stīpendia ēmerērī.
serviceable *adj* ūtilis.
servile *adj* servīlis; (*fig*) abiectus, humilis.
servility *n* adūlātiō *f*.
servitude *n* servitūs *f*.
session *n* conventus *m*; **be in** ~ sedēre.
sesterce *n* sēstertius *m*; **10** ~**s** decem sēstertiī;
10,000 ~**s** dēna sēstertia *ntpl*; **1,000,000** ~**s**
deciēs sēstertium.
set *vt* pōnere, locāre, statuere, sistere; (*bone*)
condere; (*course*) dīrigere; (*example*) dare;
(*limit*) impōnere; (*mind*) intendere; (*music*)
modulārī; (*sail*) dare; (*sentries*) dispōnere;
(*table*) īnstruere; (*trap*) parāre ♦ *vi* (*ASTRO*)
occidere; ~ **about** incipere; ~ **against**
oppōnere; ~ **apart** sēpōnere; ~ **aside**
sēpōnere; ~ **down** (*writing*) perscrībere; ~
eyes on cōnspicere; ~ **foot on** ingredī; ~ **forth**
expōnere, ēdere; ~ **free** līberāre; ~ **in motion**
movēre; ~ **in order** compōnere, dispōnere; ~
off (*decoration*) distinguere; (*art*) illūmināre;
~ **on** (*to attack*) immittere; ~ **on foot**
īnstituere; ~ **on fire** incendere; ~ **one's heart**
on exoptāre; ~ **out** *vi* proficīscī; ~ **over**
praeficere, impōnere; ~ **up** statuere; (*fig*)
cōnstituere.
set *adj* (*arrangement*) status; (*purpose*) certus;
(*rule*) praescrīptus; (*speech*) compositus; **of** ~
purpose cōnsultō ♦ *n* (*persons*) numerus *m*;
(*things*) congeriēs *f*; (*current*) cursus *m*.
setback *n* repulsa *f*.
settee *n* lectulus *m*.
setting *n* (*ASTRO*) occāsus *m*; (*event*) locus *m*.
settle *n* sella *f* ♦ *vt* statuere; (*annuity*)
praestāre; (*business*) trānsigere; (*colony*)
dēdūcere; (*debt*) exsolvere; (*decision*)
cōnstituere; (*dispute*) dēcīdere, compōnere

settled–shelve

♦ vi (abode) cōnsīdere; (agreement)
cōnstituere, convenīre; (sediment) dēsīdere;
~ in īnsidēre (dat).
settled adj certus, explōrātus.
settlement n (of a colony) dēductiō f; (colony)
colōnia f; (of dispute) dēcīsiō f, compositiō f;
(to wife) dōs f.
settler n colōnus m.
set to n pugna f.
seven num septem; ~ each septēnī; ~ times
septiēns.
seven hundred num septingentī.
seven hundredth adj septingentēsimus.
seventeen num septendecim.
seventeenth adj septimus decimus.
seventh adj septimus; for the ~ time
septimum.
seventieth adj septuāgēsimus.
seventy num septuāgintā; ~ each septuāgēnī; ~
times septuāgiēns.
sever vt incīdere, sēparāre, dīvidere.
several adj complūrēs, aliquot.
severally adv singulī.
severe adj gravis, sevērus, dūrus; (style)
austērus; (weather) asper; (pain) ācer,
gravis.
severely adv graviter, sevērē.
severity n gravitās f, asperitās f, sevēritās f.
sew vt suere; ~ up cōnsuere; ~ up in īnsuere in
(acc).
sewer n cloāca f.
sex n sexus m.
shabbily adv sordidē.
shabbiness n sordēs fpl.
shabby adj sordidus.
shackle n compēs f, vinculum nt ♦ vt impedīre,
vincīre.
shade n umbra f; (colour) color m; ~s pl mānēs
mpl; put in the ~ officere (dat) ♦ vt opācāre,
umbram adferre (dat).
shadow n umbra f.
shadowy adj obscūrus; (fig) inānis.
shady adj umbrōsus, opācus.
shaft n (missile) tēlum nt, sagitta f; (of spear)
hastīle nt; (of cart) tēmō m; (of light) radius m;
(excavation) puteus m.
shaggy adj hirsūtus.
shake vt quatere, agitāre; (structure)
labefacere, labefactāre; (belief) īnfirmāre;
(resolution) labefactāre, commovēre; ~
hands with dextram dare (dat) ♦ vi quatī,
agitārī, tremere, horrēscere; ~ off dēcutere,
excutere; ~ out excutere.
shaking n tremor m.
shaky adj īnstābilis, tremebundus.
shall aux vb = fut indic.
shallot n caepa Ascalōnia f.
shallow adj brevis, vadōsus; (fig) levis.
shallowness n vada ntpl; (fig) levitās f.
shallows n brevia ntpl, vada ntpl.
sham adj fictus, falsus, fūcōsus ♦ n simulātiō f,
speciēs f ♦ vt simulāre.
shambles n laniēna f.

shame n (feeling) pudor m; (cause) dēdecus nt,
ignōminia f; it ~s pudet (+ acc of person, gen of
thing); it is a ~ flāgitium est ♦ vt rubōrem
incutere (dat) ♦ interj prō pudor!
shamefaced adj verēcundus.
shameful adj ignōminiōsus, turpis.
shamefully adv turpiter.
shameless adj impudēns.
shamelessly adv impudenter.
shamelessness n impudentia f.
shank n crūs nt.
shape n fōrma f, figūra f ♦ vt fōrmāre, fingere;
(fig) īnfōrmāre ♦ vi: ~ well prōficere.
shapeless adj īnfōrmis, dēfōrmis.
shapelessness n dēfōrmitās f.
shapeliness n fōrma f.
shapely adj fōrmōsus.
shard n testa f.
share n pars f; (plough) vōmer m; go ~s with
inter sē partīrī ♦ vt (give) partīrī, impertīre;
(have) commūnicāre, participem esse (gen).
sharer n particeps m/f, socius m.
shark n volpēs marīna f.
sharp adj acūtus; (fig) ācer, acūtus; (bitter)
amarus.
sharpen vt acuere; (fig) exacuere.
sharply adv ācriter, acūtē.
sharpness n aciēs f; (mind) acūmen nt,
argūtiae fpl; (temper) acerbitās f.
shatter vt quassāre, perfringere, adflīgere;
(fig) frangere.
shave vt rādere; ~ off abrādere.
shavings n rāmenta ntpl.
she pron haec, ea, illa.
sheaf n manipulus m.
shear vt tondēre, dētondēre.
shears n forficēs fpl.
sheath n vāgīna f.
sheathe vt recondere.
shed vt fundere; (blood) effundere; (one's
own) profundere; (tears) effundere;
(covering) exuere; ~ light on (fig) lūmen
adhibēre (dat).
sheen n nitor m.
sheep n ovis f; (flock) pecus nt.
sheepfold n ovīle nt.
sheepish adj pudibundus.
sheepishly adv pudenter.
sheer adj (absolute) merus; (steep) praeruptus.
sheet n (cloth) linteum nt; (metal) lāmina f;
(paper) carta f, scheda f; (sail) pēs m; (water)
aequor nt.
shelf n pluteus m, pēgma nt.
shell n concha f; (egg) putāmen nt; (tortoise)
testa f.
shellfish n conchȳlium nt.
shelter n suffugium nt, tegmen nt; (refuge)
perfugium nt, asȳlum nt; (lodging) hospitium
nt; (fig) umbra f ♦ vt tegere, dēfendere;
(refugee) excipere ♦ vi latēre; ~ behind (fig)
dēlitēscere in (abl).
sheltered adj (life) umbrātilis.
shelve vt differre ♦ vi sē dēmittere.

shelving *adj* dēclīvis.
shepherd *n* pastor *m*.
shield *n* scūtum *nt*; clipeus *m*; (*small*) parma *f*; (*fig*) praesidium *nt* ♦ *vt* prōtegere, dēfendere.
shift *n* (*change*) mūtātiō *f*; (*expedient*) ars *f*, dolus *m*; **make ~ to** efficere ut; **in ~s** per vicēs ♦ *vt* mūtāre; (*move*) movēre ♦ *vi* mūtārī; discēdere.
shiftless *adj* iners, inops.
shifty *adj* vafer, versūtus.
shilling *n* solidus *m*.
shimmer *vi* micāre ♦ *n* tremulum lūmen *nt*.
shin *n* tībia *f*.
shine *vi* lūcēre, fulgēre; (*reflecting*) nitēre; (*fig*) ēminēre; **~ forth** ēlūcēre, ēnitēre; effulgēre; **~ upon** adfulgēre (*dat*) ♦ *n* nitor *m*.
shingle *n* lapillī *mpl*, glārea *f*.
shining *adj* lūcidus, splendidus; (*fig*) illūstris.
shiny *adj* nitidus.
ship *n* nāvis *f*; **admiral's ~** nāvis praetōria; **decked ~** nāvis tēcta, nāvis cōnstrāta ♦ *vt* (*cargo*) impōnere; (*to a place*) nāvī invehere.
shipowner *n* nāviculārius *m*.
shipping *n* nāvēs *fpl*.
shipwreck *n* naufragium *nt*; **suffer ~** naufragium facere.
shipwrecked *adj* naufragus.
shirk *vt* dēfugere, dētrectāre.
shirt *n* subūcula *f*.
shiver *n* horror *m* ♦ *vi* horrēre, tremere ♦ *vt* perfringere, comminuere.
shivering *n* horror *m*.
shoal *n* (*fish*) exāmen *nt*; (*water*) vadum *nt*; **~s** *pl* brevia *ntpl*.
shock *n* impulsus *m*; (*battle*) concursus *m*, cōnflīctus *m*; (*hair*) caesariēs *f*; (*mind*) offēnsiō *f* ♦ *vt* percutere, offendere.
shocking *adj* atrōx, dētestābilis, flāgitiōsus.
shoddy *adj* vīlis.
shoe *n* calceus *m*.
shoemaker *n* sūtor *m*.
shoot *n* surculus *m*; (*vine*) pampinus *m* ♦ *vi* frondēscere; (*movement*) volāre; **~ up** ēmicāre ♦ *vt* (*missile*) conicere, iaculārī; (*person*) iaculārī, trānsfīgere.
shop *n* taberna *f*.
shore *n* lītus *nt*, ōra *f* ♦ *vt* fulcīre.
short *adj* brevis; (*broken*) curtus; (*amount*) exiguus; **for a ~ time** parumper, paulisper; **~ of** (*number*) intrā (*acc*); **be ~ of** indigēre (*abl*); **cut ~** interpellāre; **in ~** ad summam, dēnique; **very ~** perbrevis; **fall ~ of** nōn pervenīre ad, abesse ab; **run ~** dēficere; **to cut a long story ~** nē multīs morer, nē multa.
shortage *n* inopia *f*.
shortcoming *n* dēlictum *nt*, culpa *f*.
short cut *n* via compendiāria *f*.
shorten *vt* curtāre, imminuere, contrahere; (*sail*) legere.
shorthand *n* notae *fpl*.
shorthand writer *n* āctuārius *m*.
short-lived *adj* brevis.

shortly *acv* (*time*) brevī; (*speak*) breviter; **~ after** paulō post, nec multō post.
shortness *n* brevitās *f*, exiguitās *f*; (*difficulty*) angustiae *fpl*.
short-sighted *adj* (*fig*) imprōvidus, imprūdēns.
short-sightedness *n* imprūdentia *f*.
short-tempered *adj* īrācundus.
shot *n* ictus *m*; (*range*) iactus *m*.
should *vi* (*duty*) dēbēre.
shoulder *n* umerus *m*; (*animal*) armus *m* ♦ *vt* (*burden*) suscipere.
shout *n* clāmor *m*, adclāmātiō *f* ♦ *vt*, *vi* clāmāre, vōciferārī; **~ down** obstrepere (*dat*); **~ out** exclāmāre.
shove *vt* trūdere, impellere.
shovel *n* rutrum *nt*.
show *n* speciēs *f*; (*entertainment*) lūdī *mpl*, spectāculum *nt*; (*stage*) lūdicrum *nt*; **for ~** in speciem; **put on a ~** spectācula dare ♦ *vt* mōnstrāre, indicāre, ostendere, ostentāre; (*point out*) dēmōnstrāre; (*qualities*) praestāre; **~ off** *vi* sē iactāre ♦ *vt* ostentāre.
shower *n* imber *m* ♦ *vt* fundere, conicere.
showery *adj* pluvius.
showiness *n* ostentātiō *f*.
showing off *n* iactātiō *f*.
showy *adj* speciōsus.
shred *n* fragmentum *nt*; **in ~s** minūtātim; **tear to ~s** dīlaniāre ♦ *vt* concīdere.
shrew *n* virāgō *f*.
shrewd *adj* acūtus, ācer, sagāx.
shrewdly *adv* acūtē, sagāciter.
shrewdness *n* acūmen *nt*, sagācitās *f*.
shriek *n* ululātus *m* ♦ *vi* ululāre.
shrill *adj* acūtus, argūtus.
shrine *n* fānum *nt*, dēlubrum *nt*.
shrink *vt* contrahere ♦ *vi* contrahī; **~ from** abhorrēre ab, refugere ab, dētrectāre.
shrivel *vt* corrūgāre ♦ *vi* exārēscere.
shroud *n* integumentum *nt*; **~s** *pl* rudentēs *mpl* ♦ *vt* involvere.
shrub *n* frutex *m*.
shrubbery *n* fruticētum *nt*.
shudder *n* horror *m* ♦ *vi* exhorrēscere; **~ at** horrēre.
shuffle *vt* miscēre ♦ *vi* claudicāre; (*fig*) tergiversārī.
shun *vt* vītāre, ēvītāre, dēfugere.
shut *vt* claudere; (*with cover*) operīre; (*hand*) comprimere; **~ in** inclūdere; **~ off** interclūdere; **~ out** exclūdere; **~ up** inclūdere.
shutter *n* foricula *f*, lūmināre *nt*.
shuttle *n* radius *m*.
shy *adj* timidus, pudibundus, verēcundus.
shyly *adv* timidē, verēcundē.
shyness *n* verēcundia *f*.
sibyl *n* sibylla *f*.
sick *adj* aeger, aegrōtus; **be ~** aegrōtāre; **feel ~** nauseāre; **I am ~ of** mē taedet (*gen*).
sicken *v* fastīdium movēre (*dat*) ♦ *vi* nauseāre, aegrōtāre.

sickle n falx f.
sickly adj invalidus.
sickness n nausea f; (illness) morbus m, aegritūdō f.
side n latus nt; (direction) pars f; (faction) partēs fpl; (kin) genus nt; **on all ~s** undique; **on both ~s** utrimque; **on one ~ unā ex parte**; **on our ~** ā nōbis; **be on the ~ of** stāre ab, sentī-e cum; **on the far ~ of** ultrā (acc); **on this ~** hīac; **on this ~ of** cis (acc), citrā (acc) ♦ vi: **~ with** stāre ab, facere cum.
sideboard n abacus m.
sidelong adj oblīquus.
sideways adv oblīquē, in oblīquum.
sidle vi oblīquō corpore incēdere.
siege n obsidiō f, oppugnātiō f; **lay ~ to** obsidēre.
siege works n opera ntpl.
siesta n merīdiātiō f; **take a ~** merīdiāre.
sieve n crībrum nt.
sigh n suspīrium nt; (loud) gemitus m ♦ vi suspīrāre, gemere.
sight n (sense) vīsus m; (process) aspec-us m; (range) cōnspectus m; (thing seen) spectāculum nt, speciēs f; **at ~ ex tempore**; **at first ~ prīmō aspectū**; **in ~ in cōnspectū**; **come into ~ in cōnspectum sē dare**; **in the ~ of in oculīs** (gen); **catch ~ of cōnspicere**; **lose ~ of ē cōnspectū āmittere**; (fig) oblīvīscī (gen) ♦ vt cōnspicārī.
sightless adj caecus.
sightly adj decōrus.
sign n signum nt, indicium nt; (distinctio) īnsigne nt; (mark) nota f; (trace) vestīgium nt; (proof) documentum nt; (portent) ōmen nt; (Zodiac) signum nt; **give a ~ innuere** ♦ vi signum dare, innuere ♦ vt subscrībere (dat); (as witness) obsignāre.
signal n signum nt; **give the ~ for retreat receptuī canere** ♦ vi signum dare ♦ adj īnsignis, ēgregius.
signalize vt nōbilitāre.
signally adv ēgregiē.
signature n nōmen nt, manus f, chīrographum nt.
signet n signum nt.
signet ring n anulus m.
significance n interpretātiō f, significātiō f, vīs f; (importance) pondus nt.
significant adj gravis, clārus.
signification n significātiō f.
signify vt significāre, velle; (omen) portendere; **it does not ~ nōn interest**.
silence n silentium nt; **in ~ per silentium** ♦ vt comprimere; (argument) refūtāre.
silent adj tacitus; (habit) taciturnus; **be ~ silēre, tacēre**; **be ~ about silēre, tacēre**; **become ~ conticēscere**.
silently adv tacitē.
silhouette n adumbrātiō f.
silk n bombȳx m; (clothes) sērica ntpl ♦ adj bombȳcinus, sēricus.
silken adj bombȳcinus.

sill n līmen nt.
silliness n stultitia f, ineptiae fpl.
silly adj fatuus, ineptus; stultus; **be ~ dēsipere**.
silt n līmus m.
silver n argentum nt ♦ adj argenteus.
silver mine n argentāria f.
silver plate n argentum nt.
silver-plated adj argentātus.
silvery adj argenteus.
similar adj similis.
similarity n similitūdō f.
similarly adv similiter.
simile n similitūdō f.
simmer vi lēniter fervēre.
simper vi molliter subrīdēre.
simple adj simplex; (mind) fatuus; (task) facilis.
simpleton n homō ineptus m.
simplicity n simplicitās f; (mind) stultitia f.
simplify vt faciliōrem reddere.
simply adv simpliciter; (merely) sōlum, tantum.
simulate vt simulāre.
simulation n simulātiō f.
simultaneously adv simul, ūnā, eōdem tempore.
sin n peccātum nt, nefās nt, dēlictum nt ♦ vi peccāre.
since adv abhinc; **long ~ iamdūdum** ♦ conj (time) ex quō tempore, postquam; (reason) cum (+ subj), quōniam; **~ he quippe quī** ♦ prep ab (abl), ex (abl), post (acc); **ever ~ usque ab**.
sincere adj sincērus, simplex, apertus.
sincerely adv sincērē, ex animō.
sincerity n fidēs f, simplicitās f.
sinew n nervus m.
sinewy adj nervōsus.
sinful adj improbus, impius, incestus.
sinfully adv improbē, impiē.
sing vt canere, cantāre; **~ of canere**.
singe vt adūrere.
singer n cantor m.
singing n cantus m ♦ adj canōrus.
single adj ūnus, sōlus, ūnicus; (unmarried) caelebs ♦ vt: **~ out ēligere, excerpere**.
single-handed adj ūnus.
singly adv singillātim, singulī.
singular adj singulāris; (strange) novus.
singularly adv singulāriter, praecipuē.
sinister adj īnfaustus, malevolus.
sink vi dēsīdere; (in water) dēmergī; **~ in inlābī, īnsīdere** ♦ vt dēprimere, mergere; (well) fodere; (fig) dēmergere.
sinless adj integer, innocēns, castus.
sinner n peccātor m.
sinuous adj sinuōsus.
sip vt gustāre, lībāre.
siphon n siphō m.
sir n (to master) ere; (to equal) vir optime; (title) eques m.
sire n pater m.
siren n sīrēn f.

sirocco n Auster m.
sister n soror f; ~'s sorōrius.
sisterhood n germānitās f; (*society*) sorōrum societās f.
sister-in-law n glōs f.
sisterly adj sorōrius.
sit vi sedēre; ~ **beside** adsidēre (*dat*); ~ **down** cōnsīdere; ~ **on** īnsidēre (*dat*); (*eggs*) incubāre; ~ **at table** accumbere; ~ **up** (*at night*) vigilāre.
site n situs m, locus m; (*for building*) ārea f.
sitting n sessiō f.
situated adj situs.
situation n situs m; (*CIRCS*) status m, condiciō f.
six num sex; ~ **each** sēnī; ~ **or seven** sex septem; ~ **times** sexiēns.
six hundred num sēscentī; ~ **each** sēscēnī; ~ **times** sēscentiēns.
six hundredth adj sēscentēsimus.
sixteen num sēdecim; ~ **each** sēnī dēnī; ~ **times** sēdeciēns.
sixteenth adj sextus decimus.
sixth adj sextus; **for the** ~ **time** sextum.
sixtieth adj sexagēsimus.
sixty num sexāgintā; ~ **each** sexāgēnī; ~ **times** sexāgiēns.
size n māgnitūdō f, amplitūdō f; (*measure*) mēnsūra f, fōrma f.
skate vi per glaciem lābī; ~ **on thin ice** (*fig*) incēdere per ignēs suppositōs cinerī dolōsō.
skein n glomus nt.
skeleton n ossa ntpl.
sketch n adumbrātiō f, dēscrīptiō f ♦ vt adumbrāre, īnfōrmāre.
skewer n verū nt.
skiff n scapha f, lēnunculus m.
skilful adj perītus, doctus, scītus; (*with hands*) habilis.
skilfully adv perītē, doctē; habiliter.
skill n ars f, perītia f, sollertia f.
skilled adj perītus, doctus; ~ **in** perītus (+ gen).
skim vt dēspūmāre; ~ **over** (*fig*) legere, perstringere.
skin n cutis f; (*animal*) pellis f ♦ vt pellem dētrahere (*dat*).
skinflint n avārus m.
skinny adj macer.
skip vi exsultāre ♦ vt praeterīre.
skipper n magister m.
skirmish n leve proelium nt ♦ vi vēlitārī.
skirmisher n vēles m, excursor m.
skirt n īnstita f; (*border*) limbus m ♦ vt contingere (*dat*); (*motion*) legere.
skittish adj lascīvus.
skulk vi latēre, dēlitēscere.
skull n caput nt.
sky n caelum nt; **of the** ~ caelestis.
skylark n alauda f.
slab n tabula f.
slack adj remissus, laxus; (*work*) piger, neglegēns.
slacken vt remittere, dētendere ♦ vi laxārī.
slackness n remissiō f; pigritia f.

slag n scōria f.
slake vt restinguere, sēdāre.
slam vt adflīgere.
slander n maledicta ntpl, obtrectātiō f; (*law*) calumnia f ♦ vt maledīcere (*dat*), īnfāmāre, obtrectāre (*dat*).
slanderer n obtrectātor m.
slanderous adj maledicus.
slang n vulgāria verba ntpl.
slant vi in trānsversum īre.
slanting adj oblīquus, trānsversus.
slantingly adv oblīquē, ex trānsversō.
slap n alapa f ♦ vt palmā ferīre.
slapdash adj praeceps, temerārius.
slash vt caedere ♦ n ictus m.
slate n (*roof*) tēgula f; (*writing*) tabula f ♦ vt increpāre.
slatternly adj sordidus, incōmptus.
slaughter n caedēs f, strāgēs f ♦ vt trucīdāre.
slaughterhouse n laniēna f.
slave n servus m; (*domestic*) famulus m; (*home-born*) verna m; **be a** ~ **to** īnservīre (*dat*); **household** ~s familia f.
slave girl n ancilla f.
slavery n servitūs f.
slavish adj servīlis.
slavishly adv servīliter.
slay vt interficere, occīdere.
slayer n interfector m.
sleek adj nitidus, pinguis.
sleep n somnus m; **go to** ~ obdormīscere ♦ vi dormīre; ~ **off** vt ēdormīre.
sleeper n dormītor m.
sleepiness n sopor m.
sleepless adj īnsomnis, vigil.
sleeplessness n īnsomnia f.
sleepy adj somniculōsus; **be** ~ dormītāre.
sleeve n manica f.
sleight of hand n praestīgiae fpl.
slender adj gracilis, exīlis.
slenderness n gracilitās f.
slice n frūstum nt ♦ vt secāre.
slide n lāpsus m ♦ vi lābī.
slight adj levis, exiguus, parvus ♦ n neglegentia f ♦ vt neglegere, offendere.
slightingly adv contemptim.
slightly adv leviter, paululum.
slightness n levitās f.
slim adj gracilis.
slime n līmus m.
slimness n gracilitās f.
slimy adj līmōsus, mūcōsus.
sling n funda f ♦ vt mittere, iaculārī.
slinger n funditor m.
slink vi sē subducere.
slip n lāpsus m; (*mistake*) offēnsiuncula f; (*plant*) surculus m ♦ vi lābī; ~ **away** ēlābī, dīlābī; ~ **out** ēlābī; (*word*) excidere; **give the** ~ **to** ēlūdere; **let** ~ āmittere, ōmittere; **there's many a** ~ **twixt the cup and the lip** inter ōs et offam multa interveniunt.
slipper n solea f.

slippery adj lūbricus.
slipshod adj neglegēns.
slit n rīma f ♦ vt findere, incīdere.
sloe n spīnus m.
slope n dēclīve nt, clīvus m; (steep) dēiectus m
 ♦ vi sē dēmittere, vergere.
sloping adj dēclīvis, dēvexus; (up) adclīvis.
slot n rīma f.
sloth n inertia f, segnitia f, dēsidia f, ignāvia f.
slothful adj ignāvus, iners, segnis.
slothfully adv ignāvē, segniter.
slouch vi languidē incēdere.
slough n (skin) exuviae fpl; (bog) palūs f.
slovenliness n ignāvia f, sordēs fpl.
slovenly adj ignāvus, sordidus.
slow adj tardus, lentus; (mind) hebes
slowly adv tardē, lentē.
slowness n tarditās f.
sludge n līmus m.
slug n līmāx f.
sluggard n homō ignāvus m.
sluggish adj piger, segnis; (mind) hebes.
sluggishly adv pigrē, segniter.
sluggishness n pigritia f, inertia f.
sluice n cataracta f.
slumber n somnus m, sopor m ♦ vi dormīre.
slump n vīlis annōna f.
slur n nota f; cast ~ on dētrectāre ♦ vt: ~ words
 balbūtīre.
sly adj astūtus, vafer, callidus; on the ~ ex
 opīnātō.
slyly adv astūtē, callidē.
slyness n astūtia f.
smack n (blow) ictus m; (with hand) alapa f;
 (boat) lēnunculus m; (taste) sapor m ♦ vt
 ferīre ♦ vi: ~ of olēre, redolēre.
small adj parvus, exiguus; how ~ quantulus,
 quantillus; so ~ tantulus; very ~ perexiguus,
 minimus; a ~ meeting of īnfrequēns.
smaller adj minor.
smallest adj minimus.
smallness n exiguitās f, brevitās f.
small talk n sermunculus m.
smart adj (action) ācer, alacer; (dress)
 concinnus, nitidus; (pace) vēlōx; (wit)
 facētus, salsus ♦ n dolor m ♦ vi dolēre (fig)
 ūrī, mordērī.
smartly adv ācriter; nitidē; vēlōciter; facētē.
smartness n alacritās f; (dress) nitor m; (wit)
 facētiae fpl, sollertia f.
smash n ruīna f ♦ vt frangere, comminuere.
smattering n: get a ~ of odōrārī, prīmīs labrīs
 attingere; with a ~ of imbūtus (abl).
smear vt oblinere, ungere.
smell n (sense) odōrātus m; (odour) odor m; (of
 cooking) nīdor m ♦ vt olfacere, odōrārī ♦ vi
 olēre.
smelly adj olidus.
smelt vt fundere.
smile n rīsus m ♦ vi subrīdēre; ~ at adrīdēre
 (dat); ~ upon rīdēre ad; (fig) secundum esse
 (dat).
smiling adj laetus.

smirk vi subrīdēre.
smith n faber m.
smithy n fabrica f.
smock n tunica f.
smoke n fūmus m ♦ vi fūmāre.
smoky adj fūmōsus.
smooth adj lēvis; (skin) glaber; (talk) blandus;
 (sea) placidus; (temper) aequus; (voice) lēvis,
 teres ♦ vt sternere, līmāre.
smoothly adv lēviter, lēniter.
smoothness n lēvitās f, lēnitās f.
smother vt opprimere, suffocāre.
smoulder vi fūmāre.
smudge n macula f.
smug adj suī contentus.
smuggle vt fūrtim importāre.
smugness n amor suī m.
smut n fūlīgō f.
snack n cēnula f; take a ~ gustāre.
snag n impedīmentum nt, scrūpulus m.
snail n cochlea f.
snake n anguis m, serpēns f.
snaky adj vīpereus.
snap vt rumpere, praerumpere; ~ the fingers
 digitīs concrepāre ♦ vi rumpī, dissilīre; ~ at
 mordēre; ~ up corripere.
snare n laqueus m, plaga f, pedica f ♦ vt inrētīre.
snarl n gannītus m ♦ vi gannīre.
snatch vt rapere, ēripere, adripere,
 corripere; ~ at captāre.
sneak n perfidus m ♦ vi conrēpere; ~ in sē
 īnsinuāre; ~ out ēlābī.
sneaking adj humilis, fūrtīvus.
sneer n irrīsiō f ♦ vi irrīdēre, dērīdēre.
sneeze n sternūtāmentum nt ♦ vi sternuere.
sniff vt odōrārī.
snip vt praecīdere, secāre.
snob n homō ambitiōsus m.
snood n mitra f.
snooze vi dormītāre.
snore vi stertere.
snoring n rhoncus m.
snort n fremitus m ♦ vi fremere.
snout n rōstrum nt.
snow n nix f ♦ vi ningere; ~ed under nive
 obrutus; it is ~ing ningit.
snowy adj nivālis; (colour) niveus.
snub vt neglegere, praeterīre.
snub-nosed adj sīmus.
snuff n (candle) fungus m.
snug adj commodus.
snugly adv commodē.
so adv (referring back) sīc; (referring forward) ita;
 (with adj and adv) tam; (with verb) adeō;
 (consequence) ergō, itaque, igitur; and ~
 itaque; ~ great tantus; so-so sīc; ~ as to ut; ~
 be it estō; ~ big tantus; ~ far usque adeō,
 adhūc; ~ far as quod; ~ far from adeō nōn; ~
 little tantillus; ~ long as dum; ~ many tot; ~
 much adj tantus ♦ adv tantum; (with compar)
 tantō; ~ often totiēns; ~ that ut (+ subj); ~ that
 ... not (purpose) nē; (result) ut nōn; and ~ on
 deinceps; not ~ very haud ita; say ~ id dīcere.

soak *vt* imbuere, madefacere.
soaking *adj* madidus.
soap *n* sapō *m*.
soar *vi* in sublīme ferrī, subvolāre; ~ **above** superāre.
sob *n* singultus *m* ♦ *vi* singultāre.
sober *adj* sobrius; (*conduct*) modestus; (*mind*) sānus.
soberly *adv* sobriē, modestē.
sobriety *n* modestia *f*, continentia *f*.
so-called *adj* quī dīcitur.
sociability *n* facilitās *f*.
sociable *adj* facilis, cōmis.
sociably *adv* faciliter, cōmiter.
social *adj* sociālis, commūnis.
socialism *n* populāris ratiō *f*.
socialist *n* homō populāris *m/f*.
society *n* societās *f*; (*class*) optimātēs *mpl*; (*being with*) convīctus *m*; **cultivate the ~ of** adsectārī; **secret** ~ sodālitās *f*.
sod *n* caespes *m*, glaeba *f*.
soda *n* nitrum *nt*.
sodden *adj* madidus.
soever *adv* -cumque.
sofa *n* lectus *m*.
soft *adj* mollis; (*fruit*) mītis; (*voice*) submissus; (*character*) dēlicātus; (*words*) blandus.
soften *vt* mollīre; (*body*) ēnervāre; (*emotion*) lēnīre, mītigāre ♦ *vi* mollēscere, mītēscere.
soft-hearted *adj* misericors.
softly *adv* molliter, lēniter; blandē.
softness *n* mollitia *f*, mollitiēs *f*.
soil *n* sōlum *nt*, humus *f* ♦ *vt* inquināre, foedāre.
sojourn *n* commorātiō *f*, mānsiō *f* ♦ *vi* commorārī.
sojourner *n* hospes *m*, hospita *f*.
solace *n* sōlātium *nt*, levātiō *f* ♦ *vt* sōlārī, cōnsōlārī.
solar *adj* sōlis.
solder *n* ferrūmen *nt* ♦ *vt* ferrūmināre.
soldier *n* mīles *m*; **be a ~** mīlitāre; **common ~** manipulāris *m*, gregārius mīles *m*; **fellow ~** commīlitō *m*; **foot ~** pedes *m*; **old ~** veterānus *m* ♦ *vi* mīlitāre.
soldierly *adj* mīlitāris.
soldiery *n* mīles *m*.
sole *adj* sōlus, ūnus, ūnicus ♦ *n* (*foot*) planta *f*; (*fish*) solea *f*.
solecism *n* soloecismus *m*.
solely *adv* sōlum, tantum, modō.
solemn *adj* gravis; (*religion*) sanctus.
solemnity *n* gravitās *f*; sanctitās *f*.
solemnize *vt* agere.
solemnly *adv* graviter; ritē.
solicit *vt* flāgitāre, obsecrāre.
solicitation *n* flāgitātiō *f*.
solicitor *n* advocātus *m*.
solicitous *adj* anxius, trepidus.
solicitously *adv* anxiē, trepidē.
solicitude *n* cūra *f*, anxietās *f*.
solid *adj* solidus; (*metal*) pūrus; (*food*) firmus; (*argument*) firmus; (*character*) cōnstāns,

spectātus; **become** ~ concrēscere; **make** ~ cōgere.
solidarity *n* societās *f*.
solidify *vt* cōgere ♦ *vi* concrēscere.
solidity *n* soliditās *f*.
solidly *adv* firmē, cōnstanter.
soliloquize *vi* sēcum loquī.
soliloquy *n* ūnīus ōrātiō *f*.
solitary *adj* sōlus, sōlitārius; (*instance*) ūnicus; (*place*) dēsertus.
solitude *n* sōlitūdō *f*.
solo *n* canticum *nt*.
solstice *n* (*summer*) sōlstitium *nt*; (*winter*) brūma *f*.
solstitial *adj* sōlstitiālis, brūmālis.
soluble *adj* dissolūbilis.
solution *n* (*of puzzle*) ēnōdātiō *f*.
solve *vt* ēnōdāre, explicāre.
solvency *n* solvendī facultās *f*.
solvent *adj*: **be ~** solvendō esse.
sombre *adj* obscūrus; (*fig*) tristis.
some *adj* aliquī; (*pl*) nonnullī, aliquot; ~ **people** sunt qui (+ *subj*); ~ ... **other** alius ... alius; **for** ~ **time** aliquamdiū; **with ~ reason** nōn sine causā ♦ *pron* aliquis; (*pl*) nonnullī, sunt quī (*subj*), erant quī (*subj*).
somebody *pron* aliquis; ~ **or other** nescioquis.
somehow *adv* quōdammodō, nescio quōmodō.
someone *pron* aliquis; (*negative*) quisquam; ~ **or other** nescioquis; ~ **else** alius.
something *pron* aliquid; ~ **or other** nescioquid; ~ **else** aliud.
sometime *adv* aliquandō; (*past*) quondam.
sometimes *adv* interdum, nonnumquam; ~ ... ~ **modo** ... **modo**.
somewhat *adv* aliquantum, nōnnihil, paulum; (*with compar*) paulō, aliquantō.
somewhere *adv* alicubi; (*to*) aliquō; ~ **else** alibī; (*to*) aliō; **from ~** alicunde; **from ~ else** aliunde.
somnolence *n* somnus *m*.
somnolent *adj* sēmisomnus.
son *n* filius *m*; **small ~** fīliolus *m*.
song *n* carmen *nt*, cantus *m*.
son-in-law *n* gener *m*.
sonorous *adj* sonōrus, canōrus.
soon *adv* mox, brevi, citō; **as ~ as** ut prīmum, cum prīmum (+ *fut perf*), simul āc/atque (+ *perf indic*); **as ~ as possible** quam prīmum; **too ~** praemātūrē, ante tempus.
sooner *adv* prius, mātūrius; (*preference*) libentius, potius; ~ **or later** sērius ōcius; **no ~ said than done** dictum factum.
soonest *adv* mātūrissimē.
soot *n* fūlīgō *f*.
soothe *vt* dēlēnīre, permulcēre.
soothing *adj* lēnis, blandus.
soothingly *adv* blandē.
soothsayer *n* hariolus *m*, vātēs *m/f*, haruspex *m*.
sooty *adj* fūmōsus.
sop *n* offa *f*; (*fig*) dēlēnīmentum *nt*.

sophism n captiō f.
sophist n sophistēs m.
sophistical adj acūleātus, captiōsus.
sophisticated adj lepidus, urbānus.
sophistry n captiō f.
soporific adj sopōrifer, somnifer.
soprano adj acūtus.
sorcerer n veneficus m.
sorceress n venefica f, saga f.
sorcery n venēficium nt; (means) venēna ntpl, carmina ntpl.
sordid adj sordidus; (conduct) illīberālis.
sordidly adv sordidē.
sordidness n sordēs fpl; illīberālitās f.
sore adj molestus, gravis, acerbus; **feel ~** dolēre ♦ n ulcus nt.
sorely adv graviter, vehementer.
sorrel n lapathus f, lapathum nt.
sorrow n dolor m, aegritūdō f; (outward) maeror m; (for death) lūctus m ♦ vi dolēre, maerere, lūgēre.
sorrowful adj maestus, tristis.
sorrowfully adv maestē.
sorry adj paenitēns; (poor) miser; **I am ~ for** (remorse) mē paenitet, mē piget (gen); (pity) mē miseret (gen).
sort n genus nt; **a ~ of** quīdam; **all ~s of** omnēs; **the ~ of** tālis; **this ~ of** huiusmodī; **the common ~** plēbs f; **I am not the ~ of man to** nōn is sum quī (+ subj); **I am out of ~s** mihī displiceō ♦ vt dīgerere, compōnere; (votes) diribēre.
sortie n excursiō f, excursus m, ēruptiō f; **make a ~** ērumpere, excurrere.
sot n ēbriōsus m.
sottish adj ēbriōsus, tēmulentus.
sottishness n vīnolentia f.
soul n anima f, animus m; (essence) vīs f; (person) caput nt; **not a ~** nēmō ūnus; **the ~ of** (fig) medulla f.
soulless adj caecus, dūrus.
sound n sonitus m, sonus m; (articulate) vōx f; (confused) strepitus m; (loud) fragor m; (strait) fretum nt ♦ vt (signal) canere; (instrument) īnflāre; (depth) scrūtārī, temptāre; (person) animum temptāre (gen) ♦ vi canere, sonāre; (seem) vidērī; **~ a retreat** receptuī canere ♦ adj sānus, salūbris; (health) firmus; (sleep) artus; (judgment) exquīsītus; (argument) vērus; **safe and ~** salvus, incolumis.
soundly adv (beat) vehementer; (sleep) artē; (study) penitus, dīligenter.
soundness n sānitās f, integritās f.
soup n iūs nt.
sour adj acerbus, amārus, acidus; **turn ~** acēscere; (fig) coacēscere ♦ vt (fig) exacerbāre.
source n fōns m; (river) caput nt; (fig) fōns m, orīgō f; **have its ~ in** orīrī ex; (fig) proficīscī ex.
sourness n acerbitās f; (temper) mōrōsitās f.
souse vt immergere.

south n merīdiēs f ♦ adj austrālis ♦ adv ad merīdiem.
south-east adv inter sōlis ortum et merīdiem.
southerly adj ad merīdiem versus.
southern adj austrālis.
south-west adv inter occāsum sōlis et merīdiem.
south wind n auster m.
souvenir n monumentum nt.
sovereign n rēx m, rēgīna f ♦ adj prīnceps, summus.
sovereignty n rēgnum nt, imperium nt, prīncipātus m; (of the people) māiestās f.
sow n scrōfa f, sūs f.
sow vt serere; (field) cōnserere ♦ vi sementem facere.
sower n sator m.
sowing n sēmentis f.
spa n aquae fpl.
space n (extension) spatium nt; (not matter) ināne nt; (room) locus m; (distance) intervallum nt; (time) spatium nt; **open ~** ārea f; **leave a ~ of** intermittere ♦ vt: **~ out** dispōnere.
spacious adj amplus, capāx.
spaciousness n amplitūdō f.
spade n pāla f, rūtrum nt.
span n (measure) palmus m; (extent) spatium nt ♦ vt iungere.
spangle n bractea f.
spangled adj distinctus.
spar n tignum nt.
spare vt parcere (dat); (to give) suppeditāre; **~ time for** vacāre (dat) ♦ adj exīlis; (extra) subsecīvus.
sparing adj parcus.
sparingly adv parcē.
spark n scintilla f; (fig) igniculus m.
sparkle vi scintillāre, nitēre, micāre.
sparrow n passer m.
sparse adj rārus.
spasm n convulsiō f.
spasmodically adv interdum.
spatter vt aspergere.
spawn n ōva ntpl.
speak vt, vi loquī; (make speech) dīcere, contiōnārī, ōrātiōnem habēre; **~ out** ēloquī; **~ to** adloquī; (converse) colloquī cum; **~ well of** bene dīcere (dat); **it ~s for itself** rēs ipsa loquitur.
speaker n ōrātor m.
speaking n: **art of ~** dīcendī ars f; **practise public ~** dēclāmāre ♦ adj: **likeness ~** vīvida imāgō.
spear n hasta f.
spearman n hastātus m.
special adj praecipuus, proprius.
speciality n proprium nt.
specially adv praecipuē, praesertim.
species n genus nt.
specific adj certus.
specification n dēsignātiō f.
specify vt dēnotāre, dēsignāre.

specimen n exemplar nt, exemplum nt.
specious adj speciōsus.
speciously adv speciōsē.
speciousness n speciēs f.
speck n macula f.
speckled adj maculīs distinctus.
spectacle n spectāculum nt.
spectacular adj spectābilis.
spectator n spectātor m.
spectral adj larvālis.
spectre n larva f.
speculate vi cōgitāre, coniectūrās facere; (COMM) forō ūtī.
speculation n cōgitātiō f, coniectūra f; (COMM) ālea f.
speculator n contemplātor m; (COMM) āleātor m.
speech n ōrātiō f; (language) sermō m, lingua f; (to people or troops) cōntiō f; **make a ~** ōrātiōnem/cōntiōnem habēre.
speechless adj ēlinguis, mūtus.
speed n celeritās f, cursus m, vēlōcitās f; **with all ~** summa celeritate; **at full ~** māgnō cursū, incitātus; (riding) citātō equō ♦ vt adcelerāre, mātūrāre ♦ vi properāre, festīnāre.
speedily adv celeriter, citō.
speedy adj celer, vēlōx, citus.
spell n carmen nt.
spellbound adj: **be ~** obstipēscere.
spelt n far nt.
spend vt impendere, īnsūmere; (public money) ērogāre; (time) agere, cōnsūmere, terere; (strength) effundere; **~ itself** (storm) dēsaevīre; **~ on** īnsūmere (acc & dat).
spendthrift n nepōs m, prōdigus m.
sphere n globus m; (of action) prōvincia f.
spherical adj globōsus.
sphinx n sphinx f.
spice n condīmentum nt; **~s** pl odōrēs mpl ♦ vt condīre.
spicy adj odōrātus; (wit) salsus.
spider n arānea f; **~'s web** arāneum nt.
spike n dēns m, clāvus m.
spikenard n nardus m.
spill vt fundere, profundere ♦ vi redundāre.
spin vt (thread) nēre, dēdūcere; (top) versāre; **~ out** (story) prōdūcere ♦ vi circumagī, versārī.
spindle n fūsus m.
spine n spīna f.
spineless adj ēnervātus.
spinster n virgō f.
spiral adj intortus ♦ n spīra f.
spire n cōnus m.
spirit n (life) anima f; (intelligence) mēns f; (soul) animus m; (vivacity) spīritus m, vigor m, vīs f; (character) ingenium nt; (intention) voluntās f; (of an age) mōrēs mpl; (ghost) anima f; **~s** pl mānēs mpl; **full of ~** alacer, animōsus.
spirited adj animōsus, ācer.
spiritless adj iners, frāctus, timidus.
spiritual adj animī.

spit n verū nt ♦ vi spuere, spūtāre; **~ on** cōnspūtāre; **~ out** exspuere.
spite n invidia f, malevolentia f, līvor m; **in ~ of me** mē invītō; **in ~ of the difficulties** in his angustiīs ♦ vt incommodāre, offendere.
spiteful adj malevolus, malignus, invidus.
spitefully adv malevolē, malignē.
spitefulness n malevolentia f.
spittle n spūtum nt.
splash n fragor m ♦ vt aspergere.
spleen n splēn m; (fig) stomachus m.
splendid adj splendidus, lūculentus; īnsignis; (person) amplus.
splendidly adv splendidē, optimē.
splendour n splendor m, fulgor m; (fig) lautitia f, adparātus m.
splenetic adj stomachōsus.
splice vt iungere.
splint n ferula f.
splinter n fragmentum nt, assula f ♦ vt findere.
split vt findere ♦ vi dissilīre ♦ adj fissus ♦ n fissum nt; (fig) dissidium nt.
splutter vi balbūtīre.
spoil n praeda f ♦ vt (rob) spoliāre; (mar) corrumpere ♦ vi corrumpī.
spoiler n spoliātor m; corruptor m.
spoils npl spolia ntpl, exuviae fpl.
spoke n radius m; **put a ~ in one's wheel** inicere scrūpulum (dat).
spokesman n interpres m, ōrātor m.
spoliation n spoliātiō f, dīreptiō f.
spondee n spondēus m.
sponge n spongia f.
sponsor n spōnsor m; (fig) auctor m.
spontaneity n impulsus m, voluntās f.
spontaneous adj voluntārius.
spontaneously adv suā sponte, ultrō.
spoon n cochlear nt.
sporadic adj rārus.
sporadically adv passim.
sport n lūdus m; (in Rome) campus m; (fun) iocus m; (ridicule) lūdibrium nt; **make ~ of** illūdere (dat) ♦ vi lūdere.
sportive adj lascīvus.
sportiveness n lascīvia f.
sportsman n vēnātor m.
sportsmanlike adj honestus, generōsus.
spot n macula f; (place) locus m; (dice) pūnctum nt; **on the ~** īlicō ♦ vt maculāre; (see) animadvertere.
spotless adj integer, pūrus; (character) castus.
spotted adj maculōsus.
spouse n coniunx m/f.
spout n (of jug) ōs nt; (pipe) canālis m ♦ vi ēmicāre.
sprain vt intorquēre.
sprawl vi sē fundere.
sprawling adj fūsus.
spray n aspergō f ♦ vt aspergere.
spread vt pandere, extendere; (news) dīvulgāre; (infection) vulgāre ♦ vi patēre; (rumour) mānāre, incrēbrēscere; (feeling) glīscere.

spreadeagle *vt* dispandere.
spreading *adj* (*tree*) patulus.
spree *n* cōmissātiō *f*.
sprig *n* virga *f*.
sprightliness *n* alacritās *f*.
sprightly *adj* alacer, hilaris.
spring *n* (*season*) vēr *nt*; (*water*) fōns *m*; (*leap*)
    saltus *m* ♦ *vi* (*grow*) crēscere, ēnāscī; (*leap*)
    salīre; ~ **from** orīrī ex, proficīscī ex; ~ **on to**
    īnsilīre in (*acc*); ~ **up** exorīrī, exsilīre ♦ *vt*: ~
    a leak rīmās agere; ~ **a surprise on**
    admīrātiōnem movēre (*dat*) ♦ *adj* vērnus.
springe *n* laqueus *m*.
sprinkle *vt* aspergere; ~ **on** īnspergere (*dat*).
sprint *vi* currere.
sprout *n* surculus *m* ♦ *vi* fruticārī.
spruce *adj* nitidus, concinnus.
sprung *adj* ortus, oriundus.
spume *n* spūma *f*.
spur *n* calcar *nt*; ~ **of a hill** prōminēns collis; **on**
    the ~ of the moment ex tempore ♦ *vt*
    incitāre; ~ **the willing horse** currentem
    incitāre; ~ **on** concitāre.
spurious *adj* falsus, fūcōsus, fictus.
spurn *vt* spernere, aspernārī, respuere.
spurt *vi* ēmicāre; (*run*) sē incitāre ♦ *n* impetus
    m.
spy *n* speculātor *m*, explōrātor *m* ♦ *vi* speculārī
    ♦ *vt* cōnspicere; ~ **out** explōrāre.
squabble *n* iūrgium *nt* ♦ *vi* rixārī.
squad *n* (*MIL*) decuria.
squadron *n* (*cavalry*) āla *f*, turma *f*; (*ships*)
    classis *f*.
squalid *adj* sordidus, dēfōrmis.
squall *n* procella *f*.
squally *adj* procellōsus.
squalor *n* sordēs *fpl*, squālor *m*.
squander *vt* dissipāre, disperdere, effundere.
squanderer *n* prōdigus *m*.
square *n* quadrātum *nt*; (*town*) ārea *f* ♦ *vt*
    quadrāre; (*account*) subdūcere ♦ *vi* cōnstāre,
    congruere ♦ *adj* quadrātus.
squash *vt* conterere, contundere.
squat *vi* subsīdere ♦ *adj* brevis atque obēsus.
squatter *n* (*on land*) agripeta *m*.
squawk *vi* crōcīre.
squeak *n* strīdor *m* ♦ *vi* strīdēre.
squeal *n* vāgītus *m* ♦ *vi* vāgīre.
squeamish *adj* fastīdiōsus; **feel ~** nauseāre,
    fastīdīre.
squeamishness *n* fastīdium *nt*, nausea *f*.
squeeze *vt* premere, comprimere; ~ **out**
    exprimere.
squint *adj* perversus ♦ *n*: **person with a ~**
    strabō *m* ♦ *vi* strabō esse.
squinter *n* strabō *m*.
squinting *adj* paetus.
squire *n* armiger *m*; (*landed*) dominus *m*.
squirm *vi* volūtārī.
squirrel *n* sciūrus *m*.
squirt *vt* ēicere, effundere ♦ *vi* ēmicāre.
stab *n* ictus *m*, vulnus *nt* ♦ *vt* fodere, ferīre,
    percutere.

stability *n* stabilitās *f*, firmitās *f*, cōnstantia *f*.
stabilize *vt* stabilīre, firmāre.
stable *adj* firmus, stabilis ♦ *n* stabulum *nt*,
    equīle *nt*; **shut the ~ door after the horse is**
    stolen clipeum post vulnera sūmere.
stack *n* acervus *m* ♦ *vt* congerere, cumulāre.
stadium *n* spatium *nt*.
staff *n* scīpiō *m*, virga *f*; (*augur's*) lituus *m*;
    (*officers*) contubernālēs *mpl*.
stag *n* cervus *m*.
stage *n* pulpitum *nt*, proscēnium *nt*; (*theatre*)
    scēna *f*, theātrum *nt*; (*scene of action*) campus
    m; (*of journey*) iter *nt*; (*of progress*) gradus *m* ♦
    adj scēnicus ♦ *vt* (*play*) dare, docēre.
stage fright *n* horror *m*.
stagger *vi* titubāre ♦ *vt* obstupefacere.
stagnant *adj* iners.
stagnate *vi* (*fig*) cessāre, refrīgēscere.
stagnation *n* cessātiō *f*, torpor *m*.
stagy *adj* scēnicus.
staid *adj* sevērus, gravis.
stain *n* macula *f*, lābēs *f*; (*fig*) dēdecus *nt*,
    ignōminia *f* ♦ *vt* maculāre, foedāre,
    contāmināre; ~ **with** īnficere (*abl*).
stainless *adj* pūrus, integer.
stair *n* scālae *fpl*, gradus *mpl*.
staircase *n* scālae *fpl*.
stake *n* pālus *m*, stīpes *m*; (*pledge*) pignus *nt*; **be**
    at ~ agī, in discrīmine esse ♦ *vt* (*wager*)
    dēpōnere.
stale *adj* obsolētus, effētus; (*wine*) vapidus.
stalemate *n*: **reach a ~** ad incitās redigī.
stalk *n* (*corn*) calamus *m*; (*plant*) stīpes *m* ♦ *vi*
    incēdere ♦ *vt* vēnārī, īnsidiārī (*dat*).
stall *n* (*animal*) stabulum *nt*; (*seat*) subsellium
    nt; (*shop*) taberna *f* ♦ *vt* stabulāre.
stallion *n* equus *m*.
stalwart *adj* ingēns, rōbustus, fortis.
stamina *n* patientia *f*.
stammer *n* haesitātiō *f* ♦ *vi* balbūtīre.
stammering *adj* balbus.
stamp *n* fōrma *f*; (*mark*) nota *f*, signum *nt*; (*of*
    feet) supplōsiō *f* ♦ *vt* imprimere; (*coin*) ferīre,
    signāre; (*fig*) inūrere; ~ **one's feet** pedem
    supplōdere; ~ **out** exstinguere.
stampede *n* discursus *m*; (*fig*) pavor *m* ♦ *vi*
    discurrere; (*fig*) expavēscere.
stance *n* status *m*.
stanchion *n* columna *f*.
stand *n* (*position*) statiō *f*, (*platform*) suggestus
    m; **make a ~** resistere, restāre ♦ *vi* stāre;
    (*remain*) manēre; (*matters*) sē habēre ♦ *vt*
    statuere; (*tolerate*) ferre, tolerāre; ~ **against**
    resistere (*dat*); ~ **aloof** abstāre; ~ **by** adsistere
    (*dat*); (*friend*) adesse (*dat*); (*promise*)
    praestāre; ~ **convicted** manifestum tenērī; ~
    down concēdere; ~ **fast** cōnsistere; ~ **one's**
    ground in locō perstāre; ~ **for** (*office*) petere;
    (*meaning*) significāre; (*policy*) postulāre; ~ **in**
    awe of in metū habēre; ~ **in need of** indigēre
    (*abl*); ~ **on** īnsistere in (*abl*); ~ **on end**
    horrēre; ~ **on one's dignity** gravitātem suam
    tuērī; ~ **out** ēminēre, exstāre; (*against*)

resistere (*dat*); (*to sea*) in altum prōvehī; ~
out of the way of dēcēdere (*dat*); ~ **over**
(*case*) ampliāre; ~ **still** cōnsistere, īnsistere;
~ **to reason** sequī; ~ **trial** reum fierī; ~ **up**
surgere, cōnsurgere; ~ **up for** dēfendere,
adesse (*dat*); ~ **up to** respōnsāre (*dat*).
standard *n* (*MIL*) signum *nt*; (*measure*) nōrma *f*;
~ **author** scrīptor classicus *m*; **up to** ~ iūstus;
judge by the ~ **of** referre ad.
standard-bearer *n* signifer *m*.
standing *adj* perpetuus ♦ *n* status *m*; (*social*)
locus *m*, ōrdō *m*; **of long** ~ inveterātus; **be of**
long ~ inveterāscere.
stand-offish *adj* tēctus.
standstill *n*: **be at a** ~ haerēre, frīgēre; **bring**
to a ~ ad incitās redigere; **come to a** ~
īnsistere.
stanza *n* tetrastichon *nt*.
staple *n* uncus *m* ♦ *adj* praecipuus.
star *n* stēlla *f*, astrum *nt*; sīdus *nt*; **shooting** ~**s**
acontiae *fpl*.
starboard *adj* dexter.
starch *n* amylum *nt*.
stare *n* obtūtus *m* ♦ *vi* intentīs oculīs intuērī,
stupēre; ~ **at** contemplārī.
stark *adj* rigidus; simplex ♦ *adv* plānē, omnīnō.
starling *n* sturnus *m*.
starry *adj* stēllātus.
start *n* initium *nt*; (*movement*) saltus *m*;
(*journey*) profectiō *f*; **by fits and** ~**s** carptim;
have a day's ~ **on** diē antecēdere ♦ *vt*
incipere, īnstituere; (*game*) excitāre;
(*process*) movēre ♦ *vi* (*with fright*) resilīre;
(*journey*) proficīscī; ~ **up** exsilīre.
starting place *n* carcerēs *mpl*.
startle *vt* excitāre, terrēre.
starvation *n* famēs *f*.
starve *vi* fāme cōnficī; (*cold*) frīgēre ♦ *vt* fāme
ēnecāre.
starveling *n* famēlicus *m*.
state *n* (*condition*) status *m*, condiciō *f*; (*pomp*)
adparātus *m*; (*POL*) cīvitās *f*, rēs pūblica *f*; **the**
~ **of affairs is** ita sē rēs habet; **I know the** ~ **of**
affairs quō in locō rēs sit sciō; **of the** ~
pūblicus ♦ *adj* pūblicus ♦ *vt* adfirmāre,
expōnere, profitērī; ~ **one's case** causam
dīcere.
stateliness *n* māiestās *f*, gravitās *f*.
stately *adj* gravis, grandis, nōbilis.
statement *n* adfirmātiō *f*, dictum *nt*; (*witness*)
testimōnium *nt*.
state of health *n* valētūdō *f*.
state of mind *n* adfectiō *f*.
statesman *n* vir reī pūblicae gerendae
perītus *m*, cōnsilī pūblicī auctor *m*.
statesmanlike *adj* prūdēns.
statesmanship *n* cīvīlis prūdentia *f*.
static *adj* stabilis.
station *n* locus *m*; (*MIL*) statiō *f*; (*social*) locus *m*,
ōrdō *m* ♦ *vt* collocāre, pōnere; (*in different*
places) dispōnere.
stationary *adj* immōtus, statārius, stabilis.
statistics *n* cēnsus *m*.

statuary *n* fictor *m*.
statute *n* statua *f*, signum *nt*, imāgō *f*.
statuette *n* sigillum *nt*.
stature *n* fōrma *f*, statūra *f*.
status *n* locus *m*.
status quo *n*: **restore the** ~ ad integrum
restituere.
statutable *adj* lēgitimus.
statute *n* lēx *f*.
staunch *vt* (*blood*) sistere ♦ *adj* fīdus,
cōnstāns.
stave *vt* perrumpere, perfringere; ~ **off**
arcēre.
stay *n* firmāmentum *nt*; (*fig*) columen *nt*;
(*sojourn*) mānsiō *f*, commorātiō *f* ♦ *vt* (*prop*)
fulcīre; (*stop*) dētinēre, dēmorārī ♦ *vi*
manēre, commorārī.
stead *n* locus *m*; **stand one in good** ~ prōdesse
(*dat*).
steadfast *adj* firmus, stabilis, cōnstāns; ~ **at**
home tenēre sē domī.
steadfastly *adv* cōnstanter.
steadfastness *n* firmitās *f*, cōnstantia *f*.
steadily *adv* firmē, cōnstanter.
steadiness *n* stabilitās *f*; (*fig*) cōnstantia *f*.
steady *adj* stabilis, firmus; (*fig*) gravis,
cōnstāns.
steak *n* offa *f*.
steal *vt* surripere, fūrārī ♦ *vi*: ~ **away** sē
subdūcere; ~ **over** subrēpere (*dat*); ~ **into** sē
īnsinuāre in (*acc*); ~ **a march on** occupāre.
stealing *n* fūrtum *nt*.
stealth *n* fūrtum *nt*; **by** ~ fūrtim, clam.
stealthily *adv* fūrtim, clam.
stealthy *adj* fūrtīvus, clandestīnus.
steam *n* aquae vapor *m*, fūmus *m* ♦ *vi* fūmāre.
steed *n* equus *m*.
steel *n* ferrum *nt*, chalybs *m* ♦ *adj* ferreus ♦ *vt*
dūrāre; ~ **oneself** obdūrēscere.
steely *adj* ferreus.
steelyard *n* statēra *f*.
steep *adj* arduus, praeceps, praeruptus;
(*slope*) dēclīvis ♦ *vt* imbuere.
steeple *n* turris *f*.
steepness *n* arduum *nt*.
steer *vi* gubernāre, regere, dīrigere ♦ *n*
iuvencus *m*.
steering *n* gubernātiō *f*.
steersman *n* gubernātor *m*; rector *m*.
stellar *adj* stēllārum.
stem *n* stīpes *m*, truncus *m*; (*ship*) prōra *f* ♦ *vt*
adversārī (*dat*); ~ **the tide of** (*fig*) obsistere
(*dat*).
stench *n* foetor *m*.
stenographer *n* exceptor *m*, āctuārius *m*.
stenography *n* notae *fpl*.
stentorian *adj* (*voice*) ingēns.
step *n* gradus *m*; (*track*) vestīgium *nt*; (*of stair*)
gradus *m*; ~ **by** ~ gradātim; **flight of** ~**s**
gradus *mpl*; **take a** ~ gradum facere; **take** ~**s**
to ratiōnem inīre ut, vidēre ut; **march in** ~ in
numerum īre; **out of** ~ extrā numerum ♦ *vi*
gradī, incēdere; ~ **aside** dēcēdere; ~ **back**

regredī; ~ **forward** prōdīre; ~ **on** insistere (*dat*).
stepdaughter *n* prīvīgna *f*.
stepfather *n* vītricus *m*.
stepmother *n* noverca *f*.
stepson *n* prīvīgnus *m*.
stereotyped *adj* trītus.
sterile *adj* sterilis.
sterility *n* sterilitās *f*.
sterling *adj* integer, probus, gravis.
stern *adj* dūrus, sevērus; (*look*) torvus ♦ *n* puppis *f*.
sternly *adv* sevērē, dūriter.
sternness *n* sevēritās *f*.
stew *vt* coquere.
steward *n* prōcūrātor *m*; (*of estate*) vīlicus *m*.
stewardship *n* prōcūrātiō *f*.
stick *n* (*for beating*) fūstis *m*; (*for walking*) baculum *nt* ♦ *vi* haerēre; ~ **at nothing** ad omnia dēscendere; ~ **fast in** inhaerēre (*dat*), inhaerēscere in (*abl*); ~ **out** ēminēre; ~ **to** adhaerēre (*dat*); ~ **up** ēminēre; ~ **up for** dēfendere ♦ *vt* (*with glue*) conglūtināre; (*with point*) fīgere; ~ **into** īnfīgere; ~ **top on** praefīgere.
stickler *n* dīligēns (*gen*).
sticky *adj* lentus, tenāx.
stiff *adj* rigidus; (*difficult*) difficilis; **be** ~ rigēre.
stiffen *vt* rigidum facere ♦ *vi* rigēre.
stiffly *adv* rigidē.
stiff-necked *adj* obstinātus.
stiffness *n* rigor *m*.
stifle *vt* suffocāre; (*fig*) opprimere, restinguere.
stigma *n* nota *f*.
stigmatize *vt* notāre.
stile *n* saepēs *f*.
still *adj* immōtus, tranquillus, quiētus; tacitus ♦ *vt* lēnīre, sēdāre ♦ *adv* etiam, adhūc, etiamnum; (*past*) etiam tum; (*with compar*) etiam; (*adversative*) tamen, nihilōminus.
stillness *n* quiēs *f*; silentium *nt*.
stilly *adj* tacitus.
stilted *adj* (*language*) īnflātus.
stilts *n* grallae *fpl*.
stimulant *n* stimulus *m*.
stimulate *vt* stimulāre, acuere, exacuere, excitāre.
stimulus *n* stimulus *m*.
sting *n* aculeus *m*; (*wound*) ictus *m*; (*fig*) aculeus *m*, morsus *m* ♦ *vt* pungere, mordēre.
stingily *adv* sordidē.
stinginess *n* avāritia *f*, sordēs *fpl*, tenācitās *f*.
stinging *adj* (*words*) aculeātus, mordāx.
stingy *adj* sordidus, tenāx.
stink *n* foetor *m* ♦ *vi* foetere; ~ **of** olēre.
stinking *adj* foetidus.
stint *n* modus *m*; **without** ~ abundē ♦ *vt* circumscrībere.
stipend *n* mercēs *f*.
stipulate *vt* pacīscī, stipulārī.
stipulation *n* condiciō *f*, pactum *nt*.
stir *n* tumultus *m* ♦ *vt* movēre, agitāre; (*fig*)

commovēre; ~ **up** excitāre, incitāre ♦ *vi* movērī.
stirring *adj* impiger, tumultuōsus; (*speech*) ārdēns.
stitch *vt* suere ♦ *n* sūtūra *f*; (*in side*) dolor *m*.
stock *n* stirps *f*, genus *nt*, gēns *f*; (*equipment*) īnstrūmenta *ntpl*; (*supply*) cōpia *f*; (*investment*) pecūniae *fpl*; **live**~ rēs pecuāria *f* ♦ *vt* īnstruere ♦ *adj* commūnis, trītus.
stockade *n* vallum *nt*.
stock dove *n* palumbēs *m/f*.
stock in trade *n* īnstrūmenta *ntpl*.
stocks *n* (*ship*) nāvālia *ntpl*; (*torture*) compedēs *fpl*.
stock-still *adj* plānē immōtus.
stocky *adj* brevis atque obēsus.
stodgy *adj* crūdus, īnsulsus.
stoic *n* Stōicus *m* ♦ *adj* Stōicus.
stoical *adj* dūrus, patiēns.
stoically *adv* patienter.
stoicism *n* Stōicōrum ratiō *f*, Stōicōrum disciplīna *f*.
stoke *vt* agitāre.
stole *n* stola *f*.
stolid *adj* stolidus.
stolidity *n* īnsulsitās *f*.
stolidly *adv* stolidē.
stomach *n* stomachus *m*; venter *m* ♦ *vt* patī, tolerāre.
stone *n* lapis *m*, saxum *nt*; (*precious*) gemma *f*, lapillus *m*; (*of fruit*) acinum *nt*; **leave no** ~ **unturned** omnia experīrī; **kill two birds with one** ~ ūnō saltū duōs aprōs capere; **hewn** ~ saxum quadrātum; **unhewn** ~ caementum *nt* ♦ *vt* lapidibus percutere ♦ *adj* lapideus; ~ **blind** plānē caecus; ~ **deaf** plānē surdus.
stonecutter *n* lapicīda *m*.
stony *adj* (*soil*) lapidōsus; (*path*) scrūpōsus; (*feeling*) dūrus, ferreus.
stool *n* sēdēcula *f*.
stoop *vi* sē dēmittere; ~ **to** dēscendere in (*acc*).
stop *n* mora *f*; (*punctuation*) pūnctum *nt*; **come to a** ~ īnsistere; **put a** ~ **to** comprimere, dirimere ♦ *vt* sistere, inhibēre, fīnīre; (*restrain*) cohibēre; (*hole*) obtūrāre; ~ **up** occlūdere, interclūdere ♦ *vi* dēsinere, dēsistere; (*motion*) īnsistere.
stopgap *n* tībīcen *m*.
stoppage *n* interclūsiō *f*, impedīmentum *nt*.
stopper *n* obtūrāmentum *nt*.
store *n* cōpia *f*; (*place*) horreum *nt*; (*for wine*) apothēca *f*; **be in** ~ **for** manēre; **set great** ~ **by** māgnī aestimāre ♦ *vt* condere, repōnere; ~ **away** recondere; ~ **up** repōnere, congerere.
storehouse *n* (*fig*) thēsaurus *m*.
storekeeper *n* cellārius *m*.
storeship *n* nāvis frūmentāria *f*.
storey *n* tabulātum *nt*.
stork *n* cicōnia *f*.
storm *n* tempestās *f*, procella *f*; **take by** ~ expugnāre ♦ *vt* (*MIL*) expugnāre ♦ *vi* saevīre; ~ **at** īnsectārī, invehī in (*acc*).

stormbound *adj* tempestāte dētentus.
stormer *n* expugnātor *m*.
storming *n* expugnātiō *f*.
stormy *adj* turbidus, procellōsus; (*fig*) turbulentus.
story *n* fābula *f*, nārrātiō *f*; (*short*) fābella *f*; (*untrue*) mendācium *nt*.
storyteller *n* nārrātor *m*; (*liar*) mendāx *m*.
stout *adj* pinguis; (*brave*) fortis; (*strong*) validus, rōbustus; (*material*) firmus.
stouthearted *adj* māgnanimus.
stoutly *adv* fortiter.
stove *n* camīnus *m*, fornāx *f*.
stow *vt* repōnere, condere; ~ **away** *vi* in nāvī dēlitēscere.
straddle *vi* vāricāre.
straggle *vi* deerrāre, pālārī.
straggler *n* pālāns *m*.
straggling *adj* dispersus, rārus.
straight *adj* rēctus, dīrēctus; (*fig*) apertus, vērāx; **in a ~ line** rēctā, ē regiōne; **set ~** dīrigere ♦ *adv* dīrēctō, rēctā.
straighten *vt* corrigere, extendere.
straightforward *adj* simplex, dīrēctus; (*easy*) facilis.
straightforwardness *n* simplicitās *f*.
straightness *n* (*fig*) integritās *f*.
straightway *adv* statim, extemplō.
strain *n* contentiō *f*; (*effort*) labor *m*; (*music*) modī *mpl*; (*breed*) genus *nt* ♦ *vt* intendere, contendere; (*injure*) nimiā contentiōne dēbilitāre; (*liquid*) dēliquāre, percōlāre ♦ *vi* ēnītī, vīrēs contendere.
strained *adj* (*language*) accessītus.
strainer *n* cōlum *nt*.
strait *adj* angustus ♦ *n* fretum *nt*; ~**s** *pl* angustiae *fpl*.
straiten *vt* coartāre, contrahere; ~**ed circumstances** angustiae *fpl*.
strait-laced *adj* tristis, sevērus.
strand *n* lītus *nt*; (*of rope*) fīlum *nt* ♦ *vt* (*ship*) ēicere.
strange *adj* novus, īnsolitus; (*foreign*) peregrīnus; (*another's*) aliēnus; (*ignorant*) rudis, expers.
strangely *adv* mīrē, mīrum in modum.
strangeness *n* novitās *f*, īnsolentia *f*.
stranger *n* (*from abroad*) advena *f*; peregrīnus *m*; (*visiting*) hospes *m*, hospita *f*; (*not of the family*) externus *m*; (*unknown*) ignōtus *m*.
strangle *vt* strangulāre, laqueō gulam frangere.
strap *n* lōrum *nt*, habēna *f*.
strapping *adj* grandis.
stratagem *n* cōnsilium *nt*, fallācia *f*.
strategic *adj* (*action*) prūdēns; (*position*) idōneus.
strategist *n* artis bellicae perītus *m*.
strategy *n* ars imperātōria *f*; cōnsilia *ntpl*.
straw *n* (*stalk*) culmus *m*; (*collective*) strāmentum *nt*; **not care a ~ for** floccī nōn facere ♦ *adj* strāmenticius.
strawberry *n* frāgum *nt*.

strawberry tree *n* arbutus *m*.
stray *vt* aberrāre, deerrāre; vagārī ♦ *adj* errābundus.
streak *n* līnea *f*, macula *f*; (*light*) radius *m*; (*character*) vēna *f* ♦ *vt* maculāre.
stream *n* flūmen *nt*, fluvius *m*; **down** ~ secundō flūmine; **up** ~ adversō flūmine ♦ *vi* fluere, sē effundere; ~ **into** īnfluere in (*acc*).
streamlet *n* rīvus *m*, rīvulus *m*.
street *n* via *f*, platea *f*.
strength *n* vīrēs *fpl*; (*of material*) firmitās *f*; (*fig*) rōbur *nt*, nervī *mpl*; (*MIL*) numerus *m*; **know the enemy's** ~ quot sint hostēs scīre; **on the** ~ **of** frētus (*abl*).
strengthen *vt* firmāre, corrōborāre; (*position*) mūnīre.
strenuous *adj* impiger, strēnuus, sēdulus.
strenuously *adv* impigrē, strēnuē.
strenuousness *n* industria *f*.
stress *n* (*words*) ictus *m*; (*meaning*) vīs *f*; (*importance*) mōmentum *nt*; (*difficulty*) labor *m*; **lay great** ~ **on** in māgnō discrīmine pōnere ♦ *vt* exprimere.
stretch *n* spatium *nt*, tractus *m*; **at a** ~ sine ullā intermissiōne ♦ *vt* tendere, intendere; (*length*) prōdūcere, extendere; (*facts*) in māius crēdere; ~ **a point** indulgēre; ~ **before** obtendere; ~ **forth** porrigere; ~ **oneself** (*on ground*) sternī; ~ **out** porrigere, extendere ♦ *vi* extendī, patēscere.
strew *vt* (*things*) sternere; (*place*) cōnsternere.
stricken *adj* saucius.
strict *adj* (*defined*) ipse, certus; (*severe*) sevērus, rigidus; (*accurate*) dīligēns.
strictly *adv* sevērē; dīligenter; ~ **speaking** scīlicet, immo.
strictness *n* sevēritās *f*; dīligentia *f*.
stricture *n* vītuperātiō *f*.
stride *n* passus *m*; **make great** ~**s** (*fig*) multum prōficere ♦ *vi* incēdere, ingentēs gradūs ferre.
strident *adj* asper.
strife *n* discordia *f*, pugna *f*.
strike *vt* ferīre, percutere; (*instrument*) pellere, pulsāre; (*sail*) subdūcere; (*tent*) dētendere; (*mind*) venīre in (*acc*); (*camp*) movēre; (*fear into*) incutere in (*acc*); ~ **against** offendere; ~ **out** dēlēre; ~ **up** (*music*) incipere; ~ **a bargain** pacīscī; **be struck** vāpulāre ♦ *vi* (*work*) cessāre.
striking *adj* īnsignis, īnsignītus, ēgregius.
strikingly *adv* īnsignītē.
string *n* (*cord*) resticula *f*; (*succession*) seriēs *f*; (*instrument*) nervus *m*; (*bow*) nervus *m*; **have two ~s to one's bow** duplicī spē ūtī ♦ *vt* (*bow*) intendere; (*together*) coniungere.
stringency *n* sevēritās *f*.
stringent *adj* sevērus.
strip *vt* nūdāre, spoliāre, dēnūdāre; ~ **off** exuere; (*leaves*) stringere, dēstringere ♦ *n* lacinia *f*.
stripe *n* virga *f*; (*on tunic*) clāvus *m*; ~**s** *pl* verbera *ntpl*.

striped *adj* virgātus.
stripling *n* adulescentulus *m.*
strive *vi* nītī, ēnītī, contendere; (*contend*) certāre.
stroke *n* ictus *m*; (*lightning*) fulmen *nt* (*oar*) pulsus *m*; (*pen*) līnea *f*; ~ **of luck** fortūna secunda *f* ♦ *vt* mulcēre, dēmulcēre.
stroll *vi* deambulāre, spatiārī.
strong *adj* fortis, validus; (*health*) rōbustus, firmus; (*material*) firmus; (*smell*) grevis; (*resources*) pollēns, potēns; (*feeling*) ācer, māgnus; (*language*) vehemēns, probrōsus; **be** ~ valēre; **be twenty** ~ vīgintī esse numerō.
strongbox *n* arca *f.*
stronghold *n* arx *f.*
strongly *adv* validē, vehementer, forciter, ācriter, graviter.
strong-minded *adj* pertināx, cōnstans.
strophe *n* stropha *f.*
structure *n* aedificium *nt*; (*form*) structūra *f*; (*arrangement*) compositiō *f.*
struggle *n* (*effort*) cōnātus *m*; (*fight*) pugna *f*, certāmen *nt* ♦ *vi* nītī; certāre, contendere; (*fight*) luctārī; ~ **upwards** ēnītī.
strut *vi* māgnificē incēdere.
stubble *n* stipula *f.*
stubborn *adj* pertināx, pervicāx.
stubbornly *adv* pertināciter, pervicāciter.
stubbornness *n* pertinācia *f*, pervicācia *f.*
stucco *n* gypsum *nt.*
stud *n* clāvus *m*; (*horses*) equī *mpl.*
studded *adj* distinctus.
student *n* discipulus *m*; **be a** ~ **of** studēre (*dat*).
studied *adj* meditātus, accūrātus; (*language*) exquīsītus.
studio *n* officīna *f.*
studious *adj* litterīs dēditus, litterārum studiōsus; (*careful*) attentus.
studiously *adv* dē industriā.
study *vt* studēre (*dat*); (*prepare*) meditārī; ~ **under** audīre ♦ *n* studium *nt*; (*room*) bibliothēca *f.*
stuff *n* māteria *f*; (*cloth*) textile *nt* ♦ *vt* farcīre, refercīre; (*with food*) sagīnāre.
stuffing *n* sagina *f*; (*of cushion*) tōmentum *nt.*
stultify *vt* ad inritum redigere.
stumble *vi* offendere; ~ **upon** incidere in (*acc*), offendere.
stumbling block *n* offēnsiō *f.*
stump *n* stīpes *m.*
stun *vt* stupefacere; (*fig*) obstupefacere, cōnfundere.
stunned *adj* attonitus.
stunt *vt* corporis auctum inhibēre.
stunted *adj* curtus.
stupefaction *n* stupor *m.*
stupefied *adj*: **be** ~ stupēre, obstupefacere.
stupefy *vt* obstupefacere.
stupendous *adj* mīrus, mīrificus.
stupid *adj* stultus, hebes, ineptus.
stupidity *n* stultitia *f.*
stupidly *adv* stultē, ineptē.
stupor *n* stupor *m.*

sturdily *adv* fortiter.
sturdiness *n* rōbur *nt*, firmitās *f.*
sturdy *adj* fortis, rōbustus.
sturgeon *n* acipēnser *m.*
stutter *vi* balbūtire.
stuttering *adj* balbus.
sty *n* hara *f.*
style *n* (*kind*) genus *nt*, ratiō *f*; (*of dress*) habitus *m*; (*of prose*) ēlocūtiō *f*, ōrātiō *f*; (*pen*) stilus *m* ♦ *vt* appellāre.
stylish *adj* ēlegāns, lautus, expolītus.
stylishly *adv* ēleganter.
suasion *n* suāsiō *f.*
suave *adj* blandus, urbānus.
suavity *n* urbānitās *f.*
subaltern *n* succenturiō *m.*
subdivide *vt* dīvidere.
subdivision *n* pars *f*, mōmentum *nt.*
subdue *vt* subigere, dēvincere, redigere, domāre; (*fig*) cohibēre.
subdued *adj* dēmissus, summissus.
subject *n* (*person*) cīvis *m/f*; (*matter*) rēs *f*; (*theme*) locus *m*, argūmentum *nt* ♦ *adj* subiectus; ~ **to** obnoxius (*dat*) ♦ *vt* subicere; obnoxium reddere.
subjection *n* servitūs *f.*
subjective *adj* proprius.
subject matter *n* māteria *f.*
subjoin *vt* subicere, subiungere.
subjugate *vt* subigere, dēbellāre, domāre.
sublime *adj* sublīmis, ēlātus, excelsus.
sublimely *adv* excelsē.
sublimity *n* altitūdō *f*, ēlātiō *f.*
submarine *adj* submersus.
submerge *vt* dēmergere; (*flood*) inundāre ♦ *vi* sē dēmergere.
submersed *adj* submersus.
submission *n* obsequium *nt*, servitium *nt*; (*fig*) patientia *f.*
submissive *adj* submissus, docilis, obtemperāns.
submissively *adv* submissē, oboedienter, patienter.
submit *vi* sē dēdere; ~ **to** pārēre (*dat*), obtemperāre (*dat*), patī, subīre ♦ *vt* (*proposal*) referre.
subordinate *adj* subiectus, secundus ♦ *vt* subiungere, subicere.
suborn *vt* subicere, subōrnāre.
subpoena *vt* testimōnium dēnūntiāre (*dat*).
subscribe *vt* (*name*) subscrībere; (*money*) cōnferre.
subscription *n* collātiō *f.*
subsequent *adj* sequēns, posterior.
subsequently *adv* posteā, mox.
subserve *vt* subvenīre (*dat*), commodāre.
subservience *n* obsequium *nt.*
subservient *adj* obsequēns; (*thing*) ūtilis, commodus.
subside *vi* dēsīdere, resīdere; (*fever*) dēcēdere; (*wind*) cadere; (*passion*) dēfervēscere.
subsidence *n* lābēs *f.*

subsidiary adj subiectus, secundus.
subsidize vt pecūniās suppeditāre (dat).
subsidy n pecūniae fpl, vectīgal nt.
subsist vi cōnstāre, sustentārī.
subsistence n vīctus m.
substance n (matter) rēs f, corpus nt; (essence) nātūra f; (gist) summa f; (reality) rēs f; (wealth) opēs fpl.
substantial adj solidus; (real) vērus; (important) gravis; (rich) opulentus, dīves.
substantially adv rē; māgnā ex parte.
substantiate vt cōnfirmāre.
substitute vt subicere, repōnere, substituere ♦ n vicārius m.
substratum n fundāmentum nt.
subterfuge n latebra f, perfugium nt.
subterranean adj subterrāneus.
subtle adj (fine) subtīlis; (shrewd) acūtus, astūtus.
subtlety n subtīlitās f; acūmen nt, astūtia f.
subtly adv subtīliter; acūtē, astūte.
subtract vt dētrahere, dēmere; (money) dēdūcere.
subtraction n dētractiō f, dēductiō f.
suburb n suburbium nt.
suburban adj suburbānus.
subvention n pecūniae fpl.
subversion n ēversiō f, ruīna f.
subversive adj sēditiōsus.
subvert vt ēvertere, subruere.
subverter n ēversor m.
succeed vi (person) rem bene gerere; (activity) prosperē ēvenīre; ~ **in obtaining** impetrāre ♦ vt īnsequī, excipere, succēdere (dat).
success n bonus ēventus m, rēs bene gesta f.
successful adj fēlīx; (thing) secundus; **be ~** rem bene gerere; (play) stāre.
successfully adv fēlīciter, prosperē, bene.
succession n (coming next) successiō f; (line) seriēs f, ōrdō m; **alternate ~** vicissitūdō f; **in ~** deinceps, ex ōrdine.
successive adj continuus, perpetuus.
successively adv deinceps, ex ōrdine; (alternately) vicissim.
successor n successor m.
succinct adj brevis, pressus.
succinctly adv breviter, pressē.
succour n auxilium nt, subsidium nt ♦ vt subvenīre (dat), succurrere (dat), opem ferre (dat).
succulence n sūcus m.
succulent adj sūcidus.
succumb vi succumbere, dēficere.
such adj tālis, ēiusmodī, hūiusmodī; (size) tantus; **at ~ a time** id temporis; **~ great** tantus.
suchlike adj hūiusmodī, ēiusdem generis.
suck vt sūgere; **~ in** sorbēre; **~ up** exsorbēre, ēbibere.
sucker n surculus m.
sucking adj (child) lactēns.
suckle vt nūtrīcārī, mammam dare (dat).
suckling n lactēns m/f.

sudden adj subitus, repentīnus.
suddenly adv subitō, repente.
sue vt in iūs vocāre, lītem intendere (dat); **~ for** rogāre, petere, ōrāre.
suffer vt patī, ferre, tolerāre; (injury) accipere; (loss) facere; (permit) patī, sinere ♦ vi dolōre adficī; **~ defeat** cladem accipere; **~ from** labōrāre ex, adficī (abl); **~ for** poenās dare (gen).
sufferable adj tolerābilis.
sufferance n patientia f, tolerantia f.
suffering n dolor m.
suffice vi sufficere, suppetere.
sufficiency n satis.
sufficient adj idōneus, satis (gen).
sufficiently adv satis.
suffocate vt suffocāre.
suffrage n suffrāgium nt.
suffuse vt suffundere.
sugar n saccharon nt.
suggest vt admonēre, inicere, subicere; **~ itself** occurrere.
suggestion n admonitiō f; **at the ~ of** admonitū (gen); **at my ~** mē auctōre.
suicidal adj fūnestus.
suicide = mors voluntāria f; **commit ~** mortem sibī cōnscīscere.
suit n (law) līs f, āctiō f; (clothes) vestītus m ♦ vt convenīre (dat), congruere (dat); (dress) sedēre (dat), decēre; **it ~s** decet; **to ~ me** dē meā sententiā.
suitability n convenientia f.
suitable adj aptus (+ acc), idōneus (+ acc).
suitably adv aptē, decenter.
suite n comitēs mpl, comitātus m.
suitor n procus m, amāns m.
sulk vi aegrē ferre, mōrōsum esse.
sulky adj mōrōsus, tristis.
sullen adj tristis, mōrōsus.
sullenness n mōrōsitās f.
sully vt īnfuscāre, contāmināre.
sulphur n sulfur nt.
sultriness n aestus m.
sultry adj aestuōsus.
sum n summa f; **~ of money** pecūnia f ♦ vt subdūcere, computāre; **~ up** summātim dēscrībere; **to ~ up** ūnō verbō, quid plūra?
summarily adv strictim, summātim; sine morā.
summarize vt summātim dēscrībere.
summary n summārium nt, epitomē f ♦ adj subitus, praesēns.
summer n aestās f ♦ adj aestīvus; **of ~** aestīvus.
summit n vertex m, culmen nt; (fig) fastīgium nt; **the ~ of** summus.
summon vt arcessere; (meeting) convocāre; (witness) citāre; **~ up courage** animum sūmere.
summons n (law) vocātiō f ♦ vt in iūs vocāre, diem dīcere (dat).
sumptuary adj sūmptuārius.
sumptuous adj sūmptuōsus, adparātus,

māgnificus, lautus.
sumptuously *adv* sūmptuōsē, māgnificē.
sun *n* sōl *m* ♦ *vt*: ~ **oneself** aprīcārī.
sunbeam *n* radius *m*.
sunburnt *adj* adūstus.
sunder *vt* sēparāre, dīvidere.
sundial *n* sōlārium *nt*.
sundry *adj* dīversī, complūrēs.
sunlight *n* sōl *m*.
sunlit *adj* aprīcus.
sunny *adj* aprīcus, serēnus.
sunrise *n* sōlis ortus *m*.
sunset *n* sōlis occāsus *m*.
sunshade *n* umbella *f*.
sunshine *n* sōl *m*.
sup *vi* cēnāre.
superabundance *n* abundantia *f*.
superabundant *adj* nimius.
superabundantly *adv* satis superque.
superannuated *adj* ēmeritus.
superb *adj* māgnificus.
superbly *adv* māgnificē.
supercilious *adj* adrogāns, superbus.
superciliously *adv* adroganter, superbē.
superciliousness *n* adrogantia *f*, fastus *m*.
supererogation *n*: **of** ~ ultrō factus.
superficial *adj* levis; **acquire a ~ knowledge of**
prīmīs labrīs gustare.
superficiality *n* levitās *f*.
superficially *adv* leviter, strictim.
superfluity *n* abundantia *f*.
superfluous *adj* supervacāneus, nimius; **be ~**
redundāre.
superhuman *adj* dīvīnus, hūmānō mācr.
superimpose *vt* superimpōnere.
superintend *vt* prōcūrāre, praeesse (*dat*).
superintendence *n* cūra *f*.
superintendent *n* cūrātor *m*, praefectus *m*.
superior *adj* melior, amplior; **be ~** praestāre,
superāre ♦ *n* prīnceps *m*, praefectus *n*.
superiority *n* praestantia *f*; **have the ~**
superāre; (*in numbers*) plūrēs esse.
superlative *adj* ēgregius, optimus.
supernatural *adj* dīvīnus.
supernaturally *adv* dīvīnitus.
supernumerary *adj* adscrīptīcius; **~ soldiers**
accēnsī *mpl*.
superscription *n* titulus *m*.
supersede *vt* succēdere (*dat*), in locum
succēdere (*gen*); **~ gold with silver** prō aurō
argentum suppōnere.
superstition *n* rēligiō *f*, superstitiō *f*.
superstitious *adj* rēligiōsus, superstitiōsus.
supervene *vi* īnsequī, succēdere.
supervise *vt* prōcūrāre.
supervision *n* cūra *f*.
supervisor *n* cūrātor *m*.
supine *adj* supīnus; (*fig*) neglegēns, segnis.
supinely *adv* segniter.
supper *n* cēna *f*; **after ~** cēnātus.
supperless *adj* iēiūnus.
supplant *vt* praevertere.
supple *adj* flexibilis, mollis.

supplement *n* appendix *f* ♦ *vt* amplificāre.
supplementary *adj* additus.
suppleness *n* mollitia *f*.
suppliant *n* supplex *m/f*.
supplicate *vt* supplicāre, obsecrāre.
supplication *n* precēs *fpl*.
supplies *npl* commeātus *m*.
supply *n* cōpia *f* ♦ *vt* suppeditāre, praebēre;
(*loss*) supplēre.
support *n* firmāmentum *nt*; (*help*) subsidium *nt*,
adiūmentum *nt*; (*food*) alimenta *ntpl*; (*of party*)
favor *m*; (*of needy*) patrōcinium *nt*; **I ~** subsidio
sum (*dat*); **lend ~ to rumours** alimenta
rūmōribus addere ♦ *vt* fulcīre; (*living*)
sustinēre, sustentāre; (*with help*) adiuvāre,
opem ferre (*dat*); (*at law*) adesse (*dat*).
supportable *adj* tolerābilis.
supporter *n* fautor *m*; (*at trial*) advocātus *m*; (*of
proposal*) auctor *m*.
supporting cast *n* adiūtōrēs *mpl*.
suppose *vi* (*assume*) pōnere; (*think*)
existimāre, opīnārī, crēdere; **~ it is true** fac
vērum esse.
supposedly *adv* ut fāma est.
supposing *conj* sī; (*for the sake of argument*) sī
iam.
supposition *n* opīniō *f*; **on this ~** hōc positō.
supposititious *adj* subditus, subditīvus.
suppress *vt* opprimere, comprimere;
(*knowledge*) cēlāre, reticēre; (*feelings*)
coercēre, reprimere.
suppression *n* (*of fact*) reticentia *f*.
supremacy *n* imperium *nt*, dominātus *m*,
prīncipātus *m*.
supreme *adj* summus; **be ~** dominārī; **~
command** imperium *nt*.
supremely *adv* ūnicē, plānē.
sure *adj* certus; (*fact*) explōrātus; (*friend*) fīdus;
be ~ of compertum habēre; **feel ~** persuāsum
habēre, haud scīre an; **pro certō habēre;
make ~ of** (*fact*) comperīre; (*action*) efficere
ut; **to be ~** quidem; **~ enough** rē vērā.
surely *adv* certō, certē, nonne; (*tentative*)
scīlicet, sānē; **~ you do not think?** num
putās?; **~ not** num.
surety *n* (*person*) vās *m*, praes *m*, spōnsor *m*;
(*deposit*) fīdūcia *f*; **be ~ for** spondēre prō.
surf *n* fluctus *m*.
surface *n* superficiēs *f*; **~ of the water** summa
aqua.
surfeit *n* satietās *f* ♦ *vt* satiāre, explēre.
surge *n* aestus *m*, fluctus *m* ♦ *vi* tumēscere.
surgeon *n* chīrurgus *m*.
surgery *n* chīrurgia *f*.
surlily *adv* mōrōsē.
surliness *n* mōrōsitās *f*.
surly *adj* mōrōsus, difficilis.
surmise *n* coniectūra *f* ♦ *vi* suspicārī,
conicere, augurārī.
surmount *vt* superāre.
surmountable *adj* superābilis.
surname *n* cognōmen *nt*.
surpass *vt* excellere, exsuperāre, antecēdere.

surpassing _adj_ excellēns.
surplus _n_ reliquum _nt_; (_money_) pecūniae residuae _fpl_.
surprise _n_ admīrātiō _f_; (_cause_) rēs inopīnāta _f_; **take by** ~ dēprehendere ♦ _adj_ subitus ♦ _vt_ dēprehendere; (_MIL_) opprimere; **be ~d** dēmīrārī; **be ~d at** admīrārī.
surprising _adj_ mīrus, mīrābilis.
surprisingly _adv_ mīrē, mīrābiliter.
surrender _vt_ dēdere, trādere, concēdere ♦ _vi_ sē dēdere; ~ **unconditionally to** sē suaque omnia potestāti permittere (_gen_) ♦ _n_ dēditiō _f_; (_legal_) cessiō _f_; **unconditional** ~ permissiō _f_.
surreptitious _adj_ fūrtīvus.
surreptitiously _adv_ fūrtim, clam; **get in** ~ inrēpere in (_acc_).
surround _vt_ circumdare, cingere, circumvenīre, circumfundere.
surrounding _adj_ circumiectus; ~**s** _n_ vīcīnia _f_.
survey _vt_ contemplārī, cōnsīderāre; (_land_) mētārī ♦ _n_ contemplātiō _f_; (_land_) mēnsūra _f_.
surveyor _n_ fīnītor _m_, agrīmēnsor _m_, mētātor _m_.
survival _n_ salūs _f_.
survive _vt_ superāre ♦ _vt_ superesse (_dat_).
survivor _n_ superstes _m/f_.
susceptibility _n_ mollitia _f_.
susceptible _adj_ mollis.
suspect _vt_ suspicārī; **be ~ed** in suspiciōnem venīre.
suspend _vt_ suspendere; (_activity_) differre; (_person_) locō movēre; **be ~ed** pendēre.
suspense _n_ dubitātiō _f_; **be in** ~ animī pendēre, haerēre.
suspicion _n_ suspiciō _f_; **direct** ~ **to** suspiciōnem adiungere ad.
suspicious _adj_ (_suspecting_) suspiciōsus; (_suspected_) dubius, anceps.
sustain _vt_ (_weight_) sustinēre; (_life_) alere, sustentāre; (_hardship_) ferre, sustinēre; (_the part of_) agere.
sustenance _n_ alimentum _nt_, vīctus _m_.
sutler _n_ lixa _m_.
suzerain _n_ dominus _m_.
swaddling clothes _n_ incūnābula _ntpl_.
swagger _vi_ sē iactāre.
swaggerer _n_ homō glōriōsus _m_.
swallow _n_ hirundō _f_ ♦ _vt_ dēvorāre; ~ **up** absorbēre.
swamp _n_ palūs _f_ ♦ _vt_ opprimere.
swampy _adj_ ūlīginōsus.
swan _n_ cycnus _m_; ~'**s** cycnēus.
swank _vi_ sē iactāre.
sward _n_ caespes _m_.
swarm _n_ exāmen _nt_; (_fig_) nūbēs _f_ ♦ _vi_: ~ **round** circumfundī.
swarthy _adj_ fuscus, aquilus.
swathe _vt_ conligāre.
sway _n_ dīciō _f_, imperium _nt_; **bring under one's** ~ suae dīciōnis facere ♦ _vt_ regere ♦ _vi_ vacillāre.
swear _vi_ iūrāre; ~ **allegiance to** iūrāre in verba (_gen_).

sweat _n_ sūdor _m_ ♦ _vi_ sūdāre.
sweep _vt_ verrere; ~ **away** rapere; ~ **out** ēverrere.
sweet _adj_ dulcis, suāvis.
sweeten _vt_ dulcem reddere.
sweetheart _n_ dēliciae _fpl_.
sweetly _adv_ dulciter, suāviter.
sweetness _n_ dulcitūdō _f_, suāvitās _f_.
sweet-tempered _adj_ suāvis, cōmis.
swell _n_ tumor _m_ ♦ _vi_ tumēre, tumēscere; (_fig_) glīscere ♦ _vt_ inflāre.
swelling _adj_ tumidus ♦ _n_ tumor _m_.
swelter _vi_ aestū labōrāre.
swerve _vi_ dēclīnāre, dēvertere ♦ _n_ dēclīnātiō _f_.
swift _adj_ celer, vēlōx, incitātus.
swiftly _adv_ celeriter, vēlōciter.
swiftness _n_ celeritās _f_, vēlōcitās _f_.
swill _vt_ (_rinse_) colluere; (_drink_) ēpōtāre.
swim _vi_ nāre, innāre; (_place_) natāre; ~ **across** trānāre; ~ **ashore** ēnāre; ~ **to** adnāre.
swimming _n_ natātiō _f_.
swindle _vt_ circumvenīre, verba dare (_dat_) ♦ _n_ fraus _f_.
swine _n_ sūs _m/f_.
swineherd _n_ subulcus _m_.
swing _n_ (_motion_) oscillātiō _f_ ♦ _vi_ oscillāre ♦ _vt_ lībrāre.
swinish _adj_ obscēnus.
swirl _n_ vertex _m_ ♦ _vi_ volūtārī.
switch _n_ virga _f_ ♦ _vt_ flectere, torquēre.
swivel _n_ cardō _f_.
swollen _adj_ tumidus, turgidus, īnflātus.
swoon _n_ dēfectiō _f_ ♦ _vi_ intermorī.
swoop _n_ impetus _m_ ♦ _vi_ lābī; ~ **down on** involāre in (_acc_).
sword _n_ gladius _m_; **put to the** ~ occīdere; **with fire and** ~ ferrō ignīque.
swordsman _n_ gladiātor _m_.
sworn _adj_ iūrātus.
sybarite _n_ dēlicātus _m_.
sycophancy _n_ adsentātiō _f_, adūlātiō _f_.
sycophant _n_ adsentātor _m_, adūlātor _m_.
syllable _n_ syllaba _f_.
syllogism _n_ ratiōcinātiō _f_.
sylvan _adj_ silvestris.
symbol _n_ signum _nt_, īnsigne _nt_.
symmetrical _adj_ concinnus, aequus.
symmetry _n_ concinnitās _f_, aequitās _f_.
sympathetic _adj_ concors, misericors.
sympathetically _adv_ misericorditer.
sympathize _vi_ cōnsentīre; ~ **with** miserērī (_gen_).
sympathy _n_ concordia _f_, cōnsēnsus _m_; misericordia _f_.
symphony _n_ concentus _m_.
symptom _n_ signum _nt_, indicium _nt_.
syndicate _n_ societās _f_.
synonym _n_ verbum idem dēclārāns _nt_.
synonymous _adj_ idem dēclārāns.
synopsis _n_ summārium _nt_.
syringe _n_ clystēr _m_.
system _n_ ratiō _f_, fōrmula _f_; (_PHILOS_) disciplīna _f_.

T, t

systematic adj ōrdinātus, cōnstāns.
systematically adv ratiōne, ōrdine.
systematize vt in ōrdinem redigere.

tabernacle n tabernāculum nt.
table n mēnsa f; (inscribed) tabula f; (list) index m; **at ~** inter cēnam; **turn the ~s on** pār parī referre.
tablet n tabula f, tabella f.
taboo n rēligiō f.
tabulate vt in ōrdinem redigere.
tacit adj tacitus.
tacitly adv tacitē.
taciturn adj taciturnus.
taciturnity n taciturnitās f.
tack n clāvulus m; (of sail) pēs m ♦ vt: **~ on** adsuere ♦ vi (ship) reciprocārī, nāvem flectere.
tackle n armāmenta ntpl ♦ vt adgredī.
tact n iūdicium nt, commūnis sēnsus m hūmānitās f.
tactful adj prūdēns, hūmānus.
tactfully adv prūdenter, hūmāniter.
tactician n reī mīlitāris perītus m.
tactics n rēs mīlitāris f, bellī ratiō f.
tactless adj ineptus.
tactlessly adv ineptē.
tadpole n rānunculus m.
tag n appendicula f.
tail n cauda f; **turn ~** terga vertere.
tailor n vestītor m.
taint n lābēs f, vitium nt ♦ vt inquināre, contāmināre, īnficere.
take vt capere, sūmere; (auspices) habēre; (disease) contrahere; (experience) ferre; (fire) concipere; (meaning) accipere, interpretārī; (in the act) dēprehendere; (person) dūcere; **~ after** similem esse (dat, gen); **~ across** trānsportāre; **~ arms** arma sūmere; **~ away** dēmere, auferre, adimere, abdūcere; **~ back** recipere; **~ by storm** expugnāre; **~ care that** curāre ut/ne (+ subj); **~ down** dētrahere; (in writing) exscrībere; **~ for** habēre prō; **~ hold of** prehendere; **~ in** (as guest) recipere; (information) percipere, comprehendere; (with deceit) dēcipere; **~ in hand** incipere, suscipere; **~ off** dēmere; (clothes) exuere; **~ on** suscipere; **~ out** eximere, extrahere; (from store) prōmere; **~ over** excipere; **~ place** fierī, accidere; **~ prisoner** capere; **~ refuge in** cōnfugere ad (+ infin); **~ the field in** aciem dēscendere; **~ to** sē dēdere (dat), amāre; **~ to oneself** suscipere; **~ up** sūmere,

tollere; (task) incipere, adgredī ad; (in turn) excipere; (room) occupāre; **~ upon oneself** recipere, sibī sūmere.
taking adj grātus ♦ n (MIL) expugnātiō f.
tale n fābula f, fābella f.
talent n (money) talentum nt; (ability) ingenium nt, indolēs f.
talented adj ingeniōsus.
talk n sermō m; (with another) colloquium nt; **common ~** fāma f; **be the ~ of the town** in ōre omnium esse ♦ vi loquī; (to one) colloquī cum; **~ down to** ad intellectum audientis dēscendere; **~ over** cōnferre, disserere dē.
talkative adj loquāx.
talkativeness n loquācitās f.
tall adj prōcērus, grandis.
tallness n prōcēritās f.
tallow n sēbum nt.
tally n tessera f ♦ vi congruere.
talon n unguis m.
tamarisk n myrīca f.
tambourine n tympanum nt.
tame vt domāre, mānsuēfacere ♦ adj mānsuētus; (character) ignāvus; (language) īnsulsus, frīgidus.
tamely adv ignāvē, lentē.
tameness n mānsuētūdō f; (fig) lentitūdō f.
tamer n domitor m.
tamper vi: **~ with** (person) sollicitāre; (writing) interpolāre.
tan vt imbuere.
tang n sapor m.
tangible adj tāctilis.
tangle n nōdus m ♦ vt implicāre.
tank n lacus m.
tanned adj (by sun) adūstus.
tanner n coriārius m.
tantalize vt lūdere.
tantamount adj pār, īdem.
tantrum n īra f.
tap n epitonium nt; (touch) plāga f ♦ vt (cask) relinere; (hit) ferīre.
tape n taenia f.
taper n cēreus m ♦ vi fastīgārī.
tapestry n aulaea ntpl.
tar n pix f.
tardily adv tardē, lentē.
tardiness n tarditās f, segnitia f.
tardy adj tardus, lentus.
tare n lolium nt.
targe n parma f.
target n scopus m.
tariff n portōrium nt.
tarn n lacus m.
tarnish vt īnfuscāre, inquināre ♦ vi īnfuscārī.
tarry vi morārī, commorārī, cunctārī.
tart adj acidus, asper ♦ n scrīblīta f.
tartly adv acerbē.
tartness n asperitās f.
task n pēnsum nt, opus nt, negōtium nt; **take to ~** obiūrgāre.
taskmaster n dominus m.
tassel n fimbriae fpl.

taste n (_sense_) gustātus m; (_flavour_) sapor m; (_artistic_) iūdicium nt, ēlegantia f; (_for rhetoric_) aurēs fpl; of ~ doctus; in good ~ ēlegāns ♦ vt gustāre, dēgustāre ♦ vi sapere; ~ of resipere.
tasteful adj ēlegāns.
tastefully adv ēleganter.
tastefulness n ēlegantia f.
tasteless adj īnsulsus, inēlegāns.
tastelessly adv īnsulsē, inēleganter.
tastelessness n īnsulsitās f.
taster n praegustātor m.
tasty adj dulcis.
tattered adj pannōsus.
tatters n pannī mpl.
tattoo vt compungere.
taunt n convīcium nt, probrum nt ♦ vt exprobrāre, obicere (_dat of pers, acc of charge_).
taunting adj contumēliōsus.
tauntingly adv contumēliōsē.
taut adj intentus; **draw** ~ addūcere.
tavern n taberna f, hospitium nt.
tawdry adj vīlis.
tawny adj fulvus.
tax n vectīgal nt, tribūtum nt; **a 5 per cent** ~ vīcēsima f; **free from** ~ immūnis ♦ vt vectīgal impōnere (_dat_); (_strength_) contendere; ~ **with** (_charge_) obicere (_acc_ & _dat_), īnsimulāre.
taxable adj vectīgālis.
taxation n vectīgālia ntpl.
tax collector n exāctor m.
tax farmer n pūblicānus m.
taxpayer n assiduus m.
teach vt docēre, ērudīre, īnstituere; (_thoroughly_) ēdocēre; (_pass_) discere; ~ **your grandmother** sūs Minervam.
teachable adj docilis.
teacher n magister m, magistra f, doctor m; (PHILOS) praeceptor m; (_of literature_) grammaticus m; (_of rhetoric_) rhētor m.
teaching n doctrīna f, disciplīna f.
team n (_animals_) iugum nt.
tear n lacrima f; **shed** ~s lacrimās effundere ♦ vt scindere; ~ **down** revellere; ~ **in pieces** dīlaniāre, discerpere, lacerāre; ~ **off** abscindere, dēripere; ~ **open** rescindere; ~ **out** ēvellere; ~ **up** convellere.
tearful adj flēbilis.
tease vt lūdere, inrītāre.
teat n mamma f.
technical adj (_term_) proprius.
technique n ars f.
tedious adj longus, lentus, odiōsus.
tediously adv molestē.
tedium n taedium nt, molestia f.
teem vi abundāre.
teeming adj fēcundus, refertus.
teens n: in one's ~ adulescentulus.
teethe vi dentīre.
tell vt (_story_) nārrāre; (_person_) dīcere (_dat_); (_number_) ēnumerāre; (_inform_) certiōrem facere; (_difference_) intellegere; (_order_) iubēre (+ _acc and infin_), imperāre (+ **ut/ne** _and subj_);

~ **the truth** vēra dīcere; ~ **lies** mentior ♦ vi valēre; ~ **the difference between** discernere; **I cannot** ~ nesciō.
telling adj validus.
temerity n temeritās f.
temper n animus m, ingenium nt; (_bad_) īra f, īrācundia f; (_of metal_) temperātiō f ♦ vt temperāre; (_fig_) moderārī (_dat_).
temperament n animī habitus m, animus m.
temperamental adj incōnstāns.
temperance n temperantia f, continentia f.
temperate adj temperātus, moderātus, sobrius.
temperately adv moderātē.
temperature n calor m, frīgus nt; **mild** ~ temperiēs f.
tempest n tempestās f, procella f.
tempestuous adj procellōsus.
temple n templum nt, aedēs f; (_head_) tempus nt.
temporal adj hūmānus, profānus.
temporarily adv ad tempus.
temporary adj brevis.
temporize vi temporis causā facere, tergiversārī.
tempt vt sollicitāre, pellicere, invītāre.
temptation n illecebra f.
tempter n impulsor m.
ten num decem; ~ **each** dēnī; ~ **times** deciēns.
tenable adj inexpugnābilis, stabilis, certus.
tenacious adj tenāx, firmus.
tenaciously adv tenāciter.
tenacity n tenācitās f.
tenant n inquilīnus m, habitātor m; (_on land_) colōnus m.
tenantry n colōnī mpl.
tend vi spectāre, pertinēre ♦ vt cūrāre, colere.
tendency n inclīnātiō f, voluntās f.
tender adj tener, mollis ♦ vt dēferre, offerre.
tenderhearted adj misericors.
tenderly adv indulgenter.
tenderness n indulgentia f, mollitia f.
tendon n nervus m.
tendril n clāviculus m.
tenement n habitātiō f; **block of** ~s īnsula f.
tenet n dogma nt, dēcrētum nt.
tennis court n sphaeristērium nt.
tenor n (_course_) tenor m; (_purport_) sententia f.
tense adj intentus ♦ n tempus nt.
tension n intentiō f.
tent n tabernāculum nt; (_general's_) praetōrium nt.
tentacle n bracchium nt.
tentatively adv experiendō.
tenterhooks n: on ~ animī suspēnsus.
tenth adj decimus; **for the** ~ **time** decimum; **men of the** ~ **legion** decumānī mpl.
tenuous adj rārus.
tenure n possessiō f.
tepid adj tepidus; **be** ~ tepēre.
tergiversation n tergiversātiō f.
term n (_limit_) terminus m; (_period_) spatium nt; (_word_) verbum nt ♦ vt appellāre, nuncupāre.

terminate *vt* termināre, fīnīre ♦ *vi* dēsinere; (*words*) cadere.
termination *n* fīnis *m*, terminus *m*.
terminology *n* vocābula *ntpl*.
terms *npl* condiciō *f*, lēx *f*; propose ~ condiciōnem ferre; be on good ~ in grātiā esse; we come to ~ inter nōs convenit.
terrain *n* ager *m*.
terrestrial *adj* terrestris.
terrible *adj* terribilis, horribilis, horrendus.
terribly *adv* horrendum in modum.
terrific *adj* formīdolōsus; vehemēns.
terrify *vt* terrēre, perterrēre, exterrēre.
terrifying *adj* formīdolōsus.
territory *n* ager *m*, fīnēs *mpl*.
terror *n* terror *m*, formīdō *f*, pavor *m*; object of ~ terror *m*; be a ~ to terrōrī esse (*dat*).
terrorize *vt* metum inicere (*dat*).
terse *adj* pressus, brevis.
tersely *adv* pressē.
terseness *n* brevitās *f*.
tessellated *adj* tessellātus.
test *n* experīmentum *nt*, probātiō *f*; (*standard*) obrussa *f*; put to the ~ experīrī, perīclitārī; stand the ~ spectārī ♦ *vt* experīrī, probāre, spectāre.
testament *n* testāmentum *nt*.
testamentary *adj* testāmentārius.
testator *n* testātor *m*.
testify *vt* testificārī.
testifying *n* testificātiō *f*.
testily *adv* stomachōsē.
testimonial *n* laudātiō *f*.
testimony *n* testimōnium *nt*.
testy *adj* difficilis, stomachōsus.
tether *n* retināculum *nt*, vinculum *nt* ♦ *vt* religāre.
tetrarch *n* tetrarchēs *m*.
tetrarchy *n* tetrarchia *f*.
text *n* verba *ntpl*.
textbook *n* ars *f*.
textile *adj* textilis.
textual *adj* verbōrum.
texture *n* textus *m*.
than *conj* quam *abl*; other ~ alius ac.
thank *vt* grātiās agere (*dat*); ~ you bene facis; no, ~ you benīgnē.
thankful *adj* grātus.
thankfully *adv* grātē.
thankfulness *n* grātia *f*.
thankless *adj* ingrātus.
thanklessly *adv* ingrātē.
thanks *n* grātiae *fpl*, grātēs *fpl*; return ~ grātiās agere, grātēs persolvere; ~ to you operā tuā, beneficiō tuō; it is ~ to sb that ... not per aliquem stat quominus (+ *subj*).
thanksgiving *n* grātulātiō *f*; (*public*) supplicātiō *f*.
that pron (*demonstrative*) ille; (*relat*) quī ♦ *conj* (*statement*) acc & *infin*; (*command, purpose, result*) ut; (*fearing*) nē; (*emotion*) quod; oh ~ utinam.
thatch *n* culmus *m*, strāmenta *ntpl* ♦ *vt* tegere,

integere.
thaw *vt* dissolvere ♦ *vi* liquēscere, tabēscere.
the art *not expressed*; (*emphatic*) ille; (*with* compar) quō ... eō.
theatre *n* theātrum *nt*.
theatrical *adj* scēnicus.
theft *n* fūrtum *nt*.
their *adj* eōrum; (*ref to subject*) suus.
theme *n* māteria *f*, argūmentum *nt*.
themselves *pron* ipsī; (*reflexive*) sē.
then *adv* (*time*) tum, tunc; (*succession*) deinde, tum, posteā; (*consequence*) igitur, ergō; now and ~ interdum; only ~ tum dēmum.
thence *adv* inde.
thenceforth *adv* inde, posteā, ex eō tempore.
theologian *n* theologus *m*.
theology *n* theologia *f*.
theorem *n* prōpositum *nt*.
theoretical *adj* contemplātīvus.
theory *n* ratiō *f*; ~ and practice ratiō atque ūsus.
there *adv* ibī, illīc; (*thither*) eō, illūc; from ~ inde, illinc; here and ~ passim; ~ is est; (*interj*) ecce.
thereabout(s) *adv* circā, circiter, prope.
thereafter *adv* deinde, posteā.
thereby *adv* eā rē, hōc factō.
therefore *adv* itaque, igitur, ergō, idcircō.
therein *adv* inibī, in eō.
thereof *adv* ēius, ēius reī.
thereon *adv* īnsuper, in eō.
thereupon *adv* deinde, statim, inde, quō facto.
therewith *adv* cum eō.
thesis *n* prōpositum *nt*.
thews *n* nervī *mpl*.
they *pron* iī, hī, illī.
thick *adj* dēnsus; (*air*) crassus.
thicken *vt* dēnsāre ♦ *vi* concrēscere.
thickening *n* concrētiō *f*.
thicket *n* dūmētum *nt*.
thickheaded *adj* stupidus, hebes.
thickly *adv* dēnsē; ~ populated frequēns.
thickness *n* crassitūdō *f*.
thickset *adj* brevis atque obēsus
thick-skinned *adj*: be ~ callēre; become ~ occallēscere.
thief *n* fūr *m*.
thieve *vt* fūrārī, surripere.
thievery *n* fūrtum *nt*.
thievish *adj* fūrāx.
thigh *n* femur *nt*.
thin *adj* exīlis, gracilis, tenuis; (*a tendance*) īnfrequēns ♦ *vt* attenuāre, extenuāre; ~ out rārefacere; ~ down dīluere.
thine *adj* tuus.
thing *n* rēs *f*; as ~s are nunc, cum haec ita sint.
think *vi* cōgitāre; (*opinion*) putāre, existimāre, arbitrārī, rērī, crēdere; as I ~ meā sententiā; ~ about cōgitāre dē; ~ highly of māgnī aestimāre; ~ nothing of nihilī facere; ~ out excōgitāre; ~ over reputāre, in mente agitāre.
thinker *n* philosophus *m*.

thinking adj sapiēns ♦ n cōgitātiō f; ~ **that** ratus, arbitratus.

thinly adv exīliter, tenuiter; rārē.

thinness n exīlitās f, gracilitās f; (person) maciēs f; (number) exiguitās f, īnfrequentia f; (air) tenuitās f.

thin-skinned adj inrītābilis.

third adj tertius; **for the** ~ **time** tertium ♦ n tertia pars f, triēns m; **two** ~**s** duae partēs, bēs m.

thirdly adv tertiō.

thirst n sitis f ♦ vi sitīre; ~ **for** sitīre.

thirstily adv sitienter.

thirsty adj sitiēns.

thirteen num tredecim; ~ **each** ternī dēnī; ~ **times** terdeciēns.

thirteenth adj tertius decimus.

thirtieth adj trīcēsimus.

thirty num trīgintā; ~ **each** trīcēnī; ~ **times** trīciēns.

this pron hīc.

thistle n carduus m.

thither adv eō, illūc.

thole n scalmus nt.

thong n lōrum nt, habēna f.

thorn n spīna f, sentis m.

thorny adj spīnōsus.

thorough adj absolūtus, germānus; (work) accūrātus.

thoroughbred adj generōsus.

thoroughfare n via f.

thoroughly adv penitus, omnīnō, funditus.

thoroughness n cūra f, diligentia f.

thou pron tū.

though conj etsī, etiamsī, quamvīs (+ subj), quamquam all (+ indic).

thought n (faculty) cōgitātiō f, mēns f, animus m; (an idea) cōgitātum nt, nōtiō f; (design) cōnsilium nt, prōpositum nt; (expressed) sententia f; (heed) cautiō f, prōvidentia f; (RHET) inventiō f; **second** ~**s** posteriōrēs cōgitātiōnēs.

thoughtful adj cōgitābundus; prōvidus.

thoughtfully adv prōvidē.

thoughtless adj incōnsīderātus, incōnsultus, imprōvidus, immemor.

thoughtlessly adv temerē, incōnsultē.

thoughtlessness n incōnsīderantia f, imprūdentia f.

thousand num mīlle; ~**s** pl mīlia (+ gen) ntpl; ~ **each** mīllēnī; ~ **times** mīlliēns; **three** ~ tria mīlia.

thousandth adj mīllēsimus.

thrall n servus m.

thraldom n servitūs f.

thrash vt verberāre.

thrashing n verbera ntpl.

thread n fīlum nt; **hang by a** ~ (fig) fīlō pendēre ♦ vt: ~ **one's way** sē īnsinuāre.

threadbare adj trītus, obsolētus.

threat n minae fpl, minātiō f.

threaten vt minārī (dat of pers), dēnūntiāre ♦ vi imminēre, impendēre.

threatening adj mināx, imminēns.

threateningly adv mināciter.

three num trēs; ~ **each** ternī; ~ **times** ter; ~ **days** trīduum nt; ~ **years** triennium nt; ~ **quarters** trēs partēs fpl, dōdrāns m.

three-cornered adj triangulus, triquetrus.

threefold adj triplex.

three hundred num trecentī; ~ **each** trecēnī; ~ **times** trecentiēns.

three hundredth adj trecentēsimus.

three-legged adj tripēs.

three-quarters n dōdrāns m, trēs partēs fpl.

thresh vt terere, exterere.

threshing floor n ārea f.

threshold n līmen nt.

thrice adv ter.

thrift n frūgālitās f, parsimōnia f.

thriftily adv frūgāliter.

thrifty adj parcus, frūgī.

thrill n horror m ♦ vt percellere, percutere ♦ vi trepidāre.

thrilling adj mīrābilis.

thrive vi vigēre, valēre, crēscere.

thriving adj valēns, vegetus; (crops) laetus.

throat n faucēs fpl, guttur nt; **cut the** ~ **of** iugulāre.

throaty adj gravis, raucus.

throb vi palpitāre, micāre ♦ n pulsus m.

throe n dolor m; **be in the** ~**s** of labōrāre ex.

throne n solium nt; (power) rēgnum nt.

throng n multitūdō f, frequentia f ♦ vt celebrāre; ~ **round** stīpāre, circumfundī (dat).

throttle vt strangulāre.

through prep per (acc); (cause) propter (acc), abl ♦ adv: ~ **and** ~ penitus; **carry** ~ exsequī, peragere; **go** ~ trānsīre; **run** ~ percurrere; **be** ~ **with** perfunctum esse (abl).

throughout adv penitus, omnīnō ♦ prep per (acc).

throw n iactus m, coniectus m ♦ vt iacere, conicere; ~ **about** iactāre; ~ **across** trāicere; ~ **away** abicere; (something precious) prōicere; ~ **back** rēicere; ~ **down** dēturbāre, dēicere; ~ **into** inicere; ~ **into confusion** perturbāre; ~ **off** excutere, exsolvere; ~ **open** patefacere; ~ **out** ēicere, prōicere; ~ **over** inicere; (fig) dēstituere; ~ **overboard** iactūram facere (gen); ~ **to** (danger) obicere; ~ **up** ēicere; (building) exstruere; ~ **a bridge over** pontem inicere (dat), pontem faciendum cūrāre in (abl); ~ **light on** (fig) lūmen adhibēre (dat); ~ **a rider** equitem excutere.

throwing n coniectiō f, iactus m.

thrum n līcium nt.

thrush n turdus m.

thrust vt trūdere, pellere, impingere; ~ **at** petere; ~ **away** dētrūdere; ~ **forward** prōtrūdere; ~ **home** dēfīgere; ~ **into** īnfīgere, impingere; ~ **out** extrūdere.

thud n gravis sonitus m.

thug n percussor m, sīcārius m.

thumb n pollex m; **have under one's ~ in** potestāte suā habēre.

thump n plāga f ♦ vt tundere, pulsāre.

thunder n tonitrus m ♦ vi tonāre, intonāre; **it ~s** tonāt.

thunderbolt n fulmen nt.

thunderer n tonāns m.

thunderstruck adj attonitus.

thus adv (referring back) sīc; (referring forward) ita; **~ far** hāctenus.

thwack vt verberāre.

thwart vt obstāre (dat), officere (dat), remorārī, frustrārī ♦ n (boat's) trānstrum nt.

thy adj tuus.

thyme n thymum nt; (wild) serpyllum nt.

tiara n diadēma nt.

ticket n tessera f.

tickle vt titillāre.

tickling n titillātiō f.

ticklish adj lūbricus.

tidal adj: **~ waters** aestuārium nt.

tide n aestus m; (time) tempus nt; **ebb ~** aestūs recessus m; **flood ~** aestūs accessus m; **turn of the ~** commūtātiō aestūs; **the ~ will turn** (fig) circumagētur hīc orbis.

tidily adv concinnē, mundē.

tidiness n concinnitās f, munditia f.

tidings n nūntius m.

tidy adj concinnus, mundus.

tie n (bond) vinculum nt, cōpula f; (kin) necessitūdō f ♦ vt ligāre; (knot) nectere; **~ fast** dēvincīre, cōnstringere; **~ on** illigāre; **~ to** adligāre; **~ together** colligāre; **~ up** adligāre; (wound) obligāre.

tier n ōrdō m.

tiff n dissēnsiō f.

tiger n tigris m, more usu f.

tight adj strictus, astrictus, intentus; (close) artus; **draw ~** intendere, addūcere.

tighten vt adstringere, contendere.

tightly adv artē, angustē.

tightrope n extentus fūnis; **~ walker** n fūnambulus m.

tigress n tigris f.

tile n tegula f, imbrex f, later nt.

till conj dum, dōnec ♦ prep usque ad (acc), in (acc); **not ~** dēmum ♦ n arca f ♦ vt colere.

tillage n cultus m.

tiller n (AGR) cultor m; (ship) clāvus m, gubernāculum nt.

tilt vt inclīnāre.

tilth n cultus m, arvum nt.

timber n (for building) māteria f; (firewood) lignum nt.

timbrel n tympanum nt.

time n tempus nt; (lifetime) aetās f; (interval) intervallum nt, spatium nt; (of day) hōra f; (leisure) ōtium nt; (rhythm) numerus m; **another ~** aliās; **at ~s** aliquandō, interdum; **at all ~s** semper; **at any ~** umquam; **at one ~ ... at another** aliās ... aliās; **at that ~** tunc, id temporis; **at the right ~** ad tempus, mātūrē, tempestīvē; **at the same ~** simul; tamen; **at**

the wrong ~ intempestīvē; **beating ~** percussiō f; **convenient ~** opportūnitās f; **for a ~** aliquantisper, parumper; **for a long ~** diū; **for some ~** aliquamdiū; **for the ~ being** ad tempus; **from ~ to ~** interdum, identidem; **have a good ~** geniō indulgēre; **have ~ for** vacāre (dat); **in ~** ad tempus, tempore; **in a short ~** brevī; **in good ~** tempestīvus; **in the ~ of** apud (acc); **keep ~** (marching) gradum cōnferre; (music) modulārī; **many ~s** saepe, saepenumerō; **pass, spend ~** tempus sūmere, dēgere; **several ~s** aliquotiēns; **some ~** aliquandō; **waste ~** tempus terere; **what is the ~?** quota hōra est?; **~ expired** ēmeritus.

time-honoured adj antīquus.

timeliness n opportūnitās f.

timely adj opportūnus, tempestīvus, mātūrus.

timid adj timidus.

timidity n timiditās f.

timidly adv timidē.

timorous adj timidus.

timorously adv timidē.

tin n stannum nt, plumbum album nt ♦ adj stanneus.

tincture n color m, sapor m ♦ vt īnficere.

tinder n fōmes m.

tinge vt imbuere, īnficere, tingere.

tingle vi horrēre.

tingling n horror m.

tinkle vi tinnīre ♦ n tinnītus m.

tinsel n bractea f; (fig) speciēs f, fūcus m.

tint n color m ♦ vt colōrāre.

tiny adj minūtus, pusillus, perexiguus.

tip n apex m, cacūmen nt, extrēmum nt; **the ~ of** prīmus, extrēmus ♦ vt praefīgere; **~ over** invertere.

tipple vi pōtāre.

tippler n pōtor m, ēbrius m.

tipsy adj tēmulentus.

tiptoes n: **on ~** suspēnsō gradū.

tirade n obiūrgātiō f, dēclāmātiō f.

tire vt fatīgāre; **~ out** dēfatīgāre ♦ vi dēfetīscī, fatīgārī; **I ~ of** mē taedet (gen); **it ~s** taedet (+ acc of person, gen of thing).

tired adj (dē)fessus, lassus; **~ out** dēfessus; **I am ~ of** mē taedet.

tiresome adj molestus, difficilis.

tiring adj labōriōsus, operōsus.

tiro n tīrō m, rudis m.

tissue n textus m.

tit n: **give ~ for tat** pār parī respondēre.

Titan n Tītān m.

titanic adj immānis.

titbit n cuppēdium nt.

tithe n decuma f.

tithe gatherer n decumānus m.

titillate vt titillāre.

titillation n titillātiō f.

title n (book) īnscrīptiō f, index m; (inscription) titulus m; (person) nōmen nt, appellātiō f; (claim) iūs nt, vindiciae fpl; **assert one's ~ to** vindicāre; **give a ~ to** īnscrībere.

titled adj nōbilis.

title deed n auctōritās f.
titter n rīsus m ♦ vi rīdēre.
tittle-tattle n sermunculus m.
titular adj nōmine.
to prep ad (acc), in (acc); (attitude) ergā (acc);
(giving) dat; (towns, small islands, domus, rūs)
acc ♦ conj (purpose) ut ♦ adv: **come** ~ animum
recipere; ~ **and fro** hūc illūc.
toad n būfō m.
toady n adsentātor m, parasītus m ♦ vt
adsentārī (dat).
toadyism n adsentātiō f.
toast n: **drink a** ~ propīnāre ♦ vt torrēre; (drink)
propīnāre (dat).
today adv hodiē; ~'s hodiernus.
toe n digitus m; **big** ~ pollex m.
toga n toga f.
together adv ūnā, simul; **bring** ~ cōgere,
congerere; **come** ~ convenīre, congregārī;
put ~ cōnferre, compōnere.
toil n labor m; (snare) rēte nt ♦ vi labōrāre; ~ **at**
ēlabōrāre in (abl).
toilet n (lady's) cultus m.
toilsome adj labōriōsus, operōsus.
toil-worn adj labōre cōnfectus.
token n īnsigne nt, signum nt, indicium nt.
tolerable adj tolerābilis, patibilis; (quality)
mediocris; (size) modicus.
tolerably adv satis, mediocriter.
tolerance n patientia f, tolerantia f.
tolerant adj indulgēns, tolerāns.
tolerantly adv indulgenter.
tolerate vt tolerāre, ferre, indulgēre (dat).
toleration n patientia f; (freedom) lībertās f.
toll n vectīgal nt; (harbour) portōrium nt.
toll collector n exāctor m; portitor m.
tomb n sepulcrum nt.
tombstone n lapis m.
tome n liber m.
tomorrow adv crās; ~'s crāstinus; **the day**
after ~ perendiē; **put off till** ~ in crāstinum
differre.
tone n sonus m, vōx f; (painting) color m.
tongs n forceps m/f.
tongue n lingua f; (shoe) ligula f; **on the tip of**
one's ~ in prīmōribus labrīs.
tongue-tied adj ēlinguis, īnfāns.
tonnage n amphorae fpl.
tonsils n tōnsillae fpl.
tonsure n rāsūra f.
too adv (also) etiam, īnsuper, quoque; (excess)
nimis ♦ compar adj: ~ **far** extrā modum; ~
much nimium; ~ **long** nimium diū; ~ **great to**
māior quam quī (subj); ~ **late** sērius; ~ **little**
parum (+ gen).
tool n īnstrūmentum nt; (AGR) ferrāmentum nt;
(person) minister m.
tooth n dēns m; ~ **and nail** tōtō corpore atque
omnibus unguīs; **cast in one's teeth**
exprobrāre, obicere; **cut teeth** dentīre; **in the**
teeth of obviam (dat), adversus (acc); **with**
the teeth mordicus.
toothache n dentium dolor m.

toothed adj dentātus.
toothless adj ēdentulus.
toothpick n dentiscalpium nt.
toothsome adj suāvis, dulcis.
top n vertex m, fastīgium nt; (tree) cacūmen nt;
(toy) turbō m; **from** ~ **to toe** ab īmīs unguibus
usque ad verticem summum; **the** ~ **of**
summus ♦ vt exsuperāre; ~ **up** supplēre ♦ adj
superior, summus.
tope vi pōtāre.
toper n pōtor m.
topiary adj topiārius. ♦ n topiārium opus nt.
topic n rēs f; (RHET) locus m; ~ **of conversation**
sermō m.
topical adj hodiernus.
topmost adj summus.
topography n dēscrīptiō f.
topple vi titubāre; ~ **over** prōlābī.
topsail n dolō m.
topsyturvy adv praeposterē; **turn** ~ sūrsum
deōrsum versāre, permiscēre.
tor n mōns m.
torch n fax f, lampas f.
torment n cruciātus m; (mind) angor m ♦ vt
cruciāre; (mind) discruciāre, excruciāre,
angere
tormentor n tortor m.
tornado n turbō m.
torpid adj torpēns; **be** ~ torpēre; **grow** ~
obtorpēscere.
torpor n torpor m, inertia f.
torrent n torrēns m.
torrid adj torridus.
torsion n tortus m.
torso n truncus m.
tortoise n testūdō f.
tortoiseshell n testūdō f.
tortuous adj flexuōsus.
torture n cruciātus m, supplicium nt;
instrument of ~ tormentum nt ♦ vt torquēre,
cruciāre, excruciāre.
torturer n tortor m, carnifex m.
toss n iactus m ♦ vt iactāre, excutere; ~ **about**
agitāre; **be** ~**ed** (at sea) fluitāre.
total adj tōtus, ūniversus ♦ n summa f.
totality n ūniversitās f.
totally adv omnīnō, plānē.
totter vi lābāre, titubāre; **make** ~ labefactāre.
tottering n titubātiō f.
touch n tāctus m; **a** ~ **of** aliquantulum (gen);
finishing ~ manus extrēma f ♦ vt tangere,
attingere; (feelings) movēre, tangere ♦ vi
inter sē contingere; ~ **at** nāvem appellere ad;
~ **on** (topic) attingere, perstringere; ~ **up**
expolīre.
touch-and-go adj anceps ♦ n discrīmen nt.
touching adj (place) contiguus; (emotion)
flexanimus ♦ prep quod attinet ad (acc).
touchstone n (fig) obrussa f.
touchy adj inrītābilis, stomachōsus.
tough adj dūrus.
toughen vt dūrāre.
toughness n dūritia f.

tour n iter nt; (abroad) peregrīnātiō f.
tourist n viātor m, peregrīnātor m.
tournament n certāmen nt.
tow n stuppa f; **of ~** stuppeus ♦ vt adnexum
  trahere, remulcō trahere.
toward(s) prep ad (acc), versus (after noun,
  acc); (feelings) in (acc), ergā (acc); (time) sub
  (acc).
towel n mantēle nt.
tower n turris f ♦ vi ēminēre.
towered adj turrītus.
town n urbs f, oppidum nt; **country ~**
  mūnicipium nt ♦ adj urbānus.
town councillor n decuriō m.
townsman n oppidānus m.
townspeople npl oppidānī mpl.
towrope n remulcum nt.
toy n crepundia ntpl ♦ vi lūdere.
trace n vestīgium nt, indicium nt ♦ vt
  investīgāre; (draw) dēscrībere; **~ out**
  dēsignāre.
track n (mark) vestīgium nt; (path) callis m,
  sēmita f; (of wheel) orbita f; (of ship) cursus m
  ♦ vt investīgāre, indāgāre.
trackless adj invius.
tract n (country) tractus m, regiō f; (book)
  libellus m.
tractable adj tractābilis, facilis, docilis.
trade n mercātūra f, mercātus m; (a business)
  ars f, quaestus m; **freedom of ~** commercium
  nt ♦ vi mercātūrās facere, negōtiārī; **~ in**
  vēndere, vēnditāre.
trader n mercātor m, negōtiātor m.
tradesman n opifex m.
tradition n fāma f, mōs māiōrum m, memoria
  f.
traditional adj ā māiōribus trāditus, patrius.
traditionally adv mōre māiōrum.
traduce vt calumniārī, obtrectāre (dat).
traducer n calumniātor m, obtrectātor m.
traffic n commercium nt; (on road) vehicula
  ntpl ♦ vi mercātūrās facere; **~ in** vēndere,
  vēnditāre.
tragedian n (author) tragoedus m; (actor) āctor
  tragicus m.
tragedy n tragoedia f; (fig) calamitās f, malum
  nt.
tragic adj tragicus; (fig) tristis.
tragically adv tragicē; male.
tragicomedy n tragicocōmoedia f.
trail n vestīgia ntpl ♦ vt trahere ♦ vi trahī.
train n (line) agmen nt, ōrdō m; (of dress) īnstita
  f; (army) impedīmenta ntpl; (followers)
  comitēs mpl, satellitēs mpl, cohors f ♦ vt
  īnstituere, īnstruere, docēre, adsuēfacere;
  exercēre; (weapon) dīrigere.
trainer n (sport) lanista m, aliptēs m.
training n disciplīna f, īnstitūtiō f; (practice)
  exercitātiō f.
trait n līneāmentum nt.
traitor n prōditor m.
traitorous adj perfidus, perfidiōsus.
traitorously adv perfidiōsē.

trammel vt impedīre.
tramp n (man) planus m; (of feet) pulsus m ♦ vi
  gradī.
trample vi: **~ on** obterere, prōterere,
  prōculcāre.
trance n stupor m; (prophetic) furor m.
tranquil adj tranquillus, placidus, quiētus,
  sēdātus.
tranquility n tranquillitās f, quiēs f, pāx f.
tranquillize vt pācāre, sēdāre.
tranquilly adv tranquillē, placidē, tranquillō
  animō.
transact vt agere, gerere, trānsigere.
transaction n rēs f, negōtium nt.
transactor n āctor m.
transalpine adj trānsalpīnus.
transcend vt superāre, excēdere.
transcendence n praestantia f.
transcendent adj eximius, ēgregius,
  excellēns.
transcendental adj dīvīnus.
transcendentally adv eximiē, ēgregiē, ūnicē.
transcribe vt dēscrībere, trānscrībere.
transcriber n librārius m.
transcript n exemplar nt, exemplum nt.
transfer n trānslātiō f; (of property) aliēnātiō f
  ♦ vt trānsferre; (troops) trādūcere; (property)
  abaliēnāre; (duty) dēlēgāre.
transference n trānslātiō f.
transfigure vt trānsfōrmāre.
transfix vt trānsfīgere, trāicere, trānsfodere;
  (mind) obstupefacere; **be ~ed** stupēre,
  stupēscere.
transform vt commūtāre, vertere.
transformation n commūtātiō f.
transgress vt violāre, perfringere ♦ vi
  dēlinquere.
transgression n dēlictum nt.
transgressor n violātor m.
transience n brevitās f.
transient adj fluxus, cadūcus, brevis.
transit n trānsitus m.
transition n mūtātiō f; (speech) trānsitus m.
transitory adj brevis, fluxus.
translate vt vertere, reddere; **~ into Latin**
  Latīnē reddere.
translation n: **a Latin ~ of Homer** Latīnē
  redditus Homērus.
translator n interpres m.
translucent adj perlūcidus.
transmarine adj trānsmarīnus.
transmission n missiō f.
transmit vt mittere; (legacy) trādere, prōdere.
transmutable adj mūtābilis.
transmutation n mūtātiō f.
transmute vt mūtāre, commūtāre.
transom n trabs f.
transparency n perlūcida nātūra f.
transparent adj perlūcidus; (fig) perspicuus.
transparently adv perspicuē.
transpire vi (get known) ēmānāre, dīvulgārī;
  (happen) ēvenīre.
transplant vt trānsferre.

transport n vectūra f; (ship) nāvis onerāria f; (emotion) ēlātiō f, summa laetitia f ♦ vt trānsportāre, trānsvehere, trānsmittere; **be ~ed** (fig) efferrī, gestīre.

transportation n vectūra f.

transpose vt invertere; (words) trāicere.

transposition n (words) trāiectiō f.

transverse adj trānsversus, oblīquus.

transversely adv in trānsversum, oblīquē.

trap n laqueus m; (fig) īnsidiae fpl ♦ vt dēcipere, excipere; (fig) inlaqueāre.

trappings n ōrnāmenta ntpl, īnsignia ntpl; (horse's) phalerae fpl.

trash n nūgae fpl.

trashy adj vīlis.

Trasimene n Trasimēnus m.

travail n labor m, sūdor m; (woman's) puerperium nt ♦ vi labōrāre, sūdāre; parturīre.

travel n itinera ntpl; (foreign) peregrīnātiō f ♦ vi iter facere; (abroad) peregrīnārī; **~ through** peragrāre; **~ to** contendere ad, in (acc), proficīscī in (acc).

traveller n viātor m; (abroad) peregrīnātor m.

traverse vt peragrāre, lūstrāre; **~ a great distance** multa mīlia passuum iter facere.

travesty n perversa imitātiō f ♦ vt perversē imitārī.

tray n ferculum nt.

treacherous adj perfidus, perfidiōsus; (ground) lūbricus.

treacherously adv perfidiōsē.

treachery n perfidia f.

tread vi incēdere, ingredī; **~ on** īnsistere (dat) ♦ n gradus m, incessus m.

treadle n (loom) īnsilia ntpl.

treadmill n pistrīnum nt.

treason n māiestās f, perduelliō f; **be charged with ~** māiestātis accūsārī; **be guilty of high ~ against** māiestātem minuere, laedere (gen).

treasonable adj perfidus, perfidiōsus.

treasure n gāza f, thēsaurus m; (person) dēliciae fpl ♦ vt māximī aestimāre, dīligere, fovēre; **~ up** condere, congerere.

treasure house n thēsaurus m.

treasurer n aerārī praefectus m; (royal) dioecētēs m.

treasury n aerārium nt; (emperor's) fiscus m.

treat n convīvium nt; dēlectātiō f ♦ vt (in any way) ūtī (abl), habēre, tractāre, accipere; (patient) cūrāre; (topic) tractāre; (with hospitality) invītāre; **~ with** agere cum; **~ as a friend** amīcī locō habēre.

treatise n liber m.

treatment n tractātiō f; (MED) cūrātiō f.

treaty n foedus nt; **make a ~** foedus ferīre.

treble adj triplus; (voice) acūtus ♦ n acūtus sonus m ♦ vt triplicāre.

tree n arbor f.

trek vi migrāre ♦ n migrātiō f.

trellis n cancellī mpl.

tremble vi tremere, horrēre.

trembling n tremor m, horror m ♦ adj tremulus.

tremendous adj immānis, ingēns, vastus.

tremendously adv immāne quantum.

tremor n tremor m.

tremulous adj tremulus.

trench n fossa f.

trenchant adj ācer.

trenchantly adv ācriter.

trend n inclīnātiō f ♦ vi vergere.

trepidation n trepidātiō f.

trespass n dēlictum nt ♦ vi dēlinquere; **~ on** (property) invādere in (acc); (patience, time, etc) abūtī (abl).

trespasser n quī iniussū dominī ingreditur.

tress n crīnis m.

trial n (essay) experientia f; (test) probātiō f; (law) iūdicium nt, quaestiō f; (trouble) labor m, aerumna f; **make ~ of** experīrī, perīculum facere (gen); **be brought to ~** in iūdicium venīre; **put on ~** in iūdicium vocāre; **hold a ~ on** quaestiōnem habēre dē (abl).

triangle n triangulum nt.

triangular adj triangulus, triquetrus.

tribe n tribus m; gēns f; (barbarian) nātiō f.

tribulation n aerumna f.

tribunal n iūdicium nt.

tribune n tribūnus m; (platform) rōstra ntpl.

tribuneship, tribunate n tribūnātus m.

tribunician adj tribūnicius.

tributary adj vectīgālis ♦ n: **be a ~ of** (river) īnfluere in (acc).

tribute n tribūtum nt, vectīgal nt; (verbal) laudātiō f; **pay a ~ to** laudāre.

trice n: **in a ~** mōmentō temporis.

trick n dolus m, fallācia f, fraus f, īnsidiae fpl, ars f; (conjurer's) praestīgiae fpl; (habit) mōs m ♦ vt fallere, dēcipere, ēlūdere; (with words) verba dare (dat); **~ out** ōrnāre, distinguere.

trickery n dolus m, fraus f, fallāciae fpl.

trickle n guttae fpl ♦ vi mānāre, dēstillāre.

trickster n fraudātor m, veterātor m.

tricky adj lūbricus, difficilis.

trident n tridēns m, fuscina f.

tried adj probātus, spectātus.

triennial adj trietēricus.

triennially adv quartō quōque annō.

trifle n nūgae fpl, paululum nt ♦ vi lūdere, nūgārī; **~ with** lūdere.

trifling adj levis, exiguus.

triflingly adv leviter.

trig adj lepidus, concinnus.

trigger n manulea f.

trim adj nitidus, concinnus ♦ vt putāre, tondēre; (lamp) oleum īnstillāre (dat) ♦ vi temporibus servīre.

trimly adv concinnē.

trimness n nitor m, munditia f.

trinket n crepundia ntpl.

trip n iter nt ♦ vt supplantāre ♦ vi lābī, titubāre; **~ along** currere; **~ over** incurrere in (acc).

tripartite adj tripartītus.

tripe n omāsum nt.
triple adj triplex, triplus ◆ vt triplicāre.
triply adv trifāriam.
tripod n tripus m.
trireme n trirēmis f.
trite adj trītus.
triumph n triumphus m; (victory) victōria f ◆ vi triumphāre; vincere; ~ over dēvincere.
triumphal adj triumphālis.
triumphant adj victor; laetus.
triumvir n triumvir m.
triumvirate n triumvirātus m.
trivial adj levis, tenuis.
triviality n nūgae fpl.
trochaic adj trochaicus.
trochee n trochaeus m.
Trojan n Trōiānus m.
troop n grex f, caterva f; (cavalry) turma f ◆ vi cōnfluere, congregārī.
trooper n eques m.
troops npl cōpiae fpl.
trope n figūra f, trānslātiō f.
trophy n tropaeum nt; **set up a** ~ tropaeum pōnere.
tropic n sōlstitiālis orbis m; ~**s** pl loca fervida ntpl.
tropical adj tropicus.
trot vi tolūtim īre.
troth n fidēs f.
trouble n incommodum nt, malum nt molestia f, labor m; (effort) opera f, negōtium nt; (disturbance) turba f, tumultus m; **take the** ~ **to** operam dare ut; **be worth the** ~ operae pretium esse ◆ vt (disturb) turbāre; (make uneasy) sollicitāre, exagitāre; (annoy) incommodāre, molestiam exhibēre (dat); ~ **oneself about** cūrāre, respicere; **be** ~**d with** labōrāre ex.
troubler n turbātor m.
troublesome adj molestus, incommodus, difficilis.
troublesomeness n molestia f.
troublous adj turbidus, turbulentus.
trough n alveus m.
trounce vt castīgāre.
troupe n grex f, caterva f.
trousered adj brācātus.
trousers n brācae fpl.
trow vi opīnārī.
truant adj tardus ◆ n cessātor m; **play** ~ cessāre, nōn compārēre.
truce n indutiae fpl.
truck n carrus m; **have no** ~ **with** nihil commercī habēre cum.
truckle vi adsentārī.
truculence n ferōcia f, asperitās f.
truculent adj truculentus, ferōx.
truculently adv ferōciter.
trudge vi rēpere, pedibus incēdere.
true adj vērus; (genuine) germānus, vērus; (loyal) fīdus, fidēlis; (exact) rēctus, iūstus.
truism n verbum trītum nt.
truly adv rēvērā, profectō, vērē.

trumpery n nūgae fpl ◆ adj vīlis.
trumpet n tuba f, būcina f.
trumpeter n būcinātor m, tubicen m.
trump up vt ēmentīrī, cōnfingere.
truncate vt praecīdere.
truncheon n fustis m, scīpiō m.
trundle vt volvere.
trunk n truncus m; (elephant's) manus f; (box) cista f.
truss n fascia f ◆ vt colligāre.
trust n fidēs f, fīdūcia f; **breach of** ~ mala fidēs; **held in** ~ fīdūciārius; **put** ~ **in** fidem habēre (dat), ◆ vt confīdere (dat), crēdere (dat); (entrust) committere, concrēdere.
trustee n tūtor m.
trusteeship n tūtēla f.
trustful adj crēdulus, fīdēns.
trustfully adv fīdenter.
trustily adv fidēliter.
trustiness n fidēs f, fidēlitās f.
trusting adj fīdēns.
trustingly adv fīdenter.
trustworthily adv fidēliter.
trustworthiness n fidēs f, integritās f.
trustworthy adj fīdus, certus; (witness) locuplēs; (authority) certus, bonus.
trusty adj fīdus, fidēlis.
truth n vēritās f, vērum nt; **in** ~ rē vērā.
truthful adj vērāx.
truthfully adv vērē.
truthfulness n fidēs f.
try vt (attempt) cōnārī; (test) experīrī, temptāre; (harass) exercēre; (judge) iūdicāre, cognōscere; ~ **for** petere, quaerere.
trying adj molestus.
tub n alveus m, cūpa f.
tubby adj obēsus.
tube n fistula f.
tufa n tōfus m.
tuft n crista f.
tug vt trahere, tractāre.
tuition n īnstitūtiō f.
tumble vi concidere, corruere, prōlābī ◆ n cāsus m.
tumbledown adj ruīnōsus.
tumbler n pōculum nt.
tumid adj tumidus, īnflātus.
tumour n tūber nt.
tumult n tumultus m, turba f; (fig) perturbātiō f.
tumultuous adj tumultuōsus, turbidus.
tumultuously adv tumultuōsē.
tumulus n tumulus m.
tun n dolium nt.
tune n modī mpl, carmen nt; **keep in** ~ concentum servāre; **out of** ~ absonus, dissonus; (strings) incontentus ◆ vt (strings) intendere.
tuneful adj canōrus.
tunefully adv numerōsē.
tunic n tunica f; **wearing a** ~ tunicātus.
tunnel n cunīculus m.
tunny n thunnus m.

turban n mitra f, mitella f.
turbid adj turbidus.
turbot n rhombus m.
turbulence n tumultus m.
turbulent adj turbulentus, turbidus.
turbulently adv turbulentē, turbidē.
turf n caespes m.
turgid adj turgidus, īnflātus.
turgidity n (RHET) ampullae fpl.
turgidly adv īnflātē.
turmoil n turba f, tumultus m; (mind) perturbātiō f.
turn n (motion) conversiō f; (bend) flexus m, ānfrāctus m; (change) commūtātiō f, vicissitūdō f; (walk) spatium nt; (of mind) adfectus m; (of language) sententia f, cōnfōrmātiō f; ~ of events mutātiō rērum f; bad ~ iniūria f; good ~ beneficium nt; ~ of the scale mōmentum nt; take a ~ for the worse in pēiōrem partem vertī; in ~s invicem, vicissim, alternī; in one's ~ locō ōrdine ♦ vt vertere, convertere, flectere; (change) vertere, mūtāre; (direct) intendere, dīrigere; (translate) vertere, reddere; (on a lathe) tornāre; ~ the edge of retundere; ~ the head mentem exturbāre; ~ the laugh against rīsum convertere in (acc); ~ the scale (fig) mōmentum habēre; ~ the stomach nauseam facere; ~ to account ūtī (abl), in rem suam convertere ♦ vi versārī, circumagī; (change) vertere, mūtārī; (crisis) pendēre; (direction) convertī; (scale) prōpendēre; ~ king's/ queen's evidence indicium profitērī; ~ against vt aliēnāre ab ♦ vi dēscīscere ab; ~ around (se) circumvertere; ~ aside vt dēflectere, dēclīnāre ♦ vi dēvertere, sē dēclīnāre; ~ away vt āvertere, dēpellere ♦ vi āversārī, discēdere; ~ back vi revertī; ~ down vt invertere; (proposal) rēicere; ~ into vi vertere in (acc), mūtārī in (acc); ~ out vt ēicere, expellere ♦ vi cadere, ēvenīre, ēvādere; ~ outside in excutere; ~ over vt ēvertere; (book) ēvolvere; (in mind) volūtāre, agitāre; ~ round vt circumagere ♦ vi convertī; ~ up vt retorquēre; (earth) versāre; (nose) corrūgāre ♦ vi adesse, intervenīre; ~ upside down invertere.
turncoat n trānsfuga m.
turning n flexus m, ānfrāctus m.
turning point n discrīmen nt, mēta f.
turnip n rāpum nt.
turpitude n turpitūdō f.
turquoise n callais f ♦ adj callainus.
turret n turris f.
turreted adj turrītus.
turtle n testūdō f; turn ~ invertī.
turtle dove n turtur m.
tusk n dēns m.
tussle n luctātiō f ♦ vi luctārī.
tutelage n tūtēla f.
tutelary adj praeses.
tutor n praeceptor m, magister m ♦ vt docēre, praecipere (dat).

tutorship n tūtēla f.
twaddle n nūgae fpl.
twang n sonus m ♦ vi increpāre.
tweak vi vellicāre.
tweezers n forceps m/f, volsella f.
twelfth adj duodecimus ♦ n duodecima pars f, ūncia f; eleven ~s deūnx m; five ~s quīncūnx m; seven ~s septūnx m.
twelve num duodecim; ~ each duodēnī; ~ times duodeciēns.
twelvemonth n annus m.
twentieth adj vīcēsimus ♦ n vīcēsima pars f; (tax) vīcēsima f.
twenty num vīgintī; ~ each vīcēnī; ~ times vīciēns.
twice adv bis; ~ as much duplus, bis tantō; ~ a day bis diē, bis in diē.
twig n virga f, rāmulus m.
twilight n (morning) dīlūculum nt; (evening) crepusculum nt.
twin adj geminus ♦ n geminus m, gemina f.
twine n resticula f ♦ vt nectere, implicāre, contexere ♦ vi sē implicāre; ~ round complectī.
twinge n dolor m.
twinkle vi micāre.
twirl vt intorquēre, contorquēre ♦ vi circumagī.
twist vt torquēre, intorquēre ♦ vi torquērī.
twit vt obicere (dat).
twitch vt vellicāre ♦ vi micāre.
twitter vi pīpilāre.
two num duo; ~ each bīnī; ~ days biduum nt; ~ years biennium nt; ~ years old bīmus; ~ by ~ bīnī; ~ feet long bipedālis; in ~ parts bifāriam, bipartītō.
two-coloured adj bicolor.
two-edged adj anceps.
twofold adj duplex, anceps.
two-footed adj bipēs.
two-headed adj biceps.
two-horned adj bicornis.
two hundred num ducentī; ~ each ducēnī; ~ times ducentiēns.
two hundredth adj ducentēsimus.
two-oared adj birēmis.
two-pronged adj bidēns, bifurcus.
two-way adj bivius.
type n (pattern) exemplar nt; (kind) genus nt.
typhoon n turbō m.
typical adj proprius, solitus.
typically adv dē mōre, ut mōs est.
typify vt exprimere.
tyrannical adj superbus, crūdēlis.
tyrannically adv superbē, crūdēliter.
tyrannize vi dominārī, rēgnāre.
tyrannous adj see **tyrannical**
tyrannously adv see **tyrannically**.
tyranny n dominātiō f, rēgnum nt.
tyrant n rēx m, crūdēlis dominus m; (Greek) tyrannus m.
tyro n tīrō m, rudis m.

U, u

ubiquitous adj omnibus locīs praesēns.
ubiquity n ūniversa praesentia f.
udder n über nt.
ugliness n foedītās f, dēfōrmitās f, turpitūdō f.
ugly adj foedus, dēfōrmis, turpis.
ulcer n ulcus nt, vomica f.
ulcerate vi ulcerārī.
ulcerous adj ulcerōsus.
ulterior adj ulterior.
ultimate adj ultimus, extrēmus.
ultimately adv tandem, ad ultimum.
umbrage n offēnsiō f; **take ~ at** indignē ferre, patī.
umbrageous adj umbrōsus.
umbrella n umbella f.
umpire n arbiter m, disceptātor m.
unabashed adj intrepidus, impudēns
unabated adj integer.
unable adj impotēns; **be ~** nōn posse, nequīre.
unacceptable adj ingrātus.
unaccompanied adj sōlus.
unaccomplished adj īnfectus, imperfectus; (person) indoctus.
unaccountable adj inexplicābilis.
unaccountably adv sine causā, repertē.
unaccustomed adj īnsuētus, īnsolitus.
unacquainted adj ignārus (gen), imperītus (gen).
unadorned adj inōrnātus, incōmptus; (speech) nūdus, ēnucleātus.
unadulterated adj sincērus, integer.
unadvisedly adv imprūdenter, incōnsultē.
unaffected adj simplex, candidus.
unaffectedly adv simpliciter.
unaided adj sine auxiliō, nūdus.
unalienable adj proprius.
unalloyed adj pūrus.
unalterable adj immūtābilis.
unaltered adj immūtātus.
unambiguous adj apertus, certus.
unambitious adj humilis, modestus.
unanimity n cōnsēnsiō f, ūnanimitās f.
unanimous adj concors, ūnanimus; **be ~** idem omnēs sentīre.
unanimously adv ūnā vōce, omnium cōnsēnsū.
unanswerable adj necessārius.
unanswerably adv sine contrōversiā.
unappreciative adj ingrātus.
unapproachable adj inaccessus; (person) difficilis.
unarmed adj inermis.
unasked adj ultrō, suā sponte.
unassailable adj inexpugnābilis.
unassailed adj intāctus, incolumis.

unassuming adj modestus, dēmissus; **~ manners** modestia f.
unassumingly adv modestē.
unattached adj līber.
unattempted adj intentātus; **leave ~** praetermittere.
unattended adj sōlus, sine comitibus.
unattractive adj invenustus.
unauthentic adj incertō auctōre.
unavailing adj inūtilis, inānis.
unavenged adj inultus.
unavoidable adj necessārius.
unavoidably adv necessāriō.
unaware adj īnscius, ignārus.
unawares adv inopīnātō, dē imprōvīsō; incautus.
unbalanced adj turbātus.
unbar vt reserāre.
unbearable adj intolerābilis, intolerandus.
unbearably adv intoleranter.
unbeaten adj invictus.
unbecoming adj indecōrus, inhonestus; **it is ~** dēdecet.
unbeknown adj ignōtus.
unbelief n diffīdentia f.
unbelievable adj incrēdibilis.
unbelievably adv incrēdibiliter.
unbelieving adj incrēdulus.
unbend vt remittere, laxāre ♦ vi animum remittere, aliquid dē sevēritāte remittere.
unbending adj inexōrābilis, sevērus.
unbiassed adj integer, incorruptus, aequus.
unbidden adj ultrō, sponte.
unbind vt solvere, resolvere.
unblemished adj pūrus, integer.
unblushing adj impudēns.
unblushingly adv impudenter.
unbolt vt reserāre.
unborn adj nōndum nātus.
unbosom vt patefacere, effundere.
unbound adj solūtus.
unbounded adj īnfīnītus, immēnsus.
unbridled adj īnfrēnātus; (fig) effrēnātus, indomitus, impotēns.
unbroken adj integer; (animal) intractātus; (friendship) inviolātus; (series) perpetuus, continuus.
unburden vt exonerāre; **~ oneself of** aperīre, patefacere.
unburied adj inhumātus, īnsepultus.
unbusinesslike adj iners.
uncalled-for adj supervacāneus.
uncanny adj mīrus, mōnstruōsus.
uncared-for adj neglectus.
unceasing adj perpetuus, adsiduus.
unceasingly adv perpetuō, adsiduē.
unceremonious adj agrestis, inurbānus.
unceremoniously adv inurbānē.
uncertain adj incertus, dubius, anceps; **be ~** dubitāre, pendēre.
uncertainly adv incertē, dubitanter.
uncertainty n incertum nt; (state) dubitātiō f.
unchangeable adj immūtābilis; (person)

cōnstāns.
unchanged _adj_ immūtātus, īdem; **remain ~**
permanēre.
uncharitable _adj_ inhūmānus, malignus.
uncharitableness _n_ inhūmānitās _f._
uncharitably _adv_ inhūmānē, malignē.
unchaste _adj_ impudīcus, libīdinōsus.
unchastely _adv_ impudīcē.
unchastity _n_ incestus _m_, libīdō _f._
unchecked _adj_ līber, indomitus.
uncivil _adj_ inurbānus, importūnus,
inhūmānus.
uncivilized _adj_ barbarus, incultus, ferus.
uncivilly _adv_ inurbānē.
uncle _n_ (_paternal_) patruus _m_; (_maternal_)
avunculus _m._
unclean _adj_ immundus; (_fig_) impūrus,
obscēnus.
uncleanly _adv_ impūrē.
uncleanness _n_ sordēs _fpl_; (_fig_) impūritās _f_,
obscēnitās _f._
unclose _vt_ aperīre.
unclothe _vt_ nūdāre, vestem dētrahere (_dat_).
unclothed _adj_ nūdus.
unclouded _adj_ serēnus.
uncoil _vt_ explicāre, ēvolvere.
uncomely _adj_ dēfōrmis, turpis.
uncomfortable _adj_ incommodus, molestus.
uncomfortably _adv_ incommodē.
uncommitted _adj_ vacuus.
uncommon _adj_ rārus, īnsolitus, inūsitātus;
(_eminent_) ēgregius, singulāris, eximius.
uncommonly _adv_ rārō; ēgregiē, ūnicō.
uncommonness _n_ īnsolentia _f._
uncommunicative _adj_ tēctus, taciturnus.
uncomplaining _adj_ patiēns.
uncompleted _adj_ imperfectus.
uncompromising _adj_ dūrus, rigidus.
unconcern _n_ sēcūritās _f._
unconcerned _adj_ sēcūrus, ōtiōsus.
unconcernedly _adv_ lentē.
uncondemned _adj_ indemnātus.
unconditional _adj_ absolūtus.
unconditionally _adv_ nullā condiciōne.
uncongenial _adj_ ingrātus.
unconnected _adj_ sēparātus, disiūnctus;
(_style_) dissolūtus.
unconquerable _adj_ invictus.
unconquered _adj_ invictus.
unconscionable _adj_ improbus.
unconscionably _adv_ improbē.
unconscious _adj_: **~ of** īnscius (_gen_), ignārus
(_gen_); **become ~** sōpīrī, animō linquī.
unconsciousness _n_ sopor _m._
unconsecrated _adj_ profānus.
unconsidered _adj_ neglectus.
unconstitutional _adj_ illicitus.
unconstitutionally _adv_ contrā lēgēs, contrā
rem pūblicam.
uncontaminated _adj_ pūrus, incorruptus,
integer.
uncontrollable _adj_ impotēns, effrēnātus.
uncontrollably _adv_ effrēnātē.

uncontrolled _adj_ līber, solūtus.
unconventional _adj_ īnsolitus, solūtus.
unconvicted _adj_ indemnātus.
unconvincing _adj_ incrēdibilis, nōn vērī
similis.
uncooked _adj_ crūdus.
uncorrupted _adj_ incorruptus, integer.
uncouple _vt_ disiungere.
uncouth _adj_ horridus, agrestis, inurbānus.
uncouthly _adv_ inurbānē.
uncouthness _n_ inhūmānitās _f_, rūsticitās _f._
uncover _vt_ dētegere, aperīre, nūdāre.
uncritical _adj_ indoctus, crēdulus.
uncultivated _adj_ incultus; (_fig_) agrestis,
rūsticus, impolītus.
uncultured _adj_ agrestis, rudis.
uncut _adj_ intōnsus.
undamaged _adj_ integer, inviolātus.
undaunted _adj_ intrepidus, fortis.
undecayed _adj_ incorruptus.
undeceive _vt_ errōrem tollere (_dat_), errōrem
ēripere (_dat_).
undecided _adj_ dubius, anceps; (_case_) integer.
undecked _adj_ (_ship_) apertus.
undefended _adj_ indēfēnsus, nūdus.
undefiled _adj_ integer, incontāminātus.
undemonstrative _adj_ taciturnus.
undeniable _adj_ certus.
undeniably _adv_ sine dubiō.
undependable _adj_ inconstāns, mōbilis.
under _adv_ īnfrā, subter ◆ _prep_ sub (_abl_), īnfrā
(_acc_); (_number_) intrā (_acc_); (_motion_) sub (_acc_);
~ arms in armīs; **~ colour** (pretext of) speciē
(_gen_), per speciem (_gen_); **~ my leadership** mē
duce; **~ the circumstances** cum haec ita sint;
labour ~ labōrāre ex; **~ the eyes of** in
cōnspectū (+ _gen_); **~ the leadership of** _abl_ +
duce.
underage _adj_ impūbēs.
undercurrent _n_: **an ~ of** lātens.
underestimate _vt_ minōris aestimāre.
undergarment _n_ subūcula _f._
undergo _vt_ subīre, patī, ferre.
underground _adj_ subterrāneus ◆ _adv_ sub
terrā.
undergrowth _n_ virgulta _ntpl._
underhand _adj_ clandestīnus, fūrtīvus ◆ _adv_
clam, fūrtim.
underline _vt_ subscrībere.
underling _n_ minister _m_, satelles _m/f._
undermine _vt_ subruere; (_fig_) labefacere,
labefactāre.
undermost _adj_ īnfimus.
underneath _adv_ īnfrā ◆ _prep_ sub (_abl_), īnfrā
(_acc_); (_motion_) sub (_acc_).
underprop _vt_ fulcīre.
underrate _vt_ obtrectāre, extenuāre, minōris
aestimāre.
understand _vt_ intellegere, comprehendere;
(_be told_) accipere, comperīre; (_in a sense_)
interpretārī; **~ Latin** Latīnē scīre.
understandable _adj_ crēdibilis.
understanding _adj_ sapiēns, perītus ◆ _n_

intellegentia f; (faculty) mēns f, intellectus m; (agreement) cōnsēnsus m; (condition) condiciō f.
undertake vt suscipere, sūmere, adīre ad; (business) condūcere; (case) agere, dēfendere; (promise) recipere, spondēre.
undertaker n dissignātor m.
undertaking n inceptum nt, inceptiō f.
undervalue vt minōris aestimāre.
underwood n virgulta ntpl.
underworld n īnferī mpl.
undeserved adj immeritus, iniūstus.
undeservedly adv immeritō, indignē.
undeserving adj indignus.
undesigned adj fortuītus.
undesignedly adv fortuītō, temerē.
undesirable adj odiōsus, ingrātus.
undeterred adj immōtus.
undeveloped adj immātūrus.
undeviating adj dīrēctus.
undigested adj crūdus.
undignified adj levis, inhonestus.
undiminished adj integer.
undiscernible adj invīsus, obscūrus.
undisciplined adj lascīvus, immoderātus; (MIL) inexercitātus.
undiscovered adj ignōtus.
undisguised adj apertus.
undisguisedly adv palam, apertē.
undismayed adj impavidus, intrepidus.
undisputed adj certus.
undistinguished adj ignōbilis, inglōrius.
undisturbed adj tranquillus, placidus.
undo vt (knot) expedīre, resolvere; (sewing) dissuere; (fig) īnfectum reddere.
undoing n ruīna f.
undone adj infectus; (ruined) perditus; **be ~** perīre, disperīre; **hopelessly ~** dēperditus.
undoubted adj certus.
undoubtedly adv sine dubiō, plānē.
undress vt exuere, vestem dētrahere (dat).
undressed adj nūdus.
undue adj nimius, immoderātus, inīquus.
undulate vi fluctuāre.
undulation n spīra f.
unduly adv nimis, plūs aequō.
undutiful adj impius.
undutifully adv impiē.
undutifulness n impietās f.
undying adj immortālis, aeternus.
unearth vt ēruere, dētegere.
unearthly adj mōnstruōsus, dīvīnus, hūmānō māior.
uneasily adv aegrē.
uneasiness n sollicitūdō f, perturbātiō f
uneasy adj sollicitus, anxius, inquiētus.
uneducated adj illitterātus, indoctus, rudis; **be ~** litterās nescīre.
unemployed adj ōtiōsus.
unemployment n cessātiō f.
unencumbered adj expedītus, līber.
unending adj perpetuus, sempiternus.
unendowed adj indōtātus.

unendurable adj intolerandus, intolerābilis.
unenjoyable adj iniūcundus, molestus.
unenlightened adj rudis, inērudītus.
unenterprising adj iners.
unenviable adj nōn invidendus.
unequal adj impār, dispār.
unequalled adj ūnicus, singulāris.
unequally adv inaequāliter, inīquē.
unequivocal adj apertus, plānus.
unerring adj certus.
unerringly adv certē.
unessential adj adventīcius, supervacāneus.
uneven adj impār; (surface) asper, inīquus, inaequābilis.
unevenly adv inīquē, inaequāliter.
unevenness n inīquitās f, asperitās f.
unexamined adj (case) incognitus.
unexampled adj inaudītus, ūnicus, singulāris.
unexceptionable adj ēmendātus; (authority) certissimus.
unexpected adj imprōvīsus, inopīnātus, īnsperātus.
unexpectedly adv dē imprōvīsō, ex īnspērātō, inopīnātō, necopīnātō.
unexplored adj inexplōrātus.
unfading adj perennis, vīvus.
unfailing adj perennis, certus, perpetuus.
unfailingly adv semper.
unfair adj inīquus, iniūstus.
unfairly adv inīquē, iniūstē.
unfairness n inīquitās f, iniūstitia f.
unfaithful adj īnfidēlis, īnfīdus, perfidus.
unfaithfully adv īnfidēliter.
unfaithfulness n īnfidēlitās f.
unfamiliar adj novus, ignōtus, īnsolēns; (sight) invīsitātus.
unfamiliarity n īnsolentia f.
unfashionable adj obsolētus.
unfasten vt solvere, refīgere.
unfathomable adj īnfīnītus, profundus.
unfavourable adj inīquus, adversus, importūnus.
unfavourably adv inīquē, male; **be ~ disposed** āversō animō esse.
unfed adj iēiūnus.
unfeeling adj dūrus, crūdēlis, ferreus.
unfeelingly adv crūdēliter.
unfeigned adj sincērus, vērus, simplex.
unfeignedly adv sincērē, vērē.
unfilial adj impius.
unfinished adj īnfectus, imperfectus.
unfit adj inūtilis, incommodus, aliēnus.
unfix vt refīgere.
unflinching adj impavidus, firmus.
unfold vt explicāre, ēvolvere; (story) expōnere, ēnārrāre.
unfolding n explicātiō f.
unforeseen adj imprōvīsus.
unforgettable adj memorābilis.
unforgiving adj implācābilis.
unformed adj īnfōrmis.
unfortified adj immūnītus, nūdus.

unfortunate adj īnfēlīx, īnfortūnātus.
unfortunately adv īnfēlīciter, male; ~ **you did not come** male accidit quod nōn vēnistī.
unfounded adj inānis, vānus.
unfrequented adj dēsertus.
unfriendliness n inimīcitia f.
unfriendly adj inimīcus, malevolus; **in an ~ manner** inimīcē.
unfruitful adj sterilis; (fig) inānis, vānus.
unfruitfulness n sterilitās f.
unfulfilled adj īnfectus, inritus.
unfurl vt explicāre, pandere.
unfurnished adj nūdus.
ungainly adj agrestis, rūsticus.
ungallant adj inurbānus, parum cōmis.
ungenerous adj illīberālis; ~ **conduct** illīberālitās f.
ungentlemanly adj illīberālis.
ungirt adj discinctus.
ungodliness n impietās f.
ungodly adj impius.
ungovernable adj impotēns, indomitus.
ungovernableness n impotentia f.
ungraceful adj inconcinnus, inēlegāns.
ungracefully adv inēleganter.
ungracious adj inhūmānus, petulāns, importūnus.
ungraciously adv acerbē.
ungrammatical adj barbarus; **be ~** soloecismum facere.
ungrateful adj ingrātus.
ungrudging adj largus, nōn invītus.
ungrudgingly adv sine invidiā.
unguarded adj intūtus; (word) incautus, incōnsultus.
unguardedly adv temerē, incōnsultē.
unguent n unguentum nt.
unhallowed adj profānus, impius.
unhand vt mittere.
unhandy adj inhabilis.
unhappily adv īnfēlīciter, miserē.
unhappiness n miseria f, tristitia f, maestitia f.
unhappy adj īnfēlix, miser, tristis.
unharmed adj incolumis, integer, salvus.
unharness vt disiungere.
unhealthiness n valētūdō f; (climate) gravitās f.
unhealthy adj invalidus, aeger; (climate) gravis, pestilens.
unheard adj inaudītus; (law) indictā causā.
unheard-of adj inaudītus.
unheeded adj neglectus.
unheeding adj immemor, sēcūrus.
unhelpful adj difficilis, invītus.
unhesitating adj audāx, prōmptus.
unhesitatingly adv sine dubitātiōne.
unhewn adj rudis.
unhindered adj expedītus.
unhinged adj mente captus.
unhistorical adj fictus, commentīcius.
unholiness n impietās f.
unholy adj impius.

unhonoured adj inhonōrātus.
unhoped-for adj īnspērātus.
unhorse vt excutere, equō dēicere.
unhurt adj integer, incolumis.
unicorn n monocerōs m.
uniform adj aequābilis, aequālis ♦ n īnsignia ntpl; (MIL) sagum nt; **in ~** sagātus; **put on ~** saga sūmere.
uniformity n aequābilitās f, cōnstantia f.
uniformly adv aequābiliter, ūnō tenōre.
unify vt coniungere.
unimaginative adj hebes, stolidus.
unimpaired adj integer, incolumis, illībātus.
unimpeachable adj (character) integer; (style) ēmendātus.
unimportant adj levis, nullīus mōmentī.
uninformed adj indoctus, ignārus.
uninhabitable adj inhabitābilis.
uninhabited adj dēsertus.
uninitiated adj profānus; (fig) rudis.
uninjured adj integer, incolumis.
unintelligent adj īnsipiēns, tardus, excors.
unintelligible adj obscūrus.
unintelligibly adv obscūrē.
unintentionally adv imprūdēns, temerē.
uninteresting adj frīgidus, āridus.
uninterrupted adj continuus, perpetuus.
uninterruptedly adv continenter, sine ullā intermissiōne.
uninvited adj invocātus; ~ **guest** umbra f.
uninviting adj iniūcundus, invenustus.
union n coniūnctiō f; (social) cōnsociātiō f, societās f; (POL) foederātae cīvitātēs fpl; (agreement) concordia f, cōnsēnsus m; (marriage) coniugium nt.
unique adj ūnicus, ēgregius, singulāris.
unison n concentus m; (fig) concordia f, cōnsēnsus m.
unit n ūniō f.
unite vt coniungere, cōnsociāre, cōpulāre ♦ vi coīre; cōnsentīre, cōnspīrāre; (rivers) cōnfluere.
unity n (concord) concordia f, cōnsēnsus m.
universal adj ūniversus, commūnis.
universally adv ūniversus, omnis; (place) ubīque.
universe n mundus m, rērum nātūra f.
university n acadēmia f.
unjust adj iniūstus, inīquus.
unjustifiable adj indignus, inexcūsābilis.
unjustly adv iniūstē, iniūriā.
unkempt adj horridus.
unkind adj inhūmānus, inīquus.
unkindly adv inhūmānē, asperē.
unkindness n inhūmānitās f.
unknowingly adv imprūdēns, īnscius.
unknown adj ignōtus, incognitus; (fame) obscūrus.
unlawful adj vetitus, iniūriōsus.
unlawfully adv iniūriōsē, iniūriā.
unlearn vt dēdiscere.
unlearned adj indoctus, inērudītus.
unless conj nisī.

unlettered adj illitterātus.
unlike adj dissimilis (+ gen or dat), dispār.
unlikely adj nōn vērīsimilis.
unlimited adj īnfīnītus, immēnsus.
unload vt exonerāre, deonerāre; (from ship) expōnere.
unlock vt reserāre, reclūdere.
unlooked-for adj īnspērātus, inexpectātus.
unloose vt solvere, exsolvere.
unlovely adj invenustus.
unluckily adv īnfēlīciter.
unlucky adj īnfēlīx, īnfortūnātus; (aay) āter.
unmake vt īnfectum reddere.
unman vt mollīre, frangere, dēbilitāre.
unmanageable adj inhabilis.
unmanly adj mollis, ēnervātus, muliebris.
unmannerliness n importūnitās f, inhūmānitās f.
unmannerly adj importūnus, inhūmānus.
unmarried adj (man) caelebs; (woman) vidua.
unmask vt nūdāre, dētegere.
unmatched adj ūnicus, singulāris.
unmeaning adj inānis.
unmeasured adj īnfīnītus, immoderātus.
unmeet adj parum idōneus.
unmelodious adj absonus, absurdus.
unmentionable adj īnfandus.
unmentioned adj indictus; **leave ~** ōmittere.
unmerciful adj immisericors, inclēmēns.
unmercifully adv inclēmenter.
unmerited adj immeritus, indignus.
unmindful adj immemor.
unmistakable adj certus, manifestus.
unmistakably adv sine dubiō, certē.
unmitigated adj merus.
unmixed adj pūrus.
unmolested adj intāctus.
unmoor vt solvere.
unmoved adj immōtus.
unmusical adj absonus, absurdus.
unmutilated adj integer.
unnatural adj (event) mōnstruōsus; (feelings) impius, inhūmānus; (style) arcessītus, pūtidus.
unnaturally adv contrā nātūram; impiē, inhūmānē; pūtidē.
unnavigable adj innāvigābilis.
unnecessarily adv nimis.
unnecessary adj inūtilis, supervacāneus.
unnerve vt dēbilitāre, frangere.
unnoticed adj: **be ~** latēre, fallere.
unnumbered adj innumerus.
unobjectionable adj honestus, culpae expers.
unobservant adj tardus.
unobserved adj: **be ~** latēre, fallere.
unobstructed adj apertus, pūrus.
unobtrusive adj verēcundus; **be ~** fallere.
unobtrusiveness n verēcundia f.
unoccupied adj vacuus, ōtiōsus.
unoffending adj innocēns.
unofficial adj prīvātus.
unorthodox adj abnōrmis.
unostentatious adj modestus, verēcundus.

unostentatiously adv nullā iactātiōne.
unpaid adj (services) grātuītus; (money) dēbitus.
unpalatable adj amārus; (fig) iniūcundus, īnsuāvis.
unparalleled adj ūnicus, inaudītus.
unpardonable adj inexcūsābilis.
unpatriotic adj impius.
unpitying adj immisericors, ferreus.
unpleasant adj iniūcundus, ingrātus, īnsuāvis, gravis, molestus.
unpleasantly adv iniūcundē, ingrātē, graviter.
unpleasantness n iniūcunditās f, molestia f.
unpleasing adj ingrātus, invenustus.
unploughed adj inarātus.
unpoetical adj pedester.
unpolished adj impolītus; (person) incultus, agrestis, inurbānus; (style) inconditus, rudis.
unpopular adj invidiōsus, invīsus.
unpopularity n invidia f, odium nt.
unpractised adj inexercitātus, imperītus.
unprecedented adj īnsolēns, novus, inaudītus.
unprejudiced adj integer, aequus.
unpremeditated adj repentīnus, subitus.
unprepared adj imparātus.
unprepossessing adj invenustus, illepidus.
unpretentious adj modestus, verēcundus.
unprincipled adj improbus, levis, prāvus.
unproductive adj infēcundus, sterilis.
unprofitable adj inūtilis, vānus.
unprofitably adv frustrā, ab rē.
unpropitious adj īnfēlīx, adversus.
unpropitiously adv malīs ōminibus.
unprotected adj indēfēnsus, intūtus, nūdus.
unprovoked adj ultrō (adv).
unpunished adj impūnītus ♦ adv impūne.
unqualified adj nōn idōneus; (unrestricted) absolūtus.
unquestionable adj certus.
unquestionably adv facile, certē.
unquestioning adj crēdulus.
unravel vt retexere; (fig) ēnōdāre, explicāre.
unready adj imparātus.
unreal adj falsus, vānus.
unreality n vānitās f.
unreasonable adj inīquus, importūnus.
unreasonableness n inīquitās f.
unreasonably adv inīquē.
unreasoning adj stolidus, temerārius.
unreclaimed adj (land) incultus.
unrefined adj impolītus, inurbānus, rudis.
unregistered adj incēnsus.
unrelated adj aliēnus.
unrelenting adj implācābilis, inexōrābilis.
unreliable adj incertus, levis.
unreliably adv leviter.
unrelieved adj perpetuus, adsiduus.
unremitting adj adsiduus.
unrequited adj inultus, inānis.
unreservedly adv apertē, sine ullā exceptiōne.

unresponsive adj hebes.
unrest n inquiēs f, sollicitūdō f.
unrestrained adj līber, impotēns, effrēnātus, immoderātus.
unrestricted adj līber, absolūtus.
unrevenged adj inultus.
unrewarded adj inhonōrātus.
unrewarding adj ingrātus, vānus.
unrighteous adj iniūstus, impius.
unrighteously adv iniūstē, impiē.
unrighteousness n impietās f.
unripe adj immātūrus, crūdus.
unrivalled adj ēgregius, singulāris, ūnicus.
unroll vt ēvolvere, explicāre.
unromantic adj pedester.
unruffled adj immōtus, tranquillus.
unruliness n licentia f, impotentia f.
unruly adj effrēnātus, impotēns, immoderātus.
unsafe adj perīculōsus, dubius; (*structure*) īnstābilis.
unsaid adj indictus.
unsatisfactorily adv nōn ex sententiā, male.
unsatisfactory adj parum idōneus, malus.
unsatisfied adj parum contenus.
unsavoury adj īnsuāvis, taeter.
unscathed adj incolumis, integer.
unschooled adj indoctus, inērudītus.
unscrupulous adj improbus, impudēns.
unscrupulously adv improbē, impudenter.
unscrupulousness n improbitās f, impudentia f.
unseal vt resignāre, solvere.
unseasonable adj intempestīvus, importūnus.
unseasonableness n incommoditās f.
unseasonably adv intempestīvē, importūnē.
unseasoned adj (*food*) nōn condītus; (*wood*) viridis.
unseat vt (*rider*) excutere.
unseaworthy adj īnfirmus.
unseeing adj caecus.
unseemly adj indecōrus.
unseen adj invīsus; (*ever before*) invīsitātus.
unselfish adj innocēns, probus, līberālis.
unselfishly adv līberāliter.
unselfishness n innocentia f, līberālitās f.
unserviceable adj inūtilis.
unsettle vt ad incertum revocāre, turbāre, sollicitāre.
unsettled adj incertus, dubius; (*mind*) sollicitus, suspēnsus; (*times*) turbidus.
unsew vt dissuere.
unshackle vt expedīre, solvere.
unshaken adj immōtus, firmus, stabilis.
unshapely adj dēfōrmis.
unshaven adj intōnsus.
unsheathe vt dēstringere, stringere.
unshod adj nūdis pedibus.
unshorn adj intōnsus.
unsightliness n dēfōrmitās f, turpitūdō f.
unsightly adj foedus, dēfōrmis.
unskilful adj indoctus, īnscītus, incallidus.

unskilfully adv indoctē, īnscītē, incallide.
unskilfulness n īnscītia f, imperītia f.
unskilled adj imperītus, indoctus; ~ **in** imperītus (+ gen).
unslaked adj (*lime*) vīvus; (*thirst*) inexplētus.
unsociable adj īnsociābilis, difficilis.
unsoiled adj integer, pūrus.
unsolicited adj voluntārius ♦ adv ultrō.
unsophisticated adj simplex, ingenuus.
unsound adj īnfirmus; (*mind*) īnsānus; (*opinion*) falsus, perversus.
unsoundness n īnfirmitās f, īnsānitās f, prāvitās f.
unsparing adj inclēmēns, immisericors; (*lavish*) prōdigus.
unsparingly adv inclēmenter; prōdigē.
unspeakable adj īnfandus, incrēdibilis.
unspeakably adv incrēdibiliter.
unspoilt adj integer.
unspoken adj indictus, tacitus.
unspotted adj integer, pūrus.
unstable adj īnstabilis; (*fig*) incōnstāns, levis.
unstained adj pūrus, incorruptus, integer.
unstatesmanlike adj illīberālis.
unsteadily adv incōnstanter; **walk** ~ titubāre.
unsteadiness n (*fig*) incōnstantia f.
unsteady adj īnstabilis; (*fig*) incōnstāns.
unstitch vt dissuere.
unstring vt retendere.
unstudied adj simplex.
unsubdued adj invictus.
unsubstantial adj levis, inānis.
unsuccessful adj īnfēlīx; (*effort*) inritus; **be** ~ offendere; **I am** ~ mihī nōn succēdit.
unsuccessfully adv īnfēlīciter, rē īnfectā.
unsuitable adj incommodus, aliēnus, importūnus; **it is** ~ dēdecet.
unsuitableness n incommoditās f.
unsuitably adv incommodē, ineptē.
unsuited adj parum idōneus.
unsullied adj pūrus, incorruptus.
unsure adj incertus, dubius.
unsurpassable adj inexsuperābilis.
unsurpassed adj ūnicus, singulāris.
unsuspected adj latēns, nōn suspectus; **be** ~ latēre, in suspiciōnem nōn venīre.
unsuspecting adj imprōvidus, imprūdēns.
unsuspicious adj nōn suspicāx, crēdulus.
unswerving adj cōnstāns.
unsworn adj iniūrātus.
unsymmetrical adj inaequālis.
untainted adj incorruptus, integer.
untamable adj indomitus.
untamed adj indomitus, ferus.
untaught adj indoctus, rudis.
unteach vt dēdocēre.
unteachable adj indocilis.
unterable adj inānis, īnfirmus.
unthankful adj ingrātus.
unthankfully adv ingrātē.
unthankfulness n ingrātus animus m.
unthinkable adj incrēdibilis.
unthinking adj incōnsīderātus, imprōvidus.

unthriftily *adv* prōdigē.
unthrifty *adj* prōdigus, profūsus.
untidily *adv* neglegenter.
untidiness *n* neglegentia *f*.
untidy *adj* neglegēns, inconcinnus, squālidus.
untie *vt* solvere.
until *conj* dum, dōnec ◆ *prep* usque ad (*acc*), in (*acc*); ~ **now** adhūc.
untilled *adj* incultus.
untimely *adj* intempestīvus, immātūrus, importūnus.
untiring *adj* impiger; (*effort*) adsiduus.
unto *prep* ad (*acc*), in (*acc*).
untold *adj* innumerus.
untouched *adj* intāctus, integer.
untoward *adj* adversus, malus.
untrained *adj* inexercitātus, imperītus, rudis.
untried *adj* intemptātus, inexpertus; (*trial*) incognitus.
untrodden *adj* āvius.
untroubled *adj* tranquillus, placidus, quiētus; (*mind*) sēcūrus.
untrue *adj* falsus, fictus; (*disloyal*) īnfīdus, īnfidēlis.
untrustworthy *adj* īnfīdus, mōbilis.
untruth *n* mendācium *nt*, falsum *nt*.
untruthful *adj* mendāx, falsus.
untruthfully *adv* falsō, falsē.
untuneful *adj* absonus.
unturned *adj*: **leave no stone** ~ nihil intemptātum relinquere, omnia experīrī.
untutored *adj* indoctus, incultus.
unused *adj* (*person*) īnsuētus, īnsolitus; (*thing*) integer.
unusual *adj* īnsolitus, inūsitātus, īnsolēns, novus.
unusually *adv* īnsolenter, praeter cōnsuētūdinem.
unusualness *n* īnsolentia *f*, novitās *f*.
unutterable *adj* īnfandus, inēnārrābilis.
unvarnished *adj* (*fig*) simplex, nūdus.
unveil *vt* (*fig*) aperīre, patefacere.
unversed *adj* ignārus (*gen*), imperītus (*gen*).
unwanted *adj* supervacāneus.
unwarily *adv* imprudenter, incautē, incōnsultē.
unwariness *n* imprūdentia *f*.
unwarlike *adj* imbellis.
unwarrantable *adj* inīquus, iniūstus.
unwarrantably *adv* iniūriā.
unwary *adj* imprūdēns, incautus, incōnsultus.
unwavering *adj* stabilis, immōtus.
unwearied, unwearying *adj* indēfessus, adsiduus.
unweave *vt* retexere.
unwedded *adj* (*man*) caelebs; (*woman*) vidua.
unwelcome *adj* ingrātus.
unwell *adj* aeger, aegrōtus.
unwept *adj* indēflētus.
unwholesome *adj* pestilēns, gravis.
unwieldy *adj* inhabilis.
unwilling *adj* invītus; **be** ~ nolle.
unwillingly *adv* invītus.

unwind *vt* ēvolvere, retexere.
unwise *adj* stultus, īnsipiēns, imprūdēns.
unwisely *adv* īnsipienter, imprūdenter.
unwittingly *adv* imprūdēns, īnsciēns.
unwonted *adj* īnsolitus, inūsitātus.
unworthily *adv* indignē.
unworthiness *n* indignitās *f*.
unworthy *adj* indignus (+ *abl*).
unwounded *adj* intāctus, integer.
unwrap *vt* ēvolvere, explicāre.
unwritten *adj* nōn scrīptus; ~ **law** mōs *m*.
unwrought *adj* īnfectus, rudis.
unyielding *adj* dūrus, firmus, inexōrābilis.
unyoke *vt* disiungere.
up *adv* sūrsum; ~ **and down** sūrsum deōrsum; ~ **to** usque ad (*acc*), tenus (*abl, after noun*); **bring** ~ subvehere; (*child*) ēducāre; **climb** ~ ēscendere; **come** ~ **to** aequāre; **lift** ~ ērigere, sublevāre; **from childhood** ~ ā puerō; **it is all** ~ **with** āctum est dē; **well** ~ **in** gnārus (*gen*), perītus (*gen*); **what is he** ~ **to?** quid struit? ◆ *prep* (*motion*) in (*acc*) ◆ *n*: ~**s and downs** (*fig*) vicissitūdinēs *fpl*.
upbraid *vt* exprobrāre (*dat pers, acc charge*); obicere (*dat and acc*), increpāre, castīgāre.
upbringing *n* ēducātiō *f*.
upheaval *n* ēversiō *f*.
upheave *vt* ēvertere.
uphill *adj* acclīvis ◆ *adv* adversō colle, in adversum collem.
uphold *vt* sustinēre, tuērī, servāre.
upholstery *r* supellex *f*.
upkeep *n* impēnsa *f*.
upland *adj* montānus.
uplift *vt* extollere, sublevāre.
upon *prep* in (*abl*), super (*abl*); (*motion*) in (*acc*), super (*acc*); (*dependence*) ex (*abl*); ~ **this** quō factō.
upper *adj* superior; **gain the** ~ **hand** superāre, vincere.
uppermost *adj* suprēmus, summus.
uppish *adj* superbus.
upright *adj* rēctus, ērēctus; (*character*) integer, probus, honestus.
uprightly *adv* rēctē; integrē.
uprightness *n* integritās *f*.
upriver *adj, adv* adversō flūmine.
uproar *n* tumultus *m*; clāmor *m*.
uproarious *adj* tumultuōsus.
uproariously *adv* tumultuōsē.
uproot *vt* ērādīcāre, exstirpāre, ēruere.
upset *vt* ēvertere, invertere, subvertere; ~ **the apple cart** plaustrum percellere ◆ *adj* (*fig*) perturbātus.
upshot *n* ēventus *m*.
upside-down *adv*: **turn** ~ ēvertere, invertere; (*fig*) miscēre.
upstart *n* novus homō *m* ◆ *adj* repentīnus.
upstream *adj, adv* adversō flūmine.
upward(s) *adv* sūrsum; ~ **of** (*number*) amplius.
urban *adj* urbānus, oppidānus.
urbane *adj* urbānus, cōmis.
urbanely *adv* urbānē, cōmiter.

V, v

urbanity n urbānitās f.
urchin n (boy) puerulus m; (animal) echīnus m.
urge vt urgēre, impellere; (speech) hortārī, incitāre; (advice) suādēre; (request) sollicitāre; ~ **on** incitāre ♦ n impulsus m; dēsīderium nt.
urgency n necessitās f.
urgent adj praesēns, gravis; **be** ~ instāre.
urgently adv graviter.
urn n urna f.
usage n mōs m, īnstitūtum nt, ūsus m.
use n ūsus m; (custom) mōs m, cōnsuētūdō f; **be of** ~ ūsuī esse, prōdesse, condūcere; **out of** ~ desuētus; **go out of** ~ exolēscere; **in common** ~ ūsitātus; **it's no** ~ nīl agis, nīl agimus ♦ vt ūtī (abl); (improperly) abūtī; (for a purpose) adhibēre; (word) ūsurpāre; ~ **up** cōnsūmere, exhaurīre; ~**d to** adsuētus (dat); solēre (+ infin); **I** ~**d to do** faciebam.
useful adj ūtilis; **be** ~ ūsuī esse.
usefully adv ūtiliter.
usefulness n ūtilitās f.
useless adj inūtilis; (thing) inānis, inritus; **be** ~ nihil valēre.
uselessly adv inūtiliter, frustrā.
uselessness n inānitās f.
usher n (court) apparitor m; (theatre) dēsignātor m ♦ vt: ~ **in** indūcere, intrōdūcere.
usual adj ūsitātus, solitus; **as** ~ ut adsolet, ut fert cōnsuētūdō, ex cōnsuētūdine; **out of the** ~ īnsolitus, extrā ōrdinem.
usually adv ferē, plērumque; **he** ~ **comes** venīre solet.
usufruct n ūsus et fructus m.
usurer n faenerātor m.
usurp vt occupāre, invādere in (acc), ūsurpāre.
usurpation n occupātō f.
usury n faenerātiō f, ūsūra f; **practise** ~ faenerārī.
utensil n īnstrūmentum nt, vās nt.
utility n ūtilitās f, commodum nt.
utilize vt ūtī (abl); (for a purpose) adhibēre.
utmost adj extrēmus, summus; **at the** ~ summum; **do one's** ~ omnibus vīribus contendere.
utter adj tōtus, extrēmus, summus ♦ vt ēmittere, ēdere, ēloquī, prōnūntiāre.
utterance n dictum nt; (process) prōnūntiātiō f.
utterly adv funditus, omnīnō, penitus.
uttermost adj extrēmus, ultimus.

vacancy n inānitās f; (office) vacuitās f; **there is a** ~ locus vacat; **elect to fill a** ~ sufficere.
vacant adj inānis, vacuus; **be** ~ vacāre.
vacate vt vacuum facere.
vacation n fēriae fpl.
vacillate vi vacillāre, dubitāre.
vacillation n dubitātiō f.
vacuity n inānitās f.
vacuous adj vacuus.
vacuum n ināne nt.
vagabond n grassātor m ♦ adj vagus.
vagary n libīdō f.
vagrancy n errātiō f.
vagrant n grassātor m, vagus m.
vague adj incertus, dubius.
vaguely adv incertē.
vain n vānus, inānis, inritus; (person) glōriōsus; **in** ~ frustrā.
vainglorious adj glōriōsus.
vainglory n glōria f, iactantia f.
vainly adv frustrā, nēquīquam.
vale n vallis f.
valet n cubiculārius m.
valiant adj fortis, ācer.
valiantly adv fortiter, ācriter.
valid adj ratus; (argument) gravis, firmus.
validity n vīs f, auctōritās f.
valley n vallis f.
valorous adj fortis.
valour n virtūs f.
valuable adj pretiōsus.
valuation n aestimātiō f.
value n pretium nt; (fig) vīs f, honor m ♦ vt aestimāre; (esteem) dīligere; ~ **highly** māgnī aestimāre; ~ **little** parvī aestimāre, parvī facere.
valueless adj vīlis, minimī pretī.
valuer n aestimātor m.
van n (in battle) prīma aciēs f; (on march) prīmum agmen nt.
vanguard n prīmum agmen nt.
vanish vi diffugere, ēvānēscere, dīlābī.
vanity n (unreality) vānitās f; (conceit) glōria f.
vanquish vt vincere, superāre, dēvincere.
vanquisher n victor m.
vantage n (ground) locus superior m.
vapid adj vapidus, īnsulsus.
vapidly adv īnsulsē.
vaporous adj nebulōsus.
vapour n vapor m, nebula f; (from earth) exhālātiō f.
variable adj varius, mūtābilis.
variableness n mūtābilitās f, incōnstantia f.
variance n discordia f, dissēnsiō f, discrepantia f; **at** ~ discors; **be at** ~ dissidēre,

inter sē discrepāre; **set at** ~ aliēnāre.
variant adj varius.
variation n varietās f, vicissitūdō f.
variegate vt variāre.
variegated adj varius.
variety n varietās f; (number) multitūdō f; (kind) genus nt; **a** ~ **of** dīversī.
various adj varius, dīversus.
variously adv variē.
varlet n verberō m.
varnish n pigmentum nt; (fig) fūcus m.
varnished adj (fig) fūcātus.
vary vt variāre, mūtāre; (decorate) dis= inguere ♦ vi mūtārī.
vase n vās nt.
vassal n ambāctus m; (fig) cliēns m.
vast adj vastus, immānis, ingēns, immēnsus.
vastly adv valdē.
vastness n māgnitūdō f, immēnsitās f.
vat n cūpa f.
vault n (ARCH) fornix f; (jump) saltus m ♦ vi salīre.
vaulted adj fornicātus.
vaunt vt iactāre, ostentāre ♦ vi sē iactāre, glōriārī.
vaunting n ostentātiō f, glōria f ♦ adj glōriōsus.
veal n vitulīna f.
vedette n excursor m.
veer vi sē vertere, flectī.
vegetable n holus nt.
vehemence n vīs f, violentia f; (passio-) ārdor m, impetus m.
vehement adj vehemēns, violentus, ācer.
vehemently adv vehementer, ācriter.
vehicle n vehiculum nt.
Veii n Veiī, Vēiorum mpl.
veil n rīca f; (bridal) flammeum nt; (fig) integumentum nt ♦ vt vēlāre, tegere.
vein n vēna f.
vellum n membrāna f.
velocity n celeritās f, vēlōcitās f.
venal adj vēnālis.
vend vt vēndere.
vendetta n simultās f.
vendor n caupō m.
veneer n (fig) speciēs f, fūcus m.
venerable adj gravis, augustus.
venerate vt colere, venerārī.
veneration n venerātiō f, cultus m.
venerator n cultor m.
vengeance n ultiō f, poena f; **take** ~ **on** ulcīscī, vindicāre in (acc); **take** ~ **for** ulcīscī, vindicāre.
vengeful adj ultor.
venial adj ignōscendus.
venison n dāma f, ferīna f.
venom n venēnum nt; (fig) vīrus nt.
venomous adj venēnātus.
vent n spīrāculum nt; (outlet) exitus m; **give** ~ **to** profundere, ēmittere ♦ vt ēmittere; (feelings on) profundere in (acc), ērumpere in (acc).

ventilate vt perflāre; (opinion) in medium prōferre, vulgāre.
ventilation n perflāre.
venture n perīculum nt; (gamble) ālea f; **at a** ~ temerē ♦ vi audēre ♦ vt perīclitārī, in āleam dare.
venturesome adj audāx, temerārius.
venturesomeness n audācia f, temeritās f.
veracious adj vērāx, vēridicus.
veracity n vēritās f, fidēs f.
verb n verbum nt.
verbally adv per colloquia; (translate) ad verbum, verbum prō verbo.
verbatim adv ad verbum, totidem verbīs.
verbiage n verba ntpl.
verbose adj verbōsus.
verbosity n loquendī prōfluentia f.
verdant adj viridis.
verdict n sententia f, iūdicium nt; **deliver a** ~ sententiam prōnūntiāre; **give a** ~ **in favour of** causam adiūdicāre (dat).
verdigris n aerūgō f.
verdure n viriditās f.
verge n ōra f; **the** ~ **of** extrēmus; **on the** ~ **of** (fig) prope (acc) ♦ vi vergere.
verification n cōnfirmātiō f.
verify vt cōnfirmāre, comprobāre.
verily adv profectō, certē.
verisimilitude n vērī similitūdō f.
veritable adj vērus.
veritably adv vērē.
verity n vēritās f.
vermilion n sandīx f.
vermin n bestiolae fpl.
vernacular adj patrius ♦ n patrius sermō m.
vernal adj vērnus.
versatile adj versūtus, varius.
versatility n versātile ingenium nt.
verse n (line) versus m; (poetry) versus mpl, carmina ntpl.
versed adj īnstructus, perītus, exercitātus.
versification n ars versūs faciendī.
versify vt versū inclūdere ♦ vi versūs facere.
version n (of story) fōrma f; **give a Latin** ~ **of** Latīnē reddere.
vertex n vertex m, fastīgium nt.
vertical adj rēctus, dīrēctus.
vertically adv ad līneam, rēctā līneā, ad perpendiculum.
vertigo n vertīgō f.
vervain n verbēna f.
verve n ācrimōnia f.
very adj ipse ♦ adv admodum, valdē, vehementer ♦ superl: **at that** ~ **moment** tum māximē; **not** ~ nōn ita.
vessel n (receptacle) vās nt; (ship) nāvigium nt.
vest n subūcula f ♦ vt: ~ **power in** imperium dēferre (dat); **~ed interests** nummī locātī mpl.
vestal adj vestālis ♦ n virgō vestālis f.
vestibule n vestibulum nt.
vestige n vestīgium nt, indicium nt.
vestment n vestīmentum nt.
vesture n vestis f.

vetch n vicia f.
veteran adj veterānus ♦ n (MIL) veterānus m; (fig) veterātor m.
veto n interdictum nt; (tribune's) intercessiō f ♦ vt interdīcere (dat); (tribune) intercēdere (dat).
vex vt vexāre, sollicitāre, stomachum movēre (dat); **be ~ed** aegrē ferre, stomachārī.
vexation n (caused) molestia f; (felt) dolor m, stomachus m.
vexatious adj odiōsus, molestus.
vexatiously adv molestē.
vexed adj īrātus; (question) anceps.
via prep per (acc).
viaduct n pōns m.
viands n cibus m.
vibrate vi vībrāre, tremere.
vibration n tremor m.
vicarious adj vicārius.
vice n (general) prāvitās f, perditī mōrēs mpl; (particular) vitium nt, flāgitium nt; (clamp) fībula f.
viceroy n prōcūrātor m.
vicinity n vīcīnia f, vīcīnitās f.
vicious adj prāvus, vitiōsus, flāgitiōsus; (temper) contumāx.
viciously adv flāgitiōsē; contumāciter.
vicissitude n vicissitūdō f; **~s** pl vicēs fpl.
victim n victima f, hostia f; (fig) piāculum nt; (exploited) praeda f; **be the ~ of** labōrāre ex; **fall a ~ to** morī (abl); (trickery) circumvenīrī (abl).
victimize vt nocēre (dat), circumvenīre.
victor n victor m.
victorious adj victor m, victrīx f; **be ~** vincere.
victory n victōria f; **win a ~** victōriam reportāre; **win a ~ over** vincere, superāre.
victory message n laureātae litterae fpl.
victory parade n triumphus m.
victual vt rem frūmentāriam suppeditāre (dat).
victualler n caupō m; (MIL) frūmentārius m.
victuals n cibus m; (MIL) frūmentum nt, commeātus m.
vie vi certāre, contendere; **~ with** aemulārī.
view n cōnspectus m; (from far) prōspectus m; (from high) dēspectus m; (opinion) sententia f; **exposed to ~** in mediō; **entertain a ~** sentīre; **in ~ of** propter (acc); **in my ~** meā sententiā, meō iūdiciō; **end in ~** prōpositum nt; **have in ~** spectāre; **point of ~** iūdicium nt; **with a ~ to** eō cōnsiliō ut ♦ vt īnspicere, spectāre, intuērī.
vigil n pervigilium nt; **keep a ~** vigilāre.
vigilance n vigilantia f, dīligentia f.
vigilant adj vigilāns, dīligēns.
vigilantly adv vigilanter, dīligenter.
vigorous adj ācer, vegetus, integer; (style) nervōsus.
vigorously adv ācriter, strēnuē.
vigour n vīs f, nervī mpl, integritās f.
vile adj turpis, impūrus, abiectus.
vilely adv turpiter, impūrē.

vileness n turpitūdō f, impūritās f.
vilification n obtrectātiō f, calumnia f.
vilify vt obtrectāre, calumniārī, maledīcere (dat).
villa n vīlla f.
village n pāgus m, vīcus m; **in every ~** pāgātim.
villager n pāgānus m, vīcānus m.
villain n furcifer m, scelerātus m.
villainous adj scelestus, scelerātus, nēquam.
villainously adv scelestē.
villainy n scelus nt, nēquitia f.
vindicate vt (right) vindicāre; (action) pūrgāre; (belief) arguere; (person) dēfendere, prōpugnāre prō (abl).
vindication n dēfēnsiō f, pūrgātiō f.
vindicator n dēfēnsor m, prōpugnātor m.
vindictive adj ultor, ulcīscendī cupidus.
vine n vītis f; **wild ~** labrusca f.
vinedresser n vīnitor m.
vinegar n acētum nt.
vineyard n vīnea f, vīnētum nt.
vintage n vindēmia f.
vintner n vīnārius m.
violate vt violāre.
violation n violātiō f.
violator n violātor m.
violence n violentia f, vīs f, iniūria f; **do ~ to** violāre; **offer ~ to** vim īnferre (dat).
violent adj violentus, vehemēns; (passion) ācer, impotēns; **~ death** nex f.
violently adv vehementer, per vim.
violet n viola f.
viper n vīpera f.
viperous adj (fig) malignus.
virgin n virgō f ♦ adj virginālis.
virginity n virginitās f.
virile adj virīlis.
virility n virtūs f.
virtually adv rē vērā, ferē.
virtue n virtūs f, honestum nt; (woman's) pudīcitia f; (power) vis f, potestās f; **by ~ of** ex (abl).
virtuous adj honestus, probus, integer.
virtuously adv honestē.
virulence n vīs f, vīrus nt.
virulent adj acerbus.
virus n vīrus nt.
visage n ōs n, faciēs f.
vis-à-vis prep exadversus (acc).
viscosity n lentor m.
viscous adj lentus, tenāx.
visible adj ēvidēns, cōnspicuus, manifestus; **be ~** appārēre.
visibly adv manifestō.
vision n (sense) vīsus m; (power) aspectus m; (apparition) vīsum nt, vīsiō f; (whim) somnium nt.
visionary adj vānus ♦ n somniāns m.
visit n adventus m; (formal) salūtātiō f; (long) commorātiō f; **pay a ~ to** invīsere ♦ vt vīsere; **~ occasionally** intervīsere; **go to ~** invīsere.
visitation n (to inspect) recēnsiō f; (to punish) animadversiō f.

visitor n hospes m, hospita f; (formal) salūtātor m.
visor n buccula f.
vista n prōspectus m.
visual adj oculōrum.
visualize vt animō cernere, ante oculōs pōnere.
visually adv oculīs.
vital adj (of life) vītālis; (essential) necessārius, māximī mōmentī.
vitality n vīs f; (style) sanguis m.
vitally adv praecipuē, imprīmīs.
vitals n viscera ntpl.
vitiate vt corrumpere, vitiāre.
vitreous adj vitreus.
vitrify vt in vitrum excoquere.
vituperate vt vituperāre, obiūrgāre.
vituperation n vituperātiō f, maledicta ntpl.
vituperative adj maledicus.
vivacious adj alacer, vegetus, hilaris.
vivaciously adv hilare.
vivacity n alacritās f, hilaritās f.
vivid adj vīvidus, ācer.
vividly adv ācriter.
vivify vt animāre.
vixen n vulpēs f.
vocabulary n verbōrum cōpia f.
vocal adj: ~ **music** vōcis cantus m.
vocation n officium nt, mūnus nt.
vociferate vt, vi vōciferārī, clāmāre.
vociferation n vōciferātiō f, clāmor m.
vociferous adj vōciferāns.
vociferously adv māgnīs clāmōribus.
vogue n mōs m; **be in ~** flōrēre, in honōre esse.
voice n vōx f ♦ vt exprimere, ēloquī.
void adj inānis, vacuus; **~ of** expers (gen); **null and ~** inritus ♦ n ināne nt ♦ vt ēvomere, ēmittere.
volatile adj levis, mōbilis.
volatility n levitās f.
volition n voluntās f.
volley n imber m.
volubility n volūbilitās f.
voluble adj volūbilis.
volume n (book) liber m; (mass) mōlēs f; (of sound) māgnitūdō f.
voluminous adj cōpiōsus.
voluntarily adv ultrō, suā sponte.
voluntary adj voluntārius; (unpaid) grātuītus.
volunteer n (MIL) ēvocātus m ♦ vt ultrō offerre ♦ vi (MIL) nōmen dare.
voluptuary n dēlicātus m, homō voluptārius m.
voluptuous adj voluptārius, mollis, dēlicātus, luxuriōsus.
voluptuously adv molliter, dēlicātē, luxuriōsē.
voluptuousness n luxuria f, libīdō f.
vomit vt vomere, ēvomere; **~ up** ēvomere.
voracious adj vorāx, edāx.
voraciously adv avidē.
voracity n edācitās f, gula f.
vortex n vertex m, turbō m.

votary n cultor m.
vote n suffrāgium nt; (opinion) sententia f; **~ for** (candidate) suffrāgārī (dat); (senator's motion) discēdere in sententiam (gen) ♦ vi (election) suffrāgium ferre; (judge) sententiam ferre; (senator) cēnsēre; **take a ~** (senate) discessiōnem facere ♦ vt (senate) dēcernere; **~ against** (bill) antīquāre.
voter n suffrāgātor m.
votive adj vōtīvus.
vouch vi spondēre; **~ for** praestāre, testificārī.
voucher n (person) auctor m; (document) auctōritās f.
vouchsafe vt concēdere.
vow n vōtum nt; (promise) fidēs f ♦ vt vovēre; (promise) spondēre.
vowel n vōcālis f.
voyage n nāvigātiō f, cursus m ♦ vi nāvigāre.
vulgar adj (common) vulgāris; (low) plēbēius, sordidus, īnsulsus.
vulgarity n sordēs fpl, īnsulsitās f.
vulgarly adv vulgō; īnsulsē.
vulnerable adj nūdus; (fig) obnoxius; **be ~** vulnerārī posse.
vulture n vultur m; (fig) vulturius m.

W, w

wad n massa f.
wade vi per vada īre; **~ across** vadō trānsīre.
waft vt ferre, vehere.
wag n facētus homō m, icculātor m ♦ vt movēre, mōtāre, agitāre ♦ vi movērī, agitārī.
wage n mercēs f; (pl) mercēs f, manupretium nt; (fig) pretium nt, praemium nt ♦ vt gerere; **~ war on** bellum īnferre (dat)/gerere.
wager n spōnsiō f ♦ vi spōnsiōnem facere ♦ vt dēpōnere, oppōnere.
waggery n facētiae fpl.
waggish adj facētus, rīdiculus.
waggle vt agitāre, mōtāre.
wagon n plaustrum nt, carrus m.
waif n inops m/f.
wail n ēiulātus m ♦ vi ēiulāre, dēplōrāre, lāmentārī.
wailing n plōrātus m, lāmentātiō f.
waist n medium corpus nt; **hold by the ~** medium tenēre.
wait n: **have a long ~** diū exspectāre; **lie in ~** īnsidiārī ♦ vi manēre, opperīrī, exspectāre; **~ for** exspectāre; **~ upon** (accompany) adsectārī, dēdūcere; (serve) famulārī (dat); (visit) salūtāre.
waiter n famulus m, minister m.

waive vt dēpōnere, remittere.
wake vt excitāre, suscitāre ◆ vi expergīscī.
wake n vestīgia ntpl; **in the ~** pōne, ā tergō; **follow in the ~ of** vestīgiīs instāre (gen).
wakeful adj vigil.
wakefulness n vigilantia f.
waken vt excitāre ◆ vi expergīscī.
walk n (act) ambulātiō f, deambulātiō f; (gait) incessus m; (place) ambulātiō f, xystus m; **~ of life** status m; **go for a ~** spatiārī, deambulāre ◆ vi ambulāre, īre, gradī; (with dignity) incēdere; **~ about** inambulāre; **~ out** ēgredī.
wall n mūrus m; (indoors) pariēs m; (afield) māceria f; **~s** pl (of town) moenia ntpl ◆ vt mūnīre, saepīre; **~ up** inaedificāre.
wallet n pēra f.
wallow vi volūtārī.
walnut n iūglāns f.
wan adj pallidus.
wand n virga f.
wander vi errāre, vagārī; (in mind) ālūcinārī; **~ over** pervagārī.
wanderer n errō m, vagus m.
wandering adj errābundus, vagus ◆ n errātiō f, error m.
wane vi dēcrēscere, senēscere.
want n inopia f, indigentia f, egestās f, pēnūria f; (craving) dēsīderium nt; **in ~** inops; **be in ~** egēre ◆ vt (lack) carēre (abl), egēre (abl), indigēre (abl); (miss) dēsīderāre; (wish) velle.
wanting adj (missing) absēns; (defective) vitiōsus, parum idōneus; **be ~** deesse, dēficere ◆ prep sine (abl).
wanton adj lascīvus, libīdinōsus ◆ vi lascīvīre.
wantonly adv lascīvē, libīdinōsē.
war n bellum nt; **regular ~** iūstum bellum; **fortunes of ~** fortūna bellī; **outbreak of ~** exortum bellum; **be at ~ with** bellum gerere cum; **declare ~** bellum indīcere; **discontinue ~** bellum dēpōnere; **end ~** (by agreement) compōnere; (by victory) cōnficere; **enter ~** bellum suscipere; **give the command of a ~** bellum mandāre; **make ~** bellum īnferre; **prolong a ~** bellum trahere; **provoke ~** bellum movēre; **wage ~** bellum gerere; **wage ~ on** bellum īnferre (dat) ◆ vi bellāre.
warble vi canere, cantāre.
warbling adj garrulus, canōrus ◆ n cantus m.
war cry n clāmor m.
ward n custōdia f; (person) pupillus m, pupilla f; (of town) regiō f ◆ vt: **~ off** arcēre, dēfendere, prōpulsāre.
warden n praefectus m.
warder n custōs m.
wardrobe n vestiārium nt.
wardship n tūtēla f.
warehouse n apothēca f.
wares n merx f, mercēs fpl.
warfare n bellum nt.
warily adv prōvidenter, cautē.
wariness n circumspectiō f, cautiō f.

warlike adj ferōx, bellicōsus.
warm adj calidus; (fig) ācer, studiōsus; **be ~** calēre; **become ~** calefierī, incalēscere; **keep ~** fovēre; **~ baths** thermae fpl ◆ vt calefacere, tepefacere, fovēre ◆ vi calefierī.
warmly adv (fig) ferventer, studiōsē.
warmth n calor m.
warn vt monēre, admonēre.
warning n (act) monitiō f; (particular) monitum nt; (lesson) documentum nt, exemplum nt.
warp n stāmina ntpl ◆ vt dēprāvāre, īnflectere.
warped adj (fig) prāvus.
warrant n auctōritās f ◆ vt praestāre.
warranty n cautiō f.
warrior n bellātor m, bellatrīx f, mīles m.
warship n nāvis longa f.
wart n verrūca f.
wary adj prōvidus, cautus, prūdēns.
wash vt lavāre; (of rivers, sea) adluere; **~ away** dīluere; **~ clean** abluere; **~ out** (fig) ēluere ◆ vi lavārī.
washbasin n aquālis m.
washing n lavātiō f.
wasp n vespa f.
waspish adj acerbus, stomachōsus.
waste n dētrīmentum nt, intertrīmentum nt; (extravagance) effūsiō f; (of time) iactūra f; (land) sōlitūdō f, vastitās f ◆ adj dēsertus, vastus; **lay ~** vastāre, populārī ◆ vt cōnsūmere, perdere, dissipāre; (time) terere, absūmere; (with disease) absūmere ◆ vi: **~ away** tābēscere, intābēscere.
wasteful adj prōdigus, profūsus; (destructive) damnōsus, perniciōsus.
wastefully adv prōdigē.
wasting n tābēs f.
wastrel n nebulō m.
watch n (being awake) vigilia f; (sentry) statiō f, excubiae fpl; **keep ~** excubāre; **keep ~ on, over** custōdīre, invigilāre (dat); **set ~** vigiliās dispōnere; **at the third ~** ad tertiam būcinam ◆ vt (guard) custōdīre; (observe) intuērī, observāre, spectāre ad (+ acc); **~ for** observāre, exspectāre; (enemy) īnsidiārī (dat); **~ closely** adservāre.
watcher n custōs m.
watchful adj vigilāns.
watchfully adv vigilanter.
watchfulness n vigilantia f.
watchman n custōs m, vigil m.
watchtower n specula f.
watchword n tessera f, signum nt.
water n aqua f; **deep ~** gurges m; **fresh ~** aqua dulcis; **high ~** māximus aestus; **running ~** aqua prōfluēns; **still ~** stagnum nt; **fetch ~** aquārī; **fetching ~** aquātiō f; **cold ~** frīgida f; **hot ~** calida f; **troubled ~s** (fig) turbidae rēs ◆ vt (land) inrigāre; (animal) adaquāre.
water carrier n aquātor m; (Zodiac) Aquārius m.
water clock n clepsydra f.
waterfall n cataracta f.
watering n aquātiō f; **~ place** n (spa) aquae fpl.

water pipe n fistula f.
watershed n aquārum dīvortium nt.
water snake n hydrus m.
water spout n prēstēr m.
watery adj aquōsus, ūmidus.
wattle n crātēs f.
wave n unda f, fluctus m ♦ vt agitāre, iactāre ♦
vi fluctuāre.
waver vi dubitāre, fluctuārī, nūtāre, vacillāre,
labāre, inclināre.
wavering adj dubius, incōnstāns ♦ n dubitātiō
f, fluctuātiō f.
wavy adj undātus; (hair) crispus.
wax n cēra f ♦ vt cērāre ♦ vi crēscere.
waxen adj cēreus.
waxy adj cērōsus.
way n via f; (route) iter nt; (method) modus m,
ratiō f; (habit) mōs m; (ship's) impetus m; **all
the ~ to, from** usque ad, ab; **by the ~**
(parenthesis) etenim; **get in the ~ of**
intervenīre (dat), impedīre; **get under ~**
nāvem solvere; **give ~** (structure) labāre; (MIL)
cēdere; **give ~ to** indulgēre (dat); **go out of
one's ~ to** do ultrō facere; **have one's ~**
imperāre; **in a ~** quōdam modō; **in this ~** ad
hunc modum; **it is not my ~ to** nōn meum est
(infin); **lose one's ~** deerrare; **make ~** dē viā
dēcēdere; **make ~ for** cēdere (dat), **make
one's ~ into** sē īnsinuāre in (acc); **on the ~**
inter viam, in itinere; **out of the ~** āvius,
dēvius; (fig) reconditus; **pave the ~ for**
praeparāre; **put out of the ~** tollere **right of ~**
iter; **stand in the ~ of** obstāre (dat); **that ~**
illāc; **this ~** hāc; **~s and means** opēs fpl,
reditūs mpl.
wayfarer n viātor m.
waylay vt īnsidiārī (dat).
wayward adj protervus, incōnstāns, levis.
waywardness n libīdō f, levitās f.
we pron nōs.
weak adj dēbilis, īnfirmus, imbēcillus; (health)
invalidus; (argument) levis, tenuis; (senses)
hebes.
weaken vt dēbilitāre, īnfirmāre; (resistance)
frangere, labefactāre ♦ vi imminuī, labāre.
weakling n imbēcillus m.
weakly adj invalidus, aeger ♦ adv īnfirmē.
weak-minded adj mollis.
weakness n dēbilitās f, īnfirmitās f; (of
argument) levitās f; (of mind) imbēcillitās f;
imbēcillitās f; (flaw) vitium nt; **have a ~ for**
delectārī (abl).
weal n salūs f, rēs f; (mark of blow) vībex f; **the
common ~** rēs pūblica f.
wealth n dīvitiae fpl, opēs fpl; **a ~ of** cōpia f,
abundantia f.
wealthy adj dīves, opulentus, locuplēs,
beātus; **make ~** locuplētāre, dītāre; **very ~**
praedīves.
wean vt lacte dēpellere; (fig) dēdocēre.
weapon n tēlum nt.
wear n (dress) habitus m; **~ and tear**
intertrīmentum nt ♦ vt gerere, gestāre; (rub)

terere, conterere; **~ out** cōnficere ♦ vi
dūrāre; **~ off** minuī.
wearily adv cum lassitūdine, languidē.
weariness n fatīgātiō f, lassitūdō f; (of)
taedium nt.
wearisome adj molestus, operōsus,
labōriōsus.
weary adj lassus, fessus, cēfessus, fatīgātus ♦
vt fatīgāre; **I am weary of** me taedet (+ gen).
weasel n mustēla f.
weather n tempestās f, caelum nt; **fine ~**
serēnitās f ♦ vt superāre.
weather-beaten adj tempestāte dūrātus.
weave vt texere.
weaver n textor m, textrix f.
web n (on loom) tēla f; (spider's) arāneum nt.
wed vt (a wife) dūcere; (a husband) nūbere
(dat).
wedding n nūptiae fpl.
wedge n cuneus m ♦ vt cuneāre.
wedlock n mātrimōnium rt.
weed n inūtilis herba f ♦ vi runcāre.
weedy adj exīlis.
week n hebdomas f.
ween vt arbitrārī, putāre.
weep vi flēre, lacrimārī; **~ for** dēflēre,
dēplōrāre.
weeping n flētus m, lacrimae fpl.
weevil n curculiō m.
weft n subtēmen nt; (web) tēla f.
weigh vt pendere, exāmināre; (anchor) tollere;
(thought) ponderāre; **~ down** dēgravāre,
opprimere; **~ out** expendere ♦ vi pendere.
weight n pondus nt; (influence) auctōritās f,
mōmentum nt; (burden) onus nt; **have great ~**
(fig) multum valēre; **he is worth his ~ in gold**
aurō contrā cōnstat.
weightily adv graviter.
weightiness n gravitās f.
weighty adj gravis.
weir n mōlēs f.
weird adj mōnstruōsus ♦ n fātum nt.
welcome adj grātus, exspectātus, acceptus ♦
n salūtātiō f ♦ vt excipere, salvēre iubēre ♦
interj salvē, salvēte.
welfare n salūs f.
well n puteus m; (spring) fōrs m ♦ vi scatēre ♦
adj salvus, sānus, valēns; **be ~** valēre ♦ adv
bene, probē; (transition) age ♦ interj
(concession) estō; (surprise) heia; **~ and good**
estō; **~ begun is half done** dīmidium factī quī
coepit habet; **~ done!** probē!; **~ met**
opportūnē venis; **~ on in years** aetāte
prōvectus; **all is ~** bene habet; **as ~** etiam; **as
~ as** cum ... tum, et ... et; **let ~ alone** quiēta
nōn movēre; **take ~** in bonam partem
accipere; **wish ~** favēre (dat); **you may ~ say**
iūre dīcis; **you might as ~ say** illud potius
dīcās.
well-advised adj prūdēns.
well-behaved adj modestus.
wellbeing n salūs f.
well-bred adj generōsus, līberālis.

well-disposed adj benevolus, amīcus.
well-informed adj ērudītus.
well-judged adj ēlegāns.
well-knit adj dēnsus.
well-known adj nōtus, nōbilis; (saying) trītus.
well-nigh adv paene.
well-off adj beātus, fortūnātus; **you are** ~ bene est tibī.
well-read adj litterātus.
well-timed adj opportūnus.
well-to-do adj beātus, dīves.
well-tried adj probātus.
well-turned adj rotundus.
well-versed adj perītus, expertus.
well-wisher n amīcus m, benevolēns m.
well-worn adj trītus.
welter n turba f ♦ vi miscērī, turbārī; (wallow) volūtārī.
wench n muliercula f.
wend vt: ~ **one's way** īre, sē ferre.
west n occidēns m, sōlis occāsus m ♦ adj occidentālis.
westerly, western adj occidentālis.
westwards adv ad occidentem.
west wind n Favōnius m.
wet adj ūmidus, madidus; **be** ~ madēre; ~ **weather** pluvia f ♦ vt madefacere.
wether n vervēx m.
wet nurse n nūtrīx f.
whack n ictus m, plāga f ♦ vt pulsāre, verberāre.
whale n bālaena f.
wharf n crepīdō f.
what pron (interrog) quid; (adj) quī; (relat) id quod, ea quae; ~ **kind of?** qualis.
whatever, whatsoever pron quidquid, quodcumque; (adj) quīcumque.
wheat n trīticum nt.
wheaten adj trīticeus.
wheedle vt blandīrī, pellicere.
wheedling adj blandus ♦ n blanditiae fpl.
wheel n rota f ♦ vt flectere, circumagere ♦ vi sē flectere, circumagī.
wheelbarrow n pabō m.
wheeze vi anhēlāre.
whelm vt obruere.
whelp n catulus m.
when adv (interrog) quandō, quō tempore ♦ conj (time) cum (+ subj), ubī (+ indic).
whence adv unde.
whenever conj quotiēns, utcumque, quandocumque, cum (+ perf/pluperf indic); (as soon as) simul āc.
where adv ubī; (to) quō; ~ ... **from** unde; ~ **to** quo (interrog and relat).
whereabouts n locus m; **your** ~ quō in locō sīs.
whereas conj quōniam; (contrast) not expressed.
whereby adv quō pāctō, quō.
wherefore adv (interrog) quārē, cūr; (relat) quamobrem, quāpropter.
wherein adv in quō, in quā.
whereof adv cūius, cūius reī.

whereon adv in quō, in quā.
whereupon adv quō factō.
wherever conj ubiubī, quācumque.
wherewith adv quī, cum quō.
wherry n linter f.
whet vt acuere; (fig) exacuere.
whether conj (interrog) utrum; (single question) num; (condition) sīve, seu; ~ ... **or** utrum ... an (in indir question); (in cond clauses) seu (sive) ... seu (sive); ~ ... **not** utrum ... necne (in indir question).
whetstone n cōs f.
whey n serum nt.
which pron (interrog) quis; (of two) uter; (relat) quī ♦ adj quī; (of two) uter.
whichever pron quisquis, quīcumque; (of two) utercumque.
whiff n odor m.
while n spatium nt, tempus nt; **for a** ~ parumper; **a little** ~ paulisper; **a long** ~ diū; **it is worth** ~ expedit, operae pretium est; **once in a** ~ interdum ♦ conj dum + pres indic (= during the time that); + imperf indic (= all the time that) ♦ vt: ~ **away** dēgere, fallere.
whilst conj dum.
whim n libīdō f, arbitrium nt.
whimper n vāgītus m ♦ vi vāgīre.
whimsical adj facētus, īnsolēns.
whimsically adv facētē.
whimsy n dēliciae fpl, facētiae fpl.
whine n quīritātiō f ♦ vi quīritāre.
whinny n hinnītus m ♦ vi hinnīre.
whip n flagellum nt, flagrum nt ♦ vt flagellāre, verberāre.
whirl n turbō m ♦ vt intorquēre contorquēre ♦ vi contorquērī.
whirlpool n vertex m, vōragō f.
whirlwind n turbō m.
whisper n susurrus m ♦ vt, vi susurrāre, īnsusurrāre; ~ **to** ad aurem admonēre, in aurem dīcere.
whistle n (instrument) fistula f; (sound) sībilus m ♦ vi sībilāre.
white adj albus; (shining) candidus; (complexion) pallidus; (hair) cānus; **turn** ~ exalbēscere ♦ n album nt; (egg) albūmen nt.
white-hot adj: **to be** ~ excandēscere.
whiten vt dealbāre ♦ vi albēscere.
whiteness n candor m.
whitewash n albārium nt ♦ vt dealbāre.
whither adv quō; ~**soever** quōcumque.
whitish adj albulus.
whizz n strīdor m ♦ vi strīdere, increpāre.
who pron quis; (relat) quī.
whoever pron quisquis, quīcumque.
whole adj tōtus, cūnctus; (unhurt) integer, incolumis; (healthy) sānus ♦ n tōtum nt, summa f, ūniversitās f; **on the** ~ plērumque.
wholehearted adj studiōsissimus.
wholeheartedly adv ex animō.
wholesale adj māgnus, cōpiōsus; ~ **business** negōtiātiō f; ~ **dealer** mercātor m, negōtiātor m.

wholesome adj salūtāris, salūbris.
wholesomeness n salūbritās f.
wholly adv omnīnō, tōtus.
whoop n ululātus m ♦ vi ululāre.
whose pron cūius.
why adv cūr, qūarē, quamobrem, qua de causa.
wick n mergulus m.
wicked adj improbus, scelestus; (to gods, kin, country) impius.
wickedly adv improbē, scelestē, impiē.
wickedness n improbitās f, scelus nt, impietās f.
wicker adj vīmineus ♦ n vīmen nt.
wide adj lātus, amplus; **be ~ of** aberrāre ab ♦ adv lātē; **far and ~** longē lātēque.
widely adv lātē; (among people) vulgō.
widen vt laxāre, dīlātāre.
widespread adj effūsus, vulgātus.
widow n vidua f.
widowed adj viduus, orbus.
widower n viduus m.
widowhood n viduitās f.
width n lātitūdō f, amplitūdō f.
wield vt tractāre, gestāre, ūtī (abl).
wife n uxor f.
wifely adj uxōrius.
wig n capillāmentum nt.
wild adj ferus, indomitus, saevus; (plant) agrestis; (land) incultus; (temper) furibundus, impotens, āmēns; (shot) temerārius; **~ state** feritās f.
wild beast n fera f.
wilderness n sōlitūdō f, loca dēserta ntpl.
wildly adv saevē.
wildness n feritās f.
wile n dolus m, ars f, fraus f.
wilful adj pervicāx, contumāx; (action) cōnsultus.
wilfully adv contumāciter; cōnsultō.
wilfulness n pervicācia f, libīdō f.
wilily adv astūtē, vafrē.
wiliness n astūtia f.
will n (faculty) voluntās f, animus m; (intent) cōnsilium nt; (decision) arbitrium nt; (of gods) nūtus m; (document) testāmentum nt; **~ and pleasure** libīdō f; **against one's ~** invītus; **at ~** ad libīdinem suam; **good ~** studium nt; **ill ~** invidia f; **with a ~** summō studiō; **without making a ~** intestātus, intestātō ♦ vt velle, fut; (legacy) lēgāre; **as you ~** ut libet.
willing adj libēns, parātus; **be ~** velle; **not be ~** nōlle.
willingly adv libenter.
willingness n voluntās f.
willow n salix f ♦ adj salignus.
willowy adj gracilis.
wilt vi flaccēscere.
wily adj astūtus, vafer, callidus.
wimple n mitra f.
win vt ferre, obtinēre, adipisci; (after effort) auferre; (victory) reportāre; (fame) cōnsequī, adsequī; (friends) sibī conciliāre; **~ the day** vincere; **~ over** dēlēnire, conciliāre ♦ vi vincere.
wince vi resilīre.
winch n māchina f, sucula f.
wind n ventus m; (north) aquilō m; (south) auster m; (east) eurus m; (west) favōnius m; **I get ~ of** subolet mihī; **run before the ~** vento sē dare; **take the ~ out of one's sails** suō sibī gladiō iugulāre; **there is something in the ~** nescioquid olet; **which way the ~ blows** quōmodo sē rēs habeat.
wind vt torquēre; **~ round** intorquēre ♦ vi flectī, sinuāre; **~ up** (speech) perōrāre.
windbag n verbōsus m.
winded adj anhēlāns.
windfall n repentīnum bonum nt.
winding adj flexuōsus, tortuōsus ♦ n flexiō f, flexus m; **~s** pl (speech) ambāgēs fpl.
windlass n māchina f, sucula f.
window n fenestra f.
windpipe n aspera artēria f.
windward adj ad ventum conversus ♦ adv: **to ~** ventum versus.
windy adj ventōsus.
wine n vīnum nt; (new) mustum nt; (undiluted) merum nt.
winebibber n vīnōsus m.
wine cellar n apothēca f.
wine merchant n vīnārius m.
wine press n prēlum nt.
wing n āla f; (MIL) cornū nt, āla f; (of bird) penna f; **take ~** ēvolāre; **take under one's ~** patrōnus fierī (gen), clientem habēre, in custōdiam recipere.
winged adj ālātus, pennātus, volucer.
wink n nictus m ♦ vi nictāre; **~ at** cōnīvēre (dat).
winner n victor m.
winning adj blandus, iūcundus.
winningly adv blandē, iūcundē.
winning post n mēta f.
winnings n lucra ntpl.
winnow vt ventilāre; (fig) excutere.
winnowing-fan n vannus f.
winsome adj blandus, suāvis.
winter n hiems f; (mid) brūma f ♦ adj hiemālis, hībernus ♦ vi hībernāre.
winter quarters n hīberna ntpl.
wintry adj hiemālis, hībernus.
wipe vt dētergēre; **~ away** abstergēre; **~ dry** siccāre; **~ off** dētergēre; **~ out** dēlēre; **~ the nose** ēmungere.
wire n fīlum aēneum nt.
wiry adj nervōsus.
wisdom n sapientia f; (in action) prūdentia f; (in judgment) cōnsilium nt.
wise adj sapiēns, prūdēns.
wisely adv sapienter, prūdenter.
wish n optātum nt, vōtum nt; (for something missing) dēsīderium nt; **~es** pl (greeting) salūs f ♦ vt optāre, cupere, velle; **~ for** exoptāre, expetere, dēsīderāre; **~ good-day** salvēre iubēre; **as you ~** ut libet; **I ~ I could** utinam

possim.
wishful adj cupidus.
wishing n optātiō f.
wisp n manipulus m.
wistful adj dēsīderī plenus.
wistfully adv cum dēsīderiō.
wistfulness n dēsīderium nt.
wit n (humour) facētiae fpl, salēs mpl; (intellect) argūtiae fpl, ingenium nt; **caustic** ~ dicācitās f; **be at one's wits' end** valdē haerēre; **be out of one's ~s** dēlīrāre; **have one's ~s about one** prūdens esse; **to** ~ nempe, dīcō.
witch n sāga f, strīga f.
witchcraft n veneficium nt, magicae artēs fpl.
with prep (person) cum (abl); (thing) abl; (in company) apud (acc); (fight) cum (abl), contrā (acc); **be angry** ~ īrāscī (dat); **begin** ~ incipere ab; **rest** ~ esse penes (acc); **end** ~ dēsinere in (acc); **what do you want** ~ **me?** quid mē vis?
withdraw vt dēdūcere, dētrahere; (fig) āvocāre; (words) retractāre ♦ vi discēdere, abscēdere, sē recipere, sē subdūcere.
withdrawal n (MIL) receptus m.
wither vt torrēre ♦ vi dēflōrēscere.
withered adj marcidus.
withhold vt abstinēre, retinēre, supprimere.
within adv intus, intrā; (motion) intrō ♦ prep intrā (acc), in (abl).
without adv extrā, forīs; **from** ~ extrīnsecus; **be** ~ vacāre (abl), carēre (abl) ♦ prep sine (abl), expers (gen); **I admire** ~ **fearing** ita laudō ut nōn timeam; ~ **breaking the law** salvīs lēgibus; **you cannot see** ~ **admiring** vidēre nōn potes quīn laudēs; **you cannot appreciate** ~ **seeing for yourself** aestimāre nōn potes nisī ipse vīderis; ~ **doubt** sine dubio; ~ **the order of** iniūssū (gen); ~ **striking a blow** rē integrā.
withstand vt resistere (dat), obsistere (dat); (attack) ferre, sustinēre.
withy n vīmen nt.
witless adj excors, ineptus, stultus.
witness n (person) testis m/f; (to a document) obsignātor m; (spectator) arbiter m; (evidence) testimōnium nt; **call as** ~ antestārī; **bear** ~ testificārī; **call to** ~ testārī ♦ vt testificārī; (see) vidēre, intuērī.
witnessing n testificātiō f.
witticism n dictum nt; ~**s** pl facētiae fpl.
wittily adv facētē, salsē.
wittingly adv sciēns.
witty adj facētus, argūtus, salsus; (caustic) dicāx.
wizard n magus m, veneficus m.
wizardry n magicae artēs fpl.
wizened adj marcidus.
woad n vitrum nt.
wobble vi titubāre; (structure) labāre.
woe n luctus m, dolor m, aerumna f; ~**s** pl mala ntpl, calamitātēs fpl; ~ **to** vae (dat).
woeful adj tristis, maestus, aerumnōsus.
woefully adv triste, miserē.
wolf n lupus m, lupa f; ~**'s** lupīnus.

woman n fēmina f, mulier f; **old** ~ anus f; **married** ~ mātrōna f; ~**'s** muliebris.
womanish adj muliebris, effēminātus.
womanly adj muliebris.
womb n uterus m.
wonder n admīrātiō f; (of a thing) admīrābilitās f; (thing) mīrāculum nt, mīrum nt, portentum nt ♦ vi mīrārī; ~ **at** admīrārī, dēmīrārī.
wonderful adj mīrus, mīrābilis, admīrābilis; ~ **to relate** mīrābile dictu.
wonderfully adv mīrē, mīrābiliter, mīrum quantum.
wonderfulness n admīrābilitās f.
wondering adj mīrābundus.
wonderment n admīrātiō f.
wondrous adj mīrus, mīrābilis.
wont n mōs m, cōnsuētūdō f.
wonted adj solitus.
woo vt petere.
wood n silva f, nemus nt; (material) lignum nt; **gather** ~ lignārī; **touch** ~**!** absit verbō invidia ♦ adj ligneus.
woodcutter n lignātor m.
wooded adj silvestris, saltuōsus.
wooden adj ligneus.
woodland n silvae fpl ♦ adj silvestris.
woodman n lignātor m.
wood nymph n dryas f.
woodpecker n pīcus m.
wood pigeon n palumbēs m/f.
woodwork n tigna ntpl.
woodworker n faber tignārius m.
woody adj silvestris, silvōsus.
wooer n procus m.
woof n subtēmen nt.
wool n lāna f.
woollen adj lāneus.
woolly adj lānātus.
word n verbum nt; (spoken) vōx f; (message) nūntius m; (promise) fidēs f; (term) vocābulum nt; ~ **for** ~ ad verbum, verbum ē verbō; **a** ~ **with you!** paucīs tē volō!; **break one's** ~ fidem fallere; **bring back** ~ renūntiāre; **by** ~ **of mouth** ōre; **fair ~s** blanditiae fpl; **give one's** ~ fidem dare; **have a** ~ **with** colloquī cum; **have ~s with** iūrgāre cum; **have a good** ~ **for** laudāre; **in a** ~ ūnō verbō, dēnique; **keep one's** ~ fidem praestāre; **of few** ~**s** taciturnus; **take at one's** ~ crēdere (dat).
wording n verba ntpl.
wordy adj verbōsus.
work n (energy) labor m, opera f; (task) opus nt; (thing done) opus nt; (book) liber m; (trouble) negōtium nt; ~**s** (MIL) opera ntpl; (mechanism) māchinātiō f; (place) officīna f ♦ vi labōrāre ♦ vt (men) exercēre; (metal) fabricārī; (soil) subigere; (results) efficere; ~ **at** ēlabōrāre; ~ **in** admiscēre; ~ **off** exhaurīre; ~ **out** ēlabōrāre; ~ **up** (emotion) efferre; ~ **one's way up** prōficere ♦ vi gerī.
workaday adj cottīdiānus.

workhouse n ergastulum nt.

working n (mechanism) māchinātiō f; (soil) cultus m.

workman n (unskilled) operārius m; (skilled) opifex m, faber m; **workmen** operae fpl.

workmanship n ars f, artificium nt.

workshop n fabrica f, officīna f.

world n (universe) mundus m; (earth) orbis terrārum m; (nature) rērum nātūra f (mankind) hominēs mpl; (masses) vulgus nt; **of the ~** mundānus; **man of the ~** homō urbānus m; **best in the ~** rērum optimus, omnium optimus; **where in the ~** ubī gentium.

worldliness n quaestūs studium nt.

worldly adj quaestuī dēditus.

worm n vermis m ♦ vi: **~ one's way** sē īnsinuāre.

worm-eaten adj vermiculōsus.

wormwood n absinthium nt.

worn adj trītus.

worried adj sollicitus, anxius.

worry n cūra f, sollicitūdō f ♦ vi sollicitārī ♦ vt vexāre, sollicitāre; (of dogs) lacerāre.

worse adj pēior, dēterior; **grow ~** ingravēscere; **make matters ~** rem exasperāre ♦ adv pēius, dēterius.

worsen vi ingravēscere, dēteriōr fieri.

worship n venerātiō f, deōrum cultus m; (rite) sacra ntpl, rēs dīvīnae fpl ♦ vt adōrāre, venerārī, colere.

worst adj pessimus, dēterrimus; **~ enemy** inimīcissimus m; **endure the ~** ultima patī; vincere.

worsted n lāna f.

worth n (value) pretium nt; (moral) dignitās f, frūgālitās f, virtūs f; (prestige) auctōritās f ♦ adj dignus; **for all one's ~** prō virīlī parte; **how much is it ~?** quanti vēnit?; **it is ~ a lot** multum valet; **it is ~ doing** operae pretium est.

worthily adv dignē, meritō.

worthiness n dignitās f.

worthless adj (person) nēquam; (thing) vīlis, inānis.

worthlessness n levitās f, nēquitia f; vīlitās f.

worthy adj dignus; (person) frūgī, honestus; **~ of** dignus (abl).

wound n vulnus nt ♦ vt vulnerāre; (feelings) offendere.

wounded adj saucius.

wrangle n iūrgium nt, rixa f ♦ vi iūrgāre, rixārī, altercārī.

wrap vt involvere, obvolvere; **~ round** intorquēre; **~ up** involvere.

wrapper n involucrum nt.

wrapping n integumentum nt.

wrath n īra f, īrācundia f.

wrathful adj īrātus.

wrathfully adv īrācundē.

wreak vt: **~ vengeance on** saevīre in (acc), ulcīscī.

wreath n corōna f, sertum nt.

wreathe vt (garland) torquēre; (object)

corōnāre.

wreck n naufragium nt ♦ vt frangere; (fig) perdere; **be ~ed** naufragium facere.

wreckage n fragmenta ntpl.

wrecked adj (person) naufragus; (ship) frāctus.

wrecker n perditor m.

wren n rēgulus m.

wrench vt intorquēre, extorquēre; **~ away** ēripere; **~ open** effringere.

wrest vt extorquēre.

wrestle vi luctārī.

wrestler n luctātor m, athlēta m.

wrestling n luctātiō f.

wretch n scelerātus m, nēquam homō m; **poor ~** miser homō m.

wretched adj īnfēlīx, miser; (pitiful) flēbilis.

wretchedly adv miserē.

wretchedness n miseria f, maestitia f.

wriggle vi sē torquēre.

wriggling adj sinuōsus.

wright n faber m.

wring vt torquēre; **~ from** extorquēre.

wrinkle n rūga f ♦ vt corrūgāre.

wrinkled adj rūgōsus.

wrist n prīma palmae pars f.

writ n (legal) auctōritās f.

write vt scrībere; (book) cōnscrībere; **~ off** indūcere; **~ on** īnscrībere (dat); **~ out** exscrībere, dēscrībere; **~ out in full** perscrībere.

writer n (lit) scrīptor m, auctor m; (clerk) scrība m.

writhe vi torquērī.

writing n (act) scrīptiō f; (result) scrīptum nt.

wrong adj falsus, perversus, prāvus; (unjust) iniūstus, inīquus; **be ~, go ~** errāre ♦ n iniūria f, culpa f, noxa f, malum nt; **do ~** peccāre, dēlinquere; **right and ~** (moral) honesta ac turpia ntpl ♦ vt laedere, nocēre (dat); (by deceit) fraudāre.

wrongdoer n, maleficus m, scelerātus m.

wrongdoing n scelus nt.

wrongful adj iniūstus, iniūriosus, inīquus.

wrongfully adv iniūriā, iniūstē, inīquē.

wrong-headed adj perversus.

wrong-headedness n perversitās f.

wrongly adv falsō, dēprāvātē, male, perperam.

wroth adj īrātus.

wrought adj factus.

wry adj dētortus; **make a ~ face** ōs dūcere.

wryness n prāvitās f.

Y, y

yacht n phasēlus m.
yard n (court) ārea f; (measure) trēs pedēs.
yardarm n antenna f.
yarn n fīlum nt; (story) fābula f.
yawn n hiātus m ♦ vi hiāre, ōscitāre; (chasm) dehiscere.
ye pron vōs.
yean vt parere.
year n annus m; **every ~** quotannīs; **for a ~** in annum; **half ~** sēmēstre spatium nt; **this ~'s** hōrnus; **twice a ~** bis annō; **two ~s** biennium nt; **three ~s** triennium nt; **four ~s** quadriennium nt; **five ~s** quinquennium nt.
yearly adj annuus, anniversārius ♦ adv quotannīs.
yearn vi: **~ for** dēsīderāre, exoptāre.
yearning n dēsīderium nt.
yeast n fermentum nt.
yell n clāmor m; (of pain) ēiulātiō f ♦ vi clāmāre, eiulāre.
yellow adj flāvus; (pale) gilvus; (deep) fulvus; (gold) luteus; (saffron) croceus.
yelp n gannītus m ♦ vi gannīre.
yeoman n colōnus m.
yes adv ita verō (est), māximē; (correcting) immo.
yesterday adv herī ♦ n hesternus diēs m; **~'s** hesternus; **the day before ~** nudius tertius.
yet adv (contrast) tamen, nihilōminus, attamen; (time) adhūc, etiam; (with compar) etiam; **and ~** atquī, quamquam; **as ~** adhūc; **not ~** nōndum.
yew n taxus f.
yield n fructus m ♦ vt (crops) ferre, efferre; (pleasure) adferre; (concession) dare, concēdere; (surrender) dēdere ♦ vi cēdere; (surrender) sē dēdere, sē trādere; **~ to the**

wishes of mōrem gerere (dat), obsequī (dat).
yielding adj (person) facilis, obsequēns; (thing) mollis ♦ n cessiō f; dēditiō f.
yoke n iugum nt ♦ vt iungere, coniungere.
yokel n agrestis m.
yolk n vitellus m.
yonder adv illīc ♦ adj ille, iste.
yore n: **of ~** quondam, ōlim.
you pron tū, vōs.
young adj iuvenis, adulēscēns; (child) parvus; **~er** iūnior, nātū minor; **~est** nātū minimus ♦ n fētus m, pullus m, catulus m.
young man n iuvenis m; adulēscēns m.
youngster n puer m.
your adj tuus, vester.
yourself pron ipse.
youth n (age) iuventūs f, adulescentia f; (person) iuvenis m, adulēscēns m; (collective) iuventūs f.
youthful adj iuvenīlis, puerīlis.
youthfully adv iuvenīliter.

Z, z

zeal n studium nt, ārdor m.
zealot n studiōsus m, fautor m.
zealous adj studiōsus, ārdēns.
zealously adv studiōsē, ārdenter.
zenith n vertex m.
zephyr n Favōnius m.
zero n nihil nt.
zest n (taste) sapor m; (fig) gustātus m, impetus m.
zigzag n ānfrāctus m ♦ adj tortuōsus.
zither n cithara f.
zodiac n signifer orbis m.
zone n cingulus m.

Grammar and Verb Tables

This book is designed to help pupils and students of Latin to understand the grammar of the language. For beginners, the book provides an introduction to and explanation of the basic forms. More advanced students will find it an invaluable guide for reference and revision.

All parts of speech (nouns, pronouns, adjectives etc) are treated separately and clearly explained for the benefit of learners. Differences in usages are illustrated by extensive examples from many Latin authors. *American students and teachers, please note: this book is designed for use by students around the world, many of whom use British case ordering (Nom, Voc, Acc, Gen, Dat, Abl).*

A special section on word order in Latin, one of the greatest problems for students and pupils, has been included to guide the learner through both simple and compound sentences.

For ease of reference, all necessary structures, such as Indirect Statement, Conditional Sentences etc, have been listed under Contents. Each is then explained, for both English and Latin usage, to show the learner how to recognize the structure and translate it into English. Further examples of all structures are provided, for practice.

Handy, practical hints are given in the section on Translation Guidelines, to highlight the more common problems that confront students, and to assist in translation.

The final part of the grammar section lists the many "false friends" or confusable words that often lead students and pupils astray when translating from Latin. This section is of particular importance for examination candidates.

Tables of regular verbs provide information on verb formation and usage, while unique verbs are given in full with their meanings. A special feature of the grammar is a list of the 400 most common verbs, both regular and irregular. Irregular parts of verbs are highlighted and the conjugation number of each listed, so that by referring to the table indicated by this number, any part of the verb may be deduced.

VERBS

Abbreviations used

abl	ablative	**m, masc**	masculine
acc	accusative	**nt, neut**	neuter
adv	adverb	**nom**	nominative
conj	conjunction	**pl**	plural
dat	dative	**plup**	pluperfect
dep	deponent	**p(p)**	page(s)
f, fem	feminine	**prep**	preposition
gen	genitive	**pron**	pronoun
indic	indicative	**sing**	singular
intrans	intransitive	**voc**	vocative

Nouns

A noun is the name of a person, thing or quality.

Gender

- In Latin, as in English, the gender of nouns, representing persons or living creatures, is decided by meaning. Nouns denoting male people and animals are masculine

vir	a man
Gaius	Gaius
cervus	stag

- Nouns denoting female people and animals are feminine

femina	a woman
Cornelia	Cornelia
cerva	doe/hind

- However, the gender of things or qualities in Latin is decided by the ending of the noun.

anulus (ring)	*masc*
sapientia (wisdom)	*fem*
barba (beard)	*fem*
gaudium (joy)	*nt*

Number

- Nouns may be singular, denoting one, or plural, denoting two or more. This is shown by change of ending

sing	*pl*
terra (land)	terrae
modus (way)	modi
opus (work)	opera

Cases

- There are six cases in Latin, expressing the relationship of the noun to the other words in the sentence.

Nominative
the subject of the verb: **Caesar** died

Vocative
addressing someone/thing: Welcome, **Alexander**

Accusative
the object of the verb: The cat ate **the mouse**

Genitive
belonging to someone/thing: The home **of my friend**

Dative
the indirect object of the verb: I gave the book **to my son**

Ablative
says by, with or from whom/what: This was agreed **by the Senate**

Declensions

- Latin nouns are divided into five groups or declensions by the ending of their stems. Each declension has six cases, both singular and plural, denoted by different endings. The endings of the genitive singular case help to distinguish the different declensions.

	STEMS	GENITIVE SINGULAR
1st Declension	-a	-ae
2nd Declension	-ŏ or u	-ī
3rd Declension	-i, u, consonant	-is
4th Declension	-ŭ	-ūs
5th Declension	-ē	-ēi

First Declension

- All nouns end in -a in the nominative case and all are feminine except when the noun indicates a male, *eg* **poēta** (a poet), **agricola** (a farmer), *etc.*

	SINGULAR		PLURAL	
Nom	fēmina	the woman	fēminae	women
Voc	fēmina	o woman	fēminae	o women
Acc	fēminam	the woman	fēminās	women
Gen	fēminae	of the woman	fēminārum	of the women
Dat	fēminae	to/for the woman	fēminīs	to/for the women
Abl	fēminā	by/with/ from the woman	fēminīs	by/with/ from the women

- Note that **dea** (goddess) and **filia** (daughter), have their dative and ablative plurals **deābus** and **filiābus**

Declensions (contd)

Second Declension

- Nouns of the second declension end in **-us**, or a few in **-er** or **-r**. All are masculine. Those few which end in **-um** are neuter.

	SINGULAR	PLURAL	
			slaves
Nom	servus	servī	
Voc	serve	servī	
Acc	servum	servōs	
Gen	servī	servōrum	
Dat	servō	servīs	
Abl	servō	servīs	
	slave		

	SINGULAR	PLURAL	
			boys
Nom	puer	puerī	
Voc	puer	puerī	
Acc	puerum	puerōs	
Gen	puerī	puerōrum	
Dat	puerō	puerīs	
Abl	puerō	puerīs	
	boy		

	SINGULAR	PLURAL	
			wars
Nom	bellum	bella	
Voc	bellum	bella	
Acc	bellum	bella	
Gen	bellī	bellōrum	
Dat	bellō	bellīs	
Abl	bellō	bellīs	
	war		

- Note that proper names ending in **-ius** have vocative in **-ī**, o Vergilī – o Virgil!

- **deus** (god), has an alternative vocative **deus**, and plural forms **dī** in nominative and **dīs** in dative and ablative.

Third Declension

This is the largest group of nouns and may be divided into two broad categories, stems ending in a consonant and those ending in **-i**. All genders in this declension must be learnt.

Consonant Stems

- ending in **-l**

consul, -is *m* (consul)

	SINGULAR	PLURAL
Nom	cōnsul	cōnsulēs
Voc	cōnsul	cōnsulēs
Acc	cōnsulem	cōnsulēs
Gen	cōnsulis	cōnsulum
Dat	cōnsulī	cōnsulibus
Abl	cōnsule	cōnsulibus

- ending in **-n**

legio, -onis *f* (legion)

	SINGULAR	PLURAL
Nom	legiō	legiōnēs
Voc	legiō	legiōnēs
Acc	legiōnem	legiōnēs
Gen	legiōnis	legiōnum
Dat	legiōnī	legiōnibus
Abl	legiōne	legiōnibus

Continued

Declensions (contd)

flumen, -inis *nt* (river)

	SINGULAR	PLURAL
Nom	flumen	flūmina
Voc	flumen	flūmina
Acc	flumen	flūmina
Gen	flūminis	flūminum
Dat	flūminī	flūminibus
Abl	flūmine	flūminibus

● Note that the genitive plural of these nouns ends in **-um**.

● Stems ending in **-i**

cīvis, -is *m/f* (citizen)

	SINGULAR	PLURAL
Nom	cīvis	cīvēs
Voc	cīvis	cīvēs
Acc	cīvem	cīvēs
Gen	cīvis	cīvium
Dat	cīvī	cīvibus
Abl	cīve	cīvibus

● Note that these nouns have genitive plural in **-ium**.

Neuter Nouns

mare, -is *nt* (sea)

	SINGULAR	PLURAL
Nom	mare	maria
Voc	mare	maria
Acc	mare	maria
Gen	maris	marium
Dat	marī	maribus
Abl	marī	maribus

animal, -is *nt* (animal)

	SINGULAR	PLURAL
Nom	animal	animālia
Voc	animal	animālia
Acc	animal	animālia
Gen	animālis	animālium
Dat	animālī	animālibus
Abl	animālī	animālibus

● Note that the ablative singular of these neuter nouns ends in **-i**.

● Nominative, vocative and accusative singular endings of neuter nouns are identical.

● Nominative, vocative and accusative plural endings of neuter nouns in **all** declensions end in **-ā**.

Continued

Declensions (contd)

Monosyllabic Consonant Stems

The following have their genitive plural in -ium:

arx, arcis *f* (citadel)	– arcium (of citadels)
gēns, gentis *f* (race)	– gentium (of races)
mōns, montis *m* (mountain)	– montium (of mountains)
nox, noctis *f* (night)	– noctium (of nights)
pōns, pontis *m* (bridge)	– pontium (of bridges)
urbs, urbis *f* (city)	– urbium (of cities)

Fourth Declension

Nouns in this declension end in -us in the nominative singular and are mainly masculine. A few end in -u and are neuter.

exercitus, -ūs *m* (army)

	SINGULAR	PLURAL
Nom	exercitus	exercitūs
Voc	exercitus	exercitūs
Acc	exercitum	exercitūs
Gen	exercitūs	exercituum
Dat	exercituī	exercitibus
Abl	exercitū	exercitibus

genū, -ūs *nt* (knee)

	SINGULAR	PLURAL
Nom	genū	genua
Voc	genū	genua
Acc	genū	genua
Gen	genūs	genuum
Dat	genū	genibus
Abl	genū	genibus

- Note that a few common nouns are feminine, *eg* **domus** (house), **manus** (hand), **Idus** (Ides *or* 15th of the month).

- The form **domī** (at home) is an old form called locative. **domō** (from home) *abl sing*, **domōs** *acc pl* and **domōrum** *gen pl* are also used besides the fourth declension forms of **domus** (house).

Fifth Declension

There are only a few nouns in this declension. All end in -ēs in the nominative case. Most are feminine, but **diēs** (day) and **merīdiēs** (midday) are masculine.

diēs, -diēī *m* (day)

	SINGULAR	PLURAL
Nom	diēs	diēs
Voc	diēs	diēs
Acc	diem	diēs
Gen	diēī	diērum
Dat	diēī	diēbus
Abl	diē	diēbus

Cases

Use Of Cases

Nominative Case

The nominative case is used where:

- the noun is the **subject** of the verb (→**1**)
- the noun is a **complement** (→**2**)
- the noun is in **apposition** to the subject (→**3**)

Accusative Case

The accusative case is used:

- for the **direct object** of the verb (→**4**)
- with verbs of teaching and asking which take accusative of person and thing (→**5**)
- Verbs of naming, making *etc* take two accusatives for the same person or thing (→**6**)
- in exclamations (→**7**)
- to show extent of space (→**8**)
- to show extent of time (→**9**)
- to show motion to a place or country usually with a preposition (→**10**)
- to show motion towards, without a preposition, before names of towns and small islands (→**11**)

  Note also: **domum** (home), **rus** (to the country), **foras** (outside)

- for an object with similar meaning to the verb (*cognate*) (→**12**)

Continued

NOUNS 17

Examples

1 **Sextus** ridet
Sextus laughs

2 Romulus **rex** factus est
Romulus was made king

3 Marcus Annius, **eques Romanus,** hoc dicit
Marcus Annius, a Roman businessman, says this

4 canis **baculum** petit
the dog fetches the stick

5 **puerum litteras** docebo
I shall teach the boy literature

6 **Ancum Martium regem** populus creavit
The people made Ancus Martius king

7 o **tempora,** o **mores**
what times, what conduct!

8 murus decem **pedes** altus est
the wall is 10 foot high

9 Troia decem **annos** obsessa est
Troy was under siege for 10 years

10 **ad Hispaniam** effugerunt
they escaped to Spain

11 **Athenas** legati missi sunt
Ambassadors were sent to Athens

12 **vitam** bonam **vixit**
he lived a good life

Cases (contd)

Dative Case

- Indirect object (*ie* to or for whom an action is performed) (→**1**)

- used with verbs of obeying (**parēre**), resisting (**resistere**), pleasing (**placēre**), ordering (**imperāre**) *etc* (→**2**)

- verb compounds (beginning **ad-**, **ob-**, **prae-**, **sub-**) denoting helping or hindering take dative (→**3**)

  adesse – come to help
  subvenire – help

- indicates possession (→**4**)

- is used with adjectives meaning "like" (**similis**), "fit" (**aptus**), "near" (**proximus**) (→**5**)

- indicates a purpose (known as *predicative dative*) (→**6**)

- shows the agent of gerund/gerundive (→**7**)

Continued

Examples

1 pecuniam **domino** dedit
he gave the money to his master

2 maria terraeque **Deo** parent
land and sea obey God

3 Pompeius **hostibus** obstitit
Pompey opposed the enemy

4 Poppaea amica est **Marciae**
Poppaea is Marcia's friend

5 feles **tigri similis** est
the cat is like a tiger

6 nemo mihi **auxilio** est
there is no-one to help me

7 omnia erant agenda **nobis**
everything had to be done by us

20 NOUNS

Cases (contd)

Genitive Case

- Indicates possession (→**1**)
- Denotes part of a whole (→**2**)
- Indicates a quality, always with an adjective (→**3**)
- Is used as a predicate, where a person represents a quality (→**4**)
- Is used with superlatives (→**5**)
- Precedes **causa** and **gratia** (for the sake of) (→**6**)
- Is used after certain adjectives (→**7**)

sciens	(knowing)
inscius	(ignorant of)
cupidus	(desiring)
particeps	(sharing) *etc*

- Is used with verbs of remembering (**memini**) and forgetting (**obliviscor**) (→**8**)
- Follows verbs of accusing, convicting *etc* (→**9**)
- Represents value or worth (→**10**)

Continued

Examples

1 domus **regis**
the king's house

uxor **Augusti**
the wife of Augustus

2 quid **novi**
what news?

plus **cibi**
more food

3 magnae **auctoritatis** es
your reputation is great

4 **stulti** est hoc facere
it is the mark of a fool to do this

5 Indus est **omnium fluminum** maximum
the Indus is the greatest of all rivers

6 tu me **amoris causa** servavisti
you saved me for love's sake

7 Verres, **cupidus pecuniae**, ex hereditate praedatus est
Verres, greedy for money, robbed the estate

8 **mortis** memento
remember death

9 ante **actarum rerum** Antonius accusatus est
Antony was accused of previous offences

10 frumentum **minimi** vendidit
he sold corn at the lowest price

flocci non facio
I don't care at all

Cases (contd)

Ablative Case

- Indicates place, usually with the preposition "in" (→**1**)
  Note, however: **totā Asiā** – throughout Asia
  terrā marīque – by land and sea

- Indicates motion from, or down from a place, usually with prepositions **ex**, **de**, **a(b)** (→**2**)

- Note prepositions are omitted before names of towns, small islands and **domo** (from home), **rure** (from the country), **foris** (from outside) (→**3**)

- Represents time when or within which something happens (→**4**)

- Indicates origin, sometimes with prepositions **in**, **ex**, **a(b)** (→**5**)

- Is used to show material from which something is made (→**6**)

- Indicates manner (how something is done), usually with **cum** when there is no adjective, and without **cum** when there is an adjective (→**7**)

- Is used with verbs of depriving, filling, needing and with **opus est** (→**8**)

- Is used with deponent verbs **utor** (use), **abutor** (abuse), **fungor** (accomplish), **potior** (gain possession of) (→**9**)

- States cause (→**10**)

- To form **ablative absolute**, where a noun in the ablative is combined with a participle or another noun or adjective in the same case, to form an idea independent of the rest of the sentence. This is equivalent to an adverbial clause (→**11**)

Examples

1 Milo **in urbe** mansit
Milo remained in the city

2 **de equo** cecidit
He fell down from his horse

praedam **ex urbe ornatissima** sustulit
He stole booty from the rich city

3 **domo** cucurrerunt servi
The slaves ran from the house

4 **hac nocte** Agricola obiit
Agricola died on this night

decem annis Lacedaimonii non haec confecerunt
The Spartans did not complete this task within 10 years

5 Romulus et Remus, **Marte nati**
Romulus and Remus, sons of Mars

flumina **in Caucaso monte** orta
Rivers rising in the Caucasus mountains

6 statua **ex auro** facta est
The statue was made of gold

7 mulieres **cum virtute** vixerunt
The women lived virtuously

summa celeritate Poeni regressi sunt
The Carthaginians retreated at top speed

8 aliquem **vita** privare
to deprive someone of life

opus est mihi **divitiis**
I need wealth

9 **vi et armis** usus est
He used force of arms

10 leo **fame** decessit
The lion died of hunger

11 **exigua parte aestatis reliqua**, Caesar in Britanniam proficisci contendit
Although only a little of the summer remained, Caesar hurried to set out for Britain

Adjectives

An adjective adds a quality to the noun. It usually follows the noun but sometimes comes before it for emphasis. The adjective agrees with its noun in number, case and gender.

Gender
vir bonus (*masc*)   a good man
fēmina pulchra (*fem*)   a beautiful woman
bellum longum (*neut*)   a long war

Number
virī bonī (*pl*)   good men
fēminae pulchrae (*pl*)   beautiful women
bella longa (*pl*)   long wars

Case
virō bonō (*dat sing*)   for a good man
fēminās pulchrās (*acc pl*)   beautiful women
bellī longī (*gen sing*)   of a long war

- Adjectives are declined like nouns and usually arranged in two groups:

1 those with endings of the first and second declensions
2 those with endings of the third declension

First and Second Declensions

bonus, bona, bonum (good)

	Masc	Fem	Neut
SINGULAR			
Nom	bonus	bona	bonum
Voc	bone	bona	bonum
Acc	bonum	bonam	bonum
Gen	bonī	bonae	bonī
Dat	bonō	bonae	bonō
Abl	bonō	bonā	bonō
PLURAL			
	Masc	Fem	Neut
Nom	bonī	bonae	bona
Voc	bonī	bonae	bona
Acc	bonōs	bonās	bona
Gen	bonōrum	bonārum	bonōrum
Dat	bonīs	bonīs	bonīs
Abl	bonīs	bonīs	bonīs

Declensions (contd)

miser, misera, miserum (unhappy)

SINGULAR

	Masc	Fem	Neut
Nom	miser	misera	miserum
Voc	miser	misera	miserum
Acc	miserum	miseram	miserum
Gen	miserī	miserae	miserī
Dat	miserō	miserae	miserō
Abl	miserō	miserā	miserō

PLURAL

	Masc	Fem	Neut
Nom	miserī	miserae	misera
Voc	miserī	miserae	misera
Acc	miserōs	miserās	misera
Gen	miserōrum	miserārum	miserōrum
Dat	miserīs	miserīs	miserīs
Abl	miserīs	miserīs	miserīs

- **liber** (free) and **tener** (tender) are declined like **miser**

pulcher, pulchra, pulchrum (beautiful)

SINGULAR

	Masc	Fem	Neut
Nom	pulcher	pulchra	pulchrum
Voc	pulcher	pulchra	pulchrum
Acc	pulchrum	pulchram	pulchrum
Gen	pulchrī	pulchrae	pulchrī
Dat	pulchrō	pulchrae	pulchrō
Abl	pulchrō	pulchrā	pulchrō

PLURAL

	Masc	Fem	Neut
Nom	pulchrī	pulchrae	pulchra
Voc	pulchrī	pulchrae	pulchra
Acc	pulchrōs	pulchrās	pulchra
Gen	pulchrōrum	pulchrārum	pulchrōrum
Dat	pulchrīs	pulchrīs	pulchrīs
Abl	pulchrīs	pulchrīs	pulchrīs

- **aeger** (sick), **crēber** (frequent), **integer** (whole), **niger** (black), **piger** (slow) and **sacer** (sacred) are declined like **pulcher**

Declensions (contd)

- The following group of adjectives form their genitive singular in -ius and dative singular in -i:

alius, -a, -ud	another
alter, altera, alterum	one of two
neuter, neutra, neutrum	neither
nūllus, -a, -um	none
sōlus, -a, -um	alone
tōtus, -a, -um	whole
ūllus, -a, -um	any
ūnus, -a, -um	one
uter, utra, utrum	which of two?

solus (alone)

SINGULAR

	Masc	Fem	Neut
Nom	solus	sola	solum
Acc	solum	solam	solum
Gen	solius	solius	solius
Dat	soli	soli	soli
Abl	solo	sola	solo

PLURAL

	Masc	Fem	Neut
Nom	soli	solae	sola
Acc	solos	solas	sola
Gen	solorum	solarum	solorum
Dat	solis	solis	solis
Abl	solis	solis	solis

Third Declension

Adjectives of the third declension, like nouns, may be divided into two broad types, those with consonant stems and those with vowel stems in -i.

Consonant Stems

These have **one** ending in nominative singular.

prūdēns (wise)

SINGULAR

	Masc	Fem	Neut
Nom	prūdēns	prūdēns	prūdēns
Voc	prūdēns	prūdēns	prūdēns
Acc	prūdentem	prūdentem	prūdēns
Gen	prūdentis	prūdentis	prūdentis
Dat	prūdentī	prūdentī	prūdentī
Abl	prūdentī	prūdentī	prūdentī

PLURAL

	Masc	Fem	Neut
Nom	prūdentēs	prūdentēs	prūdentia
Voc	prūdentēs	prūdentēs	prūdentia
Acc	prūdentēs	prūdentēs	prūdentia
Gen	prūdentium	prūdentium	prūdentium
Dat	prūdentibus	prūdentibus	prūdentibus
Abl	prūdentibus	prūdentibus	prūdentibus

- **dīligēns** (careful), **innocēns** (innocent), **frequēns** (frequent), **potēns** (powerful), **ingēns** (huge) are declined like **prūdēns**

Declensions (contd)

amāns (loving)

SINGULAR

	Masc	Fem	Neut
Nom	amāns	amāns	amāns
Voc	amāns	amāns	amāns
Acc	amantem	amantem	amāns
Gen	amantis	amantis	amantis
Dat	amantī	amantī	amantī
Abl	amante	amante	amante

PLURAL

	Masc	Fem	Neut
Nom	amantēs	amantēs	amantia
Voc	amantēs	amantēs	amantia
Acc	amantēs	amantēs	amantia
Gen	amantium	amantium	amantium
Dat	amantibus	amantibus	amantibus
Abl	amantibus	amantibus	amantibus

- All Present participles are declined like **amāns,** although Present participles of the other conjugations end in **-ēns**

- When participles are used as adjectives **-ī** is used instead of **-e** in ablative singular case

fēlix (lucky)

SINGULAR

	Masc	Fem	Neut
Nom	fēlix	fēlix	fēlix
Voc	fēlix	fēlix	fēlix
Acc	fēlicem	fēlicem	fēlix
Gen	fēlicis	fēlicis	fēlicis
Dat	fēlicī	fēlicī	fēlicī
Abl	fēlicī	fēlicī	fēlicī

PLURAL

	Masc	Fem	Neut
Nom	fēlicēs	fēlicēs	fēlicia
Voc	fēlicēs	fēlicēs	fēlicia
Acc	fēlicēs	fēlicēs	fēlicia
Gen	fēlicium	fēlicium	fēlicium
Dat	fēlicibus	fēlicibus	fēlicibus
Abl	fēlicibus	fēlicibus	fēlicibus

audāx (bold) and **ferōx** (fierce) are declined like **fēlix**

- Note that all the above adjectives have the same case endings in all genders except for the neuter accusative singular and the neuter nominative, vocative and accusative plural.

Declensions (contd)

Vowel Stems

The following adjectives have **two** endings in nominative singular, one for masculine and feminine, one for neuter.

fortis, forte (brave)

	Masc	Fem	Neut
		SINGULAR	
Nom	fortis	fortis	forte
Voc	fortis	fortis	forte
Acc	fortem	fortem	forte
Gen	fortis	fortis	fortis
Dat	fortī	fortī	fortī
Abl	fortī	fortī	fortī
		PLURAL	
Nom	fortēs	fortēs	fortia
Voc	fortēs	fortēs	fortia
Acc	fortēs	fortēs	fortia
Gen	fortium	fortium	fortium
Dat	fortibus	fortibus	fortibus
Abl	fortibus	fortibus	fortibus

- **brevis** (short), **facilis** (easy), **gravis** (heavy), **levis** (light), **omnis** (all), **tristis** (sad), **turpis** (disgraceful), **talis** (of such a kind), and **qualis** (of which kind), are declined like **fortis**.

The following adjectives have **three** endings in nominative singular.

ācer, ācris, ācre (sharp)

	Masc	Fem	Neut
		SINGULAR	
Nom	ācer	ācris	ācre
Voc	ācer	ācris	ācre
Acc	ācrem	ācrem	ācre
Gen	ācris	ācris	ācris
Dat	ācrī	ācrī	ācrī
Abl	ācrī	ācrī	ācrī
		PLURAL	
Nom	ācrēs	ācrēs	ācria
Voc	ācrēs	ācrēs	ācria
Acc	ācrēs	ācrēs	ācria
Gen	ācrium	ācrium	ācrium
Dat	ācribus	ācribus	ācribus
Abl	ācribus	ācribus	ācribus

- **alacer** (lively), **equester** (of cavalry), and **volucer** (winged), are declined like **acer**, and **celer** (swift), declines similarly, but keeps **-e-** throughout (*eg* **celer, celeris, celere**)

34 ADJECTIVES

Use of Adjectives

There are two ways of using adjectives.

- They can be used **attributively**, where the adjective in English comes before the noun: the new car

- An attributive adjective in Latin usually follows its noun but may sometimes come before it with a change of meaning (→**1**)

- They can be used **predicatively**, where the adjective comes after the verb: the car is new (→**2**)

- If an adjective describes two nouns, it agrees in gender with the nearer (→**3**)

- When an adjective describes two subjects of different sex it is often masculine plural (→**4**)

- When an adjective describes two subjects representing things without life it is often neuter plural (→**5**)

Examples ADJECTIVES 35

1 res **parvae**
small things

in **parvis rebus**
in unimportant matters

civis **Romanus** sum
I am a Roman citizen

2 Servi erant **fideles**
The slaves were faithful

3 Antonius, vir consilii **magni** et prudentiae
Antony, a man of great wisdom and prudence

4 frater et soror sunt **timidi**
Brother and sister are frightened

5 Calor et ventus per artus **praesentia** erant
Warmth and wind were present in the limbs

Comparative and Superlative

Adjectives also have comparative forms *eg* I am **luckier** than you, and superlative forms *eg* the **noblest** Roman of them all.

Formation

● The comparative is formed by adding **-ior** (*masc and fem*) and **-ius** (*neut*) to the consonant stem of the adjective and the superlative by adding **-issimus, -a, -um** to the stem:

POSITIVE

altus	high
audāx	bold
brevis	short
prūdēns	wise

COMPARATIVE

altior	higher
audācior	bolder
brevior	shorter
prūdentior	wiser

SUPERLATIVE

altissimus	highest
audācissimus	boldest
brevissimus	shortest
prūdentissimus	wisest

Continued

● If the adjective ends in **-er** (*in masc nom sing*) add **-rimus** to form the superlative.

POSITIVE

ācer	sharp
celer	swift
miser	unhappy
pulcher	beautiful

COMPARATIVE

ācrior	sharper
celerior	swifter
miserior	more unhappy
pulchrior	more beautiful

SUPERLATIVE

ācerrimus	sharpest
celerrimus	swiftest
miserrimus	most unhappy
pulcherrimus	most beautiful

● Six adjectives ending in **-ilis** (*in masc nom sing*) add **-limus** to the stem to form the superlative.

POSITIVE

facilis	easy
difficilis	difficult
similis	like
dissimilis	unlike
gracilis	slight
humilis	low

COMPARATIVE

facilior	easier
difficilior	more difficult
similior	more like
dissimilior	more unlike
gracilior	more slight
humilior	lower

SUPERLATIVE

facillimus	easiest
difficillimus	most difficult
simillimus	most like
dissimillimus	most unlike
gracillimus	most slight
humillimus	lowest

Comparative and Superlative (contd)

Irregular comparison

- Some adjectives have irregular comparative and superlative forms:

POSITIVE	
bonus	good
malus	bad
parvus	small
magnus	big
multus	much
multī	many

COMPARATIVE	
melior	better
pēior	worse
minor	smaller
māior	bigger
plūs	more
plūrēs	more

SUPERLATIVE	
optimus	best
pessimus	worst
minimus	smallest, least
māximus	biggest
plūrimus	most
plūrimī	most

Continued

- Note that all adjectives ending in **-us** preceded by a vowel (except those ending in **-quus**) form comparative and superlative thus:

idōneus	suitable
magis idōneus	more suitable
māximē idōneus	most suitable

but

antiquus	old
antiquior	older
antiquissimus	oldest

- Note the following comparatives and superlatives where there is no positive form:

exterior	outer	**extrēmus**	furthest
inferior	lower	**infimus** or **imus**	lowest
superior	upper, higher	**suprēmus** or **summus**	highest
posterior	later	**postrēmus**	latest

Comparative and Superlative (contd)

Declension of Comparative and Superlative

- All comparatives decline like adjectives of the third declension.

	SINGULAR			PLURAL	
	Masc/Fem	Neut		Masc/Fem	Neut
Nom	altior	altius		altiōrēs	altiōra
Voc	altior	altius		altiōrēs	altiōra
Acc	altiōrem	altius		altiōrēs	altiōra
Gen	altiōris	altiōris		altiōrum	altiōrum
Dat	altiōrī	altiōrī		altiōribus	altiōribus
Abl	altiōre	altiōre		altiōribus	altiōribus

- Note ablative singular in **-e**.
- All superlatives decline like adjectives of first and second declensions (*eg* **bonus, bona, bonum**).

Use

- The comparative is often followed by **quam** (than), or the thing or person compared is given in the ablative case (→**1**)

- Sometimes the comparative can be translated by "rather" or "quite" (→**2**)

- The comparative is often strengthened by "**multo**" (→**3**)

- Sometimes the superlative can be translated by "very", or even as a positive adjective in English (→**4**)

- "**quam**" with the superlative means "as … as possible" (→**5**)

Examples

1 Marcus est **altior quam soror**
Marcus est **altior sorore**
Marcus is taller than his sister

2 Gallus erat **fortior**
the Gaul was rather brave

3 **multo carior**
much dearer

4 **vir sapientissimus**
a very wise man

integerrima vita
of virtuous life

5 **quam paucissimi**
as few people as possible

42 ADVERBS

Adverbs

An adverb modifies a verb, adjective, another adverb or a noun. It answers questions such as "how?", "when?", "why?", "where?", "to what extent?".

Formation

- Some are formed from nouns *eg* **furtim** (stealthily) or pronouns **aliās** (at other times) but most are formed from adjectives.

- Accusative singular neuter of adjectives of extent:

multum	much	**nimium**	too much
paulum	a little	**aliquantum**	somewhat
prīmum	first	**cēterum**	for the rest

- Adjectives in **-us** and **-er** change to **-ē**:

altē	highly	**miserē**	wretchedly

- Ablative forms of these adjectives in **-ō** or **-ā**:

certē *or* **certō**	certainly	**vērē**	in truth
dextrā	on the right	**vērō**	certainly

- Adjectives of the third declension add **-ter/-iter**:

audacter	boldly	**celeriter**	quickly
prudenter	wisely		

Position

- An adverb comes before the verb, adjective, adverb or noun that it modifies (→**1**)

- However adverbs of time often come at the beginning of the sentence (→**2**)

Continued

---

1 **vehementer** errabas, Verres
you were making a big mistake, Verres

nimium libera respublica
too free a state

bis consul
twice consul

2 cras **mane** putat se venturum esse
He thinks he will come tomorrow morning

saepe hoc mecum cogitavi
I often thought this over by myself

Common Adverbs

● Manner – "how?"

ita	thus	crudeliter	cruelly
sīc	thus	iustē	justly
aliter	otherwise	liberē	freely
forte	by chance	repente	suddenly
magnopere	greatly		

● Time – "when?"

iam, nunc	now	(n)umquam	(n)ever
simul	at the same time	iterum	again
anteā	before	saepe	often
posteā	afterwards	hodiē	today
cotīdiē	every day	herī	yesterday
diū	for a long time	crās	tomorrow
mox	soon	postrīdiē	next day
interim or -ea	meanwhile	statim	immediately
tum	then		

● Place – "where?"

ubi?	where?	unde?	where from?	quō?	where to?
ibi	there	inde	from there	eō	to there
hic	here	hinc	from here	hūc	to here
usquam	any-where	nusquam	nowhere		

Others

etiam	also	fortasse	perhaps
quoque	also	consultō	on purpose
quidem	indeed	scīlicet	no doubt

Comparison of Adverbs

The comparative form of the adverb is the nominative singular neuter of the comparative adjective. The superlative of the adverb is formed by changing -us of the superlative adjective to -ē.

POSITIVE	COMPARATIVE	SUPERLATIVE
altē highly	**altius** more highly	**altissimē** most highly
audācter boldly	**audācius** more boldly	**audācissimē** most boldly
bene well	**melius** better	**optimē** best
breviter briefly	**brevius** more briefly	**brevissimē** most briefly
diū for a long time	**diūtius** longer	**diūtissimē** longest
facile easily	**facilius** more easily	**facillimē** most easily
magnoperē greatly	**magis** more	**maximē** most
male badly	**peius** worse	**pessimē** worst
miserē wretchedly	**miserius** more wretchedly	**miserrimē** most wretchedly
multum much	**plūs** more	**plūrimum** most
paulum a little	**minus** less	**minimē** least
prope near	**propius** nearer	**proximē** nearest
saepe often	**saepius** more often	**saepissimē** most often

- Notes on use of the comparative adjective may be applied also to the comparative adverb (*see p 40*).

rem totam brevius cognōscite
Find out about the whole matter more briefly

magis cōnsiliō quam virtūte vīcit
He won more because of his strategy than his courage

legiōnēs diūtius sine cōnsule fuērunt
The legions were too long without a consul

multō plūs
much more

optimē
very well

mihi placēbat Pompōnius maximē vel minimē
I liked Pomponius the most or disliked him the least

optimus quisque id optimē facit
All the best people do it best

quam celerrimē   as quickly as possible

Pronouns

Personal Pronouns

The pronouns **ego** (I), **nōs** (we), **tū** (you, *sing*), **vōs** (you, *pl*) decline as follows:

SINGULAR

Nom	**ego**	I	**tū**	you
Acc	**mē**	me	**tē**	you
Gen	**meī**	of me	**tuī**	of you
Dat	**mihi**	to/for me	**tibi**	to/for you
Abl	**mē**	by/with/from me	**tē**	by/with/from you

PLURAL

Nom	**nōs**	we	**vōs**	you
Acc	**nōs**	us	**vōs**	you
Gen	**nostrum**	of us	**vestrum**	of you
Dat	**nōbis**	to/for us	**vobis**	to/for you
Abl	**nōbis**	by/with/from us	**vōbis**	by/with/from you

Possessive

meus, -a, -um	my	**tuus, -a, -um**	your
noster, -ra, -rum	our	**vester, -ra, -rum**	your

- **nostri** and **vestri** are alternative forms of genitive plural.
- Possessives are sometimes used instead of the genitive of personal pronouns:

odium tuum
hatred of you

- For the third person pronoun, he/she/it, Latin uses **is, ea, id**:

SINGULAR

	Masc		Fem		Neut	
Nom	**is**	he	**ea**	she	**id**	it
Acc	**eum**	him	**eam**	her	**id**	it
Gen	**ēius**	of him	**ēius**	of her	**ēius**	of it
Dat	**eī**	to him	**eī**	to her	**eī**	to it
Abl	**eō**	by him	**eā**	by her	**eō**	by it

PLURAL

	Masc		Fem		Neut	
Nom	**eī**	they	**eae**	they	**ea**	they
Acc	**eōs**	them	**eās**	them	**ea**	them
Gen	**eōrum**	of them	**eārum**	of them	**eōrum**	of them
Dat	**eīs**	to them	**eīs**	to them	**eīs**	to them
Abl	**eīs**	by them	**eīs**	by them	**eīs**	by them

Use

- Pronouns as subjects (I, you) are not usually used in Latin. The person of the verb is indicated by the ending (*eg* **mīsimus** – we sent). **ego, nos** *etc* are used only for emphasis:

ego vulgus odi, tū amas
I hate crowds, you love them

- The genitive forms **nostrum** and **vestrum** are used partitively:

multi nostrum
many of us
pauci vestrum
a few of you

Reflexive Pronouns

Acc	mē	myself	
Gen	meī		
Dat	mihi		
Abl	mē		
	tē	yourself	
	tuī		
	tibi		
	tē		
Acc	nōs	ourselves	
Gen	nostrum		
Dat	nōbis		
Abl	nōbis		
	vōs	yourselves	
	vestrum		
	vōbis		
	vōbis		

- These are identical in form to personal pronouns.

Acc	sē	himself/herself/itself/themselves
Gen	suī	
Dat	sibi	
Abl	sē	

- Reflexive pronouns are used to refer to the subject of the sentence:

quisque se amat
everybody loves themselves

me lavo
I wash myself

Determinative Pronouns

- **is** – he/that, **ea** – she, **id** – it: as above
- **idem** (the same)

SINGULAR

	Masc	Fem	Neut
Nom	īdem	eadem	idem
Acc	eundem	eandem	idem
Gen	eiusdem	eiusdem	eiusdem
Dat	eīdem	eīdem	eīdem
Abl	eōdem	eādem	eōdem

PLURAL

	Masc	Fem	Neut
Nom	eīdem	eaedem	eadem
Acc	eōsdem	eāsdem	eadem
Gen	eōrundem	eārundem	eōrundem
Dat	eīsdem	eīsdem	eīsdem
Abl	eīsdem	eīsdem	eīsdem

- **ipse** (himself/herself/itself/themselves)

SINGULAR

	Masc	Fem	Neut
Nom	ipse	ipsa	ipsum
Acc	ipsum	ipsam	ipsum
Gen	ipsius	ipsius	ipsius
Dat	ipsī	ipsī	ipsī
Abl	ipsō	ipsā	ipsō

PLURAL

	Masc	Fem	Neut
Nom	ipsī	ipsae	ipsa
Acc	ipsōs	ipsās	ipsa
Gen	ipsōrum	ipsārum	ipsōrum
Dat	ipsīs	ipsīs	ipsīs
Abl	ipsīs	ipsīs	ipsīs

Demonstrative Pronouns

- **hic** (this/these)

	Masc	*SINGULAR* Fem	Neut
Nom	hic	haec	hōc
Acc	hunc	hanc	hōc
Gen	hūius	hūius	hūius
Dat	huic	huic	huic
Abl	hōc	hāc	hōc

	Masc	*PLURAL* Fem	Neut
Nom	hī	hae	haec
Acc	hōs	hās	haec
Gen	hōrum	hārum	hōrum
Dat	hīs	hīs	hīs
Abl	hīs	hīs	hīs

- **ille** (that/those)

	Masc	*SINGULAR* Fem	Neut
Nom	ille	illa	illud
Acc	illum	illam	illud
Gen	illīus	illīus	illīus
Dat	illī	illī	illī
Abl	illō	illā	illō

	Masc	*PLURAL* Fem	Neut
Nom	illī	illae	illa
Acc	illōs	illās	illa
Gen	illōrum	illārum	illōrum
Dat	illīs	illīs	illīs
Abl	illīs	illīs	illīs

- Note that **īdem**, **hīc**, **ille** and all their parts may be adjectives as well as pronouns

PRONOUNS 53

Examples

1 **eadem** femina
the same woman

hic puer
this boy

2 tu autem **eadem** ages?
Are you going to do the same things?

patria est carior quam **nos ipsi**
Our native land is dearer than ourselves

3 **hac** remota, quomodo **illum** aestimemus?
When she is removed, how are we to judge him?

4 **nos** oportet opus conficere
We must complete the task

5 accusatores dicunt **te ipsam** testem **eius** criminis esse
The prosecutors claim that you yourself are the witness of that crime

6 sed **haec** omitto; ad **illa** quae **me** magis moverunt respondeo
But I pass over these matters; I reply to those which have affected me more deeply

7 pax **vobiscum**
Peace be with you!

8 puella intravit; **ea mihi** litteras dedit
The girl came in; she gave me a letter

Relative Pronouns

SINGULAR

	Masc	Fem	Neut	
Nom	**quī**	**quae**		who
Acc	**quem**	**quam**		whom
Gen	**cūius**	**cūius**		whose
Dat	**cuī**	**cuī**		to whom
Abl	**quō**	**quā**		by whom

	Neut			
Nom	**quod**			which/that
Acc	**quod**			which/that
Gen	**cūius**			of which
Dat	**cuī**			to which
Abl	**quō**			by which

PLURAL

	Masc	Fem	Neut	
Nom	**quī**	**quae**		who
Acc	**quōs**	**quās**		whom
Gen	**quōrum**	**quārum**		whose
Dat	**quibus**	**quibus**		to whom
Abl	**quibus**	**quibus**		by whom

	Neut			
Nom	**quae**			which
Acc	**quae**			which
Gen	**quōrum**			of which
Dat	**quibus**			to which
Abl	**quibus**			by which

- A relative pronoun attaches a subordinate clause to a word preceding it (its antecedent). It agrees with this word in number and gender but takes its case from its own clause (→1)

- **quīdam, quaedam, quoddam** (a certain, somebody) **quīcumque, quaecumque, quodcumque** (whoever/ whatever), decline in the same way as the relative above (→2)

1 iuvenis cuius librum Sextus legit laetus erat
The young man, whose book Sextus read, was happy

Fortunāta, quae erat uxor Trimalchiōnis, saltāre coeperat
Fortunata, who was Trimalchio's wife, had begun to dance

tum duo crotalia protulit quae Fortunātae cōnsīderanda dedit
Then she brought out a pair of earrings which she gave to Fortunata to look at

2 quīdam ex lēgātīs
a certain ambassador

tu, quīcumque es
you, whoever you are

Interrogative Pronouns

SINGULAR

	Masc	Fem		
Nom	quis	quis/quae	who?	
Acc	quem	quam	whom?	
Gen	cūius	cūius	whose?	
Dat	cuī	cuī	to whom?	
Abl	quō	quā	by whom?	

	Neut		
Nom	quid	what?	
Acc	quid	what?	
Gen	cūius	of what?	

PLURAL

	Masc	Fem		
Nom	quī	quae	who?	
Acc	quōs	quās	whom?	
Gen	quōrum	quārum	whose?	
Dat	quibus	quibus	to whom?	
Abl	quibus	quibus	by whom?	

	Neut			
Nom	quae	what?	Dat	quibus to what?
Acc	quae	what?	Abl	quibus by what?
Gen	quōrum	of what?		

(for Dat/Abl in first singular block: cuī to what?, quō by what?; plural: quibus to what?, quibus by what?)

- The interrogative pronoun is used to ask questions and usually is the first word in the sentence (→**1**)

- **quisquis, quisquis, quidquid** (whoever, whatever)
  quisque, quisque, quidque (each)
  quisquam, quisquam, quicquam (anyone, anything)
  aliquis, aliquis, aliquid (someone, something)
  These pronouns decline in the same way as **quis** above
  (→**2**)

Examples

1 **quae fuit enim causa quamobrem istī mulierī venenum dare vellet Caelius?**
What was the reason why Caelius wanted to give that woman poison?

quid agam, iudices?
What am I to do, men of the jury?

quos ad cenam invitavisti?
Whom did you invite for dinner?

quorum agros Galli incenderunt?
Whose fields did the Gauls burn?

2 **quisque** is est
whoever he is

si **quemquam** video
if I see anyone

liber **alicuius**
someone's book

Prepositions

A preposition expresses the relationship of one word to another. Each Latin preposition governs a noun or pronoun in the accusative or ablative case. Some prepositions govern both cases. Some may also be used as adverbs *eg* **prope** (near).

Position

- Prepositions generally come before the noun, or an adjective or equivalent qualifying the noun *eg*

  ad villam
  to the house

  ad Ciceronis villam
  to Cicero's house

- **cum** follows a personal pronoun *eg*

  mēcum
  with me

Prepositions governing the Accusative

On the following pages you will find some of the most frequent uses of prepositions in Latin. In the list below, the broad meaning is given on the left, with examples of usage following. Prepositions are given in alphabetical order.

ad

to/towards (*a place or person*)	**oculos ad caelum sustulit** he raised his eyes to heaven
at, in the direction of, with regard to	**ad Capuam profectus sum** I set out in the direction of Capua
	ad portas at the gates
	ad duo milia occisi about 2000 were killed
	nil ad me attinet it means nothing to me

adversum (-us)

opposite	**sedens adversus te** sitting opposite you
towards	**adversus Italiam** towards (*ie* facing) Italy
against	**adversum flumen** against the stream

Continued

Prepositions governing the Accusative (contd)

ante

before (*of place and time*), used with ordinal number in dates	**ante meridiem** before midday
	ante limen before the doorway
	ante diem quintum Kalendas Ianuarias 28th December (*ie* 5th before Kalends of January)

apud

at/near (*usually with persons*)	**Crassus apud eum sedet** Crassus is sitting near him
in the writing of	**apud Platonem** in Plato's writings
before (*authorities*)	**apud pontifices** before the high priests

circum (circa)

around, about (*of place, people*)	**circum forum** around the forum
	circum Hectorem around Hector
	circa montes around the mountains
	circa decem milia Gallorum about ten thousand Gauls

contra

against	**contra hostes** against the enemy
	contra ventos against the wind
opposite	**contra Britanniam** facing Britain

extra

outside of	**extra muros** outside the walls
beyond (*of place and time*)	**extra iocum** beyond a joke

inter

between	**inter oppositos exercitus** between the opposing armies
	amans inter se loving each other
among	**inter saucios** among the wounded
	inter manus within reach
during	**inter hos annos** during these years

Continued

Prepositions governing the Accusative (contd)

intra

within (*of place and time*)

intra parietes
within the walls

intra quattuor annos
within four years

ob

on account of

quam ob rem
therefore

ob stultitiam
on account of your
foolishness

per

through

per noctem
through the night

by means of

per vos
by means of you

per aetatem periit
he died of old age

per deos iuro
I swear by the gods

post

after (*of time and place*)

post urbem conditam
after the foundation of the
city

post tergum
behind your back

praeter

beyond

praeter naturam
beyond nature

besides

**praeter se tres alios
adduxit**
he brought three others
besides himself

except for

praeter paucos
except for a few

prope

near

prope me habitavit
he lived near me

propter

on account of

propter metum mortis
on account of fear of
death

Continued

Prepositions governing the Accusative (contd)

secundum

along (*of place*)	**secundum flumen** along the river
immediately after (*time*)	**secundum quietem** on waking from sleep
according to	**secundum naturam** according to nature

trans

across	**vexillum trans vallum traicere** to take the standard across the rampart
	trans Rhenum across the Rhine

ultra

beyond (*of time, degree etc*)	**ultra vires** beyond one's power

Continued

Prepositions governing the Ablative

Those which are spatial represent the idea of rest in a place or motion from a place.

a(b)

from (*of place, people, direction, time*)	**ab arce hostes deiecti sunt** the enemy were driven from the citadel
	a nobis abesse to be distant from us
	a dextrā from the right
	a tertiā horā from the third hour
by (*agent*)	**ab amicis desertus** abandoned by friends

cum

with	**vade mecum** go with me!
	cum curā loqui to speak with care
	cum Augusto coniurare to conspire with Augustus
	summa cum laude with distinction

Continued

Prepositions governing the Ablative (contd)

dē

down from	**dē caelō dēmittere** to send down from heaven
away from	**de triclinio exire** to go away from the dining room
about	**cogitare de hāc rē** to think about this matter
	dē industriā on purpose
during *or* at (*of time*)	**dē nocte** at night, during the night

ē(x)

out of (*from*)	**ē carcere effugerunt** they escaped from prison
	ex equis desilire to jump from their horses
	quidam ex Hispania someone from Spain
	statua ex argentō facta a statue made of silver
immediately after	**ex consulatu** immediately after his consulship
from	**ex hōc diē** from that day
	ex aequō equally

pro

for/on behalf of	**pro se quisque** each one for himself/ herself
	pro patriā mori to die for one's country
according to	**pro viribus agere** to act according to one's ability
in front of	**pro rostris** in front of the rostrum

sine

without	**sine spē** without hope
	sine pecuniā without money

Prepositions governing Accusative and Ablative

in

with accusative

into   **in hanc urbem venire**
to come into the city

till   **in primam lucem dormivit**
he slept till dawn

against   **in rem publicam aggredi**
to attack the state

with ablative

in   **puella in illā domō laetē vivebat**
the girl lived happily in that house

on   **in capite coronam gerebat**
he wore a crown on his head

   in animo habere
to intend (to have in one's mind)

within (*of time*)   **in omni aetate**
within every age

in (*of condition*)   **in parte facilis, in parte difficilis**
easy in parts, difficult in others

---

sub

with accusative

beneath   **sub iugum mittere**
to send beneath the yoke (*ie* into slavery)

below (*with verb of motion*)   **sub ipsum murum**
just below the wall

before (*of time*)   **sub vesperum**
just before nightfall

with ablative

under (*of place and power*)   **sub montibus constituere**
to station under the mountains

   sub Nerone
under the power of Nero

super

with accusative

over, above (*of place*), in addition   **super capita hostium**
over the heads of the enemy

   alii, super alios, advenerunt
they arrived one after the other

with ablative

concerning/about   **super his rebus scribam**
I shall write about these matters

Numerals

Cardinal and Ordinal Numbers

		CARDINAL	ORDINAL
1	I	ūnus, -a, -um	prīmus, -a, -um
2	II	duo, -ae, -o	secundus, -a, -um
3	III	trēs, tria	tertius, -a, -um
4	IV	quattuor	quartus, -a, -um
5	V	quīnque	quīntus, -a, -um
6	VI	sex	sextus, -a, -um
7	VII	septem	septimus, -a, -um
8	VIII	octō	octāvus, -a, -um
9	IX	novem	nōnus, -a, -um
10	X	decem	decimus, -a, -um
11	XI	ūndecim	ūndecimus, -a, -um
12	XII	duodecim	duodecimus, -a, -um
13	XIII	tredecim	tertius decimus, -a, -um
14	XIV	quattuordecim	quartus decimus, -a, -um
15	XV	quīndecim	quīntus decimus, -a, -um
16	XVI	sēdecim	sextus decimus, -a, -um
17	XVII	septendecim	septimus decimus, -a, -um
18	XVIII	duodēvigintī	duodēvicēsimus, -a, -um
19	XIX	ūndēvigintī	ūndēvicēsimus, -a, -um
20	XX	vigintī	vicēsimus, -a, -um
21	XXI	vigintī ūnus	vicēsimus prīmus
30	XXX	trigintā	trīcēsimus
40	XL	quadrāgintā	quadrāgēsimus
50	L	quīnquāgintā	quīnquāgēsimus
60	LX	sexāgintā	sexāgēsimus
70	LXX	septuāgintā	septuāgēsimus
80	LXXX	octōgintā	octōgēsimus
90	XC	nōnāgintā	nōnāgēsimus
100	C	centum	centēsimus

		CARDINAL	ORDINAL
200	CC	ducentī, -ae, -a	ducentēsimus
300	CCC	trecentī, -ae, -a	trecentēsimus
400	CCCC	quadringentī, -ae, -a	quadringentēsimus
500	D (IƆ)	quīngentī, -ae, -a	quīngentēsimus
600	DC	sescentī, -ae, -a	sescentēsimus
700	DCC	septingentī, -ae, -a	septingentēsimus
800	DCCC	octingentī, -ae, -a	octingentēsimus
900	DCCCC	nōngentī, -ae, -a	nōngentēsimus
1000	M (CIƆ)	mīlle	mīllēsimus
2000	MM	duo mīlia	bis mīllēsimus
1,000,000		deciēs centēna (centum) mīlia	mīlia

- Fractions are expressed as follows:

dimidia pars	1/2
tertia pars	1/3
quārta pars	1/4

Continued

72 NUMERALS

Cardinal and Ordinal Numbers (contd)

- Ordinal numbers (→1) decline like 1st and 2nd declension adjectives

- Cardinal numbers (→2) do not decline except for **unus, duo, trēs** and hundreds (**ducenti etc**)

- **unus** declines as 1st and 2nd declension adjectives except that the genitive singular ends in **-ius** and the dative in **-i**

- **duo** (two) declines as follows:

	Masc	Fem	Neut
Nom	duo	duae	duo
Acc	duōs	duās	duo
Gen	duōrum	duārum	duōrum
Dat	duōbus	duābus	duōbus
Abl	duōbus	duābus	duōbus

ambō, -ae, -a (both) declines in the same way

- **trēs** (three) declines as follows:

	Masc	Fem	Neut
Nom	trēs	trēs	tria
Acc	trēs	trēs	tria
Gen	trium	trium	trium
Dat	tribus	tribus	tribus
Abl	tribus	tribus	tribus

- Genitive of hundreds, eg **trecentī** ends **-um** (→3)

- **mīlia** (thousands) declines as follows:

Nom	mīlia	Dat	mīlibus
Acc	mīlia	Abl	mīlibus
Gen	mīlium		

- **mīlle** (thousand) does not decline.

---

1 coquus **secundam** mensam paraverat
The cook had prepared the second course

legionis **nonae** milites magnam partem hostium interfecerunt
Soldiers of the ninth legion killed a large number of the enemy

2 **decem mīlia** passuum exercitus progressus est
The army advanced 10 miles

Cerberus, qui **tria** capita habebat, in antro recubuit
Cerberus, who had three heads, crouched in the cave

Stellae **novem** orbes confecerunt
The stars completed nine orbits

duodeviginti onerariae naves huc accedebant
Eighteen cargo ships were approaching

Caesar **trecentos** milites trans Padanum traiecit
Caesar transported three hundred soldiers across the River Po

da mi basia **mille**
Give me a thousand kisses

3 **trecentum militum**
of three hundred soldiers

4 **duo mīlia passuum** (gen)
2000 paces or 2 miles

Distributive Numerals

These are used when repetition is involved as when multi-plying (→**1**)

1	**singulī, -ae, -a**	*one each*
2	**bīnī, -ae, -a**	*two each*
3	**ternī (trīnī)**	
4	**quaternī**	
5	**quīnī**	
6	**sēnī**	
7	**septēnī**	
8	**octōnī**	
9	**novēnī**	
10	**dēnī**	

Numeral Adverbs

1	**semel**	*once*
2	**bis**	*twice*
3	**ter**	
4	**quater**	
5	**quīnquiēs**	
6	**sexiēs**	
7	**septiēs**	
8	**octiēs**	
9	**noviēs**	
10	**deciēs**	
	(→**2**)	

1 **bīnī gladiātōrēs**
(*describing pairs of gladiators*)

bīna castra
two camps

quaternōs dēnāriōs in singulās vīnī amphorās
4 denarii each for a bottle of wine

2 nōn plus quam **semel**
not more than once

deciēs centēna mīlia sestertium *or* **deciēs** sestertium
1,000,000 sesterces

ter quattuor
twelve (*three times four*)

Dates

- Events of the year were usually recorded by using the names of the consuls holding office that year (→**1**)

- From the late republic the date of the foundation of Rome was established – 753 BC and time was calculated from this date (→**2**)

- The four seasons were: (→**3**)

ver, veris (*nt*)   spring
aestās, -ātis (*f*)   summer
autumnus, -ī (*m*)   autumn
hiems, -is (*f*)   winter

- The months were refomed by Julius Caesar (7 of 31 days, 4 of 30, 1 of 28, and an extra day each leap year). Each month (mensis, -is, *m*) was identified by the following adjectives:

Iānuārius   January
Februārius   February
Martius   March
Aprīlis   April
Māius   May
Iūnius   June
Iūlius (Quīntīlis) July
Augustus (Sextīlis) August
September   September
Octōber   October
November   November
December   December

- Three important days each month were:

Kalendae, -ārum (*fpl*) Kalends *or* 1st
Nonae, -ārum (*fpl*)   Nones *or* 5th/7th
Idus, -uum (*fpl*)   Ides *or* 13th/15th

Continued

Examples

1 **Nerone iterum L. Pisone consulibus** pauca memoria digna evenerunt
Few incidents worth recording took place during the year when Nero and Lucius Piso were consuls (AD 57)

Lentulo Gaetulico C. Calvisio consulibus decreta sunt triumphi insignia Poppaeo Sabino
A triumph was voted to Poppaeus Sabinus during the consulship of Lentulus Gaetulicius and Gaius Calvisius

2 **ab urbe condita**
since the foundation of Rome

ante urbem conditam
before the foundation of the city

post urbem conditam
after the foundation of the city

3 ineunte aestate
in the beginning of summer

media aestate
midsummer

iam **hieme confecta**
when winter was already over

vere ineunte Antonius Tarentum navigavit
At the beginning of spring, Antony sailed to Tarentum

Dates (contd)

- In March, July, October and May, Nones fall on the 7th and Ides on the 15th day (5th and 13th in all other months).

- To refer to these dates, the ablative is used (→1)

- To refer to the day before these dates, use pridiē (→2)

- All other days were reckoned by counting (inclusively) the days before the next main date. "ante diem" + accusative of ordinal numbers and the next main date were used:
9th of February is 5 days before the 13th of February (counting inclusively). 28th April is 4 days before 1st May (→3)

- An easy way to work out such dates is to add one to Nones and Ides and subtract the Latin number. Add two to the number of days in the month before the Kalends, again subtracting the given Latin number. You will then have the date in English

- The day was divided into twelve hours horae, -arum (fpl). The hours of darkness into four watches of three hours each, vigiliae, -arum (fpl), from 6–9 pm, 9–12 pm, 12–3 am, 3–6 am

- Other ways of expressing time:

primā luce	at dawn
solo orto	at sunrise
solis occasu	at sunset
media nocte	at midnight
noctu, nocte	at night
mane	in the morning
meridie	at midday
sub vesperum	towards evening
vespere	in the evening (→4)

Examples

1 **Kalendīs Martiīs**
on the 1st of March

Idibus Decembribus
on the 13th of December

Idibus Martiīs Caesar a Bruto interfectus est
Caesar was killed by Brutus on the 15th of March

2 **pridiē Nonas Ianuarias (Non. Ian.)**
4th January

3 **ante diem quintum Idus Februarias**
9th February

ante diem quartum Kalendas Maias
28th April

4 **prima hora**
at the first hour (6–7 am)

tertia vigilia
during the third watch (midnight–3 am)

tertia fere vigilia navem solvit
He set sail after midnight (during the third watch)
ipse **hora circiter quarta diei** cum primis navibus Britanniam attigit
He himself reached Britain with the first ships around 10 o'clock in the morning

vespere vinum optimum convivae bibunt
In the evening, the guests drink vintage wine

Word Order

Simple Sentences

Word order in English is stricter than in Latin. The usual English order – subject + verb + object – differentiates the meaning of sentences such as, "The cat caught the mouse" and "The mouse caught the cat". Latin order is more flexible since the endings of words clearly show their function, whatever their position in the sentence.

Compare the following:

feles murem cepit   the cat caught the mouse
murem cepit feles   it was the cat that caught the mouse

The sentences are identical in meaning, although the emphasis is different. This difference in word order often makes it difficult for English translators to unravel long Latin sentences. However there are certain principles to help:

- The normal *grammatical* word order in Latin is:

  Subject first, Predicate after (by Predicate understand "verb")

- Expressions qualifying the subject (*ie* adjectives) must be near the subject

- Expressions qualifying the predicate (*eg* objects, adverbs, prepositional phrases) must be near the verb

Thus the usual word order of a simple sentence is:

(Connecting Word)
Subject
(Adjective)
Object
Adverbs *or* Prepositional Phrases
Predicate (verb) (→1)

Continued

1 at **hostes** magnam virtutem in extrema spe salutis
   praestiterunt
   But the enemy showed great courage, finally hoping
   to save themselves

   Ariovistus ad postulata Caesaris pauca **respondit**
   Ariovistus briefly replied to Caesar's demands

   iste **Hannibal** sic hanc Tertiam **dilexit**
   Thus that Hannibal loved this Tertia

Simple Sentences (contd)

- Another principle is *emphasis*, where the words are in an unusual order, eg subject last, predicate first (→**1**)

- Questions usually begin with interrogatives (→**2**)

- Adjectives may precede or follow nouns. Check agreement of endings (→**3**)

- Genitives usually follow the governing word (→**4**)

- Words in apposition usually follow one another, although "rex" often comes first (→**5**)

- Adverbs usually come before their verb, adjective or adverb (→**6**)

- Prepositions usually come before their nouns (→**7**) but note, magna **cum** cura (with great care).

- Finally, watch out for the omission of words, particularly parts of **esse** (to be) (→**8**)

1 **horum** adventu **redintegratur** | **seditio** (subject last)
On their arrival trouble broke out once more

confecerunt me | **infirmitates** meorum (verb first)
I have been upset by the illnesses of my slaves

2 **quid** hoc loco potes dicere, homo amentissime?
What can you say at this point, you madman?

quis clarior in Graecia Themistocle?
Who (is) more famous in Greece than Themistocles?

3 **bello magno** victus   **magna domus**
conquered in a great war   a large house

4 multi **nostrum**   filius **Augusti**
many of us   Augustus' son

5 Cicero, **consul**
Cicero, the consul

rex Tarquinius
King Tarquinius

6 **vix** cuiquam persuadebatur
hardly anyone could be persuaded

multo carius
much dearer

7 **in** villam
into the house

sub monte
under the mountain

8 **pudor inde et miseratio et patris Agrippae, Augusti avi memoria (est)**
A feeling of pity and shame came over them and they remembered her father Agrippa and her grandfather Augustus

Compound Sentences

A compound sentence is one with a main clause and one or more subordinate clauses. In Latin this is called a **period**, where the most important idea is kept to the end.

- conservate parenti filium, parentem filio, (1) ne aut senectutem iam prope desperatam contempsisse aut adulescentiam plenam spei maximae non modo non aluisse vos verum etiam perculisse atque adflixisse videamini (2). (Cic. – Pro Caelio 32.80)

  1. Main clause
     save a son for his father, a father for his son.
  2. Negative purpose clause
     lest you appear either to have cast aside an old man near despair or that you have failed to sustain a young man full of the highest hopes, but have even struck him down and ruined him.

  Note that this sentence builds towards a climax at the end. The most important verbs here are **perculisse** and **adflixisse** rather than **videamini** (you may seem). Notice also the rhythm of the last two words. Repetition of similar phrases is common – **parenti filium, parentem filio**. This sentence is a good illustration of an orator's style.

- Historical style is much simpler, often a subordinate clause followed by a main clause:

  cum equites nostri funditoribus sagittariisque flumen transgressi essent (1), cum equitatu proelium commiserunt

  1. Subordinate adverbial clause of time
     when our cavalry had crossed the river with slingers and archers
  2. Main clause
     they joined battle with the cavalry

- Participle phrase followed by the **main clause** and **subordinate** clause:

  nec patrum cognitionibus satiatus iudiciis (1); adsidebat in cornu tribunalis (2), ne praetorem curuli depelleret (Tac Ann I 75)

  1. Participle phrase
     nor was he (the emperor) satisfied with taking part in Senate trials
  2. Main clause
     he used to sit in the ordinary lawcourts
  3. Subordinate clause of purpose
     in case he pushed the praetor from his curule chair

Many other combinations of clauses are possible. It is important to relate the sentence to its context and to the passage as a whole as Latin sentences are linked logically. It is often helpful when translating a long sentence to pick out subjects and verbs in order to recognize the structure of the clauses and grasp the overall meaning of the sentence.

Simple Sentences

Direct Statement

The basic patterns involved in direct statement have been illustrated under **Word Order** (*see* p 80).

Direct Questions

In Latin a direct question can be expressed as follows by:

- an interrogative pronoun (→**1**)

  quis? (who?), **quid?** (what?), **cur?** (why?)

- adding -**ne** to the first word, where no definite answer is indicated (→**2**)

- **nonne**, when the expected answer is YES (→**3**)

- **num**, when the expected answer is NO (→**4**)

- **utrum** ... **an(non)**
  -ne ...**an(non)** } (whether) ... or (not)
  ... **an(non)**
  in double questions (→**5**)

Continued

1   **quis** est
     Who is it?

   quid dicit?
   What is he saying?

   cur lacrimas?
   Why are you crying?

2   timesne Verrem?
   Are you scared of Verres?

3   **nonne** cladem audivisti?
   Surely you heard of the defeat?
   or You heard of the defeat, didn't you?

4   **num** heri venisti?
   Surely you didn't come yesterday?
   or You didn't come yesterday, did you?

5   utrum has condiciones accepistis **annon**?
   Have you accepted these conditions or not?

Simple Sentences (contd)

Direct Command

- A direct command in Latin is expressed in the second person by the imperative if positive, by **noli(te)** with the present infinitive if negative (→**1**)

- A direct command in the first or third persons is expressed by the present subjunctive, with **nē** if negative (→**2**)

Wishes

- Wishes are expressed in Latin by **utinam** with the subjunctive, **utinam nē** when negative (→**3**)

- **vellem** may also be used with imperfect or pluperfect subjunctive to express wishes (→**4**)

1 **venite** mecum
come with me

noli me tangere
don't touch me

2 **vivamus** atque **amemus**
let us live and let us love

ne **fiat** lux
let there not be light

3 **utinam** frater redeat
I wish my brother would return (*future*)

utinam ne vere scriberem
I wish I were not writing the truth (*present*)

utinam brevi moratus esses
I wish you had stayed a little (*past*)

4 **vellem** me ad cenam **invitavisses**
I wish you had invited me to dinner

Compound Sentences

Indirect Statement

"You are making a mistake" is a *direct statement.* "I think that you are making a mistake" is an *indirect statement.*

- The indirect statement is the object clause of "I think". In indirect statement in Latin, the subject of the clause (*eg* te) goes into the accusative case, the verb is an infinitive (errare):

Puto **te errare**
I think that you are making a mistake

- This pattern is used after verbs of saying, thinking, perceiving, knowing (→**1**)

Examples

1	**audire**	hear	**negare**	say ... not
	cognoscere	discover	**nescire**	not to know
	credere	believe	**putare**	think
	dicere	say	**scire**	know
	intellegere	understand	**sentire**	perceive
	meminisse	remember	**videre**	see
	narrare	tell		

Continued

Indirect Statement (contd)

Translation

- The *present infinitive* refers to actions happening at the same time and may be translated – is, are, was, were.

- The *perfect infinitive* refers to prior action and may be translated – has, have, had.

- The *future infinitive* refers to future action and may be translated – will, would.

putamus	te errāre
	te errāvisse
	te errātūrum esse

We think	that you are making a mistake
	that you have made a mistake
	that you will make a mistake

putabamus	te errāre
	te errāvisse
	te errātūrum esse

We thought	that you were making a mistake
	that you had made a mistake
	that you would make a mistake

- Notice that when the main verb is *past* tense, translate the present infinitive – "was, were", the past infinitive – "had", the future infinitive – "would".

- The reflexive pronoun **sē** is used to refer to the subject of the main verb (→**1**)

- Translate **negō** – I say that ... not (→**2**)

- Verbs of promising, hoping, threatening or swearing (*eg* **promittō, polliceor, spērō, minor, iuro**) are followed by an accusative and future infinitive (→**3**)

---

1 senex dixit **se** thesaurum invenisse
The old man said that he had found treasure

2 **negavit** servum domum venturum esse
He said that the slave would not come home

3 **promisi me festinaturum esse**
I promised that I would hurry

sperabat se hoc confecturum esse
He hoped that he could complete this
or He hoped to complete this

Further Examples

creditores existimabant **eum** totam pecuniam **perdidisse**
His creditors thought that he had lost all his money

memini **simulacra** deorum de caelo **percussa esse**
I remember that the gods' statues were struck down from the heavens

vidistine **Catonem** in bibliotheca **sedere**?
Did you see Cato sitting in the library?

iuro **me** pro patria fortiter **pugnaturum esse**
I swear that I shall fight bravely for my country

iam ego credo **vos** verum **dixisse**
I now believe that you spoke the truth

negavit **nihil** umquam pulchrius statua **fuisse**
He said that nothing had ever been more beautiful than that statue

Indirect Question

"Where did he come from?" is a *direct question*. "I asked where he had come from" is an *indirect question*. Latin uses the same interrogative words (**quis** - who, **quid** - what *etc*) and the verb in indirect questions is always subjunctive

rogavi unde venisset
I asked where he had come from

- Latin uses six different forms of the subjunctive in this construction in a precise sequence depending on the main verb (→**1**)

Examples

1	rogo	**unde veniat**	(present)
		unde venerit	(perfect)
		unde venturus sit	(future)
	I ask	where he comes from	(present)
		where he has come from	(perfect)
		where he will come from	(future)
	rogavi	**unde veniret**	(imperfect)
		unde venisset	(pluperfect)
		unde venturus esset	(future perfect)
	I asked	where he was coming from	(imperfect)
		where he had come from	(pluperfect)
		where he would come from	(future perfect)

Continued

Indirect Question (contd)

Translation

Translation of tenses in indirect question is *easy*, because English uses the same tenses as Latin, as can be seen on page 94.

- The reflexive pronoun **se** is used to refer to the subject of the main verb (→**1**)

- **utrum … an** (if … or), **utrum … necne** (whether … or not) are also used in indirect questions (→**2**)

- **num** is used to mean "if" in indirect questions (→**3**)

1 rogavit **quando se visuri essemus**
He asked when we would see him

2 roga **utrum** iverit **an** manserit
Ask whether he went or stayed

roga **utrum** manserit **necne**
Ask whether he stayed or not

rogavit **utrum** Scylla infestior **esset** Charybdis **necne**
He asked whether Charybdis was more dangerous than Scylla or not

3 nescio **num** venturi sint
I don't know if they will come

Further Examples

nescimus **quid facturi simus**
We don't know what we shall do

mirum est **quanta sit Roma**
It is amazing how big Rome is
or The size of Rome is amazing

exploratores cognoverunt **quanti essent** Poeni
Scouts discovered what the numbers of the Carthaginians were

incredibile est **quomodo** talia facere **potuerit**
It is incredible how he was able to do such things

nemo audivit **quid** rex **constituisset**
No one heard what the king had decided
or No one heard the king's decision

Indirect Command

"Come here" is a *direct command.* "I ordered you to come here" is an *indirect command.* Indirect commands in Latin are expressed by **ut** (when positive) or **nē** (when negative) and have their verbs in the subjunctive (→**1**)

- Latin uses two tenses of the subjunctive, present or imperfect, in this construction. It uses the present subjunctive if the main verb is present or future tense and imperfect subjunctive if the main verb is in the past tense. (→**2**)

Translation

- The English translation of the indirect command is the same, whichever tense is used in Latin – the infinitive (*eg* to come)

- The reflexive **se** is used to refer to the subject of the main verb (→**3**)

- Common verbs introducing indirect command are:

hortor   encourage
moneo   warn
oro   beg
persuadeo persuade
rogo   ask

- *Only* **iubeo** (to order), **veto** (to tell ... not), are usually used with the infinitive in Latin (→**4**)

Examples

1 tibi imperavi **ut** venirēs
   I ordered you to come
   tibi imperavi **ne** venires
   I forbade you to come
   milites oravit **ne** in castris diutius **manerent**
   He begged his soldiers not to stay in camp any longer
   hoc rogo, mi Tiro, **ne** temere **naviges**
   I beg you, my dear Tiro, not to sail carelessly

2 tibi **impero ut** venias   (*present*)
   I order you to come
   tibi **imperavi ut venires**   (*imperfect*)
   I ordered you to come

   deos precor **ut** nobis **parcant**
   I beg the gods to spare us

   amicos roga **ut veniant**, operamque **dent**, et messim
   hanc nobis **adiuvent**
   Ask your friends to come and lend a hand and help
   us with this harvest

3 nos oravit ut **sibi** cibum daremus
   He begged us to give him food

4 **iubeo** eos **navigare**
   I order them to sail

   veto eos **navigare**
   I tell them not to sail

   mater me **vetuit** in murum **ascendere**
   Mother forbade me to climb on the wall

   Antonius eos **iussit** adventum **suum exspectare**
   Antony told them to await his arrival

Purpose or Final Clauses

There are two ways of expressing purpose in English:

> I am hurrying to the city to see the games
> I am hurrying to the city so that I may see the games

or

- In Latin **ut** is used with the present or imperfect subjunctive, to express purpose. The present subjunctive is used if the main verb is in the present or future tense and the imperfect subjunctive if the main verb is in the past tense (→**1**)

- Negative purpose clauses are introduced by **ne** which can be translated "so that ... not", "in case", "to avoid", "lest" etc (→**2**)

- If there is a comparative adjective or adverb in the Latin sentence **quō** is used instead of **ut** (→**3**)

- The relative **qui**, **quae**, **quod** may be used instead of **ut**, if it refers to an object in the main clause (→**4**)

- After negative **ne**, **quis** is used instead of **aliquis** to mean "anyone"

  Note that **se** is used to refer to the subject of the main verb (→**5**)

- **ad** is used with the gerundive to express purpose (→**6**)

- The supine -**um** is used after verbs of motion to express purpose (→**7**)

1   ad urbem festino **ut** ludos **videam**
I am hurrying to the city to see the games
ad urbem festinavi **ut** ludos **viderem**
I hurried to the city to see the games
filium multo fletu complexus, pepulit **ut abiret**
Embracing his son tearfully, he drove him to leave

2   Tiberius hoc recusavit **ne** Germanicus imperium **haberet**
Tiberius refused this lest Germanicus had power
pontem resciderunt **ne** hostes flumen **transirent**
They broke down the bridge in case the enemy crossed the river

3   puellae cantabant **quo** laetiores essent **hospites**
The girls sang to make their guests happier

4   rex sex milites delegit **qui** ad Graeciam **proficiscerentur**
The king chose six soldiers to set off for Greece

5   in silvis se abdidit **ne quis se** videret
He hid in the woods lest anyone should see him
sed **ut** venenum manifesto comprehendi **posset**, constitui locum iussit, **ut** eo **mitteret** amicos, **qui laterent**, cum venisset Licinius, venenumque traderet, comprehenderent
But *so that the poison could be seized openly*, he ordered that a place be appointed, *to send friends there, to hide.* When Licinius came to hand over the poison they could arrest him.

6   Verres ad Siciliam venit **ad urbes diripiendas**
Verres came to Sicily to plunder its cities

7   veniunt **spectatum**
They come to see

102 SENTENCES

Result or Consecutive Clauses

The road is so long that I am tired
It was so hot that we could not work

In both these sentences, a result or consequence is expressed in English by using words such as

so ... that (positive)
so that ... not (negative)

● In Latin the following words are frequently used in the main clause

adeo	to such an extent
ita	thus, so
talis	of such a kind
tam	so
tantus	so great
tot	so many

● In the result clause, **ut** (so that) and **ut ... non** (so that ... not) are used with the present or imperfect subjunctive. Present subjunctive is used where the main verb is in the present and the imperfect subjunctive is used where the main verb is past (→**1**)

● **Note** that **eum** is used to refer to "him" instead of **se** when referring to the subject of the main clause as in the first example (→**1**)

SENTENCES 103

Examples

1 Gallus **tam** ferox est **ut** omnes Romani eum **timeant**
The Gaul is so fierce that all the Romans are scared of him

tanta erat tempestas **ut** nautae navem **non solverent**
So great was the storm that the sailors could not set sail

nemo est **adeo** stultus **ut non** discere **possit**
No one is so stupid that he can't learn

tot sententiae erant **ut nemo consentiret**
There were so many opinions that no one could agree

tales nos esse putamus **ut** ab omnibus **laudemur**
We think that we are the sort of people to be praised by everyone

Verbs of Fearing

In Latin, verbs of fearing (**timeo, metuo, paveo, vereor**) are followed by **nē, nē non** or **ut** with the present and perfect, imperfect and pluperfect subjunctive according to sequence of tenses:

- The present subjunctive represents present and future tenses in English

  I am afraid he is coming
  I am afraid he will come

- The perfect subjunctive represents the past tense in English

  I am afraid that he has come

- When the verb of fearing is in the past tense, imperfect and pluperfect subjunctive are used in Latin instead (→**1**)

- **nē** is used if the fear is expressed in a positive sentence (*ie* I am afraid he will come). **nē nōn, ut** is used if the fear is expressed negatively (*ie* I am afraid that he won't come) (→**2**)

- As in English, the infinitive can follow a verb of fearing, provided that the subjects of both are the same (→**3**)

Examples

1 veritus sum **ne veniret**
    I was afraid he was coming

   veritus sum **ne venisset**
    I was afraid that he had come

2 **vereor ne** amicus **veniat**
    I am afraid lest my friend comes
   or lest my friend will come

   vereor ne amicus **non veniat**
    I am afraid that my friend won't come

   vereor ut amicus **venerit**
    I am afraid that my friend has not come

   verebar ne amicus **non venisset**
    I was afraid that my friend had not come

   metuo ne virtutis maiorum nostrum **obliviscamur**
    I am afraid that we shall forget the courage of our
    ancestors

   paves ne ducas tu illam
    You are afraid to marry her

   Verres, **veritus ne** servi bellum in Sicilia **facerent**,
    multos in vincula coniecit
    Verres, fearing that slaves might revolt in Sicily, threw
    many into prison

   Romani **verebantur ne** fortiter **non pugnavissent**
    The Romans were afraid that they had not fought
    bravely

3 timeo **abire**
    I am afraid to go away

   mulier **timebat manere** sola
    The woman was scared to remain alone

Conditional Sentences

Compare the following two sentences in English:

(a) If I tell you a lie, you will be angry
(b) If I were to tell you a lie, you would be angry

The first is a *logical statement of fact*, stating what *will* happen, the second is a *hypothesis*, stating what *would* happen.

For the first type of sentence, Latin uses the indicative mood in both main and conditional clauses. For the second type, Latin uses the subjunctive mood in both main and conditional clauses.

Translate type (a) as follows:

si hoc **dicis**, sapiens **es**
if you say this, you are wise

si hoc **dicebas**, sapiens **eras**
if you were saying this, you were wise

si hoc **dixisti**, **erravisti**
if you said this, then you made a mistake

si hoc **dixeris**, **errabis**
if you say this, you will make a mistake

Notice that the same tenses in English are used as in Latin except in the last sentence. Latin is more precise – you *will have said* this, before you make a mistake, therefore Latin uses the *future perfect* tense.

Continued

- Consider also the following sentence:

si me **amabis**, mecum **manebis**
If you love me, you will stay with me

Latin uses the *future* tense in both clauses. English uses the *present* tense in the "if" clause. Both actions, "loving" and "remaining" *logically* refer to the *future*.

Translate type (b) as follows:

(*present*)
si hoc **dicas**, **erres**
if you were to say this, you would be making a mistake

(*imperfect*)
si hoc **diceres**, **errares**
if you said (*or* were saying) that, you would be making a mistake

(*pluperfect*)
si hoc **dixisses**, **erravisses**
if you had said that, you would have made a mistake

Notice that both tenses of the subjunctive are the same in the above examples. Sometimes an imperfect may be used in one clause and the pluperfect in the other:

si pudorem **haberes**, Romā **abiisses**
if you had any sense of shame, you would have left Rome

Conditional Sentences (contd)

Negative Conditional Sentences

- **nisi** (unless) is the negative of **si** (if). (→**1**)

- **si non** (if not), is less common and negates *one* word, or is used when the same verb is repeated (→**2**)

1 nisi id statim **feceris,** ego te **tradam** magistratui
Unless you do this immediately, I shall hand you over
to the magistrate

nisi utilem **crederem,** non pacem **peterem**
Unless I thought it useful, I would not be seeking
peace

2 si me **adiuveris,** laeta **ero; si** me **non adiuveris,** tristis
ero
If you help me, I shall be happy; if you don't help me,
I shall be sad

si navigatio **non morabitur,** mox te **vid"bo**
If my sailing is not delayed, I shall see you soon

Further Examples

(b) quis illum sceleratum fuisse **putavisset, si tacuisset?**
Who would have thought he was a rascal, if he had
kept quiet?

(b) multi **agerent et pugnarent si** rei publicae **videretur**
Many would act and fight, if the state decided

(a) gaudemus si liberi in horto **ludunt**
We are happy if the children play in the garden

(b) si quis in caelum **ascendisset,** pulchritudinem side-
rum **conspexisset**
If anyone had gone up to heaven, he would have seen
the beauty of the stars

Concessive Clauses

In English, Concessive clauses usually begin with "although":

Although he is rich, he is not happy
I shall succeed although it is difficult

- **quamquam** (although) is followed by the indicative (→**1**)

  Note that **tamen** (however) is often used in the main clause in concessive sentences

- **quamvis** (although) is always followed by the subjunctive (→**2**)

- **cum** in the sense "although" is always followed by the subjunctive (→**3**)

- **etsi** (although) takes the Indicative or subjunctive according to the same rules as **si** (see p 106). The indicative is more common (→**4**)

---

1 medici **quamquam intellegunt**, numquam **tamen** aegris de morbo dicunt
Although doctors know, they never tell their patients about their illness

quamquam Aeneas dicere **volebat**, Dido solo fixos oculos aversa tenebat
Although Aeneas wished to speak, Dido turned away and kept her eyes fixed on the ground

2 **quamvis** frater **esset** molestus, Marcus eum amavit
Although his brother was a nuisance, Marcus loved him

feminae, **quamvis** in periculo **essent**, tamen liberos servaverunt
Although the women were in danger, yet they saved their children

3 **cum non didicissem** geometrias, litteras sciebam
Although I had not learnt geometry, I knew my letters

non poterant, **cum vellent**, Lucium liberare
They were not able, although they wished, to free Lucium

4 **etsi** servus **est**, certe persona est
Although he is a slave, he is a person

etsi victoriam non **reportavissetis**, tamen vos contentos esse oportebat
Although you had not won a victory, yet you should have been content

etsi domi **esset fillius iuvenis**, agros ipse colebat
Although he had a young son at home, he cultivated the fields by himself

112 SENTENCES

Causal Clauses

Clauses which begin with the words "because" or "since" and give a reason for something are often called causal clauses in English.

- Causal clauses have their verbs in the indicative when the *actual* cause is stated. They are introduced by **quod, quia** (because), and **quoniam** (since) (→**1**)

- **quod** is used with the subjunctive when the cause is only *suggested* (→**2**)

- **non quod** (+*subj*) ... **sed quia** (+ *indic*) not because ... but because ..., is used when the first reason is discarded. The true reason is expressed in the indicative (→**3**)

- **cum** (since, as) is always followed by the subjunctive (→**4**)

- **qui** with the subjunctive can be used to mean "since" (→**5**)

Examples   SENTENCES 113

1 non iratus sum **quod** in me **fuisti** asperior
I am not angry because you were too harsh towards me

in crypta Neapolitana vecti, timebamus **quia** longior et obscurior carcere **erat**
Travelling in the Naples tunnel, we were afraid because it was longer and darker than a prison

quoniam ita tu **vis**, ego Puteolos tecum proficiscar
Since you wish this, I shall set off with you to Pozzuoli

2 templa spoliare non poterant **quod** religione impedirentur
They could not plunder the temples because (they said) they were prevented by religious feelings

3 mater semper maxime laboravit **non quod** necessarium esset sed quia honestum esse **videbatur**
Mother always worked very hard, not because it was necessary but because it seemed proper

4 quae **cum** ita **sint**, Catilina, egredere ex urbe!
Since this is so, Catilina, leave the city!

Caesar, **cum** in continente hiemare **constituisset**, ad Galliam rediit
Since Caesar had decided to spend the winter on the mainland, he returned to Gaul

5 sapiens erat **qui** studiis totos annos **dedisset**
He was wise since he had devoted all his years to study

Temporal Clauses

Clauses denoting time are introduced by conjunctions, *eg* **ubi** (when) followed by verbs in the indicative. Some conjunctions, *eg* **cum** (when) may also take the subjunctive. (→**1**)

Conjunctions followed by the indicative:

ut	when, as
ubi	when
cum primum	
ubi primum	as soon as
ut primum	
simul ac	as soon as
simul atque	
quotiens	as often as, whenever
quamdiu	as long as, while
ex quo (tempore)	ever since
postquam	after (**post** or **postea**
posteaquam	may be separated from **quam**)

---

1 **ut** valetudo Germanici Romae **nuntiata est**, magna ira erat
When Germanicus' state of health was announced in Rome, there was great anger

ubi primum classis visa est, **complentur** non modo portus sed moenia ac tecta
As soon as the fleet was seen, not only the harbour but the walls and rooftops were filled (with people)

quod **ubi cognitum est** hostibus, universi nonam legionem nocte aggressi sunt
When this was discovered by the enemy, all of them attacked the ninth legion at night

quotiens proficiscor, pluit
Every time I set out, it rains

manebat **quamdiu poterat**
He stayed as long as he could

septimus annus est, milites, **ex quo** Britanniam **vicistis**
It is seven years, soldiers, since you conquered Britain

postquam vallum **intravit**, portas stationibus **confirmavit**
After entering the fortification, he strengthened the gates with guards

post tertium diem **quam redierat**, mortuus est
He died three days after his return

Continued

Temporal Clauses (contd)

Conjunctions which take the indicative or subjunctive:

cum

- **when** with indicative and often **tum** in the main clause (→**1**)

- **whenever** with the following pattern of tenses in the indicative: (→**2**)
  + **perfect** followed by **present** tense
  + **future perfect** followed by **future** tense
  + **pluperfect** followed by **imperfect** tense

- **when, as** with the imperfect or pluperfect subjunctive narrative (→**3**)

dum

- **while** with indicative

  the present tense is used when **dum** means "during the time that" (→**4**)

- Note that where the same tense (here, the future) is used in both clauses, **dum** means "all the time that". Latin uses future **vivam** more accurately than English "live" (→**5**)

Continued

Examples   SENTENCES 117

1 **cum** tu Romae **eras, tum** ego domi eram
When you were in Rome, I was then at home

2 **cum surrexerat, cadebat**
Whenever he got up, he fell down
cum domum **veni,** amicum **visito**
Whenever I come home, I visit my friend

3 Socrates, **cum** triginta tyranni **essent,** non exibat
Socrates didn't go out when there were 30 tyrants
cum id Caesari **nuntiatum esset** ab urbe profectus est
When that message had been given to Caesar, he set out from the city

4 **dum** haec **geruntur** sex milia hominum ad Rhenum contenderunt
While this was going on, 6000 men marched to the Rhine

5 **dum vivam,** laeta **ero**
While I live, I shall be happy

Temporal Clauses (contd)

Clauses which take Indicative or Subjunctive (contd)

dum, donec

● **until**   with subjunctive, often with the sense of
                     purpose or suspense (→**1**)

antequam, priusquam

● **before**   with indicative (→**2**)

● **ante** and   may be separated from **quam** especially
  prius   in negative sentences (→**3**)

● **before**   with subjunctive, usually with a sense of
                     purpose or limit (→**4**)

---

1 multa Antonio concessit **dum** interfectores patris
    ulcisceretur
    He made many concessions to Antony until he could
    avenge his father's killers

    Haterius in periculo erat **donec** Augustam auxilium
    oraret
    Haterius was in danger until he begged for Augusta's
    help

2 **antequam finiam,** hoc dicam
    Before I finish, I shall say this

    priusquam gallus **cantabit,** ter me negabis
    Before the cock crows, you will deny me three times

3 neque **prius** fugere destiterunt **quam** ad castra **per-
    venerunt**
    They didn't stop running away before reaching their
    camp

4 consul Romam festinavit **antequam** Hannibal eo **per-
    veniret**
    The consul hurried to Rome before Hannibal could
    reach it

    ita cassita nidum migravit **priusquam** agricola
    frumentum **meteret**
    And so the lark abandoned her nest before the farmer
    could reap the corn

Comparative Clauses

- These are adverbial clauses which express likeness, agreement (or the opposite) with what is stated in the main clause. (→1)

- When the comparative clause states a fact (as above) the verb is in the **indicative**. The commonest words of comparison are (→2)

ut (as), **sicut** (just as), **aliter ac**, **aliter ut** (different from), **idem ac**, **idem atque**, **qui** etc (the same as)

- When the comparative clause is purely **imaginary**, the verb is **subjunctive**. The commonest words used with this type of clause are (→3)

velut(si), **quasi**, **tamquam (si)** (as if)

Examples

1 eadem dixi ac prius dixeram
I said the same as I had said before

2 **ego ita ero, ut me esse oportet**
I shall be as I should be

sicut lupus agnos rapit, ita mater liberos servat
Just as the wolf snatches the lamb, so the mother saves her children

haud aliter se gerebat ac solebat
He behaved as he usually did
or He behaved no differently from usual

idem abierunt qui venerant
The same men vanished as came

3 **velutsi haec res nihil ad se pertinuisset, tacebat**
He remained silent, as if this thing had nothing to do with him

hic flammae Aetnae minantur quasi ad caelum sublatae sint
Here Aetna's flames threaten, as if raised to the heavens

Cleopatram salutaverunt tamquam si esset regina
They greeted Cleopatra as if she were queen

Relative Clauses

- Relative clauses are more common in Latin than in English. They are introduced by the following:

  qui, quae, quod which, who, that
  ubi where, in which
  unde from where, from which

- These relatives come at the beginning of the clause but after prepositions.

- The relative agrees with a word which precedes it – its *antecedent* – in gender and number, but takes its case from its own clause (→1)

  qui is masculine plural agreeing with antecedent **Romani**, nominative because it is the subject of **incenderunt**

  quā is feminine singular agreeing with **regio**, ablative after preposition **in** (→2)

  quos is masculine plural agreeing with **servos**, accusative because it is the object of **iudicavit** (→3)

- The relative **quod** refers to a sentence, and **id** is omitted (**id quod** – that which). This is often used in parenthesis, and not attached grammatically to the rest of the sentence

  After **cuius** (of, concerning which) the noun **laudationis** is repeated (→4)

- The relative sometimes agrees with the following word, especially with the verb **esse** (→5)

Continued

1 hi sunt Romani **qui** libros incenderunt
These are the Romans who burnt the books

2 haec est regio **in qua** ego sum natus
This is the region in which I was born

3 servos **quos** ipse iudicavit, eos sua sponte liberavit
He willingly freed those slaves whom he himself had judged

4 deinde, **quod** alio loco antea dixi, quae est ista tandem laudatio, **cuius laudationis** legati et principes et publice tibi navem aedificatam, et privatim se ipsos abs te spoliatos esse dixerunt? (**Cicero**, Verres V 58)
Well then, as I said earlier elsewhere, what does that praise consist of, namely that publicly the ambassadors and chief citizens said a ship had been built for you, but privately that they themselves had been robbed by you?

5 iusta gloria **qui** fructus virtutis est, bello quaeritur
True glory, which is the reward of courage, is looked for in war

Relative Clauses (contd)

Use Of Subjunctive In Relative Clauses

- The subjunctive is used in relative clauses dependent on infinitives or subjunctives (→**1**)

- When **qui** is used with the subjunctive, it may express cause (→**2**)

  quippe is sometimes used with **qui** in this sense

- When **qui** *etc* is used with the present or imperfect subjunctive, it may express purpose (→**3**)

- **qui** with the subjunctive is used with the following (→**4**)

dignus est **qui**	he is worthy of
idoneus est **qui**	he is fit to
sunt **qui**	there are people who
nemo est **qui**	there is no one who

- At the beginning of a sentence, any part of **qui, quae, quod** may be used as a connective (instead of the demonstrative) with the previous sentence. Translate it in English by "this" or "that" (→**5**)

Examples

1 quis sit **cui** vita talis **placeat**?
   Who is there that likes such a life?

2 multa de mea sententia questus est Caesar (**quippe**)
   qui Ravennae Crassum ante **vidisset**
   Caesar complained a lot about my decision since he
   had seen Crassus at Ravenna previously

3 legatos misit **qui** pacem **peterent**
   He sent ambassadors to ask for peace

4 **Sunt qui** dicere **timeant**
   There are some who are afraid to speak
   nemo **idoneus** aderat **qui responderet**
   There was nobody there capable of replying

5 **quod** cum **audivisset**, soror lacrimas fudit
   When she heard this, my sister shed tears
   quae cum ita **sint**, Vatinium defendam
   Since this is so, I shall defend Vatinius

Negatives

There are several ways of forming a negative in Latin.

non

- This is the common negative in the indicative and usually stands before the verb, although it may be put in front of any word for emphasis (→**1**)

- Two negatives in the same sentence make an affirmative (→**2**)

haud

- This makes a single word negative, usually an adjective or an adverb (→**3**)

- It is also used in expressions such as **haud scio an** (I don't know whether), and **haud dubito** (I don't doubt) (→**4**)

- **haudquaquam** means not at all (→**5**)

Continued

---

1   ante horam tertiam noctis de foro **non discedit**
He didn't leave the forum before nine o'clock at night

Ambarri Caesarem certiorem faciunt se, vastatis agris, **non facile** vim hostium ab oppidis prohibere
The Ambarri informed Caesar that it was **not easy** for them, since their territory was destroyed, to keep the enemy force away from their towns

Caesar **non exspectandum** sibi statuit dum Helvetii pervenirent
Caesar decided **not to wait** till the Swiss arrived

2   non possum **non facere**
I must do

non sumus **ignari**
We are well aware

3   **haud** magnus
not great

haud procul
not far away

4   **haud scio an** ire mihi liceat
I don't know whether I am allowed to go

5   homo bonus, **haudquaquam** eloquens
A good man but not at all a good speaker

128 SENTENCES

Negatives (contd)

ne

- This is the negative of the imperative and subjunctive. It is also used in many subordinate clauses where the verb is in the subjunctive (→1)

- Wishes (→2)

- Purpose (→3)

- Indirect command (→4)

- Fearing (→5)

Continued

SENTENCES 129

Examples

1 ne diutius **vivamus**
Let us **not** live any longer

2 utinam **ne** id **accidisset**
I wish that it **had not happened**

3 agnus celeriter fugit **ne** lupi se **caperent**
The lamb ran away quickly **in case** the wolves caught it

4 pater mihi imperavit **ne abirem**
Father told me **not to go away**

5 cives metuebant **ne** Tiberius libertatem sibi **non redderet**
The citizens were afraid that Tiberius **would not give** them **back** their freedom

veritus sum **ne** id quod accidit **adveniret**
I was afraid that what did in fact happen **might take place**

Negatives (contd)

Other Negatives

• **neque ... neque**	neither ... nor (→**1**)
• **neque ... quisquam**	neither anyone *or* and no one
neque ... quidquam	neither anything *or* and nothing
neque ... umquam	neither ever *or* and never
nemo ... umquam	no one ever *or* never anyone
nihil ... umquam	nothing ever *or* never anything (→**2**)

• Notice the following combinations:

nonnulli some	*but* **nulli ... non**	all
nonnihil somewhat	*but* **nihil ... non**	everything (→**3**)

non solum ... sed etiam	} not only ... but also
non solum ... sed quoque	} (→**4**)

• Roman authors repeat negatives for effect (→**5**)

Examples

1 **neque** illo adit **quisquam neque** eis ipsis **quidquam** praeter oram maritimam notum est
Neither did anyone approach that place, nor did they themselves know anything except the coast

2 **neque** post id tempus **umquam** summis nobiscum copiis hostes contenderunt
And after that the enemy never engaged in battle with us at full strength

ego **nihil umquam** feci solus
I never did anything alone

3 **nonnulli** amici
some friends

nulli amici **non** venerunt
all my friends came

4 Herennius Pontius, iam gravis annis, **non solum** militaribus **sed quoque** civilibus muneribus abscesserat
Herennius Pontius, now old, had withdrawn not only from military but also from civic duties

5 **nihil** audio quod audisse, **nihil** dico quod dixisse paeniteat; **nemo** apud me quemquam sinistris sermonibus carpit, **neminem** ipse reprehendo, **nisi** tamen me cum parum commode scribo; **nulla** spe, **nullo** timore sollicitor, **nullis** rumoribus inquietor; mecum tantum et cum libellis loquor (**Pliny** Ep 1, 9)
I hear nothing that I would regret having heard, I say nothing that I would regret having said; at home nobody nags me with vicious remarks, I don't blame anyone except myself when I write badly; no hope or fear worries me, no idle talk disturbs me; I speak only to myself and to my books

Translation Guidelines

Translating from Latin into English can be both a challenge and a pleasure. The word order of both languages is different: word order shows the relationship of words in English, in Latin it is shown by word endings. Sentences are generally shorter in English, structures simpler. Latin sentences often contain more subordinate clauses, sometimes embedded in other clauses, and often build up to form a long periodic sentence. Subject matter is two thousand years distant in time, although many ideas are still familiar to us today. The following guidelines are suggested to help in translation.

Guidelines

- *Establish the context* of the passage to be translated. Read the introduction in English carefully, find out *who* or *what* is being discussed, *when* and *where* the action took place.

- *Read through the whole passage* fairly quickly to gain some general understanding of the passage, however incomplete.

- *Focus on each sentence*, either taking each word as it comes, or establishing subject/verb/object according to your normal approach. Many find it helpful to pick out the verbs and work out the structure of the clauses. Watch for agreement of adjectives with nouns and how prepositional phrases fit in.

- *Watch conjunctions* et, sed *etc* and connectives such as **tamen** (however), and **igitur** (therefore). These help explain the logic of the passage as a whole.

- *Note punctuation.* It can be helpful in isolating clauses within the sentences, or marking off an ablative absolute.

- *Be open-minded.* Does **cum**, for example, mean "when", "since", or "although"? Don't decide till the whole sentence is worked out.

- *Use dictionaries carefully.* Check words of similar spelling, check endings. Once you have found the right Latin word, check all of its meanings before deciding on the correct translation.

- *Watch out for features of style eg* use of two adjectives with same meaning *etc.*

- Finally, *check your translation.* Does the narrative or logic of the passage seem consistent? Does your English sound natural? Does it represent the tone or style of the Latin passage? At this stage, fill in any blanks or make corrections.

Translation Problems

Finding the subject

• Look for a noun with a nominative ending. Check with verb ending for agreement. If there is no nominative, the subject will be indicated by the verb ending. Remember that, in Latin, the subject is continued from the previous sentence unless there is clear indication otherwise (→1)

Adjective agreement

• Check which adjective agrees with which noun in number, case and gender. Remember that it may be separated from its noun.

          a   b   b   a

te **flagrantis atrox hora Caniculae** nescit tangere
The blazing Dog Star's fierce daytime heat can't touch you

Passive

• Often it is better to turn a Latin passive verb into an active verb in English (→2)

Tense

• English is not so precise as Latin in its use of tenses. Use the tense that seems most natural in English, for example, English past tense for historic present in Latin, or English present tense for Latin future perfect in a conditional clause (→3)

Continued

Examples   TRANSLATION **135**

1   **consules** et armare plebem et inermem pati **timebant. sedabant** tumultum, sedando interdum **movebant.**
     The consuls were afraid both to arm the people and to leave them unarmed. **They quelled** the riot, but sometimes, in quelling it, **they stirred it up again.**

2   hoc a tu **demonstrari** et **probari** volo
     I wish you to demonstrate and prove this
or I wish this to be demonstrated and proved by you

3   hoc faciam si **potuero** (*future perfect*)
     I shall do this if I can (*present*)

Translation Problems (contd)

Ablative absolute

hostibus victis can be translated:

when the enemy had been beaten
after beating the enemy
they beat the enemy and ...
although the enemy were beaten

Choose the version that makes most sense within the context of the passage.

Omission of esse

- Parts of **esse** (to be) are often omitted and have to be supplied in English (→**1**)

Omission of small words (**ut, id, eo, hic** etc)

- Check that you do not omit to translate these words – they are often very important (→**2**)

Neuter plurals

- **omnia** (everything) and **multa** (many things) are often mistranslated.

Impersonal passives

- It is worthwhile learning these (→**3**)

Continued

Examples   TRANSLATION   **137**

1   sed Germanicus quanto (**erat**) summae spei propior,
       tanto impensius pro Tiberio niti
       But the nearer Germanicus **was** to succeeding, the
       more strenuously he exerted himself on behalf of
       Tiberius

2   **eo**   to there (*adv*), by, with *or* from
                          him (*abl of pronoun*)
       id ... quod   that which
       hic   this (*pron*), here (*adv*)
       fit ... ut   it happens ... that

3   **allatum est**   it was announced
       cognitum est   it was discovered
       pugnatum est   a battle was fought
       traditum est   it was recorded
       visum est   it seemed

Translation Problems (contd)

Similarity of English/Latin Words

A higher percentage of English words are derived from Latin than from any other source. This can be helpful when trying to deduce the meaning of a Latin word, *eg* **portus** (port). But **porta** (gate) may cause confusion. The following examples taken from actual examination scripts provide a cautionary note. The correct translation follows in brackets:

Examples

prima luce nuntius hic **Ameriam** venit
At dawn the messenger came to America
(At dawn the messenger came to Ameria)

sex et quinquaginta **milia passuum** in cisio pervolavit
56 thousand flew past in a chariot
(He quickly travelled fifty-six miles in a chariot)

ut mori **mallet**
He would rather be killed by a mallet
(To prefer to die)

legati **crediderunt**
The embassy got credit
(The ambassadors believed)

False Friends/Confusables

ad (+ acc)	to, towards
ab (+ abl)	from, by, with
adeo	to such an extent
adeō	I approach
aestās	summer
aestus	heat, tide
aetas	age
aura	breeze
aurēs (pl)	ears
aurum	gold
avis	bird
avus	grandfather
cadō	I fall
caedō	I cut, kill
cēdō	I go, yield
campus	plain
castra (pl)	camp
cēterum	but
cēterī (pl)	the rest
coepī	I began
coēgī	I forced
constituō	I decide
consistō	I stop

crīmen	charge
scelus	crime
cum (prep)	with
cum (conj)	when, since, although
dominus	master
domus	house
equitēs (pl)	horsemen
equus	horse
fama	fame, report
fames	hunger
forte	by chance
fortis	brave (not strong)
fugāre	to put to flight
fugere	to flee, escape
hōra	hour
hōrum (gen pl)	of these
iaceō	I lie
iaciō	I throw
imperātor	general (not emperor)
imperātus	ordered (past participle)
inveniō	I find (not come in)
invītō	I invite
invītus	unwilling
iter, -ineris	journey
iterum	again
lātus, -a, -um	broad
lātus, -a, -um	brought
lātus, -eris	side

Continued

False Friends/Confusables (contd)

līber, -rī	book
līber, -a, -um	free
līberī, -ōrum (pl)	children
libertus, -ī	freedman
magister, -rī	master
magistrātus	magistrate
malus, -a, -um	bad
mālum, -ī	apple
mālō, mālle	I prefer
manus, -ūs	hand, band
mānēs, -ium	spirits of dead
miser, -a, -um	unhappy
mīseram	I had sent (plup of mitto)
morior, -ī	I die
moror, -ārī	I delay
nauta	sailor
nāvis	ship
nēmō	no one
nimium	too much
occāsio	opportunity
occāsus (solis)	setting (of sun)
occidere	to fall, set
occīdere	to kill
opem	help
opera, -ae	work
opus, -eris	task
opus est	it is necessary

Continued

ōra, -ae	coast
ōrō, -āre	I pray, beg
ōs, ōris	face
ōs, ossis	bone
parcō, -ere	I spare
pareō, -ēre	I obey
pariō, -ere	I give birth to
parō, -āre	I prepare
passus, -ūs	a pace
passus, -a, -um	suffered (*past participle of* **patior**)
porta, -ae	gate
portus, -ūs	port
portō, -āre	I carry
quaerō, -ere	I seek
queror, -ī	I complain
quīdam	a certain (person)
quidem	indeed
reddō, -ere	I give back
redeō, -īre	I go back
serviō, -īre	I serve
servō, -āre	I save
sōl, -is	sun
soleō, -ēre, solitus sum	I am accustomed
solum, -ī	soil
sōlus, -a, -um	alone

False Friends/Confusables (contd)

tamen	however
tandem	at last
ut(ī)	in order that, as, when
utī (*dep*)	to use
vallis, -is	valley
vallum, -i	wall, rampart
victor	winner
victus (*past part*)	beaten
vinctus (*past part*)	bound
vīs	force
vīres, -ium	strength
vir, -ī	man
virga, -ae	stick
virgō, -inis	girl
vīta, -ae	life
vītō, -āre	I avoid

VERB TABLES

Conjugations

There are four patterns of regular Latin verbs called conjugations. Each can be identified by the ending of the
present infinitive:

- First conjugation verbs end in -**āre** (*eg* amāre – to love)

- Second conjugation verbs end in -**ēre** (*eg* habēre – to have)

- Third conjugation verbs end in -**ere** (*eg* mittere – to send)

- Fourth conjugation verbs end in -**īre** (*eg* audīre – to hear)

Each regular verb has three **stems**:

- A **present stem** which is found by cutting off -**re** from the present infinitive (*eg* amāre, habēre, mittere, audīre).

- A **perfect stem** which is formed by adding -**v** to the present stem in the first and fourth conjugations (*eg* amāvī, audīvī), and by adding -**u** to the present stem in the second conjugation (*eg* habuī).

  In the third conjugation there are several possible endings (*eg* scrīpsī, dīxī).

  Some short verbs lengthen the stem vowel (*eg* lēgī), others double the first consonant and vowel (*eg* cu-currī).

- A **supine stem** which is formed by cutting off -**um** from the supine forms (*eg* amātum, habitum, missum, audītum).

Tenses

These forms of the verb show when an action takes place, in the present, in the past or in the future.

In Latin there are six tenses:

1 Present
2 Imperfect } formed from the **present** stem
3 Future

4 Perfect
5 Pluperfect } formed from the **perfect** stem
6 Future Perfect

Tenses Formed from the Present Stem

The following endings are added to the stem:

	PRESENT	IMPERFECT	FUTURE Conj 1&2	Conj 3&4
sing				
1st person	-ō	-bam	-bō	-am
2nd person	-s	-bas	-bis	-ēs
3rd person	-t	-bat	-bit	-et
pl				
1st person	-mus	-bāmus	-bimus	-ēmus
2nd person	-tis	-bātis	-bitis	-ētis
3rd person	-nt	-bant	-bunt	-ent

Note that the above endings show the number and person of the subject of the verb. Subject pronouns are therefore not normally necessary in Latin.

Continued

Conjugations

	1	2	3	4
INFINITIVE	amāre	habēre	mittere	audīre
PRESENT STEM	amā-	habē-	mitte-	audi-
PRESENT	amō	habeō	mittō	audiō
	amās	habēs	mittis	audis
	amat	habet	mittit	audit
	amāmus	habēmus	mittimus	audīmus
	amātis	habētis	mittitis	audītis
	amant	habent	mittunt	audiunt
IMPERFECT	amābam	habēbam	mittēbam	audiēbam
	amābās	habēbās	mittēbās	audiēbās
	amābat	habēbat	mittēbat	audiēbat
	amābāmus	habēbāmus	mittēbāmus	audiēbāmus
	amābātis	habēbātis	mittēbātis	audiēbātis
	amābant	habēbant	mittēbant	audiēbant
FUTURE	amābō	habēbō	mittam	audiam
	amābis	habēbis	mittēs	audiēs
	amābit	habēbit	mittet	audiet
	amābimus	habēbimus	mittēmus	audiēmus
	amābitis	habēbitis	mittētis	audiētis
	amābunt	habēbunt	mittent	audient

150 VERBS

Tenses (contd)

Use:

The Present

In Latin, the present tense expresses what is going on now and can be translated into English in two ways (*eg laborat* – he works, he is working)

- The present is often used in Latin instead of a past tense to make the action more exciting (→1)

- Sometimes the Latin present tense is used to describe an action begun in the past and and still continuing (→2)

The Imperfect

- Describes what went on or continued for a time (→3)

- Denotes an action repeated in the past (→4)

- Is used when an action is intended or interrupted (→5)

- Is sometimes translated "had" when used with **iam** (→6)

The Future

- Is used in Latin as in English to denote what will or is going to be or to happen (→7)

- Is occasionally used as a command (→8)

- After "**si**" (if) in conditional sentences, it is sometimes translated as present tense in English (→9)

Examples

1   **prima luce Caesar Gallos oppugnat**
     Caesar attacked the Gauls at dawn

2   **Alexander iam tres annos regit**
     Alexander has been ruling for three years now

3   **pluebat** – it was raining

4   **fortiter pugnabant**
         They used to fight bravely
     or They kept fighting bravely

5   **Romam intrabam**
     I was about to enter Rome

6   **multos iam dies villam habitabat**
     He had already lived in the house for many days

7   **hoc faciemus**
         We shall do this
     or We are going to do this

     erit gloria
     There will be glory

8   **non me vocabis**
     Don't call me

9   **si id credes, errabis**
     If you believe this, you will be making a mistake

Tenses (contd)

Tenses Formed from the Perfect Stem

To the appropriate perfect stem add the following endings:

	PERFECT	PLUPERFECT	FUTURE PERFECT
sing			
1st person	-ī	-eram	-erō
2nd person	-istī	-erās	-eris
3rd person	-it	-erat	-erit
pl			
1st person	-imus	-erāmus	-erimus
2nd person	-istis	-erātis	-eritis
3rd person	-ērunt	-erant	-erint

Conjugations

	1	2	3	4
PERFECT STEM	amāv-	habu-	mīs-	audī-
PERFECT				
	amāvī	habuī	mīsī	audīvī
	amāvistī	habuistī	mīsistī	audīvistī
	amāvit	habuit	mīsit	audīvit
	amāvimus	habuimus	mīsimus	audīvimus
	amāvistis	habuistis	mīsistis	audīvistis
	amāvērunt	habuērunt	mīsērunt	audīvērunt
PLUPERFECT				
	amāveram	habueram	mīseram	audīveram
	amāverās	habuerās	mīserās	audīverās
	amāverat	habuerat	mīserat	audīverat
	amāverāmus	habuerāmus	mīserāmus	audīverāmus
	amāverātis	habuerātis	mīserātis	audīverātis
	amāverant	habuerant	mīserant	audīverant
FUTURE PERFECT				
	amāverō	habuerō	mīserō	audīverō
	amāveris	habueris	mīseris	audīveris
	amāverit	habuerit	mīserit	audīverit
	amāverimus	habuerimus	mīserimus	audīverimus
	amāveritis	habueritis	mīseritis	audīveritis
	amāverint	habuerint	mīserint	audīverint

Continued

154 VERBS

Tenses (contd)

Use:

The Perfect

- In Latin, the perfect tense is equivalent to the simple past tense (*eg* vīdī – I saw) and the perfect tense (*eg* vīdī – I have seen) in English.

- It states past action particularly in narrative (→**1**)

- Expresses an action completed in the past which still has effect in the present (→**2**)

The Pluperfect

- Denotes an action completed in the past before another past action (→**3**)

The Future Perfect

- Denotes completing something in the future (→**4**)

- Is often used with volō, possum, nolō *etc* (→**5**)

- Denotes an action which precedes another action in the future, often in a subordinate clause (→**6**)

Examples

1 **veni, vidi, vici**
I came, I saw, I conquered

2 **spem in fide alicuius habuerunt**
They place their hope in someone's good faith

3 **Mithridates urbem Asiae clarissimam obsederat quam L. Lucullus virtute liberavit**
Mithridates had besieged the most famous city in Asia that Lucius Lucullus freed by his courage

4 **id fecero**
I shall have done it

5 **si potuero, faciam**
If I can, I shall do it

6 **qui prior venerit, prior discedet**
First to come will be first to go

156 VERBS

The Passive

Verbs may be active or passive. In **active** forms of the verb, the subject carries out the action (*eg* Brutus **killed** Caesar). In **passive** forms of the verb, the subject receives the action (*eg* Caesar **was killed** by Brutus).

Conjugation

To form the passive tenses of regular verbs, substitute the following endings for those of the present, imperfect and future active tenses (conjugated on page 148):

- In the present 1st person sing the ending is **-or**.
- In the imperfect, the endings are added to **-ba**.
- In the future (conjugations 1 and 2), the endings are added to **-bo** (*1st person sing*), **-be** (*2nd person sing*), and **-bi** for other persons. In conjugations 3 and 4, the 1st person *sing* ending is **-ar**.

Continued

		1st person	-r
sing		2nd person	-ris
		3rd person	-tur
		1st person	-mur
pl		2nd person	-mini
		3rd person	-ntur

Conjugations

	1	2	3	4
PRESENT PASSIVE				
	amor	habēor	mittor	audior
	amāris	habēris	mitteris	audiris
	amātur	habētur	mittitur	auditur
	amāmur	habēmur	mittimur	audimur
	amāminī	habēminī	mittimini	audimini
	amantur	habēntur	mittuntur	audiuntur
IMPERFECT PASSIVE				
	amābar	habēbar	mittēbar	audiēbar
	amābāris	habēbāris	mittēbāris	audiēbāris
	amābātur	habēbātur	mittēbātur	audiēbātur
	amābāmur	habēbāmur	mittēbāmur	audiēbāmur
	amābāminī	habēbāminī	mittēbāminī	audiēbāminī
	amābantur	habēbantur	mittēbantur	audiēbantur
FUTURE PASSIVE				
	amābor	habēbor	mittar	audiar
	amāberis	habēberis	mittēris	audiēris
	amābitur	habēbitur	mittētur	audiētur
	amābimur	habēbimur	mittēmur	audiēmur
	amābiminī	habēbiminī	mittēminī	audiēminī
	amābuntur	habēbuntur	mittentur	audientur

The Passive (contd)

Translation

Present Passive

1. I am loved — we are loved
   you (*sing*) are loved — you (*pl*) are loved
   he/she/it is loved — they are loved
2. I am held *etc*
3. I am sent *etc*
4. I am heard *etc*

Imperfect Passive

1. I was loved — we were loved
   you (*sing*) were loved — you (*pl*) were loved
   he/she/it was loved — they were loved
2. I was held *etc*
3. I was sent *etc*
4. I was heard *etc*

Future Passive

1. I shall be loved — we shall be loved
   you (*sing*) will be loved — you (*pl*) will be loved
   he/she/it will be loved — they will be loved
2. I shall be held *etc*
3. I shall be sent *etc*
4. I shall be heard *etc*

- "going to be" may also be used to translate the future.

Continued

The Passive (contd)

Perfect, Pluperfect and Future Perfect Passive

These tenses consist of the past participle (formed from the supine stem) and tenses of the verb **sum** (to be). The past participle endings agree in number and gender with the subject of the verb.

Conjugations

1	2	3	4	
PERFECT PASSIVE				
amātus -a, -um	habitus -a, -um	missus -a, -um	audītus -a, -um	**sum** / **es** / **est**
amātī -ae, -a	habitī -ae, -a	missī -ae, -a	audītī -ae, -a	**sumus** / **estis** / **sunt**
PLUPERFECT PASSIVE				
amātus	habitus	missus	audītus	**eram** / **erās** / **erat**
amātī	habitī	missī	audītī	**erāmus** / **erātis** / **erant**
FUTURE PERFECT PASSIVE				
amātus	habitus	missus	audītus	**erō** / **eris** / **erit**
amātī	habitī	missī	audītī	**erimus** / **eritis** / **erunt**

160 VERBS

The Passive (contd)

Translation

Perfect Passive

1. I have been loved   we have been loved
   you (*sing*) have been loved   you (*pl*) have been loved
   he/she/it has been loved   they have been loved

2. I have been held *or* I was held *etc*

3. I have been sent *or* I was sent *etc*

4. I have been heard *or* I was heard *etc*

Pluperfect Passive

1. I had been loved   we had been loved
   you (*sing*) had been loved   you (*pl*) had been loved
   he/she/it had been loved   they had been loved

2. I had been held *etc*

3. I had been sent *etc*

4. I had been heard *etc*

Future Perfect Passive

1. I shall have been loved   we shall have been loved
   you (*sing*) will have been   you (*pl*) will have been
   loved   loved
   he/she/it will have been   they will have been loved
   loved

2. I shall have been held *etc*

3. I shall have been sent *etc*

4. I shall have been heard *etc*

VERBS 161

Examples

1. **milites a populo occisi sunt**
   The soldiers were killed by the people

2. **populus milites occidit**
   The people killed the soldiers

- Note that the subject of the passive verb in (1) becomes the object of the active verb in (2).

- Often in English it is better to translate the meaning actively as in (2).

- The **agent** of the action is translated by **a(b)** with the ablative case as in **a populo** (1) – by the people.

- The **thing** causing the action is translated by the ablative case alone

   saxo percussus erat
   He had been struck by a rock

The Subjunctive

So far all verbs described have belonged to the indicative mood, which states facts. The subjunctive mood represents ideas, possibilities or necessities and is often translated by auxiliary verbs such as **may**, **might**, **could**, **would**, **should** or **must**. There are four tenses active and passive – present, imperfect, perfect and pluperfect.

Formation of Active

The present subjunctive active is formed from the present stem, the imperfect from the infinitive. To these add the endings

-m, -s, -t, -mus, -tis, -nt.

- Note that in first conjugation present the preceding vowel is **-e**, and in all others **-a**.

- The present subjunctive active is sometimes translated by using **"may"** (→**1**)

- The imperfect subjunctive active is sometimes trans-lated by using **"might"** (→**2**)

Conjugations

	1	2	3	4
PRESENT SUBJUNCTIVE ACTIVE				
	amem	habeam	mittam	audiam
	amēs	habeās	mittās	audiās
	amet	habeat	mittat	audiat
	amēmus	habeāmus	mittāmus	audiāmus
	amētis	habeātis	mittātis	audiātis
	ament	habeant	mittant	audiant
IMPERFECT SUBJUNCTIVE ACTIVE				
	amārem	habērem	mitterem	audīrem
	amārēs	habērēs	mitterēs	audīrēs
	amāret	habēret	mitteret	audīret
	amārēmus	habērēmus	mitterēmus	audīrēmus
	amārētis	habērētis	mitterētis	audīrētis
	amārent	habērent	mitterent	audīrent

1 **amem** – I may love
mittas – you (*sing*) may send
habeat – he may have
audiant – they may hear

2 **mitteretis** – you (*pl*) might send
haberem – I might have
amaret – she might love
audirent – they might hear

Continued

The Subjunctive (contd)

Formation of Passive

The passive of the present and imperfect subjunctive is easily formed by substituting the normal passive endings (-r, -ris, -tur, -mur, -mini, -ntur) for the active ones.

Conjugation

1	2	3	4

PRESENT SUBJUNCTIVE PASSIVE

amer	habear	mittar	audiar
amēris	habeāris	mittāris	audiāris
amētur	habeātur	mittātur	audiātur
amēmur	habeāmur	mittāmur	audiāmur
amēminī	habeāminī	mittāminī	audiāminī
amentur	habeantur	mittantur	audiantur

IMPERFECT SUBJUNCTIVE PASSIVE

amārer	habērer	mitterer	audīrer
amārēris	habērēris	mitterēris	audīrēris
amārētur	habērētur	mitterētur	audīrētur
amārēmur	habērēmur	mitterēmur	audīrēmur
amārēminī	habērēminī	mitterēminī	audīrēminī
amārentur	habērentur	mitterentur	audīrentur

- The present subjunctive passive is sometimes translated by using "**may be**" (→1)

- The imperfect subjunctive passive is sometimes translated by using "**might be**" (→2)

Continued

Examples

1. **habeamur** – we may be held
   amer – I may be loved
   mittamini – you (*pl*) may be sent
   audiantur – they may be heard

2. **audiremini** – you (*pl*) might be heard
   amaretur – he might be loved
   haberentur – they might be held
   mitterer – I might be sent

The Subjunctive (contd)

Perfect and Pluperfect Subjunctive Active

Both perfect and pluperfect subjunctive active are formed from the perfect stem as follows:

Conjugation

1	2	3	4
PERFECT SUBJUNCTIVE ACTIVE			
amāverim	habuerim	mīserim	audīverim
amāveris	habueris	mīseris	audīveris
amāverit	habuerit	mīserit	audīverit
amāverimus	habuerimus	mīserimus	audīverimus
amāveritis	habueritis	mīseritis	audīveritis
amāverint	habuerint	mīserint	audīverint
PLUPERFECT SUBJUNCTIVE ACTIVE			
amāvissem	habuissem	mīsissem	audīvissem
amāvissēs	habuissēs	mīsissēs	audīvissēs
amāvisset	habuisset	mīsisset	audīvisset
amāvissēmus	habuissēmus	mīsissēmus	audīvissēmus
amāvissētis	habuissētis	mīsissētis	audīvissētis
amāvissent	habuissent	mīsissent	audīvissent

- The Perfect subjunctive active is sometimes translated by using **"may have"** with the past participle in English (→1)

- The Pluperfect subjunctive active is sometimes translated by using **"might have"** with the past participle in English (→2)

Continued

Examples

1 **miserit** – he may have sent
   habuerint – they may have had
   audiveris – you (*sing*) may have heard
   amaveritis – you (*pl*) may have loved

2 **amavissemus** – we might have loved
   habuisset – he might have had
   audivissent – they might have heard
   misissem – I might have sent

The Subjunctive (contd)

Perfect and Pluperfect Subjunctive Passive

Both perfect and pluperfect subjunctive passive are formed from the supine stem and the present and imperfect subjunctive of **sum** respectively:

Conjugation

	1		2	
PERFECT SUBJUNCTIVE PASSIVE				
amātus	sim	habitus	sim	
	sīs		sīs	
	sit		sit	
pl				
amātī	sīmus	habitī	sīmus	
	sītis		sītis	
	sint		sint	
PLUPERFECT SUBJUNCTIVE PASSIVE				
amātus	essem	habitus	essem	
	essēs		essēs	
	esset		esset	
pl				
amātī	essēmus	habitī	essēmus	
	essētis		essētis	
	essent		essent	

Conjugation

	3		4	
PERFECT SUBJUNCTIVE PASSIVE				
missus	sim	audītus	sim	
	sīs		sīs	
	sit		sit	
pl				
missī	sīmus	audītī	sīmus	
	sītis		sītis	
	sint		sint	
PLUPERFECT SUBJUNCTIVE PASSIVE				
missus	essem	audītus	essem	
	essēs		essēs	
	esset		esset	
pl				
missī	essēmus	audītī	essēmus	
	essētis		essētis	
	essent		essent	

Continued

Examples

The Subjunctive (contd)

- The perfect subjunctive passive is sometimes translated by using "**may have been**" with the past participle in English (→**1**)

- The pluperfect subjunctive passive is sometimes translated by using "**might have been**" with the past participle in English (→**2**)

Examples

1 **habitus sis** – you (*sing*) may have been held
missi simus – we may have been sent
auditus sim – I may have been heard
amati sint – they may have been loved

2 **amati essemus** – we might have been loved
habiti essent – they might have been held
missus esses – you (*sing*) might have been sent
auditus essem – I might have been heard

172 VERBS

The Imperative

This is the mood of command. It has two forms, 2nd person *sing* and *pl*, active (→1) and passive: (→2)

Conjugations

	1	2	3	4
IMPERATIVE ACTIVE				
sing	amā	habē	mitte	audī
pl	amāte	habēte	mittite	audīte
IMPERATIVE PASSIVE				
sing	amāre	habēre	mittere	audīre
pl	amāminī	habēminī	mittīminī	audīminī

1 **pecuniam mittite, o cives**
Citizens, send money! (active)

spem habe
Have hope! (active)

2 **in curia audimini**
Be heard in the senate! (passive)

ab omnibus semper amare, Romule
Always be loved by everyone, Romulus (passive)

The Infinitive

The infinitive was originally a noun and can be used in this way in Latin (*eg* amāre – to love *or* loving). There are three types, present, future and perfect, both active and passive, formed as follows:

Active

	1	**2**
PRESENT	amāre	habēre
FUTURE	amātūrus esse	habitūrus esse
PERFECT	amāvisse	habuisse

	3	**4**
PRESENT	mittere	audīre
FUTURE	missūrus esse	audītūrus esse
PERFECT	mīsisse	audīvisse

Translation

to love
to be going to love
to have loved

to send
to be going to send
to have sent

to have
to be going to have
to have had

to hear
to be going to hear
to have heard

Continued

Passive

	1	**2**
PRESENT	amārī	habērī
FUTURE	amātum īrī	habitum īrī
PERFECT	amātus esse	habitus esse

	3	**4**
PRESENT	mittī	audīrī
FUTURE	missum īrī	audītum īrī
PERFECT	missus esse	audītus esse

Translation

to be loved
to be going to be loved
to have been loved

to be sent
to be going to be sent
to have been sent

to be had
to be going to be had
to have been had

to be heard
to be going to be heard
to have been heard

- In the future active -urus, -a, -um and in the perfect passive -us, -a, -um agree in number and gender with the noun or pronoun in indirect speech.

176 VERBS

The Infinitive (contd)

Uses of the Infinitive

- It can be used as a neuter noun

- As the subject of the sentence (→1)

- With certain nouns such as **fas** (right), **nefas** (wrong) (→2)

- As the object of the following verbs: (→3)

volō	I wish	**cupiō**	I desire
nolō	I do not wish	**sinō**	I allow
possum	I am able to, can	**cogō**	I force
sciō	I know (how)	**audeō**	I dare
nesciō	I do not know	**conor**	I try
debeō	I ought	**desinō**	I stop
soleō	I am accustomed	**dubitō**	I hesitate
incipiō	I begin	**coepi**	I begin

- It can be used to describe a rapid series of events instead of using the perfect tense (→4)

Examples

VERBS 177

1 **errare est humanum**
  To err is human

2 **nefas est templa destruere**
  It is wrong to destroy temples

3 **volo domum redire**
  I wish to return home

  desine mortuos commemorare
  Stop remembering the dead

  Romam exstinctam esse cupit
  He wishes Rome blotted out

4 **ille non tollere oculos, non remittere stilum, tum fragor adventare et intra limen audiri**
  He did not raise his eyes nor put down his pen, then the noise came closer and could be heard inside the door.

178 VERBS

Participles

There are three participles (or verbal adjectives) in Latin: the present active, the perfect passive and the future active.

The Present Participle

This is formed from the present stem by adding **-ns** and lengthening the previous vowel. The genitive ending is **-ntis**.

Conjugation

1	2	3	4
amāns	habēns	mittēns	audiēns
loving	having	sending	hearing

- Note that these decline like group 3 adjectives ending in **-ns** with ablative singular, in **-i** when used as an adjective and in **-e** when used as a verb. They agree in number, case and gender with nouns or pronouns in the sentence.

Use

- It denotes an action going on at the same time as the main verb (→**1**)

- It can be used as a noun (→**2**)

Continued

---

1 **pro patria pugnantes iuvenes mortui sunt**
The young men died *while fighting* for their country

Romulo regnante, Roma urbs parva erat
While Romulus was ruling, Rome was a small city

2 **lacrimae adstantium**
the tears of *people standing by*

180 VERBS

Participles (contd)

The Perfect Participle

This is formed from the supine stem by adding the endings -us, -a, -m. It declines like first and second declension adjectives (see pages 25–28)

Conjugation

1	2	3	4
amātus (having been) loved	habitus (having been) held	missus (having been) sent	audītus (having been) heard

Use

- It denotes an action that is completed before that of the main verb (→**1**)
- English is less precise in the use of tenses and frequently uses a present to translate a Latin past participle.

The Future Participle

This is formed by adding -ūrus, -a, -um to the supine stem. It declines like first and second declension adjectives.

Conjugation

1	2	3	4
amātūrus going to love	habitūrus going to have	missūrus going to send	audītūrus going to hear

Use

- It denotes an action that is going to take place (→**2**)
- The forms **futurus** (going to be) and **venturus** (going to come) are often used as adjectives.

Examples

1 **equites Romani auditi ad senatum adducti sunt**
The Roman businessmen *were heard* and then were brought before the Senate

castra capta incendimus
We *captured* the camp and burnt it
or *Capturing* the camp, we burnt it

2 **nos morituri te salutamus**
We who are *about to die* salute you

Gerunds and Gerundives

The **gerund** is a **verbal noun** and is active.
The **gerundive** is a **verbal adjective** and is passive.

The gerund is formed by adding -**ndum** to the present stem. It declines like a neuter noun -**ndum**, -**ndī**, -**ndō**, -**ndō**.

The gerundive declines like first and second declension adjectives -**us**, -**a**, -**um** (A)

Conjugation

	1	2	3	4
GERUND	amandum loving	habendum having	mittendum sending	audiendum hearing
GERUNDIVE	amandus requiring to be loved	habendus requiring to be held	mittendus requiring to be sent	audiendus requiring to be heard

Gerunds and Gerundives (contd)

Use of Gerund and Gerundive

- The gerund is often used with the accusative case to express **purpose** (→**1**)

- If the verb has a direct object, the gerundive is used instead (→**2**)

- The gerund is used in the genitive case with nouns and adjectives (→**3**) such as

  ars (art), **spes** (hope), **cupidus** (eager), **peritus** (skilled)

- Both the gerund and the gerundive can be used in the genitive with **causa** to express **purpose** (→**4**)

- The gerundive can be used to imply **obligation** and the person is expressed by the dative case (→**5**)

- If the verb cannot take a direct object, the impersonal form is used (→**6**)

- Both the gerund and the gerundive can be used in the ablative case (→**7**)

Examples

1 **venit ad regnandum**
He came to rule

2 **venit ad pacem petendam**
He came to make peace

3 **spes videndi**
Hope of seeing

  peritus equitandi
Skilled in riding

4 **dicendi causa**
to speak

  pacis petendae causa
For the sake of making peace

5 **poenae nobis timendae sunt**
Punishment must be feared by us
or We must fear punishment

6 **mihi parendum est**
You must obey me

7 **docendo discimus**
We learn by teaching

  me puniendo effugit
By punishing mc he escaped

186 VERBS: IMPERSONAL

Impersonal Verbs

Impersonal verbs are used in the third person singular only

- To describe the weather (→1)

- To express feeling. The person affected appears in the accusative case and the cause in the genitive case (→2)

- To express permission or pleasure. The person affected appears in the accusative or in the dative case. The verb is often followed by a present infinitive (→3)

- To express happening, following *etc.* These are followed by **ut** with the subjunctive mood (→4)

fit ut	it happens that
accidit ut	it happens that
sequitur ut	it follows that

- Certain intransitive verbs are used impersonally in the passive (→5)

- Verbs of saying, believing *etc* are used impersonally in the perfect passive tense (→6)

- The verbs, **interest** (it is of importance), and **refert** (it is of concern), are followed usually by **meā, tuā, nostrā, vestrā** (→7)

- Sometimes **interest** is followed by genitive of the person (→8)

- The following verbs are followed by a present infinitive. The person involved appears in the accusative case (→9)

  | me decet | it is fitting for me |
  | me oportet | I must/ought |

Examples VERBS: IMPERSONAL 187

1
pluit
it is raining
tonat
there is thunder

fulgurat
there is lightning
ningit
it is snowing

2
me miseret
I am sorry for
me paenitet
I repent of

me miseret sociorum
I am sorry for my
comrades

3
mihi licet
I am allowed to
tibi videtur
it seems good to you
or you decide

nobis placet
it is pleasing to us
or we like

4
fit ut
it happens that
accidit ut
it happens that

fit ut fallar
it happens that I am
mistaken

5
pugnatum est in mari
the battle was fought at sea
vivitur in oculis omnium
life is lived in the sight of everyone

6
nuntiatum est
it has been announced
mihi dictum est Germanos transiisse Rhenum
I was told that the Germans had crossed the Rhine

7
nihil mea refert
it is of no interest to me

8
Caesaris interest
it is important to Caesar

9
nos morari oportuit
we ought to have waited

Deponent Verbs

Deponent verbs are passive in form but active in meaning. They also have present and future participles and future infinitive which are active. The perfect participle is also active in meaning. Otherwise the conjugation is similar to that of regular verbs.

1st Conjugation

conārī (to try)

INDICATIVE

PRESENT — I try *etc*

conor
conāris
conātur
conāmur
conāminī
conantur

IMPERFECT — I was trying *etc*

conābar
conābāris
conābātur
conābāmur
conābāminī
conābantur

FUTURE — I shall try *etc*

conābor
conāberis
conābitur
conābimur
conābiminī
conābuntur

SUBJUNCTIVE

PRESENT — I may try *etc*

coner
conēris
conētur
conēmur
conēminī
conentur

IMPERFECT — I might try *etc*

conārer
conārēris
conārētur
conārēmur
conārēminī
conārentur

Continued

PERFECT — I tried

conātus **sum**
-a, -um **es**   you tried *etc*

conātus **sim**   I may have tried
-a, -um **sis**   you may have tried *etc*

PLUPERFECT — I had tried

conātus **eram**
-a, -um **eras**   you had tried *etc*

conātus **essem**   I might have tried
-a, -um **esses**   you might have tried *etc*

FUTURE PERFECT — I shall have tried

conātus **ero**
-a, -um **eris**   you will have tried *etc*

IMPERATIVE

conāre   *sing*   try
conāminī   *pl*   try

INFINITIVES

present   conārī   to try
future   conātūrus esse   to be going to try
perfect   conātus esse   to have tried

PARTICIPLES

present   conāns   trying
future   conātūrus   going to try
perfect   conātus   having tried

GERUND   conāndum   trying

GERUNDIVE   conāndus   requiring to be tried

Second, Third, Fourth Conjugations

These are conjugated like the passive form of verbs of the corresponding conjugations. A summary is provided as follows:

Second Conjugation

verērī (to fear, be afraid)

INDICATIVE

Present	**vereor**	I am afraid
Imperfect	**verēbar**	I was afraid
Future	**verēbor**	I shall be afraid
Perfect	**veritus sum**	I was afraid
Pluperfect	**veritus eram**	I had been afraid
Future Perfect	**veritus erō**	I shall have been afraid

SUBJUNCTIVE

Present	**verear**	I may be afraid
Imperfect	**verērer**	I might be afraid
Perfect	**veritus sim**	I may have been afraid
Pluperfect	**veritus essem**	I might have been afraid

IMPERATIVE

Singular	**verēre**	be afraid
Plural	**verēminī**	be afraid

Continued

INFINITIVES

Present	**verērī**	to be afraid
Future	**veritūrus esse**	to be going to be afraid
Perfect	**veritus esse**	to have been afraid

PARTICIPLES

Present	**verēns**	fearing, being afraid
Future	**veritūrus**	going to fear *or* be afraid
Perfect	**veritus**	having feared *or* been afraid (active)

GERUND

	verendum	fearing

GERUNDIVE

	verendus	requiring to be feared

Second, Third, Fourth Conjugations (contd)

Third Conjugation

sequī (to follow)

INDICATIVE		
Present	sequor	I follow
Imperfect	sequēbar	I was following
Future	sequar	I shall follow
Perfect	secūtus sum	I followed
Pluperfect	secūtus eram	I had followed
Future Perfect	secūtus erō	I shall have followed
SUBJUNCTIVE		
Present	sequar	I may follow
Imperfect	sequerer	I might follow
Perfect	secūtus sim	I may have followed
Pluperfect	secūtus essem	I might have followed
IMPERATIVE		
Singular	sequere	follow
Plural	sequiminī	follow
INFINITIVES		
Present	sequī	to follow
Future	secūtūrus esse	to be going to follow
Perfect	secūtus esse	to have followed
PARTICIPLES		
Present	sequēns	following
Future	secūtūrus	going to follow
Perfect	secūtus	having followed
GERUND	sequendum	following
GERUNDIVE	sequendus	requiring to be followed

Fourth Conjugation

mentīrī (to lie)

INDICATIVE		
Present	mentior	I lie
Imperfect	mentiēbar	I was lying
Future	mentiar	I shall lie
Perfect	mentītus sum	I lied
Pluperfect	mentītus eram	I had lied
Future Perfect	mentītus erō	I shall have lied
SUBJUNCTIVE		
Present	mentiar	I may lie
Imperfect	mentīrer	I might lie
Perfect	mentītus sim	I may have lied
Pluperfect	mentītus essem	I might have lied
IMPERATIVE		
Singular	mentīre	lie
Plural	mentiminī	lie
INFINITIVES		
Present	mentīrī	to lie
Future	mentītūrus esse	to be going to lie
Perfect	mentītus esse	to have lied
PARTICIPLES		
Present	mentiēns	lying
Future	mentītūrus	going to lie
Perfect	mentītus	having lied
GERUND	mentiendum	lying
GERUNDIVE	mentiendus	requiring to be lied to

Semi-deponent Verbs

A few verbs are passive in form and active in meaning in only the perfect tenses. All other tenses are active in form and meaning. These are:

audēre	to dare
gaudēre	to be glad
solēre	to be accustomed
confīdere	to trust

INDICATIVE		
Present	audeō	I dare
Imperfect	audēbam	I was daring
Future	audēbo	I shall dare
SUBJUNCTIVE		
Present	audeam	I may dare
Imperfect	audērem	I might dare
IMPERATIVE		
Singular	audē	dare
Plural	audētē	dare
INFINITIVE		
Present	audēre	to dare
PRES PARTICIPLE	audēns	daring
GERUND	audendum	daring
GERUNDIVE	audendus	requiring to be dared

All other parts are **passive** in form:

INDICATIVE		
Perfect	**ausus sum**	I dared
Pluperfect	**ausus eram**	I had dared
Future Perfect	**ausus erō**	I shall have dared
SUBJUNCTIVE		
Perfect	**ausus sim**	I may have dared
Pluperfect	**ausus essem**	I might have dared
PARTICIPLES		
Perfect	**ausus**	having dared
Future	**ausūrus**	going to dare
INFINITIVES		
Perfect	**ausus esse**	to have dared
Future	**ausūrus esse**	to be going to dare

Unique Verbs

The following verbs are different from the conjugations described so far:

esse (to be)

Indicative

PRESENT

sum	I am
es	you (*sing*) arc
est	he/she/it is
sumus	we are
estis	you (*pl*) are
sunt	they are

IMPERFECT

eram	I was
erās	you (*sing*) were
erat	he/she/it was
erāmus	we were
erātis	you (*pl*) were
erant	they were

FUTURE

erō	I shall be
eris	you (*sing*) will bc
erit	he/she/it will be
erimus	we shall be
eritis	you (*pl*) will be
erunt	they will be

Subjunctive

PRESENT

sim	I may be
sīs	you (*sing*) may be
sit	he/she/it may be
sīmus	we may be
sītis	you (*pl*) may be
sint	they may be

IMPERFECT

essem	I might be
essēs	you (*sing*) might be
esset	he/she/it might be
essēmus	we might be
essētis	you (*pl*) might be
essent	they might be

Continued

esse (to be) (contd)

Indicative

PERFECT

fuī	I have been, was
fuistī	you (*sing*) have been/were
fuit	he/she/it has been/was
fuimus	we have been/were
fuistis	you (*pl*) have been/were
fuērunt	they have been/were

PLUPERFECT

fueram	I had been
fuerās	you (*sing*) had been
fuerat	he/she/it had been
fuerāmus	we had been
fuerātis	you (*pl*) had been
fuerant	they had been

FUTURE PERFECT

fuerō	I shall have been
fueris	you (*sing*) will have been
fuerit	he/she/it will have been
fuerimus	we shall have been
fueritis	you (*pl*) will have been
fuerint	they will have been

Subjunctive

PERFECT

fuerim	I may have been
fueris	you (*sing*) may have been
fuerit	he/she/it may have been
fuerimus	we may have been
fueritis	you (*pl*) may have been
fuerint	they may have been

PLUPERFECT

fuissem	I might have been
fuissēs	you (*sing*) might have been
fuisset	he/she/it might have been
fuissēmus	we might have been
fuissētis	you (*pl*) might have been
fuissent	they might have been

Imperative

Singular	**es**	be
Plural	**este**	be

Infinitives

Present	**esse**	to be
Future	{ **futūrus esse** **fore**	to be going to be
Perfect	**fuisse**	to have been

Participle

	futūrus	going to be

- Compounds of **esse** are listed in the principal parts page 220.

posse (to be able)

- This verb is formed from **pot-** and **-esse**. Note that **t** becomes **s** before another **s**.

Indicative

PRESENT

possum	I am able
potes	you (*sing*) are able
potest	he/she/it is able
possumus	we are able
potestis	you (*pl*) are able
possunt	they are able

IMPERFECT

poteram	I was able *etc*
poterās	
poterat	
poterāmus	
poterātis	
poterant	

FUTURE

poterō	I shall be able *etc*
poteris	
poterit	
poterimus	
poteritis	
poterunt	

Subjunctive

PRESENT

possim	I may be able *etc*
possīs	
possit	
possīmus	
possītis	
possint	

IMPERFECT

possem	I might be able *etc*
possēs	
posset	
possēmus	
possētis	
possent	

Continued

posse (to be able) (contd)

Indicative

PERFECT

potuī	I have been able *etc*
potuistī	
potuit	
potuimus	
potuistis	
potuērunt	

PLUPERFECT

potueram	I had been able *etc*
potuerās	
potuerat	
potuerāmus	
potuerātis	
potuerant	

FUTURE PERFECT

potuerō	I shall have been able *etc*
potueris	
potuerit	
potuerimus	
potueritis	
potuerint	

Subjunctive

PERFECT

potuerim	I may have been able *etc*
potueris	
potuerit	
potuerimus	
potueritis	
potuerint	

PLUPERFECT

potuissem	I might have been able *etc*
potuissēs	
potuisset	
potuissēmus	
potuissētis	
potuissent	

Infinitives

posse	to be able
potuisse	to have been able

ferre (to bear)

Active

Indicative

PRESENT
ferō I bear *etc*
fers
fert
ferimus
fertis
ferunt

IMPERFECT
ferēbam I was bearing

FUTURE
feram I shall bear

PERFECT
tulī I bore

PLUPERFECT
tuleram I had borne

FUTURE PERFECT
tulerō I shall have borne

Subjunctive

PRESENT
feram I may bear *etc*
ferās
ferat
ferāmus
ferātis
ferant

IMPERFECT
ferrem I might bear

PERFECT
tulerim I may have borne

PLUPERFECT
tulissem I might have borne

Infinitives
Present **ferre** to bear
Future **lātūrus esse** to be going to bear
Perfect **tulisse** to have borne

Imperatives
Singular **fer** bear
Plural **ferte** bear

Supine **lātum**

Continued

ferre (to bear) (contd)

Passive

Indicative

PRESENT	
feror	I am borne *etc*
ferris	
fertur	
ferimur	
feriminī	
feruntur	
IMPERFECT	
ferēbar	I was being borne
FUTURE	
ferar	I shall be borne
PERFECT	
lātus sum	I was borne
PLUPERFECT	
lātus eram	I had been borne
FUTURE PERFECT	
lātus erō	I shall have been borne

Subjunctive

PRESENT	
ferar	I may be borne *etc*
ferāris	
ferātur	
ferāmur	
ferāminī	
ferantur	
IMPERFECT	
ferrer	I might be borne
PERFECT	
lātus sim	I may have been borne
PLUPERFECT	
lātus essem	I might have been borne

Infinitives

Present	**ferrī**	to be borne
Future	**lātum īrī**	to be going to be borne
Perfect	**lātus esse**	to have been borne

Imperatives

Singular	**ferre**	be borne
Plural	**feriminī**	be borne

Participles

Present	**ferēns**	bearing
Future	**lātūrus**	going to bear
Perfect	**lātus**	having been borne/carried

Gerund	**ferendum**	bearing
Gerundive	**ferendus**	requiring to be borne

Continued

fieri (to become, be made)

- This verb is the passive form of **facere** – to make.

Indicative

PRESENT

fīō	I become
fīs	you (*sing*) become
fit	he/she/it becomes
(fīmus)	
(fītis)	
fīunt	

IMPERFECT
fīēbam I was becoming

FUTURE
fīam I shall become

PERFECT
factus sum I became

PLUPERFECT
factus eram I had become

FUTURE PERFECT
factus erō I shall have become

Subjunctive

PRESENT

fīam	I may become *etc*
fīās	
fīat	
fīāmus	
fīātis	
fīant	

IMPERFECT
fierem I might become

PERFECT
factus sim I may have become

PLUPERFECT
factus essem I might have become

Infinitives

Present	**fierī**	to become
Future	**factum īrī**	to be going to become
Perfect	**factus esse**	to have become

Participle
Perfect **factus** having become

Gerundive faciendus becoming

210 VERBS: UNIQUE

īre (to go)

• The stem is i-. Before a, o, u, it changes to e-.

Indicative

PRESENT
eō   I go *etc*
īs
it
īmus
ītis
eunt

IMPERFECT
ībam   I was going

FUTURE
ībō   I shall go

PERFECT
īvī *or* iī   I went/have gone

PLUPERFECT
īveram   I had gone

FUTURE PERFECT
īverō   I shall have gone

Subjunctive

PRESENT
eam   I may go *etc*
eās
eat
eāmus
eātis
eant

IMPERFECT
īrem   I might go

PERFECT
īverim   I may have gone

PLUPERFECT
īvissem   I might have gone

Infinitives
Present   īre   to go
Future   itūrus esse   to be going to go
Perfect   īvisse *or* īsse   to have gone

Imperative
Singular   ī   go
Plural   īte   go

Participles
Present   iēns (*gen* euntis)   going
Future   itūrus   going to go

Gerund   eundum   going

velle (to wish)

Indicative

PRESENT
volō I wish/am willing *etc*
vīs
vult
volumus
vultis
volunt

IMPERFECT
volēbam I was wishing
volēbās
volēbat
volēbāmus
volēbātis
volēbant

FUTURE
volam I shall wish

PERFECT
voluī I wished/have wished

PLUPERFECT
volueram I had wished

FUTURE PERFECT
voluerō I shall have wished

Subjunctive

PRESENT
velim I may wish
velīs
velit
velīmus
velītis
velint

IMPERFECT
vellem I might wish
vellēs
vellet
vellēmus
vellētis
vellent

PERFECT
voluerim I may have wished

PLUPERFECT
voluissem I might have wished

Infinitives
Present   **velle**   to wish
Perfect   **voluisse**   to have wished

Participle   volēns, -entis   wishing

Continued

nōlle (not to wish, to be unwilling)

● This verb was originally **nōn volo**.

Indicative

PRESENT
nolō   I do not wish *etc*
nōn vis
nōn vult
nōlumus
nōn vultis
nōlunt

IMPERFECT
nōlēbam   I was not wishing
nōlēbās
nōlēbat
nōlēbāmus
nōlēbātis
nōlēbant

FUTURE
nōlam   I shall not wish

PERFECT
nōlui   I have not wished

PLUPERFECT
nōlueram   I had not wished

FUTURE PERFECT
nōluerō   I shall not have wished

Continued

Subjunctive

PRESENT
nōlim   I may not wish
nōlis
nōlit
nōlimus
nōlitis
nōlint

IMPERFECT
nōllem   I might not wish
nōllēs
nōllet
nōllēmus
nōllētis
nōllent

PERFECT
nōluerim   I may not have wished

PLUPERFECT
nōluissem   I might not have wished

Infinitives
Present   **nōlle**   not to wish
Perfect   **nōluisse**   not to have wished

Participle   **nōlēns, -entis**   not wishing

216 VERBS: UNIQUE

mālle (to prefer)

- This verb is formed from ma volō or magis volō (I wish more).

Indicative

PRESENT

mālō	I prefer
māvīs	
māvult	
mālumus	
māvultis	
mālunt	

IMPERFECT

mālēbam	I was preferring
mālēbās	
mālēbat	
malebamus	
mālēbātis	
mālēbant	

FUTURE

mālam	I shall prefer

PERFECT

mālui	I preferred

PLUPERFECT

mālueram	I had preferred

FUTURE PERFECT

māluerō	I shall have preferred

VERBS: UNIQUE 217

Subjunctive

PRESENT

mālim	I may prefer
mālis	
mālit	
mālīmus	
mālītis	
mālint	

IMPERFECT

māllem	I might prefer
māllēs	
māllet	
māllēmus	
māllētis	
māllent	

PERFECT

māluerim	I may have preferred

PLUPERFECT

māluissem	I might have preferred

Infinitives

Present	mālle	to prefer
Perfect	māluisse	to have preferred

Defective Verbs

The following verbs have only a few forms which are used.
These are shown below.

inquam (I say)

PRESENT

inquam	
inquis	
inquit	
inquimus	
inquitis	
inquiunt	

This verb is mainly used in the third person singular

inquiēbat	he said
inquiet	he will say
inquit	he said

avēre	to hail, say "hello"
salvēre	to hail
valēre	to say goodbye

- These verbs are found mainly in infinitives as above or imperatives:

avē, salvē	hello (*sing*)
avēte, salvēte	hello (*pl*)
valē (*sing*), **valēte** (*pl*)	goodbye

- Four verbs, **ōdī, meminī, coepī, nōvī** are found only in the perfect stem but are translated as follows:

ōdī	I hate
ōderam	I hated
ōderō	I shall hate
odisse	to hate
meminī	I remember
memineram	I remembered
meminerō	I shall remember
meminisse	to remember
coepī	I begin
coeperam	I began
coeperō	I shall begin
coepisse	to begin
nōvī	I know
nōveram	I knew
nōverō	I shall know
nōvisse	to know

Likewise subjunctive:

ōderim	I may hate
ōdissem	I might hate
meminerim	I may remember
meminissem	I might remember
coeperim	I may begin
coepissem	I might begin
nōverim	I may know
nōvissem	I might know

Principal Parts of Common Verbs

Latin verbs are most usefully listed under four principal parts, from which all other tenses *etc* may be formed or recognized

	1ST PERSON PRESENT ACTIVE	PRESENT INFINITIVE	1ST PERSON PERFECT ACTIVE	SUPINE
1st Conjugation	amō	amāre	amāvī	amātum
2nd Conjugation	habeō	habēre	habuī	habitum
3rd Conjugation	mittō	mittere	mīsī	missum
4th Conjugation	audiō	audīre	audīvī	audītum

400 of the most common verbs in Latin are listed below. Included are the following:

- 120 regular verbs. Their conjugations are indicated by numbers 1–4. All parts of these verbs can be deduced from the model conjugations on pp 148–185.

- Nearly 300 verbs which are irregular in parts (highlighted in bold), mainly in the perfect and supine. Again their conjugation is indicated by the number of the group to which they belong. Regular parts of these verbs and person endings etc may be deduced from the models of conjugations 1–4. Many compound verbs are included (*eg* afficio from ad-facio).

- Eight unique verbs and their compounds. These are marked bold throughout and a page reference is given *in italics* for these.

- Defective verbs which are shown in full in the main text. Again a page reference *in italics* is provided.

	Conj Page
	3
abdō, abdere, **abdidī, abditum** hide	3
abeō, abīre, abiī, abitum go away	3
abicio, abicere, **abiēcī, abiectum** throw away	
absum, abesse, āfuī be away	3
accēdō, accēdere, **accessī, accessum** approach	3
accidō, accidere, **accidī** happen	3
accipiō, accipere, **accēpī, acceptum** receive	
accūsō, accūsāre, accūsāvī, accūsātum accuse	1
addō, addere, **addidī, additum** add	3
adeō, adīre, adiī, aditum approach	3
adimō, adimere, **adēmī, ademptum** take away	3
adiuvō, adiuvāre, **adiūvī, adiūtum** help	1
administrō, administrāre, administrāvī, administrātum administer	1
adsum, adesse, adfuī be present	
adveniō, advenīre, **advēnī, adventum** reach	4
aedificō, aedificāre, aedificāvī, aedificātum build	1
afferō, afferre, attulī, allātum bring to	
afficiō, afficere, **affēcī, affectum** affect	3
aggredior, aggredī, **aggressus sum** attack	3
agnōscō, agnōscere, **agnōvī, agnitum** recognize	3
agō, agere, **ēgī, āctum** do/drive	3
alō, alere, **aluī, altum** feed	3
ambulō, ambulāre, ambulāvī, ambulātum walk	1
āmittō, āmittere, **āmīsī, āmissum** lose	3
amō, amāre, amāvī, amātum love	1

		Conj *Page*
animadvertō, animadvertere, animadvertī, animadversum	notice	3
aperiō, aperīre, aperuī, apertum	open	4
appareō, apparēre, appāruī, apparitum	appear	2
appellō, appellāre, appellāvī, appellātum	call	1
appropinquō, appropinquāre, appropinquāvī, appropinquātum	approach	1
arbitror, arbitrārī, arbitrātus sum	think	1
arcessō, arcessere, arcessīvī, arcessītum	send for	3
ardeō, ārdēre, ārsī, ārsum	burn	2
armō, armāre, armāvī, armātum	arm	1
ascendō, ascendere, ascendī, ascēnsum	climb up	3
aspiciō, aspicere, aspexī, aspectum	look at	3
attingō, attingere, attigī, attāctum	touch	3
audeō, audēre, ausus sum	dare	2
audiō, audīre, audīvī, audītum	hear	4
auferō, auferre, abstulī, ablātum	take away	
augeō, augēre, auxī, auctum	increase	2
bibō, bibere, bibī	drink	3
cadō, cadere, cecidī, cāsum	fall	3
caedō, caedere, cecīdī, caesum	cut/kill	3
canō, canere, cecinī, cantum	sing	3
capiō, capere, cēpī, captum	take	3
careō, carēre	lack	2
carpō, carpere, carpsī, carptum	pick	3
caveō, cavēre, cāvī, cautum	beware	2
cēdō, cēdere, cessī, cessum	go/give way	3

		Conj *Page*
cēlō, cēlāre, cēlāvī, cēlātum	hide	1
cernō, cernere, crēvī, crētum	perceive	3
cieō, ciēre, cīvī, citum	rouse	2
cingō, cingere, cīnxī, cīnctum	surround	3
circumdō, circumdāre, circumdedī, circumdatum	place round	1
clāmō, clāmāre, clāmāvī, clāmātum	shout	1
claudō, claudere, clausī, clausum	close	3
coepī, coeptus	begin	219
cōgitō, cōgitāre, cōgitāvī, cōgitātum	think	1
cōgnōscō, cōgnōscere, cōgnōvī, cōgnitum	find out	3
cōgō, cōgere, coēgī, coāctum	collect/compel	3
colō, colere, coluī, cultum	look after/ worship	3
collocō, collocāre, collocāvī, collocātum	place	1
commoveō, commovēre, commōvī, commōtum	upset	2
comparō, comparāre, comparāvī, comparātum	get ready	1
comperiō, comperīre, comperī, compertum	discover	4
compleō, complēre, complēvī, complētum	fill	2
comprehendō, comprehendere, comprehendī, comprehēnsum	grasp	3
concurrō, concurrere, concurrī, concursum	run together	3
condō, condere, condidī, conditum	found	3
cōnficiō, cōnficere, cōnfēcī, cōnfectum	finish	3
cōnfīdō, cōnfīdere, cōnfīsus sum	trust	3

		Conj Page
confirmō, confirmāre, confirmāvī, confirmātum	strengthen	1
confiteor, confitērī, confessus sum	confess	2
congredior, congredī, congressus sum	meet	3
coniciō, conicere, coniēcī, coniectum	throw	3
coniungō, coniungere, coniūnxī, coniūnctum	join	3
coniūrō, coniūrāre, coniūrāvī, coniūrātum	conspire	1
conor, conārī, conātus sum	try	1
consentiō, consentīre, consēnsī, consēnsum	agree	4
consistō, consistere, constitī, constitum	stop	3
conspiciō, conspicere, conspexī, conspectum	catch sight of	3
constō, constāre, constitī	agree	1
constituō, constituere, constituī, constitūtum	decide	3
construō, construere, construxī, constructum	construct	3
consulō, consulere, consuluī, consultum	consult	3
consūmō, consūmere, consūmpsī, consūmptum	use up	3
contemnō, contemnere, contempsī, contemptum	despise	3
contendō, contendere, contendī, contentum	strive/hurry	3
contingō, contingere, contigī, contactum	touch	3

		Conj Page
conveniō, convenīre, convēnī, conventum	meet	4
corripiō, corripere, corripuī, correptum	seize	3
crēdō, crēdere, crēdidī, crēditum	believe	3
crescō, crescere, crēvī, crētum	grow	3
culpō, culpāre, culpāvī, culpātum	blame	1
cunctor, cunctārī, cunctātus sum	delay	1
cupiō, cupere, cupīvī, cupītum	desire	3
cūrō, cūrāre, cūrāvī, cūrātum	look after	1
currō, currere, cucurrī, cursum	run	3
custōdiō, custōdīre, custōdīvī, custōdītum	guard	4
damnō, damnāre, damnāvī, damnātum	condemn	1
dēbeō, dēbēre, dēbuī, dēbitum	have to/owe	2
dēdō, dēdere, dēdidī, dēditum	hand over/yield	3
dēdūcō, dēdūcere, dēdūxī, dēductum	bring/escort	3
dēfendō, dēfendere, dēfendī, dēfensum	defend	3
dēficiō, dēficere, dēfēcī, dēfectum	revolt/fail	3
dēiciō, dēicere, dēiēcī, dēiectum	throw down	3
dēlectō, dēlectāre, dēlectāvī, dēlectātum	delight	1
dēleō, dēlēre, dēlēvī, dēlētum	destroy	2
dēligō, dēligere, dēlēgī, dēlectum	choose	3
dēmōnstrō, dēmōnstrāre, dēmōnstrāvī, dēmōnstrātum	show	1
dēpōnō, dēpōnere, dēposuī, dēpositum	lay down	3

		Conj/Page
dēscendō, dēscendere, dēscendī, dēscēnsum	go down	3
dēserō, dēsere, dēseruī, dēsertum	desert	3
dēsiderō, dēsiderāre, dēsiderāvī, dēsiderātum	long for	1
dēsiliō, dēsilīre, dēsiluī, dēsultum	jump down	3
dēsinō, dēsinere, dēsiī, dēsitum	stop/leave off	3
dēsistō, dēsistere, dēstitī	stop/leave off	3
dēspērō, dēspērāre, dēspērāvī, dēspērātum	despair	1
dēstruō, dēstruere, dēstruxī, dēstructum	destroy	3
dīcō, dīcere, dīxī, dictum	tell/say	3
dīligō, dīligere, dīlexī, dīlectum	love	3
dīmittō, dīmittere, dīmīsī, dīmissum	send away	3
discēdō, discēdere, discessī, discessum	go away	3
discō, discere, didicī	learn	3
dīvidō, dīvidere, dīvīsī, dīvīsum	divide	3
dō, dāre, dedī, datum	give	1
doceō, docēre, docuī, doctum	teach	2
doleō, dolēre, doluī, dolitum	grieve	2
dormiō, dormīre, dormīvī, dormītum	sleep	4
dubitō, dubitāre, dubitāvī, dubitātum	doubt	1
dūcō, dūcere, dūxī, ductum	lead	3
edō, edere, ēdī, ēsum	eat	3
efficiō, efficere, effēcī, effectum	complete	3
effugiō, effugere, effūgī	escape	3
ēgredior, ēgredī, ēgressus sum	go out	3
ēmō, ēmere, ēmī, ēmptum	buy	3
eō, īre, īvī, ītum	go	210

		Conj/Page
errō, errāre, errāvī, errātum	wander/be wrong	1
ērumpō, ērumpere, ērūpī, ēruptum	burst out	3
excitō, excitāre, excitāvī, excitātum	arouse	1
exeō, exīre, exiī, exitum	go out	
exerceō, exercēre, exercuī, exercitum	exercise/train	2
exīstimō, exīstimāre, exīstimāvī, exīstimātum	think	1
expellō, expellere, expulī, expulsum	drive out	3
experior, experīrī, expertus sum	try/test	4
exspectō, exspectāre, exspectāvī, exspectātum	wait for	1
exuō, exuere, exuī, exūtum	take off	3
faciō, facere, fēcī, factum	do/make	3
fallō, fallere, fefellī, falsum	deceive	3
faveō, favēre, fāvī, fautum	favour	2
ferō, ferre, tulī, lātum	bring/bear	204
festīnō, festīnāre, festīnāvī, festīnātum	hurry	1
fīgō, fīgere, fīxī, fīxum	fix	3
fingō, fingere, fīnxī, fictum	invent	3
fīō, fierī, factus sum	become/happen	208
flectō, flectere, flexī, flexum	bend	3
fleō, flēre, flēvī, flētum	weep	2
fluō, fluere, flūxī, flūxum	flow	3
frangō, frangere, frēgī, frāctum	break	3
fruor, fruī, frūctus or fruitus sum	enjoy	3
fugiō, fugere, fūgī, fugitum	flee/escape	3
fugō, fugāre, fugāvī, fugātum	put to flight	1
fundō, fundere, fūdī, fūsum	pour	3
fungor, fungī, fūnctus sum	perform	3

Verb		Conj / Page
gaudeō, gaudēre, **gāvīsus sum**	be glad	2
gemō, gemere, **gemuī, genitum**	groan	3
gerō, gerere, **gessī, gestum**	carry on/ wear	3
gignō, gignere, **genuī, genitum**	produce	3
habeō, habēre, habuī, habitum	have/keep	2
habitō, habitāre, habitāvī, habitātum	live (in)	1
haereō, haerēre, **haesī, haesum**	stick	2
hauriō, haurīre, **hausī, haustum**	drain away	4
horreō, horrēre, horruī	stand on end	2
hortor, hortārī, hortātus sum	encourage	1
iaceō, iacēre, iacuī	lie down	2
iaciō, iacere, **iēcī, iactum**	throw	3
ignōscō, ignōscere, **ignōvī, ignōtum**	forgive	3
immineō, imminēre	threaten	2
impediō, impedīre, impedīvī, impedītum	hinder	4
impellō, impellere, **impulī, impulsum**	drive on	3
imperō, imperāre, imperāvī, imperātum	order	1
incendō, incendere, **incendī, incēnsum**	burn	3
incipiō, incipere, **coepī, coeptum**	begin	3
incitō, incitāre, incitāvī, incitātum	drive on	1
inclūdō, inclūdere, **inclūsī, inclūsum**	include	3
incolō, incolere, incoluī	live (in)	3
īnferō, īnferre, intulī, illātum	bring against	3
ingredior, ingredī, **ingressus sum**	enter	3

Verb		Conj / Page
īnstituō, īnstituere, **īnstituī, īnstitūtum**	set up	3
īnstruō, īnstruere, **īnstrūxī, īnstrūctum**	set/draw up	3
intellegō, intellegere, **intellēxī, intellēctum**	realize	3
interficiō, interficere, **interfēcī, interfectum**	kill	3
intersum, interesse	be among/be important	(impers)
intrō, intrāre, intrāvī, intrātum	enter	1
inveniō, invenīre, **invēnī, inventum**	come upon/ find	4
invītō, invītāre, invītāvī, invītātum	invite	1
irrumpō, irrumpere, **irrūpī, irruptum**	rush into	3
iubeō, iubēre, **iussī, iussum**	order	2
iūdicō, iūdicāre, iūdicāvī, iūdicātum	judge	1
iungō, iungere, **iūnxī, iūnctum**	join	3
iūrō, iūrāre, iūrāvī, iūrātum	swear	1
iuvō, iuvāre, **iūvī, iūtum**	help	1
lābor, lābī, **lāpsus sum**	slip	3
labōrō, labōrāre, labōrāvī, labōrātum	work	1
lacessō, lacessere, **lacessīvī, lacessītum**	harass	3
lacrimō, lacrimāre, lacrimāvī, lacrimātum	weep	1
laedō, laedere, **laesī, laesum**	hurt	3
lateō, latēre, latuī	lie hidden	2
laudō, laudāre, laudāvī, laudātum	praise	1
lavō, lavāre, **lāvī, lautum/lavātum/ lōtum**	wash	1
legō, legere, **lēgī, lēctum**	read/choose	3

		Conj	Page
levō, levāre, levāvī, levātum	lighten	1	
līberō, līberāre, līberāvī, līberātum	free	1	
licet, licēre, licuit	it is allowed	2	
locō, locāre, locāvī, locātum	place	1	
loquor, loquī, locūtus sum	speak	3	
lūdō, lūdere, lūsī, lūsum	play	3	
lustrō, lustrāre, lustrāvī, lustrātum	purify/scan	1	
mālō, mālle, māluī	prefer		216
mandō, mandāre, mandāvī, mandātum	command/trust	1	
maneō, manēre, mānsī, mānsum	remain/stay	2	
meminī, meminisse	remember		219
mentior, mentīrī, mentītus sum	tell lies	4	
metuō, metuere, metuī	fear	3	
minor, minārī, minātus sum	threaten	1	
minuō, minuere, minuī, minūtum	lessen	3	
miror, mirārī, mirātus sum	wonder (at)	1	
misceō, miscēre, miscuī, mixtum	mix	2	
misereor, miserērī, miseritus sum / miseret, miserēre, miseruit (eg me miseret tuī – I am sorry for you)	pity	2	
mittō, mittere, mīsī, missum	send	3	
mōlior, mōlīrī, mōlītus sum	strive/toil	4	
moneō, monēre, monuī, monitum	advise/warn	2	
morior, morī, mortuus sum	die	3	
moror, morārī, morātus sum	delay/loiter	1	
moveō, movēre, mōvī, mōtum	move	2	
mūniō, mūnīre, mūnīvī/mūniī, mūnītum	fortify	4	
mūtō, mūtāre, mūtāvī, mūtātum	change	1	
nancīscor, nancīscī, na(n)ctus sum	obtain	3	
nārrō, nārrāre, nārrāvī, nārrātum	tell	1	

		Conj	Page
nāscor, nāscī, nātus sum	be born	3	
nāvigō, nāvigāre, nāvigāvī, nāvigātum	sail	1	
necō, necāre, necāvī, necātum	kill	1	
negō, negāre, negāvī, negātum	refuse/deny	1	
neglegō, neglegere, neglēxī, neglēctum	neglect	3	
nesciō, nescīre, nescīvī or iī, nescītum	not to know	4	
noceō, nocēre, nocuī, nocitum	harm	2	
nōlō, nōlle, nōluī	not to wish/be unwilling		214
nōscō, nōscere, nōvī, nōtum (in perfect tenses translate as "know")	get to know	3	219
nūntiō, nūntiāre, nūntiāvī, nūntiātum	announce	1	
obeō, obīre, obīvī or iī, obitum	die		
obiciō, obicere, obiēcī, obiectum	throw to/oppose	3	
oblīvīscor, oblīvīscī, oblītus sum	forget	3	
obsideō, obsidēre, obsēdī, obsessum	besiege	2	
obtineō, obtinēre, obtinuī, obtentum	hold/obtain	2	
occīdō, occīdere, occīdī, occāsum	fall	3	
occīdō, occīdere, occīdī, occīsum	kill	3	
occupō, occupāre, occupāvī, occupātum	seize	1	
occurrō, occurrere, occurrī, occursum	meet	3	
ōdī, ōdisse	hate		219
offerō, offerre, obtulī, oblātum	present		

		Conj/Page
oportet, oportēre, oportuit	be proper/ought	2
opprimō, opprimere, **oppressī, oppressum**	crush	3
oppugnō, oppugnāre, oppugnāvī, oppugnātum	attack	1
optō, optāre, optāvī, optātum	wish	1
orior, orīrī, **ortus sum**	arise	4
ōrō, ōrāre, ōrāvī, ōrātum	beg/plead	1
ōrnō, ōrnāre, ōrnāvī, ōrnātum	decorate/equip	1
ostendō, ostendere, **ostendī, ostentum**	show	3
pācō, pācāre, pācāvī, pācātum	pacify	1
paenitet, paenitēre, paenituit	repent of	2
pandō, pandere, **pandī, passum**	spread out	3
parcō, parcere, **pepercī, parsum**	spare	3
pāreō, pārēre, pāruī	obey	2
pariō, parere, **peperī, partum**	give birth to	3
parō, parāre, parāvī, parātum	prepare	1
pāscō, pāscere, **pāvī, pāstum**	feed	3
patefaciō, patefacere, **patefēcī, patefactum**	open	3
pateō, patēre, patuī	be open	2
patior, patī, **passus sum**	suffer/allow	3
paveō, pavēre, **pāvī**	fear	2
pellō, pellere, **pepulī, pulsum**	drive	3
pendeō, pendēre, **pependī, pēnsum** (*intrans*)	hang	2
pendō, pendere, **pependī, pēnsum**	weigh/pay	3
perdō, perdere, **perdidī, perditum**	lose/destroy	3
pereō, **perīre, periī, peritum**	perish	3
perficiō, perficere, **perfēcī, perfectum**	complete	3

		Conj/Page
pergō, pergere, **perrēxī, perrēctum**	proceed	3
permittō, permittere, **permīsī, permissum**	allow	3
persuadeō, persuadēre, **persuāsī, persuāsum**	persuade	2
pertineō, pertinēre, pertinuī, **pertentum**	concern	2
perturbō, perturbāre, perturbāvī, perturbātum	confuse	1
perveniō, pervenīre, **pervēnī, perventum**	arrive at	4
petō, petere, **petīvī, petītum**	seek/ask	3
placeō, placēre, placuī, placitum	please	2
placet, placēre, placuit	it seems good	2
polliceor, pollicērī, **pollicitus sum**	promise	2
pōnō, pōnere, **posuī, positum**	place/put	3
portō, portāre, portāvī, portātum	carry	1
poscō, poscere, **poposcī**	ask for/demand	3
possum, posse, potuī	to be able	200
postulō, postulāre, postulāvī, postulātum	demand	1
potior, potīrī, potītus sum	gain possession of	4
praebeō, praebēre, praebuī, praebitum	show	2
praeficiō, praeficere, **praefēcī, praefectum**	put in command of	3
praestō, praestāre, **praestitī, praestatum**	stand out	1
premō, premere, **pressī, pressum**	press	3
prōcēdō, prōcēdere, **prōcessī, prōcessum**	advance	3

		Conj Page
prōdō, prōdere, **prōdidī, prōditum**	betray	3
prōficīscor, prōficīscī, **profectus sum**	set out	3
prōgredior, prōgredī, **progressus sum**	advance	3
prohibeō, prohibēre, prohibuī, prohibitum	prevent	2
prōmittō, prōmittere, **prōmīsī, prōmissum**	promise	3
prōvideō, prōvidēre, **prōvidī, prōvīsum**	take precautions	2
pugnō, pugnāre, pugnāvī, pugnātum	fight	1
pūniō, pūnīre, pūnīvī or iī, punītum	punish	4
putō, putāre, putāvī, putātum	think	1
quaerō, quaerere, **quaesīvī, quaesītum**	ask/seek	3
queror, querī, **questus sum**	complain	3
quiēscō, quiēscere, **quiēvī, quiētum**	keep quiet	3
rapiō, rapere, **rapuī, raptum**	snatch/seize	3
recipiō, recipere, **recēpī, receptum**	receive/recover	3
recūsō, recūsāre, recūsāvī, recūsātum	refuse	1
reddō, reddere, **reddidī, redditum**	give back/return	3
redeō, redīre, rediī, reditum	come back/return	
redūcō, redūcere, **redūxī, reductum**	bring back	3
regō, regere, **rēxī, rēctum**	rule	3
regredior, regredī, **regressus sum**	retreat	3
relinquō, relinquere, relīquī, **relictum**	leave	3

		Conj Page
remittō, remittere, **remīsī, remissum**	send back	3
reor, rērī, **ratus sum**	think	2
repellō, repellere, **reppulī, repulsum**	drive back	3
reperiō, reperīre, **repperī, repertum**	find	4
resistō, resistere, **restitī**	resist	3
respiciō, respicere, **respexī, respectum**	look back	3
respondeō, respondēre, **respondī, respōnsum**	answer	2
restō, restāre, **restitī**	remain	1
restituō, restituere, **restituī, restitūtum**	restore	3
retineō, retinēre, retinuī, **retentum**	hold back	2
rīdeō, rīdēre, **rīsī, rīsum**	laugh	2
rogō, rogāre, rogāvī, rogātum	ask	1
rumpō, rumpere, **rūpī, ruptum**	burst	3
ruō, ruere, **ruī, rutum (ruitūrus – fut part)**	rush/fall	3
sciō, scīre, **scīvī/iī, scītum**	know	4
scrībō, scrībere, **scrīpsī, scrīptum**	write	3
sēcernō, sēcernere, secrēvī, **sēcrētum**	set apart	3
secō, secāre, **secuī, sectum**	cut	1
sedeō, sedēre, **sēdī, sessum**	sit	2
sentiō, sentīre, **sēnsī, sēnsum**	feel/perceive	4
sepeliō, sepelīre, sepelīvī, **sepultum**	bury	4
sequor, sequī, **secūtus sum**	follow	3
serō, serere, **sēvī, satum**	sow	3
serviō, servīre, servīvī, servītum	serve/be a slave	4
servō, servāre, servāvī, servātum	save	1

		Conj Page
simulō, simulāre, simulāvī, simulātum	pretend	1
sinō, sinere, **sīvī, situm**	allow	3
sistō, sistere, **stitī, statum**	set up	3
soleō, solēre, **solitus sum**	be used to	2
sollicitō, sollicitāre, sollicitāvī, sollicitātum	worry	1
solvō, solvere, **solvī, solūtum**	loosen	3
sonō, sonāre, **sonuī, sonitum**	sound	1
spargō, spargere, **sparsī, sparsum**	scatter/sprinkle	3
spectō, spectāre, spectāvī, spectātum	look at	1
spērō, spērāre, spērāvī, spērātum	hope	1
spoliō, spoliāre, spoliāvī, spoliātum	rob/plunder	1
statuō, statuere, **statuī, statūtum**	set up	3
sternō, sternere, **strāvī, strātum**	cover/overthrow	3
stō, stāre, **stetī, stātum**	stand	1
struō, struere, **strūxī, strūctum**	build	3
studeō, studēre, studuī	study	2
suādeō, suādēre, **suāsī, suāsum**	advise	2
subeō, subīre, subiī, subitum	undergo	
succēdō, succēdere, **successī, successum**	go up/relieve	3
succurrō, succurrere, succurrī, succursum	help	3
sum, esse, fuī, futūrus		196
sūmō, sūmere, sūmpsī, sūmptum	take	3
superō, superāre, superāvī, superātum	overcome	1
supersum, superesse, superfuī	survive	
surgō, surgere, **surrēxī, surrēctum**	rise/get up	3
suscipiō, suscipere, suscēpī, **susceptum**	undertake	3

		Conj Page
suspicor, suspicārī, suspicātus sum	suspect	1
sustineō, sustinēre, sustinuī, **sustentum**	sustain	2
taceō, tacēre, tacuī, tacitum	be silent	2
taedet, taedēre, taeduit, **taesum est**	be tired of	2
tangō, tangere, **tetigī, tactum**	touch	3
tegō, tegere, **tēxī, tectum**	cover	3
tendō, tendere, **tetendī, tentum** or **tēnsum**	stretch	3
teneō, tenēre, tenuī, **tentum**	hold	2
terreō, terrēre, terruī, territum	terrify	2
timeō, timēre, timuī	fear	2
tollō, tollere, **sustulī, sublātum**	raise/remove	3
tonō, tonāre, **tonuī**	thunder	1
torqueō, torquēre, **torsī, tortum**	twist	2
trādō, trādere, **trādidī, trāditum**	hand over	3
trahō, trahere, **trāxī, tractum**	drag	3
traiciō, traicere, **traiēcī, traiectum**	take across	3
trānseō, trānsīre, trānsiī, trānsitum	cross over	
tueor, tuērī, tuitus sum	look at	2
ulcīscor, ulcīscī, **ultus sum**	punish/avenge	3
urgeō, urgēre, **ursī**	press/urge	2
ūrō, ūrere, **ussī, ustum**	burn	3
ūtor, ūtī, **ūsus sum**	use	3
valeō, valēre, valuī, valitum	be strong	2
vastō, vastāre, vastāvī, vastātum	destroy	1
vehō, vehere, **vēxī, vectum**	carry	3
vendō, vendere, **vendidī, venditum**	sell	3
veniō, venīre, **vēnī, ventum**	come	4
vereor, verērī, veritus sum	fear	2

	Conj *Page*
vertō, vertere, vertī, versum	turn	3
vescor, vescī	feed on	3
vetō, vetāre, vetuī, vetitum	forbid	1
videō, vidēre, vīdī, vīsum	see	2
vigilō, vigilāre, vigilāvī, vigilātum	stay awake	1
vinciō, vincīre, vīnxī, vīnctum	bind	4
vincō, vincere, vīcī, victum	defeat/conquer	3
vītō, vītāre, vītāvī, vītātum	avoid	1
vīvō, vīvere, vīxī, victum	live	3
vocō, vocāre, vocāvī, vocātum	call/invite	1
volō, velle, voluī	wish/want	212
volvō, volvere, volvī, volūtum	roll	3
voveō, vovēre, vōvī, vōtum	vow	2

The following index lists comprehensively both grammatical terms and key words in English and Latin.